WEST ACADEMIC PUBLISHING'S EMERITUS ADVISORY BOARD

JESSE H. CHOPER
Professor of Law and Dean Emeritus
University of California, Berkeley

LARRY D. KRAMER
President, William and Flora Hewlett Foundation

JAMES J. WHITE
Robert A. Sullivan Emeritus Professor of Law
University of Michigan

WEST ACADEMIC PUBLISHING'S
LAW SCHOOL ADVISORY BOARD

MARK C. ALEXANDER
Arthur J. Kania Dean and Professor of Law
Villanova University Charles Widger School of Law

JOSHUA DRESSLER
Distinguished University Professor Emeritus
Michael E. Moritz College of Law, The Ohio State University

MEREDITH J. DUNCAN
Professor of Law
University of Houston Law Center

RENÉE McDONALD HUTCHINS
Dean & Professor of Law
University of Maryland Carey School of Law

RENEE KNAKE JEFFERSON
Joanne and Larry Doherty Chair in Legal Ethics &
Professor of Law, University of Houston Law Center

ORIN S. KERR
William G. Simon Professor of Law
University of California, Berkeley

JONATHAN R. MACEY
Professor of Law,
Yale Law School

DEBORAH JONES MERRITT
Distinguished University Professor,
John Deaver Drinko/Baker & Hostetler Chair in Law Emerita
Michael E. Moritz College of Law, The Ohio State University

ARTHUR R. MILLER
University Professor and Chief Justice Warren E. Burger Professor of
Constitutional Law and the Courts, New York University

GRANT S. NELSON
Professor of Law Emeritus, Pepperdine University
Professor of Law Emeritus, University of California, Los Angeles

A. BENJAMIN SPENCER
Dean & Trustee Professor of Law
William & Mary Law School

CRIMINAL PROCEDURE
CASES AND MATERIALS

Third Edition

■ ■ ■

Cynthia Lee
Edward F. Howrey Professor of Law
The George Washington University Law School

L. Song Richardson
President
Colorado College

AMERICAN CASEBOOK SERIES®

The publisher is not engaged in rendering legal or other professional advice, and this publication is not a substitute for the advice of an attorney. If you require legal or other expert advice, you should seek the services of a competent attorney or other professional.

American Casebook Series is a trademark registered in the U.S. Patent and Trademark Office.

© 2016, 2018 LEG, Inc. d/b/a West Academic
© 2023 LEG, Inc. d/b/a West Academic
    860 Blue Gentian Road, Suite 350
    Eagan, MN 55121
    1-877-888-1330

West, West Academic Publishing, and West Academic are trademarks of West Publishing Corporation, used under license.

Printed in the United States of America

ISBN: 978-1-64708-618-3

This book is dedicated to

Kenichi Haramoto

Tuck and Dorothea Lee

Kurt Kieffer

Song Yim and Nehemiah Richardson

ACKNOWLEDGMENTS

Cynthia Lee would like to thank several people for their help in making this casebook possible. First and foremost, she thanks Matt Halldorson, who served as her Research Assistant from the summer of his first year in law school at the George Washington University Law School until he graduated in May 2016. Matt helped gather excerpts for possible inclusion in the first edition of the casebook. He put cases into casebook format, made sure the formatting was consistent throughout, edited cases, drafted the Index, and proofread numerous drafts. This casebook could not have been produced without Matt's help. Additionally, Professor Lee thanks Research Assistants Masako Yoshioka, Carrie James, and Mario Kolev, who assisted with the production of the first edition of this casebook. She thanks Research Assistants Stephanie Hansen, Leanza Bethel, and Payal Patel, who helped proofread the page proofs for the second edition of this casebook. She thanks Research Assistants Alexandra Bruer, Matthew Broussard, Robin Choi, Garrett Dowell, Julie Jones, Thomas Kang Il Lee, and Jessica Mayes who assisted with the third edition of the casebook. Finally, she thanks Administrative Assistants Katey Mason from the University of California at Hastings and Elizabeth Moulton from the George Washington University Law School, who provided administrative support to Professor Lee in the production of the first edition of this casebook, Prerna Balasundarum from the George Washington University Law School who provided administrative support in the production of the second edition of this casebook, and Sarah Prabhakar from the George Washington University Law School who provided administrative support in the production of the third edition of this casebook.

L. Song Richardson extends her deepest gratitude to her Research Assistants Sean Corpstein, Elizabeth Etchells, and Grant Lientz from the University of Iowa College of Law and Ariela-Rutkin Becker and Sierra Nelson from the University of California, Irvine School of Law who worked tirelessly to help bring this casebook to completion.

SUMMARY OF CONTENTS

ACKNOWLEDGMENTS V
TABLE OF CASES XXI

Chapter 1. Introduction to the Criminal Justice Process 1
A. Sources of Criminal Procedure Law 1
B. The Investigation of the Crime 1
C. The Arrest 2
D. Judicial Determination of Probable Cause 3
E. The Prosecutor's Decision to Charge 3
F. Initial Appearance or Arraignment on the Complaint 4
G. The Preliminary Hearing 4
H. The Grand Jury 5
I. Arraignment on the Information or Indictment 5
J. Pretrial Motions 5
K. Discovery 6
L. Plea Negotiations 6
M. Trial, Sentencing, and Appeal 6

Chapter 2. What Constitutes a Search? 9
A. The Open Fields Doctrine 17
B. The Third Party Doctrine 26
C. Electronic Surveillance 43
D. Dog Sniffs 74
E. Commentary on the "Reasonable Expectation of Privacy" Test 82

Chapter 3. Probable Cause 89

Chapter 4. Search Warrants 103

Chapter 5. Arrests 117

Chapter 6. Searches Incident to Arrest 133

Chapter 7. The Automobile Exception 169

Chapter 8. *Terry* Stops and Frisks 201

Chapter 9. The Plain View Doctrine 241

Chapter 10. Racial Profiling 255

Chapter 11. Seizures 287

Chapter 12. Police Use of Force 329

Summary of Contents

Chapter 13. Consent Searches 351

Chapter 14. Administrative Searches 371
A. Inventory Searches 372
B. Vehicle Checkpoint Searches 377
C. Strip Searches 388

Chapter 15. Exigent Circumstances 405

Chapter 16. The Exclusionary Rule 421

Chapter 17. The Right to Counsel 467

Chapter 18. Interrogations—the Due Process Voluntariness Test 487

Chapter 19. Interrogations—the Sixth Amendment Right to Counsel 503

Chapter 20. Interrogations—the *Miranda* Rule 531
A. What Constitutes "Custody" and "Interrogation" for Purposes of the *Miranda* Rule? 548
B. Can Police Try Again After a Suspect Invokes Her *Miranda* Rights? 574
C. Waiver of *Miranda* Rights 597
D. More on *Miranda* and the Fifth Amendment's Privilege Against Self-Incrimination 618
E. *Miranda* and *Massiah*: Contrasting Perspectives 660

Chapter 21. Lineups and Other Pretrial Identification Procedures 673

Chapter 22. The Prosecutor's Charging Discretion 703

Chapter 23. Grand Jury 731

Chapter 24. Bail 747

Chapter 25. The Right to a Speedy Trial 763

Chapter 26. Discovery 779

Chapter 27. Plea Bargaining 803

Chapter 28. The Right to Trial by Jury 835

Chapter 29. The Role of Criminal Defense Counsel 883

Chapter 30. The Right of Presence 931

Chapter 31. The Confrontation Clause 941

Chapter 32. Double Jeopardy 971
A. Collateral Estoppel 971
B. The "Same Offense" Requirement 976
C. The Dual Sovereignty Doctrine 987
D. Criminal Versus Civil Punishment 995
E. Mistrials 999
F. Retrial Following Acquittals, Dismissals, and Convictions 1010
G. Jury Nullification 1019

Chapter 33. Sentencing 1029

Appendix 1051

Index 1099

TABLE OF CONTENTS

ACKNOWLEDGMENTS V
TABLE OF CASES XXI

Chapter 1. Introduction to the Criminal Justice Process 1
A. Sources of Criminal Procedure Law 1
B. The Investigation of the Crime 1
C. The Arrest 2
D. Judicial Determination of Probable Cause 3
E. The Prosecutor's Decision to Charge 3
F. Initial Appearance or Arraignment on the Complaint 4
G. The Preliminary Hearing 4
H. The Grand Jury 5
I. Arraignment on the Information or Indictment 5
J. Pretrial Motions 5
K. Discovery 6
L. Plea Negotiations 6
M. Trial, Sentencing, and Appeal 6

Chapter 2. What Constitutes a Search? 9
    Katz v. United States 10
    Katz and the Origins of the "Reasonable Expectation of Privacy" Test 15
A. The Open Fields Doctrine 17
    Florida v. Riley 18
    Note 24
    Open Fields in the Inner City: Application of the Curtilage Doctrine to Urban and Suburban Areas 24
B. The Third Party Doctrine 26
    Smith v. Maryland 27
    California v. Greenwood 32
    What Is a Search? Two Conceptual Flaws in Fourth Amendment Doctrine and Some Hints of a Remedy 38
    Digital Dossiers and the Dissipation of Fourth Amendment Privacy 40
C. Electronic Surveillance 43
    United States v. White 44
    Kyllo v. United States 48
    Note 53
    United States v. Jones 54
    Note 62
    Carpenter v. United States 63
D. Dog Sniffs 74
    Florida v. Jardines 75

E. Commentary on the "Reasonable Expectation of Privacy" Test............. 82
    "One Train May Hide Another": Katz, Stonewall, and the Secret
        Subtext of Criminal Procedure 82
    The Distribution of Fourth Amendment Privacy 85

Chapter 3. Probable Cause.. 89
Spinelli v. United States... 90
Illinois v. Gates 92
Note 98
Maryland v. Pringle 99

Chapter 4. Search Warrants.. 103
Maryland v. Garrison... 103
Note 109
Richards v. Wisconsin 112
Note 115

Chapter 5. Arrests... 117
United States v. Watson 117
Payton v. New York 120
Steagald v. United States 123
Ashcroft v. Al-Kidd... 128

Chapter 6. Searches Incident to Arrest... 133
Chimel v. California.. 133
United States v. Robinson 137
Note 140
Vale v. Louisiana.. 141
Note 145
New York v. Belton 145
Note 150
Arizona v. Gant 153
Note 160
Riley v. California 161

Chapter 7. The Automobile Exception 169
California v. Carney... 169
California v. Acevedo... 175
Wyoming v. Houghton 183
The Fourth Amendment and Common Law 189
Collins v. Virginia 192

Chapter 8. *Terry* Stops and Frisks.. 201
Terry v. Ohio... 201
Note 211
Terry v. Ohio at Thirty-Five: A Revisionist View 212
Stopping the Usual Suspects: Race and the Fourth Amendment.... 215
Arrest Efficiency and the Fourth Amendment............................... 220

Florida v. J.L.	222
Illinois v. Wardlow	225
Note	230
"Black and Blue Encounters"—Some Preliminary Thoughts About Fourth Amendment Seizures: Should Race Matter?	232
Foreword: Transparent Adjudication and Social Science Research in Constitutional Criminal Procedure	233
Note	234
Michigan v. Long	235

Chapter 9. The Plain View Doctrine 241
Arizona v. Hicks	241
Minnesota v. Dickerson	249

Chapter 10. Racial Profiling 255
(E)racing the Fourth Amendment	256
United States v. Brignoni-Ponce	261
La Migra in the Mirror: Immigration Enforcement and Racial Profiling on the Texas Border	265
The Case Against Race Profiling in Immigration Enforcement	267
Note	269
Whren v. United States	270
"Driving While Black" and All Other Traffic Offenses: The Supreme Court and Pretextual Traffic Stops	274
"Walking While Black": Encounters with the Police on My Street	278
Gendered (In)security: Migration and Criminalization in the Security State	283
Profiling Terror	283

Chapter 11. Seizures 287
Immigration and Naturalization Service v. Delgado	288
Note	293
Florida v. Bostick	294
(E)racing the Fourth Amendment	299
Note	303
No Need to Shout: Bus Sweeps and the Psychology of Coercion	304
Note	308
"Black and Blue Encounters"—Some Preliminary Thoughts About Fourth Amendment Seizures: Should Race Matter?	308
Note	311
Florida v. Royer	313
Note	320
Torres v. Madrid	320

Chapter 12. Police Use of Force 329
Tennessee v. Garner	330
Graham v. Connor	335
Scott v. Harris	339

Whose Eyes Are You Going to Believe? Scott v. Harris and the Perils of
    Cognitive Illiberalism 346

Chapter 13. Consent Searches 351
Schneckloth v. Bustamonte 351
Note 357
Illinois v. Rodriguez 358
Georgia v. Randolph 362

Chapter 14. Administrative Searches 371
A. Inventory Searches 372
   Colorado v. Bertine 373
B. Vehicle Checkpoint Searches 377
   Michigan v. Sitz 377
   City of Indianapolis v. Edmond 383
C. Strip Searches 388
   Safford Unified School District #1 v. Redding 388
   Florence v. Board of Chosen Freeholders 392
   Unsexing the Fourth Amendment 400

Chapter 15. Exigent Circumstances 405
Welsh v. Wisconsin 406
Note 411
Brigham City, Utah v. Stuart 412
Kentucky v. King 415

Chapter 16. The Exclusionary Rule 421
Wolf v. Colorado 422
Mapp v. Ohio 425
The Road to Mapp v. Ohio and Beyond: The Origins, Development and
    Future of the Exclusionary Rule in Search-and-Seizure Cases 432
Dollree Mapp, 1923–2014: "The Rosa Parks of the Fourth Amendment" 433
United States v. Leon 436
Note 442
Herring v. United States 443
Note 448
Wong Sun v. United States 449
Note 453
Nix v. Williams 453
Note 456
Utah v. Strieff 457

Chapter 17. The Right to Counsel 467
Betts v. Brady 468
Note 472
Gideon v. Wainwright 473
Note 476
Scott v. Illinois 478

Note 481
The Gender of Gideon 483

Chapter 18. Interrogations—the Due Process Voluntariness Test 487
Ashcraft v. State of Tennessee 488
Spano v. New York 493
Note 497
Lisenba v. California 498

Chapter 19. Interrogations—the Sixth Amendment Right to Counsel 503
Massiah v. United States 503
Escobedo v. Illinois 507
Brewer v. Williams 513
United States v. Henry 521
Kuhlmann v. Wilson 525

Chapter 20. Interrogations—the *Miranda* Rule 531
    Miranda v. Arizona 531
    Note 547
A. What Constitutes "Custody" and "Interrogation" for Purposes of the *Miranda* Rule? 548
    1. The Meaning of "Custody" 548
        Berkemer v. McCarty 548
        J.D.B. v. North Carolina 554
        Note 559
    2. The Meaning of "Interrogation" 559
        Rhode Island v. Innis 559
        Note 567
        Illinois v. Perkins 568
B. Can Police Try Again After a Suspect Invokes Her *Miranda* Rights? 574
    Michigan v. Mosley 574
    Edwards v. Arizona 579
    Note 583
    Davis v. United States 583
    In a Different Register: The Pragmatics of Powerlessness in Police Interrogation 587
    Maryland v. Shatzer 590
C. Waiver of *Miranda* Rights 597
    North Carolina v. Butler 597
    Moran v. Burbine 601
    Berghuis v. Thompkins 609
    Colorado v. Spring 615

D. More on *Miranda* and the Fifth Amendment's Privilege Against Self-Incrimination 618
    New York v. Quarles 619
    Dickerson v. United States 626
    Note 632
    United States v. Patane 632
    Oregon v. Elstad 636
    Missouri v. Seibert 642
    Harris v. New York 651
    James v. Illinois 653
    Wrongly Accused: Is Race a Factor in Convicting the Innocent? 658
E. *Miranda* and *Massiah*: Contrasting Perspectives 660
    1. Does a Voluntary, Knowing and Intelligent Waiver of One's *Miranda* Right to Counsel Suffice to Waive One's Sixth Amendment Right to Counsel? 661
        Patterson v. Illinois 661
    2. Does Invocation of the Sixth Amendment Right to Counsel Constitute an Invocation of One's *Miranda* Right to Counsel? 664
        McNeil v. Wisconsin 664
    3. Does a Request for Counsel at an Arraignment Trigger the Protections of the *Edwards* Rule? 667
        Montejo v. Louisiana 668

Chapter 21. Lineups and Other Pretrial Identification Procedures 673
United States v. Wade 674
Kirby v. Illinois 679
Manson v. Brathwaite 683
Note 691
Eyewitness Identifications and State Courts as Guardians Against Wrongful Conviction 692
'They All Look Alike': The Other-Race Effect 693
Using an Expert to Evaluate Eyewitness Identification Evidence 695
Perry v. New Hampshire 696

Chapter 22. The Prosecutor's Charging Discretion 703
United States v. Armstrong 704
Note 712
Racial Fairness in the Criminal Justice System: The Role of the Prosecutor 712
Note 715
United States v. Goodwin 717
Note 725
United States v. Batchelder 725

Chapter 23. Grand Jury 731
Vasquez v. Hillery 732

Table of Contents

Note 737
Costello v. United States 738
United States v. Williams 740
Note 744

Chapter 24. Bail 747
Stack v. Boyle 748
United States v. Salerno 751
Note 758
"Give Us Free": Addressing Racial Disparities in Bail Determinations 760

Chapter 25. The Right to a Speedy Trial 763
Barker v. Wingo 763
Betterman v. Montana 772
United States v. Lovasco 774
Note 778

Chapter 26. Discovery 779
Brady v. Maryland 780
Note 781
United States v. Bagley 782
Note 790
Rule 3.8: Special Responsibilities of a Prosecutor 790
Note 791
Prosecutorial Discretion at the Core: The Good Prosecutor Meets Brady ... 792
Williams v. Florida 795
Note 801

Chapter 27. Plea Bargaining 803
Bordenkircher v. Hayes 804
Santobello v. New York 809
Mabry v. Johnson 812
United States v. Ruiz 814
Boykin v. Alabama 817
Henderson v. Morgan 820
North Carolina v. Alford 823
Note 827
The Advent of the "Vanishing Trial": Why Trials Matter 828
Trials Without Justice 831

Chapter 28. The Right to Trial by Jury 835
Blanton v. City of North Las Vegas 836
Note 838
Ramos v. Louisiana 838
Note 845
Empty Votes in Jury Deliberations 847
Singer v. United States 851
Taylor v. Louisiana 854

Duren v. Missouri	858
Note	862
Turner v. Murray	863
Note	868
Batson v. Kentucky	868
"Good" Reversal Followed "Unfair" Trial	875
Note	876
J.E.B. v. Alabama	877

Chapter 29. The Role of Criminal Defense Counsel ... 883

Why I Defend Guilty Clients	884
Strickland v. Washington	887
Note	894
Padilla v. Kentucky	895
Note	900
Buck v. Davis	902
Note	908
Nix v. Whiteside	910
Note	916
Wheat v. United States	917
Faretta v. California	924

Chapter 30. The Right of Presence ... 931

United States v. Gagnon	931
Taylor v. United States	934
Illinois v. Allen	936

Chapter 31. The Confrontation Clause ... 941

Crawford v. Washington	942
Note	949
Davis v. Washington	949
Note	956
Giles v. California	957
Note	963
Richardson v. Marsh	963

Chapter 32. Double Jeopardy ... 971

A. Collateral Estoppel	971
Ashe v. Swenson	972
B. The "Same Offense" Requirement	976
United States v. Dixon	976
Note	986
C. The Dual Sovereignty Doctrine	987
Heath v. Alabama	987
Note	993
D. Criminal Versus Civil Punishment	995
Hudson v. United States	995
Note	998

E.	Mistrials	999
	Arizona v. Washington	999
	Oregon v. Kennedy	1004
F.	Retrial Following Acquittals, Dismissals, and Convictions	1010
	United States v. Scott	1010
	Burks v. United States	1015
G.	Jury Nullification	1019
	Racially Based Jury Nullification: Black Power in the Criminal Justice System	1019
	The Dangers of Race-Based Jury Nullification: A Response to Professor Butler	1025

Chapter 33. Sentencing **1029**
Coker v. Georgia 1029
Note 1033
Ewing v. California 1033
Note 1039
McCleskey v. Kemp 1039

Appendix **1051**
Rule 6: The Grand Jury 1052
Rule 7: The Indictment and the Information 1057
Rule 11: Pleas 1058
Rule 12.1: Notice of an Alibi Defense 1062
Rule 16: Discovery and Inspection 1063
Rule 26.2: Producing a Witness's Statement 1067
Rule 29: Motion for a Judgment of Acquittal 1068
Federal Bail Reform Act of 1984 1070
The Jencks Act: Demands for Production of Statements and Reports of Witnesses 1078
Prosecution Function 1080
Defense Function 1089

INDEX 1099

TABLE OF CASES

The principal cases are in bold type.

Aldridge v. United States, 862
Andrews, United States v., 314
Apodaca v. Oregon, 848
Argersinger v. Hamlin, 883
Arizona v. Fulminante, 733
Arizona v. Gant, 153
Arizona v. Hicks, 241
Arizona v. Johnson, 226
Arizona v. Mauro, 567
Arizona v. United States, 269
Arizona v. Washington, 999
Arizona, United States v., 269
Armstrong, United States v., 704
Arvizu, United States v., 235
Arzberger, United States v., 1073
Ash, United States v., 691
Ashcraft v. State of Tennessee, 488
Ashcroft v. Al-Kidd, 128
Ashe v. Swenson, 972
Atwater v. City of Lago Vista, 119, 150, 152
Bagley, United States v., 782
Ballew v. Georgia, 846
Banks, United States v., 115
Barber v. Page, 946
Barker v. Wingo, 763
Batchelder, United States v., 725
Batson v. Kentucky, 868
Berghuis v. Thompkins, 609
Berkemer v. McCarty, 548
Betterman v. Montana, 772
Betts v. Brady, 468
Blanton v. City of North Las Vegas, 7, 836
Blockburger v. United States, 517
Bolton, People v., 917
Bordenkircher v. Hayes, 803, 804
Bostick v. State, 297
Boykin v. Alabama, 817
Brady v. Maryland, 780
Brendlin v. California, 289
Brewer v. Williams, 513
Brigham City, Utah v. Stuart, 412
Brignoni-Ponce, United States v., 261
Brinegar v. United States, 89
Brower v. County of Inyo, 289
Brown v. Ohio, 984
Buck v. Davis, 902
Bullcoming v. New Mexico, 956
Bumper v. North Carolina, 357

Burch v. Louisiana, 846
Burchfield v. North Dakota, 412
Burks v. United States, 1015
California v. Acevedo, 175
California v. Carney, 169
California v. Greenwood, 32
California v. Hodari D., 287, 289
Caniglia v. Strom, 413
Carpenter v. United States, 63
Chadwick, United States v., 35
Chavez v. Martinez, 625
Chimel v. California, 133
Coker v. Georgia, 1029
Colorado v. Bertine, 373
Colorado v. Connelly, 497, 541
Colorado v. Spring, 615
Costello v. United States, 738
Crawford v. Washington, 942
Currier v. Virginia, 971
Davis v. United States, 443, 583
Davis v. Washington, 949
Diaz v. United States, 986
Dickerson v. United States, 626
Dixon, United States v., 976
Doggett v. United States, 769
Drayton v. United States, 303
Duncan v. Louisiana, 835
Dunn v. United States, 19
Duren v. Missouri, 858
Edmonson v. Leesville Concrete Co., 871
Edwards v. Arizona, 579
Edwards v. Vannoy, 843
Escobedo v. Illinois, 507
Ewing v. California, 1033
Faretta v. California, 924
Fernandez v. California, 366
Florence v. Board of Chosen Freeholders, 392
Florida v. Bostick, 294
Florida v. J.L., 222
Florida v. Jardines, 25, 75
Florida v. Jimeno, 357
Florida v. Riley, 18
Florida v. Royer, 313
Floyd v. City of New York, 211, 212
Fosnight, State v., 917
Foster v. Chatman, 877
Frink v. State, 744
Gagnon, United States v., 931
Gamble v. United States, 993

Georgia v. McCollum, 870
Georgia v. Randolph, 362
Gerstein v. Pugh, 151
Gideon v. Wainwright, 473
Giglio v. United States, 785
Giles v. California, 957
Goodwin, United States v., 717
Grady v. Corbin, 980
Grady v. North Carolina, 58
Graham v. Connor, 335
Green, United States v., 803
Groh v. Ramirez, 109
Ham v. South Carolina, 862
Harlow v. Fitzgerald, 389
Harris v. New York, 651
Harris v. Oklahoma, 981
Heath v. Alabama, 987
Henderson v. Morgan, 820
Henry, United States v., 521
Herrera, State v., 744
Herring v. United States, 443
Hill v. Lockhart, 900
Horton v. California, 246
Howes v. Fields, 594
Hudson v. Michigan, 115
Hudson v. United States, 995
Hurtado v. California, 731
Illinois v. Allen, 936
Illinois v. Caballes, 74, 276
Illinois v. Gates, 92
Illinois v. Krull, 442
Illinois v. McArthur, 136
Illinois v. Perkins, 568
Illinois v. Rodriguez, 358
Illinois v. Wardlow, 225
Immigration and Naturalization Service v. Delgado, 288
Indiana v. Edwards, 928
Indianapolis, City of v. Edmond, 383
Iowa v. Tovar, 927
J.D.B. v. North Carolina, 554
J.E.B. v. Alabama, 877
Jacobsen, United States v., 75, 241
James v. Illinois, 653
Jencks v. United States, 801
Johnson v. Louisiana, 848
Johnson v. Superior Court, 744
Johnson v. Zerbst, 467
Johnson, People v., 916
Jones, United States v., 54
Karo, United States v., 54, 57
Karper, United States v., 1073
Katz v. United States, 10
Kennedy v. Louisiana, 1033
Kentucky v. King, 415
Kirby v. Illinois, 679
Knotts, United States v., 53
Knowles v. Iowa, 140

Kuhlmann v. Wilson, 525
Kyles v. Whitley, 790
Kyllo v. United States, 48
LaDeau, United States v., 725
Lafler v. Cooper, 901
Lawrence v. Texas, 83
Lee v. United States, 900
Leon, United States v., 436
Lewis v. United States, 838
Ligon v. City of New York, 211
Lisenba v. California, 498
Lovasco, United States v., 774
Lowery, People v., 917
Mabry v. Johnson, 812
Maine v. Moulton, 528
Manson v. Brathwaite, 683
Mapp v. Ohio, 425
Martinez-Fuerte, United States v., 264, 379
Maryland v. Buie, 135
Maryland v. Dyson, 173
Maryland v. Garrison, 103
Maryland v. Pringle, 99
Maryland v. Shatzer, 590
Massiah v. United States, 503
McCleskey v. Kemp, 1039
McFadyen v. Duke Univ., 792
McKaskle v. Wiggins, 928
McNeil v. Wisconsin, 571, 585, 664
Melendez-Diaz v. Massachusetts, 956
Merritt, United States v., 1073
Michigan v. Bryant, 955
Michigan v. Jackson, 667
Michigan v. Long, 235
Michigan v. Mosley, 574
Michigan v. Sitz, 371, 377
Midgett, United States v., 913
Miller-El v. Dretke, 872
Minnesota v. Dickerson, 249
Minnick v. Mississippi, 581
Miranda v. Arizona, 531
Missouri v. Frye, 803, 901
Missouri v. McNeely, 411
Missouri v. Siebert, 642
Montejo v. Louisiana, 668
Moran v. Burbine, 601
New Jersey v. T.L.O., 371
New York v. Belton, 145, 154
New York v. Quarles, 619
Nix v. Whiteside, 910
Nix v. Williams, 453
North Carolina v. Alford, 823
North Carolina v. Butler, 597
Ohio v. Clark, 954
Ohio v. Roberts, 941
Olmstead v. United States, 9
Olsen, United States v., 791
Oregon v. Bradshaw, 583
Oregon v. Elstad, 636

TABLE OF CASES

Oregon v. Kennedy, 1004
Padilla v. Commonwealth, 897
Padilla v. Kentucky, 895
Patane, United States v., 632
Patterson v. Illinois, 661
Payton v. New York, 120
Pena-Rodriguez v. Colorado, 862
Perry v. New Hampshire, 696
Place, United States v., 74, 235
Polouizzi, United States v., 1073
Powers v. Ohio, 871
Puerto Rico v. Sanchez Valle, 990
Purkett v. Elem, 871
Ramos v. Louisiana, 838
Rawlings v. Kentucky, 142
Rhode Island v. Innis, 559
Richards v. Wisconsin, 112
Richardson v. Marsh, 963
Riley v. California, 161
Ristaino v. Ross, 862
Riverside, County of v. McLaughlin, 151
Robinson, United States v., 137
Rock v. Arkansas, 911
Rodriguez v. United States, 75, 277
Roviaro v. United States, 817
Ruiz, United States v., 814
Safford Unified School District #1 v. Redding, 388
Salerno, United States v., 751
Sanborn v. State, 917
Santobello v. New York, 809
Schmerber v. California, 412
Schneckloth v. Bustamonte, 351
Scott v. Harris, 339
Scott v. Illinois, 478
Scott, United States v., 1010
Sharpe, United States v., 320
Singer v. United States, 7, 851
Skinner v. Railway Labor Executive's Association, 371
Smedley, United States v., 1073
Smith v. Maryland, 27
Spano v. New York, 493
Spinelli v. United States, 90
Stack v. Boyle, 748
Stanton v. Sims, 409
Steagald v. United States, 123
Stone v. Powell, 8
Stovall v. Denno, 684
Strickland v. Washington, 887
Sum, State v., 313
Taylor v. Louisiana, 854
Taylor v. United States, 934
Teague v. Lane, 958
Tennessee v. Garner, 330
Terry v. Ohio, 201
Texas v. Brown, 89
Texas v. Cobb, 517

Texas v. McCullough, 720
Thornton v. United States, 150, 155
Torres v. Madrid, 289
Torres, United States v., 1073
Turner v. Murray, 863
Ursery, United States v., 998
Utah v. Strieff, 457
Vale v. Louisiana, 141
Vasquez v. Hillery, 732
Virginia v. Moore, 140
Wade, United States v., 674
Warren, Commonwealth v., 231
Watson, United States v., 117, 355
Weaver, United States v., 282
Welsh v. Wisconsin, 121, 406
Westerbann-Martinez, United States v., 314
Wheat v. United States, 917
White, United States v., 44
Whren v. United States, 270
Williams v. Florida, 795, 845
Williams, United States v., 740
Willis v. Bernini, 744
Wolf v. Colorado, 422
Wong Sun v. United States, 449
Wyoming v. Houghton, 183

CRIMINAL PROCEDURE
CASES AND MATERIALS

Third Edition

CHAPTER 1

INTRODUCTION TO THE CRIMINAL JUSTICE PROCESS

■ ■ ■

A. SOURCES OF CRIMINAL PROCEDURE LAW

This casebook presents the leading Supreme Court cases on the criminal justice process. In each distinct phase of this process, procedures exist to achieve fair adjudication of criminal allegations and to prevent government oppression of liberty and privacy interests. Many of these procedures can be found in state criminal codes and the Federal Rules of Criminal Procedure. The most important criminal procedure protections, however, are found in the Bill of Rights or the first ten amendments to the U.S. Constitution. In interpreting these provisions, the Supreme Court sets a constitutional floor for government behavior. States are free to provide more protection to their citizens, but cannot provide less than the constitutional minimum. Because so much of criminal procedure derives from the U.S. Constitution, the basic criminal procedure class is often referred to as constitutional criminal procedure.

This chapter provides an overview of the criminal justice process. It is important to keep in mind that every state has its own specific procedures for the processing of a criminal defendant, so the steps outlined in this chapter may not reflect what takes place in every state. Moreover, procedures often differ depending on the seriousness of the crime. The procedures outlined in this chapter are the most common procedures in place for the processing of a person charged with a felony offense.

B. THE INVESTIGATION OF THE CRIME

It is typical for the police to conduct an investigation once a crime occurs. The police may question witnesses to the crime, take photos of the crime scene, and gather forensic evidence in the hopes of determining who committed the crime. At some point during the investigation of the crime, the police will begin to focus their attention on a suspect or several suspects.

As part of the investigation process, the police may wish to search a suspect's home, car, and other belongings. Whether such a search can take place without a warrant turns on U.S. Supreme Court case law interpreting the Fourth Amendment. These cases tell us what kind of government action constitutes a "search" within the meaning of the Fourth Amendment, the requirements for a valid search warrant, and when police can conduct a search without obtaining a search warrant in advance. When evidence is obtained in violation of the Fourth Amendment, it can be excluded at trial.

Another investigative technique is the interrogation of a suspect. Police officers will often question an individual suspected of having committed a crime in an effort to get the suspect to confess or make incriminating statements. Police who question suspects must abide by certain rules. For instance, the Supreme Court has held that it violates due process if the police beat a suspect in order to obtain a confession. The Supreme Court has also held that under certain circumstances, police may not question a suspect without the suspect's attorney being present. These and other "rules" of interrogation are examined in the cases that follow.

Police may also place a suspect in a lineup. The purpose of a lineup is to see if an eyewitness to the crime can identify the person who committed the crime. To conduct a lineup, police will usually put the suspect and other individuals who are physically similar to the suspect in a line with their backs against a wall so they are all facing towards a one-way mirror behind which is the eyewitness. Each person in the lineup is asked to step forward, and the eyewitness is asked whether the person who has stepped forward is the person who committed the crime. Sometimes, the police will show an eyewitness a photographic array—a photo of the suspect's face along with photos of the faces of other individuals with similar features—instead of conducting a live physical lineup. A positive witness identification can provide both probable cause to support an arrest and evidence at trial to support a conviction. The "rules" governing lineups are also examined within this casebook.

C. THE ARREST

An arrest is a seizure of a person who is suspected of having broken the law. If the offense in question is a minor offense, the arrestee may be released with an order to appear in court at some later date. For more serious offenses, the arrestee will remain in custody, at least temporarily.

An arrest must be based on probable cause to believe that a crime has been committed and the person being arrested committed that crime. An arrest can either be warrantless, in which case it will be based upon the police officer's determination of probable cause, or pursuant to an arrest warrant issued by a judicial magistrate. If an arrest warrant is needed, a police officer must supply a magistrate with an affidavit articulating specific facts to support a finding of probable cause prior to making the arrest. If the magistrate finds probable cause to arrest, the magistrate will issue a warrant for the suspect's arrest. You will learn about the "rules" governing arrests within.

D. JUDICIAL DETERMINATION OF PROBABLE CAUSE

If an individual is arrested and taken into custody without an arrest warrant, a prompt judicial determination of probable cause must be made after the arrest. A magistrate judge will review the facts and circumstances underlying the arrest to ensure that the officer had probable cause to support the arrest. The judicial determination of probable cause is presumed to be sufficiently prompt if it occurs within 48 hours of the arrest. If the magistrate judge finds that the arrest is not supported by probable cause, the arrestee will be released from custody.

E. THE PROSECUTOR'S DECISION TO CHARGE

Once an individual has been arrested, the prosecutor must decide whether to formally charge the arrestee. The prosecutor's charge might be the same or different from the original charge for which the individual was arrested. In some cases, the prosecutor may send the case back to the police for further investigation. In other cases, the prosecutor may simply decline to file any charges at all. If the prosecutor decides to go forward with prosecution, the prosecutor will file a criminal complaint with the court. The complaint serves as the initial charging document.

In exercising its charging discretion, the prosecutor should follow ethical obligations articulated in the Model Rules of Professional Conduct (or her state's ethics code). Section 3–1.2(b) of the ABA Criminal Justice System: Standards for the Prosecution Function reminds prosecutors of these ethical obligations:

> The primary duty of the prosecutor is to seek justice within the bounds of the law, not merely to convict. The prosecutor serves the public interest and should act with integrity and balanced judgment to increase public safety both by pursuing appropriate criminal charges of appropriate severity, and by exercising discretion to not pursue criminal charges in appropriate circumstances. The prosecutor should seek to protect the innocent and convict the guilty, consider the interests of victims and witnesses, and respect the constitutional and legal rights of all persons, including suspects and defendants.

The prosecutor's decision to charge is completely discretionary. Before the case can go to trial, however, either a magistrate judge through a preliminary hearing or a grand jury will assess the case for probable cause. The preliminary hearing and the grand jury proceeding act as checks on the prosecutor's charging discretion. Additionally, most prosecutors serve as elected officials. As such, they are subject to voter referendum for their charging decisions.

F. INITIAL APPEARANCE OR ARRAIGNMENT ON THE COMPLAINT

An arrestee who is taken into custody and charged must be brought before a magistrate judge within a short time after the arrest. At this initial appearance, sometimes called the arraignment on the complaint, the magistrate judge will inform the defendant of the charge or charges against him and of various constitutional rights, such as the right to remain silent. In many jurisdictions, the magistrate judge will also decide at this initial appearance whether to release the defendant on bail or continue to keep the defendant in custody pending trial. If the defendant is indigent and the government is seeking jail time, the magistrate judge will assign a court appointed attorney. The magistrate will also set a date for the preliminary hearing at this time.

G. THE PRELIMINARY HEARING

The preliminary hearing is an adversarial proceeding conducted by a magistrate judge who is charged with evaluating the case to determine whether there is probable cause to support the charges contained in the complaint. The defendant has a right to be present at the preliminary hearing, a right to counsel, and a right to cross-examine the prosecution's witnesses. The defendant may also testify at the preliminary hearing and present evidence. It is not common for a defendant to present a full-blown case at the preliminary hearing because the government's burden of proof is so low. The government just needs to convince the magistrate judge that there is probable cause to believe a crime has been committed and that the defendant committed it. It does not need to establish every element of the charged offense or offenses beyond a reasonable doubt as it would at trial. In most cases, the magistrate judge will find probable cause and bind the defendant over for trial.

Rather than reveal too much of its defense strategy, the defense will usually use the preliminary hearing to obtain a preview of the prosecution's case and lock in the testimony of the prosecution's witnesses. If the magistrate judge finds that the case lacks probable cause, she will dismiss the case. If the magistrate judge finds probable cause, the defendant will be bound over for trial. If grand jury review is not required, a document drafted by the prosecutor, called an information, will replace the complaint as the formal charging document in the case.

H. THE GRAND JURY

The Fifth Amendment to the U.S. Constitution gives felony defendants the right to an indictment by a grand jury. The Supreme Court has declined to apply this right to the states through the Due Process Clause of the Fourteenth Amendment. This means that in most states, it is up to the prosecutor whether to proceed by way of preliminary hearing or grand jury proceeding.

A grand jury proceeding is a one-sided proceeding at which the prosecutor presents evidence to the grand jurors without participation by defense counsel. The grand jury is tasked with deciding whether there is probable cause to support the indictment, which the prosecutor has drafted. If the grand jury does not find probable cause to support the charges, it will issue a no bill, and the charges will be dropped. If the grand jury finds probable cause, it may return the indictment, which will replace the complaint as the formal charging document in the case once it is filed with the court.

I. ARRAIGNMENT ON THE INFORMATION OR INDICTMENT

After an information or indictment has been filed, the defendant will be arraigned before the trial court. At this proceeding, the defendant will be informed of the charges against him and asked to enter a plea. The defendant may plead guilty, not guilty, or nolo contendere (no contest). If the defendant pleads guilty or nolo contendere, the judge must assure that the plea is voluntary and that the defendant understands the charges, the constitutional rights that the defendant is waiving by entering a plea, and the consequences of the plea, before accepting the plea. If the defendant pleads not guilty, the judge will set a date for trial.

J. PRETRIAL MOTIONS

In preparation for trial, both the defense and prosecution may file pretrial motions. For example, a defendant may file a motion to suppress physical evidence obtained in a police search, arguing that the government violated his Fourth Amendment rights in obtaining the evidence. The defendant may move to exclude incriminating statements he made to the police from being admitted at trial, arguing that they were obtained in violation of due process or his Fifth Amendment privilege against self-incrimination. Either side may file a motion to exclude evidence that the other side plans to present on the ground that it is not relevant or reliable.

K. DISCOVERY

Discovery is the name for the process through which prosecutors and defense attorneys share information about the case. The discovery process is predominantly governed by rules and statutes. In federal court, for instance, Rule 16 of the Federal Rules of Criminal Procedure explains the obligations of both the prosecution and the defense to disclose information. Sometimes, discovery is governed by the U.S. Constitution. For example, under what is known as the *Brady* rule, the prosecutor has a constitutional duty to disclose evidence that is both favorable to the accused and material to guilt or punishment.

Discovery in criminal cases is much more limited than discovery in civil cases, even though a defendant's liberty is often at stake in a criminal case. Regardless of the limitations set forth in the discovery rules, some prosecutor's offices engage in open-file discovery, which means the office will allow the defendant access to all of the information in its files, aside from attorney work-product. Other offices will only disclose the bare minimum required by the rules and statutes governing discovery.

L. PLEA NEGOTIATIONS

Most criminal cases are resolved by a guilty plea instead of a trial. The process of negotiating a plea, wherein the defendant usually agrees to plead guilty to a lesser offense in exchange for some concession from the prosecution, is commonly known as plea bargaining. The benefit of plea bargaining from the prosecution's standpoint is a guaranteed conviction. The benefit to the defendant is a reduction in criminal liability or jail time.

A plea bargain can be reached at any stage of the process, even as late as during jury deliberations. Most plea agreements, however, are reached prior to trial. Before a judge will accept a defendant's guilty plea, the judge will have a conversation with the defendant on the record, known as the plea colloquy, in order to make sure the defendant understands his constitutional rights and is knowingly and voluntarily waiving those rights. Additionally, the court[a] must be assured that the plea is voluntary and that the defendant has been advised by competent legal counsel.

M. TRIAL, SENTENCING, AND APPEAL

At trial, the government carries the burden of proving every element of the charged offense beyond a reasonable doubt. Although the Sixth Amendment to the U.S. Constitution guarantees a right to a trial by an impartial jury in all criminal prosecutions, the Supreme Court has held

---

[a] When you see a reference to "the court," this sometimes means the institution of the court in which the defendant is being prosecuted. At other times, "the court" is just another way of referring to the judge.

CH. 1 INTRODUCTION TO THE CRIMINAL JUSTICE PROCESS

that the jury trial right applies only to defendants charged with a non-petty offense.[b]

At the beginning of the trial, both sides will make an opening statement. The opening statement serves as a summary of what each side believes the evidence will show. The prosecutor goes first because it bears the ultimate burden of proof. After both sides have made their opening statements, the prosecution will present its case.

At the close of the prosecution's case, the defense may make a motion to dismiss the case, also known as a motion for a judgment of acquittal, arguing that no reasonable jury could find the defendant guilty beyond a reasonable doubt based on the evidence presented. In considering the motion, the court must review the evidence in the light most favorable to the prosecution. If the court grants this motion, the charges against the defendant will be dismissed, and the court will enter a judgment of acquittal. If the court denies the motion, the trial will continue and the defense will be given an opportunity to present its case. The defense is not required to present any witnesses, nor is the defendant required to testify. If the defendant elects not to testify, the court will usually instruct the jurors not to make any negative inferences from the defendant's decision not to testify. At the close of the defendant's case-in-chief, the prosecution may present rebuttal witnesses.

After both sides rest, the parties will give their closing arguments. The prosecution will present its closing argument first. The defense will follow with its closing argument. The prosecution is allowed to have the final word.

After closing arguments, the defense can renew or make a motion for a judgment of acquittal for the first time. Importantly, the failure to make such a motion can foreclose the defendant's ability to appeal a guilty verdict based on a claim that the evidence was insufficient to convict. If the motion is granted, the court will enter a judgment of acquittal. If the motion is denied, the court will proceed to instruct the jury on the law applicable to the case. The exact language of the instructions given to the jury is a matter that is litigated outside the presence of the jury. Both sides can propose jury instructions, but the judge will make the final decision as to which jury instructions will be given to the jury and the wording of those jury instructions. Any objections to the instructions will be preserved on the record in case of error and appeal.

After the judge instructs the jury, the jury will retire to deliberate on its verdict. The jury will typically enter either a verdict of guilty or not

---

[b] Blanton v. City of North Las Vegas, 489 U.S. 538 (1989). In federal court, the defendant can waive his right to a trial by jury and elect to be tried by a judge only if the prosecutor consents and the judge approves. Singer v. United States, 380 U.S. 24 (1965). A trial before a judge is called a bench trial.

guilty. The jury is not required to give an explanation for its verdict. If the verdict is not guilty, the charges will be dismissed, and the defendant will be released. As a general matter, the Double Jeopardy Clause will protect the defendant who has been acquitted from being retried for the same offense. If the verdict is guilty, the court will enter a judgment of conviction and set a date for sentencing.

In preparation for sentencing, often a probation officer will prepare a presentence report for the court. The report will provide a summary of the case, information about the defendant's criminal history, and a recommendation as to the sentence. The court has broad discretion to choose whatever it feels is the appropriate sentence, as long as it complies with any applicable statutory minimums or maximums set by the legislature. The court may sentence the defendant to a term of imprisonment and/or order the defendant to pay a fine. If the court feels a term of incarceration is unnecessary, the court may sentence the defendant to probation or order the defendant to perform community service. The court can also order the defendant to pay restitution to the victim. In federal court, the sentencing judge will usually consult the federal sentencing guidelines and sentence the defendant within the applicable guideline range.

Following sentencing, the defendant may file an appeal to the intermediate court of appeals to try to overturn his conviction. The appellate court can either affirm the conviction or reverse it. If the appellate court reverses the conviction, it will usually order a new trial. Sometimes, however, the appellate court will reverse the conviction and order the charges dismissed. If the intermediate court of appeals affirms the conviction, the defendant can try to appeal to the supreme court of the state in which he was convicted. Review by the state supreme court is completely discretionary, which means the state supreme court can choose not to hear the case without providing any reason for its action. A judgment of conviction becomes final after the highest court of the state affirms the conviction or declines to hear the case.[c]

---

[c] If the case involves an issue of broad significance, the defendant may try to appeal to the U.S. Supreme Court. Review by the U.S. Supreme Court is also completely discretionary. After exhausting the appeal process, the defendant may try to get released from custody by filing a petition for habeas corpus. A petition for habeas corpus in federal court must be based upon an alleged violation of the U.S. Constitution other than the Fourth Amendment. Stone v. Powell, 428 U.S. 465 (1976). Proceeding by way of habeas corpus is often called collateral review because it is done outside the appeal process.

CHAPTER 2

WHAT CONSTITUTES A SEARCH?

■ ■ ■

The Fourth Amendment to the U.S. Constitution provides:

The right of the people to be secure in their persons, houses, papers, and effects, against unreasonable searches and seizures, shall not be violated, and no Warrants shall issue, but upon probable cause, supported by Oath or affirmation, and particularly describing the place to be searched, and the persons or things to be seized.

The Fourth Amendment expressly proscribes unreasonable searches and seizures. Thus, as a preliminary matter, a court reviewing a defendant's claim that his Fourth Amendment rights were violated must determine whether a "search" or a "seizure" within the meaning of the Fourth Amendment took place. If the court finds that a search or seizure occurred, then it must decide whether that search or seizure was unreasonable.

The first case in this chapter, *Katz v. United States*, is the Court's seminal opinion on what constitutes a search for purposes of the Fourth Amendment. In *Katz*, the Court declines to apply the trespass doctrine, which had previously governed the question of whether a search occurred, and instead embraces a test that focuses on expectations of privacy. Under the trespass doctrine, a court trying to decide whether a search within the meaning of the Fourth Amendment had taken place would ask whether there had been a physical intrusion or trespass by government agents into a constitutionally protected area. *See, e.g.*, Olmstead v. United States, 277 U.S. 438 (1928) (finding no violation of the Fourth Amendment where the government wiretapped the defendants' telephone lines without trespassing upon any property belonging to the defendants).

In Katz *and the Origins of the "Reasonable Expectation of Privacy" Test*, Peter Winn provides us with a behind the scenes look at how the two-part test in Justice Harlan's concurring opinion, rather than language from Justice Stewart's majority opinion, became the test for deciding whether a search has occurred within the meaning of the Fourth Amendment.

In the ensuing cases, the Court relies upon a variety of considerations when deciding whether a search has taken place within the meaning of the Fourth Amendment. As you read these cases, try to figure out what factors inform the Court's determination of whether the government has conducted a search. In other words, try to discern what factors the Court thinks are relevant in deciding whether the government has intruded upon a reasonable expectation of privacy. The excerpts in this chapter by Professors Sherry Colb, Daniel Solove, and Carrie Leonetti help illuminate some of these factors.

KATZ V. UNITED STATES
Supreme Court of the United States
389 U.S. 347, 88 S. Ct. 507, 19 L. Ed. 2d 576 (1967)

JUSTICE STEWART delivered the opinion of the Court.

The petitioner was convicted * * * [of] transmitting wagering information by telephone from Los Angeles to Miami and Boston in violation of a federal statute. At trial the Government was permitted, over the petitioner's objection, to introduce evidence of the petitioner's end of telephone conversations, overheard by FBI agents who had attached an electronic listening and recording device to the outside of the public telephone booth from which he had placed his calls. In affirming his conviction, the Court of Appeals rejected the contention that the recordings had been obtained in violation of the Fourth Amendment, because "[t]here was no physical entrance into the area occupied by, (the petitioner)." We granted certiorari in order to consider the constitutional questions thus presented.

The petitioner had phrased those questions as follows:

A. Whether a public telephone booth is a constitutionally protected area so that evidence obtained by attaching an electronic listening recording device to the top of such a booth is obtained in violation of the right to privacy of the user of the booth.

B. Whether physical penetration of a constitutionally protected area is necessary before a search and seizure can be said to be violative of the Fourth Amendment to the United States Constitution.

We decline to adopt this formulation of the issues. In the first place the correct solution of Fourth Amendment problems is not necessarily promoted by incantation of the phrase "constitutionally protected area." Secondly, the Fourth Amendment cannot be translated into a general constitutional "right to privacy." That Amendment protects individual privacy against certain kinds of governmental intrusion, but its protections go further, and often have nothing to do with privacy at all. Other provisions of the Constitution protect personal privacy from other forms of governmental invasion. But the protection of a person's general right to privacy—his right to be let alone by other people—is, like the protection of his property and of his very life, left largely to the law of the individual States.

Because of the misleading way the issues have been formulated, the parties have attached great significance to the characterization of the telephone booth from which the petitioner placed his calls. The petitioner has strenuously argued that the booth was a "constitutionally protected area." The Government has maintained with equal vigor that it was not. But this effort to decide whether or not a given "area," viewed in the abstract, is "constitutionally protected" deflects attention from the problem presented by this case. For the Fourth Amendment protects people, not places. What a person knowingly exposes to the public, even in his own home or office, is not a subject of Fourth Amendment protection. But what he seeks to preserve as private, even in an area accessible to the public, may be constitutionally protected.

The Government stresses the fact that the telephone booth from which the petitioner made his calls was constructed partly of glass, so that he was as visible after he entered it as he would have been if he had remained outside. But what he sought to exclude when he entered the booth was not the intruding eye—it was the uninvited ear. He did not shed his right to do so simply because he made his calls from a place where he might be seen. No less than an individual in a business office, in a friend's apartment, or in a taxicab, a person in a telephone booth may rely upon the protection of the Fourth Amendment. One who occupies it, shuts the door behind him, and pays the toll that permits him to place a call is surely entitled to assume that the words he utters into the mouthpiece will not be broadcast to the world. To read the Constitution more narrowly is to ignore the vital role that the public telephone has come to play in private communication.

The Government contends, however, that the activities of its agents in this case should not be tested by Fourth Amendment requirements, for the surveillance technique they employed involved no physical penetration of the telephone booth from which the petitioner placed his calls. It is true that the absence of such penetration was at one time thought to foreclose further Fourth Amendment inquiry * * *. But "[t]he premise that property interests control the right of the Government to search and seize has been discredited." Thus, although a closely divided Court supposed in *Olmstead* that surveillance without any trespass and without the seizure of any material object fell outside the ambit of the Constitution, we have since departed from the narrow view on which that decision rested. * * * [O]nce it is recognized that the Fourth Amendment protects people—and not simply "areas"—against unreasonable searches and seizures it becomes clear that the reach of that Amendment cannot turn upon the presence or absence of a physical intrusion into any given enclosure.

We conclude that * * * the "trespass" doctrine * * * can no longer be regarded as controlling. The Government's activities in electronically listening to and recording the petitioner's words violated the privacy upon which he justifiably relied while using the telephone booth and thus constituted a "search and seizure" within the meaning of the Fourth Amendment. The fact that the electronic device employed to achieve that end did not happen to penetrate the wall of the booth can have no constitutional significance.

The question remaining for decision, then, is whether the search and seizure conducted in this case complied with constitutional standards. In that regard, the Government's position is that its agents acted in an entirely defensible manner: They did not begin their electronic surveillance until investigation of the petitioner's activities had established a strong probability that he was using the telephone in question to transmit gambling information to persons in other States, in violation of federal law. Moreover, the surveillance was limited, both in scope and in duration, to the specific purpose of establishing the contents of the petitioner's unlawful telephonic communications. The agents confined their surveillance to the brief periods during which he used the telephone booth, and they took great care to overhear only the conversations of the petitioner himself.

Accepting this account of the Government's actions as accurate, it is clear that this surveillance was so narrowly circumscribed that a duly authorized magistrate, properly notified of the need for such investigation, specifically informed of the basis on which it was to proceed, and clearly apprised of the precise intrusion it would entail, could constitutionally have authorized, with appropriate safeguards, the very limited search and seizure that the Government asserts in fact took place. * * * [A] judicial order could have accommodated "the legitimate needs of law enforcement" by authorizing the carefully limited use of electronic surveillance.

* * * It is apparent that the agents in this case acted with restraint. Yet the inescapable fact is that this restraint was imposed by the agents themselves, not by a judicial officer. They were not required, before commencing the search, to present their estimate of probable cause for detached scrutiny by a neutral magistrate. They were not compelled, during the conduct of the search itself, to observe precise limits established in advance by a specific court order. Nor were they directed, after the search had been completed, to notify the authorizing magistrate in detail of all that had been seized. In the absence of such safeguards, this Court has never sustained a search upon the sole ground that officers reasonably expected to find evidence of a particular crime and voluntarily confined their activities to the least intrusive means consistent with that end. Searches conducted without warrants have been held unlawful "notwithstanding facts unquestionably showing probable cause," for the Constitution requires "that the deliberate, impartial judgment of a judicial

officer * * * be interposed between the citizen and the police * * *." "Over and again this Court has emphasized that the mandate of the (Fourth) Amendment requires adherence to judicial processes," and that searches conducted outside the judicial process, without prior approval by judge or magistrate, are *per se* unreasonable under the Fourth Amendment—subject only to a few specifically established and well-delineated exceptions. * * *

The Government * * * urges the creation of a new exception to cover this case. It argues that surveillance of a telephone booth should be exempted from the usual requirement of advance authorization by a magistrate upon a showing of probable cause. We cannot agree. Omission of such authorization "bypasses the safeguards provided by an objective predetermination of probable cause, and substitutes instead the far less reliable procedure of an after-the-event justification for the * * * search, too likely to be subtly influenced by the familiar shortcomings of hindsight judgment." And bypassing a neutral predetermination of the scope of a search leaves individuals secure from Fourth Amendment violations "only in the discretion of the police."

These considerations do not vanish when the search in question is transferred from the setting of a home, an office, or a hotel room to that of a telephone booth. Wherever a man may be, he is entitled to know that he will remain free from unreasonable searches and seizures. The government agents here ignored "the procedure of antecedent justification * * * that is central to the Fourth Amendment," a procedure that we hold to be a constitutional precondition of the kind of electronic surveillance involved in this case. Because the surveillance here failed to meet that condition, and because it led to the petitioner's conviction, the judgment must be reversed. * * *

JUSTICE HARLAN concurring. * * *

As the Court's opinion states, "the Fourth Amendment protects people, not places." The question, however, is what protection it affords to those people. Generally, as here, the answer to that question requires reference to a "place." My understanding of the rule that has emerged from prior decisions is that there is a twofold requirement, first that a person have exhibited an actual (subjective) expectation of privacy and, second, that the expectation be one that society is prepared to recognize as "reasonable." Thus a man's home is, for most purposes, a place where he expects privacy, but objects, activities, or statements that he exposes to the "plain view" of outsiders are not "protected" because no intention to keep them to himself has been exhibited. On the other hand, conversations in the open would not be protected against being overheard, for the expectation of privacy under the circumstances would be unreasonable.

The critical fact in this case is that "[o]ne who occupies it (a telephone booth), shuts the door behind him, and pays the toll that permits him to place a call is surely entitled to assume" that his conversation is not being intercepted. The point is not that the booth is "accessible to the public" at other times, but that it is a temporarily private place whose momentary occupants' expectations of freedom from intrusion are recognized as reasonable. * * *

JUSTICE BLACK dissenting.

* * * [T]he language of the Amendment is the crucial place to look in construing a written document such as our Constitution. The Fourth Amendment says that

> The right of the people to be secure in their persons, houses, papers, and effects, against unreasonable searches and seizures, shall not be violated, and no Warrants shall issue, but upon probable cause, supported by Oath or affirmation, and particularly describing the place to be searched, and the persons or things to be seized.

The first clause protects "persons, houses, papers, and effects, against unreasonable searches and seizures * * *." These words connote the idea of tangible things with size, form, and weight, things capable of being searched, seized, or both. The second clause of the Amendment still further establishes its Framers' purpose to limit its protection to tangible things by providing that no warrants shall issue but those "particularly describing the place to be searched, and the persons or things to be seized." A conversation overheard by eavesdropping, whether by plain snooping or wiretapping, is not tangible and, under the normally accepted meanings of the words, can neither be searched nor seized. * * * I must conclude that the Fourth Amendment simply does not apply to eavesdropping.

Tapping telephone wires, of course, was an unknown possibility at the time the Fourth Amendment was adopted. But eavesdropping (and wiretapping is nothing more than eavesdropping by telephone) was * * * "an ancient practice which at common law was condemned as a nuisance. In those days the eavesdropper listened by naked ear under the eaves of houses or their windows, or beyond their walls seeking out private discourse." There can be no doubt that the Framers were aware of this practice, and if they had desired to outlaw or restrict the use of evidence obtained by eavesdropping, I believe that they would have used the appropriate language to do so in the Fourth Amendment. They certainly would not have left such a task to the ingenuity of language-stretching judges. * * *

[JUSTICE DOUGLAS' concurring opinion and JUSTICE WHITE's concurring opinion have been omitted.]

KATZ AND THE ORIGINS OF THE "REASONABLE EXPECTATION OF PRIVACY" TEST

Peter Winn
40 McGeorge L. Rev. 1 (2009)

Why should we care about the history of *Katz v. United States*? The 1967 Supreme Court case, of course, formulated the "reasonable expectation of privacy" test that is used to decide when a governmental intrusion constitutes a "search" under the Fourth Amendment. But the test extends beyond the confines of the Constitution; it has found its way into common law and statutes, and even the laws of other countries. In short, *Katz v. United States* represents a great touchstone in the law of privacy, and Judge [Harvey] Schneider's memoir of his experience as the lawyer for Charles Katz gives us a glimpse into the origins of an important legal doctrine and a rare peek into the human side of the development of law. * * *

Although the majority opinion is a masterful example of judicial politics, and presents a reasoned defense of the result, it is not without its flaws. It begins with a highly unusual attack on counsel—both the petitioner's attorneys as well as the government's—criticizing them for framing the issue as "whether a public telephone booth is a constitutionally protected area so that evidence obtained by attaching an electronic listening recording device to the top of such a booth is obtained in violation of the right to privacy of the user of the booth." However, this judicial "frame" was not invented by the lawyers, but had been used explicitly by the Court itself in numerous earlier Fourth Amendment cases. * * * Furthermore, when the Court granted *certiorari*, it framed the issues in precisely this manner. * * * Once the Court accepted this formulation, the parties would be expected to address only those issues in their briefs and argument. * * *

Moreover, the Court's criticism is surprisingly inaccurate. Katz's attorneys specifically argued in their opening brief that the old trespass test had been discredited and needed to be replaced with a test based not on property but on a right of privacy. Furthermore, [a] passage from the opinion * * * appears to have borrowed the specific language it used to make this point from the petitioner's brief. And one can find other echoes of the petitioner's briefs in the text of the majority opinion. Of course, it is not unusual for a court to borrow, without attribution, arguments, ideas, and even explicit passages from a brief filed by counsel. The practice exemplifies the fundamental collaborative nature of the legal process. Lawyers usually consider it a high compliment when a court borrows directly from their briefs, for it shows the court's respect for the quality of their work product. What is unusual is to see such borrowings accompanied by criticism of counsel for missing the point.

There is an even more surprising mistake in the majority opinion: When one listens to the oral argument or reads the transcript, one recognizes that it was counsel for the petitioner who first took the position that the manner in which the issues had been framed (by reference to a "constitutionally protected area") needed to be altered, and who reformulated the issues into exactly the manner ultimately adopted by the Court. It appears that the oral argument persuaded the Court to reformulate the issues. However, instead of acknowledging flaws in the earlier cases and correcting the analysis, the Court's opinion blames *counsel* for getting it wrong.

The Justices, of course, did not intentionally make what we now can see was a highly embarrassing mistake. The erroneous criticism of counsel first appears in the draft opinion prepared by Stewart's law clerk, who likely never attended the oral argument. The criticism of counsel for missing the point, after adopting arguments from the brief, is more difficult to explain. But whatever the explanation, no one appears to have noticed the problem before the opinion was published.

In addition to its embarrassing attack on counsel, the majority opinion contains an important weakness in its legal analysis. The opinion creates the impression of a revolutionary upheaval of the previous regime, while using criticism of counsel to sidestep the otherwise difficult job of addressing prior inconsistent case law with candor. * * * While announcing a new understanding of the Fourth Amendment based on a right of privacy, it says nothing about how this newfound right is to be determined. In eliminating the trespass standard of *Olmstead*, it offers nothing by way of a standard to replace it. How then, has a Supreme Court case, which contains so many mistakes and which promised a legal revolution that it ultimately could never deliver, come to occupy such an unchallenged position in the modern legal Pantheon? The short answer is that the majority opinion has been largely ignored. Instead, most courts cite to the * * * concurring opinion by Justice Harlan[.]

Within a year, the Supreme Court started to use Harlan's "reasonable expectation of privacy" test as the standard in its Fourth Amendment jurisprudence. Within a decade, Harlan's test became so familiar that the Court officially recognized it as the essence of the *Katz* decision—a rare instance where a concurrence effectively replaced a majority opinion. * * *

Where * * * did the reasonable expectation of privacy test come from? The test is not mentioned in the record of the lower courts, or in the pleadings and briefs filed in the Supreme Court. Until recently, most observers treated the test as if Harlan made it up out of thin air. However, as the few who have taken the time to read the transcripts or listen to the oral arguments know, the idea came from the lawyers—specifically one lawyer—Harvey (now Judge) Schneider who, with Burton Marks, represented the petitioner, Charles Katz.

* * * Judge Schneider * * * realized that the days of the *Olmstead* trespass standard were numbered. In the days leading up to the oral argument, the young lawyer began to rethink his strategy. He suddenly realized that expectations of privacy should be based on an objective standard, one that could be formulated using the reasonable man standard from tort law. In an act of great courage, he decided to focus all of his energy during oral argument on articulating the new standard for the Court. As we have seen, the test had not been articulated in the briefs, and presenting it at oral argument arguably constituted a breach of protocol. Only a young and inexperienced lawyer would ever have tried such a thing. * * *

The credit for the reasonable expectation of privacy test thus belongs to two men: one of them, a bright, young, and relatively inexperienced lawyer who nevertheless had great talent and nerve; the other, a wise old judge who knew how to listen. To their lasting credit, both men saw the significance of an important legal idea when few others did, and had the courage to follow through with that idea, resulting in what is now universally recognized as the great cornerstone of Fourth Amendment jurisprudence.

A. THE OPEN FIELDS DOCTRINE

In a number of cases, the Court has drawn a distinction between "curtilage" and "open fields." The home and its curtilage—roughly described as the area in immediate proximity to the home—are both protected by the Fourth Amendment. Beyond the curtilage, however, is "open fields," land that enjoys no Fourth Amendment protection. Under what has become known as the Open Fields Doctrine, law enforcement agents are permitted to enter and search property deemed "open fields" without a warrant. Even if law enforcement officers trespass onto private property that is considered an "open field," no Fourth Amendment violation has occurred. The term "open fields" is somewhat of a misnomer since land does not have to be either "open" or a "field" in order to constitute open fields.

How should courts decide whether lands surrounding a home constitutes curtilage or open fields? Is the Fourth Amendment protection provided to the curtilage as strong as that provided to the home? The next case, *Florida v. Riley*, begins to answer these questions. *Florida v. Jardines*, the last case in this chapter, also sheds light on the answers to these questions.

FLORIDA V. RILEY
Supreme Court of the United States
488 U.S. 445, 109 S. Ct. 693, 102 L. Ed. 2d 835 (1989)

JUSTICE WHITE delivered the opinion of the Court.

On certification to it by a lower state court, the Florida Supreme Court addressed the following question: "Whether surveillance of the interior of a partially covered greenhouse in a residential backyard from the vantage point of a helicopter located 400 feet above the greenhouse constitutes a 'search' for which a warrant is required under the Fourth Amendment and Article I, § 12 of the Florida Constitution." The court answered the question in the affirmative, and we granted the State's petition for certiorari challenging that conclusion.

Respondent Riley lived in a mobile home located on five acres of rural property. A greenhouse was located 10 to 20 feet behind the mobile home. Two sides of the greenhouse were enclosed. The other two sides were not enclosed but the contents of the greenhouse were obscured from view from surrounding property by trees, shrubs, and the mobile home. The greenhouse was covered by corrugated roofing panels, some translucent and some opaque. At the time relevant to this case, two of the panels, amounting to approximately 10% of the roof area, were missing. A wire fence surrounded the mobile home and the greenhouse, and the property was posted with a "DO NOT ENTER" sign.

This case originated with an anonymous tip to the Pasco County Sheriff's office that marijuana was being grown on respondent's property. When an investigating officer discovered that he could not see the contents of the greenhouse from the road, he circled twice over respondent's property in a helicopter at the height of 400 feet. With his naked eye, he was able to see through the openings in the roof and one or more of the open sides of the greenhouse and to identify what he thought was marijuana growing in the structure. A warrant was obtained based on these observations, and the ensuing search revealed marijuana growing in the greenhouse. Respondent was charged with possession of marijuana under Florida law. The trial court granted his motion to suppress; the Florida Court of Appeals reversed but certified the case to the Florida Supreme Court, which quashed the decision of the Court of Appeals and reinstated the trial court's suppression order.

We agree with the State's submission that our decision in *California v. Ciraolo,* controls this case. There, acting on a tip, the police inspected the back-yard of a particular house while flying in a fixed-wing aircraft at 1,000 feet. With the naked eye the officers saw what they concluded was marijuana growing in the yard. A search warrant was obtained on the strength of this airborne inspection, and marijuana plants were found. The trial court refused to suppress this evidence, but a state appellate court held that the inspection violated the Fourth and Fourteenth Amendments to the United States Constitution, and that the warrant was therefore invalid. We in turn reversed, holding that the inspection was not a search subject to the Fourth Amendment. We recognized that the yard was within the curtilage[a] of the house, that a fence shielded the yard from observation from the street, and that the occupant had a subjective expectation of privacy. We held, however, that such an expectation was not reasonable and not one "that society is prepared to honor." * * * "What a person knowingly exposes to the public, even in his own home or office, is not a subject of Fourth Amendment protection." As a general proposition, the police may see what may be seen "from a public vantage point where [they have] a right to be." Thus the police, like the public, would have been free to inspect the backyard garden from the street if their view had been unobstructed. They were likewise free to inspect the yard from the vantage point of an aircraft flying in the navigable airspace as this plane was. "In an age where private and commercial flight in the public airways is routine, it is unreasonable for respondent to expect that his marijuana plants were constitutionally protected from being observed with the naked eye from an altitude of 1,000 feet. The Fourth Amendment simply does not require the police traveling in the public airways at this altitude to obtain a warrant in order to observe what is visible to the naked eye."

We arrive at the same conclusion in the present case. In this case, as in *Ciraolo*, the property surveyed was within the curtilage of respondent's home. Riley no doubt intended and expected that his greenhouse would not be open to public inspection, and the precautions he took protected against ground-level observation. Because the sides and roof of his greenhouse were left partially open, however, what was growing in the greenhouse was subject to viewing from the air. Under the holding in *Ciraolo*, Riley could not reasonably have expected the contents of his greenhouse to be immune from examination by an officer seated in a fixed-wing aircraft flying in navigable airspace. * * * "[P]rivate and commercial flight [by helicopter] in the public airways is routine" in this country, and there is no indication that such flights are unheard of in Pasco County, Florida. Riley could not reasonably have expected that his greenhouse was protected from public or official observation from a helicopter had it been flying within the navigable airspace for fixed-wing aircraft.

Nor on the facts before us, does it make a difference for Fourth Amendment purposes that the helicopter was flying at 400 feet when the officer saw what was growing in the greenhouse through the partially open

---

[a] The area immediately surrounding the home is called the curtilage and is protected by the Fourth Amendment. In *Dunn v. United States*, 480 U.S. 294 (1987), the Court identified four factors a court should weigh when trying to determine whether the area in question constitutes curtilage: (1) the area's proximity to the home, (2) whether the area is within an enclosure surrounding the home, (3) the nature of the area's uses, and (4) steps taken to protect the area from observation. *Id.* at 301.

roof and sides of the structure. We would have a different case if flying at that altitude had been contrary to law or regulation. But helicopters are not bound by the lower limits of the navigable airspace allowed to other aircraft. Any member of the public could legally have been flying over Riley's property in a helicopter at the altitude of 400 feet and could have observed Riley's greenhouse. The police officer did no more. This is not to say that an inspection of the curtilage of a house from an aircraft will always pass muster under the Fourth Amendment simply because the plane is within the navigable airspace specified by law. But it is of obvious importance that the helicopter in this case was *not* violating the law, and there is nothing in the record or before us to suggest that helicopters flying at 400 feet are sufficiently rare in this country to lend substance to respondent's claim that he reasonably anticipated that his greenhouse would not be subject to observation from that altitude. Neither is there any intimation here that the helicopter interfered with respondent's normal use of the greenhouse or of other parts of the curtilage. As far as this record reveals, no intimate details connected with the use of the home or curtilage were observed, and there was no undue noise, and no wind, dust, or threat of injury. In these circumstances, there was no violation of the Fourth Amendment.

The judgment of the Florida Supreme Court is accordingly reversed.

So ordered.

JUSTICE O'CONNOR concurring in the judgment.

I concur in the judgment reversing the Supreme Court of Florida because I agree that police observation of the greenhouse in Riley's curtilage from a helicopter passing at an altitude of 400 feet did not violate an expectation of privacy "that society is prepared to recognize as 'reasonable.'" I write separately, however, to clarify the standard I believe follows from *California v. Ciraolo*. In my view, the plurality's approach rests the scope of Fourth Amendment protection too heavily on compliance with FAA regulations whose purpose is to promote air safety, not to protect "[t]he right of the people to be secure in their persons, houses, papers, and effects, against unreasonable searches and seizures." * * *

In determining whether Riley had a reasonable expectation of privacy from aerial observation, the relevant inquiry after *Ciraolo* is not whether the helicopter was where it had a right to be under FAA regulations. Rather, consistent with *Katz*, we must ask whether the helicopter was in the public airways at an altitude at which members of the public travel with sufficient regularity that Riley's expectation of privacy from aerial observation was not "one that society is prepared to recognize as 'reasonable.'" * * * If the public rarely, if ever, travels overhead at such altitudes, the observation cannot be said to be from a vantage point generally used by the public and Riley cannot be said to have "knowingly expose[d]" his greenhouse to public view. However, if the public can generally be expected to travel over residential backyards at an altitude of 400 feet, Riley cannot reasonably expect his curtilage to be free from such aerial observation.

In my view, the defendant must bear the burden of proving that his expectation of privacy was a reasonable one, and thus that a "search" within the meaning of the Fourth Amendment even took place. * * *

Because there is reason to believe that there is considerable public use of airspace at altitudes of 400 feet and above, and because Riley introduced no evidence to the contrary before the Florida courts, I conclude that Riley's expectation that his curtilage was protected from naked-eye aerial observation from that altitude was not a reasonable one. * * *

JUSTICE BRENNAN, with whom JUSTICE MARSHALL and JUSTICE STEVENS join, dissenting.

The Court holds today that police officers need not obtain a warrant based on probable cause before circling in a helicopter 400 feet above a home in order to investigate what is taking place behind the walls of the curtilage. I cannot agree that the Fourth Amendment to the Constitution, which safeguards "[t]he right of the people to be secure in their persons, houses, papers, and effects, against unreasonable searches and seizures," tolerates such an intrusion on privacy and personal security.

The opinion for a plurality of the Court reads almost as if *Katz v. United States* had never been decided. Notwithstanding the disclaimers of its final paragraph, the opinion relies almost exclusively on the fact that the police officer conducted his surveillance from a vantage point where, under applicable Federal Aviation Administration regulations, he had a legal right to be. *Katz* teaches, however, that the relevant inquiry is whether the police surveillance "violated the privacy upon which [the defendant] justifiably relied," or as Justice Harlan put it, whether the police violated an "expectation of privacy . . . that society is prepared to recognize as 'reasonable.'" * * *

The plurality * * * summarily concludes that Riley's expectation of privacy was unreasonable because "[a]ny member of the public could legally have been flying over Riley's property in a helicopter at the altitude of 400 feet and could have observed Riley's greenhouse." This observation is, in turn, based solely on the fact that the police helicopter was within the airspace within which such craft are allowed by federal safety regulations to fly.

I agree, of course, that "[w]hat a person knowingly exposes to the public . . . is not a subject of Fourth Amendment protection." But I cannot agree that one "knowingly exposes [an area] to the public" solely because a helicopter may legally fly above it. Under the plurality's exceedingly grudging Fourth Amendment theory, the expectation of privacy is defeated if a single member of the public could conceivably position herself to see into the area in question without doing anything illegal. It is defeated whatever the difficulty a person would have in so positioning herself, and however infrequently anyone would in fact do so. In taking this view the plurality ignores the very essence of *Katz*. The reason why there is no reasonable expectation of privacy in an area that is exposed to the public is that little diminution in "the amount of privacy and freedom remaining to citizens" will result from police surveillance of something that any passerby readily sees. To pretend, as the plurality opinion does, that the same is true when the police use a helicopter to peer over high fences is, at best, disingenuous. * * *

It is a curious notion that the reach of the Fourth Amendment can be so largely defined by administrative regulations issued for purposes of flight safety.[2] It is more curious still that the plurality relies to such an extent on the legality of the officer's act, when we have consistently refused to equate police violation of the law with infringement of the Fourth Amendment.[3] But the plurality's willingness to end its inquiry when it finds that the officer was in a position he had a right to be in is misguided for an even more fundamental reason. Finding determinative the fact that the officer was where he had a right to be is, at bottom, an attempt to analogize surveillance from a helicopter to surveillance by a police officer standing on a public road and viewing evidence of crime through an open window or a gap in a fence. In such a situation, the occupant of the home may be said to lack any reasonable expectation of privacy in what can be seen from that road—even if, in fact, people rarely pass that way.

The police officer positioned 400 feet above Riley's backyard was not, however, standing on a public road. The vantage point he enjoyed was not one any citizen could readily share. His ability to see over Riley's fence depended on his use of a very expensive and sophisticated piece of machinery to which few ordinary citizens have access. In such circumstances it makes no more sense to rely on the legality of the officer's position in the skies than it would to judge the constitutionality of the wiretap in *Katz* by the legality of the officer's position outside the telephone booth. The simple inquiry whether the police officer had the legal right to be in the position from which he made his observations cannot suffice, for

---

[2] The plurality's use of the FAA regulations as a means for determining whether Riley enjoyed a reasonable expectation of privacy produces an incredible result. Fixed-wing aircraft may not be operated below 500 feet (1,000 feet over congested areas), while helicopters may be operated below those levels. Therefore, whether Riley's expectation of privacy is reasonable turns on whether the police officer at 400 feet above his curtilage is seated in an airplane or a helicopter. This cannot be the law.

[3] In *Oliver v. United States*, for example, we held that police officers who trespassed upon posted and fenced private land did not violate the Fourth Amendment, despite the fact that their action was subject to criminal sanctions. We noted that the interests vindicated by the Fourth Amendment were not identical with those served by the common law of trespass. * * *

we cannot assume that Riley's curtilage was so open to the observations of passersby in the skies that he retained little privacy or personal security to be lost to police surveillance. The question before us must be not whether the police were where they had a right to be, but whether public observation of Riley's curtilage was so commonplace that Riley's expectation of privacy in his backyard could not be considered reasonable. * * *

If indeed the purpose of the restraints imposed by the Fourth Amendment is to "safeguard the privacy and security of individuals," then it is puzzling why it should be the helicopter's noise, wind, and dust that provides the measure of whether this constitutional safeguard has been infringed. Imagine a helicopter capable of hovering just above an enclosed courtyard or patio without generating any noise, wind, or dust at all—and, for good measure, without posing any threat of injury. Suppose the police employed this miraculous tool to discover not only what crops people were growing in their greenhouses, but also what books they were reading and who their dinner guests were. Suppose, finally, that the FAA regulations remained unchanged, so that the police were undeniably "where they had a right to be." Would today's plurality continue to assert that "[t]he right of the people to be secure in their persons, houses, papers, and effects, against unreasonable searches and seizures" was not infringed by such surveillance? Yet that is the logical consequence of the plurality's rule that, so long as the police are where they have a right to be under air traffic regulations, the Fourth Amendment is offended only if the aerial surveillance interferes with the use of the backyard as a garden spot. * * *

What separates me from JUSTICE O'CONNOR is essentially an empirical matter concerning the extent of public use of the airspace at that altitude, together with the question of how to resolve that issue. * * * I think we could take judicial notice that, while there may be an occasional privately owned helicopter that flies over populated areas at an altitude of 400 feet, such flights are a rarity and are almost entirely limited to approaching or leaving airports or to reporting traffic congestion near major roadways.

* * * Because the State has greater access to information concerning customary flight patterns and because the coercive power of the State ought not be brought to bear in cases in which it is unclear whether the prosecution is a product of an unconstitutional, warrantless search, the burden of proof properly rests with the State and not with the individual defendant. The State quite clearly has not carried this burden. * * *

[JUSTICE BLACKMUN's dissenting opinion has been omitted.]

NOTE

In the next excerpt, *Open Fields in the Inner City: Application of the Curtilage Doctrine to Urban and Suburban Areas*, Carrie Leonetti examines the open fields doctrine within the context of multi-occupant dwellings and urges courts to rethink the way they treat common areas in apartment buildings and public housing projects, dwellings where the middle class, the working class, and the poor tend to reside.

OPEN FIELDS IN THE INNER CITY: APPLICATION OF THE CURTILAGE DOCTRINE TO URBAN AND SUBURBAN AREAS

Carrie Leonetti
15 Geo. Mason U. Civ. Rts. L.J. 297 (2005)

The first standard for determining whether a search has occurred for Fourth Amendment purposes is whether the individual affected has a reasonable expectation of privacy in the area searched. In the case of multi-occupant dwellings, such as apartment complexes, hotels, and motels, this determination is complicated by the fact that residents do not occupy the entire dwelling and its surrounding areas alone. Instead, certain areas of the dwelling are shared among multiple residents.

* * * The Supreme Court has afforded apartments and hotel rooms status as "homes" under the Fourth Amendment. * * * Unfortunately, however, courts have also generally ended this protection at the inside of the door of an individual apartment or motel room, largely on the basis of the *Dunn* factors [(1) the proximity of the area to the home; (2) whether the area was within an enclosure surrounding the home; (3) the nature of the uses to which the area was put; and (4) the steps taken to protect the area from observation by passers-by]. * * *

This analytical loophole has encouraged the proliferation of two increasingly popular police investigatory techniques in urban areas and among multi-occupant dwellings: canine sniffs and knock-and-talks. Both canine sniffs and knock-and-talks involve an approach only to the outer door of an individual tenant's apartment or motel room, with the entry into the unit being justified later, either by consent or by probable cause developed during the initial approach of the unit. These techniques were designed by police to gain entry for a search without obtaining a warrant and, ultimately, to avoid the encumbrances caused by the protections provided by the Fourth Amendment.

The "knock-and-talk" is an investigatory method in which the police approach a dwelling, without probable cause or a warrant, knock on the door, identify themselves as police officers, and attempt to "talk" their way inside to conduct a search of the dwelling by gaining the occupant's verbal "consent." The knock-and-talk has become extremely popular with law enforcement agencies around the country, particularly in areas of high drug activity. Despite its popularity, however, few courts have addressed its constitutionality. Nonetheless, several federal circuit courts of appeal have found that the procedure does not offend the Fourth Amendment, regardless of the time of day or night at which the search takes place. * * *

Applying a similar rationale, that a resident's privacy interest begins only inside the apartment or motel-room door, [lower] courts have held that dog sniffs of the exterior of urban dwellings, for the purpose of generating probable cause for entry therein, do not constitute searches for Fourth Amendment purposes.[a] * * *

One analytical device that courts have employed in declining to suppress the fruits of these investigatory techniques, and thereby avoiding the recognition and protection of privacy rights in the curtilage of more densely populated areas, is to rely upon a quasi-trespass theory within common areas of urban dwellings that are accessible to more than one occupant or tenant. In the context of multi-occupant dwellings, in particular, courts have generally permitted knock-and-talks and dog-sniff searches in common areas based on the theory that individual tenants lack the ability to exclude other occupants from them.

The problem with the common-area theory of curtilage is that *Katz*'s reasonable-expectation-of-privacy test is not coextensive with the property concept of an exclusive right to exclude. The example of a single apartment with two roommates living in two separate bedrooms provides a useful analogy. While each roommate has a right to exclude the other from his or her bedroom, neither has a right to exclude the other from the common areas of that apartment. Nonetheless, the two tenants together have a collective right to exclude all but each other and their guests from the entire apartment. Therefore, while one roommate could consent to a search of the living room or kitchen on behalf of the other, it does not follow that the police could conduct a warrantless search of those areas of the dwelling simply because they are common to the two roommates. * * * Like the two roommates in a shared apartment, each resident of an apartment building or motel is offended by the invasion of the common premises in the same manner that each member of a single-family household is affronted by the invasion of the curtilage.

The central principle of the Fourth Amendment is that a person may "retreat into his own home and there be free from unreasonable governmental intrusion." If privacy is confined only to areas that are exclusively occupied by a single tenant, then most Americans would be left with only a few hundred square feet in which to confine themselves from

---

[a] After this Article was published, the U.S. Supreme Court held that bringing a drug-sniffing dog to a front door of a house without a warrant constitutes an unreasonable search in violation of the Fourth Amendment. Florida v. Jardines, 569 U.S. 1 (2013).

the increasing governmental intrusions of modern life. This mistakenly ignores the collective right that the residents of an apartment building, condominium complex, or hotel have to exclude all individuals that do not have a legitimate purpose there. * * *

Ultimately, it is important to remember that the *Dunn* factors were not meant to be an exhaustive list, but rather were merely meant to illustrate the primary inquiry of the curtilage doctrine-namely, whether the area sought to be protected is one that is truly tied to the intimate activities of the home. Occupants of urban, multi-unit dwellings do participate in intimate activities associated with the privacy of a home that extend beyond the doors of their apartments into the common property of the building, such as barbequing on a back patio or sunbathing on a roof deck. These activities would clearly be factors, under *Dunn*, in determining the boundaries of curtilage on a large ranch-style home. There is no principled reason why the same activities should not generate a privacy interest in an urban setting, where privacy is all the more rare and sacred. As the Court of Appeals of Indiana explained:

> Individuals who live in apartments often hang decorations on outside doors and place doormats on the ground outside the door. Further, individuals who have apartments that exit immediately outside often place and keep personal items on their steps or porches. Simply because one lives in an apartment does not mean that he or she does not at times occupy the space immediately outside of the apartment home. Thus, one who lives in an apartment also treats the area immediately outside his or her apartment home as his or her curtilage.

* * * [Courts should] recognize that residents in apartment buildings and hotels have a reasonable expectation of privacy * * * in all common areas of the dwelling in which the residents have a right to expect that none but their cohabitants and invited guests will enter. This * * * would include hallways and enclosed yards, each of which form the curtilage of an individual unit as to all but those invited there by the resident of any other unit. The police could constitutionally conduct a knock-and-talk or dog-sniff investigation in the common areas of such a dwelling, therefore, only with a warrant issued upon probable cause or consistent with one of the well-established exceptions to the warrant requirement, such as the consent of a resident or manager. * * *

B. THE THIRD PARTY DOCTRINE

In a series of cases in the 1970s, the Supreme Court established what has become known as the third party doctrine. Under this doctrine, an individual has no reasonable expectation of privacy in information or items voluntarily conveyed to a third party. The first case in this section, *Smith*

v. *Maryland*, explains the rationale behind the third party doctrine. In *California v. Greenwood*, the Court relies in part on the third party doctrine when assessing whether a search of the defendants' trash violated the Fourth Amendment. The excerpts that follow encourage us to rethink the soundness of the third party doctrine.

SMITH V. MARYLAND
Supreme Court of the United States
442 U.S. 735, 99 S. Ct. 2577, 61 L. Ed. 2d 220 (1979)

JUSTICE BLACKMUN delivered the opinion of the Court. * * *

This case presents the question whether the installation and use of a pen register[1] constitutes a "search" within the meaning of the Fourth Amendment, made applicable to the States through the Fourteenth Amendment.

On March 5, 1976, in Baltimore, Md., Patricia McDonough was robbed. She gave the police a description of the robber and of a 1975 Monte Carlo automobile she had observed near the scene of the crime. After the robbery, McDonough began receiving threatening and obscene phone calls from a man identifying himself as the robber. On one occasion, the caller asked that she step out on her front porch; she did so, and saw the 1975 Monte Carlo she had earlier described to police moving slowly past her home. On March 16, police spotted a man who met McDonough's description driving a 1975 Monte Carlo in her neighborhood. By tracing the license plate number, police learned that the car was registered in the name of petitioner, Michael Lee Smith.

The next day, the telephone company, at police request, installed a pen register at its central offices to record the numbers dialed from the telephone at petitioner's home. The police did not get a warrant or court order before having the pen register installed. The register revealed that on March 17 a call was placed from petitioner's home to McDonough's phone. On the basis of this and other evidence, the police obtained a warrant to search petitioner's residence. The search revealed that a page in petitioner's phone book was turned down to the name and number of Patricia McDonough; the phone book was seized. Petitioner was arrested, and a six-man lineup was held on March 19. McDonough identified petitioner as the man who had robbed her.

Petitioner was indicted * * * for robbery. By pretrial motion, he sought to suppress "all fruits derived from the pen register" on the ground that the

---

[1] "A pen register is a mechanical device that records the numbers dialed on a telephone by monitoring the electrical impulses caused when the dial on the telephone is released. It does not overhear oral communications and does not indicate whether calls are actually completed." A pen register is "usually installed at a central telephone facility [and] records on a paper tape all numbers dialed from [the] line" to which it is attached.

police had failed to secure a warrant prior to its installation. The trial court denied the suppression motion, holding that the warrantless installation of the pen register did not violate the Fourth Amendment. * * * Petitioner was convicted * * *. He appealed * * *.

The Court of Appeals affirmed the judgment of conviction, holding that "there is no constitutionally protected reasonable expectation of privacy in the numbers dialed into a telephone system and hence no search within the fourth amendment is implicated by the use of a pen register installed at the central offices of the telephone company." Because there was no "search," the court concluded, no warrant was needed. * * * Certiorari was granted in order to resolve indications of conflict in the decided cases as to the restrictions imposed by the Fourth Amendment on the use of pen registers.

* * * In determining whether a particular form of government-initiated electronic surveillance is a "search" within the meaning of the Fourth Amendment, our lodestar is *Katz v. United States.* * * * This [*Katz*] inquiry * * * embraces two discrete questions. The first is whether the individual, by his conduct, has "exhibited an actual (subjective) expectation of privacy,"—whether * * * the individual has shown that "he seeks to preserve [something] as private." The second question is whether the individual's subjective expectation of privacy is "one that society is prepared to recognize as 'reasonable,'"—whether * * * the individual's expectation, viewed objectively, is "justifiable" under the circumstances.

In applying the *Katz* analysis to this case, it is important to begin by specifying precisely the nature of the state activity that is challenged. The activity here took the form of installing and using a pen register. Since the pen register was installed on telephone company property at the telephone company's central offices, petitioner obviously cannot claim that his "property" was invaded or that police intruded into a "constitutionally protected area." Petitioner's claim, rather, is that, notwithstanding the absence of a trespass, the State, as did the Government in *Katz*, infringed a "legitimate expectation of privacy" that petitioner held. Yet a pen register differs significantly from the listening device employed in *Katz*, for pen registers do not acquire the *contents* of communications.

* * * [P]etitioner's argument that [the pen register's] installation and use constituted a "search" necessarily rests upon a claim that he had a "legitimate expectation of privacy" regarding the numbers he dialed on his phone. This claim must be rejected. First, we doubt that people in general entertain any actual expectation of privacy in the numbers they dial. All telephone users realize that they must "convey" phone numbers to the telephone company, since it is through telephone company switching equipment that their calls are completed. All subscribers realize, moreover, that the phone company has facilities for making permanent records of the

numbers they dial, for they see a list of their long-distance (toll) calls on their monthly bills. In fact, pen registers and similar devices are routinely used by telephone companies "for the purposes of checking billing operations, detecting fraud and preventing violations of law." * * * Although subjective expectations cannot be scientifically gauged, it is too much to believe that telephone subscribers, under these circumstances, harbor any general expectation that the numbers they dial will remain secret.

Petitioner argues, however, that, whatever the expectations of telephone users in general, he demonstrated an expectation of privacy by his own conduct here, since he "us[ed] the telephone *in his house* to the exclusion of all others." But the site of the call is immaterial for purposes of analysis in this case. Although petitioner's conduct may have been calculated to keep the *contents* of his conversation private, his conduct was not and could not have been calculated to preserve the privacy of the number he dialed. Regardless of his location, petitioner had to convey that number to the telephone company in precisely the same way if he wished to complete his call. The fact that he dialed the number on his home phone rather than on some other phone could make no conceivable difference, nor could any subscriber rationally think that it would.

Second, even if petitioner did harbor some subjective expectation that the phone numbers he dialed would remain private, this expectation is not "one that society is prepared to recognize as 'reasonable.'" This Court consistently has held that a person has no legitimate expectation of privacy in information he voluntarily turns over to third parties. In *Miller*, for example, the Court held that a bank depositor has no "legitimate 'expectation of privacy'" in financial information "voluntarily conveyed to ... banks and exposed to their employees in the ordinary course of business."

> The depositor takes the risk, in revealing his affairs to another, that the information will be conveyed by that person to the Government. . . . This Court has held repeatedly that the Fourth Amendment does not prohibit the obtaining of information revealed to a third party and conveyed by him to Government authorities, even if the information is revealed on the assumption that it will be used only for a limited purpose and the confidence placed in the third party will not be betrayed.

Because the depositor "assumed the risk" of disclosure, the Court held that it would be unreasonable for him to expect his financial records to remain private.

This analysis dictates that petitioner can claim no legitimate expectation of privacy here. When he used his phone, petitioner voluntarily conveyed numerical information to the telephone company and "exposed" that information to its equipment in the ordinary course of business. In so doing, petitioner assumed the risk that the company would reveal to police the numbers he dialed. The switching equipment that processed those numbers is merely the modern counterpart of the operator who, in an earlier day, personally completed calls for the subscriber. Petitioner concedes that if he had placed his calls through an operator, he could claim no legitimate expectation of privacy. We are not inclined to hold that a different constitutional result is required because the telephone company has decided to automate.

We therefore conclude that petitioner in all probability entertained no actual expectation of privacy in the phone numbers he dialed, and that, even if he did, his expectation was not "legitimate." The installation and use of a pen register, consequently, was not a "search," and no warrant was required. The judgment of the Maryland Court of Appeals is affirmed. * * *

JUSTICE POWELL took no part in the consideration or decision of this case.

JUSTICE STEWART, with whom JUSTICE BRENNAN joins, dissenting.

I am not persuaded that the numbers dialed from a private telephone fall outside the constitutional protection of the Fourth and Fourteenth Amendments.

In *Katz v. United States*, the Court acknowledged the "vital role that the public telephone has come to play in private communication[s]." The role played by a private telephone is even more vital. * * *

Nevertheless, the Court today says that [the] safeguards [of the Fourth Amendment] do not extend to the numbers dialed from a private telephone, apparently because when a caller dials a number the digits may be recorded by the telephone company for billing purposes. But that observation no more than describes the basic nature of telephone calls. A telephone call simply cannot be made without the use of telephone company property and without payment to the company for the service. * * * Yet we have squarely held that the user of even a public telephone is entitled "to assume that the words he utters into the mouthpiece will not be broadcast to the world."

The central question in this case is whether a person who makes telephone calls from his home is entitled to make a similar assumption about the numbers he dials. What the telephone company does or might do with those numbers is no more relevant to this inquiry than it would be in a case involving the conversation itself. It is simply not enough to say, after *Katz*, that there is no legitimate expectation of privacy in the numbers dialed because the caller assumes the risk that the telephone company will disclose them to the police. * * *

The numbers dialed from a private telephone—although certainly more prosaic than the conversation itself—are not without "content." Most private telephone subscribers may have their own numbers listed in a publicly distributed directory, but I doubt there are any who would be happy to have broadcast to the world a list of the local or long distance numbers they have called. This is not because such a list might in some sense be incriminating, but because it easily could reveal the identities of the persons and the places called, and thus reveal the most intimate details of a person's life. * * *

JUSTICE MARSHALL, with whom JUSTICE BRENNAN joins, dissenting. * * *

Applying the standards set forth in *Katz v. United States*, the Court first determines that telephone subscribers have no subjective expectations of privacy concerning the numbers they dial. To reach this conclusion, the Court posits that individuals somehow infer from the long-distance listings on their phone bills, and from the cryptic assurances of "help" in tracing obscene calls included in "most" phone books, that pen registers are regularly used for recording local calls. But even assuming, as I do not, that individuals "typically know" that a phone company monitors calls for internal reasons, it does not follow that they expect this information to be made available to the public in general or the government in particular. Privacy is not a discrete commodity, possessed absolutely or not at all. Those who disclose certain facts to a bank or phone company for a limited business purpose need not assume that this information will be released to other persons for other purposes.

The crux of the Court's holding, however, is that whatever expectation of privacy petitioner may in fact have entertained regarding his calls, it is not one "society is prepared to recognize as 'reasonable'." In so ruling, the Court determines that individuals who convey information to third parties have "assumed the risk" of disclosure to the government. This analysis is misconceived in two critical respects.

Implicit in the concept of assumption of risk is some notion of choice. At least in the third-party consensual surveillance cases, which first incorporated risk analysis into Fourth Amendment doctrine, the defendant presumably had exercised some discretion in deciding who should enjoy his confidential communications. By contrast here, unless a person is prepared to forgo use of what for many has become a personal or professional necessity, he cannot help but accept the risk of surveillance. It is idle to speak of "assuming" risks in contexts where, as a practical matter, individuals have no realistic alternative. * * *

In my view, whether privacy expectations are legitimate within the meaning of *Katz* depends not on the risks an individual can be presumed to accept when imparting information to third parties, but on the risks he should be forced to assume in a free and open society. * * * And for those "extensive intrusions that significantly jeopardize [individuals'] sense of security ... more than self-restraint by law enforcement officials is required."

The use of pen registers, I believe, constitutes such an extensive intrusion. To hold otherwise ignores the vital role telephonic communication plays in our personal and professional relationships, as well as the First and Fourth Amendment interests implicated by unfettered official surveillance. Privacy in placing calls is of value not only to those engaged in criminal activity. The prospect of unregulated governmental monitoring will undoubtedly prove disturbing even to those with nothing illicit to hide. Many individuals, including members of unpopular political organizations or journalists with confidential sources, may legitimately wish to avoid disclosure of their personal contacts. Permitting governmental access to telephone records on less than probable cause may thus impede certain forms of political affiliation and journalistic endeavor that are the hallmark of a truly free society. Particularly given the Government's previous reliance on warrantless telephonic surveillance to trace reporters' sources and monitor protected political activity, I am unwilling to insulate use of pen registers from independent judicial review.

Just as one who enters a public telephone booth is "entitled to assume that the words he utters into the mouthpiece will not be broadcast to the world," so too, he should be entitled to assume that the numbers he dials in the privacy of his home will be recorded, if at all, solely for the phone company's business purposes. Accordingly, I would require law enforcement officials to obtain a warrant before they enlist telephone companies to secure information otherwise beyond the government's reach.

CALIFORNIA V. GREENWOOD

Supreme Court of the United States
486 U.S. 35, 108 S. Ct. 1625, 100 L. Ed. 2d 30 (1988)

JUSTICE WHITE delivered the opinion of the Court.

The issue here is whether the Fourth Amendment prohibits the warrantless search and seizure of garbage left for collection outside the curtilage of a home. We conclude, in accordance with the vast majority of lower courts that have addressed the issue, that it does not.

In early 1984, Investigator Jenny Stracner of the Laguna Beach Police Department received information indicating that respondent Greenwood might be engaged in narcotics trafficking. Stracner learned that a criminal suspect had informed a federal drug enforcement agent in February 1984 that a truck filled with illegal drugs was en route to the Laguna Beach address at which Greenwood resided. In addition, a neighbor complained of heavy vehicular traffic late at night in front of Greenwood's single-family home. The neighbor reported that the vehicles remained at Greenwood's house for only a few minutes.

Stracner sought to investigate this information by conducting a surveillance of Greenwood's home. She observed several vehicles make brief stops at the house during the late-night and early morning hours, and she followed a truck from the house to a residence that had previously been under investigation as a narcotics-trafficking location.

On April 6, 1984, Stracner asked the neighborhood's regular trash collector to pick up the plastic garbage bags that Greenwood had left on the curb in front of his house and to turn the bags over to her without mixing their contents with garbage from other houses. The trash collector cleaned his truck bin of other refuse, collected the garbage bags from the street in front of Greenwood's house, and turned the bags over to Stracner. The officer searched through the rubbish and found items indicative of narcotics use. She recited the information that she had gleaned from the trash search in an affidavit in support of a warrant to search Greenwood's home.

Police officers encountered both respondents at the house later that day when they arrived to execute the warrant. The police discovered quantities of cocaine and hashish during their search of the house. Respondents were arrested on felony narcotics charges. * * *

The Superior Court dismissed the charges against respondents on the authority of *People v. Krivda*, which held that warrantless trash searches violate the Fourth Amendment and the California Constitution. The court found that the police would not have had probable cause to search the Greenwood home without the evidence obtained from the trash searches.

The Court of Appeal affirmed. * * * The California Supreme Court denied the State's petition for review of the Court of Appeal's decision. We granted certiorari and now reverse.

The warrantless search and seizure of the garbage bags left at the curb outside the Greenwood house would violate the Fourth Amendment only if respondents manifested a subjective expectation of privacy in their garbage that society accepts as objectively reasonable. Respondents do not disagree with this standard.

They assert, however, that they had, and exhibited, an expectation of privacy with respect to the trash that was searched by the police: The trash, which was placed on the street for collection at a fixed time, was contained in opaque plastic bags, which the garbage collector was expected to pick up, mingle with the trash of others, and deposit at the garbage dump. The trash was only temporarily on the street, and there was little likelihood that it would be inspected by anyone.

It may well be that respondents did not expect that the contents of their garbage bags would become known to the police or other members of the public. An expectation of privacy does not give rise to Fourth Amendment protection, however, unless society is prepared to accept that expectation as objectively reasonable.

Here, we conclude that respondents exposed their garbage to the public sufficiently to defeat their claim to Fourth Amendment protection. It is common knowledge that plastic garbage bags left on or at the side of a public street are readily accessible to animals, children, scavengers, snoops, and other members of the public. Moreover, respondents placed their refuse at the curb for the express purpose of conveying it to a third party, the trash collector, who might himself have sorted through respondents' trash or permitted others, such as the police, to do so. Accordingly, having deposited their garbage "in an area particularly suited for public inspection and, in a manner of speaking, public consumption, for the express purpose of having strangers take it," respondents could have had no reasonable expectation of privacy in the inculpatory items that they discarded.

Furthermore, as we have held, the police cannot reasonably be expected to avert their eyes from evidence of criminal activity that could have been observed by any member of the public. Hence, "[w]hat a person knowingly exposes to the public, even in his own home or office, is not a subject of Fourth Amendment protection." We held in *Smith v. Maryland*, for example, that the police did not violate the Fourth Amendment by causing a pen register to be installed at the telephone company's offices to record the telephone numbers dialed by a criminal suspect. An individual has no legitimate expectation of privacy in the numbers dialed on his telephone, we reasoned, because he voluntarily conveys those numbers to the telephone company when he uses the telephone. Again, we observed that "a person has no legitimate expectation of privacy in information he voluntarily turns over to third parties." * * *

The judgment of the California Court of Appeal is therefore reversed, and this case is remanded for further proceedings not inconsistent with this opinion.

It is so ordered.

JUSTICE KENNEDY took no part in the consideration or decision of this case.

JUSTICE BRENNAN with whom JUSTICE MARSHALL joins, dissenting.

Every week for two months, and at least once more a month later, the Laguna Beach police clawed through the trash that respondent Greenwood left in opaque, sealed bags on the curb outside his home. Complete strangers minutely scrutinized their bounty, undoubtedly dredging up intimate details of Greenwood's private life and habits. The intrusions proceeded without a warrant, and no court before or since has concluded that the police acted on probable cause to believe Greenwood was engaged in any criminal activity.

Scrutiny of another's trash is contrary to commonly accepted notions of civilized behavior. I suspect, therefore, that members of our society will be shocked to learn that the Court, the ultimate guarantor of liberty, deems unreasonable our expectation that the aspects of our private lives that are concealed safely in a trash bag will not become public.

"A container which can support a reasonable expectation of privacy may not be searched, even on probable cause, without a warrant."[a] Thus, as the Court observes, if Greenwood had a reasonable expectation that the contents of the bags that he placed on the curb would remain private, the warrantless search of those bags violated the Fourth Amendment.

*** In *Robbins v. California*, *** Justice Stewart, writing for a plurality of four, pronounced that "unless the container is such that its contents may be said to be in plain view, those contents are fully protected by the Fourth Amendment," and soundly rejected any distinction for Fourth Amendment purposes among various opaque, sealed containers:

> [E]ven if one wished to import such a distinction into the Fourth Amendment, it is difficult if not impossible to perceive any objective criteria by which that task might be accomplished. What one person may put into a suitcase, another may put into a paper bag. . . . And . . . no court, no constable, no citizen, can sensibly be asked to distinguish the relative "privacy interests" in a closed suitcase, briefcase, portfolio, duffel bag, or box. * * *

More recently, in *United States v. Ross*, the Court, relying on the "virtually unanimous agreement in *Robbins* . . . that a constitutional distinction between 'worthy' and 'unworthy' containers would be improper," held that a distinction among "paper bags, locked trunks, lunch buckets, and orange crates" would be inconsistent with

> the central purpose of the Fourth Amendment. . . [A] traveler who carries a toothbrush and a few articles of clothing in a paper bag or knotted scarf [may] claim an equal right to conceal his possessions from official inspection as the sophisticated executive with the locked attaché case. * * *

---

[a] The Supreme Court has held that if police have probable cause to believe that a container contains contraband or evidence of a crime, they may seize the container, but may not search it until they obtain a search warrant issued by a neutral and detached judicial officer. *See* United States v. Chadwick, 433 U.S. 1 (1977). This rule, which has been called the Container Doctrine, is based on two rationales: (1) individuals have heightened expectations of privacy in their luggage, purses, backpacks, and other containers, and (2) once seized, a container is not readily mobile, and therefore the officer need not worry that the owner of the container will be able to grab a weapon or destroy evidence within. Cynthia Lee, *Package Bombs, Footlockers, and Laptops: What the Disappearing Container Doctrine Can Tell Us About the Fourth Amendment*, 100 J. CRIM. L. & CRIMINOLOGY 1403, 1422 (2010).

Accordingly, we have found a reasonable expectation of privacy in the contents of a 200-pound "double-locked footlocker," a "comparatively small, unlocked suitcase," a "totebag," and "packages wrapped in green opaque plastic."

Our precedent, therefore, leaves no room to doubt that had respondents been carrying their personal effects in opaque, sealed plastic bags—identical to the ones they placed on the curb—their privacy would have been protected from warrantless police intrusion. So far as Fourth Amendment protection is concerned, opaque plastic bags are every bit as worthy as "packages wrapped in green opaque plastic" and "double-locked footlocker[s]."

Respondents deserve no less protection just because Greenwood used the bags to discard rather than to transport his personal effects. Their contents are not inherently any less private, and Greenwood's decision to discard them, at least in the manner in which he did, does not diminish his expectation of privacy.

A trash bag, like any of the above-mentioned containers, "is a common repository for one's personal effects" and, even more than many of them, is "therefore . . . inevitably associated with the expectation of privacy." A single bag of trash testifies eloquently to the eating, reading, and recreational habits of the person who produced it. A search of trash, like a search of the bedroom, can relate intimate details about sexual practices, health, and personal hygiene. Like rifling through desk drawers or intercepting phone calls, rummaging through trash can divulge the target's financial and professional status, political affiliations and inclinations, private thoughts, personal relationships, and romantic interests. It cannot be doubted that a sealed trash bag harbors telling evidence of the "intimate activity associated with the 'sanctity of a man's home and the privacies of life,'" which the Fourth Amendment is designed to protect.

The Court properly rejects the State's attempt to distinguish trash searches from other searches on the theory that trash is abandoned and therefore not entitled to an expectation of privacy. As the author of the Court's opinion observed last Term, a defendant's "property interest [in trash] does not settle the matter for Fourth Amendment purposes, for the reach of the Fourth Amendment is not determined by state property law." In evaluating the reasonableness of Greenwood's expectation that his sealed trash bags would not be invaded, the Court has held that we must look to "understandings that are recognized and permitted by society." Most of us, I believe, would be incensed to discover a meddler—whether a neighbor, a reporter, or a detective—scrutinizing our sealed trash containers to discover some detail of our personal lives. That was, quite naturally, the reaction to the sole incident on which the Court bases its conclusion that "snoops" and the like defeat the expectation of privacy in trash. When a tabloid reporter examined then-Secretary of State Henry Kissinger's trash and published his findings, Kissinger was "really revolted" by the intrusion and his wife suffered "grave anguish." The public response roundly condemning the reporter demonstrates that society not only recognized those reactions as reasonable, but shared them as well. Commentators variously characterized his conduct as "a disgusting invasion of personal privacy," "indefensible . . . as civilized behavior," and contrary to "the way decent people behave in relation to each other."

Beyond a generalized expectation of privacy, many municipalities, whether for reasons of privacy, sanitation, or both, reinforce confidence in the integrity of sealed trash containers by "prohibit[ing] anyone, except authorized employees of the Town . . . to rummage into, pick up, collect, move or otherwise interfere with articles or materials placed on . . . any public street for collection." * * *

That is not to deny that isolated intrusions into opaque, sealed trash containers occur. When, acting on their own, "animals, children, scavengers, snoops, [or] other members of the public," *actually* rummage through a bag of trash and expose its contents to plain view, "police cannot reasonably be expected to avert their eyes from evidence of criminal activity that could have been observed by any member of the public." * * *

Had Greenwood flaunted his intimate activity by strewing his trash all over the curb for all to see, or had some nongovernmental intruder invaded his privacy and done the same, I could accept the Court's conclusion that an expectation of privacy would have been unreasonable. Similarly, had police searching the city dump run across incriminating evidence that, despite commingling with the trash of others, still retained its identity as Greenwood's, we would have a different case. But all that Greenwood "exposed . . . to the public," were the exteriors of several opaque, sealed containers. * * *

The mere *possibility* that unwelcome meddlers *might* open and rummage through the containers does not negate the expectation of privacy in their contents any more than the possibility of a burglary negates an expectation of privacy in the home. * * *

Nor is it dispositive that "respondents placed their refuse at the curb for the express purpose of conveying it to a third party, . . . who might himself have sorted through respondents' trash or permitted others, such as the police, to do so." In the first place, Greenwood can hardly be faulted for leaving trash on his curb when a county ordinance commanded him to do so, and prohibited him from disposing of it in any other way. * * * More importantly, even the voluntary relinquishment of possession or control over an effect does not necessarily amount to a relinquishment of a privacy expectation in it. Were it otherwise, a letter or package would lose all Fourth Amendment protection when placed in a mailbox or other depository with the "express purpose" of entrusting it to the postal officer or a private carrier; those bailees are just as likely as trash collectors (and certainly have greater incentive) to "sor[t] through" the personal effects entrusted to them, "or permi[t] others, such as police to do so." Yet, it has been clear for at least 110 years that the possibility of such an intrusion does not justify a warrantless search by police in the first instance. * * *

I dissent.

WHAT IS A SEARCH? TWO CONCEPTUAL FLAWS IN FOURTH AMENDMENT DOCTRINE AND SOME HINTS OF A REMEDY
Sherry F. Colb
55 Stan. L. Rev. 119 (2002)

When determining what privacy the Fourth Amendment does and does not protect—what circumstances, in other words, give rise to a "reasonable expectation of privacy"—the Court asks: "What is a search?" To rule out activities that do not qualify, the Court denies privacy in whatever people "knowingly expose" to the public. If a person knowingly exposes some object or activity to the public, there has accordingly been no search. Absent a search, police may observe the thing that is "exposed" without having to obtain a warrant or otherwise justify their observations. * * *

In developing the category of things that are "knowingly exposed," and therefore not a search, the Court has repeatedly made two analytic moves that effectively rob the category of any firm boundaries: (1) It treats the risk of exposure through third-party wrongdoing as tantamount to an invitation for that exposure ("Move One"); and (2) it treats exposure to a limited audience as morally equivalent to exposure to the whole world ("Move Two").

Treating risk-taking as inviting exposure effectively excuses (and even justifies) what would otherwise be wrongful conduct by third parties, including the police. If a man lies down and falls into a deep sleep on a subway train, for example, he risks having his pocket picked. A pickpocket can easily swipe the sleeping man's wallet without encountering any resistance. We might even say colloquially that the sleeping man has "asked to have his pocket picked." This colloquialism does not, however, describe a legal justification for the pickpocket. We would not say, in other words, that the man on the train has willingly agreed to the taking of his wallet * * *. Like taking candy from a baby, taking a wallet from a sleeping man remains a crime, no matter how easy it is to accomplish.

The second of the two moves, treating exposure to a limited audience as identical to exposure to the world, means failing to recognize degrees of privacy in the Fourth Amendment context. A person going on vacation, for example, might give a neighbor the key to her house and ask him to water her plants while she is gone. The neighbor now has explicit permission to observe what would otherwise be hidden from view, namely, the inside of the vacationer's home (at least those parts visible from areas through which he must travel to reach the plants). By granting this permission, the vacationer has forfeited a measure of privacy and has thus knowingly exposed part of her home to her neighbor. Still, if the neighbor were to invite his friends or family into the apartment to see the vacationer's personal items, * * * that act would go beyond the scope of the vacationer's permission and therefore represent an invasion of her privacy. There are degrees of privacy and, accordingly, degrees of exposure, and one might choose to forfeit some of her freedom from exposure without thereby forfeiting all of it. * * *

Perhaps the leading decision equating risk and invitation is *California v. Greenwood*. Suspecting narcotics trafficking, a police officer asked a garbage collector to segregate Greenwood's trash upon collection. After separating the target's garbage, the collector then gave it to the officer to permit her to rummage through it. The Supreme Court considered the following question: "[W]hether the Fourth Amendment prohibits the warrantless search and seizure of garbage left for collection outside the curtilage of a home." Did the officer, in other words, invade any "reasonable expectation of privacy" by obtaining and rummaging through Greenwood's trash, such that a Fourth Amendment search took place, triggering the warrant requirement?

The Court answered no to these questions and concluded that when a person leaves his trash at the curb, he knowingly exposes it to the public. When Greenwood placed his garbage on the street, the Court said, he took a significant risk that the bag would be torn open and its contents revealed. "It is common knowledge," the majority explained, "that plastic garbage bags left on or at the side of a public street are readily accessible to animals, children, scavengers, snoops, and other members of the public." In other words, children, raccoons, and snoops would have had access to the garbage, sitting out in public as it was, and they could have raided it, just as the police officer did. * * *

By invoking the risk of snoops rummaging through Greenwood's garbage, the Court made Move One, described above. It treated a person who takes the risk that something might occur as having invited the materialization of that risk. Without explicitly articulating this equivalence, the Court permitted the officer to act as though the garbage, which was in fact safely enclosed within an opaque bag, had actually been strewn about by all manner of errant creatures in the neighborhood. By constructively inviting such exposure, Greenwood could not be heard to complain of the government's acceptance of the invitation.

The Supreme Court's approach to the facts of *Greenwood* was highly artificial. It is unpersuasive to argue that by putting out his garbage,

Greenwood had knowingly relinquished the secrecy of its contents. When the garbage was at the curb, Greenwood's hypothetical snoopy neighbor might have had to violate the law to rummage through it in the way that the police officer did. To say that he invited the world to rummage through it was thus to confuse the risk of exposure, one that he can perhaps be said to have knowingly taken, and exposure itself, something that the police officer brought about in a manner that would have been wrongful conduct if attempted by a private "snoop."

To see further why the Court's equation of risk and invitation in *Greenwood* is destructive of privacy, consider what else a "snoop," raccoon, or child might have done. * * * A snoop, raccoon, or child might have climbed beyond the curb, onto the curtilage, and into Greenwood's house through an open window, perhaps proceeding to remove items from the shelves. * * * The Court presumably would not suggest, however, that these possibilities might justify the police in doing the same. The suggestion is nonetheless implicit in the "risk as invitation" argument that the Court adopts in *Greenwood*. * * *

DIGITAL DOSSIERS AND THE DISSIPATION OF FOURTH AMENDMENT PRIVACY

Daniel J. Solove
75 S. Cal. L. Rev. 1083 (2002)

We live in the early stages of the Information Age, a time when technology has given us unprecedented abilities to communicate, transfer and share information, access data, and analyze a profound array of facts and ideas. The complete benefits of the Information Age do not simply come to us. We must "plug in" to join in. In other words, we must establish relationships with a panoply of companies. To connect to the Internet, we must subscribe to an ISP [internet service provider]. To be able to receive more than a few television channels, we need to open an account with a cable company. Phone service, mobile phone service, and other utilities require us to open accounts with a number of entities.

Further, life in modern society demands that we enter into numerous relationships with professionals (doctors, lawyers, accountants), businesses (restaurants, video rental stores), merchants (bookstores, mail catalog companies), publishing companies (magazines, newspapers), organizations (charities), financial institutions (banks, investment firms, credit card companies), landlords, employers, and other entities (insurance companies, security companies, travel agencies, car rental companies, hotels). Our relationships with all of these entities generate records containing personal information necessary to establish an account and record of our transactions, preferences, purchases, and activities. We are becoming a society of records, and these records are not held by us, but by third parties. * * *

These record systems are becoming increasingly useful to law enforcement officials. Personal information can help the government detect fraud, espionage, fugitives, smuggling cartels, drug distribution rings, and terrorist cells. Information about a person's financial transactions, purchases, and religious and political beliefs can assist law enforcement in investigating suspected criminals, individuals providing money and assistance to terrorists, or profiling people for more thorough searches at airports.

* * * [F]rom pen registers and trap and trace devices, the government can obtain a list of all the phone numbers dialed to or from a particular location, potentially revealing the people with whom a person associates. From bank records, which contain one's account activity and check writing, the government can discover the various companies and professionals that a person does business with (ISP, telephone company, credit card company, magazine companies, doctors, attorneys, and so on). Credit card company records can reveal where one eats and shops and which cultural events one attends. The government can obtain one's travel destinations and activities from travel agent records. From hotel records, it can discover the numbers a person dialed and the pay-per-view movies a person watched. * * * From video stores, the government can access an inventory of the videos that a person has rented. * * *

Beyond the records described above, the Internet has the potential to become one of the government's greatest information gathering tools. There are two significant aspects of the Internet that make it such a revolutionary data collection device. First, it gives many individuals a false sense of privacy. The secrecy and anonymity of the Internet is often a mirage. People are rarely truly anonymous because ISPs keep records of a subscriber's screen name and pseudonyms. ISP account information can also include the subscriber's name, address, phone numbers, passwords, information about web surfing sessions and durations, credit card and bank account information. By learning a person's screen name, the government can identify the person behind the pseudonym postings to newsgroups or chatrooms. For example, in *McVeigh v. Cohen*, AOL provided a Navy official with the identity of an individual using a pseudonym who indicated he was gay and worked in the military. Based on this information, the Navy proceeded to initiate discharge proceedings under the "Don't Ask, Don't Tell" policy. * * *

Websites often accumulate a great deal of information about their users. Through the use of a "cookie," which identifies a user by deploying a text file into the user's computer, websites can detect the previous website and parts of the site a user accessed. This data is called "clickstream data" because it records nearly every click of the mouse. Another information collection device, known as a "web bug," involves hidden pixel tags secretly planted on a user's hard drive that surreptitiously gather data about the user. Websites also collect data when people fill out online questionnaires pertaining to their hobbies, health, and interests. Further, a person's Internet postings are archived and do not readily disappear. As we invest more time on the Internet, strangers and unfamiliar organizations are keeping permanent records about our lives.

Thus, the government can glean a substantial amount of information about visitors to a particular website. For example, certain health websites ask individuals to fill out questionnaires about their symptoms to determine whether they have a disease. Other websites have questionnaires relating to psychology and personality. From Internet retailers, the government can learn about the books, videos, music, and electronics that one purchases. Some Internet retailers, such as "Amazon.com," record all the purchases a person makes throughout the many years that the person has been shopping on the website. Also, retailers use surveys to identify how a person rates books and videos. Based on this information, the government can discover a consumer's interests, sexuality, political views, religious beliefs, and lifestyle. Further, if a person buys a gift from an Internet retailer and has it mailed to a friend, the government may learn the friend's name and address and develop a list of an individual's friends and acquaintances. * * *

While life in the Information Age has brought us a dizzying amount of information, it has also placed a profound amount of information about our lives in the hands of numerous entities. These digital dossiers are increasingly becoming digital biographies, a horde of aggregated bits of information combined to reveal a portrait of who we are based upon what we buy, the organizations we belong to, how we navigate the Internet, and which shows and videos we watch. This information is not held by trusted friends or family members, but by large bureaucracies that we do not know very well or sometimes do not even know at all.

* * * [T]he Court [has] held that there is no reasonable expectation in privacy for information known or exposed to third parties. In *United States v. Miller*, federal agents presented subpoenas to two banks to produce all of the financial records of the defendant. * * * The defendant challenged the subpoenas as a violation of the Fourth Amendment. The Court held that there was no reasonable expectation of privacy in financial records maintained by a bank. "[T]he Fourth Amendment does not prohibit the obtaining of information revealed to a third party and conveyed by him to Government authorities." The Court reasoned: * * * "All of the documents obtained, including financial statements and deposit slips, contain only information voluntarily conveyed to the banks and exposed to their employees in the ordinary course of business." In *Smith v. Maryland*, * * * [t]he Court concluded that there was no reasonable expectation of privacy in pen registers. Since people "know that they must convey numerical information to the phone company" and that the phone company records

this information for billing purposes, people cannot "harbor any general expectation that the numbers they dial will remain secret."

Miller and *Smith* establish a general rule that if information is in the hands of third parties, then an individual can have no reasonable expectation of privacy in that information, which means that the Fourth Amendment does not apply. Individuals thus probably do not have a reasonable expectation of privacy in communications and records maintained by ISPs or computer network system administrators. * * *

Smith and *Miller* have been extensively criticized throughout the past several decades. However, it is only recently that we are truly beginning to see the profound implications of the Court's third party doctrine. * * * Gathering information from third party records is an emerging law enforcement practice with as many potential dangers as the wiretapping in *Olmstead*. "The progress of science in furnishing the government with means of espionage is not likely to stop with wiretapping," Justice Brandeis observed in his *Olmstead* dissent. "Ways may some day be developed by which the government, without removing papers from secret drawers, can reproduce them in court, and by which it will be enabled to expose to a jury the most intimate occurrences of the home."

That day is here. Government information gathering from the extensive dossiers being assembled with modern computer technology poses one of the most significant threats to privacy of our times. * * *

C. ELECTRONIC SURVEILLANCE

Recent advances in technology have made it easier than ever before for the government to track our movements and obtain information about us and the people with whom we correspond by e-mail or telephone. For example, cell site simulators, also known as Stingrays, mimic cell phone towers and can intercept locational and electronic identifying information from nearby cell phones. Locational information can be useful if, for example, police are trying to prove that a homicide suspect was in the neighborhood at the time of the crime. Because these devices can capture such information from any cell phone in the vicinity, the government can collect information not only from a suspect's phone but also from the cellphones of other individuals who happen to be close by. Keystroke loggers installed on a computer can give the government information about every key stroke a person types on a computer. Drones, small pilotless aircraft that can be equipped with listening devices and cameras, have the ability to fly at much lower altitudes than helicopters and airplanes and can capture information that would otherwise be fairly difficult to obtain.

Even before these technological advances, the Court chose to address questions involving the Fourth Amendment implications of electronic surveillance by the government. In the first case in this section, *United*

States v. White, the Court considers whether the government conducts a search when an agent listens in on conversations between a suspect and an informant wearing a wire. In *Kyllo v. United States*, the Court considers whether the government's use of a thermal imaging device aimed at the home of a man suspected of growing marijuana plants inside constitutes a search. In *United States v. Jones*, the Court examines whether the placement of a GPS tracking device on the underside of a vehicle and the tracking of the vehicle's movements for a period of four weeks is a search.

UNITED STATES V. WHITE
Supreme Court of the United States
401 U.S. 745, 91 S. Ct. 1122, 28 L. Ed. 2d 453 (1971)

JUSTICE WHITE delivered the opinion of the Court.

In 1966, respondent James A. White was tried and convicted under two consolidated indictments charging various illegal transactions in narcotics violative of 26 U.S.C. § 4705(a) and 21 U.S.C. § 174. He was fined and sentenced as a second offender to 25-year concurrent sentences. The issue before us is whether the Fourth Amendment bars from evidence the testimony of governmental agents who related certain conversations which had occurred between defendant White and a government informant, Harvey Jackson, and which the agents overheard by monitoring the frequency of a radio transmitter carried by Jackson and concealed on his person. On four occasions the conversations took place in Jackson's home; each of these conversations was overheard by an agent concealed in a kitchen closet with Jackson's consent and by a second agent outside the house using a radio receiver. Four other conversations—one in respondent's home, one in a restaurant, and two in Jackson's car—were overheard by the use of radio equipment. The prosecution was unable to locate and produce Jackson at the trial and the trial court overruled objections to the testimony of the agents who conducted the electronic surveillance. The jury returned a guilty verdict and defendant appealed.
* * *

Hoffa v. United States, which was left undisturbed by *Katz*, held that however strongly a defendant may trust an apparent colleague, his expectations in this respect are not protected by the Fourth Amendment when it turns out that the colleague is a government agent regularly communicating with the authorities. In these circumstances, "no interest legitimately protected by the Fourth Amendment is involved," for that amendment affords no protection to "a wrongdoer's misplaced belief that a person to whom he voluntarily confides his wrongdoing will not reveal it." No warrant to "search and seize" is required in such circumstances, nor is it when the Government sends to defendant's home a secret agent who conceals his identity and makes a purchase of narcotics from the accused, or when the same agent, unbeknown to the defendant, carries electronic equipment to record the defendant's words and the evidence so gathered is later offered in evidence. * * *

Concededly a police agent who conceals his police connections may write down for official use his conversations with a defendant and testify concerning them, without a warrant authorizing his encounters with the defendant and without otherwise violating the latter's Fourth Amendment rights. For constitutional purposes, no different result is required if the agent instead of immediately reporting and transcribing his conversations with defendant, either (1) simultaneously records them with electronic equipment which he is carrying on his person; (2) or carries radio equipment which simultaneously transmits the conversations either to recording equipment located elsewhere or to other agents monitoring the transmitting frequency. If the conduct and revelations of an agent operating without electronic equipment do not invade the defendant's constitutionally justifiable expectations of privacy, neither does a simultaneous recording of the same conversations made by the agent or by others from transmissions received from the agent to whom the defendant is talking and whose trustworthiness the defendant necessarily risks.

Our problem is not what the privacy expectations of particular defendants in particular situations may be or the extent to which they may in fact have relied on the discretion of their companions. Very probably, individual defendants neither know nor suspect that their colleagues have gone or will go to the police or are carrying recorders or transmitters. Otherwise, conversation would cease and our problem with these encounters would be nonexistent or far different from those now before us. Our problem, in terms of the principles announced in *Katz*, is what expectations of privacy are constitutionally "justifiable"—what expectations the Fourth Amendment will protect in the absence of a warrant. * * * If the law gives no protection to the wrongdoer whose trusted accomplice is or becomes a police agent, neither should it protect him when that same agent has recorded or transmitted the conversations which are later offered in evidence to prove the State's case.

Inescapably, one contemplating illegal activities must realize and risk that his companions may be reporting to the police. If he sufficiently doubts their trustworthiness, the association will very probably end or never materialize. But if he has no doubts, or allays them, or risks what doubt he has, the risk is his. In terms of what his course will be, what he will or will not do or say, we are unpersuaded that he would distinguish between probable informers on the one hand and probable informers with transmitters on the other. Given the possibility or probability that one of his colleagues is cooperating with the police, it is only speculation to assert that the defendant's utterances would be substantially different or his sense of security any less if he also thought it possible that the suspected colleague is wired for sound. At least there is no persuasive evidence that the difference in this respect between the electronically equipped and the unequipped agent is substantial enough to require discrete constitutional recognition, particularly under the Fourth Amendment which is ruled by fluid concepts of "reasonableness."

Nor should we be too ready to erect constitutional barriers to relevant and probative evidence which is also accurate and reliable. An electronic recording will many times produce a more reliable rendition of what a defendant has said than will the unaided memory of a police agent. It may also be that with the recording in existence it is less likely that the informant will change his mind, less chance that threat or injury will suppress unfavorable evidence and less chance that cross-examination will confound the testimony. Considerations like these obviously do not favor the defendant, but we are not prepared to hold that a defendant who has no constitutional right to exclude the informer's unaided testimony nevertheless has a Fourth Amendment privilege against a more accurate version of the events in question.

It is thus untenable to consider the activities and reports of the police agent himself, though acting without a warrant, to be a "reasonable" investigative effort and lawful under the Fourth Amendment but to view the same agent with a recorder or transmitter as conducting an "unreasonable" and unconstitutional search and seizure. * * *

JUSTICE DOUGLAS, dissenting.

The issue in this case is clouded and concealed by the very discussion of it in legalistic terms. What the ancients knew as "eavesdropping," we now call "electronic surveillance"; but to equate the two is to treat man's first gunpowder on the same level as the nuclear bomb. Electronic surveillance is the greatest leveler of human privacy ever known. How most forms of it can be held "reasonable" within the meaning of the Fourth Amendment is a mystery. * * *

These were wholly pre-arranged episodes of surveillance. The first was in the informant's home to which respondent had been invited. The second was also in the informer's home, the next day. The third was four days later at the home of the respondent. The fourth was in the informer's car two days later. Twelve days after that a meeting in the informer's home was intruded upon. The sixth occurred at a street rendezvous. The seventh was in the informer's home and the eighth in a restaurant owned by respondent's mother-law. So far as time is concerned there is no excuse for not seeking a warrant. And while there is always an effort involved in preparing affidavits or other evidence in support of a showing probable cause, that burden was given constitutional sanction in the Fourth Amendment against the activities of the agents of George III. It was designed not to protect criminals but to protect everyone's privacy. * * *

Monitoring, if prevalent, certainly kills free discourse and spontaneous utterances. Free discourse—a First Amendment value—may be frivolous or serious, humble or defiant, reactionary or revolutionary, profane or in good taste; but it is not free if there is surveillance. Free discourse liberates the spirit, though it may produce only froth. The individual must keep some facts concerning his thoughts within a small zone of people. At the same time he must be free to pour out his woes or inspirations or dreams to others. He remains the sole judge as to what must be said and what must remain unspoken. This is the essence of the idea of privacy implicit in the First and Fifth Amendments as well as in the Fourth. * * *

"Few conversations would be what they are if the speakers thought others were listening. Silly, secret, thoughtless and thoughtful statements would all be affected. The sheer numbers in our lives, the anonymity of urban living and the inability to influence things that are important are depersonalizing and dehumanizing factors of modern life. To penetrate the last refuge of the individual, the precious little privacy that remains, the basis of individual dignity, can have meaning to the quality of our lives that we cannot foresee. In terms of present values, that meaning cannot be good."

* * * [M]ust everyone live in fear that every word he speaks may be transmitted or recorded and later repeated to the entire world? I can imagine nothing that has a more chilling effect on people speaking their minds and expressing their views on important matters. The advocates of that regime should spend some time in totalitarian countries and learn firsthand the kind of regime they are creating here. * * *

JUSTICE HARLAN, dissenting * * *

Since it is the task of the law to form and project, as well as mirror and reflect, we should not, as judges, merely recite the expectations and risks without examining the desirability of saddling them upon society. The critical question, therefore, is whether under our system of government, as reflected in the Constitution, we should impose on our citizens the risks of the electronic listener or observer without at least the protection of a warrant requirement. * * *

The impact of the practice of third-party bugging, must, I think, be considered such as to undermine that confidence and sense of security in dealing with one another that is characteristic of individual relationships between citizens in a free society.

* * * Much offhand exchange is easily forgotten and one may count on the obscurity of his remarks, protected by the very fact of a limited audience, and the likelihood that the listener will either overlook or forget what is said, as well as the listener's inability to reformulate a conversation without having to contend with a documented record. All these values are

sacrificed by a rule of law that permits official monitoring of private discourse limited only by the need to locate a willing assistant. * * *

[JUSTICE BLACK's concurring opinion, JUSTICE BRENNAN's concurring opinion, and JUSTICE MARSHALL's dissenting opinion have been omitted.]

KYLLO V. UNITED STATES
Supreme Court of the United States
533 U.S. 27, 121 S. Ct. 2038, 150 L. Ed. 2d 94 (2001)

JUSTICE SCALIA delivered the opinion of the Court.

This case presents the question whether the use of a thermal-imaging device aimed at a private home from a public street to detect relative amounts of heat within the home constitutes a "search" within the meaning of the Fourth Amendment.

In 1991 Agent William Elliott of the United States Department of the Interior came to suspect that marijuana was being grown in the home belonging to petitioner Danny Kyllo, part of a triplex on Rhododendron Drive in Florence, Oregon. Indoor marijuana growth typically requires high-intensity lamps. In order to determine whether an amount of heat was emanating from petitioner's home consistent with the use of such lamps, at 3:20 a.m. on January 16, 1992, Agent Elliott and Dan Haas used an Agema Thermovision 210 thermal imager to scan the triplex. Thermal imagers detect infrared radiation, which virtually all objects emit but which is not visible to the naked eye. The imager converts radiation into images based on relative warmth—black is cool, white is hot, shades of gray connote relative differences; in that respect, it operates somewhat like a video camera showing heat images. The scan of Kyllo's home took only a few minutes and was performed from the passenger seat of Agent Elliott's vehicle across the street from the front of the house and also from the street in back of the house. The scan showed that the roof over the garage and a side wall of petitioner's home were relatively hot compared to the rest of the home and substantially warmer than neighboring homes in the triplex. Agent Elliott concluded that petitioner was using halide lights to grow marijuana in his house, which indeed he was. Based on tips from informants, utility bills, and the thermal imaging, a Federal Magistrate Judge issued a warrant authorizing a search of petitioner's home, and the agents found an indoor growing operation involving more than 100 plants. Petitioner was indicted on one count of manufacturing marijuana, in violation of 21 U.S.C. § 841(a)(1). He unsuccessfully moved to suppress the evidence seized from his home and then entered a conditional guilty plea. * * *

The Fourth Amendment provides that "[t]he right of the people to be secure in their persons, houses, papers, and effects, against unreasonable searches and seizures, shall not be violated." "At the very core" of the

Fourth Amendment "stands the right of a man to retreat into his own home and there be free from unreasonable governmental intrusion." With few exceptions, the question whether a warrantless search of a home is reasonable and hence constitutional must be answered no. * * *

It would be foolish to contend that the degree of privacy secured to citizens by the Fourth Amendment has been entirely unaffected by the advance of technology. * * * The question we confront today is what limits there are upon this power of technology to shrink the realm of guaranteed privacy.

The *Katz* test—whether the individual has an expectation of privacy that society is prepared to recognize as reasonable—has often been criticized as circular, and hence subjective and unpredictable. While it may be difficult to refine *Katz* when the search of areas such as telephone booths, automobiles, or even the curtilage and uncovered portions of residences is at issue, in the case of the search of the interior of homes—the prototypical and hence most commonly litigated area of protected privacy—there is a ready criterion, with roots deep in the common law, of the minimal expectation of privacy that *exists,* and that is acknowledged to be *reasonable.* To withdraw protection of this minimum expectation would be to permit police technology to erode the privacy guaranteed by the Fourth Amendment. We think that obtaining by sense-enhancing technology any information regarding the interior of the home that could not otherwise have been obtained without physical "intrusion into a constitutionally protected area," constitutes a search—at least where (as here) the technology in question is not in general public use. This assures preservation of that degree of privacy against government that existed when the Fourth Amendment was adopted. On the basis of this criterion, the information obtained by the thermal imager in this case was the product of a search.[2]

The Government maintains, however, that the thermal imaging must be upheld because it detected "only heat radiating from the external surface of the house." The dissent makes this its leading point. * * * But just as a thermal imager captures only heat emanating from a house, so also a powerful directional microphone picks up only sound emanating

---

[2] The dissent's repeated assertion that the thermal imaging did not obtain information regarding the interior of the home is simply inaccurate. A thermal imager reveals the relative heat of various rooms in the home. The dissent may not find that information particularly private or important, but there is no basis for saying it is not information regarding the interior of the home. The dissent's comparison of the thermal imaging to various circumstances in which outside observers might be able to perceive, without technology, the heat of the home—for example, by observing snowmelt on the roof,—is quite irrelevant. The fact that equivalent information could sometimes be obtained by other means does not make lawful the use of means that violate the Fourth Amendment. The police might, for example, learn how many people are in a particular house by setting up year-round surveillance; but that does not make breaking and entering to find out the same information lawful. In any event, on the night of January 16, 1992, no outside observer could have discerned the relative heat of Kyllo's home without thermal imaging.

from a house * * *. We rejected such a mechanical interpretation of the Fourth Amendment in *Katz,* where the eavesdropping device picked up only sound waves that reached the exterior of the phone booth. Reversing that approach would leave the homeowner at the mercy of advancing technology—including imaging technology that could discern all human activity in the home. While the technology used in the present case was relatively crude, the rule we adopt must take account of more sophisticated systems that are already in use or in development. * * *

The Government also contends that the thermal imaging was constitutional because it did not "detect private activities occurring in private areas." * * * The Fourth Amendment's protection of the home has never been tied to measurement of the quality or quantity of information obtained. In *Silverman,* for example, we made clear that any physical invasion of the structure of the home, "by even a fraction of an inch," was too much, and there is certainly no exception to the warrant requirement for the officer who barely cracks open the front door and sees nothing but the nonintimate rug on the vestibule floor. In the home, our cases show, *all* details are intimate details, because the entire area is held safe from prying government eyes. * * *

Limiting the prohibition of thermal imaging to "intimate details" would not only be wrong in principle; it would be impractical in application, failing to provide "a workable accommodation between the needs of law enforcement and the interests protected by the Fourth Amendment." To begin with, there is no necessary connection between the sophistication of the surveillance equipment and the "intimacy" of the details that it observes—which means that one cannot say (and the police cannot be assured) that use of the relatively crude equipment at issue here will always be lawful. The Agema Thermovision 210 might disclose, for example, at what hour each night the lady of the house takes her daily sauna and bath—a detail that many would consider "intimate"; and a much more sophisticated system might detect nothing more intimate than the fact that someone left a closet light on. We * * * would have to develop a jurisprudence specifying which home activities are "intimate" and which are not. And even when (if ever) that jurisprudence were fully developed, no police officer would be able to know *in advance* whether his through-the-wall surveillance picks up "intimate" details—and thus would be unable to know in advance whether it is constitutional. * * *

We have said that the Fourth Amendment draws "a firm line at the entrance to the house." That line, we think, must be not only firm but also bright—which requires clear specification of those methods of surveillance that require a warrant. While it is certainly possible to conclude from the videotape of the thermal imaging that occurred in this case that no "significant" compromise of the homeowner's privacy has occurred, we must take the long view, from the original meaning of the Fourth Amendment forward. * * *

Where, as here, the Government uses a device that is not in general public use, to explore details of the home that would previously have been unknowable without physical intrusion, the surveillance is a "search" and is presumptively unreasonable without a warrant. * * *

JUSTICE STEVENS, with whom THE CHIEF JUSTICE, JUSTICE O'CONNOR, and JUSTICE KENNEDY join, dissenting. * * *

There is no need for the Court to craft a new rule to decide this case, as it is controlled by established principles from our Fourth Amendment jurisprudence. One of those core principles, of course, is that "searches and seizures *inside a home* without a warrant are presumptively unreasonable." But it is equally well settled that searches and seizures of property in plain view are presumptively reasonable. Whether that property is residential or commercial, the basic principle is the same: "What a person knowingly exposes to the public, even in his own home or office, is not a subject of Fourth Amendment protection." That is the principle implicated here.

* * * [T]his case involves nothing more than off-the-wall surveillance by law enforcement officers to gather information exposed to the general public from the outside of petitioner's home. All that the infrared camera did in this case was passively measure heat emitted from the exterior surfaces of petitioner's home; all that those measurements showed were relative differences in emission levels, vaguely indicating that some areas of the roof and outside walls were warmer than others. As still images from the infrared scans show, no details regarding the interior of petitioner's home were revealed. Unlike an x-ray scan, or other possible "through-the-wall" techniques, the detection of infrared radiation emanating from the home did not accomplish "an unauthorized physical penetration into the premises," nor did it "obtain information that it could not have obtained by observation from outside the curtilage of the house."

Indeed, the ordinary use of the senses might enable a neighbor or passerby to notice the heat emanating from a building, particularly if it is vented, as was the case here. Additionally, any member of the public might notice that one part of a house is warmer than another part or a nearby building if, for example, rainwater evaporates or snow melts at different rates across its surfaces. Such use of the senses would not convert into an unreasonable search if, instead, an adjoining neighbor allowed an officer onto her property to verify her perceptions with a sensitive thermometer. Nor, in my view, does such observation become an unreasonable search if made from a distance with the aid of a device that merely discloses that the exterior of one house, or one area of the house, is much warmer than another. Nothing more occurred in this case.

Thus, the notion that heat emissions from the outside of a dwelling are a private matter implicating the protections of the Fourth Amendment (the text of which guarantees the right of people "to be secure *in* their ... houses" against unreasonable searches and seizures (emphasis added)) is not only unprecedented but also quite difficult to take seriously. Heat waves, like aromas that are generated in a kitchen, or in a laboratory or opium den, enter the public domain if and when they leave a building. A subjective expectation that they would remain private is not only implausible but also surely not "one that society is prepared to recognize as 'reasonable.'"

To be sure, the homeowner has a reasonable expectation of privacy concerning what takes place within the home, and the Fourth Amendment's protection against physical invasions of the home should apply to their functional equivalent. But the equipment in this case did not penetrate the walls of petitioner's home, and while it did pick up "details of the home" that were exposed to the public, it did not obtain "any information regarding the *interior* of the home." In the Court's own words, based on what the thermal imager "showed" regarding the outside of petitioner's home, the officers "concluded" that petitioner was engaging in illegal activity inside the home. It would be quite absurd to characterize their thought processes as "searches," regardless of whether they inferred (rightly) that petitioner was growing marijuana in his house, or (wrongly) that "the lady of the house [was taking] her daily sauna and bath." * * * For the first time in its history, the Court assumes that an inference can amount to a Fourth Amendment violation.

Notwithstanding the implications of today's decision, there is a strong public interest in avoiding constitutional litigation over the monitoring of emissions from homes, and over the inferences drawn from such monitoring. Just as "the police cannot reasonably be expected to avert their eyes from evidence of criminal activity that could have been observed by any member of the public," so too public officials should not have to avert their senses or their equipment from detecting emissions in the public domain such as excessive heat, traces of smoke, suspicious odors, odorless gases, airborne particulates, or radioactive emissions, any of which could identify hazards to the community. In my judgment, monitoring such emissions with "sense-enhancing technology," and drawing useful conclusions from such monitoring, is an entirely reasonable public service.

On the other hand, the countervailing privacy interest is at best trivial. After all, homes generally are insulated to keep heat in, rather than to prevent the detection of heat going out, and it does not seem to me that society will suffer from a rule requiring the rare homeowner who both intends to engage in uncommon activities that produce extraordinary amounts of heat, and wishes to conceal that production from outsiders, to make sure that the surrounding area is well insulated. * * *

Despite the Court's attempt to draw a line that is "not only firm but also bright," the contours of its new rule are uncertain because its protection apparently dissipates as soon as the relevant technology is "in general public use." Yet how much use is general public use is not even hinted at by the Court's opinion, which makes the somewhat doubtful assumption that the thermal imager used in this case does not satisfy that criterion.[5] In any event, putting aside its lack of clarity, this criterion is somewhat perverse because it seems likely that the threat to privacy will grow, rather than recede, as the use of intrusive equipment becomes more readily available. * * *

I respectfully dissent.

NOTE

When is a device not in "general public use"? The *Kyllo* Court found that the thermal imaging device at issue in the case was not in general public use but was it correct in doing so? Justice Stevens points out in footnote 5 of his dissent, that the thermal imaging device used by the agent "number[ed] close to a thousand manufactured units; . . . ha[d] a predecessor numbering in the neighborhood of 4,000 to 5,000 units; . . . compete[d] with a product numbering from 5,000 to 6,000 units; and . . . [was] 'readily available to the public' for commercial, personal, or law enforcement purposes." Kyllo v. United States, 533 U.S. at 47 n.5 (Stevens, J., dissenting). Justice Stevens was relying on numbers back in 2001 when *Kyllo* was decided. Presumably those numbers have increased as technology has advanced. If technology not in general public use aimed at the home constitutes a search within the meaning of the Fourth Amendment, should the Court have come out differently in *Florida v. Riley*? What if a case similar to *Florida v. Riley* were to come before the Supreme Court today?

In the next case, *United States v. Jones*, the Court addresses the question of whether the installation of a GPS tracking device on the underside of a vehicle parked in a public parking lot and the monitoring of that device by government agents for 30 days constitutes a search within the meaning of the Fourth Amendment. Prior to deciding *Jones*, the Court had held that the monitoring of a beeper, an older type of tracking device, inside a car traveling on a public road did not constitute a search because an individual traveling in a car on a public road has no reasonable expectation of privacy in his movements from one place to another. United States v. Knotts, 460 U.S. 276, 281 (1983). In a later case, the Court reaffirmed *Knotts*, but held that once a car with a beeper being monitored by the government goes from the public

---

[5] The record describes a device that numbers close to a thousand manufactured units; that has a predecessor numbering in the neighborhood of 4,000 to 5,000 units; that competes with a similar product numbering from 5,000 to 6,000 units; and that is "readily available to the public" for commercial, personal, or law enforcement purposes, and is just an 800-number away from being rented from "half a dozen national companies" by anyone who wants one. Since, by virtue of the Court's new rule, the issue is one of first impression, perhaps it should order an evidentiary hearing to determine whether these facts suffice to establish "general public use."

street into the garage of a home, the continued monitoring of the beeper constitutes a search requiring a warrant because such monitoring would reveal information about the inside of the home. United States v. Karo, 468 U.S. 705, 714–15 (1985). Given these two prior cases, many thought the Court would find that the police surveillance in *Jones* was not a search. The Court's decision was thus a surprise on many fronts.

UNITED STATES V. JONES
Supreme Court of the United States
565 U.S. 400, 132 S. Ct. 945, 181 L. Ed. 2d 911 (2012)

JUSTICE SCALIA delivered the opinion of the Court.

We decide whether the attachment of a Global-Positioning-System (GPS) tracking device to an individual's vehicle, and subsequent use of that device to monitor the vehicle's movements on public streets, constitutes a search or seizure within the meaning of the Fourth Amendment.

In 2004 respondent Antoine Jones, owner and operator of a nightclub in the District of Columbia, came under suspicion of trafficking in narcotics and was made the target of an investigation by a joint FBI and Metropolitan Police Department task force. *** Based in part on information gathered from [various investigative techniques], in 2005 the Government applied to the United States District Court for the District of Columbia for a warrant authorizing the use of an electronic tracking device on the Jeep Grand Cherokee registered to Jones's wife. A warrant issued, authorizing installation of the device in the District of Columbia and within 10 days.

On the 11th day, and not in the District of Columbia but in Maryland,[1] agents installed a GPS tracking device on the undercarriage of the Jeep while it was parked in a public parking lot. Over the next 28 days, the Government used the device to track the vehicle's movements, and once had to replace the device's battery when the vehicle was parked in a different public lot in Maryland. By means of signals from multiple satellites, the device established the vehicle's location within 50 to 100 feet, and communicated that location by cellular phone to a Government computer. It relayed more than 2,000 pages of data over the 4-week period.

The Government ultimately obtained a multiple-count indictment charging Jones and several alleged co-conspirators with, as relevant here, conspiracy to distribute and possess with intent to distribute five kilograms or more of cocaine and 50 grams or more of cocaine base. *** Jones filed a motion to suppress evidence obtained through the GPS device. The District Court granted the motion only in part, suppressing the data obtained while the vehicle was parked in the garage adjoining Jones's residence. It held

---

[1] In this litigation, the Government has conceded noncompliance with the warrant and has argued only that a warrant was not required.

the remaining data admissible, because "[a] person traveling in an automobile on public thoroughfares has no reasonable expectation of privacy in his movements from one place to another." * * * The jury returned a guilty verdict, and the District Court sentenced Jones to life imprisonment.

The United States Court of Appeals for the District of Columbia Circuit reversed the conviction because of admission of the evidence obtained by warrantless use of the GPS device which, it said, violated the Fourth Amendment. * * *

The Fourth Amendment provides in relevant part that "[t]he right of the people to be secure in their persons, houses, papers, and effects, against unreasonable searches and seizures, shall not be violated." It is beyond dispute that a vehicle is an "effect" as that term is used in the Amendment. We hold that the Government's installation of a GPS device on a target's vehicle,[2] and its use of that device to monitor the vehicle's movements, constitutes a "search."

It is important to be clear about what occurred in this case: The Government physically occupied private property for the purpose of obtaining information. We have no doubt that such a physical intrusion would have been considered a "search" within the meaning of the Fourth Amendment when it was adopted. * * * The text of the Fourth Amendment reflects its close connection to property, since otherwise it would have referred simply to "the right of the people to be secure against unreasonable searches and seizures"; the phrase "in their persons, houses, papers, and effects" would have been superfluous.

Consistent with this understanding, our Fourth Amendment jurisprudence was tied to common-law trespass, at least until the latter half of the 20th century. Thus, in *Olmstead v. United States*, we held that wiretaps attached to telephone wires on the public streets did not constitute a Fourth Amendment search because "[t]here was no entry of the houses or offices of the defendants."

Our later cases, of course, have deviated from that exclusively property-based approach. In *Katz v. United States*, we said that "the Fourth Amendment protects people, not places," and found a violation in attachment of an eavesdropping device to a public telephone booth. Our later cases have applied the analysis of Justice Harlan's concurrence in

---

[2] As we have noted, the Jeep was registered to Jones's wife. The Government acknowledged, however, that Jones was "the exclusive driver." If Jones was not the owner he had at least the property rights of a bailee. The Court of Appeals concluded that the vehicle's registration did not affect his ability to make a Fourth Amendment objection, and the Government has not challenged that determination here. We therefore do not consider the Fourth Amendment significance of Jones's status.

that case, which said that a violation occurs when government officers violate a person's "reasonable expectation of privacy."

The Government contends that the Harlan standard shows that no search occurred here, since Jones had no "reasonable expectation of privacy" in the area of the Jeep accessed by Government agents (its underbody) and in the locations of the Jeep on the public roads, which were visible to all. But we need not address the Government's contentions, because Jones's Fourth Amendment rights do not rise or fall with the *Katz* formulation. At bottom, we must "assur[e] preservation of that degree of privacy against government that existed when the Fourth Amendment was adopted." As explained, for most of our history the Fourth Amendment was understood to embody a particular concern for government trespass upon the areas ("persons, houses, papers, and effects") it enumerates.[3] *Katz* did not repudiate that understanding. * * *

More recently, in *Soldal v. Cook County*, the Court unanimously rejected the argument that although a "seizure" had occurred "in a 'technical' sense" when a trailer home was forcibly removed, no Fourth Amendment violation occurred because law enforcement had not "invade[d] the [individuals'] privacy." *Katz*, the Court explained, established that "property rights are not the sole measure of Fourth Amendment violations," but did not "snuf[f] out the previously recognized protection for property." * * * *Katz* did not narrow the Fourth Amendment's scope.[5]

The Government contends that several of our post-*Katz* cases foreclose the conclusion that what occurred here constituted a search. It relies principally on two cases in which we rejected Fourth Amendment challenges to "beepers," electronic tracking devices that represent another

---

[3] Justice Alito's concurrence (hereinafter concurrence) doubts the wisdom of our approach because "it is almost impossible to think of late-18th-century situations that are analogous to what took place in this case." But in fact it posits a situation that is not far afield—a constable's concealing himself in the target's coach in order to track its movements. There is no doubt that the information gained by that trespassory activity would be the product of an unlawful search—whether that information consisted of the conversations occurring in the coach, or of the destinations to which the coach traveled.

In any case, it is quite irrelevant whether there was an 18th-century analog. Whatever new methods of investigation may be devised, our task, *at a minimum*, is to decide whether the action in question would have constituted a "search" within the original meaning of the Fourth Amendment. Where, as here, the Government obtains information by physically intruding on a constitutionally protected area, such a search has undoubtedly occurred.

[5] The concurrence notes that post-*Katz* we have explained that "an actual trespass is neither necessary *nor sufficient* to establish a constitutional violation." That is undoubtedly true, and undoubtedly irrelevant. * * * Trespass alone does not qualify, but there must be conjoined with that what was present here: an attempt to find something or to obtain information.

Related to this, and similarly irrelevant, is the concurrence's point that, if analyzed separately, neither the installation of the device nor its use would constitute a Fourth Amendment search. Of course not. A trespass on "houses" or "effects," or a *Katz* invasion of privacy, is not alone a search unless it is done to obtain information; and the obtaining of information is not alone a search unless it is achieved by such a trespass or invasion of privacy.

form of electronic monitoring. The first case, *United States v. Knotts*, upheld against Fourth Amendment challenge the use of a "beeper" that had been placed in a container of chloroform, allowing law enforcement to monitor the location of the container. We said that there had been no infringement of Knotts' reasonable expectation of privacy since the information obtained—the location of the automobile carrying the container on public roads, and the location of the off-loaded container in open fields near Knotts' cabin—had been voluntarily conveyed to the public. * * *

The second "beeper" case, *United States v. Karo*,[a] does not suggest a different conclusion. * * *

The concurrence faults our approach for "present[ing] particularly vexing problems" in cases that do not involve physical contact, such as those that involve the transmission of electronic signals. We entirely fail to understand that point. For unlike the concurrence, which would make *Katz* the *exclusive* test, we do not make trespass the exclusive test. Situations involving merely the transmission of electronic signals without trespass would *remain* subject to *Katz* analysis.

In fact, it is the concurrence's insistence on the exclusivity of the *Katz* test that needlessly leads us into "particularly vexing problems" in the present case. This Court has to date not deviated from the understanding that mere visual observation does not constitute a search. We accordingly held in *Knotts* that "[a] person traveling in an automobile on public thoroughfares has no reasonable expectation of privacy in his movements from one place to another." Thus, even assuming that the concurrence is correct to say that "[t]raditional surveillance" of Jones for a 4-week period "would have required a large team of agents, multiple vehicles, and perhaps aerial assistance," our cases suggest that such visual observation is constitutionally permissible. It may be that achieving the same result through electronic means, without an accompanying trespass, is an unconstitutional invasion of privacy, but the present case does not require us to answer that question.

And answering it affirmatively leads us needlessly into additional thorny problems. The concurrence posits that "relatively short-term monitoring of a person's movements on public streets" is okay, but that "the use of longer term GPS monitoring in investigations *of most offenses*" is no good. That introduces yet another novelty into our jurisprudence. There is no precedent for the proposition that whether a search has occurred

---

[a] In *United States v. Karo*, 468 U.S. 705 (1984), the Court reaffirmed *Knotts*, but held that when a car with a government-installed beeper goes into a private home's garage, the continued monitoring of that beeper constitutes a "search" within the meaning of the Fourth Amendment. *Id*. at 715. The Court reasoned that once the car leaves the public roads and enters the home, the beeper is conveying private information about the home not readily observable to any member of the public. *Id*.

depends on the nature of the crime being investigated. And even accepting that novelty, it remains unexplained why a 4-week investigation is "surely" too long and why a drug-trafficking conspiracy involving substantial amounts of cash and narcotics is not an "extraordinary offens[e]" which may permit longer observation. What of a 2-day monitoring of a suspected purveyor of stolen electronics? Or of a 6-month monitoring of a suspected terrorist? We may have to grapple with these "vexing problems" in some future case where a classic trespassory search is not involved and resort must be had to *Katz* analysis; but there is no reason for rushing forward to resolve them here. * * *

The judgment of the Court of Appeals for the D.C. Circuit is affirmed.[b]

It is so ordered.

JUSTICE SOTOMAYOR, concurring.

* * * [A]s Justice Alito notes, physical intrusion is now unnecessary to many forms of surveillance. With increasing regularity, the Government will be capable of duplicating the monitoring undertaken in this case by enlisting factory- or owner-installed vehicle tracking devices or GPS-enabled smartphones. * * *

Awareness that the Government may be watching chills associational and expressive freedoms. And the Government's unrestrained power to assemble data that reveal private aspects of identity is susceptible to abuse. The net result is that GPS monitoring—by making available at a relatively low cost such a substantial quantum of intimate information about any person whom the Government, in its unfettered discretion, chooses to track—may "alter the relationship between citizen and government in a way that is inimical to democratic society."

I would take these attributes of GPS monitoring into account when considering the existence of a reasonable societal expectation of privacy in the sum of one's public movements. I would ask whether people reasonably expect that their movements will be recorded and aggregated in a manner that enables the Government to ascertain, more or less at will, their political and religious beliefs, sexual habits, and so on. * * * I would also consider the appropriateness of entrusting to the Executive, in the absence of any oversight from a coordinate branch, a tool so amenable to misuse, especially in light of the Fourth Amendment's goal to curb arbitrary exercises of police power to and prevent "a too permeating police surveillance."

---

[b] In a later case, the Court relied on *Jones* to hold that requiring a recidivist sex offender to wear an electronic tracking device at all times constitutes a "search" within the meaning of the Fourth Amendment. Grady v. North Carolina, 575 U.S. 306, 135 S. Ct. 1368 (2015). The Court declined to rule on whether this type of search was reasonable.

More fundamentally, it may be necessary to reconsider the premise that an individual has no reasonable expectation of privacy in information voluntarily disclosed to third parties. This approach is ill suited to the digital age, in which people reveal a great deal of information about themselves to third parties in the course of carrying out mundane tasks. People disclose the phone numbers that they dial or text to their cellular providers; the URLs that they visit and the e-mail addresses with which they correspond to their Internet service providers; and the books, groceries, and medications they purchase to online retailers. Perhaps, as Justice Alito notes, some people may find the "tradeoff" of privacy for convenience "worthwhile," or come to accept this "diminution of privacy" as "inevitable," and perhaps not. I for one doubt that people would accept without complaint the warrantless disclosure to the Government of a list of every Web site they had visited in the last week, or month, or year. * * * I would not assume that all information voluntarily disclosed to some member of the public for a limited purpose is, for that reason alone, disentitled to Fourth Amendment protection.

JUSTICE ALITO with whom JUSTICE GINSBURG, JUSTICE BREYER, and JUSTICE KAGAN join, concurring in the judgment.

This case requires us to apply the Fourth Amendment's prohibition of unreasonable searches and seizures to a 21st-century surveillance technique, the use of a Global Positioning System (GPS) device to monitor a vehicle's movements for an extended period of time. Ironically, the Court has chosen to decide this case based on 18th-century tort law. By attaching a small GPS device to the underside of the vehicle that respondent drove, the law enforcement officers in this case engaged in conduct that might have provided grounds in 1791 for a suit for trespass to chattels. And for this reason, the Court concludes, the installation and use of the GPS device constituted a search.

This holding, in my judgment, is unwise. It strains the language of the Fourth Amendment; it has little if any support in current Fourth Amendment case law; and it is highly artificial.

I would analyze the question presented in this case by asking whether respondent's reasonable expectations of privacy were violated by the long-term monitoring of the movements of the vehicle he drove.

The Fourth Amendment prohibits "unreasonable searches and seizures," and the Court makes very little effort to explain how the attachment or use of the GPS device fits within these terms. The Court does not contend that there was a seizure. A seizure of property occurs when there is "some meaningful interference with an individual's possessory interests in that property," and here there was none. Indeed, the success of the surveillance technique that the officers employed was dependent on the fact that the GPS did not interfere in any way with the operation of the vehicle, for if any such interference had been detected, the device might have been discovered. * * *

The Court argues—and I agree—that "we must 'assur[e] preservation of that degree of privacy against government that existed when the Fourth Amendment was adopted.'" But it is almost impossible to think of late-18th-century situations that are analogous to what took place in this case. (Is it possible to imagine a case in which a constable secreted himself somewhere in a coach and remained there for a period of time in order to monitor the movements of the coach's owner?³) The Court's theory seems to be that the concept of a search, as originally understood, comprehended any technical trespass that led to the gathering of evidence, but we know that this is incorrect. At common law, any unauthorized intrusion on private property was actionable [under tort law], but a trespass on open fields, as opposed to the "curtilage" of a home, does not fall within the scope of the Fourth Amendment because private property outside the curtilage is not part of a "hous[e]" within the meaning of the Fourth Amendment.

The Court's reasoning in this case is very similar to that in the Court's early decisions involving wiretapping and electronic eavesdropping, namely, that a technical trespass followed by the gathering of evidence constitutes a search. * * * This trespass-based rule was repeatedly criticized. In *Olmstead*, Justice Brandeis [dissenting] wrote that it was "immaterial where the physical connection with the telephone wires was made." Although a private conversation transmitted by wire did not fall within the literal words of the Fourth Amendment, he argued, the Amendment should be understood as prohibiting "every unjustifiable intrusion by the government upon the privacy of the individual."

Katz v. United States finally did away with the old approach, holding that a trespass was not required for a Fourth Amendment violation.

* * * [T]he Court's reasoning largely disregards what is really important (the *use* of a GPS for the purpose of long-term tracking) and instead attaches great significance to something that most would view as relatively minor (attaching to the bottom of a car a small, light object that does not interfere in any way with the car's operation). Attaching such an object is generally regarded as so trivial that it does not provide a basis for recovery under modern tort law.ᶜ But under the Court's reasoning, this conduct may violate the Fourth Amendment. By contrast, if long-term monitoring can be accomplished without committing a technical trespass—suppose, for example, that the Federal Government required or persuaded

---

³ The Court suggests that something like this might have occurred in 1791, but this would have required either a gigantic coach, a very tiny constable, or both—not to mention a constable with incredible fortitude and patience.

ᶜ Justice Alito explains in another part of his opinion that under trespass law today, there must be some actual damage to the property and that in this case, there was no actual damage to the Jeep.

auto manufacturers to include a GPS tracking device in every car—the Court's theory would provide no protection.

*** [T]he Court's reliance on the law of trespass will present particularly vexing problems in cases involving surveillance that is carried out by making electronic, as opposed to physical, contact with the item to be tracked. For example, suppose that the officers in the present case had followed respondent by surreptitiously activating a stolen vehicle detection system that came with the car when it was purchased. Would the sending of a radio signal to activate this system constitute a trespass to chattels? Trespass to chattels has traditionally required a physical touching of the property. ***

The *Katz* expectation-of-privacy test avoids the problems and complications noted above, but it is not without its own difficulties. *** [T]he *Katz* test rests on the assumption that this hypothetical reasonable person has a well-developed and stable set of privacy expectations. But technology can change those expectations. Dramatic technological change may lead to periods in which popular expectations are in flux and may ultimately produce significant changes in popular attitudes. New technology may provide increased convenience or security at the expense of privacy, and many people may find the tradeoff worthwhile. And even if the public does not welcome the diminution of privacy that new technology entails, they may eventually reconcile themselves to this development as inevitable. ***

Recent years have seen the emergence of many new devices that permit the monitoring of a person's movements. In some locales, closed-circuit television video monitoring is becoming ubiquitous. On toll roads, automatic toll collection systems create a precise record of the movements of motorists who choose to make use of that convenience. ***

Perhaps most significant, cell phones and other wireless devices now permit wireless carriers to track and record the location of users—and as of June 2011, it has been reported, there were more than 322 million wireless devices in use in the United States. *** [W]hen a user activates the GPS on such a phone, a provider is able to monitor the phone's location and speed of movement and can then report back real-time traffic conditions after combining ("crowdsourcing") the speed of all such phones on any particular road. *** The availability and use of these and other new devices will continue to shape the average person's expectations about the privacy of his or her daily movements.

In the pre-computer age, *** [t]raditional surveillance for any extended period of time was difficult and costly and therefore rarely undertaken. The surveillance at issue in this case—constant monitoring of the location of a vehicle for four weeks—would have required a large team of agents, multiple vehicles, and perhaps aerial assistance. Only an investigation of unusual importance could have justified such an expenditure of law enforcement resources. Devices like the one used in the present case, however, make long-term monitoring relatively easy and cheap. In circumstances involving dramatic technological change, the best solution to privacy concerns may be legislative. A legislative body is well situated to gauge changing public attitudes, to draw detailed lines, and to balance privacy and public safety in a comprehensive way.

To date, however, Congress and most States have not enacted statutes regulating the use of GPS tracking technology for law enforcement purposes. The best that we can do in this case is to apply existing Fourth Amendment doctrine and to ask whether the use of GPS tracking in a particular case involved a degree of intrusion that a reasonable person would not have anticipated.

Under this approach, relatively short-term monitoring of a person's movements on public streets accords with expectations of privacy that our society has recognized as reasonable. But the use of longer term GPS monitoring in investigations of most offenses impinges on expectations of privacy. For such offenses, society's expectation has been that law enforcement agents and others would not—and indeed, in the main, simply could not—secretly monitor and catalogue every single movement of an individual's car for a very long period. In this case, for four weeks, law enforcement agents tracked every movement that respondent made in the vehicle he was driving. We need not identify with precision the point at which the tracking of this vehicle became a search, for the line was surely crossed before the 4-week mark. Other cases may present more difficult questions. But where uncertainty exists with respect to whether a certain period of GPS surveillance is long enough to constitute a Fourth Amendment search, the police may always seek a warrant. * * *

For these reasons, I conclude that the lengthy monitoring that occurred in this case constituted a search under the Fourth Amendment. I therefore agree with the majority that the decision of the Court of Appeals must be affirmed.

NOTE

One type of electronic surveillance that has become ubiquitous in cities and states across the United States is the traffic camera, which is used to catch drivers who run red lights and drivers who drive at speeds over the speed limit. Local governments have come to depend on traffic cams to bolster their budgets as these cameras bring in millions of dollars in annual revenue. *See* Mike DeBonis, *Broken Traffic Cameras Contributed to Massive Revenue Decline, D.C. Police Say*, WASH. POST (Jan. 27, 2015) (noting that in fiscal year 2012, Washington, D.C.'s camera program raked in more than $85 million), https://www.washingtonpost.com/local/dc-politics/broken-traffic-cameras-contributed-to-massive-revenue-decline-dc-police-say/2015/01/27/773989f8-a627-11e4-a2b2-776095f393b2_story.html (https://perma.cc/QV5K-4CTS).

While many drivers hate traffic cameras, I. Bennett Capers argues for more cameras in public spaces in an effort to deracialize policing. He observes that "cameras ... do not have implicit biases. Nor do they suffer from unconscious racism." I. Bennett Capers, *Race, Policing, and Technology*, 95 N.C. L. REV. 1241, 1276 (2017) (arguing for more policing through public surveillance to reduce police discretion in the enforcement of traffic laws and bring about more equality in policing). Elizabeth Joh has similarly advocated using electronic technology to enforce the traffic laws since this would reduce police discretion in traffic enforcement. Elizabeth E. Joh, *Discretionless Policing, Technology and the Fourth Amendment*, 95 CALIF. L. REV. 199 (2007) (proposing the establishment of a nationwide network of computers and car-installed sensors, similar to the in-vehicle smart-box technology used in Israel that communicates information about a driver's speed to law enforcement and triggers the automatic issuance of a traffic ticket when the driver goes over the speed limit, to reduce police discretion in traffic enforcement).

CARPENTER V. UNITED STATES
Supreme Court of the United States
582 U.S. ___, 138 S. Ct. 2206, 201 L. Ed. 2d 507 (2018)

CHIEF JUSTICE ROBERTS delivered the opinion of the Court.

This case presents the question whether the Government conducts a search under the Fourth Amendment when it accesses historical cell phone records that provide a comprehensive chronicle of the user's past movements.

There are 396 million cell phone service accounts in the United States—for a Nation of 326 million people. Cell phones perform their wide and growing variety of functions by connecting to a set of radio antennas called "cell sites." Although cell sites are usually mounted on a tower, they can also be found on light posts, flagpoles, church steeples, or the sides of buildings. Cell sites typically have several directional antennas that divide the covered area into sectors.

Cell phones continuously scan their environment looking for the best signal, which generally comes from the closest cell site. Most modern devices, such as smartphones, tap into the wireless network several times a minute whenever their signal is on, even if the owner is not using one of the phone's features. Each time the phone connects to a cell site, it generates a time-stamped record known as cell-site location information (CSLI). The precision of this information depends on the size of the geographic area covered by the cell site. The greater the concentration of cell sites, the smaller the coverage area. As data usage from cell phones has increased, wireless carriers have installed more cell sites to handle the traffic. That has led to increasingly compact coverage areas, especially in urban areas.

Wireless carriers collect and store CSLI for their own business purposes, including finding weak spots in their network and applying "roaming" charges when another carrier routes data through their cell sites. In addition, wireless carriers often sell aggregated location records to data brokers, without individual identifying information of the sort at issue here. While carriers have long retained CSLI for the start and end of incoming calls, in recent years phone companies have also collected location information from the transmission of text messages and routine data connections. Accordingly, modern cell phones generate increasingly vast amounts of increasingly precise CSLI.

In 2011, police officers arrested four men suspected of robbing a series of Radio Shack and (ironically enough) T-Mobile stores in Detroit. One of the men confessed that, over the previous four months, the group (along with a rotating cast of getaway drivers and lookouts) had robbed nine different stores in Michigan and Ohio. The suspect identified 15 accomplices who had participated in the heists and gave the FBI some of their cell phone numbers; the FBI then reviewed his call records to identify additional numbers that he had called around the time of the robberies.

Based on that information, the prosecutors applied for court orders under the Stored Communications Act to obtain cell phone records for petitioner Timothy Carpenter and several other suspects. That statute, as amended in 1994, permits the Government to compel the disclosure of certain telecommunications records when it "offers specific and articulable facts showing that there are reasonable grounds to believe" that the records sought "are relevant and material to an ongoing criminal investigation." 18 U.S.C. § 2703(d). Federal Magistrate Judges issued two orders directing Carpenter's wireless carriers—MetroPCS and Sprint—to disclose "cell/site sector [information] for [Carpenter's] telephone[ ] at call origination and at call termination for incoming and outgoing calls" during the four-month period when the string of robberies occurred. The first order sought 152 days of cell-site records from MetroPCS, which produced records spanning 127 days. The second order requested seven days of CSLI from Sprint, which produced two days of records covering the period when Carpenter's phone was "roaming" in northeastern Ohio. Altogether the Government obtained 12,898 location points cataloging Carpenter's movements—an average of 101 data points per day.

Carpenter was charged with six counts of robbery and an additional six counts of carrying a firearm during a federal crime of violence. Prior to trial, Carpenter moved to suppress the cell-site data provided by the wireless carriers. He argued that the Government's seizure of the records violated the Fourth Amendment because they had been obtained without a warrant supported by probable cause. The District Court denied the motion.

At trial, seven of Carpenter's confederates pegged him as the leader of the operation. In addition, FBI agent Christopher Hess offered expert testimony about the cell-site data. Hess explained that each time a cell phone taps into the wireless network, the carrier logs a time-stamped record of the cell site and particular sector that were used. With this information, Hess produced maps that placed Carpenter's phone near four of the charged robberies. In the Government's view, the location records clinched the case: They confirmed that Carpenter was "right where the . . . robbery was at the exact time of the robbery." Carpenter was convicted on all but one of the firearm counts and sentenced to more than 100 years in prison.

The Court of Appeals for the Sixth Circuit affirmed. The court held that Carpenter lacked a reasonable expectation of privacy in the location information collected by the FBI because he had shared that information with his wireless carriers. Given that cell phone users voluntarily convey cell-site data to their carriers as "a means of establishing communication," the court concluded that the resulting business records are not entitled to Fourth Amendment protection.

We granted certiorari. * * *

The case before us involves the Government's acquisition of wireless carrier cell-site records revealing the location of Carpenter's cell phone whenever it made or received calls. This sort of digital data—personal location information maintained by a third party—does not fit neatly under existing precedents. Instead, requests for cell-site records lie at the intersection of two lines of cases, both of which inform our understanding of the privacy interests at stake.

The first set of cases addresses a person's expectation of privacy in his physical location and movements. * * * In *United States v. Jones,* FBI agents installed a GPS tracking device on Jones's vehicle and remotely monitored the vehicle's movements for 28 days. The Court decided the case based on the Government's physical trespass of the vehicle. At the same time, five Justices agreed that related privacy concerns would be raised by, for example, "surreptitiously activating a stolen vehicle detection system" in Jones's car to track Jones himself, or conducting GPS tracking of his cell phone. Since GPS monitoring of a vehicle tracks "every movement" a person makes in that vehicle, the concurring Justices concluded that "longer term GPS monitoring in investigations of most offenses impinges on expectations of privacy"—regardless whether those movements were disclosed to the public at large.

In a second set of decisions, the Court has drawn a line between what a person keeps to himself and what he shares with others. We have previously held that "a person has no legitimate expectation of privacy in information he voluntarily turns over to third parties." That remains true "even if the information is revealed on the assumption that it will be used only for a limited purpose." As a result, the Government is typically free to obtain such information from the recipient without triggering Fourth Amendment protections.

This third-party doctrine largely traces its roots to [*United States v.*] *Miller*. While investigating Miller for tax evasion, the Government subpoenaed his banks, seeking several months of canceled checks, deposit slips, and monthly statements. The Court rejected a Fourth Amendment challenge to the records collection. For one, Miller could "assert neither ownership nor possession" of the documents; they were "business records of the banks." For another, the nature of those records confirmed Miller's limited expectation of privacy, because the checks were "not confidential communications but negotiable instruments to be used in commercial transactions," and the bank statements contained information "exposed to [bank] employees in the ordinary course of business." The Court thus concluded that Miller had "take[n] the risk, in revealing his affairs to another, that the information [would] be conveyed by that person to the Government."

Three years later, *Smith* [*v. Maryland*] applied the same principles in the context of information conveyed to a telephone company. The Court ruled that the Government's use of a pen register—a device that recorded the outgoing phone numbers dialed on a landline telephone—was not a search. Noting the pen register's "limited capabilities," the Court "doubt[ed] that people in general entertain any actual expectation of privacy in the numbers they dial." Telephone subscribers know, after all, that the numbers are used by the telephone company "for a variety of legitimate business purposes," including routing calls. And at any rate, the Court explained, such an expectation "is not one that society is prepared to recognize as reasonable." When Smith placed a call, he "voluntarily conveyed" the dialed numbers to the phone company by "expos[ing] that information to its equipment in the ordinary course of business." Once again, we held that the defendant "assumed the risk" that the company's records "would be divulged to police." The question we confront today is how to apply the Fourth Amendment to a new phenomenon: the ability to chronicle a person's past movements through the record of his cell phone signals. Such tracking partakes of many of the qualities of the GPS monitoring we considered in *Jones*. Much like GPS tracking of a vehicle, cell phone location information is detailed, encyclopedic, and effortlessly compiled.

At the same time, the fact that the individual continuously reveals his location to his wireless carrier implicates the third-party principle of *Smith* and *Miller*. But while the third-party doctrine applies to telephone numbers and bank records, it is not clear whether its logic extends to the qualitatively different category of cell-site records. After all, when *Smith* was decided in 1979, few could have imagined a society in which a phone goes wherever its owner goes, conveying to the wireless carrier not just dialed digits, but a detailed and comprehensive record of the person's movements.

We decline to extend *Smith* and *Miller* to cover these novel circumstances. Given the unique nature of cell phone location records, the fact that the information is held by a third party does not by itself overcome the user's claim to Fourth Amendment protection. Whether the Government employs its own surveillance technology as in *Jones* or leverages the technology of a wireless carrier, we hold that an individual maintains a legitimate expectation of privacy in the record of his physical movements as captured through CSLI. The location information obtained from Carpenter's wireless carriers was the product of a search.[3]

A person does not surrender all Fourth Amendment protection by venturing into the public sphere. To the contrary, "what [one] seeks to preserve as private, even in an area accessible to the public, may be constitutionally protected." A majority of this Court has already recognized that individuals have a reasonable expectation of privacy in the whole of their physical movements. Prior to the digital age, law enforcement might have pursued a suspect for a brief stretch, but doing so "for any extended period of time was difficult and costly and therefore rarely undertaken." For that reason, "society's expectation has been that law enforcement agents and others would not—and indeed, in the main, simply could not—secretly monitor and catalogue every single movement of an individual's car for a very long period."

Allowing government access to cell-site records contravenes that expectation. Although such records are generated for commercial purposes, that distinction does not negate Carpenter's anticipation of privacy in his physical location. Mapping a cell phone's location over the course of 127 days provides an all-encompassing record of the holder's whereabouts. As with GPS information, the time-stamped data provides an intimate window into a person's life, revealing not only his particular movements, but through them his "familial, political, professional, religious, and sexual associations." These location records "hold for many Americans the 'privacies of life.'" And like GPS monitoring, cell phone tracking is remarkably easy, cheap, and efficient compared to traditional investigative tools. With just the click of a button, the Government can access each

---

[3] * * * [W]e need not decide whether there is a limited period for which the Government may obtain an individual's historical CSLI free from Fourth Amendment scrutiny, and if so, how long that period might be. It is sufficient for our purposes today to hold that accessing seven days of CSLI constitutes a Fourth Amendment search.

carrier's deep repository of historical location information at practically no expense. * * *

The Government's primary contention to the contrary is that the third-party doctrine governs this case. In its view, cell-site records are fair game because they are "business records" created and maintained by the wireless carriers. * * *

The Government's position fails to contend with the seismic shifts in digital technology that made possible the tracking of not only Carpenter's location but also everyone else's, not for a short period but for years and years. Sprint Corporation and its competitors are not your typical witnesses. Unlike the nosy neighbor who keeps an eye on comings and goings, they are ever alert, and their memory is nearly infallible. There is a world of difference between the limited types of personal information addressed in *Smith* and *Miller* and the exhaustive chronicle of location information casually collected by wireless carriers today. The Government thus is not asking for a straightforward application of the third-party doctrine, but instead a significant extension of it to a distinct category of information.

The third-party doctrine partly stems from the notion that an individual has a reduced expectation of privacy in information knowingly shared with another. But the fact of "diminished privacy interests does not mean that the Fourth Amendment falls out of the picture entirely." *Smith* and *Miller,* after all, did not rely solely on the act of sharing. Instead, they considered "the nature of the particular documents sought" to determine whether "there is a legitimate 'expectation of privacy' concerning their contents." *Smith* pointed out the limited capabilities of a pen register; as explained in *Riley,* telephone call logs reveal little in the way of "identifying information." * * * In mechanically applying the third-party doctrine to this case, the Government fails to appreciate that there are no comparable limitations on the revealing nature of CSLI. * * *

Neither does the second rationale underlying the third-party doctrine—voluntary exposure—hold up when it comes to CSLI. Cell phone location information is not truly "shared" as one normally understands the term. In the first place, cell phones and the services they provide are "such a pervasive and insistent part of daily life" that carrying one is indispensable to participation in modern society. Second, a cell phone logs a cell-site record by dint of its operation, without any affirmative act on the part of the user beyond powering up. Virtually any activity on the phone generates CSLI, including incoming calls, texts, or e-mails and countless other data connections that a phone automatically makes when checking for news, weather, or social media updates. Apart from disconnecting the phone from the network, there is no way to avoid leaving behind a trail of location data. As a result, in no meaningful sense does the user voluntarily "assume[ ] the risk" of turning over a comprehensive dossier of his physical movements.

We therefore decline to extend *Smith* and *Miller* to the collection of CSLI. Given the unique nature of cell phone location information, the fact that the Government obtained the information from a third party does not overcome Carpenter's claim to Fourth Amendment protection. The Government's acquisition of the cell-site records was a search within the meaning of the Fourth Amendment.

Our decision today is a narrow one. We do not express a view on matters not before us: real-time CSLI or "tower dumps" (a download of information on all the devices that connected to a particular cell site during a particular interval). We do not disturb the application of *Smith* and *Miller* or call into question conventional surveillance techniques and tools, such as security cameras. Nor do we address other business records that might incidentally reveal location information. Further, our opinion does not consider other collection techniques involving foreign affairs or national security. As Justice Frankfurter noted when considering new innovations in airplanes and radios, the Court must tread carefully in such cases, to ensure that we do not "embarrass the future."

Having found that the acquisition of Carpenter's CSLI was a search, we also conclude that the Government must generally obtain a warrant supported by probable cause before acquiring such records. Although the "ultimate measure of the constitutionality of a governmental search is 'reasonableness,'" our cases establish that warrantless searches are typically unreasonable where "a search is undertaken by law enforcement officials to discover evidence of criminal wrongdoing." Thus, "[i]n the absence of a warrant, a search is reasonable only if it falls within a specific exception to the warrant requirement."

The Government acquired the cell-site records pursuant to a court order issued under the Stored Communications Act, which required the Government to show "reasonable grounds" for believing that the records were "relevant and material to an ongoing investigation." That showing falls well short of the probable cause required for a warrant. The Court usually requires "some quantum of individualized suspicion" before a search or seizure may take place. Under the standard in the Stored Communications Act, however, law enforcement need only show that the cell-site evidence might be pertinent to an ongoing investigation—a "gigantic" departure from the probable cause rule, as the Government explained below. Consequently, an order issued under Section 2703(d) of the Act is not a permissible mechanism for accessing historical cell-site records. Before compelling a wireless carrier to turn over a subscriber's CSLI, the Government's obligation is a familiar one—get a warrant. * * *

[E]ven though the Government will generally need a warrant to access CSLI, case-specific exceptions may support a warrantless search of an individual's cell-site records under certain circumstances. "One well-recognized exception applies when ' "the exigencies of the situation" make the needs of law enforcement so compelling that [a] warrantless search is objectively reasonable under the Fourth Amendment.' " Such exigencies include the need to pursue a fleeing suspect, protect individuals who are threatened with imminent harm, or prevent the imminent destruction of evidence.

As a result, if law enforcement is confronted with an urgent situation, such fact-specific threats will likely justify the warrantless collection of CSLI. Lower courts, for instance, have approved warrantless searches related to bomb threats, active shootings, and child abductions. Our decision today does not call into doubt warrantless access to CSLI in such circumstances. While police must get a warrant when collecting CSLI to assist in the mine-run criminal investigation, the rule we set forth does not limit their ability to respond to an ongoing emergency.

As Justice Brandeis explained in his famous dissent, the Court is obligated—as "[s]ubtler and more far-reaching means of invading privacy have become available to the Government"—to ensure that the "progress of science" does not erode Fourth Amendment protections. Here the progress of science has afforded law enforcement a powerful new tool to carry out its important responsibilities. At the same time, this tool risks Government encroachment of the sort the Framers, "after consulting the lessons of history," drafted the Fourth Amendment to prevent.

We decline to grant the state unrestricted access to a wireless carrier's database of physical location information. In light of the deeply revealing nature of CSLI, its depth, breadth, and comprehensive reach, and the inescapable and automatic nature of its collection, the fact that such information is gathered by a third party does not make it any less deserving of Fourth Amendment protection. The Government's acquisition of the cell-site records here was a search under that Amendment.

The judgment of the Court of Appeals is reversed, and the case is remanded for further proceedings consistent with this opinion.

It is so ordered.

JUSTICE THOMAS, dissenting

This case should not turn on "whether" a search occurred. It should turn, instead, on *whose* property was searched. The Fourth Amendment guarantees individuals the right to be secure from unreasonable searches of "*their* persons, houses, papers, and effects." In other words, "*each* person has the right to be secure against unreasonable searches . . . in *his own* person, house, papers, and effects." By obtaining the cell-site records of

MetroPCS and Sprint, the Government did not search Carpenter's property. He did not create the records, he does not maintain them, he cannot control them, and he cannot destroy them. Neither the terms of his contracts nor any provision of law makes the records his. The records belong to MetroPCS and Sprint. * * *

The more fundamental problem with the Court's opinion, however, is its use of the "reasonable expectation of privacy" test, which was first articulated by Justice Harlan in *Katz v. United States*. The *Katz* test has no basis in the text or history of the Fourth Amendment. And, it invites courts to make judgments about policy, not law. Until we confront the problems with this test, *Katz* will continue to distort Fourth Amendment jurisprudence. I respectfully dissent.

Katz was the culmination of a series of decisions applying the Fourth Amendment to electronic eavesdropping. The first such decision was *Olmstead v. United States,* where federal officers had intercepted the defendants' conversations by tapping telephone lines near their homes. In an opinion by Chief Justice Taft, the Court concluded that this wiretap did not violate the Fourth Amendment. No "search" occurred, according to the Court, because the officers did not physically enter the defendants' homes. And neither the telephone lines nor the defendants' intangible conversations qualified as "persons, houses, papers, [or] effects" within the meaning of the Fourth Amendment. In the ensuing decades, this Court adhered to *Olmstead* and rejected Fourth Amendment challenges to various methods of electronic surveillance. * * *

In *Katz,* the Court rejected *Olmstead*'s * * * holding—that eavesdropping is not a search absent a physical intrusion into a constitutionally protected area. The federal officers in *Katz* had intercepted the defendant's conversations by attaching an electronic device to the outside of a public telephone booth. The Court concluded that this was a "search" because the officers "violated the privacy upon which [the defendant] justifiably relied while using the telephone booth." Although the device did not physically penetrate the booth, the Court overruled *Olmstead* and held that "the reach of [the Fourth] Amendment cannot turn upon the presence or absence of a physical intrusion." The Court did not explain what should replace *Olmstead*'s physical-intrusion requirement. It simply asserted that "the Fourth Amendment protects people, not places" and "what [a person] seeks to preserve as private ... may be constitutionally protected."

Justice Harlan's concurrence in *Katz* attempted to articulate the standard that was missing from the majority opinion. * * * Justice Harlan identified a "twofold requirement" to determine when the protections of the Fourth Amendment apply: "first that a person have exhibited an actual (subjective) expectation of privacy and, second, that the expectation be one that society is prepared to recognize as 'reasonable.' "

Justice Harlan did not cite anything for this "expectation of privacy" test, and the parties did not discuss it in their briefs. The test appears to have been presented for the first time at oral argument by one of the defendant's lawyers. The lawyer, a recent law-school graduate, apparently had an "[e]piphany" while preparing for oral argument. He conjectured that, like the "reasonable person" test from his Torts class, the Fourth Amendment should turn on "whether a reasonable person . . . could have expected his communication to be private." The lawyer presented his new theory to the Court at oral argument. After some questioning from the Justices, the lawyer conceded that his test should also require individuals to subjectively expect privacy. With that modification, Justice Harlan seemed to accept the lawyer's test almost verbatim in his concurrence.

* * * Justice Harlan's concurrence profoundly changed our Fourth Amendment jurisprudence. It took only one year for the full Court to adopt his two-pronged test. And by 1979, the Court was describing Justice Harlan's test as the "lodestar" for determining whether a "search" had occurred. * * *

Under the *Katz* test, a "search" occurs whenever "government officers violate a person's 'reasonable expectation of privacy.' " The most glaring problem with this test is that it has "no plausible foundation in the text of the Fourth Amendment." The Fourth Amendment, as relevant here, protects "[t]he right of the people to be secure in their persons, houses, papers, and effects, against unreasonable searches." By defining "search" to mean "any violation of a reasonable expectation of privacy," the *Katz* test misconstrues virtually every one of these words.

The *Katz* test distorts the original meaning of "searc[h]"—the word in the Fourth Amendment that it purports to define. Under the *Katz* test, the government conducts a search anytime it violates someone's "reasonable expectation of privacy." That is not a normal definition of the word "search."

At the founding, "search" did not mean a violation of someone's reasonable expectation of privacy. The word was probably not a term of art, as it does not appear in legal dictionaries from the era. And its ordinary meaning was the same as it is today: " '[t]o look over or through for the purpose of finding something; to explore; to examine by inspection; as, to *search* the house for a book; to *search* the wood for a thief.' " The word "search" was not associated with "reasonable expectation of privacy" until Justice Harlan coined that phrase in 1967. * * *

The *Katz* test strays even further from the text by focusing on the concept of "privacy." The word "privacy" does not appear in the Fourth Amendment (or anywhere else in the Constitution for that matter). Instead, the Fourth Amendment references "[t]he right of the people to be secure." It then qualifies that right by limiting it to "persons" and three specific types of property: "houses, papers, and effects." By connecting the right to be secure to these four specific objects, "[t]he text of the Fourth Amendment reflects its close connection to property." "[P]rivacy," by contrast, "was not part of the political vocabulary of the [founding]." * * *

In shifting the focus of the Fourth Amendment from property to privacy, the *Katz* test also reads the words "persons, houses, papers, and effects" out of the text. At its broadest formulation, the *Katz* test would find a search "*wherever* an individual may harbor a reasonable 'expectation of privacy.'" The Court today, for example, does not ask whether cell-site location records are "persons, houses, papers, [or] effects" within the meaning of the Fourth Amendment. Yet "persons, houses, papers, and effects" cannot mean "anywhere" or "anything." *Katz*'s catchphrase that "the Fourth Amendment protects people, not places," is not a serious attempt to reconcile the constitutional text. The Fourth Amendment obviously protects people; "[t]he question . . . is what protection it affords to those people." The Founders decided to protect the people from unreasonable searches and seizures of four specific things—persons, houses, papers, and effects. * * *

"[P]ersons, houses, papers, and effects" are not the only words that the *Katz* test reads out of the Fourth Amendment. The Fourth Amendment specifies that the people have a right to be secure from unreasonable searches of "their" persons, houses, papers, and effects. Although phrased in the plural, "[t]he obvious meaning of ['their'] is that *each* person has the right to be secure against unreasonable searches and seizures in *his own* person, house, papers, and effects." Stated differently, the word "their" means, at the very least, that individuals do not have Fourth Amendment rights in *someone else's* property. Yet, under the *Katz* test, individuals can have a reasonable expectation of privacy in another person's property. *See, e.g., Carter,* 525 U.S., at 89, 119 S. Ct. [at 473] (majority opinion) ("[A] person may have a legitimate expectation of privacy in the house of someone else"). Until today, our precedents have not acknowledged that individuals can claim a reasonable expectation of privacy in someone else's business records. But the Court erases that line in this case, at least for cell-site location records. In doing so, it confirms that the *Katz* test does not necessarily require an individual to prove that the government searched *his* person, house, paper, or effect.

* * * Carpenter stipulated below that the cell-site records are the business records of Sprint and MetroPCS. * * * If someone stole these records from Sprint or MetroPCS, Carpenter does not argue that he could recover in a traditional tort action. Nor do his contracts with Sprint and MetroPCS make the records his, even though such provisions could exist in the marketplace. * * *

The *Katz* test comes closer to the text of the Fourth Amendment when it asks whether an expectation of privacy is "reasonable," but it ultimately distorts that term as well. The Fourth Amendment forbids "unreasonable searches." In other words, reasonableness determines the legality of a search, not "whether a search . . . within the meaning of the Constitution has *occurred*." * * *

That the *Katz* test departs so far from the text of the Fourth Amendment is reason enough to reject it. But the *Katz* test also has proved unworkable in practice. Jurists and commentators tasked with deciphering our jurisprudence have described the *Katz* regime as "an unpredictable jumble," "a mass of contradictions and obscurities," "all over the map," "riddled with inconsistency and incoherence," "a series of inconsistent and bizarre results that [the Court] has left entirely undefended," "unstable," "chameleon-like," " 'notoriously unhelpful,' " "a conclusion rather than a starting point for analysis," "distressingly unmanageable," "a dismal failure," "flawed to the core," "unadorned fiat," and "inspired by the kind of logic that produced Rube Goldberg's bizarre contraptions." * * *

Because the *Katz* test is a failed experiment, this Court is duty bound to reconsider it. Until it does, I agree with my dissenting colleagues' reading of our precedents. Accordingly, I respectfully dissent.

[The dissenting opinions of JUSTICE KENNEDY, JUSTICE ALITO, and JUSTICE GORSUCH have been omitted.]

D. DOG SNIFFS

In several cases, beginning with *United States v. Place*, 462 U.S. 696 (1983), the Court has dealt with the question of whether a dog sniff by a police dog trained to detect contraband constitutes a search within the meaning of the Fourth Amendment. In *Place*, the Court held that a canine sniff of luggage at the airport, which does not require the opening of luggage nor the exposure of noncontraband items to public view, does not constitute a search within the meaning of the Fourth Amendment. The Court found it noteworthy that a dog sniff discloses only the presence or absence of contraband for which a suspect has no legitimate expectation of privacy. The Court made a point of stating that a canine sniff is *sui generis*. "We are aware of no other investigative procedure that is so limited both in the manner in which the information is obtained and in the content of the information revealed by the procedure." *Id.* at 707. Because the Court concluded that the dog sniff of Place's luggage did not constitute a search, the officers were not required to obtain a warrant based on probable cause.

In *Illinois v. Caballes*, 543 U.S. 405 (2004), the Court was asked to consider whether the Fourth Amendment requires police to have reasonable suspicion of criminal activity before using a drug detection dog to sniff a vehicle for narcotics during a lawful traffic stop. Echoing what it said in *Place*, the *Caballes* Court held that the use of a well-trained narcotics detection dog to reveal contraband hidden in a car during a lawful traffic stop does not implicate legitimate privacy interests. "We have held that any interest in possessing contraband cannot be deemed 'legitimate,' and thus, governmental conduct that only reveals the possession of contraband 'compromises no legitimate privacy interest.'" *Id.* at 408 (citing *United States v. Jacobsen*, 466 U.S. 109 (1984)). The *Caballes* Court concluded that the police do not need reasonable suspicion, probable cause, or a warrant to conduct a dog sniff of a car during a lawful traffic stop because a dog sniff under these circumstances does not constitute a search within the meaning of the Fourth Amendment.[a]

In the next case, *Florida v. Jardines*, the Court was asked once again to decide the constitutionality of a warrantless dog sniff. Unlike in *Place* and *Caballes*, which involved dog sniffs in clearly public places (an airport in *Place* and a road in *Caballes*), the dog sniff in *Jardines* occurred on the front porch of a home. Given the Court's previous pronouncements on the subject, many expected the Court to find that the dog sniff did not constitute a search within the meaning of the Fourth Amendment. Some were surprised to find the Court ruling in favor of the defendant in this case.

FLORIDA V. JARDINES

Supreme Court of the United States
569 U.S. 1, 133 S. Ct. 1409, 185 L. Ed. 2d 495 (2013)

JUSTICE SCALIA delivered the opinion of the Court.

We consider whether using a drug-sniffing dog on a homeowner's porch to investigate the contents of the home is a "search" within the meaning of the Fourth Amendment.

In 2006, Detective William Pedraja of the Miami-Dade Police Department received an unverified tip that marijuana was being grown in the home of respondent Joelis Jardines. One month later, the Department and the Drug Enforcement Administration sent a joint surveillance team to Jardines' home. Detective Pedraja was part of that team. He watched the home for fifteen minutes and saw no vehicles in the driveway or activity around the home, and could not see inside because the blinds were drawn. Detective Pedraja then approached Jardines' home accompanied by

---

[a] In *Rodriguez v. United States*, 575 U.S. 348 (2015), the Court was asked to decide whether a police officer may prolong a traffic stop in order to conduct a dog sniff of the car without reasonable suspicion that the driver or his passenger are involved in criminal activity. The Court held that absent reasonable suspicion, adding time to a traffic stop in order to conduct a dog sniff violates the Fourth Amendment's prohibition against unreasonable seizures. It distinguished the case before it, in which the officer had already issued the motorist a warning for driving on the shoulder of the highway before conducting the dog sniff, from the situation in *Illinois v. Caballes*, in which the dog sniff was conducted during the traffic stop.

Detective Douglas Bartelt, a trained canine handler who had just arrived at the scene with his drug-sniffing dog. The dog was trained to detect the scent of marijuana, cocaine, heroin, and several other drugs, indicating the presence of any of these substances through particular behavioral changes recognizable by his handler.

Detective Bartelt had the dog on a six-foot leash, owing in part to the dog's "wild" nature and tendency to dart around erratically while searching. As the dog approached Jardines' front porch, he apparently sensed one of the odors he had been trained to detect, and began energetically exploring the area for the strongest point source of that odor. As Detective Bartelt explained, the dog "began tracking that airborne odor by . . . tracking back and forth," engaging in what is called "bracketing," "back and forth, back and forth." Detective Bartelt gave the dog "the full six feet of the leash plus whatever safe distance [he could] give him" to do this—he testified that he needed to give the dog "as much distance as I can." And Detective Pedraja stood back while this was occurring, so that he would not "get knocked over" when the dog was "spinning around trying to find" the source.

After sniffing the base of the front door, the dog sat, which is the trained behavior upon discovering the odor's strongest point. Detective Bartelt then pulled the dog away from the door and returned to his vehicle. He left the scene after informing Detective Pedraja that there had been a positive alert for narcotics.

On the basis of what he had learned at the home, Detective Pedraja applied for and received a warrant to search the residence. When the warrant was executed later that day, Jardines attempted to flee and was arrested; the search revealed marijuana plants, and he was charged with trafficking in cannabis.

At trial, Jardines moved to suppress the marijuana plants on the ground that the canine investigation was an unreasonable search. The trial court granted the motion, and the Florida Third District Court of Appeal reversed. On a petition for discretionary review, the Florida Supreme Court quashed the decision of the Third District Court of Appeal and approved the trial court's decision to suppress, holding (as relevant here) that the use of the trained narcotics dog to investigate Jardines' home was a Fourth Amendment search unsupported by probable cause, rendering invalid the warrant based upon information gathered in that search.

We granted certiorari, limited to the question of whether the officers' behavior was a search within the meaning of the Fourth Amendment.

The Fourth Amendment provides in relevant part that the "right of the people to be secure in their persons, houses, papers, and effects, against unreasonable searches and seizures, shall not be violated." The Amendment establishes a simple baseline, one that for much of our history formed the exclusive basis for its protections: When "the Government obtains information by physically intruding" on persons, houses, papers, or effects, "a 'search' within the original meaning of the Fourth Amendment" has "undoubtedly occurred." By reason of our decision in *Katz v. United States*, property rights "are not the sole measure of Fourth Amendment violations"—but though *Katz* may add to the baseline, it does not subtract anything from the Amendment's protections "when the Government *does* engage in [a] physical intrusion of a constitutionally protected area."

That principle renders this case a straightforward one. The officers were gathering information in an area belonging to Jardines and immediately surrounding his house—in the curtilage of the house, which we have held enjoys protection as part of the home itself. And they gathered that information by physically entering and occupying the area to engage in conduct not explicitly or implicitly permitted by the homeowner.

* * * [W]hen it comes to the Fourth Amendment, the home is first among equals. At the Amendment's "very core" stands "the right of a man to retreat into his own home and there be free from unreasonable governmental intrusion." This right would be of little practical value if the State's agents could stand in a home's porch or side garden and trawl for evidence with impunity; the right to retreat would be significantly diminished if the police could enter a man's property to observe his repose from just outside the front window.

We therefore regard the area "immediately surrounding and associated with the home"—what our cases call the curtilage—as "part of the home itself for Fourth Amendment purposes." That principle has ancient and durable roots. Just as the distinction between the home and the open fields is "as old as the common law," so too is the identity of home and what Blackstone called the "curtilage or homestall," for the "house protects and privileges all its branches and appurtenan[ces]." This area around the home is "intimately linked to the home, both physically and psychologically," and is where "privacy expectations are most heightened."

While the boundaries of the curtilage are generally "clearly marked," the "conception defining the curtilage" is at any rate familiar enough that it is "easily understood from our daily experience." Here there is no doubt that the officers entered it: The front porch is the classic exemplar of an area adjacent to the home and "to which the activity of home life extends."

Since the officers' investigation took place in a constitutionally protected area, we turn to the question of whether it was accomplished through an unlicensed physical intrusion. While law enforcement officers need not "shield their eyes" when passing by the home "on public thoroughfares," an officer's leave to gather information is sharply circumscribed when he steps off those thoroughfares and enters the Fourth Amendment's protected areas. * * * As it is undisputed that the detectives had all four of their feet and all four of their companion's firmly planted on the constitutionally protected extension of Jardines' home, the only question is whether he had given his leave (even implicitly) for them to do so. He had not.

* * * We have * * * recognized that "the knocker on the front door is treated as an invitation or license to attempt an entry, justifying ingress to the home by solicitors, hawkers and peddlers of all kinds." This implicit license typically permits the visitor to approach the home by the front path, knock promptly, wait briefly to be received, and then (absent invitation to linger longer) leave. Complying with the terms of that traditional invitation does not require fine-grained legal knowledge; it is generally managed without incident by the Nation's Girl Scouts and trick-or-treaters. Thus, a police officer not armed with a warrant may approach a home and knock, precisely because that is "no more than any private citizen might do."

But introducing a trained police dog to explore the area around the home in hopes of discovering incriminating evidence is something else. There is no customary invitation to do *that*. An invitation to engage in canine forensic investigation assuredly does not inhere in the very act of hanging a knocker. To find a visitor knocking on the door is routine (even if sometimes unwelcome); to spot that same visitor exploring the front path with a metal detector, or marching his bloodhound into the garden before saying hello and asking permission, would inspire most of us to—well, call the police. The scope of a license—express or implied—is limited not only to a particular area but also to a specific purpose. Consent at a traffic stop to an officer's checking out an anonymous tip that there is a body in the trunk does not permit the officer to rummage through the trunk for narcotics. Here, the background social norms that invite a visitor to the front door do not invite him there to conduct a search. * * *

The State argues that investigation by a forensic narcotics dog by definition cannot implicate any legitimate privacy interest. The State cites for authority our decisions in *United States v. Place*, *United States v. Jacobsen*, and *Illinois v. Caballes*, which held, respectively, that canine inspection of luggage in an airport, chemical testing of a substance that had fallen from a parcel in transit, and canine inspection of an automobile during a lawful traffic stop, do not violate the "reasonable expectation of privacy" described in *Katz*.

Just last Term, we considered an argument much like this. *Jones* held that tracking an automobile's whereabouts using a physically-mounted GPS receiver is a Fourth Amendment search. The Government argued that the *Katz* standard "show[ed] that no search occurred," as the defendant had "no 'reasonable expectation of privacy'" in his whereabouts on the public roads—a proposition with at least as much support in our case law as the one the State marshals here. But because the GPS receiver had been physically mounted on the defendant's automobile (thus intruding on his "effects"), we held that tracking the vehicle's movements was a search: a person's "Fourth Amendment rights do not rise or fall with the *Katz* formulation." The *Katz* reasonable-expectations test "has been *added to,* not *substituted for,*" the traditional property-based understanding of the Fourth Amendment, and so is unnecessary to consider when the government gains evidence by physically intruding on constitutionally protected areas.

Thus, we need not decide whether the officers' investigation of Jardines' home violated his expectation of privacy under *Katz*. One virtue of the Fourth Amendment's property-rights baseline is that it keeps easy cases easy. That the officers learned what they learned only by physically intruding on Jardines' property to gather evidence is enough to establish that a search occurred. * * *

The government's use of trained police dogs to investigate the home and its immediate surroundings is a "search" within the meaning of the Fourth Amendment. The judgment of the Supreme Court of Florida is therefore affirmed.

It is so ordered.

JUSTICE KAGAN, with whom JUSTICE GINSBURG and JUSTICE SOTOMAYOR join, concurring.

For me, a simple analogy clinches this case—and does so on privacy as well as property grounds. A stranger comes to the front door of your home carrying super-high-powered binoculars. He doesn't knock or say hello. Instead, he stands on the porch and uses the binoculars to peer through your windows, into your home's furthest corners. It doesn't take long (the binoculars are really very fine): In just a couple of minutes, his uncommon behavior allows him to learn details of your life you disclose to no one. Has your "visitor" trespassed on your property, exceeding the license you have granted to members of the public to, say, drop off the mail or distribute campaign flyers? Yes, he has. And has he also invaded your "reasonable expectation of privacy," by nosing into intimacies you sensibly thought protected from disclosure? Yes, of course, he has done that too.

That case is this case in every way that matters. Here, police officers came to Joelis Jardines' door with a super-sensitive instrument, which they deployed to detect things inside that they could not perceive unassisted. The equipment they used was animal, not mineral. * * * Detective Bartelt's dog was not your neighbor's pet, come to your porch on a leisurely stroll. As this Court discussed earlier this Term, drug-detection dogs are highly trained tools of law enforcement, geared to respond in distinctive ways to specific scents so as to convey clear and reliable information to their human partners. They are to the poodle down the street as high-powered binoculars are to a piece of plain glass. Like the binoculars, a drug-detection dog is a specialized device for discovering objects not in plain view (or plain smell). And as in the hypothetical above, that device was aimed here at a home—the most private and inviolate (or so we expect) of all the places and things the Fourth Amendment protects. Was this activity a trespass? Yes, as the Court holds today. Was it also an invasion of privacy? Yes, that as well.

The Court today treats this case under a property rubric; I write separately to note that I could just as happily have decided it by looking to Jardines' privacy interests. A decision along those lines would have looked . . . well, much like this one. It would have talked about "the right of a man to retreat into his own home and there be free from unreasonable governmental intrusion." It would have insisted on maintaining the "practical value" of that right by preventing police officers from standing in an adjacent space and "trawl[ing] for evidence with impunity." It would have explained that "privacy expectations are most heightened" in the home and the surrounding area. And it would have determined that police officers invade those shared expectations when they use trained canine assistants to reveal within the confines of a home what they could not otherwise have found there.

It is not surprising that in a case involving a search of a home, property concepts and privacy concepts should so align. The law of property "naturally enough influence[s]" our "shared social expectations" of what places should be free from governmental incursions. And so the sentiment "my home is my own," while originating in property law, now also denotes a common understanding—extending even beyond that law's formal protections—about an especially private sphere. Jardines' home was his property; it was also his most intimate and familiar space. The analysis proceeding from each of those facts, as today's decision reveals, runs mostly along the same path.

I can think of only one divergence: If we had decided this case on privacy grounds, we would have realized that *Kyllo v. United States* already resolved it. The *Kyllo* Court held that police officers conducted a search when they used a thermal-imaging device to detect heat emanating from a private home, even though they committed no trespass. Highlighting our intention to draw both a "firm" and a "bright" line at "the entrance to the house," we announced the following rule:

> Where, as here, the Government uses a device that is not in general public use, to explore details of the home that would previously have been unknowable without physical intrusion, the surveillance is a "search" and is presumptively unreasonable without a warrant.

That "firm" and "bright" rule governs this case: The police officers here conducted a search because they used a "device . . . not in general public use" (a trained drug-detection dog) to "explore details of the home" (the presence of certain substances) that they would not otherwise have discovered without entering the premises.

And again, the dissent's argument that the device is just a dog cannot change the equation. As *Kyllo* made clear, the "sense-enhancing" tool at issue may be "crude" or "sophisticated," may be old or new (drug-detection dogs actually go back not "12,000 years" or "centuries," but only a few decades), may be either smaller or bigger than a breadbox; still, "at least where (as here)" the device is not "in general public use," training it on a home violates our "minimal expectation of privacy"—an expectation "that *exists*, and that is acknowledged to be *reasonable*." That does not mean the device is off-limits, as the dissent implies; it just means police officers cannot use it to examine a home without a warrant or exigent circumstance.

With these further thoughts, suggesting that a focus on Jardines' privacy interests would make an "easy cas[e] easy" twice over, I join the Court's opinion in full.

JUSTICE ALITO, with whom THE CHIEF JUSTICE, JUSTICE KENNEDY, and JUSTICE BREYER join, dissenting.

The Court's decision in this important Fourth Amendment case is based on a putative rule of trespass law that is nowhere to be found in the annals of Anglo-American jurisprudence.

The law of trespass generally gives members of the public a license to use a walkway to approach the front door of a house and to remain there for a brief time. This license is not limited to persons who intend to speak to an occupant or who actually do so. (Mail carriers and persons delivering packages and flyers are examples of individuals who may lawfully approach a front door without intending to converse.) Nor is the license restricted to categories of visitors whom an occupant of the dwelling is likely to welcome; as the Court acknowledges, this license applies even to "solicitors, hawkers and peddlers of all kinds." And the license even extends to police officers who wish to gather evidence against an occupant (by asking potentially incriminating questions).

According to the Court, however, the police officer in this case, Detective Bartelt, committed a trespass because he was accompanied during his otherwise lawful visit to the front door of respondent's house by his dog, Franky. Where is the authority evidencing such a rule? Dogs have been domesticated for about 12,000 years; they were ubiquitous in both this country and Britain at the time of the adoption of the Fourth Amendment; and their acute sense of smell has been used in law enforcement for centuries. Yet the Court has been unable to find a single case—from the

United States or any other common-law nation—that supports the rule on which its decision is based. Thus, trespass law provides no support for the Court's holding today.

The Court's decision is also inconsistent with the reasonable-expectations-of-privacy test that the Court adopted in *Katz v. United States*. A reasonable person understands that odors emanating from a house may be detected from locations that are open to the public, and a reasonable person will not count on the strength of those odors remaining within the range that, while detectible by a dog, cannot be smelled by a human.

For these reasons, I would hold that no search within the meaning of the Fourth Amendment took place in this case, and I would reverse the decision below. * * *

E. COMMENTARY ON THE "REASONABLE EXPECTATION OF PRIVACY" TEST

The Court's search jurisprudence has generated much in the way of commentary and critique. The two excerpts that conclude this chapter help us think about ways in which the reasonable expectation of privacy test helps or hurts individuals along the fault lines of class, race, and/or sexual orientation. In the first excerpt, *One Train May Hide Another:* Katz, *Stonewall, and the Secret Subtext of Criminal Procedure,* David Sklanksy talks about how the *Katz* case helped the gay pride movement. In *The Distribution of Fourth Amendment Privacy*, the late William Stuntz provides a class and race-based critique of *Katz*.

"ONE TRAIN MAY HIDE ANOTHER": KATZ, STONEWALL, AND THE SECRET SUBTEXT OF CRIMINAL PROCEDURE

David Alan Sklansky
41 U.C. Davis L. Rev. 875 (2008)

In December 1967 the Supreme Court reversed an interstate wagering conviction and $300 fine in the case of Charlie Katz, a small-time Los Angeles sports bettor who may or may not also have been operating as a bookie. The Court concluded that agents of the Federal Bureau of Investigation had violated the Fourth Amendment's prohibition against "unreasonable searches and seizures" by bugging a pair of public telephone booths from which Katz had placed his bets.

The decision was immediately seen as momentous on two different levels. First, and more specifically, it settled a decades-long controversy over the constitutional status of electronic eavesdropping. *Katz* made clear both that surveillance of this kind constituted a "search" within the meaning of the Fourth Amendment (contrary to what the Court itself had said a half century earlier in its much reviled decision in *Olmstead v. United States*). * * * Second, and more generally, *Katz* laid the groundwork for a new understanding of—or at least a new way to talk about—the Fourth Amendment's purpose and scope. Justice Stewart's majority opinion in *Katz* decisively abandoned an old view (also associated with *Olmstead*) that the Fourth Amendment protected only against physical trespasses, and replaced it with a focus on a more freewheeling, less territorial version of privacy. * * * [T]oday, four decades later, *Katz* remains a landmark both because it provides the constitutional framework that continues to govern electronic surveillance, and because it provides the modern test for a "search" within the meaning of the Fourth Amendment. A "search," today, is an infringement on a "reasonable expectation of privacy."

* * * [T]he Supreme Court's decision in *Katz* * * * had direct and important ramifications for one [police] practice: spying on men in toilet stalls. The literature on *Katz* rarely mentions men's room surveillance, probably because criminal procedure scholars think of this police tactic, if they think of it at all, as a small and squalid footnote in law enforcement history. But in 1967, when Katz was decided, spying on toilet stalls—through cracks, heating ducts, and other peepholes—was a familiar part of the pattern of harassment, humiliation, and persecution shaping the lives of gay people, particularly gay men. So the role that *Katz* played in helping to end the practice was no small thing.

The use of public washrooms as favored sites for homosexual encounters dates at least to the early twentieth century, and so do efforts by the police to combat the practice by surreptitious surveillance. Men's rooms offered "privacy in public"—a broadly accessible, readily identifiable venue where "it was easy to orchestrate sexual activity . . . so that no one uninvolved would see it." By 1967, when *Katz* was decided, the use of public restrooms for impersonal homosexual activity was widespread and well known throughout the United States, and surreptitiously monitoring restrooms, through peepholes or with undercover decoys, had become a chief tactic in the policing of homosexuality. Members of the UCLA Law Review, reviewing Los Angeles County police and court records in the mid-1960s, found that of 493 felony arrests for homosexual activity, 274 were made in public restrooms. Most of these arrests were for sexual conduct directly witnessed by the arresting officers—typically, it seems, from hidden observation posts.

Men's room spying would have accounted for an even larger share of sodomy[a] enforcement in Los Angeles County in the mid-1960s were it not

---

[a] Throughout much of the twentieth century, sodomy was a crime in many states until the Supreme Court, in *Lawrence v. Texas*, 539 U.S. 558 (2003), struck down Texas' sodomy law, which criminalized sexual intimacy between same-sex couples, but not identical behavior by opposite-sex

for a pair of state judicial decisions in 1962. In *Bielicki v. Superior Court*, the California Supreme Court threw out evidence of sodomy that Long Beach vice squad officers had obtained by spying through a pipe overlooking two closed toilet booths in an amusement park. The court reasoned, unanimously, that the spying violated the search-and-seizure provisions of both the federal and California constitutions, because it invaded the "personal right of privacy of the person occupying the stall." Several months later, in *Britt v. Superior Court*, the court reaffirmed its ruling in *Bielicki* and elaborated its rationale. "The crucial fact," the justices explained, "was neither the manner of observation alone nor the place of commission alone, but rather the manner in which the police observed a place and persons in that place which is ordinarily understood to afford personal privacy to individual occupants." The "constitutionally protected right of personal privacy" protected a person not only at home but "when as a member of the public he is temporarily occupying a room ... offered to the public for private, however transient, individual use."

This was the reasoning later adopted in *Katz*, of course. But *Bielicki* was decided half a decade before *Katz*, and the legal support network for defendants brave enough to challenge sodomy prosecutions, a network thin enough in California, was even thinner elsewhere in the country. The American Civil Liberties Union did not take a position opposing enforcement of sodomy laws until 1967. Even "homophile" organizations—the early, fragmented antecedents of the gay rights movement, which focused their efforts in the early 1960s on securing public understanding and respect for gay men and lesbians—often were uncomfortable defending defendants accused of carrying out or soliciting sex in "public." * * *

[In 1967], the Court decided *Katz*, * * * vindicating the 1962 decisions of the California Supreme Court. In the wake of *Katz*, the California Supreme Court reaffirmed and extended its earlier condemnation of toilet stall spying, and courts elsewhere in the country slowly followed suit. Not all of those courts went as far as the California justices, who found an expectation of privacy against covert surveillance even in toilet stalls without doors. But courts in a range of jurisdictions read *Katz* to provide Fourth Amendment protection at least in enclosed toilet stalls.

In doing so, they generally stressed * * * Justice Harlan's description of a telephone booth as a "temporarily private place," analogous, during its short use, to a house. "Surely," the Minnesota Supreme Court pointed out, Justice Harlan's reasoning applied to facilities that "assure the user of privacy as much as a telephone booth does." A Michigan appellate court agreed: "bathroom stalls ... like the telephone booth in Katz," are "temporarily private places whose momentary occupants' expectations of privacy are recognized by society as reasonable." An Idaho appellate court

---

couples. The Court found the sodomy statute in violation of the right to liberty under the Due Process Clause.

found "no constitutional distinction between a public telephone booth and a public restroom stall with regard to the privacy expectation generated within"; in either case, the expectation was one "society would recognize as objectively reasonable." Repeatedly, courts ruling on the constitutionality of men's room spying returned to the emphasis Justice Harlan had given to telephone booths as special, quasi-private locations, notwithstanding the insistence by the *Katz* majority that the Fourth Amendment "protects people, not places."

None of this should surprise. However strained the analogy may be between a telephone booth and a house, the analogy between a toilet stall and telephone booth is easy to draw—so easy, in fact, that the leading treatise on search-and-seizure law treats the application of *Katz* to closed restroom stalls as "clear beyond question." It is difficult to think of another space that so closely resembles a telephone booth in providing "privacy in public." (Department store fitting rooms come close, but they play a less central role in everyday life.) * * *

Thus it was inevitable that *Katz* would have large implications for the policing of homosexuality. As it turned out, those implications went beyond protecting privacy in toilet stalls, important as that was. The court victories that *Katz* made possible for gay litigants and their lawyers, like the victories made possible by other Supreme Court decisions in the late 1960s and early 1970s, helped to embolden the homophile movement, contributed to a growing sense among gay men and lesbians that they had rights they could insist on and enforce, and gave ammunition to politicians interested in getting the police out of the homosexual harassment business. In all of these ways, *Katz*, along with other decisions having nothing ostensibly to do with homosexual rights, helped pave the way to Stonewall and the gay liberation movement. * * *

THE DISTRIBUTION OF FOURTH AMENDMENT PRIVACY
William J. Stuntz
67 Geo. Wash. L. Rev. 1265 (1999)

Most of Fourth Amendment law is devoted to the regulation of searches, and searches are defined as anything agents of the government do that infringes a reasonable expectation of privacy. As every criminal procedure class learns, if the key to that definition is the word "expectation," the definition is circular. People expect what they think will happen, and what they think will happen is a function of what has happened in the past. By altering its behavior, the government can change how people expect it to behave. Thus, if the government is bound only to respect people's expectations, it is not bound at all, for it can easily condition the citizenry to expect little or no privacy.

So if it is to have any bite, Fourth Amendment privacy protection must be tied to something other than what people expect from the police. The law's solution is to tie its protection to what people expect from one another. People define, in their ordinary interactions with each other, the kinds of things they do and don't want to keep secret; once that private space has been so defined, the police should be required to respect it. This sounds like a brilliant idea, a way to permit the law to develop and adapt to changing circumstances without having judges pull their own intuitions about privacy out of thin air. * * *

The principle that * * * the police can see and hear only those things that the rest of us can see and hear—has wide application; it is not too much to call it the defining principle of Fourth Amendment doctrine. Eavesdropping on telephone conversations is a "search." Overhearing a conversation on the street isn't. Jumping over a backyard fence to look around is a "search." Viewing the same yard from an airplane window isn't. Hiding in the bushes just outside the house and looking in the living room window is a "search." Standing in the street and peering through the open curtains into the living room isn't. The pattern is clear enough: the police can infringe privacy in ways that anyone else might infringe it, but not (meaning, again, not without special justification) in ways that differ from the sorts of things ordinary people might do. All these results seem designed to take the privacy people have, and use it to define the privacy that the police cannot invade without some good cause. * * *

There are plenty of complications and counter-examples. * * * But for all its contradictions, the law retains a substantial degree of coherence. The things and places people keep secret from one another are surely more private, and hence their discovery more harmful to privacy, than the things and places people expose to the world. And among the places where people maintain their privacy, a hierarchy exists. Homes really *are* more private than other places; cars and containers we carry around are private, but less so than homes; clothing less so still. These propositions are not perfectly true, but the law must deal in generalizations, and they are good generalizations.

Perhaps *because* they are good generalizations, they have a substantial class bias. Consider how Fourth Amendment protection works in [the following] major spheres: home, * * * car, and street. Save for a small homeless population, rich and poor alike have homes. But the homes of the rich are larger and more comfortable, making it possible to live a larger portion of life in them. Privacy follows space, and people with money have more space than people without. People with more money are more likely to live in detached houses with yards; people with less money are more likely to live in apartment buildings with common hallways. Because others can hear (sometimes smell) from the hallway what goes on inside apartments, the police can too. My neighbors cannot freely surround my house to hear what is happening inside; consequently, neither can the police. * * *

With cars, the tilt is less substantial: one can enjoy as much, or as little, privacy in an old Chevrolet as in a new Lexus. Still, a substantial slice of the urban poor (in some cities, the urban middle class as well) use public transportation in place of cars. Fourth Amendment law treats passengers on subways and buses no differently than pedestrians on the street. And pedestrians receive less Fourth Amendment protection than drivers.

Which leads to the [next] sphere, the street. As with transport, there are two divides here: between cities and everyplace else, and between richer and poorer. Street life is mostly an urban phenomenon. It is also mostly a phenomenon of the lower and lower-middle classes. Again, poorer people have less comfortable homes; it is natural to want to spend less time, and do less, in them. Other forms of entertainment are more costly than sitting on a front stoop or wandering the streets and talking to friends. So among urban residential neighborhoods, one finds more pedestrian traffic in poorer neighborhoods than in wealthier ones.

And Fourth Amendment law makes it easy for police to stop and search pedestrians. Police can approach anyone and ask questions with no justification at all; as long as the encounter is no more coercive than any police-citizen encounter must be, it is deemed consensual, notwithstanding the fact that such conversations rarely seem optional to the suspect. That power is terribly important, for it gives the police the authority to initiate street encounters at will. * * *

The general picture is clear enough. Fourth Amendment privacy is unequally distributed; it more closely resembles the right to buy political advertisements, which is useful only to those with money, than the right to vote, which almost all adult citizens share. Privacy, as Fourth Amendment law defines it, is something people tend to have a lot of only when they also have a lot of other things.

The temptation is to blame this feature of Fourth Amendment law on privacy's definition. By tying the definition of "searches" to the kind of privacy people actually have, the doctrine naturally tends to favor some classes of people over others, for people who have more privacy also have more, period. The solution, one might think, is a less positive, more normative definition of privacy. Ask not what privacy we actually have with each other; rather, ask what privacy we ought to have with the police. If rich and poor deserve the same level of privacy protection from the police, perhaps the law can simply give it to them.

That task is harder than it sounds. If by "privacy" one means the interest in not being observed (seen or heard), it is impossible. The problem is that, in general, the harm from being observed declines steeply with the addition of each new observer. If my wife and I have conversations that we wish to share only with each other, it is a real injury to each of us for a third party to listen in. If we live in an apartment building where our neighbors hear all our conversations because the walls are so thin, the addition of one more pair of ears is not particularly harmful. The point is not that poor people don't care about privacy; they surely do. Rather, the point is that, much of the time, the police don't take privacy (in the Fourth Amendment sense of the word) away from poor people, because those people have already lost it, and one cannot lose it twice. However the law of police searches is defined, if its goal is to protect against the harm of being observed, it will give most of its protection to people who can afford lives that allow limited observation. That excludes the urban poor.

Note: the urban poor, not simply the poor. People who live outside cities tend to have cars whatever their income level. People in trailer parks live in places that afford almost as much privacy as detached houses. It is poor people in cities who tend to live in large apartment buildings, to travel by bus or subway, and because of a combination of income and concentrated population, to spend more time on the street than do people in other places. This urban-nonurban divide creates another divide. Poverty in America is not exclusively an urban phenomenon. Poverty among certain population groups in certain parts of the country *is* almost exclusively an urban phenomenon. Poor whites are dispersed; they do not live in close proximity to large numbers of other poor whites. Poor blacks are more likely to live in cities, surrounded by other poor blacks. If the law is tilted against the urban poor, it is bound to have a racial tilt as well. * * *

[Handwritten at top: Hunch → Bare Suspicion → PC → Preponderance of Evidence → Beyond Reasonable Doubt / Somewhere in middle]

CHAPTER 3

PROBABLE CAUSE

■ ■ ■

Recall that the Fourth Amendment requires that "no Warrants shall issue, but upon probable cause." Accordingly, before a magistrate can issue a search warrant, the magistrate must first find that the police have probable cause to believe that evidence of a crime will be found in the place to be searched. Probable cause is also required for a valid arrest with or without a warrant. To arrest an individual, an officer needs probable cause to believe a crime has been committed and that the person he is arresting committed it.

The quantum of evidence required to establish probable cause has never been crystal clear. The Court has stated that probable cause " 'means less than evidence which would justify condemnation' or conviction," but "more than bare suspicion." *Brinegar v. United States*, 338 U.S. 160, 175 (1949). This statement that "probable cause is more than a suspicion and less than beyond a reasonable doubt places it somewhere between .01% and 90%, which, when all is said and done, is not all that helpful." Craig S. Lerner, *The Reasonableness of Probable Cause*, 81 TEX. L. REV. 951, 996 (2003).

In 1983, Justice Rehnquist, writing for a plurality of the Court, suggested that probable cause requires less proof than a preponderance of the evidence, stating in dicta that probable cause "does not demand any showing that such a belief be correct or more likely true than false." *Texas v. Brown*, 460 U.S. 730, 742 (1983). According to Justice Rehnquist, probable cause can be satisfied by less certainty than the preponderance of the evidence standard that governs in civil cases.[a]

In *Spinelli v. United States*, the Court examines the factors that the trial court should consider when determining whether probable cause

---

[a] Cynthia Lee comments that:

Justice Rehnquist's view of probable cause allows, and perhaps even fosters, racial disparity in arrests. Lowering the threshold of certainty needed for probable cause makes it easier for officers to arrest individuals. Police officers, however, cannot arrest every single person for whom they have probable cause to arrest and, necessarily, will exercise their discretion in choosing who they actually arrest. Although most officers probably do not intend to discriminate on the basis of race, racial stereotypes are likely to color their perceptions of who seems suspicious and therefore, is worthy of arrest. An extremely low threshold of certainty for probable cause means the bulk of these arrests will be deemed justifiable. Racial disparity in arrests is something the law should seek to avoid.

Cynthia Lee, *Probable Cause with Teeth*, 88 GEO. WASH. L. REV. 269, 277 (2020).

exists in cases in which police rely on an informant's tip. Note that the *Spinelli* Court rejects a totality of the circumstances approach in favor of a more structured two-part test for probable cause. This two-part test became known as the *Aguilar-Spinelli* test for probable cause. In *Illinois v. Gates*, the Court reverses course but does not completely abandon the factors that the *Spinelli* Court found relevant to the probable cause determination in cases involving an informant's tip. In *Maryland v. Pringle*, the Court wrestles with the meaning of probable cause in a case not involving an informant's tip.

SPINELLI V. UNITED STATES
Supreme Court of the United States
393 U.S. 410, 89 S. Ct. 584, 21 L. Ed. 2d 637 (1969)

JUSTICE HARLAN delivered the opinion of the Court.

William Spinelli was convicted * * * of traveling to St. Louis, Missouri, from a nearby Illinois suburb with the intention of conducting gambling activities proscribed by Missouri law. * * * [P]etitioner challenged the constitutionality of the warrant which authorized the FBI search that uncovered the evidence necessary for his conviction. * * * Believing it desirable that the principles of *Aguilar* should be further explicated, we granted certiorari * * *.

In *Aguilar*, a search warrant had issued upon an affidavit of police officers who swore only that they had "received reliable information from a credible person and do believe" that narcotics were being illegally stored on the described premises. While recognizing that the constitutional requirement of probable cause can be satisfied by hearsay information, this Court held the affidavit inadequate for two reasons. First, the application failed to set forth any of the "underlying circumstances" necessary to enable the magistrate independently to judge of the validity of the informant's conclusion that the narcotics were where he said they were. Second, the affiant-officers did not attempt to support their claim that their informant was "credible" or his information "reliable." The Government is, however, quite right in saying that the FBI affidavit in the present case is more ample than that in *Aguilar*. Not only does it contain a report from an anonymous informant, but it also contains a report of an independent FBI investigation which is said to corroborate the informant's tip. We are then, required to delineate the manner in which *Aguilar's* two-pronged test should be applied in these circumstances.

In essence, the affidavit * * * contained the following allegations:

1. The FBI had kept track of Spinelli's movements on five days during the month of August 1965. On four of these occasions, Spinelli was seen crossing one of two bridges leading from Illinois into St. Louis, Missouri, between 11 a.m. and 12:15 p.m. On four

of the five days, Spinelli was also seen parking his car in a lot used by residents of an apartment house at 1108 Indian Circle Drive in St. Louis, between 3:30 p.m. and 4:45 p.m. On one day, Spinelli was followed further and seen to enter a particular apartment in the building.

2. An FBI check with the telephone company revealed that this apartment contained two telephones listed under the name of Grace P. Hagen, and carrying the numbers WYdown 4–0029 and WYdown 4–0136.

3. The application stated that "William Spinelli is known to this affiant and to federal law enforcement agents and local law enforcement agents as a bookmaker, an associate of bookmakers, a gambler, and an associate of gamblers."

4. Finally it was stated that the FBI "has been informed by a confidential reliable informant that William Spinelli is operating a handbook and accepting wagers and disseminating wagering information by means of the telephones which have been assigned the numbers WYdown 4–0029 and WYdown 4–0136."

There can be no question that the last item mentioned, detailing the informant's tip, has a fundamental place in this warrant application. Without it, probable cause could not be established. The first two items reflect only innocent-seeming activity and data. Spinelli's travels to and from the apartment building and his entry into a particular apartment on one occasion could hardly be taken as bespeaking gambling activity; and there is surely nothing unusual about an apartment containing two separate telephones. Many a householder indulges himself in this petty luxury. Finally, the allegation that Spinelli was "known" to the affiant and to other federal and local law enforcement officers as a gambler and an associate of gamblers is but a bald and unilluminating assertion of suspicion that is entitled to no weight in appraising the magistrate's decision.

So much indeed the Government does not deny. Rather, following the reasoning of the Court of Appeals, the Government claims that the informant's tip gives a suspicious color to the FBI's reports detailing Spinelli's innocent-seeming conduct and that, conversely, the FBI's surveillance corroborates the informant's tip, thereby entitling it to more weight. * * * We believe, however, that the "totality of circumstances" approach taken by the Court of Appeals paints with too broad a brush. Where, as here, the informer's tip is a necessary element in a finding of probable cause, its proper weight must be determined by a more precise analysis.

The informer's report must first be measured against *Aguilar's* standards so that its probative value can be assessed. * * * Applying these principles to the present case, we first consider the weight to be given the informer's tip when it is considered apart from the rest of the affidavit. * * * Though the affiant swore that his confidant was "reliable," he offered the magistrate no reason in support of this conclusion. Perhaps even more important is the fact that *Aguilar*'s other test has not been satisfied. The tip does not contain a sufficient statement of the underlying circumstances from which the informer concluded that Spinelli was running a bookmaking operation. We are not told how the FBI's source received his information—it is not alleged that the informant personally observed Spinelli at work or that he had ever placed a bet with him. Moreover, if the informant came by the information indirectly, he did not explain why his sources were reliable. In the absence of a statement detailing the manner in which the information was gathered, it is especially important that the tip describe the accused's criminal activity in sufficient detail that the magistrate may know that he is relying on something more substantial than a casual rumor circulating in the underworld or an accusation based merely on an individual's general reputation. * * *

We conclude, then, that in the present case the informant's tip—even when corroborated to the extent indicated—was not sufficient to provide the basis for a finding of probable cause. * * *

The judgment of the Court of Appeals is reversed.

JUSTICE MARSHALL took no part in the consideration or decision of the case.

[JUSTICE WHITE's concurring opinion, JUSTICE BLACK's dissenting opinion, JUSTICE FORTAS' dissenting opinion, and JUSTICE STEWART's dissenting opinion have been omitted.]

ILLINOIS v. GATES
Supreme Court of the United States
462 U.S. 213, 103 S. Ct. 2317, 76 L. Ed. 2d 527 (1983)

JUSTICE REHNQUIST delivered the opinion of the Court. * * *

On May 3, 1978, the Bloomingdale Police Department received by mail an anonymous handwritten letter which read as follows:

> This letter is to inform you that you have a couple in your town who strictly make their living on selling drugs. They are Sue and Lance Gates, they live on Greenway, off Bloomingdale Rd. in the condominiums. Most of their buys are done in Florida. Sue his wife drives their car to Florida, where she leaves it to be loaded up with drugs, then Lance flys [sic] down and drives it back. Sue flys [sic] back after she drops the car off in Florida. May 3 she is driving down there again and Lance will be flying down in a few days to drive it back. At the time Lance drives the car back he has the

trunk loaded with over $100,000.00 in drugs. Presently they have over $100,000.00 worth of drugs in their basement.

They brag about the fact they never have to work, and make their entire living on pushers.

I guarantee if you watch them carefully you will make a big catch. They are friends with some big drugs dealers, who visit their house often.

Lance & Susan Gates

Greenway

in Condominiums

The letter was referred by the Chief of Police of the Bloomingdale Police Department to Detective Mader, who decided to pursue the tip. Mader learned, from the office of the Illinois Secretary of State, that an Illinois driver's license had been issued to one Lance Gates, residing at a stated address in Bloomingdale. He contacted a confidential informant, whose examination of certain financial records revealed a more recent address for the Gates, and he also learned from a police officer assigned to O'Hare Airport that "L. Gates" had made a reservation on Eastern Airlines flight 245 to West Palm Beach, Fla., scheduled to depart from Chicago on May 5 at 4:15 p.m.

Mader then made arrangements with an agent of the Drug Enforcement Administration for surveillance of the May 5 Eastern Airlines flight. The agent later reported to Mader that Gates had boarded the flight, and that federal agents in Florida had observed him arrive in West Palm Beach and take a taxi to the nearby Holiday Inn. They also reported that Gates went to a room registered to one Susan Gates and that, at 7:00 a.m. the next morning, Gates and an unidentified woman left the motel in a Mercury bearing Illinois license plates and drove northbound on an interstate frequently used by travelers to the Chicago area. In addition, the DEA agent informed Mader that the license plate number on the Mercury registered to a Hornet station wagon owned by Gates. The agent also advised Mader that the driving time between West Palm Beach and Bloomingdale was approximately 22 to 24 hours.

Mader signed an affidavit setting forth the foregoing facts, and submitted it to a judge of the Circuit Court of DuPage County, together with a copy of the anonymous letter. The judge of that court thereupon issued a search warrant for the Gates' residence and for their automobile. The judge, in deciding to issue the warrant, could have determined that the *modus operandi* of the Gates had been substantially corroborated. As the anonymous letter predicted, Lance Gates had flown from Chicago to West Palm Beach late in the afternoon of May 5th, had checked into a hotel room registered in the name of his wife, and, at 7:00 a.m. the following morning, had headed north, accompanied by an unidentified woman, out of West Palm Beach on an interstate highway used by travelers from South Florida to Chicago in an automobile bearing a license plate issued to him.

At 5:15 a.m. on March 7th, only 36 hours after he had flown out of Chicago, Lance Gates, and his wife, returned to their home in Bloomingdale, driving the car in which they had left West Palm Beach some 22 hours earlier. The Bloomingdale police were awaiting them, searched the trunk of the Mercury, and uncovered approximately 350 pounds of marijuana. A search of the Gates' home revealed marijuana, weapons, and other contraband. The Illinois Circuit Court ordered suppression of all these items, on the ground that the affidavit submitted to the Circuit Judge failed to support the necessary determination of probable cause to believe that the Gates' automobile and home contained the contraband in question. This decision was affirmed in turn by the Illinois Appellate Court and by a divided vote of the Supreme Court of Illinois.

The Illinois Supreme Court concluded—and we are inclined to agree—that, standing alone, the anonymous letter sent to the Bloomingdale Police Department would not provide the basis for a magistrate's determination that there was probable cause to believe contraband would be found in the Gates' car and home. The letter provides virtually nothing from which one might conclude that its author is either honest or his information reliable; likewise, the letter gives absolutely no indication of the basis for the writer's predictions regarding the Gates' criminal activities. Something more was required, then, before a magistrate could conclude that there was probable cause to believe that contraband would be found in the Gates' home and car.

The Illinois Supreme Court also properly recognized that Detective Mader's affidavit might be capable of supplementing the anonymous letter with information sufficient to permit a determination of probable cause. In holding that the affidavit in fact did not contain sufficient additional information to sustain a determination of probable cause, the Illinois court applied a "two-pronged test," derived from our decision in *Spinelli v. United States*. The Illinois Supreme Court, like some others, apparently understood *Spinelli* as requiring that the anonymous letter satisfy each of two independent requirements before it could be relied on. According to this view, the letter, as supplemented by Mader's affidavit, first had to adequately reveal the "basis of knowledge" of the letter writer—the particular means by which he came by the information given in his report. Second, it had to provide facts sufficiently establishing either the "veracity" of the affiant's informant, or, alternatively, the "reliability" of the informant's report in this particular case. * * *

We agree with the Illinois Supreme Court that an informant's "veracity," "reliability" and "basis of knowledge" are all highly relevant in determining the value of his report. We do not agree, however, that these elements should be understood as entirely separate and independent requirements to be rigidly exacted in every case, which the opinion of the Supreme Court of Illinois would imply. Rather, as detailed below, they should be understood simply as closely intertwined issues that may usefully illuminate the commonsense, practical question whether there is "probable cause" to believe that contraband or evidence is located in a particular place.

This totality-of-the-circumstances approach is far more consistent with our prior treatment of probable cause than is any rigid demand that specific "tests" be satisfied by every informant's tip. Perhaps the central teaching of our decisions bearing on the probable cause standard is that it is a "practical, nontechnical conception." "In dealing with probable cause, . . . as the very name implies, we deal with probabilities."

* * * [P]robable cause is a fluid concept—turning on the assessment of probabilities in particular factual contexts—not readily, or even usefully, reduced to a neat set of legal rules. Informants' tips doubtless come in many shapes and sizes from many different types of persons. As we said in *Adams v. Williams*, "Informants' tips, like all other clues and evidence coming to a policeman on the scene may vary greatly in their value and reliability." Rigid legal rules are ill-suited to an area of such diversity. "One simple rule will not cover every situation."

Moreover, the "two-pronged test" directs analysis into two largely independent channels—the informant's "veracity" or "reliability" and his "basis of knowledge." There are persuasive arguments against according these two elements such independent status. Instead, they are better understood as relevant considerations in the totality-of-the-circumstances analysis that traditionally has guided probable cause determinations: a deficiency in one may be compensated for, in determining the overall reliability of a tip, by a strong showing as to the other, or by some other indicia of reliability.

If, for example, a particular informant is known for the unusual reliability of his predictions of certain types of criminal activities in a locality, his failure, in a particular case, to thoroughly set forth the basis of his knowledge surely should not serve as an absolute bar to a finding of probable cause based on his tip. Likewise, if an unquestionably honest citizen comes forward with a report of criminal activity—which if fabricated would subject him to criminal liability—we have found rigorous scrutiny of the basis of his knowledge unnecessary. Conversely, even if we entertain some doubt as to an informant's motives, his explicit and detailed description of alleged wrongdoing, along with a statement that the event was observed first-hand, entitles his tip to greater weight than might otherwise be the case. * * *

For all these reasons, we conclude that it is wiser to abandon the "two-pronged test" established by our decisions in *Aguilar* and *Spinelli*. In its place we reaffirm the totality-of-the-circumstances analysis that traditionally has informed probable cause determinations. The task of the issuing magistrate is simply to make a practical, common-sense decision whether, given all the circumstances set forth in the affidavit before him, including the "veracity" and "basis of knowledge" of persons supplying hearsay information, there is a fair probability that contraband or evidence of a crime will be found in a particular place. * * * We are convinced that this flexible, easily applied standard will better achieve the accommodation of public and private interests that the Fourth Amendment requires than does the approach that has developed from *Aguilar* and *Spinelli*.

Our earlier cases illustrate the limits beyond which a magistrate may not venture in issuing a warrant. A sworn statement of an affiant that "he has cause to suspect and does believe that" liquor illegally brought into the United States is located on certain premises will not do. An affidavit must provide the magistrate with a substantial basis for determining the existence of probable cause. * * * An officer's statement that "affiants have received reliable information from a credible person and believe" that heroin is stored in a home, is likewise inadequate. * * * [T]his is a mere conclusory statement that gives the magistrate virtually no basis at all for making a judgment regarding probable cause. Sufficient information must be presented to the magistrate to allow that official to determine probable cause; his action cannot be a mere ratification of the bare conclusions of others. * * *

Our decisions applying the totality-of-the-circumstances analysis outlined above have consistently recognized the value of corroboration of details of an informant's tip by independent police work. * * * The corroboration of the letter's predictions that the Gates' car would be in Florida, that Lance Gates would fly to Florida in the next day or so, and that he would drive the car north toward Bloomingdale all indicated, albeit not with certainty, that the informant's other assertions also were true. "Because an informant is right about some things, he is more probably right about other facts,"—including the claim regarding the Gates' illegal activity. * * *

Finally, the anonymous letter contained a range of details relating not just to easily obtained facts and conditions existing at the time of the tip, but to future actions of third parties ordinarily not easily predicted. The letter writer's accurate information as to the travel plans of each of the Gates was of a character likely obtained only from the Gates themselves, or from someone familiar with their not entirely ordinary travel plans. If the informant had access to accurate information of this type a magistrate could properly conclude that it was not unlikely that he also had access to reliable information of the Gates' alleged illegal activities. Of course, the Gates' travel plans might have been learned from a talkative neighbor or travel agent; under the "two-pronged test" developed from *Spinelli*, the character of the details in the anonymous letter might well not permit a sufficiently clear inference regarding the letter writer's "basis of knowledge." But, as discussed previously, probable cause does not demand the certainty we associate with formal trials. It is enough that there was a fair probability that the writer of the anonymous letter had obtained his entire story either from the Gates or someone they trusted. And corroboration of major portions of the letter's predictions provides just this probability. It is apparent, therefore, that the judge issuing the warrant had a "substantial basis for . . . conclud[ing]" that probable cause to search the Gates' home and car existed. The judgment of the Supreme Court of Illinois therefore must be

Reversed.

JUSTICE STEVENS, with whom JUSTICE BRENNAN joins, dissenting.

* * * [T]he anonymous informant [was] not * * * completely accurate in his or her predictions. The informant had indicated that "Sue drives their car to Florida *where she leaves it to be loaded up with drugs. . . . Sue flies back after she drops the car off in Florida.*" Yet Detective Mader's affidavit reported that she "left the West Palm Beach area driving the Mercury northbound."

The discrepancy between the informant's predictions and the facts known to Detective Mader is significant for three reasons. First, it cast doubt on the informant's hypothesis that the Gates already had "over $100,000 worth of drugs in their basement." The informant had predicted an itinerary that always kept one spouse in Bloomingdale, suggesting that the Gates did not want to leave their home unguarded because something valuable was hidden within. That inference obviously could not be drawn when it was known that the pair was actually together over a thousand miles from home.

Second, the discrepancy made the Gates' conduct seem substantially less unusual than the informant had predicted it would be. It would have been odd if, as predicted, Sue had driven down to Florida on Wednesday, left the car, and flown right back to Illinois. But the mere facts that Sue was in West Palm Beach with the car,[1] that she was joined by her husband

---

[1] The anonymous note suggested that she was going down on Wednesday, but for all the officers knew she had been in Florida for a month.

at the Holiday Inn on Friday,[2] and that the couple drove north together the next morning are neither unusual nor probative of criminal activity. * * *

Of course, the activities in this case did not stop when the magistrate issued the warrant. The Gates drove all night to Bloomingdale, the officers searched the car and found 400 pounds of marijuana, and then they searched the house. However, none of these subsequent events may be considered in evaluating the warrant, and the search of the house was legal only if the warrant was valid. I cannot accept the Court's casual conclusion that, *before the Gates arrived in Bloomingdale,* there was probable cause to justify a valid entry and search of a private home. No one knows who the informant in this case was, or what motivated him or her to write the note. Given that the note's predictions were faulty in one significant respect, and were corroborated by nothing except ordinary innocent activity, I must surmise that the Court's evaluation of the warrant's validity has been colored by subsequent events. * * *

[Except for footnote 20 in JUSTICE WHITE's concurring opinion,[20] JUSTICE WHITE's concurring opinion and JUSTICE BRENNAN's dissenting opinion have been omitted.]

NOTE

Is it really true that "because an informant is right about some things, he is more probably right about other facts"? Consider a hypothetical posed originally by Justice White, concurring in *Spinelli v. United States*, and repeated by Justice Brennan, dissenting in *Illinois v. Gates*:

> [Suppose] a reliable informant states there is gambling equipment in Apartment 607 and then proceeds to describe in detail Apartment 201, a description which is verified before applying for the warrant. He was right about 201, but that hardly makes him more believable about the equipment in 607. But what if he states that there are narcotics locked in a safe in Apartment 300, which is described in detail, and the apartment manager verifies everything but the contents of the safe? I doubt that the report about the narcotics is

---

[2] Lance does not appear to have behaved suspiciously in flying down to Florida. He made a reservation in his own name and gave an accurate home phone number to the airlines. And Detective Mader's affidavit does not report that he did any of the other things drug couriers are notorious for doing, such as paying for the ticket in cash, dressing casually, looking pale and nervous, improperly filling out baggage tags, carrying American Tourister luggage, not carrying any luggage, or changing airlines en route.

[20] The "veracity" prong is satisfied by a recitation in the affidavit that the informant previously supplied accurate information to the police, or by proof that the informant gave his information against his penal interest. The "basis of knowledge" prong is satisfied by a statement from the informant that he personally observed the criminal activity, or, if he came by the information indirectly, by a satisfactory explanation of why his sources were reliable, or, in the absence of a statement detailing the manner in which the information was gathered, by a description of the accused's criminal activity in sufficient detail that the magistrate may infer that the informant is relying on something more substantial than a casual rumor or an individual's general reputation.

made appreciably more believable by the verification. The informant could still have gotten his information concerning the safe from others about whom nothing is known or could have inferred the presence of narcotics from circumstances which a magistrate would find unacceptable.

MARYLAND V. PRINGLE
Supreme Court of the United States
540 U.S. 366, 124 S. Ct. 795, 157 L. Ed. 2d 769 (2003)

CHIEF JUSTICE REHNQUIST delivered the opinion of the Court. * * *

At 3:16 a.m. on August 7, 1999, a Baltimore County Police officer stopped a Nissan Maxima for speeding. There were three occupants in the car: Donte Partlow, the driver and owner, respondent Pringle, the front-seat passenger, and Otis Smith, the back-seat passenger. The officer asked Partlow for his license and registration. When Partlow opened the glove compartment to retrieve the vehicle registration, the officer observed a large amount of rolled-up money in the glove compartment. The officer returned to his patrol car with Partlow's license and registration to check the computer system for outstanding violations. The computer check did not reveal any violations. The officer returned to the stopped car, had Partlow get out, and issued him an oral warning.

After a second patrol car arrived, the officer asked Partlow if he had any weapons or narcotics in the vehicle. Partlow indicated that he did not. Partlow then consented to a search of the vehicle. The search yielded $763 from the glove compartment and five plastic glassine baggies containing cocaine from behind the back-seat armrest. When the officer began the search the armrest was in the upright position flat against the rear seat. The officer pulled down the armrest and found the drugs, which had been placed between the armrest and the back seat of the car.

The officer questioned all three men about the ownership of the drugs and money, and told them that if no one admitted to ownership of the drugs he was going to arrest them all. The men offered no information regarding the ownership of the drugs or money. All three were placed under arrest and transported to the police station.

Later that morning, Pringle waived his rights under *Miranda v. Arizona*, and gave an oral and written confession in which he acknowledged that the cocaine belonged to him, that he and his friends were going to a party, and that he intended to sell the cocaine or "[u]se it for sex." Pringle maintained that the other occupants of the car did not know about the drugs, and they were released.

The trial court denied Pringle's motion to suppress his confession. * * * A jury convicted Pringle of possession with intent to distribute cocaine and possession of cocaine. He was sentenced to 10 years' incarceration without the possibility of parole. * * *

The Court of Appeals of Maryland, by divided vote, reversed, holding that, absent specific facts tending to show Pringle's knowledge and dominion or control over the drugs, "the mere finding of cocaine in the back armrest when [Pringle] was a front seat passenger in a car being driven by its owner is insufficient to establish probable cause for an arrest for possession." We granted certiorari and now reverse. * * *

It is uncontested in the present case that the officer, upon recovering the five plastic glassine baggies containing suspected cocaine, had probable cause to believe a felony had been committed. The sole question is whether the officer had probable cause to believe that Pringle committed that crime. * * *

The probable-cause standard is incapable of precise definition or quantification into percentages because it deals with probabilities and depends on the totality of the circumstances. We have stated, however, that "[t]he substance of all the definitions of probable cause is a reasonable ground for belief of guilt," and that the belief of guilt must be particularized with respect to the person to be searched or seized. * * *

In this case, Pringle was one of three men riding in a Nissan Maxima at 3:16 a.m. There was $763 of rolled-up cash in the glove compartment directly in front of Pringle.[2] Five plastic glassine baggies of cocaine were behind the back-seat armrest and accessible to all three men. Upon questioning, the three men failed to offer any information with respect to the ownership of the cocaine or the money.

We think it an entirely reasonable inference from these facts that any or all three of the occupants had knowledge of, and exercised dominion and control over, the cocaine. Thus, a reasonable officer could conclude that there was probable cause to believe Pringle committed the crime of possession of cocaine, either solely or jointly.

Pringle's attempt to characterize this case as a guilt-by-association case is unavailing. His reliance on *Ybarra v. Illinois* * * * is misplaced. In *Ybarra,* police officers obtained a warrant to search a tavern and its bartender for evidence of possession of a controlled substance. Upon entering the tavern, the officers conducted patdown searches of the customers present in the tavern, including Ybarra. Inside a cigarette pack retrieved from Ybarra's pocket, an officer found six tinfoil packets containing heroin. We stated:

---

[2] The Court of Appeals of Maryland dismissed the $763 seized from the glove compartment as a factor in the probable-cause determination, stating that "[m]oney, without more, is innocuous." The court's consideration of the money in isolation, rather than as a factor in the totality of the circumstances, is mistaken in light of our precedents. We think it is abundantly clear from the facts that this case involves more than money alone.

[A] person's mere propinquity to others independently suspected of criminal activity does not, without more, give rise to probable cause to search that person. Where the standard is probable cause, a search or seizure of a person must be supported by probable cause particularized with respect to that person. This requirement cannot be undercut or avoided by simply pointing to the fact that coincidentally there exists probable cause to search or seize another or to search the premises where the person may happen to be.

We held that the search warrant did not permit body searches of all of the tavern's patrons and that the police could not pat down the patrons for weapons, absent individualized suspicion.

This case is quite different from *Ybarra*. Pringle and his two companions were in a relatively small automobile, not a public tavern. In *Wyoming v. Houghton*, we noted that "a car passenger—unlike the unwitting tavern patron in *Ybarra*—will often be engaged in a common enterprise with the driver, and have the same interest in concealing the fruits or the evidence of their wrongdoing." Here we think it was reasonable for the officer to infer a common enterprise among the three men. The quantity of drugs and cash in the car indicated the likelihood of drug dealing, an enterprise to which a dealer would be unlikely to admit an innocent person with the potential to furnish evidence against him. * * *

We hold that the officer had probable cause to believe that Pringle had committed the crime of possession of a controlled substance. Pringle's arrest therefore did not contravene the Fourth and Fourteenth Amendments. Accordingly, the judgment of the Court of Appeals of Maryland is reversed, and the case is remanded for further proceedings not inconsistent with this opinion.

It is so ordered.

Chapter 4

Search Warrants

■ ■ ■

The Fourth Amendment is quite explicit when it comes to the requirements for a valid warrant, providing that "no Warrants shall issue, but upon probable cause, supported by Oath or affirmation, and particularly describing the place to be searched, and the persons or things to be seized." From this language we can derive that a valid warrant requires at least three things. First, it must be supported by probable cause. Second, the affiant or the person applying for a warrant must affirm under oath that the facts in the affidavit are true. Third, the warrant must state with particularity the place to be searched and the items or persons to be seized. This last requirement is known as the particularity requirement. *Maryland v. Garrison* examines the meaning of the particularity requirement.

When law enforcement officers execute a search warrant at a home, not only must the warrant meet the above requirements, the execution of the warrant must also be reasonable. One rule that informs the reasonableness of the execution of a search warrant at a home is the knock-and-announce rule, also known as the knock-notice rule, which requires police to knock and announce their identity before forcibly entering a dwelling to execute a search warrant. *Richards v. Wisconsin* elaborates upon the knock-and-announce rule.

Maryland v. Garrison
Supreme Court of the United States
480 U.S. 79, 107 S. Ct. 1013, 94 L. Ed. 2d 72 (1987)

Justice Stevens delivered the opinion of the Court.

Baltimore police officers obtained and executed a warrant to search the person of Lawrence McWebb and "the premises known as 2036 Park Avenue third floor apartment." When the police applied for the warrant and when they conducted the search pursuant to the warrant, they reasonably believed that there was only one apartment on the premises described in the warrant. In fact, the third floor was divided into two apartments, one occupied by McWebb and one by respondent Garrison. Before the officers executing the warrant became aware that they were in a separate apartment occupied by respondent, they had discovered the contraband that provided the basis for respondent's conviction for violating

Maryland's Controlled Substances Act. The question presented is whether the seizure of that contraband was prohibited by the Fourth Amendment. * * *

There is no question that the warrant was valid and was supported by probable cause. * * * [A]fter making a reasonable investigation, including a verification of information obtained from a reliable informant, an exterior examination of the three-story building at 2036 Park Avenue, and an inquiry of the utility company, the officer who obtained the warrant reasonably concluded that there was only one apartment on the third floor and that it was occupied by McWebb. When six Baltimore police officers executed the warrant, they fortuitously encountered McWebb in front of the building and used his key to gain admittance to the first-floor hallway and to the locked door at the top of the stairs to the third floor. As they entered the vestibule on the third floor, they encountered respondent, who was standing in the hallway area. The police could see into the interior of both McWebb's apartment to the left and respondent's to the right, for the doors to both were open. Only after respondent's apartment had been entered and heroin, cash, and drug paraphernalia had been found did any of the officers realize that the third floor contained two apartments. As soon as they became aware of that fact, the search was discontinued. All of the officers reasonably believed that they were searching McWebb's apartment. No further search of respondent's apartment was made.

The matter on which there is a difference of opinion concerns the proper interpretation of the warrant. A literal reading of its plain language, as well as the language used in the application for the warrant, indicates that it was intended to authorize a search of the entire third floor.[3] * * *

In our view, the case presents two separate constitutional issues, one concerning the validity of the warrant and the other concerning the reasonableness of the manner in which it was executed. We shall discuss the questions separately.

The Warrant Clause of the Fourth Amendment categorically prohibits the issuance of any warrant except one "particularly describing the place to be searched and the persons or things to be seized." The manifest purpose of this particularity requirement was to prevent general searches. By limiting the authorization to search to the specific areas and things for which there is probable cause to search, the requirement ensures that the

---

[3] The warrant states:

Affidavit having been made before me by Detective Albert Marcus, Baltimore Police Department, Narcotic Unit, that he has reason to believe that on the person of Lawrence Meril McWebb . . . [and] on the premises known as 2036 Park Avenue third floor apartment, described as a three story brick dwelling with the numerals 2–0–3–6 affixed to the front of same in the City of Baltimore, there is now being concealed certain property. . . . You are therefor[e] commanded, with the necessary and proper assistants, to search forthwith the person/premises hereinabove described for the property specified, executing this warrant and making the search . . .

search will be carefully tailored to its justifications, and will not take on the character of the wide-ranging exploratory searches the Framers intended to prohibit. Thus, the scope of a lawful search is "defined by the object of the search and the places in which there is probable cause to believe that it may be found. Just as probable cause to believe that a stolen lawnmower may be found in a garage will not support a warrant to search an upstairs bedroom, probable cause to believe that undocumented aliens are being transported in a van will not justify a warrantless search of a suitcase."

In this case there is no claim that the "persons or things to be seized" were inadequately described or that there was no probable cause to believe that those things might be found in "the place to be searched" as it was described in the warrant. With the benefit of hindsight, however, we now know that the description of that place was broader than appropriate because it was based on the mistaken belief that there was only one apartment on the third floor of the building at 2036 Park Avenue. The question is whether that factual mistake invalidated a warrant that undoubtedly would have been valid if it had reflected a completely accurate understanding of the building's floor plan.

Plainly, if the officers had known, or even if they should have known, that there were two separate dwelling units on the third floor of 2036 Park Avenue, they would have been obligated to exclude respondent's apartment from the scope of the requested warrant. But we must judge the constitutionality of their conduct in light of the information available to them at the time they acted. Those items of evidence that emerge after the warrant is issued have no bearing on whether or not a warrant was validly issued. Just as the discovery of contraband cannot validate a warrant invalid when issued, so is it equally clear that the discovery of facts demonstrating that a valid warrant was unnecessarily broad does not retroactively invalidate the warrant. The validity of the warrant must be assessed on the basis of the information that the officers disclosed, or had a duty to discover and to disclose, to the issuing Magistrate.[10] On the basis

---

[10] Arguments can certainly be made that the police in this case should have been able to ascertain that there was more than one apartment on the third floor of this building. It contained seven separate dwelling units and it was surely possible that two of them might be on the third floor. But the record also establishes that Officer Marcus made specific inquiries to determine the identity of the occupants of the third-floor premises. The officer went to 2036 Park Avenue and found that it matched the description given by the informant: a three-story brick dwelling with the numerals 2–0–3–6 affixed to the front of the premises. The officer "made a check with the Baltimore Gas and Electric Company and discovered that the premises of 2036 Park Ave. third floor was in the name of Lawrence McWebb." Officer Marcus testified at the suppression hearing that he inquired of the Baltimore Gas and Electric Company in whose name the third floor apartment was listed: "I asked if there is a front or rear or middle room. They told me, one third floor was only listed to Lawrence McWebb." The officer also discovered from a check with the Baltimore Police Department that the police records of Lawrence McWebb matched the address and physical description given by the informant. The Maryland courts that are presumptively familiar with local conditions were unanimous in concluding that the officer reasonably believed

of that information, we agree with the conclusion of all three Maryland courts that the warrant, insofar as it authorized a search that turned out to be ambiguous in scope, was valid when it issued.

The question whether the execution of the warrant violated respondent's constitutional right to be secure in his home is somewhat less clear. We have no difficulty concluding that the officers' entry into the third-floor common area was legal; they carried a warrant for those premises, and they were accompanied by McWebb, who provided the key that they used to open the door giving access to the third-floor common area. If the officers had known, or should have known, that the third floor contained two apartments before they entered the living quarters on the third floor, and thus had been aware of the error in the warrant, they would have been obligated to limit their search to McWebb's apartment. Moreover, as the officers recognized, they were required to discontinue the search of respondent's apartment as soon as they discovered that there were two separate units on the third floor and therefore were put on notice of the risk that they might be in a unit erroneously included within the terms of the warrant. The officers' conduct and the limits of the search were based on the information available as the search proceeded. While the purposes justifying a police search strictly limit the permissible extent of the search, the Court has also recognized the need to allow some latitude for honest mistakes that are made by officers in the dangerous and difficult process of making arrests and executing search warrants.

* * * [T]he validity of the search of respondent's apartment pursuant to a warrant authorizing the search of the entire third floor depends on whether the officers' failure to realize the overbreadth of the warrant was objectively understandable and reasonable. Here it unquestionably was. The objective facts available to the officers at the time suggested no distinction between McWebb's apartment and the third-floor premises.[12]

For that reason, the officers properly responded to the command contained in a valid warrant even if the warrant is interpreted as authorizing a search limited to McWebb's apartment rather than the entire third floor. Prior to the officers' discovery of the factual mistake, they perceived McWebb's apartment and the third-floor premises as one and the same; therefore their execution of the warrant reasonably included the entire third floor.[13] Under either interpretation of the warrant, the officers'

McWebb was the only tenant on that floor. Because the evidence supports their conclusion, we accept that conclusion for the purpose of our decision.

[12] Nothing McWebb did or said after he was detained outside 2036 Park Avenue would have suggested to the police that there were two apartments on the third floor. McWebb provided the key that opened the doors on the first floor and on the third floor. The police could reasonably have believed that McWebb was admitting them to an undivided apartment on the third floor. When the officers entered the foyer on the third floor, neither McWebb nor Garrison informed them that they lived in separate apartments.

[13] We expressly distinguish the facts of this case from a situation in which the police know there are two apartments on a certain floor of a building, and have probable cause to believe that

conduct was consistent with a reasonable effort to ascertain and identify the place intended to be searched within the meaning of the Fourth Amendment. * * *

JUSTICE BLACKMUN, with whom JUSTICE BRENNAN and JUSTICE MARSHALL join, dissenting.

Under this Court's precedents, the search of respondent Garrison's apartment violated the Fourth Amendment. While executing a warrant specifically limited to McWebb's residence, the officers expanded their search to include respondent's adjacent apartment, an expansion made without a warrant and in the absence of exigent circumstances. In my view, Maryland's highest court correctly concluded that the trial judge should have granted respondent's motion to suppress the evidence seized as a result of this warrantless search of his apartment. * * *

The home always has received special protection in analysis under the Fourth Amendment, which protects the "right of the people to be secure in their persons, *houses*, papers, and effects, against unreasonable searches and seizures." The Fourth Amendment, in fact, was a direct response to the colonists' objection to searches of homes under general warrants or without warrants. In today's society, the protection of the Amendment of course is extended to the equivalent of the traditional single-family house, such as an apartment. * * *

The Fourth Amendment also states that "no Warrants shall issue, but upon probable cause, supported by Oath or affirmation, and *particularly describing* the place to be searched, and the persons or things to be seized" (emphasis added). The particularity-of-description requirement is satisfied where "the description is such that the officer with a search warrant can with reasonable effort ascertain and identify the place intended." In applying this requirement to searches aimed at residences within multiunit buildings, such as the search in the present case, courts have declared invalid those warrants that fail to describe the targeted unit with enough specificity to prevent a search of all the units. * * *

Applying the above principles to this case, I conclude that the search of respondent's apartment was improper. The words of the warrant were plain and distinctive: the warrant directed the officers to seize marijuana and drug paraphernalia on the person of McWebb and in *McWebb's* apartment, *i.e.*, "on the premises known as 2036 Park Avenue third floor apartment." As the Court of Appeals observed, this warrant specifically authorized a search only of McWebb's—not respondent's—residence. In its interpretation of the warrant, the majority suggests that the language of

---

drugs are being sold out of that floor, but do not know in which of the two apartments the illegal transactions are taking place. A search pursuant to a warrant authorizing a search of the entire floor under those circumstances would present quite different issues from the ones before us in this case.

this document, as well as that in the supporting affidavit, permitted a search of the *entire* third floor. It escapes me why the language in question, "third floor apartment," when used with reference to a single unit in a multiple-occupancy building and in the context of one person's residence, plainly has the meaning the majority discerns, rather than its apparent and, indeed, obvious signification—one apartment located *on* the third floor. Accordingly, if, as appears to be the case, the warrant was limited in its description to the third floor apartment of McWebb, then the search of an additional apartment—respondent's—was warrantless and is presumed unreasonable "in the absence of some one of a number of well defined 'exigent circumstances.'" Because the State has not advanced any such exception to the warrant requirement, the evidence obtained as a result of this search should have been excluded.

Because the Court cannot justify the officers' search under the "exceptional circumstances" rubric, it analyzes the police conduct here in terms of "mistake." According to the Court, hindsight makes it clear that the officers were mistaken, first, in not describing McWebb's apartment with greater specificity in the warrant, and, second, in including respondent's apartment within the scope of the execution of the warrant. * * *

Even if one accepts the majority's view that there is no Fourth Amendment violation where the officers' mistake is reasonable, it is questionable whether that standard was met in this case. * * * The "place" at issue here is a small multiple-occupancy building. * * * [A]ny analysis of the "reasonableness" of the officers' behavior here must be done with this context in mind. * * *

In my view, * * * the "objective facts" should have made the officers aware that there were two different apartments on the third floor well before they discovered the incriminating evidence in respondent's apartment. Before McWebb happened to drive up while the search party was preparing to execute the warrant, one of the officers, Detective Shea, somewhat disguised as a construction worker, was already on the porch of the row house and was seeking to gain access to the locked first-floor door that permitted entrance into the building. From this vantage point he had time to observe the seven mailboxes and bells; indeed, he rang *all* seven bells, apparently in an effort to summon some resident to open the front door to the search party. A reasonable officer in Detective Shea's position, already aware that this was a multiunit building and now armed with further knowledge of the number of units in the structure, would have conducted *at that time* more investigation to specify the exact location of McWebb's apartment before proceeding further. For example, he might have questioned another resident of the building. * * *

Moreover, a reasonable officer would have realized the mistake in the warrant during the moments following the officers' entrance to the third floor. The officers gained access to the vestibule separating McWebb's and respondent's apartments through a locked door for which McWebb supplied the key. There, in the open doorway to his apartment, they encountered respondent, clad in pajamas and wearing a half-body cast as a result of a recent spinal operation. Although the facts concerning what next occurred are somewhat in dispute, it appears that respondent, together with McWebb and the passenger from McWebb's car, were shepherded into McWebb's apartment across the vestibule from his own. Once again, the officers were curiously silent. The informant had not led the officers to believe that anyone other than McWebb lived in the third-floor apartment; the search party had McWebb, the person targeted by the search warrant, in custody when it gained access to the vestibule; yet when they met respondent on the third floor, they simply asked him who he was but never where he lived. Had they done so, it is likely that they would have discovered the mistake in the warrant before they began their search.

Finally and most importantly, even if the officers had learned nothing from respondent, they should have realized the error in the warrant from their initial security sweep. Once on the third floor, the officers first fanned out through the rooms to conduct a preliminary check for other occupants who might pose a danger to them. As the map of the third floor demonstrates, the two apartments were almost a mirror image of each other—each had a bathroom, a kitchen, a living room, and a bedroom. Given the somewhat symmetrical layout of the apartments, it is difficult to imagine that, in the initial security sweep, a reasonable officer would not have discerned that two apartments were on the third floor, realized his mistake, and then confined the ensuing search to McWebb's residence.

Accordingly, even if a reasonable error on the part of police officers prevents a Fourth Amendment violation, the mistakes here, both with respect to obtaining and executing the warrant, are not reasonable and could easily have been avoided.

I respectfully dissent.

NOTE

Although the Court in *Maryland v. Garrison* discusses the particularity requirement, it ultimately finds no particularity problem with the warrant. How then might the particularity requirement be violated? The Court answers this question in *Groh v. Ramirez*, 540 U.S. 551 (2004). In that case, a federal agent, relying on a tip from a concerned citizen who said he had seen automatic rifles, grenades, and a rocket launcher at Joseph Ramirez's ranch, prepared an application for a warrant to search Ramirez's ranch. In his affidavit, the agent stated that the search was for any automatic firearms or parts to automatic weapons, destructive devices including but not limited to grenades, grenades launchers, rocket launchers, and receipts pertaining to the purchase or manufacture of automatic weapons or explosive devices or launchers. *Id.* at 554. The search warrant authorizing a search of Ramirez's ranch, however, failed to identify any of the items described in the agent's warrant application. *Id.* Indeed, in the portion of the warrant form that called for a description of the persons or property to be seized, the agent provided a description of Ramirez's home, not the items to be seized. *Id.* Moreover, the warrant did not incorporate by reference the itemized list contained in the affidavit. *Id.* at 554–55.

A search of Ramirez's home uncovered no illegal weapons or explosives. *Id.* at 555. No charges were filed against Ramirez. *Id.* Ramirez sued the federal agents who searched his home, arguing that they violated his Fourth Amendment right to be free from unreasonable searches and seizures. *Id.* The Supreme Court agreed that Ramirez's Fourth Amendment rights were violated. The Court found the search warrant plainly invalid since it failed to describe with particularity the persons or things to be seized. *Id.* at 557. The Court further found that the fact that the application described the things to be seized did not save the warrant from its facial invalidity since the Fourth Amendment "requires particularity in the warrant, not its supporting documents." *Id.* Because the search warrant did not describe the items to be seized at all, the Court regarded the search as warrantless. *Id.* at 558. The Court left open the question whether the warrant would have been saved if it had incorporated by reference the warrant application. *Id.* ("In this case the warrant did not incorporate other documents by reference . . . Hence, we need not further explore the matter of incorporation.").

The Court addressed the purposes behind the particularity requirement, explaining that "the purpose of the particularity requirement is not limited to the prevention of general searches." *Id.* at 561. "A particular warrant also 'assures the individual whose property is searched or seized of the lawful authority of the executing officer, his need to search, and the limits of his power to search.'" *Id.*

The next case examines what is called the knock-and-announce rule. As explained below, the knock-and-announce rule is not an absolute rule. In certain circumstances, police are allowed to forcibly enter a home without knocking and announcing prior to entry. Police may even seek a no knock warrant, which authorizes their entry into a home without requiring them to knock and announce their identity in advance.[a]

No knock warrants became the subject of intense criticism after the death of Breonna Taylor in 2020. Taylor was a 26-year-old Black female EMT

---

[a] WAYNE R. LAFAVE, SEARCH & SEIZURE: A TREATISE ON THE FOURTH AMENDMENT § 4.8(g) (6th ed. 2020) (noting that "[a] small number of jurisdictions have adopted legislation permitting magistrates to issue search warrants specifically authorizing entry without prior announcement upon a sufficient showing to the magistrate of a need to do so, either to prevent destruction of evidence or to prevent harm to the executing officer").

(Emergency Medical Technician) who was killed by police executing a search warrant on her home in Louisville, Kentucky in 2020.[b]

In the early morning hours of March 13, 2020, Taylor and her boyfriend, Kenneth Walker, a 27-year-old Black man, were awoken by loud banging on the front door of Taylor's apartment. The officers claimed they knocked and shouted "Police" several times prior to entering Taylor's apartment. Walker acknowledged that he and Taylor were awoken by loud banging on the door but said he called out "Who's there?" and did not hear a response. Thinking they were about to be robbed by home invasion robbers, Walker, a licensed gun owner, grabbed his gun. When two plainclothes police officers burst through the door, Walker was in the hallway holding his gun pointed at the front door. Not realizing that the men were police officers, Walker fired one shot, which hit one of the officers in the leg. The two officers who were in the entryway and a third officer standing immediately outside the apartment returned fire. In the hail of bullets, one of their shots killed Taylor who was standing next to and slightly behind Walker in the hallway. No drugs were found in Taylor's apartment.[c]

Taylor's death, which occurred just two months before the death of George Floyd, the Black man who died after former police officer Derek Chauvin pinned his knee against Floyd's neck for at least nine-and-a-half minutes,

---

[b] The police were investigating suspected drug trafficking activity involving firearms. Breonna Taylor was not a target of the investigation, but one of the targets of the investigation was a former boyfriend of Taylor's—a man named Jamarcus Glover. Rukmini Callimachi, *Breonna Taylor's Life Was Changing. Then the Police Came to Her Door*, N.Y. TIMES (Aug. 30, 2020), https://www.nytimes.com/2020/08/30/us/breonna-taylor-police-killing.html (https://perma.cc/22PC-CEAT). Police stated in their affidavit for the search warrant for Taylor's apartment that they had verified through a postal inspector that Glover had been seen entering and leaving Taylor's apartment with a package police believed contained drugs, then driving to a "known drug house." Search Warrant for 3003 Springfield Drive #4, Louisville, KY 40214, No. 20–1371 (Mar. 12, 2020); Jaynes Aff. For Search Warrant for 3003 Springfield Drive #4, Louisville, KY 40214, No. 20–1371 (Mar. 12, 2020). In August 2022, four current and former Louisville Metro Police officers were charged with federal crimes related to Breonna Taylor's death. Billy Kobin & Andrew Wolfson, *"Breonna Taylor Should Be Alive Today": 4 Current & Ex-LMPD Officers Charged in Her Death*, LOUISVILLE COURIER J. (Aug. 5, 2022), https://www.courier-journal.com/story/news/crime/2022/08/04/ex-lmpd-detective-joshua-jaynes-charged-fbi-breonna-taylor-case/65391852007/ (https://perma.cc/TQX6-J9D3). Three of the charged officers were accused of making false statements and omitting material information on the affidavit in support of the search warrant. *Id.* (noting that "[Officer] Jaynes wrote [in the affidavit that] he'd verified through a U.S. Postal inspector that Taylor's ex-boyfriend Jamarcus Glover, a suspected drug trafficker, was having packages delivered to her apartment . . . [b]ut Jaynes had actually spoken to [Officer] Mattingly, who had gotten information from Shively Police, not the postal inspector. According to those Shively officers, postal inspectors said there were no packages.").

[c] For more information on the death of Breonna Taylor, *see* Darcy Costello & Tessa Duvall, *Minute by Minute: What Happened the Night Louisville Police Fatally Shot Breonna Taylor*, LOUISVILLE COURIER J. (May 14, 2020, 7:25 PM), https://www.courier-journal.com/story/news/2020/05/14/minute-minute-account-breonna-taylor-fatal-shooting-louisville-police/5182824002/ (https://perma.cc/L93R-6BQR) (discussing the March 13, 2020 shooting death of Breonna Taylor); Richard A. Oppel Jr. et. al., *What to Know About Breonna Taylor's Death*, N.Y. TIMES (Apr. 26, 2021), https://www.nytimes.com/article/breonna-taylor-police.html (https://perma.cc/KUV5-JQMS); *20/20: Say Her Name: Breonna Taylor*, ABC NEWS (Nov. 21, 2020), https://abc.com/shows/2020/episode-guide/2020-11/20-say-her-name-breonna-taylor (https://perma.cc/853B-8ABH).

stopping Floyd's ability to breathe, led to calls for the repeal of no knock warrants.[d]

RICHARDS V. WISCONSIN
Supreme Court of the United States
520 U.S. 385, 117 S. Ct. 1416, 137 L. Ed. 2d 615 (1997)

JUSTICE STEVENS delivered the opinion of the Court.

In *Wilson v. Arkansas*, we held that the Fourth Amendment incorporates the common law requirement that police officers entering a dwelling must knock on the door and announce their identity and purpose before attempting forcible entry. At the same time, we recognized that the "flexible requirement of reasonableness should not be read to mandate a rigid rule of announcement that ignores countervailing law enforcement interests," and left "to the lower courts the task of determining the circumstances under which an unannounced entry is reasonable under the Fourth Amendment."

In this case, the Wisconsin Supreme Court concluded that police officers are *never* required to knock and announce their presence when executing a search warrant in a felony drug investigation. * * * We disagree with the court's conclusion that the Fourth Amendment permits a blanket exception to the knock-and-announce requirement for this entire category of criminal activity. * * *

On December 31, 1991, police officers in Madison, Wisconsin, obtained a warrant to search Steiney Richards' motel room for drugs and related paraphernalia. The search warrant was the culmination of an investigation that had uncovered substantial evidence that Richards was one of several individuals dealing drugs out of motel rooms in Madison. The police requested a warrant that would have given advance authorization for a "no-knock" entry into the motel room, but the Magistrate explicitly deleted those portions of the warrant.

The officers arrived at the motel room at 3:40 a.m. Officer Pharo, dressed as a maintenance man, led the team. With him were several plainclothes officers and at least one man in uniform. Officer Pharo knocked on Richards' door and, responding to the query from inside the room, stated that he was a maintenance man. With the chain still on the door, Richards cracked it open. Although there is some dispute as to what occurred next, Richards acknowledges that when he opened the door he saw the man in uniform standing behind Officer Pharo. He quickly slammed the door closed and, after waiting two or three seconds, the

---

[d] Tessa Duvall & Darcy Costello, *In Cities and States Across the US, Breonna's Law Is Targeting Deadly No-Knock Warrants*, LOUISVILLE COURIER J. (Mar. 17, 2021), https://www.courier-journal.com/story/news/local/breonna-taylor/2021/03/12/spread-of-breonnas-law-across-us-has-become-policy-legacy/4642996001/ (https://perma.cc/D6HZ-463W).

officers began kicking and ramming the door to gain entry to the locked room. At trial, the officers testified that they identified themselves as police while they were kicking the door in. When they finally did break into the room, the officers caught Richards trying to escape through the window. They also found cash and cocaine hidden in plastic bags above the bathroom ceiling tiles.

Richards sought to have the evidence from his motel room suppressed on the ground that the officers had failed to knock and announce their presence prior to forcing entry into the room. The trial court denied the motion, concluding that the officers could gather from Richards' strange behavior when they first sought entry that he knew they were police officers and that he might try to destroy evidence or to escape. The judge emphasized that the easily disposable nature of the drugs the police were searching for further justified their decision to identify themselves as they crossed the threshold instead of announcing their presence before seeking entry. Richards appealed the decision to the Wisconsin Supreme Court and that court affirmed.

The Wisconsin Supreme Court * * * found it reasonable—after considering criminal conduct surveys, newspaper articles, and other judicial opinions—to assume that all felony drug crimes will involve "an extremely high risk of serious if not deadly injury to the police as well as the potential for the disposal of drugs by the occupants prior to entry by the police." Notwithstanding its acknowledgment that in "some cases, police officers will undoubtedly decide that their safety, the safety of others, and the effective execution of the warrant dictate that they knock and announce," the court concluded that exigent circumstances justifying a no-knock entry are always present in felony drug cases. * * * Accordingly, the court determined that police in Wisconsin do not need specific information about dangerousness, or the possible destruction of drugs in a particular case, in order to dispense with the knock-and-announce requirement in felony drug cases.

We recognized in *Wilson* that the knock-and-announce requirement could give way "under circumstances presenting a threat of physical violence," or "where police officers have reason to believe that evidence would likely be destroyed if advance notice were given." It is indisputable that felony drug investigations may frequently involve both of these circumstances. The question we must resolve is whether this fact justifies dispensing with case-by-case evaluation of the manner in which a search was executed.

The Wisconsin court explained its blanket exception as necessitated by the special circumstances of today's drug culture, and the State asserted at oral argument that the blanket exception was reasonable in "felony drug cases because of the convergence in a violent and dangerous form of commerce of weapons and the destruction of drugs." But creating exceptions to the knock-and-announce rule based on the "culture" surrounding a general category of criminal behavior presents at least two serious concerns.

First, the exception contains considerable overgeneralization. For example, while drug investigation frequently does pose special risks to officer safety and the preservation of evidence, not every drug investigation will pose these risks to a substantial degree. For example, a search could be conducted at a time when the only individuals present in a residence have no connection with the drug activity and thus will be unlikely to threaten officers or destroy evidence. Or the police could know that the drugs being searched for were of a type or in a location that made them impossible to destroy quickly. In those situations, the asserted governmental interests in preserving evidence and maintaining safety may not outweigh the individual privacy interests intruded upon by a no-knock entry. Wisconsin's blanket rule impermissibly insulates these cases from judicial review.

A second difficulty with permitting a criminal-category exception to the knock-and-announce requirement is that the reasons for creating an exception in one category can, relatively easily, be applied to others. Armed bank robbers, for example, are, by definition, likely to have weapons, and the fruits of their crime may be destroyed without too much difficulty. If a *per se* exception were allowed for each category of criminal investigation that included a considerable—albeit hypothetical—risk of danger to officers or destruction of evidence, the knock-and-announce element of the Fourth Amendment's reasonableness requirement would be meaningless.

Thus, the fact that felony drug investigations may frequently present circumstances warranting a no-knock entry cannot remove from the neutral scrutiny of a reviewing court the reasonableness of the police decision not to knock and announce in a particular case. Instead, in each case, it is the duty of a court confronted with the question to determine whether the facts and circumstances of the particular entry justified dispensing with the knock-and-announce requirement.

In order to justify a "no-knock" entry, the police must have a reasonable suspicion that knocking and announcing their presence, under the particular circumstances, would be dangerous or futile, or that it would inhibit the effective investigation of the crime by, for example, allowing the destruction of evidence. This standard—as opposed to a probable cause requirement—strikes the appropriate balance between the legitimate law enforcement concerns at issue in the execution of search warrants and the individual privacy interests affected by no-knock entries. This showing is not high, but the police should be required to make it whenever the reasonableness of a no-knock entry is challenged.

Although we reject the Wisconsin court's blanket exception to the knock-and-announce requirement, we conclude that the officers' no-knock entry into Richards' motel room did not violate the Fourth Amendment. We agree with the trial court, and with Justice Abrahamson, that the circumstances in this case show that the officers had a reasonable suspicion that Richards might destroy evidence if given further opportunity to do so.

The judge who heard testimony at Richards' suppression hearing concluded that it was reasonable for the officers executing the warrant to believe that Richards knew, after opening the door to his motel room the first time, that the men seeking entry to his room were the police. Once the officers reasonably believed that Richards knew who they were, the court concluded, it was reasonable for them to force entry immediately given the disposable nature of the drugs.

In arguing that the officers' entry was unreasonable, Richards places great emphasis on the fact that the Magistrate who signed the search warrant for his motel room deleted the portions of the proposed warrant that would have given the officers permission to execute a no-knock entry. But this fact does not alter the reasonableness of the officers' decision, which must be evaluated as of the time they entered the motel room. * * *

Accordingly, although we reject the blanket exception to the knock-and-announce requirement for felony drug investigations, the judgment of the Wisconsin Supreme Court is affirmed.[a]

It is so ordered.

NOTE

How long must police officers wait after knocking and announcing before forcibly entering a dwelling? There is no bright-line answer to this question. In *United States v. Banks*, 540 U.S. 31 (2003), a unanimous Court explained that the answer to this question depends on the totality of the circumstances.

In *Banks*, federal and local law enforcement officers went to an apartment to execute a warrant to search for cocaine. They called out, "Police. Search warrant," and knocked loudly on the door. After waiting 15 to 20 seconds and receiving no answer, the officers broke down the front door with a battering ram. Defendant Banks was in the shower and testified that he heard nothing

---

[a] In this case, the Court found that the no-knock entry was reasonable. If the Court had determined that the no-knock entry was unreasonable and therefore the officers violated the knock-and-announce rule, would the defendant's motion to suppress have been granted? In *Hudson v. Michigan*, 547 U.S. 586 (2006), the Court answered this question in the negative, holding that the exclusionary rule does not apply to violations of the knock-and-announce rule. Justice Scalia, writing for the Court, utilized a cost-benefit analysis in a case in which police failed to knock and announce prior to forcibly entering a dwelling. Justice Scalia noted that the social costs of applying the exclusionary rule to knock-and-announce violations far outweigh any deterrent value that would come from applying the exclusionary rule to such violations of the Fourth Amendment. He further opined that police officers have little incentive to disregard the knock-and-announce rule.

until the crash of the door. The search uncovered weapons, crack cocaine, and other evidence of drug dealing.

Banks moved to suppress the evidence found in his apartment, arguing that the officers executing the search warrant waited an unreasonably short amount of time before forcing entry and therefore violated his Fourth Amendment rights. Banks argued that 15 to 20 seconds was too brief since he was in the shower and did not hear the knock. He also argued that even if he had heard the knock, it would have taken him more than 20 seconds to get from the bathroom to the front door.

The Court rejected these arguments, stating that it was irrelevant that the defendant was in the shower since the reasonableness of the officers' actions must be judged from the perspective of a reasonable officer on the scene and there was no indication that the police knew the defendant was in the shower. The Court acknowledged that the defendant's argument that 20 seconds was too short for him to get to the door would have had some merit if the officers had justified their timing by claiming that the defendant's failure to open the door indicated a refusal to admit them. In this case, however, the officers claimed an exigent need to prevent the destruction of drugs. The Court noted that prudent drug dealers will often keep their stash of drugs near a toilet or kitchen sink so they can dispose of the drugs quickly should the police raid their homes. Since the typical drug dealer can flush cocaine down the drain within 15 to 20 seconds, the Court found that the 15 to 20 second wait after knocking and announcing in this case satisfied the Fourth Amendment's reasonableness requirement.

CHAPTER 5

ARRESTS

■ ■ ■

In this chapter, we will study the constitutional requirements for an arrest. Recall that the Fourth Amendment proscribes unreasonable searches and seizures. Until now, our focus has primarily been on searches and seizures of property. The Fourth Amendment also governs searches and seizures of persons. An arrest is a seizure of the person.

In the cases we have studied thus far, the Supreme Court has expressed a preference for searches conducted with a warrant based on probable cause. In the first case in this chapter, *United States v. Watson*, we see the Court taking a different approach when it comes to arrests. *Payton v. New York* and *Steagald v. United States* limit the reach of *Watson*, but the rule expressed in *Watson* remains the general rule for arrests outside the home. In *Ashcroft v. al-Kidd*, the Court considers whether the post-9/11 use of material witness warrants to detain terrorism suspects for whom the government otherwise lacks probable cause to arrest violates the Fourth Amendment.

UNITED STATES V. WATSON
Supreme Court of the United States
423 U.S. 411, 96 S. Ct. 820, 46 L. Ed. 2d 598 (1976)

JUSTICE WHITE delivered the opinion of the Court.

This case presents questions under the Fourth Amendment as to the legality of a warrantless arrest. * * *

The relevant events began on August 17, 1972, when an informant, one Khoury, telephoned a postal inspector informing him that respondent Watson was in possession of a stolen credit card and had asked Khoury to cooperate in using the card to their mutual advantage. On five to 10 previous occasions Khoury had provided the inspector with reliable information on postal inspection matters, some involving Watson. Later that day Khoury delivered the card to the inspector. On learning that Watson had agreed to furnish additional cards, the inspector asked Khoury to arrange to meet with Watson. Khoury did so, a meeting being scheduled for August 22. Watson canceled that engagement, but at noon on August 23, Khoury met with Watson at a restaurant designated by the latter. Khoury had been instructed that if Watson had additional stolen credit cards, Khoury was to give a designated signal. The signal was given, the officers closed in, and Watson was forthwith arrested. * * * Watson was charged with possessing stolen mail in violation of 18 U.S.C. § 1708.

Prior to trial, Watson moved to suppress the cards, claiming that his arrest was illegal for want of probable cause and an arrest warrant. * * * The motion was denied, and Watson was convicted of illegally possessing the two cards seized from his car.

A divided panel of the Court of Appeals for the Ninth Circuit reversed. * * * In reaching this judgment, the court decided, * * * notwithstanding its agreement with the District Court that Khoury was reliable and that there was probable cause for arresting Watson, * * * the arrest [was] unconstitutional because the postal inspector had failed to secure an arrest warrant although he concededly had time to do so. * * *

Contrary to the Court of Appeals' view, Watson's arrest was not invalid because executed without a warrant. Title 18 U.S.C. § 3061(a)(3) expressly empowers the Board of Governors of the Postal Service to authorize Postal Service officers and employees "performing duties related to the inspection of postal matters" to

> make arrests without warrant for felonies cognizable under the laws of the United States if they have reasonable grounds to believe that the person to be arrested has committed or is committing such a felony.

* * * Because there was probable cause in this case to believe that Watson had violated § 1708, the inspector and his subordinates, in arresting Watson, were acting strictly in accordance with the governing statute and regulations.

* * * Section 3061 represents a judgment by Congress that it is not unreasonable under the Fourth Amendment for postal inspectors to arrest without a warrant provided they have probable cause to do so. This was not an isolated or quixotic judgment of the legislative branch. Other federal law enforcement officers have been expressly authorized by statute for many years to make felony arrests on probable cause but without a warrant. This is true of United States marshals, and of agents of the Federal Bureau of Investigation, the Drug Enforcement Administration, the Secret Service, and the Customs Service.

Because there is a "strong presumption of constitutionality due to an Act of Congress, especially when it turns on what is 'reasonable,'" "[o]bviously the Court should be reluctant to decide that a search thus authorized by Congress was unreasonable and that the Act was therefore unconstitutional." Moreover, there is nothing in the Court's prior cases indicating that under the Fourth Amendment a warrant is required to make a valid arrest for a felony. Indeed, the relevant prior decisions are uniformly to the contrary.

"The usual rule is that a police officer may arrest without warrant one believed by the officer upon reasonable cause to have been guilty of a felony...." * * * [T]he Court "has never invalidated an arrest supported by probable cause solely because the officers failed to secure a warrant."

The cases construing the Fourth Amendment thus reflect the ancient common-law rule that a peace officer was permitted to arrest without a warrant for a misdemeanor or felony committed in his presence as well as for a felony not committed in his presence if there was reasonable ground for making the arrest. This has also been the prevailing rule under state constitutions and statutes. * * * "The public safety, and the due apprehension of criminals, charged with heinous offences, imperiously require that [felony] arrests should be made without warrant by officers of the law." * * *

The balance struck by the common law in generally authorizing felony arrests on probable cause, but without a warrant, has survived substantially intact.[a] It appears in almost all of the States in the form of express statutory authorization. * * * This is [also] the rule Congress has long directed its principal law enforcement officers to follow.

Watson's arrest did not violate the Fourth Amendment, and the Court of Appeals erred in holding to the contrary. * * *

Reversed.

JUSTICE STEVENS took no part in the consideration or decision of this case.

JUSTICE POWELL, concurring. * * *

On its face, our decision today creates a certain anomaly. There is no more basic constitutional rule in the Fourth Amendment area than that which makes a warrantless search unreasonable except in a few "jealously and carefully drawn" exceptional circumstances. * * * In short, the course of judicial development of the Fourth Amendment with respect to searches has remained true to the principles so well expressed by Mr. Justice Jackson:

> Any assumption that evidence sufficient to support a magistrate's disinterested determination to issue a search warrant will justify the officers in making a search without a warrant would reduce

---

[a] While *United States v. Watson* involved an arrest for a felony offense, the rule that police officers with probable cause to arrest may, consistent with the Fourth Amendment, arrest an individual in a public place without a warrant has been extended to arrests for misdemeanors. *See* Atwater v. City of Lago Vista, 532 U.S. 318 (2001) (holding that the Fourth Amendment does not prohibit an officer from making a warrantless arrest in public for a minor criminal offense punishable only by a fine).

the Amendment to a nullity and leave the people's homes secure only in the discretion of police officers.... When the right of privacy must reasonably yield to the right of search is, as a rule, to be decided by a judicial officer, not by a policeman or Government enforcement agent.

Since the Fourth Amendment speaks equally to both searches and seizures, and since an arrest, the taking hold of one's person, is quintessentially a seizure, it would seem that the constitutional provision should impose the same limitations upon arrests that it does upon searches. Indeed, as an abstract matter an argument can be made that the restrictions upon arrest perhaps should be greater. A search may cause only annoyance and temporary inconvenience to the law-abiding citizen, assuming more serious dimension only when it turns up evidence of criminality. An arrest, however, is a serious personal intrusion regardless of whether the person seized is guilty or innocent. Although an arrestee cannot be held for a significant period without some neutral determination that there are grounds to do so, no decision that he should go free can come quickly enough to erase the invasion of his privacy that already will have occurred. Logic therefore would seem to dictate that arrests be subject to the warrant requirement at least to the same extent as searches.

But logic sometimes must defer to history and experience. The Court's opinion emphasizes the historical sanction accorded warrantless felony arrests. * * *

In sum, the historical and policy reasons sketched above fully justify the Court's sustaining of a warrantless arrest upon probable cause, despite the resulting divergence between the constitutional rule governing searches and that now held applicable to seizures of the person. * * *

[JUSTICE STEWART's concurring opinion and JUSTICE MARSHALL's dissenting opinion have been omitted.]

PAYTON V. NEW YORK

Supreme Court of the United States
445 U.S. 573, 100 S. Ct. 1371, 63 L. Ed. 2d 639 (1980)

JUSTICE STEVENS delivered the opinion of the Court.

These appeals challenge the constitutionality of New York statutes that authorize police officers to enter a private residence without a warrant and with force, if necessary, to make a routine felony arrest.

The important constitutional question presented by this challenge has been expressly left open in a number of our prior opinions. In *United States v. Watson*, we upheld a warrantless "midday public arrest," expressly noting that the case did not pose "the still unsettled question . . . 'whether and under what circumstances an officer may enter a suspect's home to make a warrantless arrest.'" The question has been answered in different ways by other appellate courts. * * *

* * * We now reverse the New York Court of Appeals and hold that the Fourth Amendment to the United States Constitution, made applicable to the States by the Fourteenth Amendment, prohibits the police from making a warrantless and nonconsensual entry into a suspect's home in order to make a routine felony arrest.[a]

We first state the facts of both cases in some detail * * *. On January 14, 1970, after two days of intensive investigation, New York detectives had assembled evidence sufficient to establish probable cause to believe that Theodore Payton had murdered the manager of a gas station two days earlier. At about 7:30 a.m. on January 15, six officers went to Payton's apartment in the Bronx, intending to arrest him. They had not obtained a warrant. Although light and music emanated from the apartment, there was no response to their knock on the metal door. They summoned emergency assistance and, about 30 minutes later, used crowbars to break open the door and enter the apartment. No one was there. In plain view, however, was a .30-caliber shell casing that was seized and later admitted into evidence at Payton's murder trial. * * *

On March 14, 1974, Obie Riddick was arrested for the commission of two armed robberies that had occurred in 1971. He had been identified by the victims in June 1973, and in January 1974 the police had learned his address. They did not obtain a warrant for his arrest. At about noon on March 14, a detective, accompanied by three other officers, knocked on the door of the Queens house where Riddick was living. When his young son opened the door, they could see Riddick sitting in bed covered by a sheet. They entered the house and placed him under arrest. Before permitting him to dress, they opened a chest of drawers two feet from the bed in search of weapons and found narcotics and related paraphernalia. Riddick was subsequently indicted on narcotics charges. * * *

Before addressing the narrow question presented by these appeals, we put to one side other related problems that are *not* presented today. Although it is arguable that the warrantless entry to effect Payton's arrest might have been justified by exigent circumstances, none of the New York courts relied on any such justification * * *. Nor do these cases raise any question concerning the authority of the police, without either a search or arrest warrant, to enter a third party's home to arrest a suspect.* * * Finally, in both cases we are dealing with entries into homes made without the consent of any occupant.

---

[a] While *Payton v. New York* involved an arrest for a felony offense, the Court later made clear that its holding also applied to arrests for misdemeanor offenses. Welsh v. Wisconsin, 466 U.S. 740 (1984).

It is familiar history that indiscriminate searches and seizures conducted under the authority of "general warrants" were the immediate evils that motivated the framing and adoption of the Fourth Amendment. * * * The Amendment provides:

> The right of the people to be secure in their persons, houses, papers, and effects, against unreasonable searches and seizures, shall not be violated, and no Warrants shall issue, but upon probable cause, supported by Oath or affirmation, and particularly describing the place to be searched, and the persons or things to be seized.

It is thus perfectly clear that the evil the Amendment was designed to prevent was broader than the abuse of a general warrant. Unreasonable searches or seizures conducted without any warrant at all are condemned by the plain language of the first clause of the Amendment. Almost a century ago the Court stated in resounding terms that the principles reflected in the Amendment "reached farther than the concrete form" of the specific cases that gave it birth, and "apply to all invasions on the part of the government and its employés of the sanctity of a man's home and the privacies of life." Without pausing to consider whether that broad language may require some qualification, it is sufficient to note that the warrantless arrest of a person is a species of seizure required by the Amendment to be reasonable. Indeed, as Mr. Justice Powell noted in his concurrence in *United States v. Watson*, the arrest of a person is "quintessentially a seizure."

The simple language of the Amendment applies equally to seizures of persons and to seizures of property. Our analysis in this case may therefore properly commence with rules that have been well established in Fourth Amendment litigation involving tangible items. As the Court reiterated just a few years ago, the "physical entry of the home is the chief evil against which the wording of the Fourth Amendment is directed." And we have long adhered to the view that the warrant procedure minimizes the danger of needless intrusions of that sort.

It is a "basic principle of Fourth Amendment law" that searches and seizures inside a home without a warrant are presumptively unreasonable. Yet it is also well settled that objects such as weapons or contraband found in a public place may be seized by the police without a warrant. The seizure of property in plain view involves no invasion of privacy and is presumptively reasonable, assuming that there is probable cause to associate the property with criminal activity. The distinction between a warrantless seizure in an open area and such a seizure on private premises was plainly stated in *G.M. Leasing Corp. v. United States*. * * *

As the late Judge Leventhal recognized, this distinction has equal force when the seizure of a person is involved. Writing on the constitutional issue now before us for the United States Court of Appeals for the District of Columbia Circuit sitting en banc, Judge Leventhal first noted the settled rule that warrantless arrests in public places are valid. He immediately recognized, however, that

> [a] greater burden is placed . . . on officials who enter a home or dwelling without consent. Freedom from intrusion into the home or dwelling is the archetype of the privacy protection secured by the Fourth Amendment.

His analysis of this question then focused on the long-settled premise that, absent exigent circumstances, a warrantless entry to search for weapons or contraband is unconstitutional even when a felony has been committed and there is probable cause to believe that incriminating evidence will be found within. He reasoned that the constitutional protection afforded to the individual's interest in the privacy of his own home is equally applicable to a warrantless entry for the purpose of arresting a resident of the house; for it is inherent in such an entry that a search for the suspect may be required before he can be apprehended. Judge Leventhal concluded that an entry to arrest and an entry to search for and to seize property implicate the same interest in preserving the privacy and the sanctity of the home, and justify the same level of constitutional protection. * * *

We find this reasoning to be persuasive and in accord with this Court's Fourth Amendment decisions. * * * Thus, for Fourth Amendment purposes, an arrest warrant founded on probable cause implicitly carries with it the limited authority to enter a dwelling in which the suspect lives when there is reason to believe the suspect is within.

Because no arrest warrant was obtained in either of these cases, the judgments must be reversed and the cases remanded to the New York Court of Appeals for further proceedings not inconsistent with this opinion.

It is so ordered.

[JUSTICE BLACKMUN's concurring opinion, JUSTICE WHITE's dissenting opinion, and JUSTICE REHNQUIST's dissenting opinion have been omitted.]

STEAGALD V. UNITED STATES
Supreme Court of the United States
451 U.S. 204, 101 S. Ct. 1642, 68 L. Ed. 2d 38 (1981)

JUSTICE MARSHALL delivered the opinion of the Court. * * *

In early January 1978, an agent of the Drug Enforcement Administration (DEA) was contacted in Detroit, Mich., by a confidential informant who suggested that he might be able to locate Ricky Lyons, a federal fugitive wanted on drug charges. On January 14, 1978, the informant called the agent again, and gave him a telephone number in the

Atlanta, Ga., area where, according to the informant, Ricky Lyons could be reached during the next 24 hours. On January 16, 1978, the agent called fellow DEA Agent Kelly Goodowens in Atlanta and relayed the information he had obtained from the informant. Goodowens contacted Southern Bell Telephone Co., and secured the address corresponding to the telephone number obtained by the informant. Goodowens also discovered that Lyons was the subject of a 6-month-old arrest warrant.

Two days later, Goodowens and 11 other officers drove to the address supplied by the telephone company to search for Lyons. The officers observed two men standing outside the house to be searched. These men were Hoyt Gaultney and petitioner Gary Steagald. The officers approached with guns drawn, frisked both men, and, after demanding identification, determined that neither man was Lyons. Several agents proceeded to the house. Gaultney's wife answered the door, and informed the agents that she was alone in the house. She was told to place her hands against the wall and was guarded in that position while one agent searched the house. Ricky Lyons was not found, but during the search of the house the agent observed what he believed to be cocaine. Upon being informed of this discovery, Agent Goodowens sent an officer to obtain a search warrant and in the meantime conducted a second search of the house, which uncovered additional incriminating evidence. During a third search conducted pursuant to a search warrant, the agents uncovered 43 pounds of cocaine. Petitioner was arrested and indicted on federal drug charges.

Prior to trial, petitioner moved to suppress all evidence uncovered during the various searches on the ground that it was illegally obtained because the agents had failed to secure a search warrant before entering the house. Agent Goodowens testified at the suppression hearing that there had been no "physical hinderance" preventing him from obtaining a search warrant and that he did not do so because he believed that the arrest warrant for Ricky Lyons was sufficient to justify the entry and search. The District Court agreed with this view, and denied the suppression motion. Petitioner was convicted, and renewed his challenge to the search in his appeal. A divided Court of Appeals for the Fifth Circuit affirmed the District Court's denial of petitioner's suppression motion. Because the issue presented by this case is an important one that has divided the Circuits, we granted certiorari. * * *

The question before us is a narrow one. The search at issue here took place in the absence of consent or exigent circumstances. Except in such special situations, we have consistently held that the entry into a home to conduct a search or make an arrest is unreasonable under the Fourth Amendment unless done pursuant to a warrant. Thus, as we recently observed: "In terms that apply equally to seizures of property and to seizures of persons, the Fourth Amendment has drawn a firm line at the entrance to the house. Absent exigent circumstances, that threshold may not reasonably be crossed without a warrant." Here, of course, the agents had a warrant—one authorizing the arrest of Ricky Lyons. However, the Fourth Amendment claim here is not being raised by Ricky Lyons. Instead, the challenge to the search is asserted by a person not named in the warrant who was convicted on the basis of evidence uncovered during a search of his residence for Ricky Lyons. Thus, the narrow issue before us is whether an arrest warrant—as opposed to a search warrant—is adequate to protect the Fourth Amendment interests of persons not named in the warrant, when their homes are searched without their consent and in the absence of exigent circumstances.

The purpose of a warrant is to allow a neutral judicial officer to assess whether the police have probable cause to make an arrest or conduct a search. As we have often explained, the placement of this checkpoint between the Government and the citizen implicitly acknowledges that an "officer engaged in the often competitive enterprise of ferreting out crime," may lack sufficient objectivity to weigh correctly the strength of the evidence supporting the contemplated action against the individual's interests in protecting his own liberty and the privacy of his home. However, while an arrest warrant and a search warrant both serve to subject the probable cause determination of the police to judicial review, the interests protected by the two warrants differ. An arrest warrant is issued by a magistrate upon a showing that probable cause exists to believe that the subject of the warrant has committed an offense and thus the warrant primarily serves to protect an individual from an unreasonable seizure. A search warrant, in contrast is issued upon a showing of probable cause to believe that the legitimate object of a search is located in a particular place, and therefore safeguards an individual's interest in the privacy of his home and possessions against the unjustified intrusion of the police.

Thus, whether the arrest warrant issued in this case adequately safeguarded the interests protected by the Fourth Amendment depends upon what the warrant authorized the agents to do. To be sure, the warrant embodied a judicial finding that there was probable cause to believe that Ricky Lyons had committed a felony, and the warrant therefore authorized the officers to seize Lyons. However, the agents sought to do more than use the warrant to arrest Lyons in a public place or in his home; instead, they relied on the warrant as legal authority to enter the home of a third person based on their belief that Ricky Lyons might be a guest there. Regardless of how reasonable this belief might have been, it was never subjected to the detached scrutiny of a judicial officer. Thus, while the warrant in this case may have protected Lyons from an unreasonable seizure, it did absolutely nothing to protect petitioner's privacy interest in being free from an unreasonable invasion and search of his home. Instead, petitioner's only protection from an illegal entry and search was the agent's personal determination of probable cause. In the absence of exigent circumstances, we have consistently held that such judicially untested determinations are not reliable enough to justify an entry into a person's home to arrest him without a warrant, or a search of a home for objects in the absence of a search warrant. We see no reason to depart from this settled course when the search of a home is for a person rather than an object.

A contrary conclusion—that the police, acting alone and in the absence of exigent circumstances, may decide when there is sufficient justification for searching the home of a third party for the subject of an arrest warrant—would create a significant potential for abuse. Armed solely with an arrest warrant for a single person, the police could search all the homes of that individual's friends and acquaintances. Moreover, an arrest warrant may serve as the pretext for entering a home in which the police have a suspicion, but not probable cause to believe, that illegal activity is taking place. The Government recognizes the potential for such abuses, but contends that existing remedies—such as motions to suppress illegally procured evidence and damages actions for Fourth Amendment violations—provide adequate means of redress. We do not agree. As we observed on a previous occasion, "[t]he [Fourth] Amendment is designed to prevent, not simply to redress, unlawful police action." Indeed, if suppression motions and damages actions were sufficient to implement the Fourth Amendment's prohibition against unreasonable searches and seizures, there would be no need for the constitutional requirement that in the absence of exigent circumstances a warrant must be obtained for a home arrest or a search of a home for objects. We have instead concluded that in such cases the participation of a detached magistrate in the probable cause determination is an essential element of a reasonable search or seizure, and we believe that the same conclusion should apply here.

In sum, two distinct interests were implicated by the search at issue here—Ricky Lyons' interest in being free from an unreasonable seizure and petitioner's interest in being free from an unreasonable search of his home. Because the arrest warrant for Lyons addressed only the former interest, the search of petitioner's home was no more reasonable from petitioner's perspective than it would have been if conducted in the absence of any warrant. Since warrantless searches of a home are impermissible absent consent or exigent circumstances, we conclude that the instant search violated the Fourth Amendment. * * *

The Government also suggests that practical problems might arise if law enforcement officers are required to obtain a search warrant before entering the home of a third party to make an arrest. The basis of this concern is that persons, as opposed to objects, are inherently mobile, and thus officers seeking to effect an arrest may be forced to return to the magistrate several times as the subject of the arrest warrant moves from place to place. We are convinced, however, that a search warrant requirement will not significantly impede effective law enforcement efforts.

First, the situations in which a search warrant will be necessary are few. As noted in *Payton v. New York,* an arrest warrant alone will suffice to enter a suspect's own residence to effect his arrest. Furthermore, if probable cause exists, no warrant is required to apprehend a suspected felon in a public place. Thus, the subject of an arrest warrant can be readily seized before entering or after leaving the home of a third party. Finally, the exigent-circumstances doctrine significantly limits the situations in which a search warrant would be needed. For example, a warrantless entry of a home would be justified if the police were in "hot pursuit" of a fugitive. Thus, to the extent that searches for persons pose special problems, we believe that the exigent-circumstances doctrine is adequate to accommodate legitimate law enforcement needs.

Moreover, in those situations in which a search warrant is necessary, the inconvenience incurred by the police is simply not that significant. First, if the police know of the location of the felon when they obtain an arrest warrant, the additional burden of obtaining a search warrant at the same time is miniscule. The inconvenience of obtaining such a warrant does not increase significantly when an outstanding arrest warrant already exists. In this case, for example, Agent Goodowens knew the address of the house to be searched two days in advance, and planned the raid from the federal courthouse in Atlanta where, we are informed, three full-time magistrates were on duty. In routine search cases such as this, the short time required to obtain a search warrant from a magistrate will seldom hinder efforts to apprehend a felon. Finally, if a magistrate is not nearby, a telephonic search warrant can usually be obtained.

Whatever practical problems remain, however, cannot outweigh the constitutional interests at stake. Any warrant requirement impedes to some extent the vigor with which the Government can seek to enforce its laws, yet the Fourth Amendment recognizes that this restraint is necessary in some cases to protect against unreasonable searches and seizures. We conclude that this is such a case. The additional burden imposed on the police by a warrant requirement is minimal. In contrast, the right protected—that of presumptively innocent people to be secure in their homes from unjustified, forcible intrusions by the Government—is weighty. Thus, in order to render the instant search reasonable under the Fourth Amendment, a search warrant was required.

Accordingly, the judgment of the Court of Appeals is reversed, and the case is remanded to that court for further proceedings consistent with this opinion.

So ordered.

THE CHIEF JUSTICE concurs in the judgment.

JUSTICE REHNQUIST, with whom JUSTICE WHITE joins, dissenting. * * *

The government's interests in the warrantless entry of a third-party dwelling to execute an arrest warrant are compelling. The basic problem confronting police in such situations is the inherent mobility of the fugitive. By definition, the police have probable cause to believe that the fugitive is in a dwelling which is not his home. He may stay there for a week, a day, or 10 minutes. Fugitives from justice tend to be mobile, and police officers will generally have no way of knowing whether the subject of an arrest warrant will be at the dwelling when they return from seeking a search warrant. Imposition of a search warrant requirement in such circumstances will frustrate the compelling interests of the government and indeed the public in the apprehension of those subject to outstanding arrest warrants.

The Court's responses to these very real concerns are singularly unpersuasive. It first downplays them by stating that "the situations in which a search warrant will be necessary are few," because no search warrant is necessary to arrest a suspect at his home and, if the suspect is at another's home, the police need only wait until he leaves, since no search warrant is needed to arrest him in a public place. These beguilingly simpl[e] answers to a serious law enforcement problem simply will not wash. Criminals who know or suspect they are subject to arrest warrants would not be likely to return to their homes, and while "[t]he police could reduce the likelihood of escape by staking out all possible exits . . . the costs of such a stakeout seems excessive in an era of rising crime and scarce police resources." * * *

Because the burden on law enforcement officers to obtain a separate search warrant before entering the dwelling of a third party to execute a concededly valid arrest warrant is great, and carries with it a high possibility that the fugitive named in the arrest warrant will escape apprehension, I would conclude that the application of the traditional "reasonableness" standard of the Fourth Amendment does not require a separate search warrant in a case such as this. * * *

ASHCROFT V. AL-KIDD
Supreme Court of the United States
563 U.S. 731, 131 S. Ct. 2074, 179 L. Ed. 2d 1149 (2011)

JUSTICE SCALIA delivered the opinion of the Court.

We decide whether a former Attorney General enjoys immunity from suit for allegedly authorizing federal prosecutors to obtain valid material-witness warrants for detention of terrorism suspects whom they would otherwise lack probable cause to arrest.

The federal material-witness statute authorizes judges to "order the arrest of [a] person" whose testimony "is material in a criminal proceeding . . . if it is shown that it may become impracticable to secure the presence of the person by subpoena." Material witnesses enjoy the same constitutional right to pretrial release as other federal detainees, and federal law requires release if their testimony "can adequately be secured by deposition, and if further detention is not necessary to prevent a failure of justice."

Because this case arises from a motion to dismiss, we accept as true the factual allegations in Abdullah al-Kidd's complaint. The complaint alleges that, in the aftermath of the September 11th terrorist attacks, then-Attorney General John Ashcroft authorized federal prosecutors and law enforcement officials to use the material-witness statute to detain individuals with suspected ties to terrorist organizations. It is alleged that federal officials had no intention of calling most of these individuals as witnesses, and that they were detained, at Ashcroft's direction, because federal officials suspected them of supporting terrorism but lacked sufficient evidence to charge them with a crime.

It is alleged that this pretextual detention policy led to the material-witness arrest of al-Kidd, a native-born United States citizen. FBI agents apprehended him in March 2003 as he checked in for a flight to Saudi Arabia. Two days earlier, federal officials had informed a Magistrate Judge that, if al-Kidd boarded his flight, they believed information "crucial" to the prosecution of Sami Omar al-Hussayen would be lost. Al-Kidd remained in federal custody for 16 days and on supervised release until al-Hussayen's trial concluded 14 months later. Prosecutors never called him as a witness.

In March 2005, al-Kidd filed this *Bivens* action to challenge the constitutionality of Ashcroft's alleged policy. * * * Ashcroft filed a motion to dismiss based on absolute and qualified immunity, which the District Court denied. A divided panel of the United States Court of Appeals for the Ninth Circuit affirmed, holding that the Fourth Amendment prohibits pretextual arrests absent probable cause of criminal wrongdoing, and that Ashcroft could not claim qualified or absolute immunity. * * * We granted certiorari.

Qualified immunity shields federal and state officials from money damages unless a plaintiff pleads facts showing (1) that the official violated a statutory or constitutional right, and (2) that the right was "clearly established" at the time of the challenged conduct. We recently reaffirmed that lower courts have discretion to decide which of the two prongs of qualified-immunity analysis to tackle first. * * *

The Fourth Amendment protects "[t]he right of the people to be secure in their persons, houses, papers, and effects, against unreasonable searches and seizures." An arrest, of course, qualifies as a "seizure" of a "person" under this provision and so must be reasonable under the circumstances. * * *

Fourth Amendment reasonableness "is predominantly an objective inquiry." We ask whether "the circumstances, viewed objectively, justify [the challenged] action." If so, that action was reasonable "*whatever* the subjective intent" motivating the relevant officials. This approach recognizes that the Fourth Amendment regulates conduct rather than thoughts, and it promotes evenhanded, uniform enforcement of the law.

Two "limited exception[s]" to this rule are our special-needs and administrative-search cases, where "actual motivations" do matter. A judicial warrant and probable cause are not needed where the search or seizure is justified by "special needs, beyond the normal need for law enforcement," such as the need to deter drug use in public schools or the need to assure that railroad employees engaged in train operations are not under the influence of drugs or alcohol, and where the search or seizure is in execution of an administrative warrant authorizing, for example, an inspection of fire-damaged premises to determine the cause, or an inspection of residential premises to assure compliance with a housing code. But those exceptions do not apply where the officer's purpose is not to attend to the special needs or to the investigation for which the administrative inspection is justified. * * *

Apart from those cases, we have almost uniformly rejected invitations to probe subjective intent. * * * Needless to say, warrantless, "suspicionless intrusions pursuant to a general scheme," are far removed from the facts of this case. A warrant issued by a neutral Magistrate Judge authorized al-Kidd's arrest. The affidavit accompanying the warrant application (as al-Kidd concedes) gave individualized reasons to believe that he was a material witness and that he would soon disappear. The existence of a judicial warrant based on individualized suspicion takes this case outside the domain of * * * our special-needs and administrative-search cases. * * *

[The Court reviews the existing case law and concludes that former Attorney General John Ashcroft did not violate clearly established law by authorizing the use of material witness warrants to detain individuals suspected of terrorism.]

We hold that an objectively reasonable arrest and detention of a material witness pursuant to a validly obtained warrant cannot be challenged as unconstitutional on the basis of allegations that the arresting authority had an improper motive. * * * The judgment of the Court of Appeals is reversed, and the case is remanded for further proceedings consistent with this opinion.

It is so ordered.

JUSTICE KAGAN took no part in the consideration or decision of this case.

JUSTICE GINSBURG, with whom JUSTICE BREYER and JUSTICE SOTOMAYOR join, concurring in the judgment. * * *

In addressing al-Kidd's Fourth Amendment claim against Ashcroft, the Court assumes at the outset the existence of a *validly obtained* material witness warrant. That characterization is puzzling. Is a warrant "validly obtained" when the affidavit on which it is based fails to inform the issuing Magistrate Judge that "the Government has no intention of using [al-Kidd as a witness] at [another's] trial," and does not disclose that al-Kidd had cooperated with FBI agents each of the several times they had asked to interview him?

Casting further doubt on the assumption that the warrant was validly obtained, the Magistrate Judge was not told that al-Kidd's parents, wife, and children were all citizens and residents of the United States. In addition, the affidavit misrepresented that al-Kidd was about to take a one-way flight to Saudi Arabia, with a first-class ticket costing approximately $5,000; in fact, al-Kidd had a round-trip, coach-class ticket that cost $1,700. Given these omissions and misrepresentations, there is strong cause to question the Court's opening assumption—a valid material-witness warrant. * * *

I also agree with Justice KENNEDY that al-Kidd's treatment presents serious questions, unaddressed by the Court, concerning "the [legality of] the Government's use of the Material Witness Statute in this case." In addition to the questions Justice KENNEDY poses, and even if the initial material witness classification had been proper, what even arguably legitimate basis could there be for the harsh custodial conditions to which al-Kidd was subjected: Ostensibly held only to secure his testimony, al-Kidd was confined in three different detention centers during his 16 days' incarceration, kept in high-security cells lit 24 hours a day, strip-searched and subjected to body-cavity inspections on more than one occasion, and handcuffed and shackled about his wrists, legs, and waist. * * *

[Abdullah al-Kidd's] ordeal is a grim reminder of the need to install safeguards against disrespect for human dignity, constraints that will control officialdom even in perilous times.

[JUSTICE KENNEDY's concurring opinion and JUSTICE SOTOMAYOR's concurring opinion have been omitted.]

Chapter 6

Searches Incident to Arrest

■ ■ ■

Starting with this chapter, we begin our study of the various ways police may conduct warrantless searches without running afoul of the Constitution. The first of many exceptions to the warrant requirement that we will study is the search incident to arrest exception. *Chimel v. California* explains this exception and the rationales for permitting police to engage in such searches without having to seek prior judicial approval in the form of a warrant. In *Robinson v. California*, the Court elaborates upon the permissible scope of a search incident to arrest when an officer is searching the person of the arrestee. *Vale v. Louisiana* tells us more about the prerequisites for a valid search incident to arrest and the permissible scope of such a search.

In the next two cases, the Court examines the requirements for a valid search of a vehicle incident to arrest. In *New York v. Belton*, the Court establishes what appears to be a clear, bright-line test governing the search of a vehicle incident to the arrest of an occupant of that vehicle. In *Arizona v. Gant*, the Court continues its examination of searches of vehicles incident to arrest. Finally, in *Riley v. California*, the Court addresses whether an officer can search a cell phone incident to arrest without securing a warrant in advance.

Chimel v. California
Supreme Court of the United States
395 U.S. 752, 89 S. Ct. 2034, 23 L. Ed. 2d 685 (1969)

Justice Stewart delivered the opinion of the Court.

This case raises basic questions concerning the permissible scope under the Fourth Amendment of a search incident to a lawful arrest.

The relevant facts are essentially undisputed. Late in the afternoon of September 13, 1965, three police officers arrived at the Santa Ana, California, home of the petitioner with a warrant authorizing his arrest for the burglary of a coin shop. The officers knocked on the door, identified themselves to the petitioner's wife, and asked if they might come inside. She ushered them into the house, where they waited 10 or 15 minutes until the petitioner returned home from work. When the petitioner entered the house, one of the officers handed him the arrest warrant and asked for permission to "look around." The petitioner objected, but was advised that "on the basis of the lawful arrest," the officers would nonetheless conduct a search. No search warrant had been issued.

Accompanied by the petitioner's wife, the officers then looked through the entire three-bedroom house, including the attic, the garage, and a small workshop. In some rooms the search was relatively cursory. In the master bedroom and sewing room, however, the officers directed the petitioner's wife to open drawers and "to physically move contents of the drawers from side to side so that (they) might view any items that would have come from (the) burglary." After completing the search, they seized numerous items-primarily coins, but also several medals, tokens, and a few other objects. The entire search took between 45 minutes and an hour.

At the petitioner's subsequent state trial on two charges of burglary, the items taken from his house were admitted into evidence against him, over his objection that they had been unconstitutionally seized. He was convicted, and the judgments of conviction were affirmed by both the California Court of Appeal and the California Supreme Court. * * * [T]he appellate courts [held] that the search of the petitioner's home had been justified, despite the absence of a search warrant, on the ground that it had been incident to a valid arrest. We granted certiorari in order to consider the petitioner's substantial constitutional claims.

Without deciding the question, we proceed on the hypothesis that the California courts were correct in holding that the arrest of the petitioner was valid under the Constitution. This brings us directly to the question whether the warrantless search of the petitioner's entire house can be constitutionally justified as incident to that arrest. The decisions of this Court bearing upon that question have been far from consistent, as even the most cursory review makes evident.

Only last Term in *Terry* v. *Ohio*, we emphasized that "the police must, whenever practicable, obtain advance judicial approval of searches and seizures through the warrant procedure," and that "the scope of [a] search must be 'strictly tied to and justified by' the circumstances which rendered its initiation permissible. The search undertaken by the officer in that "stop and frisk" case was sustained under that test, because it was no more than a "protective . . . search for weapons."

* * *

A similar analysis underlies the "search incident to arrest" principle, and marks its proper extent. When an arrest is made, it is reasonable for the arresting officer to search the person arrested in order to remove any weapons that the latter might seek to use in order to resist arrest or effect his escape. Otherwise, the officer's safety might well be endangered, and the arrest itself frustrated. In addition, it is entirely reasonable for the arresting officer to search for and seize any evidence on the arrestee's person in order to prevent its concealment or destruction. And the area into which an arrestee might reach in order to grab a weapon or evidentiary items must, of course, be governed by a like rule. A gun on a table or in a drawer in front of one who is arrested can be as dangerous to the arresting officer as one concealed in the clothing of the person arrested. There is ample justification, therefore, for a search of the arrestee's person and the area "within his immediate control"—construing that phrase to mean the area from within which he might gain possession of a weapon or destructible evidence.

There is no comparable justification, however, for routinely searching any room other than that in which an arrest occurs—or, for that matter, for searching through all the desk drawers or other closed or concealed areas in that room itself.[a] Such searches, in the absence of well-recognized exceptions, may be made only under the authority of a search warrant. The "adherence to judicial processes" mandated by the Fourth Amendment requires no less.

* * * [H]ad [petitioner] been arrested earlier in the day, at his place of employment rather than at home, no search of his house could have been made without a search warrant. In any event, even apart from the possibility of such police tactics, the general point so forcefully made by Judge Learned Hand in *United States v. Kirschenblatt* remains:

> After arresting a man in his house, to rummage at will among his papers in search of whatever will convict him, appears to us to be indistinguishable from what might be done under a general warrant; indeed, the warrant would give more protection, for presumably it must be issued by a magistrate. True, by hypothesis the power would not exist, if the supposed offender were not found on the premises; but it is small consolation to know that one's papers are safe only so long as one is not at home.

Application of sound Fourth Amendment principles to the facts of this case produces a clear result. The search here went far beyond the petitioner's person and the area from within which he might have obtained either a weapon or something that could have been used as evidence against him. There was no constitutional justification, in the absence of a search warrant, for extending the search beyond that area. The scope of the search

---

[a] In a later case, the Court backtracked from this position. In *Maryland v. Buie*, 494 U.S. 325 (1990), the Court held that incident to arrest and without any additional probable cause or reasonable suspicion beyond the probable cause needed to arrest, a police officer may search "closets and other spaces immediately adjoining the place of arrest from which an attack could be immediately launched." *Id.* at 335. Beyond these spaces, an officer may conduct a limited protective sweep or cursory visual inspection of the rest of the house only if the officer has a reasonable suspicion, based on specific and articulable facts that the area to be swept "harbors an individual posing a danger to those on the arrest scene." *Id.* at 335, 337.

was, therefore, "unreasonable" under the Fourth and Fourteenth Amendments and the petitioner's conviction cannot stand.

Reversed.

JUSTICE WHITE with whom JUSTICE BLACK joins, dissenting.

* * * The Court has always held, and does not today deny, that when there is probable cause to search and it is "impracticable" for one reason or another to get a search warrant, then a warrantless search may be reasonable. This is the case whether an arrest was made at the time of the search or not.

* * * [I]t seems to me unreasonable to require the police to leave the scene in order to obtain a search warrant when they are already legally there to make a valid arrest, and when there must almost always be a strong possibility that confederates of the arrested man will in the meanwhile remove the items for which the police have probable cause to search. This must so often be the case that it seems to me as unreasonable to require a warrant for a search of the premises as to require a warrant for search of the person and his very immediate surroundings.

This case provides a good illustration of my point that it is unreasonable to require police to leave the scene of an arrest in order to obtain a search warrant when they already have probable cause to search and there is a clear danger that the items for which they may reasonably search will be removed before they return with a warrant. Petitioner was arrested in his home after an arrest * * * which I will now assume was valid. There was doubtless probable cause not only to arrest petitioner, but also to search his house. He had obliquely admitted, both to a neighbor and to the owner of the burglarized store, that he had committed the burglary. In light of this, and the fact that the neighbor had seen other admittedly stolen property in petitioner's house, there was surely probable cause on which a warrant could have issued to search the house for the stolen coins. Moreover, had the police simply arrested petitioner, taken him off to the station house, and later returned with a warrant, it seems very likely that petitioner's wife, who in view of petitioner's generally garrulous nature must have known of the robbery, would have removed the coins.[b] For the police to search the house while the evidence they had probable cause to search out and seize was still there cannot be considered unreasonable. * * *

[JUSTICE HARLAN's concurring opinion has been omitted.]

---

[b] Another option is reflected in *Illinois v. McArthur*, in which the Court held it reasonable for one officer to remain with the defendant at the family residence, watching him each time he entered the residence, while another officer left to obtain a search warrant. 531 U.S. 326 (2001).

UNITED STATES v. ROBINSON
Supreme Court of the United States
414 U.S. 218, 94 S. Ct. 467, 38 L. Ed. 2d 427 (1973)

JUSTICE REHNQUIST delivered the opinion of the Court. * * *

On April 23, 1968, at approximately 11 p.m., Officer Richard Jenks, a 15-year veteran of the District of Columbia Metropolitan Police Department, observed the respondent driving a 1965 Cadillac near the intersection of 8th and C Streets, N.E., in the District of Columbia. Jenks, as a result of previous investigation following a check of respondent's operator's permit four days earlier, determined there was reason to believe that respondent was operating a motor vehicle after the revocation of his operator's permit. This is an offense defined by statute in the District of Columbia which carries a mandatory minimum jail term, a mandatory minimum fine, or both.

Jenks signaled respondent to stop the automobile, which respondent did, and all three of the occupants emerged from the car. At that point Jenks informed respondent that he was under arrest for "operating after revocation and obtaining a permit by misrepresentation." It was assumed by the Court of Appeals, and is conceded by the respondent here, that Jenks had probable cause to arrest respondent, and that he effected a full custody arrest.

In accordance with procedures prescribed in police department instructions, Jenks then began to search respondent. He explained at a subsequent hearing that he was "face-to-face" with the respondent, and "placed (his) hands on (the respondent), my right-hand to his left breast like this (demonstrating) and proceeded to pat him down thus (with the right hand)." During this patdown, Jenks felt an object in the left breast pocket of the heavy coat respondent was wearing, but testified that he "couldn't tell what it was" and also that he "couldn't actually tell the size of it." Jenks then reached into the pocket and pulled out the object, which turned out to be a "crumpled up cigarette package." Jenks testified that at this point he still did not know what was in the package:

> As I felt the package I could feel objects in the package but I couldn't tell what they were. . . . I knew they weren't cigarettes.

The officer then opened the cigarette pack and found 14 gelatin capsules of white powder which he thought to be, and which later analysis proved to be, heroin. Jenks then continued his search of respondent to completion, feeling around his waist and trouser legs, and examining the remaining pockets. The heroin seized from the respondent was admitted into evidence at the trial which resulted in his conviction in the District Court. * * *

It is well settled that a search incident to a lawful arrest is a traditional exception to the warrant requirement of the Fourth Amendment. This general exception has historically been formulated into two distinct propositions. The first is that a search may be made of the person of the arrestee by virtue of the lawful arrest. The second is that a search may be made of the area within the control of the arrestee.

Examination of this Court's decisions shows that these two propositions have been treated quite differently. The validity of the search of a person incident to a lawful arrest has been regarded as settled from its first enunciation, and has remained virtually unchallenged until the present case. The validity of the second proposition, while likewise conceded in principle, has been subject to differing interpretations as to the extent of the area which may be searched. * * *

Throughout the series of cases in which the Court has addressed the second proposition relating to a search incident to a lawful arrest—the permissible area beyond the person of the arrestee which such a search may cover—no doubt has been expressed as to the unqualified authority of the arresting authority to search the person of the arrestee. * * * The justification or reason for the authority to search incident to a lawful arrest rests quite as much on the need to disarm the suspect in order to take him into custody as it does on the need to preserve evidence on his person for later use at trial. * * *

Nor are we inclined, on the basis of what seems to us to be a rather speculative judgment, to qualify the breadth of the general authority to search incident to a lawful custodial arrest on an assumption that persons arrested for the offense of driving while their licenses have been revoked are less likely to possess dangerous weapons than are those arrested for other crimes.[5] It is scarcely open to doubt that the danger to an officer is far greater in the case of the extended exposure which follows the taking of a suspect into custody and transporting him to the police station than in the case of the relatively fleeting contact resulting from the typical *Terry*-type stop. This is an adequate basis for treating all custodial arrests alike for purposes of search justification.

But quite apart from these distinctions, our more fundamental disagreement with the Court of Appeals arises from its suggestion that there must be litigated in each case the issue of whether or not there was

---

[5] Such an assumption appears at least questionable in light of the available statistical data concerning assaults on police officers who are in the course of making arrests. The danger to the police officer flows from the fact of the arrest, and its attendant proximity, stress, and uncertainty, and not from the grounds for arrest. One study concludes that approximately 30% of the shootings of police officers occur when an officer stops a person in an automobile. The Government in its brief notes that the Uniform Crime Reports, prepared by the Federal Bureau of Investigation, indicate that a significant percentage of murders of police officers occurs when the officers are making traffic stops. Those reports indicate that during January–March 1973, 35 police officers were murdered; 11 of those officers were killed while engaged in making traffic stops.

present one of the reasons supporting the authority for a search of the person incident to a lawful arrest. We do not think the long line of authorities of this Court * * * or what we can glean from the history of practice in this country and in England, requires such a case-by-case adjudication. A police officer's determination as to how and where to search the person of a suspect whom he has arrested is necessarily a quick ad hoc judgment which the Fourth Amendment does not require to be broken down in each instance into an analysis of each step in the search. The authority to search the person incident to a lawful custodial arrest, while based upon the need to disarm and to discover evidence, does not depend on what a court may later decide was the probability in a particular arrest situation that weapons or evidence would in fact be found upon the person of the suspect. A custodial arrest of a suspect based on probable cause is a reasonable intrusion under the Fourth Amendment; that intrusion being lawful, a search incident to the arrest requires no additional justification. It is the fact of the lawful arrest which establishes the authority to search, and we hold that in the case of a lawful custodial arrest a full search of the person is not only an exception to the warrant requirement of the Fourth Amendment, but is also a "reasonable" search under that Amendment.

The search of respondent's person conducted by Officer Jenks in this case and the seizure from him of the heroin, were permissible under established Fourth Amendment law. * * * Since it is the fact of custodial arrest which gives rise to the authority to search, it is of no moment that Jenks did not indicate any subjective fear of the respondent or that he did not himself suspect that respondent was armed. Having in the course of a lawful search come upon the crumpled package of cigarettes, he was entitled to inspect it; and when his inspection revealed the heroin capsules, he was entitled to seize them as "fruits, instrumentalities, or contraband" probative of criminal conduct. The judgment of the Court of Appeals holding otherwise is reversed.

JUSTICE MARSHALL with whom JUSTICE DOUGLAS and JUSTICE BRENNAN join, dissenting. * * *

The majority opinion fails to recognize that the search conducted by Officer Jenks did not merely involve a search of respondent's person. It also included a separate search of effects found on his person. And even were we to assume, arguendo, that it was reasonable for Jenks to remove the object he felt in respondent's pocket, clearly there was no justification consistent with the Fourth Amendment which would authorize his opening the package and looking inside.

To begin with, after Jenks had the cigarette package in his hands, there is no indication that he had reason to believe or did in fact believe that the package contained a weapon. More importantly, even if the crumpled-up cigarette package had in fact contained some sort of small weapon, it would have been impossible for respondent to have used it once the package was in the officer's hands. Opening the package, therefore, did not further the protective purpose of the search. Even the dissenting opinion in the Court of Appeals conceded that "since the package was now in the officer's possession, any risk of the prisoner's use of a weapon in this package had been eliminated." * * *

The Government argues that it is difficult to see what constitutionally protected "expectation of privacy" a prisoner has in the interior of a cigarette pack. One wonders if the result in this case would have been the same were respondent a businessman who was lawfully taken into custody for driving without a license and whose wallet was taken from him by the police. Would it be reasonable for the police officer, because of the possibility that a razor blade was hidden somewhere in the wallet, to open it, remove all the contents, and examine each item carefully? Or suppose a lawyer lawfully arrested for a traffic offense is found to have a sealed envelope on his person. Would it be permissible for the arresting officer to tear open the envelope in order to make sure that it did not contain a clandestine weapon—perhaps a pin or a razor blade? Would it not be more consonant with the purpose of the Fourth Amendment and the legitimate needs of the police to require the officer, if he has any question whatsoever about what the wallet or letter contains, to hold on to it until the arrestee is brought to the precinct station? * * *

The search conducted by Officer Jenks in this case went far beyond what was reasonably necessary to protect him from harm or to ensure that respondent would not effect an escape from custody. In my view, it therefore fell outside the scope of a properly drawn "search incident to arrest" exception to the Fourth Amendment's warrant requirement. I would affirm the judgment of the Court of Appeals holding that the fruits of the search should have been suppressed at respondent's trial.

NOTE

It is clear from *Chimel* and *Robinson* that a valid custodial arrest is a necessary prerequisite to a search incident to arrest. Even if the officer has the discretion to arrest or cite the offending individual, if the officer chooses to cite rather than arrest, she has no authority to conduct a search incident to an arrest. *Knowles v. Iowa*, 525 U.S. 113 (1998) (refusing to recognize a search incident to citation exception to the warrant requirement).

What if a state law prohibits the officer from making an arrest for the offense in question? If an officer arrests an individual in violation of state law, does this mean the arrest is not valid for purposes of the search incident to arrest exception? One would think that an arrest that violated state law would clearly be an invalid arrest, but a unanimous Supreme Court held otherwise in *Virginia v. Moore*, 553 U.S. 164 (2008). In *Virginia v. Moore*, the defendant was arrested for the misdemeanor of driving with a suspended license even though Virginia law required officers to issue a summons rather than arrest such individuals. After arresting Moore, the officers conducted a search incident to arrest and found 16 grams of crack cocaine on Moore's person. In finding that the arrest was valid despite being in violation of state law, Justice Scalia, writing for the Court, explained that probable cause to believe an individual has committed a crime is all that is needed for an arrest to comport with the Fourth Amendment. As for the defendant's argument that the warrantless search did not fall within the search incident to arrest exception because it did not stem from a "lawful" custodial arrest, the Court responded that the term "lawful" as used in its previous search incident to arrest decisions just meant that the arrest had to be in compliance with the Constitution. An arrest based on probable cause, the Court stated, is a lawful, i.e. constitutional, arrest even if it is in violation of state law.

VALE V. LOUISIANA
Supreme Court of the United States
399 U.S. 30, 90 S. Ct. 1969, 26 L. Ed. 2d 409 (1970)

JUSTICE STEWART delivered the opinion of the Court.

The appellant, Donald Vale, was convicted in a Louisiana court on a charge of possessing heroin and was sentenced as a multiple offender to 15 years' imprisonment at hard labor. The Louisiana Supreme Court affirmed the conviction, rejecting the claim that evidence introduced at the trial was the product of an unlawful search and seizure. * * *

The evidence adduced at the pretrial hearing on a motion to suppress showed that on April 24, 1967, officers possessing two warrants for Vale's arrest and having information that he was residing at a specified address proceeded there in an unmarked car and set up a surveillance of the house. The evidence of what then took place was summarized by the Louisiana Supreme Court as follows:

> After approximately 15 minutes the officers observed a green 1958 Chevrolet drive up and sound the horn and after backing into a parking place, again blew the horn. At this juncture Donald Vale, who was well known to Officer Brady having arrested him twice in the previous month, was seen coming out of the house and walk up to the passenger side of the Chevrolet where he had a close brief conversation with the driver; and after looking up and down the street returned inside of the house. Within a few minutes he reappeared on the porch, and again cautiously looked up and down the street before proceeding to the passenger side of the Chevrolet, leaning through the window. From this the officers were convinced a narcotics sale had taken place. They returned to their car and immediately drove toward Donald Vale, and as they reached within approximately three cars lengths from the accused, (Donald Vale) he looked up and, obviously recognizing

the officers, turned around, walking quickly toward the house. At the same time the driver of the Chevrolet started to make his get away when the car was blocked by the police vehicle. The three officers promptly alighted from the car, whereupon Officers Soule and Laumann called to Donald Vale to stop as he reached the front steps of the house, telling him he was under arrest. Officer Brady at the same time, seeing the driver of the Chevrolet, Arizzio Saucier, whom the officers knew to be a narcotic addict, place something hurriedly in his mouth, immediately placed him under arrest and joined his co-officers. Because of the transaction they had just observed they, informed Donald Vale they were going to search the house, and thereupon advised him of his constitutional rights. After they all entered the front room, Officer Laumann made a cursory inspection of the house to ascertain if anyone else was present and within about three minutes Mrs. Vale and James Vale, mother and brother of Donald Vale, returned home carrying groceries and were informed of the arrest and impending search.

The search of a rear bedroom revealed a quantity of narcotics.

The Louisiana Supreme Court held that the search of the house did not violate the Fourth Amendment because it occurred "in the immediate vicinity of the arrest" of Donald Vale and was "substantially contemporaneous therewith * * *." We cannot agree. * * *

A search may be incident to an arrest "only if it is substantially contemporaneous with the arrest[a] and is confined to the immediate vicinity of the arrest." If a search of a house is to be upheld as incident to an arrest, that arrest must take place inside the house, not somewhere outside—whether two blocks away, twenty feet away, or on the sidewalk near the front steps. "Belief, however well founded, that an article sought is concealed in a dwelling house furnishes no justification for a search of that place without a warrant." That basic rule "has never been questioned in this Court."

The Louisiana Supreme Court thought the search independently supportable because it involved narcotics, which are easily removed, hidden, or destroyed. It would be unreasonable, the Louisiana court concluded, "to require the officers under the facts of the case to first secure a search warrant before searching the premises, as time is of the essence inasmuch as the officers never know whether there is anyone on the premises to be searched who could very easily destroy the evidence." Such

---

[a] Generally speaking, a valid custodial arrest will precede the search incident to that arrest. If the officer searches first and then arrests, can the search still come within the search incident to arrest exception? In *Rawlings v. Kentucky*, 448 U.S. 98 (1980), the Court answered this question in the affirmative, explaining "where the formal arrest follow[s] quickly on the heels of the challenged search . . ., we do not believe it particularly important that the search preceded the arrest rather than vice versa" as long as the officer had probable cause to arrest prior to the search in question. *Id.* at 111.

a rationale could not apply to the present case, since by their own account the arresting officers satisfied themselves that no one else was in the house when they first entered the premises. But entirely apart from that point, our past decisions make clear that only in "a few specifically established and well-delineated" situations, may a warrantless search of a dwelling withstand constitutional scrutiny, even though the authorities have probable cause to conduct it. The burden rests on the State to show the existence of such an exceptional situation. And the record before us discloses none.

There is no suggestion that anyone consented to the search. The officers were not responding to an emergency. They were not in hot pursuit of a fleeing felon. The goods ultimately seized were not in the process of destruction. Nor were they about to be removed from the jurisdiction.

The officers were able to procure two warrants for Vale's arrest. They also had information that he was residing at the address where they found him. There is thus no reason, so far as anything before us appears, to suppose that it was impracticable for them to obtain a search warrant as well. We decline to hold that an arrest on the street can provide its own "exigent circumstance" so as to justify a warrantless search of the arrestee's house. * * *

Reversed and remanded.

JUSTICE BLACKMUN took no part in the consideration or decision of this case.

JUSTICE BLACK, with whom THE CHIEF JUSTICE joins, dissenting.

The Fourth Amendment to the United States Constitution prohibits only "unreasonable searches." A warrant has never been thought to be an absolute requirement for a constitutionally proper search. Searches, whether with or without a warrant, are to be judged by whether they are reasonable, and * * * common sense dictates that reasonableness varies with the circumstances of the search. The Louisiana Supreme Court held not only that the police action here was reasonable but also that failure to conduct an immediate search would have been unreasonable. With that view I am in complete agreement, for the following reasons.

* * * [T]he police had probable cause to believe that Vale was engaged in a narcotics transfer, and that a supply of narcotics would be found in the house, to which Vale had returned after his first conversation, from which he had emerged furtively bearing what the police could readily deduce was a supply of narcotics, and toward which he hurried after seeing the police. But the police did not know then who else might be in the house. Vale's arrest took place near the house, and anyone observing from inside would surely have been alerted to destroy the stocks of contraband which the police believed Vale had left there. The police had already seen Saucier, the

narcotics addict, apparently swallow what Vale had given him. Believing that some evidence had already been destroyed and that other evidence might well be, the police were faced with the choice of risking the immediate destruction of evidence or entering the house and conducting a search. I cannot say that their decision to search was unreasonable. Delay in order to obtain a warrant would have given an accomplice just the time he needed.

That the arresting officers did, in fact, believe that others might be in the house is attested to by their actions upon entering the door left open by Vale. The police at once checked the small house to determine if anyone else was present. Just as they discovered the house was empty, however, Vale's mother and brother arrived. Now what had been a suspicion became a certainty: Vale's relatives were in possession and knew of his arrest. To have abandoned the search at this point, and left the house with Vale, would not have been the action of reasonable police officers.

* * * [T]he circumstances here were sufficiently exceptional to justify a search, even if the search was not strictly "incidental" to an arrest. The Court recognizes that searches to prevent the destruction or removal of evidence have long been held reasonable by this Court. Whether the "exceptional circumstances" justifying such a search exist or not is a question that may be, as it is here, quite distinct from whether or not the search was incident to a valid arrest. It is thus unnecessary to determine whether the search was valid as incident to the arrest. * * *

The Court, however, finds the search here unreasonable. First, the Court suggests that the contraband was not "in the process of destruction." None of the cases cited by the Court supports the proposition that "exceptional circumstances" exist only when the process of destruction has already begun. On the contrary we implied that those circumstances did exist when "evidence or contraband was threatened with removal or destruction."

Second, the Court seems to argue that the search was unreasonable because the police officers had time to obtain a warrant. I agree that the opportunity to obtain a warrant is one of the factors to be weighed in determining reasonableness. But the record conclusively shows that there was no such opportunity here. As I noted above, once the officers had observed Vale's conduct in front of the house they had probable cause to believe that a felony had been committed and that immediate action was necessary. At no time after the events in front of Mrs. Vale's house would it have been prudent for the officers to leave the house in order to secure a warrant.

The Court asserts, however, that because the police obtained two warrants for Vale's arrest there is "no reason * * * to suppose that it was impracticable for them to obtain a search warrant as well." The difficulty is that the two arrest warrants on which the Court seems to rely so heavily were not issued because of any present misconduct of Vale's; they were issued because the bond had been increased for an earlier narcotics charge then pending against Vale. When the police came to arrest Vale, they knew only that his bond had been increased. There is nothing in the record to indicate that, absent the increased bond, there would have been probable cause for an arrest, much less a search. Probable cause for the search arose for the first time when the police observed the activity of Vale and Saucier in and around the house. * * *

NOTE

In referring to "exceptional circumstances," the dissent alludes to what is known as the exigent circumstances exception to the warrant requirement. Under this exception, which we will cover later, as a general matter, a law enforcement officer with probable cause to believe that evidence of a crime will be found in the place to be searched may conduct a warrantless search if the exigencies of the situation make getting a warrant impracticable.

NEW YORK V. BELTON
Supreme Court of the United States
453 U.S. 454, 101 S. Ct. 2860, 69 L. Ed. 2d 768 (1981)

JUSTICE STEWART delivered the opinion of the Court.

When the occupant of an automobile is subjected to a lawful custodial arrest, does the constitutionally permissible scope of a search incident to his arrest include the passenger compartment of the automobile in which he was riding? That is the question at issue in the present case.

On April 9, 1978, Trooper Douglas Nicot, a New York State policeman driving an unmarked car on the New York Thruway, was passed by another automobile traveling at an excessive rate of speed. Nicot gave chase, overtook the speeding vehicle, and ordered its driver to pull it over to the side of the road and stop. There were four men in the car, one of whom was Roger Belton, the respondent in this case. The policeman asked to see the driver's license and automobile registration, and discovered that none of the men owned the vehicle or was related to its owner. Meanwhile, the policeman had smelled burnt marihuana and had seen on the floor of the car an envelope marked "Supergold" that he associated with marihuana. He therefore directed the men to get out of the car, and placed them under arrest for the unlawful possession of marihuana. He patted down each of the men and "split them up into four separate areas of the Thruway at this time so they would not be in physical touching area of each other." He then picked up the envelope marked "Supergold" and found that it contained marihuana. After giving the arrestees the warnings required by *Miranda v. Arizona*, the state policeman searched each one of them. He then searched the passenger compartment of the car. On the back seat he found a black leather jacket belonging to Belton. He unzipped one of the pockets of the jacket and discovered cocaine. Placing the jacket in his automobile, he drove the four arrestees to a nearby police station.

Belton was subsequently indicted for criminal possession of a controlled substance. In the trial court he moved that the cocaine the trooper had seized from the jacket pocket be suppressed. The court denied the motion. Belton then pleaded guilty to a lesser included offense, but preserved his claim that the cocaine had been seized in violation of the Fourth and Fourteenth Amendments.

* * * We granted certiorari to consider the constitutionally permissible scope of a search in circumstances such as these.

It is a first principle of Fourth Amendment jurisprudence that the police may not conduct a search unless they first convince a neutral magistrate that there is probable cause to do so. This Court has recognized, however, that "the exigencies of the situation" may sometimes make exemption from the warrant requirement "imperative." Specifically, the Court held in *Chimel v. California*, that a lawful custodial arrest creates a situation which justifies the contemporaneous search without a warrant of the person arrested and of the immediately surrounding area. Such searches have long been considered valid because of the need "to remove any weapons that [the arrestee] might seek to use in order to resist arrest or effect his escape" and the need to prevent the concealment or destruction of evidence.

The Court's opinion in *Chimel* emphasized the principle that * * * "[the] scope of [a] search must be 'strictly tied to and justified by' the circumstances which rendered its initiation permissible." Thus while the Court in *Chimel* found "ample justification" for a search of "the area from within which [an arrestee] might gain possession of a weapon or destructible evidence," the Court found "no comparable justification . . . for routinely searching any room other than that in which an arrest occurs—or, for that matter, for searching through all the desk drawers or other closed or concealed areas in that room itself."

Although the principle that limits a search incident to a lawful custodial arrest may be stated clearly enough, courts have discovered the principle difficult to apply in specific cases. Yet, as one commentator has pointed out, the protection of the Fourth and Fourteenth Amendments "can only be realized if the police are acting under a set of rules which, in most instances, makes it possible to reach a correct determination beforehand as to whether an invasion of privacy is justified in the interest of law enforcement." This is because "Fourth Amendment doctrine, given force and effect by the exclusionary rule, is primarily intended to regulate the police in their day-to-day activities and thus ought to be expressed in terms that are readily applicable by the police in the context of the law enforcement activities in which they are necessarily engaged. A highly sophisticated set of rules, qualified by all sorts of ifs, ands, and buts and requiring the drawing of subtle nuances and hairline distinctions, may be the sort of heady stuff upon which the facile minds of lawyers and judges eagerly feed, but they may be 'literally impossible of application by the officer in the field.' "

In short, "[a] single, familiar standard is essential to guide police officers, who have only limited time and expertise to reflect on and balance the social and individual interests involved in the specific circumstances they confront." * * *

When a person cannot know how a court will apply a settled principle to a recurring factual situation, that person cannot know the scope of his constitutional protection, nor can a policeman know the scope of his authority. While the *Chimel* case established that a search incident to an arrest may not stray beyond the area within the immediate control of the arrestee, courts have found no workable definition of "the area within the immediate control of the arrestee" when that area arguably includes the interior of an automobile and the arrestee is its recent occupant. Our reading of the cases suggests the generalization that articles inside the relatively narrow compass of the passenger compartment of an automobile are in fact generally, even if not inevitably, within "the area into which an arrestee might reach in order to grab a weapon or evidentiary [item]." In order to establish the workable rule this category of cases requires, we read *Chimel*'s definition of the limits of the area that may be searched in light of that generalization. Accordingly, we hold that when a policeman has made a lawful custodial arrest of the occupant of an automobile, he may, as a contemporaneous incident of that arrest, search the passenger compartment of that automobile. It follows from this conclusion that the police may also examine the contents of any containers found within the passenger compartment, for if the passenger compartment is within reach of the arrestee, so also will containers in it be within his reach.[4] Such a container may, of course, be searched whether it is open or closed, since the justification for the search is not that the arrestee has no privacy interest in the container, but that the lawful custodial arrest justifies the infringement of any privacy interest the arrestee may have. Thus, while the Court in *Chimel* held that the police could not search all the drawers in an arrestee's house simply because the police had arrested him at home,

---

[4] "Container" here denotes any object capable of holding another object. It thus includes closed or open glove compartments, consoles, or other receptacles located anywhere within the passenger compartment, as well as luggage, boxes, bags, clothing, and the like. Our holding encompasses only the interior of the passenger compartment of an automobile and does not encompass the trunk.

the Court noted that drawers within an arrestee's reach could be searched because of the danger their contents might pose to the police.

It is true, of course, that these containers will sometimes be such that they could hold neither a weapon nor evidence of the criminal conduct for which the suspect was arrested. However, in *United States* v. *Robinson*, the Court rejected the argument that such a container—there a "crumpled up cigarette package"—located during a search of Robinson incident to his arrest could not be searched: "The authority to search the person incident to a lawful custodial arrest, while based upon the need to disarm and to discover evidence, does not depend on what a court may later decide was the probability in a particular arrest situation that weapons or evidence would in fact be found upon the person of the suspect. A custodial arrest of a suspect based on probable cause is a reasonable intrusion under the Fourth Amendment; that intrusion being lawful, a search incident to the arrest requires no additional justification." * * *

It is not questioned that the respondent was the subject of a lawful custodial arrest on a charge of possessing marihuana. The search of the respondent's jacket followed immediately upon that arrest. The jacket was located inside the passenger compartment of the car in which the respondent had been a passenger just before he was arrested. The jacket was thus within the area which we have concluded was "within the arrestee's immediate control" within the meaning of the *Chimel* case.[6] The search of the jacket, therefore, was a search incident to a lawful custodial arrest, and it did not violate the Fourth and Fourteenth Amendments. Accordingly, the judgment is reversed.

It is so ordered.

JUSTICE BRENNAN, with whom JUSTICE MARSHALL joins, dissenting. * * *

It has long been a fundamental principle of Fourth Amendment analysis that exceptions to the warrant requirement are to be narrowly construed. Predicated on the Fourth Amendment's essential purpose of "[shielding] the citizen from unwarranted intrusions into his privacy," this principle carries with it two corollaries. First, for a search to be valid under the Fourth Amendment, it must be " 'strictly tied to and justified by' the circumstances which rendered its initiation permissible." Second, in determining whether to grant an exception to the warrant requirement, courts should carefully consider the facts and circumstances of each search and seizure, focusing on the reasons supporting the exception rather than on any bright-line rule of general application.

---

[6] Because of this disposition of the case, there is no need here to consider whether the search and seizure were permissible under the so-called "automobile exception."

The *Chimel* exception to the warrant requirement was designed with two principal concerns in mind: the safety of the arresting officer and the preservation of easily concealed or destructible evidence. * * * The *Chimel* standard was narrowly tailored to address these concerns: it permits police officers who have effected a custodial arrest to conduct a warrantless search "of the arrestee's person and the area 'within his immediate control'—construing that phrase to mean the area from within which he might gain possession of a weapon or destructible evidence." It thus places a temporal and a spatial limitation on searches incident to arrest, excusing compliance with the warrant requirement only when the search "is substantially contemporaneous with the arrest and is confined to the *immediate* vicinity of the arrest." When the arrest has been consummated and the arrestee safely taken into custody, the justifications underlying *Chimel*'s limited exception to the warrant requirement cease to apply: at that point there is no possibility that the arrestee could reach weapons or contraband.

In its attempt to formulate a "single, familiar standard . . . to guide police officers, who have only limited time and expertise to reflect on and balance the social and individual interests involved in the specific circumstances they confront," the Court today disregards these principles, and instead adopts a fiction—that the interior of a car is *always* within the immediate control of an arrestee who has recently been in the car. The Court thus holds:

> [When] a policeman has made a lawful custodial arrest of the occupant of an automobile, he may, as a contemporaneous incident of that arrest, search the passenger compartment of that automobile . . . [and] may also examine the contents of any containers found within the passenger compartment. . . .

In so holding, the Court ignores both precedent and principle and fails to achieve its objective of providing police officers with a more workable standard for determining the permissible scope of searches incident to arrest.

As the facts of this case make clear, the Court today substantially expands the permissible scope of searches incident to arrest by permitting police officers to search areas and containers the arrestee could not possibly reach at the time of arrest. These facts demonstrate that at the time Belton and his three companions were placed under custodial arrest—which was *after* they had been removed from the car, patted down, and separated—none of them could have reached the jackets that had been left on the back seat of the car. * * *

By approving the constitutionality of the warrantless search in this case, the Court carves out a dangerous precedent that is not justified by the concerns underlying *Chimel*. Disregarding the principle "that the scope of a warrantless search must be commensurate with the rationale that excepts the search from the warrant requirement," the Court for the first time grants police officers authority to conduct a warrantless "area" search under circumstances where there is no chance that the arrestee "might gain possession of a weapon or destructible evidence." Under the approach taken today, the result would presumably be the same even if Officer Nicot had handcuffed Belton and his companions in the patrol car before placing them under arrest, and even if his search had extended to locked luggage or other inaccessible containers located in the back seat of the car. * * *

The Court seeks to justify its departure from the principles underlying *Chimel* by proclaiming the need for a new "bright-line" rule to guide the officer in the field. As we pointed out in *Mincey* v. *Arizona*, however, "the mere fact that law enforcement may be made more efficient can never by itself justify disregard of the Fourth Amendment." Moreover, the Court's attempt to forge a "bright-line" rule fails on its own terms. While the "interior/trunk" distinction may provide a workable guide in certain routine cases—for example, where the officer arrests the driver of a car and then immediately searches the seats and floor—in the long run, I suspect it will create far more problems than it solves. The Court's new approach leaves open too many questions and, more important, it provides the police and the courts with too few tools with which to find the answers. * * *

[JUSTICE WHITE's dissenting opinion has been omitted.]

NOTE

In *Thornton v. United States*, 541 U.S. 615 (2004), the Court extended the rule of *Belton* to cover recent occupants of a vehicle. Thornton was arrested after he parked his car and started walking away. He challenged the constitutionality of the ensuing search of his vehicle as not falling within the rule of *Belton* since he was not arrested while an occupant of a vehicle. The *Thornton* Court rejected his challenge, explaining that "the arrest of a suspect who is next to a vehicle presents identical concerns regarding officer safety and the destruction of evidence as the arrest of one who is inside the vehicle." 541 U.S. at 621.

Can police lawfully make a custodial arrest of an individual for a minor criminal offense for which the only possible sanction is a $50 fine? In *Atwater v. City of Lago Vista*, 532 U.S. 318 (2001), the Court continued its expansion of the search incident to arrest doctrine, answering this question in the affirmative.

Gail Atwater was pulled over for driving without a seatbelt and failing to secure her 3-year-old son and 5-year-old daughter in seatbelts. Atwater asked to take her frightened, upset, and crying children to a friend's house nearby, but the officer refused her request. Instead, the officer handcuffed Atwater, placed her in his squad car, and drove her to the local police station where she was placed in a jail cell for about an hour before being released on bond.

Atwater was charged with driving without a seatbelt fastened, failing to secure her children in seatbelts, driving without a license, and failing to provide proof of insurance. She pled no contest to the misdemeanor seatbelt offenses and paid a $50 fine. The other charges were dismissed.

Atwater filed a lawsuit against the officer and the City of Lago Vista, arguing that her Fourth Amendment right to be free from unreasonable seizure was violated when the officer arrested her and took her into custody for a minor fine-only criminal offense. The Court ruled against Atwater, noting that as long as an officer "has probable cause to believe that an individual has committed even a very minor criminal offense in his presence, he may, without violating the Fourth Amendment, arrest the offender." *Id.* at 354. Since the officer had probable cause to believe Atwater had committed a crime (failing to wear a seatbelt and failing to secure her children with seatbelts), he was authorized to make a custodial arrest.

Justice O'Connor, dissenting in *Atwater*, felt Atwater's custodial arrest for a minor fine-only offense was constitutionally unreasonable, noting that even a brief custodial arrest implicates significant privacy and liberty interests. Justice O'Connor explained:

> A custodial arrest exacts an obvious toll on an individual's liberty and privacy, even when the period of custody is relatively brief. The arrestee is subject to a full search of her person and confiscation of her possessions. If the arrestee is the occupant of a car, the entire passenger compartment of the car, including packages therein, is subject to search as well. The arrestee may be detained for up to 48 hours without having a magistrate determine whether there in fact was probable cause for the arrest.[a] Because people arrested for all types of violent and nonviolent offenses may be housed together awaiting such review, this detention period is potentially dangerous. And once the period of custody is over, the fact of the arrest is a permanent part of the public record. * * *
>
> Giving police officers constitutional carte blanche to effect an arrest whenever there is probable cause to believe a fine-only misdemeanor has been committed is irreconcilable with the Fourth Amendment's command that seizures be reasonable. * * * The majority insists that a bright-line rule focused on probable cause is necessary to vindicate the State's interest in easily administrable law enforcement rules. * * * While clarity is certainly a value worthy of consideration in our Fourth Amendment jurisprudence, it by no means trumps the values

---

[a] In *Gerstein v. Pugh*, 420 U.S. 103 (1975), the Court held that "the Fourth Amendment requires a judicial determination of probable cause as a prerequisite to extended restraint of liberty following [a warrantless] arrest." *Id.* at 114. This judicial determination of probable cause can be conducted ex parte without an adversary proceeding. *See id.* at 120. Later, the Court held that this judicial determination of probable cause will be presumed reasonable if made within 48 hours of a warrantless arrest. County of Riverside v. McLaughlin, 500 U.S. 44, 56 (1991).

of liberty and privacy at the heart of the Amendment's protections.[b]
* * *

Justice O'Connor then continued to explain the choices an officer can make and the things an officer can do once the officer has made a lawful custodial arrest:

> Under today's holding, when a police officer has probable cause to believe that a fine-only misdemeanor offense has occurred, that officer may stop the suspect, issue a citation, and let the person continue on her way. Or, if a traffic violation, the officer may stop the car, arrest the driver, search the driver, search the entire passenger compartment of the car including any purse or package inside, and impound the car and inventory all of its contents. Although the Fourth Amendment expressly requires that the latter course be a reasonable and proportional response to the circumstances of the offense, the majority gives officers unfettered discretion to choose that course without articulating a single reason why such action is appropriate.[c]

Finally, Justice O'Connor critiqued the decision for its impact on the practice of racial profiling:

> Such unbounded discretion carries with it grave potential for abuse. The majority takes comfort in the lack of evidence of "an epidemic of unnecessary minor-offense arrests." But the relatively small number of published cases dealing with such arrests proves little and should provide little solace. Indeed, as the recent debate over racial profiling demonstrates all too clearly, a relatively minor traffic infraction may often serve as an excuse for stopping and harassing an individual. After today, the arsenal available to any officer extends to a full arrest and the searches permissible concomitant to that arrest.[d] * * *

Frank Rudy Cooper commends Justice O'Connor for her critique of the *Atwater* decision, observing that "Justice O'Connor's *Atwater* dissent entered racial profiling into the Court's explicit discussion about searches incident to arrest."[e]

In the next case, the Court appears to pull back from the broad discretion it allowed officers in *New York v. Belton* without explicitly overruling *Belton*.

---

[b] Atwater v. City of Lago Vista, 532 U.S. 318, 364, 365–66 (2001) (O'Connor, J., dissenting). Justice O'Connor would have imposed a different rule. She would have held "that when there is probable cause to believe that a fine-only offense has been committed, the police officer should issue a citation unless the officer is 'able to point to specific and articulable facts which, taken together with rational inferences from those facts, reasonably warrant [the additional] intrusion' of a full custodial arrest." *Id.* at 366.

[c] *Id.* at 372.

[d] *Id.*

[e] Frank Rudy Cooper, *Post-Racialism and Searches Incident to Arrest*, 44 ARIZ. ST. L. J. 113, 147 (2012).

Does the Court strike the right balance and adequately rein in the discretion afforded officers when they arrest an occupant or recent occupant of a vehicle?

ARIZONA V. GANT

Supreme Court of the United States
556 U.S. 332, 129 S. Ct. 1710, 173 L. Ed. 2d 485 (2009)

JUSTICE STEVENS delivered the opinion of the Court. * * *

On August 25, 1999, acting on an anonymous tip that the residence at 2524 North Walnut Avenue was being used to sell drugs, Tucson police officers Griffith and Reed knocked on the front door and asked to speak to the owner. Gant answered the door and, after identifying himself, stated that he expected the owner to return later. The officers left the residence and conducted a records check, which revealed that Gant's driver's license had been suspended and there was an outstanding warrant for his arrest for driving with a suspended license.

When the officers returned to the house that evening, they found a man near the back of the house and a woman in a car parked in front of it. After a third officer arrived, they arrested the man for providing a false name and the woman for possessing drug paraphernalia. Both arrestees were handcuffed and secured in separate patrol cars when Gant arrived. The officers recognized his car as it entered the driveway, and Officer Griffith confirmed that Gant was the driver by shining a flashlight into the car as it drove by him. Gant parked at the end of the driveway, got out of his car, and shut the door. Griffith, who was about 30 feet away, called to Gant, and they approached each other, meeting 10-to-12 feet from Gant's car. Griffith immediately arrested Gant and handcuffed him.

Because the other arrestees were secured in the only patrol cars at the scene, Griffith called for backup. When two more officers arrived, they locked Gant in the backseat of their vehicle. After Gant had been handcuffed and placed in the back of a patrol car, two officers searched his car: One of them found a gun, and the other discovered a bag of cocaine in the pocket of a jacket on the backseat.

Gant was charged with two offenses—possession of a narcotic drug for sale and possession of drug paraphernalia (*i.e.*, the plastic bag in which the cocaine was found). He moved to suppress the evidence seized from his car on the ground that the warrantless search violated the Fourth Amendment. * * *

The trial court * * * denied the motion to suppress. * * * [T]he court held that the search was permissible as a search incident to arrest. A jury found Gant guilty on both drug counts, and he was sentenced to a 3-year term of imprisonment. * * *

Consistent with our precedent, our analysis begins, as it should in every case addressing the reasonableness of a warrantless search, with the basic rule that "searches conducted outside the judicial process, without prior approval by judge or magistrate, are *per se* unreasonable under the Fourth Amendment—subject only to a few specifically established and well-delineated exceptions." Among the exceptions to the warrant requirement is a search incident to a lawful arrest. The exception derives from interests in officer safety and evidence preservation that are typically implicated in arrest situations.

In *Chimel*, we held that a search incident to arrest may only include "the arrestee's person and the area 'within his immediate control'— construing that phrase to mean the area from within which he might gain possession of a weapon or destructible evidence." That limitation, which continues to define the boundaries of the exception, ensures that the scope of a search incident to arrest is commensurate with its purposes of protecting arresting officers and safeguarding any evidence of the offense of arrest that an arrestee might conceal or destroy. If there is no possibility that an arrestee could reach into the area that law enforcement officers seek to search, both justifications for the search-incident-to-arrest exception are absent and the rule does not apply.

In *Belton*, we considered *Chimel*'s application to the automobile context. A lone police officer in that case stopped a speeding car in which Belton was one of four occupants. While asking for the driver's license and registration, the officer smelled burnt marijuana and observed an envelope on the car floor marked "Supergold"—a name he associated with marijuana. Thus having probable cause to believe the occupants had committed a drug offense, the officer ordered them out of the vehicle, placed them under arrest, and patted them down. Without handcuffing the arrestees,[1] the officer "split them up into four separate areas of the Thruway . . . so they would not be in physical touching area of each other" and searched the vehicle, including the pocket of a jacket on the backseat, in which he found cocaine.

*** *Belton* *** has been widely understood to allow a vehicle search incident to the arrest of a recent occupant even if there is no possibility the arrestee could gain access to the vehicle at the time of the search. This reading may be attributable to Justice Brennan's dissent in *Belton*, in which he characterized the Court's holding as resting on the "fiction . . . that the interior of a car is *always* within the immediate control of an arrestee who has recently been in the car." Under the majority's approach, he argued, "the result would presumably be the same even if [the officer]

---

[1] The officer was unable to handcuff the occupants because he had only one set of handcuffs. See Brief for Petitioner in *New York v. Belton*, O.T.1980, No. 80–328, p. 3 (hereinafter Brief in No. 80–328).

had handcuffed Belton and his companions in the patrol car" before conducting the search.

Since we decided *Belton*, Courts of Appeals have given different answers to the question whether a vehicle must be within an arrestee's reach to justify a vehicle search incident to arrest, but Justice Brennan's reading of the Court's opinion has predominated. * * *

Under this broad reading of *Belton*, a vehicle search would be authorized incident to every arrest of a recent occupant notwithstanding that in most cases the vehicle's passenger compartment will not be within the arrestee's reach at the time of the search. To read *Belton* as authorizing a vehicle search incident to every recent occupant's arrest would thus untether the rule from the justifications underlying the *Chimel* exception—a result clearly incompatible with our statement in *Belton* that it "in no way alters the fundamental principles established in the *Chimel* case regarding the basic scope of searches incident to lawful custodial arrests." Accordingly, we reject this reading of *Belton* and hold that the *Chimel* rationale authorizes police to search a vehicle incident to a recent occupant's arrest only when the arrestee is unsecured and within reaching distance of the passenger compartment at the time of the search.

Although it does not follow from *Chimel*, we also conclude that circumstances unique to the vehicle context justify a search incident to a lawful arrest when it is "reasonable to believe evidence relevant to the crime of arrest might be found in the vehicle." In many cases, as when a recent occupant is arrested for a traffic violation, there will be no reasonable basis to believe the vehicle contains relevant evidence. But in others, * * * the offense of arrest will supply a basis for searching the passenger compartment of an arrestee's vehicle and any containers therein.[a]

Neither the possibility of access nor the likelihood of discovering offense-related evidence authorized the search in this case. Unlike in *Belton,* which involved a single officer confronted with four unsecured arrestees, the five officers in this case outnumbered the three arrestees, all of whom had been handcuffed and secured in separate patrol cars before the officers searched Gant's car. Under those circumstances, Gant clearly

---

[a] In authorizing a search of the vehicle incident to arrest when it is "reasonable to believe evidence relevant to the crime of arrest might be found in the vehicle," the *Gant* Court endorsed an interpretation of *Belton* first suggested by Justice Scalia, who concurred in *United States v. Thornton*, 541 U.S. 615, 632 (2004). In his concurring opinion, Justice Scalia noted that it was extremely unlikely that Thornton, who was handcuffed and secured in the back of a police car at the time of the search, could have escaped and retrieved a weapon or evidence from his vehicle unless he possessed the skill of Houdini and the strength of Hercules. *Id.* at 625–26. From this, Justice Scalia argued that *Belton* searches were justifiable not because the arrestee might grab a weapon or evidentiary item from the car, but simply because the car might contain evidence relevant to the crime for which he was arrested. *Id.* at 629. Justice Scalia concluded that he "would therefore limit *Belton* searches to cases where it is reasonable to believe evidence relevant to the crime of arrest might be found in the vehicle." *Id.* at 632.

was not within reaching distance of his car at the time of the search. An evidentiary basis for the search was also lacking in this case. Whereas Belton and Thornton were arrested for drug offenses, Gant was arrested for driving with a suspended license—an offense for which police could not expect to find evidence in the passenger compartment of Gant's car. Because police could not reasonably have believed either that Gant could have accessed his car at the time of the search or that evidence of the offense for which he was arrested might have been found therein, the search in this case was unreasonable.

The State does not seriously disagree with the * * * conclusion that Gant could not have accessed his vehicle at the time of the search, but it nevertheless asks us to uphold the search of his vehicle under the broad reading of *Belton* discussed above. The State argues that *Belton* searches are reasonable regardless of the possibility of access in a given case because that expansive rule correctly balances law enforcement interests, including the interest in a bright-line rule, with an arrestee's limited privacy interest in his vehicle.

For several reasons, we reject the State's argument. First, the State seriously undervalues the privacy interests at stake. Although we have recognized that a motorist's privacy interest in his vehicle is less substantial than in his home, the former interest is nevertheless important and deserving of constitutional protection. It is particularly significant that *Belton* searches authorize police officers to search not just the passenger compartment but every purse, briefcase, or other container within that space. A rule that gives police the power to conduct such a search whenever an individual is caught committing a traffic offense, when there is no basis for believing evidence of the offense might be found in the vehicle, creates a serious and recurring threat to the privacy of countless individuals. Indeed, the character of that threat implicates the central concern underlying the Fourth Amendment—the concern about giving police officers unbridled discretion to rummage at will among a person's private effects. * * *

Contrary to the State's suggestion, a broad reading of *Belton* is also unnecessary to protect law enforcement safety and evidentiary interests. * * * Other established exceptions to the warrant requirement authorize a vehicle search under additional circumstances when safety or evidentiary concerns demand. For instance, *Michigan v. Long* permits an officer to search a vehicle's passenger compartment when he has reasonable suspicion that an individual, whether or not the arrestee, is "dangerous" and might access the vehicle to "gain immediate control of weapons." If there is probable cause to believe a vehicle contains evidence of criminal activity, *United States v. Ross* authorizes a search of any area of the vehicle in which the evidence might be found. * * *

Our dissenting colleagues argue that the doctrine of *stare decisis* requires adherence to a broad reading of *Belton* even though the justifications for searching a vehicle incident to arrest are in most cases absent. The doctrine of *stare decisis* is of course "essential to the respect accorded to the judgments of the Court and to the stability of the law," but it does not compel us to follow a past decision when its rationale no longer withstands "careful analysis."

We have never relied on *stare decisis* to justify the continuance of an unconstitutional police practice. And we would be particularly loath to uphold an unconstitutional result in a case that is so easily distinguished from the decisions that arguably compel it. The safety and evidentiary interests that supported the search in *Belton* simply are not present in this case. Indeed, it is hard to imagine two cases that are factually more distinct, as *Belton* involved one officer confronted by four unsecured arrestees suspected of committing a drug offense and this case involves several officers confronted with a securely detained arrestee apprehended for driving with a suspended license. * * *

The experience of the 28 years since we decided *Belton* has shown that the generalization underpinning the broad reading of that decision is unfounded. We now know that articles inside the passenger compartment are rarely "within 'the area into which an arrestee might reach,'" and blind adherence to *Belton*'s faulty assumption would authorize myriad unconstitutional searches. The doctrine of *stare decisis* does not require us to approve routine constitutional violations.

Police may search a vehicle incident to a recent occupant's arrest only if the arrestee is within reaching distance of the passenger compartment at the time of the search or it is reasonable to believe the vehicle contains evidence of the offense of arrest. When these justifications are absent, a search of an arrestee's vehicle will be unreasonable unless police obtain a warrant or show that another exception to the warrant requirement applies. * * *

ALITO, J. with whom THE CHIEF JUSTICE and JUSTICE KENNEDY join, and with whom JUSTICE BREYER joins except as to Part II-E, dissenting.

Twenty-eight years ago, in *New York v. Belton*, this Court held that "when a policeman has made a lawful custodial arrest of the occupant of an automobile, he may, as a contemporaneous incident of that arrest, search the passenger compartment of that automobile." Five years ago, in *Thornton v. United States*, * * * the Court not only reaffirmed but extended the holding of *Belton*, making it applicable to recent occupants. Today's decision effectively overrules those important decisions, even though respondent Gant has not asked us to do so.

To take the place of the overruled precedents, the Court adopts a new two-part rule under which a police officer who arrests a vehicle occupant or recent occupant may search the passenger compartment if (1) the arrestee is within reaching distance of the vehicle at the time of the search or (2) the officer has reason to believe that the vehicle contains evidence of the offense of arrest. The first part of this new rule may endanger arresting officers and is truly endorsed by only four Justices; Justice Scalia joins solely for the purpose of avoiding a "4-to-1-to-4 opinion." The second part of the new rule is taken from Justice Scalia's separate opinion in *Thornton* without any independent explanation of its origin or justification and is virtually certain to confuse law enforcement officers and judges for some time to come. * * *

Although the Court refuses to acknowledge that it is overruling *Belton* and *Thornton*, there can be no doubt that it does so. * * *

The precise holding in *Belton* could not be clearer. The Court stated unequivocally: "[W]e hold that when a policeman has made a lawful custodial arrest of the occupant of an automobile, he may, as a contemporaneous incident of that arrest, search the passenger compartment of that automobile."

Despite this explicit statement, the opinion of the Court in the present case curiously suggests that *Belton* may reasonably be read as adopting a holding that is narrower than the one explicitly set out in the *Belton* opinion, namely, that an officer arresting a vehicle occupant may search the passenger compartment "*when* the passenger compartment is within an arrestee's reaching distance." According to the Court, the broader reading of *Belton* that has gained wide acceptance "may be attributable to Justice Brennan's dissent."

Contrary to the Court's suggestion, however, Justice Brennan's *Belton* dissent did not mischaracterize the Court's holding in that case or cause that holding to be misinterpreted. As noted, the *Belton* Court explicitly stated precisely what it held. * * *

Prior to *Chimel*, the Court's precedents permitted an arresting officer to search the area within an arrestee's "possession" and "control" for the purpose of gathering evidence. Based on this "abstract doctrine," the Court had sustained searches that extended far beyond an arrestee's grabbing area.

The *Chimel* Court, in an opinion written by Justice Stewart, overruled these cases. Concluding that there are only two justifications for a warrantless search incident to arrest—officer safety and the preservation of evidence—the Court stated that such a search must be confined to "the arrestee's person" and "the area from within which he might gain possession of a weapon or destructible evidence."

Unfortunately, *Chimel* did not say whether "the area from within which [an arrestee] might gain possession of a weapon or destructible evidence" is to be measured at the time of the arrest or at the time of the search, but unless the *Chimel* rule was meant to be a specialty rule, applicable to only a few unusual cases, the Court must have intended for this area to be measured at the time of arrest.

This is so because the Court can hardly have failed to appreciate the following two facts. First, in the great majority of cases, an officer making an arrest is able to handcuff the arrestee and remove him to a secure place before conducting a search incident to the arrest. Second, because it is safer for an arresting officer to secure an arrestee before searching, it is likely that this is what arresting officers do in the great majority of cases. (And it appears, not surprisingly, that this is in fact the prevailing practice.) Thus, if the area within an arrestee's reach were assessed, not at the time of arrest, but at the time of the search, the *Chimel* rule would rarely come into play.

Moreover, if the applicability of the *Chimel* rule turned on whether an arresting officer chooses to secure an arrestee prior to conducting a search, rather than searching first and securing the arrestee later, the rule would "create a perverse incentive for an arresting officer to prolong the period during which the arrestee is kept in an area where he could pose a danger to the officer." * * *

I do not think that this is what the *Chimel* Court intended. Handcuffs were in use in 1969. The ability of arresting officers to secure arrestees before conducting a search—and their incentive to do so—are facts that can hardly have escaped the Court's attention. I therefore believe that the *Chimel* Court intended that its new rule apply in cases in which the arrestee is handcuffed before the search is conducted.

The *Belton* Court, in my view, proceeded on the basis of this interpretation of *Chimel*. Again speaking through Justice Stewart, the *Belton* Court reasoned that articles in the passenger compartment of a car are "generally, even if not inevitably" within an arrestee's reach. This is undoubtedly true at the time of the arrest of a person who is seated in a car but plainly not true when the person has been removed from the car and placed in handcuffs. Accordingly, the *Belton* Court must have proceeded on the assumption that the *Chimel* rule was to be applied at the time of arrest. And that is why the *Belton* Court was able to say that its decision "in no way alter[ed] the fundamental principles established in the *Chimel* case regarding the basic scope of searches incident to lawful custodial arrests." Viewing *Chimel* as having focused on the time of arrest, *Belton*'s only new step was to eliminate the need to decide on a case-by-case basis whether a particular person seated in a car actually could have reached the part of the passenger compartment where a weapon or evidence was hidden. * * *

The Court * * * leaves the law relating to searches incident to arrest in a confused and unstable state. The first part of the Court's new two-part rule—which permits an arresting officer to search the area within an arrestee's reach at the time of the search—applies, at least for now, only to vehicle occupants and recent occupants, but there is no logical reason why the same rule should not apply to all arrestees.

The second part of the Court's new rule, which the Court takes uncritically from Justice Scalia's separate opinion in *Thornton,* raises doctrinal and practical problems that the Court makes no effort to address. Why, for example, is the standard for this type of evidence-gathering search "reason to believe" rather than probable cause? And why is this type of search restricted to evidence of the offense of arrest? It is true that an arrestee's vehicle is probably more likely to contain evidence of the crime of arrest than of some other crime, but if reason-to-believe is the governing standard for an evidence-gathering search incident to arrest, it is not easy to see why an officer should not be able to search when the officer has reason to believe that the vehicle in question possesses evidence of a crime other than the crime of arrest.

Nor is it easy to see why an evidence-gathering search incident to arrest should be restricted to the passenger compartment. The *Belton* rule was limited in this way because the passenger compartment was considered to be the area that vehicle occupants can generally reach, but since the second part of the new rule is not based on officer safety or the preservation of evidence, the ground for this limitation is obscure.

Respondent in this case has not asked us to overrule *Belton,* much less *Chimel.* * * * I would therefore leave any reexamination of our prior precedents for another day, if such a reexamination is to be undertaken at all. In this case, I would simply apply *Belton* and reverse the judgment below.

[JUSTICE SCALIA's concurring opinion has been omitted.]

NOTE

In the next case, the Court considers whether an officer may, incident to a lawful custodial arrest, seize a cellphone found in an arrestee's pocket. One might have thought the *Robinson v. California* decision answered this question, but the Court surprised many with its decision in *Riley v. California.*

RILEY V. CALIFORNIA
Supreme Court of the United States
573 U.S. 373, 134 S. Ct. 2473, 189 L. Ed. 2d 430 (2014)

CHIEF JUSTICE ROBERTS delivered the opinion of the Court.

* * * [P]etitioner David Riley was stopped by a police officer for driving with expired registration tags. In the course of the stop, the officer also learned that Riley's license had been suspended. The officer impounded Riley's car, pursuant to department policy, and another officer conducted an inventory search of the car. Riley was arrested for possession of concealed and loaded firearms when that search turned up two handguns under the car's hood.

An officer searched Riley incident to the arrest and found items associated with the "Bloods" street gang. He also seized a cell phone from Riley's pants pocket. According to Riley's uncontradicted assertion, the phone was a "smart phone," a cell phone with a broad range of other functions based on advanced computing capability, large storage capacity, and Internet connectivity. The officer accessed information on the phone and noticed that some words (presumably in text messages or a contacts list) were preceded by the letters "CK"—a label that, he believed, stood for "Crip Killers," a slang term for members of the Bloods gang.

At the police station about two hours after the arrest, a detective specializing in gangs further examined the contents of the phone. The detective testified that he "went through" Riley's phone "looking for evidence, because . . . gang members will often video themselves with guns or take pictures of themselves with the guns." Although there was "a lot of stuff" on the phone, particular files that "caught [the detective's] eye" included videos of young men sparring while someone yelled encouragement using the moniker "Blood." The police also found photographs of Riley standing in front of a car they suspected had been involved in a shooting a few weeks earlier.

Riley was ultimately charged, in connection with that earlier shooting, with firing at an occupied vehicle, assault with a semiautomatic firearm, and attempted murder. The State alleged that Riley had committed those crimes for the benefit of a criminal street gang, an aggravating factor that carries an enhanced sentence. Prior to trial, Riley moved to suppress all evidence that the police had obtained from his cell phone. He contended that the searches of his phone violated the Fourth Amendment because they had been performed without a warrant and were not otherwise justified by exigent circumstances. The trial court rejected that argument. At Riley's trial, police officers testified about the photographs and videos found on the phone, and some of the photographs were admitted into evidence. Riley was convicted on all three counts and received an enhanced sentence of 15 years to life in prison.

The California Court of Appeal affirmed. The California Supreme Court denied Riley's petition for review, and we granted certiorari. * * *

The [case] before us concern[s] the reasonableness of a warrantless search incident to a lawful arrest. In 1914, this Court first acknowledged in dictum "the right on the part of the Government * * * to search the person of the accused when legally arrested to discover and seize the fruits or evidences of crime." Since that time, it has been well accepted that such a search constitutes an exception to the warrant requirement. Indeed, the label "exception" is something of a misnomer in this context, as warrantless searches incident to arrest occur with far greater frequency than searches conducted pursuant to a warrant.

Although the existence of the exception for such searches has been recognized for a century, its scope has been debated for nearly as long. That debate has focused on the extent to which officers may search property found on or near the arrestee. Three related precedents set forth the rules governing such searches:

The first, *Chimel v. California*, laid the groundwork for most of the existing search incident to arrest doctrine. Police officers in that case arrested Chimel inside his home and proceeded to search his entire three-bedroom house, including the attic and garage. In particular rooms, they also looked through the contents of drawers. The Court crafted the following rule for assessing the reasonableness of a search incident to arrest:

> When an arrest is made, it is reasonable for the arresting officer to search the person arrested in order to remove any weapons that the latter might seek to use in order to resist arrest or effect his escape. Otherwise, the officer's safety might well be endangered, and the arrest itself frustrated. In addition, it is entirely reasonable for the arresting officer to search for and seize any evidence on the arrestee's person in order to prevent its concealment or destruction . . . . There is ample justification, therefore, for a search of the arrestee's person and the area "within his immediate control"—construing that phrase to mean the area from within which he might gain possession of a weapon or destructible evidence. * * *

Four years later, in *United States v. Robinson*, the Court applied the *Chimel* analysis in the context of a search of the arrestee's person. A police officer had arrested Robinson for driving with a revoked license. The officer conducted a patdown search and felt an object that he could not identify in Robinson's coat pocket. He removed the object, which turned out to be a crumpled cigarette package, and opened it. Inside were 14 capsules of heroin.

*** This Court *** reject[ed] the notion that "case-by-case adjudication" was required to determine "whether or not there was present one of the reasons supporting the authority for a search of the person incident to a lawful arrest." *** The Court thus concluded that the search of *Robinson* was reasonable even though there was no concern about the loss of evidence, and the arresting officer had no specific concern that *Robinson* might be armed. ***

The search incident to arrest trilogy concludes with *Gant,* which analyzed searches of an arrestee's vehicle. *Gant,* like *Robinson,* recognized that the *Chimel* concerns for officer safety and evidence preservation underlie the search incident to arrest exception. As a result, the Court concluded that *Chimel* could authorize police to search a vehicle "only when the arrestee is unsecured and within reaching distance of the passenger compartment at the time of the search." *Gant* added, however, an independent exception for a warrantless search of a vehicle's passenger compartment "when it is 'reasonable to believe evidence relevant to the crime of arrest might be found in the vehicle.'" That exception stems not from *Chimel,* the Court explained, but from "circumstances unique to the vehicle context."

These cases require us to decide how the search incident to arrest doctrine applies to modern cell phones, which are now such a pervasive and insistent part of daily life that the proverbial visitor from Mars might conclude they were an important feature of human anatomy. A smart phone of the sort taken from Riley was unheard of ten years ago; a significant majority of American adults now own such phones. ***

We first consider each *Chimel* concern in turn. *** Digital data stored on a cell phone cannot itself be used as a weapon to harm an arresting officer or to effectuate the arrestee's escape. Law enforcement officers remain free to examine the physical aspects of a phone to ensure that it will not be used as a weapon—say, to determine whether there is a razor blade hidden between the phone and its case. Once an officer has secured a phone and eliminated any potential physical threats, however, data on the phone can endanger no one. ***

The United States and California both suggest that a search of cell phone data might help ensure officer safety in more indirect ways, for example by alerting officers that confederates of the arrestee are headed to the scene. There is undoubtedly a strong government interest in warning officers about such possibilities, but neither the United States nor California offers evidence to suggest that their concerns are based on actual experience. The proposed consideration would also represent a broadening of *Chimel*'s concern that an *arrestee himself* might grab a weapon and use it against an officer "to resist arrest or effect his escape." And any such threats from outside the arrest scene do not "lurk[ ] in all custodial arrests."

Accordingly, the interest in protecting officer safety does not justify dispensing with the warrant requirement across the board. * * *

The United States and California focus primarily on the second *Chimel* rationale: preventing the destruction of evidence. The United States and California argue that information on a cell phone may * * * be vulnerable to two types of evidence destruction unique to digital data—remote wiping and data encryption. Remote wiping occurs when a phone, connected to a wireless network, receives a signal that erases stored data. * * * Encryption is a security feature that some modern cell phones use in addition to password protection. When such phones lock, data becomes protected by sophisticated encryption that renders a phone all but "unbreakable" unless police know the password.

As an initial matter, these broader concerns about the loss of evidence are distinct from *Chimel*'s focus on a defendant who responds to arrest by trying to conceal or destroy evidence within his reach. With respect to remote wiping, the Government's primary concern turns on the actions of third parties who are not present at the scene of arrest. And data encryption is even further afield. There, the Government focuses on the ordinary operation of a phone's security features, apart from *any* active attempt by a defendant or his associates to conceal or destroy evidence upon arrest.

* * * Remote wiping can be fully prevented by disconnecting a phone from the network. There are at least two simple ways to do this: First, law enforcement officers can turn the phone off or remove its battery. Second, if they are concerned about encryption or other potential problems, they can leave a phone powered on and place it in an enclosure that isolates the phone from radio waves. Such devices are commonly called "Faraday bags," after the English scientist Michael Faraday. They are essentially sandwich bags made of aluminum foil: cheap, lightweight, and easy to use. They may not be a complete answer to the problem, but at least for now they provide a reasonable response. In fact, a number of law enforcement agencies around the country already encourage the use of Faraday bags.

To the extent that law enforcement still has specific concerns about the potential loss of evidence in a particular case, there remain more targeted ways to address those concerns. If "the police are truly confronted with a 'now or never' situation,"—for example, circumstances suggesting that a defendant's phone will be the target of an imminent remote-wipe attempt—they may be able to rely on exigent circumstances to search the phone immediately. * * *

The United States asserts that a search of all data stored on a cell phone is "materially indistinguishable" from searches of * * * physical items. That is like saying a ride on horseback is materially indistinguishable from a flight to the moon. Both are ways of getting from point A to point B, but little else justifies lumping them together. Modern cell phones, as a category, implicate privacy concerns far beyond those implicated by the search of a cigarette pack, a wallet, or a purse. * * *

One of the most notable distinguishing features of modern cell phones is their immense storage capacity. Before cell phones, a search of a person was limited by physical realities and tended as a general matter to constitute only a narrow intrusion on privacy. Most people cannot lug around every piece of mail they have received for the past several months, every picture they have taken, or every book or article they have read—nor would they have any reason to attempt to do so. And if they did, they would have to drag behind them a trunk of the sort held to require a search warrant in *Chadwick*, rather than a container the size of the cigarette package in *Robinson*.

But the possible intrusion on privacy is not physically limited in the same way when it comes to cell phones. The current top-selling smart phone has a standard capacity of 16 gigabytes (and is available with up to 64 gigabytes). Sixteen gigabytes translates to millions of pages of text, thousands of pictures, or hundreds of videos. Cell phones couple that capacity with the ability to store many different types of information: Even the most basic phones that sell for less than $20 might hold photographs, picture messages, text messages, Internet browsing history, a calendar, a thousand-entry phone book, and so on. We expect that the gulf between physical practicability and digital capacity will only continue to widen in the future.

The storage capacity of cell phones has several interrelated consequences for privacy. First, a cell phone collects in one place many distinct types of information—an address, a note, a prescription, a bank statement, a video—that reveal much more in combination than any isolated record. Second, a cell phone's capacity allows even just one type of information to convey far more than previously possible. The sum of an individual's private life can be reconstructed through a thousand photographs labeled with dates, locations, and descriptions; the same cannot be said of a photograph or two of loved ones tucked into a wallet. Third, the data on a phone can date back to the purchase of the phone, or even earlier. A person might carry in his pocket a slip of paper reminding him to call Mr. Jones; he would not carry a record of all his communications with Mr. Jones for the past several months, as would routinely be kept on a phone. * * *

Although the data stored on a cell phone is distinguished from physical records by quantity alone, certain types of data are also qualitatively different. An Internet search and browsing history, for example, can be found on an Internet-enabled phone and could reveal an individual's private interests or concerns—perhaps a search for certain symptoms of disease, coupled with frequent visits to WebMD. Data on a cell phone can also reveal where a person has been. Historic location information is a standard feature on many smart phones and can reconstruct someone's specific movements down to the minute, not only around town but also within a particular building. * * *

Apart from their arguments for a direct extension of *Robinson,* the United States and California offer various fallback options for permitting warrantless cell phone searches under certain circumstances. Each of the proposals is flawed and contravenes our general preference to provide clear guidance to law enforcement through categorical rules. * * *

The United States first proposes that the *Gant* standard be imported from the vehicle context, allowing a warrantless search of an arrestee's cell phone whenever it is reasonable to believe that the phone contains evidence of the crime of arrest. But *Gant* relied on "circumstances unique to the vehicle context" to endorse a search solely for the purpose of gathering evidence. Justice Scalia's *Thornton* opinion, on which *Gant* was based, explained that those unique circumstances are "a reduced expectation of privacy" and "heightened law enforcement needs" when it comes to motor vehicles. For reasons that we have explained, cell phone searches bear neither of those characteristics.

At any rate, a *Gant* standard would prove no practical limit at all when it comes to cell phone searches. In the vehicle context, *Gant* generally protects against searches for evidence of past crimes. In the cell phone context, however, it is reasonable to expect that incriminating information will be found on a phone regardless of when the crime occurred. Similarly, in the vehicle context *Gant* restricts broad searches resulting from minor crimes such as traffic violations. That would not necessarily be true for cell phones. It would be a particularly inexperienced or unimaginative law enforcement officer who could not come up with several reasons to suppose evidence of just about any crime could be found on a cell phone. Even an individual pulled over for something as basic as speeding might well have locational data dispositive of guilt on his phone. An individual pulled over for reckless driving might have evidence on the phone that shows whether he was texting while driving. The sources of potential pertinent information are virtually unlimited, so applying the *Gant* standard to cell phones would in effect give "police officers unbridled discretion to rummage at will among a person's private effects." * * *

We also reject the United States' final suggestion that officers should always be able to search a phone's call log. * * * The Government relies on *Smith v. Maryland,* which held that no warrant was required to use a pen register at telephone company premises to identify numbers dialed by a particular caller. The Court in that case, however, concluded that the use of a pen register was not a "search" at all under the Fourth Amendment.

There is no dispute here that the officers engaged in a search. * * * Moreover, call logs typically contain more than just phone numbers; they include any identifying information that an individual might add. * * *

We cannot deny that our decision today will have an impact on the ability of law enforcement to combat crime. Cell phones have become important tools in facilitating coordination and communication among members of criminal enterprises, and can provide valuable incriminating information about dangerous criminals. Privacy comes at a cost.

Our holding, of course, is not that the information on a cell phone is immune from search; it is instead that a warrant is generally required before such a search, even when a cell phone is seized incident to arrest. Our cases have historically recognized that the warrant requirement is "an important working part of our machinery of government," not merely "an inconvenience to be somehow 'weighed' against the claims of police efficiency." Recent technological advances similar to those discussed here have, in addition, made the process of obtaining a warrant itself more efficient. *See McNeely*, 569 U.S., at ___ (Roberts, C.J., concurring in part and dissenting in part) (describing jurisdiction where "police officers can e-mail warrant requests to judges' iPads [and] judges have signed such warrants and e-mailed them back to officers in less than 15 minutes").

Modern cell phones are not just another technological convenience. With all they contain and all they may reveal, they hold for many Americans "the privacies of life." The fact that technology now allows an individual to carry such information in his hand does not make the information any less worthy of the protection for which the Founders fought. Our answer to the question of what police must do before searching a cell phone seized incident to an arrest is accordingly simple—get a warrant. * * *

It is so ordered.

[JUSTICE ALITO's concurring opinion has been omitted.]

Chapter 7

The Automobile Exception

■ ■ ■

In this chapter, we will study the automobile exception to the warrant requirement. In *California v. Carney,* the Court discusses the rationales behind the automobile exception and considers whether a motor home ought to be considered a vehicle for purposes of the automobile exception. In *California v. Acevedo,* the Court examines whether an officer with probable cause to believe evidence of a crime is within a container that happens to be in a car may search that container without a warrant under the automobile exception. In *Wyoming v. Houghton,* the Court decides whether the warrantless search of a passenger's purse found in a vehicle is justified under the automobile exception. Almost as interesting as the Court's answer to this question is the way the Court arrives at its conclusion. In *The Fourth Amendment and Common Law,* David Sklansky critiques the Court's increasing focus on whether the government action in question constituted a search at early common law to resolve the question of whether that action constitutes a search within the meaning of the Fourth Amendment today. In the last case in this chapter, *Collins v. Virginia,* the Court considers whether the automobile exception allows an officer to enter the curtilage to search a vehicle parked therein.

California v. Carney
Supreme Court of the United States
471 U.S. 386, 105 S. Ct. 2066, 85 L. Ed. 2d 406 (1985)

Chief Justice Burger delivered the opinion of the Court.

We granted certiorari to decide whether law enforcement agents violated the Fourth Amendment when they conducted a warrantless search, based on probable cause, of a fully mobile "motor home" located in a public place.

On May 31, 1979, Drug Enforcement Agency Agent Robert Williams watched respondent, Charles Carney, approach a youth in downtown San Diego. The youth accompanied Carney to a Dodge Mini Motor Home parked in a nearby lot. Carney and the youth closed the window shades in the motor home, including one across the front window. Agent Williams had previously received uncorroborated information that the same motor home was used by another person who was exchanging marihuana for sex. Williams, with assistance from other agents, kept the motor home under surveillance for the entire one and one-quarter hours that Carney and the youth remained inside. When the youth left the motor home, the agents followed and stopped him. The youth told the agents that he had received marijuana in return for allowing Carney sexual contacts.

At the agents' request, the youth returned to the motor home and knocked on its door; Carney stepped out. The agents identified themselves as law enforcement officers. Without a warrant or consent, one agent entered the motor home and observed marihuana, plastic bags, and a scale of the kind used in weighing drugs on a table. Agent Williams took Carney into custody and took possession of the motor home. A subsequent search of the motor home at the police station revealed additional marihuana in the cupboards and refrigerator.

Respondent was charged with possession of marihuana for sale. At a preliminary hearing, he moved to suppress the evidence discovered in the motor home. The Magistrate denied the motion. * * * Respondent * * * pleaded *nolo contendere* to the charges against him, and was placed on probation for three years. * * *

The California Supreme Court reversed the conviction. * * * The California Supreme Court held that the expectations of privacy in a motor home are more like those in a dwelling than in an automobile because the primary function of motor homes is not to provide transportation but to "provide the occupant with living quarters."

We granted certiorari. We reverse.

The Fourth Amendment protects the "right of the people to be secure in their persons, houses, papers, and effects, against unreasonable searches and seizures." This fundamental right is preserved by a requirement that searches be conducted pursuant to a warrant issued by an independent judicial officer. There are, of course, exceptions to the general rule that a warrant must be secured before a search is undertaken; one is the so-called "automobile exception" at issue in this case. This exception to the warrant requirement was first set forth by the Court 60 years ago in *Carroll v. United States*. There, the Court recognized that the privacy interests in an automobile are constitutionally protected; however, it held that the ready mobility of the automobile justifies a lesser degree of protection of those interests. * * *

The capacity to be "quickly moved" was clearly the basis of the holding in *Carroll,* and our cases have consistently recognized ready mobility as one of the principal bases of the automobile exception. * * * The mobility of automobiles, we have observed, "creates circumstances of such exigency that, as a practical necessity, rigorous enforcement of the warrant requirement is impossible."

However, although ready mobility alone was perhaps the original justification for the vehicle exception, our later cases have made clear that ready mobility is not the only basis for the exception. The reasons for the vehicle exception, we have said, are twofold. "Besides the element of mobility, less rigorous warrant requirements govern because the expectation of privacy with respect to one's automobile is significantly less than that relating to one's home or office."

Even in cases where an automobile was not immediately mobile, the lesser expectation of privacy resulting from its use as a readily mobile vehicle justified application of the vehicular exception. In some cases, the configuration of the vehicle contributed to the lower expectations of privacy; for example, we held in *Cardwell v. Lewis* that, because the passenger compartment of a standard automobile is relatively open to plain view, there are lesser expectations of privacy. But even when enclosed "repository" areas have been involved, we have concluded that the lesser expectations of privacy warrant application of the exception. We have applied the exception in the context of a locked car trunk, a sealed package in a car trunk, a closed compartment under the dashboard, the interior of a vehicle's upholstery, or sealed packages inside a covered pickup truck.

These reduced expectations of privacy derive not from the fact that the area to be searched is in plain view, but from the pervasive regulation of vehicles capable of traveling on the public highways. As we explained in *South Dakota v. Opperman,* an inventory search case:

> Automobiles, unlike homes, are subjected to pervasive and continuing governmental regulation and controls, including periodic inspection and licensing requirements. As an everyday occurrence, police stop and examine vehicles when license plates or inspection stickers have expired, or if other violations, such as exhaust fumes or excessive noise, are noted, or if headlights or other safety equipment are not in proper working order.

The public is fully aware that it is accorded less privacy in its automobiles because of this compelling governmental need for regulation. * * * In short, the pervasive schemes of regulation, which necessarily lead to reduced expectations of privacy, and the exigencies attendant to ready mobility justify searches without prior recourse to the authority of a magistrate so long as the overriding standard of probable cause is met.

When a vehicle is being used on the highways, or if it is readily capable of such use and is found stationary in a place not regularly used for residential purposes—temporary or otherwise—the two justifications for the vehicle exception come into play. First, the vehicle is obviously readily mobile by the turn of an ignition key, if not actually moving. Second, there is a reduced expectation of privacy stemming from its use as a licensed motor vehicle subject to a range of police regulation inapplicable to a fixed dwelling. At least in these circumstances, the overriding societal interests in effective law enforcement justify an immediate search before the vehicle and its occupants become unavailable.

While it is true that respondent's vehicle possessed some, if not many of the attributes of a home, it is equally clear that the vehicle falls clearly within the scope of the exception laid down in *Carroll* and applied in succeeding cases. Like the automobile in *Carroll*, respondent's motor home was readily mobile. Absent the prompt search and seizure, it could readily have been moved beyond the reach of the police. Furthermore, the vehicle was licensed to "operate on public streets; [was] serviced in public places; . . . and [was] subject to extensive regulation and inspection." And the vehicle was so situated that an objective observer would conclude that it was being used not as a residence, but as a vehicle.

Respondent urges us to distinguish his vehicle from other vehicles within the exception because it was *capable of functioning as a home.* In our increasingly mobile society, many vehicles used for transportation can be and are being used not only for transportation but for shelter, *i.e.,* as a "home" or "residence." To distinguish between respondent's motor home and an ordinary sedan for purposes of the vehicle exception would require that we apply the exception depending upon the size of the vehicle and the quality of its appointments. Moreover, to fail to apply the exception to vehicles such as a motor home ignores the fact that a motor home lends itself easily to use as an instrument of illicit drug traffic and other illegal activity. In *United States v. Ross,* we declined to distinguish between "worthy" and "unworthy" containers, noting that "the central purpose of the Fourth Amendment forecloses such a distinction." We decline today to distinguish between "worthy" and "unworthy" vehicles which are either on the public roads and highways, or situated such that it is reasonable to conclude that the vehicle is not being used as a residence.

Our application of the vehicle exception has never turned on the other uses to which a vehicle might be put. The exception has historically turned on the ready mobility of the vehicle, and on the presence of the vehicle in a setting that objectively indicates that the vehicle is being used for transportation.[3] These two requirements for application of the exception ensure that law enforcement officials are not unnecessarily hamstrung in their efforts to detect and prosecute criminal activity, and that the legitimate privacy interests of the public are protected.[a] Applying the

---

[3] We need not pass on the application of the vehicle exception to a motor home that is situated in a way or place that objectively indicates that it is being used as a residence. Among the factors that might be relevant in determining whether a warrant would be required in such a circumstance is its location, whether the vehicle is readily mobile or instead, for instance, elevated on blocks, whether the vehicle is licensed, whether it is connected to utilities, and whether it has convenient access to a public road.

[a] This language in *California v. Carney* seems to suggest that "ready mobility" is a prerequisite to application of the automobile exception. In a later case, however, the Court made

vehicle exception in these circumstances allows the essential purposes served by the exception to be fulfilled, while assuring that the exception will acknowledge legitimate privacy interests. * * *

The judgment of the California Supreme Court is reversed, and the case is remanded for further proceedings not inconsistent with this opinion.

It is so ordered.

JUSTICE STEVENS, with whom JUSTICE BRENNAN and JUSTICE MARSHALL join, dissenting.

* * * Motor homes, by their common use and construction, afford their owners a substantial and legitimate expectation of privacy when they dwell within. When a motor home is parked in a location that is removed from the public highway, I believe that society is prepared to recognize that the expectations of privacy within it are not unlike the expectations one has in a fixed dwelling. As a general rule, such places may only be searched with a warrant based upon probable cause. Warrantless searches of motor homes are only reasonable when the motor home is traveling on the public streets or highways, or when exigent circumstances otherwise require an immediate search without the expenditure of time necessary to obtain a warrant. * * *

In this case, the motor home was parked in an off-the-street lot only a few blocks from the courthouse in downtown San Diego where dozens of magistrates were available to entertain a warrant application. The officers clearly had the element of surprise with them, and with curtains covering the windshield, the motor home offered no indication of any imminent departure. The officers plainly had probable cause to arrest the respondent and search the motor home, and on this record, it is inexplicable why they eschewed the safe harbor of a warrant.

In the absence of any evidence of exigency in the circumstances of this case, the Court relies on the inherent mobility of the motor home to create a conclusive presumption of exigency. This Court, however, has squarely held that mobility of the place to be searched is not a sufficient justification for abandoning the warrant requirement. In *United States v. Chadwick*, the Court held that a warrantless search of a footlocker violated the Fourth Amendment even though there was ample probable cause to believe it contained contraband. The Government had argued that the [ready mobility] rationale of the automobile exception applied to movable containers in general, and that the warrant requirement should be limited to searches of homes and other "core" areas of privacy. We categorically rejected the Government's argument, observing that there are greater

---

clear that ready mobility is merely a justification for, not a required element of, the automobile exception. *Maryland v. Dyson*, 527 U.S. 465 (1999) (finding that the automobile exception to the warrant requirement does not have a separate exigency requirement and that probable cause is all that is required to satisfy this exception).

privacy interests associated with containers than with automobiles, and that there are less practical problems associated with the temporary detention of a container than with the detention of an automobile. * * *

It is perfectly obvious that the citizen has a much greater expectation of privacy concerning the interior of a mobile home than of a piece of luggage such as a footlocker. If "inherent mobility" does not justify warrantless searches of containers, it cannot rationally provide a sufficient justification for the search of a person's dwelling place.

Unlike a brick bungalow or a frame Victorian, a motor home seldom serves as a permanent lifetime abode. The motor home in this case, however, was designed to accommodate a breadth of ordinary everyday living. Photographs in the record indicate that its height, length, and beam provided substantial living space inside: stuffed chairs surround a table; cupboards provide room for storage of personal effects; bunk beds provide sleeping space; and a refrigerator provides ample space for food and beverages. Moreover, curtains and large opaque walls inhibit viewing the activities inside from the exterior of the vehicle. The interior configuration of the motor home establishes that the vehicle's size, shape, and mode of construction should have indicated to the officers that it was a vehicle containing mobile living quarters.

The State contends that officers in the field will have an impossible task determining whether or not other vehicles contain mobile living quarters. It is not necessary for the Court to resolve every unanswered question in this area in a single case, but common English usage suggests that we already distinguish between a "motor home" which is "equipped as a self-contained traveling home," a "camper" which is only equipped for "casual travel and camping," and an automobile which is "designed for passenger transportation." Surely the exteriors of these vehicles contain clues about their different functions which could alert officers in the field to the necessity of a warrant. * * *

In my opinion, searches of places that regularly accommodate a wide range of private human activity are fundamentally different from searches of automobiles which primarily serve a public transportation function. Although it may not be a castle, a motor home is usually the functional equivalent of a hotel room, a vacation and retirement home, or a hunting and fishing cabin. These places may be as spartan as a humble cottage when compared to the most majestic mansion, but the highest and most legitimate expectations of privacy associated with these temporary abodes should command the respect of this Court. In my opinion, a warrantless search of living quarters in a motor home is "presumptively unreasonable absent exigent circumstances."

I respectfully dissent.

CALIFORNIA V. ACEVEDO
Supreme Court of the United States
500 U.S. 565, 111 S. Ct. 1982, 114 L. Ed. 2d 619 (1991)

JUSTICE BLACKMUN delivered the opinion of the Court.

This case requires us once again to consider the so-called "automobile exception" to the warrant requirement of the Fourth Amendment and its application to the search of a closed container in the trunk of a car.

On October 28, 1987, Officer Coleman of the Santa Ana, Cal., Police Department received a telephone call from a federal drug enforcement agent in Hawaii. The agent informed Coleman that he had seized a package containing marijuana which was to have been delivered to the Federal Express Office in Santa Ana and which was addressed to J.R. Daza at 805 West Stevens Avenue in that city. The agent arranged to send the package to Coleman instead. Coleman then was to take the package to the Federal Express office and arrest the person who arrived to claim it.

Coleman received the package on October 29, verified its contents, and took it to the Senior Operations Manager at the Federal Express office. At about 10:30 a.m. on October 30, a man, who identified himself as Jamie Daza, arrived to claim the package. He accepted it and drove to his apartment on West Stevens. He carried the package into the apartment.

At 11:45 a.m., officers observed Daza leave the apartment and drop the box and paper that had contained the marijuana into a trash bin. Coleman at that point left the scene to get a search warrant. About 12:05 p.m., the officers saw Richard St. George leave the apartment carrying a blue knapsack which appeared to be half full. The officers stopped him as he was driving off, searched the knapsack, and found 1 ½ pounds of marijuana.

At 12:30 p.m., respondent Charles Steven Acevedo arrived. He entered Daza's apartment, stayed for about 10 minutes, and reappeared carrying a brown paper bag that looked full. The officers noticed that the bag was the size of one of the wrapped marijuana packages sent from Hawaii. Acevedo walked to a silver Honda in the parking lot. He placed the bag in the trunk of the car and started to drive away. Fearing the loss of evidence, officers in a marked police car stopped him. They opened the trunk and the bag, and found marijuana.

Respondent was charged in state court with possession of marijuana for sale. * * * He moved to suppress the marijuana found in the car. The motion was denied. He then pleaded guilty but appealed the denial of the suppression motion.

The California Court of Appeal, Fourth District, concluded that the marijuana found in the paper bag in the car's trunk should have been suppressed. The court concluded that the officers had probable cause to believe that the paper bag contained drugs but lacked probable cause to suspect that Acevedo's car, itself, otherwise contained contraband. Because the officers' probable cause was directed specifically at the bag, the court held that the case was controlled by *United States v. Chadwick* rather than by *United States v. Ross*. Although the court agreed that the officers could seize the paper bag, it held that, under *Chadwick,* they could not open the bag without first obtaining a warrant for that purpose. The court then recognized "the anomalous nature" of the dichotomy between the rule in *Chadwick* and the rule in *Ross*. That dichotomy dictates that if there is probable cause to search a car, then the entire car—including any closed container found therein—may be searched without a warrant, but if there is probable cause only as to a container in the car, the container may be held but not searched until a warrant is obtained. * * *

We granted certiorari, to reexamine the law applicable to a closed container in an automobile, a subject that has troubled courts and law enforcement officers since it was first considered in *Chadwick*.

The Fourth Amendment protects the "right of the people to be secure in their persons, houses, papers, and effects, against unreasonable searches and seizures." Contemporaneously with the adoption of the Fourth Amendment, the First Congress, and, later, the Second and Fourth Congresses, distinguished between the need for a warrant to search for contraband concealed in "a dwelling house or similar place" and the need for a warrant to search for contraband concealed in a movable vessel. In *Carroll*, this Court established an exception to the warrant requirement for moving vehicles, for it recognized

> a necessary difference between a search of a store, dwelling house or other structure in respect of which a proper official warrant readily may be obtained, and a search of a ship, motor boat, wagon or automobile, for contraband goods, where it is not practicable to secure a warrant because the vehicle can be quickly moved out of the locality or jurisdiction in which the warrant must be sought.

It therefore held that a warrantless search of an automobile, based upon probable cause to believe that the vehicle contained evidence of crime in the light of an exigency arising out of the likely disappearance of the vehicle, did not contravene the Warrant Clause of the Fourth Amendment. * * *

In *United States v. Ross*, decided in 1982, we held that a warrantless search of an automobile under the *Carroll* doctrine could include a search of a container or package found inside the car when such a search was supported by probable cause. * * * Thus, "[i]f probable cause justifies the search of a lawfully stopped vehicle, it justifies the search of every part of the vehicle and its contents that may conceal the object of the search." In *Ross*, therefore, we clarified the scope of the *Carroll* doctrine as properly including a "probing search" of compartments and containers within the automobile so long as the search is supported by probable cause.

In addition to this clarification, *Ross* distinguished the *Carroll* doctrine from the separate rule that governed the search of closed containers. The Court had announced this separate rule, unique to luggage and other closed packages, bags, and containers, in *United States v. Chadwick*. In *Chadwick*, federal narcotics agents had probable cause to believe that a 200-pound double-locked footlocker contained marijuana. The agents tracked the locker as the defendants removed it from a train and carried it through the station to a waiting car. As soon as the defendants lifted the locker into the trunk of the car, the agents arrested them, seized the locker, and searched it. In this Court, the United States did not contend that the locker's brief contact with the automobile's trunk sufficed to make the *Carroll* doctrine applicable. Rather, the United States urged that the search of movable luggage could be considered analogous to the search of an automobile.

The Court rejected this argument because, it reasoned, a person expects more privacy in his luggage and personal effects than he does in his automobile. Moreover, it concluded that as "may often not be the case when automobiles are seized," secure storage facilities are usually available when the police seize luggage.

In *Arkansas v. Sanders*, the Court extended *Chadwick*'s rule to apply to a suitcase actually being transported in the trunk of a car. In *Sanders*, the police had probable cause to believe a suitcase contained marijuana. They watched as the defendant placed the suitcase in the trunk of a taxi and was driven away. The police pursued the taxi for several blocks, stopped it, found the suitcase in the trunk, and searched it. * * * Again, the *Sanders* majority stressed the heightened privacy expectation in personal luggage and concluded that the presence of luggage in an automobile did not diminish the owner's expectation of privacy in his personal items.

In *Ross*, the Court endeavored to distinguish between *Carroll*, which governed the *Ross* automobile search, and *Chadwick*, which governed the *Sanders* automobile search. It held that the *Carroll* doctrine covered searches of automobiles when the police had probable cause to search an entire vehicle, but that the *Chadwick* doctrine governed searches of luggage when the officers had probable cause to search only a container within the vehicle. Thus, in a *Ross* situation, the police could conduct a reasonable search under the Fourth Amendment without obtaining a warrant, whereas in a *Sanders* situation, the police had to obtain a warrant before they searched.

* * * We now must decide the question deferred in *Ross*: whether the Fourth Amendment requires the police to obtain a warrant to open the sack

in a movable vehicle simply because they lack probable cause to search the entire car. We conclude that it does not. * * *

The line between probable cause to search a vehicle and probable cause to search a package in that vehicle is not always clear, and separate rules that govern the two objects to be searched may enable the police to broaden their power to make warrantless searches and disserve privacy interests. * * * If the police know that they may open a bag only if they are actually searching the entire car, they may search more extensively than they otherwise would in order to establish the general probable cause required by *Ross*. * * * We cannot see the benefit of a rule that requires law enforcement officers to conduct a more intrusive search in order to justify a less intrusive one.

To the extent that the *Chadwick-Sanders* rule protects privacy, its protection is minimal. Law enforcement officers may seize a container and hold it until they obtain a search warrant. "Since the police, by hypothesis, have probable cause to seize the property, we can assume that a warrant will be routinely forthcoming in the overwhelming majority of cases." And the police often will be able to search containers without a warrant, despite the *Chadwick-Sanders* rule, as a search incident to a lawful arrest. * * *

Finally, the search of a paper bag intrudes far less on individual privacy than does the incursion sanctioned long ago in *Carroll*. In that case, prohibition agents slashed the upholstery of the automobile. This Court nonetheless found their search to be reasonable under the Fourth Amendment. If destroying the interior of an automobile is not unreasonable, we cannot conclude that looking inside a closed container is. In light of the minimal protection to privacy afforded by the *Chadwick-Sanders* rule, and our serious doubt whether that rule substantially serves privacy interests, we now hold that the Fourth Amendment does not compel separate treatment for an automobile search that extends only to a container within the vehicle. * * *

Although we have recognized firmly that the doctrine of *stare decisis* serves profoundly important purposes in our legal system, this Court has overruled a prior case on the comparatively rare occasion when it has bred confusion or been a derelict or led to anomalous results. *Sanders* was explicitly undermined in *Ross* and the existence of the dual regimes for automobile searches that uncover containers has proved as confusing as the *Chadwick* and *Sanders* dissenters predicted. We conclude that it is better to adopt one clear-cut rule to govern automobile searches and eliminate the warrant requirement for closed containers set forth in *Sanders*.

The interpretation of the *Carroll* doctrine set forth in *Ross* now applies to all searches of containers found in an automobile. * * * The Court in *Ross* put it this way: * * * "Probable cause to believe that a container placed in

the trunk of a taxi contains contraband or evidence does not justify a search of the entire cab." We reaffirm that principle. In the case before us, the police had probable cause to believe that the paper bag in the automobile's trunk contained marijuana. That probable cause now allows a warrantless search of the paper bag. The facts in the record reveal that the police did not have probable cause to believe that contraband was hidden in any other part of the automobile and a search of the entire vehicle would have been without probable cause and unreasonable under the Fourth Amendment.
* * *

Until today, this Court has drawn a curious line between the search of an automobile that coincidentally turns up a container and the search of a container that coincidentally turns up in an automobile. The protections of the Fourth Amendment must not turn on such coincidences. We therefore interpret *Carroll* as providing one rule to govern all automobile searches. The police may search an automobile and the containers within it where they have probable cause to believe contraband or evidence is contained.
* * *

It is so ordered.

JUSTICE SCALIA, concurring in the judgment.

I agree with the dissent that it is anomalous for a briefcase to be protected by the "general requirement" of a prior warrant when it is being carried along the street, but for that same briefcase to become unprotected as soon as it is carried into an automobile. On the other hand, I agree with the Court that it would be anomalous for a locked compartment in an automobile to be unprotected by the "general requirement" of a prior warrant, but for an unlocked briefcase within the automobile to be protected. I join in the judgment of the Court because I think its holding is more faithful to the text and tradition of the Fourth Amendment, and if these anomalies in our jurisprudence are ever to be eliminated that is the direction in which we should travel.

The Fourth Amendment does not by its terms require a prior warrant for searches and seizures; it merely prohibits searches and seizures that are "unreasonable." * * * Although the Fourth Amendment does not explicitly impose the requirement of a warrant, it is of course textually possible to consider that implicit within the requirement of reasonableness. For some years after the (still continuing) explosion in Fourth Amendment litigation that followed our announcement of the exclusionary rule in *Weeks v. United States*, our jurisprudence lurched back and forth between imposing a categorical warrant requirement and looking to reasonableness alone.

* * * Even before today's decision, the "warrant requirement" had become so riddled with exceptions that it was basically unrecognizable. In 1985, one commentator cataloged nearly 20 such exceptions, including

"searches incident to arrest ... automobile searches ... border searches ... administrative searches of regulated businesses ... exigent circumstances ... search[es] incident to nonarrest when there is probable cause to arrest ... boat boarding for document checks ... welfare searches ... inventory searches ... airport searches ... school search[es] ...." * * * Our intricate body of law regarding "reasonable expectation of privacy" has been developed largely as a means of creating these exceptions, enabling a search to be denominated not a Fourth Amendment "search" and therefore not subject to the general warrant requirement.

Unlike the dissent, therefore, I do not regard today's holding as some momentous departure, but rather as merely the continuation of an inconsistent jurisprudence that has been with us for years. Cases like *United States v. Chadwick* and *Arkansas v. Sanders* have taken the "preference for a warrant" seriously, while cases like *United States v. Ross* and *Carroll v. United States* have not. There can be no clarity in this area unless we make up our minds, and unless the principles we express comport with the actions we take.

In my view, the path out of this confusion should be sought by returning to the first principle that the "reasonableness" requirement of the Fourth Amendment affords the protection that the common law afforded. * * * [T]he supposed "general rule" that a warrant is always required does not appear to have any basis in the common law, and confuses rather than facilitates any attempt to develop rules of reasonableness in light of changed legal circumstances, as the anomaly eliminated and the anomaly created by today's holding both demonstrate.

And there are more anomalies still. Under our precedents (as at common law), a person may be arrested outside the home on the basis of probable cause, without an arrest warrant. Upon arrest, the person, as well as the area within his grasp, may be searched for evidence related to the crime. Under these principles, if a known drug dealer is carrying a briefcase reasonably believed to contain marijuana (the unauthorized possession of which is a crime), the police may arrest him and search his person on the basis of probable cause alone. And, under our precedents, upon arrival at the station house, the police may inventory his possessions, including the briefcase, even if there is no reason to suspect that they contain contraband. According to our current law, however, the police may not, on the basis of the same probable cause, take the less intrusive step of stopping the individual on the street and demanding to see the contents of his briefcase. That makes no sense *a priori,* and in the absence of any common-law tradition supporting such a distinction, I see no reason to continue it. * * *

JUSTICE STEVENS, with whom JUSTICE MARSHALL joins, dissenting. * * *

The Fourth Amendment is a restraint on Executive power. The Amendment constitutes the Framers' direct constitutional response to the unreasonable law enforcement practices employed by agents of the British Crown. Over the years—particularly in the period immediately after World War II and particularly in opinions authored by Justice Jackson after his service as a special prosecutor at the Nuremburg trials—the Court has recognized the importance of this restraint as a bulwark against police practices that prevail in totalitarian regimes.

This history is, however, only part of the explanation for the warrant requirement. The requirement also reflects the sound policy judgment that, absent exceptional circumstances, the decision to invade the privacy of an individual's personal effects should be made by a neutral magistrate rather than an agent of the Executive. In his opinion for the Court in *Johnson v. United States*, Justice Jackson explained:

> The point of the Fourth Amendment, which often is not grasped by zealous officers, is not that it denies law enforcement the support of the usual inferences which reasonable men draw from evidence. Its protection consists in requiring that those inferences be drawn by a neutral and detached magistrate instead of being judged by the officer engaged in the often competitive enterprise of ferreting out crime.

Our decisions have always acknowledged that the warrant requirement imposes a burden on law enforcement. And our cases have not questioned that trained professionals normally make reliable assessments of the existence of probable cause to conduct a search. We have repeatedly held, however, that these factors are outweighed by the individual interest in privacy that is protected by advance judicial approval. The Fourth Amendment dictates that the privacy interest is paramount, no matter how marginal the risk of error might be if the legality of warrantless searches were judged only after the fact. * * *

In *Chadwick*, the Department of Justice had mounted a frontal attack on the warrant requirement. The Government's principal contention was that "the Fourth Amendment Warrant Clause protects only interests traditionally identified with the home." We categorically rejected that contention. * * * We also rejected the Government's alternative argument that the rationale of our automobile search cases demonstrated the reasonableness of permitting warrantless searches of luggage.

We concluded that neither of the justifications for the automobile exception could support a similar exception for luggage. We first held that the privacy interest in luggage is "substantially greater than in an automobile." Unlike automobiles and their contents, we reasoned, "[l]uggage contents are not open to public view, except as a condition to a border entry or common carrier travel; nor is luggage subject to regular inspections and official scrutiny on a continuing basis." Indeed, luggage is specifically intended to safeguard the privacy of personal effects, unlike an automobile, "whose primary function is transportation."

We then held that the mobility of luggage did not justify creating an additional exception to the Warrant Clause. Unlike an automobile, luggage can easily be seized and detained pending judicial approval of a search. Once the police have luggage "under their exclusive control, there [i]s not the slightest danger that the [luggage] or its contents could [be] removed before a valid search warrant could be obtained.... With the [luggage] safely immobilized, it [i]s unreasonable to undertake the additional and greater intrusion of a search without a warrant." * * *

In its opinion today, the Court recognizes that the police did not have probable cause to search respondent's vehicle and that a search of anything but the paper bag that respondent had carried from Daza's apartment and placed in the trunk of his car would have been unconstitutional. Moreover, as I read the opinion, the Court assumes that the police could not have made a warrantless inspection of the bag before it was placed in the car. Finally, the Court also does not question the fact that, under our prior cases, it would have been lawful for the police to seize the container and detain it (and respondent) until they obtained a search warrant. * * *

The Court does not attempt to identify any exigent circumstances that would justify its refusal to apply the general rule against warrantless searches. Instead, it advances these three arguments: First, the rules identified in the foregoing cases are confusing and anomalous. Second, the rules do not protect any significant interest in privacy. And, third, the rules impede effective law enforcement. None of these arguments withstands scrutiny. * * *

To the extent there was any "anomaly" in our prior jurisprudence, the Court has "cured" it at the expense of creating a more serious paradox. For surely it is anomalous to prohibit a search of a briefcase while the owner is carrying it exposed on a public street yet to permit a search once the owner has placed the briefcase in the locked trunk of his car. One's privacy interest in one's luggage can certainly not be diminished by one's removing it from a public thoroughfare and placing it—out of sight—in a privately owned vehicle. Nor is the danger that evidence will escape increased if the luggage is in a car rather than on the street. In either location, if the police have probable cause, they are authorized to seize the luggage and to detain it until they obtain judicial approval for a search. Any line demarking an exception to the warrant requirement will appear blurred at the edges, but the Court has certainly erred if it believes that, by erasing one line and drawing another, it has drawn a clearer boundary. * * *

To support its argument that today's holding works only a minimal intrusion on privacy, the Court suggests that "[i]f the police know that they may open a bag only if they are actually searching the entire car, they may search more extensively than they otherwise would in order to establish the general probable cause required by *Ross*." * * * [T]his fear is unexplained and inexplicable. Neither evidence uncovered in the course of a search nor the scope of the search conducted can be used to provide *post hoc* justification for a search unsupported by probable cause at its inception. * * *

Even if the warrant requirement does inconvenience the police to some extent, that fact does not distinguish this constitutional requirement from any other procedural protection secured by the Bill of Rights. It is merely a part of the price that our society must pay in order to preserve its freedom. Thus, in a unanimous opinion that relied on both *Johnson* and *Chadwick*, Justice Stewart wrote:

> Moreover, the mere fact that law enforcement may be made more efficient can never by itself justify disregard of the Fourth Amendment. The investigation of crime would always be simplified if warrants were unnecessary. But the Fourth Amendment reflects the view of those who wrote the Bill of Rights that the privacy of a person's home and property may not be totally sacrificed in the name of maximum simplicity in enforcement of the criminal law.

It is too early to know how much freedom America has lost today. The magnitude of the loss is, however, not nearly as significant as the Court's willingness to inflict it without even a colorable basis for its rejection of prior law.

I respectfully dissent.

[JUSTICE WHITE's dissenting opinion has been omitted.]

WYOMING V. HOUGHTON
Supreme Court of the United States
526 U.S. 295, 119 S. Ct. 1297, 143 L. Ed. 2d 408 (1999)

JUSTICE SCALIA delivered the opinion of the Court.

This case presents the question whether police officers violate the Fourth Amendment when they search a passenger's personal belongings inside an automobile that they have probable cause to believe contains contraband.

In the early morning hours of July 23, 1995, a Wyoming Highway Patrol officer stopped an automobile for speeding and driving with a faulty brake light. There were three passengers in the front seat of the car: David Young (the driver), his girlfriend, and respondent. While questioning Young, the officer noticed a hypodermic syringe in Young's shirt pocket. He left the occupants under the supervision of two backup officers as he went to get gloves from his patrol car. Upon his return, he instructed Young to step out of the car and place the syringe on the hood. The officer then asked Young why he had a syringe; with refreshing candor, Young replied that he used it to take drugs.

At this point, the backup officers ordered the two female passengers out of the car and asked them for identification. Respondent falsely identified herself as "Sandra James" and stated that she did not have any identification. Meanwhile, in light of Young's admission, the officer searched the passenger compartment of the car for contraband. On the back seat, he found a purse, which respondent claimed as hers. He removed from the purse a wallet containing respondent's driver's license, identifying her properly as Sandra K. Houghton. When the officer asked her why she had lied about her name, she replied: "In case things went bad."

Continuing his search of the purse, the officer found a brown pouch and a black wallet-type container. Respondent denied that the former was hers, and claimed ignorance of how it came to be there; it was found to contain drug paraphernalia and a syringe with 60 ccs of methamphetamine. Respondent admitted ownership of the black container, which was also found to contain drug paraphernalia, and a syringe (which respondent acknowledged was hers) with 10 ccs of methamphetamine—an amount insufficient to support the felony conviction at issue in this case. The officer also found fresh needle-track marks on respondent's arms. He placed her under arrest.

The State of Wyoming charged respondent with felony possession of methamphetamine in a liquid amount greater than three-tenths of a gram. After a hearing, the trial court denied her motion to suppress all evidence obtained from the purse as the fruit of a violation of the Fourth and Fourteenth Amendments. The court held that the officer had probable cause to search the car for contraband, and, by extension, any containers therein that could hold such contraband. A jury convicted respondent as charged.

The Wyoming Supreme Court, by divided vote, reversed the conviction. * * * The court held that the search of respondent's purse violated the Fourth and Fourteenth Amendments because the officer "knew or should have known that the purse did not belong to the driver, but to one of the passengers," and because "there was no probable cause to search the passengers' personal effects and no reason to believe that contraband had been placed within the purse." We granted certiorari.

The Fourth Amendment protects "[t]he right of the people to be secure in their persons, houses, papers, and effects, against unreasonable searches and seizures." In determining whether a particular governmental action violates this provision, we inquire first whether the action was regarded as an unlawful search or seizure under the common law when the

Amendment was framed. Where that inquiry yields no answer, we must evaluate the search or seizure under traditional standards of reasonableness by assessing, on the one hand, the degree to which it intrudes upon an individual's privacy and, on the other, the degree to which it is needed for the promotion of legitimate governmental interests.

It is uncontested in the present case that the police officers had probable cause to believe there were illegal drugs in the car. *Carroll v. United States* similarly involved the warrantless search of a car that law enforcement officials had probable cause to believe contained contraband—in that case, bootleg liquor. The Court concluded that the Framers would have regarded such a search as reasonable in light of legislation enacted by Congress from 1789 through 1799—as well as subsequent legislation from the founding era and beyond—that empowered customs officials to search any ship or vessel without a warrant if they had probable cause to believe that it contained goods subject to a duty. Thus, the Court held that "contraband goods concealed and illegally transported in an automobile or other vehicle may be searched for without a warrant" where probable cause exists.

We have furthermore read the historical evidence to show that the Framers would have regarded as reasonable (if there was probable cause) the warrantless search of containers *within* an automobile. In *Ross*, we upheld as reasonable the warrantless search of a paper bag and leather pouch found in the trunk of the defendant's car by officers who had probable cause to believe that the trunk contained drugs. * * *

Ross summarized its holding as follows: "If probable cause justifies the search of a lawfully stopped vehicle, it justifies the search of *every part of the vehicle and its contents* that may conceal the object of the search." And our later cases describing *Ross* have characterized it as applying broadly to *all* containers within a car, without qualification as to ownership. * * *

To be sure, there was no passenger in *Ross,* and it was not claimed that the package in the trunk belonged to anyone other than the driver. Even so, if the rule of law that *Ross* announced were limited to contents belonging to the driver, or contents other than those belonging to passengers, one would have expected that substantial limitation to be expressed. * * *

In sum, neither *Ross* itself nor the historical evidence it relied upon admits of a distinction among packages or containers based on ownership. When there is probable cause to search for contraband in a car, it is reasonable for police officers—like customs officials in the founding era—to examine packages and containers without a showing of individualized probable cause for each one. A passenger's personal belongings, just like the driver's belongings or containers attached to the car like a glove compartment, are "in" the car, and the officer has probable cause to search for contraband *in* the car.

Even if the historical evidence, as described by *Ross*, were thought to be equivocal, we would find that the balancing of the relative interests weighs decidedly in favor of allowing searches of a passenger's belongings. Passengers, no less than drivers, possess a reduced expectation of privacy with regard to the property that they transport in cars, which "trave[l] public thoroughfares," "seldom serv[e] as . . . the repository of personal effects," are subjected to police stop and examination to enforce "pervasive" governmental controls "[a]s an everyday occurrence," and finally, are exposed to traffic accidents that may render all their contents open to public scrutiny.

In this regard—the degree of intrusiveness upon personal privacy and indeed even personal dignity—the two cases the Wyoming Supreme Court found dispositive differ substantially from the package search at issue here. *United States v. Di Re* held that probable cause to search a car did not justify a body search of a passenger. And *Ybarra v. Illinois* held that a search warrant for a tavern and its bartender did not permit body searches of all the bar's patrons. These cases turned on the unique, significantly heightened protection afforded against searches of one's person. "Even a limited search of the outer clothing . . . constitutes a severe, though brief, intrusion upon cherished personal security, and it must surely be an annoying, frightening, and perhaps humiliating experience." Such traumatic consequences are not to be expected when the police examine an item of personal property found in a car.

Whereas the passenger's privacy expectations are, as we have described, considerably diminished, the governmental interests at stake are substantial. Effective law enforcement would be appreciably impaired without the ability to search a passenger's personal belongings when there is reason to believe contraband or evidence of criminal wrongdoing is hidden in the car. As in all car-search cases, the "ready mobility" of an automobile creates a risk that the evidence or contraband will be permanently lost while a warrant is obtained. In addition, a car passenger—unlike the unwitting tavern patron in *Ybarra*—will often be engaged in a common enterprise with the driver, and have the same interest in concealing the fruits or the evidence of their wrongdoing. A criminal might be able to hide contraband in a passenger's belongings as readily as in other containers in the car, perhaps even surreptitiously, without the passenger's knowledge or permission. (This last possibility provided the basis for respondent's defense at trial; she testified that most of the seized contraband must have been placed in her purse by her traveling companions at one or another of various times, including the time she was "half asleep" in the car.)

To be sure, these factors favoring a search will not always be present, but the balancing of interests must be conducted with an eye to the generality of cases. To require that the investigating officer have positive reason to believe that the passenger and driver were engaged in a common enterprise, or positive reason to believe that the driver had time and occasion to conceal the item in the passenger's belongings, surreptitiously or with friendly permission, is to impose requirements so seldom met that a "passenger's property" rule would dramatically reduce the ability to find and seize contraband and evidence of crime. * * * [O]nce a "passenger's property" exception to car searches became widely known, one would expect passenger-confederates to claim everything as their own. And one would anticipate a bog of litigation—in the form of both civil lawsuits and motions to suppress in criminal trials—involving such questions as whether the officer should have believed a passenger's claim of ownership, whether he should have inferred ownership from various objective factors, whether he had probable cause to believe that the passenger was a confederate, or to believe that the driver might have introduced the contraband into the package with or without the passenger's knowledge. When balancing the competing interests, our determinations of "reasonableness" under the Fourth Amendment must take account of these practical realities. We think they militate in favor of the needs of law enforcement, and against a personal-privacy interest that is ordinarily weak. * * *

We hold that police officers with probable cause to search a car may inspect passengers' belongings found in the car that are capable of concealing the object of the search. The judgment of the Wyoming Supreme Court is reversed.

It is so ordered.

JUSTICE BREYER, concurring.

I join the Court's opinion with the understanding that history is meant to inform, but not automatically to determine, the answer to a Fourth Amendment question. I also agree with the Court that when a police officer has probable cause to search a car, say, for drugs, it is reasonable for that officer also to search containers within the car. If the police must establish a container's ownership prior to the search of that container (whenever, for example, a passenger says "that's mine"), the resulting uncertainty will destroy the workability of the bright-line rule set forth in *United States v. Ross*. * * *

At the same time, I would point out certain limitations upon the scope of the bright-line rule that the Court describes. Obviously, the rule applies only to automobile searches. Equally obviously, the rule applies only to containers found within automobiles. And it does not extend to the search of a person found in that automobile. As the Court notes, * * * the search of a person, including even "a limited search of the outer clothing," is a very different matter in respect to which the law provides "significantly heightened protection."

Less obviously, but in my view also important, is the fact that the container here at issue, a woman's purse, was found at a considerable distance from its owner, who did not claim ownership until the officer discovered her identification while looking through it. Purses are special containers. They are repositories of especially personal items that people generally like to keep with them at all times. So I am tempted to say that a search of a purse involves an intrusion so similar to a search of one's person that the same rule should govern both. However, given this Court's prior cases, I cannot argue that the fact that the container was a purse *automatically* makes a legal difference, for the Court has warned against trying to make that kind of distinction. But I can say that it would matter if a woman's purse, like a man's billfold, were attached to her person. It might then amount to a kind of "outer clothing," which under the Court's cases would properly receive increased protection. In this case, the purse was separate from the person, and no one has claimed that, under those circumstances, the type of container makes a difference. For that reason, I join the Court's opinion.

JUSTICE STEVENS, with whom JUSTICE SOUTER and JUSTICE GINSBURG join, dissenting.

* * * In light of our established preference for warrants and individualized suspicion, I would respect the result reached by the Wyoming Supreme Court and affirm its judgment.

In all of our prior cases applying the automobile exception to the Fourth Amendment's warrant requirement, either the defendant was the operator of the vehicle and in custody of the object of the search, or no question was raised as to the defendant's ownership or custody. In the only automobile case confronting the search of a passenger defendant—*United States v. Di Re*—the Court held that the exception to the warrant requirement did not apply. In *Di Re,* as here, the information prompting the search directly implicated the driver, not the passenger. Today, instead of adhering to the settled distinction between drivers and passengers, the Court fashions a new rule that is based on a distinction between property contained in clothing worn by a passenger and property contained in a passenger's briefcase or purse. * * *

Nor am I persuaded that the mere spatial association between a passenger and a driver provides an acceptable basis for presuming that they are partners in crime or for ignoring privacy interests in a purse. Whether or not the Fourth Amendment required a warrant to search Houghton's purse, at the very least the trooper in this case had to have probable cause to believe that her purse contained contraband. The Wyoming Supreme Court concluded that he did not.

Finally, in my view, the State's legitimate interest in effective law enforcement does not outweigh the privacy concerns at issue.[3] * * * Certainly the ostensible clarity of the Court's rule is attractive. But that virtue is insufficient justification for its adoption. Moreover, a rule requiring a warrant or individualized probable cause to search passenger belongings is every bit as simple as the Court's rule; it simply protects more privacy. * * *

I respectfully dissent.

THE FOURTH AMENDMENT AND COMMON LAW
David A. Sklansky
100 Colum. L. Rev. 1739 (2000)

Famously short on specifics, the opening clause of the Fourth Amendment guarantees "[t]he right of the people to be secure in their persons, houses, papers, and effects, against unreasonable searches and seizures." For most of the past half-century, the interpretation of this guarantee has had little to do with its origins. To identify "searches and seizures" governed by the Amendment, the Supreme Court since *Katz v. United States* has asked whether a particular investigative technique invades an "expectation of privacy . . . that society is prepared to recognize as 'reasonable' "—a standard that pointedly directs attention to the present, not to the past. * * *

Within the past decade, though, the * * * tide has turned. History, as one leading scholar has noted, "is becoming the dominant subject matter" of Fourth Amendment studies, and of writings on criminal procedure more broadly. * * *

So perhaps it is unsurprising that the Supreme Court itself recently has turned back to history for guidance in interpreting the Fourth Amendment. * * * The Court * * * has made the principal criterion for identifying violations of the Fourth Amendment "whether a particular governmental action . . . was regarded as an unlawful search or seizure under the common law when the Amendment was framed."

Novelty aside, this is a curious reading in at least two respects. First, the Fourth Amendment on its face says nothing about common law, but bans all unreasonable searches and seizures, whether or not they were legal before the Amendment was adopted. Second, the chief proponent of the Court's new understanding of the Fourth Amendment has been Justice

---

[3] To my knowledge, we have never restricted ourselves to a two-step Fourth Amendment approach wherein the privacy and governmental interests at stake must be considered only if 18th-century common law "yields no answer." Neither the precedent cited by the Court, nor the majority's opinion in this case, mandate that approach.

Scalia, who is also its most vocal advocate of giving constitutional and statutory provisions their "plain meaning."

* * * Justice Scalia's commitment to eighteenth-century common law as the measure of Fourth Amendment protection [is reflected] in * * * his concurrence in *Minnesota v. Dickerson*. The defendant in *Dickerson* had been stopped for brief questioning and frisked for weapons under the rule of *Terry v. Ohio*. After satisfying himself that the defendant was unarmed, the officer nonetheless continued his tactile inspection of the defendant's clothing, eventually recovering a lump of crack cocaine. Reasoning much as it had in *Arizona v. Hicks*, the Court found the additional search unlawful without a warrant. Justice Scalia joined the Court's opinion but wrote separately to voice reservations about even the frisk permitted by *Terry*.

The purpose of the Fourth Amendment, Scalia declared, was "to preserve that degree of respect for the privacy of persons and the inviolability of their property that existed when the provision was adopted." He therefore had little use for the analysis in *Terry*, because the Court had "made no serious attempt to determine compliance with traditional standards," but instead simply had asked what "was 'reasonable' by current estimations"—applying what Scalia derided as "the original-meaning-is-irrelevant, good-policy-is-constitutional-law school of jurisprudence."

* * * Scalia wrote only for himself in *Dickerson*. And even Professor Amar, who applauded Justice Scalia's opinion in *Acevedo*, was given pause by the concurrence in *Dickerson*, which Amar thought flirted with a " 'frozen in amber' approach to Fourth Amendment reasonableness." Within two years, however, there were signs of sympathy elsewhere on the Court for Scalia's interpretive method. The evidence came in *Wilson v. Arkansas*, in which Justice Thomas wrote for a unanimous court. The holding was almost humdrum: a search of a home can be rendered "unreasonable" for purposes of the Fourth Amendment if the officers fail to knock and to announce their presence before entering—unless, under the circumstances, it is reasonable to dispense with the warning. What was noteworthy about the opinion was its reasoning. To support the Court's conclusion that "the reasonableness of a search of a dwelling may depend in part on whether law enforcement officers announced their presence and authority prior to entering," Justice Thomas reviewed common-law decisions dating from the early seventeenth century up through the 1800s. Ignoring *Terry* and *Katz*—indeed, ignoring almost all search-and-seizure decisions from the second half of the twentieth century—Justice Thomas suggested that in determining the scope of the Fourth Amendment "we have looked to the traditional protections against unreasonable searches and seizures afforded by the common law at the time of the framing." To be sure, "the underlying command of the Fourth Amendment is always that searches and seizures be reasonable," but "our effort to give content to this term may be guided by the meaning ascribed to it by the Framers of the Amendment." Remarkably, no member of the Court objected to the importance Justice Thomas gave common law in assessing the constitutionality of searches and seizures. * * *

The full Court had hinted at sympathy for Scalia's new Fourth Amendment originalism in *Wilson v. Arkansas*, and finally embraced it in *Wyoming v. Houghton*. The question in *Houghton* was whether a warrantless search of an automobile based on probable cause could include a search of a passenger's purse; the Court ruled that it could. That result followed easily enough from *Acevedo*, but Justice Scalia, writing for a majority of six, took the opportunity to sweep more broadly. In applying the Fourth Amendment, he explained, the Court asks first whether the challenged conduct "was regarded as an unlawful search or seizure under the common law when the Amendment was framed." Only if "that inquiry yields no answer" will the Court assess the search or seizure "under traditional standards of reasonableness," balancing the intrusion on privacy against the promotion of legitimate government interests. This was a good deal more emphatic than the suggestion in *Wilson v. Arkansas* that eighteenth-century understandings "may" give content to the Fourth Amendment, and it drew an objection from Justice Stevens: "To my knowledge, we have never restricted ourselves to a two-step Fourth Amendment approach wherein the privacy and governmental interests at stake must be considered only if 18th-century common law 'yields no answer.'" But only Justice Souter and Justice Ginsburg joined his dissent.

Strictly speaking, no "18th-century common law" was found applicable by the Court in *Houghton*. Instead the majority relied on federal legislation in the late-eighteenth century authorizing warrantless inspections of ships by customs officers with probable cause to suspect the presence of contraband. The Court had cited this same legislation when first authorizing warrantless searches of automobiles based on probable cause, and later when extending that authorization to include containers found in automobiles. As in those earlier decisions, the majority in *Houghton* inferred from the Founding-era legislation that "the Framers" would have thought the challenged search "reasonable."

* * * [O]ver the long term the new Fourth Amendment originalism could well have substantive consequences. I argue below that "the common law" will rarely if ever provide a determinate answer to modern search-and-seizure questions. But the rhetoric of the new Fourth Amendment originalism legitimizes some outcomes more easily than others and is relatively uncongenial to certain broad uses to which the Fourth Amendment might otherwise be put. The problem is not so much the answers provided by eighteenth-century common law—those are rare—but rather the limited range of the questions it asked.

To take perhaps the most obvious example, of late the Supreme Court has studiously avoided considerations of equality in assessing the reasonableness of searches and seizures. Constitutional challenges to discrimination, the Court has explained, should be raised under "the Equal Protection Clause, not the Fourth Amendment." Nevertheless even Professor Amar, who echoes Justice Scalia's call to return Fourth Amendment law to "first principles," suggests that constitutional reasonableness today may depend in part on considerations of race, class, and gender equity. These concerns, however, are difficult to read into the common law of 1791. Indeed, as I discuss later, eighteenth-century rules of search and seizure, far from reflecting a broad commitment to equality, systematically codified class privilege. So although the new Fourth Amendment originalism may not be to blame for the absence of race, class, and gender considerations from current search-and-seizure doctrine, the rhetoric of the new originalism makes correction of the absence less likely.

* * * [T]he structural case for the new Fourth Amendment originalism has at least two serious weaknesses. The first * * * is that it shares some of the evil it seeks to remedy: the untethered exercise of judicial power. By its terms the Fourth Amendment does not codify eighteenth-century common law, and the available evidence suggests that was not its purpose. For courts to read common law into the provision, in order to let it better accomplish what they take to be its basic function, is to engage in precisely what Scalia condemns: de facto amendment of the Constitution by unelected judges. * * *

The second weakness * * * is that common law is a far less secure tether for Fourth Amendment rights than Scalia has suggested. * * * More often than not, eighteenth-century "common law" itself is wildly indeterminate—so much so that the new Fourth Amendment originalism may make search-and-seizure law more rather than less responsive to the vicissitudes of judicial predisposition. * * *

COLLINS V. VIRGINIA

Supreme Court of the United States
584 U. S. ___, 138 S. Ct. 1663, 201 L. Ed. 2d 9 (2018)

JUSTICE SOTOMAYOR delivered the opinion of the Court.

This case presents the question whether the automobile exception to the Fourth Amendment permits a police officer, uninvited and without a warrant, to enter the curtilage of a home in order to search a vehicle parked therein. It does not.

Officer Matthew McCall of the Albemarle County Police Department in Virginia saw the driver of an orange and black motorcycle with an extended frame commit a traffic infraction. The driver eluded Officer McCall's attempt to stop the motorcycle. A few weeks later, Officer David

Rhodes of the same department saw an orange and black motorcycle traveling well over the speed limit, but the driver got away from him, too. The officers compared notes and concluded that the two incidents involved the same motorcyclist.

Upon further investigation, the officers learned that the motorcycle likely was stolen and in the possession of petitioner Ryan Collins. After discovering photographs on Collins' Facebook profile that featured an orange and black motorcycle parked at the top of the driveway of a house, Officer Rhodes tracked down the address of the house, drove there, and parked on the street. It was later established that Collins' girlfriend lived in the house and that Collins stayed there a few nights per week.[1]

From his parked position on the street, Officer Rhodes saw what appeared to be a motorcycle with an extended frame covered with a white tarp, parked at the same angle and in the same location on the driveway as in the Facebook photograph. Officer Rhodes, who did not have a warrant, exited his car and walked toward the house. He stopped to take a photograph of the covered motorcycle from the sidewalk, and then walked onto the residential property and up to the top of the driveway to where the motorcycle was parked. In order "to investigate further," Officer Rhodes pulled off the tarp, revealing a motorcycle that looked like the one from the speeding incident. He then ran a search of the license plate and vehicle identification numbers, which confirmed that the motorcycle was stolen. After gathering this information, Officer Rhodes took a photograph of the uncovered motorcycle, put the tarp back on, left the property, and returned to his car to wait for Collins.

Shortly thereafter, Collins returned home. Officer Rhodes walked up to the front door of the house and knocked. Collins answered, agreed to speak with Officer Rhodes, and admitted that the motorcycle was his and that he had bought it without title. Officer Rhodes then arrested Collins.

Collins was indicted by a Virginia grand jury for receiving stolen property. He filed a pretrial motion to suppress the evidence that Officer Rhodes had obtained as a result of the warrantless search of the motorcycle. Collins argued that Officer Rhodes had trespassed on the curtilage of the house to conduct an investigation in violation of the Fourth Amendment. The trial court denied the motion and Collins was convicted.

The Court of Appeals of Virginia affirmed. * * * It * * * concluded that Officer Rhodes' actions were lawful under the Fourth Amendment even absent a warrant because "numerous exigencies justified both his entry onto the property and his moving the tarp to view the motorcycle and record its identification number."

---

[1] Virginia does not dispute that Collins has Fourth Amendment standing.

The Supreme Court of Virginia affirmed on different reasoning. It explained that the case was most properly resolved with reference to the Fourth Amendment's automobile exception. Under that framework, it held that Officer Rhodes had probable cause to believe that the motorcycle was contraband, and that the warrantless search therefore was justified. We granted certiorari, and now reverse.

The Fourth Amendment provides in relevant part that the "right of the people to be secure in their persons, houses, papers, and effects, against unreasonable searches and seizures, shall not be violated." This case arises at the intersection of two components of the Court's Fourth Amendment jurisprudence: the automobile exception to the warrant requirement and the protection extended to the curtilage of a home.

The Court has held that the search of an automobile can be reasonable without a warrant. * * * The "ready mobility" of vehicles served as the core justification for the automobile exception for many years. Later cases then introduced an additional rationale based on "the pervasive regulation of vehicles capable of traveling on the public highways." * * *

In announcing each of these two justifications, the Court took care to emphasize that the rationales applied only to automobiles and not to houses, and therefore supported "treating automobiles differently from houses" as a constitutional matter.

When these justifications for the automobile exception "come into play," officers may search an automobile without having obtained a warrant so long as they have probable cause to do so.

Like the automobile exception, the Fourth Amendment's protection of curtilage has long been black letter law. "[W]hen it comes to the Fourth Amendment, the home is first among equals." "At the Amendment's 'very core' stands 'the right of a man to retreat into his own home and there be free from unreasonable governmental intrusion.'" To give full practical effect to that right, the Court considers curtilage—"the area 'immediately surrounding and associated with the home'—to be 'part of the home itself for Fourth Amendment purposes'" "The protection afforded the curtilage is essentially a protection of families and personal privacy in an area intimately linked to the home, both physically and psychologically, where privacy expectations are most heightened."

When a law enforcement officer physically intrudes on the curtilage to gather evidence, a search within the meaning of the Fourth Amendment has occurred. Such conduct thus is presumptively unreasonable absent a warrant.

With this background in mind, we turn to the application of these doctrines in the instant case. As an initial matter, we decide whether the part of the driveway where Collins' motorcycle was parked and subsequently searched is curtilage.

According to photographs in the record, the driveway runs alongside the front lawn and up a few yards past the front perimeter of the house. The top portion of the driveway that sits behind the front perimeter of the house is enclosed on two sides by a brick wall about the height of a car and on a third side by the house. A side door provides direct access between this partially enclosed section of the driveway and the house. A visitor endeavoring to reach the front door of the house would have to walk partway up the driveway, but would turn off before entering the enclosure and instead proceed up a set of steps leading to the front porch. When Officer Rhodes searched the motorcycle, it was parked inside this partially enclosed top portion of the driveway that abuts the house.

The " 'conception defining the curtilage' is . . . familiar enough that it is 'easily understood from our daily experience.' " Just like the front porch, side garden, or area "outside the front window," the driveway enclosure where Officer Rhodes searched the motorcycle constitutes "an area adjacent to the home and 'to which the activity of home life extends,' " and so is properly considered curtilage.

In physically intruding on the curtilage of Collins' home to search the motorcycle, Officer Rhodes not only invaded Collins' Fourth Amendment interest in the item searched, *i.e.*, the motorcycle, but also invaded Collins' Fourth Amendment interest in the curtilage of his home. The question before the Court is whether the automobile exception justifies the invasion of the curtilage.[2] The answer is no.

Applying the relevant legal principles to a slightly different factual scenario confirms that this is an easy case. Imagine a motorcycle parked inside the living room of a house, visible through a window to a passerby on the street. Imagine further that an officer has probable cause to believe that the motorcycle was involved in a traffic infraction. Can the officer, acting without a warrant, enter the house to search the motorcycle and confirm whether it is the right one? Surely not.

The reason is that the scope of the automobile exception extends no further than the automobile itself. Virginia asks the Court to expand the scope of the automobile exception to permit police to invade any space outside an automobile even if the Fourth Amendment protects that space. Nothing in our case law, however, suggests that the automobile exception gives an officer the right to enter a home or its curtilage to access a vehicle without a warrant. Expanding the scope of the automobile exception in this

---

[2] Helpfully, the parties have simplified matters somewhat by each making a concession. Petitioner concedes "for purposes of this appeal" that Officer Rhodes had probable cause to believe that the motorcycle was the one that had eluded him, and Virginia concedes that "Officer Rhodes searched the motorcycle."

way would both undervalue the core Fourth Amendment protection afforded to the home and its curtilage and "untether" the automobile exception "from the justifications underlying" it.

The Court already has declined to expand the scope of other exceptions to the warrant requirement to permit warrantless entry into the home. The reasoning behind those decisions applies equally well in this context. For instance, under the plain-view doctrine, "any valid warrantless seizure of incriminating evidence" requires that the officer "have a lawful right of access to the object itself." A plain-view seizure thus cannot be justified if it is effectuated "by unlawful trespass." Had Officer Rhodes seen illegal drugs through the window of Collins' house, for example, assuming no other warrant exception applied, he could not have entered the house to seize them without first obtaining a warrant.

Similarly, it is a "settled rule that warrantless arrests in public places are valid," but, absent another exception such as exigent circumstances, officers may not enter a home to make an arrest without a warrant, even when they have probable cause. That is because being "arrested in the home involves not only the invasion attendant to all arrests but also an invasion of the sanctity of the home." Likewise, searching a vehicle parked in the curtilage involves not only the invasion of the Fourth Amendment interest in the vehicle but also an invasion of the sanctity of the curtilage.

Just as an officer must have a lawful right of access to any contraband he discovers in plain view in order to seize it without a warrant, and just as an officer must have a lawful right of access in order to arrest a person in his home, so, too, an officer must have a lawful right of access to a vehicle in order to search it pursuant to the automobile exception.

* * * To allow an officer to rely on the automobile exception to gain entry into a house or its curtilage for the purpose of conducting a vehicle search would unmoor the exception from its justifications, render hollow the core Fourth Amendment protection the Constitution extends to the house and its curtilage, and transform what was meant to be an exception into a tool with far broader application. Indeed, its name alone should make all this clear enough: It is, after all, an exception for automobiles.[3]

---

[3] The dissent concedes that "the degree of the intrusion on privacy" is relevant in determining whether a warrant is required to search a motor vehicle "located on private property." Yet it puzzlingly asserts that the "privacy interests at stake" here are no greater than when a motor vehicle is searched "on public streets." "An ordinary person of common sense," however, clearly would understand that the privacy interests at stake in one's private residential property are far greater than on a public street. Contrary to the dissent's suggestion, it is of no significance that the motorcycle was parked just a "short walk up the driveway." The driveway was private, not public, property, and the motorcycle was parked in the portion of the driveway beyond where a neighbor would venture, in an area "intimately linked to the home, . . . where privacy expectations are most heightened." Nor does it matter that Officer Rhodes "did not damage any property," for an officer's care in conducting a search does not change the character of the place being searched.

Given the centrality of the Fourth Amendment interest in the home and its curtilage and the disconnect between that interest and the justifications behind the automobile exception, we decline Virginia's invitation to extend the automobile exception to permit a warrantless intrusion on a home or its curtilage. * * *

For the foregoing reasons, we conclude that the automobile exception does not permit an officer without a warrant to enter a home or its curtilage in order to search a vehicle therein. We leave for resolution on remand whether Officer Rhodes' warrantless intrusion on the curtilage of Collins' house may have been reasonable on a different basis, such as the exigent circumstances exception to the warrant requirement. The judgment of the Supreme Court of Virginia is therefore reversed, and the case is remanded for further proceedings not inconsistent with this opinion.

It is so ordered.

JUSTICE ALITO, dissenting.

The Fourth Amendment prohibits "unreasonable" searches. What the police did in this case was entirely reasonable. The Court's decision is not.

On the day in question, Officer David Rhodes was standing at the curb of a house where petitioner, Ryan Austin Collins, stayed a couple of nights a week with his girlfriend. From his vantage point on the street, Rhodes saw an object covered with a tarp in the driveway, just a car's length or two from the curb. It is undisputed that Rhodes had probable cause to believe that the object under the tarp was a motorcycle that had been involved a few months earlier in a dangerous highway chase, eluding the police at speeds in excess of 140 mph. Rhodes also had probable cause to believe that petitioner had been operating the motorcycle[1] and that a search of the motorcycle would provide evidence that the motorcycle had been stolen.[2]

If the motorcycle had been parked at the curb, instead of in the driveway, it is undisputed that Rhodes could have searched it without obtaining a warrant. Nearly a century ago, this Court held that officers with probable cause may search a motor vehicle without obtaining a warrant. The principal rationale for this so-called automobile or motor vehicle exception to the warrant requirement is the risk that the vehicle will be moved during the time it takes to obtain a warrant. We have also observed that the owner of an automobile has a diminished expectation of privacy in its contents.

So why does the Court come to the conclusion that Officer Rhodes needed a warrant in this case? Because, in order to reach the motorcycle,

---

[1] Petitioner had a photo on his Facebook profile of a motorcycle that resembled the unusual motorcycle involved in the prior highway chase.

[2] Rhodes suspected the motorcycle was stolen based on a conversation he had with the man who had sold the motorcycle to petitioner.

he had to walk 30 feet or so up the driveway of the house rented by petitioner's girlfriend, and by doing that, Rhodes invaded the home's "curtilage." The Court does not dispute that the motorcycle, when parked in the driveway, was just as mobile as it would have been had it been parked at the curb. Nor does the Court claim that Officer Rhodes's short walk up the driveway did petitioner or his girlfriend any harm. Rhodes did not damage any property or observe anything along the way that he could not have seen from the street. But, the Court insists, Rhodes could not enter the driveway without a warrant, and therefore his search of the motorcycle was unreasonable and the evidence obtained in that search must be suppressed.

An ordinary person of common sense would react to the Court's decision the way Mr. Bumble famously responded when told about a legal rule that did not comport with the reality of everyday life. If that is the law, he exclaimed, "the law is a[n] ass—a[n] idiot." C. Dickens, Oliver Twist 277 (1867).

The Fourth Amendment is neither an "ass" nor an "idiot." Its hallmark is reasonableness, and the Court's strikingly unreasonable decision is based on a misunderstanding of Fourth Amendment basics. * * *

In this case, there is no dispute that the search of the motorcycle was governed by the Fourth Amendment, and therefore whether or not it occurred within the curtilage is not of any direct importance. The question before us is not whether there was a Fourth Amendment search but whether the search was reasonable. And the only possible argument as to why it might not be reasonable concerns the need for a warrant. For nearly a century, however, it has been well established that officers do not need a warrant to search a motor vehicle on public streets so long as they have probable cause. Thus, the issue here is whether there is any good reason why this same rule should not apply when the vehicle is parked in plain view in a driveway just a few feet from the street.

In considering that question, we should ask whether the reasons for the "automobile exception" are any less valid in this new situation. Is the vehicle parked in the driveway any less mobile? Are any greater privacy interests at stake? If the answer to those questions is "no," then the automobile exception should apply. And here, the answer to each question is emphatically "no." The tarp-covered motorcycle parked in the driveway could have been uncovered and ridden away in a matter of seconds. And Officer Rhodes's brief walk up the driveway impaired no real privacy interests. * * *

This does not mean, however, that a warrant is never needed when officers have probable cause to search a motor vehicle, no matter where the vehicle is located. While a case-specific inquiry regarding *exigency* would be inconsistent with the rationale of the motor-vehicle exception, a case-specific inquiry regarding *the degree of intrusion on privacy* is entirely appropriate when the motor vehicle to be searched is located on private property. After all, the ultimate inquiry under the Fourth Amendment is whether a search is reasonable, and that inquiry often turns on the degree of the intrusion on privacy. Thus, contrary to the opinion of the Court, an affirmance in this case would not mean that officers could perform a warrantless search if a motorcycle were located inside a house. In that situation, the intrusion on privacy would be far greater than in the present case, where the real effect, if any, is negligible.

I would affirm the decision below and therefore respectfully dissent.

[JUSTICE THOMAS' concurrence has been omitted.]

Chapter 8

Terry Stops and Frisks

■ ■ ■

This chapter examines stops and frisks by police. Until this point, the exceptions to the warrant requirement we have studied have required probable cause even while dispensing with the warrant requirement. For example, probable cause to arrest is required to support a warrantless search under the search incident to arrest exception. Probable cause to search is required to support a warrantless search under the automobile exception. In *Terry v. Ohio*, the Court decides whether and when the police practice of stopping and frisking individuals without a warrant or probable cause comports with the Fourth Amendment. The excerpts by Lewis Katz, Anthony Thompson, and L. Song Richardson that follow *Terry* highlight some troubling implications of the *Terry* decision.

Florida v. J.L. and *Illinois v. Wardlow* reflect the Court's attempts to provide guidance to lower courts on how to determine whether police have what is necessary to support a stop or frisk. The two excerpts that follow *Wardlow*, one by Tracey Maclin and another by Tracey Meares and Bernard Harcourt, question whether flight from police is a reliable indicator of criminal activity. In *Michigan v. Long*, the Court extends *Terry* to vehicles and allows police to conduct a "frisk" of a car under certain limited circumstances.

Terry v. Ohio
Supreme Court of the United States
392 U.S. 1, 88 S. Ct. 1868, 20 L. Ed. 2d 889 (1968)

CHIEF JUSTICE WARREN delivered the opinion of the Court.

This case presents serious questions concerning the role of the Fourth Amendment in the confrontation on the street between the citizen and the policeman investigating suspicious circumstances.

Petitioner Terry was convicted of carrying a concealed weapon and sentenced to the statutorily prescribed term of one to three years in the penitentiary. Following the denial of a pretrial motion to suppress, the prosecution introduced in evidence two revolvers and a number of bullets seized from Terry and a codefendant, Richard Chilton, by Cleveland Police Detective Martin McFadden. At the hearing on the motion to suppress this evidence, Officer McFadden testified that while he was patrolling in plain clothes in downtown Cleveland at approximately 2:30 in the afternoon of October 31, 1963, his attention was attracted by two men, Chilton and Terry, standing on the corner of Huron Road and Euclid Avenue. He had never seen the two men before, and he was unable to say precisely what first drew his eye to them. However, he testified that he had been a policeman for 39 years and a detective for 35 and that he had been assigned to patrol this vicinity of downtown Cleveland for shoplifters and pickpockets for 30 years. He explained that he had developed routine habits of observation over the years and that he would "stand and watch people or walk and watch people at many intervals of the day." He added: "Now, in this case when I looked over they didn't look right to me at the time."

His interest aroused, Officer McFadden took up a post of observation in the entrance to a store 300 to 400 feet away from the two men. * * * He saw one of the men leave the other one and walk southwest on Huron Road, past some stores. The man paused for a moment and looked in a store window, then walked on a short distance, turned around and walked back toward the corner, pausing once again to look in the same store window. He rejoined his companion at the corner, and the two conferred briefly. Then the second man went through the same series of motions, strolling down Huron Road, looking in the same window, walking on a short distance, turning back, peering in the store window again, and returning to confer with the first man at the corner. The two men repeated this ritual alternately between five and six times apiece—in all, roughly a dozen trips. At one point, while the two were standing together on the corner, a third man approached them and engaged them briefly in conversation. This man then left the two others and walked west on Euclid Avenue. Chilton and Terry resumed their measured pacing, peering and conferring. After this had gone on for 10 to 12 minutes, the two men walked off together, heading west on Euclid Avenue, following the path taken earlier by the third man.

By this time Officer McFadden had become thoroughly suspicious. He testified that after observing their elaborately casual and oft-repeated reconnaissance of the store window on Huron Road, he suspected the two men of "casing a job, a stick-up," and that he considered it his duty as a police officer to investigate further. He added that he feared "they may have a gun." Thus, Officer McFadden followed Chilton and Terry and saw them stop in front of Zucker's store to talk to the same man who had conferred with them earlier on the street corner. Deciding that the situation was ripe for direct action, Officer McFadden approached the three men, identified himself as a police officer and asked for their names. At this point his knowledge was confined to what he had observed. He was not acquainted with any of the three men by name or by sight, and he had received no information concerning them from any other source. When the men "mumbled something" in response to his inquiries, Officer McFadden

grabbed petitioner Terry, spun him around so that they were facing the other two, with Terry between McFadden and the others, and patted down the outside of his clothing. In the left breast pocket of Terry's overcoat Officer McFadden felt a pistol. He reached inside the overcoat pocket, but was unable to remove the gun. At this point, keeping Terry between himself and the others, the officer ordered all three men to enter Zucker's store. As they went in, he removed Terry's overcoat completely, removed a .38-caliber revolver from the pocket and ordered all three men to face the wall with their hands raised. Officer McFadden proceeded to pat down the outer clothing of Chilton and the third man, Katz. He discovered another revolver in the outer pocket of Chilton's overcoat, but no weapons were found on Katz. The officer testified that he only patted the men down to see whether they had weapons, and that he did not put his hands beneath the outer garments of either Terry or Chilton until he felt their guns. So far as appears from the record, he never placed his hands beneath Katz' outer garments. Officer McFadden seized Chilton's gun, asked the proprietor of the store to call a police wagon, and took all three men to the station, where Chilton and Terry were formally charged with carrying concealed weapons.
* * *

After the court denied their motion to suppress, Chilton and Terry waived jury trial and pleaded not guilty. The court adjudged them guilty. * * * We granted certiorari to determine whether the admission of the revolvers in evidence violated petitioner's rights under the Fourth Amendment, made applicable to the States by the Fourteenth. We affirm the conviction.

The Fourth Amendment provides that "the right of the people to be secure in their persons, houses, papers, and effects, against unreasonable searches and seizures, shall not be violated * * *." This inestimable right of personal security belongs as much to the citizen on the streets of our cities as to the homeowner closeted in his study to dispose of his secret affairs. For, as this Court has always recognized, "No right is held more sacred, or is more carefully guarded, by the common law, than the right of every individual to the possession and control of his own person, free from all restraint or interference of others, unless by clear and unquestionable authority of law."

* * * Of course, the specific content and incidents of this right must be shaped by the context in which it is asserted. For "what the Constitution forbids is not all searches and seizures, but unreasonable searches and seizures." Unquestionably petitioner was entitled to the protection of the Fourth Amendment as he walked down the street in Cleveland. The question is whether in all the circumstances of this on-the-street encounter, his right to personal security was violated by an unreasonable search and seizure.

We would be less than candid if we did not acknowledge that this question thrusts to the fore difficult and troublesome issues regarding a sensitive area of police activity—issues which have never before been squarely presented to this Court. Reflective of the tensions involved are the practical and constitutional arguments pressed with great vigor on both sides of the public debate over the power of the police to "stop and frisk"— as it is sometimes euphemistically termed—suspicious persons.

* * * [W]e approach the issues in this case mindful of the limitations of the judicial function in controlling the myriad daily situations in which policemen and citizens confront each other on the street. The State has characterized the issue here as "the right of a police officer * * * to make an on-the-street stop, interrogate and pat down for weapons (known in street vernacular as 'stop and frisk')." But this is only partly accurate. For the issue is not the abstract propriety of the police conduct, but the admissibility against petitioner of the evidence uncovered by the search and seizure. Ever since its inception, the rule excluding evidence seized in violation of the Fourth Amendment has been recognized as a principal mode of discouraging lawless police conduct. Thus its major thrust is a deterrent one, and experience has taught that it is the only effective deterrent to police misconduct in the criminal context, and that without it the constitutional guarantee against unreasonable searches and seizures would be a mere "form of words." The rule also serves another vital function—"the imperative of judicial integrity." Courts which sit under our Constitution cannot and will not be made party to lawless invasions of the constitutional rights of citizens by permitting unhindered governmental use of the fruits of such invasions. * * *

The exclusionary rule has its limitations, however, as a tool of judicial control. * * * Regardless of how effective the rule may be where obtaining convictions is an important objective of the police, it is powerless to deter invasions of constitutionally guaranteed rights where the police either have no interest in prosecuting or are willing to forgo successful prosecution in the interest of serving some other goal.

Proper adjudication of cases in which the exclusionary rule is invoked demands a constant awareness of these limitations. The wholesale harassment by certain elements of the police community, of which minority groups, particularly Negroes, frequently complain, will not be stopped by the exclusion of any evidence from any criminal trial. Yet a rigid and unthinking application of the exclusionary rule, in futile protest against practices which it can never be used effectively to control, may exact a high toll in human injury and frustration of efforts to prevent crime. * * *

Having thus roughly sketched the perimeters of the constitutional debate over the limits on police investigative conduct in general and the background against which this case presents itself, we turn our attention to the quite narrow question posed by the facts before us: whether it is always unreasonable for a policeman to seize a person and subject him to a limited search for weapons unless there is probable cause for an arrest. * * *

Our first task is to establish at what point in this encounter the Fourth Amendment becomes relevant. That is, we must decide whether and when Officer McFadden "seized" Terry and whether and when he conducted a "search." * * *. It is quite plain that the Fourth Amendment governs 'seizures' of the person which do not eventuate in a trip to the station house and prosecution for crime—'arrests' in traditional terminology. It must be recognized that whenever a police officer accosts an individual and restrains his freedom to walk away, he has "seized" that person. And it is nothing less than sheer torture of the English language to suggest that a careful exploration of the outer surfaces of a person's clothing all over his or her body in an attempt to find weapons is not a "search." Moreover, it is simply fantastic to urge that such a procedure performed in public by a policeman while the citizen stands helpless, perhaps facing a wall with his hands raised, is a "petty indignity." It is a serious intrusion upon the sanctity of the person, which may inflict great indignity and arouse strong resentment, and it is not to be undertaken lightly. * * *

In this case there can be no question, then, that Officer McFadden "seized" petitioner and subjected him to a "search" when he took hold of him and patted down the outer surfaces of his clothing. We must decide whether at that point it was reasonable for Officer McFadden to have interfered with petitioner's personal security as he did.[16] And in determining whether the seizure and search were "unreasonable" our inquiry is a dual one—whether the officer's action was justified at its inception, and whether it was reasonably related in scope to the circumstances which justified the interference in the first place.

If this case involved police conduct subject to the Warrant Clause of the Fourth Amendment, we would have to ascertain whether "probable cause" existed to justify the search and seizure which took place. However, that is not the case. We do not retreat from our holdings that the police must, whenever practicable, obtain advance judicial approval of searches and seizures through the warrant procedure, or that in most instances failure to comply with the warrant requirement can only be excused by exigent circumstances. But we deal here with an entire rubric of police conduct—necessarily swift action predicated upon the on-the-spot observations of the officer on the beat—which historically has not been, and as a practical matter could not be, subjected to the warrant procedure. Instead, the conduct involved in this case must be tested by the Fourth

---

[16] * * * Obviously, not all personal intercourse between policemen and citizens involves "seizures" of persons. Only when the officer, by means of physical force or show of authority, has in some way restrained the liberty of a citizen may we conclude that a "seizure" has occurred. * * *

Amendment's general proscription against unreasonable searches and seizures.

Nonetheless, the notions which underlie both the warrant procedure and the requirement of probable cause remain fully relevant in this context. In order to assess the reasonableness of Officer McFadden's conduct as a general proposition, it is necessary "first to focus upon the governmental interest which allegedly justifies official intrusion upon the constitutionally protected interests of the private citizen," for there is "no ready test for determining reasonableness other than by balancing the need to search (or seize) against the invasion which the search (or seizure) entails." And in justifying the particular intrusion the police officer must be able to point to specific and articulable facts which, taken together with rational inferences from those facts, reasonably warrant that intrusion. * * * And in making that assessment it is imperative that the facts be judged against an objective standard: would the facts available to the officer at the moment of the seizure or the search "warrant a man of reasonable caution in the belief" that the action taken was appropriate? Anything less would invite intrusions upon constitutionally guaranteed rights based on nothing more substantial than inarticulate hunches, a result this Court has consistently refused to sanction. * * *

Applying these principles to this case, we consider first the nature and extent of the governmental interests involved. One general interest is of course that of effective crime prevention and detection; it is this interest which underlies the recognition that a police officer may in appropriate circumstances and in an appropriate manner approach a person for purposes of investigating possibly criminal behavior even though there is no probable cause to make an arrest. It was this legitimate investigative function Officer McFadden was discharging when he decided to approach petitioner and his companions. He had observed Terry, Chilton, and Katz go through a series of acts, each of them perhaps innocent in itself, but which taken together warranted further investigation. There is nothing unusual in two men standing together on a street corner, perhaps waiting for someone. Nor is there anything suspicious about people in such circumstances strolling up and down the street, singly or in pairs. Store windows, moreover, are made to be looked in. But the story is quite different where, as here, two men hover about a street corner for an extended period of time, at the end of which it becomes apparent that they are not waiting for anyone or anything; where these men pace alternately along an identical route, pausing to stare in the same store window roughly 24 times; where each completion of this route is followed immediately by a conference between the two men on the corner; where they are joined in one of these conferences by a third man who leaves swiftly; and where the two men finally follow the third and rejoin him a couple of blocks away. It would have been poor police work indeed for an officer of 30 years' experience in the detection of thievery from stores in this same neighborhood to have failed to investigate this behavior further.

The crux of this case, however, is not the propriety of Officer McFadden's taking steps to investigate petitioner's suspicious behavior, but rather, whether there was justification for McFadden's invasion of Terry's personal security by searching him for weapons in the course of that investigation. We are now concerned with more than the governmental interest in investigating crime; in addition, there is the more immediate interest of the police officer in taking steps to assure himself that the person with whom he is dealing is not armed with a weapon that could unexpectedly and fatally be used against him. Certainly it would be unreasonable to require that police officers take unnecessary risks in the performance of their duties. American criminals have a long tradition of armed violence, and every year in this country many law enforcement officers are killed in the line of duty, and thousands more are wounded. Virtually all of these deaths and a substantial portion of the injuries are inflicted with guns and knives.

In view of these facts, we cannot blind ourselves to the need for law enforcement officers to protect themselves and other prospective victims of violence in situations where they may lack probable cause for an arrest. When an officer is justified in believing that the individual whose suspicious behavior he is investigating at close range is armed and presently dangerous to the officer or to others, it would appear to be clearly unreasonable to deny the officer the power to take necessary measures to determine whether the person is in fact carrying a weapon and to neutralize the threat of physical harm. * * *

Our evaluation of the proper balance that has to be struck in this type of case leads us to conclude that there must be a narrowly drawn authority to permit a reasonable search for weapons for the protection of the police officer, where he has reason to believe that he is dealing with an armed and dangerous individual, regardless of whether he has probable cause to arrest the individual for a crime. The officer need not be absolutely certain that the individual is armed; the issue is whether a reasonably prudent man in the circumstances would be warranted in the belief that his safety or that of others was in danger. And in determining whether the officer acted reasonably in such circumstances, due weight must be given, not to his inchoate and unparticularized suspicion or "hunch," but to the specific reasonable inferences which he is entitled to draw from the facts in light of his experience.

We must now examine the conduct of Officer McFadden in this case to determine whether his search and seizure of petitioner were reasonable, both at their inception and as conducted. He had observed Terry, together with Chilton and another man, acting in a manner he took to be preface to a "stick-up." We think on the facts and circumstances Officer McFadden detailed before the trial judge a reasonably prudent man would have been warranted in believing petitioner was armed and thus presented a threat to the officer's safety while he was investigating his suspicious behavior. The actions of Terry and Chilton were consistent with McFadden's hypothesis that these men were contemplating a daylight robbery—which, it is reasonable to assume, would be likely to involve the use of weapons—and nothing in their conduct from the time he first noticed them until the time he confronted them and identified himself as a police officer gave him sufficient reason to negate that hypothesis. Although the trio had departed the original scene, there was nothing to indicate abandonment of an intent to commit a robbery at some point. Thus, when Officer McFadden approached the three men gathered before the display window at Zucker's store he had observed enough to make it quite reasonable to fear that they were armed; and nothing in their response to his hailing them, identifying himself as a police officer, and asking their names served to dispel that reasonable belief. We cannot say his decision at that point to seize Terry and pat his clothing for weapons was the product of a volatile or inventive imagination, or was undertaken simply as an act of harassment; the record evidences the tempered act of a policeman who in the course of an investigation had to make a quick decision as to how to protect himself and others from possible danger, and took limited steps to do so. * * *

Suffice it to note that [a protective frisk], unlike a search without a warrant incident to a lawful arrest, is not justified by any need to prevent the disappearance or destruction of evidence of crime. The sole justification of the search in the present situation is the protection of the police officer and others nearby, and it must therefore be confined in scope to an intrusion reasonably designed to discover guns, knives, clubs, or other hidden instruments for the assault of the police officer.

The scope of the search in this case presents no serious problem in light of these standards. Officer McFadden patted down the outer clothing of petitioner and his two companions. He did not place his hands in their pockets or under the outer surface of their garments until he had felt weapons, and then he merely reached for and removed the guns. He never did invade Katz' person beyond the outer surfaces of his clothes, since he discovered nothing in his patdown which might have been a weapon. Officer McFadden confined his search strictly to what was minimally necessary to learn whether the men were armed and to disarm them once he discovered the weapons. He did not conduct a general exploratory search for whatever evidence of criminal activity he might find.

We conclude that the revolver seized from Terry was properly admitted in evidence against him. At the time he seized petitioner and searched him for weapons, Officer McFadden had reasonable grounds to believe that petitioner was armed and dangerous, and it was necessary for the protection of himself and others to take swift measures to discover the true facts and neutralize the threat of harm if it materialized. The policeman carefully restricted his search to what was appropriate to the discovery of the particular items which he sought. Each case of this sort will, of course, have to be decided on its own facts. We merely hold today that where a police officer observes unusual conduct which leads him reasonably to conclude in light of his experience that criminal activity may be afoot and that the persons with whom he is dealing may be armed and presently dangerous, where in the course of investigating this behavior he identifies himself as a policeman and makes reasonable inquiries, and where nothing in the initial stages of the encounter serves to dispel his reasonable fear for his own or others' safety, he is entitled for the protection of himself and others in the area to conduct a carefully limited search of the outer clothing of such persons in an attempt to discover weapons which might be used to assault him. Such a search is a reasonable search under the Fourth Amendment, and any weapons seized may properly be introduced in evidence against the person from whom they were taken.

Affirmed.

JUSTICE HARLAN, concurring.

While I unreservedly agree with the Court's ultimate holding in this case, I am constrained to fill in a few gaps, as I see them, in its opinion. I do this because what is said by this Court today will serve as initial guidelines for law enforcement authorities and courts throughout the land as this important new field of law develops. * * *

The holding has * * * two logical corollaries that I do not think the Court has fully expressed.

In the first place, if the frisk is justified in order to protect the officer during an encounter with a citizen, the officer must first have constitutional grounds to insist on an encounter, to make a forcible stop. * * * If and when a policeman has a right * * * to disarm such a person for his own protection, he must first have a right not to avoid him but to be in his presence. * * * I would make it perfectly clear that the right to frisk in this case depends upon the reasonableness of a forcible stop to investigate a suspected crime.

Where such a stop is reasonable, however, the right to frisk must be immediate and automatic if the reason for the stop is, as here, an articulable suspicion of a crime of violence. * * * There is no reason why an officer, rightfully but forcibly confronting a person suspected of a serious crime, should have to ask one question and take the risk that the answer might be a bullet.

Upon the foregoing premises, I join the opinion of the Court.

JUSTICE WHITE, concurring.

* * * I think an additional word is in order concerning the matter of interrogation during an investigative stop. There is nothing in the Constitution which prevents a policeman from addressing questions to anyone on the streets. Absent special circumstances, the person approached may not be detained or frisked but may refuse to cooperate and go on his way. However, given the proper circumstances, such as those in this case, it seems to me the person may be briefly detained against his will while pertinent questions are directed to him. Of course, the person stopped is not obliged to answer, answers may not be compelled, and refusal to answer furnishes no basis for an arrest, although it may alert the officer to the need for continued observation. * * *

JUSTICE DOUGLAS, dissenting.

I agree that petitioner was "seized" within the meaning of the Fourth Amendment. I also agree that frisking petitioner and his companions for guns was a "search." But it is a mystery how that "search" and that "seizure" can be constitutional by Fourth Amendment standards, unless there was "probable cause" to believe that (1) a crime had been committed or (2) a crime was in the process of being committed or (3) a crime was about to be committed.

The opinion of the Court disclaims the existence of "probable cause." If loitering were in issue and that was the offense charged, there would be "probable cause" shown. But the crime here is carrying concealed weapons; and there is no basis for concluding that the officer had "probable cause" for believing that that crime was being committed. Had a warrant been sought, a magistrate would, therefore, have been unauthorized to issue one, for he can act only if there is a showing of "probable cause." We hold today that the police have greater authority to make a "seizure" and conduct a "search" than a judge has to authorize such action. We have said precisely the opposite over and over again. * * *

The infringement on personal liberty of any "seizure" of a person can only be "reasonable" under the Fourth Amendment if we require the police to possess "probable cause" before they seize him. Only that line draws a meaningful distinction between an officer's mere inkling and the presence of facts within the officer's personal knowledge which would convince a reasonable man that the person seized has committed, is committing, or is about to commit a particular crime.

To give the police greater power than a magistrate is to take a long step down the totalitarian path. Perhaps such a step is desirable to cope with modern forms of lawlessness. But if it is taken, it should be the deliberate choice of the people through a constitutional amendment. Until the Fourth Amendment * * * is rewritten, the person and the effects of the individual are beyond the reach of all government agencies until there are reasonable grounds to believe (probable cause) that a criminal venture has been launched or is about to be launched. * * *

[JUSTICE BLACK's concurring opinion has been omitted.]

NOTE

In recent years, police stops and frisks have come under increasing public scrutiny and criticism. For example, in 2008, thirteen Blacks and Latinos initiated a class-action lawsuit against the City of New York, alleging that the New York City Police Department's stop and frisk policy violated their rights under the Fourth Amendment and the Equal Protection Clause of the Fourteenth Amendment. *Floyd v. City of New York*, 959 F. Supp. 2d 540 (S.D.N.Y. 2013); Joseph Goldstein, *Trial to Start in Class-Action Suit on Constitutionality of Stop-and-Frisk Tactic*, N.Y. TIMES, Mar. 18, 2013, at A15.

During the course of the lawsuit, plaintiffs presented findings from an empirical study by Columbia law professor Jeffrey Fagan, showing that between January 2004 and June 2012, the New York City Police Department ("NYPD") conducted more than 4.4 million *Terry* stops. Second Supplemental Report of Jeffrey Fagan, Ph.D. at 10, Table 1, Floyd v. City of New York, 959 F. Supp. 2d 540 (S.D.N.Y. 2013) (No. 08 Civ. 01034) [Fagan Report]; *Floyd*, 959 F. Supp. 2d at 556. Over 80% of these 4.4 million stops were of Blacks or Hispanics.[a] Despite this massive effort, contraband was seized in only 1.06% of the stops of Black individuals and 1.25% of stops of Hispanic individuals and weapons were seized in only 1.79% of the stops of Black individuals and 1.73% of the stops of Hispanic individuals. Fagan Report at 35 Table 15.

In a 198 page opinion, Judge Scheindlin held that the NYPD's stop and frisk policy resulted in the disproportionate and discriminatory stopping of Blacks and Hispanics in violation of the Equal Protection Clause and the Fourth Amendment. 959 F. Supp. 2d at 562. According to Judge Scheindlin, NYPD's policy violated the Equal Protection Clause because it subjected all members of a racially defined group to heightened police enforcement simply because some members of that group are criminals. *Id.* It also violated the Fourth Amendment rights of the plaintiffs because the stops lacked individualized reasonable suspicion.[b]

---

[a] Even though Blacks constituted 23% and Latinos constituted 29% of New York City's population at the time, 52% of the 4.4 million individuals stopped by NYPD officers were Black and 31% were Latinos. *Floyd*, 959 F. Supp. 2d at 558–59. Whites, who made up 33% of New York City's population, constituted only 10% of the individuals stopped. *Id.* at 559.

[b] *Id.* at 660. The City appealed Judge Scheindlin's ruling. On October 31, 2013, the Second Circuit Court of Appeals stayed Judge Scheindlin's ruling, suggesting that she misapplied a local rule regarding transfer of related cases and violated ethics rules by giving media interviews responding to criticism of the District Court. *Ligon v. City of New York*, 538 Fed. Appx. 101, 102–03 (2d Cir. 2013). The Second Circuit, however, did not rule on the merits of the appeal. *Id.* at 103. In February 2014, the Second Circuit lifted the stay and remanded the case back to the District Court so that the parties could engage in settlement discussions. *Ligon v. City of New York*, 743 F.3d 362 (2d Cir. 2014). In March 2014, the City and the plaintiffs reached agreement on a settlement whereby the City, under then newly elected Mayor Bill de Blasio, would enact reforms including "training, supervision, monitoring and discipline regarding stop-and-frisk" policies.

In the next excerpt, *Terry v. Ohio at Thirty-Five: a Revisionist View*, Lewis Katz shares insights from the police report prepared by Officer McFadden and Officer McFadden's testimony at the suppression hearing and at trial. These documents suggest problems with the Supreme Court's opinion. Katz also critiques the standard of reasonable suspicion that has become associated with *Terry* stops and frisks. In *Stopping the Usual Suspects: Race and the Fourth Amendment*, Anthony Thompson provides a cogent racial critique of the *Terry v. Ohio* opinion. In *Arrest Efficiency and the Fourth Amendment*, L. Song Richardson explains how stereotypes about Black men and implicit biases can encourage police officers to stop and frisk Black individuals more often than other individuals.

TERRY V. OHIO AT THIRTY-FIVE: A REVISIONIST VIEW

Lewis R. Katz
74 Miss. L.J. 423 (2004)

On Halloween mid-afternoon in 1963, Martin McFadden, a plain clothes Cleveland Police detective, was patrolling his regular beat in downtown Cleveland. He was looking for shoplifters and pickpockets, as he had done for over 35 years. McFadden testified "that he had developed routine habits of observation over the years and that he would 'stand and watch people or walk and watch people at many intervals of the day.'"

Officer McFadden observed two black men, John Terry and Richard Chilton. He testified that when he looked at Terry and Chilton standing on the street, "they didn't look right to me at the time," although he was not acquainted with either man by name or sight, and he had received "[a]bsolutely no information regarding (the) men at all." Officer McFadden did not explain what about the two men "didn't look right" to him. The two men were dressed in topcoats, the standard dress of the day. They were engaged in no unusual behavior when they initially attracted McFadden's attention. When pressed on what about the two men attracted his interest and whether he would pursue them as he did if he saw them that day across from the court house, Officer McFadden replied, "I really don't know."

What happened as McFadden studied Terry and Chilton depends upon which version of Officer McFadden's statement of the facts one reads and in which court opinion the facts appear. McFadden watched the men over a period [of] ten minutes. He watched as one of the two men left the other and walked down the street and looked inside a shop window and continued walking, and then walked back to the other man, again looking in the shop window. The second man then repeated the same behavior. That behavior is the critical conduct which gives rise to the stop in this case. If they did it

---

Floyd v. City of New York, 302 F.R.D. 69, 80 (S.D.N.Y. 2014). In return, the City dismissed its appeal on the constitutionality of stop and frisk. *Floyd v. City of New York*, 770 F.3d 1051, 1056–57 (2d Cir. 2014).

once or twice each, their behavior was pretty unremarkable. So, how many times they looked in the store window is crucial. In the police report filed the same day as the incident, Officer McFadden wrote that the men did this "about three times each." Between the day of the event when he wrote the police report and his memory was freshest, and the suppression hearing, which was almost one year to the day after the event, Officer McFadden's memory changed. At the suppression hearing three times each became "at least four or five times apiece," which later turned into four to six trips each. Moreover, at trial, when asked how many trips he observed, Officer McFadden replied, "about four trips, three to four trips, maybe four to five trips, maybe a little more, it might be a little less. I don't know, I didn't count the trips." The Ohio Court of Appeals decision in the case picked up on the uncertainty and asserted that the men separated and looked in the window "at least two to five times" each. However, by the time the fact worked its way into Chief Justice Warren's majority opinion in the Supreme Court, the number expands exponentially. He wrote that the men did this "between five or six times apiece—in all roughly a dozen trips." Later in the majority opinion, Chief Justice Warren came up with still another number when he described Terry and Chilton's behavior: "where these men pace alternately along an identical route, pausing to stare in the same store window roughly twenty-four times." The body of law which stems from *Terry* is dependent upon this single fact.

Officer McFadden was never sure which store was the subject of the suspects' attention. At the suppression hearing he admitted he had no experience in observing the activities of individuals who were "casing" a store for a robbery. In the police report, Officer McFadden indicated that they were looking in an airline ticket office; at the suppression hearing, the Detective mentioned an airline office or a jewelry store. Chief Justice Warren (wisely) chose not to focus on this issue. If the men were "casing a . . . stickup," as Officer McFadden believed, a downtown airline office would be unlikely to produce significant cash. Even in 1963, airline tickets were rarely purchased with cash. A jewelry store would be a more lucrative target. Terry and Chilton's street behavior and the supposed target of their interest are extremely important issues because they are all that set apart these suspects from any other two people on the street, unless it was their race.

The third man, Carl Katz, a white man, approached Terry and Chilton in conversation. McFadden did not know the white man either. McFadden suspected that the two black men were "casing a job, a stick-up," and he feared they may have a gun. Cleveland was a segregated city, and police lore had it that the only time whites and blacks congregated was to plan or commit a crime. When Terry and Chilton walked on, turning a corner and walking down the street, they stopped in front of Zucker's, a men's clothing store, where they met up again with Katz. At that point, McFadden decided to act.

Officer McFadden walked over to the three men, identified himself as a police officer, and asked for their names. McFadden testified that he received a mumbled response to his inquiry. McFadden then immediately grabbed Terry, spun him around, and "patted down the outside of his clothing." When Officer McFadden felt a pistol in the inside breast pocket of Terry's overcoat, the Supreme Court reported that McFadden, then, reached inside the overcoat to retrieve the pistol but was unable to do so. He ordered all three men into the clothing store where he removed Terry's overcoat and removed a .38-caliber automatic pistol. He then ordered all three men to face the wall, and proceeded to pat-down "the outer clothing of Chilton and the third man, Katz," finding a .38-caliber revolver in Chilton's pocket, but no weapon on Carl Katz. * * *

Chief Justice Warren's majority opinion [in *Terry v. Ohio*] never used the term "reasonable suspicion," instead writing of "unusual conduct" which leads a police officer "reasonably to conclude in light of his experience that criminal activity may be afoot." It was only in Justice Harlan's concurring opinion in *Sibron* that the "reasonable suspicion" standard was articulated. In applying this diluted-cause standard, the Warren Court claimed the need to distinguish facts and circumstances from inarticulate hunches, but failed to do so when they validated the stop of Terry and Chilton based on Officer McFadden's statements that the two "didn't look right" and that McFadden "just didn't like 'em." Thus, the current standard for a stop was forever grounded upon the very type of inarticulate hunch that the Court said was an insufficient basis for a *Terry* stop. * * *

In the years since *Terry*, the standard of reasonable suspicion has become more problematic by the emphasis upon two factors. The first is the officer's experience. In *Terry*, the Court said that Officer McFadden's conclusion that criminal activity was afoot was reasonable "in light of his experience." However, Chief Justice Warren failed to elaborate on the relevant experience. Officer McFadden, an expert at identifying shoplifters and pickpockets, testified that he had never apprehended a robber. * * *

The second problematic factor is the weight given to the locale where the stop takes place. The Supreme Court has made it clear that the neighborhood where a suspect is found is not enough, alone, to justify an investigatory stop. In *Brown v. Texas,* the Court said that "(appellant's being) in a neighborhood frequented by drug users, standing alone, is not a basis for concluding that appellant himself was engaged in criminal conduct."

Nonetheless, the Supreme Court has used locale as an appropriate element in the *Terry* equation. * * * In *Illinois v. Wardlow*, Chief Justice

Rehnquist wrote that "[a]n individual's presence" in a high crime area "standing alone, is not enough to support a reasonable, particularized suspicion that the person is committing a crime" but immediately undermined that statement:

> But officers are not required to ignore the relevant characteristics of a location in determining whether the circumstances are sufficiently suspicious to warrant further investigation. Accordingly, we have previously noted the fact that the stop occurred in a "high crime area" among the relevant contextual considerations in a *Terry* analysis.

> * * * The clear message is that in "high crime" or "high drug activity" areas, i.e. the inner city, the possibility of criminal activity is so substantial as to make everyone in the area subject to police inquiry.

Consequently, lower courts give enormous weight to this collateral factor, often requiring little more than some other innocuous bits of information to fulfill the reasonable suspicion requirement justifying a stop. Thus, "high crime area" becomes a centerpiece of the *Terry* analysis, serving almost as a talismanic signal justifying investigative stops. Location in America, in this context, is a proxy for race or ethnicity. By sanctioning investigative stops on little more than the area in which the stop takes place, the phrase "high crime area" has the effect of criminalizing race. It is as though a black man standing on a street corner or sitting in a legally parked car has become the equivalent to "driving while black" for motorists. * * *

STOPPING THE USUAL SUSPECTS: RACE AND THE FOURTH AMENDMENT

Anthony C. Thompson
74 N.Y.U. L. Rev. 956 (1999)

The Supreme Court's decision in *Terry v. Ohio* is well known for the Fourth Amendment rule it announced: The police can conduct limited seizures of the person (now commonly known as "Terry stops") and limited patdowns of a person ("Terry frisks") based on a quantum of suspicion that is less substantial than the "probable cause" standard that the police must satisfy when conducting full-blown arrests and equivalent seizures of the person. In reading the decision, one would see no reason to view the case as relevant to the issue of racially motivated searches and seizures. Yet, closer review of the case—especially when supplemented with an examination of the briefs and the trial court record in the case—reveals an important racial dimension.

In the majority opinion's statement of facts, Chief Justice Warren described Detective Martin McFadden's observations of two men, John Terry and Richard Chilton, standing on a street corner in "downtown

Cleveland." There is no mention of the race of any of these individuals. The decision states that McFadden "had never seen the two men before, and he was unable to say precisely what first drew his eye to them." McFadden (who was in plain clothes) watched first one individual, then the other, walk back and forth in front of a store window and look in the window as they passed. At one point in this sequence of events, as the two individuals were standing together on the corner, "a third man approached them and engaged them briefly in conversation" then "left the two others and walked west on Euclid Avenue"; after again "pacing, peering, and conferring," Chilton and Terry headed "west on Euclid Avenue, following the path taken earlier by the third man." The Court's decision also does not mention the race of "the third man."

Having concluded that Chilton and Terry were in the process of "casing a job, a stick-up," McFadden followed them down the street. He observed them "stop . . . to talk to the same man who had conferred with them earlier on the street corner." "Deciding that the situation was ripe for direct action," McFadden approached the group, identified himself as a police officer and asked for their names. The men "'mumbled something' in response to [the officer's] inquiries," which caused the officer to "grab[ ] petitioner Terry, sp[i]n him around so they were facing the other two, . . . and pat[ ] down the outside of his clothing." Finding a gun on Terry, the officer patted down the other two and also found a gun in Chilton's overcoat.

The Court presented the foregoing facts, which represent the key portions of the *Terry* opinion's factual presentation, in entirely race-neutral terms. When treatises recite the facts of *Terry*, they generally follow the Court's lead. But an examination of the trial court record reveals that John Terry and Richard Chilton were African American; "the third man," Katz, was white; Detective McFadden also was white.

The Court's legal analysis was almost entirely devoid of references to race. * * * The Court's discussion focused almost exclusively on doctrinal aspects of Fourth Amendment law and practical considerations in adapting Fourth Amendment rules to "the need for law enforcement officers to protect themselves and other prospective victims of violence." * * *

When one adds the missing racial element to the Court's statement of facts, certain otherwise inexplicable events suddenly become much more comprehensible. Detective McFadden's assertion that "he was unable to say precisely what first drew his eye to [Terry and Chilton]," an assertion accepted by the trial court and uncritically recited by the Supreme Court, assumes a new meaning when one views *Terry* as a case in which a white detective noticed—and then focused his attention on—two black men who were doing nothing more than standing on a street corner in downtown Cleveland in the middle of the afternoon. The Court quoted Detective

McFadden's statement that "they didn't look right to me at the time," but gave no explanation for what "didn't look right" meant to McFadden because he himself had offered no such explanation in his testimony.

With the element of race restored to the case, it is more readily apparent why these two men "didn't look right" to him. This inference becomes even clearer when one considers the officer's elaboration on this point in his testimony at the trial:

> Q. Well, at what point did you consider their actions unusual?
>
> A. Well, to be truthful with you, I didn't like them. I was just attracted to them, and I surmised that there was something going on when one of them left the other one and did the walking up, walk up past the store and stopped and looked in and come back again. * * *

The Court stripped away the racial dimension of the case by removing all references to the participants' race. Although one cannot, of course, reconstruct the reasons for this rhetorical choice, it seems evident at least that this was a conscious choice. In his suppression hearing testimony, Detective McFadden repeatedly referred to the "third man" (Katz) as a "white man"; the lawyers who questioned McFadden did so as well. Yet, the Court's opinion refers to him only as "the third man" or by name.

The removal of race from the case presented the Court with a dilemma, however. To determine whether to uphold McFadden's actions under the new "stop and frisk" doctrine, the Court had to ascertain precisely why McFadden stopped and frisked Terry. After all, an essential element of pre-*Terry* "probable cause" doctrine—and one the Court carried forward to the new "stop and frisk" rule—was that a search and seizure had to be supported by specific facts that could be weighed by an objective magistrate. But, with race eliminated from the case, the most obvious explanation for McFadden's suspicions and his subsequent actions was unavailable. The Court was left with McFadden's testimony that "he was unable to say precisely what first drew his eye to them." * * *

What the Court did to "make sense" of McFadden's actions is best understood in the terms of narrative theory. As others have explained, a sound judicial opinion requires coherent factual and legal narratives. Such narratives permit the judges to clarify the events in their own minds and to present the facts and law in a manner that the legal community will generally accept. In *Terry*, the narrative upon which the Court settled was one of the "police officer as expert." To explain Detective McFadden's immediate distrust of the two men on the street corner, the Court stated:

> He had never seen the two men before, and he was unable to say precisely what first drew his eye to them. However, he testified that he had been a policeman for 39 years and a detective for 35 and that he had been assigned to patrol this vicinity of downtown

Cleveland for shoplifters and pickpockets for 30 years. He explained . . . that he would "stand and watch people or walk and watch people at many intervals of the day." He added: "Now, in this case when I looked over they didn't look right to me at the time."

The Court took McFadden's statement that could easily be construed in racial terms ("they didn't look right to me") and transformed it into a highly skilled officer's instinctive assessment that something in the situation seemed awry and worthy of investigation. And the [C]ourt accomplished this transformation in a manner quite familiar to those who study narrative: not explicitly (which would have been impossible since McFadden's testimony lacked such a direct link) but by juxtaposing two apparently unconnected subjects.

After acknowledging that each of the acts observed by McFadden was "perhaps innocent in itself" and consistent with the actions of individuals who are not engaged in criminal activity, the Court invoked the expertise of the detective to declare that "[i]t would have been poor police work indeed for an officer of 30 years' experience in the detection of thievery from stores in this same neighborhood to have failed to investigate this behavior further." * * *

An independent examination of McFadden's suppression hearing testimony provides cause to be skeptical of the Court's characterizations of his expertise. Of course, the Court in the *Terry* opinion does not claim for McFadden any experience in recognizing "casing," for the Court could not have done so. Instead, it implies such expertise by saying that McFadden "testified that he had been a policeman for 39 years and a detective for 35 and that he had been assigned to patrol this vicinity of downtown Cleveland for shoplifters and pickpockets for 30 years." * * * The "police officer as expert" narrative allowed the Court in *Terry* to present a coherent, raceless narrative about why McFadden acted as he did. Moreover, and more important for the broader canvas of Fourth Amendment jurisprudence on which the Court was painting, this device permitted the Court to denounce judicial reliance on police "hunches" in a case in which the Court was doing the very thing it was nominally condemning. * * *

In stripping away race from the case and substituting the officer-as-expert narrative, the Court in *Terry* essentially created a conceptual construct: an officer who was unaffected by considerations of race and who could be trusted even in a race-laden case like *Terry* to be acting on the basis of legitimate indicia of criminal activity. Such an officer could be trusted with the expanded powers conferred by the *Terry* opinion. * * *

Of course, even if the "Detective McFaddens" of the world could be trusted to perform in a race-neutral manner, that still left the other kind of officer * * *: the officer who would abuse expanded search and seizure powers unjustly to stop and frisk African Americans and other members of "unpopular racial and religious minorities." To deal with this concern, the Court once again constructed a narrative. This time, the Court's narrative focused on the Court itself describing the limits of judicial power, and specifically the limitations of lawmakers in construing the Fourth Amendment. The Court stated:

> The wholesale harassment by certain elements of the police community, of which minority groups, particularly Negroes, frequently complain, will not be stopped by the exclusion of any evidence from any criminal trial. Yet a rigid and unthinking application of the exclusionary rule in futile protest against practices which it can never be used effectively to control, may exact a high toll in human injury and frustration of efforts to prevent crime.

Although the Court in this passage appears to accept the validity of the complaints of "wholesale harassment" of "minority groups," the Court attributes these abuses to "certain elements of the police community." In essence, the Court divides the world of police officers into "good cops" (the "Detective McFaddens" of the world, who can be trusted) and "rogue cops" (the ones who might be expected to abuse whatever powers have been delegated to them). * * *

Although the Court appeared to assume in *Terry* * * * that police officers can make assessments of criminality independent of whatever attitudes the officers may have about race, the social scientific research shows that the stereotypic judgments and biases that an individual brings to an event fundamentally shape perception. Research suggests that negative attitudes toward African Americans create a perceptual norm of viewing African Americans as more prone to criminal conduct. * * *

The effects of these phenomena are not limited to police officers whom one can easily characterize as "biased." Of course, some law enforcement officers consciously act on the basis of racial bias in denominating behavior as "suspicious." Such officers embrace stereotypes and allow personal biases to dictate their behavior. But "dominative racists" are not the only class of discriminators. Especially as it has become less socially acceptable to acknowledge racial prejudices and because people increasingly tend to view themselves as egalitarian, discriminatory treatment is often the product of unconscious racism. * * *

ARREST EFFICIENCY AND THE FOURTH AMENDMENT
L. Song Richardson
95 Minn. L. Rev. 2035 (2011)

Research in the field of implicit social cognition repeatedly demonstrates that individuals of all races have implicit biases against Blacks. These take the form of nonconscious stereotypes and prejudices that might conflict with a person's explicit or consciously held thoughts and feelings. * * * [O]nce activated, these biases can negatively and nonconsciously influence judgments and behaviors towards Blacks in ways that a person is unaware of and largely unable to control. * * *

Black men are stereotyped as violent, criminal, and dangerous. These cultural stereotypes affect the evaluation of behaviors performed by Blacks. This was powerfully demonstrated in a study that required participants to rate an ambiguous physical contact between two people. Researchers had subjects watch a video of two men engaged in a discussion that grew increasingly heated. The subjects were unaware that the men were actors following a script. Instead, they were told that they were observing a discussion occurring in another room. Researchers asked the subjects to rate the behavior of the two men at various points during the discussion. Eventually, one man pushed the other and the subjects had the option of rating the contact as horsing around, dramatic, aggressive, or violent. Researchers manipulated the race of the pusher and the victim to test whether race would affect the subjects' perceptions.

Remarkably, the actor's race significantly influenced how subjects evaluated the contact. When the victim was White and the person initiating the physical contact was Black, seventy-five percent of the subjects interpreted the shove as violent. However, when the victim was Black and the pusher was White, only seventeen percent of the subjects labeled the contact as violent. Finally, when the two actors were Black, the perpetrator's behavior was rated as more aggressive than when the two individuals were White—sixty-nine percent versus thirteen percent. The researchers concluded that negative stereotypes associating Blacks with violence explained why the subjects evaluated ambiguous behaviors as more aggressive when performed by a Black actor as opposed to a White actor.

Other studies support the finding that individuals evaluate Blacks more negatively than Whites engaged in identical behavior. In one study, Black and White school age children rated an ambiguous bump in the hallway as more aggressive when performed by a Black actor rather than a White actor. In another, subjects evaluated the same facial expression as more hostile on a Black face than on a White face. In a third study using buttons labeled "shoot" and "don't shoot" as a weapon's trigger, the nonconscious activation of negative Black stereotypes caused individuals more quickly to shoot a potentially hostile Black than a potentially hostile White. * * *

Negative stereotypes and unfavorable attitudes towards Blacks can cause individuals to treat them differently than non-stereotyped group members. One experiment demonstrating this involved White subjects interviewing "job applicants." Researchers trained the applicants to respond to interview questions in a standard format so that any differences in the treatment they received from the interviewer would be attributable to race. The results demonstrated that White interviewers treated Black and White job applicants differently. With Black applicants, the interviewer maintained greater physical distance, made more speech errors, and ended the interview sooner than with White applicants. Researchers concluded that these differences resulted from the negative stereotypical beliefs held by the interviews of the Black job applicants.

Receiving negative treatment can cause individuals to respond in kind. This is known as the self-fulfilling prophecy or behavioral confirmation effect. Numerous researchers note that the originators of negative behavior will likely be completely unaware of the role their own behavior played in triggering the negative response. Hence, the behavioral confirmation effect "provide[s] a powerful mechanism by which stereotypes and prejudicial behavior are maintained" since "the perceiver interprets the target's behavior in line with the expectancy and encodes yet another instance of stereotype-consistent behavior." * * *

Based on the science, it is reasonable to conclude that the operation of implicit biases can cause the police to target, stop, and search Blacks more often than Whites. Police attention may be drawn to Black individuals in general, and to young Black men in particular, regardless of whether these individuals are engaged in suspicious behavior. Once their attention is captured, automatic stereotype activation can cause officers to interpret behavior as aggressive, violent, or suspicious even if identical behavior performed by a white individual would not be so interpreted. When officers approach the individual to confirm or dispel their suspicions, implicit biases can cause officers to behave aggressively without realizing it. The confronted individual may respond in kind, fulfilling officers' beliefs that the individual is suspicious and aggressive. This entire series of events, triggered not by conscious racial animus but by implicit racial biases, will likely result in officers conducting a frisk. All the while, officers will be unaware that the behavioral effects of their implicit bias triggered the entire chain of events. In the end, officers may stop and frisk Black individuals, whom they would not have deemed suspicious if they had been White, not because of bigotry or conscious considerations of race, but because of implicit cognitions. * * *

The behavioral assumption underlying the reasonable suspicion test is that a well-intentioned officer is capable of interpreting identical behavior similarly, regardless of the race of the individual they are observing. While this behavioral assumption is intuitively appealing, it does not withstand scientific scrutiny. Nonconscious stereotype activation in the presence of Black individuals may cause officers to interpret their ambiguous behaviors as suspicious, aggressive, and dangerous while similar behaviors engaged in by Whites would go unnoticed. Upon feeling suspicious, an officer can easily articulate the specific facts that he believes led him to feel suspicious without realizing that his initial feelings of suspicion may have been caused by the operation of implicit racial bias.

FLORIDA V. J.L.
Supreme Court of the United States
529 U.S. 266, 120 S. Ct. 1375, 146 L. Ed. 2d 254 (2000)

JUSTICE GINSBURG delivered the opinion of the Court.

The question presented in this case is whether an anonymous tip that a person is carrying a gun is, without more, sufficient to justify a police officer's stop and frisk of that person. We hold that it is not.

On October 13, 1995, an anonymous caller reported to the Miami-Dade Police that a young black male standing at a particular bus stop and wearing a plaid shirt was carrying a gun. So far as the record reveals, there is no audio recording of the tip, and nothing is known about the informant. Sometime after the police received the tip—the record does not say how long—two officers were instructed to respond. They arrived at the bus stop about six minutes later and saw three black males "just hanging out [there]." One of the three, respondent J.L., was wearing a plaid shirt. Apart from the tip, the officers had no reason to suspect any of the three of illegal conduct. The officers did not see a firearm, and J.L. made no threatening or otherwise unusual movements. One of the officers approached J.L., told him to put his hands up on the bus stop, frisked him, and seized a gun from J.L.'s pocket. The second officer frisked the other two individuals, against whom no allegations had been made, and found nothing.

J.L., who was at the time of the frisk "10 days shy of his 16th birthday [day]," was charged under state law with carrying a concealed firearm without a license and possessing a firearm while under the age of 18. He moved to suppress the gun as the fruit of an unlawful search, and the trial court granted his motion. The intermediate appellate court reversed, but the Supreme Court of Florida quashed that decision and held the search invalid under the Fourth Amendment. * * *

We granted certiorari, and now affirm the judgment of the Florida Supreme Court.

Our "stop and frisk" decisions begin with *Terry v. Ohio*. This Court held in *Terry*:

> [W]here a police officer observes unusual conduct which leads him reasonably to conclude in light of his experience that criminal activity may be afoot and that the persons with whom he is dealing may be armed and presently dangerous, where in the course of investigating this behavior he identifies himself as a policeman and makes reasonable inquiries, and where nothing in the initial stages of the encounter serves to dispel his reasonable fear for his own or others' safety, he is entitled for the protection of himself and others in the area to conduct a carefully limited search of the outer clothing of such persons in an attempt to discover weapons which might be used to assault him.

In the instant case, the officers' suspicion that J.L. was carrying a weapon arose not from any observations of their own but solely from a call made from an unknown location by an unknown caller. Unlike a tip from a known informant whose reputation can be assessed and who can be held responsible if her allegations turn out to be fabricated, "an anonymous tip alone seldom demonstrates the informant's basis of knowledge or veracity." As we have recognized, however, there are situations in which an anonymous tip, suitably corroborated, exhibits "sufficient indicia of reliability to provide reasonable suspicion to make the investigatory stop." The question we here confront is whether the tip pointing to J.L. had those indicia of reliability.

In [*Alabama v.*] *White*, the police received an anonymous tip asserting that a woman was carrying cocaine and predicting that she would leave an apartment building at a specified time, get into a car matching a particular description, and drive to a named motel. Standing alone, the tip would not have justified a *Terry* stop. Only after police observation showed that the informant had accurately predicted the woman's movements, we explained, did it become reasonable to think the tipster had inside knowledge about the suspect and therefore to credit his assertion about the cocaine. Although the Court held that the suspicion in *White* became reasonable after police surveillance, we regarded the case as borderline. Knowledge about a person's future movements indicates some familiarity with that person's affairs, but having such knowledge does not necessarily imply that the informant knows, in particular, whether that person is carrying hidden contraband. We accordingly classified *White* as a "close case."

The tip in the instant case lacked the moderate indicia of reliability present in *White* and essential to the Court's decision in that case. The anonymous call concerning J.L. provided no predictive information and therefore left the police without means to test the informant's knowledge or credibility. That the allegation about the gun turned out to be correct does not suggest that the officers, prior to the frisks, had a reasonable basis for suspecting J.L. of engaging in unlawful conduct: The reasonableness of official suspicion must be measured by what the officers knew before they conducted their search. All the police had to go on in this case was the bare report of an unknown, unaccountable informant who neither explained how he knew about the gun nor supplied any basis for believing he had inside information about J.L. If *White* was a close case on the reliability of anonymous tips, this one surely falls on the other side of the line.

Florida contends that the tip was reliable because its description of the suspect's visible attributes proved accurate: There really was a young black male wearing a plaid shirt at the bus stop. The United States as *amicus curiae* makes a similar argument, proposing that a stop and frisk should be permitted "when (1) an anonymous tip provides a description of a particular person at a particular location illegally carrying a concealed firearm, (2) police promptly verify the pertinent details of the tip except the existence of the firearm, and (3) there are no factors that cast doubt on the reliability of the tip...." These contentions misapprehend the reliability needed for a tip to justify a *Terry* stop.

An accurate description of a subject's readily observable location and appearance is of course reliable in this limited sense: It will help the police correctly identify the person whom the tipster means to accuse. Such a tip, however, does not show that the tipster has knowledge of concealed criminal activity. The reasonable suspicion here at issue requires that a tip be reliable in its assertion of illegality, not just in its tendency to identify a determinate person.

A second major argument advanced by Florida and the United States as *amicus* is, in essence, that the standard *Terry* analysis should be modified to license a "firearm exception." Under such an exception, a tip alleging an illegal gun would justify a stop and frisk even if the accusation would fail standard pre-search reliability testing. We decline to adopt this position.

Firearms are dangerous, and extraordinary dangers sometimes justify unusual precautions. Our decisions recognize the serious threat that armed criminals pose to public safety; *Terry*'s rule, which permits protective police searches on the basis of reasonable suspicion rather than demanding that officers meet the higher standard of probable cause, responds to this very concern. But an automatic firearm exception to our established reliability analysis would rove too far. Such an exception would enable any person seeking to harass another to set in motion an intrusive, embarrassing police search of the targeted person simply by placing an anonymous call falsely reporting the target's unlawful carriage of a gun. Nor could one securely confine such an exception to allegations involving firearms. Several Courts of Appeals have held it *per se* foreseeable for people carrying significant amounts of illegal drugs to be carrying guns as well. If police officers may properly conduct *Terry* frisks on the basis of bare-boned tips about guns, it would be reasonable to maintain under the above-cited decisions that the police should similarly have discretion to frisk based on bare-boned tips about narcotics. * * *

The facts of this case do not require us to speculate about the circumstances under which the danger alleged in an anonymous tip might be so great as to justify a search even without a showing of reliability. We do not say, for example, that a report of a person carrying a bomb need bear the indicia of reliability we demand for a report of a person carrying a firearm before the police can constitutionally conduct a frisk. Nor do we hold that public safety officials in quarters where the reasonable expectation of Fourth Amendment privacy is diminished, such as airports and schools, cannot conduct protective searches on the basis of information insufficient to justify searches elsewhere.

Finally, the requirement that an anonymous tip bear standard indicia of reliability in order to justify a stop in no way diminishes a police officer's prerogative, in accord with *Terry,* to conduct a protective search of a person who has already been legitimately stopped. We speak in today's decision only of cases in which the officer's authority to make the initial stop is at issue. In that context, we hold that an anonymous tip lacking indicia of reliability of the kind contemplated in * * * *White* does not justify a stop and frisk whenever and however it alleges the illegal possession of a firearm.

The judgment of the Florida Supreme Court is affirmed.

It is so ordered.

[JUSTICE KENNEDY's concurring opinion has been omitted.]

ILLINOIS V. WARDLOW
Supreme Court of the United States
528 U.S. 119, 120 S. Ct. 673, 145 L. Ed. 2d 570 (2000)

CHIEF JUSTICE REHNQUIST delivered the opinion of the Court. * * *

On September 9, 1995, Officers Nolan and Harvey were working as uniformed officers in the special operations section of the Chicago Police Department. The officers were driving the last car of a four-car caravan converging on an area known for heavy narcotics trafficking in order to investigate drug transactions. The officers were traveling together because they expected to find a crowd of people in the area, including lookouts and customers.

As the caravan passed 4035 West Van Buren, Officer Nolan observed respondent Wardlow[a] standing next to the building holding an opaque bag. Respondent looked in the direction of the officers and fled. Nolan and Harvey turned their car southbound, watched him as he ran through the gangway and an alley, and eventually cornered him on the street. Nolan then exited his car and stopped respondent. He immediately conducted a protective patdown search for weapons because in his experience it was common for there to be weapons in the near vicinity of narcotics transactions. During the frisk, Officer Nolan squeezed the bag respondent was carrying and felt a heavy, hard object similar to the shape of a gun. The officer then opened the bag and discovered a .38-caliber handgun with five live rounds of ammunition. The officers arrested Wardlow.

The Illinois trial court denied respondent's motion to suppress, finding the gun was recovered during a lawful stop and frisk. Following a stipulated bench trial, Wardlow was convicted of unlawful use of a weapon by a felon. The Illinois Appellate Court reversed Wardlow's conviction, concluding that the gun should have been suppressed because Officer Nolan did not have reasonable suspicion sufficient to justify an investigative stop pursuant to *Terry v. Ohio.*

The Illinois Supreme Court agreed. * * * [T]he Illinois Supreme Court determined that sudden flight in [a high crime] area does not create a reasonable suspicion justifying a *Terry* stop. * * * Finding no independently suspicious circumstances to support an investigatory detention, the court held that the stop and subsequent arrest violated the Fourth Amendment. We granted certiorari and now reverse.

This case, involving a brief encounter between a citizen and a police officer on a public street, is governed by the analysis we first applied in *Terry.* In *Terry,* we held that an officer may, consistent with the Fourth Amendment, conduct a brief, investigatory stop when the officer has a reasonable, articulable suspicion that criminal activity is afoot.[b] While "reasonable suspicion" is a less demanding standard than probable cause and requires a showing considerably less than preponderance of the evidence, the Fourth Amendment requires at least a minimal level of objective justification for making the stop. The officer must be able to articulate more than an "inchoate and unparticularized suspicion or 'hunch'" of criminal activity.

---

[a] According to David Seawell, Sam Wardlow, the respondent in this case, was a 44-year-old African American man. David Seawell, *Wardlow's Case: A Call to Broaden the Perspective of American Criminal Law*, 78 DENV. U. L. REV. 1119 (2000).

[b] In a later case, *Arizona v. Johnson*, 555 U.S. 323 (2009), the Court suggested that an officer may conduct a patdown frisk of an occupant of a vehicle that has been lawfully stopped for a minor traffic violation as long as the officer has a reasonable suspicion that the person being frisked is armed and dangerous. *Id.* at 332–34. As long as the officer has lawfully stopped the vehicle, the officer can conduct such a frisk even if she does not have reasonable suspicion to believe that the occupant is involved in criminal activity. *Id.*

Nolan and Harvey were among eight officers in a four-car caravan that was converging on an area known for heavy narcotics trafficking, and the officers anticipated encountering a large number of people in the area, including drug customers and individuals serving as lookouts. It was in this context that Officer Nolan decided to investigate Wardlow after observing him flee. An individual's presence in an area of expected criminal activity, standing alone, is not enough to support a reasonable, particularized suspicion that the person is committing a crime. But officers are not required to ignore the relevant characteristics of a location in determining whether the circumstances are sufficiently suspicious to warrant further investigation. Accordingly, we have previously noted the fact that the stop occurred in a "high crime area" among the relevant contextual considerations in a *Terry* analysis.

In this case, moreover, it was not merely respondent's presence in an area of heavy narcotics trafficking that aroused the officers' suspicion, but his unprovoked flight upon noticing the police. Our cases have also recognized that nervous, evasive behavior is a pertinent factor in determining reasonable suspicion. Headlong flight—wherever it occurs—is the consummate act of evasion: It is not necessarily indicative of wrongdoing, but it is certainly suggestive of such. In reviewing the propriety of an officer's conduct, courts do not have available empirical studies dealing with inferences drawn from suspicious behavior, and we cannot reasonably demand scientific certainty from judges or law enforcement officers where none exists. Thus, the determination of reasonable suspicion must be based on commonsense judgments and inferences about human behavior. We conclude Officer Nolan was justified in suspecting that Wardlow was involved in criminal activity, and, therefore, in investigating further.

Such a holding is entirely consistent with our decision in *Florida v. Royer*, where we held that when an officer, without reasonable suspicion or probable cause, approaches an individual, the individual has a right to ignore the police and go about his business. And any "refusal to cooperate, without more, does not furnish the minimal level of objective justification needed for a detention or seizure." But unprovoked flight is simply not a mere refusal to cooperate. Flight, by its very nature, is not "going about one's business"; in fact, it is just the opposite. Allowing officers confronted with such flight to stop the fugitive and investigate further is quite consistent with the individual's right to go about his business or to stay put and remain silent in the face of police questioning.

Respondent and *amici* also argue that there are innocent reasons for flight from police and that, therefore, flight is not necessarily indicative of ongoing criminal activity. This fact is undoubtedly true, but does not establish a violation of the Fourth Amendment. Even in *Terry,* the conduct justifying the stop was ambiguous and susceptible of an innocent explanation. The officer observed two individuals pacing back and forth in front of a store, peering into the window and periodically conferring. All of this conduct was by itself lawful, but it also suggested that the individuals were casing the store for a planned robbery. *Terry* recognized that the officers could detain the individuals to resolve the ambiguity. * * *

The judgment of the Supreme Court of Illinois is reversed, and the case is remanded for further proceedings not inconsistent with this opinion.

It is so ordered.

JUSTICE STEVENS, with whom JUSTICE SOUTER, JUSTICE GINSBURG, and JUSTICE BREYER join, concurring in part and dissenting in part.

The State of Illinois asks this Court to announce a "bright-line rule" authorizing the temporary detention of anyone who flees at the mere sight of a police officer. Respondent counters by asking us to adopt the opposite *per se* rule—that the fact that a person flees upon seeing the police can never, by itself, be sufficient to justify a temporary investigative stop of the kind authorized by *Terry v. Ohio.*

The Court today wisely endorses neither *per se* rule. Instead, it rejects the proposition that "flight is . . . necessarily indicative of ongoing criminal activity," adhering to the view that "[t]he concept of reasonable suspicion . . . is not readily, or even usefully, reduced to a neat set of legal rules," but must be determined by looking to "the totality of the circumstances—the whole picture." Abiding by this framework, the Court concludes that "Officer Nolan was justified in suspecting that Wardlow was involved in criminal activity."

Although I agree with the Court's rejection of the *per se* rules proffered by the parties, unlike the Court, I am persuaded that in this case the brief testimony of the officer who seized respondent does not justify the conclusion that he had reasonable suspicion to make the stop. * * *

The question in this case concerns "the degree of suspicion that attaches to" a person's flight—or, more precisely, what "commonsense conclusions" can be drawn respecting the motives behind that flight. A pedestrian may break into a run for a variety of reasons—to catch up with a friend a block or two away, to seek shelter from an impending storm, to arrive at a bus stop before the bus leaves, to get home in time for dinner, to resume jogging after a pause for rest, to avoid contact with a bore or a bully, or simply to answer the call of nature—any of which might coincide with the arrival of an officer in the vicinity. A pedestrian might also run because he or she has just sighted one or more police officers. In the latter instance, the State properly points out "that the fleeing person may be, *inter alia,* (1) an escapee from jail; (2) wanted on a warrant; (3) in possession of contraband, (i.e. drugs, weapons, stolen goods, etc.); or (4) someone who has just committed another type of crime." In short, there are does not say whether the caravan, or any part of it, had already passed Wardlow by before he began to run.

Indeed, the Appellate Court thought the record was even "too vague to support the inference that ... defendant's flight was related to his expectation of police focus on him." Presumably, respondent did not react to the first three cars, and we cannot even be sure that he recognized the occupants of the fourth as police officers. The adverse inference is based entirely on the officer's statement: "He looked in our direction and began fleeing."

No other factors sufficiently support a finding of reasonable suspicion. Though respondent was carrying a white, opaque bag under his arm, there is nothing at all suspicious about that. Certainly the time of day—shortly after noon—does not support Illinois' argument. Nor were the officers "responding to any call or report of suspicious activity in the area." * * *

The State, along with the majority of the Court, relies as well on the assumption that this flight occurred in a high crime area. Even if that assumption is accurate, it is insufficient because even in a high crime neighborhood unprovoked flight does not invariably lead to reasonable suspicion. On the contrary, because many factors providing innocent motivations for unprovoked flight are concentrated in high crime areas, the character of the neighborhood arguably makes an inference of guilt less appropriate, rather than more so. Like unprovoked flight itself, presence in a high crime neighborhood is a fact too generic and susceptible to innocent explanation to satisfy the reasonable suspicion inquiry.

It is the State's burden to articulate facts sufficient to support reasonable suspicion. In my judgment, Illinois has failed to discharge that burden. I am not persuaded that the mere fact that someone standing on a sidewalk looked in the direction of a passing car before starting to run is sufficient to justify a forcible stop and frisk.

I therefore respectfully dissent from the Court's judgment to reverse the court below.

NOTE

Shortly after the police shooting of Michael Brown in Ferguson, Missouri roiled the nation, Kimberly Jade Norwood, a law professor at Washington University in St. Louis, Missouri, met with a group of her 13-year-old son's teenage friends to discuss the shooting. Kimberly Jade Norwood, *The Far-Reaching Shadow Cast by Ferguson*, 46 WASH. U. J.L. & POL'Y 1, 16 (2014). Professor Norwood asked the boys, all Black male teenagers, what they would do if a police officer started walking towards them and was shocked by their response. All of her son's friends told her they would turn around and run even though none of them had ever been in trouble with the law before. *Id.* at 16–17.

unquestionably circumstances in which a person's flight is suspicious, and undeniably instances in which a person runs for entirely innocent reasons. * * *

Even assuming we know that a person runs because he sees the police, the inference to be drawn may still vary from case to case. Flight to escape police detection, we have said, may have an entirely innocent motivation:

> [I]t is a matter of common knowledge that men who are entirely innocent do sometimes fly from the scene of a crime through fear of being apprehended as the guilty parties, or from an unwillingness to appear as witnesses. * * *

In addition to these concerns, a reasonable person may conclude that an officer's sudden appearance indicates nearby criminal activity. And where there is criminal activity there is also a substantial element of danger—either from the criminal or from a confrontation between the criminal and the police. These considerations can lead to an innocent and understandable desire to quit the vicinity with all speed.

Among some citizens, particularly minorities and those residing in high crime areas, there is also the possibility that the fleeing person is entirely innocent, but, with or without justification, believes that contact with the police can itself be dangerous, apart from any criminal activity associated with the officer's sudden presence. For such a person, unprovoked flight is neither "aberrant" nor "abnormal." * * *

"Unprovoked flight," in short, describes a category of activity too broad and varied to permit a *per se* reasonable inference regarding the motivation for the activity. While the innocent explanations surely do not establish that the Fourth Amendment is always violated whenever someone is stopped solely on the basis of an unprovoked flight, neither do the suspicious motivations establish that the Fourth Amendment is never violated when a *Terry* stop is predicated on that fact alone. For these reasons, the Court is surely correct in refusing to embrace either *per se* rule advocated by the parties. The totality of the circumstances, as always, must dictate the result.

Guided by that totality-of-the-circumstances test, the Court concludes that Officer Nolan had reasonable suspicion to stop respondent. In this respect, my view differs from the Court's. The entire justification for the stop is articulated in the brief testimony of Officer Nolan. * * *

[Officer Nolan's] testimony is most noticeable for what it fails to reveal. Though asked whether he was in a marked or unmarked car, Officer Nolan could not recall the answer. He was not asked whether any of the other three cars in the caravan were marked, or whether any of the other seven officers were in uniform. * * * Officer Nolan's testimony also does not * * * indicate whether he saw respondent notice the other patrol cars. And it

Although the *Wardlow* Court accepts unprovoked flight in a high crime neighborhood as a valid factor supporting a finding of reasonable suspicion that crime is afoot, a state court case highlights that in cases with African-American male suspects, the reasons for fleeing the police could just as equally be connected to the suspect's fear of racial profiling as it could be to consciousness of guilt from criminal activity. In *Commonwealth v. Warren*, 475 Mass. 530 (2016), the Supreme Judicial Court of Massachusetts relied on empirical data from the Boston Police Department to articulate its view on the appropriate analysis of flight in the equation of reasonable suspicion, explaining:

> . . . where the suspect is a black male stopped by the police on the streets of Boston, the analysis of flight as a factor in the reasonable suspicion calculus cannot be divorced from the findings in a recent Boston Police Department (department) report documenting a pattern of racial profiling of black males in the city of Boston. According to the study, based on FIO [Field Interrogation and Observation] data collected by the department, black men in the city of Boston were more likely to be targeted for police-civilian encounters such as stops, frisks, searches, observations, and interrogations. Black men were also disproportionally targeted for repeat police encounters.
>
> We do not eliminate flight as a factor in the reasonable suspicion analysis whenever a black male is the subject of an investigatory stop. However, in such circumstances, flight is not necessarily probative of a suspect's state of mind or consciousness of guilt. Rather, the finding that black males in Boston are disproportionately and repeatedly targeted for FIO encounters suggests a reason for flight totally unrelated to consciousness of guilt. Such an individual, when approached by the police, might just as easily be motivated by the desire to avoid the recurring indignity of being racially profiled as by the desire to hide criminal activity. Given this reality for black males in the city of Boston, a judge should, in appropriate cases, consider the report's findings in weighing flight as a factor in the reasonable suspicion calculus.

475 Mass. at 539–40. Of the approximately 205,000 Boston Police Department field interrogation and observation reports studied, 89.0 percent of the subjects were male, 54.7 percent were age 24 or younger, and 63.3 percent were Black. See FINAL REPORT, AN ANALYSIS OF RACE AND ETHNICITY PATTERNS IN BOSTON POLICE DEPARTMENT FIELD INTERROGATION, OBSERVATION, FRISK, AND/OR SEARCH REPORTS 2 (June 15, 2015).

The excerpts that follow critique the presumption that an individual's flight from police gives rise to a reasonable suspicion of criminal activity.

"BLACK AND BLUE ENCOUNTERS"—SOME PRELIMINARY THOUGHTS ABOUT FOURTH AMENDMENT SEIZURES: SHOULD RACE MATTER?

Tracey Maclin
26 Val. U. L. Rev. 243 (1991)

[In *California v. Hodari D.*], Justice Scalia intimated that it is reasonable to detain young men who "Scatter in panic upon the mere sighting of the police." For Scalia, * * * proverbial common sense [indicates that] "The wicked flee when no man pursueth."

From a police perspective, Justice Scalia's remarks may make sense. * * * Of course, this viewpoint, never considers that Hodari, a black youth, may have had alternative reasons for wanting to avoid the cops. Many persons who have never committed a crime have ambivalent or negative attitudes about the police. Perhaps, a youth like Hodari flees at the sight of police because he does not wish to drop his pants, as many black youths in Boston have been forced to do, just because cops suspect he belongs to a gang or is selling drugs.

Or maybe Hodari has had an older sibling or friend roughed up by the police, and does not wish to undergo a similar experience with the approaching officers. Perhaps Hodari has seen the video-tape of the Los Angeles police beating and kicking Rodney King, or he has seen the NBC video of Don Jackson, a former police officer himself, being pushed through a store window by Long Beach, California police officers for no reason. Maybe Hodari believed that the officer who wants to ask him "What's going on here?" may engage in similar brutality in his case. As California Assemblyman Curtis Tucker was quoted as saying: "When black people in Los Angeles see a police car approaching, 'They don't know whether justice will be meted out or whether judge, jury and executioner is pulling up behind them.'" * * *

Thus, it comes as no surprise that some black men go out of their way to be calm and extremely congenial when approached by a police officer. A black man's silence in the face of police demands should not be interpreted as cooperation, however. His silent exterior masks a complex reaction of fear, anger and distrust that must be kept under wraps in order to avoid a more intense and violent confrontation than history has too often shown places the black man in an overmatched and vulnerable position. * * *

FOREWORD: TRANSPARENT ADJUDICATION AND SOCIAL SCIENCE RESEARCH IN CONSTITUTIONAL CRIMINAL PROCEDURE

Tracey L. Meares & Bernard E. Harcourt
90 J. Crim. L. & Criminology 733 (2000)

* * *

Writing for the Court in *Wardlow* * * *, the Chief Justice acknowledged the empirical nature of the question—whether flight from a police officer amounted to reasonable suspicion—but stated that there were "no available empirical studies dealing with inferences drawn from suspicious behavior." As a result, the Chief Justice maintained, the Court had to rely on its own "commonsense judgments about human behavior." In the Court's opinion, "headlong flight—wherever it occurs—is the consummate act of evasion." These types of assertions, however, are not self-evident, common sense, or simple "facts of life." They are contested empirical claims that are hotly debated in legal and social scientific circles.

* * * [A]t the heart of *Wardlow* is the degree of suspicion that attaches to a person's flight. Specifically, the case turns on how reliably flight indicates guilt. * * * A pathbreaking study of street stops in New York City released on December 1, 1999, about six weeks before *Wardlow* was published, provides critical insight to the central question in *Wardlow*. While a study of Chicago street stops would have been more apt, this study of police activity in a major urban area contains information directly pertinent to the central legal and empirical question in *Wardlow* and surely constitutes social authority for the case. * * * Particularly notable for our purposes is data collected in the study connecting the rate of stops made by police and subsequent arrests.

The relationship between stops and arrests is a potential method of determining how good an indicator a particular factor for police action must be. The relevance of this relationship was noted by Justice Stevens in dissent. Justice Stevens pointed in passing to a newspaper article reporting that in 1997, New York City's Street Crimes Unit made 45,000 stops, only 20% of which resulted in arrests. Justice Stevens then wrote, "even if these data were race neutral they would still indicate that society as a whole is paying a significant cost in infringement in liberty by these virtually random stops." * * *

The New York OAG [Office of Attorney General] Report collects, in addition to racial breakdowns on stops and frisks, a measure of how "good" those stops are: how many of the stops lead to an arrest. Citywide, that ratio was 9:1. That is, nine stops were made by the NYPD for every eventual arrest. Here, then, is empirical confirmation of the jurisprudential gap between the reasonable suspicion and probable cause standards. * * *

The citywide ratio masks a great deal. It masks variation in ratios from as low as 6.3:1 for highway and traffic to 26.7:1 for the narcotics task force. It also masks racial differences in stop-to-arrest ratios. After controlling for crime rates—measured in this study by arrest rates for various offenses—and precinct composition, researchers found that, whether the relevant precinct was majority or minority Black, the comparison between the stop-to-arrest rates for Blacks and the same rates for whites was almost always 2:1.

This analysis provides an even stronger case for the claim made by the *Wardlow* amici that minority individuals have more encounters with police that do not always trigger an initiation of the criminal justice process than do whites. This information, together with that cited by the dissenters, suggests that minority individuals have a relationship with the police that makes interpretation of flight extremely difficult. * * *

With respect to the particular issue presented in *Wardlow*, the [data] provides a fascinating picture of police work. Stops reported as undertaken because the suspect fled the scene result in a very high stop-to-arrest ratio—a ratio of 26:1. This ratio is quite close to that of stops based on factors generally understood to fail to satisfy the reasonable suspicion test. Note that even when flight in a high crime area is considered, the ratio between stops and arrests lowers, but it does not lower by much. It stands at 20.3:1. These data support the *Wardlow* dissenters' argument that flight may be caused by a whole host of reasons that are not indicative of criminal activity.

Importantly, however, the *Wardlow* Court did not discuss merely the suspicious nature of flight generally; rather, the Court assessed whether flight "upon noticing the police" or "flight [that] was motivated by the presence of a police officer" was suspicious enough to justify a police stop. * * * The ratio between stops and arrests with respect to flight to elude the police [is] 15.8:1 * * *. When the data on flight to elude police are confined to high crime areas—the very context presented by the facts in *Wardlow*—a different relationship between stops and arrests emerges. These data reveal a stop-to-arrest ratio of 45:1.

This astoundingly high [inverse] relationship between stops and arrests is suggestive that in high-crime urban communities where the population is disproportionately minority, flight from an identifiable police officer is a very poor indicator that crime is afoot. * * *

NOTE

How should courts go about deciding whether reasonable suspicion to stop or frisk an individual exists? The Court has stated that reviewing courts should look to the "totality of the circumstances" of each case to decide whether the officer had a particularized and objective basis for suspecting the individual of criminal activity. *See United States v. Arvizu*, 534 U.S. 266, 273 (2002). Where on the spectrum of levels of justification does reasonable suspicion lie? The Court has declined to measure reasonable suspicion in terms of percentages, explaining only that the officer needs more than a mere hunch to justify a stop, but the likelihood of criminal activity does not have to rise to the level of probable cause nor even a preponderance of the evidence. *Id.* at 274.

In later cases, the Court extended the *Terry* doctrine in various ways. In *United States v. Place*, 462 U.S. 696 (1983), for example, the Court extended *Terry* to cover brief, investigatory detentions of property, holding that law enforcement officials may temporarily seize luggage based upon reasonable suspicion that the luggage contains contraband or evidence of a crime. In the next case, the Court extends the *Terry* doctrine to cover a limited search of the vehicle under certain circumstances.

MICHIGAN V. LONG
Supreme Court of the United States
463 U.S. 1032, 103 S. Ct. 3469, 77 L. Ed. 2d 1201 (1983)

JUSTICE O'CONNOR delivered the opinion of the Court. * * *

Deputies Howell and Lewis were on patrol in a rural area one evening when, shortly after midnight, they observed a car traveling erratically and at excessive speed.[1] The officers observed the car turning down a side road, where it swerved off into a shallow ditch. The officers stopped to investigate. Long, the only occupant of the automobile, met the deputies at the rear of the car, which was protruding from the ditch onto the road. The door on the driver's side of the vehicle was left open.

Deputy Howell requested Long to produce his operator's license, but he did not respond. After the request was repeated, Long produced his license. Long again failed to respond when Howell requested him to produce the vehicle registration. After another repeated request, Long, whom Howell thought "appeared to be under the influence of something," turned from the officers and began walking toward the open door of the vehicle. The officers followed Long and both observed a large hunting knife on the floorboard of the driver's side of the car. The officers then stopped Long's progress and subjected him to a *Terry* protective pat-down, which revealed no weapons.

Long and Deputy Lewis then stood by the rear of the vehicle while Deputy Howell shined his flashlight into the interior of the vehicle, but did

---

[1] It is clear, and the respondent concedes, that if the officers had arrested Long for speeding or for driving while intoxicated, they could have searched the passenger compartment under *New York v. Belton*, and the trunk under *United States v. Ross*, if they had probable cause to believe that the trunk contained contraband. However, at oral argument, the State informed us that while Long could have been arrested for a speeding violation under Michigan law, he was *not* arrested because "[a]s a matter of practice," police in Michigan do not arrest for speeding violations unless "more" is involved. * * *

not actually enter it. The purpose of Howell's action was "to search for other weapons." The officer noticed that something was protruding from under the armrest on the front seat. He knelt in the vehicle and lifted the armrest. He saw an open pouch on the front seat, and upon flashing his light on the pouch, determined that it contained what appeared to be marijuana. After Deputy Howell showed the pouch and its contents to Deputy Lewis, Long was arrested for possession of marijuana. A further search of the interior of the vehicle, including the glovebox, revealed neither more contraband nor the vehicle registration. The officers decided to impound the vehicle. Deputy Howell opened the trunk, which did not have a lock, and discovered inside it approximately 75 pounds of marijuana.

The Barry County Circuit Court denied Long's motion to suppress the marijuana taken from both the interior of the car and its trunk. He was subsequently convicted of possession of marijuana. The Michigan Court of Appeals affirmed Long's conviction, holding that the search of the passenger compartment was valid as a protective search under *Terry*, and that the search of the trunk was valid as an inventory search. * * * The Michigan Supreme Court reversed. * * *

We granted certiorari in this case to consider the important question of the authority of a police officer to protect himself by conducting a *Terry*-type search of the passenger compartment of a motor vehicle during the lawful investigatory stop of the occupant of the vehicle. * * *

The court below held, and respondent Long contends, that Deputy Howell's entry into the vehicle cannot be justified under the principles set forth in *Terry* because "*Terry* authorized only a limited pat-down search of a *person* suspected of criminal activity" rather than a search of an area. Although *Terry* did involve the protective frisk of a person, we believe that the police action in this case is justified by the principles that we have already established in *Terry* and other cases. * * * Contrary to Long's view, *Terry* need not be read as restricting the preventative search to the person of the detained suspect.

* * * [W]e [have] recognized [in prior cases] that investigative detentions involving suspects in vehicles are especially fraught with danger to police officers. In *Pennsylvania v. Mimms*, we held that police may order persons out of an automobile during a stop for a traffic violation, and may frisk those persons for weapons if there is a reasonable belief that they are armed and dangerous. Our decision rested in part on the "inordinate risk confronting an officer as he approaches a person seated in an automobile."[a] * * *

---

[a] "The narrative that routine traffic stops are fraught with danger to the police is longstanding." Jordan Blair Woods, *Policing, Danger Narratives, and Routine Traffic Stops*, 117 MICH. L. REV. 635, 639 (2019). While any traffic stop can turn violent and end in an officer's death, violence against officers may not be as widespread as commonly assumed. According to an empirical study by Professor Woods that looked at thousands of traffic stops that resulted in

Our past cases indicate then that protection of police and others can justify protective searches when police have a reasonable belief that the suspect poses a danger, that roadside encounters between police and suspects are especially hazardous, and that danger may arise from the possible presence of weapons in the area surrounding a suspect. These principles compel our conclusion that the search of the passenger compartment of an automobile, limited to those areas in which a weapon may be placed or hidden, is permissible if the police officer possesses a reasonable belief based on "specific and articulable facts which, taken together with the rational inferences from those facts, reasonably warrant" the officers in believing that the suspect is dangerous and the suspect may gain immediate control of weapons. "[T]he issue is whether a reasonably prudent man in the circumstances would be warranted in the belief that his safety or that of others was in danger." If a suspect is "dangerous," he is no less dangerous simply because he is not arrested. If, while conducting a legitimate *Terry* search of the interior of the automobile, the officer should, as here, discover contraband other than weapons, he clearly cannot be required to ignore the contraband, and the Fourth Amendment does not require its suppression in such circumstances.

The circumstances of this case clearly justified Deputies Howell and Lewis in their reasonable belief that Long posed a danger if he were permitted to reenter his vehicle. The hour was late and the area rural. Long was driving his automobile at excessive speed, and his car swerved into a ditch. The officers had to repeat their questions to Long, who appeared to be "under the influence" of some intoxicant. Long was not frisked until the officers observed that there was a large knife in the interior of the car into which Long was about to reenter. The subsequent search of the car was restricted to those areas to which Long would generally have immediate control, and that could contain a weapon. The trial court determined that the leather pouch containing marijuana could have contained a weapon. It is clear that the intrusion was "strictly circumscribed by the exigencies which justifi[ed] its initiation."

In evaluating the validity of an officer's investigative or protective conduct under *Terry*, the "[t]ouchstone of our analysis . . . is always 'the reasonableness in all circumstances of the particular governmental intrusion of a citizen's personal security.'" In this case, the officers did not act unreasonably in taking preventive measures to ensure that there were no other weapons within Long's immediate grasp before permitting him to reenter his automobile. Therefore, the balancing required by *Terry* clearly weighs in favor of allowing the police to conduct an area search of the

---

violence against officers across more than 200 law enforcement agencies in Florida over a 10-year period, "the rate for a felonious killing of an officer during a routine traffic stop was 1 in every 6.5 million stops," "[t]he rate for an assault that results in serious injury to an officer was only 1 in every 361,111 stops," and "the rate for an assault (whether it results in officer injury or not) was 1 in every 6,959 stops." *Id.* at 683.

passenger compartment to uncover weapons, as long as they possess an articulable and objectively reasonable belief that the suspect is potentially dangerous.

The Michigan Supreme Court appeared to believe that it was not reasonable for the officers to fear that Long could injure them, because he was effectively under their control during the investigative stop and could not get access to any weapons that might have been located in the automobile. This reasoning is mistaken in several respects. During any investigative detention, the suspect is "in the control" of the officers in the sense that he "may be briefly detained against his will . . . ." Just as a *Terry* suspect on the street may, despite being under the brief control of a police officer, reach into his clothing and retrieve a weapon, so might a *Terry* suspect in Long's position break away from police control and retrieve a weapon from his automobile. * * *[16]

The trial court and the court of appeals upheld the search of the trunk as a valid inventory search. * * * Our holding that the initial search was justified under *Terry* makes it necessary to determine whether the trunk search was permissible under the Fourth Amendment. However, we decline to address this question because it was not passed upon by the Michigan Supreme Court, whose decision we review in this case. We remand this issue to the court below, to enable it to determine whether the trunk search was permissible. * * *

The decision of the Michigan Supreme Court is reversed, and the case is remanded for further proceedings not inconsistent with this opinion.

It is so ordered.

JUSTICE BRENNAN, with whom JUSTICE MARSHALL joins, dissenting. * * *

It is clear that *Terry* authorized only limited searches of the person for weapons. In light of what *Terry* said, relevant portions of which the Court neglects to quote, the Court's suggestion that "*Terry* need not be read as restricting the preventive search to the person of the detained suspect," can only be described as disingenuous. Nothing in *Terry* authorized police officers to search a suspect's car based on reasonable suspicion. * * *

The Court suggests no limit on the "area search" it now authorizes. The Court states that a "search of the passenger compartment of an automobile, limited to those areas in which a weapon may be placed or hidden, is permissible if the police officer possesses a reasonable belief based on 'specific and articulable facts which, taken together with the

---

[16] Long * * * argues that there cannot be a legitimate *Terry* search based on the discovery of the hunting knife because Long possessed that weapon legally. Assuming *arguendo* that Long possessed the knife lawfully, we have expressly rejected the view that the validity of a *Terry* search depends on whether the weapon is possessed in accordance with state law. * * *

rational inferences from those facts, reasonably warrant' the officers to believe that the suspect is dangerous and the suspect may gain immediate control of weapons." Presumably a weapon "may be placed or hidden" anywhere in a car. A weapon also might be hidden in a container in the car. In this case, the Court upholds the officer's search of a leather pouch because it "could have contained a weapon." In addition, the Court's requirement that an officer have a reasonable suspicion that a suspect is armed and dangerous does little to check the initiation of an area search. In this case, the officers saw a hunting knife in the car, but the Court does not base its holding that the subsequent search was permissible on the ground that possession of the knife may have been illegal under state law. An individual can lawfully possess many things that can be used as weapons. A hammer, or a baseball bat, can be used as a very effective weapon. Finally, the Court relies on the following facts to conclude that the officers had a reasonable suspicion that respondent was presently dangerous: the hour was late; the area was rural; respondent had been driving at an excessive speed; he had been involved in an accident; he was not immediately responsive to the officers' questions; and he appeared to be under the influence of some intoxicant. Based on these facts, one might reasonably conclude that respondent was drunk. A drunk driver is indeed dangerous while driving, but not while stopped on the roadside by the police. Even when an intoxicated person lawfully has in his car an object that could be used as a weapon, it requires imagination to conclude that he is presently dangerous. Even assuming that the facts in this case justified the officers' initial "frisk" of respondent, they hardly provide adequate justification for a search of a suspect's car and the containers within it. This represents an intrusion not just different in degree, but in kind, from the intrusion sanctioned by *Terry*. In short, the implications of the Court's decision are frightening. * * *

[JUSTICE STEVENS' dissenting opinion and JUSTICE BLACKMUN's concurring opinion have been omitted.]

CHAPTER 9

THE PLAIN VIEW DOCTRINE

■ ■ ■

Thus far, we have focused primarily on searches of property. We have studied how the Court decides what constitutes a search within the meaning of the Fourth Amendment and whether evidence obtained as the result of an unlawful search must be excluded as a constitutional matter. The Fourth Amendment, however, prohibits not only unreasonable searches, but also unreasonable seizures. A "seizure" of property occurs when there has been some meaningful interference by the government with an individual's possessory interests in the property in question. United States v. Jacobsen, 466 U.S. 109, 113 (1984).

Just as warrantless searches of property are presumed to be in violation of the Fourth Amendment unless an exception to the warrant requirement applies, seizures of property, at least when found in the home, are generally considered unreasonable if not supported by a warrant based upon probable cause. Under the plain view doctrine, however, police officers may search or seize items they see in plain view during the course of a lawful search even if they have not secured a warrant in advance for those items as long as they comply with certain requirements. In *Arizona v. Hicks*, the Court considers whether probable cause is one of those requirements. In *Minnesota v. Dickerson*, the Court decides whether to extend the plain view doctrine to cases involving the sense of touch.

ARIZONA V. HICKS
Supreme Court of the United States
480 U.S. 321, 107 S. Ct. 1149, 94 L. Ed. 2d 347 (1987)

JUSTICE SCALIA delivered the opinion of the Court.

In *Coolidge v. New Hampshire*, we said that in certain circumstances a warrantless seizure by police of an item that comes within plain view during their lawful search of a private area may be reasonable under the Fourth Amendment. We granted certiorari in the present case to decide whether this "plain view" doctrine may be invoked when the police have less than probable cause to believe that the item in question is evidence of a crime or is contraband.

On April 18, 1984, a bullet was fired through the floor of respondent's apartment, striking and injuring a man in the apartment below. Police officers arrived and entered respondent's apartment to search for the shooter, for other victims, and for weapons. They found and seized three weapons, including a sawed-off rifle, and in the course of their search also discovered a stocking-cap mask.

One of the policemen, Officer Nelson, noticed two sets of expensive stereo components, which seemed out of place in the squalid and otherwise ill-appointed four-room apartment. Suspecting that they were stolen, he read and recorded their serial numbers—moving some of the components, including a Bang and Olufsen turntable, in order to do so—which he then reported by phone to his headquarters. On being advised that the turntable had been taken in an armed robbery, he seized it immediately. It was later determined that some of the other serial numbers matched those on other stereo equipment taken in the same armed robbery, and a warrant was obtained and executed to seize that equipment as well. Respondent was subsequently indicted for the robbery.

The state trial court granted respondent's motion to suppress the evidence that had been seized. The Court of Appeals of Arizona affirmed. * * * The Arizona Supreme Court denied review, and the State filed this petition.

As an initial matter, the State argues that Officer Nelson's actions constituted neither a "search" nor a "seizure" within the meaning of the Fourth Amendment. We agree that the mere recording of the serial numbers did not constitute a seizure. * * * In and of itself, * * * it did not "meaningfully interfere" with respondent's possessory interest in either the serial numbers or the equipment, and therefore did not amount to a seizure.

Officer Nelson's moving of the equipment, however, did constitute a "search" separate and apart from the search for the shooter, victims, and weapons that was the lawful objective of his entry into the apartment. Merely inspecting those parts of the turntable that came into view during the latter search would not have constituted an independent search, because it would have produced no additional invasion of respondent's privacy interest. But taking action, unrelated to the objectives of the authorized intrusion, which exposed to view concealed portions of the apartment or its contents, did produce a new invasion of respondent's privacy unjustified by the exigent circumstance that validated the entry. This is why, contrary to Justice Powell's suggestion, the "distinction between 'looking' at a suspicious object in plain view and 'moving' it even a few inches" is much more than trivial for purposes of the Fourth Amendment. It matters not that the search uncovered nothing of any great personal value to respondent—serial numbers rather than (what might conceivably have been hidden behind or under the equipment) letters or photographs. A search is a search, even if it happens to disclose nothing but the bottom of a turntable.

The remaining question is whether the search was "reasonable" under the Fourth Amendment.

On this aspect of the case we reject, at the outset, the apparent position of the Arizona Court of Appeals that because the officers' action directed to the stereo equipment was unrelated to the justification for their entry into respondent's apartment, it was *ipso facto* unreasonable. That lack of relationship *always* exists with regard to action validated under the "plain view" doctrine; where action is taken for the purpose justifying the entry, invocation of the doctrine is superfluous. * * *

We turn, then, to application of the doctrine to the facts of this case. "It is well established that under certain circumstances the police may *seize* evidence in plain view without a warrant." Those circumstances include situations "[w]here the initial intrusion that brings the police within plain view of such [evidence] is supported . . . by one of the recognized exceptions to the warrant requirement," such as the exigent-circumstances intrusion here. It would be absurd to say that an object could lawfully be seized and taken from the premises, but could not be moved for closer examination. It is clear, therefore, that the search here was valid if the "plain view" doctrine would have sustained a seizure of the equipment.

There is no doubt it would have done so if Officer Nelson had probable cause to believe that the equipment was stolen. The State has conceded, however, that he had only a "reasonable suspicion," by which it means something less than probable cause. We have not ruled on the question whether probable cause is required in order to invoke the "plain view" doctrine. * * *

We now hold that probable cause is required. To say otherwise would be to cut the "plain view" doctrine loose from its theoretical and practical moorings. The theory of that doctrine consists of extending to nonpublic places such as the home, where searches and seizures without a warrant are presumptively unreasonable, the police's longstanding authority to make warrantless seizures in public places of such objects as weapons and contraband. And the practical justification for that extension is the desirability of sparing police, whose viewing of the object in the course of a lawful search is as legitimate as it would have been in a public place, the inconvenience and the risk—to themselves or to preservation of the evidence—of going to obtain a warrant. Dispensing with the need for a warrant is worlds apart from permitting a lesser standard of *cause* for the seizure than a warrant would require, *i.e.*, the standard of probable cause. No reason is apparent why an object should routinely be seizable on lesser grounds, during an unrelated search and seizure, than would have been needed to obtain a warrant for that same object if it had been known to be on the premises.

We do not say, of course, that a seizure can never be justified on less than probable cause. We have held that it can—where, for example, the seizure is minimally intrusive and operational necessities render it the only practicable means of detecting certain types of crime. No special operational necessities are relied on here, however—but rather the mere fact that the items in question came lawfully within the officer's plain view. That alone cannot supplant the requirement of probable cause. * * *

Justice O'Connor's dissent suggests that we uphold the action here on the ground that it was a "cursory inspection" rather than a "full-blown search," and could therefore be justified by reasonable suspicion instead of probable cause. As already noted, a truly cursory inspection—one that involves merely looking at what is already exposed to view, without disturbing it—is not a "search" for Fourth Amendment purposes, and therefore does not even require reasonable suspicion. We are unwilling to send police and judges into a new thicket of Fourth Amendment law, to seek a creature of uncertain description that is neither a "plain view" inspection nor yet a "full-blown search." Nothing in the prior opinions of this Court supports such a distinction. * * *

Justice Powell's dissent reasonably asks what it is we would have had Officer Nelson do in these circumstances. The answer depends, of course, upon whether he had probable cause to conduct a search, a question that was not preserved in this case. If he had, then he should have done precisely what he did. If not, then he should have followed up his suspicions, if possible, by means other than a search—just as he would have had to do if, while walking along the street, he had noticed the same suspicious stereo equipment sitting inside a house a few feet away from him, beneath an open window. It may well be that, in such circumstances, no effective means short of a search exist. But there is nothing new in the realization that the Constitution sometimes insulates the criminality of a few in order to protect the privacy of us all. Our disagreement with the dissenters pertains to where the proper balance should be struck; we choose to adhere to the textual and traditional standard of probable cause. * * *

For the reasons stated, the judgment of the Court of Appeals of Arizona is

Affirmed.

JUSTICE POWELL, with whom THE CHIEF JUSTICE and JUSTICE O'CONNOR join, dissenting. * * *

Today the Court holds for the first time that the requirement of probable cause operates as a separate limitation on the application of the plain-view doctrine. * * *

The officers' suspicion that the stereo components at issue were stolen was both reasonable and based on specific, articulable facts. Indeed, the State was unwise to concede the absence of probable cause. The police lawfully entered respondent's apartment under exigent circumstances that arose when a bullet fired through the floor of the apartment struck a man in the apartment below. What they saw in the apartment hardly suggested that it was occupied by law-abiding citizens. A .25-caliber automatic pistol lay in plain view on the living room floor. During a concededly lawful search, the officers found a .45-caliber automatic, a .22-caliber, sawed-off rifle, and a stocking-cap mask. The apartment was littered with drug paraphernalia. The officers also observed two sets of expensive stereo components of a type that frequently was stolen.

It is fair to ask what Officer Nelson should have done in these circumstances. Accepting the State's concession that he lacked probable cause, he could not have obtained a warrant to seize the stereo components. Neither could he have remained on the premises and forcibly prevented their removal. Officer Nelson's testimony indicates that he was able to read some of the serial numbers without moving the components.[3] To read the serial number on a Bang and Olufsen turntable, however, he had to "turn it around or turn it upside down." Officer Nelson noted the serial numbers on the stereo components and telephoned the National Crime Information Center to check them against the Center's computerized listing of stolen property. The computer confirmed his suspicion that at least the Bang and Olufsen turntable had been stolen. On the basis of this information, the officers obtained a warrant to seize the turntable and other stereo components that also proved to be stolen.

The Court holds that there was an unlawful search of the turntable. It agrees that the "mere recording of the serial numbers did not constitute a seizure." Thus, if the computer had identified as stolen property a component with a visible serial number, the evidence would have been admissible. But the Court further holds that "Officer Nelson's moving of the equipment ... did constitute a 'search'...." It perceives a constitutional distinction between reading a serial number on an object and moving or picking up an identical object to see its serial number. To make its position unmistakably clear, the Court concludes that a "search is a search, even if it happens to disclose nothing but the bottom of a turntable." With all respect, this distinction between "looking" at a suspicious object in plain view and "moving" it even a few inches trivializes the Fourth

---

[3] Officer Nelson testified that there was an opening of about a foot between the back of one set of stereo equipment and the wall. Presumably this opening was large enough to permit Officer Nelson to view serial numbers on the backs of the components without moving them.

Amendment.[4] The Court's new rule will cause uncertainty, and could deter conscientious police officers from lawfully obtaining evidence necessary to convict guilty persons. Apart from the importance of rationality in the interpretation of the Fourth Amendment, today's decision may handicap law enforcement without enhancing privacy interests. Accordingly, I dissent.

JUSTICE O'CONNOR, with whom THE CHIEF JUSTICE and JUSTICE POWELL join, dissenting.

The Court today gives the right answer to the wrong question. The Court asks whether the police must have probable cause before either seizing an object in plain view or conducting a full-blown search of that object, and concludes that they must. I agree. In my view, however, this case presents a different question: whether police must have probable cause before conducting a cursory inspection of an item in plain view. Because I conclude that such an inspection is reasonable if the police are aware of facts or circumstances that justify a reasonable suspicion that the item is evidence of a crime, I would reverse the judgment of the Arizona Court of Appeals, and therefore dissent.

In *Coolidge v. New Hampshire*, Justice Stewart summarized three requirements that the plurality thought must be satisfied for a plain-view search or seizure. First, the police must lawfully make an initial intrusion or otherwise be in a position from which they can view a particular area. Second, the officer must discover incriminating evidence "inadvertently."[a] Third, it must be "immediately apparent" to the police that the items they observe may be evidence of a crime, contraband, or otherwise subject to seizure. As another plurality observed in *Texas v. Brown,* these three requirements have never been expressly adopted by a majority of this Court, but "as the considered opinion of four Members of this Court [the *Coolidge* plurality] should obviously be the point of reference for further discussion of the issue." There is no dispute in this case that the first two requirements have been satisfied. The officers were lawfully in the apartment pursuant to exigent circumstances, and the discovery of the stereo was inadvertent—the officers did not " 'know in advance the location of [certain] evidence and intend to seize it,' relying on the plain-view

---

[4] Numerous articles that frequently are stolen have identifying numbers, including expensive watches and cameras, and also credit cards. Assume for example that an officer reasonably suspects that two identical watches, both in plain view, have been stolen. Under the Court's decision, if one watch is lying face up and the other lying face down, reading the serial number on one of the watches would not be a search. But turning over the other watch to read its serial number would be a search. Moreover, the officer's ability to read a serial number may depend on its location in a room and light conditions at a particular time. Would there be a constitutional difference if an officer, on the basis of a reasonable suspicion, used a pocket flashlight or turned on a light to read a number rather than moving the object to a point where a serial number was clearly visible?

[a] In a subsequent case, the Court held that inadvertent discovery is not a necessary condition for a plain view seizure. *Horton v. California*, 496 U.S. 128 (1990).

doctrine only as a pretext." Instead, the dispute in this case focuses on the application of the "immediately apparent" requirement; at issue is whether a police officer's reasonable suspicion is adequate to justify a cursory examination of an item in plain view.

The purpose of the "immediately apparent" requirement is to prevent "general, exploratory rummaging in a person's belongings." If an officer could indiscriminately search every item in plain view, a search justified by a limited purpose—such as exigent circumstances—could be used to eviscerate the protections of the Fourth Amendment. In order to prevent such a general search, therefore, we require that the relevance of the item be "immediately apparent." As Justice Stewart explained: "Of course, the extension of the original justification [for being present] is legitimate only where it is immediately apparent to the police that they have evidence before them; the 'plain view' doctrine may not be used to extend a general exploratory search from one object to another until something incriminating at last emerges."

Thus, I agree with the Court that even under the plain-view doctrine, probable cause is required before the police seize an item, or conduct a full-blown search of evidence in plain view. Such a requirement of probable cause will prevent the plain-view doctrine from authorizing general searches. This is not to say, however, that even a mere inspection of a suspicious item must be supported by probable cause. When a police officer makes a cursory inspection of a suspicious item in plain view in order to determine whether it is indeed evidence of a crime, there is no "exploratory rummaging." Only those items that the police officer "reasonably suspects" as evidence of a crime may be inspected, and perhaps more importantly, the scope of such an inspection is quite limited. In short, if police officers have a reasonable, articulable suspicion that an object they come across during the course of a lawful search is evidence of crime, in my view they may make a cursory examination of the object to verify their suspicion. If the officers wish to go beyond such a cursory examination of the object, however, they must have probable cause.

*** [T]he overwhelming majority of both state and federal courts have held that probable cause is not required for a minimal inspection of an item in plain view. As Professor LaFave summarizes the view of these courts, "the minimal additional intrusion which results from an inspection or examination of an object in plain view is reasonable if the officer was first aware of some facts and circumstances which justify a reasonable suspicion (not probable cause, in the traditional sense) that the object is or contains a fruit, instrumentality, or evidence of crime." Thus, while courts require probable cause for more extensive examination, cursory inspections—including picking up or moving objects for a better view—require only a reasonable suspicion.

Indeed, several state courts have applied a reasonable-suspicion standard in factual circumstances almost identical to this case.

This distinction between searches based on their relative intrusiveness—and its subsequent adoption by a consensus of American courts—is entirely consistent with our Fourth Amendment jurisprudence. We have long recognized that searches can vary in intrusiveness, and that some brief searches "may be so minimally intrusive of Fourth Amendment interests that strong countervailing governmental interests will justify a [search] based only on specific articulable facts" that the item in question is contraband or evidence of a crime. * * *

In my view, the balance of the governmental and privacy interests strongly supports a reasonable-suspicion standard for the cursory examination of items in plain view. The additional intrusion caused by an inspection of an item in plain view for its serial number is miniscule. Indeed, the intrusion in this case was even more transitory and less intrusive than the seizure of luggage from a suspected drug dealer in *United States v. Place, supra,* and the "severe, though brief, intrusion upon cherished personal security" in *Terry v. Ohio.*

Weighed against this minimal additional invasion of privacy are rather major gains in law enforcement. The use of identification numbers in tracing stolen property is a powerful law enforcement tool. Serial numbers are far more helpful and accurate in detecting stolen property than simple police recollection of the evidence. Given the prevalence of mass produced goods in our national economy, a serial number is often the only sure method of detecting stolen property. The balance of governmental and private interests strongly supports the view accepted by a majority of courts that a standard of reasonable suspicion meets the requirements of the Fourth Amendment. * * *

Even if probable cause were the appropriate standard, I have little doubt that it was satisfied here. When police officers, during the course of a search inquiring into grievously unlawful activity, discover the tools of a thief (a sawed-off rifle and a stocking mask) and observe in a small apartment *two* sets of stereo equipment that are both inordinately expensive in relation to their surroundings and known to be favored targets of larcenous activity, the "flexible, common-sense standard" of probable cause has been satisfied.

Because the Court today ignores the existence of probable cause, and in doing so upsets a widely accepted body of precedent on the standard of reasonableness for the cursory examination of evidence in plain view, I respectfully dissent.

[JUSTICE WHITE's concurring opinion has been omitted.]

MINNESOTA V. DICKERSON
Supreme Court of the United States
508 U.S. 366, 113 S. Ct. 2130, 124 L. Ed. 2d 334 (1993)

JUSTICE WHITE delivered the opinion of the Court.

In this case, we consider whether the Fourth Amendment permits the seizure of contraband detected through a police officer's sense of touch during a protective patdown search.

On the evening of November 9, 1989, two Minneapolis police officers were patrolling an area on the city's north side in a marked squad car. At about 8:15 p.m., one of the officers observed respondent leaving a 12-unit apartment building on Morgan Avenue North. The officer, having previously responded to complaints of drug sales in the building's hallways and having executed several search warrants on the premises, considered the building to be a notorious "crack house." According to testimony credited by the trial court, respondent began walking toward the police but, upon spotting the squad car and making eye contact with one of the officers, abruptly halted and began walking in the opposite direction. His suspicion aroused, this officer watched as respondent turned and entered an alley on the other side of the apartment building. Based upon respondent's seemingly evasive actions and the fact that he had just left a building known for cocaine traffic, the officers decided to stop respondent and investigate further.

The officers pulled their squad car into the alley and ordered respondent to stop and submit to a patdown search. The search revealed no weapons, but the officer conducting the search did take an interest in a small lump in respondent's nylon jacket. The officer later testified: "[A]s I pat-searched the front of his body, I felt a lump, a small lump, in the front pocket. I examined it with my fingers and it slid and it felt to be a lump of crack cocaine in cellophane."

The officer then reached into respondent's pocket and retrieved a small plastic bag containing one fifth of one gram of crack cocaine. Respondent was arrested and charged in Hennepin County District Court with possession of a controlled substance.

Before trial, respondent moved to suppress the cocaine. The trial court first concluded that the officers were justified under *Terry v. Ohio* in stopping respondent to investigate whether he might be engaged in criminal activity. The court further found that the officers were justified in frisking respondent to ensure that he was not carrying a weapon. Finally, analogizing to the "plain view" doctrine, under which officers may make a warrantless seizure of contraband found in plain view during a lawful search for other items, the trial court ruled that the officers' seizure of the cocaine did not violate the Fourth Amendment:

To this Court there is no distinction as to which sensory perception the officer uses to conclude that the material is contraband. An experienced officer may rely upon his sense of smell in DWI stops or in recognizing the smell of burning marijuana in an automobile. The sound of a shotgun being racked would clearly support certain reactions by an officer. The sense of touch, grounded in experience and training, is as reliable as perceptions drawn from other senses. "Plain feel," therefore, is no different than plain view and will equally support the seizure here.

His suppression motion having failed, respondent proceeded to trial and was found guilty.

On appeal, the Minnesota Court of Appeals reversed. The court agreed with the trial court that the investigative stop and protective patdown search of respondent were lawful under *Terry* because the officers had a reasonable belief based on specific and articulable facts that respondent was engaged in criminal behavior and that he might be armed and dangerous. The court concluded, however, that the officers had overstepped the bounds allowed by *Terry* in seizing the cocaine. In doing so, the Court of Appeals "decline[d] to adopt the plain feel exception" to the warrant requirement.

The Minnesota Supreme Court affirmed. * * * We granted certiorari to resolve a conflict among the state and federal courts over whether contraband detected through the sense of touch during a patdown search may be admitted into evidence. * * *

The Fourth Amendment, made applicable to the States by way of the Fourteenth Amendment, guarantees "[t]he right of the people to be secure in their persons, houses, papers, and effects, against unreasonable searches and seizures." Time and again, this Court has observed that searches and seizures "conducted outside the judicial process, without prior approval by judge or magistrate, are *per se* unreasonable under the Fourth Amendment—subject only to a few specifically established and well delineated exceptions." One such exception was recognized in *Terry v. Ohio*, which held that "where a police officer observes unusual conduct which leads him reasonably to conclude in light of his experience that criminal activity may be afoot . . . ," the officer may briefly stop the suspicious person and make "reasonable inquiries" aimed at confirming or dispelling his suspicions.

Terry further held that "[w]hen an officer is justified in believing that the individual whose suspicious behavior he is investigating at close range is armed and presently dangerous to the officer or to others," the officer may conduct a patdown search "to determine whether the person is in fact carrying a weapon." "The purpose of this limited search is not to discover evidence of crime, but to allow the officer to pursue his investigation without fear of violence...." Rather, a protective search—permitted without a warrant and on the basis of reasonable suspicion less than probable cause—must be strictly "limited to that which is necessary for the discovery of weapons which might be used to harm the officer or others nearby." If the protective search goes beyond what is necessary to determine if the suspect is armed, it is no longer valid under *Terry* and its fruits will be suppressed.

These principles were settled 25 years ago. * * * The question presented today is whether police officers may seize nonthreatening contraband detected during a protective patdown search of the sort permitted by *Terry*. We think the answer is clearly that they may, so long as the officers' search stays within the bounds marked by *Terry*.

We have already held that police officers, at least under certain circumstances, may seize contraband detected during the lawful execution of a *Terry* search. In *Michigan v. Long*, for example, police approached a man who had driven his car into a ditch and who appeared to be under the influence of some intoxicant. As the man moved to reenter the car from the roadside, police spotted a knife on the floorboard. The officers stopped the man, subjected him to a patdown search, and then inspected the interior of the vehicle for other weapons. During the search of the passenger compartment, the police discovered an open pouch containing marijuana and seized it. This Court upheld the validity of the search and seizure under *Terry*. The Court held first that, in the context of a roadside encounter, where police have reasonable suspicion based on specific and articulable facts to believe that a driver may be armed and dangerous, they may conduct a protective search for weapons not only of the driver's person but also of the passenger compartment of the automobile. Of course, the protective search of the vehicle, being justified solely by the danger that weapons stored there could be used against the officers or bystanders, must be "limited to those areas in which a weapon may be placed or hidden." The Court then held: "If, while conducting a legitimate *Terry* search of the interior of the automobile, the officer should, as here, discover contraband other than weapons, he clearly cannot be required to ignore the contraband, and the Fourth Amendment does not require its suppression in such circumstances."

The Court in *Long* justified this latter holding by reference to our cases under the "plain view" doctrine. Under that doctrine, if police are lawfully in a position from which they view an object, if its incriminating character is immediately apparent, and if the officers have a lawful right of access to the object, they may seize it without a warrant. If, however, the police lack probable cause to believe that an object in plain view is contraband without conducting some further search of the object—*i.e.*, if "its incriminating character [is not] 'immediately apparent,' " the plain view doctrine cannot justify its seizure.

We think that this doctrine has an obvious application by analogy to cases in which an officer discovers contraband through the sense of touch during an otherwise lawful search. The rationale of the plain view doctrine is that if contraband is left in open view and is observed by a police officer from a lawful vantage point, there has been no invasion of a legitimate expectation of privacy and thus no "search" within the meaning of the Fourth Amendment—or at least no search independent of the initial intrusion that gave the officers their vantage point. The warrantless seizure of contraband that presents itself in this manner is deemed justified by the realization that resort to a neutral magistrate under such circumstances would often be impracticable and would do little to promote the objectives of the Fourth Amendment. The same can be said of tactile discoveries of contraband. If a police officer lawfully pats down a suspect's outer clothing and feels an object whose contour or mass makes its identity immediately apparent, there has been no invasion of the suspect's privacy beyond that already authorized by the officer's search for weapons; if the object is contraband, its warrantless seizure would be justified by the same practical considerations that inhere in the plain view context.

The Minnesota Supreme Court rejected an analogy to the plain view doctrine on two grounds: first, its belief that "the sense of touch is inherently less immediate and less reliable than the sense of sight," and second, that "the sense of touch is far more intrusive into the personal privacy that is at the core of the [F]ourth [A]mendment." We have a somewhat different view. First, *Terry* itself demonstrates that the sense of touch is capable of revealing the nature of an object with sufficient reliability to support a seizure. The very premise of *Terry*, after all, is that officers will be able to detect the presence of weapons through the sense of touch and *Terry* upheld precisely such a seizure. Even if it were true that the sense of touch is generally less reliable than the sense of sight, that only suggests that officers will less often be able to justify seizures of unseen contraband. Regardless of whether the officer detects the contraband by sight or by touch, however, the Fourth Amendment's requirement that the officer have probable cause to believe that the item is contraband before seizing it ensures against excessively speculative seizures. The court's second concern—that touch is more intrusive into privacy than is sight—is inapposite in light of the fact that the intrusion the court fears has already been authorized by the lawful search for weapons. The seizure of an item whose identity is already known occasions no further invasion of privacy. Accordingly, the suspect's privacy interests are not advanced by a categorical rule barring the seizure of contraband plainly detected through the sense of touch.

It remains to apply these principles to the facts of this case. Respondent has not challenged the finding made by the trial court and affirmed by both the Court of Appeals and the State Supreme Court that the police were justified under *Terry* in stopping him and frisking him for weapons. Thus, the dispositive question before this Court is whether the officer who conducted the search was acting within the lawful bounds marked by *Terry* at the time he gained probable cause to believe that the lump in respondent's jacket was contraband. * * * The Minnesota Supreme Court, after "a close examination of the record," held that the officer's own testimony "belies any notion that he 'immediately' " recognized the lump as crack cocaine. Rather, the court concluded, the officer determined that the lump was contraband only after "squeezing, sliding and otherwise manipulating the contents of the defendant's pocket"—a pocket which the officer already knew contained no weapon.

Under the State Supreme Court's interpretation of the record before it, it is clear that the court was correct in holding that the police officer in this case overstepped the bounds of the "strictly circumscribed" search for weapons allowed under *Terry*. Where, as here, "an officer who is executing a valid search for one item seizes a different item," this Court rightly "has been sensitive to the danger . . . that officers will enlarge a specific authorization, furnished by a warrant or an exigency, into the equivalent of a general warrant to rummage and seize at will." Here, the officer's continued exploration of respondent's pocket after having concluded that it contained no weapon was unrelated to "[t]he sole justification of the search [under *Terry*:] . . . the protection of the police officer and others nearby." It therefore amounted to the sort of evidentiary search that *Terry* expressly refused to authorize, and that we have condemned in subsequent cases.

Once again, the analogy to the plain view doctrine is apt. In *Arizona v. Hicks*, this Court held invalid the seizure of stolen stereo equipment found by police while executing a valid search for other evidence. Although the police were lawfully on the premises, they obtained probable cause to believe that the stereo equipment was contraband only after moving the equipment to permit officers to read its serial numbers. The subsequent seizure of the equipment could not be justified by the plain view doctrine, this Court explained, because the incriminating character of the stereo equipment was not immediately apparent; rather, probable cause to believe that the equipment was stolen arose only as a result of a further search—the moving of the equipment—that was not authorized by a search warrant or by any exception to the warrant requirement. The facts of this case are very similar. Although the officer was lawfully in a position to feel the lump in respondent's pocket, because *Terry* entitled him to place his hands upon respondent's jacket, the court below determined that the incriminating character of the object was not immediately apparent to him. Rather, the officer determined that the item was contraband only after conducting a further search, one not authorized by *Terry* or by any other exception to the warrant requirement. Because this further search of respondent's pocket was constitutionally invalid, the seizure of the cocaine that followed is likewise unconstitutional.

For these reasons, the judgment of the Minnesota Supreme Court is

Affirmed.

[CHIEF JUSTICE REHNQUIST's opinion, concurring in part and dissenting in part, and JUSTICE SCALIA's concurring opinion have been omitted.]

CHAPTER 10

RACIAL PROFILING

■ ■ ■

This chapter focuses on racial and other kinds of profiling. To set the scene, the chapter starts with an excerpt from *(E)racing the Fourth Amendment*. In this excerpt, Devon Carbado, a law professor at UCLA School of Law, writes about two unnerving encounters he had with the police when he was new to the United States.

The first case in the chapter, *United States v. Brignoni-Ponce*, is often read as an opinion that reflects the Court's sensitivity to the difficulty of balancing law enforcement needs against the harm to individuals who may be suspected of criminal activity because of their race or ethnicity. The two excerpts that follow take a less charitable view of the opinion. In *La Migra in the Mirror: Immigration Enforcement and Racial Profiling on the Texas Border*, César Cuauhtémoc García Hernández argues that while appearing to be sensitive to the problem of racial profiling, the *Brignoni-Ponce* Court in fact endorses racial profiling in the immigration context. In *The Case against Race Profiling in Immigration Enforcement*, Kevin Johnson points out how the opinion reinforces negative stereotypes about individuals of Mexican ancestry and other Latinos.

In *Whren v. United States*, the Court considers whether the Fourth Amendment is violated if a police officer stops an individual for a traffic violation he has observed but otherwise lacks either probable cause to arrest or reasonable suspicion of criminal activity, which is the minimum required to temporarily detain an individual. In *"Driving While Black" and All Other Traffic Offenses: The Supreme Court and Pretextual Traffic Stops*, David Harris critiques the *Whren* decision, arguing that it gives police officers cover to engage in racial profiling of Blacks and Latinos, a practice commonly called "Driving While Black" or "Driving While Brown." In *"Walking While Black": Encounters with the Police on My Street*, law professor Paul Butler writes about the experience of being followed and questioned by police who thought he was a burglary suspect when he was walking home from work one evening.

The last two excerpts examine profiling in other contexts. In *Gendered (In)security: Immigration and Criminalization in the Security State*, Pooja Gehi writes about "Walking While Trans," shorthand for the notion that transgender people are often profiled as prostitutes. In *Profiling Terror*,

Sharon Davies condemns the post-9/11 profiling of dark-skinned individuals perceived to be Arab or from the Middle East as terrorists.

(E)RACING THE FOURTH AMENDMENT
Devon W. Carbado
100 Mich. L. Rev. 946 (2002)

It's been almost two years since I pledged allegiance to the United States of America—that is to say, became an American citizen. Before that, I was a permanent resident of America and a citizen of the United Kingdom.

Yet, I became a black American long before I acquired American citizenship. Unlike citizenship, black racial naturalization was always available to me, even as I tried to make myself unavailable for that particular Americanization process. Given the negative images of black Americans on 1970s British television and the intra-racial tensions between blacks in the U.K. and blacks in America, I was not eager, upon my arrival to the United States, to assert a black American identity. * * *

But I became a black American anyway. Before I freely embraced that identity it was ascribed to me. * * * I was closely followed or completely ignored when I visited department stores. Women clutched their purses upon encountering me in elevators. People crossed the street to avoid me. The seat beside me on the bus was almost always racially available for another black person. Already I wanted to be a black American no more. * * *

Like many black Americans, I developed the ability to cope with, manage, and sometimes even normalize certain micro-aggressive racial encounters. * * *

I have not, however, been able to normalize my experiences with the police. They continue to jar me. The very sight of the police in my rear view mirror is unnerving. Far from comforting, this sight of justice (the paradigmatic site for injustice) engenders feelings of vulnerability: How will I be over-policed this time? Do I have my driver's license, insurance, etc.? How am I dressed? * * * How will I make the officers comfortable? * * * Will they perceive me to be a good or a bad black?

These questions are part of black people's collective consciousness. They are symptomatic of a particular colorline anxiety: a police state of mind. This racial dis-ease is inflicted on black people ostensibly to cure the problem of crime. Its social effect, however, is to make * * * black people feel bad about, and uncomfortable with, being black.

My first racial episode with over-policing occurred only two weeks after I purchased my first car: a $1500 yellow, convertible Triumph Spit Fire. I had been living in America for a year; my brother had been in the States for under a month. It was about nine p.m., and we were on our way to a friend's house.

Our trip was interrupted by the blare of a siren. We were in Inglewood, a predominantly black neighborhood south of Los Angeles; a police car had signaled us to pull over. One officer approached my window; the other stationed himself beside the passenger door. He directed his flashlight into the interior of the car, locating its beam, alternatively, on our faces. The characters: two black boys. The racial stage was set.

"Anything wrong, officers?" I asked, attempting to discern the face behind the flashlight. Neither officer responded. Against my racial script, I inquired again as to whether we had done anything wrong. Again, no response. Instead, one of the officers instructed, "Step outside the car with your hands on your heads." Effectively rehearsing our blackness, we did as he asked. He then told us to sit on the side of the curb. Grudgingly, we complied. Though we were both learning our parts, the racial theater was well underway.

As we sat on the pavement, "racially exposed," our backs to the officers, our feet in the road, I asked a third time whether we had done anything wrong. One officer responded, rather curtly, that I should "shut up and not make any trouble." Perhaps foolishly, I insisted on knowing why we were being stopped. "We have a right to know, don't we? We're not criminals, after all."

Today I might have acted differently, less defiantly. But my strange career with race, at least in America, had only just begun. In other words, I had not yet lived in America long enough to learn the ways of the police, the racial conventions of black and white police encounters, the so-called rules of the game: "Don't move. Don't turn around. Don't give some rookie an excuse to shoot you." No one had explained to me that "if you get pulled over by the police never get into a verbal confrontation . . . Never! Comply with the officer. If it means getting down on the ground, then get down on the ground. Comply with *whatever* the officer is asking you to do." It had not occurred to me that my encounter with these officers was potentially life threatening. This was one of my many racial blind spots. Eventually, I would develop my second sight.

The officer discerned that I was not American. Presumably, my accent provided the clue, although my lack of racial etiquette—mouthing off to white police officers in a "high-crime" area in the middle of the night—might have suggested that I was an outsider to the racial dynamics of police encounters. My assertion of my rights, my attempts to maintain my dignity, my confronting authority (each a function of my pre-invisibility blackness) might have signaled that I was not from here and, more importantly, that I had not been racially socialized into, or internalized the racial survival strategy of, performing obedience for the police. From the officer's perspective, we were, in that moment, defiant ones.

The officer looked at my brother and me, seemingly puzzled. He needed more information racially to process us, to make sense of what he might have experienced as a moment of racial incongruity. While there was no disjuncture between how we looked and the phenotypic cues for black identity, our performance of blackness could have created a racial indeterminacy problem that had to be fixed. That is, to the extent that the officers harbored an a priori investment in our blackness (that we were criminals or thugs), our English accents might have challenged it. * * *

"Where are you guys from?"

"The U.K.," my brother responded.

"The what?"

"England."

"England?"

"Yes, England."

"You were born in England?"

"Yes."

"What part?"

"Birmingham."

"Uhmm. . . ." We were strange fruit. Our racial identity had to be grounded.

"Where are your parents from?"

"The West Indies."

We were at last racially intelligible. Our English identity had been dislocated, falsified—or at least buried among our diasporic roots.

"How long has he been in America?" the officer wanted to know, pointing at me.

"About a year," my brother responded.

"Well, tell him that if he doesn't want to find himself in jail, he should shut the fuck up."

The history of racial violence in his words existentially moved us. We were now squarely within a sub-region of the borders of American Blackness. Our rite of passage was almost complete.

My brother nudged me several times with his elbows. "Cool it," he muttered under his breath. The intense look in his eyes inflected his words. "Don't provoke them."

By this time, my brother needn't have said anything. I was beginning to see the white over black racial picture. We had the right to do whatever they wanted us to do, a reasonable expectation of uncertainty. With that awareness, I simply sat there. Quietly. My brother did the same. We were in a racial state of rightlessness, effectively outside the reach of the Fourth Amendment. The experience, in other words, was disciplinary. Although I didn't know it at the time, we were one step closer to becoming black Americans. * * *

Without our consent, one of the officers rummaged through the entire car—no doubt in search of ex post probable cause; the other watched over us. The search yielded nothing. (No drugs.) (No stolen property.) (No weapons.) Ostensibly, we were free to leave.

But what if the search had resulted in the production of incriminating evidence? That is, what if the officers' racial suspicions were confirmed? Would that have rendered their conduct legitimate? Would they thereby become "good" cops? Would that have made us "bad" blacks—blacks who confirm negative stereotypes, blacks who are undeserving of public sympathy, blacks who discredit the race? * * *

The officers requested that we stand up, which we did. * * * [T]hey forced us against the side of the patrol car. Spread-eagled, they frisked and searched us. (Still no guns.) (Still no drugs.) (Still no stolen property.)

The entire incident lasted approximately twenty minutes. Neither officer provided us with an explanation as to why we were stopped. Nor did either officer apologize. * * * The encounter ended when one of the officers muttered through the back of his head, "You're free to go."

"Pardon?"

"I said you can go now."

And that was that. * * * I wanted to say something like, "Are you absolutely certain, Officer? We really don't mind the intrusion, Officer. Do carry on with the search. Honest." But the burden of blackness in that moment rendered those thoughts unspeakable. Thus, I simply watched in silence as they left.

The encounter left us more racially aware and less racially intact. In other words, we were growing into our American profile. Still, the officers did not physically abuse us, we did not "kiss concrete," and we managed to escape jail. Relative to some black and Blue encounters, and considering my initial racial faux pas—questioning authority/asserting rights—we got off easy.

Subsequent to that experience, I have had several other incidents with the police. In this respect, and like many black people, I am a repeat player. * * * I shall recount only one more here. * * *

Two of my brothers and my brother-in-law had just arrived from England. On our way from the airport, we stopped at my sister's apartment, which was in a predominantly white neighborhood. After letting us in, my sister left to perform errands. It was about two o'clock in the afternoon; my brothers wanted some tea. I showed one of them to the kitchen. After about five minutes, we heard the kettle whistling. "Get the kettle, will you." There was no answer. My other brother went to see what was going on. Finally the kettle stopped whistling, but he never returned. My brother-in-law and I were convinced that my brothers were engaged in some sort of prank. "What are they doing in there?" Together, we went into the kitchen. At the door were two police officers. Guns drawn, they instructed us to exit the apartment. With our hands in the air, we did so.

Outside, both of my brothers were pinned against the wall at gunpoint. There were eight officers. Each was visibly edgy, nervous and apprehensive. * * * The racial product was a familiar public spectacle: white law enforcement officers disciplining black men. * * *

The officers wanted to know whether there was anyone else inside. We answered in the negative. "What's going on?" my brother-in-law inquired. The officer responded that they had received a call from a neighbor reporting that several black men had entered an apartment with guns. "Rubbish, we're just coming in from the airport."

"Do you have any drugs?"

"Of course not. Look, this is a mistake." The officers did not believe us. * * * The body of evidence—that is to say, our race—was uncontestable. * * *

"May we look inside the apartment?"

"Sure," my brother in-law "consented." "Whatever it takes to get this over."

Two officers entered the apartment. After about two minutes, they came out shaking their heads, presumably signaling that they were not at a crime scene. In fact, we were not criminals. Based on "bad" information— but information that was presumed to be good—they had made an "error." "Sometimes these things happen." At least, they were willing to apologize.

"Look, we're really sorry about this, but when we get a call that there are [black] men with guns, we take it quite seriously. Again, we really are sorry for the inconvenience." With that apology, the officers departed. Our privacy had been invaded, we experienced a loss of dignity, and our blackness had been established—once more—as a crime of identity. But * * * the police were simply doing their job: acting on racial intelligence. And we were simply shouldering our racial burden: disconfirming the assumption that we were criminals. No one was really injured. Presumably, the neighbors felt a little safer.

My eyes followed each officer into his car. As they drove off, one of them turned his head to witness the after-spectacle: the four of us (racially) traumatized in the gunned-down position they had left us. Our eyes met for a couple of seconds, and then he looked away. It was over. * * * Another day in the life, for the police and for us.

Simple injustice.

We went inside, drank our tea, and didn't much talk about what had transpired. Perhaps we didn't know how to talk about it. Perhaps we were too shocked. Perhaps we wanted to put the incident behind us—to move on, to start forgetting. Perhaps we needed time to recover our dignity, to repossess our bodies. * * *

We relayed the incident to my sister. She was furious. "Bloody bastards!" She lodged a complaint with the Beverly Hills Police Department. She called the local paper. She contacted the NAACP. "No, nobody was shot." "No, they were not physically abused." "Yes, I suppose everyone is alright."

Of course, nothing became of her complaints. After all, the police were "protecting and serving." We, like other blacks in America, were the unfortunate but necessary casualties of the war against crime.

UNITED STATES V. BRIGNONI-PONCE
Supreme Court of the United States
422 U.S. 873, 95 S. Ct. 2574, 45 L. Ed. 2d 607 (1975)

JUSTICE POWELL delivered the opinion of the Court.

As a part of its regular traffic-checking operations in southern California, the Border Patrol operates a fixed checkpoint on Interstate Highway 5 south of San Clemente. On the evening of March 11, 1973, the checkpoint was closed because of inclement weather, but two officers were observing northbound traffic from a patrol car parked at the side of the highway. The road was dark, and they were using the patrol car's headlights to illuminate passing cars. They pursued respondent's car and stopped it, saying later that their only reason for doing so was that its three occupants appeared to be of Mexican descent. The officers questioned respondent and his two passengers about their citizenship and learned that the passengers were aliens who had entered the country illegally. All three were then arrested, and respondent was charged with two counts of knowingly transporting illegal immigrants. * * * At trial respondent moved to suppress the testimony of and about the two passengers, claiming that this evidence was the fruit of an illegal seizure. The trial court denied the motion, the aliens testified at trial, and respondent was convicted on both counts.

*** [T]he Court of Appeals for the Ninth Circuit *** held that the Fourth Amendment *** forbids stopping a vehicle, even for the limited purpose of questioning its occupants, unless the officers have a "founded suspicion" that the occupants are aliens illegally in the country. The court refused to find that Mexican ancestry alone supported such a "founded suspicion" and held that respondent's motion to suppress should have been granted. We granted certiorari.

*** The only issue presented for decision is whether a roving patrol may stop a vehicle in an area near the border and question its occupants when the only ground for suspicion is that the occupants appear to be of Mexican ancestry.[a] For the reasons that follow, we affirm the decision of the Court of Appeals. ***

The Fourth Amendment applies to all seizures of the person, including seizures that involve only a brief detention short of traditional arrest. "[W]henever a police officer accosts an individual and restrains his freedom to walk away, he has 'seized' that person," and the Fourth Amendment requires that the seizure be "reasonable." As with other categories of police action subject to Fourth Amendment constraints, the reasonableness of such seizures depends on a balance between the public interest and the individual's right to personal security free from arbitrary interference by law officers.

The Government makes a convincing demonstration that the public interest demands effective measures to prevent the illegal entry of aliens at the Mexican border. Estimates of the number of illegal immigrants in the United States vary widely. A conservative estimate in 1972 produced a figure of about one million, but the INS now suggests there may be as many as 10 or 12 million aliens illegally in the country. Whatever the number, these aliens create significant economic and social problems, competing with citizens and legal resident aliens for jobs, and generating extra demand for social services. The aliens themselves are vulnerable to exploitation because they cannot complain of substandard working conditions without risking deportation.

The Government has estimated that 85% of the aliens illegally in the country are from Mexico. The Mexican border is almost 2,000 miles long, and even a vastly reinforced Border Patrol would find it impossible to prevent illegal border crossings. Many aliens cross the Mexican border on foot, miles away from patrolled areas, and then purchase transportation from the border area to inland cities, where they find jobs and elude the immigration authorities. Others gain entry on valid temporary border-crossing permits, but then violate the conditions of their entry. Most of

---

[a] Felix Humberto Brignoni-Ponce was actually a U.S. citizen of Puerto Rican (not Mexican) descent. Kevin R. Johnson, *How Racial Profiling in America Became the Law of the Land:* United States v. Brignoni-Ponce *and* Whren v. United States *and the Need for Truly Rebellious Lawyering*, 98 GEO. L.J. 1005, 1012 (2010).

these aliens leave the border area in private vehicles, often assisted by professional "alien smugglers." The Border Patrol's traffic-checking operations are designed to prevent this inland movement. They succeed in apprehending some illegal entrants and smugglers, and they deter the movement of others by threatening apprehension and increasing the cost of illegal transportation. [Public Interest = stemming illegal alien smuggling]

Against this valid public interest we must weigh the interference with individual liberty that results when an officer stops an automobile and questions its occupants. The intrusion is modest. The Government tells us that a stop by a roving patrol "usually consumes no more than a minute." There is no search of the vehicle or its occupants, and the visual inspection is limited to those parts of the vehicle that can be seen by anyone standing alongside. According to the Government, "[a]ll that is required of the vehicle's occupants is a response to a brief question or two and possibly the production of a document evidencing a right to be in the United States."

* * * [I]n appropriate circumstances the Fourth Amendment allows a properly limited "search" or "seizure" on facts that do not constitute probable cause to arrest or to search for contraband or evidence of crime. * * * [B]ecause of the importance of the governmental interest at stake, the minimal intrusion of a brief stop, and the absence of practical alternatives for policing the border, we hold that when an officer's observations lead him reasonably to suspect that a particular vehicle may contain aliens who are illegally in the country, he may stop the car briefly and investigate the circumstances that provoke suspicion. * * * [T]he stop and inquiry must be "reasonably related in scope to the justification for their initiation." The officer may question the driver and passengers about their citizenship and immigration status, and he may ask them to explain suspicious circumstances, but any further detention or search must be based on consent or probable cause.

We are unwilling to let the Border Patrol dispense entirely with the requirement that officers must have a reasonable suspicion to justify roving-patrol stops. In the context of border area stops, the reasonableness requirement of the Fourth Amendment demands something more than the broad and unlimited discretion sought by the Government. Roads near the border carry not only aliens seeking to enter the country illegally, but a large volume of legitimate traffic as well. * * * To approve roving-patrol stops of all vehicles in the border area, without any suspicion that a particular vehicle is carrying illegal immigrants, would subject the residents of these and other areas to potentially unlimited interference with their use of the highways, solely at the discretion of Border Patrol officers.[b] * * *

---

[b] In a later case, however, the Court held that the Fourth Amendment is not violated by a permanent immigration checkpoint approximately 66 miles north of the Mexican border in which all cars must stop for an initial screening and some cars are pulled off to the side and detained for

We are not convinced that the legitimate needs of law enforcement require this degree of interference with lawful traffic. * * * [T]he nature of illegal alien traffic and the characteristics of smuggling operations tend to generate articulable grounds for identifying violators. Consequently, a requirement of reasonable suspicion for stops allows the Government adequate means of guarding the public interest and also protects residents of the border areas from indiscriminate official interference. * * * Except at the border and its functional equivalents, officers on roving patrol may stop vehicles only if they are aware of specific articulable facts, together with rational inferences from those facts, that reasonably warrant suspicion that the vehicles contain aliens who may be illegally in the country.

Any number of factors may be taken into account in deciding whether there is reasonable suspicion to stop a car in the border area. Officers may consider the characteristics of the area in which they encounter a vehicle. Its proximity to the border, the usual patterns of traffic on the particular road, and previous experience with alien traffic are all relevant. They also may consider information about recent illegal border crossings in the area. The driver's behavior may be relevant, as erratic driving or obvious attempts to evade officers can support a reasonable suspicion. Aspects of the vehicle itself may justify suspicion. For instance, officers say that certain station wagons, with large compartments for fold-down seats or spare tires, are frequently used for transporting concealed aliens. The vehicle may appear to be heavily loaded, it may have an extraordinary number of passengers, or the officers may observe persons trying to hide. The Government also points out that trained officers can recognize the characteristic appearance of persons who live in Mexico, relying on such factors as the mode of dress and haircut. In all situations the officer is entitled to assess the facts in light of his experience in detecting illegal entry and smuggling.

In this case the officers relied on a single factor to justify stopping respondent's car: the apparent Mexican ancestry of the occupants. We cannot conclude that this furnished reasonable grounds to believe that the three occupants were aliens. At best the officers had only a fleeting glimpse of the persons in the moving car, illuminated by headlights. Even if they

---

secondary screening for the purpose of catching undocumented immigrants who have unlawfully entered the United States, even if there is no articulable suspicion to support these detentions. United States v. Martinez-Fuerte, 428 U.S. 543, 547 (1976) (noting that the Government "concedes that none of the three stops at issue . . . was based on any articulable suspicion"). After highlighting how difficult it is to stem the flow of illegal immigration from Mexico, the Court opines that "[a] requirement that stops on major routes inland always be based on reasonable suspicion would be impractical . . ." *Id.* at 557. In contrast to its position in *Brignoni-Ponce*, the *Martinez-Fuerte* Court made clear that there is no Fourth Amendment violation even if the primary reason a car is pulled to the side for secondary inspection is the apparent Mexican ancestry of its occupants, writing, "[E]ven if it be assumed that such referrals [for secondary inspection] are made largely on the basis of Mexican ancestry, we perceive no constitutional violation. . . . Border Patrol officers must have wide discretion in selecting the motorists to be diverted for the brief questioning involved." *Id.* at 563–64.

saw enough to think that the occupants were of Mexican descent, this factor alone would justify neither a reasonable belief that they were aliens, nor a reasonable belief that the car concealed other aliens who were illegally in the country. Large numbers of native-born and naturalized citizens have the physical characteristics identified with Mexican ancestry, and even in the border area a relatively small proportion of them are aliens. The likelihood that any given person of Mexican ancestry is an alien is high enough to make Mexican appearance a relevant factor, but standing alone it does not justify stopping all Mexican-Americans to ask if they are aliens.

The judgment of the Court of Appeals is affirmed.

Affirmed.

[JUSTICE REHNQUIST's concurring opinion and JUSTICE DOUGLAS' concurring opinion have been omitted.]

LA MIGRA IN THE MIRROR: IMMIGRATION ENFORCEMENT AND RACIAL PROFILING ON THE TEXAS BORDER
César Cuauhtémoc García Hernández
23 Notre Dame J.L. Ethics & Pub. Pol'y 167 (2009)

In the most egregious and wide-reaching example of the Supreme Court's unwillingness to extend important constitutional protections to non-citizens, the Court in a 1975 decision firmly approved racial profiling in the immigration policing context. The Court allowed racial profiling—that is, "the formal and informal targeting of African Americans, Latinos, and other racial minorities for investigation on account of their race"—even though such practices remain taboo policy in the traditional constitutional framework in which allegations of race-based decision-making are scrutinized under the Equal Protection Clause.

In this decision, *United States v. Brignoni-Ponce*, a case in which the Court directly addressed the Border Patrol's authority to stop and question people who appear to be Mexican, the Supreme Court explained, "The Government makes a convincing demonstration that the public interest demands effective measures to prevent the illegal entry of aliens at the Mexican border.... [T]hese aliens create significant economic and social problems, competing with citizens and legal residents for jobs, and generating extra demand for social services." Embracing the tired refrain that immigrants are a drain to the nation's economic stability and national security, the Supreme Court positioned itself to condone an unwavering record of governmental attacks on migrants.

Perhaps in recognition of the accepted constitutional wisdom that racial profiling is both unconstitutional and not sound policy, Justice Lewis F. Powell closed the Court's decision in *Brignoni-Ponce* with an attempt at limiting its embrace of race-based immigration enforcement: "The likelihood that any given person of Mexican ancestry is an alien is high enough to make Mexican appearance a relevant factor, but standing alone does not justify stopping all Mexican-Americans to ask if they are aliens." This apparent limitation was in fact specious.

* * * Border Patrol agents are empowered with an array of tools, many of which enable racial profiling. "Officers may consider the characteristics of the area in which they encounter a vehicle. Its proximity to the border, the usual patterns of traffic on the particular road, and previous experience with alien traffic are all relevant," wrote Justice Powell in *Brignoni-Ponce*. At least one of these criteria is always guaranteed in the Texas borderlands—proximity to the border, where 90% of the population would "appear" to be of Mexican ancestry. * * *

They may also consider information about recent illegal border crossings in the area. The driver's behavior may be relevant, as erratic driving or obvious attempts to evade officers can support a reasonable suspicion. Aspects of the vehicle itself may justify suspicion. For instance, officers say that certain station wagons, with large compartments for fold-down seats or spare tires, are frequently used for transporting concealed aliens. The vehicle may appear to be heavily loaded, it may have an extraordinary number of passengers, or the officers may observe persons trying to hide. The Government also points out that trained officers can recognize that characteristic appearance of persons who live in Mexico, relying on such factors as the mode of dress and haircut.

In essence, the *Brignoni-Ponce* Court allow[s] individual immigration agents to use ingrained stereotypes about appearance and innocuous information about the smuggler's preferred vehicle and unrelated traffic on a particular road to target anyone they choose who happens to be near the border.

The significance of the language in *Brignoni-Ponce*—"Mexican appearance"—* * * cannot be overstated. With those words the Supreme Court launched the modern immigration control regime in which the targeting of anyone who appears "Mexican" is sanctioned. It then became the role of immigration officers to determine exactly what it means to be of "Mexican appearance." Rereading Justice Powell's words in *Brignoni-Ponce* * * * I am reminded of how broad these factors reach. Recently, my family and I were in Seattle celebrating my brother's graduation from law school. Ten of us were crammed into a seven-person van, including two of us who were crouched in the rear cargo compartment. Many of us were born in México and lived there at least a few years of our lives. A few of us currently live directly on the border. Our driver, my oldest brother, was unfamiliar with the Seattle neighborhood in which we were traveling. After the graduation ceremony, on our way back to the large house that we rented for the weekend, he got lost and circled an industrial waterfront neighborhood full of warehouses and cargo ports. I can only imagine how erratic and heavily loaded our oversized vehicle looked, and how "Mexican" its passengers appeared. I can only be grateful that we were not near "the border and its functional equivalents" where immigration officers have the Supreme Court's seal of constitutional approval to stop and question families like mine—too large, too Mexican, too lost—who are riding in a suspicious vehicle, an enormous blue van with sliding doors, fold-down seats, spare tires, and out-of-state license plates—to blend into the landscape. * * *

[handwritten annotation: L wants something more than "reasonable suspicion" to stop and ask about immigration status]

THE CASE AGAINST RACE PROFILING IN IMMIGRATION ENFORCEMENT

Kevin R. Johnson
78 Wash. U. L.Q. 675 (2000)

In *United States v. Brignoni-Ponce*, the Supreme Court applied the Fourth Amendment reasonable suspicion standard used in police investigatory stops and held that Border Patrol officers on roving patrols may stop persons "only if they are aware of specific articulable facts, together with rational inferences from those facts, that reasonably warrant suspicion that the vehicles contain aliens who may be illegally in the country." In so doing, the Court found that the stop in question violated the Fourth Amendment because Border Patrol officers relied exclusively on "the apparent Mexican ancestry" of the occupants in the automobile. The Court further stated, however, that "[t]*he likelihood that any given person of Mexican ancestry is an alien is high enough to make Mexican appearance a relevant factor*, but standing alone it does not justify stopping all Mexican Americans to ask if they are aliens."

The last sentence from *Brignoni-Ponce* has greatly shaped immigration enforcement in the United States over the past twenty-five years. Yet consider how the same sentence from *Brignoni-Ponce* would read as applied to African Americans in the criminal law enforcement context. Could we imagine the Supreme Court stating that "[t]he likelihood that any given person of [African American] ancestry is [a criminal] is high enough to make [African American] appearance a relevant factor" in a criminal stop? Such a clearly discriminatory statement would provoke justified outrage. Nevertheless, the use of race in immigration stops to this point has not been carefully scrutinized. * * *

In vesting the Border Patrol with the discretion to consider "Mexican appearance" in immigration stops, the Supreme Court relied on the government's assertion that eighty-five percent of the undocumented population in the United States was of Mexican ancestry. Assuming that it is relevant to the inquiry, this figure bears no resemblance to the best available evidence today and in all likelihood was inaccurate in 1975. In 1981, the final report of the U.S. Select Commission on Immigration and

Refugee Policy summarizing U.S. Bureau of the Census data reported that "Mexican nationals probably account *for less than half* of the undocumented/illegal population." According to the latest INS estimates, Mexican citizens comprise roughly one-half of the undocumented population, a far cry from the unsubstantiated estimate that the government provided the Supreme Court in 1975.

In any event, rather than considering the percentage of undocumented persons of Mexican ancestry in the country, the Supreme Court should have considered the percentage of the total Hispanic population in the United States with lawful immigration statuses. This represents the group of individuals subject to the injuries inflicted by race profiling in immigration enforcement, harms never considered seriously by the Court in *Brignoni-Ponce*. The population of persons of "Hispanic appearance" residing *lawfully* in the United States and subject to race-based immigration stops is extensive, having grown substantially since 1975. In 1997, nearly thirty million people of Hispanic ancestry—over eleven percent of the total U.S. population—lived in the United States. * * * In contrast, as of October 1996, barely over three million undocumented Mexican and Central American immigrants lived in the United States. A crude estimate from these figures reveals that the vast majority (about ninety percent) of Hispanics in the United States are lawful immigrants or citizens. * * *

Although stops and interrogations about citizenship may appear to be minimal intrusions to people unlikely to be stopped and interrogated, such enforcement practices affect the sense of belonging to U.S. society of Latino citizens and immigrants. Especially in the Southwest, immigration enforcement regularly imposes indignities on citizens and lawful immigrants of Mexican ancestry that are not imposed on Anglos. * * * "Border Patrol officers who stop cars based in substantial part on whether the occupants 'look Mexican' infringe on the freedom of movement of Latinos who are permanent resident aliens and citizens as well as those who are undocumented." * * *

Border Patrol reliance on race also reinforces negative, ill-conceived stereotypes about "Hispanic appearance." References to "Hispanic appearance" is problematic given the fact that the phenotype varies widely among persons of Latin American ancestry. For example, "[m]ost [persons of Mexican ancestry] are of dark complexion with black hair. . . . [b]ut many are blond, blue-eyed and 'white,' while others have red hair and hazel eyes." The stereotype of the dark haired, brown skinned (often linked to "dirty") "Mexican" ignores the rich diversity of physical appearances among Latinos. Racially discriminatory immigration enforcement may encourage Latinos to, among other things, attempt to change their physical appearance and seek to "pass" as Spanish or white, with damaging personal consequences. The diversity among Latinos also suggests that room for error exists when Border Patrol officers seek to detect undocumented persons by focusing on the stereotypical "Hispanic appearance." In this respect, the classification is under-inclusive as well as over-inclusive. * * *

NOTE

In April 2010, Arizona enacted the "Support Our Law Enforcement and Safe Neighborhoods Act," commonly referred to as Senate Bill 1070. The Act was designed to "discourage and deter the unlawful entry and presence of aliens" in the United States.[a] One of S.B. 1070's most controversial provisions was § 2(B), which requires law enforcement officers to make a reasonable attempt to determine the immigration status of anyone they have lawfully detained "where reasonable suspicion exists that the person is an alien who is unlawfully present in the United States."[b] This provision drew intense criticism from civil rights groups on the ground that it not only authorizes, but also arguably mandates, racial profiling of Hispanics.[c]

The U.S. Department of Justice (DOJ) under the Obama Administration sought an injunction against four provisions of S.B. 1070, arguing that federal immigration law preempts Arizona state law. The District Court agreed with the DOJ and enjoined S.B. 1070 from taking effect.[d] The Supreme Court, in a 5 to 4 ruling, affirmed the injunction against three out of the four contested provisions, but upheld § 2(B), the provision requiring police officers with reasonable suspicion to believe that an individual is an undocumented immigrant to verify the person's immigration status.[e]

---

[a] S.B. 1070, 49th Leg., 2d Reg. Sess. (Ariz. 2010). For an in depth look at the central legal issues involving this legislation, *see* Gabriel Chin, et al., *A Legal Labyrinth: Issues Raised by Arizona Senate Bill 1070*, 25 GEO. IMMIGR. L.J. 47, 65–68 (2011).

[b] ARIZ. REV. STAT. ANN. § 11–1051(B) (2011) (West).

[c] Nicholas Riccardi, *Arizona Passes Strict Illegal Immigration Act*, L.A. TIMES (Apr. 13, 2010), http://articles.latimes.com/2010/apr/13/nation/la-na-arizona-immigration14-2010apr14.

[d] United States v. Arizona, 703 F. Supp. 2d 980, 991, 1008 (D. Ariz. 2010). The Ninth Circuit affirmed the injunction. United States v. Arizona, 641 F.3d 339 (9th Cir. 2011).

[e] Arizona v. United States, 567 U.S. 387, 415–16 (2012). The three provisions of S.B. 1070 that were struck down by the Supreme Court were the parts: (1) making it a state crime for an alien to be in the United States without proper authorization, ARIZ. REV. STAT. ANN. § 13–1509(A) (2011) (West); (2) making it a state crime for any undocumented alien to apply for work in Arizona, ARIZ. REV. STAT. ANN. § 13–2928(C) (2011) (West); and (3) authorizing law enforcement officers to arrest, without a warrant, anyone so long as the officer has probable cause to believe that the person "has committed any public offense" which would make the person deportable, ARIZ. REV. STAT. ANN. § 13–3883(A)(5) (2011) (West). *Id.* at 416.

WHREN v. UNITED STATES
Supreme Court of the United States
517 U.S. 806, 116 S. Ct. 1769, 135 L. Ed. 2d 89 (1996)

JUSTICE SCALIA delivered the opinion of the Court.

In this case we decide whether the temporary detention of a motorist who the police have probable cause to believe has committed a civil traffic violation is inconsistent with the Fourth Amendment's prohibition against unreasonable seizures unless a reasonable officer would have been motivated to stop the car by a desire to enforce the traffic laws.

On the evening of June 10, 1993, plainclothes vice-squad officers of the District of Columbia Metropolitan Police Department were patrolling a "high drug area" of the city in an unmarked car. Their suspicions were aroused when they passed a dark Pathfinder truck with temporary license plates and youthful occupants waiting at a stop sign, the driver looking down into the lap of the passenger at his right. The truck remained stopped at the intersection for what seemed an unusually long time—more than 20 seconds. When the police car executed a U-turn in order to head back toward the truck, the Pathfinder turned suddenly to its right, without signaling, and sped off at an "unreasonable" speed. The policemen followed, and in a short while overtook the Pathfinder when it stopped behind other traffic at a red light. They pulled up alongside, and Officer Ephraim Soto stepped out and approached the driver's door, identifying himself as a police officer and directing the driver, petitioner Brown, to put the vehicle in park. When Soto drew up to the driver's window, he immediately observed two large plastic bags of what appeared to be crack cocaine in petitioner Whren's hands. Petitioners were arrested, and quantities of several types of illegal drugs were retrieved from the vehicle.

Petitioners were charged in a four-count indictment with violating various federal drug laws, including 21 U.S.C. §§ 844(a) and 860(a). At a pretrial suppression hearing, they challenged the legality of the stop and the resulting seizure of the drugs. They argued that the stop had not been justified by probable cause to believe, or even reasonable suspicion, that petitioners were engaged in illegal drug-dealing activity; and that Officer Soto's asserted ground for approaching the vehicle—to give the driver a warning concerning traffic violations—was pretextual. The District Court denied the suppression motion. * * *

Petitioners were convicted of the counts at issue here. The Court of Appeals affirmed the convictions, holding with respect to the suppression issue that, "regardless of whether a police officer subjectively believes that the occupants of an automobile may be engaging in some other illegal behavior, a traffic stop is permissible as long as a reasonable officer in the same circumstances *could have* stopped the car for the suspected traffic violation." We granted certiorari.

The Fourth Amendment guarantees "[t]he right of the people to be secure in their persons, houses, papers, and effects, against unreasonable searches and seizures." Temporary detention of individuals during the stop of an automobile by the police, even if only for a brief period and for a limited purpose, constitutes a "seizure" of "persons" within the meaning of this provision. An automobile stop is thus subject to the constitutional imperative that it not be "unreasonable" under the circumstances. As a general matter, the decision to stop an automobile is reasonable where the police have probable cause to believe that a traffic violation has occurred.

Petitioners accept that Officer Soto had probable cause to believe that various provisions of the District of Columbia traffic code had been violated. They argue, however, that "in the unique context of civil traffic regulations" probable cause is not enough. Since, they contend, the use of automobiles is so heavily and minutely regulated that total compliance with traffic and safety rules is nearly impossible, a police officer will almost invariably be able to catch any given motorist in a technical violation. This creates the temptation to use traffic stops as a means of investigating other law violations, as to which no probable cause or even articulable suspicion exists. Petitioners, who are both black, further contend that police officers might decide which motorists to stop based on decidedly impermissible factors, such as the race of the car's occupants. To avoid this danger, they say, the Fourth Amendment test for traffic stops should be not * * * whether probable cause existed to justify the stop, but rather, whether a police officer, acting reasonably, would have made the stop for the reason given.

Petitioners contend that the standard they propose is consistent with our past cases' disapproval of police attempts to use valid bases of action against citizens as pretexts for pursuing other investigatory agendas. We are reminded that in *Florida v. Wells*, we stated that "an inventory search must not be a ruse for a general rummaging in order to discover incriminating evidence"; that in *Colorado v. Bertine*, in approving an inventory search, we apparently thought it significant that there had been "no showing that the police, who were following standardized procedures, acted in bad faith or for the sole purpose of investigation"; and that in *New York v. Burger,* we observed, in upholding the constitutionality of a warrantless administrative inspection, that the search did not appear to be "a 'pretext' for obtaining evidence of . . . violation of . . . penal laws."[a] But

---

[a] The Court has recognized an inventory search exception to the warrant requirement under which police officers may conduct an inventory search of an individual's possessions without a warrant or even probable cause to believe a crime is committed by the individual as long as the officers are following standardized procedures that limit their discretion and are not using the inventory as a pretext to search for evidence of a crime. *Florida v. Wells* and *Colorado v. Bertine* recognized this inventory exception. The inventory search exception is a subset of a broader exception to the warrant requirement known as the special needs or administrative search exception. *New York v. Burger* reflects the Court's endorsement of this administrative search exception.

only an undiscerning reader would regard these cases as endorsing the principle that ulterior motives can invalidate police conduct that is justifiable on the basis of probable cause to believe that a violation of law has occurred. In each case we were addressing the validity of a search conducted in the *absence* of probable cause. Our quoted statements simply explain that the exemption from the need for probable cause (and warrant), which is accorded to searches made for the purpose of inventory or administrative regulation, is not accorded to searches that are *not* made for those purposes.

* * * Not only have we never held, outside the context of inventory search or administrative inspection (discussed above), that an officer's motive invalidates objectively justifiable behavior under the Fourth Amendment; but we have repeatedly held and asserted the contrary. In *United States v. Villamonte-Marquez*, [w]e flatly dismissed the idea that an ulterior motive might serve to strip the agents of their legal justification. In *United States v. Robinson*, we held that a traffic-violation arrest (of the sort here) would not be rendered invalid by the fact that it was "a mere pretext for a narcotics search." * * * And in *Scott v. United States*, * * * we said that "[s]ubjective intent alone ... does not make otherwise lawful conduct illegal or unconstitutional." We described *Robinson* as having established that "the fact that the officer does not have the state of mind which is hypothecated by the reasons which provide the legal justification for the officer's action does not invalidate the action taken as long as the circumstances, viewed objectively, justify that action."

We think these cases foreclose any argument that the constitutional reasonableness of traffic stops depends on the actual motivations of the individual officers involved. We of course agree with petitioners that the Constitution prohibits selective enforcement of the law based on considerations such as race. But the constitutional basis for objecting to intentionally discriminatory application of laws is the Equal Protection Clause, not the Fourth Amendment. Subjective intentions play no role in ordinary, probable-cause Fourth Amendment analysis.

Recognizing that we have been unwilling to entertain Fourth Amendment challenges based on the actual motivations of individual officers, petitioners disavow any intention to make the individual officer's subjective good faith the touchstone of "reasonableness." They insist that the standard they have put forward—whether the officer's conduct deviated materially from usual police practices, so that a reasonable officer in the same circumstances would not have made the stop for the reasons given—is an "objective" one.

But although framed in empirical terms, this approach is plainly and indisputably driven by subjective considerations. Its whole purpose is to prevent the police from doing under the guise of enforcing the traffic code what they would like to do for different reasons. Petitioners' proposed standard may not use the word "pretext," but it is designed to combat nothing other than the perceived "danger" of the pretextual stop, albeit only indirectly and over the run of cases.

* * * [I]t seems to us somewhat easier to figure out the intent of an individual officer than to plumb the collective consciousness of law enforcement in order to determine whether a "reasonable officer" would have been moved to act upon the traffic violation. While police manuals and standard procedures may sometimes provide objective assistance, ordinarily one would be reduced to speculating about the hypothetical reaction of a hypothetical constable—an exercise that might be called virtual subjectivity.

Moreover, police enforcement practices, even if they could be practicably assessed by a judge, vary from place to place and from time to time. We cannot accept that the search and seizure protections of the Fourth Amendment are so variable, and can be made to turn upon such trivialities. The difficulty is illustrated by petitioners' arguments in this case. Their claim that a reasonable officer would not have made this stop is based largely on District of Columbia police regulations which permit plainclothes officers in unmarked vehicles to enforce traffic laws "only in the case of a violation that is so grave as to pose an *immediate threat* to the safety of others." This basis of invalidation would not apply in jurisdictions that had a different practice. And it would not have applied even in the District of Columbia, if Officer Soto had been wearing a uniform or patrolling in a marked police cruiser. * * *

Petitioners urge as an extraordinary factor in this case that the "multitude of applicable traffic and equipment regulations" is so large and so difficult to obey perfectly that virtually everyone is guilty of violation, permitting the police to single out almost whomever they wish for a stop. But we are aware of no principle that would allow us to decide at what point a code of law becomes so expansive and so commonly violated that infraction itself can no longer be the ordinary measure of the lawfulness of enforcement. And even if we could identify such exorbitant codes, we do not know by what standard (or what right) we would decide, as petitioners would have us do, which particular provisions are sufficiently important to merit enforcement.

For the run-of-the-mine case, which this surely is, we think there is no realistic alternative to the traditional common-law rule that probable cause justifies a search and seizure. Here the District Court found that the officers had probable cause to believe that petitioners had violated the traffic code. That rendered the stop reasonable under the Fourth Amendment, the evidence thereby discovered admissible, and the upholding of the convictions by the Court of Appeals for the District of Columbia Circuit correct. The judgment is

Affirmed.

"DRIVING WHILE BLACK" AND ALL OTHER TRAFFIC OFFENSES: THE SUPREME COURT AND PRETEXTUAL TRAFFIC STOPS

David A. Harris[a]
87 J. Crim. L. & Criminology 544 (1997)

The Supreme Court's decision in *Whren v. United States* * * * approves two alarming law enforcement practices. * * * [B]oth represent profoundly dangerous developments for a free society, especially one dedicated to the equal treatment of all citizens. First, the comprehensive scope of state traffic codes makes them extremely powerful tools under *Whren*. These codes regulate the details of driving in ways both big and small, obvious and arcane. In the most literal sense, no driver can avoid violating some traffic law during a short drive, even with the most careful attention. Fairly read, *Whren* says that any traffic violation can support a stop, no matter what the real reason for it is; this makes any citizen fair game for a stop, almost anytime, anywhere, virtually at the whim of police. Given how important an activity driving has become in American society, *Whren* changes the Fourth Amendment's rule that police must have a reason to forcibly interfere in our business—some basis to suspect wrongdoing that is more than a hunch. Simply put, that rule no longer applies when a person drives a car.

This alone should worry us, but the second police practice *Whren* approves is in fact far worse. It is this: Police will not subject all drivers to traffic stops in the way *Whren* allows. Rather, if past practice is any indication, they will use the traffic code to stop a hugely disproportionate number of African-Americans and Hispanics. We know this because it is exactly what has been happening already, even before receiving the Supreme Court's imprimatur in *Whren*. In fact, the stopping of black drivers, just to see what officers can find, has become so common in some places that this practice has its own name: * * * "driving while black." With *Whren*, we should expect African-Americans and Hispanics to experience an even greater number of pretextual traffic stops. And once police stop a car, they often search it, either by obtaining consent, using a drug sniffing dog, or by some other means. In fact, searching cars for narcotics is perhaps the major motivation for making these stops.

---

[a] David Harris, the Sally Ann Semenko Endowed Chair and Professor of Law at the University of Pittsburgh School of Law, holds the copyright to this article, which is reprinted by his permission.

Under a Constitution that restrains the government vis-a-vis the individual and that puts some limits on what the authorities may do in the pursuit of the guilty, the power of the police to stop any particular driver, at almost any time, seems oddly out of place. And with the words "equal justice under law" carved into the stone of the Supreme Court itself, one might think that the use of police power in one of its rawest forms against members of particular racial or ethnic groups might prompt the Court to show some interest in curbing such abuses. The defendant-petitioners presented both of these arguments. * * * Yet the Court paid little attention to these obvious implications of its decision. * * *

Here are [several] different stories of pretextual stops. They originate from different areas of the country: Florida in the South, Maryland in the Northeast, Illinois in the Midwest, and Colorado in the West. All involve independent police agencies. Other stories of this type of police activity exist, but those presented here are among the best documented. Each of them teaches the same lesson. And with *Whren* on the books, we should expect more of what these stories tell, not less.

a. Volusia County, Florida

Located in central Florida, Volusia County surrounds a busy stretch of Interstate 95. In the late 1980's, this portion of highway became the focus of Sheriff Bob Vogel and his deputies. Using a group of officers called the Selective Enforcement Team, Vogel operated a major drug interdiction effort against drivers moving narcotics by car through his jurisdiction. The deputies aimed not only to make arrests, but to make seizures of cash and vehicles, which their agency would keep.

As with most police agencies, the Volusia County Sheriff's Department did not keep records of stops and searches in which no arrests or seizures occurred in the three years that the Selective Enforcement Team operated. Thus no one might ever have learned about the Selective Enforcement Team's practices, except for one thing: Volusia County deputies' were cars fitted with video cameras. Deputies taped some of the I-95 stops; using Florida's public records law, The Orlando Sentinel obtained 148 hours of the videotapes. * * * [T]he tapes the newspaper obtained documented almost 1,100 stops, and they showed a number of undeniable patterns.

First, even though African-Americans and Hispanics make up only about five percent of the drivers on the county's stretch of I-95, more than seventy percent of all drivers stopped were either African-American or Hispanic. The tapes put this in stark terms. One African-American man said he was stopped seven times by police; another said that he was stopped twice within minutes. Looking at figures for all of Florida, seventy percent is vastly out of proportion to the percentage of Blacks among Floridians of driving age (11.7 percent), the percentage of Blacks among all Florida drivers convicted of traffic offenses in 1991 (15.1 percent), or to the percentage of Blacks in the nation's population as a whole (12 percent). * * * Second, the deputies not only stopped black and Hispanic drivers more often than whites; they also stopped them for longer periods of time. According to the videotapes, deputies detained Blacks and Hispanics for twice as long as they detained whites. Third, the tapes showed that police followed a stop with a search roughly half the time; eighty percent of the cars searched belonged to Black or Hispanic drivers.

It should not surprise anyone to know that deputies said they made these 1,100 stops based on "legitimate traffic violations." Violations ranged from "swerving" (243), to exceeding the speed limit by up to ten miles per hour (128), burned-out license tag lights (71), improper license tags (46), failure to signal before a lane change (45), to a smattering of others. Even so, only nine of the nearly eleven hundred drivers stopped—considerably less than one percent—received tickets, and deputies even released several drivers who admitted to crimes, including drunk driving, without any charges. The tapes also showed that the seizure of cash remained an important goal of the stops, with deputies seizing money almost three times as often as they arrested anyone for drugs. With regard to the seizures of cash, race also played a role: Ninety percent of the drivers from whom cash was taken, but who were not arrested, were Black or Hispanic. * * *

b. Robert Wilkins and the Maryland State Police

In the early morning hours of May 8, 1992, a Maryland State Police officer stopped a new rental car carrying four African-Americans on Interstate 68. The four, all relatives, were returning to the Washington, D.C. area from a family member's funeral in Chicago. After obtaining the driver's license, the officer asked the driver to step out of the car and sign a form giving consent to a search. At that point, Robert Wilkins, one of the passengers in the car, identified himself as an attorney with a 9:30 a.m. court appearance in the District of Columbia Superior Court. Wilkins told the officer that he had no right to search the car without arresting the driver; the officer replied that such searches were "routine." After all, the officer said, if Wilkins and his relatives had "nothing to hide, then what [was] the problem?" Another officer joined the first, and they detained the group for an additional half hour while other officers brought a drug-sniffing dog to the scene. The driver asked whether he would receive a ticket; the officer said he would only give the driver a warning. The driver asked that the warning be written so that the group could leave, and Wilkins asserted that continued detention in order to bring the dog violated the Constitution;[b] the officer ignored both of them. When the dog arrived,

---

[b] In 2005, the Supreme Court held that bringing a drug-sniffing dog to check for drugs after a traffic stop does not constitute a search within the meaning of the Fourth Amendment as long as it does not unreasonably prolong the traffic stop. Illinois v. Caballes, 543 U.S. 405 (2005). The Court reasoned that the possession of contraband is something in which one cannot have a reasonable expectation of privacy. In a later case, the Court ruled that an officer may not prolong a traffic stop in order to conduct a dog sniff of the car without reasonable suspicion that any of the

the officers ordered Wilkins and his relatives out of the car, despite their expressed fears of the dog and the fact that it was raining. They were forced to stand in the rain as the dog sniffed in and around the car. When the dog failed to react in any way, Wilkins and the others were then allowed back in the car—while the officer who had stopped them wrote the driver a $105 speeding ticket.

Civil rights lawyers sometimes say that despite the volume of complaints they receive about racially biased traffic stops, victims of this treatment feel reluctant to become plaintiffs in legal actions for redress. Perhaps they fear retaliation; others may want to avoid the hassle of becoming involved in a very public way in complex and often politically charged litigation. Still others may fear that opposing lawyers may discover dirt in their pasts and use it against them. Not so with Robert Wilkins. A Harvard Law School graduate, Wilkins worked as a public defender for the highly-regarded Public Defender Service in Washington, D.C. As an attorney with an active practice in criminal law, he was no doubt thoroughly familiar with the law that governed the situation in which he and his family members found themselves. The prospect of public litigation against a police agency obviously did not scare him. Individually and on behalf of a class of all others treated similarly, he and his family members sued the Maryland State Police, supervisory and command personnel at the agency, and the individual officers involved. They alleged civil rights violations and other wrongs, stating that the officers had illegally stopped and detained them on the basis of a "profile" that targeted people based on their race. State Police officials denied Wilkins' allegations; a spokesman said the practice of stopping a disproportionate number of blacks simply represented "an unfortunate byproduct of sound police policies." The implication was clear: African-Americans commit the most crime; to stop crime, we must stop African-Americans. Officials maintained this supposedly race-neutral explanation even in the face of an official document that surfaced during litigation. Dated just days before the State Police officers stopped Wilkins and his family members, it warned officers operating in Allegheny County—the very county in which police stopped the Wilkins group—to watch for "dealers and couriers (traffickers) [who] are predominantly black males and black females. . . . utilizing Interstate 68 . . ."

The case eventually produced a settlement, in which the Maryland State Police agreed not to use any race-based drug courier profiles and to cease using "race as a factor for the development of policies for stopping, detaining, and searching motorists." The State Police also agreed to conduct training that would reflect the prohibition on the use of race as both departmental policy and state law, and to pay monetary damages and

---

occupants of the car are involved in criminal activity. Rodriguez v. United States, 575 U.S. 348 (2015).

attorney's fees. Perhaps more significantly, the State Police agreed that for a period of three years, they would:

> maintain computer records of all stops in which a consent to search was given by a motorist stopped on any Maryland roadway by the Maryland State Police and all stops on any Maryland roadway by Maryland State Police in which a search by a drug-detecting dog is made. * * *

The State Police have, in fact, maintained these records, and submitted them to the court. The latest figures * * * bear a striking similarity to the information revealed by the Volusia County videotapes. Of the 732 citizens detained and searched by the Maryland State Police, 75% were African-Americans, and 5% were Hispanics. * * * Sad to say, the numbers show that very little has changed, despite the Wilkins suit and the Settlement Agreement. * * *

"WALKING WHILE BLACK": ENCOUNTERS WITH THE POLICE ON MY STREET

Paul Butler
Legal Times, Nov. 10, 1997, at 23[a]

Sometimes being a scholar of criminal procedure and a black man seems redundant.

I am walking in the most beautiful neighborhood in the District of Columbia. Though I'm coming home from work, I feel as though I'm on a nature walk: I spy deer and raccoons and hear ridiculously noisy birds. And even more unusual in Washington: black *and* white people. Living next door to each other. It's more like Disney World than the stereotypical image of Washington, D.C.

It is the neighborhood where I am fortunate enough to reside, and I am ashamed that the walk is unfamiliar; it is occasioned by my broken car. The time is about 9 p.m., and the streets are mostly deserted. When I'm about three blocks from home, a Metropolitan Police car, passing by, slows down. I keep walking, and the car makes a right turn, circles the block, and meets me. There are three officers inside. Their greeting is, "Do you live around here?"

I have been in this place before. I know that answering the question will be the beginning, not the end, of an unpleasant conversation—"Where

---

[a] On May 3, 2011, The Atlantic Philanthropies and The New Press (http://thenewpress.com/) hosted a discussion about racial profiling in the United States. You can hear and see Professor Paul Butler narrating *"Walking While Black": Encounters with the Police on My Street,* in this 9 minute YouTube video available at Paul Butler, *Profiled on My Own Street,* https://www.youtube.com/watch?v=pl7cT-O_b0E&ab_channel=atlanticphil (https://perma.cc/J8QK-Y6PH).

do you live?" "It's kind of cold to be walking, isn't it?" "Can I see some I.D.?"—that I don't feel like having.

So I ask a question instead: "Why do you want to know?" The three officers exchange a glance—the "we got a smartass on our hands" glance. I get it a lot.

"Is it against the law to walk on the sidewalk if I don't live around here?" When no response is immediately forthcoming, I say, "Have a nice evening, officers," and head toward home.

The police now use an investigative technique that probably has a name other than cat-and-mouse, but that is the most accurate description. They park their car on the side of the road, turn off their lights, and watch me walk. When I pass out of their range of vision, they zip the car up to where they can see me.

In this fashion we arrive on the block where I live. I have a question, and so I stop and wait. For once, I have the power to summon the police immediately, quicker even than the president, who lives about seven miles away. Sure enough, as soon as I pause, the car does too. The police and I have a conversation, consisting mostly of questions.

"Why are you following me?"

"Why won't you tell us where you live?"

"What made you stop me?"

"We don't see a lot of people walking in this neighborhood."

"Are you following me because I'm black?"

"No, we're black too."

This answer is true, but it is not responsive. I ask the officers if they have ever been followed around a store by a security guard. They all say yes. The senior officer—a sergeant—says that it doesn't bother her because she knows she's not a thief.

I ask if that's how the kid in the Eddie Bauer case should have felt. A Prince George's County police officer, moonlighting as a security guard, made an African-American teenager take off the shirt he was wearing and go home to get a receipt in order to prove that he had not stolen the shirt from the store. Testifying about how that made him feel, the black man-child cried. The case had been in the news the previous week because a jury awarded the boy $850,000. Nonetheless, the sergeant says she isn't aware of it.

The officers tell me that they're suspicious because this is not a neighborhood where they usually see people walking. Furthermore, they know everybody who lives in the neighborhood and they don't know me. I ask if they know who lives there, pointing down the road to the house where I have lived for 14 months. Yes, they answer, yes, they do.

And so I walk. I walk up my stairs. I sit on my porch. I wait. I wait because I am a professor of criminal procedure. I wait because I remember the last time, with different officers, in a different place, when I "cooperated." Which meant that I let them search my car. Or rather, I let one search while the other watched me. With his hand resting near his gun. On 16th Street. Cars whizzed by. I pretended that I was invisible.

Now the officers park their car and position its spotlight on my face. All three of them join me on my porch.

"Do you live here?"

"Yes, I do."

"Can we see some identification?"

"No, you may not."

During the antebellum period of our nation's history, blacks were required to carry proof of their status, slave or free, at all times. Any black unsupervised by a white was suspect. In North Carolina, to make it easier for law enforcement, nonslave blacks had to wear shoulder patches with the word "free."

The District of Columbia, through its three agents standing on my porch, tells me: "If you live here, go inside. It's too cold to be out."

I am content where I am. So, the police announce, are they. They will not leave me until I produce some I.D. or enter the house.

I have arrived home late because I worked late, writing about a book for the *Harvard Law Review*. The book, which I'm carrying in my knapsack, is *Race, Crime and the Law*, by Randall Kennedy. Since apparently none of us has anything better to do, I take the book out of my sack and show the officers Chapter 4, "Race, Law, and Suspicion: Using Color as a Proxy for Dangerousness." The chapter contains several stories just like this one. It quotes Harvard Professor Henry Louis Gates Jr. * * * "There's a moving violation that many African-Americans know as D.W.B.: Driving While Black."

But this, I announce, is the first time I've ever heard of "walking while black." I point to the big window of my beautiful house. I tell the police that I have seen people, mostly white, walking down the street at all times of the day and night, and I have never heard them questioned about their right to be there. That is why I will not show them my identification. This is not apartheid South Africa, and I don't need a pass card.

The officers are not interested. In fact, they announce, they're getting angry. There have been burglaries in this neighborhood and car vandalism.

The police are just doing their job, and I—I am wasting the taxpayers' money. One officer theorizes that I'm homeless. Another believes that I'm on drugs. The one thing of which they are certain is that I don't live here in the house on whose porch I sit. And when they find out who I "really" am, I will be guilty of unlawful entry, a misdemeanor. * * *

The sergeant tells me that since I'm being "evasive," she will interview my neighbors. The two officers who remain radio for backup. They give the dispatcher the wrong address, and I correct them. Soon a second patrol car, with two more officers, arrives. I am cold but stubborn.

Finally, my neighbor comes outside and identifies me. I'm free now—free to be left alone. Free to walk on a public street. Free to sit on my porch, even if it is cold.

But first, we—the five law enforcement officers and I—look to my neighbor for vindication, a moral to justify the last hour of our lives. My neighbor is black like us. He says that he is always happy to see police patrolling the neighborhood. But, he adds, many white people walk late at night, and they are not questioned about their right to be there. My neighbor tells the officers that they are always welcome to stop by his house for coffee. And he goes home. The sergeant invites me to a crime prevention meeting at the police station in a few weeks. Then the five officers get into their two cars and drive away.

As for me, I'm still searching for a moral. My neighborhood does not seem so beautiful anymore. I got my car repaired right away: I had enjoyed the walk, but I dreaded the next set of officers. Sometimes I prefer to leave criminal procedure at the office. Sometimes I like a walk to be simply a walk.

But sometimes I am willing for my walk to serve as a hypothetical, for the police, and for you, reader, about the Fourth Amendment and its protection against unreasonable government intrusion. If I had a television show, I would say, "Kids, don't try this at home." It is unfortunate, but other uppity Negroes have gotten themselves shot for less than what I did. The officers I encountered were professional, even if the male officers were not especially polite. They never led me to believe that they would physically harm me or even falsely arrest me. It is sad that I should feel grateful for that, but I do.

One reason that I felt safer with the officers was because they were African-American. They might stop me because I'm black, but I didn't think they would be as quick on the draw as nonblack officers, who are more susceptible to the hype. The black officer's construct of me—a black man walking in a neighborhood where people don't often walk at night—was burglary suspect, or homeless person, or drug addict. The white officer's construct—even during a traffic stop—is violent black man. At least that is what is communicated by the approach with the hand on the gun, the order to exit the car, and the patdown search. Not every time, but often enough.

Because the officers were black, I was especially angry. They should've known better.

What is reasonable law enforcement? There are neighborhoods in this city that covet police officers as concerned about crime prevention as these officers seemed to be. Like my neighbor, I had been pleased to see police patrols—at least until the police patrolled me. Still, I could excuse the intrusion as the price of life in the big city if everybody had to pay the price. But everybody does not. Ultimately, my protest is less about privacy and more about discrimination.

Most courts say that police may consider race in assessing suspicion. It is probably true that there are more black than white burglars and car thieves in the District. In *United States v. Weaver*, 966 F. 2d 391 (1992), the U.S. Court of Appeals for the 8th Circuit said of racial profiles:

> [F]acts are not to be ignored simply because they may be unpleasant.... [R]ace, when coupled with other factors [is a lawful] factor in the decision to approach and ultimately detain a [suspect]. We wish it were otherwise, but we take the facts as they are presented to us, not as we would like them to be.

But the fact is also that most of the black people who walk in my neighborhood are, like me, law-abiding. And the fact is that some white people are not law-abiding. Race is so imprecise a proxy for criminality that it is, in the end, useless.

The police officers made me an offer before they left. If I wanted to know when they stopped white people who walked in my neighborhood, they would tell me. They would ring my doorbell any time, day or night, to let me know.

Ironically, considering the officers' lack of interest in Professor Kennedy's book, their offer is also his suggestion. Kennedy believes in colorblindness, including in assessments of suspicion. He writes:

> [I]nstead of placing a racial tax on [minorities], government should, if necessary, increase taxes across the board.... [It] should be forced to inconvenience everyone ... by subjecting all ... to questioning. The reform I support, in other words, does not entail lessened policing. It only insists that the costs of policing be allocated on a nonracial basis.

I turned down the offer, thinking that the police might begin to question every walker in my neighborhood just to make a point. That would not make me feel any safer, and it would inconvenience the neighbors.

In retrospect, I made the wrong decision. I hadn't wanted to draw the enmity of my neighbors by causing them to be treated like criminal suspects. Or like black men. Sometimes the law gets me confused about the difference. Kennedy is correct: It is a confusion everyone should share.

GENDERED (IN)SECURITY: MIGRATION AND CRIMINALIZATION IN THE SECURITY STATE

Pooja Gehi
35 Harv. J. L. & Gender 357 (2012)

B. *Walking While Trans: Police Profiling and Fourth Amendment Stops*

While some transgender people do engage in criminalized work to survive, transgender people are also commonly profiled by the police as criminals whether or not they are actually committing any crimes. * * * For transgender people living in poverty who also identify as people of color, * * * policing stops are almost inevitable. Transgender people of color often even describe the consequential arrests stemming from these police interactions as "walking while trans." * * *

The legal standard for law enforcement to stop and interrogate people on the street is so vague and deferential that it offers no protection against such discrimination. For example, pursuant to the Fourth Amendment, local law enforcement is subject to a standard that demands a "reasonable, articulable suspicion that crime is afoot." This standard, however, is so unclear that a person may be stopped for almost any reason and, in particular, for reasons relating to one's race, gender identity, and/or perceived sexual orientation. For example, in *People v. Lomiller*, the First Department held that "a man carrying a purse" [met] this standard. * * * Wearing tight clothing or too much makeup is seen as a reasonable, articulable suspicion of solicitation for the purposes of prostitution, especially for people whose gender expression appears "wrong" or "suspicious" to police enforcement. Similarly, in my clients' experience, not making eye contact is often used as an indication of drug use, and holding hands with someone perceived to be of the same sex or different gender expression may be considered indication of prostitution. According to my clients, using the bathroom that a police officer perceives as "the wrong bathroom" is often used as an indication of lewd conduct. * * *

PROFILING TERROR

Sharon L. Davies
1 Ohio St. J. Crim. L. 45 (2003)

Following the attack on the World Trade Center on September 11, 2001, the nation's debate over racial profiling turned an abrupt corner. In the wake of the horrendous events of that day and the sudden loss of thousands of innocent lives, the public's view of racial profiling lurched from dramatically against the practice to decidedly in its favor. As fear of additional terrorist attacks gripped the nation and public anger over the acts grew, worried citizens began to reconsider their prior opposition to racial profiling, and proposals that actively urged law enforcement agents to take an especially hard look at persons of Middle Eastern descent abounded. These included calls for the initiation of national identification cards, the enhanced surveillance of Arab-appearing persons in airports and flight schools, the reduction or discontinuation of student visas for nationals of Middle Eastern states, the expansion of governmental authority to arrest immigrants with "links" to terrorist organizations and to accelerate their deportation, the enhancement of governmental authority to intercept privileged attorney-client communications, and the establishment of military tribunals to prosecute suspected terrorists free of the process burdens and defense rights that apply in federal court.

A new label—"ethnic profiling"—quickly emerged and the practice it described was met with shrugs of resignation rather than shouts of protest, signaling a sea change in the nation's thinking about profiling practices from its new, post-9/11 perspective. Perhaps most tellingly, the sentiment favoring this ostensibly new breed of profiling seeped even across racial lines, appealing to those who had resented being the objects of the reviled practice only days before.

In the face of this sudden shift in popular thinking, racial profiling opponents feared that the government would use the public's new tolerance for race-conscious policing as a reason to renegotiate commitments it had only recently made to oppose racial profiling practices. In the days immediately following the attacks, however, government officials struck a more cautionary chord, at least in public. Even as legal commentators could find no constitutional obstacle to ethnic profiling practices, the United States Attorney General proclaimed the government's determination to abide by its commitment to oppose race or ethnic conscious policing practices. And the Department of Transportation issued a directive to all airlines warning that targeting Arab Americans, Muslims or Sikhs would violate federal law.

Despite the government's assurances, however, fear for the rights of Arab-Americans grew as the soothing words of these public officials began to collide with information that federal agents had in fact begun to round up persons of Middle-Eastern descent and place them under arrest. In a little over a month, the number of people taken into federal custody mushroomed from dozens, to hundreds, to over one thousand. And despite round-the-clock news coverage of every conceivable aspect of the September 11 story, remarkably little was known publicly about the identity of those prisoners, the grounds for their detention, the nature of the legal charges against them, or what had led federal agents to arrest them.

If any doubts remained about the ethnic premises underlying the government's 9/11 investigation, those doubts were eliminated as information about the identity of those arrested after September 11 began to emerge, and the Attorney General announced the government's plan to interview more than five thousand persons of Middle Eastern ancestry in search of information about al Qaeda and other terrorist organizations. The Department of Justice expanded this group of interviewees four months later to include approximately 3,000 additional men who had entered the United States on non-immigrant visas from countries with an al Qaeda presence. The interview campaign made clear that the government, too, had concluded that shared heritage with the suicide bombers made individuals fair targets of suspicion after all.

And there was broad-based support for the view that it should. Even as it became apparent that ethnicity figured more heavily into the government's post-9/11 investigation than it at first cared to admit, one popular reaction was: so what? After all, all nineteen of the 9/11 suicide hijackers were nationals of Middle Eastern states. Didn't simple common sense mandate that government investigators of the events factor the shared ethnicity of additional suspects into their decisions of whom to question, detain, arrest or search? Post-9/11 polls showed that many believed the answer was yes, and that continued loyalty to an anti-profiling position after the attacks would impose senseless costs on a nation suddenly at war with terrorism.

Before long, leading criminal justice scholars began to concur, if somewhat apologetically. The gravity of the danger posed by future terrorist threats justified some degree of ethnic profiling, these experts counseled, though for different reasons. The profiling of Arabs and Muslims is distinguishable from profiling of African Americans and Latinos, some argued. An across-the-board opposition to profiling practices may be inadvisable, others wrote, particularly in times of grave national peril. Attempts to prohibit profiling outright have always been futile, still another argued, thus the best we can hope to do is to trim the resentment caused by race-based practices by more closely monitoring how aggressively the police interact with those targeted. All of these scholars acknowledged that ethnic profiling would impose costs on innocent targets, but each believed that nation's security demanded such costs, provided that safeguards were adopted to protect against police excesses.

This Article rejects the suggestion that Arab or Middle Eastern heritage provides an appropriate basis of suspicion of individuals in the aftermath of the September 11 attacks. In a nation that claims upwards of 3.5 million persons of Arab ancestry, the ethnic characteristic of Arab descent, standing alone, possesses no useful predictive power for separating the September 11 terrorists' accomplices and other terrorist wannabees from innocent Americans. * * *

The collection of terrorist acts that have occurred on American soil should make any careful thinker hesitate before concluding that persons of Middle Eastern origins are in fact more likely to be terrorists than others. Several "home-grown" terrorists belie this claim. Timothy McVeigh, a white male from upstate New York, committed an act of terrorism responsible for the loss of 168 innocent lives, and over 500 injuries. Had he had his way, the death toll would have been much higher. It was purely and simply a fortuity not in any way creditable to him that more people were not killed when he detonated the bomb outside the Murrah Federal Building. When asked if he had any regrets, McVeigh replied that his only regret was that the building had not collapsed completely. Before the events of September 11, McVeigh's malicious and premeditated crime was frequently referred to as "the deadliest act of terrorism ever committed on American soil." Nevertheless, no one suggested after the bombing of the Alfred P. Murrah Federal Building in Oklahoma City that the effort to bring to justice those responsible for that bombing and the deaths of 168 innocents could properly involve acts of police profiling that would subject to extra scrutiny young, closely-cropped, white males simply because they shared those physical characteristics with McVeigh. And why not? I suspect that it is because, when we are faced with the criminality of a white suspect who may have accomplices, we do not fall prey to the same tortured reasoning to which we seem so easily to fall prey when we are faced with a minority suspect. In such a setting, we seem instinctively to know that the odds of capturing additional culprits by treating all young, white males with suspicion are so astronomically small, and the burdens we place on innocent white males in the process are so astronomically large, that it is a course of investigative conduct that makes no logical sense.

Additional examples provide further reason to doubt [the premise that Middle Easterners are more likely to commit acts of terror than non-Middle Easterners]. Like Tim McVeigh, Ted Kaczynski also fails to fit the currently popular stereotype of the Arab or Muslim terrorist. Kaczynski, another native of upstate New York and a White American, was responsible for a string of bombings occurring over the course of seventeen years which resulted in the deaths of three people and injuries of twenty-three others. Unlike the Post-9/11 reaction, however, one would search in vain for calls for increased surveillance of scrubby, white male recluses after Kaczynski's reign of terror. * * *

CHAPTER 11

SEIZURES

■ ■ ■

The Fourth Amendment prohibits both unreasonable searches and seizures. In Chapter 2, we learned what type of government action constitutes a "search." This chapter examines what type of government action constitutes a "seizure" of the person.

A "seizure" of the person requires either the application of physical force or "submission to the assertion of authority." California v. Hodari D., 499 U.S. 621, 626 (1991). To determine whether an individual who has submitted to the assertion of governmental authority has been "seized," courts usually apply what has been called the "free to leave" test, first enunciated by Justice Stewart in *United States v. Mendenhall*. The "free to leave" test is explained and applied in the first case in this chapter, *Immigration and Naturalization Service v. Delgado*.

In *Florida v. Bostick*, the Court modifies the "free to leave" test in a case involving a bus sweep. In *(E)Racing the Fourth Amendment*, Devon Carbado critiques Justice O'Connor's colorblind analysis in *Florida v. Bostick*, showing how consideration of Bostick's race and the race of the officers could change the seizure analysis. In *No Need to Shout*, Janice Nadler uses empirical research on compliance with authority to question the Court's conclusion in another bus sweep case that the defendants were not seized and that they voluntarily consented to the searches that led to the discovery of contraband. In *"Black and Blue Encounters"—Some Preliminary Thoughts about Fourth Amendment Seizures: Should Race Matter?*, Tracey Maclin argues that courts should consider the race of the person confronted by police when applying the "free to leave" test.

In *Florida v. Royer*, the Court tries to provide guidance to lower courts on when a seizure of the person is merely a *Terry* stop for which a reasonable suspicion is required and when it constitutes a de facto arrest, requiring probable cause. While the *Royer* Court does not provide lower courts with a clear, bright line test for making this determination, it suggests several factors that are relevant to the inquiry. Try to discern these factors when you read *Royer*. Finally, in *Torres v. Madrid*, the Court addresses whether a seizure occurs when an officer applies physical force to an individual who does not submit to the officer's authority and control.

IMMIGRATION AND NATURALIZATION SERVICE v. DELGADO
Supreme Court of the United States
466 U.S. 210, 104 S. Ct. 1758, 80 L. Ed. 2d 247 (1984)

JUSTICE REHNQUIST delivered the opinion of the court. * * *

[The INS conducted surveys of the work forces at three garment factories in search of undocumented immigrants.] At the beginning of the surveys several agents positioned themselves near the buildings' exits, while other agents dispersed throughout the factory to question most, but not all, employees at their work stations. The agents displayed badges, carried walkie-talkies, and were armed, although at no point during any of the surveys was a weapon ever drawn. Moving systematically through the factory, the agents approached employees and, after identifying themselves, asked them from one to three questions relating to their citizenship. If the employee gave a credible reply that he was a United States citizen, the questioning ended, and the agent moved on to another employee. If the employee gave an unsatisfactory response or admitted that he was an alien, the employee was asked to produce his immigration papers. During the survey, employees continued with their work and were free to walk around within the factory.

Respondents are four employees questioned in one of the three surveys. In 1978 respondents and their union representative, the International Ladies Garment Workers' Union, filed two actions, later consolidated, in the United States District Court for the Central District of California challenging the constitutionality of INS factory surveys and seeking declaratory and injunctive relief. Respondents argued that the factory surveys violated their Fourth Amendment right to be free from unreasonable searches or seizures and the equal protection component of the Due Process Clause of the Fifth Amendment.

The District Court * * * ruled that none of the respondents had been detained under the Fourth Amendment during the factory surveys. * * * Accordingly, it granted summary judgment in favor of the INS.

The Court of Appeals reversed. Applying the standard first enunciated by a Member of this Court in *United States v. Mendenhall* (opinion of Stewart, J.), the Court of Appeals concluded that the entire work forces were seized for the duration of each survey, which lasted from one to two hours, because the stationing of agents at the doors to the buildings meant that "a reasonable worker 'would have believed that he was not free to leave.'" * * * [T]he Court of Appeals * * * further held that under the Fourth Amendment individual employees could be questioned only on the basis of a reasonable suspicion that a particular employee being questioned was an alien illegally in the country. A reasonable suspicion or probable cause to believe that a number of illegal aliens were working at a particular factory site was insufficient to justify questioning any individual employee.

Consequently, it also held that the individual questioning of respondents violated the Fourth Amendment because there had been no such reasonable suspicion or probable cause as to any of them.

We granted certiorari to review the decision of the Court of Appeals, because it has serious implications for the enforcement of the immigration laws. * * *

The Fourth Amendment does not proscribe all contact between the police and citizens. * * * As we have noted elsewhere: "Obviously, not all personal intercourse between policemen and citizens involves 'seizures' of persons. Only when the officer, by means of physical force or show of authority, has restrained the liberty of a citizen may we conclude that a 'seizure' has occurred."[a] While applying such a test is relatively straightforward in a situation resembling a traditional arrest, the protection against unreasonable seizures also extends to "seizures that involve only a brief detention short of traditional arrest." What has evolved from our cases is a determination that an initially consensual encounter between a police officer and a citizen can be transformed into a seizure or detention within the meaning of the Fourth Amendment, "if, in view of all

---

[a] This language suggests that a Fourth Amendment seizure of the person occurs only when an officer has restrained the liberty of a citizen, but this is not completely true. Later Supreme Court cases have clarified that there are different ways an individual can be seized for purposes of the Fourth Amendment.

In *California v. Hodari D.*, the Court noted that a "seizure" of the person requires either physical force or "submission to the assertion of authority." California v. Hodari D., 499 U.S. 621, 626 (1991). If an officer asserts a show of authority but the individual refuses to submit to that officer's authority, the officer has not seized the person. Thus, no seizure occurs when an officer yells "Stop, in the name of the law!" at a fleeing suspect who continues to flee. *Id.* The individual has to submit to the officer's show of authority in order to be seized.

Another example of a seizure by submission to authority is when the government intentionally terminates an individual's freedom of movement and thereby forces that individual to submit to the government's authority. The mere fact that there has been a governmentally caused termination of an individual's freedom of movement, however, is not sufficient to constitute a seizure for Fourth Amendment purposes. A seizure of the person through termination of freedom of movement occurs "only when there is a governmental termination of freedom of movement *through means intentionally applied.*" Brower v. County of Inyo, 489 U.S. 593, 597 (1989) (holding that setting up a roadblock for the purpose of stopping a fleeing suspect and succeeding in doing so constituted a "seizure" within the meaning of the Fourth Amendment). An accidental termination of an individual's freedom of movement by government agents would not constitute a Fourth Amendment seizure.

A person can also be seized when an officer applies physical force to the body of a person with intent to restrain that person. When there is an application of physical force, a seizure has occurred even if the officer's force is not successful in subduing the person. Torres v. Madrid, 592 U.S. ___ (2021) (finding that a woman, shot 13 times by officers trying to restrain her, was seized even though she eluded capture and was able to drive away).

As Orin Kerr explains, the "free to leave" test applies in "submission to authority" types of seizures as opposed to in cases involving the application of physical force. Orin Kerr, *What Is a Fourth Amendment 'Seizure' After* Torres v. Madrid, REASON.COM: VOLOKH CONSPIRACY (Mar. 26, 2021) ("When a person responds to a show of authority, as opposed to physical force, the test is that a seizure occurs if 'in view of all the circumstances surrounding the incident, a reasonable person would have believed that he was not free to leave.' "), https://reason.com/volokh/2021/03/26/what-is-a-fourth-amendment-seizure-after-torres-v-madrid/ (https://perma.cc/6PEE-FPES) (citing Brendlin v. California, 551 U.S. 249, 255 (2007)).

the circumstances surrounding the incident, a reasonable person would have believed that he was not free to leave." * * *

The Court of Appeals held that "the manner in which the factory surveys were conducted in this case constituted a seizure of the workforce" under the Fourth Amendment. * * * [T]he pivotal factor in its decision was the stationing of INS agents near the exits of the factory buildings. According to the Court of Appeals, the stationing of agents near the doors meant that "departures were not to be contemplated," and thus, workers were "not free to leave." In support of the decision below, respondents argue that the INS created an intimidating psychological environment when it intruded unexpectedly into the workplace with such a show of officers. Besides the stationing of agents near the exits, respondents add that the length of the survey and the failure to inform workers they were free to leave resulted in a Fourth Amendment seizure of the entire work force.

We reject the claim that the entire work forces of the two factories were seized for the duration of the surveys when the INS placed agents near the exits of the factory sites. Ordinarily, when people are at work their freedom to move about has been meaningfully restricted, not by the actions of law enforcement officials, but by the workers' voluntary obligations to their employers. The record indicates that when these surveys were initiated, the employees went about their ordinary business, operating machinery and performing other job assignments. While the surveys did cause some disruption, including the efforts of some workers to hide, the record also indicates that workers were not prevented by the agents from moving about the factories.

Respondents argue, however, that the stationing of agents near the factory doors showed the INS's intent to prevent people from leaving. But there is nothing in the record indicating that this is what the agents at the doors actually did. The obvious purpose of the agents' presence at the factory doors was to insure [sic] that all persons in the factories were questioned. The record indicates that the INS agents' conduct in this case consisted simply of questioning employees and arresting those they had probable cause to believe were unlawfully present in the factory. This conduct should have given respondents no reason to believe that they would be detained if they gave truthful answers to the questions put to them or if they simply refused to answer. * * *

The Court of Appeals also held that "detentive questioning" of individuals could be conducted only if INS agents could articulate "objective facts providing investigators with a reasonable suspicion that each questioned person, so detained, is an alien illegally in this country." Under our analysis, however, since there was no seizure of the work forces by virtue of the method of conducting the factory surveys, the only way the issue of individual questioning could be presented would be if one of the named respondents had in fact been seized or detained. * * * [W]e conclude that none were. * * *

Accordingly, the judgment of the Court of Appeals is

Reversed.

JUSTICE BRENNAN, with whom JUSTICE MARSHALL joins, concurring in part and dissenting in part. * * *

At first blush, the Court's opinion appears unremarkable. But what is striking about today's decision is its studied air of unreality. Indeed, it is only through a considerable feat of legerdemain that the Court is able to arrive at the conclusion that the respondents were not seized. The success of the Court's sleight of hand turns on the proposition that the interrogations of respondents by the INS were merely brief, "consensual encounters," that posed no threat to respondents' personal security and freedom. The record, however, tells a far different story. * * *

Although it was joined at the time by only one other Member of this Court, Part IIA of Justice Stewart's opinion in *United States v. Mendenhall*, offered a helpful, preliminary distillation of [the Court's cases on the meaning of a "seizure" of the person.] Justice Stewart explained that "a person has been 'seized' within the meaning of the Fourth Amendment only if, in view of all of the circumstances surrounding the incident, a reasonable person would have believed that he was not free to leave." The opinion also suggested that such circumstances might include "the threatening presence of several officers, the display of a weapon by an officer, some physical touching of the person of the citizen, or the use of language or tone of voice indicating that compliance with the officer's request might be compelled."

A majority of the Court has since adopted that formula as the appropriate standard for determining when inquiries made by the police cross the boundary separating merely consensual encounters from forcible stops to investigate a suspected crime. This rule properly looks not to the subjective impressions of the person questioned but rather to the objective characteristics of the encounter which may suggest whether or not a reasonable person would believe that he remained free during the course of the questioning to disregard the questions and walk away. * * *

Applying these principles to the facts of this case, I have no difficulty concluding that respondents were seized within the meaning of the Fourth Amendment when they were accosted by the INS agents and questioned concerning their right to remain in the United States. Although none of the respondents was physically restrained by the INS agents during the questioning, it is nonetheless plain beyond cavil that the manner in which the INS conducted these surveys demonstrated a "show of authority" of sufficient size and force to overbear the will of any reasonable person.

Faced with such tactics, a reasonable person could not help but feel compelled to stop and provide answers to the INS agents' questions. * * *

The Court's eagerness to conclude that these interrogations did not represent seizures is to some extent understandable, of course, because such a conclusion permits the Court to avoid the imposing task of justifying these seizures on the basis of reasonable, objective criteria as required by the Fourth Amendment.

* * * Repeatedly, we have insisted that police may not detain and interrogate an individual unless they have reasonable grounds for suspecting that the person is involved in some unlawful activity. * * * This requirement of particularized suspicion provides the chief protection of lawful citizens against unwarranted governmental interference with their personal security and privacy.

* * * [T]he INS agents involved in this case apparently were instructed, in the words of the INS Assistant District Director in charge of the operations, to interrogate "virtually all persons employed by a company." Consequently, all workers, irrespective of whether they were American citizens, permanent resident aliens,[b] or deportable aliens, were subjected to questioning by INS agents concerning their right to remain in the country. * * * [M]any of the employees in the surveyed factories who are lawful residents of the United States may have been born in Mexico, have a Latin appearance, or speak Spanish while at work. What this means, of course, is that the many lawful workers who constitute the clear majority at the surveyed workplaces are subjected to surprise questioning under intimidating circumstances by INS agents who have no reasonable basis for suspecting that they have done anything wrong. To say that such an indiscriminate policy of mass interrogation is constitutional makes a mockery of the words of the Fourth Amendment.

* * * [T]here is no reliable way to distinguish with a reasonable degree of accuracy between native-born and naturalized [U.S.] citizens[c] of Mexican ancestry on the one hand, and [undocumented] aliens of Mexican ancestry on the other. Indeed, the record in this case clearly demonstrates this danger, since respondents Correa and Delgado, although both American citizens, were subjected to questioning during the INS surveys.

---

[b] The term "permanent resident alien" refers to an individual who was born in another country, immigrated to the United States, and resides lawfully in the United States. A permanent resident has not undergone the process of naturalization and therefore is not a U.S. citizen.

[c] A native-born U.S. citizen is a person who was born in the United States and is a U.S. citizen by birth. A naturalized citizen is a person who was born in another country and becomes a U.S. citizen through the naturalization process, which involves a residency requirement, a civics test, a moral character requirement, and an interview. The term "alien" is used to refer to an immigrant to the United States, i.e., someone who was born in another country and immigrated to the United States. An undocumented "alien" of Mexican ancestry is an immigrant from Mexico who is in the United States without authorization from the United States government.

Moreover, the mere fact that a person is believed to be an alien provides no immediate grounds for suspecting any illegal activity. * * * In contexts such as these factory surveys, where it is virtually impossible to distinguish fairly between citizens and aliens, the threat to vital civil rights of American citizens would soon become intolerable if we simply permitted the INS to question persons solely on account of suspected alienage. Therefore, in order to protect both American citizens and lawful resident aliens, who are also protected by the Fourth Amendment, the INS must tailor its enforcement efforts to focus only on those workers who are reasonably suspected of being illegal aliens. * * *

No one doubts that the presence of large numbers of undocumented aliens in this country creates law enforcement problems of titanic proportions for the INS. Nor does anyone question that this agency must be afforded considerable latitude in meeting its delegated enforcement responsibilities. I am afraid, however, that the Court has become so mesmerized by the magnitude of the problem that it has too easily allowed Fourth Amendment freedoms to be sacrificed. * * * The answer to these problems, I suggest, does not lie in abandoning our commitment to protecting the cherished rights secured by the Fourth Amendment, but rather may be found by reexamining our immigration policy.

I dissent.

[JUSTICE STEVENS' concurring opinion and JUSTICE POWELL's concurring opinion have been omitted.]

NOTE

In finding that the workers at the factories were not seized, Justice Rehnquist states, "The record indicates that the INS agents' conduct in this case consisted simply of questioning employees and arresting those they had probable cause to believe were unlawfully present in the factory. This conduct should have given respondents no reason to believe that they would be detained if they gave truthful answers to the questions put to them or if they simply refused to answer."

In *Undocumented Criminal Procedure*, 58 UCLA L. REV. 1543 (2011), Devon Carbado and Cheryl Harris critique Justice Rehnquist's characterization of the surveys:

> Justice Rehnquist's account sanitizes the episode, which involved between twenty and thirty INS agents. These agents wore their INS badges, carried handcuffs—and they were armed. Some of the agents guarded the exits; others moved systematically through the factory, row by row, "in para-military formation." The entire episode lasted between one and two hours. At no time during any of this did the agents inform the workers that they were free to leave. Presumably,

the workers inferred just the opposite, especially since the INS arrested several of the workers who attempted to exit the factory.

Carbado and Harris also call attention to Justice Rehnquist's lack of engagement with the issue of race, noting:

> Significantly, at no point in Justice Rehnquist's opinion does he engage race, notwithstanding that race figured prominently in Delgado's brief. According to Delgado:
>
>> [I]nnocuous conduct does not become suspect merely because the person observed is nonwhite. Yet that is precisely what occurs during these raids. Every Latin[x] is suspected of being an undocumented alien due to his or her race. Members of a distinct minority characterized by immutable traits are singled out because they are suspected to be illegal aliens. As a result, innocent members of the class suffer an impairment of their privacy (a loss not suffered by members of the white or Black community) because the standard applied fails to distinguish in any meaningful way between the guilty and the innocent.

Devon W. Carbado and Cheryl I. Harris, *Undocumented Criminal Procedure*, 58 UCLA L. Rev. 1543 (2011). Can similar critiques be lodged against the Court's analysis in the next case?

FLORIDA V. BOSTICK

Supreme Court of the United States
501 U.S. 429, 111 S. Ct. 2382, 115 L. Ed. 2d 389 (1991)

JUSTICE O'CONNOR delivered the opinion of the Court. * * *

In this case, two [Broward County Sheriff's Department] officers discovered cocaine when they searched a suitcase belonging to Terrance Bostick. The underlying facts of the search are in dispute, but the Florida Supreme Court, whose decision we review here, stated explicitly the factual premise for its decision:

> Two officers, complete with badges, insignia and one of them holding a recognizable zipper pouch, containing a pistol, boarded a bus bound from Miami to Atlanta during a stopover in Fort Lauderdale. Eyeing the passengers, the officers, admittedly without articulable suspicion, picked out the defendant passenger and asked to inspect his ticket and identification. The ticket, from Miami to Atlanta, matched the defendant's identification and both were immediately returned to him as unremarkable. However, the two police officers persisted and explained their presence as narcotics agents on the lookout for illegal drugs. In pursuit of that aim, they then requested the defendant's consent to search his luggage. Needless to say, there is a conflict in the evidence about whether the defendant consented to the search of the second bag

in which the contraband was found and as to whether he was informed of his right to refuse consent. However, any conflict must be resolved in favor of the state, it being a question of fact decided by the trial judge.

Two facts are particularly worth noting. First, the police specifically advised Bostick that he had the right to refuse consent. Bostick appears to have disputed the point, but * * * the trial court resolved this evidentiary conflict in the State's favor. Second, at no time did the officers threaten Bostick with a gun. * * * [O]ne officer carried a zipper pouch containing a pistol—the equivalent of carrying a gun in a holster—but the [Florida Supreme Court] did not suggest that the gun was ever removed from its pouch, pointed at Bostick, or otherwise used in a threatening manner. The dissent's characterization of the officers as "gun-wielding inquisitor[s]," is colorful, but lacks any basis in fact.

Bostick was arrested and charged with trafficking in cocaine. He moved to suppress the cocaine on the grounds that it had been seized in violation of his Fourth Amendment rights. The trial court denied the motion but made no factual findings. Bostick subsequently entered a plea of guilty, but reserved the right to appeal the denial of the motion to suppress. * * *

The sole issue presented for our review is whether a police encounter on a bus of the type described above necessarily constitutes a "seizure" within the meaning of the Fourth Amendment. The State concedes, and we accept for purposes of this decision, that the officers lacked the reasonable suspicion required to justify a seizure and that, if a seizure took place, the drugs found in Bostick's suitcase must be suppressed as tainted fruit.

Our cases make it clear that a seizure does not occur simply because a police officer approaches an individual and asks a few questions. So long as a reasonable person would feel free "to disregard the police and go about his business," the encounter is consensual and no reasonable suspicion is required. * * *

There is no doubt that if this same encounter had taken place before Bostick boarded the bus or in the lobby of the bus terminal, it would not rise to the level of a seizure. The Court has dealt with similar encounters in airports and has found them to be "the sort of consensual encounter[s] that implicat[e] no Fourth Amendment interest." We have stated that even when officers have no basis for suspecting a particular individual, they may generally ask questions of that individual; ask to examine the individual's identification; and request consent to search his or her luggage—as long as the police do not convey a message that compliance with their requests is required.

Bostick insists that this case is different because it took place in the cramped confines of a bus. A police encounter is much more intimidating in this setting, he argues, because police tower over a seated passenger and there is little room to move around. Bostick claims to find support in language from *Michigan v. Chesternut* and other cases, indicating that a seizure occurs when a reasonable person would believe that he or she is not "free to leave." Bostick maintains that a reasonable bus passenger would not have felt free to leave under the circumstances of this case because there is nowhere to go on a bus. Also, the bus was about to depart. Had Bostick disembarked, he would have risked being stranded and losing whatever baggage he had locked away in the luggage compartment.

The Florida Supreme Court found this argument persuasive, so much so that it adopted a *per se* rule prohibiting the police from randomly boarding buses as a means of drug interdiction. The state court erred, however, in focusing on whether Bostick was "free to leave" rather than on the principle that those words were intended to capture. When police attempt to question a person who is walking down the street or through an airport lobby, it makes sense to inquire whether a reasonable person would feel free to continue walking. But when the person is seated on a bus and has no desire to leave, the degree to which a reasonable person would feel that he or she could leave is not an accurate measure of the coercive effect of the encounter.

Here, for example, the mere fact that Bostick did not feel free to leave the bus does not mean that the police seized him. Bostick was a passenger on a bus that was scheduled to depart. He would not have felt free to leave the bus even if the police had not been present. Bostick's movements were "confined" in a sense, but this was the natural result of his decision to take the bus; it says nothing about whether or not the police conduct at issue was coercive.

* * * Bostick's freedom of movement was restricted by a factor independent of police conduct—*i.e.,* by his being a passenger on a bus. Accordingly, the "free to leave" analysis on which Bostick relies is inapplicable. In such a situation, the appropriate inquiry is whether a reasonable person would feel free to decline the officers' requests or otherwise terminate the encounter. This formulation follows logically from prior cases and breaks no new ground. We have said before that the crucial test is whether, taking into account all of the circumstances surrounding the encounter, the police conduct would "have communicated to a reasonable person that he was not at liberty to ignore the police presence and go about his business." Where the encounter takes place is one factor, but it is not the only one. And, as the Solicitor General correctly observes, an individual may decline an officer's request without fearing prosecution. We have consistently held that a refusal to cooperate, without more, does not furnish the minimal level of objective justification needed for a detention or seizure.

The facts of this case, as described by the Florida Supreme Court, leave some doubt whether a seizure occurred. Two officers walked up to Bostick on the bus, asked him a few questions, and asked if they could search his bags. As we have explained, no seizure occurs when police ask questions of an individual, ask to examine the individual's identification, and request consent to search his or her luggage—so long as the officers do not convey a message that compliance with their requests is required. Here, the facts recited by the Florida Supreme Court indicate that the officers did not point guns at Bostick or otherwise threaten him and that they specifically advised Bostick that he could refuse consent.

Nevertheless, we refrain from deciding whether or not a seizure occurred in this case. * * * We remand so that the Florida courts may evaluate the seizure question under the correct legal standard.[a] We do reject, however, Bostick's argument that he must have been seized because no reasonable person would freely consent to a search of luggage that he or she knows contains drugs. This argument cannot prevail because the "reasonable person" test presupposes an *innocent* person.

The dissent * * * attempts to characterize our decision as applying a lesser degree of constitutional protection to those individuals who travel by bus, rather than by other forms of transportation. This, too, is an erroneous characterization. Our Fourth Amendment inquiry in this case—whether a reasonable person would have felt free to decline the officers' requests or otherwise terminate the encounter—applies equally to police encounters that take place on trains, planes, and city streets. It is the dissent that would single out this particular mode of travel for differential treatment by adopting a *per se* rule that random bus searches are unconstitutional. * * *

We adhere to the rule that, in order to determine whether a particular encounter constitutes a seizure, a court must consider all the circumstances surrounding the encounter to determine whether the police conduct would have communicated to a reasonable person that the person was not free to decline the officers' requests or otherwise terminate the encounter. That rule applies to encounters that take place on a city street or in an airport lobby, and it applies equally to encounters on a bus. The Florida Supreme Court erred in adopting a *per se* rule.

The judgment of the Florida Supreme Court is reversed, and the case is remanded for further proceedings not inconsistent with this opinion.

It is so ordered.

---

[a] On remand, the Florida Supreme Court did not evaluate whether Bostick was seized under the modified test for a seizure established by the U.S. Supreme Court. Instead, it simply affirmed the district court's denial of Bostick's motion to suppress in a per curiam opinion. Bostick v. State, 593 So.2d 494, 495 (Fla. 1992) (per curiam).

JUSTICE MARSHALL, with whom JUSTICE BLACKMUN and JUSTICE STEVENS join, dissenting. * * *

I have no objection to the manner in which the majority frames the test for determining whether a suspicionless bus sweep amounts to a Fourth Amendment "seizure." I agree that the appropriate question is whether a passenger who is approached during such a sweep "would feel free to decline the officers' requests or otherwise terminate the encounter." What I cannot understand is how the majority can possibly suggest an affirmative answer to this question.

* * * Two officers boarded the Greyhound bus on which respondent was a passenger while the bus, en route from Miami to Atlanta, was on a brief stop to pick up passengers in Fort Lauderdale. The officers made a visible display of their badges and wore bright green "raid" jackets bearing the insignia of the Broward County Sheriff's Department; one held a gun in a recognizable weapons pouch. These facts alone constitute an intimidating "show of authority." Once on board, the officers approached respondent, who was sitting in the back of the bus, identified themselves as narcotics officers and began to question him. One officer stood in front of respondent's seat, partially blocking the narrow aisle through which respondent would have been required to pass to reach the exit of the bus.

* * * Apart from trying to accommodate the officers, respondent had only two options. First, he could have remained seated while obstinately refusing to respond to the officers' questioning. But in light of the intimidating show of authority that the officers made upon boarding the bus, respondent reasonably could have believed that such behavior would only arouse the officers' suspicions and intensify their interrogation. Indeed, officers who carry out bus sweeps like the one at issue here frequently admit that this is the effect of a passenger's refusal to cooperate. The majority's observation that a mere refusal to answer questions, "without more," does not give rise to a reasonable basis for seizing a passenger, is utterly beside the point, because a passenger unadvised of his rights and otherwise unversed in constitutional law *has no reason to know* that the police cannot hold his refusal to cooperate against him.

Second, respondent could have tried to escape the officers' presence by leaving the bus altogether. But because doing so would have required respondent to squeeze past the gun-wielding inquisitor who was blocking the aisle of the bus, this hardly seems like a course that respondent reasonably would have viewed as available to him. The majority lamely protests that nothing in the stipulated facts shows that the questioning officer "*point*[ed] [his] gu[n] at [respondent] or otherwise *threaten*[ed] him" with the weapon. Our decisions recognize the obvious point, however, that the choice of the police to "display" their weapons during an encounter exerts significant coercive pressure on the confronted citizen. We have never suggested that the police must go so far as to put a citizen in immediate apprehension of *being shot* before a court can take account of the intimidating effect of being questioned by an officer with weapon in hand. * * *

Rather than requiring the police to justify the coercive tactics employed here, the majority blames respondent for his own sensation of constraint. The majority concedes that respondent "did not feel free to leave the bus" as a means of breaking off the interrogation by the Broward County officers. But this experience of confinement, the majority explains, "was the natural result of *his* decision to take the bus." Thus, in the majority's view, because respondent's "freedom of movement was restricted by a factor independent of police conduct—*i.e.*, by his being a passenger on a bus"—respondent was not seized for purposes of the Fourth Amendment.

This reasoning borders on sophism and trivializes the values that underlie the Fourth Amendment. Obviously, a person's "voluntary decision" to place himself in a room with only one exit does not authorize the police to force an encounter upon him by placing themselves in front of the exit. * * * By consciously deciding to single out persons who have undertaken interstate or intrastate travel, officers who conduct suspicionless, dragnet-style sweeps put passengers to the choice of cooperating or of exiting their buses and possibly being stranded in unfamiliar locations. It is exactly because this "choice" is no "choice" at all that police engage this technique.

In my view, the Fourth Amendment clearly condemns the suspicionless, dragnet-style sweep of intrastate or interstate buses. * * *

I dissent.

(E)RACING THE FOURTH AMENDMENT
Devon W. Carbado
100 Mich. L. Rev. 946 (2002)

The "free to leave" test—the test the Supreme Court applies to determine whether a particular police activity is a seizure of the person that implicates the Fourth Amendment—constitutes a specific doctrinal site within which the construction of race exploits and exacerbates existing racial inequalities. Two cases in particular bear this out: *Florida v. Bostick* and *INS v. Delgado*. * * * [T]o the extent that scholars engage either of these cases, they pay almost no attention to the race-constructing ideologies that underlie them. The dominant way of understanding *Bostick*, for example, is that it constitutes an instance in which the Supreme Court ignores race. While not entirely inaccurate, this understanding obscures the racial productivity of *Bostick*—that is, the Court's construction and reification of race in that case. Re-reading *Bostick* and *Delgado* as cases that are actively engaged in constructing race helps to make the point that colorblindness is not in fact race neutral, but instead reflects a particular racial preference that systematically burdens nonwhites.[a] * * *

In *Bostick*, two armed Broward County Sheriff officers wearing bright green "raid" jackets boarded a Greyhound bus at Fort Lauderdale. The bus had made a temporary stop on its way from Miami to Atlanta. When the officers entered the bus, the bus driver exited, closing the door behind him. Without suspecting any individual passenger of wrongdoing, the officers approached Terrance Bostick, who was asleep in the back of the bus. One of the officers asked to see Bostick's ticket and a piece of identification. Bostick obliged, providing the officer with a Florida driver's license and a ticket stub, both of which the officer returned to Bostick. The officers then explained that they were narcotics agents and asked for Bostick's permission to search his luggage. Upon searching Bostick's luggage the officers found approximately one pound of cocaine, and they arrested him. Subsequently, Bostick was charged with trafficking in narcotics, and he pleaded no contest.

Writing for the Court, Justice O'Connor "refrain[ed] from deciding whether or not a seizure occurred in this case." She maintained, however, that the facts left "some doubt" that Bostick was seized. In other words, she implicitly suggested that the encounter was consensual; that at all times, Bostick was free to leave. Central to her analysis is the notion that an individual's interaction with the police does not become a seizure simply because the officer asks that individual a few questions, requests that the individual produce identification, or seeks permission to search the individual's personal effects. "[A]s long as the police do not convey a message that compliance with their request is required," a seizure has not occurred. Justice O'Connor's opinion invites the conclusion that neither the officers' communication nor their conduct toward Bostick conveyed a message of compulsory compliance.

* * * Nowhere in Justice O'Connor's opinion does she entertain the possibility that Bostick may have been targeted because he is black. In fact, Justice O'Connor does not even mention Bostick's race. Nor does she mention the race of the officers. In this sense, an argument can be made that Justice O'Connor's analysis ignores race. This argument, however, is only partially correct. That is, while it is fair to say that Justice O'Connor's analysis ignores the fact that Bostick is black and the officers are white, it is more accurate to say that her analysis constructs Bostick and the officers with the racial ideology of colorblindness. In other words, the problem is not that Justice O'Connor does not see race, but rather that she sees race

---

[a] Ibram X. Kendi makes a similar point in his 2019 New York Times bestseller book, *How to Be an Antiracist*, writing, "The common idea of claiming 'color blindness' is akin to the notion of being 'not racist'—as with the 'not racist,' the colorblind individual, by consistently failing to see race, fails to see racism and falls into racist passivity. The language of colorblindness—like the language of 'not racist'—is a mask to hide racism." IBRAM X. KENDI, HOW TO BE AN ANTIRACIST (One World Press 2019).

in a particular way. Her decision to see Bostick as a man and not as a black man does not ignore race; it constructs race. * * *

That Justice O'Connor is of the view that, by and large, race does not and should not matter is clear from her race jurisprudence in the Fourteenth Amendment context. According to Justice O'Connor, "[r]acial classifications of any sort pose the risk of lasting harm to our society. They reinforce the belief, held by too many for too much of our history, that individuals should be judged by the color of their skin." For Justice O'Connor, "the individual is important, not his race, his creed, or his color." This normative commitment about race, although articulated in a different doctrinal context, helps to explain Justice O'Connor's construction of Bostick and the police officers. From Justice O'Connor's perspective, textually referencing their respective racial identities would entrench existing negative racial impressions of—that is, stigmatize—both. The thinking might be that, because of stereotypes, the starting point for conceptualizing an interaction between a black man and a white police officer might be that the former is a criminal and the latter a racist. To disrupt these social meanings, and to prevent the attribution of them to Bostick and the police officers, Justice O'Connor constructs these parties as "individuals." * * *

Justice O'Connor's commitment to individualism (not race) obscures the fact that individualism as an ideological concept is itself racializing and thus race-constructing. To appreciate how, assume that Justice O'Connor's construction of Bostick and the police officers as individuals without races disrupts both the social meaning of Bostick as a criminal and the social meaning of the police as racist cops. This disruption does not eliminate race; Bostick remains black and the police officers remain white. The disruption merely re-defines what blackness vis-à-vis Bostick and whiteness vis-à-vis the police officers signify. Under this redefinition, Bostick becomes a black man without the presumption of criminality and the police become white officers without the presumption of a racist identity. In the abstract, both disruptions might make sense. But in the context of *Bostick*, they obscure that Bostick may have held and acted on a racial presumption that the police officers were racists and the police may have held and acted on a racial presumption that Bostick was a criminal. * * *

The more fundamental problem with Justice O'Connor's analysis is that it does not explicitly engage race. Throughout her opinion, race remains unspeakable. A more careful analysis would, at the very least, have racialized Bostick's interaction with the officers. * * * Part of the circumstances of the encounter was race—more particularly, Bostick's race and the race of the police officers. The interaction of black male identity with white male police authority creates a physically confining social situation every bit as real as (and operating independently from) being on a bus. Most, if not all, black people—especially black men—are apprehensive about police encounters. They grow up with racial stories of police abuse—witnessing them as public spectacles in the media, observing them firsthand in their communities, and experiencing them as daily realities. Put another way, race-based policing is part of black people's collective consciousness. Thus, when black people encounter the police, "[t]hey don't know whether justice will be meted out or whether judge, jury and executioner is pulling up behind them." Yet, Justice O'Connor situates her seizure analysis outside of this racial reality. She removes Bostick and the police officers from a social context in which race is material to a discursive, socially constructed world in which it is not. At no time does Justice O'Connor consider how Bostick, or a man in his racial position, might have experienced two white police officers crowded around him on a bus. She race neutralizes the encounter. Bostick's race, the race of the officers, and the relationship between the two receive no textual engagement in her analysis. * * *

Perhaps Justice O'Connor does not discuss the racial dimensions of the encounter for the same reason that she discounts the coercive aspects of police encounters on buses. With respect to the latter, she argued that, to the extent that "Bostick's movements were 'confined' . . . this was the natural result of his decision to take the bus; it says nothing about whether or not the police conduct at issue was coercive." In other words, "Bostick's freedom of movement was restricted by a factor independent of police conduct—*i.e.*, by his being a passenger on a bus." Given this fact, Justice O'Connor's test for whether Bostick was seized is not whether a person in his position would have felt free to leave, but rather whether that person would have felt free to terminate the encounter. The Court's analysis reflects the idea that because Bostick chose to board the Greyhound bus, and because the police had nothing to do with that decision, it is constitutionally permissible for the officers to exploit Bostick's vulnerability as a bus passenger.

A similar argument about police culpability—or the lack thereof—can be made more broadly with respect to race and racial vulnerability. The argument would be that to the extent that Bostick's encounter with the officers reflects a degree of coercion that derived from the black/white racial interaction between Bostick's race and the race of the officers, that coercion existed apart from the conduct of the officers. "[I]t says nothing about whether or not [their] conduct . . . was coercive." The police officers did not make Bostick black. They found him that way. Nor did they make themselves white. Finally, neither officer is to be blamed for black people's general distrust of and apprehensions about the police. They have a right simply to do their jobs without being burdened by contemporary racial realities. Finally, to the extent that police officers, like the officers in

Bostick, merely exploit or take advantage of (racial) circumstances they did not themselves create, no Fourth Amendment problem exists. * * *

NOTE

In 2002, the Court considered another bus sweep case, with facts strikingly similar to *Florida v. Bostick*. In *Drayton v. United States*, 536 U.S. 194 (2002), three plainclothes officers from the Tallahassee Police Department boarded a bus bound for Detroit, Michigan. One of the officers knelt on the driver's seat and faced the rear of the bus, a second officer stayed at the rear of the bus, while the third officer, Officer Lang, worked his way towards the front of the bus, speaking with the passengers without informing them of their right to decline his request or leave. When Officer Lang reached defendants Drayton and Brown, he held up his badge and asked the men if he could check their bags. A search of one of their bags revealed no contraband. Officer Lang noticed that both men were wearing heavy jackets and baggy pants despite the warm weather, so he asked Brown, "Do you mind if I check your person?" without telling Brown that he had a right to refuse consent to search. Brown replied, "Sure," leaned up in his seat, and opened his jacket. Officer Lang patted down Brown's jacket and pockets, including his waist area, sides, and upper thighs. During the patdown, the officer felt hard objects in both thigh areas, which he suspected contained drugs. He arrested and handcuffed Brown, who was escorted from the bus. Officer Lang then asked Drayton if he could search him. Drayton responded by lifting his hands about eight inches above his legs. Officer Lang conducted a patdown of Drayton and detected hard objects similar to those found on Brown. Drayton was arrested and escorted him from the bus. The hard objects found on Drayton and Brown were plastic bundles of powder cocaine.

Applying the modified test for a seizure announced in *Florida v. Bostick*, the Court found that Drayton and Brown were not seized within the meaning of the Fourth Amendment. The Court found significant the fact that Officer Lang, the officer who searched the defendants after asking for their permission to search, did not brandish a weapon or make any intimidating movements. "There was no application of force, no intimidating movement, no overwhelming show of force, no brandishing of weapons, no blocking of exits, no threat, no command, not even an authoritative tone of voice."

Justice Souter, dissenting, objected to the majority's reliance upon Officer Lang's quiet tone of voice to conclude that a reasonable bus passenger would have felt free to decline the officer's requests or terminate the encounter. Justice Souter noted that "[a] police officer who is certain to get his way has no need to shout." In the next excerpt, Janice Nadler examines empirical research that supports Justice Souter's telling statement that a police officer who knows that a citizen will not refuse his requests has "no need to shout."

No Need to Shout: Bus Sweeps and the Psychology of Coercion

Janice Nadler
Supreme Court Review 2002[a]

The "free to terminate the encounter" test evolved from the basic proposition that the Fourth Amendment does not prohibit law enforcement officers from approaching citizens on the street and asking questions, even in the absence of individualized suspicion. So long as the encounter remains consensual, then no Fourth Amendment interests are implicated. * * *

This standard demands both consideration of the totality of the circumstances and a determination of the citizen's voluntary consent: either consent to engage in the encounter or consent to have the police search. The standard thus requires an examination of the following question: How would a reasonable person in these circumstances feel? Would a reasonable person * * * feel free to terminate the encounter, or to say no to the request to search? Note that the question of whether a reasonable person would feel free to terminate the encounter, or refuse the request to search, must necessarily be answered from the perspective of the citizen. By necessity, to answer the "free to refuse" question, the focus cannot be on the police perspective, and what the police did or could have done differently, and whether what the police did seems reasonable. The police could honestly view their actions as restrained and discreet in a situation where, at the same time, a reasonable person would feel coerced.

This distinction between citizen perspective and police perspective is a crucial one. As I shall demonstrate later, the Court's analysis * * * in *Drayton* is at bottom based on a judgment about the reasonableness of police conduct under the circumstances. * * * [T]he Court's real (but unstated) concern was whether the police conduct was acceptable (in a general policy sense) under the circumstances (no guns drawn, no explicit threats uttered). Having been satisfied implicitly that the police did not engage in abusive conduct, the Court then directly concluded that there must have been no seizure and no unconsented search.

Although the police conduct in * * * *Drayton* may have been reasonable under the circumstances, it does not follow that there was no seizure and no unconsented search for Fourth Amendment purposes. The standard for determining whether a citizen has been seized or subjected to an involuntary search focuses on whether a reasonable person in the situation would feel free to refuse the police requests. * * * [E]mpirical evidence suggests that reasonable citizens in the same situation in which Drayton

---

[a] Supreme Court Review, 2002: 160, 162–63, 173–74, 175–77, 186–90.

and Brown found themselves would not, in fact, feel free to refuse the police requests. * * *

Whether a request results in acquiescence depends a great deal on whether the requester is a legitimately constituted authority. As a general matter, persons with such authority exert an enormous amount of influence over our decisions. In many ways, it is logical that this is the case: the reason for their inordinate influence is that their position of authority signals that they possess information and power that is greater than our own. Throughout the course of our lives we learn that taking the advice of people like parents, teachers, supervisors, oncologists, and plumbers is beneficial for us, both because of their ability to enlighten us and because we depend on their good graces. * * *

Perhaps the most well-known scientific study of compliance with authority is the set of obedience studies conducted by Stanley Milgram, who investigated the extent to which people would comply with a request to perform an apparently harmful action. Milgram's subjects, who were adults from all walks of life, were informed that they would be participating in an experiment on the effects of punishment on learning. Upon arrival in the laboratory, the subject was assigned (through an apparently random procedure) to assume the role of "teacher," while the other "subject" (actually a confederate of the experimenter) was assigned to be the "learner." The subject was informed that it is his or her job to teach a series of word pairs to the learner. In full view of the subject, the learner was then strapped into a chair, and an electrode was taped to his wrist. As teacher, the subject's job was to administer shocks to the learner, by pressing switches on a shock generator, each time the learner made an error in recalling a word. Before beginning the learning task, the experimenter asked the subject to press the electrode to his or her own arm to experience a mild (but real) shock such as the one the learner would receive.

The subject was then led to an adjacent room where he or she could hear, but not see, the learner. The subject was seated in front of the shock generator, which was a box with 30 lever switches, labeled in 15-volt increments from 15 to 450 volts. The levers were also labeled with accompanying descriptions of the shock intensities, ranging from "slight shock" to "danger: severe shock." The last two switches were labeled "XXX." The experimenter informed the subject that he or she was to increase the shock level by 15 volts with each incorrect answer given by the learner.

After administering the first few shocks, the subject hears the learner protest about the painfulness of the shocks. When the shock level reaches 300 volts, the learner pounds on the wall in protest and stops participating in the word-recall task. The learner protests that his heart is bothering him, and his verbal protests become agonizing screams. Eventually, there is complete silence after each shock. Throughout the experiment, if the subject questions the procedure because of the learner's reaction, the experimenter responds by saying, "Please continue." If the subject expresses reluctance to continue, the experimenter says, "The experiment requires that you continue." If the subject becomes very insistent, the experimenter says, "You have no choice; you must go on."

Unbeknownst to the subjects, the shocks delivered to the learner are not real. Even though they believed they were delivering real shocks, most people participating in this experiment (over 65%) continued on until the very end, beyond the "danger: severe shock" level and all the way to "XXX." One hundred percent of all participants continued shocking the learner even after he protested that he was in pain.

There are obvious differences between the situation in which Milgram's subjects found themselves and the situation of the passengers on Drayton and Brown's bus. Most prominently, unlike in the Milgram experiments, no one was telling the bus passengers "you must continue." But there are similarities also. Instead of an experimenter in a white lab coat expecting cooperation, the bus passengers faced a police officer with a badge (and a gun) expecting cooperation. Like the role of the white lab coat in the Milgram experiments, the role of the police officer's displayed badge in *Drayton* should not be underestimated. In *Drayton*, Officer Lang leaned in at close range and held up his badge. Despite Milgram's empirical demonstration of the power of authorities to command compliance, the Court flatly rejected the notion that a police badge exerts pressure on passengers, holding that factors such as the presence of badges, uniforms, or guns "should have little weight in the analysis." At the same time that one officer leaned in close to passengers and displayed his badge, another officer had taken the driver's seat. With one officer in the back, one in the driver's seat, and another displaying his badge, the officers had essentially commandeered the bus. From the passengers' perspective, the message was clear that the bus was going nowhere until the officers were satisfied that they had received cooperation. Aside from the obvious message that the continuation of the trip was dependent on the officers achieving their goal of receiving passenger cooperation, the more subtle message was conveyed through symbols of authority such as the officers' positioning on the bus and the display of the badge 12–18 inches from each passenger's face. Even though the police were not in uniform, the symbols of authority were quite strong. The main point here is that in both situations, people are coerced to comply when they would prefer to refuse. * * *

In its analysis of the totality of the circumstances, the *Drayton* opinion focused heavily on the tone of the conversation between the police officer and the citizens. * * * Focusing narrowly on the tone and language used by the police makes plausible the notion that voluntary cooperation and consent were the only thoughts on the minds of passengers on the bus that day. But the Court's intense focus on precisely what Officer Lang did and did not say is problematic, because in doing so it neglected what the passengers actually experienced when they listened to the officers' polite tone and requests for permission. * * *

From the passengers' perspective, the officers appeared to board the bus with a specific goal in mind. The fact that a police officer was occupying the driver's seat in the absence of the driver gives rise to the natural inference that the officers intend to achieve their goal before the bus would continue on its regular route. * * * Officer Lang announced his goal at the outset, and the meaning of the speaker's intentions was therefore clear to the passenger: he is a police officer (an authority) and intends to look for illegal contraband.

Having understood the speaker's meaning and intentions, the next thing that the passengers heard was an indirect request: "Would you mind if I searched your bag?" Phrased directly, the request would be something like: "Let me search your bag." The question "Would you mind if . . . " is interpreted as the same thing as the direct request, but phrased more politely. The indirect request is more polite because it threatens the listener's status less than the direct request. So in all likelihood, this statement was interpreted by passengers as the officers informing the passenger what he would do, albeit in a polite fashion.

The context of discourse is crucial in the understanding of it; this is especially true when the speaker is making a request. Perceived coercion is determined by the speaker's authority and the speaker's language working together. Because authorities such as police officers direct the actions of others, the listener is likely to conclude that an utterance is in fact a directive, or an order to be followed. For example, citizens generally do not interpret "Can I please see your license and registration?" as spoken by a police officer as a genuine request; it is a command, and everyone understands this. * * *

The influence of the speaker's authority on perceived meaning has been demonstrated empirically. In one study, participants assumed the role of an employee who was late for work. The employee was advised, either by her boss or by her co-worker, not to be late anymore. The results revealed that when a peer is speaking, the listener perceives imperatives ("don't be late again") as more coercive than suggestions ("try not to be late again"). But when an authority (such as the boss) is speaking, there is no such difference in perceived coercion—forcefulness of language does not matter. The authors conclude, "those who have authority apparently need not activate coercive potential through their discourse. Their roles are sufficient to do so." So, when authorities use softened discourse—suggestions rather than imperatives—they can exert control without being face-threatening. * * *

NOTE

In the next excerpt, Tracey Maclin critiques the reasonable person test for assessing whether an individual has been seized for Fourth Amendment purposes and suggests courts should incorporate the race of the defendant into the "free to leave" test for a seizure of the person.

"BLACK AND BLUE ENCOUNTERS"—SOME PRELIMINARY THOUGHTS ABOUT FOURTH AMENDMENT SEIZURES: SHOULD RACE MATTER?

Tracey Maclin
26 Val. U. L. Rev. 243 (1991)

Currently, the Court supposes that there is an *average, hypothetical, reasonable person* out there to serve as the model for deciding Fourth Amendment cases. For example, the Court has said that a reasonable person will not feel coerced when federal drug agents accost her in an airport and ask to see her identification and airline ticket. The Court takes this position even when the person approached has not been expressly informed of her right to decline to cooperate with agents' inquiries. Similarly, no seizure occurs, according to the Court, when federal agents enter a factory to systematically question workers about their citizenship while other agents are positioned at the exits of the factory. * * *

I have argued elsewhere that the Court's definition of seizure is wholly unrealistic. The average, reasonable individual—whether he or she be found on the street, in an airport lobby, inside a factory, or seated on a bus or train—will not feel free to walk away from a typical police confrontation. Common sense teaches that most of us do not have the chutzpuh or stupidity to tell a police officer to "get lost" after he has stopped us and asked for identification or questioned us about possible criminal conduct. Indeed, practically every constitutional scholar who has considered the issue has agreed that the average, reasonable person will not feel free to leave a law enforcement official who has approached and addressed questions to them.

But even if I am mistaken in saying that the current state of the law is out of touch with the perspective of the *average, hypothetical, reasonable* person that the Court has in mind when it formulates the Fourth Amendment standards, I submit that the dynamics surrounding an encounter between a police officer and a black male are quite different from those that surround an encounter between an officer and the so-called average, reasonable person. My tentative proposal is that the Court should disregard the notion that there is an average, hypothetical, reasonable person out there by which to judge the constitutionality of police encounters. When assessing the coercive nature of an encounter, the Court should consider the race of the person confronted by the police, and how that person's race might have influenced his attitude toward the encounter.[a]

*** Currently, the Court assesses the coercive nature of a police encounter by considering the *totality of the circumstances* surrounding the confrontation. All I want the Court to do is to consider the role race might play, along with the other factors it considers, when judging the constitutionality of the encounter.

Some will no doubt object to the explicit use of race in deciding constitutional questions. Understandably, some will ask: If we really wish to live in a future non-racial society, shouldn't we be moving away from procedures and decisions in which people are classified by their race?

I too would like to see a future in which decision-makers will not have to consider the race of individuals in deciding important legal and constitutional questions. But in *today's* world, where the anger and distrust between black males and the police is rising, not decreasing, we must recall Justice Blackmun's familiar stance in the affirmative action debate. "In order to get beyond racism, we must first take account of race. There is no other way."

A harmonious future will not be achieved by ignoring the realities of today. Many black males, especially black teenagers, still view police officers as oppressors and part of a system designed to keep them in their place. * * *

A second objection I have heard against my thesis is that my solution is a form of "affirmative action" for black males. This criticism apparently stems from the notion that black men are some how receiving special advantage or benefit under a theory that considers their race in assessing the coerciveness of a police encounter. Some see my proposal as creating a separate Fourth Amendment standard for black men. Nothing could be further from the truth.

---

[a] Twenty-six years later, Devon Carbado echoed Tracey Maclin's call, urging the Court to take race into account when assessing whether an individual has been seized for Fourth Amendment purposes. Devon W. Carbado, *From Stopping Black People to Killing Black People*, 105 CAL. L. REV. 125, 143 (2017). In his Article, Carbado observes that Fourth Amendment law facilitates the space between stopping black people and killing black people by "permit[ting] police officers to force interactions with African Americans with little or no basis" and suggests that "[t]his 'front-end' police contact—which Fourth Amendment law enables—is often the predicate to 'back-end' police violence—which Fourth Amendment law should help to prevent." *Id.* at 125, 127.

I. Bennett Capers echoes these concerns, writing:

> . . . [A]s someone who has thought and written about policing for a decade now, I know that police violence is not the disease, but rather a symptom of the far larger problem of racialized policing more generally. Every police shooting, after all, begins with a look, a suspicion, or an encounter. We can do little to address racialized police violence if we do nothing to address the far broader issue of racialized looks and encounters.

I. Bennett Capers, *Race, Policing, and Technology*, 95 N.C. L. REV. 1241, 1245 (2017).

Under my approach, black males would only receive what the Fourth Amendment already guarantees them. That is, their constitutional right not to be stopped and detained by police officers who lack objective reasons for the seizure. The Court currently measures that right by assessing the coercive character of the police confrontation.

My position simply recognizes that, for most black men, the typical police confrontation is not a consensual encounter. Black men simply do not trust police officers to respect their rights. Although many black men *know* of their right to walk away from a police encounter, I submit that most do not trust the police to respect their decision to do so. I only propose that the Court consider race when assessing the coercive nature of a police confrontation. Indeed, why would the Court *want* to ignore this reality? If the Court were to acknowledge and take account of the coercive dynamics that surround police confrontations involving black males, it would only be enforcing what the Constitution already establishes. Black men would get no special treatment under this approach, they would only receive what the Fourth Amendment guarantees them.

This leads to a third objection to my thesis. This objection claims that if the Court were to acknowledge the role race plays in police confrontations with black males, it might be forced to do the same in the case of Hispanics, Asian-Americans, women, and other ethnic and social groups who has run-ins with the police.

You will pardon me if I label this objection a "fear of too much justice." At bottom, this rejection does not refute my main point—which is that police confrontations involving black males ordinarily are coercive—but instead, seeks to dismiss it by arguing that recognition of this reality may cause the Court to address the claims of other groups.

If my thesis compels the Court at some future date to face the fact that, for example, Mexican-Americans, Native Americans, or some other ethnic group experience tensions with the law enforcement officials, then so much the better. In the meantime, it strikes me as curious why society and the Court would want to deny the fact that one group, black males, currently experiences real tensions between themselves and the police. Just because similar claims may be presented by other groups today or at some future date is no reason not to consider the case of black males who have sufficient cause for complaint now.

A more substantive objection to my thesis is that it relies too heavily on the subjective perceptions of black males. Professor Wayne LaFave, the nation's foremost search and seizure scholar, has eschewed a Fourth Amendment standard that measures the seizure question by the subjective perceptions of the person confronted. In his view, "any test intended to determine what street encounters are not seizures must be expressed in terms that can be understood and applied by the officer." Asking a police officer to decide or guess whether a person feels free to leave would require predictive skills that neither the police nor anyone else possesses.

I must admit that this objection does cause me trouble. It troubles me not because it casts doubt on my original premise that police confrontations are inherently coercive. It is troubling because of the deep roots in our justice system that require lawyers to address legal questions in the framework of the average, hypothetical, reasonable person. But the Court claims to be committed to considering the totality of the circumstances in deciding whether a police confrontation constitutes a seizure. If this is true, the Court should include the consideration of race in order to gain a full view of the circumstances and dynamics surrounding the encounter.

Moreover, just as logic suggests that in evaluating the severity and pervasiveness of a sexual harassment complaint a "reasonable woman" standard makes more sense than a "reasonable person" standard, so too in assessing the coerciveness surrounding a police encounter, the Court should focus on the perspective of the person who is on the other side of the police confrontation. Continued use of a reasonable person test runs the risk that majoritarian values and perceptions of police practices will go unchallenged. * * *

The Fourth Amendment, after all, guarantees the rights of persons, not the police. While it is important for the Court to provide guidance to the officer on the beat, it is equally, if not more important, to consider the perspective of the individual who is the subject of a police intrusion. Recently, however, it seems the Rehnquist Court is more concerned about the needs and interests of police officers, than the rights of individuals. This is regrettable. As Professor Yale Kamisar asked me once, "Whose Amendment is it, anyway?" * * *

NOTE

Building on Maclin's critique of the way courts have applied the test for a seizure of the person, Kris Henning argues courts should consider both the race and the age of the individual and apply a "Reasonable Black Child" standard when deciding whether a Black youth has been seized within the meaning of the Fourth Amendment.[a] She starts by explaining and critiquing the test for a seizure of the person:

> In analyzing the legality of an officer's on-the-street encounter with a civilian, courts will first call upon the reasonable man in deciding whether the Fourth Amendment has even been implicated —that is, whether a person has been seized. As the Supreme Court articulated in *United States v. Mendenhall*: "[A] person has been 'seized' within the meaning of the Fourth Amendment only if, in view

---

[a] Kristin N. Henning, *The Reasonable Black Child: Race, Adolescence, and the Fourth Amendment*, 67 AM. U. L. REV. 1513 (2018).

of all the circumstances surrounding the incident, a reasonable person would have believed that he was not free to leave." * * *

* * * As many commentators have noted, in reality very few people—adult or child—feel free to walk away from an officer's questions without consequences. Research finding that people tend to "interpret questions or suggestions as orders when they come from a person of authority" confirms that many people feel compelled to cooperate with police.[b]

Henning then explains why young people may feel more compulsion to comply with police than adults:

This compulsion to comply is exacerbated for youth . . . . Youth are not only socialized to comply with adult authority figures, such as parents, teachers, and police, but they also have less experience to draw upon than adults, especially in the legal arena. Today, much of a youth's knowledge of the police comes from television, Internet, and social media, which provide them with little reason to believe they can decline to engage with an officer who approaches them. Even when young people know their rights, research demonstrates that adolescents are especially vulnerable to coercive circumstances and "may respond adversely to external pressures that adults are able to resist." * * * [In 2011, in *J.D.B. v. North Carolina*,] the Court first articulated an explicit "reasonable child" standard.[c]

She then explains why race, as well as age, matters in the seizure analysis:

Despite its profound impact on criminal law and procedure, the reasonable child standard may not be sufficient to protect a [Black] child . . . if it fails to account for race. * * * Experience suggests that a child's race would have as much impact on a child's perception of whether he was free to leave as would his age. Throughout American history, blacks have had a tenuous relationship with police. In every critical era—slavery, Jim Crow, lynching, and the contemporary era of mass incarceration—blacks have perceived police to be proponents of discrimination and subordination through violence and intimidation. Today, it is difficult to imagine any black person who is immune from the persistent national coverage of police-on-black killings. * * *

This Article contends that a black child's experience is unique. That is, a black child's perception of the police arises not only from his blackness, but also from his youth. * * * Black youths' perceptions of law enforcement are shaped by the vicarious and collective experiences of their friends and family members, especially those who have been verbally or physically abused by the police. Black families have long been proactive in transmitting norms on dealing with the

---

[b] *Id.* at 1521, 1522–23.

[c] *Id.* at 1523, 1525.

police to their children. Black parents tell her children to keep their hands where police can see them, avoid sudden movements, and behave in a courteous and respectful manner towards officers. For some black youth, these lessons mean the difference between life and death. For many black youths, they also transfer negative attitudes and resentment about the police from one generation to the next as youth internalized the negative experiences of their community.[d]

Adding disability as a concern, Jamelia Morgan suggests that disability should factor into assessments of whether an individual with a disability has been seized.[e] Morgan observes that "nothing in the legal test [for a seizure of the person] provides a mechanism to ensure that courts meaningfully consider how disability informs whether that particular disabled person feels free to leave or otherwise terminate the encounter" and concludes that "[a]s a result, this test fails to adequately protect the Fourth Amendment rights of disabled people."[f]

In 2022, the Supreme Court of Washington was asked to consider whether the race and ethnicity of an allegedly seized person are relevant to the determination of whether a seizure occurred. The court answered this question in the affirmative, holding that "courts [in the state of Washington] must consider the race and ethnicity of the allegedly seized person as part of the totality of the circumstances when deciding whether there was a seizure." State v. Sum, No. 99730-6, 2022 WL 2071560, at *14 (Wash. June 9, 2022). Do you think courts should incorporate race, age, or disability into the reasonable person test for a seizure of the person?

* * *

The next case suggests factors a court can consider when trying to determine whether a seizure of the person constitutes an investigatory detention (or *Terry* stop) or an arrest. Both are seizures of the person, but one—the *Terry* stop—requires only reasonable suspicion of criminal activity while the other—an arrest—requires probable cause.

FLORIDA V. ROYER
Supreme Court of the United States
460 U.S. 491, 103 S. Ct. 1319, 75 L. Ed. 2d 229 (1983)

JUSTICE WHITE announced the judgment of the Court and delivered an opinion in which JUSTICES MARSHALL, POWELL and STEVENS joined.

On January 3, 1978, Royer was observed at Miami International Airport by two plain-clothes detectives of the Dade County, Florida, Public Safety Department assigned to the County's Organized Crime Bureau,

---

[d] *Id.* at 1529, 1530–31.

[e] Jamelia Morgan, *Disability's Fourth Amendment*, 122 COLUM. L. REV. 489, 516 (2022) (arguing that "the reasonable person standard in the Court's test for whether a seizure has occurred does not adequately take into consideration disability").

[f] *Id.*

Narcotics Investigation Section. Detectives Johnson and Magdalena believed that Royer's appearance, mannerisms, luggage, and actions fit the so-called "drug courier profile."[a] Royer, apparently unaware of the attention he had attracted, purchased a one-way ticket to New York City and checked his two suitcases, placing on each suitcase an identification tag bearing the name "Holt" and the destination, "LaGuardia." As Royer made his way to the concourse which led to the airline boarding area, the two detectives approached him, identified themselves as policemen working out of the sheriff's office, and asked if Royer had a "moment" to speak with them; Royer said "Yes."

Upon request, but without oral consent, Royer produced for the detectives his airline ticket and his driver's license. The airline ticket, like the baggage identification tags, bore the name "Holt," while the driver's license carried respondent's correct name, "Royer." When the detectives asked about the discrepancy, Royer explained that a friend had made the reservation in the name of "Holt." Royer became noticeably more nervous during this conversation, whereupon the detectives informed Royer that they were in fact narcotics investigators and that they had reason to suspect him of transporting narcotics.

The detectives did not return his airline ticket and identification but asked Royer to accompany them to a room, approximately forty feet away, adjacent to the concourse. Royer said nothing in response but went with the officers as he had been asked to do. The room was later described by Detective Johnson as a "large storage closet," located in the stewardesses' lounge and containing a small desk and two chairs. Without Royer's consent or agreement, Detective Johnson, using Royer's baggage check stubs, retrieved the "Holt" luggage from the airline and brought it to the room where respondent and Detective Magdalena were waiting. Royer was asked if he would consent to a search of the suitcases. Without orally responding to this request, Royer produced a key and unlocked one of the suitcases, which the detective then opened without seeking further assent from Royer. Drugs were found in that suitcase. According to Detective

---

[a] According to the "drug courier profile" developed in the 1970s by Special Agent Paul Markonni of the Drug Enforcement Agency, drug couriers will typically travel with little or no luggage from a "source" city, i.e., a city known as a major narcotics distribution center such as Los Angeles, San Diego, Miami, and New York, and exhibit signs of nervousness. Philip S. Greene & Brian W. Wice, *The DEA Drug Courier Profile: History and Analysis*, 22 S. TEX. L.J. 261, 271 (1982). In addition, according to the profile, a drug courier will often make a phone call immediately upon deplaning and exclusively use public transportation after leaving the airport. *Id.* at 272. Given these factors, many law-abiding citizens could easily fit the description of a drug courier. As one court noted, "Los Angeles may indeed be a major narcotics distribution center, but the probability that any given airplane passenger from that city is a drug courier is infinitely small. Such a flimsy factor should not be allowed to justify or help justify the stopping of travelers from the nation's third largest city." *United States v. Andrews*, 600 F.2d 563, 566 (6th Cir. 1979). Another court commented, "[A]pparent nervousness in an airport is not necessarily a sign of suspicious behavior; it may result from an innate personality syndrome or from a disorientation from a fear of flying or from having disembarked at a strange airport." *United States v. Westerbann-Martinez*, 435 F. Supp. 690, 699 (E.D.N.Y. 1977).

Johnson, Royer stated that he did not know the combination to the lock on the second suitcase. When asked if he objected to the detective opening the second suitcase, Royer said "no, go ahead," and did not object when the detective explained that the suitcase might have to be broken open. The suitcase was pried open by the officers and more marihuana was found. Royer was then told that he was under arrest. Approximately fifteen minutes had elapsed from the time the detectives initially approached respondent until his arrest upon the discovery of the contraband.

Prior to his trial for felony possession of marihuana, Royer made a motion to suppress the evidence obtained in the search of the suitcases. The trial court [denied Royer's motion.] Following the denial of the motion to suppress, Royer changed his plea from "not guilty" to "nolo contendere," specifically reserving the right to appeal the denial of the motion to suppress. Royer was convicted.

The District Court of Appeal, sitting en banc, reversed Royer's conviction. The court held that Royer had been involuntarily confined within the small room without probable cause; that the involuntary detention had exceeded the limited restraint permitted by *Terry v. Ohio,* * * * and that the consent to search was therefore invalid because tainted by the unlawful confinement. * * * We granted the State's petition for certiorari and now affirm.

* * * [L]aw enforcement officers do not violate the Fourth Amendment by merely approaching an individual on the street or in another public place, by asking him if he is willing to answer some questions, by putting questions to him if the person is willing to listen, or by offering in evidence in a criminal prosecution his voluntary answers to such questions. Nor would the fact that the officer identifies himself as a police officer, without more, convert the encounter into a seizure requiring some level of objective justification. The person approached, however, need not answer any question put to him; indeed, he may decline to listen to the questions at all and may go on his way. He may not be detained even momentarily without reasonable, objective grounds for doing so; and his refusal to listen or answer does not, without more, furnish those grounds. If there is no detention—no seizure within the meaning of the Fourth Amendment—then no constitutional rights have been infringed.

* * * [I]t is also clear that not all seizures of the person must be justified by probable cause to arrest for a crime. * * * *Terry* created a limited exception to this general rule: certain seizures are justifiable under the Fourth Amendment if there is articulable suspicion that a person has committed or is about to commit a crime. * * *

The predicate permitting seizures on suspicion short of probable cause is that law enforcement interests warrant a limited intrusion on the personal security of the suspect. The scope of the intrusion permitted will vary to some extent with the particular facts and circumstances of each case. This much, however, is clear: an investigative detention must be temporary and last no longer than is necessary to effectuate the purpose of the stop. Similarly, the investigative methods employed should be the least intrusive means reasonably available to verify or dispel the officer's suspicion in a short period of time. It is the State's burden to demonstrate that the seizure it seeks to justify on the basis of a reasonable suspicion was sufficiently limited in scope and duration to satisfy the conditions of an investigative seizure. * * *

The State proffers three reasons for holding that when Royer consented to the search of his luggage, he was not being illegally detained. First, it is submitted that the entire encounter was consensual and hence Royer was not being held against his will at all. We find this submission untenable. Asking for and examining Royer's ticket and his driver's license were no doubt permissible in themselves, but when the officers identified themselves as narcotics agents, told Royer that he was suspected of transporting narcotics, and asked him to accompany them to the police room, while retaining his ticket and driver's license and without indicating in any way that he was free to depart, Royer was effectively seized for the purposes of the Fourth Amendment. These circumstances surely amount to a show of official authority such that "a reasonable person would have believed he was not free to leave."

Second, the State submits that if Royer was seized, there existed reasonable, articulable suspicion to justify a temporary detention and that the limits of a *Terry*-type stop were never exceeded. We agree with the State that when the officers discovered that Royer was travelling under an assumed name, this fact, and the facts already known to the officers—paying cash for a one-way ticket, the mode of checking the two bags, and Royer's appearance and conduct in general—were adequate grounds for suspecting Royer of carrying drugs and for temporarily detaining him and his luggage while they attempted to verify or dispel their suspicions in a manner that did not exceed the limits of an investigative detention. * * * We have concluded, however, that at the time Royer produced the key to his suitcase, the detention to which he was then subjected was a more serious intrusion on his personal liberty than is allowable on mere suspicion of criminal activity.

By the time Royer was informed that the officers wished to examine his luggage, * * * [t]he officers [had] informed him they were narcotics agents and had reason to believe that he was carrying illegal drugs. They requested him to accompany them to the police room. Royer went with them. He found himself in a small room—a large closet—equipped with a desk and two chairs. He was alone with two police officers who again told him that they thought he was carrying narcotics. He also found that the officers, without his consent, had retrieved his checked luggage from the airlines. What had begun as a consensual inquiry in a public place had escalated into an investigatory procedure in a police interrogation room, where the police, unsatisfied with previous explanations, sought to confirm their suspicions. The officers had Royer's ticket, they had his identification, and they had seized his luggage. Royer was never informed that he was free to board his plane if he so chose, and he reasonably believed that he was being detained. * * * As a practical matter, Royer was under arrest. * * *

We also think that the officers' conduct was more intrusive than necessary to effectuate an investigative detention otherwise authorized by the *Terry* line of cases. First, by returning his ticket and driver's license, and informing him that he was free to go if he so desired, the officers may have obviated any claim that the encounter was anything but a consensual matter from start to finish. Second, there are undoubtedly reasons of safety and security that would justify moving a suspect from one location to another during an investigatory detention, such as from an airport concourse to a more private area. There is no indication in this case that such reasons prompted the officers to transfer the site of the encounter from the concourse to the interrogation room. * * * The record does not reflect any facts which would support a finding that the legitimate law enforcement purposes which justified the detention in the first instance were furthered by removing Royer to the police room prior to the officer's attempt to gain his consent to a search of his luggage. * * *

Third, the State has not touched on the question whether it would have been feasible to investigate the contents of Royer's bags in a more expeditious way. The courts are not strangers to the use of trained dogs to detect the presence of controlled substances in luggage. There is no indication here that this means was not feasible and available. If it had been used, Royer and his luggage could have been momentarily detained while this investigative procedure was carried out. Indeed, it may be that no detention at all would have been necessary. A negative result would have freed Royer in short order; a positive result would have resulted in his justifiable arrest on probable cause. * * *

The State's third and final argument is that Royer was not being illegally held when he gave his consent because there was probable cause to arrest him at that time. Officer Johnson testified at the suppression hearing and the Florida Court of Appeal held that there was no probable cause to arrest until Royer's bags were opened, but the fact that the officers did not believe there was probable cause and proceeded on a consensual or *Terry*-stop rationale would not foreclose the State from justifying Royer's custody by proving probable cause and hence removing any barrier to relying on Royer's consent to search. We agree with the Florida Court of Appeal, however, that probable cause to arrest Royer did not exist at the time he consented to the search of his luggage. The facts are that a nervous young man with two American Tourister bags paid cash for an airline ticket to a "target city." These facts led to inquiry, which in turn revealed that the ticket had been bought under an assumed name. The proffered explanation did not satisfy the officers. We cannot agree with the State, if this is its position, that every nervous young man paying cash for a ticket to New York City under an assumed name and carrying two heavy American Tourister bags may be arrested and held to answer for a serious felony charge. * * *

Affirmed.

JUSTICE BRENNAN, concurring in the result.

* * * I dissent from the plurality's view that the initial stop of Royer was legal. For plainly Royer was "seized" for purposes of the Fourth Amendment when the officers asked him to produce his driver's license and airline ticket. *Terry* stated that "whenever a police officer accosts an individual and restrains his freedom to walk away, he has 'seized' that person." Although I agree that "not all personal intercourse between policemen and citizens involves 'seizures' of persons," and that policemen may approach citizens on the street and ask them questions without "seizing" them for purposes of the Fourth Amendment, once an officer has identified himself and asked a traveller for identification and his airline ticket, the traveller has been "seized" within the meaning of the Fourth Amendment. By identifying themselves and asking for Royer's airline ticket and driver's license the officers, as a practical matter, engaged in a "show of authority" and "restrained [Royer's] liberty." It is simply wrong to suggest that a traveller feels free to walk away when he has been approached by individuals who have identified themselves as police officers and asked for, and received, his airline ticket and driver's license.

* * * In this case, the officers decided to approach Royer because he was carrying American Tourister luggage, which appeared to be heavy; he was young; he was casually dressed; he appeared to be pale and nervous and was looking around at other people; he paid for his airline ticket in cash with a large number of bills; and he did not completely fill out the identification tags for his luggage, which was checked to New York. These facts clearly are not sufficient to provide the reasonable suspicion of criminal activity necessary to justify the officers' subsequent seizure of Royer. Indeed, considered individually or collectively, they are perfectly consistent with innocent behavior and cannot possibly give rise to any inference supporting a reasonable suspicion of criminal activity. The officers' seizure of Royer, therefore, was illegal. * * *

JUSTICE REHNQUIST, with whom THE CHIEF JUSTICE and JUSTICE O'CONNOR join, dissenting. * * *

The point at which I part company with the plurality's opinion is in the assessment of the reasonableness of the officers' conduct following their initial conversation with Royer. The plurality focuses on the transfer of the place of the interview from the main concourse of the airport to the room off the concourse and observes that Royer "found himself in a small room—a large closet—equipped with a desk and two chairs. He was alone with two police officers who again told him that they thought he was carrying narcotics. He also found that the officers, without his consent, had retrieved his checked luggage from the airlines."

Obviously, this quoted language is intended to convey stern disapproval of the described conduct of the officers. To my mind, it merits no such disapproval and was eminently reasonable. * * * Would it have been more "reasonable" to interrogate Royer about the contents of his suitcases, and to seek his permission to open the suitcases when they were retrieved, in the busy main concourse of the Miami Airport, rather than to find a room off the concourse where the confrontation would surely be less embarrassing to Royer? If the room had been large and spacious, rather than small, if it had possessed three chairs rather than two, would the officers' conduct have been made reasonable by these facts?

The plurality's answers to these questions, to the extent that it attempts any, are scarcely satisfying. It commences with the observation that "the officers' conduct was more intrusive than necessary to effectuate an investigative detention otherwise authorized by the *Terry* line of cases." * * *

All of this to my mind adds up to little more than saying that if my aunt were a man, she would be my uncle. The officers might have taken different steps than they did to investigate Royer, but the same may be said of virtually every investigative encounter that has more than one step to it. The question we must decide is what was *unreasonable* about the steps which *these officers* took with respect to *this* suspect in the Miami Airport on this particular day. On this point, the plurality stutters, fudges, and hedges. * * *

Since the plurality concedes the existence of "articulable suspicion" at least after the initial conversation with Royer, the only remaining question is whether the detention of Royer during that period of time was permissible under the rule enunciated in *Terry v. Ohio*. * * * I think the articulable suspicion which concededly focused upon Royer justified the length and nature of his detention.

* * * [I]f Royer was legally approached in the first instance and consented to accompany the detectives to the room, it does not follow that his consent went up in smoke and he was "arrested" upon entering the room. * * *

For any of these several reasons, I would reverse the judgment of the Florida District Court of Appeal.

[JUSTICE POWELL's concurring opinion and JUSTICE BLACKMUN's dissenting opinion have been omitted.]

NOTE

The Court suggests in *Royer* that if police do not use the least intrusive means readily available to confirm or deny their suspicions, the encounter is more likely to be seen as a *de facto* arrest rather than a *Terry* stop. In other contexts, the Court has been critical of a "less intrusive means" standard. For example, in *United States v. Sharpe*, 470 U.S. 675 (1985), the Court stated:

> A creative judge engaged in *post hoc* evaluation of police conduct can almost always imagine some alternative means by which the objectives of the police might have been accomplished. But "[the] fact that the protection of the public might, in the abstract, have been accomplished by 'less intrusive' means does not, by itself, render the search unreasonable." The question is not simply whether some other alternative was available, but whether the police acted unreasonably in failing to recognize or pursue it.

Id. at 686–87.

TORRES V. MADRID

Supreme Court of the United States
592 U. S. ___, 141 S. Ct. 989, 209 L. Ed. 2d 190 (2021)

CHIEF JUSTICE ROBERTS delivered the opinion of the Court.

* * *

At dawn on July 15, 2014, four New Mexico State Police officers arrived at an apartment complex in Albuquerque to execute an arrest warrant for a woman accused of white collar crimes, but also "suspected of having been involved in drug trafficking, murder, and other violent crimes." What happened next is hotly contested. We recount the facts in the light most favorable to petitioner Roxanne Torres because the court below granted summary judgment to Officers Janice Madrid and Richard Williamson, the two respondents here.

The officers observed Torres standing with another person near a Toyota FJ Cruiser in the parking lot of the complex. Officer Williamson concluded that neither Torres nor her companion was the target of the warrant. As the officers approached the vehicle, the companion departed, and Torres—at the time experiencing methamphetamine withdrawal—got into the driver's seat. The officers attempted to speak with her, but she did not notice their presence until one of them tried to open the door of her car.

Although the officers wore tactical vests marked with police identification, Torres saw only that they had guns. She thought the officers were carjackers trying to steal her car, and she hit the gas to escape them.

Neither Officer Madrid nor Officer Williamson, according to Torres, stood in the path of the vehicle, but both fired their service pistols to stop her. All told, the two officers fired 13 shots at Torres, striking her twice in the back and temporarily paralyzing her left arm.

Steering with her right arm, Torres accelerated through the fusillade of bullets, exited the apartment complex, drove a short distance, and stopped in a parking lot. After asking a bystander to report an attempted carjacking, Torres stole a Kia Soul that happened to be idling nearby and drove 75 miles to Grants, New Mexico. The good news for Torres was that the hospital in Grants was able to airlift her to another hospital where she could receive appropriate care. The bad news was that the hospital was back in Albuquerque, where the police arrested her the next day. She pleaded no contest to aggravated fleeing from a law enforcement officer, assault on a peace officer, and unlawfully taking a motor vehicle.

Torres later sought damages from Officers Madrid and Williamson under 42 U. S. C. § 1983, which provides a cause of action for the deprivation of constitutional rights by persons acting under color of state law. She claimed that the officers applied excessive force, making the shooting an unreasonable seizure under the Fourth Amendment. The District Court granted summary judgment to the officers, and the Court of Appeals for the Tenth Circuit affirmed on the ground that "a suspect's continued flight after being shot by police negates a Fourth Amendment excessive-force claim." * * * We granted certiorari.

The Fourth Amendment protects "[t]he right of the people to be secure in their persons, houses, papers, and effects, against unreasonable searches and seizures." This case concerns the "seizure" of a "person," which can take the form of "physical force" or a "show of authority" that "in some way restrain[s] the liberty" of the person. The question before us is whether the application of physical force is a seizure if the force, despite hitting its target, fails to stop the person.

We largely covered this ground in *California* v. *Hodari D.* There we interpreted the term "seizure" by consulting the common law of arrest, the "quintessential 'seizure of the person' under our Fourth Amendment jurisprudence." As Justice Scalia explained for himself and six other Members of the Court, the common law treated "the mere grasping or application of physical force with lawful authority" as an arrest, "whether or not it succeeded in subduing the arrestee." * * *

The common law distinguished the application of force from a show of authority, such as an order for a suspect to halt. The latter does not become an arrest unless and until the arrestee complies with the demand. As the Court explained in *Hodari D.*, "[a]n arrest requires *either* physical force . . . *or*, where that is absent, *submission* to the assertion of authority."

Hodari D. articulates two pertinent principles. First, common law arrests are Fourth Amendment seizures. And second, the common law considered the application of force to the body of a person with intent to restrain to be an arrest, no matter whether the arrestee escaped. * * *

At the adoption of the Fourth Amendment, a "seizure" was the "act of taking by warrant" or "of laying hold on suddenly"—for example, when an "officer seizes a thief." A seizure did not necessarily result in actual control or detention. It is true that, when speaking of property, "[f]rom the time of the founding to the present, the word 'seizure' has meant a 'taking possession.'" But the Framers selected a term—seizure—broad enough to apply to all the concerns of the Fourth Amendment: "persons," as well as "houses, papers, and effects." As applied to a person, "[t]he word 'seizure' readily bears the meaning of a laying on of hands or application of physical force to restrain movement, even when it is ultimately unsuccessful." Then, as now, an ordinary user of the English language could remark: "She seized the purse-snatcher, but he broke out of her grasp." * * *

The common law rule identified in *Hodari D.*—that the application of force gives rise to an arrest, even if the officer does not secure control over the arrestee—achieved recognition to such an extent that English lawyers could confidently (and accurately) proclaim that "[a]ll the authorities, from the earliest time to the present, establish that a corporal touch is sufficient to constitute an arrest, even though the defendant do not submit." The slightest application of force could satisfy this rule. * * *

Early American courts adopted this mere-touch rule from England, just as they embraced other common law principles of search and seizure. * * * State courts agreed that "any touching, however slight, is enough," provided the officer made his intent to arrest clear. Courts continued to hold that an arrest required only the application of force—not control or custody—through the framing of the Fourteenth Amendment, which incorporated the protections of the Fourth Amendment against the States. * * *

This case, of course, does not involve "laying hands," but instead a shooting. Neither the parties nor the United States as *amicus curiae* suggests that the officers' use of bullets to restrain Torres alters the analysis in any way. And we are aware of no common law authority addressing an arrest under such circumstances, or indeed any case involving an application of force from a distance.

* * * [W]e see no basis for drawing an artificial line between grasping with a hand and other means of applying physical force to effect an arrest. The dissent (though not the officers) argues that the common law limited arrests by force to the literal placement of hands on the suspect, because no court published an opinion discussing a suspect who continued to flee after being hit with a bullet or some other weapon. This objection calls to

mind the unavailing defense of the person who "persistently denied that he had laid hands upon a priest, for he had only cudgelled and kicked him." The required "corporal seising or touching the defendant's body" can be as readily accomplished by a bullet as by the end of a finger.

We will not carve out this greater intrusion on personal security from the mere-touch rule just because founding-era courts did not confront apprehension by firearm. While firearms have existed for a millennium and were certainly familiar at the founding, we have observed that law enforcement did not carry handguns until the latter half of the 19th century, at which point "it bec[a]me possible to use deadly force from a distance as a means of apprehension." So it should come as no surprise that neither we nor the dissent has located a common law case in which an officer used a gun to apprehend a suspect. But the focus of the Fourth Amendment is "the privacy and security of individuals," not the particular manner of "arbitrary invasion[ ] by governmental officials." * * * There is nothing subtle about a bullet, but the Fourth Amendment preserves personal security with respect to methods of apprehension old and new.

We stress, however, that the application of the common law rule does not transform every physical contact between a government employee and a member of the public into a Fourth Amendment seizure. A seizure requires the use of force *with intent to restrain*. Accidental force will not qualify. Nor will force intentionally applied for some other purpose satisfy this rule. * * *

Moreover, the appropriate inquiry is whether the challenged conduct *objectively* manifests an intent to restrain, for we rarely probe the subjective motivations of police officers in the Fourth Amendment context. Only an objective test "allows the police to determine in advance whether the conduct contemplated will implicate the Fourth Amendment." While a mere touch can be enough for a seizure, the amount of force remains pertinent in assessing the objective intent to restrain. A tap on the shoulder to get one's attention will rarely exhibit such an intent.

Nor does the seizure depend on the subjective perceptions of the seized person. Here, for example, Torres claims to have perceived the officers' actions as an attempted carjacking. But the conduct of the officers—ordering Torres to stop and then shooting to restrain her movement—satisfies the objective test for a seizure, regardless whether Torres comprehended the governmental character of their actions.

The rule we announce today is narrow. In addition to the requirement of intent to restrain, a seizure by force—absent submission—lasts only as long as the application of force. That is to say that the Fourth Amendment does not recognize any "*continuing* arrest during the period of fugitivity." The fleeting nature of some seizures by force undoubtedly may inform what damages a civil plaintiff may recover, and what evidence a criminal defendant may exclude from trial. But brief seizures are seizures all the same. Applying these principles to the facts viewed in the light most favorable to Torres, the officers' shooting applied physical force to her body and objectively manifested an intent to restrain her from driving away. We therefore conclude that the officers seized Torres for the instant that the bullets struck her. * * *

The dissent argues that we advance a "schizophrenic reading of the word 'seizure.'" But our cases demonstrate the unremarkable proposition that the nature of a seizure can depend on the nature of the object being seized. It is not surprising that the concept of constructive detention or the mere-touch rule developed in the context of seizures of a person—capable of fleeing and with an interest in doing so—rather than seizures of "houses, papers, and effects." * * *

We hold that the application of physical force to the body of a person with intent to restrain is a seizure even if the person does not submit and is not subdued. Of course, a seizure is just the first step in the analysis. The Fourth Amendment does not forbid all or even most seizures—only unreasonable ones. All we decide today is that the officers seized Torres by shooting her with intent to restrain her movement. We leave open on remand any questions regarding the reasonableness of the seizure, the damages caused by the seizure, and the officers' entitlement to qualified immunity.

The judgment of the Court of Appeals is vacated, and the case is remanded for further proceedings consistent with this opinion.

It is so ordered.

JUSTICE BARRETT took no part in the consideration or decision of this case.

JUSTICE GORSUCH, with whom JUSTICE THOMAS and JUSTICE ALITO join, dissenting.

The majority holds that a criminal suspect can be simultaneously seized and roaming at large. On the majority's account, a Fourth Amendment "seizure" takes place whenever an officer "merely touches" a suspect. It's a seizure even if the suspect refuses to stop, evades capture, and rides off into the sunset never to be seen again. That view is as mistaken as it is novel.

Until today, a Fourth Amendment "seizure" has required taking possession of someone or something. To reach its contrary judgment, * * * the majority must disregard the Constitution's original and ordinary meaning, dispense with our conventional interpretive rules, and bypass the main currents of the common law. * * *

Now before us, Ms. Torres argues that this Court's decision in *California v. Hodari D.* "compel[s] reversal." As she reads it, *Hodari D.* held that a Fourth Amendment seizure takes place whenever an officer shoots or even "mere[ly] touch[es]" an individual with the intent to restrain.

Whatever one thinks of Ms. Torres's argument, one thing is certain: *Hodari D.* has generated considerable confusion. There, officers chased a suspect on foot. Later, the suspect argued that he was "seized" for purposes of the Fourth Amendment the moment the chase began. Though *he* fled, the suspect argued, a "reasonable person" would not have felt at liberty given the officers' "show of authority," so a Fourth Amendment seizure had occurred.

The Court rejected this argument. In doing so, it explained that, "[f]rom the time of the founding to the present, the word 'seizure' has meant a 'taking possession.'" Because the defendant did not submit to the officers' show of authority, the Court reasoned, the officers' conduct amounted at most to an attempted seizure. And "neither usage nor common-law tradition makes an *attempted* seizure a seizure."

At the same time, and as Ms. Torres emphasizes, the Court didn't end its discussion there. It proceeded to imagine a different and hypothetical case, one in which the officers not only chased the suspect but also "appl[ied] physical force" to him. In these circumstances, the Court suggested, "merely touching" a suspect, even when officers fail to gain possession, might qualify as a seizure.

Unsurprisingly, these dueling passages in *Hodari D.* led to a circuit split. For the first time, some lower courts began holding that a "mere touch" constitutes a Fourth Amendment "seizure." Others, however, continued to adhere to the view, taken "[f]rom the time of the founding to the present," that the word "seizure" means "taking possession." We took this case to sort out the confusion.

As an initial matter, Ms. Torres is mistaken that *Hodari D.*'s discussion of "mere touch" seizures compels a ruling in her favor. Under the doctrine of *stare decisis*, we normally afford prior holdings of this Court considerable respect. But, in the course of issuing their holdings, judges sometimes include a "witty opening paragraph, the background information on how the law developed," or "digressions speculating on how similar hypothetical cases might be resolved." Such asides are dicta. * * * [D]icta cannot bind future courts. * * *

[T]he majority picks up where *Hodari D.*'s dicta left off. It contends that an officer "seizes" a person by merely touching him with an "intent to restrain." We are told that a touch is a seizure even if the suspect never stops or slows down; it's a seizure even if he evades capture. * * * [T]he Fourth Amendment's text, its history, and our precedent all confirm that "seizing" something doesn't mean touching it; it means taking possession.

Start with the text. The Fourth Amendment guarantees that "[t]he right of the people to be secure in their persons, houses, papers, and effects, against unreasonable searches and seizures, shall not be violated." And at least part of *Hodari D.* recognized, "[f]rom the time of the founding to the present," the key term here–"seizure"–has always meant "taking possession."

Countless contemporary dictionaries define a "seizure" or the act of "seizing" in terms of possession. This Court's early cases reflect the same understanding. Just sixteen years after the Fourth Amendment's adoption, Congress passed a statute regulating the "seizure" of ships. This Court interpreted the term to require "an open, visible possession claimed," so that those previously possessing the ship "understand that they are dispossessed, and that they are no longer at liberty to exercise any dominion on board of the ship." * * *

Today's majority disputes none of this. It accepts that a seizure of the inanimate objects mentioned in the Fourth Amendment (houses, papers, and effects) requires possession. And when it comes to persons, the majority agrees (as *Hodari D.* held) that a seizure in response to a "show of authority" takes place if and when the suspect submits to an officer's possession. The majority insists that a different rule should apply *only* in cases where an officer "touches" the suspect. Here—and here alone— possession is not required. * * *

The majority's need to resort to such a schizophrenic reading of the word "seizure" should be a signal that something has gone seriously wrong. The Fourth Amendment's Search and Seizure Clause uses the word "seizures" once in connection with four objects (persons, houses, papers, and effects). The text thus suggests parity, not disparity, in meaning. It is close to canon that when a provision uses the same word multiple times, courts must give it the same meaning each time. * * * To "[a]scrib[e] various meanings" to a single word, we have observed, is to "render meaning so malleable" that written laws risk "becom[ing] susceptible to individuated interpretation." * * *

Then there's the question what kind of "touching" will suffice. Imagine that, with an objective intent to detain a suspect, officers deploy pepper spray that enters a suspect's lungs as he sprints away. Does the application of the pepper spray count? Suppose that, intending to capture a fleeing suspect, officers detonate flash-bang grenades that are so loud they damage the suspect's eardrum, even though he manages to run off. Or imagine an officer shines a laser into a suspect's eyes to get him to stop, but the suspect is able to drive away with now-damaged retinas. Are these "touchings"? What about an officer's bullet that shatters the driver's windshield, a piece of which cuts her as she speeds away? Maybe the officer didn't touch the suspect, but he set in motion a series of events that yielded a touching.

Does that count? While assuring us that its new rule will prove easy to administer, the majority refuses to confront its certain complications. Lower courts and law enforcement won't have that luxury. * * *

Respectfully, I dissent.

CHAPTER 12

POLICE USE OF FORCE

■ ■ ■

When a police officer uses deadly force to apprehend a suspect, there is no question that a "seizure" of the person for Fourth Amendment purposes has taken place. Whether that seizure comports with the Fourth Amendment's command that searches and seizures not be unreasonable is another question. The cases in this chapter examine whether and when police use of force violates the Fourth Amendment.

In the first case in this chapter, *Tennessee v. Garner*, a police officer investigating a burglary call shot and killed an unarmed 15-year-old African-American male in the back of the head as the teen was trying to escape over a fence. The officer who shot Garner admitted that he saw no sign of a weapon and was reasonably certain Garner was unarmed when he shot him. He shot the teen anyway because he was convinced that if Garner made it over the fence, he would succeed in eluding capture. The next case, *Graham v. Connor*, is the leading Supreme Court case on when police use of force is excessive and therefore in violation of the Fourth Amendment.

In the final case in this chapter, *Scott v. Harris*, a police officer rammed his patrol car into the rear of a vehicle after a high-speed chase, causing the vehicle to crash and rendering the driver, a 19-year-old African American male, a quadriplegic. Justice Scalia, writing for the Court, suggests that no reasonable jury watching the dash-cam video of the high-speed chase could find that the officer used excessive force. In *"Whose Eyes Are You Going to Believe?"* Scott v. Harris *and the Perils of Cognitive Illiberalism*, Dan Kahan, David Hoffman, and Donald Braman present the results of an empirical study, showing that far from being an open and shut case, the reasonableness of the police action in *Scott v. Harris* is perceived differently by individuals depending on their cultural values. The Kahan study suggests one reason why lower courts should err on the side of permitting juries to decide cases in which reasonable minds can and will likely disagree, rather than summarily dismissing such cases.

TENNESSEE V. GARNER
Supreme Court of the United States
471 U.S. 1, 105 S. Ct. 1694, 85 L. Ed. 2d 1 (1985)

JUSTICE WHITE delivered the opinion of the Court.

At about 10:45 p.m. on October 3, 1974, Memphis Police Officers Elton Hymon and Leslie Wright were dispatched to answer a "prowler inside call." Upon arriving at the scene they saw a woman standing on her porch and gesturing toward the adjacent house. She told them she had heard glass breaking and that "they" or "someone" was breaking in next door. While Wright radioed the dispatcher to say that they were on the scene, Hymon went behind the house. He heard a door slam and saw someone run across the backyard. The fleeing suspect, who was appellee-respondent's decedent, Edward Garner,[a] stopped at a 6-feet-high chain link fence at the edge of the yard. With the aid of a flashlight, Hymon was able to see Garner's face and hands. He saw no sign of a weapon, and, though not certain, was "reasonably sure" and "figured" that Garner was unarmed. He thought Garner was 17 or 18 years old and about 5'5" or 5'7" tall.[2] While Garner was crouched at the base of the fence, Hymon called out "police, halt" and took a few steps toward him. Garner then began to climb over the fence. Convinced that if Garner made it over the fence he would elude capture, Hymon shot him. The bullet hit Garner in the back of the head. Garner was taken by ambulance to a hospital, where he died on the operating table. Ten dollars and a purse taken from the house were found on his body.

In using deadly force to prevent the escape, Hymon was acting under the authority of a Tennessee statute and pursuant to Police Department policy. The statute provides that "[i]f, after notice of the intention to arrest the defendant, he either flee or forcibly resist, the officer may use all the necessary means to effect the arrest." The Department policy was slightly more restrictive than the statute, but still allowed the use of deadly force in cases of burglary. The incident was reviewed by the Memphis Police Firearm's Review Board and presented to a grand jury. Neither took any action.

Garner's father then brought this action in the Federal District Court for the Western District of Tennessee, seeking damages under 42 U.S.C. § 1983 for asserted violations of Garner's constitutional rights. * * * It named as defendants Officer Hymon, the Police Department, its Director,

---

[a] The *Tennessee v. Garner* Court never mentions Garner's race in its opinion, but sources report that Edward Garner was Black. Mary Maxwell Thomas, *The African American Male: Communication Gap Converts Justice Into "Just Us" System*, 13 HARV. BLACKLETTER L. J. 1, 6 (1997); Jerry R. Sparger & David J. Giacopassi, *Memphis Revisited: A Reexamination of Police Shootings After the* Garner *Decision*, 9 JUST. Q. 211, 212 (1992).

[2] In fact, Garner, an eighth-grader, was 15. He was 5' 4" tall and weighed somewhere around 100 or 110 pounds.

and the Mayor and city of Memphis. After a 3-day bench trial, the District Court entered judgment for all defendants. * * * It * * * concluded that Hymon's actions were authorized by the Tennessee statute, which in turn was constitutional.

* * * The Court of Appeals reversed and remanded. It reasoned that the killing of a fleeing suspect is a "seizure" under the Fourth Amendment, and is therefore constitutional only if "reasonable." The Tennessee statute failed as applied to this case because it did not adequately limit the use of deadly force by distinguishing between felonies of different magnitudes * * *. Officers cannot resort to deadly force unless they "have probable cause . . . to believe that the suspect [has committed a felony and] poses a threat to the safety of the officers or a danger to the community if left at large."

The State of Tennessee, which had intervened to defend the statute, appealed to this Court. The city filed a petition for certiorari. We noted probable jurisdiction in the appeal and granted the petition.

Whenever an officer restrains the freedom of a person to walk away, he has seized that person. While it is not always clear just when minimal police interference becomes a seizure, there can be no question that apprehension by the use of deadly force is a seizure subject to the reasonableness requirement of the Fourth Amendment.

* * * To determine the constitutionality of a seizure "[w]e must balance the nature and quality of the intrusion on the individual's Fourth Amendment interests against the importance of the governmental interests alleged to justify the intrusion." We have described "the balancing of competing interests" as "the key principle of the Fourth Amendment." Because one of the factors is the extent of the intrusion, it is plain that reasonableness depends on not only when a seizure is made, but also how it is carried out. * * *

[This] balancing process * * * demonstrates that, notwithstanding probable cause to seize a suspect, an officer may not always do so by killing him. The intrusiveness of a seizure by means of deadly force is unmatched. The suspect's fundamental interest in his own life need not be elaborated upon. The use of deadly force also frustrates the interest of the individual, and of society, in judicial determination of guilt and punishment. Against these interests are ranged governmental interests in effective law enforcement. It is argued that overall violence will be reduced by encouraging the peaceful submission of suspects who know that they may be shot if they flee. Effectiveness in making arrests requires the resort to deadly force, or at least the meaningful threat thereof. * * *

Without in any way disparaging the importance of these goals, we are not convinced that the use of deadly force is a sufficiently productive means of accomplishing them to justify the killing of nonviolent suspects. The use of deadly force is a self-defeating way of apprehending a suspect and so setting the criminal justice mechanism in motion. If successful, it guarantees that that mechanism will not be set in motion. And while the meaningful threat of deadly force might be thought to lead to the arrest of more live suspects by discouraging escape attempts, the presently available evidence does not support this thesis. The fact is that a majority of police departments in this country have forbidden the use of deadly force against nonviolent suspects. If those charged with the enforcement of the criminal law have abjured the use of deadly force in arresting nondangerous felons, there is a substantial basis for doubting that the use of such force is an essential attribute of the arrest power in all felony cases. Petitioners and appellant have not persuaded us that shooting nondangerous fleeing suspects is so vital as to outweigh the suspect's interest in his own life.

The use of deadly force to prevent the escape of all felony suspects, whatever the circumstances, is constitutionally unreasonable. It is not better that all felony suspects die than that they escape. Where the suspect poses no immediate threat to the officer and no threat to others, the harm resulting from failing to apprehend him does not justify the use of deadly force to do so. It is no doubt unfortunate when a suspect who is in sight escapes, but the fact that the police arrive a little late or are a little slower afoot does not always justify killing the suspect. A police officer may not seize an unarmed, nondangerous suspect by shooting him dead. The Tennessee statute is unconstitutional insofar as it authorizes the use of deadly force against such fleeing suspects.

It is not, however, unconstitutional on its face. Where the officer has probable cause to believe that the suspect poses a threat of serious physical harm, either to the officer or to others, it is not constitutionally unreasonable to prevent escape by using deadly force. Thus, if the suspect threatens the officer with a weapon or there is probable cause to believe that he has committed a crime involving the infliction or threatened infliction of serious physical harm, deadly force may be used if necessary to prevent escape, and if, where feasible, some warning has been given. * * *

In reversing, the Court of Appeals accepted the District Court's factual conclusions and held that "the facts, as found, did not justify the use of deadly force." We agree. Officer Hymon could not reasonably have believed that Garner—young, slight, and unarmed—posed any threat. Indeed, Hymon never attempted to justify his actions on any basis other than the need to prevent an escape. * * * [T]he fact that Garner was a suspected burglar could not * * * automatically justify the use of deadly force. Hymon did not have probable cause to believe that Garner, whom he correctly believed to be unarmed, posed any physical danger to himself or others.

The dissent argues that the shooting was justified by the fact that Officer Hymon had probable cause to believe that Garner had committed a nighttime burglary. While we agree that burglary is a serious crime, we cannot agree that it is so dangerous as automatically to justify the use of deadly force. The FBI classifies burglary as a "property" rather than a "violent" crime. Although the armed burglar would present a different situation, the fact that an unarmed suspect has broken into a dwelling at night does not automatically mean he is physically dangerous. This case demonstrates as much. In fact, the available statistics demonstrate that burglaries only rarely involve physical violence. During the 10-year period from 1973–1982, only 3.8% of all burglaries involved violent crime. * * *

The judgment of the Court of Appeals is affirmed, and the case is remanded for further proceedings consistent with this opinion.

So ordered.

JUSTICE O'CONNOR, with whom THE CHIEF JUSTICE and JUSTICE REHNQUIST join, dissenting. * * *

For purposes of Fourth Amendment analysis, I agree with the Court that Officer Hymon "seized" Garner by shooting him. Whether that seizure was reasonable and therefore permitted by the Fourth Amendment requires a careful balancing of the important public interest in crime prevention and detection and the nature and quality of the intrusion upon legitimate interests of the individual. * * *

The public interest involved in the use of deadly force as a last resort to apprehend a fleeing burglary suspect relates primarily to the serious nature of the crime. Household burglaries not only represent the illegal entry into a person's home, but also "pos[e] real risk of serious harm to others." According to recent Department of Justice statistics, "[t]hree-fifths of all rapes in the home, three-fifths of all home robberies, and about a third of home aggravated and simple assaults are committed by burglars." During the period 1973–1982, 2.8 million such violent crimes were committed in the course of burglaries. Victims of a forcible intrusion into their home by a nighttime prowler will find little consolation in the majority's confident assertion that "burglaries only rarely involve physical violence." Moreover, even if a particular burglary, when viewed in retrospect, does not involve physical harm to others, the "harsh potentialities for violence" inherent in the forced entry into a home preclude characterization of the crime as "innocuous, inconsequential, minor, or 'nonviolent.'"

Because burglary is a serious and dangerous felony, the public interest in the prevention and detection of the crime is of compelling importance. Where a police officer has probable cause to arrest a suspected burglar, the use of deadly force as a last resort might well be the only means of apprehending the suspect. With respect to a particular burglary, subsequent investigation simply cannot represent a substitute for immediate apprehension of the criminal suspect at the scene. Indeed, the Captain of the Memphis Police Department testified that in his city, if apprehension is not immediate, it is likely that the suspect will not be caught. * * *

Against the strong public interests justifying the conduct at issue here must be weighed the individual interests implicated in the use of deadly force by police officers. The majority declares that "[t]he suspect's fundamental interest in his own life need not be elaborated upon." * * * Without questioning the importance of a person's interest in his life, I do not think this interest encompasses a right to flee unimpeded from the scene of a burglary. The legitimate interests of the suspect in these circumstances are adequately accommodated by the Tennessee statute: to avoid the use of deadly force and the consequent risk to his life, the suspect need merely obey the valid order to halt.

A proper balancing of the interests involved suggests that use of deadly force as a last resort to apprehend a criminal suspect fleeing from the scene of a nighttime burglary is not unreasonable within the meaning of the Fourth Amendment. Admittedly, the events giving rise to this case are in retrospect deeply regrettable. No one can view the death of an unarmed and apparently nonviolent 15-year-old without sorrow, much less disapproval. Nonetheless, the reasonableness of Officer Hymon's conduct for purposes of the Fourth Amendment cannot be evaluated by what later appears to have been a preferable course of police action. The officer pursued a suspect in the darkened backyard of a house that from all indications had just been burglarized. The police officer was not certain whether the suspect was alone or unarmed; nor did he know what had transpired inside the house. He ordered the suspect to halt, and when the suspect refused to obey and attempted to flee into the night, the officer fired his weapon to prevent escape. The reasonableness of this action for purposes of the Fourth Amendment is not determined by the unfortunate nature of this particular case; instead, the question is whether it is constitutionally impermissible for police officers, as a last resort, to shoot a burglary suspect fleeing the scene of the crime.

Even if I agreed that the Fourth Amendment was violated under the circumstances of this case, I would be unable to join the Court's opinion. * * * Relying on the Fourth Amendment, the majority asserts that it is constitutionally unreasonable to *use* deadly force against fleeing criminal suspects who do not appear to pose a threat of serious physical harm to others. By declining to limit its holding to the use of firearms, the Court unnecessarily implies that the Fourth Amendment constrains the use of any police practice that is potentially lethal, no matter how remote the risk.

*** Whatever the constitutional limits on police use of deadly force in order to apprehend a fleeing felon, I do not believe they are exceeded in a case in which a police officer has probable cause to arrest a suspect at the scene of a residential burglary, orders the suspect to halt, and then fires his weapon as a last resort to prevent the suspect's escape into the night. I respectfully dissent.

GRAHAM V. CONNOR

Supreme Court of the United States
490 U.S. 386, 109 S. Ct. 1865, 104 L. Ed. 2d 443 (1989)

CHIEF JUSTICE REHNQUIST delivered the opinion of the Court.

This case requires us to decide what constitutional standard governs a free citizen's claim that law enforcement officials used excessive force in the course of making an arrest, investigatory stop, or other "seizure" of his person. We hold that such claims are properly analyzed under the Fourth Amendment's "objective reasonableness" standard, rather than under a substantive due process standard.

In this action under 42 U.S.C. § 1983, petitioner Dethorne Graham[a] seeks to recover damages for injuries allegedly sustained when law enforcement officers used physical force against him during the course of an investigatory stop. *** On November 12, 1984, Graham, a diabetic, felt the onset of an insulin reaction. He asked a friend, William Berry, to drive him to a nearby convenience store so he could purchase some orange juice to counteract the reaction. Berry agreed, but when Graham entered the store, he saw a number of people ahead of him in the checkout line. Concerned about the delay, he hurried out of the store and asked Berry to drive him to a friend's house instead.

Respondent Connor, an officer of the Charlotte, North Carolina, Police Department, saw Graham hastily enter and leave the store. The officer became suspicious that something was amiss and followed Berry's car. About one-half mile from the store, he made an investigative stop. Although Berry told Connor that Graham was simply suffering from a "sugar reaction," the officer ordered Berry and Graham to wait while he found out what, if anything, had happened at the convenience store. When Officer Connor returned to his patrol car to call for backup assistance, Graham got out of the car, ran around it twice, and finally sat down on the curb, where he passed out briefly.

In the ensuing confusion, a number of other Charlotte police officers arrived on the scene in response to Officer Connor's request for backup. One of the officers rolled Graham over on the sidewalk and cuffed his hands

---

[a] While the Supreme Court's opinion does not mention Graham's race, at least one source describes Graham as a Black man. *Court v. Cop Misconduct*, ELYRIA CHRONICLE TELEGRAM, Oct. 13, 1989 at A4 ("Graham, who is black, says police handcuffed him, then dumped him in his yard").

tightly behind his back, ignoring Berry's pleas to get him some sugar. Another officer said: "I've seen a lot of people with sugar diabetes that never acted like this. Ain't nothing wrong with the M.F. but drunk. Lock the S.B. up." Several officers then lifted Graham up from behind, carried him over to Berry's car, and placed him face down on its hood. Regaining consciousness, Graham asked the officers to check in his wallet for a diabetic decal that he carried. In response, one of the officers told him to "shut up" and shoved his face down against the hood of the car. Four officers grabbed Graham and threw him headfirst into the police car. A friend of Graham's brought some orange juice to the car, but the officers refused to let him have it. Finally, Officer Connor received a report that Graham had done nothing wrong at the convenience store, and the officers drove him home and released him.

At some point during his encounter with the police, Graham sustained a broken foot, cuts on his wrists, a bruised forehead, and an injured shoulder; he also claims to have developed a loud ringing in his right ear that continues to this day. He commenced this action under 42 U.S.C. § 1983 against the individual officers involved in the incident, all of whom are respondents here, alleging that they had used excessive force in making the investigatory stop, in violation of "rights secured to him under the Fourteenth Amendment to the United States Constitution and 42 U.S.C. § 1983." The case was tried before a jury. At the close of petitioner's evidence, respondents moved for a directed verdict. In ruling on that motion, the District Court considered the following four factors, which it identified as "[t]he factors to be considered in determining when the excessive use of force gives rise to a cause of action under § 1983": (1) the need for the application of force; (2) the relationship between that need and the amount of force that was used; (3) the extent of the injury inflicted; and (4) "[w]hether the force was applied in a good faith effort to maintain and restore discipline or maliciously and sadistically for the very purpose of causing harm." Finding that the amount of force used by the officers was "appropriate under the circumstances," that "[t]here was no discernable injury inflicted," and that the force used "was not applied maliciously or sadistically for the very purpose of causing harm," but in "a good faith effort to maintain or restore order in the face of a potentially explosive situation," the District Court granted respondents' motion for a directed verdict.

A divided panel of the Court of Appeals for the Fourth Circuit affirmed. The majority ruled first that the District Court had applied the correct legal standard in assessing petitioner's excessive force claim. * * * [T]he majority [also] held that a reasonable jury applying the four-part test it had just endorsed to petitioner's evidence "could not find that the force applied was constitutionally excessive." * * * We granted certiorari and now reverse.

Fifteen years ago, in *Johnson v. Glick*, the Court of Appeals for the Second Circuit addressed a § 1983 damages claim filed by a pretrial detainee who claimed that a guard had assaulted him without justification. In evaluating the detainee's claim, Judge Friendly applied neither the Fourth Amendment nor the Eighth, the two most textually obvious sources of constitutional protection against physically abusive governmental conduct. Instead, he looked to "substantive due process," holding that "quite apart from any 'specific' of the Bill of Rights, application of undue force by law enforcement officers deprives a suspect of liberty without due process of law." * * * Judge Friendly went on to set forth four factors to guide courts in determining "whether the constitutional line has been crossed" by a particular use of force—the same four factors relied upon by the courts below in this case.

In the years following *Johnson v. Glick,* the vast majority of lower federal courts have applied its four-part "substantive due process" test indiscriminately to all excessive force claims lodged against law enforcement and prison officials under § 1983, without considering whether the particular application of force might implicate a more specific constitutional right governed by a different standard. * * *

We reject this notion that all excessive force claims brought under § 1983 are governed by a single generic standard. As we have said many times, § 1983 "is not itself a source of substantive rights," but merely provides "a method for vindicating federal rights elsewhere conferred." In addressing an excessive force claim brought under § 1983, analysis begins by identifying the specific constitutional right allegedly infringed by the challenged application of force. In most instances, that will be either the Fourth Amendment's prohibition against unreasonable seizures of the person, or the Eighth Amendment's ban on cruel and unusual punishments, which are the two primary sources of constitutional protection against physically abusive governmental conduct. The validity of the claim must then be judged by reference to the specific constitutional standard which governs that right, rather than to some generalized "excessive force" standard.

Where, as here, the excessive force claim arises in the context of an arrest or investigatory stop of a free citizen, it is most properly characterized as one invoking the protections of the Fourth Amendment, which guarantees citizens the right "to be secure in their persons . . . against unreasonable . . . seizures" of the person. This much is clear from our decision in *Tennessee v. Garner.* In *Garner,* we addressed a claim that the use of deadly force to apprehend a fleeing suspect who did not appear to be armed or otherwise dangerous violated the suspect's constitutional rights, notwithstanding the existence of probable cause to arrest. Though the complaint alleged violations of both the Fourth Amendment and the Due Process Clause, we analyzed the constitutionality of the challenged application of force solely by reference to the Fourth Amendment's prohibition against unreasonable seizures of the person, holding that the "reasonableness" of a particular seizure depends not only on *when* it is made, but also on *how* it is carried out. Today we make explicit what was implicit in *Garner*'s analysis, and hold that *all* claims that law enforcement officers have used excessive force—deadly or not—in the course of an arrest, investigatory stop, or other "seizure" of a free citizen should be analyzed under the Fourth Amendment and its "reasonableness" standard, rather than under a "substantive due process" approach. Because the Fourth Amendment provides an explicit textual source of constitutional protection against this sort of physically intrusive governmental conduct, that Amendment, not the more generalized notion of "substantive due process," must be the guide for analyzing these claims.

Determining whether the force used to effect a particular seizure is "reasonable" under the Fourth Amendment requires a careful balancing of "the nature and quality of the intrusion on the individual's Fourth Amendment interests" against the countervailing governmental interests at stake. Our Fourth Amendment jurisprudence has long recognized that the right to make an arrest or investigatory stop necessarily carries with it the right to use some degree of physical coercion or threat thereof to effect it. Because "[t]he test of reasonableness under the Fourth Amendment is not capable of precise definition or mechanical application," however, its proper application requires careful attention to the facts and circumstances of each particular case, including the severity of the crime at issue, whether the suspect poses an immediate threat to the safety of the officers or others, and whether he is actively resisting arrest or attempting to evade arrest by flight.

The "reasonableness" of a particular use of force must be judged from the perspective of a reasonable officer on the scene, rather than with the 20/20 vision of hindsight. The Fourth Amendment is not violated by an arrest based on probable cause, even though the wrong person is arrested, nor by the mistaken execution of a valid search warrant on the wrong premises. With respect to a claim of excessive force, the same standard of reasonableness at the moment applies: "Not every push or shove, even if it may later seem unnecessary in the peace of a judge's chambers," violates the Fourth Amendment. The calculus of reasonableness must embody allowance for the fact that police officers are often forced to make split-second judgments—in circumstances that are tense, uncertain, and rapidly evolving—about the amount of force that is necessary in a particular situation.

As in other Fourth Amendment contexts, however, the "reasonableness" inquiry in an excessive force case is an objective one: the question is whether the officers' actions are "objectively reasonable" in light of the facts and circumstances confronting them, without regard to their underlying intent or motivation. An officer's evil intentions will not make a Fourth Amendment violation out of an objectively reasonable use of force;

nor will an officer's good intentions make an objectively unreasonable use of force constitutional.

Because petitioner's excessive force claim is one arising under the Fourth Amendment, the Court of Appeals erred in analyzing it under the four-part *Johnson v. Glick* test. That test, which requires consideration of whether the individual officers acted in "good faith" or "maliciously and sadistically for the very purpose of causing harm," is incompatible with a proper Fourth Amendment analysis. We do not agree with the Court of Appeals' suggestion, that the "malicious and sadistic" inquiry is merely another way of describing conduct that is objectively unreasonable under the circumstances. Whatever the empirical correlations between "malicious and sadistic" behavior and objective unreasonableness may be, the fact remains that the "malicious and sadistic" factor puts in issue the subjective motivations of the individual officers, which our prior cases make clear has no bearing on whether a particular seizure is "unreasonable" under the Fourth Amendment. * * *

Because the Court of Appeals reviewed the District Court's ruling on the motion for directed verdict under an erroneous view of the governing substantive law, its judgment must be vacated and the case remanded to that court for reconsideration of that issue under the proper Fourth Amendment standard.

It is so ordered.

[JUSTICE BLACKMUN's concurring opinion has been omitted.]

SCOTT V. HARRIS
Supreme Court of the United States
550 U.S. 372, 127 S. Ct. 1769, 167 L. Ed. 2d 686 (2007)

JUSTICE SCALIA delivered the opinion of the Court. * * *

In March 2001, a Georgia county deputy clocked respondent's vehicle traveling at 73 miles per hour on a road with a 55-mile-per-hour speed limit. The deputy activated his blue flashing lights indicating that respondent should pull over. Instead, respondent sped away, initiating a chase down what is in most portions a two-lane road, at speeds exceeding 85 miles per hour. The deputy radioed his dispatch to report that he was pursuing a fleeing vehicle, and broadcast its license plate number. Petitioner, Deputy Timothy Scott, heard the radio communication and joined the pursuit along with other officers. In the midst of the chase, respondent pulled into the parking lot of a shopping center and was nearly boxed in by the various police vehicles. Respondent evaded the trap by making a sharp turn, colliding with Scott's police car, exiting the parking lot, and speeding off once again down a two-lane highway.

Following respondent's shopping center maneuvering, which resulted in slight damage to Scott's police car, Scott took over as the lead pursuit vehicle. Six minutes and nearly 10 miles after the chase had begun, Scott decided to attempt to terminate the episode by employing a "Precision Intervention Technique ('PIT') maneuver, which causes the fleeing vehicle to spin to a stop." Having radioed his supervisor for permission, Scott was told to "[g]o ahead and take him out." Instead, Scott applied his push bumper to the rear of respondent's vehicle. As a result, respondent lost control of his vehicle, which left the roadway, ran down an embankment, overturned, and crashed. Respondent was badly injured and was rendered a quadriplegic.[a]

Respondent filed suit against Deputy Scott and others under 42 U.S.C. § 1983, alleging, *inter alia,* a violation of his federal constitutional rights, viz. use of excessive force resulting in an unreasonable seizure under the Fourth Amendment. In response, Scott filed a motion for summary judgment based on an assertion of qualified immunity. The District Court denied the motion. * * * [T]he United States Court of Appeals for the Eleventh Circuit affirmed the District Court's decision to allow respondent's Fourth Amendment claim against Scott to proceed to trial. Taking respondent's view of the facts as given, the Court of Appeals concluded that Scott's actions could constitute "deadly force" under *Tennessee v. Garner*, and that the use of such force in this context "would violate [respondent's] constitutional right to be free from excessive force during a seizure. Accordingly, a reasonable jury could find that Scott violated [respondent's] Fourth Amendment rights." * * * We granted certiorari, and now reverse. * * *

The first step in assessing the constitutionality of Scott's actions is to determine the relevant facts. As this case was decided on summary judgment, there have not yet been factual findings by a judge or jury, and respondent's version of events (unsurprisingly) differs substantially from Scott's version. When things are in such a posture, courts are required to view the facts and draw reasonable inferences "in the light most favorable to the party opposing the [summary judgment] motion." In qualified immunity cases, this usually means adopting (as the Court of Appeals did here) the plaintiff's version of the facts.

There is, however, an added wrinkle in this case: existence in the record of a videotape capturing the events in question. There are no allegations or indications that this videotape was doctored or altered in any way, nor any contention that what it depicts differs from what actually

---

[a] The *Scott v. Harris* Court never mentions Victor Harris' race, but Harris is described as a 19-year-old African American male in other sources. Ann C. McGinley, *Cognitive Illiberalism, Summary Judgment, and Title VII: An Examination of* Ricci v. DeStefano, 57 N.Y.L. SCH. L. REV. 865, 871 (2013). *See also Why I Ran* (interview with Victor Harris, explaining why he fled from police) *available at* https://www.youtube.com/watch?v=JATVLUOjzvM.

happened. The videotape quite clearly contradicts the version of the story told by respondent and adopted by the Court of Appeals.[5] For example, the Court of Appeals adopted respondent's assertions that, during the chase, "there was little, if any, actual threat to pedestrians or other motorists, as the roads were mostly empty and [respondent] remained in control of his vehicle." Indeed, reading the lower court's opinion, one gets the impression that respondent, rather than fleeing from police, was attempting to pass his driving test. * * *

The videotape tells quite a different story. There we see respondent's vehicle racing down narrow, two-lane roads in the dead of night at speeds that are shockingly fast. We see it swerve around more than a dozen other cars, cross the double-yellow line, and force cars traveling in both directions to their respective shoulders to avoid being hit. We see it run multiple red lights and travel for considerable periods of time in the occasional center left-turn-only lane, chased by numerous police cars forced to engage in the same hazardous maneuvers just to keep up. Far from being the cautious and controlled driver the lower court depicts, what we see on the video more closely resembles a Hollywood-style car chase of the most frightening sort, placing police officers and innocent bystanders alike at great risk of serious injury.

At the summary judgment stage, facts must be viewed in the light most favorable to the nonmoving party only if there is a "genuine" dispute as to those facts. * * * When opposing parties tell two different stories, one of which is blatantly contradicted by the record, so that no reasonable jury could believe it, a court should not adopt that version of the facts for purposes of ruling on a motion for summary judgment.

That was the case here with regard to the factual issue whether respondent was driving in such fashion as to endanger human life. Respondent's version of events is so utterly discredited by the record that no reasonable jury could have believed him. The Court of Appeals should not have relied on such visible fiction; it should have viewed the facts in the light depicted by the videotape.

Judging the matter on that basis, we think it is quite clear that Deputy Scott did not violate the Fourth Amendment. Scott does not contest that his decision to terminate the car chase by ramming his bumper into respondent's vehicle constituted a "seizure." "[A] Fourth Amendment seizure [occurs] . . . when there is a governmental termination of freedom of movement through means intentionally applied." It is also conceded, by

---

[5] * * * We are happy to allow the videotape to speak for itself. See Record 36, Exh. A, available at http://www.supremecourtus.gov/opinions/video/scott_v_harris.html and in Clerk of Court's case file. [Because the url provided by the Court in this footnote no longer works, the authors of the casebook found another url depicting the high-speed chase: https://www.youtube.com/watch?v=qrVKSgRZ2GY (also available at https://perma.cc/YYM9-JYMV).]

both sides, that a claim of "excessive force in the course of making [a] . . . 'seizure' of [the] person . . . [is] properly analyzed under the Fourth Amendment's 'objective reasonableness' standard." The question we need to answer is whether Scott's actions were objectively reasonable. * * *

Respondent urges us to analyze this case as we analyzed *Garner*. We must first decide, he says, whether the actions Scott took constituted "deadly force." (He defines "deadly force" as "any use of force which creates a substantial likelihood of causing death or serious bodily injury.") If so, respondent claims that *Garner* prescribes certain preconditions that must be met before Scott's actions can survive Fourth Amendment scrutiny: (1) The suspect must have posed an immediate threat of serious physical harm to the officer or others; (2) deadly force must have been necessary to prevent escape; and (3) where feasible, the officer must have given the suspect some warning. Since these *Garner* preconditions for using deadly force were not met in this case, Scott's actions were *per se* unreasonable.

Respondent's argument falters at its first step; *Garner* did not establish a magical on/off switch that triggers rigid preconditions whenever an officer's actions constitute "deadly force." *Garner* was simply an application of the Fourth Amendment's "reasonableness" test to the use of a particular type of force in a particular situation. * * *

In determining the reasonableness of the manner in which a seizure is effected, "[w]e must balance the nature and quality of the intrusion on the individual's Fourth Amendment interests against the importance of the governmental interests alleged to justify the intrusion." * * * [I]n judging whether Scott's actions were reasonable, we must consider the risk of bodily harm that Scott's actions posed to respondent in light of the threat to the public that Scott was trying to eliminate. Although there is no obvious way to quantify the risks on either side, it is clear from the videotape that respondent posed an actual and imminent threat to the lives of any pedestrians who might have been present, to other civilian motorists, and to the officers involved in the chase. It is equally clear that Scott's actions posed a high likelihood of serious injury or death to respondent—though not the near *certainty* of death posed by, say, shooting a fleeing felon in the back of the head or pulling alongside a fleeing motorist's car and shooting the motorist. So how does a court go about weighing the perhaps lesser probability of injuring or killing numerous bystanders against the perhaps larger probability of injuring or killing a single person? We think it appropriate in this process to take into account not only the number of lives at risk, but also their relative culpability. It was respondent, after all, who intentionally placed himself and the public in danger by unlawfully engaging in the reckless, high-speed flight that ultimately produced the choice between two evils that Scott confronted. Multiple police cars, with blue lights flashing and sirens blaring, had been chasing respondent for nearly 10 miles, but he ignored their warning to stop. By contrast, those who might have been harmed had Scott not taken the action he did were entirely innocent. We have little difficulty in concluding it was reasonable for Scott to take the action that he did.

But wait, says respondent: Couldn't the innocent public equally have been protected, and the tragic accident entirely avoided, if the police had simply ceased their pursuit? We think the police need not have taken that chance and hoped for the best. Whereas Scott's action—ramming respondent off the road—was *certain* to eliminate the risk that respondent posed to the public, ceasing pursuit was not. First of all, there would have been no way to convey convincingly to respondent that the chase was off, and that he was free to go. Had respondent looked in his rearview mirror and seen the police cars deactivate their flashing lights and turn around, he would have had no idea whether they were truly letting him get away, or simply devising a new strategy for capture. Perhaps the police knew a shortcut he didn't know, and would reappear down the road to intercept him; or perhaps they were setting up a roadblock in his path. Given such uncertainty, respondent might have been just as likely to respond by continuing to drive recklessly as by slowing down and wiping his brow.

Second, we are loath to lay down a rule requiring the police to allow fleeing suspects to get away whenever they drive *so recklessly* that they put other people's lives in danger. It is obvious the perverse incentives such a rule would create: Every fleeing motorist would know that escape is within his grasp, if only he accelerates to 90 miles per hour, crosses the double-yellow line a few times, and runs a few red lights. The Constitution assuredly does not impose this invitation to impunity-earned-by-recklessness. Instead, we lay down a more sensible rule: A police officer's attempt to terminate a dangerous high-speed car chase that threatens the lives of innocent bystanders does not violate the Fourth Amendment, even when it places the fleeing motorist at risk of serious injury or death.

The car chase that respondent initiated in this case posed a substantial and immediate risk of serious physical injury to others; no reasonable jury could conclude otherwise. Scott's attempt to terminate the chase by forcing respondent off the road was reasonable, and Scott is entitled to summary judgment. The Court of Appeals' judgment to the contrary is reversed.

It is so ordered.

JUSTICE STEVENS, dissenting.

Today, the Court asks whether an officer may "take actions that place a fleeing motorist at risk of serious injury or death in order to stop the motorist's flight from endangering the lives of innocent bystanders." * * *

Relying on a *de novo* review of a videotape of a portion of a nighttime chase on a lightly traveled road in Georgia where no pedestrians or other "bystanders" were present, buttressed by uninformed speculation about the possible consequences of discontinuing the chase, eight of the jurors on this Court reach a verdict that differs from the views of the judges on both the District Court and the Court of Appeals who are surely more familiar with the hazards of driving on Georgia roads than we are. The Court's justification for this unprecedented departure from our well-settled standard of review of factual determinations made by a district court and affirmed by a court of appeals is based on its mistaken view that the Court of Appeals' description of the facts was "blatantly contradicted by the record" and that respondent's version of the events was "so utterly discredited by the record that no reasonable jury could have believed him."

Rather than supporting the conclusion that what we see on the video "resembles a Hollywood-style car chase of the most frightening sort," the tape actually confirms, rather than contradicts, the lower courts' appraisal of the factual questions at issue. More importantly, it surely does not provide a principled basis for depriving the respondent of his right to have a jury evaluate the question whether the police officers' decision to use deadly force to bring the chase to an end was reasonable.

Omitted from the Court's description of the initial speeding violation is the fact that respondent was on a four-lane portion of Highway 34 when the officer clocked his speed at 73 miles per hour and initiated the chase. More significantly—and contrary to the Court's assumption that respondent's vehicle "force[d] cars traveling in both directions to their respective shoulders to avoid being hit"—a fact unmentioned in the text of the opinion explains why those cars pulled over prior to being passed by respondent. The sirens and flashing lights on the police cars following respondent gave the same warning that a speeding ambulance or fire engine would have provided. The 13 cars that respondent passed on his side of the road before entering the shopping center, and both of the cars that he passed on the right after leaving the center, no doubt had already pulled to the side of the road or were driving along the shoulder because they heard the police sirens or saw the flashing lights before respondent or the police cruisers approached. A jury could certainly conclude that those motorists were exposed to no greater risk than persons who take the same action in response to a speeding ambulance, and that their reactions were fully consistent with the evidence that respondent, though speeding, retained full control of his vehicle. * * *

I recognize, of course, that even though respondent's original speeding violation on a four-lane highway was rather ordinary, his refusal to stop and subsequent flight was a serious offense that merited severe punishment. It was not, however, a capital offense, or even an offense that justified the use of deadly force rather than an abandonment of the chase. The Court's concern about the "imminent threat to the lives of any pedestrians who might have been present," while surely valid in an appropriate case, should be discounted in a case involving a nighttime chase in an area where no pedestrians were present.

What would have happened if the police had decided to abandon the chase? We now know that they could have apprehended respondent later because they had his license plate number. Even if that were not true, and even if he would have escaped any punishment at all, the use of deadly force in this case was no more appropriate than the use of a deadly weapon against a fleeing felon in *Tennessee v. Garner.* * * * The Court attempts to avoid the conclusion that deadly force was unnecessary by speculating that if the officers had let him go, respondent might have been "just as likely" to continue to drive recklessly as to slow down and wipe his brow. That speculation is unconvincing as a matter of common sense and improper as a matter of law. * * * Indeed, rules adopted by countless police departments throughout the country are based on a judgment that differs from the Court's. *See, e.g.,* App. to Brief for Georgia Association of Chiefs of Police, Inc., as *Amicus Curiae* A-52 ("During a pursuit, * * * [w]hen the immediate danger to the public created by the pursuit is greater than the immediate or potential danger to the public should the suspect remain at large, then the pursuit should be discontinued or terminated. . . . [P]ursuits should usually be discontinued when the violator's identity has been established to the point that later apprehension can be accomplished without danger to the public"). * * *

Whether a person's actions have risen to a level warranting deadly force is a question of fact best reserved for a jury. Here, the Court has usurped the jury's factfinding function and, in doing so, implicitly labeled the four other judges to review the case unreasonable. It chastises the Court of Appeals for failing to "vie[w] the facts in the light depicted by the videotape" and implies that no reasonable person could view the videotape and come to the conclusion that deadly force was unjustified. However, the three judges on the Court of Appeals panel apparently did view the videotapes entered into evidence and described a very different version of events:

> At the time of the ramming, apart from speeding and running two red lights, Harris was driving in a non-aggressive fashion (i.e., without trying to ram or run into the officers). Moreover, . . . Scott's path on the open highway was largely clear. The videos introduced into evidence show little to no vehicular (or pedestrian) traffic, allegedly because of the late hour and the police blockade of the nearby intersections. Finally, Scott issued absolutely no warning (e.g., over the loudspeaker or otherwise) prior to using deadly force.

If two groups of judges can disagree so vehemently about the nature of the pursuit and the circumstances surrounding that pursuit, it seems eminently likely that a reasonable juror could disagree with this Court's characterization of events. * * *

The Court today sets forth a *per se* rule that presumes its own version of the facts: "A police officer's attempt to terminate a dangerous high-speed car chase that threatens the lives of innocent bystanders does not violate the Fourth Amendment, even when it places the fleeing motorist at risk of serious injury or death." Not only does that rule fly in the face of the flexible and case-by-case "reasonableness" approach applied in *Garner* * * *, but it is also arguably inapplicable to the case at hand, given that it is not clear that this chase threatened the life of any "innocent bystande[r]." In my view, the risks inherent in justifying unwarranted police conduct on the basis of unfounded assumptions are unacceptable, particularly when less drastic measures—in this case, the use of stop sticks or a simple warning issued from a loudspeaker—could have avoided such a tragic result. In my judgment, jurors in Georgia should be allowed to evaluate the reasonableness of the decision to ram respondent's speeding vehicle in a manner that created an obvious risk of death and has in fact made him a quadriplegic at the age of 19.

I respectfully dissent.

[JUSTICE GINSBURG's concurring opinion and JUSTICE BREYER's concurring opinion have been omitted.]

WHOSE EYES ARE YOU GOING TO BELIEVE? SCOTT V. HARRIS AND THE PERILS OF COGNITIVE ILLIBERALISM
Dan M. Kahan, David A. Hoffman, Donald Braman
122 Harv. L. Rev. 837 (2009)

When [*Scott v. Harris*] was handed down * * *, a majority of Justices * * * decided to "call it" as they "saw it." Acknowledging that although normally "courts are required to view the facts and draw reasonable inferences 'in the light most favorable to the party opposing the [summary judgment] motion,'" Justice Scalia, writing for an eight-Justice majority, stated, "[t]here is . . . an added wrinkle in this case: existence in the record of a videotape capturing the events in question." * * * "Respondent's version of events is so utterly discredited by the record that no reasonable jury could have believed him."

Somewhat inconveniently for the majority, however, one Justice who had watched the tape had in fact taken Harris's view. "[T]he tape actually confirms, rather than contradicts, the lower courts' appraisal of the factual questions at issue," Justice Stevens announced in dissent.

* * * [T]he majority saw no need to resort to reasoned elaboration of its position to rebut Stevens's [arguments in dissent]. Instead, creating the Court's first (and so far only) multimedia cyber-opinion, it supplied a URL

for a digital rendering of the tape that had been uploaded to the Court's website. "We are happy," Scalia wrote, "to allow the videotape to speak for itself."

Well, does the *Scott v. Harris* tape speak for itself? If so, what does it say?

We decided to conduct an empirical study to answer these questions. We showed the video to a diverse sample of approximately 1350 Americans. We then asked them to tell us what they saw, and give us their views on the issues that the Court had identified as dispositive.

Our subjects didn't see things eye to eye. A fairly substantial majority did interpret the facts the way the Court did. But members of various subcommunities did not. African Americans, low-income workers, and residents of the Northeast, for example, tended to form more pro-plaintiff views of the facts than did the Court. So did individuals who characterized themselves as liberals and Democrats.

Individuals with these characteristics tend to share a cultural orientation that prizes egalitarianism and social solidarity. Various highly salient, "symbolic" political issues—from gun control to affirmative action, from the death penalty to environmental protection—feature conflict between persons who share this recognizable cultural profile and those who hold an opposing one that features hierarchical and individualistic values. We found that persons who subscribed to the former style tended to perceive less danger in Harris's flight, to attribute more responsibility to the police for creating the risk for the public, and to find less justification in the use of deadly force to end the chase. Indeed, these individuals were much more likely to see the police, rather than Harris, as the source of the danger posed by the flight and to find the deliberate ramming of Harris's vehicle unnecessary to avert risk to the public.

Thus, the question posed by the data is not, as Justice Breyer asked, whether to believe one's eyes, but rather whose eyes the law should believe when identifiable groups of citizens form competing factual perceptions. * * * Although an admitted minority of American society, citizens disposed to see the facts differently from the *Scott* majority share a perspective founded on common experiences and values. By insisting that a case like *Scott* be decided summarily, the Court not only denied those citizens an opportunity, in the context of jury deliberations, to inform and possibly change the view of citizens endowed with a different perspective. It also needlessly bound the result in the case to a process of decisionmaking that deprived the decision of any prospect of legitimacy in the eyes of that subcommunity whose members saw the facts differently.

* * * The Court's mistake * * * reflects a type of decisionmaking hubris that has cognitive origins and that has deleterious consequences * * *. Social psychology teaches us that our perceptions of fact are pervasively

shaped by our commitments to shared but contested views of individual virtue and social justice. It also tells us that although our ability to perceive this type of value-motivated cognition in others is quite acute, our power to perceive it in ourselves tends to be quite poor. We thus simultaneously experience overconfidence in the unassailable correctness of the factual perceptions we hold in common with our confederates and unwarranted contempt for the perceptions associated with our opposites. When these dispositions become integrated into law—as we believe they did in *Scott*—they generate needless cultural and political conflict that enervates the law's political legitimacy. Judges, legislators, and ordinary citizens should therefore always be alert to the influence of this species of "cognitive illiberalism" and take the precautions necessary to minimize it.

* * * Were a case like *Scott* to be submitted to a jury, of course, the jury would be called upon to decide (in the form of a general verdict) all the issues that the Court identified as decisive to its analysis. That is, in considering whether the use of deadly force to terminate the chase was reasonable, the jury would be required not only to gauge the degree of risk that the fleeing driver's behavior imposed on the public and the police, but also to assess the "relative culpability" of the fleeing driver and the pursuing police officer for creating that risk.

As a result of the Court's decision in *Scott*, though, in no case will a jury be permitted to decide any of those issues. The Court's decision effectively determined that, regardless of whatever other evidence might be presented in the case and whatever might transpire in the course of jury deliberations, there could be no room for "reasonable" disagreement on either the magnitude of the risks involved in the case or the role of the police in reducing or exacerbating those risks.

* * * The vast majority of citizens in our society do not desire to impose their values on others. They accept the basic liberal premise that law and policy should be confined to attainment of secular goods—security, health, prosperity—that are fully accessible to persons of all cultural outlooks. But because the factual beliefs they form about the sorts of behavior that threaten those goods are (subconsciously) motivated by their cultural appraisals of those activities, such citizens naturally divide into opposing cultural factions on the policies the law should pursue to achieve their common welfare. * * *

We argue that the decision in *Scott* reflects and reinforces these dynamics. The Justices in the majority couldn't literally have perceived that no one could see the facts on the tape differently from how they saw them. The evidence that some citizens might was staring them, literally, in the face: Justice Stevens, who presumably indicated even in conference that he was not of the view that the case was fit for summary disposition. Even apart from Justice Stevens's interpretation of the tape, though, the case was replete with cues that a decision on the grounds the Court settled on would provoke at least some generalized societal dissent. It involved a coercive, near-deadly encounter between police and a citizen, always a potentially divisive matter in our society; numerous public interest groups had filed briefs in support of the respondent; coverage of the case in the media, too, suggested the decision would be controversial.

* * * [W]e recommend that a judge engage in a sort of mental double check when ruling on a motion that would result in summary adjudication. * * * [A]lmost any time a judge does conclude that there is no genuine dispute about some set of material facts, she will be able to anticipate that some small percentage of actual jurors would nevertheless dispute them. Before concluding, then, that no reasonable juror could find such facts, the judge should try to imagine who those potential jurors might be. If, as will usually be true, she cannot identify them, or can conjure only the random faces of imaginary statistical outliers, she should proceed to decide the case summarily. But if instead she can form a concrete picture of the dissenting jurors, and they are people who bear recognizable identity-defining characteristics—demographic, cultural, political, or otherwise—she should stop and think hard. Due humility obliges her to consider whether privileging her own view of the facts risks conveying a denigrating and exclusionary message to members of such subcommunities. If it does, she should choose a different path. * * *

CHAPTER 13

CONSENT SEARCHES

∎ ∎ ∎

Amongst the various ways police can search and seize property without securing a warrant based on probable cause is the consent search. While "[t]here is no national clearinghouse for statistics on the number of times police ask for consent to search,"[a] some estimate that over 90 percent of warrantless searches are based upon the consent exception.[b] In *Schneckloth v. Bustamonte*, the Court explains what is necessary for a valid consent search. *Schneckloth* also tells us who bears the burden of proving that the requirements for a valid consent search have been satisfied.

When one thinks about police asking for consent to search, one likely envisions a police officer asking the person who is the target of the investigation for consent. Police, however, may also obtain consent to search from someone other than the target of the investigation. Under the third party consent doctrine (not to be confused with the third party doctrine studied earlier this semester, *see Smith v. Maryland, supra*), police may search property without a search warrant if they obtain the consent of a co-occupant with "common authority" over those premises or that property. In *Illinois v. Rodriguez*, we learn what "common authority" means. Watch carefully how the Court in *Illinois v. Rodriguez* broadens the third party consent doctrine. In *Georgia v. Randolph*, the Court considers another question related to the scope of the third party consent doctrine: how to resolve a split of authority in the lower courts over whether an occupant of the premises may give law enforcement officers consent to search the premises over the objection of a co-occupant who is present and objecting.

SCHNECKLOTH V. BUSTAMONTE
Supreme Court of the United States
412 U.S. 218, 93 S. Ct. 2041, 36 L. Ed. 2d 851 (1973)

JUSTICE STEWART delivered the opinion of the Court.

It is well settled under the Fourth and Fourteenth Amendments that a search conducted without a warrant issued upon probable cause is "per se unreasonable . . . subject only to a few specifically established and well-

---

[a] Marcy Strauss, *Reconstructing Consent*, 92 J. CRIM. L. & CRIMINOLOGY 211, 214 n.7 (2001).
[b] Ric Simmons, *Not Voluntary but Still Reasonable*, 80 IND. L.J. 773, 773 n.1 (2005).

delineated exceptions." It is equally well settled that one of the specifically established exceptions to the requirements of both a warrant and probable cause is a search that is conducted pursuant to consent. The constitutional question in the present case concerns the definition of "consent" in this Fourth and Fourteenth Amendment context. * * *

The respondent was brought to trial in a California court upon a charge of possessing a check with intent to defraud. He moved to suppress the introduction of certain material as evidence against him on the ground that the material had been acquired through an unconstitutional search and seizure. In response to the motion, the trial judge conducted an evidentiary hearing where it was established that the material in question had been acquired by the State under the following circumstances:

While on routine patrol in Sunnyvale, California, at approximately 2:40 in the morning, Police Officer James Rand stopped an automobile when he observed that one headlight and its license plate light were burned out. Six men were in the vehicle. Joe Alcala and the respondent, Robert Bustamonte, were in the front seat with Joe Gonzales, the driver. Three older men were seated in the rear. When, in response to the policeman's question, Gonzales could not produce a driver's license, Officer Rand asked if any of the other five had any evidence of identification. Only Alcala produced a license, and he explained that the car was his brother's. After the six occupants had stepped out of the car at the officer's request and after two additional policemen had arrived, Officer Rand asked Alcala if he could search the car. Alcala replied, "Sure, go ahead." Prior to the search no one was threatened with arrest and, according to Officer Rand's uncontradicted testimony, it "was all very congenial at this time." Gonzales testified that Alcala actually helped in the search of the car, by opening the trunk and glove compartment. In Gonzales' words: "[T]he police officer asked Joe [Alcala], he goes, 'Does the trunk open?' And Joe said, 'Yes.' He went to the car and got the keys and opened up the trunk." Wadded up under the left rear seat, the police officers found three checks that had previously been stolen from a car wash.

The trial judge denied the motion to suppress, and the checks in question were admitted in evidence at Bustamonte's trial. On the basis of this and other evidence he was convicted, and the California Court of Appeal for the First Appellate District affirmed the conviction. * * * The California Supreme Court denied review.

* * * The respondent concedes that a search conducted pursuant to a valid consent is constitutionally permissible. * * * [T]he State concedes that "[w]hen a prosecutor seeks to rely upon consent to justify the lawfulness of a search, he has the burden of proving that the consent was, in fact, freely and voluntarily given."

CH. 13   CONSENT SEARCHES   353

The precise question in this case, then, is what must the prosecution prove to demonstrate that a consent was "voluntarily" given. And upon that question there is a square conflict of views between the state and federal courts that have reviewed the search involved in the case before us. The Court of Appeals for the Ninth Circuit concluded that it is an essential part of the State's initial burden to prove that a person knows he has a right to refuse consent. * * *

The most extensive judicial exposition of the meaning of "voluntariness" has been developed in those cases in which the Court has had to determine the "voluntariness" of a defendant's confession for purposes of the Fourteenth Amendment. Almost 40 years ago, in *Brown v. Mississippi*, the Court held that a criminal conviction based upon a confession obtained by brutality and violence was constitutionally invalid under the Due Process Clause of the Fourteenth Amendment. In some 30 different cases decided during the era that intervened between *Brown* and *Escobedo v. Illinois*, the Court was faced with the necessity of determining whether in fact the confessions in issue had been "voluntarily" given. It is to that body of case law to which we turn for initial guidance on the meaning of "voluntariness" in the present context. * * *

The significant fact about all of these decisions is that none of them turned on the presence or absence of a single controlling criterion; each reflected a careful scrutiny of all the surrounding circumstances. In none of them did the Court rule that the Due Process Clause required the prosecution to prove as part of its initial burden that the defendant knew he had a right to refuse to answer the questions that were put. While the state of the accused's mind, and the failure of the police to advise the accused of his rights, were certainly factors to be evaluated in assessing the "voluntariness" of an accused's responses, they were not in and of themselves determinative.

Similar considerations lead us to [conclude] that the question whether a consent to a search was in fact "voluntary" or was the product of duress or coercion, express or implied, is a question of fact to be determined from the totality of all the circumstances. While knowledge of the right to refuse consent is one factor to be taken into account, the government need not establish such knowledge as the *sine qua non* of an effective consent. * * *

In situations where the police have some evidence of illicit activity, but lack probable cause to arrest or search, a search authorized by a valid consent may be the only means of obtaining important and reliable evidence. * * * And in those cases where there is probable cause to arrest or search, but where the police lack a warrant, a consent search may still be valuable. If the search is conducted and proves fruitless, that in itself may convince the police that an arrest with its possible stigma and embarrassment is unnecessary, or that a far more extensive search pursuant to a warrant is not justified. In short, a search pursuant to consent may result in considerably less inconvenience for the subject of the search, and, properly conducted, is a constitutionally permissible and wholly legitimate aspect of effective police activity.

But the Fourth and Fourteenth Amendments require that a consent not be coerced, by explicit or implicit means, by implied threat or covert force. For, no matter how subtly the coercion was applied, the resulting "consent" would be no more than a pretext for the unjustified police intrusion against which the Fourth Amendment is directed.

* * * In examining all the surrounding circumstances to determine if in fact the consent to search was coerced, account must be taken of subtly coercive police questions, as well as the possibly vulnerable subjective state of the person who consents. Those searches that are the product of police coercion can thus be filtered out without undermining the continuing validity of consent searches. In sum, there is no reason for us to depart in the area of consent searches, from the traditional definition of "voluntariness."

The approach of the Court of Appeals for the Ninth Circuit finds no support in any of our decisions that have attempted to define the meaning of "voluntariness." Its ruling, that the State must affirmatively prove that the subject of the search knew that he had a right to refuse consent, would, in practice, create serious doubt whether consent searches could continue to be conducted. * * *

The very object of the inquiry—the nature of a person's subjective understanding—underlines the difficulty of the prosecution's burden under the rule applied by the Court of Appeals in this case. Any defendant who was the subject of a search authorized solely by his consent could effectively frustrate the introduction into evidence of the fruits of that search by simply failing to testify that he in fact knew he could refuse to consent. * * *

One alternative that would go far toward proving that the subject of a search did know he had a right to refuse consent would be to advise him of that right before eliciting his consent. That, however, is a suggestion that has been almost universally repudiated by both federal and state courts, and, we think, rightly so. For it would be thoroughly impractical to impose on the normal consent search the detailed requirements of an effective warning. Consent searches * * * normally occur on the highway, or in a person's home or office, and under informal and unstructured conditions. * * * These situations are a far cry from the structured atmosphere of a trial where, assisted by counsel if he chooses, a defendant is informed of his trial rights. * * *

It is said, however, that a "consent" is a "waiver" of a person's rights under the Fourth and Fourteenth Amendments. The argument is that by allowing the police to conduct a search, a person "waives" whatever right he had to prevent the police from searching. It is argued that under the doctrine of *Johnson v. Zerbst*, to establish such a "waiver" the State must demonstrate "an intentional relinquishment or abandonment of a known right or privilege." * * *

Almost without exception, the requirement of a knowing and intelligent waiver has been applied only to those rights which the Constitution guarantees to a criminal defendant in order to preserve a fair trial. * * * The protections of the Fourth Amendment are of a wholly different order, and have nothing whatever to do with promoting the fair ascertainment of truth at a criminal trial. Rather, as Mr. Justice Frankfurter's opinion for the Court put it in *Wolf v. Colorado*, the Fourth Amendment protects the "security of one's privacy against arbitrary intrusion by the police." * * *

It is also argued that the failure to require the Government to establish knowledge as a prerequisite to a valid consent, will relegate the Fourth Amendment to the special province of "the sophisticated, knowledgeable and the privileged." We cannot agree. The traditional definition of voluntariness we accept today has always taken into account evidence of minimal schooling, low intelligence, and the lack of any effective warnings to a person of his rights; and the voluntariness of any statement taken under those conditions has been carefully scrutinized to determine whether it was in fact voluntarily given.

Our decision today is a narrow one. We hold only that when the subject of a search is not in custody[a] and the State attempts to justify a search on the basis of his consent, the Fourth and Fourteenth Amendments require that it demonstrate that the consent was in fact voluntarily given, and not the result of duress or coercion, express or implied. Voluntariness is a question of fact to be determined from all the circumstances, and while the subject's knowledge of a right to refuse is a factor to be taken into account, the prosecution is not required to demonstrate such knowledge as a prerequisite to establishing a voluntary consent. * * *

JUSTICE MARSHALL, dissenting.

Several years ago, Mr. Justice Stewart reminded us that "[t]he Constitution guarantees ... a society of free choice. Such a society presupposes the capacity of its members to choose." I would have thought that the capacity to choose necessarily depends upon knowledge that there

---

[a] While this language seems to suggest that a different rule might apply to an individual who is in police custody, in a later case involving a suspect who was in custody at the time he consented to a post-arrest search of his car, the Court followed *Schneckloth*, noting that the fact that the suspect was not informed of his right to refuse consent did not render the search invalid. United States v. Watson, 423 U.S. 411, 424 (1976) ("under *Schneckloth*, the absence of proof that Watson knew he could withhold his consent, though it may be a factor in the overall judgment, is not to be given controlling significance").

is a choice to be made. But today the Court reaches the curious result that one can choose to relinquish a constitutional right—the right to be free of unreasonable searches—without knowing that he has the alternative of refusing to accede to a police request to search. I cannot agree, and therefore dissent. * * *

If consent to search means that a person has chosen to forgo his right to exclude the police from the place they seek to search, it follows that his consent cannot be considered a meaningful choice unless he knew that he could in fact exclude the police. * * * I would therefore hold, at a minimum, that the prosecution may not rely on a purported consent to search if the subject of the search did not know that he could refuse to give consent. * * *

The burden on the prosecutor would disappear, of course, if the police, at the time they requested consent to search, also told the subject that he had a right to refuse consent and that his decision to refuse would be respected. The Court's assertions to the contrary notwithstanding, there is nothing impractical about this method of satisfying the prosecution's burden of proof. * * *

The Court contends that if an officer paused to inform the subject of his rights, the informality of the exchange would be destroyed. I doubt that a simple statement by an officer of an individual's right to refuse consent would do much to alter the informality of the exchange, except to alert the subject to a fact that he surely is entitled to know. It is not without significance that for many years the agents of the Federal Bureau of Investigation have routinely informed subjects of their right to refuse consent, when they request consent to search. * * * What evidence there is, then, rather strongly suggests that nothing disastrous would happen if the police, before requesting consent, informed the subject that he had a right to refuse consent and that his refusal would be respected.

I must conclude with some reluctance that when the Court speaks of practicality, what it really is talking of is the continued ability of the police to capitalize on the ignorance of citizens so as to accomplish by subterfuge what they could not achieve by relying only on the knowing relinquishment of constitutional rights. Of course it would be "practical" for the police to ignore the commands of the Fourth Amendment, if by practicality we mean that more criminals will be apprehended, even though the constitutional rights of innocent people also go by the board. But such a practical advantage is achieved only at the cost of permitting the police to disregard the limitations that the Constitution places on their behavior, a cost that a constitutional democracy cannot long absorb. * * *

[JUSTICE BLACKMUN's concurring opinion, JUSTICE POWELL's concurring opinion, JUSTICE DOUGLAS' dissenting opinion, and JUSTICE BRENNAN's dissenting opinion have been omitted.]

NOTE

Acquiescence to a claim of lawful authority does not constitute valid consent to search. *See Bumper v. North Carolina*, 391 U.S. 543, 549 (1968) (the prosecutor's "burden [to prove that consent was freely and voluntarily given] cannot be discharged by showing no more than acquiescence to a claim of lawful authority."). This is because consent must be voluntarily given in order to be valid. As the *Bumper* Court explained, when an officer tells someone that he has a search warrant and asks for permission to search, the officer is effectively telling the occupant that she has no right to refuse the search. *Id.* at 550. Accordingly, consent procured by a law enforcement officer who says he has a warrant to search the house is not a valid consent even if the officer does have a warrant. *Id.* at 549 n.14 (noting that "[o]ne is not held to have consented to the search of his premises where it is accomplished pursuant to an apparently valid search warrant" and that "[t]he presentation of a search warrant . . . by one authorized to serve it, is tinged with coercion . . .").

An otherwise valid consent search can be invalidated if the officer exceeds the scope of the consent given. How should a court go about determining the scope of a particular consent to search? In *Florida v. Jimeno*, 500 U.S. 248 (1991),[a] the Court held that the scope of a consent search is determined by

---

[a] In *Florida v. Jimeno*, an officer overheard Jimeno making what he thought was a drug transaction over the telephone. The officer followed Jimeno and pulled him over after observing a traffic violation. The officer told Jimeno that he had reason to believe Jimeno was carrying narcotics in his car and asked for his permission to search the car for drugs. He also told Jimeno that Jimeno did not have to consent to the search of his car. After Jimeno gave the officer permission to search the car, the officer picked up a folded brown paper bag on the floor of the front passenger side floorboard, opened it, and found a kilogram of cocaine within. Jimeno was charged with possession of cocaine with intent to distribute. He moved to suppress the cocaine, arguing that his consent to search the car did not extend to a search of the closed paper bag. The Supreme Court disagreed and held that the officer did not exceed the scope of the consent provided by Jimeno because a reasonable person would have understood that the consent Jimeno provided included permission to look into a closed paper bag that could have contained the object of the search. The Court explained:

> The scope of a search is generally defined by its expressed object. In this case, the terms of the search's authorization were simple. Respondent granted Officer Trujillo permission to search his car, and did not place any explicit limitation on the scope of the search. Trujillo had informed Jimeno that he believed Jimeno was carrying narcotics, and that he would be looking for narcotics in the car. We think that it was objectively reasonable for the police to conclude that the general consent to search respondents' car included consent to search containers within that car which might bear drugs.

500 U.S. at 251.

Interestingly, the Court suggested in dicta that a reasonable person would *not* have understood Jimeno's consent to include consent to open a locked briefcase found in the car. *Id.* at 252 ("It is very likely unreasonable to think that a suspect, by consenting to the search of his trunk, has agreed to the breaking open of a locked briefcase within the trunk, but it is otherwise with respect to a closed paper bag.").

Justice Marshall, dissenting, reminded the majority that in previous cases, it had refused to draw a distinction between worthy and unworthy containers:

> . . . [A]n individual's heightened expectation of privacy [does not] turn on the type of container in which he stores his possessions. Notwithstanding the majority's suggestion to the contrary, this Court has soundly rejected any distinction between "worthy" containers, like locked briefcases, and "unworthy" containers, like paper bags.
>
> Even though such a distinction perhaps could evolve in a series of cases in which paper bags, locked trunks, lunch buckets, and orange crates were placed on one side of the line

asking "what would the reasonable person have understood by the exchange between the officer and the suspect?" *Id.* at 251.

ILLINOIS V. RODRIGUEZ
Supreme Court of the United States
497 U.S. 177, 110 S. Ct. 2793, 111 L. Ed. 2d 148 (1990)

JUSTICE SCALIA delivered the opinion of the Court. * * *

Respondent Edward Rodriguez was arrested in his apartment by law enforcement officers and charged with possession of illegal drugs. The police gained entry to the apartment with the consent and assistance of Gail Fischer, who had lived there with respondent for several months. The relevant facts leading to the arrest are as follows.

On July 26, 1985, police were summoned to the residence of Dorothy Jackson on South Wolcott in Chicago. They were met by Ms. Jackson's daughter, Gail Fischer, who showed signs of a severe beating. She told the officers that she had been assaulted by respondent Edward Rodriguez earlier that day in an apartment on South California. Fischer stated that Rodriguez was then asleep in the apartment, and she consented to travel there with the police in order to unlock the door with her key so that the officers could enter and arrest him. During this conversation, Fischer several times referred to the apartment on South California as "our" apartment, and said that she had clothes and furniture there. It is unclear whether she indicated that she currently lived at the apartment, or only that she used to live there.

The police officers drove to the apartment on South California, accompanied by Fischer. They did not obtain an arrest warrant for Rodriguez, nor did they seek a search warrant for the apartment. At the apartment, Fischer unlocked the door with her key and gave the officers permission to enter. They moved through the door into the living room, where they observed in plain view drug paraphernalia and containers filled with white powder that they believed (correctly, as later analysis showed) to be cocaine. They proceeded to the bedroom, where they found Rodriguez asleep and discovered additional containers of white powder in two open attaché cases. The officers arrested Rodriguez and seized the drugs and related paraphernalia.

Rodriguez was charged with possession of a controlled substance with intent to deliver. He moved to suppress all evidence seized at the time of

---

or the other, the central purpose of the Fourth Amendment forecloses such a distinction. For just as the most frail cottage in the kingdom is absolutely entitled to the same guarantees of privacy as the most majestic mansion, so also may a traveler who carries a toothbrush and a few articles of clothing in a paper bag or knotted scarf claim an equal right to conceal his possessions from official inspection as the sophisticated executive with the locked attaché case.

Id. at 553–54 (Marshall, J., dissenting).

his arrest, claiming that Fischer had vacated the apartment several weeks earlier and had no authority to consent to the entry. The Cook County Circuit Court granted the motion, holding that at the time she consented to the entry Fischer did not have common authority over the apartment. The Court concluded that Fischer was not a "usual resident" but rather an "infrequent visitor" at the apartment on South California, based upon its findings that Fischer's name was not on the lease, that she did not contribute to the rent, that she was not allowed to invite others to the apartment on her own, that she did not have access to the apartment when respondent was away, and that she had moved some of her possessions from the apartment. The Circuit Court also rejected the State's contention that, even if Fischer did not possess common authority over the premises, there was no Fourth Amendment violation if the police *reasonably believed* at the time of their entry that Fischer possessed the authority to consent.

The Appellate Court of Illinois affirmed the Circuit Court in all respects. The Illinois Supreme Court denied the State's petition for leave to appeal, and we granted certiorari.

The Fourth Amendment generally prohibits the warrantless entry of a person's home, whether to make an arrest or to search for specific objects. The prohibition does not apply, however, to situations in which voluntary consent has been obtained, either from the individual whose property is searched, or from a third party who possesses common authority over the premises. The State of Illinois contends that that exception applies in the present case.

As we stated in *Matlock,* "[c]ommon authority" rests "on mutual use of the property by persons generally having joint access or control for most purposes . . . ." The burden of establishing that common authority rests upon the State. On the basis of this record, it is clear that burden was not sustained. The evidence showed that although Fischer, with her two small children, had lived with Rodriguez beginning in December 1984, she had moved out on July 1, 1985, almost a month before the search at issue here, and had gone to live with her mother. She took her and her children's clothing with her, though leaving behind some furniture and household effects. During the period after July 1 she sometimes spent the night at Rodriguez's apartment, but never invited her friends there, and never went there herself when he was not home. Her name was not on the lease nor did she contribute to the rent. She had a key to the apartment, which she said at trial she had taken without Rodriguez's knowledge (though she testified at the preliminary hearing that Rodriguez had given her the key). On these facts the State has not established that, with respect to the South California apartment, Fischer had "joint access or control for most purposes." To the contrary, the Appellate Court's determination of no common authority over the apartment was obviously correct.

The State contends that, even if Fischer did not in fact have authority to give consent, it suffices to validate the entry that the law enforcement officers reasonably believed she did. *** On the merits of the issue, respondent asserts that permitting a reasonable belief of common authority to validate an entry would cause a defendant's Fourth Amendment rights to be "vicariously waived." We disagree. ***

What Rodriguez *** is assured by the Fourth Amendment itself *** is not that no government search of his house will occur unless he consents; but that no such search will occur that is "unreasonable." There are various elements, of course, that can make a search of a person's house "reasonable"—one of which is the consent of the person or his cotenant. The essence of respondent's argument is that we should impose upon this element a requirement that we have not imposed upon other elements that regularly compel government officers to exercise judgment regarding the facts: namely, the requirement that their judgment be not only responsible but correct.

*** It is apparent that in order to satisfy the "reasonableness" requirement of the Fourth Amendment, what is generally demanded of the many factual determinations that must regularly be made by agents of the government—whether the magistrate issuing a warrant, the police officer executing a warrant, or the police officer conducting a search or seizure under one of the exceptions to the warrant requirement—is not that they always be correct, but that they always be reasonable. As we put it in *Brinegar v. United States*:

> Because many situations which confront officers in the course of executing their duties are more or less ambiguous, room must be allowed for some mistakes on their part. But the mistakes must be those of reasonable men, acting on facts leading sensibly to their conclusions of probability.

We see no reason to depart from this general rule with respect to facts bearing upon the authority to consent to a search. Whether the basis for such authority exists is the sort of recurring factual question to which law enforcement officials must be expected to apply their judgment; and all the Fourth Amendment requires is that they answer it reasonably. The Constitution is no more violated when officers enter without a warrant because they reasonably (though erroneously) believe that the person who has consented to their entry is a resident of the premises, than it is violated when they enter without a warrant because they reasonably (though erroneously) believe they are in pursuit of a violent felon who is about to escape.

*** [W]hat we hold today does not suggest that law enforcement officers may always accept a person's invitation to enter premises. Even when the invitation is accompanied by an explicit assertion that the person lives there, the surrounding circumstances could conceivably be such that a reasonable person would doubt its truth and not act upon it without further inquiry. As with other factual determinations bearing upon search and seizure, determination of consent to enter must "be judged against an objective standard: would the facts available to the officer at the moment . . . 'warrant a man of reasonable caution in the belief' " that the consenting party had authority over the premises? If not, then warrantless entry without further inquiry is unlawful unless authority actually exists. But if so, the search is valid.

In the present case, the Appellate Court found it unnecessary to determine whether the officers reasonably believed that Fischer had the authority to consent, because it ruled as a matter of law that a reasonable belief could not validate the entry. Since we find that ruling to be in error, we remand for consideration of that question. The judgment of the Illinois Appellate Court is reversed, and the case is remanded for further proceedings not inconsistent with this opinion.

So ordered.

JUSTICE MARSHALL, with whom JUSTICE BRENNAN and JUSTICE STEVENS join, dissenting. * * *

The majority agrees with the Illinois Appellate Court's determination that Fischer did not have authority to consent to the officers' entry of Rodriguez's apartment. The Court holds that the warrantless entry into Rodriguez's home was nonetheless valid if the officers reasonably believed that Fischer had authority to consent. The majority's defense of this position rests on a misconception of the basis for third-party consent searches. * * * [S]uch searches [rest] * * * on the premise that a person may voluntarily limit his expectation of privacy by allowing others to exercise authority over his possessions. If an individual has not so limited his expectation of privacy, the police may not dispense with the safeguards established by the Fourth Amendment.

Our cases demonstrate that third-party consent searches are free from constitutional challenge only to the extent that they rest on consent by a party empowered to do so. The majority's conclusion to the contrary ignores the legitimate expectations of privacy on which individuals are entitled to rely. That a person who allows another joint access to his property thereby limits his expectation of privacy does not justify trampling the rights of a person who has not similarly relinquished any of his privacy expectation. * * *

GEORGIA V. RANDOLPH
Supreme Court of the United States
547 U.S. 103, 126 S. Ct. 1515, 164 L. Ed. 2d 208 (2006)

JUSTICE SOUTER delivered the opinion of the Court.

The Fourth Amendment recognizes a valid warrantless entry and search of premises when police obtain the voluntary consent of an occupant who shares, or is reasonably believed to share, authority over the area in common with a co-occupant who later objects to the use of evidence so obtained. The question here is whether such an evidentiary seizure is likewise lawful with the permission of one occupant when the other, who later seeks to suppress the evidence, is present at the scene and expressly refuses to consent. * * *

Respondent Scott Randolph and his wife, Janet, separated in late May 2001, when she left the marital residence in Americus, Georgia, and went to stay with her parents in Canada, taking their son and some belongings. In July, she returned to the Americus house with the child, though the record does not reveal whether her object was reconciliation or retrieval of remaining possessions.

On the morning of July 6, Janet Randolph complained to the police that after a domestic dispute her husband took their son away, and when officers reached the house she told them that her husband was a cocaine user whose habit had caused financial troubles. She mentioned the marital problems and said that she and their son had only recently returned after a stay of several weeks with her parents. Shortly after the police arrived, Scott Randolph returned and explained that he had removed the child to a neighbor's house out of concern that his wife might take the boy out of the country again; he denied cocaine use, and countered that it was in fact his wife who abused drugs and alcohol.

One of the officers, Sergeant Murray, went with Janet Randolph to reclaim the child, and when they returned she not only renewed her complaints about her husband's drug use, but also volunteered that there were "items of drug evidence" in the house. Sergeant Murray asked Scott Randolph for permission to search the house, which he unequivocally refused.

The sergeant turned to Janet Randolph for consent to search, which she readily gave. She led the officer upstairs to a bedroom that she identified as Scott's, where the sergeant noticed a section of a drinking straw with a powdery residue he suspected was cocaine. He then left the house to get an evidence bag from his car and to call the district attorney's office, which instructed him to stop the search and apply for a warrant. When Sergeant Murray returned to the house, Janet Randolph withdrew her consent. The police took the straw to the police station, along with the Randolphs. After getting a search warrant, they returned to the house and seized further evidence of drug use, on the basis of which Scott Randolph was indicted for possession of cocaine.

He moved to suppress the evidence, as products of a warrantless search of his house unauthorized by his wife's consent over his express refusal. The trial court denied the motion, ruling that Janet Randolph had common authority to consent to the search. * * *

We granted certiorari to resolve a split of authority on whether one occupant may give law enforcement effective consent to search shared premises, as against a co-tenant who is present and states a refusal to permit the search. * * *

To the Fourth Amendment rule ordinarily prohibiting the warrantless entry of a person's house as unreasonable *per se*, one "jealously and carefully drawn" exception recognizes the validity of searches with the voluntary consent of an individual possessing authority. That person might be the householder against whom evidence is sought, or a fellow occupant who shares common authority over property, when the suspect is absent, and the exception for consent extends even to entries and searches with the permission of a co-occupant whom the police reasonably, but erroneously, believe to possess shared authority as an occupant. None of our co-occupant consent-to-search cases, however, has presented the further fact of a second occupant physically present and refusing permission to search, and later moving to suppress evidence so obtained. The significance of such a refusal turns on the underpinnings of the co-occupant consent rule, as recognized since *Matlock*.

The defendant in that case was arrested in the yard of a house where he lived with a Mrs. Graff and several of her relatives, and was detained in a squad car parked nearby. When the police went to the door, Mrs. Graff admitted them and consented to a search of the house. In resolving the defendant's objection to use of the evidence taken in the warrantless search, we said that "the consent of one who possesses common authority over premises or effects is valid as against the absent, nonconsenting person with whom that authority is shared." Consistent with our prior understanding that Fourth Amendment rights are not limited by the law of property, we explained that the third party's "common authority" is not synonymous with a technical property interest:

> The authority which justifies the third-party consent does not rest upon the law of property, with its attendant historical and legal refinements, but rests rather on mutual use of the property by persons generally having joint access or control for most purposes, so that it is reasonable to recognize that any of the co-inhabitants has the right to permit the inspection in his own right and that the others have assumed the risk that one of their number might permit the common area to be searched. * * *

The constant element in assessing Fourth Amendment reasonableness in the consent cases, then, is the great significance given to widely shared social expectations, which are naturally enough influenced by the law of property, but not controlled by its rules. * * *

Matlock's example of common understanding is readily apparent. When someone comes to the door of a domestic dwelling with a baby at her hip, as Mrs. Graff did, she shows that she belongs there, and that fact standing alone is enough to tell a law enforcement officer or any other visitor that if she occupies the place along with others, she probably lives there subject to the assumption tenants usually make about their common authority when they share quarters. They understand that any one of them may admit visitors, with the consequence that a guest obnoxious to one may nevertheless be admitted in his absence by another. As *Matlock* put it, shared tenancy is understood to include an "assumption of risk," on which police officers are entitled to rely, and although some group living together might make an exceptional arrangement that no one could admit a guest without the agreement of all, the chance of such an eccentric scheme is too remote to expect visitors to investigate a particular household's rules before accepting an invitation to come in. * * *

It is also easy to imagine different facts on which, if known, no common authority could sensibly be suspected. A person on the scene who identifies himself, say, as a landlord or a hotel manager calls up no customary understanding of authority to admit guests without the consent of the current occupant. A tenant in the ordinary course does not take rented premises subject to any formal or informal agreement that the landlord may let visitors into the dwelling, and a hotel guest customarily has no reason to expect the manager to allow anyone but his own employees into his room. In these circumstances, neither state-law property rights, nor common contractual arrangements, nor any other source points to a common understanding of authority to admit third parties generally without the consent of a person occupying the premises. And when it comes to searching through bureau drawers, there will be instances in which even a person clearly belonging on premises as an occupant may lack any perceived authority to consent; "a child of eight might well be considered to have the power to consent to the police crossing the threshold into that part of the house where any caller, such as a pollster or salesman, might well be admitted," but no one would reasonably expect such a child to be in a position to authorize anyone to rummage through his parents' bedroom.

* * * [I]t is fair to say that a caller standing at the door of shared premises would have no confidence that one occupant's invitation was a sufficiently good reason to enter when a fellow tenant stood there saying, "stay out." Without some very good reason, no sensible person would go inside under those conditions. * * *

The visitor's reticence without some such good reason would show not timidity but a realization that when people living together disagree over the use of their common quarters, a resolution must come through voluntary accommodation, not by appeals to authority. Unless the people living together fall within some recognized hierarchy, like a household of parent and child or barracks housing military personnel of different grades, there is no societal understanding of superior and inferior, a fact reflected in a standard formulation of domestic property law, that "[e]ach cotenant . . . has the right to use and enjoy the entire property as if he or she were the sole owner, limited only by the same right in the other cotenants." * * * In sum, there is no common understanding that one co-tenant generally has a right or authority to prevail over the express wishes of another, whether the issue is the color of the curtains or invitations to outsiders.

Since the co-tenant wishing to open the door to a third party has no recognized authority in law or social practice to prevail over a present and objecting co-tenant, his disputed invitation, without more, gives a police officer no better claim to reasonableness in entering than the officer would have in the absence of any consent at all. Accordingly, in the balancing of competing individual and governmental interests entailed by the bar to unreasonable searches, the cooperative occupant's invitation adds nothing to the government's side to counter the force of an objecting individual's claim to security against the government's intrusion into his dwelling place. Since we hold to the "centuries-old principle of respect for the privacy of the home," "it is beyond dispute that the home is entitled to special protection as the center of the private lives of our people." We have, after all, lived our whole national history with an understanding of "the ancient adage that a man's house is his castle [to the point that t]he poorest man may in his cottage bid defiance to all the forces of the Crown."

Disputed permission is thus no match for this central value of the Fourth Amendment, and the State's other countervailing claims do not add up to outweigh it. * * * Nor should this established policy of Fourth Amendment law be undermined by the principal dissent's claim that it shields spousal abusers and other violent co-tenants who will refuse to allow the police to enter a dwelling when their victims ask the police for help. It is not that the dissent exaggerates violence in the home; we recognize that domestic abuse is a serious problem in the United States.

But this case has no bearing on the capacity of the police to protect domestic victims. * * * No question has been raised, or reasonably could be, about the authority of the police to enter a dwelling to protect a resident from domestic violence; so long as they have good reason to believe such a threat exists, it would be silly to suggest that the police would commit a tort by entering, say, to give a complaining tenant the opportunity to collect belongings and get out safely, or to determine whether violence (or threat of violence) has just occurred or is about to (or soon will) occur, however much a spouse or other co-tenant objected. Thus, the question whether the police might lawfully enter over objection in order to provide any protection that might be reasonable is easily answered yes.[a] The undoubted right of the police to enter in order to protect a victim, however, has nothing to do with the question in this case, whether a search with the consent of one co-tenant is good against another, standing at the door and expressly refusing consent.

* * * We therefore hold that a warrantless search of a shared dwelling for evidence over the express refusal of consent by a physically present resident cannot be justified as reasonable as to him on the basis of consent given to the police by another resident. * * * [W]e have to admit that we are drawing a fine line; if a potential defendant with self-interest in objecting is in fact at the door and objects, the co-tenant's permission does not suffice for a reasonable search, whereas the potential objector, nearby but not invited to take part in the threshold colloquy, loses out.

This is the line we draw, and we think the formalism is justified. So long as there is no evidence that the police have removed the potentially objecting tenant from the entrance for the sake of avoiding a possible objection,[b] there is practical value in the simple clarity of complementary rules, one recognizing the co-tenant's permission when there is no fellow occupant on hand, the other according dispositive weight to the fellow occupant's contrary indication when he expresses it. * * * [W]e think it would needlessly limit the capacity of the police to respond to ostensibly legitimate opportunities in the field if we were to hold that reasonableness required the police to take affirmative steps to find a potentially objecting co-tenant before acting on the permission they had already received. There is no ready reason to believe that efforts to invite a refusal would make a difference in many cases, whereas every co-tenant consent case would turn into a test about the adequacy of the police's efforts to consult with a potential objector. * * * The pragmatic decision to accept the simplicity of

---

[a] The Court seems to be alluding here to the exigent circumstances exception, which permits police to enter a dwelling without a search warrant when the exigencies of the situation make it impractical for police to secure a warrant.

[b] In *Fernandez v. California*, 571 U.S. 292 (2014), the Supreme Court addressed whether police are permitted to enter a home without a search warrant after arresting and removing a physically present and objecting tenant from the entrance if a co-tenant subsequently consents. The defendant argued that this language in *Georgia v. Randolph* ("So long as there is no evidence that the police have removed the potentially objecting tenant for the sake of avoiding a potential objection . . .") invalidated the warrantless search since the police had removed him after hearing his objection. Justice Alito, writing for the Court, rejected the defendant's argument, calling this language dictum. Justice Alito went on to explain that this "dictum" was "best understood not to require an inquiry into the subjective intent of officers who detain or arrest a potential objector but instead refer to situations in which the removal of the potential objector is not objectively reasonable." *Id.* at 302. Since police had probable cause to arrest Fernandez for domestic violence, his removal from the premises was objectively reasonable and it was irrelevant whether the officers removed him to avoid having him physically present and objecting when they went back to seek his co-tenant's consent to enter. *Fernandez v. California* thus stands for the proposition that "an occupant who is absent due to a lawful detention or arrest stands in the same shoes as an occupant who is absent for any other reason." *Id.* at 303.

this line is, moreover, supported by the substantial number of instances in which suspects who are asked for permission to search actually consent, albeit imprudently, a fact that undercuts any argument that the police should try to locate a suspected inhabitant because his denial of consent would be a foregone conclusion.

This case invites a straightforward application of the rule that a physically present inhabitant's express refusal of consent to a police search is dispositive as to him, regardless of the consent of a fellow occupant. Scott Randolph's refusal is clear, and nothing in the record justifies the search on grounds independent of Janet Randolph's consent. The State does not argue that she gave any indication to the police of a need for protection inside the house that might have justified entry into the portion of the premises where the police found the powdery straw (which, if lawfully seized, could have been used when attempting to establish probable cause for the warrant issued later). Nor does the State claim that the entry and search should be upheld under the rubric of exigent circumstances, owing to some apprehension by the police officers that Scott Randolph would destroy evidence of drug use before any warrant could be obtained. * * *

JUSTICE ALITO took no part in the consideration or decision of this case.

CHIEF JUSTICE ROBERTS, with whom JUSTICE SCALIA joins, dissenting.

The Court creates constitutional law by surmising what is typical when a social guest encounters an entirely atypical situation. The rule the majority fashions does not implement the high office of the Fourth Amendment to protect privacy, but instead provides protection on a random and happenstance basis, protecting, for example, a co-occupant who happens to be at the front door when the other occupant consents to a search, but not one napping or watching television in the next room. And the cost of affording such random protection is great, as demonstrated by the recurring cases in which abused spouses seek to authorize police entry into a home they share with a nonconsenting abuser.

The correct approach to the question presented is clearly mapped out in our precedents: The Fourth Amendment protects privacy. If an individual shares information, papers, *or places* with another, he assumes the risk that the other person will in turn share access to that information or those papers *or places* with the government. And just as an individual who has shared illegal plans or incriminating documents with another cannot interpose an objection when that other person turns the information over to the government, just because the individual happens to be present at the time, so too someone who shares a place with another cannot interpose an objection when that person decides to grant access to the police, simply because the objecting individual happens to be present.

A warrantless search is reasonable if police obtain the voluntary consent of a person authorized to give it. Co-occupants have "assumed the risk that one of their number might permit [a] common area to be searched." Just as Mrs. Randolph could walk upstairs, come down, and turn her husband's cocaine straw over to the police, she can consent to police entry and search of what is, after all, her home, too.

* * * [T]he majority is confident in assuming—confident enough to incorporate its assumption into the Constitution—that an invited social guest who arrives at the door of a shared residence, and is greeted by a disagreeable co-occupant shouting "stay out," would simply go away. The Court observes that "no sensible person would go inside under those conditions," and concludes from this that the inviting co-occupant has no "authority" to insist on getting her way over the wishes of her co-occupant. But it seems equally accurate to say—based on the majority's conclusion that one does not have a right to prevail over the express wishes of his co-occupant—that the objector has no "authority" to insist on getting *his* way over his co-occupant's wish that her guest be admitted.

The fact is that a wide variety of differing social situations can readily be imagined, giving rise to quite different social expectations. A relative or good friend of one of two feuding roommates might well enter the apartment over the objection of the other roommate. The reason the invitee appeared at the door also affects expectations: A guest who came to celebrate an occupant's birthday, or one who had traveled some distance for a particular reason, might not readily turn away simply because of a roommate's objection. The nature of the place itself is also pertinent: Invitees may react one way if the feuding roommates share one room, differently if there are common areas from which the objecting roommate could readily be expected to absent himself. Altering the numbers might well change the social expectations: Invitees might enter if two of three co-occupants encourage them to do so, over one dissenter.

The possible scenarios are limitless, and slight variations in the fact pattern yield vastly different expectations about whether the invitee might be expected to enter or to go away. Such shifting expectations are not a promising foundation on which to ground a constitutional rule, particularly because the majority has no support for its basic assumption—that an invited guest encountering two disagreeing co-occupants would flee—beyond a hunch about how people would typically act in an atypical situation. * * *

While the majority's rule protects something random, its consequences are particularly severe. * * * What does the majority imagine will happen, in a case in which the consenting co-occupant is concerned about the other's criminal activity, once the door clicks shut? The objecting co-occupant may pause briefly to decide whether to destroy any evidence of wrongdoing or to inflict retribution on the consenting co-occupant first, but there can be little doubt that he will attend to both in short order. * * *

Perhaps the most serious consequence of the majority's rule is its operation in domestic abuse situations, a context in which the present question often arises. While people living together might typically be accommodating to the wishes of their co-tenants, requests for police assistance may well come from co-inhabitants who are having a disagreement. The Court concludes that because "no sensible person would go inside" in the face of disputed consent, and the consenting co-tenant thus has "no recognized authority" to insist on the guest's admission, a "police officer [has] no better claim to reasonableness in entering than the officer would have in the absence of any consent at all." But the police officer's superior claim to enter is obvious: Mrs. Randolph did not invite the police to join her for dessert and coffee; the officer's precise purpose in knocking on the door was to assist with a dispute between the Randolphs—one in which Mrs. Randolph felt the need for the protective presence of the police. The majority's rule apparently forbids police from entering to assist with a domestic dispute if the abuser whose behavior prompted the request for police assistance objects. * * *

I respectfully dissent.

[JUSTICE STEVENS' concurring opinion, JUSTICE BREYER's concurring opinion, JUSTICE SCALIA's dissenting opinion, and JUSTICE THOMAS' dissenting opinion have been omitted.]

CHAPTER 14

ADMINISTRATIVE SEARCHES

■ ■ ■

In this chapter, we will study administrative searches. The administrative search exception to the warrant requirement encompasses many different kinds of searches that do not require a warrant or probable cause. In some administrative search cases, the Supreme Court has even eliminated the requirement for individualized suspicion of criminal activity. Unfortunately, the Court has never been terribly clear about what qualifies as an administrative search.

In the late 1980s, the Court began to formulate what has become known as the "special needs" test for administrative searches. Under this test, the threshold question is whether "special needs" beyond the normal need for law enforcement make the warrant and probable cause requirements impracticable. *New Jersey v. T.L.O.*, 480 U.S. 709 (1987). If there are special needs, then the Court will balance the government's interests in conducting the search against the individual's interest in privacy.

For example, the Court has found that when railroad employees are forced to engage in drug testing following a major accident pursuant to federal regulations, this kind of drug testing implicates special needs because it is done to protect the public's interest in safety, not merely to obtain evidence of criminal activity. *Skinner v. Railway Labor Executive's Association*, 489 U.S. 602, 620 (1989). Stopping drivers at sobriety checkpoints is considered a special needs search because the purpose of such checkpoints is highway safety, not merely to prosecute drunk drivers. *Michigan v. Sitz*, 496 U.S. 444 (1990). In each of these two cases, the Supreme Court went on to balance the interests and found that the government's interests outweighed the interest in privacy held by the individuals subjected to the government action.

The Court does not always engage in special needs analysis. Sometimes, it does not even use the words "special needs" in its opinions, but instead infers that a special need justifies the warrantless government action. For example, in *Safford v. Redding, infra,* the Court never mentions the words "special needs," but the opinion is widely seen as an example of a special needs search.

The first case in this chapter, *Colorado v. Bertine*, examines the inventory search, one type of administrative search. As you will see, the

Supreme Court has decided that there are special needs above and beyond the need for law enforcement that justify inventory searches. It has also done the balancing of governmental versus individual interests—deciding that the governmental interests outweigh the individual's interests. Consequently, lower courts do not need to engage this balancing test and can take as a given that law enforcement officers may engage in inventory searches without obtaining a search warrant in advance as long as certain requirements are met. *Colorado v. Bertine* explains the requirements necessary for a search to qualify as an inventory search.

The next two cases in this chapter involve vehicle checkpoints. In *Michigan v. Sitz*, the Court considers the constitutionality of a sobriety checkpoint program designed to catch drunk drivers. In *City of Indianapolis v. Edmond*, the Court considers the constitutionality of a vehicle checkpoint designed to interdict unlawful drugs. The Court finds one checkpoint program unconstitutional and the other constitutional. Is there a principled reason to treat the two types of vehicle checkpoints differently? Does the Court provide sufficient guidance to lower courts so they can figure out assess the constitutionality of other kinds of vehicle checkpoints?

The final two cases in the chapter, *Safford v. Redding* and *Florence v. Board of Chosen Freeholders*, involve strip searches. The Court finds one type of strip search unconstitutional and the other constitutional. Are you persuaded that the Court came out correctly in both cases?

The chapter ends with an article by I. Bennett Capers. In *Unsexing the Fourth Amendment,* Professor Capers examines the use of sex and gender to inform Fourth Amendment decisions about the reasonableness of certain kinds of searches of the person, including strip searches in prisons and schools. He argues that the current preference for same-gender searches reinforces stereotypes about men as predators and women as vulnerable victims.

A. INVENTORY SEARCHES

In previous chapters, we learned about different ways the police can search our vehicles without a warrant. The case below illustrates yet another way police can search a vehicle without a warrant. Notice that the Court in *Colorado v. Bertine* not only explains the justifications or rationales behind the inventory search exception, it also discusses the conditions that must be present in order for a search to be considered a valid inventory search. The Court tells us that the officer must have been acting in accordance with standardized criteria that limit the officer's discretion. Additionally, the officer must not have been acting in bad faith or using the inventory for the sole purpose of investigation, i.e., as a pretext to search for evidence of criminal activity.

CH. 14   ADMINISTRATIVE SEARCHES   373

The inventory search exception is used not only to justify searches of vehicles, but also to justify searches of personal property, like the backpack that was searched in the case below. It is also used to justify such as searches of arrestees when they are booked and taken into custody at a jail.

COLORADO V. BERTINE
Supreme Court of the United States
479 U.S. 367, 107 S. Ct. 138, 93 L. Ed. 2d 739 (1986)

CHIEF JUSTICE REHNQUIST delivered the opinion of the Court.

On February 10, 1984, a police officer in Boulder, Colorado, arrested respondent Steven Lee Bertine for driving while under the influence of alcohol. After Bertine was taken into custody and before the arrival of a tow truck to take Bertine's van to an impoundment lot, a backup officer inventoried the contents of the van. The officer opened a closed backpack in which he found controlled substances, cocaine paraphernalia, and a large amount of cash. Bertine was subsequently charged with driving while under the influence of alcohol, unlawful possession of cocaine with intent to dispense, sell, and distribute, and unlawful possession of methaqualone. We are asked to decide whether the Fourth Amendment prohibits the State from proving these charges with the evidence discovered during the inventory of Bertine's van. We hold that it does not.

The backup officer inventoried the van in accordance with local police procedures, which require a detailed inspection and inventory of impounded vehicles. He found the backpack directly behind the frontseat of the van. Inside the pack, the officer observed a nylon bag containing metal canisters. Opening the canisters, the officer discovered that they contained cocaine, methaqualone tablets, cocaine paraphernalia, and $700 in cash. In an outside zippered pouch of the backpack, he also found $210 in cash in a sealed envelope. After completing the inventory of the van, the officer had the van towed to an impound lot and brought the backpack, money, and contraband to the police station.

After Bertine was charged with the offenses described above, he moved to suppress the evidence found during the inventory search on the ground, *inter alia*, that the search of the closed backpack and containers exceeded the permissible scope of such a search under the Fourth Amendment. The Colorado trial court * * * determined that the inventory search did not violate Bertine's rights under the Fourth Amendment of the United States Constitution. The court, nevertheless, granted Bertine's motion to suppress, holding that the inventory search violated the Colorado Constitution.

On the State's interlocutory appeal, the Supreme Court of Colorado affirmed. In contrast to the District Court, however, the Colorado Supreme Court premised its ruling on the United States Constitution. The court recognized that in *South Dakota v. Opperman,* we had held inventory searches of automobiles to be consistent with the Fourth Amendment, and that in *Illinois v. Lafayette,* we had held that the inventory search of personal effects of an arrestee at a police station was also permissible under that Amendment. The Supreme Court of Colorado felt, however, that our decisions in *Arkansas v. Sanders* and *United States v. Chadwick,* holding searches of closed trunks and suitcases to violate the Fourth Amendment, meant that *Opperman* and *Lafayette* did not govern this case.

We granted certiorari to consider the important and recurring question of federal law decided by the Colorado Supreme Court. As that court recognized, inventory searches are now a well-defined exception to the warrant requirement of the Fourth Amendment. The policies behind the warrant requirement are not implicated in an inventory search, nor is the related concept of probable cause. * * *

For these reasons, the Colorado Supreme Court's reliance on *Arkansas v. Sanders* and *United States v. Chadwick* was incorrect. Both of these cases concerned searches solely for the purpose of investigating criminal conduct, with the validity of the searches therefore dependent on the application of the probable-cause and warrant requirements of the Fourth Amendment.

By contrast, an inventory search may be "reasonable" under the Fourth Amendment even though it is not conducted pursuant to a warrant based upon probable cause. In *Opperman,* this Court assessed the reasonableness of an inventory search of the glove compartment in an abandoned automobile impounded by the police. We found that inventory procedures serve to protect an owner's property while it is in the custody of the police, to insure against claims of lost, stolen, or vandalized property, and to guard the police from danger. In light of these strong governmental interests and the diminished expectation of privacy in an automobile, we upheld the search. In reaching this decision, we observed that our cases accorded deference to police caretaking procedures designed to secure and protect vehicles and their contents within police custody.

In our more recent decision, *Lafayette,* a police officer conducted an inventory search of the contents of a shoulder bag in the possession of an individual being taken into custody. In deciding whether this search was reasonable, we recognized that the search served legitimate governmental interests similar to those identified in *Opperman.* We determined that those interests outweighed the individual's Fourth Amendment interests and upheld the search.

In the present case, as in *Opperman* and *Lafayette,* there was no showing that the police, who were following standardized procedures, acted in bad faith or for the sole purpose of investigation. In addition, the governmental interests justifying the inventory searches in *Opperman* and

CH. 14 ADMINISTRATIVE SEARCHES

Lafayette are nearly the same as those which obtain here. In each case, the police were potentially responsible for the property taken into their custody. By securing the property, the police protected the property from unauthorized interference. Knowledge of the precise nature of the property helped guard against claims of theft, vandalism, or negligence. Such knowledge also helped to avert any danger to police or others that may have been posed by the property. * * *

The Supreme Court of Colorado * * * expressed the view that the search in this case was unreasonable because Bertine's van was towed to a secure, lighted facility and because Bertine himself could have been offered the opportunity to make other arrangements for the safekeeping of his property. But the security of the storage facility does not completely eliminate the need for inventorying; the police may still wish to protect themselves or the owners of the lot against false claims of theft or dangerous instrumentalities. And while giving Bertine an opportunity to make alternative arrangements would undoubtedly have been possible, we said in *Lafayette*:

> * * * The reasonableness of any particular governmental activity does not necessarily or invariably turn on the existence of alternative "less intrusive" means.
>
> We conclude that here, as in *Lafayette*, reasonable police regulations relating to inventory procedures administered in good faith satisfy the Fourth Amendment, even though courts might as a matter of hindsight be able to devise equally reasonable rules requiring a different procedure. * * *

Bertine finally argues that the inventory search of his van was unconstitutional because departmental regulations gave the police officers discretion to choose between impounding his van and parking and locking it in a public parking place. The Supreme Court of Colorado did not rely on this argument in reaching its conclusion, and we reject it. Nothing in *Opperman* or *Lafayette* prohibits the exercise of police discretion so long as that discretion is exercised according to standard criteria and on the basis of something other than suspicion of evidence of criminal activity. Here, the discretion afforded the Boulder police was exercised in light of standardized criteria, related to the feasibility and appropriateness of parking and locking a vehicle rather than impounding it. There was no showing that the police chose to impound Bertine's van in order to investigate suspected criminal activity.

* * * The judgment of the Supreme Court of Colorado is therefore Reversed.

JUSTICE MARSHALL, with whom JUSTICE BRENNAN joins, dissenting.

376   ADMINISTRATIVE SEARCHES   CH. 14

* * * This search—it cannot legitimately be labeled an inventory—was unreasonable and violated the Fourth Amendment. Unlike the inventories in *South Dakota v. Opperman* and *Illinois v. Lafayette*, it was not conducted according to standardized procedures. * * *

As the Court acknowledges, inventory searches are reasonable only if conducted according to standardized procedures. * * * In assessing the reasonableness of searches conducted in limited situations such as these, where we do not require probable cause or a warrant, we have consistently emphasized the need for such set procedures: "standardless and unconstrained discretion is the evil the Court has discerned when in previous cases it has insisted that the discretion of the official in the field be circumscribed, at least to some extent."

The Court today attempts to evade these clear prohibitions on unfettered police discretion by declaring that "the discretion afforded the Boulder police was exercised in light of standardized criteria, related to the feasibility and appropriateness of parking and locking a vehicle rather than impounding it." This vital assertion is flatly contradicted by the record in this case. The officer who conducted the inventory, Officer Reichenbach, testified at the suppression hearing that the decision not to "park and lock" respondent's vehicle was his "own individual discretionary decision." * * *

Indeed, the record indicates that *no* standardized criteria limit a Boulder police officer's discretion. According to a departmental directive, after placing a driver under arrest, an officer has three options for disposing of the vehicle. First, he can allow a third party to take custody. Second, the officer or the driver (depending on the nature of the arrest) may take the car to the nearest public parking facility, lock it, and take the keys. Finally, the officer can do what was done in this case: impound the vehicle, and search and inventory its contents, including closed containers.

Under the first option, the police have no occasion to search the automobile. Under the "park and lock" option, "[c]losed containers that give no indication of containing either valuables or a weapon *may not be opened and the contents searched* (i.e., inventoried)." Only if the police choose the third option are they entitled to search closed containers in the vehicle. Where the vehicle is not itself evidence of a crime, as in this case, the police apparently have totally unbridled discretion as to which procedure to use. Consistent with this conclusion, Officer Reichenbach testified that such decisions were left to the discretion of the officer on the scene.

Once a Boulder police officer has made this initial completely discretionary decision to impound a vehicle, he is given little guidance as to which areas to search and what sort of items to inventory. The arresting officer, Officer Toporek, testified at the suppression hearing as to what items would be inventoried: "That would I think be very individualistic as far as what an officer may or may not go into. I think whatever arouses his suspicious [sic] as far as what may be contained in any type of article in the car." In application, these so-called procedures left the breadth of the "inventory" to the whim of the individual officer. * * *

Inventory searches are not subject to the warrant requirement because they are conducted by the government as part of a "community caretaking" function, "totally divorced from the detection, investigation, or acquisition of evidence relating to the violation of a criminal statute." Standardized procedures are necessary to ensure that this narrow exception is not improperly used to justify, after the fact, a warrantless investigative foray. Accordingly, to invalidate a search that is conducted without established procedures, it is not necessary to establish that the police actually acted in bad faith, or that the inventory was in fact a "pretext." By allowing the police unfettered discretion, Boulder's discretionary scheme * * * is unreasonable because of the " 'grave danger' of abuse of discretion." * * *

[JUSTICE BLACKMUN's concurring opinion has been omitted.]

B. VEHICLE CHECKPOINT SEARCHES

The next two cases deal with vehicle checkpoint searches, another type of administrative search. In *Michigan v. Sitz*, the Court addresses the constitutionality of a sobriety checkpoint. In *City of Indianapolis v. Edmond*, the Court addresses the constitutionality of a narcotics interdiction checkpoint. You may find it surprising that the Court reaches opposite conclusions despite the obvious similarities between these two types of checkpoints.

Edmond reminds us that when dealing with searches that purportedly fall under the administrative search exception, the Court usually starts by assessing whether there is a "special need" above and beyond the normal need for law enforcement that makes obtaining a warrant or showing individualized suspicion impracticable.

MICHIGAN V. SITZ
Supreme Court of the United States
496 U.S. 444, 110 S. Ct. 2481, 110 L. Ed. 2d 412 (1990)

JUSTICE REHNQUIST delivered the opinion of the Court.

* * * Petitioners, the Michigan Department of State Police and its Director, established a sobriety checkpoint pilot program in early 1986. The Director appointed a Sobriety Checkpoint Advisory Committee comprising representatives of the State Police force, local police forces, state prosecutors, and the University of Michigan Transportation Research Institute. Pursuant to its charge, the Advisory Committee created guidelines setting forth procedures governing checkpoint operations, site selection, and publicity.

Under the guidelines, checkpoints would be set up at selected sites along state roads. All vehicles passing through a checkpoint would be stopped and their drivers briefly examined for signs of intoxication. In cases where a checkpoint officer detected signs of intoxication, the motorist would be directed to a location out of the traffic flow where an officer would check the motorist's driver's license and car registration and, if warranted, conduct further sobriety tests. Should the field tests and the officer's observations suggest that the driver was intoxicated, an arrest would be made. All other drivers would be permitted to resume their journey immediately.

The first—and to date the only—sobriety checkpoint operated under the program was conducted in Saginaw County with the assistance of the Saginaw County Sheriff's Department. During the hour-and-fifteen-minute duration of the checkpoint's operation, 126 vehicles passed through the checkpoint. The average delay for each vehicle was approximately 25 seconds. Two drivers were detained for field sobriety testing, and one of the two was arrested for driving under the influence of alcohol. A third driver who [drove] through without stopping was pulled over by an officer in an observation vehicle and arrested for driving under the influence.

On the day before the operation of the Saginaw County checkpoint, respondents filed a complaint in the Circuit Court of Wayne County seeking declaratory and injunctive relief from potential subjection to the checkpoints. Each of the respondents "is a licensed driver in the State of Michigan . . . who regularly travels throughout the State in his automobile." * * *

After the trial, at which the court heard extensive testimony concerning, *inter alia*, the "effectiveness" of highway sobriety checkpoint programs, the court ruled that the Michigan program violated the Fourth Amendment. * * * On appeal, the Michigan Court of Appeals affirmed the holding that the program violated the Fourth Amendment. * * * After the Michigan Supreme Court denied petitioners' application for leave to appeal, we granted certiorari.

To decide this case the trial court performed a balancing test. * * * As described by the Court of Appeals, the test involved "balancing the state's interest in preventing accidents caused by drunk drivers, the effectiveness of sobriety checkpoints in achieving that goal, and the level of intrusion on an individuals' privacy caused by the checkpoints." * * *

As characterized by the Court of Appeals, the trial court's findings with respect to the balancing factors were that the State has "a grave and legitimate" interest in curbing drunken driving; that sobriety checkpoint programs are generally "ineffective" and, therefore, do not significantly further that interest; and that the checkpoints' "subjective intrusion" on individual liberties is substantial. * * *

* * * Respondents maintain that the analysis must proceed from a basis of probable cause or reasonable suspicion and rely for support on language from our decision last Term in *Treasury Employees v. Von Raab*. We said in *Von Raab*:

> Where a Fourth Amendment intrusion serves special governmental needs, beyond the normal need for law enforcement, it is necessary to balance the individual's privacy expectations against the Government's interests to determine whether it is impractical to require a warrant or some level of individualized suspicion in the particular context.

* * *

Petitioners concede, correctly in our view, that a Fourth Amendment "seizure" occurs when a vehicle is stopped at a checkpoint. The question thus becomes whether such seizures are "reasonable" under the Fourth Amendment. * * *

No one can seriously dispute the magnitude of the drunken driving problem or the States' interest in eradicating it. Media reports of alcohol-related death and mutilation on the Nation's roads are legion. The anecdotal is confirmed by the statistical. "Drunk drivers cause an annual death toll of over 25,000 and in the same time span cause nearly one million personal injuries and more than five billion dollars in property damage." * * *

Conversely, the weight bearing on the other scale—the measure of the intrusion on motorists stopped briefly at sobriety checkpoints—is slight. We reached a similar conclusion as to the intrusion on motorists subjected to a brief stop at a highway checkpoint for detecting illegal aliens.[a] We see virtually no difference between the levels of intrusion on law-abiding motorists from the brief stops necessary to the effectuation of these two types of checkpoints, which to the average motorist would seem identical save for the nature of the questions the checkpoint officers might ask. * * *

With respect to what it perceived to be the "subjective" intrusion on motorists, however, the Court of Appeals found such intrusion substantial. The court first affirmed the trial court's finding that the guidelines governing checkpoint operation minimize the discretion of the officers on the scene. But the court also agreed with the trial court's conclusion that

---

[a] Here the Court is referring to *United States v. Martinez-Fuerte*, 428 U.S. 543 (1976). In *Martinez-Fuerte*, the Court upheld the constitutionality of a permanent vehicle checkpoint on Interstate 5 near San Clemente, California, approximately 66 miles north of the border between the United States and Mexico, requiring all drivers to stop so immigration officials could check their cars for undocumented immigrants. *Id.* at 545. In balancing the governmental interests against the interests of the motorists who had to stop if they wanted to proceed along the highway, the Court found that the governmental interest in curbing the flow of undocumented immigrants from Mexico into the United States was legitimate and necessary while the intrusion on motorists from having to stop at the checkpoint was minimal. *Id.* at 562.

the checkpoints have the potential to generate fear and surprise in motorists. This was so because the record failed to demonstrate that approaching motorists would be aware of their option to make U-turns or turnoffs to avoid the checkpoints. On that basis, the court deemed the subjective intrusion from the checkpoints unreasonable.

We believe the Michigan courts misread our cases concerning the degree of "subjective intrusion" and the potential for generating fear and surprise. The "fear and surprise" to be considered are not the natural fear of one who has been drinking over the prospect of being stopped at a sobriety checkpoint but, rather, the fear and surprise engendered in law abiding motorists by the nature of the stop. * * *

Here, checkpoints are selected pursuant to the guidelines, and uniformed police officers stop every approaching vehicle. * * *

The Court of Appeals went on to consider as part of the balancing analysis the "effectiveness" of the proposed checkpoint program. Based on extensive testimony in the trial record, the court concluded that the checkpoint program failed the "effectiveness" part of the test, and that this failure materially discounted petitioners' strong interest in implementing the program. We think the Court of Appeals was wrong on this point as well.

* * * Experts in police science might disagree over which of several methods of apprehending drunken drivers is preferrable as an ideal. But for purposes of Fourth Amendment analysis, the choice among such reasonable alternatives remains with the governmental officials who have a unique understanding of, and a responsibility for, limited public resources, including a finite number of police officers. * * *

* * * During the operation of the Saginaw County checkpoint, the detention of each of the 126 vehicles that entered the checkpoint resulted in the arrest of two drunken drivers. Stated as a percentage, approximately 1.5 percent of the drivers passing through the checkpoint were arrested for alcohol impairment. In addition, an expert witness testified at the trial that experience in other States demonstrated that, on the whole, sobriety checkpoints resulted in drunken driving arrests of around 1 percent of all motorists stopped. By way of comparison, the record from one of the consolidated cases in *Martinez-Fuerte*, showed that in the associated checkpoint, illegal aliens were found in only 0.12 percent of the vehicles passing through the checkpoint. The ratio of illegal aliens detected to vehicles stopped (considering that on occasion two or more illegal aliens were found in a single vehicle) was approximately 0.5 percent. We concluded that this "record ... provides a rather complete picture of the effectiveness of the San Clemente checkpoint", and we sustained its constitutionality. We see no justification for a different conclusion here.

In sum, the balance of the State's interest in preventing drunken driving, the extent to which this system can reasonably be said to advance that interest, and the degree of intrusion upon individual motorists who are briefly stopped, weighs in favor of the state program. We therefore hold that it is consistent with the Fourth Amendment. The judgment of the Michigan Court of Appeals is accordingly reversed, and the cause is remanded for further proceedings not inconsistent with this opinion.

Reversed.

JUSTICE STEVENS, with whom JUSTICE BRENNAN and JUSTICE MARSHALL join as to Parts I and II, dissenting.

A sobriety checkpoint is usually operated at night at an unannounced location. Surprise is crucial to its method. The test operation conducted by the Michigan State Police and the Saginaw County Sheriff's Department began shortly after midnight and lasted until about 1 a.m. During that period, the 19 officers participating in the operation made two arrests and stopped and questioned 125 other unsuspecting and innocent drivers. It is, of course, not known how many arrests would have been made during that period if those officers had been engaged in normal patrol activities. However, the findings of the trial court, based on an extensive record and affirmed by the Michigan Court of Appeals, indicate that the net effect of sobriety checkpoints on traffic safety is infinitesimal and possibly negative.
* * *

* * * The Court overvalues the law enforcement interest in using sobriety checkpoints, undervalues the citizen's interest in freedom from random, unannounced investigatory seizures, and mistakenly assumes that there is "virtually no difference" between a routine stop at a permanent, fixed checkpoint and a surprise stop at a sobriety checkpoint.
* * *

There is a critical difference between a seizure that is preceded by fair notice and one that is effected by surprise. That is one reason why a border search, or indeed any search at a permanent and fixed checkpoint, is much less intrusive than a random stop. A motorist with advance notice of the location of a permanent checkpoint has an opportunity to avoid the search entirely, or at least to prepare for, and limit, the intrusion on her privacy.

No such opportunity is available in the case of a random stop or a temporary checkpoint, which both depend for their effectiveness on the element of surprise. A driver who discovers an unexpected checkpoint on a familiar local road will be startled and distressed. She may infer, correctly, that the checkpoint is not simply "business as usual," and may likewise infer, again correctly, that the police have made a discretionary decision to focus their law enforcement efforts upon her and others who pass the chosen point.

This element of surprise is the most obvious distinction between the sobriety checkpoints permitted by today's majority and the interior border checkpoints approved by this Court in *Martinez-Fuerte*. The distinction casts immediate doubt upon the majority's argument, for *Martinez-Fuerte* is the only case in which we have upheld suspicionless seizures of motorists. But the difference between notice and surprise is only one of the important reasons for distinguishing between permanent and mobile checkpoints. With respect to the former, there is no room for discretion in either the timing or the location of the stop—it is a permanent part of the landscape. In the latter case, however, although the checkpoint is most frequently employed during the hours of darkness on weekends (because that is when drivers with alcohol in their blood are most apt to be found on the road), the police have extremely broad discretion in determining the exact timing and placement of the roadblock.

There is also a significant difference between the kind of discretion that the officer exercises after the stop is made. A check for a driver's license, or for identification papers at an immigration checkpoint, is far more easily standardized than is a search for evidence of intoxication. A Michigan officer who questions a motorist at a sobriety checkpoint has virtually unlimited discretion to detain the driver on the basis of the slightest suspicion. A ruddy complexion, an unbuttoned shirt, bloodshot eyes or a speech impediment may suffice to prolong the detention. Any driver who had just consumed a glass of beer, or even a sip of wine, would almost certainly have the burden of demonstrating to the officer that her driving ability was not impaired.

Finally, it is significant that many of the stops at permanent checkpoints occur during daylight hours, whereas the sobriety checkpoints are almost invariably operated at night. A seizure followed by interrogation and even a cursory search at night is surely more offensive than a daytime stop that is almost as routine as going through a toll gate. * * *

These fears are not, as the Court would have it, solely the lot of the guilty. To be law abiding is not necessarily to be spotless, and even the most virtuous can be unlucky. Unwanted attention from the local police need not be less discomforting simply because one's secrets are not the stuff of criminal prosecutions. Moreover, those who have found—by reason of prejudice or misfortune—that encounters with the police may become adversarial or unpleasant without good cause will have grounds for worrying at any stop designed to elicit signs of suspicious behavior. Being stopped by the police is distressing even when it should not be terrifying, and what begins mildly may by happenstance turn severe. * * *

The gravity of the public concern with highway safety that is implicated by this case is, of course, undisputed. Yet, that same grave concern was implicated in [other cases in which the Court has found that

the individual's liberty interest outweighs the governmental interests].
* * *

On the degree to which the sobriety checkpoint seizures advance the public interest, however, the Court's position is wholly indefensible. The Court's analysis of this issue resembles a business decision that measures profits by counting gross receipts and ignoring expenses. The evidence in this case indicates that sobriety checkpoints result in the arrest of a fraction of one percent of the drivers who are stopped, but there is absolutely no evidence that this figure represents an increase over the number of arrests that would have been made by using the same law enforcement resources in conventional patrols. Thus, although the gross number of arrests is more than zero, there is a complete failure of proof on the question whether the wholesale seizures have produced any net advance in the public interest in arresting intoxicated drivers. * * *

The most disturbing aspect of the Court's decision today is that it appears to give no weight to the citizen's interest in freedom from suspicionless unannounced investigatory seizures. * * * [T]he Court places a heavy thumb on the law enforcement interest by looking only at gross receipts instead of net benefits. * * *

This is a case that is driven by nothing more than symbolic state action—an insufficient justification for an otherwise unreasonable program of random seizures. Unfortunately, the Court is transfixed by the wrong symbol—the illusory prospect of punishing countless intoxicated motorists—when it should keep its eyes on the road plainly marked by the Constitution.

I respectfully dissent.

[JUSTICE BLACKMUN's concurrence and JUSTICE BRENNAN's dissent have been omitted.]

CITY OF INDIANAPOLIS V. EDMOND
Supreme Court of the United States
531 U.S. 32, 121 S. Ct. 447, 148 L. Ed. 2d 333 (2000)

JUSTICE O'CONNOR delivered the opinion of the Court. * * *

In August 1998, the city of Indianapolis began to operate vehicle checkpoints on Indianapolis roads in an effort to interdict unlawful drugs. The city conducted six such roadblocks between August and November that year, stopping 1,161 vehicles and arresting 104 motorists. Fifty-five arrests were for drug-related crimes, while 49 were for offenses unrelated to drugs. The overall "hit rate" of the program was thus approximately nine percent.

The parties stipulated to the facts concerning the operation of the checkpoints by the Indianapolis Police Department (IPD) for purposes of the preliminary injunction proceedings instituted below. At each checkpoint location, the police stop a predetermined number of vehicles. Approximately 30 officers are stationed at the checkpoint. Pursuant to written directives issued by the chief of police, at least one officer approaches the vehicle, advises the driver that he or she is being stopped briefly at a drug checkpoint, and asks the driver to produce a license and registration. The officer also looks for signs of impairment and conducts an open-view examination of the vehicle from the outside. A narcotics-detection dog walks around the outside of each stopped vehicle.

The directives instruct the officers that they may conduct a search only by consent or based on the appropriate quantum of particularized suspicion. The officers must conduct each stop in the same manner until particularized suspicion develops, and the officers have no discretion to stop any vehicle out of sequence. * * *

* * * [C]heckpoint locations are selected weeks in advance based on such considerations as area crime statistics and traffic flow. The checkpoints are generally operated during daylight hours and are identified with lighted signs reading, "NARCOTICS CHECKPOINT ___ MILE AHEAD, NARCOTICS K-9 IN USE, BE PREPARED TO STOP." Once a group of cars has been stopped, other traffic proceeds without interruption until all the stopped cars have been processed or diverted for further processing. Sergeant DePew also stated that the average stop for a vehicle not subject to further processing lasts two to three minutes or less.

Respondents James Edmond and Joell Palmer were each stopped at a narcotics checkpoint in late September 1998. Respondents then filed a lawsuit on behalf of themselves and the class of all motorists who had been stopped or were subject to being stopped in the future at the Indianapolis drug checkpoints. Respondents claimed that the roadblocks violated the Fourth Amendment of the United States Constitution and the search and seizure provision of the Indiana Constitution. * * *

The Fourth Amendment requires that searches and seizures be reasonable. A search or seizure is ordinarily unreasonable in the absence of individualized suspicion of wrongdoing. While such suspicion is not an "irreducible" component of reasonableness, we have recognized only limited circumstances in which the usual rule does not apply. For example, we have upheld certain regimes of suspicionless searches where the program was designed to serve "special needs, beyond the normal need for law enforcement." See, e.g., Vernonia School Dist. (random drug testing of student-athletes); Treasury Employees v. Von Raab (drug tests for United States Customs Service employees seeking transfer or promotion to certain positions); Skinner v. Railway Labor Executives' Assn. (drug and alcohol tests for railway employees involved in train accidents or found to be in violation of particular safety regulations). * * *

In *Martinez-Fuerte*, we entertained Fourth Amendment challenges to stops at two permanent immigration checkpoints located on major United States highways less than 100 miles from the Mexican border. We noted at the outset the particular context in which the constitutional question arose, describing in some detail the "formidable law enforcement problems" posed by the northbound tide of illegal entrants into the United States. These problems had also been the focus of several earlier cases addressing the constitutionality of other Border Patrol traffic-checking operations. In *Martinez-Fuerte*, we found that the balance tipped in favor of the Government's interests in policing the Nation's borders. * * *

In [*Michigan v.*] *Sitz,* we evaluated the constitutionality of a Michigan highway sobriety checkpoint program. The *Sitz* checkpoint involved brief, suspicionless stops of motorists so that police officers could detect signs of intoxication and remove impaired drivers from the road. Motorists who exhibited signs of intoxication were diverted for a license and registration check and, if warranted, further sobriety tests. This checkpoint program was clearly aimed at reducing the immediate hazard posed by the presence of drunk drivers on the highways, and there was an obvious connection between the imperative of highway safety and the law enforcement practice at issue. The gravity of the drunk driving problem and the magnitude of the State's interest in getting drunk drivers off the road weighed heavily in our determination that the program was constitutional. * * *

It is well established that a vehicle stop at a highway checkpoint effectuates a seizure within the meaning of the Fourth Amendment. * * * [W]hat principally distinguishes these [narcotics interdiction] checkpoints from those we have previously approved is their primary purpose.

As petitioners concede, the Indianapolis checkpoint program unquestionably has the primary purpose of interdicting illegal narcotics. In their stipulation of facts, the parties repeatedly refer to the checkpoints as "drug checkpoints" and describe them as "being operated by the City of Indianapolis in an effort to interdict unlawful drugs in Indianapolis." * * * [B]oth the District Court and the Court of Appeals recognized that the primary purpose of the roadblocks is the interdiction of narcotics.

We have never approved a checkpoint program whose primary purpose was to detect evidence of ordinary criminal wrongdoing. Rather, our checkpoint cases have recognized only limited exceptions to the general rule that a seizure must be accompanied by some measure of individualized suspicion. * * * [E]ach of the checkpoint programs that we have approved was designed primarily to serve purposes closely related to the problems of policing the border or the necessity of ensuring roadway safety. Because the primary purpose of the Indianapolis narcotics checkpoint program is to uncover evidence of ordinary criminal wrongdoing, the program contravenes the Fourth Amendment.

Petitioners propose several ways in which the narcotics-detection purpose of the instant checkpoint program may instead resemble the primary purposes of the checkpoints in *Sitz* and *Martinez-Fuerte*. Petitioners state that the checkpoints in those cases had the same ultimate purpose of arresting those suspected of committing crimes. Securing the border and apprehending drunk drivers are, of course, law enforcement activities, and law enforcement officers employ arrests and criminal prosecutions in pursuit of these goals. If we were to rest the case at this high level of generality, there would be little check on the ability of the authorities to construct roadblocks for almost any conceivable law enforcement purpose. Without drawing the line at roadblocks designed primarily to serve the general interest in crime control, the Fourth Amendment would do little to prevent such intrusions from becoming a routine part of American life. * * *

Nor can the narcotics-interdiction purpose of the checkpoints be rationalized in terms of a highway safety concern similar to that present in *Sitz*. The detection and punishment of almost any criminal offense serves broadly the safety of the community, and our streets would no doubt be safer but for the scourge of illegal drugs. Only with respect to a smaller class of offenses, however, is society confronted with the type of immediate, vehicle-bound threat to life and limb that the sobriety checkpoint in *Sitz* was designed to eliminate. * * *

The primary purpose of the Indianapolis narcotics checkpoints is in the end to advance "the general interest in crime control." We decline to suspend the usual requirement of individualized suspicion where the police seek to employ a checkpoint primarily for the ordinary enterprise of investigating crimes. We cannot sanction stops justified only by the generalized and ever-present possibility that interrogation and inspection may reveal that any given motorist has committed some crime.

Of course, there are circumstances that may justify a law enforcement checkpoint where the primary purpose would otherwise, but for some emergency, relate to ordinary crime control. For example, as the Court of Appeals noted, the Fourth Amendment would almost certainly permit an appropriately tailored roadblock set up to thwart an imminent terrorist attack or to catch a dangerous criminal who is likely to flee by way of a particular route. The exigencies created by these scenarios are far removed from the circumstances under which authorities might simply stop cars as a matter of course to see if there just happens to be a felon leaving the jurisdiction. While we do not limit the purposes that may justify a checkpoint program to any rigid set of categories, we decline to approve a program whose primary purpose is ultimately indistinguishable from the general interest in crime control. * * *

Petitioners argue that the Indianapolis checkpoint program is justified by its lawful secondary purposes of keeping impaired motorists off the road and verifying licenses and registrations. If this were the case, however, law enforcement authorities would be able to establish checkpoints for virtually any purpose so long as they also included a license or sobriety check. For this reason, we examine the available evidence to determine the primary purpose of the checkpoint program. While we recognize the challenges inherent in a purpose inquiry, courts routinely engage in this enterprise in many areas of constitutional jurisprudence as a means of sifting abusive governmental conduct from that which is lawful. As a result, a program driven by an impermissible purpose may be proscribed while a program impelled by licit purposes is permitted, even though the challenged conduct may be outwardly similar. While reasonableness under the Fourth Amendment is predominantly an objective inquiry, our special needs and administrative search cases demonstrate that purpose is often relevant when suspicionless intrusions pursuant to a general scheme are at issue.

It goes without saying that our holding today does nothing to alter the constitutional status of the sobriety and border checkpoints that we approved in *Sitz* and *Martinez-Fuerte* * * *. When law enforcement authorities pursue primarily general crime control purposes at checkpoints such as here, however, stops can only be justified by some quantum of individualized suspicion. * * *

Because the primary purpose of the Indianapolis checkpoint program is ultimately indistinguishable from the general interest in crime control, the checkpoints violate the Fourth Amendment. The judgment of the Court of Appeals is, accordingly, affirmed.

It is so ordered.

CHIEF JUSTICE REHNQUIST, with whom JUSTICE THOMAS joins, and with whom JUSTICE SCALIA joins as to Part I, dissenting. * * *

As it is nowhere to be found in the Court's opinion, I begin with blackletter roadblock seizure law. "The principal protection of Fourth Amendment rights at checkpoints lies in appropriate limitations on the scope of the stop." Roadblock seizures are consistent with the Fourth Amendment if they are "carried out pursuant to a plan embodying explicit, neutral limitations on the conduct of individual officers." Specifically, the constitutionality of a seizure turns upon "a weighing of the gravity of the public concerns served by the seizure, the degree to which the seizure advances the public interest, and the severity of the interference with individual liberty." * * *

This case follows naturally from *Martinez-Fuerte* and *Sitz*. Petitioners acknowledge that the "primary purpose" of these roadblocks is to interdict illegal drugs, but this fact should not be controlling. * * * The District Court found that another "purpose of the checkpoints is to check driver's licenses and vehicle registrations," and the written directives state that the police officers are to "[l]ook for signs of impairment." The use of roadblocks to look for signs of impairment was validated by *Sitz,* and the use of roadblocks to check for driver's licenses and vehicle registrations was expressly recognized in *Delaware v. Prouse.* That the roadblocks serve these legitimate state interests cannot be seriously disputed, as the 49 people arrested for offenses unrelated to drugs can attest. * * *

With these checkpoints serving two important state interests, the remaining prongs of the * * * balancing test are easily met. The seizure is objectively reasonable as it lasts, on average, two to three minutes and does not involve a search. The subjective intrusion is likewise limited as the checkpoints are clearly marked and operated by uniformed officers who are directed to stop every vehicle in the same manner. * * *

These stops effectively serve the State's legitimate interests; they are executed in a regularized and neutral manner; and they only minimally intrude upon the privacy of the motorists. They should therefore be constitutional. * * *

[JUSTICE THOMAS' dissenting opinion has been omitted.]

C. STRIP SEARCHES

The next two cases involve strip searches. The term "strip search" is commonly understood to mean a search that requires the removal of a person's clothing to allow the inspection of normally private parts of the person's body. The first case, *Safford Unified School District #1 v. Redding,* involves the search of the bra and underpants of a 13-year-old middle school student suspected of bringing forbidden prescription and over-the-counter drugs to school. The second case, *Florence v. Board of Chosen Freeholders,* involves a correctional facility's visual search of the anus of a man who was mistakenly arrested and taken into custody.

SAFFORD UNIFIED SCHOOL DISTRICT #1 V. REDDING
Supreme Court of the United States
557 U.S. 364, 129 S. Ct. 2633, 174 L. Ed. 2d 354 (2009)

JUSTICE SOUTER delivered the opinion of the Court.

The issue here is whether a 13-year-old student's Fourth Amendment right was violated when she was subjected to a search of her bra and underpants by school officials acting on reasonable suspicion that she had brought forbidden prescription and over-the-counter drugs to school. Because there were no reasons to suspect the drugs presented a danger or were concealed in her underwear, we hold that the search did violate the Constitution, but because there is reason to question the clarity with which the right was established, the official who ordered the unconstitutional search is entitled to qualified immunity from liability.[a]

The events immediately prior to the search in question began in 13-year-old Savana Redding's math class at Safford Middle School one October day in 2003. The assistant principal of the school, Kerry Wilson, came into the room and asked Savana to go to his office. There, he showed her a day planner, unzipped and open flat on his desk, in which there were several knives, lighters, a permanent marker, and a cigarette. Wilson asked Savana whether the planner was hers; she said it was, but that a few days before she had lent it to her friend, Marissa Glines. Savana stated that none of the items in the planner belonged to her.

Wilson then showed [13-year-old] Savana [Redding] four white prescription-strength ibuprofen 400-mg pills, and one over-the-counter blue naproxen 200-mg pill, all used for pain and inflammation but banned under school rules without advance permission. He asked Savana if she knew anything about the pills. Savana answered that she did not. Wilson then told Savana that he had received a report that she was giving these pills to fellow students; Savana denied it and agreed to let Wilson search her belongings. Helen Romero, an administrative assistant, came into the office, and together with Wilson they searched Savana's backpack, finding nothing.

At that point, Wilson instructed Romero to take Savana to the school nurse's office to search her clothes for pills. Romero and the nurse, Peggy Schwallier, asked Savana to remove her jacket, socks, and shoes, leaving her in stretch pants and a T-shirt (both without pockets), which she was then asked to remove. Finally, Savana was told to pull her bra out and to the side and shake it, and to pull out the elastic on her underpants, thus exposing her breasts and pelvic area to some degree. No pills were found.

Savana's mother filed suit against Safford Unified School District #1, Wilson, Romero, and Schwallier for conducting a strip search in violation of Savana's Fourth Amendment rights. * * *

In *T.L.O.*, we recognized that the school setting "requires some modification of the level of suspicion of illicit activity needed to justify a search," and held that for searches by school officials "a careful balancing of governmental and private interests suggests that the public interest is best served by a Fourth Amendment standard of reasonableness that stops short of probable cause." We have thus applied a standard of reasonable suspicion to determine the legality of a school administrator's search of a student, and have held that a school search "will be permissible in its scope

---

[a] Qualified immunity is an affirmative defense that protects government officials "from liability for civil damages insofar as their conduct does not violate clearly established statutory or constitutional rights of which a reasonable person would have known." Harlow v. Fitzgerald, 457 U.S. 800, 818 (1982).

when the measures adopted are reasonably related to the objectives of the search and not excessively intrusive in light of the age and sex of the student and the nature of the infraction." * * *

In this case, the school's policies strictly prohibit the nonmedical use, possession, or sale of any drug on school grounds, including "[a]ny prescription or over-the-counter drug, except those for which permission to use in school has been granted pursuant to Board policy." A week before Savana was searched, another student, Jordan Romero (no relation of the school's administrative assistant), told the principal and Assistant Principal Wilson that "certain students were bringing drugs and weapons on campus," and that he had been sick after taking some pills that "he got from a classmate." On the morning of October 8, the same boy handed Wilson a white pill that he said Marissa Glines had given him. He told Wilson that students were planning to take the pills at lunch.

Wilson learned * * * that the pill was Ibuprofen 400 mg, available only by prescription. Wilson then called Marissa out of class. * * * Wilson escorted Marissa back to his office.

In the presence of Helen Romero, Wilson requested Marissa to turn out her pockets and open her wallet. Marissa produced a blue pill, several white ones, and a razor blade. Wilson asked where the blue pill came from, and Marissa answered, "I guess it slipped in when *she* gave me the IBU 400s." When Wilson asked whom she meant, Marissa replied, "Savana Redding." * * *

This suspicion of Wilson's was enough to justify a search of Savana's backpack and outer clothing. If a student is reasonably suspected of giving out contraband pills, she is reasonably suspected of carrying them on her person and in the carryall that has become an item of student uniform in most places today. If Wilson's reasonable suspicion of pill distribution were not understood to support searches of outer clothes and backpack, it would not justify any search worth making. And the look into Savana's bag, in her presence and in the relative privacy of Wilson's office, was not excessively intrusive, any more than Romero's subsequent search of her outer clothing.

* * * Savana[ ] claim[s] that extending the search at Wilson's behest to the point of making her pull out her underwear was constitutionally unreasonable. The exact label for this final step in the intrusion is not important, though strip search is a fair way to speak of it. Romero and Schwallier directed Savana to remove her clothes down to her underwear, and then "pull out" her bra and the elastic band on her underpants. Although Romero and Schwallier stated that they did not see anything when Savana followed their instructions, we would not define strip search and its Fourth Amendment consequences in a way that would guarantee litigation about who was looking and how much was seen. The very fact of Savana's pulling her underwear away from her body in the presence of the

two officials who were able to see her necessarily exposed her breasts and pelvic area to some degree, and both subjective and reasonable societal expectations of personal privacy support the treatment of such a search as categorically distinct, requiring distinct elements of justification on the part of school authorities for going beyond a search of outer clothing and belongings.

Savana's subjective expectation of privacy against such a search is inherent in her account of it as embarrassing, frightening, and humiliating. The reasonableness of her expectation (required by the Fourth Amendment standard) is indicated by the consistent experiences of other young people similarly searched, whose adolescent vulnerability intensifies the patent intrusiveness of the exposure. The common reaction of these adolescents simply registers the obviously different meaning of a search exposing the body from the experience of nakedness or near undress in other school circumstances. Changing for gym is getting ready for play; exposing for a search is responding to an accusation reserved for suspected wrongdoers and fairly understood as so degrading that a number of communities have decided that strip searches in schools are never reasonable and have banned them no matter what the facts may be[.]

The indignity of the search does not, of course, outlaw it, but it does implicate the rule of reasonableness as stated in *T.L.O.*, that "the search as actually conducted [be] reasonably related in scope to the circumstances which justified the interference in the first place." The scope will be permissible, that is, when it is "not excessively intrusive in light of the age and sex of the student and the nature of the infraction."

Here, the content of the suspicion failed to match the degree of intrusion. Wilson knew beforehand that the pills were prescription-strength ibuprofen and over-the-counter naproxen, common pain relievers equivalent to two Advil, or one Aleve. He must have been aware of the nature and limited threat of the specific drugs he was searching for, and while just about anything can be taken in quantities that will do real harm, Wilson had no reason to suspect that large amounts of the drugs were being passed around, or that individual students were receiving great numbers of pills.

Nor could Wilson have suspected that Savana was hiding common painkillers in her underwear. * * * [N]ondangerous school contraband does not raise the specter of stashes in intimate places, and there is no evidence in the record of any general practice among Safford Middle School students of hiding that sort of thing in underwear; neither Jordan nor Marissa suggested to Wilson that Savana was doing that, and the preceding search of Marissa that Wilson ordered yielded nothing. * * *

In sum, what was missing from the suspected facts that pointed to Savana was any indication of danger to the students from the power of the drugs or their quantity, and any reason to suppose that Savana was carrying pills in her underwear. We think that the combination of these deficiencies was fatal to finding the search reasonable.

In so holding, we mean to cast no ill reflection on the assistant principal, for the record raises no doubt that his motive throughout was to eliminate drugs from his school and protect students from what Jordan Romero had gone through. Parents are known to overreact to protect their children from danger, and a school official with responsibility for safety may tend to do the same. The Fourth Amendment places limits on the official, even with the high degree of deference that courts must pay to the educator's professional judgment.

We do mean, though, to make it clear that the *T.L.O.* concern to limit a school search to reasonable scope requires the support of reasonable suspicion of danger or of resort to underwear for hiding evidence of wrongdoing before a search can reasonably make the quantum leap from outer clothes and backpacks to exposure of intimate parts. The meaning of such a search, and the degradation its subject may reasonably feel, place a search that intrusive in a category of its own demanding its own specific suspicions.

* * * The strip search of Savana Redding was unreasonable and a violation of the Fourth Amendment * * *.

It is so ordered.

[JUSTICE GINSBURG's opinion, concurring in part and dissenting in part, has been omitted; JUSTICE STEVENS' opinion, concurring in part and dissenting in part, has been omitted; and JUSTICE THOMAS' opinion, concurring in part and dissenting in part, has been omitted.]

FLORENCE V. BOARD OF CHOSEN FREEHOLDERS

Supreme Court of the United States
566 U.S. 318, 132 S. Ct. 1510, 182 L. Ed. 2d 566 (2012)

JUSTICE KENNEDY delivered the opinion of the Court, except as to Part IV.

In 1998, seven years before the incidents at issue, petitioner Albert Florence was arrested after fleeing from police officers in Essex County, New Jersey. He was charged with obstruction of justice and use of a deadly weapon. Petitioner entered a plea of guilty to two lesser offenses and was sentenced to pay a fine in monthly installments. In 2003, after he fell behind on his payments and failed to appear at an enforcement hearing, a bench warrant was issued for his arrest. He paid the outstanding balance less than a week later; but, for some unexplained reason, the warrant remained in a statewide computer database.

Two years later, in Burlington County, New Jersey, petitioner and his wife were stopped in their automobile by a state trooper. Based on the outstanding warrant in the computer system, the officer arrested petitioner and took him to the Burlington County Detention Center. He was held there for six days and then was transferred to the Essex County Correctional Facility. It is not the arrest or confinement but the search process at each jail that gives rise to the claims before the Court.

Burlington County jail procedures required every arrestee to shower with a delousing agent. Officers would check arrestees for scars, marks, gang tattoos, and contraband as they disrobed. Petitioner claims he was also instructed to open his mouth, lift his tongue, hold out his arms, turn around, and lift his genitals. * * *

The Essex County Correctional Facility, where petitioner was taken after six days, is the largest county jail in New Jersey. * * * When petitioner was transferred there, all arriving detainees * * * were instructed to remove their clothing while an officer looked for body markings, wounds, and contraband. * * * [W]ithout touching the detainees, an officer looked at their ears, nose, mouth, hair, scalp, fingers, hands, arms, armpits, and other body openings. This policy applied regardless of the circumstances of the arrest, the suspected offense, or the detainee's behavior, demeanor, or criminal history. Petitioner alleges he was required to lift his genitals, turn around, and cough in a squatting position as part of the process. * * * He was released the next day, when the charges against him were dismissed.

Petitioner sued the governmental entities that operated the jails, one of the wardens, and certain other defendants. * * * Seeking relief under 42 U.S.C. § 1983 for violations of his Fourth and Fourteenth Amendment rights, petitioner maintained that persons arrested for a minor offense could not be required to remove their clothing and expose the most private areas of their bodies to close visual inspection as a routine part of the intake process. Rather, he contended, officials could conduct this kind of search only if they had reason to suspect a particular inmate of concealing a weapon, drugs, or other contraband. * * *

After discovery, the [District Court] granted petitioner's motion for summary judgment on the unlawful search claim. It concluded that any policy of "strip searching" nonindictable offenders without reasonable suspicion violated the Fourth Amendment. A divided panel of the United States Court of Appeals for the Third Circuit reversed, holding that the procedures described by the District Court struck a reasonable balance between inmate privacy and the security needs of the two jails. * * *

The Federal Courts of Appeal have come to differing conclusions as to whether the Fourth Amendment requires correctional officials to exempt some detainees who will be admitted to a jail's general population from the searches here at issue. This Court granted certiorari to address the question.

The difficulties of operating a detention center must not be underestimated by the courts. Jails (in the stricter sense of the term, excluding prison facilities) admit more than 13 million inmates a year. * * * Maintaining safety and order at these institutions requires the expertise of correctional officials, who must have substantial discretion to devise reasonable solutions to the problems they face. The Court has confirmed the importance of deference to correctional officials and explained that a regulation impinging on an inmate's constitutional rights must be upheld "if it is reasonably related to legitimate penological interests."

The Court's opinion in *Bell v. Wolfish* is the starting point for understanding how this framework applies to Fourth Amendment challenges. That case addressed a rule requiring pretrial detainees in any correctional facility run by the Federal Bureau of Prisons "to expose their body cavities for visual inspection as a part of a strip search conducted after every contact visit with a person from outside the institution." Inmates at the federal Metropolitan Correctional Center in New York City argued there was no security justification for these searches. Officers searched guests before they entered the visiting room, and the inmates were under constant surveillance during the visit. There had been but one instance in which an inmate attempted to sneak contraband back into the facility. The Court nonetheless upheld the search policy. It deferred to the judgment of correctional officials that the inspections served not only to discover but also to deter the smuggling of weapons, drugs, and other prohibited items inside. The Court explained that there is no mechanical way to determine whether intrusions on an inmate's privacy are reasonable. The need for a particular search must be balanced against the resulting invasion of personal rights.

Policies designed to keep contraband out of jails and prisons have been upheld in cases decided since *Bell*. In *Block v. Rutherford,* for example, the Court concluded that the Los Angeles County Jail could ban all contact visits because of the threat they posed. * * * In *Hudson v. Palmer,* the Court upheld the constitutionality of random searches of inmate lockers and cells even without reason to suspect a particular individual of concealing a prohibited item.

These cases establish that correctional officials must be permitted to devise reasonable search policies to detect and deter the possession of contraband in their facilities. The task of determining whether a policy is reasonably related to legitimate security interests is "peculiarly within the province and professional expertise of corrections officials." This Court has repeated the admonition that, "in the absence of substantial evidence in the record to indicate that the officials have exaggerated their response to these considerations courts should ordinarily defer to their expert judgment in such matters." * * *

Persons arrested for minor offenses may be among the detainees processed at these facilities. This is, in part, a consequence of the exercise of state authority that was the subject of *Atwater v. Lago Vista*. *Atwater* * * * involved a woman who was arrested after a police officer noticed neither she nor her children were wearing their seatbelts. * * * The Court held * * * that officers may make an arrest based upon probable cause to believe the person has committed a [fine-only] criminal offense in their presence. * * *

Correctional officials have a significant interest in conducting a thorough search as a standard part of the intake process. The admission of inmates creates numerous risks for facility staff, for the existing detainee population, and for a new detainee himself or herself. The danger of introducing lice or contagious infections, for example, is well documented. The Federal Bureau of Prisons recommends that staff screen new detainees for these conditions. Persons just arrested may have wounds or other injuries requiring immediate medical attention. It may be difficult to identify and treat these problems until detainees remove their clothes for a visual inspection.

Jails and prisons also face grave threats posed by the increasing number of gang members who go through the intake process. "Gang rivalries spawn a climate of tension, violence, and coercion." The groups recruit new members by force, engage in assaults against staff, and give other inmates a reason to arm themselves. Fights among feuding gangs can be deadly, and the officers who must maintain order are put in harm's way. These considerations provide a reasonable basis to justify a visual inspection for certain tattoos and other signs of gang affiliation as part of the intake process. The identification and isolation of gang members before they are admitted protects everyone in the facility.

Detecting contraband concealed by new detainees, furthermore, is a most serious responsibility. Weapons, drugs, and alcohol all disrupt the safe operation of a jail. Correctional officers have had to confront arrestees concealing knives, scissors, razor blades, glass shards, and other prohibited items on their person, including in their body cavities. They have also found crack, heroin, and marijuana. The use of drugs can embolden inmates in aggression toward officers or each other; and, even apart from their use, the trade in these substances can lead to violent confrontations.

There are many other kinds of contraband. The textbook definition of the term covers any unauthorized item. Everyday items can undermine security if introduced into a detention facility:

Lighters and matches are fire and arson risks or potential weapons. Cell phones are used to orchestrate violence and criminality both within and without jailhouse walls. Pills and medications enhance suicide risks. Chewing gum can block locking devices; hairpins can open handcuffs; wigs can conceal drugs and weapons.

Something as simple as an overlooked pen can pose a significant danger. Inmates commit more than 10,000 assaults on correctional staff every year and many more among themselves. * * *

Petitioner acknowledges that correctional officials must be allowed to conduct an effective search during the intake process and that this will require at least some detainees to lift their genitals or cough in a squatting position. These procedures, similar to the ones upheld in *Bell,* are designed to uncover contraband that can go undetected by a patdown, metal detector, and other less invasive searches. Petitioner maintains there is little benefit to conducting these more invasive steps on a new detainee who has not been arrested for a serious crime or for any offense involving a weapon or drugs. In his view these detainees should be exempt from this process unless they give officers a particular reason to suspect them of hiding contraband. * * *

People detained for minor offenses can turn out to be the most devious and dangerous criminals. Hours after the Oklahoma City bombing, Timothy McVeigh was stopped by a state trooper who noticed he was driving without a license plate. Police stopped serial killer Joel Rifkin for the same reason. One of the terrorists involved in the September 11 attacks was stopped and ticketed for speeding just two days before hijacking Flight 93. Reasonable correctional officials could conclude these uncertainties mean they must conduct the same thorough search of everyone who will be admitted to their facilities.

Experience shows that people arrested for minor offenses have tried to smuggle prohibited items into jail, sometimes by using their rectal cavities or genitals for the concealment. They may have some of the same incentives as a serious criminal to hide contraband. A detainee might risk carrying cash, cigarettes, or a penknife to survive in jail. Others may make a quick decision to hide unlawful substances to avoid getting in more trouble at the time of their arrest. * * *

Even if people arrested for a minor offense do not themselves wish to introduce contraband into a jail, they may be coerced into doing so by others. This could happen any time detainees are held in the same area, including in a van on the way to the station or in the holding cell of the jail. If, for example, a person arrested and detained for unpaid traffic citations is not subject to the same search as others, this will be well known to other detainees with jail experience. A hardened criminal or gang member can, in just a few minutes, approach the person and coerce him into hiding the fruits of a crime, a weapon, or some other contraband. * * * Exempting people arrested for minor offenses from a standard search protocol thus may put them at greater risk and result in more contraband being brought into the detention facility. This is a substantial reason not to mandate the exception petitioner seeks as a matter of constitutional law.

It also may be difficult, as a practical matter, to classify inmates by their current and prior offenses before the intake search. Jails can be even more dangerous than prisons because officials there know so little about the people they admit at the outset. An arrestee may be carrying a false ID or lie about his identity. The officers who conduct an initial search often do not have access to criminal history records. And those records can be inaccurate or incomplete. Petitioner's rap sheet is an example. It did not reflect his previous arrest for possession of a deadly weapon. In the absence of reliable information it would be illogical to require officers to assume the arrestees in front of them do not pose a risk of smuggling something into the facility. * * *

One of the central principles in *Atwater* applies with equal force here. Officers who interact with those suspected of violating the law have an "essential interest in readily administrable rules." The officials in charge of the jails in this case urge the Court to reject any complicated constitutional scheme requiring them to conduct less thorough inspections of some detainees based on their behavior, suspected offense, criminal history, and other factors. * * *

Even assuming all the facts in favor of petitioner, the search procedures at the Burlington County Detention Center and the Essex County Correctional Facility struck a reasonable balance between inmate privacy and the needs of the institutions. The Fourth and Fourteenth Amendments do not require adoption of the framework of rules petitioner proposes.

The judgment of the Court of Appeals for the Third Circuit is affirmed.

It is so ordered.

JUSTICE BREYER with whom JUSTICE GINSBURG, JUSTICE SOTOMAYOR, and JUSTICE KAGAN join, dissenting.

The petition for certiorari asks us to decide "[w]hether the Fourth Amendment permits a . . . suspicionless strip search of every individual arrested for any minor offense . . . ." This question is phrased more broadly than what is at issue. The case is limited to strip searches of those arrestees entering a jail's general population. And the kind of strip search in question involves more than undressing and taking a shower (even if guards monitor the shower area for threatened disorder). Rather, the searches here involve close observation of the private areas of a person's body and for that reason constitute a far more serious invasion of that person's privacy. * * *

In my view, such a search of an individual arrested for a minor offense that does not involve drugs or violence—say a traffic offense, a regulatory offense, an essentially civil matter, or any other such misdemeanor—is an "unreasonable searc[h]" forbidden by the Fourth Amendment, unless prison authorities have reasonable suspicion to believe that the individual possesses drugs or other contraband. And I dissent from the Court's contrary determination. * * *

A strip search that involves a stranger peering without consent at a naked individual, and in particular at the most private portions of that person's body, is a serious invasion of privacy. * * * The Courts of Appeals have more directly described the privacy interests at stake, writing, for example, that practices similar to those at issue here are "demeaning, dehumanizing, undignified, humiliating, terrifying, unpleasant, embarrassing, [and] repulsive, signifying degradation and submission." * * * Even when carried out in a respectful manner, and even absent any physical touching, such searches are inherently harmful, humiliating, and degrading. And the harm to privacy interests would seem particularly acute where the person searched may well have no expectation of being subject to such a search, say, because she had simply received a traffic ticket for failing to buckle a seatbelt, because he had not previously paid a civil fine, or because she had been arrested for a minor trespass. * * *

The petitioner, Albert W. Florence, states that his present arrest grew out of an (erroneous) report that he had failed to pay a minor civil fine previously assessed because he had hindered a prosecution (by fleeing police officers in his automobile). He alleges * * * that he was subjected to two strip searches of the kind in question.

The majority, like the respondents, argues that strip searches are needed (1) to detect injuries or diseases, such as lice, that might spread in confinement, (2) to identify gang tattoos, which might reflect a need for special housing to avoid violence, and (3) to detect contraband, including drugs, guns, knives, and even pens or chewing gum, which might prove harmful or dangerous in prison. In evaluating this argument, I, like the majority, recognize: that managing a jail or prison is an "inordinately difficult undertaking," that prison regulations that interfere with important constitutional interests are generally valid as long as they are "reasonably related to legitimate penological interests," that finding injuries and preventing the spread of disease, minimizing the threat of gang violence, and detecting contraband are "legitimate penological interests," and that we normally defer to the expertise of jail and prison administrators in such matters.

Nonetheless, the "particular" invasion of interests, must be "reasonably related" to the justifying "penological interest" and the need must not be "exaggerated." It is at this point that I must part company with the majority. I have found no convincing reason indicating that, in the absence of reasonable suspicion, involuntary strip searches of those arrested for minor offenses are necessary in order to further the penal interests mentioned. And there are strong reasons to believe they are not justified.

The lack of justification is fairly obvious with respect to the first two penological interests advanced. The searches already employed at Essex and Burlington include: (a) pat-frisking all inmates; (b) making inmates go through metal detectors (including the Body Orifice Screening System (BOSS) chair used at Essex County Correctional Facility that identifies metal hidden within the body); (c) making inmates shower and use particular delousing agents or bathing supplies; and (d) searching inmates' clothing. In addition, petitioner concedes that detainees could be lawfully subject to being viewed in their undergarments by jail officers or during showering (for security purposes). No one here has offered any reason, example, or empirical evidence suggesting the inadequacy of such practices for detecting injuries, diseases, or tattoos. In particular, there is no connection between the genital lift and the "squat and cough" that Florence was allegedly subjected to and health or gang concerns.

The lack of justification for such a strip search is less obvious but no less real in respect to the third interest in detecting contraband. The information demonstrating the lack of justification is of three kinds. First, there are empirically based conclusions reached in specific cases. The New York Federal District Court * * * conducted a study of 23,000 persons admitted to the Orange County correctional facility between 1999 and 2003. These 23,000 persons underwent a strip search of the kind described. Of these 23,000 persons, the court wrote, "the County encountered three incidents of drugs recovered from an inmate's anal cavity and two incidents of drugs falling from an inmate's underwear during the course of a strip search." The court added that in four of these five instances there may have been "reasonable suspicion" to search, leaving only one instance in 23,000 in which the strip search policy "arguably" detected additional contraband. The study is imperfect, for search standards changed during the time it was conducted. But the large number of inmates, the small number of "incidents," and the District Court's own conclusions make the study probative though not conclusive. * * *

Moreover, many correctional facilities apply a reasonable suspicion standard before strip searching inmates entering the general jail population, including the U.S. Marshals Service, the Immigration and Customs Service, and the Bureau of Indian Affairs. The Federal Bureau of Prisons (BOP) itself forbids suspicionless strip searches for minor offenders, though it houses separately (and does not admit to the general jail population) a person who does not consent to such a search. * * *

Indeed, neither the majority's opinion nor the briefs set forth any clear example of an instance in which contraband was smuggled into the general jail population during intake that could not have been discovered if the jail was employing a reasonable suspicion standard. * * *

For the reasons set forth, I cannot find justification for the strip search policy at issue here—a policy that would subject those arrested for minor offenses to serious invasions of their personal privacy. I consequently dissent.

[CHIEF JUSTICE ROBERTS' concurring opinion and JUSTICE ALITO's concurring opinion have been omitted.]

UNSEXING THE FOURTH AMENDMENT
I. Bennett Capers
48 U.C. Davis L. Rev. 855 (2015)

One of the main arguments raised in support of barring cross-gender searches is that it is particularly harmful to women, who may experience cross-gender searches as sexual violations. * * * The argument is raised in a range of searches, from *Terry* frisks to airport pat downs to prison strip searches and school searches. As Justice Ginsburg famously remarked about her fellow Justices after the Court decided *Redding*, "They have never been a 13-year-old girl. . . . It's a very sensitive age for a girl." * * *

These concerns are not without merit. However, they do deserve further scrutiny. Perhaps most problematic, this line of thinking engages in precisely the same type of sex stereotyping that feminists have fought hard to eradicate. It stereotypes women as vulnerable victims, reifying a trope that many feminists have long fought to retire. It casts women "as constitutively vulnerable to sexualized attack, and as essentially and necessarily modest in a way that resonates with tendencies to propertize women and deny them sexual agency."

To be clear, the sexual assault of women is real. But the leap from the observation that women are subject to sexual assault to the conclusion that cross-gender searches should be prohibited is a large leap indeed. It is also a retrogressive one. It casts women not only as likely targets of sexual harassment, but also as likely *victims*. By this, I mean that it stereotypes women as likely to *experience* cross-gender searches as sexually assaultive, debilitating, and paralyzing. It evokes the image of woman as the archetypal victim, as the weaker sex, and trades on her designation as sexual object. * * * It brings to mind the outdated thinking of cases like *Muller v. Oregon*, which deemed women as fragile beings "needing especial care," and *Bradwell v. Illinois*, which touted the "natural and proper timidity and delicacy which belongs to the female sex." * * *

Second, any policy or judicial preference for same-gender searches, in order to protect women, stereotypes men. To borrow from Amy Kapczynski, it is nothing short of "sexual profiling." It prefigures men as sexual predators, incapable of controlling their sexual urges, and incapable of conducting an authorized search within the parameters of the law. It buys into the notion that all men are potential rapists, and indeed adds to its currency. Two things are particularly troubling about such stereotyping. One, we apply this stereotype not only to men in general, but also to men who are police officers, school officials, corrections officers, and TSA employees. Stated differently, it seems strange that we paint with the same broad-brush individuals who are ethically and professionally obligated to protect us, and in whom we have entrusted such protection. Two, it is particularly troubling that so many of us who have fought against the reliance on gender-based stereotypes * * * would so casually stereotype men. * * *

In the end, though, this stereotyping of men as sexual predators and women as vulnerable victims only begins to capture the range of stereotype harms associated with juridical and policy preferences for same-gender searches. For starters, this preference renders transgender individuals invisible, failing to consider the special issues that attend a same-gender requirement for transgender individuals. It also assumes that both the person conducting the search, and the person being searched, are heterosexual. * * *

Along similar lines, creating policy or determining Fourth Amendment reasonableness on the basis of notions of male aggressiveness and female vulnerability erases other victims. * * * Reports * * * suggest that one in thirty-three men in the United States has been the victim of rape or attempted rape. Even in the military, where sexual assaults on women have gained much attention, male victimization is significant. In fact, of the 26,000 reports of unwanted sexual assault in the military in 2012, 53% involved sexual attacks on men, mostly by other men. As the *New York Times* has reported, the "majority of service members who are sexually assaulted each year are men." In short, the fact that a growing number of men have been sexually victimized, mostly by other men, undercuts part of the rationale for same-gender searches. Given this background, it is not surprising that, as Paul Butler has written, many men experience even same-sex searches as sexual, or that the "Don't Touch My Junk" movement was initiated by a searched male, or that even Justice Scalia has expressed unease with the "indignity" suffered by men during a pat-down. * * *

There is a related problem to that of stereotyping. The stereotype—that casts men as sexual aggressors and women as vulnerable victims—falsely simplifies interactions that are far more complex. Indeed, when examined closely, such assumptions about male-female interactions are often wrong. * * * In favoring same-gender searches, we conveniently sidestep the fact that men may be sexually victimized by other men, and that women may be sexually victimized by other women. This is particularly evident when it comes to limiting cross-gender pat downs and surveillance in prison. * * *

Consider the evidence from women's prisons. The assumption for women's prisons is that, like a scene from the *Orange is the New Black* in which an officer dubbed "Pornstache" gropes a female inmate, "the main threat of sexual abuse comes from male guards." Data contradict this assumption. While sexual abuse from male staff does exist, recent data reveal that the far greater threat of sexual abuse comes [from] other women, specifically female inmates. Surveys uniformly show that women inmates report twice as much female-on-female sexual victimization as victimization by male staff.

The evidence of sexual abuse from men's prisons and jails is equally counter-stereotypical. To be sure, there is male-on-male sexual violence. This alone throws a wrench into the narrative that women, not men, are vulnerable. Mounting evidence complicates this picture even more. Growing evidence suggests that women can be, and often are, sexually aggressive, too. Kim Shayo Buchanan observes:

> [D]espite the focus of prison rape discourse on fellow inmates as the source of sexual threat in men's prisons, these surveys found that incarcerated men report much higher rates of sexual abuse by staff than by fellow inmates, and found that a large majority of staff perpetrators of sexual abuse are women. . . . In total, 85 percent of male inmates who had had sex with staff reported a female perpetrator.

Quite simply, "since the publication of the first methodologically rigorous victimization surveys in 2007 and 2008, the results have consistently pointed to women staff as the main perpetrators of sexual victimization in jails and prisons for men." Of course, sexual victimization may take many forms, as female soldier Lynndie England's sexual torture of male Abu Ghraib prisoners should remind us. * * *

To be clear, I am not suggesting that the risk of being sexually assaulted is distributed equally among men and women. Nor am I suggesting that women are as likely to be perpetrators of sexual assault as are men. What I am suggesting, however, is that the trope of male perpetrator/female victim * * * is essentialist and under-inclusive insofar as it obscures other combinations of victimization, such as men being victimized by other men or women, or women being victimized by other women. More problematic, to focus exclusively on gender tropes obscures the power imbalance that lies at the heart of sexual assault, a power imbalance that may overlap with gender, but is not coterminous with it. If the real source of sexual threat stems from power imbalances, we do ourselves a disservice when we substitute gender-based proxies for actual power. We do ourselves a disservice, and we do a disservice to the goal of gender equality. * * *

CHAPTER 15

EXIGENT CIRCUMSTANCES

■ ■ ■

Many of the exceptions to the warrant requirement that we have studied thus far are motivated by exigency concerns. The automobile exception, for example, allows police to search a vehicle without a warrant, at least in part, because motor vehicles are readily mobile. A car could be moved quickly out of the jurisdiction and evidence within the car lost if police were always required to seek a warrant in advance of searching cars. The Court permits *Terry* stops and frisks without a warrant because of the need for police on the street to act quickly to confirm or dispel a particularized suspicion of criminal activity. Searches incident to arrest are permitted without a search warrant because of the concern that an arrestee could grab a weapon and use it against the officer or destroy evidence.

Because the established exceptions to the warrant requirement cannot possibly cover all of the various scenarios in which the exigencies of the situation make it impractical for police to obtain a warrant in advance of the search, the Court has recognized a catch-all exception for cases in which the exigencies of the situation make getting a warrant impracticable. This exception is called the exigent circumstances exception to the warrant requirement.

Joshua Dressler and Alan Michaels explain that "cases that fall within this exception typically involve situations in which the police act without a warrant because they reasonably believe that criminal evidence will be destroyed or a suspect will avoid capture if they take the time to seek a warrant."[a] In such cases, the exigency that justifies the warrantless action restricts the scope of the search.

For example, if the exigency is that a fugitive may elude capture if the police stop to get a warrant, the police may search places where a person might be hiding, but not a small suitcase or desk drawer. Once the exigency ends, the police may not continue searching without a warrant unless another exception to the warrant requirement applies.

While the exigent circumstances exception dispenses with the warrant requirement, it does not eliminate the probable cause requirement.[b] As a

---

[a] JOSHUA DRESSLER & ALAN C. MICHAELS, UNDERSTANDING CRIMINAL PROCEDURE, VOLUME I: INVESTIGATIONS 179 (6th ed. 2016).

[b] *Id.* at 180.

general matter, the police still need probable cause to believe evidence of a crime will be found in the place to be searched for an exigent circumstances search to be valid.

Aside from theses generalizations, the Court has never clearly delineated in one place exactly what is necessary for a search to come within the exigent circumstances exception to the warrant requirement. The cases in this chapter help us discern what types of factors are relevant to the exigent circumstances inquiry.

In *Welsh v. Wisconsin*, the Court considers whether the gravity of the underlying offense should play a role in the exigent circumstances analysis. In *Brigham City, Utah v. Stuart*, we learn about the application of the exigent circumstances doctrine in emergency aid situations. While probable cause is usually required for an exigent circumstances entry, when the police are responding to an emergency aid situation, they do not need probable cause to conduct a warrantless entry into a home.

Finally, in *Kentucky v. King*, the Court considers whether to adopt an exception to the exigent circumstances rule developed by lower courts called the "police-created exigency" doctrine. Under this doctrine, the exigent circumstances exception does not apply if the police create the very exigency that triggers the need to prevent imminent destruction of evidence.

WELSH V. WISCONSIN
Supreme Court of the United States
466 U.S. 740, 104 S. Ct. 2091, 80 L. Ed. 2d 732 (1984)

JUSTICE BRENNAN delivered the opinion of the Court.

Payton v. New York held that, absent probable cause and exigent circumstances, warrantless arrests in the home are prohibited by the Fourth Amendment. But the Court in that case explicitly refused "to consider the sort of emergency or dangerous situation, described in our cases as 'exigent circumstances,' that would justify a warrantless entry into a home for the purpose of either arrest or search." Certiorari was granted in this case to decide at least one aspect of the unresolved question: whether, and if so under what circumstances, the Fourth Amendment prohibits the police from making a warrantless night entry of a person's home in order to arrest him for a nonjailable traffic offense.

Shortly before 9 o'clock on the rainy night of April 24, 1978, a lone witness, Randy Jablonic, observed a car being driven erratically. After changing speeds and veering from side to side, the car eventually swerved off the road and came to a stop in an open field. No damage to any person or property occurred. Concerned about the driver and fearing that the car would get back on the highway, Jablonic drove his truck up behind the car so as to block it from returning to the road. Another passerby also stopped at the scene, and Jablonic asked her to call the police. Before the police arrived, however, the driver of the car emerged from his vehicle, approached Jablonic's truck, and asked Jablonic for a ride home. Jablonic instead suggested that they wait for assistance in removing or repairing the car. Ignoring Jablonic's suggestion, the driver walked away from the scene.

A few minutes later, the police arrived and questioned Jablonic. He told one officer what he had seen, specifically noting that the driver was either very inebriated or very sick. The officer checked the motor vehicle registration of the abandoned car and learned that it was registered to the petitioner, Edward G. Welsh. In addition, the officer noted that the petitioner's residence was a short distance from the scene, and therefore easily within walking distance.

Without securing any type of warrant, the police proceeded to the petitioner's home, arriving about 9 p.m. When the petitioner's stepdaughter answered the door, the police gained entry into the house.[1] Proceeding upstairs to the petitioner's bedroom, they found him lying naked in bed. At this point, the petitioner was placed under arrest for driving or operating a motor vehicle while under the influence of an intoxicant. * * * The petitioner was taken to the police station, where he refused to submit to a breath-analysis test. * * *

It is axiomatic that the "physical entry of the home is the chief evil against which the wording of the Fourth Amendment is directed." And a principal protection against unnecessary intrusions into private dwellings is the warrant requirement imposed by the Fourth Amendment on agents of the government who seek to enter the home for purposes of search or arrest. It is not surprising, therefore, that the Court has recognized, as "a 'basic principle of Fourth Amendment law[,]' that searches and seizures inside a home without a warrant are presumptively unreasonable."

Consistently with these long-recognized principles, the Court decided in *Payton v. New York*, that warrantless felony arrests in the home are prohibited by the Fourth Amendment, absent probable cause and exigent circumstances. At the same time, the Court declined to consider the scope of any exception for exigent circumstances that might justify warrantless home arrests, thereby leaving to the lower courts the initial application of the exigent-circumstances exception. Prior decisions of this Court, however, have emphasized that exceptions to the warrant requirement are

---

[1] The state trial court never decided whether there was consent to the entry because it deemed decision of that issue unnecessary in light of its finding that exigent circumstances justified the warrantless arrest. After reversing the lower court's finding of exigent circumstances, the Wisconsin Court of Appeals remanded for full consideration of the consent issue. That remand never occurred, however, because the Supreme Court of Wisconsin reversed the Court of Appeals and reinstated the trial court's judgment. For purposes of this decision, therefore, we assume that there was no valid consent to enter the petitioner's home.

"few in number and carefully delineated," and that the police bear a heavy burden when attempting to demonstrate an urgent need that might justify warrantless searches or arrests. Indeed, the Court has recognized only a few such emergency conditions, and has actually applied only the "hot pursuit" doctrine to arrests in the home.

Our hesitation in finding exigent circumstances, especially when warrantless arrests in the home are at issue, is particularly appropriate when the underlying offense for which there is probable cause to arrest is relatively minor. Before agents of the government may invade the sanctity of the home, the burden is on the government to demonstrate exigent circumstances that overcome the presumption of unreasonableness that attaches to all warrantless home entries. When the government's interest is only to arrest for a minor offense, that presumption of unreasonableness is difficult to rebut, and the government usually should be allowed to make such arrests only with a warrant issued upon probable cause by a neutral and detached magistrate.

This is not a novel idea. Writing in concurrence in *McDonald v. United States*, Justice Jackson explained why a finding of exigent circumstances to justify a warrantless home entry should be severely restricted when only a minor offense has been committed:

> * * * This method of law enforcement displays a shocking lack of all sense of proportion. Whether there is reasonable necessity for a search without waiting to obtain a warrant certainly depends somewhat upon the gravity of the offense thought to be in progress as well as the hazards of the method of attempting to reach it. . . . It is to me a shocking proposition that private homes, even quarters in a tenement, may be indiscriminately invaded at the discretion of any suspicious police officer engaged in following up offenses that involve no violence or threats of it. * * *

Consistently with this approach, the lower courts have looked to the nature of the underlying offense as an important factor to be considered in the exigent-circumstances calculus. In a leading federal case defining exigent circumstances, for example, the en banc United States Court of Appeals for the District of Columbia Circuit recognized that the gravity of the underlying offense was a principal factor to be weighed. Without approving all of the factors included in the standard adopted by that court, it is sufficient to note that many other lower courts have also considered the gravity of the offense an important part of their constitutional analysis. * * *

We therefore conclude that the common-sense approach utilized by most lower courts is required by the Fourth Amendment prohibition on "unreasonable searches and seizures," and hold that an important factor to be considered when determining whether any exigency exists is the gravity of the underlying offense for which the arrest is being made. Moreover, * * * application of the exigent-circumstances exception in the context of a home entry should rarely be sanctioned when there is probable cause to believe that only a minor offense, such as the kind at issue in this case, has been committed.[a]

Application of this principle to the facts of the present case is relatively straightforward. The petitioner was arrested in the privacy of his own bedroom for a noncriminal, traffic offense. The State attempts to justify the arrest by relying on the hot-pursuit doctrine, on the threat to public safety, and on the need to preserve evidence of the petitioner's blood-alcohol level. On the facts of this case, however, the claim of hot pursuit is unconvincing because there was no immediate or continuous pursuit of the petitioner from the scene of a crime. Moreover, because the petitioner had already arrived home, and had abandoned his car at the scene of the accident, there was little remaining threat to the public safety. Hence, the only potential emergency claimed by the State was the need to ascertain the petitioner's blood-alcohol level.

Even assuming, however, that the underlying facts would support a finding of this exigent circumstance, mere similarity to other cases involving the imminent destruction of evidence is not sufficient. The State of Wisconsin has chosen to classify the first offense for driving while intoxicated as a noncriminal, civil forfeiture offense for which no imprisonment is possible. This is the best indication of the State's interest in precipitating an arrest, and is one that can be easily identified both by the courts and by officers faced with a decision to arrest. Given this expression of the State's interest, a warrantless home arrest cannot be upheld simply because evidence of the petitioner's blood-alcohol level might have dissipated while the police obtained a warrant.[14] To allow a warrantless home entry on these facts would be to approve unreasonable police behavior that the principles of the Fourth Amendment will not sanction.

---

[a] In a short per curiam opinion in 2013, the Court retreated from its suggestion in *Welsh v. Wisconsin* that the exigent circumstances exception does not apply when the offense in question is only a minor offense. In *Stanton v. Sims*, 571 U.S. 3 (2013), the Court granted qualified immunity to a police officer who kicked open a gate to a home in pursuit of an individual who had merely disobeyed the officer's order to stop, a misdemeanor under the California Penal Code. Siding with the officer, the Court held that the law was not clearly established on whether a warrantless entry into a home in hot pursuit of a suspect who is committing only a misdemeanor offense violates the Fourth Amendment. The *Sims* Court explained, "we did not [in *Welsh v. Wisconsin*] lay down a categorical rule for all cases involving minor offenses, saying only that a warrant is 'usually' required." *Id.* at 8.

[14] Nor do we mean to suggest that the prevention of drunken driving is not properly of major concern to the States. The State of Wisconsin, however, along with several other States, has chosen to limit severely the penalties that may be imposed after a first conviction for driving while intoxicated. Given that the classification of state crimes differs widely among the States, the penalty that may attach to any particular offense seems to provide the clearest and most consistent indication of the State's interest in arresting individuals suspected of committing that offense.

The Supreme Court of Wisconsin let stand a warrantless, nighttime entry into the petitioner's home to arrest him for a civil traffic offense. Such an arrest, however, is clearly prohibited by the special protection afforded the individual in his home by the Fourth Amendment. The petitioner's arrest was therefore invalid, the judgment of the Supreme Court of Wisconsin is vacated, and the case is remanded for further proceedings not inconsistent with this opinion.

It is so ordered.

JUSTICE WHITE, with whom JUSTICE REHNQUIST joins, dissenting. * * *

The gravity of the underlying offense is, I concede, a factor to be considered in determining whether the delay that attends the warrant-issuance process will endanger officers or other persons. The seriousness of the offense with which a suspect may be charged also bears on the likelihood that he will flee and escape apprehension if not arrested immediately. But if, under all the circumstances of a particular case, an officer has probable cause to believe that the delay involved in procuring an arrest warrant will gravely endanger the officer or other persons or will result in the suspect's escape, I perceive no reason to disregard those exigencies on the ground that the offense for which the suspect is sought is a "minor" one.

* * * [N]othing in our previous decisions suggests that the fact that a State has defined an offense as a misdemeanor for a variety of social, cultural, and political reasons necessarily requires the conclusion that warrantless in-home arrests designed to prevent the imminent destruction or removal of evidence of that offense are always impermissible. * * *

A test under which the existence of exigent circumstances turns on the perceived gravity of the crime would significantly hamper law enforcement and burden courts with pointless litigation concerning the nature and gradation of various crimes. * * * The decision to arrest without a warrant typically is made in the field under less-than-optimal circumstances; officers have neither the time nor the competence to determine whether a particular offense for which warrantless arrests have been authorized by statute is serious enough to justify a warrantless home entry to prevent the imminent destruction or removal of evidence. * * *

Even if the Court were correct in concluding that the gravity of the offense is an important factor to consider in determining whether a warrantless in-home arrest is justified by exigent circumstances, it has erred in assessing the seriousness of the civil-forfeiture offense for which the officers thought they were arresting Welsh. As the Court observes, the statutory scheme in force at the time of Welsh's arrest provided that the first offense for driving under the influence of alcohol involved no potential incarceration. Nevertheless, this Court has long recognized the compelling state interest in highway safety, the Supreme Court of Wisconsin identified a number of factors suggesting a substantial and growing governmental interest in apprehending and convicting intoxicated drivers and in deterring alcohol-related offenses, and recent actions of the Wisconsin Legislature evince its "belief that significant benefits, in the reduction of the costs attributable to drunk driving, may be achieved by the increased apprehension and conviction of even first time . . . offenders." * * *

In short, the fact that Wisconsin has chosen to punish the first offense for driving under the influence with a fine rather than a prison term does not demand the conclusion that the State's interest in punishing first offenders is insufficiently substantial to justify warrantless in-home arrests under exigent circumstances. As the Supreme Court of Wisconsin observed, "[t]his is a model case demonstrating the urgency involved in arresting the suspect in order to preserve evidence of the statutory violation." We have previously recognized that "the percentage of alcohol in the blood begins to diminish shortly after drinking stops, as the body functions to eliminate it from the system." * * * I would hold that the need to prevent the imminent and ongoing destruction of evidence of a serious violation of Wisconsin's traffic laws provided an exigent circumstance justifying the warrantless in-home arrest.

I respectfully dissent.

[JUSTICE BLACKMUN's concurring opinion has been omitted.]

NOTE

In 2013, the Court decided another case involving a man suspected of driving while intoxicated. In *Missouri v. McNeely*, 569 U.S. 141 (2013), an officer observed a truck being driven by Tyler McNeely exceeding the speed limit and repeatedly crossing the centerline. After stopping McNeely, the officer saw that McNeely's eyes were bloodshot, his speech was slurred, and he had the smell of alcohol on his breath. After McNeely performed poorly on a series of field sobriety tests and refused to take a breathalyzer test, the officer arrested him and took him to a nearby hospital where he asked McNeely to consent to a blood test. When McNeely refused, the officer directed a lab technician to take a blood sample from McNeely. A test of the sample showed McNeely's blood alcohol content was well over the legal limit.

The government argued that the warrantless blood test was justified under the exigent circumstances exception to the warrant requirement and that the natural dissipation of alcohol from the bloodstream justified a per se rule allowing warrantless blood testing in all cases where an officer has probable cause to believe an individual has been driving under the influence of alcohol. The Court refused to adopt such a per se rule, explaining that "while the natural dissipation of alcohol in the blood may support a finding of exigency in a specific case, as it did in *Schmerber*,[a] it does not do so categorically. Whether a warrantless blood test of a drunk-driving suspect is reasonable must be determined case by case based on the totality of the circumstances."[b]

BRIGHAM CITY, UTAH V. STUART
Supreme Court of the United States
547 U.S. 398, 126 S. Ct. 1943, 164 L. Ed. 2d 650 (2006)

CHIEF JUSTICE ROBERTS delivered the opinion of the Court.

In this case we consider whether police may enter a home without a warrant when they have an objectively reasonable basis for believing that an occupant is seriously injured or imminently threatened with such injury. We conclude that they may.

This case arises out of a melee that occurred in a Brigham City, Utah, home in the early morning hours of July 23, 2000. At about 3 a.m., four police officers responded to a call regarding a loud party at a residence. Upon arriving at the house, they heard shouting from inside, and proceeded down the driveway to investigate. There, they observed two juveniles drinking beer in the backyard. They entered the backyard, and saw—through a screen door and windows—an altercation taking place in the kitchen of the home. According to the testimony of one of the officers, four adults were attempting, with some difficulty, to restrain a juvenile. The juvenile eventually "broke free, swung a fist and struck one of the adults in the face." The officer testified that he observed the victim of the blow spitting blood into a nearby sink. The other adults continued to try to restrain the juvenile, pressing him up against a refrigerator with such force that the refrigerator began moving across the floor. At this point, an officer opened the screen door and announced the officers' presence. Amid the tumult, nobody noticed. The officer entered the kitchen and again cried out,

---

[a] In *Schmerber v. California*, 384 U.S. 757 (1966), an officer directed hospital personnel to take a blood sample from a driver who had been arrested for driving under the influence of alcohol and was receiving treatment for injuries from a car crash, over the driver's objection. The Court found that the officer "might reasonably have believed that he was confronted with an emergency" that left no time to seek a warrant because "the percentage of alcohol in the blood begins to diminish shortly after drinking stops." *Id.* at 770. The Court further found that *"in a case such as this*, where time had to be taken to bring the accused to a hospital and to investigate the scene of the accident, there was no time to seek out a magistrate and secure a warrant." *Id.* at 771 (emphasis added). The Court concluded "that the attempt to secure evidence of blood-alcohol content *in this case* was an appropriate incident to petitioner's arrest" and therefore the officer's actions did not violate the Fourth Amendment despite the absence of a warrant. *Id.* (emphasis added).

[b] *Id.* at 156. Later, in *Burchfield v. North Dakota*, 579 U.S. 438 (2016), the Court addressed whether warrantless blood or breath tests are categorically permissible as searches incident to lawful arrest. Acknowledging that blood tests are "significantly more intrusive than blowing into a tube," *id.* at 464, the Court held that the search incident to arrest doctrine does not permit warrantless blood tests of motorists who have been lawfully arrested on suspicion of drunk driving. *Id.* at 476. Conversely, the Court held that police may administer a warrantless breath test as part of a search incident to a lawful arrest for drunk driving. *Id.*

CH. 15 EXIGENT CIRCUMSTANCES 413

and as the occupants slowly became aware that the police were on the scene, the altercation ceased.

The officers subsequently arrested respondents and charged them with contributing to the delinquency of a minor, disorderly conduct, and intoxication. In the trial court, respondents filed a motion to suppress all evidence obtained after the officers entered the home, arguing that the warrantless entry violated the Fourth Amendment. The court granted the motion, and the Utah Court of Appeals affirmed.

Before the Supreme Court of Utah, Brigham City argued that although the officers lacked a warrant, their entry was nevertheless reasonable on either of two grounds. The court rejected both contentions and, over two dissenters, affirmed. First, the court held that the injury caused by the juvenile's punch was insufficient to trigger the so-called "emergency aid doctrine"[c] because it did not give rise to an "objectively reasonable belief that an unconscious, semi-conscious, or missing person feared injured or dead [was] in the home." Furthermore, the court suggested that the doctrine was inapplicable because the officers had not sought to assist the injured adult, but instead had acted "exclusively in their law enforcement capacity."

The court also held that the entry did not fall within the exigent circumstances exception to the warrant requirement. * * * Although it found the case "a close and difficult call," the court nevertheless concluded that the officers' entry was not justified by exigent circumstances.

We granted certiorari, in light of differences among state courts and the Courts of Appeals concerning the appropriate Fourth Amendment standard governing warrantless entry by law enforcement in an emergency situation.

It is a "basic principle of Fourth Amendment law that searches and seizures inside a home without a warrant are presumptively unreasonable." Nevertheless, because the ultimate touchstone of the Fourth Amendment is "reasonableness," the warrant requirement is subject to certain exceptions. We have held, for example, that law enforcement officers may make a warrantless entry onto private property to fight a fire and investigate its cause, to prevent the imminent

---

[c] In a 2021 opinion, Justice Thomas, writing for the Court, rejected the idea that a standalone "community caretaking" doctrine justifies warrantless searches and seizures in the home. Caniglia v. Strom, 141 S. Ct. 1596 (2021). Apparently worried that the opinion might be interpreted as rejecting the idea that police are allowed to conduct warrantless searches to render emergency aid, Chief Justice Roberts wrote in a concurring opinion that it is still the case that "[a] warrant to enter a home is not required . . . when there is a 'need to assist persons who are seriously injured or threated with such injury.'" Id. at 1600 (Roberts, C.J., concurring). Similarly, Justice Kavanaugh wrote in a separate concurring opinion that the exigent circumstances doctrine applies to many different types of emergency aid situations, permitting "warrantless entries when police officers have an objectively reasonable basis to believe that there is a current, ongoing crisis for which it is reasonable to act now." Id. at 1604 (Kavanaugh, J., concurring).

destruction of evidence, or to engage in "hot pursuit" of a fleeing suspect. "[W]arrants are generally required to search a person's home or his person unless 'the exigencies of the situation' make the needs of law enforcement so compelling that the warrantless search is objectively reasonable under the Fourth Amendment."

One exigency obviating the requirement of a warrant is the need to assist persons who are seriously injured or threatened with such injury. "The need to protect or preserve life or avoid serious injury is justification for what would be otherwise illegal absent an exigency or emergency." Accordingly, law enforcement officers may enter a home without a warrant to render emergency assistance to an injured occupant or to protect an occupant from imminent injury.

Respondents do not take issue with these principles, but instead advance two reasons why the officers' entry here was unreasonable. First, they argue that the officers were more interested in making arrests than quelling violence. They urge us to consider, in assessing the reasonableness of the entry, whether the officers were "indeed motivated primarily by a desire to save lives and property." The Utah Supreme Court also considered the officers' subjective motivations relevant.

Our cases have repeatedly rejected this approach. An action is "reasonable" under the Fourth Amendment, regardless of the individual officer's state of mind, "as long as the circumstances, viewed *objectively*, justify [the] action." The officer's subjective motivation is irrelevant. It therefore does not matter here—even if their subjective motives could be so neatly unraveled—whether the officers entered the kitchen to arrest respondents and gather evidence against them or to assist the injured and prevent further violence. * * *

We think the officers' entry here was plainly reasonable under the circumstances. The officers were responding, at 3 o'clock in the morning, to complaints about a loud party. As they approached the house, they could hear from within "an altercation occurring, some kind of a fight." "It was loud and it was tumultuous." The officers heard "thumping and crashing" and people yelling "stop, stop" and "get off me." As the trial court found, "it was obvious that . . . knocking on the front door" would have been futile. The noise seemed to be coming from the back of the house; after looking in the front window and seeing nothing, the officers proceeded around back to investigate further. They found two juveniles drinking beer in the backyard. From there, they could see that a fracas was taking place inside the kitchen. A juvenile, fists clenched, was being held back by several adults. As the officers watch, he breaks free and strikes one of the adults in the face, sending the adult to the sink spitting blood.

In these circumstances, the officers had an objectively reasonable basis for believing both that the injured adult might need help and that the violence in the kitchen was just beginning. Nothing in the Fourth Amendment required them to wait until another blow rendered someone "unconscious" or "semi-conscious" or worse before entering. The role of a peace officer includes preventing violence and restoring order, not simply rendering first aid to casualties; an officer is not like a boxing (or hockey) referee, poised to stop a bout only if it becomes too one-sided. * * *

Accordingly, we reverse the judgment of the Supreme Court of Utah, and remand the case for further proceedings not inconsistent with this opinion.

It is so ordered.

[JUSTICE STEVENS' concurring opinion has been omitted.]

KENTUCKY V. KING

Supreme Court of the United States
563 U.S. 452, 131 S. Ct. 1849, 179 L. Ed. 2d 865 (2011)

JUSTICE ALITO delivered the opinion of the Court.

It is well established that "exigent circumstances," including the need to prevent the destruction of evidence, permit police officers to conduct an otherwise permissible search without first obtaining a warrant. In this case, we consider whether this rule applies when police, by knocking on the door of a residence and announcing their presence, cause the occupants to attempt to destroy evidence. The Kentucky Supreme Court held that the exigent circumstances rule does not apply in the case at hand because the police should have foreseen that their conduct would prompt the occupants to attempt to destroy evidence. We reject this interpretation of the exigent circumstances rule. The conduct of the police prior to their entry into the apartment was entirely lawful. They did not violate the Fourth Amendment or threaten to do so. In such a situation, the exigent circumstances rule applies.

This case concerns the search of an apartment in Lexington, Kentucky. Police officers set up a controlled buy of crack cocaine outside an apartment complex. Undercover Officer Gibbons watched the deal take place from an unmarked car in a nearby parking lot. After the deal occurred, Gibbons radioed uniformed officers to move in on the suspect. He told the officers that the suspect was moving quickly toward the breezeway of an apartment building, and he urged them to "hurry up and get there" before the suspect entered an apartment.

In response to the radio alert, the uniformed officers drove into the nearby parking lot, left their vehicles, and ran to the breezeway. Just as they entered the breezeway, they heard a door shut and detected a very strong odor of burnt marijuana. At the end of the breezeway, the officers saw two apartments, one on the left and one on the right, and they did not know which apartment the suspect had entered. Gibbons had radioed that the suspect was running into the apartment on the right, but the officers did not hear this statement because they had already left their vehicles. Because they smelled marijuana smoke emanating from the apartment on the left, they approached the door of that apartment.

Officer Steven Cobb, one of the uniformed officers who approached the door, testified that the officers banged on the left apartment door "as loud as [they] could" and announced, "This is the police" or "Police, police, police." Cobb said that "[a]s soon as [the officers] started banging on the door," they "could hear people inside moving," and "[i]t sounded as [though] things were being moved inside the apartment." These noises, Cobb testified, led the officers to believe that drug-related evidence was about to be destroyed.

At that point, the officers announced that they "were going to make entry inside the apartment." Cobb then kicked in the door, the officers entered the apartment, and they found three people in the front room: respondent Hollis King, respondent's girlfriend, and a guest who was smoking marijuana. The officers performed a protective sweep of the apartment during which they saw marijuana and powder cocaine in plain view. In a subsequent search, they also discovered crack cocaine, cash, and drug paraphernalia.

Police eventually entered the apartment on the right. Inside, they found the suspected drug dealer who was the initial target of their investigation.

In the Fayette County Circuit Court, a grand jury charged respondent with trafficking in marijuana, first-degree trafficking in a controlled substance, and second-degree persistent felony offender status. Respondent filed a motion to suppress the evidence from the warrantless search, but the Circuit Court denied the motion. The Circuit Court concluded that the officers had probable cause to investigate the marijuana odor and that the officers "properly conducted [the investigation] by initially knocking on the door of the apartment unit and awaiting the response or consensual entry." Exigent circumstances justified the warrantless entry, the court held, because "there was no response at all to the knocking," and because "Officer Cobb heard movement in the apartment which he reasonably concluded were persons in the act of destroying evidence, particularly narcotics because of the smell." Respondent then entered a conditional guilty plea, reserving his right to appeal the denial of his suppression motion. The court sentenced respondent to 11 years' imprisonment. [The Supreme Court of Kentucky reversed.] * * *

Over the years, lower courts have developed an exception to the exigent circumstances rule, the so-called "police-created exigency" doctrine.

Under this doctrine, police may not rely on the need to prevent destruction of evidence when that exigency was "created" or "manufactured" by the conduct of the police.

In applying this exception for the "creation" or "manufacturing" of an exigency by the police, courts require something more than mere proof that fear of detection by the police caused the destruction of evidence. An additional showing is obviously needed because * * * "in some sense the police always create the exigent circumstances." That is to say, in the vast majority of cases in which evidence is destroyed by persons who are engaged in illegal conduct, the reason for the destruction is fear that the evidence will fall into the hands of law enforcement. * * * Consequently, a rule that precludes the police from making a warrantless entry to prevent the destruction of evidence whenever their conduct causes the exigency would unreasonably shrink the reach of this well-established exception to the warrant requirement.

Presumably for the purpose of avoiding such a result, the lower courts have held that the police-created exigency doctrine requires more than simple causation, but the lower courts have not agreed on the test to be applied. Indeed, the petition in this case maintains that "[t]here are currently five different tests being used by the United States Courts of Appeals," and that some state courts have crafted additional tests.

Despite the welter of tests devised by the lower courts, the answer to the question presented in this case follows directly and clearly from the principle that permits warrantless searches in the first place. As previously noted, warrantless searches are allowed when the circumstances make it reasonable, within the meaning of the Fourth Amendment, to dispense with the warrant requirement. Therefore, the answer to the question before us is that the exigent circumstances rule justifies a warrantless search when the conduct of the police preceding the exigency is reasonable in the same sense. Where, as here, the police did not create the exigency by engaging or threatening to engage in conduct that violates the Fourth Amendment, warrantless entry to prevent the destruction of evidence is reasonable and thus allowed.[1] * * *

Some lower courts have adopted a rule that is similar to the one that we recognize today. But others, including the Kentucky Supreme Court, have imposed additional requirements that are unsound and that we now reject.

---

[1] There is a strong argument to be made that, at least in most circumstances, the exigent circumstances rule should not apply where the police, without a warrant or any legally sound basis for a warrantless entry, threaten that they will enter without permission unless admitted. In this case, however, no such actual threat was made, and therefore we have no need to reach that question.

Bad faith. Some courts, including the Kentucky Supreme Court, ask whether law enforcement officers "deliberately created the exigent circumstances with the bad faith intent to avoid the warrant requirement."

This approach is fundamentally inconsistent with our Fourth Amendment jurisprudence. "Our cases have repeatedly rejected" a subjective approach, asking only whether "the circumstances, viewed *objectively*, justify the action." Indeed, we have never held, outside limited contexts such as an "inventory search or administrative inspection . . . , that an officer's motive invalidates objectively justifiable behavior under the Fourth Amendment." * * *

Reasonable foreseeability. Some courts, again including the Kentucky Supreme Court, hold that police may not rely on an exigency if "it was reasonably foreseeable that the investigative tactics employed by the police would create the exigent circumstances." Courts applying this test have invalidated warrantless home searches on the ground that it was reasonably foreseeable that police officers, by knocking on the door and announcing their presence, would lead a drug suspect to destroy evidence.

* * * The reasonable foreseeability test would create unacceptable and unwarranted difficulties for law enforcement officers who must make quick decisions in the field, as well as for judges who would be required to determine after the fact whether the destruction of evidence in response to a knock on the door was reasonably foreseeable based on what the officers knew at the time.

Probable cause and time to secure a warrant. Some courts, in applying the police-created exigency doctrine, fault law enforcement officers if, after acquiring evidence that is sufficient to establish probable cause to search particular premises, the officers do not seek a warrant but instead knock on the door and seek either to speak with an occupant or to obtain consent to search.

This approach unjustifiably interferes with legitimate law enforcement strategies. There are many entirely proper reasons why police may not want to seek a search warrant as soon as the bare minimum of evidence needed to establish probable cause is acquired. Without attempting to provide a comprehensive list of these reasons, we note a few.

First, the police may wish to speak with the occupants of a dwelling before deciding whether it is worthwhile to seek authorization for a search. * * * Second, the police may want to ask an occupant of the premises for consent to search because doing so is simpler, faster, and less burdensome than applying for a warrant. * * * Third, law enforcement officers may wish to obtain more evidence before submitting what might otherwise be considered a marginal warrant application. Fourth, prosecutors may wish to wait until they acquire evidence that can justify a search that is broader in scope than the search that a judicial officer is likely to authorize based on the evidence then available. And finally, * * * law enforcement may not want to execute a search that will disclose the existence of an investigation because doing so may interfere with the acquisition of additional evidence against those already under suspicion or evidence about additional but as yet unknown participants in a criminal scheme. * * *

Standard or good investigative tactics. Finally, some lower court cases suggest that law enforcement officers may be found to have created or manufactured an exigency if the court concludes that the course of their investigation was "contrary to standard or good law enforcement practices (or to the policies or practices of their jurisdictions)." This approach fails to provide clear guidance for law enforcement officers and authorizes courts to make judgments on matters that are the province of those who are responsible for federal and state law enforcement agencies. * * *

For these reasons, we conclude that the exigent circumstances rule applies when the police do not gain entry to premises by means of an actual or threatened violation of the Fourth Amendment. This holding provides ample protection for the privacy rights that the Amendment protects.

When law enforcement officers who are not armed with a warrant knock on a door, they do no more than any private citizen might do. And whether the person who knocks on the door and requests the opportunity to speak is a police officer or a private citizen, the occupant has no obligation to open the door or to speak. When the police knock on a door but the occupants choose not to respond or to speak, "the investigation will have reached a conspicuously low point," and the occupants "will have the kind of warning that even the most elaborate security system cannot provide." And even if an occupant chooses to open the door and speak with the officers, the occupant need not allow the officers to enter the premises and may refuse to answer any questions at any time.

Occupants who choose not to stand on their constitutional rights but instead elect to attempt to destroy evidence have only themselves to blame for the warrantless exigent-circumstances search that may ensue.

We now apply our interpretation of the police-created exigency doctrine to the facts of this case. * * * In this case, we see no evidence that the officers either violated the Fourth Amendment or threatened to do so prior to the point when they entered the apartment. Officer Cobb testified without contradiction that the officers "banged on the door as loud as [they] could" and announced either "Police, police, police" or "This is the police." This conduct was entirely consistent with the Fourth Amendment, and we are aware of no other evidence that might show that the officers either violated the Fourth Amendment or threatened to do so. * * *

Like the court below, we assume for purposes of argument that an exigency existed. Because the officers in this case did not violate or threaten to violate the Fourth Amendment prior to the exigency, we hold that the exigency justified the warrantless search of the apartment.

The judgment of the Kentucky Supreme Court is reversed, and the case is remanded for further proceedings not inconsistent with this opinion.

It is so ordered.

JUSTICE GINSBURG, dissenting.

The Court today arms the police with a way routinely to dishonor the Fourth Amendment's warrant requirement in drug cases. In lieu of presenting their evidence to a neutral magistrate, police officers may now knock, listen, then break the door down, never mind that they had ample time to obtain a warrant. I dissent from the Court's reduction of the Fourth Amendment's force. * * *

CHAPTER 16

THE EXCLUSIONARY RULE

■ ■ ■

Since 1914, exclusion of evidence obtained in violation of the Fourth Amendment at trial has been the primary remedy for a violation of the Fourth Amendment in federal criminal court. Whether the exclusionary rule should apply to the states through the Due Process Clause has been the subject of vigorous debate since the Fourth Amendment does not specify the remedy for a violation of its mandates. In *Wolf v. Colorado*, the Court comes out one way in this debate. A mere twelve years later, the Court comes out the opposite way in *Mapp v. Ohio*.

Following *Mapp v. Ohio* are two excerpts. One is an article by former Supreme Court Justice Potter Stewart, defending the Court's decision in *Mapp* to apply the exclusionary rule to the states. Justice Stewart's article is particularly interesting because Justice Stewart did not join the majority opinion in *Mapp*. The second is an article about the life of Dollree Mapp, the Black woman at the center of the *Mapp* case who has been called the "Rosa Parks of the Fourth Amendment."

In *United States v. Leon*, we see the Court start to backtrack from its embrace of the exclusionary rule in *Mapp*. The Court in *Leon* creates a good-faith exception to the exclusionary rule, permitting the admission of illegally seized evidence when the officer reasonably relies on a search warrant later deemed invalid because it was lacking in probable cause. Since *Leon*, the Court has expanded the good faith exception, permitting the admission of evidence seized in violation of the Fourth Amendment in many other contexts. *Herring v. United States* represents an example of this trend.

The last three cases in this chapter introduce us to the fruit of the poisonous tree doctrine. The fruit of the poisonous tree doctrine extends the exclusionary rule, requiring that in addition to evidence obtained directly from a constitutional violation, any evidence *derived* from that illegally obtained evidence must also be excluded at trial. In *Wong Sun v. United States*, we see the Court applying the fruit of the poisonous tree doctrine and learn there are exceptions to this rule of exclusion. *Nix v. Williams* discusses two of those exceptions—the inevitable discovery exception and the independent source doctrine. *Utah v. Strieff* explains a third exception, the attenuation doctrine.

WOLF v. COLORADO
Supreme Court of the United States
338 U.S. 25, 69 S. Ct. 1359, 93 L. Ed. 1782 (1949)

JUSTICE FRANKFURTER delivered the opinion of the Court.

The precise question for consideration is this: Does a conviction by a State court for a State offense deny the "due process of law" required by the Fourteenth Amendment, solely because evidence that was admitted at the trial was obtained under circumstances which would have rendered it inadmissible in a prosecution for violation of a federal law in a court of the United States because there deemed to be an infraction of the Fourth Amendment. * * *

The security of one's privacy against arbitrary intrusion by the police—which is at the core of the Fourth Amendment—is basic to a free society. It is therefore implicit in "the concept of ordered liberty" and as such enforceable against the States through the Due Process Clause. The knock at the door, whether by day or by night, as a prelude to a search, without authority of law but solely on the authority of the police, did not need the commentary of recent history to be condemned as inconsistent with the conception of human rights enshrined in the history and the basic constitutional documents of English-speaking peoples.

Accordingly, we have no hesitation in saying that were a State affirmatively to sanction such police incursion into privacy it would run counter to the guaranty of the Fourteenth Amendment. But the ways of enforcing such a basic right raise questions of a different order. How such arbitrary conduct should be checked, what remedies against it should be afforded, the means by which the right should be made effective, are all questions that are not to be so dogmatically answered as to preclude the varying solutions which spring from an allowable range of judgment on issues not susceptible of quantitative solution.

In *Weeks v. United States*, this Court held that in a federal prosecution the Fourth Amendment barred the use of evidence secured through an illegal search and seizure. This ruling * * * was not derived from the explicit requirements of the Fourth Amendment; it was not based on legislation expressing Congressional policy in the enforcement of the Constitution. The decision was a matter of judicial implication. Since then it has been frequently applied and we stoutly adhere to it. But the immediate question is whether the basic right to protection against arbitrary intrusion by the police demands the exclusion of logically relevant evidence obtained by an unreasonable search and seizure because, in a federal prosecution for a federal crime, it would be excluded. As a matter of inherent reason, one would suppose this to be an issue to which men with complete devotion to the protection of the right of privacy might give different answers. When we find that in fact most of the English-speaking world does not regard as vital to such protection the exclusion of evidence thus obtained, we must hesitate to treat this remedy as an essential ingredient of the right. The contrariety of views of the States is particularly impressive in view of the careful reconsideration which they have given the problem in the light of the *Weeks* decision. * * *

As of today 30 States reject the *Weeks* doctrine, 17 States are in agreement with it. Of 10 jurisdictions within the United Kingdom and the British Commonwealth of Nations which have passed on the question, none has held evidence obtained by illegal search and seizure inadmissible.

The jurisdictions which have rejected the *Weeks* doctrine have not left the right to privacy without other means of protection. Indeed, the exclusion of evidence is a remedy which directly serves only to protect those upon whose person or premises something incriminating has been found. We cannot, therefore, regard it as a departure from basic standards to remand such persons, together with those who emerge scatheless from a search, to the remedies of private action and such protection as the internal discipline of the police, under the eyes of an alert public opinion, may afford. Granting that in practice the exclusion of evidence may be an effective way of deterring unreasonable searches, it is not for this Court to condemn as falling below the minimal standards assured by the Due Process Clause a State's reliance upon other methods which, if consistently enforced, would be equally effective. * * * The public opinion of a community can far more effectively be exerted against oppressive conduct on the part of police directly responsible to the community itself than can local opinion, sporadically aroused, be brought to bear upon remote authority pervasively exerted throughout the country.

We hold, therefore, that in a prosecution in a State court for a State crime the Fourteenth Amendment does not forbid the admission of evidence obtained by an unreasonable search and seizure. * * *

JUSTICE BLACK, concurring. * * *

I agree with what appears to be a plain implication of the Court's opinion that the federal exclusionary rule is not a command of the Fourth Amendment but is a judicially created rule of evidence which Congress might negate. * * *

JUSTICE DOUGLAS, dissenting.

I believe for the reasons stated by Mr. Justice Black in his dissent in *Adamson v. California*, that the Fourth Amendment is applicable to the States. I agree with Mr. Justice Murphy that the evidence obtained in violation of it must be excluded in state prosecutions as well as in federal prosecutions, since in absence of that rule of evidence the Amendment would have no effective sanction. I also agree with him that under that test this evidence was improperly admitted and that the judgments of conviction must be reversed.

JUSTICE MURPHY with whom JUSTICE RUTLEDGE joins, dissenting.

It is disheartening to find so much that is right in an opinion which seems to me so fundamentally wrong. Of course I agree with the Court that the Fourteenth Amendment prohibits activities which are proscribed by the search and seizure clause of the Fourth Amendment. * * *

Imagination and zeal may invent a dozen methods to give content to the commands of the Fourth Amendment. But this Court is limited to the remedies currently available. It cannot legislate the ideal system. If we would attempt the enforcement of the search and seizure clause in the ordinary case today, we are limited to three devices: judicial exclusion of the illegally obtained evidence; criminal prosecution of violators; and civil action against violators in the action of trespass.

* * * [T]here is but one alternative to the rule of exclusion. That is no sanction at all. This has been perfectly clear since 1914, when a unanimous Court decided *Weeks v. United States*. "If letters and private documents can thus be seized and held and used in evidence against a citizen accused of an offense," we said, "the protection of the 4th Amendment, declaring his right to be secure against such searches and seizures, is of no value, and, so far as those thus placed are concerned, might as well be stricken from the Constitution." "It would reduce the Fourth Amendment to a form of words."

Today the Court wipes those statements from the books with its bland citation of "other remedies." Little need be said concerning the possibilities of criminal prosecution. Self-scrutiny is a lofty ideal, but its exaltation reaches new heights if we expect a District Attorney to prosecute himself or his associates for well-meaning violations of the search and seizure clause during a raid the District Attorney or his associates have ordered. But there is an appealing ring in another alternative. A trespass action for damages is a venerable means of securing reparation for unauthorized invasion of the home. Why not put the old writ to a new use? When the Court cites cases permitting the action, the remedy seems complete.

But what an illusory remedy this is, if by "remedy" we mean a positive deterrent to police and prosecutors tempted to violate the Fourth Amendment. The appealing ring softens when we recall that in a trespass action the measure of damages is simply the extent of the injury to physical property. If the officer searches with care, he can avoid all but nominal damages—a penny, or a dollar. Are punitive damages possible? Perhaps. But a few states permit none, whatever the circumstances. In those that do, the plaintiff must show the real ill will or malice of the defendant, and surely it is not unreasonable to assume that one in honest pursuit of crime bears no malice toward the search victim. If that burden is carried, recovery may yet be defeated by the rule that there must be physical damages before punitive damages may be awarded. In addition, some states limit punitive damages to the actual expenses of litigation. * * * Even assuming the ill will of the officer, his reasonable grounds for belief that the home he searched harbored evidence of crime is admissible in mitigation of punitive damages. The bad reputation of the plaintiff is likewise admissible. If the evidence seized was actually used at a trial, that fact has been held a complete justification of the search, and a defense against the trespass action. And even if the plaintiff hurdles all these obstacles, and gains a substantial verdict, the individual officer's finances may well make the judgment useless—for the municipality, of course, is not liable without its consent. Is it surprising that there is so little in the books concerning trespass actions for violation of the search and seizure clause?

[JUSTICE RUTLEDGE's dissenting opinion has been omitted.]

MAPP V. OHIO
Supreme Court of the United States
367 U.S. 643, 81 S. Ct. 1684, 6 L. Ed. 2d 1081 (1961)

JUSTICE CLARK delivered the opinion of the Court.

Appellant stands convicted of knowingly having had in her possession and under her control certain lewd and lascivious books, pictures, and photographs in violation of § 2905.34 of Ohio's Revised Code. [T]he Supreme Court of Ohio found that her conviction was valid though "based primarily upon the introduction in evidence of lewd and lascivious books and pictures unlawfully seized during an unlawful search of defendant's home...."

On May 23, 1957, three Cleveland police officers arrived at appellant's residence in that city pursuant to information that "a person [was] hiding out in the home, who was wanted for questioning in connection with a recent bombing, and that there was a large amount of policy paraphernalia being hidden in the home." Miss Mapp and her daughter by a former marriage lived on the top floor of the two-family dwelling. Upon their arrival at that house, the officers knocked on the door and demanded entrance but appellant, after telephoning her attorney, refused to admit them without a search warrant. They advised their headquarters of the situation and undertook a surveillance of the house.

The officers again sought entrance some three hours later when four or more additional officers arrived on the scene. When Miss Mapp did not come to the door immediately, at least one of the several doors to the house was forcibly opened and the policemen gained admittance. Meanwhile Miss Mapp's attorney arrived, but the officers, having secured their own entry, and continuing in their defiance of the law, would permit him neither to see Miss Mapp nor to enter the house. It appears that Miss Mapp was halfway down the stairs from the upper floor to the front door when the officers, in this highhanded manner, broke into the hall. She demanded to see the search warrant. A paper, claimed to be a warrant, was held up by one of the officers. She grabbed the "warrant" and placed it in her bosom. A struggle ensued in which the officers recovered the piece of paper and as a result of which they handcuffed appellant because she had been "belligerent" in resisting their official rescue of the "warrant" from her person. Running roughshod over appellant, a policeman "grabbed" her, "twisted [her] hand," and she "yelled [and] pleaded with him" because "it was hurting." Appellant, in handcuffs, was then forcibly taken upstairs to her bedroom where the officers searched a dresser, a chest of drawers, a closet and some suitcases. They also looked into a photo album and through personal papers belonging to the appellant. The search spread to the rest of the second floor including the child's bedroom, the living room, the kitchen and a dinette. The basement of the building and a trunk found therein were also searched. The obscene materials for possession of which she was ultimately convicted were discovered in the course of that widespread search.

At the trial no search warrant was produced by the prosecution, nor was the failure to produce one explained or accounted for. At best, "There is, in the record, considerable doubt as to whether there ever was any warrant for the search of defendant's home." * * *

The State says that even if the search were made without authority, or otherwise unreasonably, it is not prevented from using the unconstitutionally seized evidence at trial, citing *Wolf v. Colorado* in which this Court did indeed hold "that in a prosecution in a State court for a State crime the Fourteenth Amendment does not forbid the admission of evidence obtained by an unreasonable search and seizure." On this appeal, * * * it is urged once again that we review that holding. * * *

In 1949, * * * this Court, in *Wolf v. People of State of Colorado*, * * * discussed the effect of the Fourth Amendment upon the States through the operation of the Due Process Clause of the Fourteenth Amendment. It said: "[W]e have no hesitation in saying that were a State affirmatively to sanction such police incursion into privacy it would run counter to the guaranty of the Fourteenth Amendment."

Nevertheless, after declaring that the "security of one's privacy against arbitrary intrusion by the police" is "implicit in 'the concept of ordered liberty' and as such enforceable against the States through the Due Process Clause,'" and announcing that it "stoutly adhere(d)" to the *Weeks* decision, the Court decided that the *Weeks* exclusionary rule would not then be imposed upon the States as "an essential ingredient of the right." The Court's reasons for not considering essential to the right to privacy, as a curb imposed upon the States by the Due Process Clause, that which decades before had been posited as part and parcel of the Fourth Amendment's limitations upon federal encroachment of individual privacy, were bottomed on factual considerations. * * *

The Court in *Wolf* first stated that "[t]he contrariety of views of the States" on the adoption of the exclusionary rule of *Weeks* was "particularly impressive" and, in this connection that it could not "brush aside the experience of States which deem the incidence of such conduct by the police too slight to call for a deterrent remedy ... by overriding the [States'] relevant rules of evidence." While in 1949, prior to the *Wolf* case, almost two-thirds of the States were opposed to the use of the exclusionary rule, now, despite the *Wolf* case, more than half of those since passing upon it, by their own legislative or judicial decision, have wholly or partly adopted or adhered to the *Weeks* rule. Significantly, among those now following the rule is California, which, according to its highest court, was "compelled to reach that conclusion because other remedies have completely failed to secure compliance with the constitutional provisions...." In connection with this California case, we note that the second basis elaborated in *Wolf* in support of its failure to enforce the exclusionary doctrine against the States was that "other means of protection" have been afforded "the right to privacy." The experience of California that such other remedies have been worthless and futile is buttressed by the experience of other States.

* * * Today we once again examine *Wolf*'s constitutional documentation of the right to privacy free from unreasonable state intrusion, and, after its dozen years on our books, are led by it to close the only courtroom door remaining open to evidence secured by official lawlessness in flagrant abuse of that basic right, reserved to all persons as a specific guarantee against that very same unlawful conduct. We hold that all evidence obtained by searches and seizures in violation of the Constitution is, by that same authority, inadmissible in a state court.

Since the Fourth Amendment's right of privacy has been declared enforceable against the States through the Due Process Clause of the Fourteenth, it is enforceable against them by the same sanction of exclusion as is used against the Federal Government. Were it otherwise, then just as without the *Weeks* rule the assurance against unreasonable federal searches and seizures would be "a form of words," valueless and undeserving of mention in a perpetual charter of inestimable human liberties, so too, without that rule the freedom from state invasions of privacy would be so ephemeral and so neatly severed from its conceptual nexus with the freedom from all brutish means of coercing evidence as not to merit this Court's high regard as a freedom "implicit in 'the concept of ordered liberty.'" At the time that the Court held in *Wolf* that the Amendment was applicable to the States through the Due Process Clause, the cases of this Court, as we have seen, had steadfastly held that as to federal officers the Fourth Amendment included the exclusion of the evidence seized in violation of its provisions. Even *Wolf* "stoutly adhered" to that proposition. * * * [I]n extending the substantive protections of due process to all constitutionally unreasonable searches—state or federal—it was logically and constitutionally necessary that the exclusion doctrine— an essential part of the right to privacy—be also insisted upon as an essential ingredient of the right newly recognized by the *Wolf* case. In short, the admission of the new constitutional right by *Wolf* could not consistently tolerate denial of its most important constitutional privilege, namely, the exclusion of the evidence which an accused had been forced to give by reason of the unlawful seizure. To hold otherwise is to grant the right but in reality to withhold its privilege and enjoyment. Only last year the Court itself recognized that the purpose of the exclusionary rule "is to deter—to compel respect for the constitutional guaranty in the only effectively available way—by removing the incentive to disregard it." * * *

Moreover, our holding that the exclusionary rule is an essential part of both the Fourth and Fourteenth Amendments is not only the logical dictate of prior cases, but it also makes very good sense. There is no war between the Constitution and common sense. Presently, a federal prosecutor may make no use of evidence illegally seized, but a State's attorney across the street may, although he supposedly is operating under the enforceable prohibitions of the same Amendment. Thus the State, by admitting evidence unlawfully seized, serves to encourage disobedience to the Federal Constitution which it is bound to uphold. Moreover, as was said in *Elkins*, "the very essence of a healthy federalism depends upon the avoidance of needless conflict between state and federal courts." * * *

There are those who say, as did Justice (then Judge) Cardozo, that under our constitutional exclusionary doctrine "the criminal is to go free because the constable has blundered." In some cases this will undoubtedly be the result. But, as was said in *Elkins*, "there is another consideration— the imperative of judicial integrity." The criminal goes free, if he must, but it is the law that sets him free. Nothing can destroy a government more quickly than its failure to observe its own laws, or worse, its disregard of the charter of its own existence. As Mr. Justice Brandeis, dissenting, said in *Olmstead v. United States*: "Our government is the potent, the omnipresent teacher. For good or for ill, it teaches the whole people by its example. . . . If the government becomes a lawbreaker, it breeds contempt for law; it invites every man to become a law unto himself; it invites anarchy." Nor can it lightly be assumed that, as a practical matter, adoption of the exclusionary rule fetters law enforcement. Only last year this Court expressly considered that contention and found that "pragmatic evidence of a sort" to the contrary was not wanting. The Court noted that

> The federal courts themselves have operated under the exclusionary rule of *Weeks* for almost half a century; yet it has not

been suggested either that the Federal Bureau of Investigation has thereby been rendered ineffective, or that the administration of criminal justice in the federal courts has thereby been disrupted. * * *

The ignoble shortcut to conviction left open to the State tends to destroy the entire system of constitutional restraints on which the liberties of the people rest. Having once recognized that the right to privacy embodied in the Fourth Amendment is enforceable against the States, and that the right to be secure against rude invasions of privacy by state officers is, therefore, constitutional in origin, we can no longer permit that right to remain an empty promise. Because it is enforceable in the same manner and to like effect as other basic rights secured by the Due Process Clause, we can no longer permit it to be revocable at the whim of any police officer who, in the name of law enforcement itself, chooses to suspend its enjoyment. Our decision, founded on reason and truth, gives to the individual no more than that which the Constitution guarantees him, to the police officer no less than that to which honest law enforcement is entitled, and, to the courts, that judicial integrity so necessary in the true administration of justice. * * *

Reversed and remanded.

JUSTICE DOUGLAS, concurring. * * *

I believe that this is an appropriate case in which to put an end to the asymmetry which *Wolf* imported into the law. * * *

Memorandum of JUSTICE STEWART. * * *

I express no view as to the merits of the constitutional issue which the Court today decides. * * *

JUSTICE HARLAN whom JUSTICE FRANKFURTER and JUSTICE WHITTAKER join, dissenting.

In overruling the *Wolf* case the Court, in my opinion, has forgotten the sense of judicial restraint which, with due regard for *stare decisis*, is one element that should enter into deciding whether a past decision of this Court should be overruled. Apart from that I also believe that the *Wolf* rule represents sounder Constitutional doctrine than the new rule which now replaces it.

* * * [T]he new and pivotal issue brought to the Court by this appeal is whether § 2905.34 of the Ohio Revised Code making criminal the mere knowing possession or control of obscene material, and under which appellant has been convicted, is consistent with the rights of free thought and expression assured against state action by the Fourteenth Amendment. That was the principal issue which was decided by the Ohio

Supreme Court, which was tendered by appellant's Jurisdictional Statement, and which was briefed and argued in this Court.

In this posture of things, I think it fair to say that five members of this Court have simply "reached out" to overrule *Wolf*. With all respect for the views of the majority, and recognizing that *stare decisis* carries different weight in Constitutional adjudication than it does in nonconstitutional decision, I can perceive no justification for regarding this case as an appropriate occasion for re-examining *Wolf*. * * *

The occasion which the Court has taken here is in the context of a case where the question was briefed not at all and argued only extremely tangentially. The unwisdom of overruling *Wolf* without full-dress argument is aggravated by the circumstance that that decision is a comparatively recent one (1949) to which three members of the present majority have at one time or other expressly subscribed, one to be sure with explicit misgivings. I would think that our obligation to the States, on whom we impose this new rule, as well as the obligation of orderly adherence to our own processes would demand that we seek that aid which adequate briefing and argument lends to the determination of an important issue. It certainly has never been a postulate of judicial power that mere altered disposition, or subsequent membership on the Court, is sufficient warrant for overturning a deliberately decided rule of Constitutional law.

* * * [W]hat the Court is now doing is to impose upon the States not only federal substantive standards of "search and seizure" but also the basic federal remedy for violation of those standards. For I think it entirely clear that the *Weeks* exclusionary rule is but a remedy which, by penalizing past official misconduct, is aimed at deterring such conduct in the future.

I would not impose upon the States this federal exclusionary remedy. The reasons given by the majority for now suddenly turning its back on *Wolf* seem to me notably unconvincing.

First, it is said that "the factual grounds upon which *Wolf* was based" have since changed, in that more States now follow the *Weeks* exclusionary rule than was so at the time *Wolf* was decided. While that is true, a recent survey indicates that at present one-half of the States still adhere to the common-law non-exclusionary rule, and one, Maryland, retains the rule as to felonies. But in any case surely all this is beside the point, as the majority itself indeed seems to recognize. Our concern here, as it was in *Wolf*, is not with the desirability of that rule but only with the question whether the States are Constitutionally free to follow it or not as they may themselves determine, and the relevance of the disparity of views among the States on this point lies simply in the fact that the judgment involved is a debatable one. * * *

The preservation of a proper balance between state and federal responsibility in the administration of criminal justice demands patience on the part of those who might like to see things move faster among the States in this respect. Problems of criminal law enforcement vary widely from State of State. One State, in considering the totality of its legal picture, may conclude that the need for embracing the *Weeks* rule is pressing because other remedies are unavailable or inadequate to secure compliance with the substantive Constitutional principle involved. Another, though equally solicitous of Constitutional rights, may choose to pursue one purpose at a time, allowing all evidence relevant to guilt to be brought into a criminal trial, and dealing with Constitutional infractions by other means. Still another may consider the exclusionary rule too rough-and-ready a remedy, in that it reaches only unconstitutional intrusions which eventuate in criminal prosecution of the victims. Further, a State after experimenting with the *Weeks* rule for a time may, because of unsatisfactory experience with it, decide to revert to a non-exclusionary rule. And so on. * * * For us the question remains, as it has always been, one of state power, not one of passing judgment on the wisdom of one state course or another. In my view this Court should continue to forbear from fettering the States with an adamant rule which may embarrass them in coping with their own peculiar problems in criminal law enforcement.

Further, we are told that imposition of the *Weeks* rule on the States makes "very good sense," in that it will promote recognition by state and federal officials of their "mutual obligation to respect the same fundamental criteria" in their approach to law enforcement, and will avoid "needless conflict between state and federal courts." * * *

An approach which regards the issue as one of achieving procedural symmetry or of serving administrative convenience surely disfigures the boundaries of this Court's functions in relation to the state and federal courts. Our role in promulgating the *Weeks* rule and its extensions * * * was quite a different one than it is here. There, in implementing the Fourth Amendment, we occupied the position of a tribunal having the ultimate responsibility for developing the standards and procedures of judicial administration within the judicial system over which it presides. Here we review state procedures whose measure is to be taken not against the specific substantive commands of the Fourth Amendment but under the flexible contours of the Due Process Clause. I do not believe that the Fourteenth Amendment empowers this Court to mould [sic] state remedies effectuating the right to freedom from "arbitrary intrusion by the police" to suit its own notions of how things should be done. * * *

[JUSTICE BLACK's concurring opinion has been omitted.]

THE ROAD TO MAPP V. OHIO AND BEYOND: THE ORIGINS, DEVELOPMENT AND FUTURE OF THE EXCLUSIONARY RULE IN SEARCH-AND-SEIZURE CASES

Potter Stewart
83 Colum. L. Rev. 1365 (1983)

Let us pick up the threads of our story at the home of Dollree Mapp, in Cleveland, Ohio, on May 27, 1957. Mapp lived on the second floor of a two-family brick house and rented out rooms to boarders. In mid-May, three police officers appeared at her home and demanded entrance, explaining that they were searching for a man in connection with a recent bombing. After consulting by telephone with her attorney, Mapp refused to admit them without a search warrant. The officers returned later, with others, and forced their way in. After Mapp asked to see the officers' search warrant, the officers produced a piece of paper, which Mapp grabbed and placed down the front of her blouse. A fracas ensued when one of the officers tried to retrieve the piece of paper. After handcuffing Mapp, the officers searched the house. No bombing suspect was ever found and no search warrant was ever produced. The officers did, however, find four books—*Affairs of a Troubadour, Little Darlings, London Stage Affairs*, and *Memories of a Hotel Man*—as well as a hand-drawn picture described in the state's brief as being "of a very obscene nature."

Dollree Mapp was arrested, tried for and convicted of possession of obscene materials. After the Ohio Court of Appeals and the Supreme Court of Ohio affirmed her conviction, Mapp appealed to the United States Supreme Court.

* * * The substantial federal question that prompted the Supreme Court to hear the appeal was whether the Ohio statute was vague and overbroad in violation of the first and fourteenth amendments' free press guarantee; the overwhelming portion of the briefs and virtually all of the oral argument were devoted to this issue.

In fact, until the circulation of the first draft of the majority opinion, the issue that the Court ultimately was to decide had been mentioned only by an amicus curiae, the ACLU. Its twenty-page brief included only a three-sentence paragraph at the very end asking the Court to overrule its 1949 decision in *Wolf v. Colorado*, which had held that state courts were not required to exclude evidence seized in violation of the fourth and fourteenth amendments. That the ACLU's argument was not regarded by the parties as even a remotely important issue in the case was made clear at the oral argument. The appellant's lawyer was asked whether he was requesting the Court to overrule the *Wolf* case and, thus, to exclude the fruits of an illegal search at a state trial. He answered, quite candidly, that he had never heard of the *Wolf* case.

In any event, Dollree Mapp was to go free. At the conference following the argument, a majority of the Justices agreed that the Ohio statute violated the *first* and fourteenth amendments. Justice Tom Clark was assigned the job of writing the opinion of the Court.

What transpired in the month following our conference on the case is really a matter of speculation on my part, but I have always suspected that the members of the soon-to-be *Mapp* majority had met in what I affectionately call a "rump caucus" to discuss a different basis for their decision. But regardless of how they reached their decision, five Justices of the Court concluded that the fourth and fourteenth amendments required that evidence seized in an illegal search be excluded from state trials as well as federal ones. *Wolf* was to be overruled.

I was shocked when Justice Clark's proposed Court opinion reached my desk. I immediately wrote him a note expressing my surprise and questioning the wisdom of overruling an important doctrine in a case in which the issue was not briefed, argued, or discussed by the state courts, by the parties' counsel, or at our conference following the oral argument. After my shock subsided, I wrote a brief memorandum concurring in the judgment on first and fourteenth amendment grounds, and agreeing with Justice Harlan's dissent that the issue which the majority decided was not properly before the Court. The *Mapp* majority stood its ground, however; only Justices Frankfurter and Whittaker joined Justice Harlan's dissent.

The case of *Mapp v. Ohio* provides significant insight into the judicial process and the evolution of law—a first amendment controversy was transformed into perhaps the most important search-and-seizure decision in history. * * *

DOLLREE MAPP, 1923–2014: "THE ROSA PARKS OF THE FOURTH AMENDMENT"

Ken Armstrong
The Marshall Project filed December 8, 2014

Time is not always kind to the people whose names get attached to landmark legal cases. Ernesto Miranda, the defendant whose 1966 Supreme Court case forced police to inform suspects of their basic rights ("You have the right to remain silent . . . ") was stabbed to death in a skid-row bar. Clarence Gideon won a 1963 Supreme Court case, *Gideon v. Wainwright*, that established the right of poor defendants to court-appointed lawyers. When he died a decade later the former mayor of his hometown recalled him as a "no-good punk." It fell to the American Civil Liberties Union to put a marker on his grave.

Before the *Gideon* ruling, before *Miranda*, there was *Mapp v. Ohio*, the 1961 Supreme Court decision some legal scholars credit with launching a "due process revolution" in American law. The *Mapp* ruling changed policing in America by requiring state courts to throw out evidence if it had been seized illegally. The woman behind the ruling, Dollree "Dolly" Mapp, died six weeks ago in a small town in Georgia, with virtually no notice paid. She was 91, as best we can tell.

Mapp's life was as colorful and momentous as her death was quiet. She went from being a single teenage mother in Mississippi to associating with renowned boxers and racketeers in Cleveland to making her way in New York City, where she launched one business after another. "Some of them were legitimate, and some of them were whatever they were," said her niece, Carolyn Mapp, who looked after her aunt in her final years. Along the way she tangled with police, and when she stood up to them in Cleveland—a black woman, staring down a phalanx of white officers in the 1950s—she made history.

Wayne LaFave, professor of law emeritus at the University of Illinois and a leading scholar on search and seizure, called her the "Rosa Parks of the Fourth Amendment." From talking to Mapp's family and friends, it's clear that she wasn't always easy to get along with. "She could be difficult, OK?" said Deidra Smith, a friend of about 40 years who adds: "She was brilliant and beautiful and bold." It was Mapp's boldness—"strong willed," is how she's described, time and again—that most defined and served her as she confronted illegal police tactics and draconian laws. Mapp was at her most determined "if you told her no. That just meant yes to her," said Carolyn Mapp, who lives in Georgia. "She didn't let go of anything."

In 1957, Dollree Mapp, an African American woman then in her 30s, rented half of a two-family house in Cleveland, where she lived with her daughter. Although she had no criminal record, she had ties to Cleveland's underworld. Mapp was divorced from Jimmy Bivins, a great boxer of the era who defeated eight world champions but never got a title fight. Mapp had accused Bivins of beating her—"I had to leave him or kill him, and I wasn't ready to kill him," she would later tell one author. (Bivins had accused Mapp of trying to destroy his career by feeding him fatty foods.) After the split Mapp had been briefly engaged to boxer Archie Moore, the light heavyweight champion. But they never married, and she later sued for breach of promise.

In May of that year, police were investigating a bombing at the house of Don King—a numbers racketeer who later became a famed boxing promoter—when they received a tip that a suspect might be hiding in Mapp's home. Three officers showed up at Mapp's place, demanding to be let in. Mapp refused. She called a lawyer, who advised her to relent only if police produced a warrant. Even then, the lawyer told her, she should make sure to read it. About three hours later, the police, now between 10 and 15 in number, pried a door to force their way in. A lieutenant, waving a piece of paper, said they had a warrant. Mapp asked to see it. The lieutenant told

CH. 16   THE EXCLUSIONARY RULE   435

her no. So Mapp grabbed the paper from him and stuffed it down the front of her blouse. She would later testify to what happened next:

"What are we going to do now?" one of the officers asked.

"I'm going down after it," a sergeant said.

"No, you are not," Mapp told the sergeant.

But the sergeant "went down anyway," grabbing the paper back and keeping Mapp from ever reading it. In years to come, she would say she suspected the paper was blank.

The police found the man they were looking for (although he was later cleared in the bombing). But the search didn't end there. Led by the sergeant who had retrieved the dubious warrant—a man who would later say Mapp had "a swagger about her"—police searched every room, upstairs and down, rummaging through boxes and drawers. During this search they found a pencil sketch of a nude and four books considered obscene, with titles that included "Memoirs of a Hotel Man" and "Affairs of a Troubadour." Mapp told police the materials belonged to a former roomer, for whom she had stored them. But she was charged under an Ohio law that made possession of obscene material a felony. At trial, Mapp testified that when an officer found the books, "I told him not to look at them, they might embarrass him." The jury took 20 minutes to convict, after which Mapp was sentenced to up to seven years.

Out on bond, Mapp appealed—first to the Ohio Supreme Court, where she lost, then to the U.S. Supreme Court, which agreed to hear her case. Oral argument can be a dry affair. But Mapp's case was an exception. The justices drew laughs from the courtroom gallery while leaving no doubt how absurd they found Ohio's obscenity statute. They took turns toying with the lawyer for the state, asking, if mere possession of obscene material constituted a crime, why the clerk of court had not been indicted, or the administrators at certain university libraries, or psychologists, or bibliophiles.

When Mapp's attorney, Alexander L. Kearns, presented his case, he spoke with "all the bravado of a Clarence Darrow and the inflection of W.C. Fields," according to one book.

In their initial consideration of the case all nine justices agreed that the obscenity law violated the First Amendment. But when Associate Justice Tom C. Clark drafted the majority opinion, he shifted the focus of the case to the Fourth Amendment, which prohibits unreasonable search and seizure. By the time Mapp's case reached the Supreme Court, it had become clear that the police never had obtained a warrant to search Mapp's home. Lewis Katz, a law professor at Case Western Reserve University in Cleveland, would later write: "The illegal entry of Mapp's house by the police was nothing extraordinary; it was an everyday fact of life for blacks and other racial minorities. Police throughout America were part of the machinery of keeping blacks 'in their place,' ignoring constitutional guarantees against unreasonable arrests and searches and those that barred use of 'third-degree' tactics when questioning suspects."

Ohio, like many states at the time, allowed evidence to be used even if it had been seized illegally. That turned the prohibition against unreasonable searches into a right without a remedy, making it hardly any right at all. In Mapp's case, five Supreme Court justices decided to change that. They threw out Mapp's conviction and declared that the rule excluding illegally obtained evidence would now apply in all the states—a judicial thunderclap that served notice of a court that would be reining in police in the years to come.

After her conviction was vacated, Mapp moved to Queens, New York. In 1971 police searched her home—this time, with a valid warrant—and found $150,000 worth of heroin and some stolen property. She was convicted of possession of drugs and, under new tough-on-crime laws signed by Gov. Nelson Rockefeller, received a mandatory sentence of 20 years to life. Mapp would later claim that the police had set her up due to her notoriety.

Mapp served time at the Bedford Hills Correctional Facility for Women. * * * In 1980 Gov. Hugh Carey, no fan of the state's unforgiving drug laws, commuted Mapp's sentence, and she was paroled soon after.

After her release, Mapp worked for a non-profit that provided legal assistance to inmates. A talented seamstress and dressmaker, she also threw herself into a variety of businesses, from beauty supplies to furniture upholstery to real estate. She spoke at law schools about *Mapp v. Ohio* and was interviewed for several books.

* * * Dollree Mapp died October 31 in Conyers, Georgia. Her family plans to spread her ashes in the front yard of her home in Queens.

UNITED STATES v. LEON
Supreme Court of the United States
468 U.S. 897, 104 S. Ct. 3405, 82 L. Ed. 2d 677 (1984)

JUSTICE WHITE delivered the opinion of the Court.

This case presents the question whether the Fourth Amendment exclusionary rule should be modified so as not to bar the use in the prosecution's case in chief of evidence obtained by officers acting in reasonable reliance on a search warrant issued by a detached and neutral magistrate but ultimately found to be unsupported by probable cause. To resolve this question, we must consider once again the tension between the sometimes competing goals of, on the one hand, deterring official misconduct and removing inducements to unreasonable invasions of privacy and, on the other, establishing procedures under which criminal defendants are "acquitted or convicted on the basis of all the evidence which exposes the truth." * * *

The Fourth Amendment contains no provision expressly precluding the use of evidence obtained in violation of its commands, and an examination of its origin and purposes makes clear that the use of fruits of a past unlawful search or seizure "work[s] no new Fourth Amendment wrong." The wrong condemned by the Amendment is "fully accomplished" by the unlawful search or seizure itself, and the exclusionary rule is neither intended nor able to "cure the invasion of the defendant's rights which he has already suffered." The rule thus operates as "a judicially created remedy designed to safeguard Fourth Amendment rights generally through its deterrent effect, rather than a personal constitutional right of the party aggrieved."

Whether the exclusionary sanction is appropriately imposed in a particular case * * * must be resolved by weighing the costs and benefits of preventing the use in the prosecution's case in chief of inherently trustworthy tangible evidence obtained in reliance on a search warrant issued by a detached and neutral magistrate that ultimately is found to be defective.

The substantial social costs exacted by the exclusionary rule for the vindication of Fourth Amendment rights have long been a source of concern. "Our cases have consistently recognized that unbending application of the exclusionary sanction to enforce ideals of governmental rectitude would impede unacceptably the truth-finding functions of judge and jury." An objectionable collateral consequence of this interference with the criminal justice system's truth-finding function is that some guilty defendants may go free or receive reduced sentences as a result of favorable plea bargains. Particularly when law enforcement officers have acted in objective good faith or their transgressions have been minor, the magnitude of the benefit conferred on such guilty defendants offends basic concepts of the criminal justice system. * * *

As yet, we have not recognized any form of good-faith exception to the Fourth Amendment exclusionary rule. But the balancing approach that has evolved during the years of experience with the rule provides strong support for the modification currently urged upon us. * * * [O]ur evaluation of the costs and benefits of suppressing reliable physical evidence seized by officers reasonably relying on a warrant issued by a detached and neutral magistrate leads to the conclusion that such evidence should be admissible in the prosecution's case in chief. * * * [The Court suggests that the main benefit of the exclusionary rule, deterring police from violating the Fourth Amendment, is outweighed by its costs.]

To the extent that proponents of exclusion rely on its behavioral effects on judges and magistrates * * *, their reliance is misplaced. First, the exclusionary rule is designed to deter police misconduct rather than to punish the errors of judges and magistrates. Second, there exists no evidence suggesting that judges and magistrates are inclined to ignore or subvert the Fourth Amendment or that lawlessness among these actors requires application of the extreme sanction of exclusion.

Third, and most important, we discern no basis, and are offered none, for believing that exclusion of evidence seized pursuant to a warrant will have a significant deterrent effect on the issuing judge or magistrate. * * * Judges and magistrates are not adjuncts to the law enforcement team; as neutral judicial officers, they have no stake in the outcome of particular criminal prosecutions. The threat of exclusion thus cannot be expected significantly to deter them. Imposition of the exclusionary sanction is not necessary meaningfully to inform judicial officers of their errors, and we cannot conclude that admitting evidence obtained pursuant to a warrant while at the same time declaring that the warrant was somehow defective will in any way reduce judicial officers' professional incentives to comply with the Fourth Amendment, encourage them to repeat their mistakes, or lead to the granting of all colorable warrant requests. * * *

We have frequently questioned whether the exclusionary rule can have any deterrent effect when the offending officers acted in the objectively reasonable belief that their conduct did not violate the Fourth Amendment. "No empirical researcher, proponent or opponent of the rule, has yet been able to establish with any assurance whether the rule has a deterrent effect. . . ." But even assuming that the rule effectively deters some police misconduct and provides incentives for the law enforcement profession as a whole to conduct itself in accord with the Fourth Amendment, it cannot be expected, and should not be applied, to deter objectively reasonable law enforcement activity.

This is particularly true, we believe, when an officer acting with objective good faith has obtained a search warrant from a judge or magistrate and acted within its scope. In most such cases, there is no police illegality and thus nothing to deter. It is the magistrate's responsibility to determine whether the officer's allegations establish probable cause and, if so, to issue a warrant comporting in form with the requirements of the Fourth Amendment. In the ordinary case, an officer cannot be expected to question the magistrate's probable-cause determination or his judgment that the form of the warrant is technically sufficient. "[O]nce the warrant issues, there is literally nothing more the policeman can do in seeking to comply with the law." Penalizing the officer for the magistrate's error, rather than his own, cannot logically contribute to the deterrence of Fourth Amendment violations.

We conclude that the marginal or nonexistent benefits produced by suppressing evidence obtained in objectively reasonable reliance on a subsequently invalidated search warrant cannot justify the substantial costs of exclusion. We do not suggest, however, that exclusion is always inappropriate in cases where an officer has obtained a warrant and abided by its terms. * * * [T]he officer's reliance on the magistrate's probable-cause determination and on the technical sufficiency of the warrant he issues must be objectively reasonable,[23] and it is clear that in some circumstances the officer[24] will have no reasonable grounds for believing that the warrant was properly issued.

Suppression therefore remains an appropriate remedy if the magistrate or judge in issuing a warrant was misled by information in an affidavit that the affiant knew was false or would have known was false except for his reckless disregard of the truth. The exception we recognize today will also not apply in cases where the issuing magistrate wholly abandoned his judicial role in the manner condemned in *Lo-Ji Sales, Inc. v. New York*; in such circumstances, no reasonably well trained officer should rely on the warrant. Nor would an officer manifest objective good faith in relying on a warrant based on an affidavit "so lacking in indicia of probable cause as to render official belief in its existence entirely unreasonable." Finally, depending on the circumstances of the particular case, a warrant may be so facially deficient—i.e., in failing to particularize the place to be searched or the things to be seized—that the executing officers cannot reasonably presume it to be valid.

In so limiting the suppression remedy, we leave untouched the probable-cause standard and the various requirements for a valid warrant. * * * The good-faith exception for searches conducted pursuant to warrants is not intended to signal our unwillingness strictly to enforce the requirements of the Fourth Amendment, and we do not believe that it will have this effect. * * *

JUSTICE BRENNAN, with whom JUSTICE MARSHALL joins, dissenting. * * *

At bottom, the Court's decision turns on the proposition that the exclusionary rule is merely a "judicially created remedy designed to

---

[23] [O]ur good-faith inquiry is confined to the objectively ascertainable question whether a reasonably well trained officer would have known that the search was illegal despite the magistrate's authorization. In making this determination, all of the circumstances—including whether the warrant application had previously been rejected by a different magistrate—may be considered.

[24] References to "officer" throughout this opinion should not be read too narrowly. It is necessary to consider the objective reasonableness, not only of the officers who eventually executed a warrant, but also of the officers who originally obtained it or who provided information material to the probable-cause determination. Nothing in our opinion suggests, for example, that an officer could obtain a warrant on the basis of a "bare bones" affidavit and then rely on colleagues who are ignorant of the circumstances under which the warrant was obtained to conduct the search.

safeguard Fourth Amendment rights generally through its deterrent effect, rather than a personal constitutional right." The germ of that idea is found in *Wolf v. Colorado*, and although I had thought that such a narrow conception of the rule had been forever put to rest by our decision in *Mapp v. Ohio*, it has been revived by the present Court and reaches full flower with today's decision. The essence of this view * * * is that the sole "purpose of the Fourth Amendment is to prevent unreasonable governmental intrusions into the privacy of one's person, house, papers, or effects. The wrong condemned is the unjustified governmental invasion of these areas of an individual's life. That wrong . . . is fully accomplished by the original search without probable cause." * * * Because the only constitutionally cognizable injury has already been "fully accomplished" by the police by the time a case comes before the courts, the Constitution is not itself violated if the judge decides to admit the tainted evidence. * * *

Such a reading appears plausible, because, as critics of the exclusionary rule never tire of repeating, the Fourth Amendment makes no express provision for the exclusion of evidence secured in violation of its commands. A short answer to this claim, of course, is that many of the Constitution's most vital imperatives are stated in general terms and the task of giving meaning to these precepts is therefore left to subsequent judicial decisionmaking in the context of concrete cases. The nature of our Constitution, as Chief Justice Marshall long ago explained, "requires that only its great outlines should be marked, its important objects designated, and the minor ingredients which compose those objects be deduced from the nature of the objects themselves."

A more direct answer may be supplied by recognizing that the Amendment, like other provisions of the Bill of Rights, restrains the power of the government as a whole; it does not specify only a particular agency and exempt all others. The judiciary is responsible, no less than the executive, for ensuring that constitutional rights are respected.

When that fact is kept in mind, the role of the courts and their possible involvement in the concerns of the Fourth Amendment comes into sharper focus. Because seizures are executed principally to secure evidence, and because such evidence generally has utility in our legal system only in the context of a trial supervised by a judge, it is apparent that the admission of illegally obtained evidence implicates the same constitutional concerns as the initial seizure of that evidence. Indeed, by admitting unlawfully seized evidence, the judiciary becomes a part of what is in fact a single governmental action prohibited by the terms of the Amendment. * * * The Amendment therefore must be read to condemn not only the initial unconstitutional invasion of privacy—which is done, after all, for the purpose of securing evidence—but also the subsequent use of any evidence so obtained. * * *

At the outset, the Court suggests that society has been asked to pay a high price—in terms either of setting guilty persons free or of impeding the proper functioning of trials—as a result of excluding relevant physical evidence in cases where the police, in conducting searches and seizing evidence, have made only an "objectively reasonable" mistake concerning the constitutionality of their actions. But what evidence is there to support such a claim?

* * * [R]ecent studies have demonstrated that the "costs" of the exclusionary rule—calculated in terms of dropped prosecutions and lost convictions—are quite low. Contrary to the claims of the rule's critics that exclusion leads to "the release of countless guilty criminals," these studies have demonstrated that federal and state prosecutors very rarely drop cases because of potential search and seizure problems. For example, a 1979 study prepared at the request of Congress by the General Accounting Office reported that only 0.4% of all cases actually declined for prosecution by federal prosecutors were declined primarily because of illegal search problems. If the GAO data are restated as a percentage of all arrests, the study shows that only 0.2% of all felony arrests are declined for prosecution because of potential exclusionary rule problems. Of course, these data describe only the costs attributable to the exclusion of evidence in all cases; the costs due to the exclusion of evidence in the narrower category of cases where police have made objectively reasonable mistakes must necessarily be even smaller. * * *

What then supports the Court's insistence that this evidence be admitted? Apparently, the Court's only answer is that even though the costs of exclusion are not very substantial, the potential deterrent effect in these circumstances is so marginal that exclusion cannot be justified.

* * * [W]hat the Court overlooks is that the deterrence rationale for the rule is not designed to be, nor should it be thought of as, a form of "punishment" of individual police officers for their failures to obey the restraints imposed by the Fourth Amendment. Instead, the chief deterrent function of the rule is its tendency to promote institutional compliance with Fourth Amendment requirements on the part of law enforcement agencies generally. * * *

If the overall educational effect of the exclusionary rule is considered, application of the rule to even those situations in which individual police officers have acted on the basis of a reasonable but mistaken belief that their conduct was authorized can still be expected to have a considerable long-term deterrent effect. If evidence is consistently excluded in these circumstances, police departments will surely be prompted to instruct their officers to devote greater care and attention to providing sufficient information to establish probable cause when applying for a warrant, and to review with some attention the form of the warrant that they have been issued, rather than automatically assuming that whatever document the magistrate has signed will necessarily comport with Fourth Amendment requirements.

After today's decisions, however, that institutional incentive will be lost. Indeed, the Court's "reasonable mistake" exception to the exclusionary rule will tend to put a premium on police ignorance of the law. Armed with the assurance provided by today's decisions that evidence will always be admissible whenever an officer has "reasonably" relied upon a warrant, police departments will be encouraged to train officers that if a warrant has simply been signed, it is reasonable, without more, to rely on it. Since in close cases there will no longer be any incentive to err on the side of constitutional behavior, police would have every reason to adopt a "let's-wait-until-it's-decided" approach in situations in which there is a question about a warrant's validity or the basis for its issuance.

Although the Court brushes these concerns aside, a host of grave consequences can be expected to result from its decision to carve this new exception out of the exclusionary rule. A chief consequence of today's decisions will be to convey a clear and unambiguous message to magistrates that their decisions to issue warrants are now insulated from subsequent judicial review. Creation of this new exception for good-faith reliance upon a warrant implicitly tells magistrates that they need not take much care in reviewing warrant applications, since their mistakes will from now on have virtually no consequence: If their decision to issue a warrant was correct, the evidence will be admitted; if their decision was incorrect but the police relied in good faith on the warrant, the evidence will also be admitted. Inevitably, the care and attention devoted to such an inconsequential chore will dwindle. * * *

I dissent.

[JUSTICE STEVENS' opinion concurring in part and dissenting in part and JUSTICE BLACKMUN's concurring opinion have been omitted.]

NOTE

After deciding *Leon*, the Court continued to limit the exclusionary rule by recognizing a good faith exception to the exclusionary rule in other contexts. For example, in *Illinois v. Krull*, 480 U.S. 340 (1987), the Court applied *Leon* to a case in which police relied upon a statute authorizing warrantless searches of car dealerships and auto wrecking yards that was later invalidated. In addition to finding that the police officer's reliance on the statute authorizing warrantless inspections was objectively reasonable, the Court opined that excluding evidence in this situation would have little deterrent effect because "an officer cannot be expected to question the judgment of the legislature that passed the law." *Id.* at 349–50.

In *Davis v. United States*, 564 U.S. 229 (2011), the Court again applied the reasoning of *Leon* to a case in which a police officer conducted a warrantless search of a vehicle, relying upon then binding appellate precedent, i.e. existing appellate case law that the lower courts are obliged to follow, that was later overruled. Noting that "exclusion would come at a high cost to both the truth and the public safety," the Court held that "searches conducted in objectively reasonable reliance on binding appellate precedent are not subject to the exclusionary rule." *Id.* at 232. *Herring v. United States* is yet another case in which the Court applies the reasoning of *Leon* to limit the exclusionary rule.

HERRING V. UNITED STATES
Supreme Court of the United States
555 U.S. 135, 129 S. Ct. 695, 172 L. Ed. 2d 496 (2009)

CHIEF JUSTICE ROBERTS delivered the opinion of the Court.

The Fourth Amendment forbids "unreasonable searches and seizures," and this usually requires the police to have probable cause or a warrant before making an arrest. What if an officer reasonably believes there is an outstanding arrest warrant, but that belief turns out to be wrong because of a negligent bookkeeping error by another police employee? The parties here agree that the ensuing arrest is still a violation of the Fourth Amendment, but dispute whether contraband found during a search incident to that arrest must be excluded in a later prosecution.

Our cases establish that such suppression is not an automatic consequence of a Fourth Amendment violation. Instead, the question turns on the culpability of the police and the potential of exclusion to deter wrongful police conduct. Here the error was the result of isolated negligence attenuated from the arrest. We hold that in these circumstances the jury should not be barred from considering all the evidence.

On July 7, 2004, Investigator Mark Anderson learned that Bennie Dean Herring had driven to the Coffee County Sheriff's Department to retrieve something from his impounded truck. Herring was no stranger to law enforcement, and Anderson asked the county's warrant clerk, Sandy Pope, to check for any outstanding warrants for Herring's arrest. When she found none, Anderson asked Pope to check with Sharon Morgan, her counterpart in neighboring Dale County. After checking Dale County's computer database, Morgan replied that there was an active arrest warrant for Herring's failure to appear on a felony charge. Pope relayed the information to Anderson and asked Morgan to fax over a copy of the warrant as confirmation. Anderson and a deputy followed Herring as he left the impound lot, pulled him over, and arrested him. A search incident to the arrest revealed methamphetamine in Herring's pocket, and a pistol (which as a felon he could not possess) in his vehicle.

There had, however, been a mistake about the warrant. The Dale County sheriff's computer records are supposed to correspond to actual arrest warrants, which the office also maintains. But when Morgan went to the files to retrieve the actual warrant to fax to Pope, Morgan was unable to find it. She called a court clerk and learned that the warrant had been recalled five months earlier. Normally when a warrant is recalled the court clerk's office or a judge's chambers calls Morgan, who enters the information in the sheriff's computer database and disposes of the physical copy. For whatever reason, the information about the recall of the warrant for Herring did not appear in the database. Morgan immediately called Pope to alert her to the mixup, and Pope contacted Anderson over a secure radio. This all unfolded in 10 to 15 minutes, but Herring had already been arrested and found with the gun and drugs, just a few hundred yards from the sheriff's office.

Herring was indicted in the District Court for the Middle District of Alabama for illegally possessing the gun and drugs. He moved to suppress the evidence on the ground that his initial arrest had been illegal because the warrant had been rescinded. * * * The District Court [denied Herring's motion to suppress], and the Court of Appeals for the Eleventh Circuit affirmed. * * *

We now affirm the Eleventh Circuit's judgment.

The fact that a Fourth Amendment violation occurred—*i.e.*, that a search or arrest was unreasonable—does not necessarily mean that the exclusionary rule applies. * * * [O]ur precedents establish important principles that constrain application of the exclusionary rule.

First, the exclusionary rule is not an individual right and applies only where it "result[s] in appreciable deterrence." * * * In addition, the benefits of deterrence must outweigh the costs. * * * "[T]o the extent that application of the exclusionary rule could provide some incremental deterrent, that possible benefit must be weighed against [its] substantial social costs." The principal cost of applying the rule is, of course, letting guilty and possibly dangerous defendants go free—something that "offends basic concepts of the criminal justice system." * * *

When police act under a warrant that is invalid for lack of probable cause, the exclusionary rule does not apply if the police acted "in objectively reasonable reliance" on the subsequently invalidated search warrant. We (perhaps confusingly) called this objectively reasonable reliance "good faith."

* * * [I]n *Evans*, we applied this good-faith rule to police who reasonably relied on mistaken information in a court's database that an arrest warrant was outstanding. We held that a mistake made by a judicial employee could not give rise to exclusion for three reasons: The exclusionary rule was crafted to curb police rather than judicial

misconduct; court employees were unlikely to try to subvert the Fourth Amendment; and "most important, there [was] no basis for believing that application of the exclusionary rule in [those] circumstances" would have any significant effect in deterring the errors. *Evans* left unresolved "whether the evidence should be suppressed if police personnel were responsible for the error," an issue not argued by the State in that case, but one that we now confront.

The extent to which the exclusionary rule is justified by these deterrence principles varies with the culpability of the law enforcement conduct. As we said in *Leon*, "an assessment of the flagrancy of the police misconduct constitutes an important step in the calculus" of applying the exclusionary rule. * * *

Indeed, the abuses that gave rise to the exclusionary rule featured intentional conduct that was patently unconstitutional. In *Weeks*, a foundational exclusionary rule case, the officers had broken into the defendant's home (using a key shown to them by a neighbor), confiscated incriminating papers, then returned again with a U.S. Marshal to confiscate even more. Not only did they have no search warrant, which the Court held was required, but they could not have gotten one had they tried. * * *

Equally flagrant conduct was at issue in *Mapp v. Ohio*, which overruled *Wolf v. Colorado*, and extended the exclusionary rule to the States. Officers forced open a door to Ms. Mapp's house, kept her lawyer from entering, brandished what the court concluded was a false warrant, then forced her into handcuffs and canvassed the house for obscenity. An error that arises from nonrecurring and attenuated negligence is thus far removed from the core concerns that led us to adopt the rule in the first place. * * *

To trigger the exclusionary rule, police conduct must be sufficiently deliberate that exclusion can meaningfully deter it, and sufficiently culpable that such deterrence is worth the price paid by the justice system. As laid out in our cases, the exclusionary rule serves to deter deliberate, reckless, or grossly negligent conduct, or in some circumstances recurring or systemic negligence. The error in this case does not rise to that level. * * *

We do not suggest that all recordkeeping errors by the police are immune from the exclusionary rule. * * * If the police have been shown to be reckless in maintaining a warrant system, or to have knowingly made false entries to lay the groundwork for future false arrests, exclusion would certainly be justified under our cases should such misconduct cause a Fourth Amendment violation.

* * * Officer Anderson testified that he had never had reason to question information about a Dale County warrant, and both Sandy Pope

and Sharon Morgan testified that they could remember no similar miscommunication ever happening on their watch.

* * * [W]e conclude that when police mistakes are the result of negligence such as that described here, rather than systemic error or reckless disregard of constitutional requirements, any marginal deterrence does not "pay its way." In such a case, the criminal should not "go free because the constable has blundered."

The judgment of the Court of Appeals for the Eleventh Circuit is affirmed.

It is so ordered.

JUSTICE GINSBURG, with whom JUSTICE STEVENS, JUSTICE SOUTER, and JUSTICE BREYER join, dissenting.

Petitioner Bennie Dean Herring was arrested, and subjected to a search incident to his arrest, although no warrant was outstanding against him, and the police lacked probable cause to believe he was engaged in criminal activity. The arrest and ensuing search therefore violated Herring's Fourth Amendment right "to be secure . . . against unreasonable searches and seizures." The Court of Appeals so determined, and the Government does not contend otherwise. The exclusionary rule provides redress for Fourth Amendment violations by placing the government in the position it would have been in had there been no unconstitutional arrest and search. The rule thus strongly encourages police compliance with the Fourth Amendment in the future. The Court, however, holds the rule inapplicable because careless recordkeeping by the police—not flagrant or deliberate misconduct—accounts for Herring's arrest.

I would not so construct the domain of the exclusionary rule and would hold the rule dispositive of this case. * * * The unlawful search in this case was contested in court because the police found methamphetamine in Herring's pocket and a pistol in his truck. But the "most serious impact" of the Court's holding will be on innocent persons "wrongfully arrested based on erroneous information [carelessly maintained] in a computer data base." * * *

The exclusionary rule, it bears emphasis, is often the only remedy effective to redress a Fourth Amendment violation. Civil liability will not lie for "the vast majority of [F]ourth [A]mendment violations—the frequent infringements motivated by commendable zeal, not condemnable malice." Criminal prosecutions or administrative sanctions against the offending officers and injunctive relief against widespread violations are an even farther cry.

The Court maintains that Herring's case is one in which the exclusionary rule could have scant deterrent effect and therefore would not "pay its way." I disagree.

That the mistake here involved the failure to make a computer entry hardly means that application of the exclusionary rule would have minimal value. "Just as the risk of *respondeat superior* liability encourages employers to supervise . . . their employees' conduct [more carefully], so the risk of exclusion of evidence encourages policymakers and systems managers to monitor the performance of the systems they install and the personnel employed to operate those systems."

Consider the potential impact of a decision applying the exclusionary rule in this case. As earlier observed, the record indicates that there is no electronic connection between the warrant database of the Dale County Sheriff's Department and that of the County Circuit Clerk's office, which is located in the basement of the same building. When a warrant is recalled, one of the "many different people that have access to th[e] warrants," must find the hard copy of the warrant in the "two or three different places" where the Department houses warrants, return it to the Clerk's office, and manually update the Department's database. The record reflects no routine practice of checking the database for accuracy, and the failure to remove the entry for Herring's warrant was not discovered until Investigator Anderson sought to pursue Herring five months later. Is it not altogether obvious that the Department could take further precautions to ensure the integrity of its database? The Sheriff's Department "is in a position to remedy the situation and might well do so if the exclusionary rule is there to remove the incentive to do otherwise."

Is the potential deterrence here worth the costs it imposes? In light of the paramount importance of accurate recordkeeping in law enforcement, I would answer yes, and next explain why, as I see it, Herring's motion presents a particularly strong case for suppression.

Electronic databases form the nervous system of contemporary criminal justice operations. In recent years, their breadth and influence have dramatically expanded. Police today can access databases that include not only the updated National Crime Information Center (NCIC), but also terrorist watchlists, the Federal Government's employee eligibility system, and various commercial databases. Moreover, States are actively expanding information sharing between jurisdictions. As a result, law enforcement has an increasing supply of information within its easy electronic reach.

The risk of error stemming from these databases is not slim. Herring's *amici* warn that law enforcement databases are insufficiently monitored and often out of date. Government reports describe, for example, flaws in NCIC databases, terrorist watchlist databases, and databases associated with the Federal Government's employment eligibility verification system.

Inaccuracies in expansive, interconnected collections of electronic information raise grave concerns for individual liberty. "The offense to the dignity of the citizen who is arrested, handcuffed, and searched on a public street simply because some bureaucrat has failed to maintain an accurate computer data base" is evocative of the use of general warrants that so outraged the authors of our Bill of Rights.

The Court assures that "exclusion would certainly be justified" if "the police have been shown to be reckless in maintaining a warrant system, or to have knowingly made false entries to lay the groundwork for future false arrests." This concession provides little comfort.

First, by restricting suppression to bookkeeping errors that are deliberate or reckless, the majority leaves Herring, and others like him, with no remedy for violations of their constitutional rights. * * * Second, I doubt that police forces already possess sufficient incentives to maintain up-to-date records. The Government argues that police have no desire to send officers out on arrests unnecessarily, because arrests consume resources and place officers in danger. The facts of this case do not fit that description of police motivation. Here the officer wanted to arrest Herring and consulted the Department's records to legitimate his predisposition. * * *

For the reasons stated, I would reverse the judgment of the Eleventh Circuit.

[JUSTICE BREYER's dissenting opinion has been omitted.]

NOTE

As we have learned in this chapter, under the exclusionary rule, evidence seized in violation of the Fourth Amendment will ordinarily be excluded from trial. The exclusionary rule, which applies to the states as well as the federal government, serves as the primary remedy for a violation of the Fourth Amendment.

Under what is known as the fruit of the poisonous tree doctrine, not only will evidence seized as a direct result of a violation of the Fourth Amendment or any other provision of the U.S. Constitution be excluded at trial, but evidence that is derived from that initial constitutional violation—so called fruit of the poisonous tree—will also be excluded as a general matter. The next few cases focus on different aspects of the fruit of the poisonous tree doctrine.

To understand the "fruit of the poisonous tree" metaphor, we can think about the constitutional violation as the poisoned tree. Because the tree is poisoned, so is its fruit. Fruit of the poisonous tree will be excluded at trial unless one of the following exceptions to the fruit of the poisonous tree doctrine applies: (1) the independent source doctrine, (2) the inevitable discovery doctrine, or (3) attenuation.

For example, let's say the police violate the Fourth Amendment by entering a home without a search warrant, and no exception to the warrant requirement applies. Under the exclusionary rule, any evidence they find

CH. 16   THE EXCLUSIONARY RULE   449

inside that home—such as drugs, guns, computers, cellphones, diaries, and calendars—will be excluded at trial under the exclusionary rule unless the *Leon* good faith exception to the exclusionary rule or one of *Leon*'s progeny applies. In addition, evidence derived from the initially seized evidence—like the statements of a witness whose name and email address were found on the suspect's computer—will also be inadmissible as fruit of the poisonous tree unless the government can show that the evidence falls within one of the exceptions to the fruit of the poisonous tree doctrine. The cases below explain the doctrine and its exceptions in more detail.

WONG SUN V. UNITED STATES
Supreme Court of the United States
371 U.S. 471, 83 S. Ct. 407, 9 L. Ed. 2d 441 (1963)

JUSTICE BRENNAN delivered the opinion of the Court.

The petitioners were tried without a jury in the District Court for the Northern District of California under a two-count indictment for violation of the Federal Narcotics Laws. They were * * * convicted under the second count which charged the substantive offense of fraudulent and knowing transportation and concealment of illegally imported heroin. The Court of Appeals for the Ninth Circuit * * * affirmed the convictions. We granted certiorari. * * *

About 2 a.m. on the morning of June 4, 1959, federal narcotics agents in San Francisco, after having had one Hom Way under surveillance for six weeks, arrested him and found heroin in his possession. Hom Way * * * stated after his arrest that he had bought an ounce of heroin the night before from one known to him only as "Blackie Toy," proprietor of a laundry on Leavenworth Street.

About 6 a.m. that morning six or seven federal agents went to a laundry at 1733 Leavenworth Street. The sign above the door of this establishment said "Oye's Laundry." It was operated by the petitioner James Wah Toy. There is, however, nothing in the record which identifies James Wah Toy and "Blackie Toy" as the same person. * * * Agent Alton Wong, who was of Chinese ancestry, rang the bell. When petitioner Toy appeared and opened the door, Agent Wong told him that he was calling for laundry and dry cleaning. Toy replied that he didn't open until 8 o'clock * * *. Toy started to close the door. Agent Wong thereupon took his badge from his pocket and said, "I am a federal narcotics agent." Toy immediately "slammed the door and started running" down the hallway through the laundry to his living quarters at the back where his wife and child were sleeping in a bedroom. Agent Wong and the other federal officers broke open the door and followed Toy down the hallway to the living quarters and into the bedroom. Toy reached into a nightstand drawer. Agent Wong thereupon drew his pistol, pulled Toy's hand out of the drawer, placed him under arrest and handcuffed him. There was nothing in the drawer and a search of the premises uncovered no narcotics.

One of the agents said to Toy " . . . [Hom Way] says he got narcotics from you." Toy responded, "No, I haven't been selling any narcotics at all. However, I do know somebody who has." When asked who that was, Toy said, "I only know him as Johnny. I don't know his last name." However, Toy described a house on Eleventh Avenue where he said Johnny lived; he also described a bedroom in the house where he said "Johnny kept about a piece"[2] of heroin, and where he and Johnny had smoked some of the drug the night before. The agents left immediately for Eleventh Avenue and located the house. They entered and found one Johnny Yee in the bedroom. After a discussion with the agents, Yee took from a bureau drawer several tubes containing in all just less than one ounce of heroin, and surrendered them. Within the hour Yee and Toy were taken to the Office of the Bureau of Narcotics. Yee there stated that the heroin had been brought to him some four days earlier by petitioner Toy and another Chinese known to him only as "Sea Dog."

Toy was questioned as to the identity of "Sea Dog" and said that "Sea Dog" was Wong Sun. Some agents, including Agent Alton Wong, took Toy to Wong Sun's neighborhood where Toy pointed out a multifamily dwelling where he said Wong Sun lived. Agent Wong rang a downstairs door bell and a buzzer sounded, opening the door. The officer identified himself as a narcotics agent to a woman on the landing and asked "for Mr. Wong." The woman was the wife of petitioner Wong Sun. She said that Wong Sun was "in the back room sleeping." Alton Wong and some six other officers climbed the stairs and entered the apartment. One of the officers went into the back room and brought petitioner Wong Sun from the bedroom in handcuffs. A thorough search of the apartment followed, but no narcotics were discovered.

Petitioner Toy and Johnny Yee were arraigned before a United States Commissioner on June 4 * * *. Later that day, each was released on his own recognizance. Petitioner Wong Sun was arraigned on a similar complaint filed the next day and was also released on his own recognizance. Within a few days, both petitioners and Yee were interrogated at the office of the Narcotics Bureau by Agent William Wong, also of Chinese ancestry. The agent advised each of the three of his right to withhold information which might be used against him, and stated to each that he was entitled to the advice of counsel * * *.

The agent interrogated each of the three separately. After each had been interrogated the agent prepared a statement in English from rough notes. The agent read petitioner Toy's statement to him in English and interpreted certain portions of it for him in Chinese. Toy also read the

---

[2] A "piece" is approximately one ounce.

statement in English aloud to the agent, said there were corrections to be made, and made the corrections in his own hand. Toy would not sign the statement, however; in the agent's words "he wanted to know first if the other persons involved in the case had signed theirs." Wong Sun had considerable difficulty understanding the statement in English and the agent restated its substance in Chinese. Wong Sun refused to sign the statement although he admitted the accuracy of its contents.

Hom Way did not testify at petitioners' trial. The Government offered Johnny Yee as its principal witness but excused him after he invoked the privilege against self-incrimination and flatly repudiated the statement he had given to Agent William Wong. That statement was not offered in evidence nor was any testimony elicited from him identifying either petitioner as the source of the heroin in his possession, or otherwise tending to support the charges against the petitioners.

The statute expressly provides that proof of the accused's possession of the drug will support a conviction under the statute unless the accused satisfactorily explains the possession. The Government's evidence tending to prove the petitioners' possession (the petitioners offered no exculpatory testimony) consisted of four items which the trial court admitted * * *: (1) the statements made orally by petitioner Toy in his bedroom at the time of his arrest; (2) the heroin surrendered to the agents by Johnny Yee; (3) petitioner Toy's pretrial unsigned statement; and (4) petitioner Wong Sun's similar statement. The dispute below and here has centered around the correctness of the rulings of the trial judge allowing these items in evidence. * * *

We believe that significant differences between the cases of the two petitioners require separate discussion of each. We shall first consider the case of petitioner Toy. * * * [W]e conclude that the Court of Appeals' finding that the officers' uninvited entry into Toy's living quarters was unlawful and that the bedroom arrest which followed was likewise unlawful, was fully justified on the evidence. It remains to be seen what consequences flow from this conclusion.

It is conceded that Toy's declarations in his bedroom are to be excluded if they are held to be "fruits" of the agents' unlawful action. * * * [V]erbal evidence which derives so immediately from an unlawful entry and an unauthorized arrest as the officers' action in the present case is no less the "fruit" of official illegality than the more common tangible fruits of the unwarranted intrusion. * * *

We now consider whether the exclusion of Toy's declarations requires also the exclusion of the narcotics taken from Yee, to which those declarations led the police. The prosecutor candidly told the trial court that "we wouldn't have found those drugs except that Mr. Toy helped us to." Hence this is not the case envisioned by this Court where the exclusionary rule has no application because the Government learned of the evidence "from an independent source," nor is this a case in which the connection between the lawless conduct of the police and the discovery of the challenged evidence has "become so attenuated as to dissipate the taint." We need not hold that all evidence is "fruit of the poisonous tree" simply because it would not have come to light but for the illegal actions of the police. Rather, the more apt question in such a case is "whether, granting establishment of the primary illegality, the evidence to which instant objection is made has been come at by exploitation of that illegality or instead by means sufficiently distinguishable to be purged of the primary taint." We think it clear that the narcotics were "come at by the exploitation of that illegality" and hence that they may not be used against Toy.

It remains only to consider Toy's unsigned statement. We need not decide whether, in light of the fact that Toy was free on his own recognizance when he made the statement, that statement was a fruit of the illegal arrest.[a] * * *

We turn now to the case of the other petitioner, Wong Sun. We have no occasion to disagree with the finding of the Court of Appeals that his arrest, also, was without probable cause or reasonable grounds. At all events no evidentiary consequences turn upon that question. For Wong Sun's unsigned confession was not the fruit of that arrest, and was therefore properly admitted at trial. On the evidence that Wong Sun had been released on his own recognizance after a lawful arraignment, and had returned voluntarily several days later to make the statement, we hold that the connection between the arrest and the statement had "become so attenuated as to dissipate the taint." The fact that the statement was unsigned, whatever bearing this may have upon its weight and credibility, does not render it inadmissible; Wong Sun understood and adopted its substance, though he could not comprehend the English words. The petitioner has never suggested any impropriety in the interrogation itself which would require the exclusion of this statement.

We must then consider the admissibility of the narcotics surrendered by Yee. Our holding * * * that this ounce of heroin was inadmissible against Toy does not compel a like result with respect to Wong Sun. The exclusion of the narcotics as to Toy was required solely by their tainted relationship to information unlawfully obtained from Toy, and not by any official impropriety connected with their surrender by Yee. The seizure of this heroin invaded no right of privacy of person or premises which would entitle Wong Sun to object to its use at his trial. * * *

---

[a] Toy's unsigned statement was excluded on other grounds. Since all evidence against Toy was excluded, his conviction was set aside.

The judgment of the Court of Appeals is reversed and the case is remanded to the District Court for further proceedings consistent with this opinion.

It is so ordered.

[JUSTICE DOUGLAS' concurring opinion and JUSTICE CLARK's dissenting opinion have been omitted.]

NOTE

The next case explains the independent source doctrine and the inevitable discovery doctrine. These are two different ways that "fruit of the poisonous tree" can be admitted into evidence at trial.

As you read *Nix v. Williams*, try to distinguish between the evidence that was the direct result of the constitutional violation, i.e., the evidence that was excluded under the exclusionary rule, and the evidence that constituted fruit of the poisonous tree, i.e., the evidence that the government was seeking to have admitted under one of the exceptions to the fruit of the poisonous tree doctrine.

NIX V. WILLIAMS

Supreme Court of the United States
467 U.S. 431, 104 S. Ct. 2501, 81 L. Ed. 2d 377 (1984)

CHIEF JUSTICE BURGER delivered the opinion of the Court.

We granted certiorari to consider whether, at respondent Williams' second murder trial in state court, evidence pertaining to the discovery and condition of the victim's body was properly admitted on the ground that it would ultimately or inevitably have been discovered even if no violation of any constitutional or statutory provision had taken place.

On December 24, 1968, 10-year-old Pamela Powers disappeared from a YMCA building in Des Moines, Iowa, where she had accompanied her parents to watch an athletic contest. Shortly after she disappeared, Williams was seen leaving the YMCA carrying a large bundle wrapped in a blanket; a 14-year-old boy who had helped Williams open his car door reported that he had seen "two legs in it and they were skinny and white." * * *

Police surmised that Williams had left Pamela Powers or her body somewhere between Des Moines and the Grinnell rest stop where some of the young girl's clothing had been found. On December 26, the Iowa Bureau of Criminal Investigation initiated a large-scale search. Two hundred volunteers divided into teams began the search 21 miles east of Grinnell, covering an area several miles to the north and south of Interstate 80. * * * Searchers were instructed to check all roads, abandoned farm buildings, ditches, culverts, and any other place in which the body of a small child could be hidden.

Meanwhile, Williams surrendered to local police in Davenport, where he was promptly arraigned. Williams contacted a Des Moines attorney who arranged for an attorney in Davenport to meet Williams at the Davenport police station. Des Moines police informed counsel they would pick Williams up in Davenport and return him to Des Moines without questioning him. Two Des Moines detectives then drove to Davenport, took Williams into custody, and proceeded to drive him back to Des Moines.

During the return trip, one of the policemen, Detective Leaming, began a conversation with Williams. * * * Leaming told Williams he knew the body was in the area of Mitchellville—a town they would be passing on the way to Des Moines.[a]

* * * As they continued to drive to Des Moines, Williams asked whether the blanket had been found and then directed the officers to a rest area in Grinnell where he said he had disposed of the blanket; they did not find the blanket. At this point Leaming and his party were joined by the officers in charge of the search. As they approached Mitchellville, Williams, without any further conversation, agreed to direct the officers to the child's body.

The officers directing the search had called off the search at 3 p.m., when they left the Grinnell Police Department to join Leaming at the rest area. At that time, one search team near the Jasper County-Polk County line was only two and one-half miles from where Williams soon guided Leaming and his party to the body. The child's body was found next to a culvert in a ditch beside a gravel road in Polk County, about two miles south of Interstate 80, and essentially within the area to be searched. * * *

At Williams' * * * trial in 1977 in the Iowa court, the prosecution did not offer Williams' statements into evidence, nor did it seek to show that Williams had directed the police to the child's body. However, evidence of the condition of her body as it was found, articles and photographs of her clothing, and the results of post mortem medical and chemical tests on the body were admitted. The trial court concluded that the State had proved by a preponderance of the evidence that, if the search had not been suspended and Williams had not led the police to the victim, her body would have been discovered "within a short time" in essentially the same condition as it was actually found. The trial court also ruled that if the police had not located the body, "the search would clearly have been taken

---

[a] In *Brewer v. Williams, supra*, the U.S. Supreme Court held that the police violated Williams' Sixth Amendment right to counsel when Detective Leaming gave what has been called "The Christian Burial Speech" to Williams, addressing Williams as Reverend and telling him that the victim deserved a Christian burial, which prompted Williams to tell police where he had hidden Pamela Powers' body. *See supra.*

up again where it left off, given the extreme circumstances of this case and the body would [have] been found in short order."

*** The challenged evidence was admitted and the jury *** found Williams guilty of first-degree murder; he was sentenced to life in prison. On appeal, the Supreme Court of Iowa *** affirmed. *** The Iowa court *** concluded that the State had shown by a preponderance of the evidence that, even if Williams had not guided police to the child's body, it would inevitably have been found by lawful activity of the search party before its condition had materially changed.

In 1980 Williams renewed his attack on the state-court conviction by seeking a writ of habeas corpus in the United States District Court for the Southern District of Iowa. *** The District Court denied Williams' petition.

The Court of Appeals for the Eighth Circuit reversed ***. That court assumed, without deciding, that there is an inevitable discovery exception to the exclusionary rule and that the Iowa Supreme Court correctly stated that exception to require proof that the police did not act in bad faith and that the evidence would have been discovered absent any constitutional violation. In reversing the District Court's denial of habeas relief, the Court of Appeals stated: "We hold that the State has not met the first requirement." ***

We granted the State's petition for certiorari and we reverse.

The Iowa Supreme Court correctly stated that the "vast majority" of all courts, both state and federal, recognize an inevitable discovery exception to the exclusionary rule. We are now urged to adopt and apply the so-called ultimate or inevitable discovery exception to the exclusionary rule.

*** The independent source doctrine allows admission of evidence that has been discovered by means wholly independent of any constitutional violation. That doctrine, although closely related to the inevitable discovery doctrine, does not apply here; Williams' statements to Leaming indeed led police to the child's body, but that is not the whole story. The independent source doctrine teaches us that the interest of society in deterring unlawful police conduct and the public interest in having juries receive all probative evidence of a crime are properly balanced by putting the police in the same, not a worse, position that they would have been in if no police error or misconduct had occurred. When the challenged evidence has an independent source, exclusion of such evidence would put the police in a worse position than they would have been in absent any error or violation. There is a functional similarity between these two doctrines in that exclusion of evidence that would inevitably have been discovered would also put the government in a worse position, because the police would have obtained that evidence if no misconduct had taken place.

Thus, while the independent source exception would not justify admission of evidence in this case, its rationale is wholly consistent with and justifies our adoption of the ultimate or inevitable discovery exception to the exclusionary rule.

It is clear that the cases implementing the exclusionary rule "begin with the premise that the challenged evidence is in some sense the product of illegal governmental activity." Of course, this does not end the inquiry. If the prosecution can establish by a preponderance of the evidence that the information ultimately or inevitably would have been discovered by lawful means—here the volunteers' search—then the deterrence rationale has so little basis that the evidence should be received. Anything less would reject logic, experience, and common sense.

The requirement that the prosecution must prove the absence of bad faith, imposed here by the Court of Appeals, would place courts in the position of withholding from juries relevant and undoubted truth that would have been available to police absent any unlawful police activity. Of course, that view would put the police in a worse position than they would have been in if no unlawful conduct had transpired. And, of equal importance, it wholly fails to take into account the enormous societal cost of excluding truth in the search for truth in the administration of justice. Nothing in this Court's prior holdings supports any such formalistic, pointless, and punitive approach. * * *

The Court of Appeals did not find it necessary to consider whether the record fairly supported the finding that the volunteer search party would ultimately or inevitably have discovered the victim's body. However, three courts independently reviewing the evidence have found that the body of the child inevitably would have been found by the searchers. * * *

On this record it is clear that the search parties were approaching the actual location of the body, and we are satisfied, along with three courts earlier, that the volunteer search teams would have resumed the search had Williams not earlier led the police to the body and the body inevitably would have been found. * * *

The judgment of the Court of Appeals is reversed, and the case is remanded for further proceedings consistent with this opinion.

It is so ordered.

[JUSTICE WHITE's concurring opinion, JUSTICE STEVENS' concurring opinion, and JUSTICE BRENNAN's dissenting opinion have been omitted.]

NOTE

Nix v. Williams explained the independent source doctrine and the inevitable discovery doctrine, two exceptions to the fruit of the poisonous tree doctrine. The next case, *Utah v. Strieff,* explains the attenuation doctrine, a

CH. 16   THE EXCLUSIONARY RULE   457

third way that "fruit of the poisonous tree" can be admitted into evidence. As you read the case, try to identify the factors that courts should consider when applying the attenuation doctrine. Pay careful attention to Justice Sotomayor's dissent, which has been called "an effective rebuttal to the *Strieff* majority" and "a reminder that [the] weakening of Fourth Amendment freedoms has especially dire consequences for America's minority and low-income communities."a *Utah v. Strieff* has become well-known primarily because of Justice Sotomayor's dissent.

UTAH V. STRIEFF
Supreme Court of the United States
579 U.S. 232, 136 S. Ct. 2056, 195 L. Ed. 2d 400 (2016)

JUSTICE THOMAS delivered the opinion of the Court. * * *

This case began with an anonymous tip. In December 2006, someone called the South Salt Lake City police's drug-tip line to report "narcotics activity" at a particular residence. Narcotics detective Douglas Fackrell investigated the tip. Over the course of about a week, Officer Fackrell conducted intermittent surveillance of the home. He observed visitors who left a few minutes after arriving at the house. These visits were sufficiently frequent to raise his suspicion that the occupants were dealing drugs.

One of those visitors was respondent Edward Strieff. Officer Fackrell observed Strieff exit the house and walk toward a nearby convenience store. In the store's parking lot, Officer Fackrell detained Strieff, identified himself, and asked Strieff what he was doing at the residence.

As part of the stop, Officer Fackrell requested Strieff's identification, and Strieff produced his Utah identification card. Officer Fackrell relayed Strieff's information to a police dispatcher, who reported that Strieff had an outstanding arrest warrant for a traffic violation. Officer Fackrell then arrested Strieff pursuant to that warrant. When Officer Fackrell searched Strieff incident to the arrest, he discovered a baggie of methamphetamine and drug paraphernalia.

The State charged Strieff with unlawful possession of methamphetamine and drug paraphernalia. Strieff moved to suppress the evidence, arguing that the evidence was inadmissible because it was derived from an unlawful investigatory stop. At the suppression hearing, the prosecutor conceded that Officer Fackrell lacked reasonable suspicion for the stop but argued that the evidence should not be suppressed because

---

   a   *See* Mark Joseph Stern, *Read Sonia Sotomayor's Atomic Bomb of a Dissent Slamming Racial Profiling and Mass Imprisonment*, SLATE (June 20, 2016), https://slate.com/news-and-politics/2016/06/sonia-sotomayor-dissent-in-utah-v-strieff-takes-on-police-misconduct.html (https://perma.cc/ZH8E-BLLZ). *See also* Matt Ford, *Justice Sotomayor's Ringing Dissent*, ATLANTIC (June 20, 2016), https://www.theatlantic.com/politics/archive/2016/06/utah-strieff-sotomayor/487922/ (https://perma.cc/U4QY-RNFR).

the existence of a valid arrest warrant attenuated the connection between the unlawful stop and the discovery of the contraband.

The trial court agreed with the State and admitted the evidence. * * * Strieff conditionally pleaded guilty to reduced charges of attempted possession of a controlled substance and possession of drug paraphernalia, but reserved his right to appeal the trial court's denial of the suppression motion. The Utah Court of Appeals affirmed. * * *

We granted certiorari to resolve disagreement about how the attenuation doctrine applies where an unconstitutional detention leads to the discovery of a valid arrest warrant. We now reverse.

The Fourth Amendment protects "[t]he right of the people to be secure in their persons, houses, papers, and effects, against unreasonable searches and seizures." * * * In the 20th century, * * * the exclusionary rule—the rule that often requires trial courts to exclude unlawfully seized evidence in a criminal trial—became the principal judicial remedy to deter Fourth Amendment violations.

Under the Court's precedents, the exclusionary rule encompasses both the "primary evidence obtained as a direct result of an illegal search or seizure" and, relevant here, "evidence later discovered and found to be derivative of an illegality," the so-called "fruit of the poisonous tree." But the significant costs of this rule have led us to deem it "applicable only . . . where its deterrence benefits outweigh its substantial social costs."

We have accordingly recognized several exceptions to the rule. Three of these exceptions involve the causal relationship between the unconstitutional act and the discovery of evidence. First, the independent source doctrine allows trial courts to admit evidence obtained in an unlawful search if officers independently acquired it from a separate, independent source. Second, the inevitable discovery doctrine allows for the admission of evidence that would have been discovered even without the unconstitutional source. Third, and at issue here, is the attenuation doctrine: Evidence is admissible when the connection between unconstitutional police conduct and the evidence is remote or has been interrupted by some intervening circumstance, so that "the interest protected by the constitutional guarantee that has been violated would not be served by suppression of the evidence obtained."

Turning to the application of the attenuation doctrine to this case, we * * * [need] to address whether the discovery of a valid arrest warrant was a sufficient intervening event to break the causal chain between the unlawful stop and the discovery of drug-related evidence on Strieff's person. The three factors articulated in *Brown v. Illinois*, guide our analysis. First, we look to the "temporal proximity" between the unconstitutional conduct and the discovery of evidence to determine how closely the discovery of evidence followed the unconstitutional search.

Second, we consider "the presence of intervening circumstances." Third, and "particularly" significant, we examine "the purpose and flagrancy of the official misconduct." In evaluating these factors, we assume without deciding (because the State conceded the point) that Officer Fackrell lacked reasonable suspicion to initially stop Strieff. * * *

The first factor, temporal proximity between the initially unlawful stop and the search, favors suppressing the evidence. Our precedents have declined to find that this factor favors attenuation unless "substantial time" elapses between an unlawful act and when the evidence is obtained. Here, however, Officer Fackrell discovered drug contraband on Strieff's person only minutes after the illegal stop. As the Court explained in *Brown*, such a short time interval counsels in favor of suppression; there, we found that the confession should be suppressed, relying in part on the "less than two hours" that separated the unconstitutional arrest and the confession.

In contrast, the second factor, the presence of intervening circumstances, strongly favors the State. In *Segura*, the Court addressed similar facts to those here and found sufficient intervening circumstances to allow the admission of evidence. There, agents had probable cause to believe that apartment occupants were dealing cocaine. They sought a warrant. In the meantime, they entered the apartment, arrested an occupant, and discovered evidence of drug activity during a limited search for security reasons. The next evening, the Magistrate Judge issued the search warrant. This Court deemed the evidence admissible notwithstanding the illegal search because the information supporting the warrant was "wholly unconnected with the [arguably illegal] entry and was known to the agents well before the initial entry."

Segura, of course, applied the independent source doctrine because the unlawful entry "did not contribute in any way to discovery of the evidence seized under the warrant." But the *Segura* Court suggested that the existence of a valid warrant favors finding that the connection between unlawful conduct and the discovery of evidence is "sufficiently attenuated to dissipate the taint." That principle applies here.

In this case, the warrant was valid, it predated Officer Fackrell's investigation, and it was entirely unconnected with the stop. And once Officer Fackrell discovered the warrant, he had an obligation to arrest Strieff. "A warrant is a judicial mandate to an officer to conduct a search or make an arrest, and the officer has a sworn duty to carry out its provisions." Officer Fackrell's arrest of Strieff thus was a ministerial act that was independently compelled by the pre-existing warrant. And once Officer Fackrell was authorized to arrest Strieff, it was undisputedly lawful to search Strieff as an incident of his arrest to protect Officer Fackrell's safety.

Finally, the third factor, "the purpose and flagrancy of the official misconduct," also strongly favors the State. The exclusionary rule exists to deter police misconduct. The third factor of the attenuation doctrine reflects that rationale by favoring exclusion only when the police misconduct is most in need of deterrence—that is, when it is purposeful or flagrant.

Officer Fackrell was at most negligent. In stopping Strieff, Officer Fackrell made two good-faith mistakes. First, he had not observed what time Strieff entered the suspected drug house, so he did not know how long Strieff had been there. Officer Fackrell thus lacked a sufficient basis to conclude that Strieff was a short-term visitor who may have been consummating a drug transaction. Second, because he lacked confirmation that Strieff was a short-term visitor, Officer Fackrell should have asked Strieff whether he would speak with him, instead of demanding that Strieff do so. Officer Fackrell's stated purpose was to "find out what was going on [in] the house." Nothing prevented him from approaching Strieff simply to ask. But these errors in judgment hardly rise to a purposeful or flagrant violation of Strieff's Fourth Amendment rights.

While Officer Fackrell's decision to initiate the stop was mistaken, his conduct thereafter was lawful. The officer's decision to run the warrant check was a "negligibly burdensome precautio[n]" for officer safety. And Officer Fackrell's actual search of Strieff was a lawful search incident to arrest.

Moreover, there is no indication that this unlawful stop was part of any systemic or recurrent police misconduct. To the contrary, all the evidence suggests that the stop was an isolated instance of negligence that occurred in connection with a bona fide investigation of a suspected drug house. * * *

Applying these factors, we hold that the evidence discovered on Strieff's person was admissible because the unlawful stop was sufficiently attenuated by the preexisting arrest warrant. Although the illegal stop was close in time to Strieff's arrest, that consideration is outweighed by two factors supporting the State. The outstanding arrest warrant for Strieff's arrest is a critical intervening circumstance that is wholly independent of the illegal stop. The discovery of that warrant broke the causal chain between the unconstitutional stop and the discovery of evidence by compelling Officer Fackrell to arrest Strieff. And, it is especially significant that there is no evidence that Officer Fackrell's illegal stop reflected flagrantly unlawful police misconduct.

* * * Strieff argues that, because of the prevalence of outstanding arrest warrants in many jurisdictions, police will engage in dragnet searches if the exclusionary rule is not applied. We think that this outcome is unlikely. Such wanton conduct would expose police to civil liability. And

in any event, the *Brown* factors take account of the purpose and flagrancy of police misconduct. Were evidence of a dragnet search presented here, the application of the *Brown* factors could be different. But there is no evidence that the concerns that Strieff raises with the criminal justice system are present in South Salt Lake City, Utah.

* * * We hold that the evidence Officer Fackrell seized as part of his search incident to arrest is admissible because his discovery of the arrest warrant attenuated the connection between the unlawful stop and the evidence seized from Strieff incident to arrest. The judgment of the Utah Supreme Court, accordingly, is reversed.

It is so ordered.

JUSTICE SOTOMAYOR, with whom JUSTICE GINSGBURG joins as to Parts I, II, and III, dissenting.

The Court today holds that the discovery of a warrant for an unpaid parking ticket will forgive a police officer's violation of your Fourth Amendment rights. Do not be soothed by the opinion's technical language: This case allows the police to stop you on the street, demand your identification, and check it for outstanding traffic warrants—even if you are doing nothing wrong. If the officer discovers a warrant for a fine you forgot to pay, courts will now excuse his illegal stop and will admit into evidence anything he happens to find by searching you after arresting you on the warrant. Because the Fourth Amendment should prohibit, not permit, such misconduct, I dissent.

It is tempting in a case like this, where illegal conduct by an officer uncovers illegal conduct by a civilian, to forgive the officer. After all, his instincts, although unconstitutional, were correct. But a basic principle lies at the heart of the Fourth Amendment: Two wrongs don't make a right. When "lawless police conduct" uncovers evidence of lawless civilian conduct, this Court has long required later criminal trials to exclude the illegally obtained evidence. For example, if an officer breaks into a home and finds a forged check lying around, that check may not be used to prosecute the homeowner for bank fraud. We would describe the check as "fruit of the poisonous tree." Fruit that must be cast aside includes not only evidence directly found by an illegal search but also evidence "come at by exploitation of that illegality." * * *

Applying the exclusionary rule, the Utah Supreme Court correctly decided that Strieff's drugs must be excluded because the officer exploited his illegal stop to discover them. The officer found the drugs only after learning of Strieff's traffic violation; and he learned of Strieff's traffic violation only because he unlawfully stopped Strieff to check his driver's license.

Causal chain is uninterrupted

The court also correctly rejected the State's argument that the officer's discovery of a traffic warrant unspoiled the poisonous fruit. The State analogizes finding the warrant to one of our earlier decisions, *Wong Sun v. United States*. There, an officer illegally arrested a person who, days later, voluntarily returned to the station to confess to committing a crime. Even though the person would not have confessed "but for the illegal actions of the police," we noted that the police did not exploit their illegal arrest to obtain the confession. Because the confession was obtained by "means sufficiently distinguishable" from the constitutional violation, we held that it could be admitted into evidence. The State contends that the search incident to the warrant-arrest here is similarly distinguishable from the illegal stop.

But *Wong Sun* explains why Strieff's drugs must be excluded. We reasoned that a Fourth Amendment violation may not color every investigation that follows but it certainly stains the actions of officers who exploit the infraction. We distinguished evidence obtained by innocuous means from evidence obtained by exploiting misconduct after considering a variety of factors: whether a long time passed, whether there were "intervening circumstances," and whether the purpose or flagrancy of the misconduct was "calculated" to procure the evidence.

These factors confirm that the officer in this case discovered Strieff's drugs by exploiting his own illegal conduct. The officer did not ask Strieff to volunteer his name only to find out, days later, that Strieff had a warrant against him. The officer illegally stopped Strieff and immediately ran a warrant check. The officer's discovery of a warrant was not some intervening surprise that he could not have anticipated. Utah lists over 180,000 misdemeanor warrants in its database, and at the time of the arrest, Salt Lake County had a "backlog of outstanding warrants" so large that it faced the "potential for civil liability."

The officer's violation was also calculated to procure evidence. His sole reason for stopping Strieff, he acknowledged, was investigative—he wanted to discover whether drug activity was going on in the house Strieff had just exited.

The warrant check, in other words, was not an "intervening circumstance" separating the stop from the search for drugs. It was part and parcel of the officer's illegal "expedition for evidence in the hope that something might turn up." Under our precedents, because the officer found Strieff's drugs by exploiting his own constitutional violation, the drugs should be excluded.

The Court sees things differently. * * * To explain its reasoning, the Court relies on *Segura v. United States*. * * * According to the majority, *Segura* involves facts "similar" to this case and "suggest[s]" that a valid warrant will clean up whatever illegal conduct uncovered it. It is difficult to understand this interpretation. In *Segura,* the agents' illegal conduct in entering the apartment had nothing to do with their procurement of a search warrant. Here, the officer's illegal conduct in stopping Strieff was essential to his discovery of an arrest warrant. *Segura* would be similar only if the agents used information they illegally obtained from the apartment to procure a search warrant or discover an arrest warrant. Precisely because that was not the case, the Court admitted the untainted evidence.

The majority likewise misses the point when it calls the warrant check here a "negligibly burdensome precautio[n]" taken for the officer's "safety." Remember, the officer stopped Strieff without suspecting him of committing any crime. By his own account, the officer did not fear Strieff. * * * Surely we would not allow officers to warrant-check random joggers, dog walkers, and lemonade vendors just to ensure they pose no threat to anyone else.

The majority also posits that the officer could not have exploited his illegal conduct because he did not violate the Fourth Amendment on purpose. Rather, he made "good-faith mistakes." Never mind that the officer's sole purpose was to fish for evidence. The majority casts his unconstitutional actions as "negligent" and therefore incapable of being deterred by the exclusionary rule.

But the Fourth Amendment does not tolerate an officer's unreasonable searches and seizures just because he did not know any better. Even officers prone to negligence can learn from courts that exclude illegally obtained evidence. Indeed, they are perhaps the most in need of the education, whether by the judge's opinion, the prosecutor's future guidance, or an updated manual on criminal procedure. If the officers are in doubt about what the law requires, exclusion gives them an "incentive to err on the side of constitutional behavior."

Most striking about the Court's opinion is its insistence that the event here was "isolated," with "no indication that this unlawful stop was part of any systemic or recurrent police misconduct." Respectfully, nothing about this case is isolated.

Outstanding warrants are surprisingly common. When a person with a traffic ticket misses a fine payment or court appearance, a court will issue a warrant. When a person on probation drinks alcohol or breaks curfew, a court will issue a warrant. The States and Federal Government maintain databases with over 7.8 million outstanding warrants, the vast majority of which appear to be for minor offenses. Even these sources may not track the "staggering" numbers of warrants, "drawers and drawers" full, that many cities issue for traffic violations and ordinance infractions. The county in this case has had a "backlog" of such warrants. The Department of Justice recently reported that in the town of Ferguson, Missouri, with a population of 21,000, 16,000 people had outstanding warrants against them.

Justice Department investigations across the country have illustrated how these astounding numbers of warrants can be used by police to stop people without cause. In a single year in New Orleans, officers "made nearly 60,000 arrests, of which about 20,000 were of people with outstanding traffic or misdemeanor warrants from neighboring parishes for such infractions as unpaid tickets." In the St. Louis metropolitan area, officers "routinely" stop people—on the street, at bus stops, or even in court—for no reason other than "an officer's desire to check whether the subject had a municipal arrest warrant pending." In Newark, New Jersey, officers stopped 52,235 pedestrians within a 4-year period and ran warrant checks on 39,308 of them. The Justice Department analyzed these warrant-checked stops and reported that "approximately 93% of the stops would have been considered unsupported by articulated reasonable suspicion."

I do not doubt that most officers act in "good faith" and do not set out to break the law. That does not mean these stops are "isolated instance[s] of negligence," however. Many are the product of institutionalized training procedures. The New York City Police Department long trained officers to, in the words of a District Judge, "stop and question first, develop reasonable suspicion later." The Utah Supreme Court described as "routine procedure" or "common practice" the decision of Salt Lake City police officers to run warrant checks on pedestrians they detained without reasonable suspicion. In the related context of traffic stops, one widely followed police manual instructs officers looking for drugs to "run at least a warrants check on all drivers you stop.* * *."

* * * [U]nlawful "stops" have severe consequences much greater than the inconvenience suggested by the name. * * * [The officer] may order you to stand "helpless, perhaps facing a wall with [your] hands raised." If the officer thinks you might be dangerous, he may then "frisk" you for weapons. This involves more than just a pat down. As onlookers pass by, the officer may "feel with sensitive fingers every portion of [your] body. A thorough search [may] be made of [your] arms and armpits, waistline and back, the groin and area about the testicles, and entire surface of the legs down to the feet."

The officer's control over you does not end with the stop. If the officer chooses, he may handcuff you and take you to jail for doing nothing more than speeding, jaywalking, or "driving [your] pickup truck . . . with [your] 3-year-old son and 5-year-old daughter . . . without [your] seatbelt fastened." At the jail, he can fingerprint you, swab DNA from the inside of your mouth, and force you to "shower with a delousing agent" while you "lift [your] tongue, hold out [your] arms, turn around, and lift [your] genitals." Even if you are innocent, you will now join the 65 million

Americans with an arrest record and experience the "civil death" of discrimination by employers, landlords, and whoever else conducts a background check. And, of course, if you fail to pay bail or appear for court, a judge will issue a warrant to render you "arrestable on sight" in the future.

This case involves a *suspicionless* stop, one in which the officer initiated this chain of events without justification. As the Justice Department notes, many innocent people are subjected to the humiliations of these unconstitutional searches. The white defendant in this case shows that anyone's dignity can be violated in this manner. But it is no secret that people of color are disproportionate victims of this type of scrutiny. For generations, black and brown parents have given their children "the talk"—instructing them never to run down the street; always keep your hands where they can be seen; do not even think of talking back to a stranger—all out of fear of how an officer with a gun will react to them.

By legitimizing the conduct that produces this double consciousness, this case tells everyone, white and black, guilty and innocent, that an officer can verify your legal status at any time. It says that your body is subject to invasion while courts excuse the violation of your rights. It implies that you are not a citizen of a democracy but the subject of a carceral state, just waiting to be cataloged.

We must not pretend that the countless people who are routinely targeted by police are "isolated." They are the canaries in the coal mine whose deaths, civil and literal, warn us that no one can breathe in this atmosphere. They are the ones who recognize that unlawful police stops corrode all our civil liberties and threaten all our lives. Until their voices matter too, our justice system will continue to be anything but.

* * * I dissent.

[JUSTICE KAGAN's dissent has been omitted.]

CHAPTER 17

THE RIGHT TO COUNSEL

■ ■ ■

The Sixth Amendment to the U.S. Constitution provides, "In all criminal prosecutions, the accused shall . . . have the Assistance of Counsel for his defence." In *Johnson v. Zerbst*, 304 U.S. 458 (1938), the U.S. Supreme Court held that the Sixth Amendment requires federal courts to provide an indigent defendant with counsel unless the defendant waives the right to counsel. The Court explained:

> [The Sixth Amendment] embodies a realistic recognition of the obvious truth that the average defendant does not have the professional legal skill to protect himself when brought before a tribunal with power to take his life or liberty, wherein the prosecution is presented by experienced and learned counsel. That which is simple, orderly and necessary to the lawyer, to the untrained layman may appear intricate, complex and mysterious. . . . Even the intelligent and educated layman has small and sometimes no skill in the science of law. If charged with crime, he is incapable, generally, of determining for himself whether the indictment is good or bad. He is unfamiliar with the rules of evidence. Left without the aid of counsel he may be put on trial without a proper charge, and convicted upon incompetent evidence, or evidence irrelevant to the issue or otherwise inadmissible. He lacks both the skill and knowledge adequately to prepare his defen[s]e, even though he ha[s] a perfect one. He requires the guiding hand of counsel at every step in the proceedings against him.

Id. at 462–63.

The cases in this chapter examine whether the right to counsel found in the Sixth Amendment applies to the states as well as the federal government, and whether the right to counsel applies to all defendants, or just those charged with serious offenses.

In *Betts v. Brady*, the first case in this chapter, the Court provides historical context regarding the right to counsel. In *Gideon v. Wainwright*, the Court reconsiders its ruling in *Betts*. In both cases, the central question is whether the right to counsel found in the Sixth Amendment applies to the states through the Due Process Clause of the Fourteenth Amendment. In other words, does the Fourteenth Amendment's Due Process Clause incorporate the Sixth Amendment's right to counsel and make that right applicable to the States? To answer this question, the Court in each case has to decide whether it believes the right to counsel is fundamental to a fair trial.

While the Court in *Gideon v. Wainwright* answered the question of whether the Sixth Amendment applied to the States, it left open other questions. One question *Gideon* did not answer was whether the right to counsel applies to defendants in all cases regardless of the seriousness of the offense charged. *Scott v. Illinois* reflects the Court's answers to this and other questions. A later chapter, entitled "The Role of Criminal Defense Counsel," explores issues concerning the right to effective assistance of counsel, the right to counsel of one's choice, and the right to represent oneself at trial. In the last excerpt in the chapter, *The Gender of Gideon*, Professors Kathryn Sabbeth and Jessica Steinberg show how the constitutional right to counsel largely accrues to the benefit of men over women.

BETTS V. BRADY
Supreme Court of the United States
316 U.S. 455, 62 S. Ct. 1252, 86 L. Ed. 1595 (1942)

JUSTICE ROBERTS delivered the opinion of the Court.

The petitioner was indicted for robbery in the Circuit Court of Carroll County, Maryland. Due to lack of funds, he was unable to employ counsel, and so informed the judge at his arraignment. He requested that counsel be appointed for him. The judge advised him that this could not be done, as it was not the practice in Carroll County to appoint counsel for indigent defendants, save in prosecutions for murder and rape.

Without waiving his asserted right to counsel, the petitioner pleaded not guilty and elected to be tried without a jury. At his request witnesses were summoned in his behalf. He cross-examined the State's witnesses and examined his own. The latter gave testimony tending to establish an alibi. Although afforded the opportunity, he did not take the witness stand. The judge found him guilty and imposed a sentence of eight years. * * *

Was the petitioner's conviction and sentence a deprivation of his liberty without due process of law, in violation of the Fourteenth Amendment, because of the court's refusal to appoint counsel at his request?

The Sixth Amendment of the national Constitution applies only to trials in federal courts. The due process clause of the Fourteenth Amendment does not incorporate, as such, the specific guarantees found in the Sixth Amendment, although a denial by a State of rights or privileges specifically embodied in that and others of the first eight amendments may, in certain circumstances, or in connection with other elements, operate, in a given case, to deprive a litigant of due process of law in violation of the Fourteenth. Due process of law is secured against invasion by the federal Government by the Fifth Amendment and is safeguarded against state action in identical words by the Fourteenth. The phrase formulates a concept less rigid and more fluid than those envisaged in other specific and particular provisions of the Bill of Rights. * * * Asserted denial is to be tested by an appraisal of the totality of facts in a given case. That which may, in one setting, constitute a denial of fundamental fairness, shocking to the universal sense of justice, may, in other circumstances, and in the light of other considerations, fall short of such denial. * * *

The petitioner, in this instance, asks us, in effect, to apply a rule in the enforcement of the due process clause. He says the rule to be deduced from our former decisions is that, in every case, whatever the circumstances, one charged with crime, who is unable to obtain counsel, must be furnished counsel by the State. * * *

In *Powell v. Alabama*, ignorant and friendless negro youths, strangers in the community, without friends or means to obtain counsel, were hurried to trial for a capital offense without effective appointment of counsel on whom the burden of preparation and trial would rest, and without adequate opportunity to consult even the counsel casually appointed to represent them.[a] This occurred in a State whose statute law required the appointment of counsel for indigent defendants prosecuted for the offense charged. Thus the trial was conducted in disregard of every principle of fairness and in disregard of that which was declared by the law of the State a requisite of fair trial. This court held the resulting convictions were without due process of law. It said that, in the light of all the facts, the failure of the trial court to afford the defendants reasonable time and opportunity to secure counsel as a clear denial of due process. The court stated further that "under the circumstances * * * the necessity of counsel was so vital and imperative that the failure of the trial court to make an effective appointment of counsel was likewise a denial of due process," but added:

> whether this would be so in other criminal prosecutions, or under other circumstances, we need not determine. All that it is

---

[a] Professor Shaun Ossei-Owusu provides us with a bit more detail about the 1932 case of *Powell v. Alabama*:

> Nine black boys in the Depression-era South were accused of raping two white girls on a train and arrested in Scottsboro, Alabama. The defendants—who are commonly referred to as the 'Scottsboro Boys'—were rushed through trials that were dominated by mobs, entailed minimal counsel, and were decided by all-white juries. The Supreme Court overturned their convictions and, for the first time, required states to appoint counsel for indigent capital defendants. It ruled that the Due Process Clause of the Fourteenth Amendment required such appointments.

Shaun Ossei-Owusu, The Sixth Amendment Façade: The Racial Evolution of the Right to Counsel, 167 U. PA. L. REV. 1161, 1192–93 (2019).

necessary now to decide, as we do decide, is that in a capital case, where the defendant is unable to employ counsel, and is incapable adequately of making his own defense because of ignorance, feeblemindedness, illiteracy, or the like, it is the duty of the court, whether requested or not, to assign counsel for him as a necessary requisite of due process of law * * *.

* * * The question we are now to decide is whether due process of law demands that in every criminal case, whatever the circumstances, a state must furnish counsel to an indigent defendant. Is the furnishing of counsel in all cases whatever dictated by natural, inherent, and fundamental principles of fairness? * * * [T]he question recurs whether the constraint laid by the amendment upon the national courts expresses a rule so fundamental and essential to a fair trial, and so, to due process of law, that it is made obligatory upon the States by the Fourteenth Amendment.

* * * [I]n the great majority of the States, it has been the considered judgment of the people, their representatives and their courts that appointment of counsel is not a fundamental right, essential to a fair trial. * * * In light of this evidence, we are unable to say that the concept of due process incorporated in the Fourteenth Amendment obligates the States, whatever may be their own views, to furnish counsel in every such case. * * *

In this case there was no question of the commission of a robbery. The State's case consisted of evidence identifying the petitioner as the perpetrator. The defense was an alibi. Petitioner called and examined witnesses to prove that he was at another place at the time of the commission of the offence. The simple issue was the veracity of the testimony for the State and that for the defendant. As Judge Bond says, the accused was not helpless, but was a man forty-three years old, of ordinary intelligence and ability to take care of his own interests on the trial of that narrow issue. He had once before been in a criminal court, pleaded guilty to larceny and served a sentence and was not wholly unfamiliar with criminal procedure. It is quite clear that in Maryland, if the situation had been otherwise and it had appeared that the petitioner was, for any reason, at a serious disadvantage by reason of the lack of counsel, a refusal to appoint would have resulted in the reversal of a judgment of conviction. Only recently the Court of Appeals has reversed a conviction because it was convinced on the whole record that an accused tried without counsel had been handicapped by the lack of representation.

To deduce from the due process clause a rule binding upon the States in this matter would be to impose upon them, as Judge Bond points out, a requirement without distinction between criminal charges of different magnitude or in respect of courts of varying jurisdiction. As he says: "Charges of small crimes tried before justices of the peace and capital charges tried in the higher courts would equally require the appointment of counsel. Presumably it would be argued that trials in the Traffic Court would require it." And indeed it was said by petitioner's counsel both below and in this court, that as the Fourteenth Amendment extends the protection of due process to property as well as to life and liberty, if we hold with the petitioner logic would require the furnishing of counsel in civil cases involving property.

As we have said, the Fourteenth Amendment prohibits the conviction and incarceration of one whose trial is offensive to the common and fundamental ideas of fairness and right, and while want of counsel in a particular case may result in a conviction lacking in such fundamental fairness, we cannot say that the amendment embodies an inexorable command that no trial for any offense, or in any court, can be fairly conducted and justice accorded a defendant who is not represented by counsel.

The judgment is affirmed. * * *

JUSTICE BLACK, dissenting, with whom JUSTICE DOUGLAS and JUSTICE MURPHY concur.

To hold that the petitioner had a constitutional right to counsel in this case does not require us to say that "no trial for any offense, or in any court, can be fairly conducted and justice accorded a defendant who is not represented by counsel." This case can be determined by resolution of a narrower question: whether in view of the nature of the offense and the circumstances of his trial and conviction, this petitioner was denied the procedural protection which is his right under the Federal Constitution. I think he was.

The petitioner, a farm hand, out of a job and on relief, was indicted in a Maryland state court on a charge of robbery. He was too poor to hire a lawyer. He so informed the court and requested that counsel be appointed to defend him. His request was denied. Put to trial without a lawyer, he conducted his own defense, was found guilty, and was sentenced to eight years' imprisonment. The court below found that the petitioner had "at least an ordinary amount of intelligence." It is clear from his examination of witnesses that he was a man of little education. * * *

If this case had come to us from a federal court, it is clear we should have to reverse it, because the Sixth Amendment makes the right to counsel in criminal cases inviolable by the Federal Government. I believe that the Fourteenth Amendment made the Sixth applicable to the states. But this view, although often urged in dissents, has never been accepted by a majority of this Court and is not accepted today. * * * I believe, however, that, under the prevailing view of due process, as reflected in the opinion just announced, * * * the judgment below should be reversed.

A practice cannot be reconciled with "common and fundamental ideas of fairness and right," which subjects innocent men to increased dangers of conviction merely because of their poverty. Whether a man is innocent cannot be determined from a trial in which, as here, denial of counsel has made it impossible to conclude, with any satisfactory degree of certainty, that the defendant's case was adequately presented. * * *

Denial to the poor of the request for counsel in proceedings based on charges of serious crime has long been regarded as shocking to the "universal sense of justice" throughout this country. In 1854, for example, the Supreme Court of Indiana said:

> It is not to be thought of, in a civilized community, for a moment, that any citizen put in jeopardy of life or liberty should be debarred of counsel because he was too poor to employ such aid. No Court could be respected, or respect itself, to sit and hear such a trial. The defence of the poor, in such cases, is a duty resting somewhere, which will be at once conceded as essential to the accused, to the Court, and to the public.

And most of the other States have shown their agreement by constitutional provisions, statutes, or established practice judicially approved which assure that no man shall be deprived of counsel merely because of his poverty. Any other practice seems to me to defeat the promise of our democratic society to provide equal justice under the law.

NOTE

Although the Court never explicitly used the words "special circumstances," *Betts v. Brady* is often remembered as the case in which the Court adopted a "special circumstances" test for the right to counsel in non-capital cases. Since the *Betts* Court held that the Sixth Amendment did not apply to the states through the Fourteenth Amendment's Due Process Clause, this meant that the states were not required to provide appointed counsel to indigent defendants in all criminal cases. Instead, states were only required to provide appointed counsel in cases involving "special circumstances," i.e., circumstances that would make it difficult for the defendant to receive a fair trial without the assistance of counsel.[a] Special circumstances might, for example, exist if the personal characteristics of the defendant, such as illiteracy or mental illness, made it unlikely that the defendant could prepare an adequate defense on his own or if the case was unusually complex.[b]

---

[a] Bruce R. Jacob, *50 Years Later: Memories of* Gideon v. Wainwright, 87 FLA. BAR J. 10 (Mar. 2013).

[b] In addition to a defendant's illiteracy or mental illness, race appears to have been another factor that courts in the pre-*Gideon* era considered when applying the special circumstance test. As Shaun Ossei-Owusu notes:

> Throughout the 1940s and 1950s, illiterate black defendants were the most common parties in Supreme Court right to counsel cases. The frequency of such cases is a sign of race's importance in influencing the Court's jurisprudence during this period . . . In a two-

In the next case, the Court reconsiders its ruling in *Betts v. Brady.*

GIDEON V. WAINWRIGHT
Supreme Court of the United States
372 U.S. 335, 83 S. Ct. 792, 9 L. Ed. 2d 799 (1963)

JUSTICE BLACK delivered the opinion of the Court.

Petitioner was charged in a Florida state court with having broken and entered a poolroom with intent to commit a misdemeanor. This offense is a felony under Florida law. Appearing in court without funds and without a lawyer, petitioner asked the court to appoint counsel for him, whereupon the following colloquy took place:

> The COURT: Mr. Gideon, I am sorry, but I cannot appoint Counsel to represent you in this case. Under the laws of the State of Florida, the only time the Court can appoint Counsel to represent a Defendant is when that person is charged with a capital offense. I am sorry, but I will have to deny your request to appoint Counsel to defend you in this case.
>
> The DEFENDANT: The United States Supreme Court says I am entitled to be represented by Counsel.

Put to trial before a jury, Gideon conducted his defense about as well as could be expected from a layman. He made an opening statement to the jury, cross-examined the State's witnesses, presented witnesses in his own defense, declined to testify himself, and made a short argument "emphasizing his innocence to the charge contained in the Information filed in this case." The jury returned a verdict of guilty, and petitioner was sentenced to serve five years in the state prison. Later, petitioner filed in the Florida Supreme Court this habeas corpus petition attacking his conviction and sentence on the ground that the trial court's refusal to appoint counsel for him denied him rights "guaranteed by the Constitution and the Bill of Rights by the United States Government." Treating the petition for habeas corpus as properly before it, the State Supreme Court, "upon consideration thereof" but without an opinion, denied all relief. Since 1942, when *Betts v. Brady,* was decided by a divided Court, the problem of a defendant's federal constitutional right to counsel in a state court has been a continuing source of controversy and litigation in both state and federal courts. To give this problem another review here, we granted certiorari. Since Gideon was proceeding in forma pauperis, we appointed counsel to represent him and requested both sides to discuss in their briefs

---

decade span, the Court decided ten cases involving poor, black, illiterate, and uncounseled defendants and was quite explicit about its approach; these were the "special circumstances" that the *Betts* decision seem[ed] to demand for judicial scrutiny.

Shaun Ossei-Owusu, The Sixth Amendment Façade: The Racial Evolution of the Right to Counsel, 167 U. PA. L. REV. 1161, 1197 (2019).

and oral arguments the following: "Should this Court's holding in *Betts v. Brady*, be reconsidered?"

We accept *Betts v. Brady*'s assumption, based as it was on our prior cases, that a provision of the Bill of Rights which is "fundamental and essential to a fair trial" is made obligatory upon the States by the Fourteenth Amendment. We think the Court in *Betts* was wrong, however, in concluding that the Sixth Amendment's guarantee of counsel is not one of these fundamental rights. Ten years before *Betts v. Brady*, this Court, after full consideration of all the historical data examined in *Betts*, had unequivocally declared that "the right to the aid of counsel is of this fundamental character." *Powell v. Alabama*. While the Court at the close of its *Powell* opinion did by its language, as this Court frequently does, limit its holding to the particular facts and circumstances of that case, its conclusions about the fundamental nature of the right to counsel are unmistakable. Several years later, in 1936, the Court reemphasized what it had said about the fundamental nature of the right to counsel in this language:

> We concluded that certain fundamental rights, safeguarded by the first eight amendments against federal action, were also safeguarded against state action by the due process of law clause of the Fourteenth Amendment, and among them the fundamental right of the accused to the aid of counsel in a criminal prosecution.

And again in 1938 this Court said:

> [The assistance of counsel] is one of the safeguards of the Sixth Amendment deemed necessary to insure [sic] fundamental human rights of life and liberty. * * * The Sixth Amendment stands as a constant admonition that if the constitutional safeguards it provides be lost, justice will not "still be done."

* * * The fact is that in deciding as it did—that "appointment of counsel is not a fundamental right, essential to a fair trial"—the Court in *Betts v. Brady* made an abrupt break with its own well-considered precedents. In returning to these old precedents, sounder we believe than the new, we but restore constitutional principles established to achieve a fair system of justice. Not only these precedents but also reason and reflection require us to recognize that in our adversary system of criminal justice, any person haled into court, who is too poor to hire a lawyer, cannot be assured a fair trial unless counsel is provided for him. This seems to us to be an obvious truth. Governments, both state and federal, quite properly spend vast sums of money to establish machinery to try defendants accused of crime. Lawyers to prosecute are everywhere deemed essential to protect the public's interest in an orderly society. Similarly, there are few defendants charged with crime, few indeed, who fail to hire the best lawyers they can get to prepare and present their defenses. That

government hires lawyers to prosecute and defendants who have the money hire lawyers to defend are the strongest indications of the widespread belief that lawyers in criminal courts are necessities, not luxuries. The right for one charged with crime to counsel may not be deemed fundamental and essential to fair trials in some countries, but it is in ours. From the very beginning, our state and national constitutions and laws have laid great emphasis on procedural and substantive safeguards designed to assure fair trials before impartial tribunals in which every defendant stands equal before the law. This noble ideal cannot be realized if the poor man charged with crime has to face his accusers without a lawyer to assist him. A defendant's need for a lawyer is nowhere better stated than in the moving words of Mr. Justice Sutherland in *Powell v. Alabama*:

> The right to be heard would be, in many cases, of little avail if it did not comprehend the right to be heard by counsel. Even the intelligent and educated layman has small and sometimes no skill in the science of law. If charged with crime, he is incapable, generally, of determining for himself whether the indictment is good or bad. He is unfamiliar with the rules of evidence. Left without the aid of counsel he may be put on trial without a proper charge, and convicted upon incompetent evidence, or evidence irrelevant to the issue or otherwise inadmissible. He lacks both the skill and knowledge adequately to prepare his defense, even though he have [sic] a perfect one. He requires the guiding hand of counsel at every step in the proceedings against him. Without it, though he be not guilty, he faces the danger of conviction because he does not know how to establish his innocence.

The Court in *Betts v. Brady* departed from the sound wisdom upon which the Court's holding in *Powell v. Alabama* rested. Florida, supported by two other States, has asked that *Betts v. Brady* be left intact. Twenty-two States, as friends of the Court, argue that *Betts* was "an anachronism when handed down" and that it should now be overruled. We agree.

The judgment is reversed and the cause is remanded to the Supreme Court of Florida for further action not inconsistent with this opinion.

Reversed.

JUSTICE CLARK, concurring in the result. * * *

That the Sixth Amendment requires appointment of counsel in "all criminal prosecutions" is clear, both from the language of the Amendment and from this Court's interpretation. It is equally clear * * * that the Fourteenth Amendment requires such appointment in all prosecutions for capital crimes. The Court's decision today, then, does no more than erase a distinction which has no basis in logic and an increasingly eroded basis in authority.

*** [T]he Constitution makes no distinction between capital and noncapital cases. The Fourteenth Amendment requires due process of law for the deprival of "liberty" just as for deprival of "life," and there cannot constitutionally be a difference in the quality of the process based merely upon a supposed difference in the sanction involved. How can the Fourteenth Amendment tolerate a procedure which it condemns in capital cases on the ground that deprival of liberty may be less onerous than deprival of life—a value judgment not universally accepted—or that only the latter deprival is irrevocable? I can find no acceptable rationalization for such a result, and I therefore concur in the judgment of the Court.

JUSTICE HARLAN, concurring.

I agree that *Betts v. Brady* should be overruled, but consider it entitled to a more respectful burial than has been accorded. ***

In noncapital cases, the "special circumstances" rule has continued to exist in form while its substance has been substantially and steadily eroded. In the first decade after *Betts*, there were cases in which the Court found special circumstances to be lacking, but usually by a sharply divided vote. However, no such decision has been cited to us, and I have found none after *** 1950. At the same time, there have been not a few cases in which special circumstances were found in little or nothing more than the "complexity" of the legal questions presented, although those questions were often of only routine difficulty. The Court has come to recognize, in other words, that the mere existence of a serious criminal charge constituted in itself special circumstances requiring the services of counsel at trial. In truth the *Betts v. Brady* rule is no longer a reality. ***

The special circumstances rule has been formally abandoned in capital cases, and the time has now come when it should be similarly abandoned in noncapital cases, at least as to offenses which, as the one involved here, carry the possibility of a substantial prison sentence. (Whether the rule should extend to all criminal cases need not now be decided.) This indeed does no more than to make explicit something that has long since been foreshadowed in our decisions. ***

On these premises I join in the judgment of the Court.

[JUSTICE DOUGLAS' concurring opinion has been omitted.]

NOTE

Gideon v. Wainright is not usually thought of in racial terms because the defendant in this case, Clarence Earl Gideon, was a white man. Gideon's race, however, was likely one of the reasons the Supreme Court picked his case as the vehicle for overruling *Betts v. Brady*. As Professor Shaun Ossei-Owusu notes:

Gideon was seen as a sympathetic figure; he was a poor white man who cycled in and out of prison and was denied justice.... [I]t is difficult to think of any convicted felon ... who has received such sympathy in the popular imagination and in legal lore. As one commentator notes, "[t]hough he is now a folk-hero for indigent defense, Clarence Gideon was no choir boy. In one case he admitted to stealing guns, robbing stores and planning a bank heist." ... Kim Taylor-Thompson astutely observes that the American public may have warmly embraced the outcome, "[b]ut it is unlikely that most Americans viewed the average accused criminal quite so sympathetically."[a]

Choosing a case with a white man as the defendant allowed the Warren Court to address the fact that under the law as it existed prior to *Gideon*, poor Black men were seldom afforded counsel—without appearing to be deciding the case on racial grounds.[b]

Gideon v. Wainright has not fulfilled its early promise of justice and equality for indigent defendants, most of whom are Black or brown.[c] In large part, this is because counsel representing indigent defendants receive very little compensation for their efforts. Fifty years after *Gideon* was decided, the National Association of Criminal Defense Lawyers (NACDL) undertook a 50-state survey to assess the rates of compensation paid to appointed counsel in both misdemeanor and noncapital felony criminal cases. It found that the average rate of compensation for felony cases was less than $65 an hour in the 30 states that have established a statewide compensation rate, with some states paying as little as $40 an hour.[d]

NACDL also found that 26 states had established caps or statutory limits on the total amount of compensation an appointed attorney could receive for work on any given case.[e] For example, fees for a misdemeanor case in Virginia are capped at $158.[f] For lower tier felony charges, appointed counsel in

---

[a] Shaun Ossei-Owusu, *The Sixth Amendment Façade: The Racial Evolution of the Right to Counsel*, 167 U. PA. L. REV. 1161, 1207 (2019).

[b] *Id.* at 1206.

[c] Professor Gabriel Jack Chin observes that while one of the Court's goals in *Gideon* was to ameliorate the widespread discrimination faced by African Americans in the criminal justice system, *Gideon*'s ruling establishing a constitutional right to appointed counsel has not ameliorated racial disparity in arrests, prosecutions, and punishment. Gabriel J. Chin, *Race and the Disappointing Right to Counsel*, 122 YALE L. J. 2236, 2239 (2013).

[d] JOHN P. GROSS, GIDEON AT 50: A THREE-PART EXAMINATION OF INDIGENT DEFENSE IN AMERICA, PART I—RATIONING JUSTICE: THE UNDERFUNDING OF ASSIGNED COUNSEL SYSTEMS 8 (Mar. 2013). As recently as 2019, appointed attorneys in Wisconsin were being paid only $40 per hour. WIS. STAT. § 977.08(4m)(c) (2021) ("for cases assigned on or after July 29, 1995, and before January 1, 2020, private local attorneys shall be paid $40 per hour for time spent related to a case, excluding travel, and $25 per hour for time spent in travel"). Appointed counsel in Wisconsin are now being paid $70 an hour. WIS. STAT. § 977.08(4m)(d) (2021) ("for cases assigned on or after January 1, 2020, private local attorneys shall be paid $70 per hour for time spent related to a case").

[e] GROSS, GIDEON AT 50, *supra* note d, at 9.

[f] *See* VA. CODE ANN. § 19.2–163 (2022).

Virginia can only be paid a maximum of $445.[g] For felonies punishable by more than 20 years in prison, the maximum compensation for appointed counsel is $1,235, which amounts to about 14 hours of work if one is being paid little more than $88 an hour.[h] Can one adequately defend a client charged with a serious felony in fourteen hours?

SCOTT V. ILLINOIS
Supreme Court of the United States
440 U.S. 367, 99 S. Ct. 1158, 59 L. Ed. 2d 383 (1979)

JUSTICE REHNQUIST delivered the opinion of the Court.

We granted certiorari in this case to resolve a conflict among state and lower federal courts regarding the proper application of our decision in *Argersinger v. Hamlin*. Petitioner Scott [who could not afford an attorney and was not appointed counsel to represent him at trial] was convicted of theft and fined $50 after a bench trial in the Circuit Court of Cook County, Ill. His conviction was affirmed by the state intermediate appellate court and then by the Supreme Court of Illinois, over Scott's contention that the Sixth and Fourteenth Amendments to the United States Constitution required that Illinois provide trial counsel to him at its expense.

Petitioner Scott was convicted of shoplifting merchandise valued at less than $150. The applicable Illinois statute set the maximum penalty for such an offense at a $500 fine or one year in jail, or both. The petitioner argues that a line of this Court's cases culminating in *Argersinger v. Hamlin*, requires state provision of counsel whenever imprisonment is an authorized penalty. * * *

In his petition for certiorari, petitioner referred to the issue in this case as "the question left open in *Argersinger v. Hamlin*." Whether this question was indeed "left open" in *Argersinger* depends upon whether one considers that opinion to be a point in a moving line or a holding that the States are required to go only so far in furnishing counsel to indigent defendants. * * *

In *Powell v. Alabama*, the Court held that Alabama was obligated to appoint counsel for the Scottsboro defendants, phrasing the inquiry as "whether the defendants were in substance denied the right of counsel, and if so, whether such denial infringes the due process clause of the Fourteenth Amendment." * * *

Betts v. Brady held that not every indigent defendant accused in a state criminal prosecution was entitled to appointment of counsel. A determination had to be made in each individual case whether failure to

---

[g] *Id.*

[h] Editorial, *Virginia Should Lift Rate Caps for Court-Appointed Lawyers, Boost Public Defenders' Pay*, DAILY PRESS, May 23, 2016.

appoint counsel was a denial of fundamental fairness. *Betts* was in turn overruled in *Gideon v. Wainwright.* * * *

Several Terms [sic] later the Court held in *Duncan v. Louisiana*, that the right to jury trial in federal court guaranteed by the Sixth Amendment was applicable to the States by virtue of the Fourteenth Amendment. The Court held, however: "It is doubtless true that there is a category of petty crimes or offenses which is not subject to the Sixth Amendment jury trial provision and should not be subject to the Fourteenth Amendment jury trial requirement here applied to the States. Crimes carrying possible penalties up to six months do not require a jury trial if they otherwise qualify as petty offenses . . . ." In *Baldwin v. New York*, the controlling opinion of Mr. Justice White concluded that "no offense can be deemed 'petty' for purposes of the right to trial by jury where imprisonment for more than six months is authorized."

In *Argersinger* [where the defendant was charged with a petty offense], the State of Florida urged that a similar dichotomy be employed in the right-to-counsel area: Any offense punishable by less than six months in jail should not require appointment of counsel for an indigent defendant. The *Argersinger* Court rejected this analogy, however, observing that "the right to trial by jury has a different genealogy and is brigaded with a system of trial to a judge alone." * * *

In *Argersinger* the Court [concluded] that incarceration was so severe a sanction that it should not be imposed as a result of a criminal trial unless an indigent defendant had been offered appointed counsel to assist in his defense, regardless of the cost to the States implicit in such a rule. The Court in its opinion repeatedly referred to trials "where an accused is deprived of his liberty," and to "a case that actually leads to imprisonment even for a brief period."

* * * [W]e believe that the central premise of *Argersinger*—that actual imprisonment is a penalty different in kind from fines or the mere threat of imprisonment—is eminently sound and warrants adoption of actual imprisonment as the line defining the constitutional right to appointment of counsel. * * * We therefore hold that the Sixth and Fourteenth Amendments to the United States Constitution require only that no indigent criminal defendant be sentenced to a term of imprisonment unless the State has afforded him the right to assistance of appointed counsel in his defense. The judgment of the Supreme Court of Illinois is accordingly

Affirmed.

JUSTICE POWELL, concurring.

For the reasons stated in my opinion in *Argersinger v. Hamlin*, I do not think the rule adopted by the Court in that case is required by the Constitution. * * * The *Argersinger* rule also tends to impair the proper functioning of the criminal justice system in that trial judges, in advance of hearing any evidence and before knowing anything about the case except the charge, all too often will be compelled to forgo the legislatively granted option to impose a sentence of imprisonment upon conviction. Preserving this option by providing counsel often will be impossible or impracticable—particularly in congested urban courts where scores of cases are heard in a single sitting, and in small and rural communities where lawyers may not be available. * * *

JUSTICE BRENNAN, with whom JUSTICE MARSHALL and JUSTICE STEVENS join, dissenting. * * *

This case presents the question whether the right to counsel extends to a person accused of an offense that, although punishable by incarceration, is actually punished only by a fine. * * *

* * * Earlier precedents had recognized that the assistance of appointed counsel was critical, not only to equalize the sides in an adversary criminal process, but also to give substance to other constitutional and procedural protections afforded criminal defendants.

* * * *Argersinger* held only that an indigent defendant is entitled to appointed counsel, even in petty offenses punishable by six months of incarceration or less, if he is likely to be sentenced to incarceration for any time if convicted. The question of the right to counsel in cases in which incarceration was authorized but would not be imposed was expressly reserved. * * *

* * * [T]he Court today retreats to the indefensible position that the *Argersinger* "actual imprisonment" standard is the *only* test for determining the boundary of the Sixth Amendment right to appointed counsel in state misdemeanor cases, thus necessarily deciding that in many cases (such as this one) a defendant will have no right to appointed counsel even when he has a constitutional right to a jury trial. This is simply an intolerable result. Not only is the "actual imprisonment" standard unprecedented as the exclusive test, but also the problems inherent in its application demonstrate the superiority of an "authorized imprisonment" standard that would require the appointment of counsel for indigents accused of any offense for which imprisonment for any time is authorized. * * *

Perhaps the strongest refutation of respondent's alarmist prophecies that an authorized imprisonment standard would wreak havoc on the States is that the standard has not produced that result in the substantial number of States that already provide counsel in all cases where imprisonment is authorized—States that include a large majority of the country's population and a great diversity of urban and rural environments. Moreover, of those States that do not yet provide counsel in all cases where *any* imprisonment is authorized, many provide counsel when periods of imprisonment longer than 30 days, 3 months, or 6 months are authorized. In fact, Scott would be entitled to appointed counsel under the current laws of at least 33 States. * * *

The Court's opinion * * * restricts the right to counsel, perhaps the most fundamental Sixth Amendment right, more narrowly than the admittedly less fundamental right to jury trial. * * * Today's decision reminds one of Mr. Justice Black's description [in *Gideon v. Wainwright*] of *Betts v. Brady*: "an anachronism when handed down" that "ma[kes] an abrupt break with its own well-considered precedents."

JUSTICE BLACKMUN, dissenting.

For substantially the reasons stated by Mr. Justice Brennan * * *, I would hold that the right to counsel secured by the Sixth and Fourteenth Amendments extends at least as far as the right to jury trial secured by those Amendments. Accordingly, I would hold that an indigent defendant in a state criminal case must be afforded appointed counsel whenever the defendant is prosecuted for a nonpetty criminal offense, that is, one punishable by more than six months' imprisonment, *or* whenever the defendant is convicted of an offense and is actually subjected to a term of imprisonment.

This resolution, I feel, would provide the "bright line" that defendants, prosecutors, and trial and appellate courts all deserve and, at the same time, would reconcile on a principled basis the important considerations that led to the decisions in *Duncan, Baldwin,* and *Argersinger*. * * *

NOTE

The *Scott* Court never mentions the fact that Mr. Scott was a Black man, so the case appears to be devoid of racial implications. Professor Shaun Ossei-Owusu, however, points out:

> Aubrey Scott was a fifty-two-year-old black man who was arrested for theft of a briefcase and an address book from a Woolworth's in downtown Chicago. Unrepresented during his bench trial, Scott was convicted. The punishment for the crime was a fine. He appealed and argued that he should have been appointed an attorney. The court ruled that the appointment of counsel is limited to cases in which defendants are actually imprisoned; appointment was not constitutionally required in cases involving a fine.[a]

Providing important historical context for the decision, Ossei-Owusu notes that *Scott v. Illinois* was decided "during a moment of stagflation in the American economy."[b] "During this period, some people believed that the

---

[a] Shaun Ossei-Owusu, *The Sixth Amendment Façade: The Racial Evolution of the Right to Counsel*, 167 U. PA. L. REV. 1161, 1217 (2019).

[b] *Id.*

welfare state was bloated."c "Ronald Reagan, who was on the campaign trail during the *Scott* litigation, 'rode into office backed by a largely white middle-class tax revolt, resentful of what it perceived as state largesse for undeserving, lazy, and crime-prone Black and Brown people.' "d

As Ossei-Owusu notes, the racial ramifications of the *Scott* decision have, until recently, eluded scholars. One scholar who has written about how *Scott* has impacted racial minorities today is Beth Colgan. Ossei-Owusu explains:

> Beth Colgan offers a valuable and contemporary analysis of *Scott* and the punitive fees and fines that were at the Center of the Ferguson reporte . . . Colgan suggests that lack of access to counsel may have helped produce some of Ferguson's problems. "Had people subjected to Ferguson's Municipal Court scheme been afforded indigent defense representation," she argues, "they would have been better able to challenge violations of numerous procedural and substantive constitutional rights, making many of the abuses that occurred illegal and fiscally impossible." *Scott*'s conclusion, that counsel is only constitutionally necessary in cases involving incarceration, helps make better sense of the Ferguson debacle.f

Race is not the only issue that is often overlooked in criminal procedure cases. Gender is often overlooked as well. In the next excerpt, Professors Kathryn Sabbeth and Jessica Steinberg argue that the right to counsel adopted by the Supreme Court in *Gideon v. Wainright* accrues largely to the benefit of men. Putting gender at the center of their analysis, they argue that the constitutional right to counsel is gendered, pointing to the uncontroverted fact that "the vast majority of criminal defendants with a constitutional right to counsel are men" while women "appear much more often as defendants in civil proceedings, where they enjoy no such right." Regardless of whether you agree with their claim that the right to counsel is gendered, do you think civil litigants should have a right to appointed counsel?

---

c *Id.*

d *Id.* at 1218.

e In the wake of the highly controversial police shooting of Michael Brown, an 18-year-old Black male, by former Ferguson, Missouri police officer Darren Wilson, the U.S. Department of Justice investigated both the shooting and the system of law enforcement in the City of Ferguson, Missouri. *See* Mark Berman & Wesley Lowery, *The 12 Key Highlights From the DOJ's Scathing Ferguson Report*, WASH. POST (Mar. 4, 2015), https://www.washingtonpost.com/news/post-nation/wp/2015/03/04/the-12-key-highlights-from-the-dojs-scathing-ferguson-report/ (https://perma.cc/4QSG-ZMLQ) (noting that in its report on Ferguson, Missouri, the U.S. Department of Justice "determined that in 'nearly every aspect of Ferguson's law enforcement system,' African Americans are impacted a severely disproportionate amount" and found "racist e-mails sent by police and municipal court supervisors, repeated examples of bias in law enforcement and a system that seemed built upon using arrest warrants to squeeze money out of residents").

f Ossei-Owusu, *supra* note a, at 1220, *citing* Beth A. Colgan, *Fines, Fees, and Forfeitures*, REFORMING CRIM. JUST. 205, 225 (2017) and Beth A. Colgan, *Lessons from Ferguson on Individual Defense Representation as a Tool of Systemic Racism*, 58 WM. & MARY L. REV. 1171, 1178 (2017).

THE GENDER OF GIDEON
Kathryn A. Sabbeth & Jessica K. Steinberg
69 UCLA L. Rev. __ (2022)

This Article introduces the phenomenon of the gendered right to counsel. The Supreme Court's famous decision in *Gideon v. Wainwright* guaranteed a federal constitutional right to counsel for criminal defendants facing incarceration. Advocates have pressed for an extension of that right to civil matters in which fundamental interests are stake, but the Supreme Court has demurred. The American Bar Association and other prominent groups have since questioned the Supreme Court's conclusion that criminal defense is uniquely important, particularly in comparison with the defense of shelter, sustenance, safety, healthcare, and parental rights. The economic fallout of the pandemic has put many of these interests at the center of national dialogue, and, increasingly, elected officials have acknowledged the importance of a right to counsel for those in distress. In both advocacy and academic literature, however, one consideration that has received surprisingly little attention is gender.

In this Article, we make a simple claim that has been overlooked for decades and yet has enormous symbolic, theoretical, and real-world significance: the constitutional guarantee of counsel accrues largely to the benefit of men. The vast majority of criminal defendants with a constitutional right to counsel are men. Women, in contrast, appear much more often as defendants in civil proceedings, where they enjoy no such right.

The absence of a right to counsel in civil cases has significant implications for racial justice as well as gender justice. Scholars have produced a great deal of important research on the role of race in the criminal justice system, but the literature has devoted less attention to race in the civil justice system. Why? Because, we argue, the individuals most affected are women. As one of us has noted previously, in both criminal and civil proceedings, the defendants unable to afford counsel are disproportionately people of color. Yet, in civil proceedings, they are also disproportionately women. * * * This Article is the first to present data to show that, across case types, gender is extremely significant with respect to who benefits from the right to counsel. We refer to this phenomenon, whereby one set of defendants enjoys a constitutionally guaranteed right while the other does not, as the gendered right to counsel, or, the "gender of Gideon."

* * *

[R]ight-to-counsel jurisprudence offers an important but overlooked illustration of the Supreme Court prioritizing the interests of men while marginalizing the interests of women, particularly Black women. The two key cases on the right to counsel are *Gideon v. Wainwright* and *Lassiter v.*

Department of Social Services. In one, a white man fought for his physical liberty, and in the other, a Black woman fought to maintain a connection to her child. The former was celebrated but the latter dismissed. These cases have shaped modern doctrine from the inception of a constitutional right to counsel, to the present.

Clarence Gideon's Liberty Interest

The Supreme Court has historically approached the right to counsel as a question of liberty. In 1932, the Supreme Court ruled in *Powell v. Alabama* that capital prosecution without appointed counsel violated the Fourteenth Amendment. The opinion explained that "the right involved is of such a character that it cannot be denied without violating those fundamental principles of liberty and justice which lie at the base of all our civil and political institutions." The Justices [in *Johnson v. Zerbst*] broadened the right beyond capital crimes to all federal criminal cases that threatened "fundamental human rights of life and liberty." In 1963, in *Gideon v. Wainwright*, the Court extended the rule to state cases, solidifying the right to appointment of counsel across the land. * * * *Gideon* was grounded in the Justices' conception of basic fairness.

The decision reflected the judges' sympathy for Clarence Gideon's position. The State of Florida had charged Mr. Gideon, a poor white man, with a felony, specifically breaking into a pool hall with the intent to commit a misdemeanor. Explaining regretfully that appointment of counsel was only for capital offenses, the trial judge apologized repeatedly to Mr. Gideon for the state of the law. Mr. Gideon continued pro se and was convicted by a jury. While serving his sentence, he filed a habeas corpus petition. The Supreme Court chose to hear his case.

Importantly, the Justices not only granted certiorari—deeming the case worthy of a hearing—but also appointed counsel on appeal. They provided representation for Mr. Gideon so that they, and he, would have the benefit of an attorney to fully brief the issues they were to consider. It is difficult to imagine how they would have handled the proceeding without first appointing an attorney. Yet they did appoint an attorney, and with that benefit, the Court ruled in his favor.

Gideon established the rule familiar today: an indigent criminal defendant facing the threat of incarceration is entitled to appointment of counsel. The *Gideon* Court's decision did not depend on weighing the defendant's liberty interest against countervailing factors. Nor did it depend on the length of time of the contemplated prison sentence. Rather, the Court concluded that the criminal defendant's right to appointment of counsel is fundamental.

Abby Gail Lassiter's Liberty Interest

The Supreme Court has only once considered a right-to-counsel argument presented on behalf of a woman. It decided *Lassiter v. Department of Social Services* in 1981, half a century after *Powell v. Alabama*. Like Clarence Gideon, Abby Gail Lassiter raised a Fourteenth Amendment due process argument, but the Court approached the two cases quite differently. That difference is not explained by the text of the Constitution but by the difference in who and what came before the Court.

Ms. Lassiter, a Black woman, was the mother of five children. A social worker took her second youngest, Billy, when he was an infant. The Durham County Department of Social Services then sought to terminate the mother-son relationship permanently. At the hearing regarding termination, the Department of Social Services was represented by a practiced assistant district attorney, while Ms. Lassiter was pro se. In contrast to Mr. Gideon's experience, the trial judge in Ms. Lassiter's case was not troubled by the defendant's lack of counsel. The attorney for the state offered to postpone the matter so that Ms. Lassiter could seek representation, but the judge announced that if Ms. Lassiter had wanted a lawyer, she would have obtained one, and he began the process of terminating her parental rights without delay. The hearing transcript reveals a family court judge alarmingly unconcerned about the evidentiary foundations missing from the state's case—the party with the burden of proof—while laser-focused on failures of form by the unrepresented, Black, female defendant. Not surprisingly, when the hearing concluded, the judge announced from the bench that he would sign the termination order, and Ms. Lassiter's relationship with Billy ended immediately. Ms. Lassiter appealed, contesting the denial of her right to appointed counsel.

When the case reached the Supreme Court, the majority did not see in Ms. Lassiter's situation any of the unfairness that informed its prior right-to-counsel opinions, and it did not take up any consideration of gender equity in its deliberations. It decreed that "fundamental fairness" was implicated only "where a litigant may lose his physical liberty if he loses the litigation." Moreover, the majority fashioned a new "presumption that an indigent litigant has a right to appointed counsel only when, if he loses, he may be deprived of his physical liberty." As the key language in the opinion demonstrates, the decision was reached at a time when it was still acceptable for male pronouns to be used as if neutral. Indeed, the presumption of a male subject taking center stage in constitutional law was so engrained that the opinion in *Lassiter* repeatedly (and awkwardly) refers to the female appellant as "he." It is not a stretch to suppose that the Justices, all men, saw the prototypical beneficiary of constitutional rights as a man.

After reemphasizing the newly constructed presumption that a man's physical liberty is the only interest important enough to trigger a right to counsel, the Court then weighed the costs and benefits of appointing a lawyer in Ms. Lassiter's case. The use of a cost-benefit analysis for a fundamental right is itself worthy of critique, but for our purposes what should be recognized is the establishment of a two-track system of analysis. In one set of cases, the right to counsel is guaranteed (to a white man) by what the Court identified as "fundamental principles of liberty and justice," while in a parallel set of cases, the right to counsel is only available (to a Black woman) if it outweighs other social concerns. In Ms. Lassiter's case, when the majority invoked the three-factor test of *Mathews v. Eldridge*—comparing the individual's interests, the risk of error without the requested intervention, and the state's interests—it was forced to acknowledge the social importance of parental rights. Despite this acknowledgement, the Court deprived Ms. Lassiter of appointed counsel nonetheless. In sum, the Court flatly concluded that the right to parent was categorically less important than physical liberty.

Chapter 18

Interrogations—The Due Process Voluntariness Test

■ ■ ■

This chapter and the next two chapters examine the rules governing police interrogations. Confessions resulting from police interrogations may be challenged under three constitutional provisions: the Due Process Clause, the Sixth Amendment's right to counsel provision, and the Fifth Amendment's privilege against self-incrimination. The cases in this chapter consider when police interrogation practices violate due process. The cases in Chapter 19 consider when confessions obtained by the police violate a defendant's Sixth Amendment right to counsel. The cases in Chapter 20 focus on when a suspect's statements violate the *Miranda* rule, which is based on the Fifth Amendment's privilege against self-incrimination.

The Fourteenth Amendment to the U.S. Constitution, which applies to state and local governments, provides in relevant part that no state shall "deprive any person of life, liberty, or property, without due process of law." Similarly, the Fifth Amendment, which applies to the federal government, provides, that "[n]o person shall . . . be deprived of life, liberty, or property, without due process of law." According to the Supreme Court, a defendant is denied due process of law if police coerce a statement from the defendant. A statement that is the product of police coercion rather than the individual's free choice is considered an involuntary statement and must be excluded at trial. The voluntariness of a confession is assessed by considering the totality of all the circumstances. The cases in this chapter help us understand what factors are relevant to the voluntariness inquiry.

In *Ashcraft v. Tennessee*, the Court considers whether a non-stop, 36 hour interrogation that results in a confession to murder is so inherently coercive that the use of that confession at trial violates due process. In *Spano v. New York*, the Court considers whether the use of a "false friend" to extract a confession renders that confession involuntary. Finally, in *Lisenba v. California*, the Court determines whether a confession following a lengthy interrogation that included at least one slap is involuntary. As you read the cases in this chapter, try to discern what motivates the Court's concerns about involuntary confessions. Is it that involuntary confessions are untrustworthy or do the Court's concerns transcend the truth or falsity of the confession? Additionally, what role does or should a suspect's individual characteristics play in the Court's voluntariness inquiry?

ASHCRAFT V. STATE OF TENNESSEE
Supreme Court of the United States
322 U.S. 143, 64 S. Ct. 921, 88 L. Ed. 1192 (1944)

JUSTICE BLACK delivered the opinion of the Court.

About three o'clock on the morning of Thursday, June 5, 1941, Mrs. Zelma Ida Ashcraft got in her automobile at her home in Memphis, Tennessee, and set out on a trip to visit her mother's home in Kentucky. Late in the afternoon of the same day her car was observed a few miles out of Memphis, standing on the wrong side of a road which she would likely have taken on her journey. Just off the road, in a slough, her lifeless body was found. On her head were cut places inflicted by blows sufficient to have caused her death. Petitioner Ware, age 20, a Negro, was indicted in a state court and found guilty of her murder. Petitioner Ashcraft, age 45, a white man, husband of the deceased, charged with having hired Ware to commit the murder, was tried jointly with Ware and convicted as an accessory before the fact. Both were sentenced to ninety-nine years in the state penitentiary. The Supreme Court of Tennessee affirmed the convictions.

In applying to us for certiorari, Ware and Ashcraft urged that alleged confessions were used at their trial which had been extorted from them by state law enforcement officers in violation of the Fourteenth Amendment. * * * Tennessee's legal representatives * * * defended their use [of the confessions] upon the ground that they were not compelled but were "freely and voluntarily made."

* * * Ashcraft was born on an Arkansas farm. At the age of eleven he left the farm and became a farm hand working for others. Years later he gravitated into construction work, finally becoming a skilled dragline and steam shovel operator. Uncontradicted evidence in the record was that he had acquired for himself "an excellent reputation." In 1929 he married the deceased Zelma Ida Ashcraft. Childless, they accumulated, apparently through Ashcraft's earnings, a very modest amount of jointly held property including bank accounts and an equity in the home in which they lived. The Supreme Court of Tennessee found "nothing to show but [that] the home life of Ashcraft and the deceased was pleasant and happy." Several of Mrs. Ashcraft's friends who were guests at the Ashcraft home on the night before her tragic death testified that both husband and wife appeared to be in a happy frame of mind.

The officers first talked to Ashcraft about 6 P.M. on the day of his wife's murder as he was returning home from work. Informed by them of the tragedy, he was taken to an undertaking establishment to identify her body which previously had been identified only by a driver's license. From there he was taken to the county jail where he conferred with the officers until about 2 A.M. No clues of ultimate value came from this conference, though it did result in the officers' holding and interrogating the Ashcrafts' maid and several of her friends. During the following week the officers made extensive investigations in Ashcraft's neighborhood and elsewhere and further conferred with Ashcraft himself on several occasions, but none of these activities produced tangible evidence pointing to the identity of the murderer.

Then, early in the evening of Saturday, June 14, the officers came to Ashcraft's home and "took him into custody." In the words of the Tennessee Supreme Court,

> They took him to an office or room on the northwest corner of the fifth Floor of the Shelby County jail. This office is equipped with all sorts of crime and detective devices such as a fingerprint outfit, cameras, high-powered lights, and such other devices as might be found in a homicide investigating office. * * * It appears that the officers placed Ashcraft at a table in this room on the fifth floor of the county jail with a light over his head and began to quiz him. They questioned him in relays until the following Monday morning, June 16, 1941, around nine-thirty or ten o'clock. It appears that Ashcraft from Saturday evening at seven o'clock until Monday morning at approximately nine-thirty never left this homicide room of the fifth floor.

Testimony of the officers shows that the reason they questioned Ashcraft "in relays" was that they became so tired they were compelled to rest. But from 7:00 Saturday evening until 9:30 Monday morning Ashcraft had no rest. One officer did say that he gave the suspect a single five minutes' respite, but except for this five minutes the procedure consisted of one continuous stream of questions.

As to what happened in the fifth-floor jail room during this thirty-six hour secret examination the testimony follows the usual pattern and is in hopeless conflict. Ashcraft swears that the first thing said to him when he was taken into custody was, "Why in hell did you kill your wife?"; that during the course of the examination he was threatened and abused in various ways; and that as the hours passed his eyes became blinded by a powerful electric light, his body became weary, and the strain on his nerves became unbearable. The officers, on the other hand, swear that throughout the questioning they were kind and considerate. They say that they did not accuse Ashcraft of the murder until four hours after he was brought to the jail building, though they freely admit that from that time on their barrage of questions was constantly directed at him on the assumption that he was the murderer. Together with other persons whom they brought in on Monday morning to witness the culmination of the thirty-six hour ordeal the officers declare that at that time Ashcraft was "cool," "calm," "collected," "normal"; that his vision was unimpaired and his eyes not bloodshot; and that he showed no outward signs of being tired or sleepy.

As to whether Ashcraft actually confessed, there is a similar conflict of testimony. Ashcraft maintains that although the officers incessantly attempted by various tactics of intimidation to entrap him into a confession, not once did he admit knowledge concerning or participation in the crime. And he specifically denies the officers' statements that he accused Ware of the crime, insisting that in response to their questions he merely gave them the name of Ware as one of several men who occasionally had ridden with him to work. The officers' version of what happened, however, is that about 11 P.M. on Sunday night, after twenty-eight hours' constant questioning, Ashcraft made a statement that Ware had overpowered him at his home and abducted the deceased, and was probably the killer. About midnight the officers found Ware and took him into custody, and, according to their testimony, Ware made a self-incriminating statement as of early Monday morning, and at 5:40 A.M. signed by mark a written confession in which appeared the statement that Ashcraft had hired him to commit the murder. This alleged confession of Ware was read to Ashcraft about six o'clock Monday morning, whereupon Ashcraft is said substantially to have admitted its truth in a detailed statement taken down by a reporter. About 9:30 Monday morning a transcript of Ashcraft's purported statement was read to him. The State's position is that he affirmed its truth but refused to sign the transcript, saying that he first wanted to consult his lawyer. As to this latter 9:30 episode the officers' testimony is reinforced by testimony of the several persons whom they brought in to witness the end of the examination.[a]

In reaching our conclusion as to the validity of Ashcraft's confession we do not resolve any of the disputed questions of fact relating to the details of what transpired within the confession chamber of the jail or whether Ashcraft actually did confess. Such disputes, we may say, are an inescapable consequence of secret inquisitorial practices. * * *

Our conclusion is that if Ashcraft made a confession it was not voluntary but compelled. We reach this conclusion from facts which are not in dispute at all. Ashcraft, a citizen of excellent reputation, was taken into custody by police officers. Ten days' examination of the Ashcrafts' maid, and of several others, in jail where they were held, had revealed nothing whatever against Ashcraft. Inquiries among his neighbors and business associates likewise had failed to unearth one single tangible clue pointing to his guilt. For thirty-six hours after Ashcraft's seizure during which

---

[a] One of the witnesses to Ashcraft's admission of guilt was his own family physician, two were disinterested and well-respected businessmen, another was an experienced court reporter who had long held this position of considerable trust, and the final witness was a member of the bar.

period he was held incommunicado, without sleep or rest, relays of officers, experienced investigators, and highly trained lawyers questioned him without respite. From the beginning of the questioning at 7 o'clock on Saturday evening until 6 o'clock on Monday morning Ashcraft denied that he had anything to do with the murder of his wife. And at a hearing before a magistrate about 8:30 Monday morning Ashcraft pleaded not guilty to the charge of murder which the officers had sought to make him confess during the previous thirty-six hours.

We think a situation such as that here shown by uncontradicted evidence is so inherently coercive that its very existence is irreconcilable with the possession of mental freedom by a lone suspect against whom its full coercive force is brought to bear. It is inconceivable that any court of justice in the land, conducted as our courts are, open to the public, would permit prosecutors serving in relays to keep a defendant witness under continuous cross examination for thirty-six hours without rest or sleep in an effort to extract a "voluntary" confession. Nor can we, consistently with Constitutional due process of law, hold voluntary a confession where prosecutors do the same thing away from the restraining influences of a public trial in an open court room.

The Constitution of the United States stands as a bar against the conviction of any individual in an American court by means of a coerced confession. There have been, and are now, certain foreign nations with governments dedicated to an opposite policy: governments which convict individuals with testimony obtained by police organizations possessed of an unrestrained power to seize persons suspected of crimes against the state, hold them in secret custody, and wring from them confessions by physical or mental torture. So long as the Constitution remains the basic law of our Republic, America will not have that kind of government. * * *

JUSTICE JACKSON, dissenting. * * *

This Court never yet has held that the Constitution denies a State the right to use a confession just because the confessor was questioned in custody where it did not also find other circumstances that deprived him of a "free choice to admit, to deny, or to refuse to answer." The Constitution requires that a conviction rest on a fair trial. Forced confessions are ruled out of a fair trial. They are ruled out because they have been wrung from a prisoner by measures which are offensive to concepts of fundamental fairness. Different courts have used different terms to express the test by which to judge the inadmissibility of a confession, such as "forced," "coerced," "involuntary," "extorted," "loss of freedom of will." But always where we have professed to speak with the voice of the due process clause, the test, in whatever words stated, has been applied to the particular confessor at the time of confession.

It is for this reason that American courts hold almost universally and very properly that a confession obtained during or shortly after the confessor has been subjected to brutality, torture, beating, starvation, or physical pain of any kind is prima facie "involuntary." The effect of threats alone may depend more on individual susceptibility to fear. But men are so constituted that many will risk the postponed consequences of yielding to a demand for a confession in order to be rid of present or imminent physical suffering. Actual or threatened violence have no place in eliciting truth and it is fair to assume that no officer of the law will resort to cruelty if truth is what he is seeking. We need not be too exacting about proof of the effects of such violence on the individual involved, for their effect on the human personality is invariably and seriously demoralizing.

When, however, we consider a confession obtained by questioning, even if persistent and prolonged, we are in a different field. Interrogation per se is not, while violence per se is, an outlaw. Questioning is an indispensable instrumentality of justice. It may be abused, of course, * * * but the principles by which we may adjudge when it passes constitutional limits are quite different from those that condemn police brutality, and are far more difficult to apply. * * *

The duration and intensity of an examination or inquisition always have been regarded as one of the relevant and important considerations in estimating its effect on the will of the individual involved. Thirty-six hours is a long stretch of questioning. That the inquiry was prolonged and persistent is a factor that in any calculation of its effect on Ashcraft would count heavily against the confession. But some men would withstand for days pressures that would destroy the will of another in hours. Always heretofore the ultimate question has been whether the confessor was in possession of his own will and self-control at the time of confession. For its bearing on this question the Court always has considered the confessor's strength or weakness, whether he was educated or illiterate, intelligent or moronic, well or ill, Negro or white. * * *

If the constitutional admissibility of a confession is no longer to be measured by the mental state of the individual confessor but by a general doctrine dependent on the clock, it should be capable of statement in definite terms. If thirty-six hours is more than is permissible, what about 24? or 12? or 6? or 1? All are "inherently coercive." * * *

This is not the case of an ignorant and unrepresented defendant who has been the victim of prejudice. Ashcraft was a white man of good reputation, good position, and substantial property. For a week after this crime was discovered he was not detained, although his stories to the officers did not hang together, but was at large, free to consult his friends and counsel. There was no indecent haste, but on the contrary evident deliberation, in suspecting and accusing him. * * *

SPANO V. NEW YORK
Supreme Court of the United States
360 U.S. 315, 79 S. Ct. 1202, 3 L. Ed. 2d 1265 (1959)

CHIEF JUSTICE WARREN delivered the opinion of the Court.

This is another in the long line of cases presenting the question whether a confession was properly admitted into evidence under the Fourteenth Amendment. As in all such cases, we are forced to resolve a conflict between two fundamental interests of society; its interest in prompt and efficient law enforcement, and its interest in preventing the rights of its individual members from being abridged by unconstitutional methods of law enforcement. * * *

The State's evidence reveals the following: Petitioner Vincent Joseph Spano is a derivative citizen of this country, having been born in Messina, Italy. He was 25 years old at the time of the shooting in question and had graduated from junior high school. He had a record of regular employment. The shooting took place on January 22, 1957.

On that day, petitioner was drinking in a bar. The decedent, a former professional boxer weighing almost 200 pounds who had fought in Madison Square Garden, took some of petitioner's money from the bar. Petitioner followed him out of the bar to recover it. A fight ensued, with the decedent knocking petitioner down and then kicking him in the head three or four times. Shock from the force of these blow caused petitioner to vomit. After the bartender applied some ice to his head, petitioner left the bar, walked to his apartment, secured a gun, and walked eight or nine blocks to a candy store where the decedent was frequently to be found. He entered the store in which decedent, three friends of decedent * * * and a boy who was supervising the store were present. He fired five shots, two of which entered the decedent's body, causing his death. * * *

On February 1, 1957, the Bronx County Grand Jury returned an indictment for first-degree murder against petitioner. * * * On February 3, 1957, petitioner called one Gaspar Bruno, a close friend of 8 or 10 years' standing who had attended school with him. Bruno was a fledgling police officer[.] * * * According to Bruno's testimony, petitioner told him "that he took a terrific beating, that the deceased hurt him real bad and he dropped him a couple of times and he was dazed; he didn't know what he was doing and that he went and shot at him." Petitioner told Bruno that he intended to get a lawyer and give himself up. Bruno relayed this information to his superiors.

The following day, February 4, at 7:10 p.m., petitioner, accompanied by counsel, surrendered himself to the authorities[.] * * * His attorney had cautioned him to answer no questions, and left him in the custody of the officers. He was promptly taken to the office of the Assistant District Attorney and at 7:15 p.m. the questioning began[.] * * * The record reveals that the questioning was both persistent and continuous. Petitioner, in accordance with his attorney's instructions, steadfastly refused to answer. * * * Detective Farrell testified:

    Q. And you started to interrogate him?

    A. That is right.

    Q. What did he say?

    A. He said "you would have to see my attorney. I tell you nothing but my name."

    Q. Did you continue to examine him?

    A. Verbally, yes, sir.

He asked one officer, Detective Ciccone, if he could speak to his attorney, but that request was denied. Detective Ciccone testified that he could not find the attorney's name in the telephone book.[4] * * *

At 12:15 a.m. on the morning of February 5, after five hours of questioning * * *, on the Assistant District Attorney's orders petitioner was transferred to the 46th Squad, Ryer Avenue Police Station. The Assistant District Attorney also went to the police station and to some extent continued to participate in the interrogation. Petitioner arrived at 12:30 and questioning was resumed at 12:40.

* * * [P]etitioner persisted in his refusal to answer, and again requested permission to see his attorney. * * * His request was again denied.

It was then that those in charge of the investigation decided that petitioner's close friend, Bruno, could be of use. * * * Although, in fact, his job was in no way threatened, Bruno was told to tell petitioner that petitioner's telephone call had gotten him "in a lot of trouble," and that he should seek to extract sympathy from petitioner for Bruno's pregnant wife and three children. Bruno developed this theme with petitioner without success, and petitioner, also without success, again sought to see his attorney, a request which Bruno relayed unavailingly to his superiors. After this first session with petitioner, Bruno was again directed by Lt. Gannon to play on petitioner's sympathies, but again no confession was forthcoming. But the Lieutenant a third time ordered Bruno falsely to importune his friend to confess but again petitioner clung to his attorney's advice. Inevitably, in the fourth such session directed by the Lieutenant, lasting a full hour, petitioner succumbed to his friend's prevarications and agreed to make a statement. * * *

---

    [4] How this could be so when the attorney's name, Tobias Russo, was concededly in the telephone book does not appear. * * *

At the trial, the confession was introduced in evidence over appropriate objections. The jury was instructed that it could rely on it only if it was found to be voluntary. The jury returned a guilty verdict and petitioner was sentenced to death. The New York Court of Appeals affirmed the conviction * * * and we granted certiorari. * * *

The abhorrence of society to the use of involuntary confessions does not turn alone on their inherent untrustworthiness. It also turns on the deep-rooted feeling that the police must obey the law while enforcing the law; that in the end life and liberty can be as much endangered from illegal methods used to convict those thought to be criminals as from the actual criminals themselves. * * * The facts of no case recently in this Court have quite approached the brutal beatings in *Brown v. State of Mississippi* or the 36 consecutive hours of questioning present in *Ashcraft v. State of Tennessee*. But as law enforcement officers become more responsible, and the methods used to extract confessions more sophisticated, our duty to enforce federal constitutional protections does not cease. * * * Our judgment here is that, on all the facts, this conviction cannot stand.

Petitioner was a foreign-born young man of 25 with no past history of law violation or of subjection to official interrogation, at least insofar as the record shows. He had progressed only one-half year into high school and the record indicates that he had a history of emotional instability. He did not make a narrative statement, but was subject to the leading questions of a skillful prosecutor in a question and answer confession. He was subjected to questioning not by a few men, but by many. * * * All played some part, and the effect of such massive official interrogation must have been felt. Petitioner was questioned for virtually eight straight hours before he confessed, with his only respite being a transfer to an arena presumably considered more appropriate by the police for the task at hand. Nor was the questioning conducted during normal business hours, but began in early evening, continued into the night, and did not bear fruition until the not-too-early morning. The drama was not played out, with the final admissions obtained, until almost sunrise. In such circumstances slowly mounting fatigue does, and is calculated to, play its part. The questioners persisted in the face of his repeated refusals to answer on the advice of his attorney, and they ignored his reasonable requests to contact the local attorney whom he had already retained and who had personally delivered him into the custody of these officers in obedience to the bench warrant.

The use of Bruno, characterized in this Court by counsel for the State as a "childhood friend" of petitioner's, is another factor which deserves mention in the totality of the situation. Bruno's was the one face visible to petitioner in which he could put some trust. There was a bond of friendship between them going back a decade into adolescence. It was with this material that the officers felt that they could overcome petitioner's will.

They instructed Bruno falsely to state that petitioner's telephone call had gotten him into trouble, that his job was in jeopardy, and that loss of his job would be disastrous to his three children, his wife and his unborn child. And Bruno played this part of a worried father, harried by his superiors, in not one, but four different acts, the final one lasting an hour. Petitioner was apparently unaware of John Gay's famous couplet: "An open foe may prove a curse, But a pretended friend is worse," and he yielded to his false friend's entreaties.

We conclude that petitioner's will was overborne by official pressure, fatigue and sympathy falsely aroused after considering all the facts. * * * Here a grand jury had already found sufficient cause to require petitioner to face trial on a charge of first-degree murder, and the police had an eyewitness to the shooting. The police were not therefore merely trying to solve a crime, or even to absolve a suspect. * * * They were rather concerned primarily with securing a statement from defendant on which they could convict him. The undeviating intent of the officers to extract a confession from petitioner is therefore patent. When such an intent is shown, this Court has held that the confession obtained must be examined with the most careful scrutiny, and has reversed a conviction on facts less compelling than these. Accordingly, we hold that petitioner's conviction cannot stand under the Fourteenth Amendment. * * *

JUSTICE DOUGLAS, with whom JUSTICE BLACK and JUSTICE BRENNAN join, concurring. * * *

We have often divided on whether state authorities may question a suspect for hours on end when he has no lawyer present and when he has demanded that he have the benefit of legal advice. But here we deal not with a suspect but with a man who has been formally charged with a crime. The question is whether after the indictment and before the trial the Government can interrogate the accused in secret when he asked for his lawyer and when his request was denied. * * *

Depriving a person, formally charged with a crime, of counsel during the period prior to trial may be more damaging than denial of counsel during the trial itself. * * * [W]hat use is a defendant's right to effective counsel at every stage of a criminal case if, while he is held awaiting trial, he can be questioned in the absence of counsel until he confesses? In that event the secret trial in the police precincts effectively supplants the public trial guaranteed by the Bill of Rights.

JUSTICE STEWART, whom JUSTICE DOUGLAS and JUSTICE BRENNAN join, concurring. * * *

Let it be emphasized at the outset that this is not a case where the police were questioning a suspect in the course of investigating an unsolved crime. When the petitioner surrendered to the New York authorities he was under indictment for first degree murder.

Under our system of justice an indictment is supposed to be followed by an arraignment and a trial. At every stage in those proceedings the accused has an absolute right to a lawyer's help if the case is one in which a death sentence may be imposed.

What followed the petitioner's surrender in this case was not arraignment in a court of law, but an all-night inquisition in a prosecutor's office, a police station, and an automobile. Throughout the night the petitioner repeatedly asked to be allowed to send for his lawyer, and his requests were repeatedly denied. He finally was induced to make a confession. That confession was used to secure a verdict sending him to the electric chair.

Our Constitution guarantees the assistance of counsel to a man on trial for his life in an orderly courtroom, presided over by a judge, open to the public, and protected by all the procedural safeguards of the law. Surely a Constitution which promises that much can vouchsafe no less to the same man under midnight inquisition in the squad room of a police station.

NOTE

The totality of the circumstances test suggests that any and all factors, including the defendant's mental capacity, are relevant when a court is trying to decide whether a defendant's statements to the police were "voluntary." The Court, however, seems to consider some factors more relevant than others. In *Colorado v. Connelly*, 479 U.S. 157 (1986), for example, the Court held that a confession to murder was voluntary even though the defendant, who had been a patient in several mental hospitals, suffered from chronic schizophrenia and was in a psychotic state the day before he confessed to police. A summary of this case is provided below.

On August 18, 1983, Francis Connelly approached a Denver police officer and, without any prompting from the officer, confessed to murder. After being advised of his *Miranda* rights and being told numerous times that he did not need to answer questions, Connelly again confessed and led police to the murder scene. It was later revealed that Connelly was following the "voice of God" when he confessed. At a pre-trial hearing, a psychiatrist employed by the State hospital testified that Connelly's psychosis prevented him from making a free and rational choice. Connelly thought God had instructed him to either confess to the killing or commit suicide. Based on this testimony, the trial court suppressed both the initial confession and post-*Miranda* statements, finding them to be involuntary.

The Supreme Court reversed. In an opinion written by Justice Rehnquist, the Court held that "coercive police activity is a necessary predicate to [a] finding that a confession is not 'voluntary' within the meaning of the Due Process Clause." The Court noted that over the past 50 years, all of the cases in which it found the defendant's confession to be involuntary and thus in violation of due process involved "the crucial element of police overreaching."

While acknowledging that although a defendant's mental condition "is surely relevant to an individual's susceptibility to police coercion," the Court concluded that "this fact does not justify a conclusion that a defendant's mental condition, by itself and apart from its relation to official coercion, should ever dispose of the inquiry into constitutional 'voluntariness.'"

LISENBA V. CALIFORNIA
Supreme Court of the United States
314 U.S. 219, 62 S. Ct. 280, 86 L. Ed. 166 (1941)

JUSTICE ROBERTS delivered the opinion of the Court.

* * * The petitioner, * * * Robert S. James * * *, and one Hope were indicted May 6, 1936, for the murder of James' wife on August 5, 1935. Hope pleaded guilty and was sentenced to life imprisonment. James pleaded not guilty, was tried, convicted, and sentenced to death. * * * The State's theory is that the petitioner conceived the plan of marrying, insuring his wife's life by policies providing double indemnity for accidental death, killing her in a manner to give the appearance of accident, and collecting double indemnity.

James employed Mary E. Busch as a manicurist in his barber shop in March, 1935, and, about a month later, went through a marriage ceremony with her. * * * While they were affianced, insurance was negotiated on her life, with James as beneficiary. * * *

The allegation is that James enlisted one Hope in a conspiracy to do away with Mary and collect and divide the insurance on her life. Hope testified that, at James' instigation, he procured rattlesnakes which were to bite and kill Mary; that they appeared not to be sufficiently venomous for the purpose but he ultimately purchased others and delivered them to James; that James, on August 4, 1935, blindfolded his wife's eyes, tied her to a table, had Hope bring one of the snakes into the room and caused the reptile to bite her foot; that, during the night James told Hope the bite did not have the desired effect and, in the early morning of August 5, he told Hope that he was going to drown his wife; that later * * * at [James'] request, Hope aided him in carrying the body to the yard, and James placed the body face down at the edge of a fish pond with the head and shoulders in the water.

James was at his barber shop on August 5. On that evening he took two friends home for dinner. When they arrived the house was dark and empty, and, upon a search of the grounds, his wife's body was found in the position indicated. An autopsy showed the lungs were almost filled with water. The left great toe showed a puncture and the left leg was greatly swollen and almost black. Nothing came of the investigation of the death.

James attempted to collect double indemnity; the insurers refused to pay; suits were instituted and one of them settled. As a result of this activity, a fresh investigation of Mary James' death was instituted. On April 19, 1936, officers arrested James for the crime of incest. He was booked on this charge on the morning of April 21, was given a hearing and remanded to jail. On May 2 and 3 he made statements respecting his wife's death to the prosecuting officials. * * *

James' statements were offered in evidence. * * * Objection was made that they were not voluntary. Before they were admitted the trial judge heard testimony offered by the State and the defendant on that issue. He ruled that the confessions were admissible, and they were received in evidence.

The petitioner [contends] based upon the Fourteenth Amendment, * * * that his conviction deprived him of his life without due process * * * because physical violence, threats, and other coercive means produced the confessions. * * *

The petitioner, while having almost no formal education, is a man of intelligence and business experience. After his arrest, on the charge of incest, on the morning of Sunday, April 19, 1936, he was taken for a short time to the adjoining house and [then] brought to the District Attorney's offices where he was lodged in the Bureau of Investigation. * * * He was questioned for about an hour. * * *

He was held in the District Attorney's suite until 5 or 6 o'clock, was given supper at a cafe, and then conducted to the house next door to his home, where he arrived about 7 or 7:30. Various officers questioned him there in relays throughout the night concerning his wife's death. He sat in a chair fully dressed and had no sleep. Monday morning he was taken out for breakfast and went with the officers to point out to them a house at 9th and Alvarado Streets, after which he was taken to the District Attorney's offices. He was brought back to the house next door to his home and the questioning was resumed, and continued until about 3 o'clock Tuesday morning when, he says, he fainted, and others present say he fell asleep and slept until 7 or 8 o'clock. After he had breakfasted he was booked at the jail, arraigned before a magistrate, and committed on the incest charge.

James testified that about 10 P.M. Monday, April 20, the officers began to beat him; that his body was made black and blue; that the beating impaired his hearing, and caused a hernia; that later that night an Assistant District Attorney questioned him and that, after this ordeal, he collapsed. It is admitted that an officer slapped his face that night. This is said to have occurred as the result of an offensive remark James made concerning his wife; he denies having made the remark. In corroboration of James' testimony two witnesses said they noticed that one or both of his ears were bruised and swollen when he was lodged in the jail. All of this testimony is contradicted by numerous witnesses for the State, save only that it is admitted James was repeatedly and persistently questioned at intervals during the period from Sunday night until Tuesday morning. It is testified that, except for the one slap, no one laid a hand on James; that no inducement was held out to him; that no threats were made; that he answered questions freely and intelligently; and that he was at ease, cool, and collected. He admits that no promises or threats were made or maltreatment administered on the occasions when he was in the District Attorney's office. It is significant that James stated to one of the other officers that Officer Southard had slapped him and that when, May 2, the District Attorney asked how he had been treated he again referred to the slap. In neither case did he say anything of any other mistreatment. During the period April 19–21 James made no incriminating admission or confession. * * *

There is no claim that from April 21, when he was lodged in the jail, until May 2, he was interviewed, questioned, threatened, or mistreated by anyone. During this period his attorney told him that he would be indicted for his wife's murder and should not answer any questions unless his attorney was present.

* * * On the morning of May 2, James was brought from his cell to the chaplain's room in the prison and confronted with Hope. An Assistant District Attorney outlined Hope's story and asked James whether he had anything to say, to which he replied: "Nothing."

He went back to his cell and, about noon, an order of court was obtained to remove him from the prison. He was taken to his former home by two deputy sheriffs. The evidence does not disclose clearly either the purpose or the incidents of this trip. He was then brought to the District Attorney's office. * * *

The District Attorney and, at times, others questioned James until supper time. Sandwiches and coffee were procured. James says he had coffee but someone took his sandwiches. There is testimony that he had them. The questioning * * * was continued into the night without James having refused to answer questions or having made any incriminating answers.

There is a sharp conflict as to how the session terminated. James says that Officer Southard, who had struck him on April 20, occupied the room alone with him, all others having left; that the officer told him he had been lying all evening and that if he did not tell the truth the officer would take him back to the house and beat him; that this so frightened him that he agreed to do his best to recite to the District Attorney the same story Hope had told. There is much evidence that no such incident occurred. Deputy Sheriff Killion says that sometime before midnight the others had left petitioner alone with him and that petitioner turned to him and said something to the effect: "Why can't we go out and get something to eat; if we do I'll tell you the story." To this Killion replied that they could go out.

Killion and another Deputy Sheriff, Gray, a lady friend, and another person accompanied petitioner to a public cafe where they had a supper and afterwards had cigars. James testified that neither Killion nor Gray nor the District Attorney ever laid hand on him, threatened him or offered him any inducement to confess.

The State's evidence is that after they started to smoke James told a story of which Killion took notes. * * * The party returned to the District Attorney's office and there, responding to a question by the District Attorney, James said he had told Killion the story and, in answer to questions, he repeated that story. The interview was stenographically recorded. * * *

The failure of the arresting officers promptly to produce the petitioner before an examining magistrate, their detention of him in their custody from Sunday morning to Tuesday morning, and any assault committed upon him, were violations of state statutes and criminal offenses. * * * The denial of opportunity to consult counsel, requested on May 2nd, was a misdemeanor. * * *

But illegal acts, as such, committed in the course of obtaining a confession, whatever their effect on its admissibility under local law, do not furnish an answer to the constitutional question we must decide. The effect of the officers' conduct must be appraised by other considerations in determining whether the use of the confessions was a denial of due process. * * * The gravamen of his complaint is the unfairness of the use of his confessions, and what occurred in their procurement is relevant only as it bears on that issue.

* * * The aim of the rule that a confession is inadmissible unless it was voluntarily made is to exclude false evidence. * * * The aim of the requirement of due process is not to exclude presumptively false evidence, but to prevent fundamental unfairness in the use of evidence whether true or false. * * *

As applied to a criminal trial, denial of due process is the failure to observe that fundamental fairness essential to the very concept of justice. In order to declare a denial of it we must find that the absence of that fairness fatally infected the trial; the acts complained of must be of such quality as necessarily prevents a fair trial. Such unfairness exists when a coerced confession is used as a means of obtaining a verdict of guilt. * * *

To extort testimony from a defendant by physical torture in the very presence of the trial tribunal is not due process. The case stands no better if torture induces an extrajudicial confession which is used as evidence in the courtroom. * * *

The concept of due process would void a trial in which, by threats or promises in the presence of court and jury, a defendant was induced to testify against himself. The case can stand no better if, by resort to the same means, the defendant is induced to confess and his confession is given in evidence.

* * * [W]e disapprove the violations of law involved in the treatment of the petitioner, and we think it right to add that where a prisoner held incommunicado is subjected to questioning by officers for long periods, and deprived of the advice of counsel, we shall scrutinize the record with care to determine whether, by the use of his confession, he is deprived of liberty or life through tyrannical or oppressive means. * * * But on the facts as we have endeavored fairly to set them forth, and in the light of the findings in the State courts, we cannot hold that the illegal conduct in which the law enforcement officers of California indulged by the prolonged questioning of the prisoner before arraignment, and in the absence of counsel, or their questioning on May 2, coerced the confessions, the introduction of which is the infringement of due process of which the petitioner complains. The petitioner * * * admits that no threats, promises, or acts of physical violence were offered him during this questioning or for eleven days preceding it. Counsel had been afforded full opportunity to see him and had advised him. He exhibited a self-possession, a coolness, and an acumen throughout his questioning, and at his trial, which negatives the view that he had so lost his freedom of action that the statements made were not his but were the result of the deprivation of his free choice to admit, to deny, or to refuse to answer. * * *

[JUSTICE BLACK's dissenting opinion has been omitted.]

CHAPTER 19

INTERROGATIONS—THE SIXTH AMENDMENT RIGHT TO COUNSEL

■ ■ ■

The Sixth Amendment to the U.S. Constitution provides in relevant part:

In all criminal prosecutions, the accused shall enjoy the right . . . to have the Assistance of Counsel for his defence.

In *Massiah v. United States*, the Court explains what is required for a statement to be ruled inadmissible because it was obtained in violation of the Sixth Amendment right to counsel. In *Escobedo v. Illinois*, the Court considers whether a suspect's Sixth Amendment right to counsel attaches prior to the filing of an indictment.

Brewer v. Williams is famous for Detective Leaming's "Christian burial speech." The case can be somewhat confusing because the Court utilizes the term "interrogation" in its analysis, a term that is typically used when courts are deciding the admissibility of a confession under the *Miranda* rule, as opposed to the Sixth Amendment. After assessing whether Detective Leaming deliberately elicited incriminating statements from the defendant, the Court evaluates whether the defendant validly waived his Sixth Amendment right to counsel. Try to discern whether the majority and dissenting opinions agree on what is necessary for a valid waiver. Which opinion has the better argument on the waiver question?

In the last two cases in this section, *United States v. Henry* and *Kulhman v. Wilson*, the Court addresses whether a suspect's Sixth Amendment right to counsel is violated when the suspect speaks with a jailhouse informant. Pay close attention to the way the Court in *Henry* describes the meaning of "deliberate elicitation" in the jailhouse informant context.

MASSIAH V. UNITED STATES
Supreme Court of the United States
377 U.S. 201, 84 S. Ct. 1199, 12 L. Ed. 2d 246 (1964)

JUSTICE STEWART delivered the opinion of the Court.

The petitioner was indicted for violating the federal narcotics laws. He retained a lawyer, pleaded not guilty, and was released on bail. While he was free on bail a federal agent succeeded by surreptitious means in listening to incriminating statements made by him. Evidence of these statements was introduced against the petitioner at his trial over his objection. He was convicted, and the Court of Appeals affirmed. We granted certiorari to consider whether, under the circumstances here presented, the prosecution's use at the trial of evidence of the petitioner's own incriminating statements deprived him of any right secured to him under the Federal Constitution.

The petitioner, a merchant seaman, was in 1958 a member of the crew of the S. S. Santa Maria. In April of that year federal customs officials in New York received information that he was going to transport a quantity of narcotics aboard that ship from South America to the United States. As a result of this and other information, the agents searched the Santa Maria upon its arrival in New York and found * * * five packages containing about three and a half pounds of cocaine. They also learned of circumstances, not here relevant, tending to connect the petitioner with the cocaine. He was arrested, promptly arraigned, and subsequently indicted for possession of narcotics aboard a United States vessel. In July a superseding indictment was returned, charging the petitioner and a man named Colson with the same substantive offense, and in separate counts charging the petitioner, Colson, and others with having conspired to possess narcotics aboard a United States vessel, and to import, conceal, and facilitate the sale of narcotics. The petitioner, who had retained a lawyer, pleaded not guilty and was released on bail, along with Colson.

A few days later, and quite without the petitioner's knowledge, Colson decided to cooperate with the government agents in their continuing investigation of the narcotics activities in which the petitioner, Colson, and others had allegedly been engaged. Colson permitted an agent named Murphy to install a Schmidt radio transmitter under the front seat of Colson's automobile, by means of which Murphy, equipped with an appropriate receiving device, could overhear from some distance away conversations carried on in Colson's car.

On the evening of November 19, 1959, Colson and the petitioner held a lengthy conversation while sitting in Colson's automobile, parked on a New York street. By prearrangement with Colson, and totally unbeknown to the petitioner, the agent Murphy sat in a car parked out of sight down the street and listened over the radio to the entire conversation. The petitioner made several incriminating statements during the course of this conversation. At the petitioner's trial these incriminating statements were brought before the jury through Murphy's testimony, despite the insistent objection of defense counsel. The jury convicted the petitioner of several related narcotics offenses, and the convictions were affirmed by the Court of Appeals.

The petitioner argues that it was an error of constitutional dimensions to permit the agent Murphy at the trial to testify to the petitioner's incriminating statements which Murphy had overheard under the circumstances disclosed by this record. * * * [I]t is said that the petitioner's Fifth and Sixth Amendment rights were violated by the use in evidence against him of incriminating statements which government agents had deliberately elicited from him after he had been indicted and in the absence of his retained counsel. Because of the way we dispose of the case, we do not reach the Fourth Amendment issue.

In *Spano*, this Court reversed a state criminal conviction because a confession had been wrongly admitted into evidence against the defendant at his trial. In that case the defendant had already been indicted for first-degree murder at the time he confessed. The Court held that the defendant's conviction could not stand under the Fourteenth Amendment. While the Court's opinion relied upon the totality of the circumstances under which the confession had been obtained, four concurring Justices pointed out that the Constitution required reversal of the conviction upon the sole and specific ground that the confession had been deliberately elicited by the police after the defendant had been indicted, and therefore at a time when he was clearly entitled to a lawyer's help. It was pointed out that under our system of justice the most elemental concepts of due process of law contemplate that an indictment be followed by a trial, "in an orderly courtroom, presided over by a judge, open to the public, and protected by all the procedural safeguards of the law." It was said that a Constitution which guarantees a defendant the aid of counsel at such a trial could surely vouchsafe no less to an indicted defendant under interrogation by the police in a completely extrajudicial proceeding. Anything less, it was said, might deny a defendant "effective representation by counsel at the only stage when legal aid and advice would help him."

Ever since this Court's decision in the *Spano* case, the New York courts have unequivocally followed this constitutional rule. Any secret interrogation of the defendant, from and after the finding of the indictment, without the protection afforded by the presence of counsel, contravenes the basic dictates of fairness in the conduct of criminal cases and the fundamental rights of persons charged with crime. * * *

Here we deal not with a state court conviction, but with a federal case, where the specific guarantee of the Sixth Amendment directly applies. We hold that the petitioner was denied the basic protections of that guarantee when there was used against him at his trial evidence of his own incriminating words, which federal agents had deliberately elicited from him after he had been indicted and in the absence of his counsel. It is true that in the *Spano* case the defendant was interrogated in a police station, while here the damaging testimony was elicited from the defendant without his knowledge while he was free on bail. But, as Judge Hays pointed out in his dissent in the Court of Appeals, "if such a rule is to have any efficacy it must apply to indirect and surreptitious interrogations as well as those conducted in the jailhouse. In this case, Massiah was more seriously imposed upon * * * because he did not even know that he was under interrogation by a government agent."

The Solicitor General, in his brief and oral argument, has strenuously contended that the federal law enforcement agents had the right, if not indeed the duty, to continue their investigation of the petitioner and his alleged criminal associates even though the petitioner had been indicted. * * * [T]he Solicitor General concludes that the Government agents were completely "justified in making use of Colson's cooperation by having Colson continue his normal associations and by surveilling them."

We may accept and, at least for present purposes, completely approve all that this argument implies, Fourth Amendment problems to one side. We do not question that in this case, as in many cases, it was entirely proper to continue an investigation of the suspected criminal activities of the defendant and his alleged confederates, even though the defendant had already been indicted. All that we hold is that the defendant's own incriminating statements, obtained by federal agents under the circumstances here disclosed, could not constitutionally be used by the prosecution as evidence against him at his trial.

Reversed.

JUSTICE WHITE, with whom JUSTICE CLARK and JUSTICE HARLAN join, dissenting.

* * * In my view, a civilized society must maintain its capacity to discover transgressions of the law and to identify those who flout it. This much is necessary even to know the scope of the problem, much less to formulate intelligent counter-measures. It will just not do to sweep these disagreeable matters under the rug or to pretend they are not there at all.

It is therefore a rather portentous occasion when a constitutional rule is established barring the use of evidence which is relevant, reliable and highly probative of the issue which the trial court has before it—whether the accused committed the act with which he is charged. Without the evidence, the quest for truth may be seriously impeded and in many cases the trial court, although aware of proof showing defendant's guilt, must nevertheless release him because the crucial evidence is deemed inadmissible. This result is entirely justified in some circumstances because exclusion serves other policies of overriding importance, as where evidence seized in an illegal search is excluded, not because of the quality of the proof, but to secure meaningful enforcement of the Fourth Amendment. But this only emphasizes that the soundest of reasons is necessary to warrant the exclusion of evidence otherwise admissible and the creation of another area of privileged testimony. With all due deference, I am not at all convinced that the additional barriers to the pursuit of truth which the Court today erects rest on anything like the solid foundations which decisions of this gravity should require. * * *

Whatever the content or scope of the rule may prove to be, I am unable to see how this case presents an unconstitutional interference with Massiah's right to counsel. Massiah was not prevented from consulting with counsel as often as he wished. No meetings with counsel were disturbed or spied upon. Preparation for trial was in no way obstructed. It is only a sterile syllogism—an unsound one, besides—to say that because Massiah had a right to counsel's aid before and during the trial, his out-of-court conversations and admissions must be excluded if obtained without counsel's consent or presence. The right to counsel has never meant as much before, and its extension in this case requires some further explanation, so far unarticulated by the Court. * * *

Applying the new exclusionary rule is peculiarly inappropriate in this case. At the time of the conversation in question, petitioner was not in custody but free on bail. He was not questioned in what anyone could call an atmosphere of official coercion. What he said was said to his partner in crime who had also been indicted. There was no suggestion or any possibility of coercion. What petitioner did not know was that Colson had decided to report the conversation to the police. Had there been no prior arrangements between Colson and the police, had Colson simply gone to the police after the conversation had occurred, his testimony relating Massiah's statements would be readily admissible at the trial, as would a recording which he might have made of the conversation. In such event, it would simply be said that Massiah risked talking to a friend who decided to disclose what he knew of Massiah's criminal activities. But, if, as occurred here, Colson had been cooperating with the police prior to his meeting with Massiah, both his evidence and the recorded conversation are somehow transformed into inadmissible evidence despite the fact that the hazard to Massiah remains precisely the same—the defection of a confederate in crime. * * *

ESCOBEDO V. ILLINOIS

Supreme Court of the United States
378 U.S. 478, 84 S. Ct. 1758, 12 L. Ed. 2d 977 (1964)

JUSTICE GOLDBERG delivered the opinion of the Court.

The critical question in this case is whether, under the circumstances, the refusal by the police to honor petitioner's request to consult with his lawyer during the course of an interrogation constitutes a denial of "the Assistance of Counsel" in violation of the Sixth Amendment to the Constitution as "made obligatory upon the States by the Fourteenth

Amendment," and thereby renders inadmissible in a state criminal trial any incriminating statement elicited by the police during the interrogation.

On the night of January 19, 1960, petitioner's brother-in-law was fatally shot. In the early hours of the next morning, at 2:30 a.m., petitioner was arrested without a warrant and interrogated. Petitioner made no statement to the police and was released at 5 that afternoon pursuant to a state court writ of habeas corpus obtained by Mr. Warren Wolfson, a lawyer who had been retained by petitioner.

On January 30, Benedict DiGerlando, who was then in police custody and who was later indicted for the murder along with petitioner, told the police that petitioner had fired the fatal shots. Between 8 and 9 that evening, petitioner and his sister, the widow of the deceased, were arrested and taken to police headquarters. En route to the police station, the police "had handcuffed the defendant behind his back," and "one of the arresting officers told defendant that DiGerlando had named him as the one who shot" the deceased. Petitioner testified, without contradiction, that the "detective said they had us pretty well, up pretty tight, and we might as well admit to this crime," and that he replied, "I am sorry but I would like to have advice from my lawyer." A police officer testified that although petitioner was not formally charged "he was in custody" and "couldn't walk out the door."

Shortly after petitioner reached police headquarters, his retained lawyer arrived. The lawyer described the ensuing events in the following terms:

> On that day I received a phone call [from "the mother of another defendant"] and pursuant to that phone call I went to the Detective Bureau at 11th and State. The first person I talked to was * * * Sergeant Pidgeon. I asked Sergeant Pidgeon for permission to speak to my client, Danny Escobedo. * * * Sergeant Pidgeon made a call to the Bureau lockup and informed me that the boy had been taken from the lockup to the Homicide Bureau. This was between 9:30 and 10:00 in the evening. Before I went anywhere, he called the Homicide Bureau and told them there was an attorney waiting to see Escobedo. He told me I could not see him. Then I went upstairs to the Homicide Bureau. There were several Homicide Detectives around and I talked to them. I identified myself as Escobedo's attorney and asked permission to see him. They said I could not. * * * The police officer told me to see Chief Flynn who was on duty. I identified myself to Chief Flynn and asked permission to see my client. He said I could not. * * * I think it was approximately 11:00 o'clock. He said I couldn't see him because they hadn't completed questioning. * * * [F]or a second or two I spotted him in an office in the Homicide Bureau.

The door was open and I could see through the office. * * * I waved to him and he waved back and then the door was closed, by one of the officers at Homicide. There were four or five officers milling around the Homicide Detail that night. * * * I waited around for another hour or two and went back again and renewed [m]y request to see my client. He again told me I could not. * * * I filed an official complaint with Commissioner Phelan of the Chicago Police Department. I had a conversation with every police officer I could find. I was told at Homicide that I couldn't see him and I would have to get a writ of habeas corpus. * * * I had no opportunity to talk to my client that night. * * *

Petitioner testified that during the course of the interrogation he repeatedly asked to speak to his lawyer and that the police said that his lawyer "didn't want to see" him. The testimony of the police officers confirmed these accounts in substantial detail.

Notwithstanding repeated requests by each, petitioner and his retained lawyer were afforded no opportunity to consult during the course of the entire interrogation. * * * Petitioner testified that "he heard a detective telling the attorney the latter would not be allowed to talk to [him] 'until they were done' and that he heard the attorney being refused permission to remain in the adjoining room." A police officer testified that he had told the lawyer that he could not see petitioner until "we were through interrogating" him.

There is testimony by the police that during the interrogation, petitioner, a 22-year-old of Mexican extraction with no record of previous experience with the police, "was handcuffed" in a standing position and that he "was nervous, he had circles under his eyes and he was upset" and was "agitated" because "he had not slept well in over a week."

It is undisputed that during the course of the interrogation Officer Montejano, who "grew up" in petitioner's neighborhood, who knew his family, and who uses "Spanish language in [his] police work," conferred alone with petitioner "for about a quarter of an hour * * *." Petitioner testified that the officer said to him "in Spanish that my sister and I could go home if I pinned it on Benedict DiGerlando," that "he would see to it that we would go home and be held only as witnesses, if anything, if we had made a statement against DiGerlando * * *, that we would be able to go home that night." Petitioner testified that he made the statement in issue because of this assurance. Officer Montejano denied offering any such assurance.

A police officer testified that during the interrogation the following occurred:

I informed him of what DiGerlando told me and when I did, he told me that DiGerlando was [lying] and I said, "Would you care to tell DiGerlando that?" and he said, "Yes, I will." So, I brought * * * Escobedo in and he confronted DiGerlando and he told him that he was lying and said, "I didn't shoot Manuel, you did it."

In this way, petitioner, for the first time admitted to some knowledge of the crime. After that he made additional statements further implicating himself in the murder plot. At this point an Assistant State's Attorney, Theodore J. Cooper, was summoned "to take" a statement. Mr. Cooper, an experienced lawyer who was assigned to the Homicide Division * * *, "took" petitioner's statement by asking carefully framed questions apparently designed to assure the admissibility into evidence of the resulting answers. Mr. Cooper testified that he did not advise petitioner of his constitutional rights, and it is undisputed that no one during the course of the interrogation so advised him.

Petitioner moved both before and during trial to suppress the incriminating statement, but the motions were denied. Petitioner was convicted of murder and he appealed the conviction. * * * We granted a writ of certiorari to consider whether the petitioner's statement was constitutionally admissible at his trial. We conclude, for the reasons stated below, that it was not and, accordingly, we reverse the judgment of conviction.

In *Massiah,* this Court observed that "a Constitution which guarantees a defendant the aid of counsel at * * * trial could surely vouchsafe no less to an indicted defendant under interrogation by the police in a completely extrajudicial proceeding. Anything less * * * might deny a defendant effective representation by counsel at the only stage when legal aid and advice would help him."

The interrogation here was conducted before petitioner was formally indicted. But in the context of this case, that fact should make no difference. When petitioner requested, and was denied, an opportunity to consult with his lawyer, the investigation had ceased to be a general investigation of "an unsolved crime." Petitioner had become the accused, and the purpose of the interrogation was to "get him" to confess his guilt despite his constitutional right not to do so. * * *

Petitioner, a layman, was undoubtedly unaware that under Illinois law an admission of "mere" complicity in the murder plot was legally as damaging as an admission of firing of the fatal shots. The "guiding hand of counsel" was essential to advise petitioner of his rights in this delicate situation. This was the "stage when legal aid and advice" were most critical to petitioner. * * * What happened at this interrogation could certainly "affect the whole trial," since rights "may be as irretrievably lost, if not then and there asserted, as they are when an accused represented by counsel waives a right for strategic purposes." It would exalt form over substance to make the right to counsel, under these circumstances, depend on whether at the time of the interrogation, the authorities had secured a formal indictment. Petitioner had, for all practical purposes, already been charged with murder. * * *

In *Gideon*, we held that every person accused of a crime, whether state or federal, is entitled to a lawyer at trial. The rule sought by the State here, however, would make the trial no more than an appeal from the interrogation; and the "right to use counsel at the formal trial [would be] a very hollow thing [if], for all practical purposes, the conviction is already assured by pretrial examination." "One can imagine a cynical prosecutor saying: 'Let them have the most illustrious counsel, now. They can't escape the noose. There is nothing that counsel can do for them at the trial.'"

It is argued that if the right to counsel is afforded prior to indictment, the number of confessions obtained by the police will diminish significantly, because most confessions are obtained during the period between arrest and indictment, and "any lawyer worth his salt will tell the suspect in no uncertain terms to make no statement to police under any circumstances." This argument, of course, cuts two ways. The fact that many confessions are obtained during this period points up its critical nature as a "stage when legal aid and advice" are surely needed. The right to counsel would indeed be hollow if it began at a period when few confessions were obtained. There is necessarily a direct relationship between the importance of a stage to the police in their quest for a confession and the criticalness of that stage to the accused in his need for legal advice. Our Constitution, unlike some others, strikes the balance in favor of the right of the accused to be advised by his lawyer of his privilege against self-incrimination.

We have learned the lesson of history, ancient and modern, that a system of criminal law enforcement which comes to depend on the "confession" will, in the long run, be less reliable and more subject to abuses than a system which depends on extrinsic evidence independently secured through skillful investigation. * * * This Court also has recognized that "history amply shows that confessions have often been extorted to save law enforcement officials the trouble and effort of obtaining valid and independent evidence * * *."

We have also learned the companion lesson of history that no system of criminal justice can, or should, survive if it comes to depend for its continued effectiveness on the citizens' abdication through unawareness of their constitutional rights. No system worth preserving should have to fear that if an accused is permitted to consult with a lawyer, he will become aware of, and exercise, these rights. If the exercise of constitutional rights will thwart the effectiveness of a system of law enforcement, then there is something very wrong with that system.

We hold, therefore, that where, as here, the investigation is no longer a general inquiry into an unsolved crime but has begun to focus on a particular suspect, the suspect has been taken into police custody, the police carry out a process of interrogations that lends itself to eliciting incriminating statements, the suspect has requested and been denied an opportunity to consult with his lawyer, and the police have not effectively warned him of his absolute constitutional right to remain silent, the accused has been denied "The Assistance of Counsel" in violation of the Sixth Amendment to the Constitution as "made obligatory upon the States by the Fourteenth Amendment," and that no statement elicited by the police during the interrogation may be used against him at a criminal trial. * * *

Nothing we have said today affects the powers of the police to investigate "an unsolved crime," by gathering information from witnesses and by other "proper investigative efforts." We hold only that when the process shifts from investigatory to accusatory—when its focus is on the accused and its purpose is to elicit a confession—our adversary system begins to operate, and, under the circumstances here, the accused must be permitted to consult with his lawyer.

The judgment of the Illinois Supreme Court is reversed and the case remanded for proceedings not inconsistent with this opinion. * * *

JUSTICE STEWART, dissenting.

In *Massiah v. United States*, * * * a federal grand jury had indicted Massiah. He had retained a lawyer and entered a formal plea of not guilty. * * * Massiah was released on bail, and thereafter agents of the Federal Government deliberately elicited incriminating statements from him in the absence of his lawyer. We held that the use of these statements against him at his trial denied him the basic protections of the Sixth Amendment guarantee. * * * Putting to one side the fact that the case now before us is not a federal case, the vital fact remains that this case does not involve the deliberate interrogation of a defendant after the initiation of judicial proceedings against him. The Court disregards this basic difference between the present case and Massiah's, with the bland assertion that "that fact should make no difference."

It is "that fact," I submit, which makes all the difference. Under our system of criminal justice, the institution of formal, meaningful judicial proceedings, by way of indictment, information, or arraignment, marks the point at which a criminal investigation has ended and adversary proceedings have commenced. It is at this point that the constitutional guarantees attach which pertain to a criminal trial. * * *

The confession which the Court today holds inadmissible was a voluntary one. It was given during the course of a perfectly legitimate police investigation of an unsolved murder. The Court says that what happened during this investigation "affected" the trial. I had always supposed that the whole purpose of a police investigation of a murder was to "affect" the trial of the murderer, and that it would be only an incompetent, unsuccessful, or corrupt investigation which would not do so. * * *

Supported by no stronger authority than its own rhetoric, the Court today converts a routine police investigation of an unsolved murder into a distorted analogue of a judicial trial. It imports into this investigation constitutional concepts historically applicable only after the onset of formal prosecutorial proceedings. By doing so, I think the Court perverts those precious constitutional guarantees, and frustrates the vital interests of society in preserving the legitimate and proper function of honest and purposeful police investigation. * * *

JUSTICE WHITE, with whom JUSTICE CLARK and JUSTICE STEWART join, dissenting.

In *Massiah*, the Court held that as of the date of the indictment the prosecution is disentitled to secure admissions from the accused. The Court now moves that date back to the time when the prosecution begins to "focus" on the accused. Although the opinion purports to be limited to the facts of this case, it would be naive to think that the new constitutional right announced will depend upon whether the accused has retained his own counsel, or has asked to consult with counsel in the course of interrogation. At the very least the Court holds that once the accused becomes a suspect and, presumably, is arrested, any admission made to the police thereafter is inadmissible in evidence unless the accused has waived his right to counsel. The decision is thus another major step in the direction of the goal which the Court seemingly has in mind—to bar from evidence all admissions obtained from an individual suspected of crime, whether involuntarily made or not. * * * I reject this step and the invitation to go farther which the Court has now issued. * * *

[JUSTICE HARLAN's dissenting opinion and JUSTICE STEWART's dissenting opinion have been omitted.]

BREWER V. WILLIAMS

Supreme Court of the United States
430 U.S. 387, 97 S. Ct. 1232, 51 L. Ed. 2d 424 (1977)

JUSTICE STEWART delivered the opinion of the Court. * * *

On the afternoon of December 24, 1968, a 10-year-old girl named Pamela Powers went with her family to the YMCA in Des Moines, Iowa, to watch a wrestling tournament in which her brother was participating. When she failed to return from a trip to the washroom, a search for her began. The search was unsuccessful.

Robert Williams, who had recently escaped from a mental hospital, was a resident of the YMCA. Soon after the girl's disappearance Williams was seen in the YMCA lobby carrying some clothing and a large bundle wrapped in a blanket. He obtained help from a 14-year-old boy in opening the street door of the YMCA and the door to his automobile parked outside. When Williams placed the bundle in the front seat of his car the boy "saw two legs in it and they were skinny and white." Before anyone could see what was in the bundle Williams drove away. His abandoned car was found the following day in Davenport, Iowa, roughly 160 miles east of Des Moines. A warrant was then issued in Des Moines for his arrest on a charge of abduction.

On the morning of December 26, a Des Moines lawyer named Henry McKnight went to the Des Moines police station and informed the officers present that he had just received a long-distance call from Williams, and that he had advised Williams to turn himself in to the Davenport police. Williams did surrender that morning to the police in Davenport, and they booked him on the charge specified in the arrest warrant and gave him the warnings required by *Miranda*. The Davenport police then telephoned their counterparts in Des Moines to inform them that Williams had surrendered. McKnight, the lawyer, was still at the Des Moines police headquarters, and Williams conversed with McKnight on the telephone. In the presence of the Des Moines chief of police and a police detective named Leaming, McKnight advised Williams that Des Moines police officers would be driving to Davenport to pick him up, that the officers would not interrogate him or mistreat him, and that Williams was not to talk to the officers about Pamela Powers until after consulting with McKnight upon his return to Des Moines. As a result of these conversations, it was agreed between McKnight and the Des Moines police officials that Detective Leaming and a fellow officer would drive to Davenport to pick up Williams, that they would bring him directly back to Des Moines, and that they would not question him during the trip.

In the meantime Williams was arraigned before a judge in Davenport on the outstanding arrest warrant. The judge advised him of his *Miranda* rights and committed him to jail. Before leaving the courtroom, Williams conferred with a lawyer named Kelly, who advised him not to make any statements until consulting with McKnight back in Des Moines.

Detective Leaming and his fellow officer arrived in Davenport about noon to pick up Williams and return him to Des Moines. Soon after their arrival they met with Williams and Kelly, who, they understood, was acting as Williams' lawyer. Detective Leaming repeated the *Miranda* warnings, and told Williams:

[W]e both know that you're being represented here by Mr. Kelly and you're being represented by Mr. McKnight in Des Moines, and

. . . I want you to remember this because we'll be visiting between here and Des Moines.

Williams then conferred again with Kelly alone, and after this conference Kelly reiterated to Detective Leaming that Williams was not to be questioned about the disappearance of Pamela Powers until after he had consulted with McKnight back in Des Moines. When Leaming expressed some reservations, Kelly firmly stated that the agreement with McKnight was to be carried out that there was to be no interrogation of Williams during the automobile journey to Des Moines. Kelly was denied permission to ride in the police car back to Des Moines with Williams and the two officers.

The two detectives, with Williams in their charge, then set out on the 160-mile drive. At no time during the trip did Williams express a willingness to be interrogated in the absence of an attorney. Instead, he stated several times that "[w]hen I get to Des Moines and see Mr. McKnight, I am going to tell you the whole story." Detective Leaming knew that Williams was a former mental patient, and knew also that he was deeply religious.

The detective and his prisoner soon embarked on a wide-ranging conversation covering a variety of topics, including the subject of religion. Then, not long after leaving Davenport and reaching the interstate highway, Detective Leaming delivered what has been referred to in the briefs and oral arguments as the "Christian burial speech." Addressing Williams as "Reverend," the detective said:

> I want to give you something to think about while we're traveling down the road . . . . Number one, I want you to observe the weather conditions, it's raining, it's sleeting, it's freezing, driving is very treacherous, visibility is poor. * * * They are predicting several inches of snow for tonight, and I feel that you yourself are the only person that knows where this little girl's body is. * * * And, since we will be going right past the area on the way into Des Moines, I feel that we could stop and locate the body, that the parents of this little girl should be entitled to a Christian burial for the little girl who was snatched away from them on Christmas [E]ve and murdered. And I feel we should stop and locate it on the way in rather than waiting until morning and trying to come back out after a snow storm and possibly not being able to find it at all.

Williams asked Detective Leaming why he thought their route to Des Moines would be taking them past the girl's body, and Leaming responded that he knew the body was in the area of Mitchellville a town they would be passing on the way to Des Moines.[1] Leaming then stated: "I do not want

---

[1] The fact of the matter, of course, was that Detective Leaming possessed no such knowledge.

you to answer me. I don't want to discuss it any further. Just think about it as we're riding down the road."

As the car approached Grinnell, a town approximately 100 miles west of Davenport, Williams asked whether the police had found the victim's shoes. When Detective Leaming replied that he was unsure, Williams directed the officers to a service station where he said he had left the shoes; a search for them proved unsuccessful. As they continued towards Des Moines, Williams asked whether the police had found the blanket, and directed the officers to a rest area where he said he had disposed of the blanket. Nothing was found. The car continued towards Des Moines, and as it approached Mitchellville, Williams said that he would show the officers where the body was. He then directed the police to the body of Pamela Powers.

Williams was indicted for first-degree murder. Before trial, his counsel moved to suppress all evidence relating to or resulting from any statements Williams had made during the automobile ride from Davenport to Des Moines. After an evidentiary hearing the trial judge denied the motion. * * *

The evidence in question was introduced over counsel's continuing objection at the subsequent trial. The jury found Williams guilty of murder, and the judgment of conviction was affirmed by the Iowa Supreme Court. * * *

Williams then petitioned for a writ of habeas corpus in the United States District Court for the Southern District of Iowa. * * * The District Court * * * concluded as a matter of law that the evidence in question had been wrongly admitted at Williams' trial.

The Court of Appeals for the Eighth Circuit, with one judge dissenting, affirmed this judgment. * * * We granted certiorari to consider the constitutional issues presented.

* * * [T]here is no need to review in this case the doctrine of *Miranda v. Arizona*, a doctrine designed to secure the constitutional privilege against compulsory self-incrimination. It is equally unnecessary to evaluate the ruling of the District Court that Williams' self-incriminating statements were, indeed, involuntarily made. For it is clear that the judgment before us must in any event be affirmed upon the ground that Williams was deprived of a different constitutional right [—] the right to the assistance of counsel.

This right, guaranteed by the Sixth and Fourteenth Amendments, is indispensable to the fair administration of our adversary system of criminal justice. * * * Whatever else it may mean, the right to counsel granted by the Sixth and Fourteenth Amendments means at least that a person is entitled to the help of a lawyer at or after the time that judicial proceedings have been initiated against him "whether by way of formal charge, preliminary hearing, indictment, information, or arraignment."

There can be no doubt in the present case that judicial proceedings had been initiated against Williams before the start of the automobile ride from Davenport to Des Moines. A warrant had been issued for his arrest, he had been arraigned on that warrant before a judge in a Davenport courtroom, and he had been committed by the court to confinement in jail.[a] The State does not contend otherwise.

There can be no serious doubt, either, that Detective Leaming deliberately and designedly set out to elicit information from Williams just as surely as—and perhaps more effectively than—if he had formally interrogated him. Detective Leaming was fully aware before departing for Des Moines that Williams was being represented in Davenport by Kelly and in Des Moines by McKnight. Yet he purposely sought during Williams' isolation from his lawyers to obtain as much incriminating information as possible. Indeed, Detective Leaming conceded as much when he testified at Williams' trial:

> Q. In fact, Captain, whether he was a mental patient or not, you were trying to get all the information you could before he got to his lawyer, weren't you?
>
> A. I was sure hoping to find out where that little girl was, yes, sir.
>
> Q. Well, I'll put it this way: You was [sic] hoping to get all the information you could before Williams got back to McKnight, weren't you?
>
> A. Yes, sir.

The circumstances of this case are * * * constitutionally indistinguishable from those presented in *Massiah*. * * * That the incriminating statements were elicited surreptitiously in the *Massiah* case, and otherwise here, is constitutionally irrelevant. Rather, the clear rule of *Massiah* is that once adversary proceedings have commenced against an individual, he has a right to legal representation when the government interrogates him. * * *

---

[a] In *Texas v. Cobb*, 532 U.S. 162 (2001), the Court affirmed that the Sixth Amendment right to counsel is offense specific and thus attaches only with respect to offenses for which judicial proceedings have commenced. The Court, however, acknowledged that the definition of the term "offense" is "not necessarily limited to the four corners of a charging instrument." Borrowing from its double jeopardy jurisprudence, the Court held "that when the Sixth Amendment right to counsel attaches, it does encompass offenses that, even if not formally charged, would be considered the same offense under the *Blockburger* test." Under the *Blockburger* test, two offenses are not the same offense for double jeopardy purposes if each requires proof of an element that is not required by the other. *Blockburger v. United States*, 284 U.S. 299, 304 (1932).

The Iowa courts recognized that Williams had been denied the constitutional right to the assistance of counsel. They held, however, that he had waived that right during the course of the automobile trip from Davenport to Des Moines. The state trial court explained its determination of waiver as follows:

> The time element involved on the trip, the general circumstances of it, and more importantly the absence on the Defendant's part of any assertion of his right or desire not to give information absent the presence of his attorney, are the main foundations for the Court's conclusion that he voluntarily waived such right. * * *

The District Court and the Court of Appeals were * * * correct in their understanding of the proper standard to be applied in determining the question of waiver as a matter of federal constitutional law—that it was incumbent upon the State to prove "an intentional relinquishment or abandonment of a known right or privilege."

* * * [T]he record in this case falls far short of sustaining [the State's] burden. It is true that Williams had been informed of and appeared to understand his right to counsel. But waiver requires not merely comprehension but relinquishment, and Williams' consistent reliance upon the advice of counsel in dealing with the authorities refutes any suggestion that he waived that right. * * * His statements while in the car that he would tell the whole story after seeing McKnight in Des Moines were the clearest expressions by Williams himself that he desired the presence of an attorney before any interrogation took place. But even before making these statements, Williams had effectively asserted his right to counsel by having secured attorneys at both ends of the automobile trip, both of whom, acting as his agents, had made clear to the police that no interrogation was to occur during the journey. Williams knew of that agreement and, particularly in view of his consistent reliance on counsel, there is no basis for concluding that he disavowed it.

Despite Williams' express and implicit assertions of his right to counsel, Detective Leaming proceeded to elicit incriminating statements from Williams. Leaming did not preface this effort by telling Williams that he had a right to the presence of a lawyer, and made no effort at all to ascertain whether Williams wished to relinquish that right. The circumstances of record in this case thus provide no reasonable basis for finding that Williams waived his right to the assistance of counsel. * * *

The crime of which Williams was convicted was senseless and brutal, calling for swift and energetic action by the police to apprehend the perpetrator and gather evidence with which he could be convicted. No mission of law enforcement officials is more important. Yet "[d]isinterested zeal for the public good does not assure either wisdom or right in the methods it pursues." Although we do not lightly affirm the issuance of a writ of habeas corpus in this case, so clear a violation of the Sixth and Fourteenth Amendments as here occurred cannot be condoned. The pressures on state executive and judicial officers charged with the administration of the criminal law are great, especially when the crime is murder and the victim a small child. But it is precisely the predictability of those pressures that makes imperative a resolute loyalty to the guarantees that the Constitution extends to us all.

The judgment of the Court of Appeals is affirmed.[12] It is so ordered.

JUSTICE MARSHALL, concurring.

I concur wholeheartedly in my Brother Stewart's opinion for the Court, but add these words in light of the dissenting opinions filed today. The dissenters have, I believe, lost sight of the fundamental constitutional backbone of our criminal law. They seem to think that Detective Leaming's actions were perfectly proper, indeed laudable, examples of "good police work." In my view, good police work is something far different from catching the criminal at any price. It is equally important that the police, as guardians of the law, fulfill their responsibility to obey its commands scrupulously. For "in the end life and liberty can be as much endangered from illegal methods used to convict those thought to be criminals as from the actual criminals themselves." * * *

CHIEF JUSTICE BURGER, dissenting.

The result in this case ought to be intolerable in any society which purports to call itself an organized society. It continues the Court by the narrowest margin on the much-criticized course of punishing the public for the mistakes and misdeeds of law enforcement officers, instead of punishing the officer directly, if in fact he is guilty of wrongdoing. It mechanically and blindly keeps reliable evidence from juries whether the claimed constitutional violation involves gross police misconduct or honest human error.

Williams is guilty of the savage murder of a small child; no member of the Court contends he is not. While in custody, and after no fewer than five warnings of his rights to silence and to counsel, he led police to the concealed body of his victim. The Court concedes Williams was not threatened or coerced and that he spoke and acted voluntarily and with full awareness of his constitutional rights. In the face of all this, the Court now

---

[12] The District Court stated that its decision "does not touch upon the issue of what evidence, if any, beyond the incriminating statements themselves must be excluded as 'fruit of the poisonous tree.'" We, too, have no occasion to address this issue. * * * While neither Williams' incriminating statements themselves nor any testimony describing his having led the police to the victim's body can constitutionally be admitted into evidence, evidence of where the body was found and of its condition might well be admissible on the theory that the body would have been discovered in any event, even had incriminating statements not been elicited from Williams. In the event that a retrial is instituted, it will be for the state courts in the first instance to determine whether particular items of evidence may be admitted.

holds that because Williams was prompted by the detective's statement, not interrogation but a statement, the jury must not be told how the police found the body. * * *

JUSTICE WHITE, with whom JUSTICE BLACKMUN and JUSTICE REHNQUIST join, dissenting.

* * * In order to show that a right has been waived under [the *Johnson v. Zerbst*] test, the State must prove "an intentional relinquishment or abandonment of a known right or privilege." The majority creates no new rule preventing an accused who has retained a lawyer from waiving his right to the lawyer's presence during questioning. The majority simply finds that no waiver was proved in this case. I disagree. That respondent knew of his right not to say anything to the officers without advice and presence of counsel is established on this record to a moral certainty. He was advised of the right by three officials of the State—telling at least one that he understood the right—and by two lawyers. * * * [H]e further demonstrated his knowledge of the right by informing the police that he would tell them the story in the presence of McKnight when they arrived in Des Moines. The issue in this case, then, is whether respondent relinquished that right intentionally.

Respondent relinquished his right not to talk to the police about his crime when the car approached the place where he had hidden the victim's clothes. Men usually intend to do what they do, and there is nothing in the record to support the proposition that respondent's decision to talk was anything but an exercise of his own free will. Apparently, without any prodding from the officers, respondent—who had earlier said that he would tell the whole story when he arrived in Des Moines—spontaneously changed his mind about the timing of his disclosures when the car approached the places where he had hidden the evidence. However, even if his statements were influenced by Detective Leaming's [Christian Burial Speech], respondent's decision to talk in the absence of counsel can hardly be viewed as the product of an overborne will. The statement by Leaming was not coercive; it was accompanied by a request that respondent not respond to it; and it was delivered hours before respondent decided to make any statement. Respondent's waiver was thus knowing and intentional.

The majority's contrary conclusion seems to rest on the fact that respondent "asserted" his right to counsel by retaining and consulting with one lawyer and by consulting with another. How this supports the conclusion that respondent's later relinquishment of his right not to talk in the absence of counsel was unintentional is a mystery. The fact that respondent consulted with counsel on the question whether he should talk to the police in counsel's absence makes his later decision to talk in counsel's absence better informed and, if anything, more intelligent. * * *

[JUSTICE POWELL's concurring opinion, JUSTICE STEVENS' concurring opinion, and JUSTICE BLACKMUN's dissenting opinion have been omitted.]

UNITED STATES V. HENRY

Supreme Court of the United States
447 U.S. 264, 100 S. Ct. 2183, 65 L. Ed. 2d 115 (1980)

CHIEF JUSTICE BURGER delivered the opinion of the Court.

We granted certiorari to consider whether respondent's Sixth Amendment right to the assistance of counsel was violated by the admission at trial of incriminating statements made by respondent to his cellmate, an undisclosed Government informant, after indictment and while in custody.

The Janaf Branch of the United Virginia Bank/Seaboard National in Norfolk, Va., was robbed in August 1972. Witnesses saw two men wearing masks and carrying guns enter the bank while a third man waited in the car. No witnesses were able to identify respondent Henry as one of the participants. About an hour after the robbery, the getaway car was discovered. Inside was found a rent receipt signed by one "Allen R. Norris." * * *

Government agents traced the rent receipt to Henry; on the basis of this information, Henry was arrested in Atlanta, Ga., in November 1972. Two weeks later he was indicted for armed robbery under 18 U.S.C. §§ 2113(a) and (d). He was held pending trial in the Norfolk city jail. Counsel was appointed on November 27.

On November 21, 1972, shortly after Henry was incarcerated, Government agents working on the Janaf robbery contacted one Nichols, an inmate at the Norfolk city jail, who for some time prior to this meeting had been engaged to provide confidential information to the Federal Bureau of Investigation as a paid informant. Nichols was then serving a sentence on local forgery charges. * * *

Nichols informed the agent that he was housed in the same cellblock with several federal prisoners awaiting trial, including Henry. The agent told him to be alert to any statements made by the federal prisoners, but not to initiate any conversation with or question Henry regarding the bank robbery. In early December, after Nichols had been released from jail, the agent again contacted Nichols, who reported that he and Henry had engaged in conversation and that Henry had told him about the robbery of the Janaf bank. Nichols was paid for furnishing the information. * * *

Nichols testified at trial that he had "an opportunity to have some conversations with Mr. Henry while he was in the jail," and that Henry told him that on several occasions he had gone to the Janaf Branch to see which employees opened the vault. Nichols also testified that Henry described to him the details of the robbery and stated that the only evidence connecting him to the robbery was the rental receipt. The jury was not informed that Nichols was a paid Government informant.

On the basis of this testimony, Henry was convicted of bank robbery and sentenced to a term of imprisonment of 25 years. * * * On August 28, 1975, Henry moved to vacate his sentence * * *. Henry contended that the introduction of Nichols' testimony violated his Sixth Amendment right to the assistance of counsel. * * *

The District Court [concluded] that Nichols' testimony at trial did not violate Henry's Sixth Amendment right to counsel. The Court of Appeals reversed and remanded, holding that the actions of the Government impaired the Sixth Amendment rights of the defendant under *Massiah*. * * *

The question here is whether under the facts of this case a Government agent "deliberately elicited" incriminating statements from Henry within the meaning of *Massiah*. Three factors are important. First, Nichols was acting under instructions as a paid informant for the Government; second, Nichols was ostensibly no more than a fellow inmate of Henry; and third, Henry was in custody and under indictment at the time he was engaged in conversation by Nichols.

The Court of Appeals viewed the record as showing that Nichols deliberately used his position to secure incriminating information from Henry when counsel was not present and held that conduct attributable to the Government. Nichols had been a paid Government informant for more than a year; moreover, the FBI agent was aware that Nichols had access to Henry and would be able to engage him in conversations without arousing Henry's suspicion. The arrangement between Nichols and the agent was on a contingent-fee basis; Nichols was to be paid only if he produced useful information. This combination of circumstances is sufficient to support the Court of Appeals' determination. Even if the agent's statement that he did not intend that Nichols would take affirmative steps to secure incriminating information is accepted, he must have known that such propinquity likely would lead to that result.

The Government argues that the federal agents instructed Nichols not to question Henry about the robbery. Yet according to his own testimony, Nichols was not a passive listener; rather, he had "some conversations with Mr. Henry" while he was in jail and Henry's incriminatory statements were "the product of this conversation." * * *

It is quite a different matter when the Government uses undercover agents to obtain incriminating statements from persons not in custody but suspected of criminal activity prior to the time charges are filed. In *Hoffa*, for example, this Court held that "no interest legitimately protected by the Fourth Amendment is involved" because "the Fourth Amendment [does not protect] a wrongdoer's misplaced belief that a person to whom he voluntarily confides his wrongdoing will not reveal it." Similarly, the Fifth Amendment has been held not to be implicated by the use of undercover Government agents before charges are filed because of the absence of the potential for compulsion. But the Fourth and Fifth Amendment claims made in those cases are not relevant to the inquiry under the Sixth Amendment here—whether the Government has interfered with the right to counsel of the accused by "deliberately eliciting" incriminating statements. Our holding today does not modify *White* or *Hoffa*.

* * * Henry was unaware of Nichols' role as a Government informant. The Government argues that this Court should apply a less rigorous standard under the Sixth Amendment where the accused is prompted by an undisclosed undercover informant than where the accused is speaking in the hearing of persons he knows to be Government officers. That line of argument, however, seeks to infuse Fifth Amendment concerns against compelled self-incrimination into the Sixth Amendment protection of the right to the assistance of counsel. * * *

When the accused is in the company of a fellow inmate who is acting by prearrangement as a Government agent, * * * [c]onversation stimulated in such circumstances may elicit information that an accused would not intentionally reveal to persons known to be Government agents. Indeed, the *Massiah* Court noted that if the Sixth Amendment "is to have any efficacy it must apply to indirect and surreptitious interrogations as well as those conducted in the jailhouse." The Court pointedly observed that Massiah was more seriously imposed upon because he did not know that his codefendant was a Government agent.

Moreover, the concept of a knowing and voluntary waiver of Sixth Amendment rights does not apply in the context of communications with an undisclosed undercover informant acting for the Government. In that setting, Henry, being unaware that Nichols was a Government agent expressly commissioned to secure evidence, cannot be held to have waived his right to the assistance of counsel. * * *

Under the strictures of the Court's holdings on the exclusion of evidence, we conclude that the Court of Appeals did not err in holding that Henry's statements to Nichols should not have been admitted at trial. By intentionally creating a situation likely to induce Henry to make incriminating statements without the assistance of counsel, the Government violated Henry's Sixth Amendment right to counsel. This is not a case where, in Justice Cardozo's words, "the constable . . . blundered"; rather, it is one where the "constable" planned an impermissible interference with the right to the assistance of counsel.

The judgment of the Court of Appeals for the Fourth Circuit is

Affirmed.

JUSTICE BLACKMUN, with whom JUSTICE WHITE joins, dissenting. * * *

Massiah mandates exclusion only if a federal agent "deliberately elicited" statements from the accused in the absence of counsel. The word "deliberately" denotes intent. *Massiah* ties this intent to the act of elicitation, that is, to conduct that draws forth a response. Thus *Massiah*, by its own terms, covers only action undertaken with the specific intent to evoke an inculpatory disclosure.

Faced with Agent Coughlin's unequivocal expression of an intent not to elicit statements from respondent Henry, but merely passively to receive them, the Court, in its decision to affirm the judgment of the Court of Appeals, has no choice but to depart from the natural meaning of the *Massiah* formulation. The Court deems it critical that informant Nichols had been a paid informant; that Agent Coughlin was aware that Nichols "had access" to Henry and "would be able to engage him in conversations without arousing Henry's suspicion"; and that payment to Nichols was on a contingent-fee basis. * * * Later, the Court goes even further, characterizing this as a case of "intentionally creating a situation likely to induce Henry to make incriminating statements." This determination, coupled with the statement that Nichols "prompted" respondent Henry's remarks, leads the Court to find a *Massiah* violation.

Thus, while claiming to retain the "deliberately elicited" test, the Court really forges a new test that saps the word "deliberately" of all significance. The Court's extension of *Massiah* would cover even a "negligent" triggering of events resulting in reception of disclosures. This approach, in my view, is unsupported and unwise. * * *

The Court does more than rely on dubious factors in finding that Coughlin's actions were "likely to induce" Nichols' successful prompting of Henry; it fails to focus on facts that cut strongly against that conclusion. The Court ignores Coughlin's specific instruction to Nichols that he was not to question Henry or to initiate conversation with him about the robbery. Nor does it note Nichols' likely assumption that he would not be remunerated, but reprimanded and possibly penalized, if he violated Coughlin's orders. In addition, the record shows that Nichols had worked as an FBI informant for four years and that Coughlin and Nichols had worked together for about a year on several matters. It makes sense, given Nichols' experience and Coughlin's willingness to renew their working relationship, to conclude that Nichols would follow Coughlin's instruction. Finally, it is worth noting that Henry was only one of several federal detainees to whom Nichols was to pay attention; this is not a case in which officers singled out a specific target. On these facts, I cannot agree that Coughlin "must have known that [it was] likely" that Nichols would seek to elicit information from Henry.

Under the Court's analysis, it is not enough that Coughlin should have anticipated disobedience by Nichols; it must also be shown that his actions were "likely to induce" Henry to talk. In my view, however, there was little reason to believe that even the most aggressive efforts by Nichols would lead to disclosures by Henry. Nothing in the record suggests that Henry and Nichols knew each other, far less that they had the type of relationship that would lead Henry to discuss freely a crime for which he had not yet been tried. In this respect, the case stands in stark contrast to *Massiah*, where the informant had collaborated with Massiah in a drug smuggling operation and was a codefendant in the resulting and pending prosecution. Moreover, "[t]here is nothing in the record to suggest that ... [the defendant] was peculiarly susceptible [to approaches by cellmates or that he] was unusually disoriented or upset." On these facts, it seems to me extremely unlikely that Coughlin's actions would lead to Henry's statements. * * *

In sum, I think this is an unfortunate decision, which disregards precedent and stretches to the breaking point a virtually silent record. Whatever the bounds of *Massiah*, that case does not justify exclusion of the proof challenged here.

[JUSTICE POWELL's concurring opinion, JUSTICE REHNQUIST's dissenting opinion, and JUSTICE BLACKMUN's dissenting opinion have been omitted.]

KUHLMANN V. WILSON

Supreme Court of the United States
477 U.S. 436, 106 S. Ct. 2616, 91 L. Ed. 2d 364 (1986)

JUSTICE POWELL announced the judgment of the Court and delivered the opinion of the Court * * *.

In the early morning of July 4, 1970, respondent and two confederates robbed the Star Taxicab Garage in the Bronx, New York, and fatally shot the night dispatcher. * * * After eluding the police for four days, respondent turned himself in. Respondent admitted that he had been present when the crimes took place, claimed that he had witnessed the robbery, gave the police a description of the robbers, but denied knowing them. * * *

After his arraignment, respondent was confined in the Bronx House of Detention, where he was placed in a cell with a prisoner named Benny Lee. Unknown to respondent, Lee had agreed to act as a police informant. Respondent made incriminating statements that Lee reported to the police. Prior to trial, respondent moved to suppress the statements on the ground that they were obtained in violation of his right to counsel. * * * [T]he statements were made under the following circumstances.

Before respondent arrived in the jail, Lee had entered into an arrangement with Detective Cullen, according to which Lee agreed to listen to respondent's conversations and report his remarks to Cullen. Since the police had positive evidence of respondent's participation, the purpose of placing Lee in the cell was to determine the identities of respondent's confederates. Cullen instructed Lee not to ask respondent any questions, but simply to "keep his ears open" for the names of the other perpetrators. Respondent first spoke to Lee about the crimes after he looked out the cellblock window at the Star Taxicab Garage, where the crimes had occurred. Respondent said, "someone's messing with me," and began talking to Lee about the robbery, narrating the same story that he had given the police at the time of his arrest. Lee advised respondent that this explanation "didn't sound too good," but respondent did not alter his story. Over the next few days, however, respondent changed details of his original account. Respondent then received a visit from his brother, who mentioned that members of his family were upset because they believed that respondent had murdered the dispatcher. After the visit, respondent again described the crimes to Lee. Respondent now admitted that he and two other men, whom he never identified, had planned and carried out the robbery, and had murdered the dispatcher. Lee informed Cullen of respondent's statements and furnished Cullen with notes that he had written surreptitiously while sharing the cell with respondent. * * *

The jury convicted respondent of common-law murder and felonious possession of a weapon. On May 18, 1972, the trial court sentenced him to a term of 20 years to life on the murder count and to a concurrent term of up to 7 years on the weapons count. * * *

Following this Court's decision in *United States v. Henry*, which applied the *Massiah* test to suppress statements made to a paid jailhouse informant, respondent decided to relitigate his Sixth Amendment claim. * * * The District Court * * * decided that *Henry* did not undermine the Court of Appeals' prior disposition of respondent's Sixth Amendment claim. * * * A different, and again divided, panel of the Court of Appeals reversed. * * * The court * * * reasoned that the circumstances under which respondent made his incriminating statements to Lee were indistinguishable from the facts of Henry. * * *

We granted certiorari to consider the Court of Appeals' . . . application of our decision in *Henry* to the facts of this case. We now reverse. * * *

In *United States v. Henry*, the Court applied the *Massiah* test to incriminating statements made to a jailhouse informant. The Court of Appeals in that case found a violation of *Massiah* because the informant had engaged the defendant in conversations and "had developed a relationship of trust and confidence with [the defendant] such that [the defendant] revealed incriminating information." This Court affirmed, holding that the Court of Appeals reasonably concluded that the Government informant "deliberately used his position to secure incriminating information from [the defendant] when counsel was not present." Although the informant had not questioned the defendant, the informant had "stimulated" conversations with the defendant in order to "elicit" incriminating information. The Court emphasized that those facts, like the facts of *Massiah,* amounted to "indirect and surreptitious interrogatio[n]" of the defendant.

As our recent examination of this Sixth Amendment issue in *Moulton* makes clear, the primary concern of the *Massiah* line of decisions is secret interrogation by investigatory techniques that are the equivalent of direct police interrogation. Since "the Sixth Amendment is not violated whenever—by luck or happenstance—the State obtains incriminating statements from the accused after the right to counsel has attached," a defendant does not make out a violation of that right simply by showing that an informant, either through prior arrangement or voluntarily, reported his incriminating statements to the police. Rather, the defendant must demonstrate that the police and their informant took some action, beyond merely listening, that was designed deliberately to elicit incriminating remarks.

It is thus apparent that the Court of Appeals erred in concluding that respondent's right to counsel was violated under the circumstances of this case. * * *

The state court found that Officer Cullen had instructed Lee only to listen to respondent for the purpose of determining the identities of the other participants in the robbery and murder. The police already had solid evidence of respondent's participation. The court further found that Lee followed those instructions, that he "at no time asked any questions" of respondent concerning the pending charges, and that he "only listened" to respondent's "spontaneous" and "unsolicited" statements. The only remark made by Lee that has any support in this record was his comment that respondent's initial version of his participation in the crimes "didn't sound too good." * * *

The judgment of the Court of Appeals is reversed, and the case is remanded for further proceedings consistent with this opinion.

It is so ordered.

JUSTICE BRENNAN, with whom JUSTICE MARSHALL joins, dissenting. * * *

The Sixth Amendment guarantees an accused, at least after the initiation of formal charges, the right to rely on counsel as the "medium" between himself and the State. Accordingly, the Sixth Amendment "imposes on the State an affirmative obligation to respect and preserve the accused's choice to seek [the assistance of counsel]," and therefore "[t]he determination whether particular action by state agents violates the accused's right to . . . counsel must be made in light of this obligation." To be sure, the Sixth Amendment is not violated whenever, "by luck or happenstance," the State obtains incriminating statements from the accused after the right to counsel has attached. It is violated, however, when "the State obtains incriminating statements by knowingly circumventing the accused's right to have counsel present in a confrontation between the accused and a state agent."[a] As we explained in *Henry,* where the accused has not waived his right to counsel, the government knowingly circumvents the defendant's right to counsel where it "deliberately elicit[s]" inculpatory admissions, that is, "intentionally creat[es] a situation likely to induce [the accused] to make incriminating statements without the assistance of counsel." * * *

In the instant case, as in *Henry,* the accused was incarcerated and therefore was "susceptible to the ploys of undercover Government agents." Like Nichols, Lee was a secret informant, usually received consideration for the services he rendered the police, and therefore had an incentive to produce the information which he knew the police hoped to obtain. Just as Nichols had done, Lee obeyed instructions not to question respondent and to report to the police any statements made by the respondent in Lee's presence about the crime in question. And, like Nichols, Lee encouraged respondent to talk about his crime by conversing with him on the subject over the course of several days and by telling respondent that his exculpatory story would not convince anyone without more work. However, unlike the situation in *Henry,* a disturbing visit from respondent's brother, rather than a conversation with the informant, seems to have been the immediate catalyst for respondent's confession to Lee. While it might appear from this sequence of events that Lee's comment regarding respondent's story and his general willingness to converse with respondent about the crime were not the *immediate* causes of respondent's admission, I think that the deliberate-elicitation standard requires consideration of the entire course of government behavior.

The State intentionally created a situation in which it was foreseeable that respondent would make incriminating statements without the assistance of counsel. [I]t assigned respondent to a cell overlooking the

---

[a] Here, Justice Brennan is referring to language in *Maine v. Moulton,* 474 U.S. 159 (1985). In that case, the Court found that by recommending to one defendant that he use a body wire when speaking with the other defendant, the police "intentionally created a situation that they knew, or should have known, was likely to result in Moulton's making incriminating statements." *Id.* at 168. The Court explained that "knowing exploitation by the State of an opportunity to confront the accused without counsel being present is as much a breach of the State's obligation not to circumvent the right to the assistance of counsel as is the intentional creation of such an opportunity. Accordingly, the Sixth Amendment is violated when the State obtains incriminating statements by knowingly circumventing the accused's right to have counsel present in a confrontation between the accused and a state agent." *Id.* at 176.

scene of the crime and designated a secret informant to be respondent's cellmate. The informant, while avoiding direct questions, nonetheless developed a relationship of cellmate camaraderie with respondent and encouraged him to talk about his crime. While the *coup de grace* was delivered by respondent's brother, the groundwork for respondent's confession was laid by the State. Clearly the State's actions had a sufficient nexus with respondent's admission of guilt to constitute deliberate elicitation within the meaning of *Henry*. I would affirm the judgment of the Court of Appeals.

[JUSTICE STEVENS' dissenting opinion has been omitted.]

CHAPTER 20

INTERROGATIONS—THE *MIRANDA* RULE

■ ■ ■

The Fifth Amendment to the U.S. Constitution provides in relevant part:

No person ... shall be compelled in any criminal case to be a witness against himself ....

In *Miranda v. Arizona*, the Supreme Court created a set of procedural safeguards to protect the Fifth Amendment privilege against self-incrimination. Anyone who watches television is familiar with the *Miranda* warnings that begin with: "You have the right to remain silent. Anything you say can and will be used against you." The average layperson, however, does not realize that the Court's *Miranda* decision generated a number of thorny questions. These questions are explored in the cases that follow.

MIRANDA V. ARIZONA
Supreme Court of the United States
384 U.S. 436, 86 S. Ct. 1602, 16 L. Ed. 2d 694 (1966)

CHIEF JUSTICE WARREN delivered the opinion of the Court.

The cases before us raise questions which go to the roots of our concepts of American criminal jurisprudence: the restraints society must observe consistent with the Federal Constitution in prosecuting individuals for crime. More specifically, we deal with the admissibility of statements obtained from an individual who is subjected to custodial police interrogation and the necessity for procedures which assure that the individual is accorded his privilege under the Fifth Amendment to the Constitution not to be compelled to incriminate himself. * * *

We start here, as we did in *Escobedo*, with the premise that our holding is not an innovation in our jurisprudence, but is an application of principles long recognized and applied in other settings. We have undertaken a thorough re-examination of the *Escobedo* decision and the principles it announced, and we reaffirm it. That case was but an explication of basic rights that are enshrined in our Constitution—that "No person * * * shall be compelled in any criminal case to be a witness against himself,"[a] and

---

[a] Justice Harlan, dissenting, objected to the majority's characterization of *Escobedo* as a Fifth Amendment case, stating that *Escobedo* "contains no reasoning or even general conclusions addressed to the Fifth Amendment and indeed its citation in this regard seems surprising in view

that "the accused shall * * * have the Assistance of Counsel"—rights which were put in jeopardy in that case through official overbearing. These precious rights were fixed in our Constitution only after centuries of persecution and struggle. And in the words of Chief Justice Marshall, they were secured "for ages to come, and ... designed to approach immortality as nearly as human institutions can approach it." * * *

Our holding will be spelled out with some specificity in the pages which follow but briefly stated it is this: the prosecution may not use statements, whether exculpatory or inculpatory, stemming from custodial interrogation of the defendant unless it demonstrates the use of procedural safeguards effective to secure the privilege against self-incrimination. By custodial interrogation, we mean questioning initiated by law enforcement officers after a person has been taken into custody or otherwise deprived of his freedom of action in any significant way. As for the procedural safeguards to be employed, unless other fully effective means are devised to inform accused persons of their right of silence and to assure a continuous opportunity to exercise it, the following measures are required. Prior to any questioning, the person must be warned that he has a right to remain silent, that any statement he does make may be used as evidence against him, and that he has a right to the presence of an attorney, either retained or appointed. The defendant may waive effectuation of these rights, provided the waiver is made voluntarily, knowingly and intelligently. If, however, he indicates in any manner and at any stage of the process that he wishes to consult with an attorney before speaking there can be no questioning. Likewise, if the individual is alone and indicates in any manner that he does not wish to be interrogated, the police may not question him. The mere fact that he may have answered some questions or volunteered some statements on his own does not deprive him of the right to refrain from answering any further inquiries until he has consulted with an attorney and thereafter consents to be questioned.

The constitutional issue we decide in each of these cases is the admissibility of statements obtained from a defendant questioned while in custody or otherwise deprived of his freedom of action in any significant way. In each, the defendant was questioned by police officers, detectives, or a prosecuting attorney in a room in which he was cut off from the outside world. In none of these cases was the defendant given a full and effective warning of his rights at the outset of the interrogation process. In all the cases, the questioning elicited oral admissions, and in three of them, signed statements as well which were admitted at their trials. They all thus share salient features—incommunicado interrogation of individuals in a police-dominated atmosphere, resulting in self-incriminating statements without full warnings of constitutional rights.

---

of *Escobedo*'s primary reliance on the Sixth Amendment." 384 U.S. at 512 n.9 (Harlan, J., dissenting).

An understanding of the nature and setting of this in-custody interrogation is essential to our decisions today. The difficulty in depicting what transpires at such interrogations stems from the fact that in this country they have largely taken place incommunicado. From extensive factual studies undertaken in the early 1930's, * * * it is clear that police violence and the "third degree" flourished at that time. * * * [T]he police resorted to physical brutality—beatings, hanging, whipping—and to sustained and protracted questioning incommunicado in order to extort confessions. * * * The use of physical brutality and violence is not, unfortunately, relegated to the past or to any part of the country. Only recently in Kings County, New York, the police brutally beat, kicked and placed lighted cigarette butts on the back of a potential witness under interrogation for the purpose of securing a statement incriminating a third party.

* * * [T]he modern practice of in-custody interrogation is psychologically rather than physically oriented. As we have stated before, this Court has recognized that coercion can be mental as well as physical, and that the blood of the accused is not the only hallmark of an unconstitutional inquisition. Interrogation still takes place in privacy. Privacy results in secrecy and this in turn results in a gap in our knowledge as to what in fact goes on in the interrogation rooms. A valuable source of information about present police practices, however, may be found in various police manuals and texts which document procedures employed with success in the past, and which recommend various other effective tactics. These texts are used by law enforcement agencies themselves as guides.[5] It should be noted that these texts professedly present the most enlightened and effective means presently used to obtain statements through custodial interrogation. By considering these texts and other data, it is possible to describe procedures observed and noted around the country.

The officers are told by the manuals that the "principal psychological factor contributing to a successful interrogation is privacy—being alone with the person under interrogation." The efficacy of this tactic has been explained as follows:

> If at all practicable, the interrogation should take place in the investigator's office or at least in a room of his own choice. The

---

[5] The methods described in Inbau & Reid, CRIMINAL INTERROGATION AND CONFESSIONS (1962), are a revision and enlargement of material presented in three prior editions of a predecessor text, LIE DETECTION AND CRIMINAL INTERROGATION (3d ed. 1953). The authors and their associates are officers of the Chicago Police Scientific Crime Detection Laboratory and have had extensive experience in writing, lecturing and speaking to law enforcement authorities over a 20-year period. They say that the techniques portrayed in their manuals reflect their experiences and are the most effective psychological stratagems to employ during interrogations. Similarly, the techniques described in O'Hara, FUNDAMENTALS OF CRIMINAL INVESTIGATION (1956), were gleaned from long service as observer, lecturer in police science, and work as a federal criminal investigator. All these texts have had rather extensive use among law enforcement agencies and among students of police science, with total sales and circulation of over 44,000.

subject should be deprived of every psychological advantage. In his own home he may be confident, indignant, or recalcitrant. He is more keenly aware of his rights and more reluctant to tell of his indiscretions of criminal behavior within the walls of his home. Moreover his family and other friends are nearby, their presence lending moral support. In his office, the investigator possesses all the advantages. The atmosphere suggests the invincibility of the forces of the law.

To highlight the isolation and unfamiliar surroundings, the manuals instruct the police to display an air of confidence in the suspect's guilt and from outward appearance to maintain only an interest in confirming certain details. The guilt of the subject is to be posited as a fact. The interrogator should direct his comments toward the reasons why the subject committed the act, rather than court failure by asking the subject whether he did it. Like other men, perhaps the subject has had a bad family life, had an unhappy childhood, had too much to drink, had an unrequited desire for women. The officers are instructed to minimize the moral seriousness of the offense, to cast blame on the victim or on society. These tactics are designed to put the subject in a psychological state where his story is but an elaboration of what the police purport to know already—that he is guilty. Explanations to the contrary are dismissed and discouraged.

The texts thus stress that the major qualities an interrogator should possess are patience and perseverance. One writer describes the efficacy of these characteristics in this manner:

> In the preceding paragraphs emphasis has been placed on kindness and stratagems. The investigator will, however, encounter many situations where the sheer weight of his personality will be the deciding factor. Where emotional appeals and tricks are employed to no avail, he must rely on an oppressive atmosphere of dogged persistence. He must interrogate steadily and without relent, leaving the subject no prospect of surcease. He must dominate his subject and overwhelm him with his inexorable will to obtain the truth. He should interrogate for a spell of several hours pausing only for the subject's necessities in acknowledgment of the need to avoid a charge of duress that can be technically substantiated. In a serious case, the interrogation may continue for days, with the required intervals for food and sleep, but with no respite from the atmosphere of domination. It is possible in this way to induce the subject to talk without resorting to duress or coercion. The method should be used only when the guilt of the subject appears highly probable.

CH. 20 INTERROGATIONS—THE MIRANDA RULE

The manuals suggest that the suspect be offered legal excuses for his actions in order to obtain an initial admission of guilt. Where there is a suspected revenge-killing, for example, the interrogator may say:

> Joe, you probably didn't go out looking for this fellow with the purpose of shooting him. My guess is, however, that you expected something from him and that's why you carried a gun—for your own protection. You knew him for what he was, no good. Then when you met him he probably started using foul, abusive language and he gave some indication that he was about to pull a gun on you, and that's when you had to act to save your own life. That's about it, isn't it, Joe?

Having then obtained the admission of shooting, the interrogator is advised to refer to circumstantial evidence which negates the self-defense explanation. This should enable him to secure the entire story. * * *

When the techniques described above prove unavailing, the texts recommend they be alternated with a show of some hostility. One ploy often used has been termed the "friendly-unfriendly" or the "Mutt and Jeff" act:

> * * * In this technique, two agents are employed. Mutt, the relentless investigator, who knows the subject is guilty and is not going to waste any time. He's sent a dozen men away for this crime and he's going to send the subject away for the full term. Jeff, on the other hand, is obviously a kindhearted man. He has a family himself. He has a brother who was involved in a little scrape like this. He disapproves of Mutt and his tactics and will arrange to get him off the case if the subject will cooperate. He can't hold Mutt off for very long. The subject would be wise to make a quick decision. The technique is applied by having both investigators present while Mutt acts out his role. Jeff may stand by quietly and demur at some of Mutt's tactics. When Jeff makes his plea for cooperation, Mutt is not present in the room.

The interrogators sometimes are instructed to induce a confession out of trickery. The technique here is quite effective in crimes which require identification or which run in series. In the identification situation, the interrogator may take a break in his questioning to place the subject among a group of men in a line-up. "The witness or complainant (previously coached, if necessary) studies the line-up and confidently points out the subject as the guilty party." Then the questioning resumes "as though there were now no doubt about the guilt of the subject." A variation on this technique is called the "reverse line-up":

> The accused is placed in a line-up, but this time he is identified by several fictitious witnesses or victims who associated him with different offenses. It is expected that the subject will become

desperate and confess to the offense under investigation in order to escape from the false accusations.

The manuals also contain instructions for police on how to handle the individual who refuses to discuss the matter entirely, or who asks for an attorney or relatives. The examiner is to concede him the right to remain silent. "This usually has a very undermining effect. First of all, he is disappointed in his expectation of an unfavorable reaction on the part of the interrogator. Secondly, a concession of this right to remain silent impresses the subject with the apparent fairness of his interrogator." After this psychological conditioning, however, the officer is told to point out the incriminating significance of the suspect's refusal to talk:

> Joe, you have a right to remain silent. That's your privilege and I'm the last person in the world who'll try to take it away from you. If that's the way you want to leave this, O.K. But let me ask you this. Suppose you were in my shoes and I were in yours and you called me in to ask me about this and I told you, "I don't want to answer any of your questions." You'd think I had something to hide, and you'd probably be right in thinking that. That's exactly what I'll have to think about you, and so will everybody else. So let's sit here and talk this whole thing over.

Few will persist in their initial refusal to talk, it is said, if this monologue is employed correctly. * * *

From these representative samples of interrogation techniques, the setting prescribed by the manuals and observed in practice becomes clear. In essence, it is this: To be alone with the subject is essential to prevent distraction and to deprive him of any outside support. The aura of confidence in his guilt undermines his will to resist. He merely confirms the preconceived story the police seek to have him describe. Patience and persistence, at times relentless questioning, are employed. To obtain a confession, the interrogator must "patiently maneuver himself or his quarry into a position from which the desired objective may be attained." When normal procedures fail to produce the needed result, the police may resort to deceptive stratagems such as giving false legal advice. It is important to keep the subject off balance, for example, by trading on his insecurity about himself or his surroundings. The police then persuade, trick, or cajole him out of exercising his constitutional rights.

Even without employing brutality, the "third degree" or the specific stratagems described above, the very fact of custodial interrogation exacts a heavy toll on individual liberty and trades on the weakness of individuals.

* * * In other settings, these individuals might have exercised their constitutional rights. In the incommunicado police-dominated atmosphere, they succumbed.

In the cases before us today, * * * we might not find the defendants' statements to have been involuntary in traditional terms. Our concern for adequate safeguards to protect precious Fifth Amendment rights is, of course, not lessened in the slightest. In each of the cases, the defendant was thrust into an unfamiliar atmosphere and run through menacing police interrogation procedures. The potentiality for compulsion is forcefully apparent, for example, in *Miranda*, where the indigent Mexican defendant was a seriously disturbed individual with pronounced sexual fantasies, and in *Stewart*, in which the defendant was an indigent Los Angeles Negro who had dropped out of school in the sixth grade. To be sure, the records do not evince overt physical coercion or patent psychological ploys. The fact remains that in none of these cases did the officers undertake to afford appropriate safeguards at the outset of the interrogation to insure [sic] that the statements were truly the product of free choice.

It is obvious that such an interrogation environment is created for no purpose other than to subjugate the individual to the will of his examiner. This atmosphere carries its own badge of intimidation. To be sure, this is not physical intimidation, but it is equally destructive of human dignity. The current practice of incommunicado interrogation is at odds with one of our Nation's most cherished principles—that the individual may not be compelled to incriminate himself. Unless adequate protective devices are employed to dispel the compulsion inherent in custodial surroundings, no statement obtained from the defendant can truly be the product of his free choice.

From the foregoing, we can readily perceive an intimate connection between the privilege against self-incrimination and police custodial questioning. It is fitting to turn to history and precedent underlying the Self-Incrimination Clause to determine its applicability in this situation.

* * * Those who framed our Constitution and the Bill of Rights were ever aware of subtle encroachments on individual liberty. They knew that "illegitimate and unconstitutional practices get their first footing * * * by silent approaches and slight deviations from legal modes of procedure." The privilege was elevated to constitutional status and has always been "as broad as the mischief against which it seeks to guard." We cannot depart from this noble heritage.

Thus we may view the historical development of the privilege as one which groped for the proper scope of governmental power over the citizen. * * * [T]he constitutional foundation underlying the privilege is the respect a government—state or federal—must accord to the dignity and integrity of its citizens. To maintain a "fair state-individual balance," to require the government "to shoulder the entire load," to respect the inviolability of the human personality, our accusatory system of criminal justice demands that the government seeking to punish an individual produce the evidence against him by its own independent labors, rather than by the cruel, simple expedient of compelling it from his own mouth. In sum, the privilege is fulfilled only when the person is guaranteed the right "to remain silent unless he chooses to speak in the unfettered exercise of his own will."

The question in these cases is whether the privilege is fully applicable during a period of custodial interrogation. In this Court, the privilege has consistently been accorded a liberal construction. We are satisfied that all the principles embodied in the privilege apply to informal compulsion exerted by law-enforcement officers during in-custody questioning. An individual swept from familiar surroundings into police custody, surrounded by antagonistic forces, and subjected to the techniques of persuasion described above cannot be otherwise than under compulsion to speak. As a practical matter, the compulsion to speak in the isolated setting of the police station may well be greater than in courts or other official investigations, where there are often impartial observers to guard against intimidation or trickery. * * *

Today, then, there can be no doubt that the Fifth Amendment privilege is available outside of criminal court proceedings and serves to protect persons in all settings in which their freedom of action is curtailed in any significant way from being compelled to incriminate themselves. We have concluded that without proper safeguards the process of in-custody interrogation of persons suspected or accused of crime contains inherently compelling pressures which work to undermine the individual's will to resist and to compel him to speak where he would not otherwise do so freely. In order to combat these pressures and to permit a full opportunity to exercise the privilege against self-incrimination, the accused must be adequately and effectively apprised of his rights and the exercise of those rights must be fully honored.

It is impossible for us to foresee the potential alternatives for protecting the privilege which might be devised by Congress or the States in the exercise of their creative rule-making capacities. Therefore we cannot say that the Constitution necessarily requires adherence to any particular solution for the inherent compulsions of the interrogation process as it is presently conducted. Our decision in no way creates a constitutional straitjacket which will handicap sound efforts at reform, nor is it intended to have this effect. * * * However, unless we are shown other procedures which are at least as effective in apprising accused persons of their right of silence and in assuring a continuous opportunity to exercise it, the following safeguards must be observed.

At the outset, if a person in custody is to be subjected to interrogation, he must first be informed in clear and unequivocal terms that he has the right to remain silent. For those unaware of the privilege, the warning is needed simply to make them aware of it—the threshold requirement for an intelligent decision as to its exercise. More important, such a warning is an absolute prerequisite in overcoming the inherent pressures of the interrogation atmosphere. It is not just the subnormal or woefully ignorant who succumb to an interrogator's imprecations, whether implied or expressly stated, that the interrogation will continue until a confession is obtained or that silence in the face of accusation is itself damning and will bode ill when presented to a jury. Further, the warning will show the individual that his interrogators are prepared to recognize his privilege should he choose to exercise it.

The Fifth Amendment privilege is so fundamental to our system of constitutional rule and the expedient of giving an adequate warning as to the availability of the privilege so simple, we will not pause to inquire in individual cases whether the defendant was aware of his rights without a warning being given. Assessments of the knowledge the defendant possessed, based on information as to his age, education, intelligence, or prior contact with authorities, can never be more than speculation; a warning is a clearcut fact. More important, whatever the background of the person interrogated, a warning at the time of the interrogation is indispensable to overcome its pressures and to insure [sic] that the individual knows he is free to exercise the privilege at that point in time.

The warning of the right to remain silent must be accompanied by the explanation that anything said can and will be used against the individual in court. This warning is needed in order to make him aware not only of the privilege, but also of the consequences of forgoing it. It is only through an awareness of these consequences that there can be any assurance of real understanding and intelligent exercise of the privilege. Moreover, this warning may serve to make the individual more acutely aware that he is faced with a phase of the adversary system—that he is not in the presence of persons acting solely in his interest.

The circumstances surrounding in-custody interrogation can operate very quickly to overbear the will of one merely made aware of his privilege by his interrogators. Therefore, the right to have counsel present at the interrogation is indispensable to the protection of the Fifth Amendment privilege under the system we delineate today. Our aim is to assure that the individual's right to choose between silence and speech remains unfettered throughout the interrogation process. A once-stated warning, delivered by those who will conduct the interrogation, cannot itself suffice to that end among those who most require knowledge of their rights. A mere warning given by the interrogators is not alone sufficient to accomplish that end. Prosecutors themselves claim that the admonishment of the right to remain silent without more "will benefit only the recidivist and the professional." Even preliminary advice given to the accused by his own attorney can be swiftly overcome by the secret interrogation process.

Thus, the need for counsel to protect the Fifth Amendment privilege comprehends not merely a right to consult with counsel prior to questioning, but also to have counsel present during any questioning if the defendant so desires.

The presence of counsel at the interrogation may serve several significant subsidiary functions as well. If the accused decides to talk to his interrogators, the assistance of counsel can mitigate the dangers of untrustworthiness. With a lawyer present the likelihood that the police will practice coercion is reduced, and if coercion is nevertheless exercised the lawyer can testify to it in court. The presence of a lawyer can also help to guarantee that the accused gives a fully accurate statement to the police and that the statement is rightly reported by the prosecution at trial.

An individual need not make a pre-interrogation request for a lawyer. While such request affirmatively secures his right to have one, his failure to ask for a lawyer does not constitute a waiver. No effective waiver of the right to counsel during interrogation can be recognized unless specifically made after the warnings we here delineate have been given. The accused who does not know his rights and therefore does not make a request may be the person who most needs counsel. * * *

Accordingly we hold that an individual held for interrogation must be clearly informed that he has the right to consult with a lawyer and to have the lawyer with him during interrogation under the system for protecting the privilege we delineate today. As with the warnings of the right to remain silent and that anything stated can be used in evidence against him, this warning is an absolute prerequisite to interrogation. No amount of circumstantial evidence that the person may have been aware of this right will suffice to stand in its stead. Only through such a warning is there ascertainable assurance that the accused was aware of this right.

If an individual indicates that he wishes the assistance of counsel before any interrogation occurs, the authorities cannot rationally ignore or deny his request on the basis that the individual does not have or cannot afford a retained attorney. The financial ability of the individual has no relationship to the scope of the rights involved here. The privilege against self-incrimination secured by the Constitution applies to all individuals. The need for counsel in order to protect the privilege exists for the indigent as well as the affluent. In fact, were we to limit these constitutional rights to those who can retain an attorney, our decisions today would be of little significance. The cases before us as well as the vast majority of confession cases with which we have dealt in the past involve those unable to retain counsel. While authorities are not required to relieve the accused of his poverty, they have the obligation not to take advantage of indigence in the administration of justice. * * *

In order fully to apprise a person interrogated of the extent of his rights under this system then, it is necessary to warn him not only that he has the right to consult with an attorney, but also that if he is indigent a lawyer will be appointed to represent him. Without this additional warning, the admonition of the right to consult with counsel would often be understood as meaning only that he can consult with a lawyer if he has one or has the funds to obtain one. The warning of a right to counsel would be hollow if not couched in terms that would convey to the indigent—the person most often subjected to interrogation—the knowledge that he too has a right to have counsel present. As with the warnings of the right to remain silent and of the general right to counsel, only by effective and express explanation to the indigent of this right can there be assurance that he was truly in a position to exercise it.

Once warnings have been given, the subsequent procedure is clear. If the individual indicates in any manner, at any time prior to or during questioning, that he wishes to remain silent, the interrogation must cease.[44] At this point he has shown that he intends to exercise his Fifth Amendment privilege; any statement taken after the person invokes his privilege cannot be other than the product of compulsion, subtle or otherwise. Without the right to cut off questioning, the setting of in-custody interrogation operates on the individual to overcome free choice in producing a statement after the privilege has been once invoked. If the individual states that he wants an attorney, the interrogation must cease until an attorney is present. At that time, the individual must have an opportunity to confer with the attorney and to have him present during any subsequent questioning. If the individual cannot obtain an attorney and he indicates that he wants one before speaking to police, they must respect his decision to remain silent. * * *

If the interrogation continues without the presence of an attorney and a statement is taken, a heavy burden rests on the government to demonstrate that the defendant knowingly and intelligently waived his privilege against self-incrimination and his right to retained or appointed counsel. This Court has always set high standards of proof for the waiver of constitutional rights and we reassert these standards as applied to in custody interrogation.[b] Since the State is responsible for establishing the isolated circumstances under which the interrogation takes place and has the only means of making available corroborated evidence of warnings

---

[44] If an individual indicates his desire to remain silent, but has an attorney present, there may be some circumstances in which further questioning would be permissible. In the absence of evidence of overbearing, statements then made in the presence of counsel might be free of the compelling influence of the interrogation process and might fairly be construed as a waiver of the privilege for purposes of these statements.

[b] In *Colorado v. Connelly*, 479 U.S. 157 (1986), the Supreme Court held that the State must demonstrate a waiver of *Miranda* rights by a preponderance of the evidence.

given during incommunicado interrogation, the burden is rightly on its shoulders.

An express statement that the individual is willing to make a statement and does not want an attorney followed closely by a statement could constitute a waiver. But a valid waiver will not be presumed simply from the silence of the accused after warnings are given or simply from the fact that a confession was in fact eventually obtained. A statement we made in *Carnley v. Cochran* is applicable here:

> Presuming waiver from a silent record is impermissible. The record must show, or there must be an allegation and evidence which show, that an accused was offered counsel but intelligently and understandingly rejected the offer. Anything less is not waiver.

Moreover, where in-custody interrogation is involved, there is no room for the contention that the privilege is waived if the individual answers some questions or gives some information on his own prior to invoking his right to remain silent when interrogated.

Whatever the testimony of the authorities as to waiver of rights by an accused, the fact of lengthy interrogation or incommunicado incarceration before a statement is made is strong evidence that the accused did not validly waive his rights. In these circumstances the fact that the individual eventually made a statement is consistent with the conclusion that the compelling influence of the interrogation finally forced him to do so. It is inconsistent with any notion of a voluntary relinquishment of the privilege. Moreover, any evidence that the accused was threatened, tricked, or cajoled into a waiver will, of course, show that the defendant did not voluntarily waive his privilege. The requirement of warnings and waiver of rights is fundamental with respect to the Fifth Amendment privilege and not simply a preliminary ritual to existing methods of interrogation.

The warnings required and the waiver necessary in accordance with our opinion today are, in the absence of a fully effective equivalent, prerequisites to the admissibility of any statement made by a defendant. No distinction can be drawn between statements which are direct confessions and statements which amount to "admissions" of part or all of an offense. The privilege against self-incrimination protects the individual from being compelled to incriminate himself in any manner; it does not distinguish degrees of incrimination. Similarly, for precisely the same reason, no distinction may be drawn between inculpatory statements and statements alleged to be merely "exculpatory." If a statement made were in fact truly exculpatory it would, of course, never be used by the prosecution. In fact, statements merely intended to be exculpatory by the defendant are often used to impeach his testimony at trial or to demonstrate untruths in the statement given under interrogation and thus to prove guilt by implication. These statements are incriminating in any meaningful sense of the word and may not be used without the full warnings and effective waiver required for any other statement. In *Escobedo* itself, the defendant fully intended his accusation of another as the slayer to be exculpatory as to himself.

The principles announced today deal with the protection which must be given to the privilege against self-incrimination when the individual is first subjected to police interrogation while in custody at the station or otherwise deprived of his freedom of action in any significant way. It is at this point that our adversary system of criminal proceedings commences[.]
* * *

Our decision is not intended to hamper the traditional function of police officers in investigating crime. When an individual is in custody on probable cause, the police may, of course, seek out evidence in the field to be used at trial against him. Such investigation may include inquiry of persons not under restraint. General on-the-scene questioning as to facts surrounding a crime or other general questioning of citizens in the fact-finding process is not affected by our holding. It is an act of responsible citizenship for individuals to give whatever information they may have to aid in law enforcement. In such situations the compelling atmosphere inherent in the process of in-custody interrogation is not necessarily present.

In dealing with statements obtained through interrogation, we do not purport to find all confessions inadmissible. Confessions remain a proper element in law enforcement. Any statement given freely and voluntarily without any compelling influences is, of course, admissible in evidence. The fundamental import of the privilege while an individual is in custody is not whether he is allowed to talk to the police without the benefit of warnings and counsel, but whether he can be interrogated. There is no requirement that police stop a person who enters a police station and states that he wishes to confess to a crime, or a person who calls the police to offer a confession or any other statement he desires to make. Volunteered statements of any kind are not barred by the Fifth Amendment and their admissibility is not affected by our holding today.

To summarize, we hold that when an individual is taken into custody or otherwise deprived of his freedom by the authorities in any significant way and is subjected to questioning, the privilege against self-incrimination is jeopardized. Procedural safeguards must be employed to protect the privilege and unless other fully effective means are adopted to notify the person of his right of silence and to assure that the exercise of the right will be scrupulously honored, the following measures are required. He must be warned prior to any questioning that he has the right to remain silent, that anything he says can be used against him in a court of law, that he has the right to the presence of an attorney, and that if he cannot afford an attorney one will be appointed for him prior to any questioning if he so desires. Opportunity to exercise these rights must be afforded to him throughout the interrogation. After such warnings have been given, and such opportunity afforded him, the individual may knowingly and intelligently waive these rights and agree to answer questions or make a statement. But unless and until such warnings and waiver are demonstrated by the prosecution at trial, no evidence obtained as a result of interrogation can be used against him.

A recurrent argument made in these cases is that society's need for interrogation outweighs the privilege. This argument is not unfamiliar to this Court. The whole thrust of our foregoing discussion demonstrates that the Constitution has prescribed the rights of the individual when confronted with the power of government when it provided in the Fifth Amendment that an individual cannot be compelled to be a witness against himself. * * *

In this connection, one of our country's distinguished jurists has pointed out: "The quality of a nation's civilization can be largely measured by the methods it uses in the enforcement of its criminal law." * * *

In announcing these principles, we are not unmindful of the burdens which law enforcement officials must bear, often under trying circumstances. We also fully recognize the obligation of all citizens to aid in enforcing the criminal laws. This Court, while protecting individual rights, has always given ample latitude to law enforcement agencies in the legitimate exercise of their duties. The limits we have placed on the interrogation process should not constitute an undue interference with a proper system of law enforcement. As we have noted, our decision does not in any way preclude police from carrying out their traditional investigatory functions. Although confessions may play an important role in some convictions, the cases before us present graphic examples of the overstatement of the "need" for confessions. In each case authorities conducted interrogations ranging up to five days in duration despite the presence, through standard investigating practices, of considerable evidence against each defendant. * * *

JUSTICE CLARK, dissenting in Nos. 759, 760, and 761, and concurring in the result in No. 584.

* * * Rather than employing the arbitrary Fifth Amendment rule which the Court lays down I would follow the more pliable dictates of the Due Process Clauses of the Fifth and Fourteenth Amendments which we are accustomed to administering and which we know from our cases are effective instruments in protecting persons in police custody. In this way we would not be acting in the dark nor in one full sweep changing the traditional rules of custodial interrogation which this Court has for so long

recognized as a justifiable and proper tool in balancing individual rights against the rights of society. It will be soon enough to go further when we are able to appraise with somewhat better accuracy the effect of such a holding. * * *

JUSTICE HARLAN, whom JUSTICE STEWART and JUSTICE WHITE join, dissenting. * * *

While the fine points of this scheme are far less clear than the Court admits, the tenor is quite apparent. The new rules are not designed to guard against police brutality or other unmistakably banned forms of coercion. Those who use third-degree tactics and deny them in court are equally able and destined to lie as skillfully about warnings and waivers. Rather, the thrust of the new rules is to negate all pressures, to reinforce the nervous or ignorant suspect, and ultimately to discourage any confession at all. The aim in short is toward "voluntariness" in a utopian sense, or to view it from a different angle, voluntariness with a vengeance.

* * * [T]he Court's asserted reliance on the Fifth Amendment [is] an approach which I frankly regard as a *trompe l'oeil*. The Court's opinion in my view reveals no adequate basis for extending the Fifth Amendment's privilege against self-incrimination to the police station. Far more important, it fails to show that the Court's new rules are well supported, let alone compelled, by Fifth Amendment precedents. Instead, the new rules actually derive from quotation and analogy drawn from precedents under the Sixth Amendment, which should properly have no bearing on police interrogation. * * *

Without at all subscribing to the generally black picture of police conduct painted by the Court, I think it must be frankly recognized at the outset that police questioning allowable under due process precedents may inherently entail some pressure on the suspect and may seek advantage in his ignorance or weaknesses. The atmosphere and questioning techniques, proper and fair though they be, can in themselves exert a tug on the suspect to confess, and in this light "[t]o speak of any confessions of crime made after arrest as being 'voluntary' or 'uncoerced' is somewhat inaccurate, although traditional. A confession is wholly and incontestably voluntary only if a guilty person gives himself up to the law and becomes his own accuser." Until today, the role of the Constitution has been only to sift out undue pressure, not to assure spontaneous confessions. * * *

What the Court largely ignores is that its rules impair, if they will not eventually serve wholly to frustrate, an instrument of law enforcement that has long and quite reasonably been thought worth the price paid for it. There can be little doubt that the Court's new code would markedly decrease the number of confessions.

* * * The social costs of crime are too great to call the new rules anything but a hazardous experimentation.

While passing over the costs and risks of its experiment, the Court portrays the evils of normal police questioning in terms which I think are exaggerated. Albeit stringently confined by the due process standards interrogation is no doubt often inconvenient and unpleasant for the suspect. However, it is no less so for a man to be arrested and jailed, to have his house searched, or to stand trial in court, yet all this may properly happen to the most innocent given probable cause, a warrant, or an indictment. Society has always paid a stiff price for law and order, and peaceful interrogation is not one of the dark moments of the law. * * *

JUSTICE WHITE, with whom JUSTICE HARLAN and JUSTICE STEWART join, dissenting.

The proposition that the privilege against self-incrimination forbids in-custody interrogation without the warnings specified in the majority opinion and without a clear waiver of counsel has no significant support in the history of the privilege or in the language of the Fifth Amendment.

* * * To reach the result announced on the grounds it does, the Court must stay within the confines of the Fifth Amendment, which forbids self-incrimination only if compelled. Hence the core of the Court's opinion is that because of the "compulsion inherent in custodial surroundings, no statement obtained from [a] defendant [in custody] can truly be the product of his free choice," absent the use of adequate protective devices as described by the Court. However, the Court does not point to any sudden inrush of new knowledge requiring the rejection of 70 years' experience. * * * Rather than asserting new knowledge, the Court concedes that it cannot truly know what occurs during custodial questioning, because of the innate secrecy of such proceedings. It extrapolates a picture of what it conceives to be the norm from police investigatorial manuals, published in 1959 and 1962 or earlier, without any attempt to allow for adjustments in police practices that may have occurred in the wake of more recent decisions of state appellate tribunals or this Court. But even if the relentless application of the described procedures could lead to involuntary confessions, it most assuredly does not follow that each and every case will disclose this kind of interrogation or this kind of consequence. * * *

Although in the Court's view in-custody interrogation is inherently coercive, the Court says that the spontaneous product of the coercion of arrest and detention is still to be deemed voluntary. An accused, arrested on probable cause, may blurt out a confession which will be admissible despite the fact that he is alone and in custody, without any showing that he had any notion of his right to remain silent or of the consequences of his admission. Yet, under the Court's rule, if the police ask him a single question such as "Do you have anything to say?" or "Did you kill your wife?" his response, if there is one, has somehow been compelled, even if the accused has been clearly warned of his right to remain silent. Common sense informs us to the contrary. While one may say that the response was "involuntary" in the sense the question provoked or was the occasion for the response and thus the defendant was induced to speak out when he might have remained silent if not arrested and not questioned, it is patently unsound to say the response is compelled. * * *

The obvious underpinning of the Court's decision is a deep-seated distrust of all confessions. * * * This is the not so subtle overtone of the opinion—that it is inherently wrong for the police to gather evidence from the accused himself. And this is precisely the nub of this dissent. I see nothing wrong or immoral, and certainly nothing unconstitutional, in the police's asking a suspect whom they have reasonable cause to arrest whether or not he killed his wife or in confronting him with the evidence on which the arrest was based, at least where he has been plainly advised that he may remain completely silent. Until today, "the admissions or confessions of the prisoner, when voluntarily and freely made, have always ranked high in the scale of incriminating evidence." * * *

The most basic function of any government is to provide for the security of the individual and of his property. These ends of society are served by the criminal laws which for the most part are aimed at the prevention of crime. Without the reasonably effective performance of the task of preventing private violence and retaliation, it is idle to talk about human dignity and civilized values. * * *

At the same time, the Court's per se approach may not be justified on the ground that it provides a "bright line" permitting the authorities to judge in advance whether interrogation may safely be pursued without jeopardizing the admissibility of any information obtained as a consequence. * * * Today's decision leaves open such questions as whether the accused was in custody, whether his statements were spontaneous or the product of interrogation, whether the accused has effectively waived his rights, and whether nontestimonial evidence introduced at trial is the fruit of statements made during a prohibited interrogation, all of which are certain to prove productive of uncertainty during investigation and litigation during prosecution. For all these reasons, if further restrictions on police interrogation are desirable at this time, a more flexible approach makes much more sense than the Court's constitutional straitjacket which forecloses more discriminating treatment by legislative or rule-making pronouncements. * * *

NOTE

After the *Miranda v. Arizona* opinion, Ernesto Miranda capitalized on his newfound fame by printing and selling "Miranda cards" for $2 each. He ended up getting stabbed to death ten years after the *Miranda* decision. In a twist of fate, a Miranda card that Ernesto Miranda was carrying on his person the night he was killed was used to advise one of the men suspected of killing

Miranda of his *Miranda* rights. JETHRO K. LIEBERMAN, MILESTONES! 200 YEARS OF AMERICAN LAW: MILESTONES IN OUR LEGAL HISTORY 343 (1976).

A. WHAT CONSTITUTES "CUSTODY" AND "INTERROGATION" FOR PURPOSES OF THE *MIRANDA* RULE?

Because the *Miranda* warnings are required prior to custodial interrogation, the next four cases address what constitutes "custody" and what constitutes "interrogation." In *Berkemer v. McCarty*, the Court considers whether a motorist who is questioned by an officer during a traffic stop is "in custody" for purposes of the *Miranda* rule. *JDB v. North Carolina* decides whether the age of the suspect should inform the custody analysis. In *Rhode Island v. Innis*, the Court explains the meaning of interrogation for purposes of the *Miranda* rule. Finally, in *Illinois v. Perkins*, the Court considers whether an undercover law enforcement officer must give *Miranda* warnings to an incarcerated suspect before asking him questions that may elicit an incriminating response.

1. THE MEANING OF "CUSTODY"

BERKEMER V. MCCARTY
Supreme Court of the United States
468 U.S. 420, 104 S. Ct. 3138, 82 L. Ed. 2d 317 (1984)

JUSTICE MARSHALL delivered the opinion of the Court.

This case presents two related questions: First, does our decision in *Miranda v. Arizona* govern the admissibility of statements made during custodial interrogation by a suspect accused of a misdemeanor traffic offense? Second, does the roadside questioning of a motorist detained pursuant to a traffic stop constitute custodial interrogation for the purposes of the doctrine enunciated in *Miranda*?

* * * On the evening of March 31, 1980, Trooper Williams of the Ohio State Highway Patrol observed respondent's car weaving in and out of a lane on Interstate Highway 270. After following the car for two miles, Williams forced respondent to stop and asked him to get out of the vehicle. When respondent complied, Williams noticed that he was having difficulty standing. At that point, "Williams concluded that [respondent] would be charged with a traffic offense and, therefore, his freedom to leave the scene was terminated." However, respondent was not told that he would be taken into custody. Williams then asked respondent to perform a field sobriety test, commonly known as a "balancing test." Respondent could not do so without falling.

While still at the scene of the traffic stop, Williams asked respondent whether he had been using intoxicants. Respondent replied that "he had consumed two beers and had smoked several joints of marijuana a short time before." Respondent's speech was slurred, and Williams had difficulty understanding him. Williams thereupon formally placed respondent under arrest and transported him in the patrol car to the Franklin County Jail.

At the jail, respondent was given an intoxilyzer test to determine the concentration of alcohol in his blood. The test did not detect any alcohol whatsoever in respondent's system. Williams then resumed questioning respondent in order to obtain information for inclusion in the State Highway Patrol Alcohol Influence Report. Respondent answered affirmatively a question whether he had been drinking. When then asked if he was under the influence of alcohol, he said, "I guess, barely." * * *

At no point in this sequence of events did Williams or anyone else tell respondent that he had a right to remain silent, to consult with an attorney, and to have an attorney appointed for him if he could not afford one.

Respondent was charged with operating a motor vehicle while under the influence of alcohol and/or drugs in violation of Ohio Rev. Code Ann. § 4511.19. Under Ohio law, that offense is a first-degree misdemeanor and is punishable by fine or imprisonment for up to six months. * * *

Respondent moved to exclude the various incriminating statements he had made to Trooper Williams on the ground that introduction into evidence of those statements would violate the Fifth Amendment insofar as he had not been informed of his constitutional rights prior to his interrogation. When the trial court denied the motion, respondent pleaded "no contest" and was found guilty. * * *

On appeal to the Franklin County Court of Appeals, respondent renewed his constitutional claim. Relying on a prior decision by the Ohio Supreme Court, which held that the rule announced in *Miranda* "is not applicable to misdemeanors," the Court of Appeals rejected respondent's argument and affirmed his conviction. * * *

We granted certiorari to resolve confusion in the federal and state courts regarding the applicability of our ruling in *Miranda* to interrogations involving minor offenses and to questioning of motorists detained pursuant to traffic stops. * * *

In *Miranda v. Arizona*, the Court addressed the problem of how the privilege against compelled self-incrimination guaranteed by the Fifth Amendment could be protected from the coercive pressures that can be brought to bear upon a suspect in the context of custodial interrogation. * * *

In the years since the decision in *Miranda*, we have frequently reaffirmed the central principle established by that case: if the police take a suspect into custody and then ask him questions without informing him of the [*Miranda*] rights * * *, his responses cannot be introduced into evidence to establish his guilt.

Petitioner asks us to carve an exception out of the foregoing principle. When the police arrest a person for allegedly committing a misdemeanor traffic offense and then ask him questions without telling him his constitutional rights, petitioner argues, his responses should be admissible against him. We cannot agree.

One of the principal advantages of the doctrine that suspects must be given warnings before being interrogated while in custody is the clarity of that rule. * * * The exception to *Miranda* proposed by petitioner would substantially undermine this crucial advantage of the doctrine. The police often are unaware when they arrest a person whether he may have committed a misdemeanor or a felony. Consider, for example, the reasonably common situation in which the driver of a car involved in an accident is taken into custody. Under Ohio law, both driving while under the influence of intoxicants and negligent vehicular homicide are misdemeanors, while reckless vehicular homicide is a felony. When arresting a person for causing a collision, the police may not know which of these offenses he may have committed. Indeed, the nature of his offense may depend upon circumstances unknowable to the police, such as whether the suspect has previously committed a similar offense or has a criminal record of some other kind. It may even turn upon events yet to happen, such as whether a victim of the accident dies. It would be unreasonable to expect the police to make guesses as to the nature of the criminal conduct at issue before deciding how they may interrogate the suspect.

Equally importantly, the doctrinal complexities that would confront the courts if we accepted petitioner's proposal would be Byzantine. Difficult questions quickly spring to mind: For instance, investigations into seemingly minor offenses sometimes escalate gradually into investigations into more serious matters; at what point in the evolution of an affair of this sort would the police be obliged to give *Miranda* warnings to a suspect in custody? * * * The litigation necessary to resolve such matters would be time-consuming and disruptive of law enforcement. And the end result would be an elaborate set of rules, interlaced with exceptions and subtle distinctions, discriminating between different kinds of custodial interrogations. Neither the police nor criminal defendants would benefit from such a development. * * *

Petitioner's second argument is that law enforcement would be more expeditious and effective in the absence of a requirement that persons arrested for traffic offenses be informed of their rights. Again, we are unpersuaded. The occasions on which the police arrest and then interrogate someone suspected only of a misdemeanor traffic offense are rare. The police are already well accustomed to giving *Miranda* warnings to persons taken into custody. Adherence to the principle that *all* suspects must be given such warnings will not significantly hamper the efforts of the police to investigate crimes.

We hold therefore that a person subjected to custodial interrogation is entitled to the benefit of the procedural safeguards enunciated in *Miranda*, regardless of the nature or severity of the offense of which he is suspected or for which he was arrested.

The implication of this holding is that the Court of Appeals was correct in ruling that the statements made by respondent at the County Jail were inadmissible. There can be no question that respondent was "in custody" at least as of the moment he was formally placed under arrest and instructed to get into the police car. Because he was not informed of his constitutional rights at that juncture, respondent's subsequent admissions should not have been used against him.

To assess the admissibility of the self-incriminating statements made by respondent prior to his formal arrest, we are obliged to address a second issue concerning the scope of our decision in *Miranda*: whether the roadside questioning of a motorist detained pursuant to a routine traffic stop should be considered "custodial interrogation." Respondent urges that it should, on the ground that *Miranda* by its terms applies whenever "a person has been taken into custody or otherwise deprived of his freedom of action in any significant way." * * *

It must be acknowledged at the outset that a traffic stop significantly curtails the "freedom of action" of the driver and the passengers, if any, of the detained vehicle. Under the law of most States, it is a crime either to ignore a policeman's signal to stop one's car or, once having stopped, to drive away without permission. Certainly few motorists would feel free either to disobey a directive to pull over or to leave the scene of a traffic stop without being told they might do so. Partly for these reasons, we have long acknowledged that "stopping an automobile and detaining its occupants constitute a 'seizure' within the meaning of [the Fourth] Amendmen[t], even though the purpose of the stop is limited and the resulting detention quite brief."

However, we decline to accord talismanic power to the phrase in the *Miranda* opinion emphasized by respondent. Fidelity to the doctrine announced in *Miranda* requires that it be enforced strictly, but only in those types of situations in which the concerns that powered the decision are implicated. Thus, we must decide whether a traffic stop exerts upon a detained person pressures that sufficiently impair his free exercise of his privilege against self-incrimination to require that he be warned of his constitutional rights.

Two features of an ordinary traffic stop mitigate the danger that a person questioned will be induced "to speak where he would not otherwise do so freely." First, detention of a motorist pursuant to a traffic stop is presumptively temporary and brief. The vast majority of roadside detentions last only a few minutes. A motorist's expectations, when he sees a policeman's light flashing behind him, are that he will be obliged to spend a short period of time answering questions and waiting while the officer checks his license and registration, that he may then be given a citation, but that in the end he most likely will be allowed to continue on his way. In this respect, questioning incident to an ordinary traffic stop is quite different from stationhouse interrogation, which frequently is prolonged, and in which the detainee often is aware that questioning will continue until he provides his interrogators the answers they seek.

Second, circumstances associated with the typical traffic stop are not such that the motorist feels completely at the mercy of the police. To be sure, the aura of authority surrounding an armed, uniformed officer and the knowledge that the officer has some discretion in deciding whether to issue a citation, in combination, exert some pressure on the detainee to respond to questions. But other aspects of the situation substantially offset these forces. Perhaps most importantly, the typical traffic stop is public, at least to some degree. Passersby, on foot or in other cars, witness the interaction of officer and motorist. This exposure to public view both reduces the ability of an unscrupulous policeman to use illegitimate means to elicit self-incriminating statements and diminishes the motorist's fear that, if he does not cooperate, he will be subjected to abuse. The fact that the detained motorist typically is confronted by only one or at most two policemen further mutes his sense of vulnerability. In short, the atmosphere surrounding an ordinary traffic stop is substantially less "police dominated" than that surrounding the kinds of interrogation at issue in *Miranda* itself, and in the subsequent cases in which we have applied *Miranda*.

In both of these respects, the usual traffic stop is more analogous to a so-called "*Terry* stop," than to a formal arrest. Under the Fourth Amendment, we have held, a policeman who lacks probable cause but whose "observations lead him reasonably to suspect" that a particular person has committed, is committing, or is about to commit a crime, may detain that person briefly in order to "investigate the circumstances that provoke suspicion." "[The] stop and inquiry must be 'reasonably related in scope to the justification for their initiation.'" Typically, this means that the officer may ask the detainee a moderate number of questions to determine his identity and to try to obtain information confirming or dispelling the officer's suspicions. But the detainee is not obliged to respond. And, unless the detainee's answers provide the officer with probable cause to arrest him, he must then be released. The comparatively nonthreatening character of detentions of this sort explains the absence of any suggestion in our opinions that *Terry* stops are subject to the dictates of *Miranda*. The similarly noncoercive aspect of ordinary traffic stops prompts us to hold that persons temporarily detained pursuant to such stops are not "in custody" for the purposes of *Miranda*.

Respondent contends that to "exempt" traffic stops from the coverage of *Miranda* will open the way to widespread abuse. Policemen will simply delay formally arresting detained motorists, and will subject them to sustained and intimidating interrogation at the scene of their initial detention. The net result, respondent contends, will be a serious threat to the rights that the *Miranda* doctrine is designed to protect.

We are confident that the state of affairs projected by respondent will not come to pass. It is settled that the safeguards prescribed by *Miranda* become applicable as soon as a suspect's freedom of action is curtailed to a "degree associated with formal arrest." If a motorist who has been detained pursuant to a traffic stop thereafter is subjected to treatment that renders him "in custody" for practical purposes, he will be entitled to the full panoply of protections prescribed by *Miranda*.

Admittedly, our adherence to the doctrine just recounted will mean that the police and lower courts will continue occasionally to have difficulty deciding exactly when a suspect has been taken into custody. Either a rule that *Miranda* applies to all traffic stops or a rule that a suspect need not be advised of his rights until he is formally placed under arrest would provide a clearer, more easily administered line. However, each of these two alternatives has drawbacks that make it unacceptable. The first would substantially impede the enforcement of the Nation's traffic laws—by compelling the police either to take the time to warn all detained motorists of their constitutional rights or to forgo use of self-incriminating statements made by those motorists—while doing little to protect citizens' Fifth Amendment rights. The second would enable the police to circumvent the constraints on custodial interrogations established by *Miranda*.

Turning to the case before us, we find nothing in the record that indicates that respondent should have been given *Miranda* warnings at any point prior to the time Trooper Williams placed him under arrest. For the reasons indicated above, we reject the contention that the initial stop of respondent's car, by itself, rendered him "in custody." And respondent has failed to demonstrate that, at any time between the initial stop and the arrest, he was subjected to restraints comparable to those associated with a formal arrest. Only a short period of time elapsed between the stop and the arrest. At no point during that interval was respondent informed that his detention would not be temporary. Although Trooper Williams apparently decided as soon as respondent stepped out of his car that respondent would be taken into custody and charged with a traffic offense,

Williams never communicated his intention to respondent. A policeman's unarticulated plan has no bearing on the question whether a suspect was "in custody" at a particular time; the only relevant inquiry is how a reasonable man in the suspect's position would have understood his situation. Nor do other aspects of the interaction of Williams and respondent support the contention that respondent was exposed to "custodial interrogation" at the scene of the stop. From aught that appears in the stipulation of facts, a single police officer asked respondent a modest number of questions and requested him to perform a simple balancing test at a location visible to passing motorists. Treatment of this sort cannot fairly be characterized as the functional equivalent of formal arrest.

We conclude, in short, that respondent was not taken into custody for the purposes of *Miranda* until Williams arrested him. Consequently, the statements respondent made prior to that point were admissible against him. * * *

J.D.B. v. NORTH CAROLINA
Supreme Court of the United States
564 U.S. 261, 131 S. Ct. 2394, 180 L. Ed. 2d 310 (2011)

JUSTICE SOTOMAYOR delivered the opinion of the Court.

This case presents the question whether the age of a child subjected to police questioning is relevant to the custody analysis of *Miranda v. Arizona.* * * * [W]e hold that a child's age properly informs the *Miranda* custody analysis.

Petitioner J.D.B. was a 13-year-old, seventh-grade student attending class at Smith Middle School in Chapel Hill, North Carolina when he was removed from his classroom by a uniformed police officer, escorted to a closed-door conference room, and questioned by police for at least half an hour.

This was the second time that police questioned J.D.B. in the span of a week. Five days earlier, two home break-ins occurred, and various items were stolen. Police stopped and questioned J.D.B. after he was seen behind a residence in the neighborhood where the crimes occurred. That same day, police also spoke to J.D.B.'s grandmother—his legal guardian—as well as his aunt.

Police later learned that a digital camera matching the description of one of the stolen items had been found at J.D.B.'s middle school and seen in J.D.B.'s possession. Investigator DiCostanzo, the juvenile investigator with the local police force who had been assigned to the case, went to the school to question J.D.B. * * * Although DiCostanzo asked the school administrators to verify J.D.B.'s date of birth, address, and parent contact information from school records, neither the police officers nor the school administrators contacted J.D.B.'s grandmother.

The uniformed officer interrupted J.D.B.'s afternoon social studies class, removed J.D.B. from the classroom, and escorted him to a school conference room. There, J.D.B. was met by DiCostanzo, the assistant principal, and the administrative intern. The door to the conference room was closed. With the two police officers and the two administrators present, J.D.B. was questioned for the next 30 to 45 minutes. Prior to the commencement of questioning, J.D.B. was given neither *Miranda* warnings nor the opportunity to speak to his grandmother. Nor was he informed that he was free to leave the room.

Questioning began with small talk—discussion of sports and J.D.B.'s family life. DiCostanzo asked, and J.D.B. agreed, to discuss the events of the prior weekend. * * *

Eventually, J.D.B. asked whether he would "still be in trouble" if he returned the "stuff." In response, DiCostanzo explained that return of the stolen items would be helpful, but "this thing is going to court" regardless. DiCostanzo then warned that he may need to seek a secure custody order if he believed that J.D.B. would continue to break into other homes. When J.D.B. asked what a secure custody order was, DiCostanzo explained that "it's where you get sent to juvenile detention before court."

After learning of the prospect of juvenile detention, J.D.B. confessed that he and a friend were responsible for the break-ins. DiCostanzo only then informed J.D.B. that he could refuse to answer the investigator's questions and that he was free to leave. Asked whether he understood, J.D.B. nodded and provided further detail, including information about the location of the stolen items. Eventually J.D.B. wrote a statement, at DiCostanzo's request. When the bell rang indicating the end of the schoolday [sic], J.D.B. was allowed to leave to catch the bus home.

Two juvenile petitions were filed against J.D.B., each alleging one count of breaking and entering and one count of larceny. J.D.B.'s public defender moved to suppress his statements and the evidence derived therefrom, arguing that suppression was necessary because J.D.B. had been "interrogated by police in a custodial setting without being afforded *Miranda* warning[s]" and because his statements were involuntary under the totality of the circumstances test. After a suppression hearing at which DiCostanzo and J.D.B. testified, the trial court denied the motion, deciding that J.D.B. was not in custody at the time of the schoolhouse interrogation and that his statements were voluntary. * * *

A divided panel of the North Carolina Court of Appeals affirmed. The North Carolina Supreme Court held, over two dissents, that J.D.B. was not in custody when he confessed, "declin[ing] to extend the test for custody to include consideration of the age . . . of an individual subjected to questioning by police."

We granted certiorari to determine whether the *Miranda* custody analysis includes consideration of a juvenile suspect's age. * * *

By its very nature, custodial police interrogation entails "inherently compelling pressures." Even for an adult, the physical and psychological isolation of custodial interrogation can "undermine the individual's will to resist and . . . compel him to speak where he would not otherwise do so freely." Indeed, the pressure of custodial interrogation is so immense that it "can induce a frighteningly high percentage of people to confess to crimes they never committed." That risk is all the more troubling—and recent studies suggest, all the more acute—when the subject of custodial interrogation is a juvenile. * * *

Recognizing that the inherently coercive nature of custodial interrogation "blurs the line between voluntary and involuntary statements," this Court in *Miranda* adopted a set of prophylactic measures designed to safeguard the constitutional guarantee against self-incrimination. * * *

Because these measures protect the individual against the coercive nature of custodial interrogation, they are required "only where there has been such a restriction on a person's freedom as to render him in custody." As we have repeatedly emphasized, whether a suspect is "in custody" is an objective inquiry. * * *

The State and its *amici* contend that a child's age has no place in the custody analysis, no matter how young the child subjected to police questioning. We cannot agree. In some circumstances, a child's age "would have affected how a reasonable person" in the suspect's position "would perceive his or her freedom to leave." That is, a reasonable child subjected to police questioning will sometimes feel pressured to submit when a reasonable adult would feel free to go. We think it clear that courts can account for that reality without doing any damage to the objective nature of the custody analysis.

* * * We have observed that children "generally are less mature and responsible than adults," that they "often lack the experience, perspective, and judgment to recognize and avoid choices that could be detrimental to them," that they "are more vulnerable or susceptible to . . . outside pressures" than adults, and so on. Addressing the specific context of police interrogation, we have observed that events that "would leave a man cold and unimpressed can overawe and overwhelm a lad in his early teens." Describing no one child in particular, these observations restate what "any parent knows"—indeed, what any person knows—about children generally. * * *

As this discussion establishes, "[o]ur history is replete with laws and judicial recognition" that children cannot be viewed simply as miniature adults. We see no justification for taking a different course here. So long as the child's age was known to the officer at the time of the interview, or would have been objectively apparent to any reasonable officer, including age as part of the custody analysis requires officers neither to consider circumstances "unknowable" to them, nor to "anticipat[e] the frailties or idiosyncrasies" of the particular suspect whom they question. * * *

Reviewing the question *de novo* today, we hold that so long as the child's age was known to the officer at the time of police questioning, or would have been objectively apparent to a reasonable officer, its inclusion in the custody analysis is consistent with the objective nature of that test.[8] This is not to say that a child's age will be a determinative, or even a significant, factor in every case. It is, however, a reality that courts cannot simply ignore. * * *

The question remains whether J.D.B. was in custody when police interrogated him. We remand for the state courts to address that question, this time taking account of all of the relevant circumstances of the interrogation, including J.D.B.'s age at the time. The judgment of the North Carolina Supreme Court is reversed, and the case is remanded for proceedings not inconsistent with this opinion.

It is so ordered.

JUSTICE ALITO, with whom THE CHIEF JUSTICE, JUSTICE SCALIA, and JUSTICE THOMAS join, dissenting.

The Court's decision in this case may seem on first consideration to be modest and sensible, but in truth it is neither. It is fundamentally inconsistent with one of the main justifications for the *Miranda* rule: the perceived need for a clear rule that can be easily applied in all cases. * * *

Miranda's prophylactic regime places a high value on clarity and certainty. Dissatisfied with the highly fact-specific constitutional rule against the admission of involuntary confessions, the *Miranda* Court set down rigid standards that often require courts to ignore personal characteristics that may be highly relevant to a particular suspect's actual susceptibility to police pressure. This rigidity, however, has brought with it one of *Miranda*'s principal strengths—"the ease and clarity of its application" by law enforcement officials and courts. A key contributor to

---

[8] This approach does not undermine the basic principle that an interrogating officer's unarticulated, internal thoughts are never—in and of themselves—objective circumstances of an interrogation. Unlike a child's youth, an officer's purely internal thoughts have no conceivable effect on how a reasonable person in the suspect's position would understand his freedom of action. Rather than "overtur[n]" that settled principle, the limitation that a child's age may inform the custody analysis only when known or knowable simply reflects our unwillingness to require officers to "make guesses" as to circumstances "unknowable" to them in deciding when to give *Miranda* warnings.

this clarity, at least up until now, has been *Miranda*'s objective reasonable-person test for determining custody. * * *

The Court's rationale for importing age into the custody standard is that minors tend to lack adults' "capacity to exercise mature judgment" and that failing to account for that "reality" will leave some minors unprotected under *Miranda* in situations where they perceive themselves to be confined. I do not dispute that many suspects who are under 18 will be more susceptible to police pressure than the average adult. * * * It is no less a "reality," however, that many persons over the age of 18 are also more susceptible to police pressure than the hypothetical reasonable person. Yet the Miranda custody standard has never accounted for the personal characteristics of these or any other individual defendants.

Indeed, it has always been the case under *Miranda* that the unusually meek or compliant are subject to the same fixed rules, including the same custody requirement, as those who are unusually resistant to police pressure. *Miranda*'s rigid standards are both overinclusive and underinclusive. They are overinclusive to the extent that they provide a windfall to the most hardened and savvy of suspects, who often have no need for *Miranda*'s protections. Compare *Orozco v. Texas* (White, J., dissenting) ("Where the defendant himself [w]as a lawyer, policeman, professional criminal, or otherwise has become aware of what his right to silence is, it is sheer fancy to assert that his answer to every question asked him is compelled unless he is advised of those rights with which he is already intimately familiar"). And *Miranda*'s requirements are underinclusive to the extent that they fail to account for "frailties," "idiosyncrasies," and other individualized considerations that might cause a person to bend more easily during a confrontation with the police. * * *

That is undoubtedly why this Court's *Miranda* cases have never before mentioned "the suspect's age" or any other individualized consideration in applying the custody standard. And unless the *Miranda* custody rule is now to be radically transformed into one that takes into account the wide range of individual characteristics that are relevant in determining whether a confession is voluntary, the Court must shoulder the burden of explaining why age is different from these other personal characteristics.

Why, for example, is age different from intelligence? Suppose that an officer, upon going to a school to question a student, is told by the principal that the student has an I.Q. of 75 and is in a special-education class. Are those facts more or less important than the student's age in determining whether he or she "felt . . . at liberty to terminate the interrogation and leave"? * * *

How about the suspect's cultural background? Suppose the police learn (or should have learned) that a suspect they wish to question is a recent immigrant from a country in which dire consequences often befall any person who dares to attempt to cut short any meeting with the police. Is this really less relevant than the fact that a suspect is a month or so away from his 18th birthday? * * *

In time, the Court will have to confront these issues, and it will be faced with a difficult choice. It may choose to distinguish today's decision and adhere to the arbitrary proclamation that "age . . . is different." Or it may choose to extend today's holding and, in doing so, further undermine the very rationale for the *Miranda* regime. * * *

NOTE

Empirical research suggests that people tend to think Black kids are older than their actual age. In one study, Philip Atiba Goff showed individuals pictures of boys of various ages and races, told them that the boys were suspected of a particular crime, and then asked the subjects to guess the ages of the boys in the photos. *See, e.g.,* Philip Atiba Goff et al., *The Essence of Innocence: Consequences of Dehumanizing Black Children*, 106 J. OF PERSONALITY & SOC. PSYCHOL. 526 (2014). In case after case, the subjects thought the Black kids were much older than the White and Latino kids of the same age who were suspected of the same crime. *Id.* at 532. Individuals also thought the Black kids were more blameworthy for their actions than the White or Latino kids. *Id.* Goff did the same experiment on police officers and found that police officers also overestimated the age of Black and Latino kids who were suspected of having participated in criminal activity, while not overestimating the age of White children suspected of criminal activity. *Id.* at 535. Black 13-year-old kids were repeatedly perceived to be adults. *Id.* Does this research suggest any problems with the Court's test for "custody"?

2. THE MEANING OF "INTERROGATION"

RHODE ISLAND V. INNIS
Supreme Court of the United States
446 U.S. 291, 100 S. Ct. 1682, 64 L. Ed. 2d 297 (1980)

JUSTICE STEWART delivered the opinion of the Court.

In *Miranda v. Arizona*, the Court held that, once a defendant in custody asks to speak with a lawyer, all interrogation must cease until a lawyer is present. The issue in this case is whether the respondent was "interrogated" in violation of the standards promulgated in the *Miranda* opinion.

On the night of January 12, 1975, John Mulvaney, a Providence, R.I., taxicab driver, disappeared after being dispatched to pick up a customer. His body was discovered four days later buried in a shallow grave in Coventry, R.I. He had died from a shotgun blast aimed at the back of his head.

On January 17, 1975, shortly after midnight, the Providence police received a telephone call from Gerald Aubin, also a taxicab driver, who reported that he had just been robbed by a man wielding a sawed-off shotgun. * * * While at the Providence police station waiting to give a statement, Aubin noticed a picture of his assailant on a bulletin board. Aubin so informed one of the police officers present. * * * That person was the respondent. * * *

At approximately 4:30 a. m. on the same date, Patrolman Lovell, while cruising the streets of Mount Pleasant in a patrol car, spotted the respondent standing in the street facing him. When Patrolman Lovell stopped his car, the respondent walked towards it. Patrolman Lovell then arrested the respondent, who was unarmed, and advised him of his so-called *Miranda* rights. While the two men waited in the patrol car for other police officers to arrive, Patrolman Lovell did not converse with the respondent other than to respond to the latter's request for a cigarette.

Within minutes, Sergeant Sears arrived at the scene of the arrest, and he also gave the respondent the *Miranda* warnings. Immediately thereafter, Captain Leyden and other police officers arrived. Captain Leyden advised the respondent of his *Miranda* rights. The respondent stated that he understood those rights and wanted to speak with a lawyer. Captain Leyden then directed that the respondent be placed in a "caged wagon," a four-door police car with a wire screen mesh between the front and rear seats, and be driven to the central police station. Three officers, Patrolmen Gleckman, Williams, and McKenna, were assigned to accompany the respondent to the central station. They placed the respondent in the vehicle and shut the doors. Captain Leyden then instructed the officers not to question the respondent or intimidate or coerce him in any way. The three officers then entered the vehicle, and it departed.

While en route to the central station, Patrolman Gleckman initiated a conversation with Patrolman McKenna concerning the missing shotgun. As Patrolman Gleckman later testified:

A. At this point, I was talking back and forth with Patrolman McKenna stating that I frequent this area while on patrol and [that because a school for handicapped children is located nearby,] there's a lot of handicapped children running around in this area, and God forbid one of them might find a weapon with shells and they might hurt themselves. * * *

While Patrolman Williams said nothing, he overheard the conversation between the two officers:

A. He [Gleckman] said it would be too bad if the little—I believe he said a girl—would pick up the gun, maybe kill herself.

The respondent then interrupted the conversation, stating that the officers should turn the car around so he could show them where the gun was located. At this point, Patrolman McKenna radioed back to Captain Leyden that they were returning to the scene of the arrest and that the respondent would inform them of the location of the gun. At the time the respondent indicated that the officers should turn back, they had traveled no more than a mile, a trip encompassing only a few minutes.

The police vehicle then returned to the scene of the arrest where a search for the shotgun was in progress. There, Captain Leyden again advised the respondent of his *Miranda* rights. The respondent replied that he understood those rights but that he "wanted to get the gun out of the way because of the kids in the area in the school." The respondent then led the police to a nearby field, where he pointed out the shotgun under some rocks by the side of the road.

* * * Before trial, the respondent moved to suppress the shotgun and the statements he had made to the police regarding it. After an evidentiary hearing at which the respondent elected not to testify, the trial judge found that the respondent had been "repeatedly and completely advised of his *Miranda* rights." He further found that it was "entirely understandable that [the officers in the police vehicle] would voice their concern [for the safety of the handicapped children] to each other." The judge then concluded that the respondent's decision to inform the police of the location of the shotgun was "a waiver, clearly, and on the basis of the evidence that I have heard, and [sic] intelligent waiver, of his [*Miranda*] right to remain silent." Thus, without passing on whether the police officers had in fact "interrogated" the respondent, the trial court sustained the admissibility of the shotgun and testimony related to its discovery. That evidence was later introduced at the respondent's trial, and the jury returned a verdict of guilty on all counts.

On appeal, the Rhode Island Supreme Court, in a 3–2 decision, set aside the respondent's conviction. * * * Having concluded that both the shotgun and testimony relating to its discovery were obtained in violation of the *Miranda* standards and therefore should not have been admitted into evidence, the Rhode Island Supreme Court held that the respondent was entitled to a new trial.

We granted certiorari to address for the first time the meaning of "interrogation" under *Miranda v. Arizona*. * * *

In the present case, the parties are in agreement that the respondent was fully informed of his *Miranda* rights and that he invoked his *Miranda* right to counsel when he told Captain Leyden that he wished to consult with a lawyer. It is also uncontested that the respondent was "in custody" while being transported to the police station.

The issue, therefore, is whether the respondent was "interrogated" by the police officers in violation of the respondent's undisputed right under *Miranda* to remain silent until he had consulted with a lawyer. In resolving this issue, we first define the term "interrogation" under *Miranda* before turning to a consideration of the facts of this case.

The starting point for defining "interrogation" in this context is, of course, the Court's *Miranda* opinion. There the Court observed that "[b]y custodial interrogation, we mean questioning initiated by law enforcement officers after a person has been taken into custody or otherwise deprived of his freedom of action in any significant way." This passage and other references throughout the opinion to "questioning" might suggest that the *Miranda* rules were to apply only to those police interrogation practices that involve express questioning of a defendant while in custody.

We do not, however, construe the *Miranda* opinion so narrowly. The concern of the Court in *Miranda* was that the "interrogation environment" created by the interplay of interrogation and custody would "subjugate the individual to the will of his examiner" and thereby undermine the privilege against compulsory self-incrimination. The police practices that evoked this concern included several that did not involve express questioning [such as] the so-called "reverse line-up" in which a defendant would be identified by coached witnesses as the perpetrator of a fictitious crime, with the object of inducing him to confess to the actual crime of which he was suspected in order to escape the false prosecution. The Court in *Miranda* also included in its survey of interrogation practices the use of psychological ploys, such as to "posi[t]" "the guilt of the subject," to "minimize the moral seriousness of the offense," and "to cast blame on the victim or on society." It is clear that these techniques of persuasion, no less than express questioning, were thought, in a custodial setting, to amount to interrogation.

This is not to say, however, that all statements obtained by the police after a person has been taken into custody are to be considered the product of interrogation. * * * "Interrogation," as conceptualized in the *Miranda* opinion, must reflect a measure of compulsion above and beyond that inherent in custody itself.[4]

---

[4] There is language in the opinion of the Rhode Island Supreme Court in this case suggesting that the definition of "interrogation" under *Miranda* is informed by this Court's decision in *Brewer v. Williams*. This suggestion is erroneous. Our decision in *Brewer* rested solely on the Sixth and Fourteenth Amendment right to counsel. That right, as we held in *Massiah v. United States*, prohibits law enforcement officers from "deliberately elicit[ing]" incriminating information from a defendant in the absence of counsel after a formal charge against the defendant has been filed. Custody in such a case is not controlling; indeed, the petitioner in *Massiah* was not in custody. By contrast, the right to counsel at issue in the present case is based not on the Sixth and Fourteenth Amendments, but rather on the Fifth and Fourteenth Amendments as interpreted in the *Miranda* opinion. The definitions of "interrogation" under the Fifth and Sixth Amendments, if indeed the term "interrogation" is even apt in the Sixth Amendment context, are not necessarily interchangeable, since the policies underlying the two constitutional protections are quite distinct.

We conclude that the *Miranda* safeguards come into play whenever a person in custody is subjected to either express questioning or its functional equivalent. That is to say, the term "interrogation" under *Miranda* refers not only to express questioning, but also to any words or actions on the part of the police (other than those normally attendant to arrest and custody) that the police should know are reasonably likely to elicit an incriminating response[5] from the suspect. The latter portion of this definition focuses primarily upon the perceptions of the suspect, rather than the intent of the police. This focus reflects the fact that the *Miranda* safeguards were designed to vest a suspect in custody with an added measure of protection against coercive police practices, without regard to objective proof of the underlying intent of the police. A practice that the police should know is reasonably likely to evoke an incriminating response from a suspect thus amounts to interrogation.[7] But, since the police surely cannot be held accountable for the unforeseeable results of their words or actions, the definition of interrogation can extend only to words or actions on the part of police officers that they should have known were reasonably likely to elicit an incriminating response.[8]

Turning to the facts of the present case, we conclude that the respondent was not "interrogated" within the meaning of *Miranda*. It is undisputed that the first prong of the definition of "interrogation" was not satisfied, for the conversation between Patrolmen Gleckman and McKenna included no express questioning of the respondent. Rather, that conversation was, at least in form, nothing more than a dialogue between the two officers to which no response from the respondent was invited.

Moreover, it cannot be fairly concluded that the respondent was subjected to the "functional equivalent" of questioning. It cannot be said, in short, that Patrolmen Gleckman and McKenna should have known that their conversation was reasonably likely to elicit an incriminating response from the respondent. There is nothing in the record to suggest that the officers were aware that the respondent was peculiarly susceptible to an appeal to his conscience concerning the safety of handicapped children. Nor

---

[5] By "incriminating response" we refer to any response—whether inculpatory or exculpatory—that the prosecution may seek to introduce at trial.

[7] This is not to say that the intent of the police is irrelevant, for it may well have a bearing on whether the police should have known that their words or actions were reasonably likely to evoke an incriminating response. In particular, where a police practice is designed to elicit an incriminating response from the accused, it is unlikely that the practice will not also be one which the police should have known was reasonably likely to have that effect.

[8] Any knowledge the police may have had concerning the unusual susceptibility of a defendant to a particular form of persuasion might be an important factor in determining whether the police should have known that their words or actions were reasonably likely to elicit an incriminating response from the suspect.

is there anything in the record to suggest that the police knew that the respondent was unusually disoriented or upset at the time of his arrest.[9]

The case thus boils down to whether, in the context of a brief conversation, the officers should have known that the respondent would suddenly be moved to make a self-incriminating response. Given the fact that the entire conversation appears to have consisted of no more than a few off hand remarks, we cannot say that the officers should have known that it was reasonably likely that Innis would so respond. This is not a case where the police carried on a lengthy harangue in the presence of the suspect. Nor does the record support the respondent's contention that, under the circumstances, the officers' comments were particularly "evocative." It is our view, therefore, that the respondent was not subjected by the police to words or actions that the police should have known were reasonably likely to elicit an incriminating response from him.

The Rhode Island Supreme Court erred, in short, in equating "subtle compulsion" with interrogation. That the officers' comments struck a responsive chord is readily apparent. Thus, it may be said, as the Rhode Island Supreme Court did say, that the respondent was subjected to "subtle compulsion." But that is not the end of the inquiry. It must also be established that a suspect's incriminating response was the product of words or actions on the part of the police that they should have known were reasonably likely to elicit an incriminating response.[10] This was not established in the present case.

For the reasons stated, the judgment of the Supreme Court of Rhode Island is vacated, and the case is remanded to that court for further proceedings not inconsistent with this opinion.

It is so ordered.

JUSTICE MARSHALL, with whom JUSTICE BRENNAN joins, dissenting.

I am substantially in agreement with the Court's definition of "interrogation" within the meaning of *Miranda v. Arizona*. In my view, the *Miranda* safeguards apply whenever police conduct is intended or likely to produce a response from a suspect in custody. * * * Thus, the Court requires an objective inquiry into the likely effect of police conduct on a typical individual, taking into account any special susceptibility of the

---

[9] The record in no way suggests that the officers' remarks were *designed* to elicit a response. It is significant that the trial judge, after hearing the officers' testimony, concluded that it was "entirely understandable that [the officers] would voice their concern [for the safety of the handicapped children] to each other."

[10] By way of example, if the police had done no more than to drive past the site of the concealed weapon while taking the most direct route to the police station, and if the respondent, upon noticing for the first time the proximity of the school for handicapped children, had blurted out that he would show the officers where the gun was located, it could not seriously be argued that this "subtle compulsion" would have constituted "interrogation" within the meaning of the *Miranda* opinion.

suspect to certain kinds of pressure of which the police know or have reason to know.

I am utterly at a loss, however, to understand how this objective standard as applied to the facts before us can rationally lead to the conclusion that there was no interrogation. * * *

One can scarcely imagine a stronger appeal to the conscience of a suspect—any suspect—than the assertion that if the weapon is not found an innocent person will be hurt or killed. And not just any innocent person, but an innocent child—a little girl—a helpless, handicapped little girl on her way to school. The notion that such an appeal could not be expected to have any effect unless the suspect were known to have some special interest in handicapped children verges on the ludicrous. As a matter of fact, the appeal to a suspect to confess for the sake of others, to "display some evidence of decency and honor," is a classic interrogation technique.

Gleckman's remarks would obviously have constituted interrogation if they had been explicitly directed to respondent, and the result should not be different because they were nominally addressed to McKenna. This is not a case where police officers speaking among themselves are accidentally overheard by a suspect. These officers were "talking back and forth" in close quarters with the handcuffed suspect, traveling past the very place where they believed the weapon was located. They knew respondent would hear and attend to their conversation, and they are chargeable with knowledge of and responsibility for the pressures to speak which they created.

I firmly believe that this case is simply an aberration, and that in future cases the Court will apply the standard adopted today in accordance with its plain meaning.

JUSTICE STEVENS, dissenting.

* * * In my view any statement that would normally be understood by the average listener as calling for a response is the functional equivalent of a direct question, whether or not it is punctuated by a question mark. The Court, however, takes a much narrower view. It holds that police conduct is not the "functional equivalent" of direct questioning unless the police should have known that what they were saying or doing was likely to elicit an incriminating response from the suspect. This holding represents a plain departure from the principles set forth in *Miranda*. * * *

In short, in order to give full protection to a suspect's right to be free from any interrogation at all, the definition of "interrogation" must include any police statement or conduct that has the same purpose or effect as a direct question. Statements that appear to call for a response from the suspect, as well as those that are designed to do so, should be considered interrogation. By prohibiting only those relatively few statements or actions that a police officer should know are likely to elicit an incriminating response, the Court today accords a suspect considerably less protection. Indeed, since I suppose most suspects are unlikely to incriminate themselves even when questioned directly, this new definition will almost certainly exclude every statement that is not punctuated with a question mark from the concept of "interrogation."

The difference between the approach required by a faithful adherence to *Miranda* and the stinted test applied by the Court today can be illustrated by comparing three different ways in which Officer Gleckman could have communicated his fears about the possible dangers posed by the shotgun to handicapped children. He could have:

(1) directly asked Innis:

Will you please tell me where the shotgun is so we can protect handicapped school children from danger?

(2) announced to the other officers in the wagon:

If the man sitting in the back seat with me should decide to tell us where the gun is, we can protect handicapped children from danger.

Or (3) stated to the other officers:

It would be too bad if a little handicapped girl would pick up the gun that this man left in the area and maybe kill herself.

In my opinion, all three of these statements should be considered interrogation because all three appear to be designed to elicit a response from anyone who in fact knew where the gun was located. Under the Court's test, on the other hand, the form of the statements would be critical. The third statement would not be interrogation because in the Court's view there was no reason for Officer Gleckman to believe that Innis was susceptible to this type of an implied appeal, therefore, the statement would not be reasonably likely to elicit an incriminating response. Assuming that this is true, then it seems to me that the first two statements, which would be just as unlikely to elicit such a response, should also not be considered interrogation. But, because the first statement is clearly an express question, it would be considered interrogation under the Court's test. The second statement, although just as clearly a deliberate appeal to Innis to reveal the location of the gun, would presumably not be interrogation because (a) it was not in form a direct question and (b) it does not fit within the "reasonably likely to elicit an incriminating response" category that applies to indirect interrogation.

As this example illustrates, the Court's test creates an incentive for police to ignore a suspect's invocation of his rights in order to make continued attempts to extract information from him. If a suspect does not appear to be susceptible to a particular type of psychological pressure, the police are apparently free to exert that pressure on him despite his request for counsel, so long as they are careful not to punctuate their statements with question marks. And if, contrary to all reasonable expectations, the suspect makes an incriminating statement, that statement can be used against him at trial. The Court thus turns *Miranda*'s unequivocal rule against any interrogation at all into a trap in which unwary suspects may be caught by police deception. * * *

In any event, I think the Court is clearly wrong in holding, as a matter of law, that Officer Gleckman should not have realized that his statement was likely to elicit an incriminating response. * * *

The Court's assumption that criminal suspects are not susceptible to appeals to conscience is directly contrary to the teachings of police interrogation manuals, which recommend appealing to a suspect's sense of morality as a standard and often successful interrogation technique. Surely the practical experience embodied in such manuals should not be ignored in a case such as this in which the record is devoid of any evidence—one way or the other—as to the susceptibility of suspects in general or of Innis in particular.

NOTE

Is the *Innis* test for interrogation easy to apply? Consider *Arizona v. Mauro*, 481 U.S. 250 (1987), a case in which a man was taken into custody after he freely admitted to police officers that he killed his son. After being advised of his *Miranda* rights at the police station, Mauro told police officers that he did not want to talk any more without a lawyer present. All questioning of Mauro immediately ceased. At around the same time, another officer was questioning Mauro's wife in another interrogation room. Mrs. Mauro asked if she could speak with her husband. The officer questioning Mrs. Mauro was reluctant to allow such a meeting, but after consulting with his supervisor, took Mrs. Mauro to her husband, seated himself at a desk in the room, and placed a tape recorder in plain view on the desk. He then listened to and recorded the brief conversation between Mauro and his wife in which Mauro told Mrs. Mauro several times to "shut up." Mauro also advised his wife not to answer any questions until she spoke with an attorney.

At Mauro's trial for the murder of his son, Mauro claimed he was insane at the time of the crime. To rebut Mauro's claim of insanity, the government introduced the taped conversation. Mauro sought to suppress the tape recording on the ground that it was the result of an interrogation in violation of his *Miranda* rights. The trial court refused to suppress the recording, and Mauro was convicted and sentenced to death. The Arizona Supreme Court reversed Mauro's conviction, noting that because Mauro had invoked his right to counsel, police were not supposed to interrogate him any further until counsel was present. The court also noted that the detectives acknowledged that they knew it was possible Mauro might make incriminating statements if he met with his wife. The Arizona Supreme Court concluded that the police had engaged in an interrogation since they knew that if they put Mauro and his wife in the same room, incriminating statements were likely to be made.

In an opinion written by Justice Powell, the U.S. Supreme Court reversed, holding that the officer's actions did not constitute interrogation or its "functional equivalent." The police officer did not ask any questions of Mauro and there was no evidence that the police arranged the conversation for the purpose of obtaining incriminating statements. Even though the officers were aware of the possibility that Mauro would make incriminating statements if he met with his wife, the Court explained that a mere possibility was insufficient to meet the *Rhode Island v. Innis* standard of "any words or actions on the part of the police (other than those normally attendant to arrest and custody) that the police should know are reasonably likely to elicit an incriminating response." In concluding that the actions of the police in this case did not constitute an interrogation, the Court stated, "officers do not interrogate a suspect simply by hoping that he will incriminate himself."

ILLINOIS V. PERKINS
Supreme Court of the United States
496 U.S. 292, 110 S. Ct. 2394, 110 L. Ed. 2d 243 (1990)

JUSTICE KENNEDY delivered the opinion of the Court.

An undercover government agent was placed in the cell of respondent Perkins, who was incarcerated on charges unrelated to the subject of the agent's investigation. Respondent made statements that implicated him in the crime that the agent sought to solve. Respondent claims that the statements should be inadmissible because he had not been given *Miranda* warnings by the agent. We hold that the statements are admissible. *Miranda* warnings are not required when the suspect is unaware that he is speaking to a law enforcement officer and gives a voluntary statement.

In November 1984, Richard Stephenson was murdered in a suburb of East St. Louis, Illinois. The murder remained unsolved until March 1986, when one Donald Charlton told police that he had learned about a homicide from a fellow inmate at the Graham Correctional Facility, where Charlton had been serving a sentence for burglary. The fellow inmate was Lloyd Perkins, who is the respondent here. Charlton told police that, while at Graham, he had befriended respondent, who told him in detail about a murder that respondent had committed in East St. Louis. On hearing Charlton's account, the police recognized details of the Stephenson murder that were not well known, and so they treated Charlton's story as a credible one.

By the time the police heard Charlton's account, respondent had been released from Graham, but police traced him to a jail in Montgomery

County, Illinois, where he was being held pending trial on a charge of aggravated battery, unrelated to the Stephenson murder. The police wanted to investigate further respondent's connection to the Stephenson murder, but feared that the use of an eavesdropping device would prove impracticable and unsafe. They decided instead to place an undercover agent in the cellblock with respondent and Charlton. The plan was for Charlton and undercover agent John Parisi to pose as escapees from a work release program who had been arrested in the course of a burglary. Parisi and Charlton were instructed to engage respondent in casual conversation and report anything he said about the Stephenson murder.

Parisi, using the alias "Vito Bianco," and Charlton, both clothed in jail garb, were placed in the cellblock with respondent at the Montgomery County jail. * * * Respondent greeted Charlton who, after a brief conversation with respondent, introduced Parisi by his alias. Parisi told respondent that he "wasn't going to do any more time" and suggested that the three of them escape. Respondent replied that the Montgomery County jail was "rinky-dink" and that they could "break out." * * * Parisi asked respondent if he had ever "done" anybody. Respondent said that he had and proceeded to describe at length the events of the Stephenson murder. * * * Parisi did not give respondent *Miranda* warnings before the conversations.

Respondent was charged with the Stephenson murder. Before trial, he moved to suppress the statements made to Parisi in the jail. The trial court granted the motion to suppress, and the State appealed. The Appellate Court of Illinois affirmed, holding that *Miranda* prohibits all undercover contacts with incarcerated suspects that are reasonably likely to elicit an incriminating response.

We granted certiorari to decide whether an undercover law enforcement officer must give *Miranda* warnings to an incarcerated suspect before asking him questions that may elicit an incriminating response. We now reverse.

In *Miranda,* the Court held that the Fifth Amendment privilege against self-incrimination prohibits admitting statements given by a suspect during "custodial interrogation" without a prior warning. Custodial interrogation means "questioning initiated by law enforcement officers after a person has been taken into custody. . . ." The warning mandated by *Miranda* was meant to preserve the privilege during "incommunicado interrogation of individuals in a police-dominated atmosphere." * * * "Fidelity to the doctrine announced in *Miranda* requires that it be enforced strictly, but only in those types of situations in which the concerns that powered the decision are implicated."

Conversations between suspects and undercover agents do not implicate the concerns underlying *Miranda.* The essential ingredients of a "police-dominated atmosphere" and compulsion are not present when an incarcerated person speaks freely to someone whom he believes to be a fellow inmate. Coercion is determined from the perspective of the suspect. When a suspect considers himself in the company of cellmates and not officers, the coercive atmosphere is lacking. There is no empirical basis for the assumption that a suspect speaking to those whom he assumes are not officers will feel compelled to speak by the fear of reprisal for remaining silent or in the hope of more lenient treatment should he confess.

It is the premise of *Miranda* that the danger of coercion results from the interaction of custody and official interrogation. We reject the argument that *Miranda* warnings are required whenever a suspect is in custody in a technical sense and converses with someone who happens to be a government agent. Questioning by captors, who appear to control the suspect's fate, may create mutually reinforcing pressures that the Court has assumed will weaken the suspect's will, but where a suspect does not know that he is conversing with a government agent, these pressures do not exist. * * *

Miranda forbids coercion, not mere strategic deception by taking advantage of a suspect's misplaced trust in one he supposes to be a fellow prisoner. * * * Ploys to mislead a suspect or lull him into a false sense of security that do not rise to the level of compulsion or coercion to speak are not within *Miranda*'s concerns.

Miranda was not meant to protect suspects from boasting about their criminal activities in front of persons whom they believe to be their cellmates. This case is illustrative. Respondent had no reason to feel that undercover agent Parisi had any legal authority to force him to answer questions or that Parisi could affect respondent's future treatment. Respondent viewed the cellmate-agent as an equal and showed no hint of being intimidated by the atmosphere of the jail. In recounting the details of the Stephenson murder, respondent was motivated solely by the desire to impress his fellow inmates. He spoke at his own peril. * * *

This Court's Sixth Amendment decisions in *Massiah v. United States*, *United States v. Henry*, and *Maine v. Moulton* also do not avail respondent. We held in those cases that the government may not use an undercover agent to circumvent the Sixth Amendment right to counsel once a suspect has been charged with the crime. After charges have been filed, the Sixth Amendment prevents the government from interfering with the accused's right to counsel. In the instant case no charges had been filed on the subject of the interrogation, and our Sixth Amendment precedents are not applicable.[a] * * *

---

[a] The Court hints in this paragraph that the Sixth Amendment only applies to deliberate elicitation of incriminating statements about charged offenses, not deliberate elicitation of incriminating statements about uncharged offenses. One year later, the Court explicitly held that the Sixth Amendment right to counsel is offense specific, i.e. that the Sixth Amendment prohibits only the deliberate elicitation of incriminating statements about a charged offense in the absence

We hold that an undercover law enforcement officer posing as a fellow inmate need not give *Miranda* warnings to an incarcerated suspect before asking questions that may elicit an incriminating response. The statements at issue in this case were voluntary, and there is no federal obstacle to their admissibility at trial. We now reverse and remand for proceedings not inconsistent with our opinion.

It is so ordered.

JUSTICE MARSHALL, dissenting.

* * * The conditions that require the police to apprise a defendant of his constitutional rights—custodial interrogation conducted by an agent of the police—were present in this case. Because Lloyd Perkins received no *Miranda* warnings before he was subjected to custodial interrogation, his confession was not admissible.

The Court reaches the contrary conclusion by fashioning an exception to the *Miranda* rule that applies whenever "an undercover law enforcement officer posing as a fellow inmate ... ask[s] questions that may elicit an incriminating response" from an incarcerated suspect. This exception is inconsistent with the rationale supporting *Miranda* and allows police officers intentionally to take advantage of suspects unaware of their constitutional rights. I therefore dissent.

The Court does not dispute that the police officer here conducted a custodial interrogation of a criminal suspect. Perkins was incarcerated in county jail during the questioning at issue here; under these circumstances, he was in custody as that term is defined in *Miranda*. The United States argues that Perkins was not in custody for purpose of *Miranda* because he was familiar with the custodial environment as a result of being in jail for two days and previously spending time in prison. Perkins' familiarity with confinement, however, does not transform his incarceration into some sort of noncustodial arrangement.

While Perkins was confined, an undercover police officer, with the help of a police informant, questioned him about a serious crime. Although the Court does not dispute that Perkins was interrogated, it downplays the nature of the 35-minute questioning by disingenuously referring to it as a "conversatio[n]." The officer's narration of the "conversation" at Perkins' suppression hearing however, reveals that it clearly was an interrogation.

[Agent:] You ever do anyone?

[Perkins:] Yeah, once in East St. Louis, in a rich white neighborhood.

---

of counsel. *See McNeil v. Wisconsin*, 501 U.S. 171, 175 (1991). No Sixth Amendment violation occurs if a government agent deliberately elicits incriminating statements regarding an uncharged offense or, more accurately, an offense for which formal judicial proceedings have not yet commenced. *Id.*

[Informant:] I didn't know they had any rich white neighborhoods in East St. Louis.

[Perkins:] It wasn't in East St. Louis, it was by a race track in Fairview Heights. . . .

[Agent]: You did a guy in Fairview Heights?

[Perkins:] Yeah in a rich white section where most of the houses look the same.

[Informant]: If all the houses look the same, how did you know you had the right house?

[Perkins:] Me and two guys cased the house for about a week. I knew exactly which house, the second house on the left from the corner.

[Agent]: How long ago did this happen?

[Perkins:] Approximately about two years ago. I got paid $5,000 for that job.

[Agent]: How did it go down?

[Perkins:] I walked up [to] this guy['s] house with a sawed-off under my trench coat.

[Agent]: What type gun[?]

[Perkins:] A .12 gauge Remmington [*sic*] Automatic Model 1100 sawed-off.

The police officer continued the inquiry, asking a series of questions designed to elicit specific information about the victim, the crime scene, the weapon, Perkins' motive, and his actions during and after the shooting. This interaction was not a "conversation"; Perkins, the officer, and the informant were not equal participants in a free-ranging discussion, with each man offering his views on different topics. Rather, it was an interrogation: Perkins was subjected to express questioning likely to evoke an incriminating response.

Because Perkins was interrogated by police while he was in custody, *Miranda* required that the officer inform him of his rights. In rejecting that conclusion, the Court finds that "conversations" between undercover agents and suspects are devoid of the coercion inherent in station house interrogations conducted by law enforcement officials who openly represent the State. *Miranda* was not, however, concerned solely with police *coercion*. It dealt with *any* police tactics that may operate to compel a suspect in custody to make incriminating statements without full awareness of his constitutional rights. Thus, when a law enforcement agent structures a custodial interrogation so that a suspect feels compelled to reveal incriminating information, he must inform the suspect of his constitutional rights and give him an opportunity to decide whether or not to talk.

The compulsion proscribed by *Miranda* includes deception by the police. See *Miranda* (indicting police tactics "to induce a confession out of trickery," such as using fictitious witnesses or false accusations); *Berkemer* ("The purposes of the safeguards prescribed by *Miranda* are to ensure that the police do not coerce *or* trick captive suspects into confessing"). * * * Perkins, however, was interrogated while incarcerated. As the Court has acknowledged in the Sixth Amendment context: "[T]he mere fact of custody imposes pressures on the accused; confinement may bring into play subtle influences that will make him particularly susceptible to the ploys of undercover Government agents."

Custody works to the State's advantage in obtaining incriminating information. The psychological pressures inherent in confinement increase the suspect's anxiety, making him likely to seek relief by talking with others. The inmate is thus more susceptible to efforts by undercover agents to elicit information from him. Similarly, where the suspect is incarcerated, the constant threat of physical danger peculiar to the prison environment may make him demonstrate his toughness to other inmates by recounting or inventing past violent acts. "Because the suspect's ability to select people with whom he can confide is completely within their control, the police have a unique opportunity to exploit the suspect's vulnerability. In short, the police can insure [sic] that if the pressures of confinement lead the suspect to confide in anyone, it will be a police agent." In this case, the police deceptively took advantage of Perkins' psychological vulnerability by including him in a sham escape plot, a situation in which he would feel compelled to demonstrate his willingness to shoot a prison guard by revealing his past involvement in a murder. * * *

The Court's adoption of an exception to the *Miranda* doctrine is incompatible with the principle, consistently applied by this Court, that the doctrine should remain simple and clear. * * * The Court's adoption of the "undercover agent" exception to the *Miranda* rule * * * is necessarily also the adoption of a substantial loophole in our jurisprudence protecting suspects' Fifth Amendment rights.

I dissent.

[JUSTICE BRENNAN's concurring opinion, suggesting that the deception and manipulation practiced upon Perkins raised a substantial claim that his confession was obtained in violation of the Due Process Clause, has been omitted.]

B. CAN POLICE TRY AGAIN AFTER A SUSPECT INVOKES HER *MIRANDA* RIGHTS?

The cases in this section address whether police officers can interrogate suspects after they have invoked either their *Miranda* right to silence or their *Miranda* right to counsel. The two main cases on this subject are *Michigan v. Mosley* and *Edwards v. Arizona*. In *Michigan v. Mosley*, the Court focuses on whether law enforcement officers can interrogate a suspect who has invoked her *Miranda* right to silence. In *Edwards v. Arizona*, the Court describes the procedures that police officers must follow when a suspect invokes her *Miranda* right to counsel. This set of procedures has been called the *Edwards* rule.

In *Davis v. United States*, the Court addresses whether the *Edwards* rule applies when a suspect does not clearly invoke her right to counsel. Janet Ainsworth's article, *In a Different Register: The Pragmatics of Powerlessness in Police Interrogation*, considers whether the Court's invocation jurisprudence adequately accounts for different communication styles.

The final case in this section, *Maryland v. Shatzer*, examines whether law enforcement officers are permanently barred from attempting to obtain a waiver of the right to counsel from a suspect who has invoked this right on a prior occasion. As you read the cases in this section, consider whether the Court's reasoning is consistent with its decision in *Miranda*.

MICHIGAN V. MOSLEY
Supreme Court of the United States
423 U.S. 96, 96 S. Ct. 321, 46 L. Ed. 2d 313 (1975)

JUSTICE STEWART delivered the opinion of the Court.

The respondent, Richard Bert Mosley, was arrested in Detroit, Mich., in the early afternoon of April 8, 1971, in connection with robberies that had recently occurred at the Blue Goose Bar and the White Tower Restaurant on that city's lower east side. The arresting officer, Detective James Cowie of the Armed Robbery Section of the Detroit Police Department, was acting on a tip implicating Mosley and three other men in the robberies. After effecting the arrest, Detective Cowie brought Mosley to the Robbery, Breaking and Entering Bureau of the Police Department, located on the fourth floor of the departmental headquarters building. The officer advised Mosley of his rights under this Court's decision in *Miranda v. Arizona*, and had him read and sign the department's constitutional rights notification certificate. After filling out the necessary arrest papers, Cowie began questioning Mosley about the robbery of the White Tower Restaurant. When Mosley said he did not want to answer any questions about the robberies, Cowie promptly ceased the interrogation. The completion of the arrest papers and the questioning of Mosley together took approximately 20 minutes. At no time during the questioning did Mosley indicate a desire to consult with a lawyer, and there is no claim that the procedures followed to this point did not fully comply with the strictures of the *Miranda* opinion. Mosley was then taken to a ninth-floor cell block.

Shortly after 6 p. m., Detective Hill of the Detroit Police Department Homicide Bureau brought Mosley from the cell block to the fifth-floor office of the Homicide Bureau for questioning about the fatal shooting of a man named Leroy Williams. Williams had been killed on January 9, 1971, during a holdup attempt outside the 101 Ranch Bar in Detroit. Mosley had not been arrested on this charge or interrogated about it by Detective Cowie. Before questioning Mosley about this homicide, Detective Hill carefully advised him of his "*Miranda* rights." Mosley read the notification form both silently and aloud, and Detective Hill then read and explained the warnings to him and had him sign the form. Mosley at first denied any involvement in the Williams murder, but after the officer told him that Anthony Smith had confessed to participating in the slaying and had named him as the "shooter," Mosley made a statement implicating himself in the homicide. The interrogation by Detective Hill lasted approximately 15 minutes, and at no time during its course did Mosley ask to consult with a lawyer or indicate that he did not want to discuss the homicide. In short, there is no claim that the procedures followed during Detective Hill's interrogation of Mosley, standing alone, did not fully comply with the strictures of the *Miranda* opinion.

Mosley was subsequently charged in a one-count information with first-degree murder. Before the trial he moved to suppress his incriminating statement on a number of grounds, among them the claim that under the doctrine of the *Miranda* case it was constitutionally impermissible for Detective Hill to question him about the Williams murder after he had told Detective Cowie that he did not want to answer any questions about the robberies. The trial court denied the motion to suppress after an evidentiary hearing, and the incriminating statement was subsequently introduced in evidence against Mosley at his trial. The jury convicted Mosley of first-degree murder, and the court imposed a mandatory sentence of life imprisonment.

On appeal to the Michigan Court of Appeals, Mosley renewed his previous objections to the use of his incriminating statement in evidence. The appellate court reversed the judgment of conviction, holding that Detective Hill's interrogation of Mosley had been a per se violation of the *Miranda* doctrine. * * * We granted the writ because of the important constitutional question presented.

* * * The issue in this case * * * is whether the conduct of the Detroit police that led to Mosley's incriminating statement did in fact violate the

Miranda "guidelines," so as to render the statement inadmissible in evidence against Mosley at his trial. Resolution of the question turns almost entirely on the interpretation of a single passage in the *Miranda* opinion, upon which the Michigan appellate court relied in finding a per se violation of *Miranda*:

> Once warnings have been given, the subsequent procedure is clear. If the individual indicates in any manner, at any time prior to or during questioning, that he wishes to remain silent, the interrogation must cease. At this point he has shown that he intends to exercise his Fifth Amendment privilege; any statement taken after the person invokes his privilege cannot be other than the product of compulsion, subtle or otherwise. Without the right to cut off questioning, the setting of in-custody interrogation operates on the individual to overcome free choice in producing a statement after the privilege has been once invoked.[7]

This passage states that "the interrogation must cease" when the person in custody indicates that "he wishes to remain silent." It does not state under what circumstances, if any, a resumption of questioning is permissible. The passage could be literally read to mean that a person who has invoked his "right to silence" can never again be subjected to custodial interrogation by any police officer at any time or place on any subject. * * * Or the passage could be interpreted to require only the immediate cessation of questioning, and to permit a resumption of interrogation after a momentary respite.

It is evident that any of these possible literal interpretations would lead to absurd and unintended results. To permit the continuation of custodial interrogation after a momentary cessation would clearly frustrate the purposes of *Miranda* by allowing repeated rounds of questioning to undermine the will of the person being questioned. At the other extreme, a blanket prohibition against the taking of voluntary statements or a permanent immunity from further interrogation, regardless of the circumstances, would transform the *Miranda* safeguards into wholly irrational obstacles to legitimate police investigative activity, and deprive suspects of an opportunity to make informed and intelligent assessments of their interests. Clearly, therefore, neither this passage nor any other passage in the *Miranda* opinion can sensibly be read to create a per se proscription of indefinite duration upon any further questioning by any police officer on any subject, once the person in custody has indicated a desire to remain silent.

A reasonable and faithful interpretation of the *Miranda* opinion must rest on the intention of the Court in that case to adopt "fully effective means

---

[7] The present case does not involve the procedures to be followed if the person in custody asks to consult with a lawyer, since Mosley made no such request at any time. * * *

... to notify the person of his right of silence and to assure that the exercise of the right will be scrupulously honored . . . ." The critical safeguard identified in the passage at issue is a person's "right to cut off questioning." Through the exercise of his option to terminate questioning he can control the time at which questioning occurs, the subjects discussed, and the duration of the interrogation. The requirement that law enforcement authorities must respect a person's exercise of that option counteracts the coercive pressures of the custodial setting. We therefore conclude that the admissibility of statements obtained after the person in custody has decided to remain silent depends under *Miranda* on whether his "right to cut off questioning" was "scrupulously honored."[10]

A review of the circumstances leading to Mosley's confession reveals that his "right to cut off questioning" was fully respected in this case. Before his initial interrogation, Mosley was carefully advised that he was under no obligation to answer any questions and could remain silent if he wished. He orally acknowledged that he understood the *Miranda* warnings and then signed a printed notification-of-rights form. When Mosley stated that he did not want to discuss the robberies, Detective Cowie immediately ceased the interrogation and did not try either to resume the questioning or in any way to persuade Mosley to reconsider his position. After an interval of more than two hours, Mosley was questioned by another police officer at another location about an unrelated holdup murder. He was given full and complete *Miranda* warnings at the outset of the second interrogation. He was thus reminded again that he could remain silent and could consult with a lawyer, and was carefully given a full and fair opportunity to exercise these options. * * *

This is not a case, therefore, where the police failed to honor a decision of a person in custody to cut off questioning, either by refusing to discontinue the interrogation upon request or by persisting in repeated efforts to wear down his resistance and make him change his mind. In contrast to such practices, the police here immediately ceased the interrogation, resumed questioning only after the passage of a significant period of time and the provision of a fresh set of warnings, and restricted the second interrogation to a crime that had not been a subject of the earlier interrogation. * * *

For these reasons, we conclude that the admission in evidence of Mosley's incriminating statement did not violate the principles of *Miranda v. Arizona*. Accordingly, the judgment of the Michigan Court of Appeals is

---

[10] The dissenting opinion asserts that *Miranda* established a requirement that once a person has indicated a desire to remain silent, questioning may be resumed only when counsel is present. But clearly the Court in *Miranda* imposed no such requirement, for it distinguished between the procedural safeguards triggered by a request to remain silent and a request for an attorney and directed that "the interrogation must cease until an attorney is present" only "[i]f the individual states that he wants an attorney."

vacated, and the case is remanded to that court for further proceedings not inconsistent with this opinion.

It is so ordered.

Judgment vacated and case remanded.

JUSTICE BRENNAN, with whom JUSTICE MARSHALL joins, dissenting.

* * * [T]he process of eroding *Miranda* rights, begun with *Harris v. New York*,[a] continues with today's holding that police may renew the questioning of a suspect who has once exercised his right to remain silent, provided the suspect's right to cut off questioning has been "scrupulously honored." Today's distortion of *Miranda*'s constitutional principals [sic] can be viewed only as yet another step in the erosion and, I suppose, ultimate overruling of *Miranda*'s enforcement of the privilege against self-incrimination.

* * * The language which the Court finds controlling in this case teaches that renewed questioning itself is part of the process which invariably operates to overcome the will of a suspect. That teaching is embodied in the form of a proscription on any further questioning once the suspect has exercised his right to remain silent. Today's decision uncritically abandons that teaching. * * *

I agree that *Miranda* is not to be read, on the one hand, to impose an absolute ban on resumption of questioning "at any time or place on any subject," or on the other hand, "to permit a resumption of interrogation after a momentary respite." But this surely cannot justify adoption of a vague and ineffective procedural standard that falls somewhere between those absurd extremes, for *Miranda* in flat and unambiguous terms requires that questioning "cease" when a suspect exercises the right to remain silent. *Miranda*'s terms, however, are not so uncompromising as to preclude the fashioning of guidelines to govern this case. * * *

The fashioning of guidelines for this case is an easy task. Adequate procedures are readily available. * * * [A] requirement that resumption of questioning should await appointment and arrival of counsel for the suspect would be an acceptable and readily satisfied precondition to resumption. *Miranda* expressly held that "[t]he presence of counsel . . . would be the adequate protective device necessary to make the process of police interrogation conform to the dictates of the privilege [against self-incrimination]." * * *

My concern with the Court's opinion does not end with its treatment of *Miranda*, but extends to its treatment of the facts in this case. The Court's effort to have the Williams homicide appear as "an unrelated

---

[a] In *Harris v. New York, infra*, the Court held that statements taken in violation of *Miranda*, while not admissible in the prosecution's case-in-chief, may be used to impeach a defendant who takes the stand to testify in his defense.

holdup murder," is patently unsuccessful. The anonymous tip received by Detective Cowie, conceded by the Court to be the sole basis for Mosley's arrest embraced both the robberies covered in Cowie's interrogation and the robbery-murder of Williams about which Detective Hill questioned Mosley. Thus, when Mosley was apprehended, Cowie suspected him of being involved in the Williams robbery in addition to the robberies about which he tried to examine Mosley. On another matter, the Court treats the second interrogation as being "at another location." Yet the fact is that it was merely a different floor of the same building. * * *

[JUSTICE WHITE's concurring opinion has been omitted.]

EDWARDS V. ARIZONA
Supreme Court of the United States
451 U.S. 477, 101 S. Ct. 1880, 68 L. Ed. 2d 378 (1981)

JUSTICE WHITE delivered the opinion of the Court.

We granted certiorari in this case, limited to Question 1 presented in the petition, which in relevant part was "whether the Fifth, Sixth, and Fourteenth Amendments require suppression of a post-arrest confession, which was obtained after Edwards had invoked his right to consult counsel before further interrogation . . ." * * *

On January 19, 1976, a sworn complaint was filed against Edwards in Arizona state court charging him with robbery, burglary, and first-degree murder. An arrest warrant was issued pursuant to the complaint, and Edwards was arrested at his home later that same day. At the police station, he was informed of his rights as required by *Miranda v. Arizona*. Petitioner stated that he understood his rights, and was willing to submit to questioning. After being told that another suspect already in custody had implicated him in the crime, Edwards denied involvement and gave a taped statement presenting an alibi defense. He then sought to "make a deal." The interrogating officer told him that he wanted a statement, but that he did not have the authority to negotiate a deal. The officer provided Edwards with the telephone number of a county attorney. Petitioner made the call, but hung up after a few moments. Edwards then said: "I want an attorney before making a deal." At that point, questioning ceased and Edwards was taken to county jail.

At 9:15 the next morning, two detectives, colleagues of the officer who had interrogated Edwards the previous night, came to the jail and asked to see Edwards. When the detention officer informed Edwards that the detectives wished to speak with him, he replied that he did not want to talk to anyone. The guard told him that "he had" to talk and then took him to meet with the detectives. The officers identified themselves, stated they wanted to talk to him, and informed him of his *Miranda* rights. Edwards was willing to talk, but he first wanted to hear the taped statement of the alleged accomplice who had implicated him. After listening to the tape for several minutes, petitioner said that he would make a statement so long as it was not tape-recorded. The detectives informed him that the recording was irrelevant since they could testify in court concerning whatever he said. Edwards replied: "I'll tell you anything you want to know, but I don't want it on tape." He thereupon implicated himself in the crime.

Prior to trial, Edwards moved to suppress his confession on the ground that his *Miranda* rights had been violated when the officers returned to question him after he had invoked his right to counsel. The trial court initially granted the motion to suppress, but reversed its ruling when presented with a supposedly controlling decision of a higher Arizona court. The court stated without explanation that it found Edwards' statement to be voluntary. Edwards was tried twice and convicted. Evidence concerning his confession was admitted at both trials.

On appeal, the Arizona Supreme Court held that Edwards had invoked both his right to remain silent and his right to counsel during the interrogation conducted on the night of January 19. The court then went on to determine, however, that Edwards had waived both rights during the January 20 meeting when he voluntarily gave his statement to the detectives after again being informed that he need not answer questions and that he need not answer without the advice of counsel. * * *

Because the use of Edwards' confession against him at his trial violated his rights under the Fifth and Fourteenth Amendments as construed in *Miranda v. Arizona*, we reverse the judgment of the Arizona Supreme Court.[7] * * *

In *Miranda v. Arizona*, the Court determined that the Fifth and Fourteenth Amendments' prohibition against compelled self-incrimination required that custodial interrogation be preceded by advice to the putative defendant that he has the right to remain silent and also the right to the presence of an attorney. The Court also indicated the procedures to be followed subsequent to the warnings. If the accused indicates that he wishes to remain silent, "the interrogation must cease." If he requests counsel, "the interrogation must cease until an attorney is present."

Miranda thus declared that an accused has a Fifth and Fourteenth Amendment right to have counsel present during custodial interrogation. Here, the critical facts as found by the Arizona Supreme Court are that Edwards asserted his right to counsel and his right to remain silent on January 19, but that the police, without furnishing him counsel, returned the next morning to confront him and as a result of the meeting secured

---

[7] We thus need not decide Edwards' claim that the State deprived him of his right to counsel under the Sixth and Fourteenth Amendments as construed and applied in *Massiah v. United States*. * * * The Arizona Supreme Court did not address the Sixth Amendment question, nor do we.

incriminating oral admissions. Contrary to the holdings of the state courts, Edwards insists that having exercised his right on the 19th to have counsel present during interrogation, he did not validly waive that right on the 20th. For the following reasons, we agree.

First, the Arizona Supreme Court applied an erroneous standard for determining waiver where the accused has specifically invoked his right to counsel. It is reasonably clear under our cases that waivers of counsel must not only be voluntary, but must also constitute a knowing and intelligent relinquishment or abandonment of a known right or privilege, a matter which depends in each case "upon the particular facts and circumstances surrounding that case, including the background, experience, and conduct of the accused."

Considering the proceedings in the state courts in the light of this standard, we note that in denying petitioner's motion to suppress, the trial court found the admission to have been "voluntary," without separately focusing on whether Edwards had knowingly and intelligently relinquished his right to counsel.

* * * Here, however sound the conclusion of the state courts as to the voluntariness of Edwards' admission may be, neither the trial court nor the Arizona Supreme Court undertook to focus on whether Edwards understood his right to counsel and intelligently and knowingly relinquished it. It is thus apparent that the decision below misunderstood the requirement for finding a valid waiver of the right to counsel, once invoked.

Second, although we have held that after initially being advised of his *Miranda* rights, the accused may himself validly waive his rights and respond to interrogation, * * * additional safeguards are necessary when the accused asks for counsel; and we now hold that when an accused has invoked his right to have counsel present during custodial interrogation, a valid waiver of that right cannot be established by showing only that he responded to further police-initiated custodial interrogation even if he has been advised of his rights. We further hold that an accused, such as Edwards, having expressed his desire to deal with the police only through counsel, is not subject to further interrogation by the authorities until counsel has been made available to him,[a] unless the accused himself initiates further communication, exchanges, or conversations with the police.

---

[a] One question raised by this language in *Edwards v. Arizona* is whether allowing a suspect to consult with an attorney would be sufficient to satisfy the requirement that an accused who has requested counsel not be subjected to further interrogation "until counsel *has been made available to him.*" (emphasis added). In *Minnick v. Mississippi*, the Court answered this question in the negative, holding "that when counsel is requested, interrogation must cease, and officials may not reinitiate interrogation without counsel present, whether or not the accused has consulted with his attorney." 498 U.S. 146, 153 (1990).

Miranda itself indicated that the assertion of the right to counsel was a significant event and that once exercised by the accused, "the interrogation must cease until an attorney is present." Our later cases have not abandoned that view. * * *

In concluding that the fruits of the interrogation initiated by the police on January 20 could not be used against Edwards, we do not hold or imply that Edwards was powerless to countermand his election or that the authorities could in no event use any incriminating statements made by Edwards prior to his having access to counsel. Had Edwards initiated the meeting on January 20, nothing in the Fifth and Fourteenth Amendments would prohibit the police from merely listening to his voluntary, volunteered statements and using them against him at the trial. The Fifth Amendment right identified in *Miranda* is the right to have counsel present at any custodial interrogation. Absent such interrogation, there would have been no infringement of the right that Edwards invoked and there would be no occasion to determine whether there had been a valid waiver.

But this is not what the facts of this case show. Here, the officers conducting the interrogation on the evening of January 19 ceased interrogation when Edwards requested counsel as he had been advised he had the right to do. The Arizona Supreme Court was of the opinion that this was a sufficient invocation of his *Miranda* rights, and we are in accord. It is also clear that without making counsel available to Edwards, the police returned to him the next day. This was not at his suggestion or request. Indeed, Edwards informed the detention officer that he did not want to talk to anyone. At the meeting, the detectives told Edwards that they wanted to talk to him and again advised him of his *Miranda* rights. Edwards stated that he would talk, but what prompted this action does not appear. He listened at his own request to part of the taped statement made by one of his alleged accomplices and then made an incriminating statement, which was used against him at his trial. We think it is clear that Edwards was subjected to custodial interrogation on January 20 within the meaning of *Rhode Island v. Innis*, and that this occurred at the instance of the authorities. His statement made without having had access to counsel, did not amount to a valid waiver and hence was inadmissible.

Accordingly, the holding of the Arizona Supreme Court that Edwards had waived his right to counsel was infirm, and the judgment of that court is reversed.

So ordered.

[CHIEF JUSTICE BURGER's concurring opinion and JUSTICE POWELL's concurring opinion have been omitted.]

NOTE

In *Edwards v. Arizona*, the Court held that an accused, "having expressed his desire to deal with the police only through counsel, is not subject to further interrogation by the authorities until counsel has been made available to him, unless the accused himself *initiates* further communication, exchanges, or conversations with the police." In *Oregon v. Bradshaw*, 462 U.S. 1039 (1983), a plurality of the Court defined "initiation" for purposes of the *Edwards* rule as a statement or question by the suspect that indicates a desire to open up a more generalized discussion relating to the investigation. According to *Bradshaw*, "There are some inquiries, such as a request for a drink of water or a request to use the telephone that are so routine that they cannot be fairly said to represent a desire on the part of the accused to open up a more generalized discussion relating . . . to the investigation." *Id.* at 1045. The *Bradshaw* plurality, however, found that Bradshaw's asking the officer, "What's going to happen to me now?," just before or during his transport from the police station to the jail, constituted initiation, allowing the officer to proceed with interrogation. The dissenting Justices (Marshall, Brennan, Blackmun, and Stevens) agreed with the plurality's definition of initiation, but were baffled at the plurality's conclusion that Bradshaw's question constituted initiation. To the dissent, it was plain that Bradshaw's only desire was to find out where the police were going to take him, not to open up a more generalized discussion relating to the investigation.

DAVIS V. UNITED STATES
Supreme Court of the United States
512 U.S. 452, 114 S. Ct. 2350, 129 L. Ed. 2d 362 (1994)

JUSTICE O'CONNOR delivered the opinion of the Court.

In *Edwards v. Arizona*, we held that law enforcement officers must immediately cease questioning a suspect who has clearly asserted his right to have counsel present during custodial interrogation. In this case we decide how law enforcement officers should respond when a suspect makes a reference to counsel that is insufficiently clear to invoke the *Edwards* prohibition on further questioning.

Pool brought trouble—not to River City, but to the Charleston Naval Base. Petitioner, a member of the United States Navy, spent the evening of October 2, 1988, shooting pool at a club on the base. Another sailor, Keith Shackleton, lost a game and a $30 wager to petitioner, but Shackleton refused to pay. After the club closed, Shackleton was beaten to death with a pool cue on a loading dock behind the commissary. The body was found early the next morning.

The investigation by the Naval Investigative Service (NIS) gradually focused on petitioner. Investigative agents determined that petitioner was at the club that evening, and that he was absent without authorization from his duty station the next morning. The agents also learned that only privately owned pool cues could be removed from the club premises, and that petitioner owned two cues—one of which had a bloodstain on it. The agents were told by various people that petitioner either had admitted committing the crime or had recounted details that clearly indicated his involvement in the killing.

On November 4, 1988, petitioner was interviewed at the NIS office. As required by military law, the agents advised petitioner that he was a suspect in the killing, that he was not required to make a statement, that any statement could be used against him at a trial by court-martial, and that he was entitled to speak with an attorney and have an attorney present during questioning. Petitioner waived his rights to remain silent and to counsel, both orally and in writing.

About an hour and a half into the interview, petitioner said, "Maybe I should talk to a lawyer." According to the uncontradicted testimony of one of the interviewing agents, the interview then proceeded as follows:

> [We m]ade it very clear that we're not here to violate his rights, that if he wants a lawyer, then we will stop any kind of questioning with him, that we weren't going to pursue the matter unless we have it clarified is he asking for a lawyer or is he just making a comment about a lawyer, and he said, ["]No, I'm not asking for a lawyer," and then he continued on, and said, "No, I don't want a lawyer."

After a short break, the agents reminded petitioner of his rights to remain silent and to counsel. The interview then continued for another hour, until petitioner said, "I think I want a lawyer before I say anything else." At that point, questioning ceased.

At his general court-martial, petitioner moved to suppress statements made during the November 4 interview. The Military Judge denied the motion * * *. Petitioner was convicted on one specification of unpremeditated murder * * *. He was sentenced to confinement for life, a dishonorable discharge, forfeiture of all pay and allowances, and a reduction to the lowest pay grade. * * *

Although we have twice previously noted the varying approaches the lower courts have adopted with respect to ambiguous or equivocal references to counsel during custodial interrogation, we have not addressed the issue on the merits. We granted certiorari to do so.

The Sixth Amendment right to counsel attaches only at the initiation of adversary criminal proceedings, and before proceedings are initiated a suspect in a criminal investigation has no constitutional right to the assistance of counsel. Nevertheless, we held in *Miranda v. Arizona* that a suspect subject to custodial interrogation has the right to consult with an attorney and to have counsel present during questioning, and that the police must explain this right to him before questioning begins. The right to counsel established in *Miranda* was one of a "series of recommended 'procedural safeguards'... [that] were not themselves rights protected by the Constitution but were instead measures to insure [sic] that the right against compulsory self-incrimination was protected."

The right to counsel recognized in *Miranda* is sufficiently important to suspects in criminal investigations, we have held, that it "require[s] the special protection of the knowing and intelligent waiver standard." If the suspect effectively waives his right to counsel after receiving the *Miranda* warnings, law enforcement officers are free to question him. But if a suspect requests counsel at any time during the interview, he is not subject to further questioning until a lawyer has been made available or the suspect himself reinitiates conversation. This "second layer of prophylaxis for the *Miranda* right to counsel," is "designed to prevent police from badgering a defendant into waiving his previously asserted *Miranda* rights." To that end, we have held that a suspect who has invoked the right to counsel cannot be questioned regarding any offense unless an attorney is actually present. * * *

The applicability of the "'rigid' prophylactic rule" of *Edwards* requires courts to "determine whether the accused *actually invoked* his right to counsel." To avoid difficulties of proof and to provide guidance to officers conducting interrogations, this is an objective inquiry. Invocation of the *Miranda* right to counsel "requires, at a minimum, some statement that can reasonably be construed to be an expression of a desire for the assistance of an attorney." But if a suspect makes a reference to an attorney that is ambiguous or equivocal in that a reasonable officer in light of the circumstances would have understood only that the suspect *might* be invoking the right to counsel, our precedents do not require the cessation of questioning.

Rather, the suspect must unambiguously request counsel. As we have observed, "a statement either is such an assertion of the right to counsel or it is not." Although a suspect need not "speak with the discrimination of an Oxford don," he must articulate his desire to have counsel present sufficiently clearly that a reasonable police officer in the circumstances would understand the statement to be a request for an attorney.[a] If the

---

[a] In *McNeil v. Wisconsin*, 501 U.S. 171 (1991), the Supreme Court held that a suspect's request for appointed counsel at an initial appearance on a charged offense does not constitute an invocation of his *Miranda* right to counsel. Justice Scalia, writing for the Court, explained that different interests are protected by the Sixth Amendment right to counsel and the *Miranda* right to counsel:

> The purpose of the Sixth Amendment counsel guarantee * * * is to "protect the unaided layman at critical confrontations" with his "expert adversary," the government, *after* "the adverse positions of government and defendant have solidified" with respect to a particular alleged crime. The purpose of the *Miranda-Edwards* guarantee, on the other hand, * * * is to protect a quite different interest: the suspect's "desire to deal with the

statement fails to meet the requisite level of clarity, *Edwards* does not require that the officers stop questioning the suspect.

We decline petitioner's invitation to extend *Edwards* and require law enforcement officers to cease questioning immediately upon the making of an ambiguous or equivocal reference to an attorney. The rationale underlying *Edwards* is that the police must respect a suspect's wishes regarding his right to have an attorney present during custodial interrogation. But when the officers conducting the questioning reasonably do not know whether or not the suspect wants a lawyer, a rule requiring the immediate cessation of questioning "would transform the *Miranda* safeguards into wholly irrational obstacles to legitimate police investigative activity," because it would needlessly prevent the police from questioning a suspect in the absence of counsel even if the suspect did not wish to have a lawyer present. * * *

We recognize that requiring a clear assertion of the right to counsel might disadvantage some suspects who—because of fear, intimidation, lack of linguistic skills, or a variety of other reasons—will not clearly articulate their right to counsel although they actually want to have a lawyer present. But the primary protection afforded suspects subject to custodial interrogation is the *Miranda* warnings themselves. "[F]ull comprehension of the rights to remain silent and request an attorney [is] sufficient to dispel whatever coercion is inherent in the interrogation process." * * * Although *Edwards* provides an additional protection—if a suspect subsequently requests an attorney, questioning must cease—it is one that must be affirmatively invoked by the suspect.

In considering how a suspect must invoke the right to counsel, we must consider the other side of the *Miranda* equation: the need for effective law enforcement. Although the courts ensure compliance with the *Miranda* requirements through the exclusionary rule, it is police officers who must actually decide whether or not they can question a suspect. The *Edwards* rule—questioning must cease if the suspect asks for a lawyer—provides a bright line that can be applied by officers in the real world of investigation and interrogation without unduly hampering the gathering of information. But if we were to require questioning to cease if a suspect makes a statement that *might* be a request for an attorney, this clarity and ease of application would be lost. Police officers would be forced to make difficult judgment calls about whether the suspect in fact wants a lawyer even though he has not said so, with the threat of suppression if they guess

---

police only through counsel." This is in one respect narrower than the interest protected by the Sixth Amendment guarantee (because it relates only to custodial interrogation) and in another respect broader (because it relates to interrogation regarding *any* suspected crime and attaches whether or not the "adversarial relationship" produced by a pending prosecution has yet arisen). To invoke the Sixth Amendment interest is, as a matter of *fact, not* to invoke the *Miranda-Edwards* interest.

Id. at 178.

wrong. We therefore hold that, after a knowing and voluntary waiver of the *Miranda* rights, law enforcement officers may continue questioning until and unless the suspect clearly requests an attorney.

Of course, when a suspect makes an ambiguous or equivocal statement it will often be good police practice for the interviewing officers to clarify whether or not he actually wants an attorney. That was the procedure followed by the NIS agents in this case. Clarifying questions help protect the rights of the suspect by ensuring that he gets an attorney if he wants one, and will minimize the chance of a confession being suppressed due to subsequent judicial second-guessing as to the meaning of the suspect's statement regarding counsel. But we decline to adopt a rule requiring officers to ask clarifying questions. If the suspect's statement is not an unambiguous or unequivocal request for counsel, the officers have no obligation to stop questioning him.

To recapitulate: We held in *Miranda* that a suspect is entitled to the assistance of counsel during custodial interrogation even though the Constitution does not provide for such assistance. We held in *Edwards* that if the suspect invokes the right to counsel at any time, the police must immediately cease questioning him until an attorney is present. But we are unwilling to create a third layer of prophylaxis to prevent police questioning when the suspect *might* want a lawyer. Unless the suspect actually requests an attorney, questioning may continue.

The courts below found that petitioner's remark to the NIS agents—"Maybe I should talk to a lawyer"—was not a request for counsel, and we see no reason to disturb that conclusion. The NIS agents therefore were not required to stop questioning petitioner, though it was entirely proper for them to clarify whether petitioner in fact wanted a lawyer. Because there is no ground for suppression of petitioner's statements, the judgment of the Court of Military Appeals is

Affirmed.

[JUSTICE SCALIA's concurring opinion and JUSTICE SOUTER's concurring opinion have been omitted.]

IN A DIFFERENT REGISTER: THE PRAGMATICS OF POWERLESSNESS IN POLICE INTERROGATION

Janet E. Ainsworth
103 Yale L.J. 259 (1993)

* * *

Invocation doctrines that favor direct speech operate to the detriment of certain groups within society. Sociolinguistic research has demonstrated that discrete segments of the population—particularly women and ethnic minorities—are far more likely than others to adopt indirect speech patterns. An indirect mode of expression is characteristic of the language used by powerless persons, both those who are members of certain groups that have historically been powerless within society as well as those who are powerless because of the particular situation in which they find themselves. Because criminal suspects confronted with police interrogation may feel powerless, they will often attempt to invoke their rights by using speech patterns that the law currently refuses to recognize. * * *

The inadequacy of the majority legal approach to the invocation of *Miranda* rights is symptomatic of a more general phenomenon within the law: the incorporation of unconscious androcentric[a] assumptions into legal doctrine. * * * [R]ecent works in feminist jurisprudence have examined a variety of legal doctrines and practices that seem on the surface to be gender-neutral, and have discovered gender bias through the use of one of the primary methodological tools of feminist theory—asking the "woman question." As framed in feminist jurisprudence, the "woman question" asks, "What would law be like if women had been considered by the drafters and interpreters of the law?" Asking the "woman question" forces us to imagine a counterfactual world in which women's experiences, perspectives, and behavior were taken into account in constructing the legal order. By measuring the actual legal order against this imagined world, feminist methodology exposes assumptions that are deeply embedded within the law, assumptions that influence the shape of legal doctrine and the dynamics of legal practice.

In the case of *Miranda* rights, asking the "woman question" means asking whether a legal doctrine preferring direct and unqualified assertions of the right to counsel takes into account the speech patterns of women as well as other powerless groups. As I will detail, sociolinguistic research on typical male and female speech patterns indicates that men tend to use direct and assertive language, whereas women more often adopt indirect and deferential speech patterns. Because majority legal doctrine governing a person's rights during police interrogation favors linguistic behavior more typical of men than of women, asking the "woman question" reveals a hidden bias in this ostensibly gender-neutral doctrine.

The sociolinguistic evidence that women disproportionately adopt indirect speech patterns predicts that legal rules requiring the use of direct and unqualified language will adversely affect female defendants more often than male defendants. The real world consequences of such a bias are by no means trivial. If women are indeed disadvantaged by this doctrine, then the law has compromised the ability of millions of women arrestees to exercise their constitutional rights.

---

[a] The Merriam-Webster Dictionary defines "androcentric" as "dominated by or emphasizing masculine interests or a masculine point of view." *See* https://www.merriam-webster.com/dictionary/androcentric.

The detrimental consequences of interrogation law, however, are not limited to female defendants. Asking the "woman question" provokes related inquiry into whether legal doctrine may similarly fail to incorporate the experiences and perspectives of other marginalized groups. The fact that asking the "woman question" can prompt fruitful inquiry into other missing perspectives is what Katherine Bartlett calls "[c]onverting the [w]oman [q]uestion into the [q]uestion of the [e]xcluded." Although the sociolinguistic research on speech patterns of various ethnic groups in the United States is less extensive than that detailing gender-linked differences in language use, the available evidence demonstrates that there are a number of ethnic speech communities whose members habitually adopt a speech register including indirect and qualified modes of expression very much like those observed in typical female language use.

Even within communities whose speech is not characterized by indirect modes of expression, individual speakers who are socially or situationally powerless frequently adopt an indirect speech register. In fact, several prominent researchers have concluded that the use of this characteristically "female" speech style correlates better with powerlessness than with gender. The psychosocial dynamics of the police interrogation setting inherently involve an imbalance of power between the suspect, who is situationally powerless, and the interrogator, whose role entails the exercise of power. Such asymmetries of power in the interrogation session increase the likelihood that a particular suspect will adopt an indirect, and thus seemingly equivocal, mode of expression.

* * * From a feminist perspective, the characteristically masculine preference for assertive speech can be seen as simply one instance of a more generalized masculine preference for assertive behavior. Such a critique would lead one to ask why the law should obligate suspects in police custody affirmatively to invoke the right to counsel at all. Instead of requiring the suspect to confront police by asserting her rights, why not automatically provide arrested suspects with counsel to be consulted before interrogation begins?

This is not so radical a proposal as it might seem. The law already recognizes certain instances in which an accused's right to counsel attaches whether or not he acts to assert that right. Extending these precedents to the context of custodial interrogation is admittedly a large step beyond *Miranda*, but not an unwarranted one. * * *

An inquiry prompted by feminist theory suggests that any version of legal doctrine that requires the express invocation of a right will disadvantage those who are uncomfortable asserting themselves in the adversarial atmosphere of police interrogation. Just as the current doctrinal preference for unqualified assertions of the right to counsel tends disproportionately to impair exercise of their rights by those who use the female speech register, so too a doctrine that demands affirmative assertion of the right may well tend to favor those who generally display assertive behavior and disadvantage those who do not.

MARYLAND V. SHATZER
Supreme Court of the United States
559 U.S. 98, 130 S. Ct. 1213, 175 L. Ed. 2d 1045 (2009)

JUSTICE SCALIA delivered the opinion of the Court.

We consider whether a break in custody ends the presumption of involuntariness established in *Edwards v. Arizona*.

In August 2003, a social worker assigned to the Child Advocacy Center in the Criminal Investigation Division of the Hagerstown Police Department referred to the department allegations that respondent Michael Shatzer, Sr., had sexually abused his 3-year-old son. At that time, Shatzer was incarcerated at the Maryland Correctional Institution-Hagerstown, serving a sentence for an unrelated child-sexual-abuse offense. Detective Shane Blankenship was assigned to the investigation and interviewed Shatzer at the correctional institution on August 7, 2003. Before asking any questions, Blankenship reviewed Shatzer's *Miranda* rights with him, and obtained a written waiver of those rights. When Blankenship explained that he was there to question Shatzer about sexually abusing his son, Shatzer expressed confusion—he had thought Blankenship was an attorney there to discuss the prior crime for which he was incarcerated. Blankenship clarified the purpose of his visit, and Shatzer declined to speak without an attorney. Accordingly, Blankenship ended the interview, and Shatzer was released back into the general prison population. Shortly thereafter, Blankenship closed the investigation.

Two years and six months later, the same social worker referred more specific allegations to the department about the same incident involving Shatzer. Detective Paul Hoover, from the same division, was assigned to the investigation. He and the social worker interviewed the victim, then eight years old, who described the incident in more detail. With this new information in hand, on March 2, 2006, they went to the Roxbury Correctional Institute, to which Shatzer had since been transferred, and interviewed Shatzer in a maintenance room outfitted with a desk and three chairs. Hoover explained that he wanted to ask Shatzer about the alleged incident involving Shatzer's son. Shatzer was surprised because he thought that the investigation had been closed, but Hoover explained they had opened a new file. Hoover then read Shatzer his *Miranda* rights and obtained a written waiver on a standard department form.

Hoover interrogated Shatzer about the incident for approximately 30 minutes. Shatzer denied ordering his son to perform fellatio on him, but admitted to masturbating in front of his son from a distance of less than three feet. Before the interview ended, Shatzer agreed to Hoover's request that he submit to a polygraph examination. At no point during the interrogation did Shatzer request to speak with an attorney or refer to his prior refusal to answer questions without one.

Five days later, on March 7, 2006, Hoover and another detective met with Shatzer at the correctional facility to administer the polygraph examination. After reading Shatzer his *Miranda* rights and obtaining a written waiver, the other detective administered the test and concluded that Shatzer had failed. When the detectives then questioned Shatzer, he became upset, started to cry, and incriminated himself by saying, "I didn't force him. I didn't force him." After making this inculpatory statement, Shatzer requested an attorney, and Hoover promptly ended the interrogation.

The State's Attorney for Washington County charged Shatzer with second-degree sexual offense, sexual child abuse, second-degree assault, and contributing to conditions rendering a child in need of assistance. Shatzer moved to suppress his March 2006 statements pursuant to *Edwards*. The trial court held a suppression hearing and later denied Shatzer's motion. * * * Over the dissent of two judges, the Court of Appeals of Maryland reversed and remanded. * * * We granted certiorari.

The Fifth Amendment, which applies to the States by virtue of the Fourteenth Amendment, provides that "[n]o person . . . shall be compelled in any criminal case to be a witness against himself." In *Miranda*, the Court adopted a set of prophylactic measures to protect a suspect's Fifth Amendment right from the "inherently compelling pressures" of custodial interrogation. * * *

To counteract the coercive pressure, *Miranda* announced that police officers must warn a suspect prior to questioning that he has a right to remain silent, and a right to the presence of an attorney. After the warnings are given, if the suspect indicates that he wishes to remain silent, the interrogation must cease. Similarly, if the suspect states that he wants an attorney, the interrogation must cease until an attorney is present. Critically, however, a suspect can waive these rights. To establish a valid waiver, the State must show that the waiver was knowing, intelligent, and voluntary under the "high standar[d] of proof for the waiver of constitutional rights [set forth in] *Johnson v. Zerbst*."

In *Edwards*, the Court determined that *Zerbst*'s traditional standard for waiver was not sufficient to protect a suspect's right to have counsel present at a subsequent interrogation if he had previously requested counsel; "additional safeguards" were necessary. The Court therefore superimposed a "second layer of prophylaxis." *Edwards* held:

> [W]hen an accused has invoked his right to have counsel present during custodial interrogation, a valid waiver of that right cannot

be established by showing only that he responded to further police-initiated custodial interrogation even if he has been advised of his rights. . . . [He] is not subject to further interrogation by the authorities until counsel has been made available to him, unless the accused himself initiates further communication, exchanges, or conversations with the police. * * *

The rationale of *Edwards* is that once a suspect indicates that "he is not capable of undergoing [custodial] questioning without advice of counsel," "any subsequent waiver that has come at the authorities' behest, and not at the suspect's own instigation, is itself the product of the 'inherently compelling pressures' and not the purely voluntary choice of the suspect." Under this rule, a voluntary *Miranda* waiver is sufficient at the time of an initial attempted interrogation to protect a suspect's right to have counsel present, but it is not sufficient at the time of subsequent attempts if the suspect initially requested the presence of counsel. * * *

We have frequently emphasized that the *Edwards* rule is not a constitutional mandate, but judicially prescribed prophylaxis. Because *Edwards* is "our rule, not a constitutional command," "it is our obligation to justify its expansion."

A judicially crafted rule is "justified only by reference to its prophylactic purpose" and applies only where its benefits outweigh its costs. We begin with the benefits. * * * [The *Edwards* rule's] fundamental purpose * * * is to "[p]reserv[e] the integrity of an accused's choice to communicate with police only through counsel" by "prevent[ing] police from badgering a defendant into waiving his previously asserted *Miranda* rights." * * *

When * * * a suspect has been released from his pretrial custody and has returned to his normal life for some time before the later attempted interrogation, there is little reason to think that his change of heart regarding interrogation without counsel has been coerced. He has no longer been isolated. He has likely been able to seek advice from an attorney, family members, and friends. And he knows from his earlier experience that he need only demand counsel to bring the interrogation to a halt; and that investigative custody does not last indefinitely. In these circumstances, it is farfetched to think that a police officer's asking the suspect whether he would like to waive his *Miranda* rights will any more "wear down the accused," than did the first such request at the original attempted interrogation—which is of course not deemed coercive. His change of heart is less likely attributable to "badgering" than it is to the fact that further deliberation in familiar surroundings has caused him to believe (rightly or wrongly) that cooperating with the investigation is in his interest. * * *

At the same time that extending the *Edwards* rule [to all cases in which there has been a break in custody] yields diminished benefits, extending the rule also increases its costs: the in-fact voluntary confessions it excludes from trial, and the voluntary confessions it deters law enforcement officers from even trying to obtain. * * *

We conclude that such an extension of *Edwards* is not justified; we have opened its "protective umbrella" far enough. The protections offered by *Miranda*, which we have deemed sufficient to ensure that the police respect the suspect's desire to have an attorney present the first time police interrogate him, adequately ensure that result when a suspect who initially requested counsel is reinterrogated after a break in custody that is of sufficient duration to dissipate its coercive effects.

If Shatzer's return to the general prison population qualified as a break in custody, there is no doubt that it lasted long enough (2½ years) to meet that durational requirement. But what about a break that has lasted only one year? Or only one week? It is impractical to leave the answer to that question for clarification in future case-by-case adjudication; law enforcement officers need to know, with certainty and beforehand, when renewed interrogation is lawful.

* * * We think it appropriate to specify a period of time to avoid the consequence that continuation of the *Edwards* presumption "will not reach the correct result most of the time." It seems to us that period is 14 days. That provides plenty of time for the suspect to get reacclimated to his normal life, to consult with friends and counsel, and to shake off any residual coercive effects of his prior custody. * * *

The 14-day limitation meets Shatzer's concern that a break-in-custody rule lends itself to police abuse. He envisions that once a suspect invokes his *Miranda* right to counsel, the police will release the suspect briefly (to end the *Edwards* presumption) and then promptly bring him back into custody for reinterrogation. But once the suspect has been out of custody long enough (14 days) to eliminate its coercive effect, there will be nothing to gain by such gamesmanship—nothing, that is, except the entirely appropriate gain of being able to interrogate a suspect who has made a valid waiver of his *Miranda* rights.

The facts of this case present an additional issue. No one questions that Shatzer was in custody for *Miranda* purposes during the interviews with Detective Blankenship in 2003 and Detective Hoover in 2006. Likewise, no one questions that Shatzer triggered the *Edwards* protections when, according to Detective Blankenship's notes of the 2003 interview, he stated that "he would not talk about this case without having an attorney present." After the 2003 interview, Shatzer was released back into the general prison population where he was serving an unrelated sentence. The issue is whether that constitutes a break in *Miranda* custody.

We have never decided whether incarceration constitutes custody for *Miranda* purposes, and have indeed explicitly declined to address the issue.[a] * * * To determine whether a suspect was in *Miranda* custody we have asked whether "there is a 'formal arrest or restraint on freedom of movement' of the degree associated with a formal arrest." This test, no doubt, is satisfied by all forms of incarceration. Our cases make clear, however, that the freedom-of-movement test identifies only a necessary and not a sufficient condition for *Miranda* custody. We have declined to accord it "talismanic power," because *Miranda* is to be enforced "only in those types of situations in which the concerns that powered the decision are implicated." * * *

Here, we are addressing the interim period during which a suspect was not interrogated, but was subject to a baseline set of restraints imposed pursuant to a prior conviction. Without minimizing the harsh realities of incarceration, we think lawful imprisonment imposed upon conviction of a crime does not create the coercive pressures identified in *Miranda*.

Interrogated suspects who have previously been convicted of crime live in prison. When they are released back into the general prison population, they return to their accustomed surroundings and daily routine—they regain the degree of control they had over their lives prior to the interrogation. Sentenced prisoners, in contrast to the *Miranda* paradigm, are not isolated with their accusers. They live among other inmates, guards, and workers, and often can receive visitors and communicate with people on the outside by mail or telephone. * * *

Shatzer's experience illustrates the vast differences between *Miranda* custody and incarceration pursuant to conviction. At the time of the 2003 attempted interrogation, Shatzer was already serving a sentence for a prior conviction. After that, he returned to the general prison population in the Maryland Correctional Institution-Hagerstown and was later transferred, for unrelated reasons, down the street to the Roxbury Correctional Institute. Both are medium-security state correctional facilities. Inmates in these facilities generally can visit the library each week, have regular exercise and recreation periods, can participate in basic adult education and occupational training, are able to send and receive mail, and are allowed to receive visitors twice a week. His continued detention after the 2003 interrogation did not depend on what he said (or did not say) to Detective Blankenship, and he has not alleged that he was placed in a higher level of security or faced any continuing restraints as a result of the

---

[a] In *Howes v. Fields*, 565 U.S. 499 (2012), the Court answered this question. Writing for the Court, Justice Alito noted that "standard conditions of confinement and associated restrictions on freedom will not necessarily implicate the same interests that the Court sought to protect when it afforded special safeguards to persons subjected to custodial interrogation." He concluded that "service of a term of imprisonment, without more, is not enough to constitute *Miranda* custody."

2003 interrogation. The "inherently compelling pressures" of custodial interrogation ended when he returned to his normal life. * * *

Because Shatzer experienced a break in *Miranda* custody lasting more than two weeks between the first and second attempts at interrogation, *Edwards* does not mandate suppression of his March 2006 statements. Accordingly, we reverse the judgment of the Court of Appeals of Maryland, and remand the case for further proceedings not inconsistent with this opinion.

It is so ordered.

JUSTICE STEVENS, concurring in the judgment.

While I agree that the presumption from *Edwards v. Arizona* is not "eternal," and does not mandate suppression of Shatzer's statement made after a 2½-year break in custody, I do not agree with the Court's newly announced rule: that *Edwards* always ceases to apply when there is a 14-day break in custody.

* * * A 14-day break in custody does not change the fact that custodial interrogation is inherently compelling. It is unlikely to change the fact that a detainee "considers himself unable to deal with the pressures of custodial interrogation without legal assistance." [I]n some instances, a 14-day break in custody may make matters worse "[w]hen a suspect understands his (expressed) wishes to have been ignored" and thus "may well see further objection as futile and confession (true or not) as the only way to end his interrogation."

The Court * * * speculates * * * that once a suspect has been out of *Miranda* custody for 14 days, "[h]e has likely been able to seek advice from an attorney, family members, and friends." This speculation, however, is overconfident and only questionably relevant. As a factual matter, we do not know whether the defendant has been able to seek advice: First of all, suspects are told that if they cannot afford a lawyer, one will be provided for them. * * * Second, even suspects who are not indigent cannot necessarily access legal advice (or social advice as the Court presumes) within 14 days. Third, suspects may not realize that they need to seek advice from an attorney. Unless police warn suspects that the interrogation will resume in 14 days, why contact a lawyer? When a suspect is let go, he may assume that the police were satisfied. In any event, it is not apparent why interim advice matters. In *Minnick v. Mississippi*, we held that it is not sufficient that a detainee happened to speak at some point with a lawyer. If the actual interim advice of an attorney is not sufficient, the hypothetical, interim advice of "an attorney, family members, and friends," is not enough.

The many problems with the Court's new rule are exacerbated in the very situation in this case: a suspect who is in prison. Even if, as the Court assumes, a trip to one's home significantly changes the *Edwards* calculus, a trip to one's prison cell is not the same. A prisoner's freedom is severely limited, and his entire life remains subject to government control. Such an environment is not conducive to "shak[ing] off any residual coercive effects of his prior custody." Nor can a prisoner easily "seek advice from an attorney, family members, and friends," especially not within 14 days; prisoners are frequently subject to restrictions on communications. Nor, in most cases, can he live comfortably knowing that he cannot be badgered by police; prison is not like a normal situation in which a suspect "is in control, and need only shut his door or walk away to avoid police badgering." Indeed, for a person whose every move is controlled by the State, it is likely that "his sense of dependence on, and trust in, counsel as the guardian of his interests in dealing with government officials intensified." The Court ignores these realities of prison, and instead rests its argument on the supposition that a prisoner's "detention . . . is relatively disconnected from their prior unwillingness to cooperate in an investigation." But that is not necessarily the case. Prisoners are uniquely vulnerable to the officials who control every aspect of their lives; prison guards may not look kindly upon a prisoner who refuses to cooperate with police. And cooperation frequently is relevant to whether the prisoner can obtain parole. Moreover, even if it is true as a factual matter that a prisoner's fate is not controlled by the police who come to interrogate him, how is the prisoner supposed to know that? * * * [W]hen a guard informs a suspect that he must go speak with police, it will "appear" to the prisoner that the guard and police are not independent.

* * * I cannot join the Court's opinion. I concur in today's judgment, however, on another ground: Even if Shatzer could not consult a lawyer and the police never provided him one, the 2½-year break in custody is a basis for treating the second interrogation as no more coercive than the first. * * * [C]ertain things change over time. An indigent suspect who took police at their word that they would provide an attorney probably will feel that he has "been denied the counsel he has clearly requested," when police begin to question him, without a lawyer, only 14 days later. But, when a suspect has been left alone for a significant period of time, he is not as likely to draw such conclusions when the police interrogate him again. It is concededly "impossible to determine with precision" where to draw such a line. In the case before us, however, the suspect was returned to the general prison population for 2½ years. I am convinced that this period of time is sufficient. I therefore concur in the judgment.

[JUSTICE THOMAS' opinion, concurring in part and concurring in the judgment, has been omitted.]

C. WAIVER OF *MIRANDA* RIGHTS

The cases in this section focus on questions surrounding the waiver of *Miranda* rights. In *North Carolina v. Butler*, the Court considers whether a suspect must explicitly waive her *Miranda* rights to silence and/or counsel in order for that waiver to be valid. In *Moran v. Burbine*, the Court decides whether police misrepresentations to a suspect's attorney or their failure to inform the suspect of his lawyer's attempts to reach him will invalidate the suspect's waiver of his *Miranda* rights. In *Berghuis v. Thompkins,* the Court addresses several important issues involving both invocation and waiver of the right to silence. Finally, in *Colorado v. Spring*, the Court addresses whether a suspect must be made aware of all the crimes about which he may be interrogated in order to knowingly and intelligently waive his *Miranda* rights.

NORTH CAROLINA V. BUTLER
Supreme Court of the United States
441 U.S. 369, 99 S. Ct. 1755, 60 L. Ed. 2d 286 (1979)

JUSTICE STEWART delivered the opinion of the Court.

In evident conflict with the present view of every other court that has considered the issue, the North Carolina Supreme Court has held that *Miranda v. Arizona*, requires that no statement of a person under custodial interrogation may be admitted in evidence against him unless, at the time the statement was made, he explicitly waived the right to the presence of a lawyer. We granted certiorari to consider whether this per se rule reflects a proper understanding of the *Miranda* decision.

The respondent was convicted in a North Carolina trial court of kidnaping, armed robbery, and felonious assault. The evidence at his trial showed that he and a man named Elmer Lee had robbed a gas station in Goldsboro, N.C., in December 1976, and had shot the station attendant as he was attempting to escape. The attendant was paralyzed, but survived to testify against the respondent.

* * * FBI Agent Martinez testified that at the time of the arrest he fully advised the respondent of the rights delineated in the *Miranda* case. According to the uncontroverted testimony of Martinez, the agents then took the respondent to the FBI office in nearby New Rochelle, N. Y. There, after the agents determined that the respondent had an 11th grade education and was literate, he was given the Bureau's "Advice of Rights" form which he read. When asked if he understood his rights, he replied that he did. The respondent refused to sign the waiver at the bottom of the form. He was told that he need neither speak nor sign the form, but that the agents would like him to talk to them. The respondent replied: "I will talk to you but I am not signing any form." He then made inculpatory

statements.[2] Agent Martinez testified that the respondent said nothing when advised of his right to the assistance of a lawyer. At no time did the respondent request counsel or attempt to terminate the agents' questioning.

At the conclusion of this testimony the respondent moved to suppress the evidence of his incriminating statements on the ground that he had not waived his right to the assistance of counsel at the time the statements were made. The court denied the motion, finding that

> the statement made by the defendant, William Thomas Butler, to Agent David C. Martinez, was made freely and voluntarily to said agent after having been advised of his rights as required by the Miranda ruling, including his right to an attorney being present at the time of the inquiry and that the defendant, Butler, understood his rights; [and] that he effectively waived his rights, including the right to have an attorney present during the questioning by his indication that he was willing to answer questions, having read the rights form together with the Waiver of Rights * * *.

The respondent's statements were then admitted into evidence, and the jury ultimately found the respondent guilty of each offense charged.

On appeal, the North Carolina Supreme Court reversed the convictions and ordered a new trial. It found that the statements had been admitted in violation of the requirements of the *Miranda* decision, noting that the respondent had refused to waive in writing his right to have counsel present and that there had not been a specific oral waiver. As it had in at least two earlier cases, the court read the *Miranda* opinion as provid[ing] in plain language that waiver of the right to counsel during interrogation will not be recognized unless such waiver is "specifically made" after the *Miranda* warnings have been given.

We conclude that the North Carolina Supreme Court erred in its reading of the *Miranda* opinion. There, this Court said:

> If the interrogation continues without the presence of an attorney and a statement is taken, a heavy burden rests on the government to demonstrate that the defendant knowingly and intelligently waived his privilege against self-incrimination and his right to retained or appointed counsel.

The Court's opinion went on to say:

> An express statement that the individual is willing to make a statement and does not want an attorney followed closely by a

---

[2] The respondent admitted to the agents that he and Lee had been drinking heavily on the day of the robbery. He acknowledged that they had decided to rob a gas station, but denied that he had actually participated in the robbery. His friend, he said, had shot the attendant.

statement could constitute a waiver. But a valid waiver will not be presumed simply from the silence of the accused after warnings are given or simply from the fact that a confession was in fact eventually obtained.

Thus, the Court held that an express statement can constitute a waiver, and that silence alone after such warnings cannot do so. But the Court did not hold that such an express statement is indispensable to a finding of waiver.

An express written or oral statement of waiver of the right to remain silent or of the right to counsel is usually strong proof of the validity of that waiver, but is not inevitably either necessary or sufficient to establish waiver. The question is not one of form, but rather whether the defendant in fact knowingly and voluntarily waived the rights delineated in the *Miranda* case. As was unequivocally said in *Miranda*, mere silence is not enough. That does not mean that the defendant's silence, coupled with an understanding of his rights and a course of conduct indicating waiver, may never support a conclusion that a defendant has waived his rights. The courts must presume that a defendant did not waive his rights; the prosecution's burden is great; but in at least some cases waiver can be clearly inferred from the actions and words of the person interrogated.

* * * There is no doubt that this respondent was adequately and effectively apprised of his rights. The only question is whether he waived the exercise of one of those rights, the right to the presence of a lawyer. Neither the state court nor the respondent has offered any reason why there must be a negative answer to that question in the absence of an express waiver. * * * [T]he question of waiver must be determined on "the particular facts and circumstances surrounding that case, including the background, experience, and conduct of the accused."

We see no reason to discard that standard and replace it with an inflexible per se rule in a case such as this. * * * By creating an inflexible rule that no implicit waiver can ever suffice, the North Carolina Supreme Court has gone beyond the requirements of federal organic law. It follows that its judgment cannot stand. * * *

Accordingly, the judgment is vacated, and the case is remanded to the North Carolina Supreme Court for further proceedings not inconsistent with this opinion.

It is so ordered.

JUSTICE POWELL took no part in the consideration or decision of this case.

JUSTICE BRENNAN, with whom JUSTICE MARSHALL and JUSTICE STEVENS joins, dissenting.

Miranda v. Arizona held that "[n]o effective waiver of the right to counsel during interrogation can be recognized unless specifically made after the warnings we here delineate have been given." * * *

The rule announced by the Court today allows a finding of waiver based upon "infer[ence] from the actions and words of the person interrogated." The Court thus shrouds in half-light the question of waiver, allowing courts to construct inferences from ambiguous words and gestures. But the very premise of *Miranda* requires that ambiguity be interpreted against the interrogator. That premise is the recognition of the "compulsion inherent in custodial" interrogation, and of its purpose "to subjugate the individual to the will of [his] examiner." Under such conditions, only the most explicit waivers of rights can be considered knowingly and freely given.

The instant case presents a clear example of the need for an express waiver requirement. As the Court acknowledges, there is a disagreement over whether respondent was orally advised of his rights at the time he made his statement. The fact that Butler received a written copy of his rights is deemed by the Court to be sufficient basis to resolve the disagreement. But, unfortunately, there is also a dispute over whether Butler could read. And, obviously, if Butler did not have his rights read to him, and could not read them himself, there could be no basis upon which to conclude that he knowingly waived them. Indeed, even if Butler could read there is no reason to believe that his oral statements, which followed a refusal to sign a written waiver form, were intended to signify relinquishment of his rights.

Faced with "actions and words" of uncertain meaning, some judges may find waivers where none occurred. Others may fail to find them where they did. In the former case, the defendant's rights will have been violated; in the latter, society's interest in effective law enforcement will have been frustrated. A simple prophylactic rule requiring the police to obtain an express waiver of the right to counsel before proceeding with interrogation eliminates these difficulties. And since the Court agrees that *Miranda* requires the police to obtain some kind of waiver—whether express or implied—the requirement of an express waiver would impose no burden on the police not imposed by the Court's interpretation. It would merely make that burden explicit. Had Agent Martinez simply elicited a clear answer from Willie Butler to the question, "Do you waive your right to a lawyer?" this journey through three courts would not have been necessary.

[JUSTICE BLACKMUN's concurring opinion has been omitted.]

MORAN V. BURBINE
Supreme Court of the United States
475 U.S. 412, 106 S. Ct. 1135, 89 L. Ed. 2d 410 (1986)

JUSTICE O'CONNOR delivered the opinion of the Court. * * *

On the morning of March 3, 1977, Mary Jo Hickey was found unconscious in a factory parking lot in Providence, Rhode Island. Suffering from injuries to her skull apparently inflicted by a metal pipe found at the scene, she was rushed to a nearby hospital. Three weeks later she died from her wounds.

Several months after her death, the Cranston, Rhode Island, police arrested respondent and two others in connection with a local burglary. Shortly before the arrest, Detective Ferranti of the Cranston police force had learned from a confidential informant that the man responsible for Ms. Hickey's death lived at a certain address and went by the name of "Butch." Upon discovering that respondent lived at that address and was known by that name, Detective Ferranti informed respondent of his *Miranda* rights. When respondent refused to execute a written waiver, Detective Ferranti spoke separately with the two other suspects arrested on the breaking and entering charge and obtained statements further implicating respondent in Ms. Hickey's murder. At approximately 6 p.m., Detective Ferranti telephoned the police in Providence to convey the information he had uncovered. An hour later, three officers from that department arrived at the Cranston headquarters for the purpose of questioning respondent about the murder.

That same evening, at about 7:45 p.m., respondent's sister telephoned the Public Defender's Office to obtain legal assistance for her brother. Her sole concern was the breaking and entering charge, as she was unaware that respondent was then under suspicion for murder. She asked for Richard Casparian who had been scheduled to meet with respondent earlier that afternoon to discuss another charge unrelated to either the break-in or the murder. As soon as the conversation ended, the attorney who took the call attempted to reach Mr. Casparian. When those efforts were unsuccessful, she telephoned Allegra Munson, another Assistant Public Defender, and told her about respondent's arrest and his sister's subsequent request that the office represent him.

At 8:15 p.m., Ms. Munson telephoned the Cranston police station and asked that her call be transferred to the detective division. In the words of the Supreme Court of Rhode Island, whose factual findings we treat as presumptively correct, the conversation proceeded as follows:

> A male voice responded with the word "Detectives." Ms. Munson identified herself and asked if Brian Burbine was being held; the person responded affirmatively. Ms. Munson explained to the person that Burbine was represented by attorney Casparian who

was not available; she further stated that she would act as Burbine's legal counsel in the event that the police intended to place him in a lineup or question him. The unidentified person told Ms. Munson that the police would not be questioning Burbine or putting him in a lineup and that they were through with him for the night. Ms. Munson was not informed that the Providence Police were at the Cranston police station or that Burbine was a suspect in Mary's murder.

At all relevant times, respondent was unaware of his sister's efforts to retain counsel and of the fact and contents of Ms. Munson's telephone conversation.

Less than an hour later, the police brought respondent to an interrogation room and conducted the first of a series of interviews concerning the murder. Prior to each session, respondent was informed of his *Miranda* rights, and on three separate occasions he signed a written form acknowledging that he understood his right to the presence of an attorney and explicitly indicating that he "[did] not want an attorney called or appointed for [him]" before he gave a statement. Uncontradicted evidence at the suppression hearing indicated that at least twice during the course of the evening, respondent was left in a room where he had access to a telephone, which he apparently declined to use. Eventually, respondent signed three written statements fully admitting to the murder.

Prior to trial, respondent moved to suppress the statements. The court denied the motion, finding that respondent had received the *Miranda* warnings and had "knowingly, intelligently, and voluntarily waived his privilege against self-incrimination [and] his right to counsel." * * * The Court of Appeals for the First Circuit * * * reversed, [holding] that the police's conduct had fatally tainted respondent's "otherwise valid" waiver of his Fifth Amendment privilege against self-incrimination and right to counsel. The court reasoned that by failing to inform respondent that an attorney had called and that she had been assured that no questioning would take place until the next day, the police had deprived respondent of information crucial to his ability to waive his rights knowingly and intelligently. The court also found that the record would support "no other explanation for the refusal to tell Burbine of Attorney Munson's call than ... deliberate or reckless irresponsibility." This kind of "blameworthy action by the police," the court concluded, together with respondent's ignorance of the telephone call, "vitiate[d] any claim that [the] waiver of counsel was knowing and voluntary."

We granted certiorari to decide whether a prearraignment confession preceded by an otherwise valid waiver must be suppressed either because the police misinformed an inquiring attorney about their plans concerning the suspect or because they failed to inform the suspect of the attorney's efforts to reach him.

In *Miranda v. Arizona*, the Court recognized that custodial interrogations, by their very nature, generate "compelling pressures which work to undermine the individual's will to resist and to compel him to speak where he would not otherwise do so freely." To combat this inherent compulsion, and thereby protect the Fifth Amendment privilege against self-incrimination, *Miranda* imposed on the police an obligation to follow certain procedures in their dealings with the accused. * * *

Respondent does not dispute that the Providence police followed these procedures with precision. * * * He contends instead that the confessions must be suppressed because the police's failure to inform him of the attorney's telephone call deprived him of information essential to his ability to knowingly waive his Fifth Amendment rights. In the alternative, he suggests that to fully protect the Fifth Amendment values served by *Miranda*, we should extend that decision to condemn the conduct of the Providence police. We address each contention in turn. * * *

Echoing the standard first articulated in *Johnson v. Zerbst*, *Miranda* holds that "[t]he defendant may waive effectuation" of the rights conveyed in the warnings "provided the waiver is made voluntarily, knowingly and intelligently." The inquiry has two distinct dimensions. First, the relinquishment of the right must have been voluntary in the sense that it was the product of a free and deliberate choice rather than intimidation, coercion, or deception. Second, the waiver must have been made with a full awareness of both the nature of the right being abandoned and the consequences of the decision to abandon it. Only if the "totality of the circumstances surrounding the interrogation" reveal both an uncoerced choice and the requisite level of comprehension may a court properly conclude that the *Miranda* rights have been waived.

Under this standard, we have no doubt that respondent validly waived his right to remain silent and to the presence of counsel. The voluntariness of the waiver is not at issue. As the Court of Appeals correctly acknowledged, the record is devoid of any suggestion that police resorted to physical or psychological pressure to elicit the statements. Indeed it appears that it was respondent, and not the police, who spontaneously initiated the conversation that led to the first and most damaging confession. Nor is there any question about respondent's comprehension of the full panoply of rights set out in the *Miranda* warnings and of the potential consequences of a decision to relinquish them. * * *

Events occurring outside of the presence of the suspect and entirely unknown to him surely can have no bearing on the capacity to comprehend and knowingly relinquish a constitutional right. Under the analysis of the Court of Appeals, the same defendant, armed with the same information and confronted with precisely the same police conduct, would have knowingly waived his *Miranda* rights had a lawyer not telephoned the police station to inquire about his status. Nothing in any of our waiver decisions or in our understanding of the essential components of a valid waiver requires so incongruous a result. No doubt the additional information would have been useful to respondent; perhaps even it might have affected his decision to confess. But we have never read the Constitution to require that the police supply a suspect with a flow of information to help him calibrate his self-interest in deciding whether to speak or stand by his rights. Once it is determined that a suspect's decision not to rely on his rights was uncoerced, that he at all times knew he could stand mute and request a lawyer, and that he was aware of the State's intention to use his statements to secure a conviction, the analysis is complete and the waiver is valid as a matter of law. The Court of Appeals' conclusion to the contrary was in error.

Nor do we believe that the level of the police's culpability in failing to inform respondent of the telephone call has any bearing on the validity of the waivers. In light of the state-court findings that there was no "conspiracy or collusion" on the part of the police, we have serious doubts about whether the Court of Appeals was free to conclude that their conduct constituted "deliberate or reckless irresponsibility." But whether intentional or inadvertent, the state of mind of the police is irrelevant to the question of the intelligence and voluntariness of respondent's election to abandon his rights. Although highly inappropriate, even deliberate deception of an attorney could not possibly affect a suspect's decision to waive his *Miranda* rights unless he were at least aware of the incident. * * * Nor was the failure to inform respondent of the telephone call the kind of "trick[ery]" that can vitiate the validity of a waiver. Granting that the "deliberate or reckless" withholding of information is objectionable as a matter of ethics, such conduct is only relevant to the constitutional validity of a waiver if it deprives a defendant of knowledge essential to his ability to understand the nature of his rights and the consequences of abandoning them. Because respondent's voluntary decision to speak was made with full awareness and comprehension of all the information *Miranda* requires the police to convey, the waivers were valid.

* * * Regardless of any issue of waiver, he urges, the Fifth Amendment requires the reversal of a conviction if the police are less than forthright in their dealings with an attorney or if they fail to tell a suspect of a lawyer's unilateral efforts to contact him. Because the proposed modification ignores the underlying purposes of the *Miranda* rules and because we think that the decision as written strikes the proper balance between society's legitimate law enforcement interests and the protection of the defendant's Fifth Amendment rights, we decline the invitation to further extend *Miranda*'s reach.

At the outset, while we share respondent's distaste for the deliberate misleading of an officer of the court, reading *Miranda* to forbid police deception of an *attorney* "would cut [the decision] completely loose from its own explicitly stated rationale." * * * Clearly, a rule that focuses on how the police treat an attorney—conduct that has no relevance at all to the degree of compulsion experienced by the defendant during interrogation—would ignore both *Miranda*'s mission and its only source of legitimacy.

Nor are we prepared to adopt a rule requiring that the police inform a suspect of an attorney's efforts to reach him. While such a rule might add marginally to *Miranda*'s goal of dispelling the compulsion inherent in custodial interrogation, overriding practical considerations counsel against its adoption. As we have stressed on numerous occasions, "[o]ne of the principal advantages" of *Miranda* is the ease and clarity of its application. We have little doubt that the approach urged by respondent and endorsed by the Court of Appeals would have the inevitable consequence of muddying *Miranda*'s otherwise relatively clear waters. The legal questions it would spawn are legion: To what extent should the police be held accountable for knowing that the accused has counsel? Is it enough that someone in the station house knows, or must the interrogating officer himself know of counsel's efforts to contact the suspect? Do counsel's efforts to talk to the suspect concerning one criminal investigation trigger the obligation to inform the defendant before interrogation may proceed on a wholly separate matter? We are unwilling to modify *Miranda* in a manner that would so clearly undermine the decision's central "virtue of informing police and prosecutors with specificity." * * *

Respondent also contends that the Sixth Amendment requires exclusion of his three confessions. * * * The difficulty for respondent is that the interrogation sessions that yielded the inculpatory statements took place before the initiation of "adversary judicial proceedings." He contends, however, that this circumstance is not fatal to his Sixth Amendment claim. * * * Placing principal reliance on a footnote in *Miranda*, and on *Escobedo v. Illinois*, he maintains that * * * [t]he right to noninterference with an attorney's dealings with a criminal suspect * * * arises the moment that the relationship is formed, or, at the very least, once the defendant is placed in custodial interrogation.

We are not persuaded. At the outset, subsequent decisions foreclose any reliance on *Escobedo* and *Miranda* for the proposition that the Sixth Amendment right, in any of its manifestations, applies prior to the initiation of adversary judicial proceedings. Although *Escobedo* was originally decided as a Sixth Amendment case, "the Court in retrospect perceived that the 'prime purpose' of *Escobedo* was not to vindicate the constitutional right to counsel as such, but, like *Miranda*, 'to guarantee full effectuation of the privilege against self-incrimination . . . .'" Clearly then, *Escobedo* provides no support for respondent's argument. Nor, of course, does *Miranda*, the holding of which rested exclusively on the Fifth Amendment. * * *

Questions of precedent to one side, we find respondent's understanding of the Sixth Amendment both practically and theoretically unsound. As a practical matter, it makes little sense to say that the Sixth Amendment right to counsel attaches at different times depending on the fortuity of whether the suspect or his family happens to have retained counsel prior to interrogation. More importantly, the suggestion that the existence of an attorney-client relationship itself triggers the protections of the Sixth Amendment misconceives the underlying purposes of the right to counsel. The Sixth Amendment's intended function is not to wrap a protective cloak around the attorney-client relationship for its own sake any more than it is to protect a suspect from the consequences of his own candor. Its purpose, rather, is to assure that in any "criminal [prosecution]," the accused shall not be left to his own devices in facing the " 'prosecutorial forces of organized society.' " By its very terms, it becomes applicable only when the government's role shifts from investigation to accusation. For it is only then that the assistance of one versed in the "intricacies . . . of law," is needed to assure that the prosecution's case encounters "the crucible of meaningful adversarial testing." * * *

Because, as respondent acknowledges, the events that led to the inculpatory statements preceded the formal initiation of adversary judicial proceedings, we reject the contention that the conduct of the police violated his rights under the Sixth Amendment. * * *

Finally, respondent contends that the conduct of the police was so offensive as to deprive him of the fundamental fairness guaranteed by the Due Process Clause of the Fourteenth Amendment. Focusing primarily on the impropriety of conveying false information to an attorney, he invites us to declare that such behavior should be condemned as violative of canons fundamental to the " 'traditions and conscience of our people.' " We do not question that on facts more egregious than those presented here police deception might rise to a level of a due process violation. * * * We hold only that, on these facts, the challenged conduct falls short of the kind of misbehavior that so shocks the sensibilities of civilized society as to warrant a federal intrusion into the criminal processes of the States.

We hold therefore that the Court of Appeals erred in finding that the Federal Constitution required the exclusion of the three inculpatory statements. Accordingly, we reverse and remand for proceedings consistent with this opinion.

So ordered.

JUSTICE STEVENS, with whom JUSTICE BRENNAN and JUSTICE MARSHALL join, dissenting. * * *

Well-settled principles of law lead inexorably to the conclusion that the failure to inform Burbine of the call from his attorney makes the subsequent waiver of his constitutional rights invalid. Analysis should begin with an acknowledgment that the burden of proving the validity of a waiver of constitutional rights is always on the *government*. When such a waiver occurs in a custodial setting, that burden is an especially heavy one.

* * * *Miranda* clearly condemns threats or trickery that cause a suspect to make an unwise waiver of his rights even though he fully understands those rights. In my opinion there can be no constitutional distinction—as the Court appears to draw—between a deceptive misstatement and the concealment by the police of the critical fact that an attorney retained by the accused or his family has offered assistance, either by telephone or in person. * * *

As the Court notes, the question is whether the deceptive police conduct "deprives a defendant of knowledge essential to his ability to understand the nature of his rights and the consequences of abandoning them." This question has been resoundingly answered time and time again by the state courts. * * * Unlike the majority, the state courts have realized that attorney communication to the police about the client is an event that has a direct "bearing" on the knowing and intelligent waiver of constitutional rights. As the Oregon Supreme Court has explained: "To pass up an abstract offer to call some unknown lawyer is very different from refusing to talk with an identified attorney actually available to provide at least initial assistance and advice, whatever might be arranged in the long run. A suspect indifferent to the first offer may well react quite differently to the second."

In short, settled principles about construing waivers of constitutional rights and about the need for strict presumptions in custodial interrogations, as well as a plain reading of the *Miranda* opinion itself, overwhelmingly support the conclusion reached by almost every state court that has considered the matter—a suspect's waiver of his right to counsel is invalid if police refuse to inform the suspect of his counsel's communications. * * *

At the time attorney Munson made her call to the Cranston police station, she was acting as Burbine's attorney. Under ordinary principles of agency law the deliberate deception of Munson was tantamount to deliberate deception of her client. If an attorney makes a mistake in the course of her representation of her client, the client must accept the consequences of that mistake. It is equally clear that when an attorney makes an inquiry on behalf of her client, the client is entitled to a truthful answer. Surely the client must have the same remedy for a false representation to his lawyer that he would have if he were acting *pro se* and had propounded the question himself. * * *

In my view, as a matter of law, the police deception of Munson was tantamount to deception of Burbine himself. It constituted a violation of Burbine's right to have an attorney present during the questioning that began shortly thereafter. * * *

The possible reach of the Court's opinion is stunning. For the majority seems to suggest that police may deny counsel all access to a client who is being held. At least since *Escobedo v. Illinois*, it has been widely accepted that police may not simply deny attorneys access to their clients who are in custody. This view has survived the recasting of *Escobedo* from a Sixth Amendment to a Fifth Amendment case that the majority finds so critically important. That this prevailing view is shared *by the police* can be seen in the state-court opinions detailing various forms of police deception of attorneys. For, if there were no obligation to give attorneys access, there would be no need to take elaborate steps to avoid access, such as shuttling the suspect to a different location, or taking the lawyer to different locations; police could simply refuse to allow the attorneys to see the suspects. But the law enforcement profession has apparently believed, quite rightly in my view, that denying lawyers access to their clients is impermissible. The Court today seems to assume that this view was error—that, from the federal constitutional perspective, the lawyer's access is, as a question from the Court put it in oral argument, merely "a matter of prosecutorial grace." * * *

The Court devotes precisely five sentences to its conclusion that the police interference in the attorney's representation of Burbine did not violate the Due Process Clause. In the majority's view, the due process analysis is a simple "shock the conscience" test. Finding its conscience troubled, but not shocked, the majority rejects the due process challenge. * * *

In my judgment, police interference in the attorney-client relationship is the type of governmental misconduct on a matter of central importance to the administration of justice that the Due Process Clause prohibits. Just as the police cannot impliedly promise a suspect that his silence will not be used against him and then proceed to break that promise, so too police cannot tell a suspect's attorney that they will not question the suspect and then proceed to question him. Just as the government cannot conceal from a suspect material and exculpatory evidence, so too the government cannot conceal from a suspect the material fact of his attorney's communication.

Police interference with communications between an attorney and his client violates the due process requirement of fundamental fairness. Burbine's attorney was given completely false information about the lack of questioning; moreover, she was not told that her client would be questioned regarding a murder charge about which she was unaware. Burbine, in turn, was not told that his attorney had phoned and that she had been informed that he would not be questioned. Quite simply, the Rhode Island police effectively drove a wedge between an attorney and a suspect through misinformation and omissions.

The majority does not "question that on facts more egregious than those presented here police deception might rise to a level of a due process violation." In my view, the police deception disclosed by this record plainly does rise to that level.

This case turns on a proper appraisal of the role of the lawyer in our society. If a lawyer is seen as a nettlesome obstacle to the pursuit of wrongdoers—as in an inquisitorial society—then the Court's decision today makes a good deal of sense. If a lawyer is seen as an aid to the understanding and protection of constitutional rights—as in an accusatorial society—then today's decision makes no sense at all. * * *

I respectfully dissent.

BERGHUIS V. THOMPKINS

Supreme Court of the United States
560 U.S. 370, 130 S. Ct. 2250, 176 L. Ed. 2d 1098 (2010)

JUSTICE KENNEDY delivered the opinion of the Court. * * *

On January 10, 2000, a shooting occurred outside a mall in Southfield, Michigan. Among the victims was Samuel Morris, who died from multiple gunshot wounds. The other victim, Frederick France, recovered from his injuries and later testified. Thompkins, who was a suspect, fled. About one year later he was found in Ohio and arrested there.

Two Southfield police officers traveled to Ohio to interrogate Thompkins, then awaiting transfer to Michigan. The interrogation began around 1:30 p.m. and lasted about three hours. * * * At the beginning of the interrogation, one of the officers, Detective Helgert, presented Thompkins with a form derived from the *Miranda* rule. It stated:

NOTIFICATION OF CONSTITUTIONAL RIGHTS AND STATEMENT

1. You have the right to remain silent.

2. Anything you say can and will be used against you in a court of law.

3. You have a right to talk to a lawyer before answering any questions and you have the right to have a lawyer present with you while you are answering any questions.

4. If you cannot afford to hire a lawyer, one will be appointed to represent you before any questioning, if you wish one.

5. You have the right to decide at any time before or during questioning to use your right to remain silent and your right to talk with a lawyer while you are being questioned.

Helgert asked Thompkins to read the fifth warning out loud. Thompkins complied. Helgert later said this was to ensure that Thompkins could read, and Helgert concluded that Thompkins understood English. Helgert then read the other four *Miranda* warnings out loud and asked Thompkins to sign the form to demonstrate that he understood his rights. Thompkins declined to sign the form. The record contains conflicting evidence about whether Thompkins then verbally confirmed that he understood the rights listed on the form. * * *

Officers began an interrogation. At no point during the interrogation did Thompkins say that he wanted to remain silent, that he did not want to talk with the police, or that he wanted an attorney. Thompkins was "[l]argely" silent during the interrogation, which lasted about three hours. He did give a few limited verbal responses, however, such as "yeah," "no," or "I don't know." And on occasion he communicated by nodding his head. Thompkins also said that he "didn't want a peppermint" that was offered to him by the police and that the chair he was "sitting in was hard."

About 2 hours and 45 minutes into the interrogation, Helgert asked Thompkins, "Do you believe in God?" Thompkins made eye contact with Helgert and said "Yes," as his eyes "well[ed] up with tears." Helgert asked, "Do you pray to God?" Thompkins said "Yes." Helgert asked, "Do you pray to God to forgive you for shooting that boy down?" Thompkins answered "Yes" and looked away. Thompkins refused to make a written confession, and the interrogation ended about 15 minutes later.

Thompkins was charged with first-degree murder, assault with intent to commit murder, and certain firearms-related offenses. He moved to suppress the statements made during the interrogation. He argued that he had invoked his Fifth Amendment right to remain silent, requiring police to end the interrogation at once, that he had not waived his right to remain silent, and that his inculpatory statements were involuntary. The trial court denied the motion. * * * The jury found Thompkins guilty on all counts. * * *

Thompkins makes various arguments that his answers to questions from the detectives were inadmissible. He first contends that he "invoke[d] his privilege" to remain silent by not saying anything for a sufficient period of time, so the interrogation should have "cease[d]" before he made his inculpatory statements.

This argument is unpersuasive. In the context of invoking the *Miranda* right to counsel, the Court in *Davis v. United States* held that a suspect must do so "unambiguously." If an accused makes a statement concerning the right to counsel "that is ambiguous or equivocal" or makes no statement, the police are not required to end the interrogation or ask questions to clarify whether the accused wants to invoke his or her *Miranda* rights.

The Court has not yet stated whether an invocation of the right to remain silent can be ambiguous or equivocal, but there is no principled reason to adopt different standards for determining when an accused has invoked the *Miranda* right to remain silent and the *Miranda* right to counsel at issue in *Davis*. Both protect the privilege against compulsory self-incrimination by requiring an interrogation to cease when either right is invoked.

There is good reason to require an accused who wants to invoke his or her right to remain silent to do so unambiguously. A requirement of an unambiguous invocation of *Miranda* rights results in an objective inquiry that "avoid[s] difficulties of proof and * * * provide[s] guidance to officers" on how to proceed in the face of ambiguity. If an ambiguous act, omission, or statement could require police to end the interrogation, police would be required to make difficult decisions about an accused's unclear intent and face the consequence of suppression "if they guess wrong." Suppression of a voluntary confession in these circumstances would place a significant burden on society's interest in prosecuting criminal activity. * * *

Thompkins did not say that he wanted to remain silent or that he did not want to talk with the police. Had he made either of these simple, unambiguous statements, he would have invoked his "right to cut off questioning." Here he did neither, so he did not invoke his right to remain silent.

We next consider whether Thompkins waived his right to remain silent. Even absent the accused's invocation of the right to remain silent, the accused's statement during a custodial interrogation is inadmissible at trial unless the prosecution can establish that the accused "in fact knowingly and voluntarily waived [*Miranda*] rights" when making the statement. The waiver inquiry "has two distinct dimensions": waiver must be "voluntary in the sense that it was the product of a free and deliberate choice rather than intimidation, coercion, or deception," and "made with a full awareness of both the nature of the right being abandoned and the consequences of the decision to abandon it."

Some language in *Miranda* could be read to indicate that waivers are difficult to establish absent an explicit written waiver or a formal, express oral statement. *Miranda* said "a valid waiver will not be presumed simply from the silence of the accused after warnings are given or simply from the fact that a confession was in fact eventually obtained." 384 U.S. at 475 ("No effective waiver . . . can be recognized unless specifically made after the [*Miranda*] warnings . . . have been given"). In addition, the *Miranda* Court stated that "a heavy burden rests on the government to demonstrate that the defendant knowingly and intelligently waived his privilege against self-incrimination and his right to retained or appointed counsel."

The course of decisions since *Miranda*, [however], demonstrates that waivers can be established even absent formal or express statements of waiver that would be expected in, say, a judicial hearing to determine if a guilty plea has been properly entered. * * *

One of the first cases to decide the meaning and import of *Miranda* with respect to the question of waiver was *North Carolina v. Butler*. * * * *Butler* interpreted the *Miranda* language concerning the "heavy burden" to show waiver. * * * And in a later case, the Court stated that this "heavy burden" is not more than the burden to establish waiver by a preponderance of the evidence.

The prosecution * * * does not need to show that a waiver of *Miranda* rights was express. An "implicit waiver" of the "right to remain silent" is sufficient to admit a suspect's statement into evidence. *Butler* made clear that a waiver of *Miranda* rights may be implied through "the defendant's silence, coupled with an understanding of his rights and a course of conduct indicating waiver." The Court in *Butler* therefore "retreated" from the "language and tenor of the *Miranda* opinion," which "suggested that the Court would require that a waiver . . . be 'specifically made.'"

If the State establishes that a *Miranda* warning was given and the accused made an uncoerced statement, this showing, standing alone, is insufficient to demonstrate "a valid waiver" of *Miranda* rights. The prosecution must make the additional showing that the accused understood these rights. Where the prosecution shows that a *Miranda* warning was given and that it was understood by the accused, an accused's uncoerced statement establishes an implied waiver of the right to remain silent. * * *

The record in this case shows that Thompkins waived his right to remain silent. There is no basis in this case to conclude that he did not understand his rights; and on these facts it follows that he chose not to invoke or rely on those rights when he did speak. First, there is no contention that Thompkins did not understand his rights; and from this it follows that he knew what he gave up when he spoke. There was more than enough evidence in the record to conclude that Thompkins understood his *Miranda* rights. Thompkins received a written copy of the *Miranda* warnings; Detective Helgert determined that Thompkins could read and understand English; and Thompkins was given time to read the warnings. Thompkins, furthermore, read aloud the fifth warning, which stated that "you have the right to decide at any time before or during questioning to use your right to remain silent and your right to talk with a lawyer while you are being questioned." * * * Helgert, moreover, read the warnings aloud.

Second, Thompkins's answer to Detective Helgert's question about whether Thompkins prayed to God for forgiveness for shooting the victim is a "course of conduct indicating waiver" of the right to remain silent. If Thompkins wanted to remain silent, he could have said nothing in response to Helgert's questions, or he could have unambiguously invoked his *Miranda* rights and ended the interrogation. * * * Thompkins's answer to Helgert's question about praying to God for forgiveness for shooting the victim was sufficient to show a course of conduct indicating waiver. * * *

Third, there is no evidence that Thompkins's statement was coerced. Thompkins does not claim that police threatened or injured him during the interrogation or that he was in any way fearful. The interrogation was conducted in a standard-sized room in the middle of the afternoon. It is true that apparently he was in a straight-backed chair for three hours, but there is no authority for the proposition that an interrogation of this length is inherently coercive. * * * In these circumstances, Thompkins knowingly and voluntarily made a statement to police, so he waived his right to remain silent.

Thompkins next argues that, even if his answer to Detective Helgert could constitute a waiver of his right to remain silent, the police were not allowed to question him until they obtained a waiver first. *Butler* forecloses this argument. The *Butler* Court held that courts can infer a waiver of *Miranda* rights "from the actions and words of the person interrogated." This principle would be inconsistent with a rule that requires a waiver at the outset. * * * This holding also makes sense given that "the primary protection afforded suspects subject[ed] to custodial interrogation is the *Miranda* warnings themselves."

* * * Thus, after giving a *Miranda* warning, police may interrogate a suspect who has neither invoked nor waived his or her *Miranda* rights. On these premises, it follows the police were not required to obtain a waiver of Thompkins's *Miranda* rights before commencing the interrogation.

In sum, a suspect who has received and understood the *Miranda* warnings, and has not invoked his *Miranda* rights, waives the right to remain silent by making an uncoerced statement to the police. Thompkins did not invoke his right to remain silent and stop the questioning. Understanding his rights in full, he waived his right to remain silent by making a voluntary statement to the police. The police, moreover, were not required to obtain a waiver of Thompkins's right to remain silent before interrogating him. * * *

JUSTICE SOTOMAYOR, with whom JUSTICE STEVENS, JUSTICE GINSBURG, and JUSTICE BREYER join, dissenting.

The Court concludes today that a criminal suspect waives his right to remain silent if, after sitting tacit and uncommunicative through nearly three hours of police interrogation, he utters a few one-word responses. The

Court also concludes that a suspect who wishes to guard his right to remain silent against such a finding of "waiver" must, counterintuitively, speak—and must do so with sufficient precision to satisfy a clear-statement rule that construes ambiguity in favor of the police. Both propositions mark a substantial retreat from the protection against compelled self-incrimination that *Miranda v. Arizona* has long provided during custodial interrogation. * * *

The strength of Thompkins' *Miranda* claims depends in large part on the circumstances of the 3-hour interrogation, at the end of which he made inculpatory statements later introduced at trial. The Court's opinion downplays record evidence that Thompkins remained almost completely silent and unresponsive throughout that session. * * *

As to the interrogation itself, Helgert candidly characterized it as "very, very one-sided" and "nearly a monologue." Thompkins was "[p]eculiar," "[s]ullen," and "[g]enerally quiet." Helgert and his partner "did most of the talking," as Thompkins was "not verbally communicative" and "[l]argely" remained silent.

* * * I begin with the question whether Thompkins waived his right to remain silent. Even if Thompkins did not invoke that right, he is entitled to relief because Michigan did not satisfy its burden of establishing waiver. * * *

Rarely do this Court's precedents provide clearly established law so closely on point with the facts of a particular case. Together, *Miranda* and *Butler* establish that a court "must presume that a defendant did not waive his right[s]"; the prosecution bears a "heavy burden" in attempting to demonstrate waiver; the fact of a "lengthy interrogation" prior to obtaining statements is "strong evidence" against a finding of valid waiver; "mere silence" in response to questioning is "not enough"; and waiver may not be presumed "simply from the fact that a confession was in fact eventually obtained."

It is undisputed here that Thompkins never expressly waived his right to remain silent. * * * *Miranda* and *Butler* expressly preclude the possibility that the inculpatory statements themselves are sufficient to establish waiver.

[Moreover], Thompkins' "actions and words" preceding the inculpatory statements simply do not evidence a "course of conduct indicating waiver" sufficient to carry the prosecution's burden. * * * Unlike in *Butler*, Thompkins made no initial declaration akin to "I will talk to you." Indeed, Michigan and the United States concede that no waiver occurred in this case until Thompkins responded "yes" to the questions about God. I believe it is objectively unreasonable under our clearly established precedents to conclude the prosecution met its "heavy burden" of proof on a record consisting of three one-word answers, following 2 hours and 45 minutes of silence punctuated by a few largely nonverbal responses to unidentified questions.

* * * I [also] cannot agree with the Court's much broader ruling that a suspect must clearly invoke his right to silence by speaking. Taken together with the Court's reformulation of the prosecution's burden of proof as to waiver, today's novel clear-statement rule for invocation invites police to question a suspect at length—notwithstanding his persistent refusal to answer questions—in the hope of eventually obtaining a single inculpatory response which will suffice to prove waiver of rights. Such a result bears little semblance to the "fully effective" prophylaxis that *Miranda* requires. * * *

Davis' clear-statement rule is * * * a poor fit for the right to silence. Advising a suspect that he has a "right to remain silent" is unlikely to convey that he must speak (and must do so in some particular fashion) to ensure the right will be protected. * * *

[T]he Court's concern that police will face "difficult decisions about an accused's unclear intent" and suffer the consequences of "guess[ing] wrong," is misplaced. If a suspect makes an ambiguous statement or engages in conduct that creates uncertainty about his intent to invoke his right, police can simply ask for clarification. It is hardly an unreasonable burden for police to ask a suspect, for instance, "Do you want to talk to us?" * * * Police may well prefer not to seek clarification of an ambiguous statement out of fear that a suspect will invoke his rights. But "our system of justice is not founded on a fear that a suspect will exercise his rights. 'If the exercise of constitutional rights will thwart the effectiveness of a system of law enforcement, then there is something very wrong with that system.'" * * *

Today's decision turns *Miranda* upside down. Criminal suspects must now unambiguously invoke their right to remain silent—which, counterintuitively, requires them to speak. At the same time, suspects will be legally presumed to have waived their rights even if they have given no clear expression of their intent to do so. Those results, in my view, find no basis in *Miranda* or our subsequent cases and are inconsistent with the fair-trial principles on which those precedents are grounded. * * * I respectfully dissent.

COLORADO V. SPRING

Supreme Court of the United States
479 U.S. 564, 107 S. Ct. 851, 93 L. Ed. 2d 954 (1987)

JUSTICE POWELL delivered the opinion of the Court.

In *Miranda*, the Court held that a suspect's waiver of the Fifth Amendment privilege against self-incrimination is valid only if it is made voluntarily, knowingly, and intelligently. This case presents the question whether the suspect's awareness of all the crimes about which he may be questioned is relevant to determining the validity of his decision to waive the Fifth Amendment privilege.

In February 1979, respondent John Leroy Spring and a companion shot and killed Donald Walker during a hunting trip in Colorado. * * * On March 30, 1979, ATF agents arrested Spring [on unrelated firearms charges].

An ATF agent on the scene of the arrest advised Spring of his *Miranda* rights. Spring was advised of his *Miranda* rights a second time after he was transported to the ATF office in Kansas City. At the ATF office, the agents also advised Spring that he had the right to stop the questioning at any time or to stop the questioning until the presence of an attorney could be secured. Spring then signed a written form stating that he understood and waived his rights, and that he was willing to make a statement and answer questions.

ATF agents first questioned Spring about the firearms transactions that led to his arrest. They then asked Spring if he had a criminal record. He admitted that he had a juvenile record for shooting his aunt when he was 10 years old. The agents asked if Spring had ever shot anyone else. Spring ducked his head and mumbled, "I shot another guy once." The agents asked Spring if he had ever been to Colorado. Spring said no. The agents asked Spring whether he had shot a man named Walker in Colorado and thrown his body into a snowbank. Spring paused and then ducked his head again and said no. The interview ended at this point.

On May 26, 1979, Colorado law enforcement officials visited Spring while he was in jail in Kansas City pursuant to his arrest on the firearms offenses. The officers gave Spring the *Miranda* warnings, and Spring again signed a written form indicating that he understood his rights and was willing to waive them. The officers informed Spring that they wanted to question him about the Colorado homicide. Spring indicated that he "wanted to get it off his chest." In an interview that lasted approximately 1½ hours, Spring confessed to the Colorado murder. During that time, Spring talked freely to the officers, did not indicate a desire to terminate the questioning, and never requested counsel. The officers prepared a written statement summarizing the interview. Spring read, edited, and signed the statement.

Spring was charged in Colorado state court with first-degree murder. Spring moved to suppress both statements on the ground that his waiver of *Miranda* rights was invalid. The trial court found that the ATF agents' failure to inform Spring before the March 30 interview that they would question him about the Colorado murder did not affect his waiver of his *Miranda* rights * * *.

Accordingly, the trial court concluded that the March 30 statement should not be suppressed on Fifth Amendment grounds. The trial court [suppressed the statement on other grounds]. The court concluded that the May 26 statement "was made freely, voluntarily, and intelligently, after [Spring's] being properly and fully advised of his rights, and that the statement should not be suppressed, but should be admitted in evidence." * * * Spring was convicted of first-degree murder.

Spring argued on appeal that his waiver of *Miranda* rights before the March 30 statement was invalid because he was not informed that he would be questioned about the Colorado murder. Although this statement was not introduced at trial, he claimed that its validity was relevant because the May 26 statement that was admitted against him was the illegal "fruit" of the March 30 statement and therefore should have been suppressed. The Colorado Court of Appeals agreed with Spring * * *. The Colorado Supreme Court affirmed the judgment of the Court of Appeals * * *. We granted certiorari [and we] now reverse.

There is no dispute that the police obtained the May 26 confession after complete *Miranda* warnings and after informing Spring that he would be questioned about the Colorado homicide. The Colorado Supreme Court nevertheless held that the confession should have been suppressed because it was the illegal "fruit" of the March 30 statement. A confession cannot be "fruit of the poisonous tree" if the tree itself is not poisonous. Our inquiry, therefore, centers on the validity of the March 30 statement.

The Fifth Amendment of the United States Constitution provides that no person "shall be compelled in any criminal case to be a witness against himself." * * * In *Miranda,* the Court concluded that "without proper safeguards the process of in-custody interrogation of persons suspected or accused of crime contains inherently compelling pressures which work to undermine the individual's will to resist and to compel him to speak where he would not otherwise do so freely." * * *

Consistent with this purpose, a suspect may waive his Fifth Amendment privilege, "provided the waiver is made voluntarily, knowingly and intelligently." In this case, the law enforcement officials twice informed Spring of his Fifth Amendment privilege in precisely the manner specified by *Miranda.* As we have noted, Spring indicated that he understood the enumerated rights and signed a written form expressing his intention to waive his Fifth Amendment privilege. The trial court specifically found that "there was no element of duress or coercion used to induce Spring's statements [on March 30, 1978]." Despite the explicit warnings and the finding by the trial court, Spring argues that his March 30 statement was in effect compelled in violation of his Fifth Amendment privilege because he signed the waiver form without being aware that he would be questioned about the Colorado homicide. Spring's argument strains the meaning of compulsion past the breaking point.

A statement is not "compelled" within the meaning of the Fifth Amendment if an individual "voluntarily, knowingly and intelligently" waives his constitutional privilege. * * * There is no doubt that Spring's decision to waive his Fifth Amendment privilege was voluntary. He alleges no "coercion of a confession by physical violence or other deliberate means calculated to break [his] will," and the trial court found none. His allegation that the police failed to supply him with certain information does not relate to any of the traditional indicia of coercion: "the duration and conditions of detention . . . , the manifest attitude of the police toward him, his physical and mental state, the diverse pressures which sap or sustain his powers of resistance and self-control." * * *

There also is no doubt that Spring's waiver of his Fifth Amendment privilege was knowingly and intelligently made: that is, that Spring understood that he had the right to remain silent and that anything he said could be used as evidence against him. The Constitution does not require that a criminal suspect know and understand every possible consequence of a waiver of the Fifth Amendment privilege. * * *

This Court's holding in *Miranda* specifically required that the police inform a criminal suspect that he has the right to remain silent and that *anything* he says may be used against him. There is no qualification of this broad and explicit warning. The warning, as formulated in *Miranda,* conveys to a suspect the nature of his constitutional privilege and the consequences of abandoning it. Accordingly, we hold that a suspect's awareness of all the possible subjects of questioning in advance of interrogation is not relevant to determining whether the suspect voluntarily, knowingly, and intelligently waived his Fifth Amendment privilege.

The judgment of the Colorado Supreme Court is reversed, and the case is remanded for further proceedings not inconsistent with this opinion.

It is so ordered.

[JUSTICE MARSHALL's dissenting opinion has been omitted.]

D. MORE ON *MIRANDA* AND THE FIFTH AMENDMENT'S PRIVILEGE AGAINST SELF-INCRIMINATION

In the next set of cases contained in this chapter, we see the Court continuing to shape the contours of the *Miranda* rule. In *New York v. Quarles*, the Court considers whether to adopt a public safety exception to the *Miranda* rule. In *Dickerson v. United States*, the Court has the opportunity to overrule *Miranda*, but declines to do so. In *United States v.*

Patane, the Court decides whether physical evidence obtained as a result of a *Miranda* violation must be suppressed.

The next two cases, *Oregon v. Elstad* and *Missouri v. Seibert*, address two-stage interrogations. These are situations in which there is an initial failure by law enforcement to administer the *Miranda* warnings, even though the warnings should have been given, that results in the suspect making an incriminating statement. This first unwarned interrogation is followed by a second interrogation in which the *Miranda* warnings are given, and the suspect repeats the incriminating statement given earlier. The question before the Court in both cases is whether the initial failure to warn taints subsequent admissions made after the suspect was given the required *Miranda* warnings.

In *Harris v. New York* and *James v. Illinois*, the Court considers whether statements and evidence obtained in violation of *Miranda* can be used for impeachment purposes. Finally, in *Wrongly Accused: Is Race a Factor in Convicting the Innocent?*, Andrew Taslitz describes social science research that questions whether police officers are better than ordinary laypersons at making reliable credibility determinations.

NEW YORK V. QUARLES
Supreme Court of the United States
467 U.S. 649, 104 S. Ct. 2626, 81 L. Ed. 2d 550 (1984)

JUSTICE REHNQUIST delivered the opinion of the Court.

Respondent Benjamin Quarles was charged in the New York trial court with criminal possession of a weapon. The trial court suppressed the gun in question, and a statement made by respondent, because the statement was obtained by police before they read respondent his "*Miranda* rights." That ruling was affirmed on appeal through the New York Court of Appeals. We granted certiorari, and we now reverse. We conclude that under the circumstances involved in this case, overriding considerations of public safety justify the officer's failure to provide *Miranda* warnings before he asked questions devoted to locating the abandoned weapon.

On September 11, 1980, at approximately 12:30 a.m., Officer Frank Kraft and Officer Sal Scarring were on road patrol in Queens, N.Y., when a young woman approached their car. She told them that she had just been raped by a black male, approximately six feet tall, who was wearing a black jacket with the name "Big Ben" printed in yellow letters on the back. She told the officers that the man had just entered an A & P supermarket located nearby and that the man was carrying a gun.

The officers drove the woman to the supermarket, and Officer Kraft entered the store while Officer Scarring radioed for assistance. Officer

Kraft quickly spotted respondent, who matched the description given by the woman, approaching a checkout counter. Apparently upon seeing the officer, respondent turned and ran toward the rear of the store, and Officer Kraft pursued him with a drawn gun. When respondent turned the corner at the end of an aisle, Officer Kraft lost sight of him for several seconds, and upon regaining sight of respondent, ordered him to stop and put his hands over his head.

Although more than three other officers had arrived on the scene by that time, Officer Kraft was the first to reach respondent. He frisked him and discovered that he was wearing a shoulder holster which was then empty. After handcuffing him, Officer Kraft asked him where the gun was. Respondent nodded in the direction of some empty cartons and responded, "the gun is over there." Officer Kraft thereafter retrieved a loaded .38-caliber revolver from one of the cartons, formally placed respondent under arrest, and read him his *Miranda* rights from a printed card. Respondent indicated that he would be willing to answer questions without an attorney present. Officer Kraft then asked respondent if he owned the gun and where he had purchased it. Respondent answered that he did own it and that he had purchased it in Miami, Fla.

In the subsequent prosecution of respondent for criminal possession of a weapon,[1] the judge excluded the statement, "the gun is over there," and the gun because the officer had not given respondent the warnings required by our decision in *Miranda v. Arizona*, before asking him where the gun was located. The judge excluded the other statements about respondent's ownership of the gun and the place of purchase, as evidence tainted by the prior *Miranda* violation. The Appellate Division of the Supreme Court of New York affirmed without opinion.

The Court of Appeals granted leave to appeal and affirmed by a 4–3 vote. * * * For the reasons which follow, we believe that this case presents a situation where concern for public safety must be paramount to adherence to the literal language of the prophylactic rules enunciated in *Miranda*. * * *

In this case we have before us no claim that respondent's statements were actually compelled by police conduct which overcame his will to resist. Thus the only issue before us is whether Officer Kraft was justified in failing to make available to respondent the procedural safeguards associated with the privilege against compulsory self-incrimination since *Miranda*.

The Fifth Amendment guarantees that "[no] person ... shall be compelled in any criminal case to be a witness against himself." In *Miranda* this Court for the first time extended the Fifth Amendment privilege

---

[1] The State originally charged respondent with rape, but the record provides no information as to why the State failed to pursue that charge.

against compulsory self-incrimination to individuals subjected to custodial interrogation by the police. The Fifth Amendment itself does not prohibit all incriminating admissions; "[absent] some officially *coerced* self-accusation, the Fifth Amendment privilege is not violated by even the most damning admissions." The *Miranda* Court, however, presumed that interrogation in certain custodial circumstances is inherently coercive and held that statements made under those circumstances are inadmissible unless the suspect is specifically informed of his *Miranda* rights and freely decides to forgo those rights. The prophylactic *Miranda* warnings therefore are "not themselves rights protected by the Constitution but [are] instead measures to insure [sic] that the right against compulsory self-incrimination [is] protected." Requiring *Miranda* warnings before custodial interrogation provides "practical reinforcement" for the Fifth Amendment right.

The New York Court of Appeals was undoubtedly correct in deciding that the facts of this case come within the ambit of the *Miranda* decision as we have subsequently interpreted it. We agree that respondent was in police custody because we have noted that "the ultimate inquiry is simply whether there is a 'formal arrest or restraint on freedom of movement' of the degree associated with a formal arrest." Here Quarles was surrounded by at least four police officers and was handcuffed when the questioning at issue took place. As the New York Court of Appeals observed, there was nothing to suggest that any of the officers were any longer concerned for their own physical safety. * * *

We hold that on these facts there is a "public safety" exception to the requirement that *Miranda* warnings be given before a suspect's answers may be admitted into evidence, and that the availability of that exception does not depend upon the motivation of the individual officers involved. In a kaleidoscopic situation such as the one confronting these officers, where spontaneity rather than adherence to a police manual is necessarily the order of the day, the application of the exception which we recognize today should not be made to depend on post hoc findings at a suppression hearing concerning the subjective motivation of the arresting officer. Undoubtedly most police officers, if placed in Officer Kraft's position, would act out of a host of different, instinctive, and largely unverifiable motives—their own safety, the safety of others, and perhaps as well the desire to obtain incriminating evidence from the suspect.

Whatever the motivation of individual officers in such a situation, we do not believe that the doctrinal underpinnings of *Miranda* require that it be applied in all its rigor to a situation in which police officers ask questions reasonably prompted by a concern for the public safety. * * *

The police in this case, in the very act of apprehending a suspect, were confronted with the immediate necessity of ascertaining the whereabouts of a gun which they had every reason to believe the suspect had just removed from his empty holster and discarded in the supermarket. So long as the gun was concealed somewhere in the supermarket, with its actual whereabouts unknown, it obviously posed more than one danger to the public safety: an accomplice might make use of it, a customer or employee might later come upon it.

In such a situation, if the police are required to recite the familiar *Miranda* warnings before asking the whereabouts of the gun, suspects in Quarles' position might well be deterred from responding. * * * Here, had *Miranda* warnings deterred Quarles from responding to Officer Kraft's question about the whereabouts of the gun, the cost would have been something more than merely the failure to obtain evidence useful in convicting Quarles. Officer Kraft needed an answer to his question not simply to make his case against Quarles but to insure [sic] that further danger to the public did not result from the concealment of the gun in a public area.

We conclude that the need for answers to questions in a situation posing a threat to the public safety outweighs the need for the prophylactic rule protecting the Fifth Amendment's privilege against self-incrimination. We decline to place officers such as Officer Kraft in the untenable position of having to consider, often in a matter of seconds, whether it best serves society for them to ask the necessary questions without the *Miranda* warnings and render whatever probative evidence they uncover inadmissible, or for them to give the warnings in order to preserve the admissibility of evidence they might uncover but possibly damage or destroy their ability to obtain that evidence and neutralize the volatile situation confronting them.[7]

* * * The exception which we recognize today, far from complicating the thought processes and the on-the-scene judgments of police officers, will simply free them to follow their legitimate instincts when confronting situations presenting a danger to the public safety.

We hold that the Court of Appeals in this case erred in excluding the statement, "the gun is over there," and the gun because of the officer's failure to read respondent his *Miranda* rights before attempting to locate the weapon. Accordingly we hold that it also erred in excluding the

---

[7] The dissent argues that a public safety exception to *Miranda* is unnecessary because in every case an officer can simply ask the necessary questions to protect himself or the public, and then the prosecution can decline to introduce any incriminating responses at a subsequent trial. But [since the Fifth Amendment prohibits compelled self-incrimination] absent actual coercion by the officer, there is no constitutional imperative requiring the exclusion of the evidence that results from police inquiry of this kind; and we do not believe that the doctrinal underpinnings of *Miranda* require us to exclude the evidence, thus penalizing officers for asking the very questions which are the most crucial to their efforts to protect themselves and the public.

subsequent statements as illegal fruits of a *Miranda* violation.[9] We therefore reverse and remand for further proceedings not inconsistent with this opinion. * * *

JUSTICE O'CONNOR, concurring in the judgment in part and dissenting in part.

In *Miranda v. Arizona*, the Court held unconstitutional, because inherently compelled, the admission of statements derived from in-custody questioning not preceded by an explanation of the privilege against self-incrimination and the consequences of forgoing it. Today, the Court concludes that overriding considerations of public safety justify the admission of evidence—oral statements and a gun—secured without the benefit of such warnings. In so holding, the Court acknowledges that it is departing from prior precedent, and that it is "[lessening] the desirable clarity of [the *Miranda*] rule." Were the Court writing from a clean slate, I could agree with its holding. But *Miranda* is now the law and, in my view, the Court has not provided sufficient justification for departing from it or for blurring its now clear strictures. Accordingly, I would require suppression of the initial statement taken from respondent in this case. On the other hand, nothing in *Miranda* or the privilege itself requires exclusion of nontestimonial evidence derived from informal custodial interrogation, and I therefore agree with the Court that admission of the gun in evidence is proper. * * *

In my view, a "public safety" exception unnecessarily blurs the edges of the clear line heretofore established and makes *Miranda*'s requirements more difficult to understand. In some cases, police will benefit because a reviewing court will find that an exigency excused their failure to administer the required warnings. But in other cases, police will suffer because, though they thought an exigency excused their noncompliance, a reviewing court will view the "objective" circumstances differently and require exclusion of admissions thereby obtained. The end result will be a finespun new doctrine on public safety exigencies incident to custodial interrogation, complete with the hair-splitting distinctions that currently plague our Fourth Amendment jurisprudence.

The justification the Court provides for upsetting the equilibrium that has finally been achieved—that police cannot and should not balance considerations of public safety against the individual's interest in avoiding compulsory testimonial self-incrimination—really misses the critical question to be decided. *Miranda* has never been read to prohibit the police from asking questions to secure the public safety. Rather, the critical question *Miranda* addresses is who shall bear the cost of securing the

---

[9] Because we hold that there is no violation of *Miranda* in this case, we have no occasion to reach arguments made by the State and the United States as amicus curiae that the gun is admissible either because it is non-testimonial or because the police would inevitably have discovered it absent their questioning.

public safety when such questions are asked and answered: the defendant or the State. *Miranda*, for better or worse, found the resolution of that question implicit in the prohibition against compulsory self-incrimination and placed the burden on the State. When police ask custodial questions without administering the required warnings, *Miranda* quite clearly requires that the answers received be presumed compelled and that they be excluded from evidence at trial. * * *

JUSTICE MARSHALL, with whom JUSTICE BRENNAN and JUSTICE STEVENS join, dissenting. * * *

The majority's entire analysis rests on the factual assumption that the public was at risk during Quarles' interrogation. This assumption is completely in conflict with the facts as found by New York's highest court. Before the interrogation began, Quarles had been "reduced to a condition of physical powerlessness." Contrary to the majority's speculations, Quarles was not believed to have, nor did he in fact have, an accomplice to come to his rescue. When the questioning began, the arresting officers were sufficiently confident of their safety to put away their guns. As Officer Kraft acknowledged at the suppression hearing, "the situation was under control." Based on Officer Kraft's own testimony, the New York Court of Appeals found: "Nothing suggests that any of the officers was by that time concerned for his own physical safety." The Court of Appeals also determined that there was no evidence that the interrogation was prompted by the arresting officers' concern for the public's safety.

The majority attempts to slip away from these unambiguous findings of New York's highest court by proposing that danger be measured by objective facts rather than the subjective intentions of arresting officers. Though clever, this ploy was anticipated by the New York Court of Appeals: "[T]here is no evidence in the record before us that there were exigent circumstances posing a risk to the public safety . . . ." * * *

The New York court's conclusion that neither Quarles nor his missing gun posed a threat to the public's safety is amply supported by the evidence presented at the suppression hearing. Again contrary to the majority's intimations, no customers or employees were wandering about the store in danger of coming across Quarles' discarded weapon. Although the supermarket was open to the public, Quarles' arrest took place during the middle of the night when the store was apparently deserted except for the clerks at the checkout counter. The police could easily have cordoned off the store and searched for the missing gun. Had they done so, they would have found the gun forthwith. The police were well aware that Quarles had discarded his weapon somewhere near the scene of the arrest. As the State acknowledged before the New York Court of Appeals: "After Officer Kraft had handcuffed and frisked the defendant in the supermarket, he knew with a high degree of certainty that the defendant's gun was within the immediate vicinity of the encounter. He undoubtedly would have searched for it in the carton a few feet away without the defendant having looked in that direction and saying that it was there." * * *

The irony of the majority's decision is that the public's safety can be perfectly well protected without abridging the Fifth Amendment. If a bomb is about to explode or the public is otherwise imminently imperiled, the police are free to interrogate suspects without advising them of their constitutional rights. Such unconsented questioning may take place not only when police officers act on instinct but also when higher faculties lead them to believe that advising a suspect of his constitutional rights might decrease the likelihood that the suspect would reveal life-saving information. If trickery is necessary to protect the public, then the police may trick a suspect into confessing. While the Fourteenth Amendment sets limits on such behavior, nothing in the Fifth Amendment or our decision in *Miranda v. Arizona* proscribes this sort of emergency questioning. All the Fifth Amendment forbids is the introduction of coerced statements at trial.[a]

To a limited degree, the majority is correct that there is a cost associated with the Fifth Amendment's ban on introducing coerced self-incriminating statements at trial. Without a "public-safety" exception, there would be occasions when a defendant incriminated himself by revealing a threat to the public, and the State was unable to prosecute because the defendant retracted his statement after consulting with counsel and the police cannot find independent proof of guilt. Such occasions would not, however, be common. The prosecution does not always lose the use of incriminating information revealed in these situations. After consulting with counsel, a suspect may well volunteer to repeat his statement in hopes of gaining a favorable plea bargain or more lenient sentence. The majority thus overstates its case when it suggests that a police officer must necessarily choose between public safety and admissibility.

But however frequently or infrequently such cases arise, their regularity is irrelevant. The Fifth Amendment prohibits compelled self-incrimination. As the Court has explained on numerous occasions, this prohibition is the mainstay of our adversarial system of criminal justice. Not only does it protect us against the inherent unreliability of compelled testimony, but it also ensures that criminal investigations will be conducted with integrity and that the judiciary will avoid the taint of official lawlessness. The policies underlying the Fifth Amendment's

---

[a] In *Chavez v. Martinez*, 538 U.S. 760 (2003), the Court held that the Fifth Amendment is not violated until statements compelled by police interrogation are actually used in a criminal case. "Statements compelled by police interrogations of course may not be used against a defendant at trial, but it is not until their use in a criminal case that a violation of the Self-Incrimination Clause occurs."

privilege against self-incrimination are not diminished simply because testimony is compelled to protect the public's safety. The majority should not be permitted to elude the Amendment's absolute prohibition simply by calculating special costs that arise when the public's safety is at issue. Indeed, were constitutional adjudication always conducted in such an ad hoc manner, the Bill of Rights would be a most unreliable protector of individual liberties.

DICKERSON V. UNITED STATES
Supreme Court of the United States
530 U.S. 428, 120 S. Ct. 2326, 147 L. Ed. 2d 405 (2000)

CHIEF JUSTICE REHNQUIST delivered the opinion of the Court.

In *Miranda v. Arizona*, we held that certain warnings must be given before a suspect's statement made during custodial interrogation could be admitted in evidence. In the wake of that decision, Congress enacted 18 U.S.C. § 3501, which in essence laid down a rule that the admissibility of such statements should turn only on whether or not they were voluntarily made. We hold that *Miranda*, being a constitutional decision of this Court, may not be in effect overruled by an Act of Congress, and we decline to overrule *Miranda* ourselves. We therefore hold that *Miranda* and its progeny in this Court govern the admissibility of statements made during custodial interrogation in both state and federal courts.

Petitioner Dickerson was indicted for bank robbery, conspiracy to commit bank robbery, and using a firearm in the course of committing a crime of violence, all in violation of the applicable provisions of Title 18 of the United States Code. Before trial, Dickerson moved to suppress a statement he had made at a Federal Bureau of Investigation field office, on the grounds that he had not received "*Miranda* warnings" before being interrogated. The District Court granted his motion to suppress, and the Government took an interlocutory appeal to the United States Court of Appeals for the Fourth Circuit. That court, by a divided vote, reversed the District Court's suppression order. It agreed with the District Court's conclusion that petitioner had not received *Miranda* warnings before making his statement. But it went on to hold that § 3501, which in effect makes the admissibility of statements such as Dickerson's turn solely on whether they were made voluntarily, was satisfied in this case. It then concluded that our decision in *Miranda* was not a constitutional holding, and that, therefore, Congress could by statute have the final say on the question of admissibility.

Because of the importance of the questions raised by the Court of Appeals' decision, we granted certiorari, and now reverse. * * *

We begin with a brief historical account of the law governing the admission of confessions. Prior to *Miranda*, we evaluated the admissibility of a suspect's confession under a voluntariness test. * * * We have never abandoned this due process jurisprudence, and thus continue to exclude confessions that were obtained involuntarily. But our decisions in *Malloy v. Hogan* and *Miranda* changed the focus of much of the inquiry in determining the admissibility of suspects' incriminating statements. In *Malloy*, we held that the Fifth Amendment's Self-incrimination Clause is incorporated in the Due Process Clause of the Fourteenth Amendment and thus applies to the States.

In *Miranda*, we noted that the advent of modern custodial police interrogation brought with it an increased concern about confessions obtained by coercion. Because custodial police interrogation, by its very nature, isolates and pressures the individual, we stated that "[e]ven without employing brutality, the 'third degree' or [other] specific stratagems, * * * custodial interrogation exacts a heavy toll on individual liberty and trades on the weakness of individuals." We concluded that the coercion inherent in custodial interrogation blurs the line between voluntary and involuntary statements, and thus heightens the risk that an individual will not be "accorded his privilege under the Fifth Amendment . . . not to be compelled to incriminate himself." Accordingly, we laid down "concrete constitutional guidelines for law enforcement agencies and courts to follow." Those guidelines established that the admissibility in evidence of any statement given during custodial interrogation of a suspect would depend on whether the police provided the suspect with four warnings. * * *

Two years after *Miranda* was decided, Congress enacted § 3501. That section provides, in relevant part:

(a) In any criminal prosecution brought by the United States or by the District of Columbia, a confession . . . shall be admissible in evidence if it is voluntarily given. Before such confession is received in evidence, the trial judge shall, out of the presence of the jury, determine any issue as to voluntariness. If the trial judge determines that the confession was voluntarily made it shall be admitted in evidence and the trial judge shall permit the jury to hear relevant evidence on the issue of voluntariness and shall instruct the jury to give such weight to the confession as the jury feels it deserves under all the circumstances.

(b) The trial judge in determining the issue of voluntariness shall take into consideration all the circumstances surrounding the giving of the confession, including (1) the time elapsing between arrest and arraignment of the defendant making the confession, if it was made after arrest and before arraignment, (2) whether such defendant knew the nature of the offense with which he was charged or of which he was suspected at the time of making the confession, (3) whether or not such defendant was advised or knew that he was not required to make any statement and that any such statement could be used against him, (4) whether or not such defendant had been advised prior to questioning of his right to the assistance of counsel; and (5) whether or not such defendant was without the assistance of counsel when questioned and when giving such confession.

The presence or absence of any of the above-mentioned factors to be taken into consideration by the judge need not be conclusive on the issue of voluntariness of the confession.

Given § 3501's express designation of voluntariness as the touchstone of admissibility, its omission of any warning requirement, and the instruction for trial courts to consider a nonexclusive list of factors relevant to the circumstances of a confession, we agree with the Court of Appeals that Congress intended by its enactment to overrule *Miranda*. Because of the obvious conflict between our decision in *Miranda* and § 3501, we must address whether Congress has constitutional authority to thus supersede *Miranda*. If Congress has such authority, § 3501's totality-of-the-circumstances approach must prevail over *Miranda's* requirement of warnings; if not, that section must yield to *Miranda's* more specific requirements.

The law in this area is clear. This Court has supervisory authority over the federal courts, and we may use that authority to prescribe rules of evidence and procedure that are binding in those tribunals. However, the power to judicially create and enforce nonconstitutional "rules of procedure and evidence for the federal courts exists only in the absence of a relevant Act of Congress." Congress retains the ultimate authority to modify or set aside any judicially created rules of evidence and procedure that are not required by the Constitution.

But Congress may not legislatively supersede our decisions interpreting and applying the Constitution. This case therefore turns on whether the *Miranda* Court announced a constitutional rule or merely exercised its supervisory authority to regulate evidence in the absence of congressional direction. * * * Relying on the fact that we have created several exceptions to *Miranda's* warnings requirement and that we have repeatedly referred to the *Miranda* warnings as "prophylactic," and "not themselves rights protected by the Constitution," the Court of Appeals concluded that the protections announced in *Miranda* are not constitutionally required.

We disagree with the Court of Appeals' conclusion, although we concede that there is language in some of our opinions that supports the view taken by that court. But first and foremost of the factors on the other side—that *Miranda* is a constitutional decision—is that both *Miranda* and two of its companion cases applied the rule to proceedings in state courts—to wit, Arizona, California, and New York. Since that time, we have consistently applied *Miranda*'s rule to prosecutions arising in state courts. It is beyond dispute that we do not hold a supervisory power over the courts of the several States. With respect to proceedings in state courts, our "authority is limited to enforcing the commands of the United States Constitution."

The *Miranda* opinion itself begins by stating that the Court granted certiorari "to explore some facets of the problems * * * of applying the privilege against self-incrimination to in-custody interrogation, and to give concrete constitutional guidelines for law enforcement agencies and courts to follow." In fact, the majority opinion is replete with statements indicating that the majority thought it was announcing a constitutional rule. * * *

Additional support for our conclusion that *Miranda* is constitutionally based is found in the *Miranda* Court's invitation for legislative action to protect the constitutional right against coerced self-incrimination. * * * [T]he Court emphasized that * * * the Constitution would not preclude legislative solutions that differed from the prescribed *Miranda* warnings but which were "at least as effective in apprising accused persons of their right of silence and in assuring a continuous opportunity to exercise it."

The Court of Appeals also relied on the fact that we have, after our *Miranda* decision, made exceptions from its rule in cases such as *New York v. Quarles*, and *Harris v. New York*. * * * These decisions illustrate the principle—not that *Miranda* is not a constitutional rule—but that no constitutional rule is immutable. No court laying down a general rule can possibly foresee the various circumstances in which counsel will seek to apply it, and the sort of modifications represented by these cases are as much a normal part of constitutional law as the original decision.

The Court of Appeals also noted that in *Oregon v. Elstad*, we stated that "[t]he *Miranda* exclusionary rule * * * serves the Fifth Amendment and sweeps more broadly than the Fifth Amendment itself." Our decision in that case—refusing to apply the traditional "fruits" doctrine developed in Fourth Amendment cases—does not prove that *Miranda* is a nonconstitutional decision, but simply recognizes the fact that unreasonable searches under the Fourth Amendment are different from unwarned interrogation under the Fifth Amendment. * * *

The dissent argues that it is judicial overreaching for this Court to hold § 3501 unconstitutional unless we hold that the *Miranda* warnings are required by the Constitution, in the sense that nothing else will suffice to satisfy constitutional requirements. But we need not go further than *Miranda* to decide this case. In *Miranda*, the Court noted that reliance on the traditional totality-of-the-circumstances test raised a risk of overlooking an involuntary custodial confession, a risk that the Court found unacceptably great when the confession is offered in the case in chief to prove guilt. The Court therefore concluded that something more than the totality test was necessary. As discussed above, § 3501 reinstates the totality test as sufficient. Section 3501 therefore cannot be sustained if *Miranda* is to remain the law.

Whether or not we would agree with *Miranda*'s reasoning and its resulting rule, were we addressing the issue in the first instance, the principles of *stare decisis* weigh heavily against overruling it now. * * *

We do not think there is such justification for overruling *Miranda*. *Miranda* has become embedded in routine police practice to the point where the warnings have become part of our national culture. * * * While we have overruled our precedents when subsequent cases have undermined their doctrinal underpinnings, we do not believe that this has happened to the *Miranda* decision. If anything, our subsequent cases have reduced the impact of the *Miranda* rule on legitimate law enforcement while reaffirming the decision's core ruling that unwarned statements may not be used as evidence in the prosecution's case in chief.

The disadvantage of the *Miranda* rule is that statements which may be by no means involuntary, made by a defendant who is aware of his "rights," may nonetheless be excluded and a guilty defendant go free as a result. But experience suggests that the totality-of-the-circumstances test which § 3501 seeks to revive is more difficult than *Miranda* for law enforcement officers to conform to, and for courts to apply in a consistent manner. The requirement that *Miranda* warnings be given does not, of course, dispense with the voluntariness inquiry. But as we said in *Berkemer v. McCarty*, "[c]ases in which a defendant can make a colorable argument that a self-incriminating statement was 'compelled' despite the fact that the law enforcement authorities adhered to the dictates of *Miranda* are rare."

In sum, we conclude that *Miranda* announced a constitutional rule that Congress may not supersede legislatively. Following the rule of *stare decisis*, we decline to overrule *Miranda* ourselves. * * *

JUSTICE SCALIA, with whom JUSTICE THOMAS joins, dissenting. * * *

Marbury v. Madison held that an Act of Congress will not be enforced by the courts if what it prescribes violates the Constitution of the United States. That was the basis on which *Miranda* was decided. One will search today's opinion in vain, however, for a statement (surely simple enough to make) that what 18 U.S.C. § 3501 prescribes—the use at trial of a voluntary confession, even when a *Miranda* warning or its equivalent has failed to be given—violates the Constitution. The reason the statement does not appear is not only (and perhaps not so much) that it would be absurd, inasmuch as § 3501 excludes from trial precisely what the

Constitution excludes from trial, viz., compelled confessions; but also that Justices whose votes are needed to compose today's majority are on record as believing that a violation of Miranda is not a violation of the Constitution. And so, to justify today's agreed-upon result, the Court must adopt a significant new, if not entirely comprehensible, principle of constitutional law. As the Court chooses to describe that principle, statutes of Congress can be disregarded, not only when what they prescribe violates the Constitution, but when what they prescribe contradicts a decision of this Court that "announced a constitutional rule." As I shall discuss in some detail, the only thing that can possibly mean in the context of this case is that this Court has the power, not merely to apply the Constitution but to expand it, imposing what it regards as useful "prophylactic" restrictions upon Congress and the States. That is an immense and frightening antidemocratic power, and it does not exist.

It takes only a small step to bring today's opinion out of the realm of power-judging and into the mainstream of legal reasoning: The Court need only go beyond its carefully couched iterations that "*Miranda* is a constitutional decision," that "*Miranda* is constitutionally based," that *Miranda* has "constitutional underpinnings," and come out and say quite clearly: "We reaffirm today that custodial interrogation that is not preceded by *Miranda* warnings or their equivalent violates the Constitution of the United States." It cannot say that, because a majority of the Court does not believe it. The Court therefore acts in plain violation of the Constitution when it denies effect to this Act of Congress. * * *

Today's judgment converts *Miranda* from a milestone of judicial overreaching into the very Cheops' Pyramid (or perhaps the Sphinx would be a better analogue) of judicial arrogance. In imposing its Court-made code upon the States, the original opinion at least asserted that it was demanded by the Constitution. Today's decision does not pretend that it is—and yet still asserts the right to impose it against the will of the people's representatives in Congress. Far from believing that *stare decisis* compels this result, I believe we cannot allow to remain on the books even a celebrated decision—especially a celebrated decision—that has come to stand for the proposition that the Supreme Court has power to impose extraconstitutional constraints upon Congress and the States. This is not the system that was established by the Framers, or that would be established by any sane supporter of government by the people.

I dissent from today's decision, and, until § 3501 is repealed, will continue to apply it in all cases where there has been a sustainable finding that the defendant's confession was voluntary.

NOTE

On October 6, 2000, Charles Dickerson was found guilty of conspiracy, bank robbery, and a gun charge after a retrial before an Alexandria, Virginia jury. Brooke A. Masters, *Miranda Win Fails to Free Robber: Va. Jury Convicts Man on 3 Counts*, WASH. POST, Oct. 7, 2000, at B1. The jury found that Dickerson conspired with his cousin's husband, James Rochester, to rob banks and served as the getaway driver for the robbery of an Old Town Alexandria bank, but acquitted Dickerson of four other counts involving the robbery of two other banks and two related gun charges after hearing him testify that he was somewhere else at the time of these crimes. *Id.* Ironically, the incriminating statement that was the center of attention before the Supreme Court ended up being admitted at Dickerson's retrial because Dickerson's attorneys decided to have him take the stand and testify in his defense to rebut allegations made by Rochester that Dickerson was his regular "wheel man." *Id.* at B5. Because the Supreme Court has held that statements in violation of *Miranda*, while ordinarily inadmissible, can be admitted to impeach a defendant's testimony, Dickerson's statement to a detective after being told that the FBI was going to search his house ("you're going to find some dye-stained money and a silver .48 caliber gun") was admitted into evidence. *Id.*

UNITED STATES v. PATANE
Supreme Court of the United States
542 U.S. 630, 124 S. Ct. 2620, 159 L. Ed. 2d 667 (2004)

JUSTICE THOMAS announced the judgment of the Court and delivered an opinion, in which THE CHIEF JUSTICE and JUSTICE SCALIA join.

In this case we must decide whether a failure to give a suspect the warnings prescribed by *Miranda* requires suppression of the physical fruits of the suspect's unwarned but voluntary statements. * * * Because the *Miranda* rule protects against violations of the Self-Incrimination Clause, which, in turn, is not implicated by the introduction at trial of physical evidence resulting from voluntary statements, we answer the question presented in the negative.

In June 2001, respondent, Samuel Francis Patane, was arrested for harassing his ex-girlfriend, Linda O'Donnell. He was released on bond, subject to a temporary restraining order that prohibited him from contacting O'Donnell. Respondent apparently violated the restraining order by attempting to telephone O'Donnell. On June 6, 2001, Officer Tracy Fox of the Colorado Springs Police Department began to investigate the matter. On the same day, a county probation officer informed an agent of the Bureau of Alcohol, Tobacco and Firearms (ATF), that respondent, a convicted felon, illegally possessed a .40 Glock pistol. The ATF relayed this information to Detective Josh Benner, who worked closely with the ATF. Together, Detective Benner and Officer Fox proceeded to respondent's residence.

After reaching the residence and inquiring into respondent's attempts to contact O'Donnell, Officer Fox arrested respondent for violating the restraining order. Detective Benner attempted to advise respondent of his *Miranda* rights but got no further than the right to remain silent. At that point, respondent interrupted, asserting that he knew his rights, and neither officer attempted to complete the warning.[1]

Detective Benner then asked respondent about the Glock. Respondent was initially reluctant to discuss the matter, stating: "I am not sure I should tell you anything about the Glock because I don't want you to take it away from me." Detective Benner persisted, and respondent told him that the pistol was in his bedroom. Respondent then gave Detective Benner permission to retrieve the pistol. Detective Benner found the pistol and seized it.

A grand jury indicted respondent for possession of a firearm by a convicted felon, in violation of 18 U.S.C. § 922(g)(1). The District Court granted respondent's motion to suppress the firearm, reasoning that the officers lacked probable cause to arrest respondent for violating the restraining order. It therefore declined to rule on respondent's alternative argument that the gun should be suppressed as the fruit of an unwarned statement.

The Court of Appeals reversed the District Court's ruling with respect to probable cause but affirmed the suppression order on respondent's alternative theory. * * * We granted certiorari.

As we explain below, the *Miranda* rule is a prophylactic employed to protect against violations of the Self-Incrimination Clause. The Self-Incrimination Clause, however, is not implicated by the admission into evidence of the physical fruit of a voluntary statement. Accordingly, there is no justification for extending the *Miranda* rule to this context. And just as the Self-Incrimination Clause primarily focuses on the criminal trial, so too does the *Miranda* rule. The *Miranda* rule is not a code of police conduct, and police do not violate the Constitution (or even the *Miranda* rule, for that matter) by mere failures to warn. For this reason, the exclusionary rule * * * does not apply. * * *

The Self-Incrimination Clause provides: "No person ... shall be compelled in any criminal case to be a witness against himself." We need not decide here the precise boundaries of the Clause's protection. For present purposes, it suffices to note that the core protection afforded by the Self-Incrimination Clause is a prohibition on compelling a criminal defendant to testify against himself at trial. The Clause cannot be violated

---

[1] The Government concedes that respondent's answers to subsequent on-the-scene questioning are inadmissible at trial under *Miranda* despite the partial warning and respondent's assertions that he knew his rights.

by the introduction of nontestimonial evidence obtained as a result of voluntary statements.

To be sure, the Court has recognized and applied several prophylactic rules designed to protect the core privilege against self-incrimination. For example, although the text of the Self-Incrimination Clause at least suggests that "its coverage [is limited to] compelled testimony that is used against the defendant in the trial itself," potential suspects may, at times, assert the privilege in proceedings in which answers might be used to incriminate them in a subsequent criminal case. We have explained that "[t]he natural concern which underlies [these] decisions is that an inability to protect the right at one stage of a proceeding may make its invocation useless at a later stage."

Similarly, in *Miranda*, the Court concluded that the possibility of coercion inherent in custodial interrogations unacceptably raises the risk that a suspect's privilege against self-incrimination might be violated. To protect against this danger, the *Miranda* rule creates a presumption of coercion, in the absence of specific warnings, that is generally irrebuttable for purposes of the prosecution's case in chief.

But because these prophylactic rules * * * necessarily sweep beyond the actual protections of the Self-Incrimination Clause, any further extension of these rules must be justified by its necessity for the protection of the actual right against compelled self-incrimination. Indeed, at times the Court has declined to extend *Miranda* even where it has perceived a need to protect the privilege against self-incrimination. * * *

[N]othing in *Dickerson*, including its characterization of *Miranda* as announcing a constitutional rule, changes any of these observations. Indeed, in *Dickerson*, the Court specifically noted that the Court's "subsequent cases have reduced the impact of the *Miranda* rule on legitimate law enforcement while reaffirming [*Miranda*]'s core ruling that unwarned statements may not be used as evidence in the prosecution's case in chief." This description of *Miranda*, especially the emphasis on the use of "unwarned statements . . . in the prosecution's case in chief," makes clear our continued focus on the protections of the Self-Incrimination Clause. * * * In short, nothing in *Dickerson* calls into question our continued insistence that the closest possible fit be maintained between the Self-Incrimination Clause and any rule designed to protect it.

* * * *Dickerson*'s characterization of *Miranda* as a constitutional rule does not lessen the need to maintain the closest possible fit between the Self-Incrimination Clause and any judge-made rule designed to protect it. And there is no such fit here. Introduction of the nontestimonial fruit of a voluntary statement, such as respondent's Glock, does not implicate the Self-Incrimination Clause. The admission of such fruit presents no risk that a defendant's coerced statements (however defined) will be used

against him at a criminal trial. In any case, "[t]he exclusion of unwarned statements ... is a complete and sufficient remedy" for any perceived *Miranda* violation. There is simply no need to extend (and therefore no justification for extending) the prophylactic rule of *Miranda* to this context. * * *

Accordingly, we reverse the judgment of the Court of Appeals and remand the case for further proceedings.

It is so ordered.

JUSTICE SOUTER, with whom JUSTICE STEVENS and JUSTICE GINSBURG join, dissenting.

The plurality repeatedly says that the Fifth Amendment does not address the admissibility of nontestimonial evidence, an overstatement that is beside the point. The issue actually presented today is whether courts should apply the fruit of the poisonous tree doctrine lest we create an incentive for the police to omit *Miranda* warnings, before custodial interrogation. In closing their eyes to the consequences of giving an evidentiary advantage to those who ignore *Miranda*, the plurality adds an important inducement for interrogators to ignore the rule in that case.

Miranda rested on insight into the inherently coercive character of custodial interrogation and the inherently difficult exercise of assessing the voluntariness of any confession resulting from it. Unless the police give the prescribed warnings meant to counter the coercive atmosphere, a custodial confession is inadmissible, there being no need for the previous time-consuming and difficult enquiry into voluntariness. That inducement to forestall involuntary statements and troublesome issues of fact can only atrophy if we turn around and recognize an evidentiary benefit when an unwarned statement leads investigators to tangible evidence. There is, of course, a price for excluding evidence, but the Fifth Amendment is worth a price, and in the absence of a very good reason, the logic of *Miranda* should be followed: a *Miranda* violation raises a presumption of coercion, and the Fifth Amendment privilege against compelled self-incrimination extends to the exclusion of derivative evidence. * * *

There is no way to read this case except as an unjustifiable invitation to law enforcement officers to flout *Miranda* when there may be physical evidence to be gained. * * * I respectfully dissent.

[JUSTICE KENNEDY's concurring opinion, in which JUSTICE O'CONNOR joined, and JUSTICE BREYER's dissenting opinion have been omitted.]

OREGON v. ELSTAD
Supreme Court of the United States
470 U.S. 298, 105 S. Ct. 1285, 84 L. Ed. 2d 222 (1985)

JUSTICE O'CONNOR delivered the opinion of the Court.

This case requires us to decide whether an initial failure of law enforcement officers to administer the warnings required by *Miranda v. Arizona*, without more, "taints" subsequent admissions made after a suspect has been fully advised of and has waived his *Miranda* rights. Respondent, Michael James Elstad, was convicted of burglary by an Oregon trial court. The Oregon Court of Appeals reversed, holding that respondent's signed confession, although voluntary, was rendered inadmissible by a prior remark made in response to questioning without benefit of *Miranda* warnings. We granted certiorari, and we now reverse.

In December 1981, the home of Mr. and Mrs. Gilbert Gross, in the town of Salem, Polk County, Ore., was burglarized. Missing were art objects and furnishings valued at $150,000. A witness to the burglary contacted the Polk County Sheriff's Office, implicating respondent Michael Elstad, an 18-year-old neighbor and friend of the Gross' teenage son. Thereupon, Officers Burke and McAllister went to the home of respondent Elstad, with a warrant for his arrest. Elstad's mother answered the door. She led the officers to her son's room where he lay on his bed, clad in shorts and listening to his stereo. The officers asked him to get dressed and to accompany them into the living room. Officer McAllister asked respondent's mother to step into the kitchen, where he explained that they had a warrant for her son's arrest for the burglary of a neighbor's residence. Officer Burke remained with Elstad in the living room. He later testified:

> I sat down with Mr. Elstad and I asked him if he was aware of why Detective McAllister and myself were there to talk with him. He stated no, he had no idea why we were there. I then asked him if he knew a person by the name of Gross, and he said yes, he did, and also added that he heard that there was a robbery at the Gross house. And at that point I told Mr. Elstad that I felt he was involved in that, and he looked at me and stated, "Yes, I was there."

The officers then escorted Elstad to the back of the patrol car. * * * Elstad was transported to the Sheriff's headquarters and approximately one hour later, Officers Burke and McAllister joined him in McAllister's office. McAllister then advised respondent for the first time of his *Miranda* rights, reading from a standard card. Respondent indicated he understood his rights, and, having these rights in mind, wished to speak with the officers. Elstad gave a full statement, explaining that he had known that the Gross family was out of town and had been paid to lead several acquaintances to the Gross residence and show them how to gain entry through a defective sliding glass door. The statement was typed, reviewed by respondent, read back to him for correction, initialed and signed by Elstad and both officers. As an afterthought, Elstad added and initialed the sentence, "After leaving the house Robby & I went back to [the] van & Robby handed me a small bag of grass." Respondent concedes that the officers made no threats or promises either at his residence or at the Sheriff's office.

Respondent was charged with first-degree burglary. * * * Respondent moved at once to suppress his oral statement and signed confession. He contended that the statement he made in response to questioning at his house "let the cat out of the bag," and tainted the subsequent confession as "fruit of the poisonous tree" * * *. The judge ruled that the statement, "I was there," had to be excluded because the defendant had not been advised of his *Miranda* rights. The written confession taken after Elstad's arrival at the Sheriff's office, however, was admitted in evidence. * * * Elstad was found guilty of burglary in the first degree.

* * * This Court granted certiorari to consider the question whether the Self-Incrimination Clause of the Fifth Amendment requires the suppression of a confession, made after proper *Miranda* warnings and a valid waiver of rights, solely because the police had obtained an earlier voluntary but unwarned admission from the defendant.

The arguments advanced in favor of suppression of respondent's written confession rely heavily on metaphor. One metaphor, familiar from the Fourth Amendment context, would require that respondent's confession, regardless of its integrity, voluntariness, and probative value, be suppressed as the "tainted fruit of the poisonous tree" of the *Miranda* violation. A second metaphor questions whether a confession can be truly voluntary once the "cat is out of the bag." Taken out of context, each of these metaphors can be misleading. They should not be used to obscure fundamental differences between the role of the Fourth Amendment exclusionary rule and the function of *Miranda* in guarding against the prosecutorial use of compelled statements as prohibited by the Fifth Amendment. * * *

Respondent's contention that his confession was tainted by the earlier failure of the police to provide *Miranda* warnings and must be excluded as "fruit of the poisonous tree" assumes the existence of a constitutional violation. This figure of speech is drawn from *Wong Sun v. United States*, in which the Court held that evidence and witnesses discovered as a result of a search in violation of the Fourth Amendment must be excluded from evidence. The *Wong Sun* doctrine applies as well when the fruit of the Fourth Amendment violation is a confession. * * *

But * * * a procedural *Miranda* violation differs in significant respects from violations of the Fourth Amendment, which have traditionally mandated a broad application of the "fruits" doctrine. The purpose of the Fourth Amendment exclusionary rule is to deter unreasonable searches, no matter how probative their fruits. * * * Where a Fourth Amendment violation "taints" the confession, * * * the prosecution must show a sufficient break in events to undermine the inference that the confession was caused by the Fourth Amendment violation.

The *Miranda* exclusionary rule, however, serves the Fifth Amendment and sweeps more broadly than the Fifth Amendment itself. It may be triggered even in the absence of a Fifth Amendment violation. The Fifth Amendment prohibits use by the prosecution in its case in chief only of compelled testimony. Failure to administer *Miranda* warnings creates a presumption of compulsion. Consequently, unwarned statements that are otherwise voluntary within the meaning of the Fifth Amendment must nevertheless be excluded from evidence under *Miranda*. * * *

But the *Miranda* presumption, though irrebuttable for purposes of the prosecution's case in chief, does not require that the statements and their fruits be discarded as inherently tainted. Despite the fact that patently voluntary statements taken in violation of *Miranda* must be excluded from the prosecution's case, the presumption of coercion does not bar their use for impeachment purposes on cross-examination.

* * * It is an unwarranted extension of *Miranda* to hold that a simple failure to administer the warnings, unaccompanied by any actual coercion or other circumstances calculated to undermine the suspect's ability to exercise his free will, so taints the investigatory process that a subsequent voluntary and informed waiver is ineffective for some indeterminate period. Though *Miranda* requires that the unwarned admission must be suppressed, the admissibility of any subsequent statement should turn in these circumstances solely on whether it is knowingly and voluntarily made.

* * * The failure of police to administer *Miranda* warnings does not mean that the statements received have actually been coerced, but only that courts will presume the privilege against compulsory self-incrimination has not been intelligently exercised. * * * In these circumstances, a careful and thorough administration of *Miranda* warnings serves to cure the condition that rendered the unwarned statement inadmissible. The warning conveys the relevant information and thereafter the suspect's choice whether to exercise his privilege to remain silent should ordinarily be viewed as an "act of free will."

The Oregon court nevertheless identified a subtle form of lingering compulsion, the psychological impact of the suspect's conviction that he has let the cat out of the bag and, in so doing, has sealed his own fate. But endowing the psychological effects of voluntary unwarned admissions with constitutional implications would, practically speaking, disable the police from obtaining the suspect's informed cooperation even when the official coercion proscribed by the Fifth Amendment played no part in either his warned or unwarned confessions. * * *

This Court has never held that the psychological impact of voluntary disclosure of a guilty secret qualifies as state compulsion or compromises the voluntariness of a subsequent informed waiver. * * * When neither the initial nor the subsequent admission is coerced, little justification exists for permitting the highly probative evidence of a voluntary confession to be irretrievably lost to the factfinder.

* * * We must conclude that, absent deliberately coercive or improper tactics in obtaining the initial statement, the mere fact that a suspect has made an unwarned admission does not warrant a presumption of compulsion. A subsequent administration of *Miranda* warnings to a suspect who has given a voluntary but unwarned statement ordinarily should suffice to remove the conditions that precluded admission of the earlier statement. In such circumstances, the finder of fact may reasonably conclude that the suspect made a rational and intelligent choice whether to waive or invoke his rights.

Though belated, the reading of respondent's rights was undeniably complete. McAllister testified that he read the *Miranda* warnings aloud from a printed card and recorded Elstad's responses. There is no question that respondent knowingly and voluntarily waived his right to remain silent before he described his participation in the burglary. It is also beyond dispute that respondent's earlier remark was voluntary, within the meaning of the Fifth Amendment. Neither the environment nor the manner of either "interrogation" was coercive. The initial conversation took place at midday, in the living room area of respondent's own home, with his mother in the kitchen area, a few steps away. Although in retrospect the officers testified that respondent was then in custody, at the time he made his statement he had not been informed that he was under arrest. The arresting officers' testimony indicates that the brief stop in the living room before proceeding to the station house was not to interrogate the suspect but to notify his mother of the reason for his arrest.

The State has conceded the issue of custody and thus we must assume that Burke breached *Miranda* procedures in failing to administer *Miranda* warnings before initiating the discussion in the living room. * * * Whatever the reason for Burke's oversight, the incident had none of the earmarks of coercion. Nor did the officers exploit the unwarned admission to pressure respondent into waiving his right to remain silent.

Respondent, however, has argued that he was unable to give a fully informed waiver of his rights because he was unaware that his prior statement could not be used against him. Respondent suggests that Officer McAllister, to cure this deficiency, should have added an additional warning to those given him at the Sheriff's office. Such a requirement is neither practicable nor constitutionally necessary. In many cases, a breach of *Miranda* procedures may not be identified as such until long after full *Miranda* warnings are administered and a valid confession obtained. The standard *Miranda* warnings explicitly inform the suspect of his right to consult a lawyer before speaking. Police officers are ill-equipped to pinch-hit for counsel, construing the murky and difficult questions of when "custody" begins or whether a given unwarned statement will ultimately be held admissible.

* * * The Court today in no way retreats from the bright-line rule of *Miranda*. * * * [But] there is no warrant for presuming coercive effect where the suspect's initial inculpatory statement, though technically in violation of *Miranda*, was voluntary. The relevant inquiry is whether, in fact, the second statement was also voluntarily made. As in any such inquiry, the finder of fact must examine the surrounding circumstances and the entire course of police conduct with respect to the suspect in evaluating the voluntariness of his statements. The fact that a suspect chooses to speak after being informed of his rights is, of course, highly probative. We find that the dictates of *Miranda* and the goals of the Fifth Amendment proscription against use of compelled testimony are fully satisfied in the circumstances of this case by barring use of the unwarned statement in the case in chief. No further purpose is served by imputing "taint" to subsequent statements obtained pursuant to a voluntary and knowing waiver. We hold today that a suspect who has once responded to unwarned yet uncoercive questioning is not thereby disabled from waiving his rights and confessing after he has been given the requisite *Miranda* warnings.

The judgment of the Court of Appeals of Oregon is reversed, and the case is remanded for further proceedings not inconsistent with this opinion.

It is so ordered.

JUSTICE BRENNAN, with whom JUSTICE MARSHALL joins, dissenting.

* * * [T]he Court has engaged of late in a studied campaign to strip the *Miranda* decision piecemeal and to undermine the rights *Miranda* sought to secure. Today's decision not only extends this effort a further step, but delivers a potentially crippling blow to *Miranda* and the ability of courts to safeguard the rights of persons accused of crime. For at least with respect to successive confessions, the Court today appears to strip remedies for *Miranda* violations of the "fruit of the poisonous tree" doctrine prohibiting the use of evidence presumptively derived from official illegality. * * *

The threshold question is this: What effect should an admission or confession of guilt obtained in violation of an accused's *Miranda* rights be presumed to have upon the voluntariness of subsequent confessions that are preceded by *Miranda* warnings? Relying on the "cat out of the bag" analysis * * *, the Oregon Court of Appeals held that the first confession presumptively taints subsequent confessions in such circumstances. * * *

The Court today sweeps aside this common-sense approach as "speculative" reasoning, adopting instead a rule that "the psychological impact of voluntary disclosure of a guilty secret" neither "qualifies as state compulsion" nor "compromises the voluntariness" of subsequent confessions. So long as a suspect receives the usual *Miranda* warnings before further interrogation, the Court reasons, the fact that he "is free to exercise his own volition in deciding whether or not to make" further confessions "ordinarily" is a sufficient "cure" and serves to break any causal connection between the illegal confession and subsequent statements.

The Court's marble-palace psychoanalysis is tidy, but it flies in the face of our own precedents, demonstrates a startling unawareness of the realities of police interrogation, and is completely out of tune with the experience of state and federal courts over the last 20 years. * * *

This Court has had long experience with the problem of confessions obtained after an earlier confession has been illegally secured. Subsequent confessions in these circumstances are not *per se* inadmissible, but the prosecution must demonstrate facts "sufficient to insulate the [subsequent] statement from the effect of all that went before." * * *

One of the factors that can vitiate the voluntariness of a subsequent confession is the hopeless feeling of an accused that he has nothing to lose by repeating his confession, even where the circumstances that rendered his first confession illegal have been removed. As the Court observed in *United States v. Barker*:

> [A]fter an accused has once let the cat out of the bag by confessing, no matter what the inducement, he is never thereafter free of the psychological and practical disadvantages of having confessed. He can never get the cat back in the bag. The secret is out for good. In such a sense, a later confession always may be looked upon as a fruit of the first.

* * * Although we have * * * rejected a *per se* rule forbidding the introduction of subsequent statements in these circumstances, we have emphasized that the psychological impact of admissions and confessions of criminal guilt nevertheless can have a decisive impact in undermining the voluntariness of a suspect's responses to continued police interrogation and must be accounted for in determining their admissibility. As Justice Harlan explained in his separate *Darwin* opinion: "A principal reason why a suspect might make a second or third confession is simply that, having already confessed once or twice, he might think he has little to lose by repetition." * * *

The correct approach, administered for almost 20 years by most courts with no untoward results, is to presume that an admission or confession obtained in violation of *Miranda* taints a subsequent confession unless the prosecution can show that the taint is so attenuated as to justify admission of the subsequent confession. * * *

The Court clearly errs in suggesting that suppression of the "unwarned admission" alone will provide meaningful deterrence. The experience of lower courts demonstrates that the police frequently have refused to comply with *Miranda* precisely in order to obtain incriminating statements that will undermine the voluntariness of the accused's decision to speak again once he has received the usual warnings.

* * * How can the Court possibly expect the authorities to obey *Miranda* when they have every incentive now to interrogate suspects without warnings or an effective waiver, knowing that the fruits of such interrogations "ordinarily" will be admitted, that an admissible subsequent confession "ordinarily" can be obtained simply by reciting the *Miranda* warnings shortly after the first has been procured and asking the accused to repeat himself, and that unless the accused can demonstrate otherwise his confession will be viewed as an "act of free will" in response to "legitimate law enforcement activity"? By condoning such a result, the Court today encourages practices that threaten to reduce *Miranda* to a mere "form of words," and it is shocking that the Court nevertheless disingenuously purports that it "in no way retreats" from the *Miranda* safeguards. * * * I dissent.

[JUSTICE STEVENS' dissenting opinion has been omitted.]

MISSOURI V. SEIBERT
Supreme Court of the United States
542 U.S. 600, 124 S. Ct. 2601, 159 L. Ed. 2d 643 (2004)

JUSTICE SOUTER announced the judgment of the Court and delivered the opinion, in which JUSTICE STEVENS, JUSTICE GINSBURG, and JUSTICE BREYER join.

This case tests a police protocol for custodial interrogation that calls for giving no warnings of the rights to silence and counsel until interrogation has produced a confession. Although such a statement is generally inadmissible, since taken in violation of *Miranda v. Arizona*, the interrogating officer follows it with *Miranda* warnings and then leads the suspect to cover the same ground a second time. The question here is the admissibility of the repeated statement. Because this midstream recitation of warnings after interrogation and unwarned confession could not effectively comply with *Miranda's* constitutional requirement, we hold that a statement repeated after a warning in such circumstances is inadmissible.

Respondent Patrice Seibert's 12-year-old son Jonathan had cerebral palsy, and when he died in his sleep she feared charges of neglect because of bedsores on his body. In her presence, two of her teenage sons and two of their friends devised a plan to conceal the facts surrounding Jonathan's death by incinerating his body in the course of burning the family's mobile home, in which they planned to leave Donald Rector, a mentally ill teenager living with the family, to avoid any appearance that Jonathan had been unattended. Seibert's son Darian and a friend set the fire, and Donald died.

Five days later, the police awakened Seibert at 3 a.m. at a hospital where Darian was being treated for burns. In arresting her, Officer Kevin Clinton followed instructions from Rolla, Missouri, Officer Richard Hanrahan that he refrain from giving *Miranda* warnings. After Seibert had been taken to the police station and left alone in an interview room for 15 to 20 minutes, Officer Hanrahan questioned her without *Miranda* warnings for 30 to 40 minutes, squeezing her arm and repeating "Donald was also to die in his sleep." After Seibert finally admitted she knew Donald was meant to die in the fire, she was given a 20-minute coffee and cigarette break. Officer Hanrahan then turned on a tape recorder, gave Seibert the *Miranda* warnings, and obtained a signed waiver of rights from her. He resumed the questioning with "Ok, 'trice, we've been talking for a little while about what happened on Wednesday the twelfth, haven't we?" and confronted her with her prewarning statements:

Hanrahan: "Now, in discussion you told us, you told us that there was a[n] understanding about Donald."

Seibert: "Yes."

Hanrahan: "Did that take place earlier that morning?"

Seibert: "Yes."

Hanrahan: "And what was the understanding about Donald?"

Seibert: "If they could get him out of the trailer, to take him out of the trailer."

Hanrahan: "And if they couldn't?"

Seibert: "I, I never even thought about it. I just figured they would."

Hanrahan: " 'Trice, didn't you tell me that he was supposed to die in his sleep?"

Seibert: "If that would happen, 'cause he was on that new medicine, you know. . . ."

Hanrahan: "The Prozac? And it makes him sleepy. So he was supposed to die in his sleep?"

Seibert: "Yes."

After being charged with first-degree murder for her role in Donald's death, Seibert sought to exclude both her prewarning and postwarning statements. At the suppression hearing, Officer Hanrahan testified that he made a "conscious decision" to withhold *Miranda* warnings, thus resorting to an interrogation technique he had been taught: question first, then give the warnings, and then repeat the question "until I get the answer that she's already provided once." He acknowledged that Seibert's ultimate statement was "largely a repeat of information * * * obtained" prior to the warning.

The trial court suppressed the prewarning statement but admitted the responses given after the *Miranda* recitation. A jury convicted Seibert of second-degree murder. On appeal, the Missouri Court of Appeals affirmed, treating this case as indistinguishable from *Oregon v. Elstad*.

The Supreme Court of Missouri reversed, holding that "[i]n the circumstances here, where the interrogation was nearly continuous, * * * the second statement, clearly the product of the invalid first statement, should have been suppressed." * * *

We granted certiorari, to resolve a split in the Courts of Appeals. We now affirm.

In *Miranda*, we * * * conditioned the admissibility at trial of any custodial confession on warning a suspect of his rights: failure to give the prescribed warnings and obtain a waiver of rights before custodial questioning generally requires exclusion of any statements obtained. * * *

The technique of interrogating in successive, unwarned and warned phases raises a new challenge to *Miranda*. Although we have no statistics on the frequency of this practice, it is not confined to Rolla, Missouri. An officer of that police department testified that the strategy of withholding *Miranda* warnings until after interrogating and drawing out a confession was promoted not only by his own department, but by a national police training organization and other departments in which he had worked. * * * The upshot of all this advice is a question-first practice of some popularity, as one can see from the reported cases describing its use, sometimes in obedience to departmental policy.

* * * The object of question-first is to render *Miranda* warnings ineffective by waiting for a particularly opportune time to give them, after the suspect has already confessed.

* * * [I]t would be absurd to think that mere recitation of the litany suffices to satisfy *Miranda* in every conceivable circumstance. "The inquiry is simply whether the warnings reasonably 'conve[y] to [a suspect] his rights as required by *Miranda*.'" The threshold issue when interrogators question first and warn later is thus whether it would be reasonable to find

that in these circumstances the warnings could function "effectively" as *Miranda* requires. Could the warnings effectively advise the suspect that he had a real choice about giving an admissible statement at that juncture? Could they reasonably convey that he could choose to stop talking even if he had talked earlier? For unless the warnings could place a suspect who has just been interrogated in a position to make such an informed choice, there is no practical justification for accepting the formal warnings as compliance with *Miranda*, or for treating the second stage of interrogation as distinct from the first, unwarned and inadmissible segment.[4]

* * * By any objective measure, applied to circumstances exemplified here, it is likely that if the interrogators employ the technique of withholding warnings until after interrogation succeeds in eliciting a confession, the warnings will be ineffective in preparing the suspect for successive interrogation, close in time and similar in content. After all, the reason that question-first is catching on is as obvious as its manifest purpose, which is to get a confession the suspect would not make if he understood his rights at the outset; the sensible underlying assumption is that with one confession in hand before the warnings, the interrogator can count on getting its duplicate, with trifling additional trouble. Upon hearing warnings only in the aftermath of interrogation and just after making a confession, a suspect would hardly think he had a genuine right to remain silent, let alone persist in so believing once the police began to lead him over the same ground again. A more likely reaction on a suspect's part would be perplexity about the reason for discussing rights at that point, bewilderment being an unpromising frame of mind for knowledgeable decision. What is worse, telling a suspect that "anything you say can and will be used against you," without expressly excepting the statement just given, could lead to an entirely reasonable inference that what he has just said will be used, with subsequent silence being of no avail. Thus, when *Miranda* warnings are inserted in the midst of coordinated and continuing interrogation, they are likely to mislead and "depriv[e] a defendant of knowledge essential to his ability to understand the nature of his rights and the consequences of abandoning them." * * *

---

[4] Respondent Seibert argues that her second confession should be excluded from evidence under the doctrine known by the metaphor of the "fruit of the poisonous tree," developed in the Fourth Amendment context in *Wong Sun v. United States*: evidence otherwise admissible but discovered as a result of an earlier violation is excluded as tainted, lest the law encourage future violations. But the Court in *Elstad* rejected the *Wong Sun* fruits doctrine for analyzing the admissibility of a subsequent warned confession following "an initial failure . . . to administer the warnings required by *Miranda*." * * * *Elstad* held that "a suspect who has once responded to unwarned yet uncoercive questioning is not thereby disabled from waiving his rights and confessing after he has been given the requisite *Miranda* warnings." In a sequential confession case, clarity is served if the later confession is approached by asking whether in the circumstances the *Miranda* warnings given could reasonably be found effective. If yes, a court can take up the standard issues of voluntary waiver and voluntary statement; if no, the subsequent statement is inadmissible for want of adequate *Miranda* warnings, because the earlier and later statements are realistically seen as parts of a single, unwarned sequence of questioning.

Missouri argues that a confession repeated at the end of an interrogation sequence envisioned in a question-first strategy is admissible on the authority of *Oregon v. Elstad*, but the argument disfigures that case. * * *

The contrast between *Elstad* and this case reveals a series of relevant facts that bear on whether *Miranda* warnings delivered midstream could be effective enough to accomplish their object: the completeness and detail of the questions and answers in the first round of interrogation, the overlapping content of the two statements, the timing and setting of the first and the second, the continuity of police personnel, and the degree to which the interrogator's questions treated the second round as continuous with the first. In *Elstad*, it was not unreasonable to see the occasion for questioning at the station house as presenting a markedly different experience from the short conversation at home; since a reasonable person in the suspect's shoes could have seen the station house questioning as a new and distinct experience, the *Miranda* warnings could have made sense as presenting a genuine choice whether to follow up on the earlier admission.

At the opposite extreme are the facts here, which by any objective measure reveal a police strategy adapted to undermine the *Miranda* warnings.[6] The unwarned interrogation was conducted in the station house, and the questioning was systematic, exhaustive, and managed with psychological skill. When the police were finished there was little, if anything, of incriminating potential left unsaid. The warned phase of questioning proceeded after a pause of only 15 to 20 minutes, in the same place as the unwarned segment When the same officer who had conducted the first phase recited the *Miranda* warnings, he said nothing to counter the probable misimpression that the advice that anything Seibert said could be used against her also applied to the details of the inculpatory statement previously elicited. In particular, the police did not advise that her prior statement could not be used. Nothing was said or done to dispel the oddity of warning about legal rights to silence and counsel right after the police had led her through a systematic interrogation, and any uncertainty on her part about a right to stop talking about matters previously discussed would only have been aggravated by the way Officer Hanrahan set the scene by saying "we've been talking for a little while about what happened on Wednesday the twelfth, haven't we?" The impression that the further questioning was a mere continuation of the earlier questions and responses was fostered by references back to the confession already given. It would have been reasonable to regard the two sessions as parts of a continuum, in which it would have been unnatural to

---

[6] Because the intent of the officer will rarely be as candidly admitted as it was here (even as it is likely to determine the conduct of the interrogation), the focus is on facts apart from intent that show the question-first tactic at work.

refuse to repeat at the second stage what had been said before. These circumstances must be seen as challenging the comprehensibility and efficacy of the *Miranda* warnings to the point that a reasonable person in the suspect's shoes would not have understood them to convey a message that she retained a choice about continuing to talk.

* * * Because the question-first tactic effectively threatens to thwart *Miranda*'s purpose of reducing the risk that a coerced confession would be admitted, and because the facts here do not reasonably support a conclusion that the warnings given could have served their purpose, Seibert's postwarning statements are inadmissible. The judgment of the Supreme Court of Missouri is affirmed.

It is so ordered.

JUSTICE BREYER, concurring.

In my view, the following simple rule should apply to the two-stage interrogation technique: Courts should exclude the "fruits" of the initial unwarned questioning unless the failure to warn was in good faith. I believe this is a sound and workable approach to the problem this case presents. Prosecutors and judges have long understood how to apply the "fruits" approach, which they use in other areas of law. And in the workaday world of criminal law enforcement the administrative simplicity of the familiar has significant advantages over a more complex exclusionary rule.

I believe the plurality's approach in practice will function as a "fruits" test. The truly "effective" *Miranda* warnings on which the plurality insists, will occur only when certain circumstances—a lapse in time, a change in location or interrogating officer, or a shift in the focus of the questioning—intervene between the unwarned questioning and any postwarning statement.

I consequently join the plurality's opinion in full. I also agree with Justice Kennedy's opinion insofar as it is consistent with this approach and makes clear that a good-faith exception applies.

JUSTICE KENNEDY, concurring in the judgment.

The interrogation technique used in this case is designed to circumvent *Miranda v. Arizona*. It undermines the *Miranda* warning and obscures its meaning. The plurality opinion is correct to conclude that statements obtained through the use of this technique are inadmissible. Although I agree with much in the careful and convincing opinion for the plurality, my approach does differ in some respects, requiring this separate statement. * * *

In my view, *Elstad* was correct in its reasoning and its result. *Elstad* reflects a balanced and pragmatic approach to enforcement of the *Miranda* warning. An officer may not realize that a suspect is in custody and warnings are required. The officer may not plan to question the suspect or may be waiting for a more appropriate time. Skilled investigators often interview suspects multiple times, and good police work may involve referring to prior statements to test their veracity or to refresh recollection. In light of these realities it would be extravagant to treat the presence of one statement that cannot be admitted under *Miranda* as sufficient reason to prohibit subsequent statements preceded by a proper warning. * * *

This case presents different considerations. The police used a two-step questioning technique based on a deliberate violation of *Miranda*. The *Miranda* warning was withheld to obscure both the practical and legal significance of the admonition when finally given.

* * * When an interrogator uses this deliberate, two-step strategy, predicated upon violating *Miranda* during an extended interview, postwarning statements that are related to the substance of prewarning statements must be excluded absent specific, curative steps.

The plurality concludes that whenever a two-stage interview occurs, admissibility of the postwarning statement should depend on "whether [the] *Miranda* warnings delivered midstream could have been effective enough to accomplish their object" given the specific facts of the case. This test envisions an objective inquiry from the perspective of the suspect, and applies in the case of both intentional and unintentional two-stage interrogations. In my view, this test cuts too broadly. *Miranda's* clarity is one of its strengths, and a multifactor test that applies to every two-stage interrogation may serve to undermine that clarity. I would apply a narrower test applicable only in the infrequent case, such as we have here, in which the two-step interrogation technique was used in a calculated way to undermine the *Miranda* warning.

The admissibility of postwarning statements should continue to be governed by the principles of *Elstad* unless the deliberate two-step strategy was employed. If the deliberate two-step strategy has been used, postwarning statements that are related to the substance of prewarning statements must be excluded unless curative measures are taken before the postwarning statement is made. Curative measures should be designed to ensure that a reasonable person in the suspect's situation would understand the import and effect of the *Miranda* warning and of the *Miranda* waiver. For example, a substantial break in time and circumstances between the prewarning statement and the *Miranda* warning may suffice in most circumstances, as it allows the accused to distinguish the two contexts and appreciate that the interrogation has taken a new turn. Alternatively, an additional warning that explains the likely inadmissibility of the prewarning custodial statement may be sufficient. No curative steps were taken in this case, however, so the postwarning statements are inadmissible and the conviction cannot stand.

For these reasons, I concur in the judgment of the Court.

JUSTICE O'CONNOR, with whom the CHIEF JUSTICE, JUSTICE SCALIA, and JUSTICE THOMAS join, dissenting.

The plurality devours *Oregon v. Elstad*, even as it accuses petitioner's argument of "disfigur[ing]" that decision. I believe that we are bound by *Elstad* to reach a different result, and I would vacate the judgment of the Supreme Court of Missouri.

On two preliminary questions I am in full agreement with the plurality. First, the plurality appropriately follows *Elstad* in concluding that Seibert's statement cannot be held inadmissible under a "fruit of the poisonous tree" theory. Second, the plurality correctly declines to focus its analysis on the subjective intent of the interrogating officer. * * *

Although the analysis the plurality ultimately espouses examines the same facts and circumstances that a "fruits" analysis would consider (such as the lapse of time between the two interrogations and change of questioner or location), it does so for entirely different reasons. The fruits analysis would examine those factors because they are relevant to the balance of deterrence value versus the "drastic and socially costly course" of excluding reliable evidence. The plurality, by contrast, looks to those factors to inform the psychological judgment regarding whether the suspect has been informed effectively of her right to remain silent. The analytical underpinnings of the two approaches are thus entirely distinct, and they should not be conflated just because they function similarly in practice.

The plurality's rejection of an intent-based test is also, in my view, correct. Freedom from compulsion lies at the heart of the Fifth Amendment, and requires us to assess whether a suspect's decision to speak truly was voluntary. Because voluntariness is a matter of the suspect's state of mind, we focus our analysis on the way in which suspects experience interrogation.

Thoughts kept inside a police officer's head cannot affect that experience. * * * A suspect who experienced exactly the same interrogation as Seibert, save for a difference in the undivulged, subjective intent of the interrogating officer when he failed to give *Miranda* warnings, would not experience the interrogation any differently.

* * * [R]ecognizing an exception to *Elstad* for intentional violations would require focusing constitutional analysis on a police officer's subjective intent, an unattractive proposition that we all but uniformly avoid. In general, "we believe that 'sending state and federal courts on an expedition into the minds of police officers would produce a grave and

fruitless misallocation of judicial resources.'" This case presents the uncommonly straightforward circumstance of an officer openly admitting that the violation was intentional. But the inquiry will be complicated in other situations probably more likely to occur. * * *

For these reasons, I believe that the approach espoused by Justice Kennedy is ill advised. Justice Kennedy would extend *Miranda's* exclusionary rule to any case in which the use of the "two-step interrogation technique" was "deliberate" or "calculated." * * * Far from promoting "clarity," the approach will add a third step to the suppression inquiry. In virtually every two-stage interrogation case, in addition to addressing the standard *Miranda* and voluntariness questions, courts will be forced to conduct the kind of difficult, state-of-mind inquiry that we normally take pains to avoid.

The plurality's adherence to *Elstad*, and mine to the plurality, end there. Our decision in *Elstad* rejected two lines of argument advanced in favor of suppression. The first was based on the "fruit of the poisonous tree" doctrine, discussed above. The second was the argument that the "lingering compulsion" inherent in a defendant's having let the "cat out of the bag" required suppression. * * *

We rejected this [cat out of the bag] theory outright. We did so not because we refused to recognize the "psychological impact of the suspect's conviction that he has let the cat out of the bag," but because we refused to "endo[w]" those "psychological effects" with "constitutional implications." * * *

I would analyze the two-step interrogation procedure under the voluntariness standards central to the Fifth Amendment and reiterated in *Elstad*. *Elstad* commands that if Seibert's first statement is shown to have been involuntary, the court must examine whether the taint dissipated through the passing of time or a change in circumstances: "When a prior statement is actually coerced, the time that passes between confessions, the change in place of interrogations, and the change in identity of the interrogators all bear on whether that coercion has carried over into the second confession." In addition, Seibert's second statement should be suppressed if she showed that it was involuntary despite the *Miranda* warnings. * * *

Because I believe that the plurality gives insufficient deference to *Elstad* and that Justice Kennedy places improper weight on subjective intent, I respectfully dissent.

HARRIS v. NEW YORK
Supreme Court of the United States
401 U.S. 222, 91 S. Ct. 643, 28 L. Ed. 2d 1 (1971)

CHIEF JUSTICE BURGER delivered the opinion of the Court.

We granted the writ in this case to consider petitioner's claim that a statement made by him to police under circumstances rendering it inadmissible to establish the prosecution's case in chief under *Miranda* may not be used to impeach his credibility.

The State of New York charged petitioner in a two-count indictment with twice selling heroin to an undercover police officer. At a subsequent jury trial the officer was the State's chief witness, and he testified as to details of the two sales. A second officer verified collateral details of the sales, and a third offered testimony about the chemical analysis of the heroin.

Petitioner took the stand in his own defense. He admitted knowing the undercover police officer but denied a sale on January 4, 1966. He admitted making a sale of contents of a glassine bag to the officer on January 6 but claimed it was baking powder and part of a scheme to defraud the purchaser.

On cross-examination petitioner was asked seriatim whether he had made specified statements to the police immediately following his arrest on January 7—statements that partially contradicted petitioner's direct testimony at trial. In response to the cross-examination, petitioner testified that he could not remember virtually any of the questions or answers recited by the prosecutor. At the request of petitioner's counsel the written statement from which the prosecutor had read questions and answers in his impeaching process was placed in the record for possible use on appeal; the statement was not shown to the jury.

The trial judge instructed the jury that the statements attributed to petitioner by the prosecution could be considered only in passing on petitioner's credibility and not as evidence of guilt. In closing summations both counsel argued the substance of the impeaching statements. The jury then found petitioner guilty on the second count of the indictment. The New York Court of Appeals affirmed in a per curiam opinion.

At trial the prosecution made no effort in its case in chief to use the statements allegedly made by petitioner, conceding that they were inadmissible under *Miranda*. The transcript of the interrogation used in the impeachment, but not given to the jury, shows that no warning of a right to appointed counsel was given before questions were put to petitioner when he was taken into custody. Petitioner makes no claim that the statements made to the police were coerced or involuntary.

Some comments in the *Miranda* opinion can indeed be read as indicating a bar to use of an uncounseled statement for any purpose, but discussion of that issue was not at all necessary to the Court's holding and cannot be regarded as controlling. *Miranda* barred the prosecution from making its case with statements of an accused made while in custody prior to having or effectively waiving counsel. It does not follow from *Miranda* that evidence inadmissible against an accused in the prosecution's case in chief is barred for all purposes, provided of course that the trustworthiness of the evidence satisfies legal standards.

* * * Petitioner's testimony in his own behalf concerning the events of January 7 contrasted sharply with what he told the police shortly after his arrest. The impeachment process here undoubtedly provided valuable aid to the jury in assessing petitioner's credibility, and the benefits of this process should not be lost, in our view, because of the speculative possibility that impermissible police conduct will be encouraged thereby. Assuming that the exclusionary rule has a deterrent effect on proscribed police conduct, sufficient deterrence flows when the evidence in question is made unavailable to the prosecution in its case in chief.

Every criminal defendant is privileged to testify in his own defense, or to refuse to do so. But that privilege cannot be construed to include the right to commit perjury. Having voluntarily taken the stand, petitioner was under an obligation to speak truthfully and accurately, and the prosecution here did no more than utilize the traditional truth-testing devices of the adversary process. Had inconsistent statements been made by the accused to some third person, it could hardly be contended that the conflict could not be laid before the jury by way of cross-examination and impeachment.

The shield provided by *Miranda* cannot be perverted into a license to use perjury by way of a defense, free from the risk of confrontation with prior inconsistent utterances. We hold, therefore, that petitioner's credibility was appropriately impeached by use of his earlier conflicting statements.

Affirmed.

JUSTICE BLACK dissents.

JUSTICE BRENNAN, with whom JUSTICE DOUGLAS and JUSTICE MARSHALL, join, dissenting.

It is conceded that the question-and-answer statement used to impeach petitioner's direct testimony was, under *Miranda* constitutionally inadmissible as part of the State's direct case against petitioner. I think that the Constitution also denied the State the use of the statement on cross-examination to impeach the credibility of petitioner's testimony given in his own defense. * * *

The objective of deterring improper police conduct is only part of the larger objective of safeguarding the integrity of our adversary system. The "essential mainstay" of that system is the privilege against self-incrimination, which for that reason has occupied a central place in our jurisprudence since before the Nation's birth. Moreover, "we may view the historical development of the privilege as one which groped for the proper scope of governmental power over the citizen. * * * [T]he constitutional foundation underlying the privilege is the respect a government * * * must accord to the dignity and integrity of its citizens." These values are plainly jeopardized if an exception against admission of tainted statements is made for those used for impeachment purposes. Moreover, it is monstrous that courts should aid or abet the law-breaking police officer. It is abiding truth that "nothing can destroy a government more quickly than its failure to observe its own laws, or worse, its disregard of the charter of its own existence." Thus even to the extent that *Miranda* was aimed at deterring police practices in disregard of the Constitution, I fear that today's holding will seriously undermine the achievement of that objective. The Court today tells the police that they may freely interrogate an accused incommunicado and without counsel and know that although any statement they obtain in violation of *Miranda* cannot be used on the State's direct case, it may be introduced if the defendant has the temerity to testify in his own defense. This goes far toward undoing much of the progress made in conforming police methods to the Constitution. I dissent.

JAMES V. ILLINOIS
Supreme Court of the United States
493 U.S. 307, 110 S. Ct. 648, 107 L. Ed. 2d 676 (1990)

JUSTICE BRENNAN delivered the opinion of the Court.

The impeachment exception to the exclusionary rule permits the prosecution in a criminal proceeding to introduce illegally obtained evidence to impeach the defendant's own testimony. The Illinois Supreme Court extended this exception to permit the prosecution to impeach the testimony of *all* defense witnesses with illegally obtained evidence. Finding this extension inconsistent with the balance of values underlying our previous applications of the exclusionary rule, we reverse.

On the night of August 30, 1982, eight young boys returning home from a party were confronted by a trio of other boys who demanded money. When the eight boys refused to comply, one member of the trio produced a gun and fired into the larger group, killing one boy and seriously injuring another. When the police arrived, the remaining members of the larger group provided eyewitness accounts of the event and descriptions of the perpetrators.

The next evening, two detectives of the Chicago Police Department took 15-year-old Darryl James into custody as a suspect in the shooting. James was found at his mother's beauty parlor sitting under a hair dryer; when he emerged, his hair was black and curly. After placing James in their car, the detectives questioned him about his prior hair color. He responded that the previous day his hair had been reddish brown, long, and combed straight back. The detectives questioned James again later at the police station, and he further stated that he had gone to the beauty parlor in order to have his hair "dyed black and curled in order to change his appearance."

The State subsequently indicted James for murder and attempted murder. Prior to trial, James moved to suppress the statements regarding his hair, contending that they were the fruit of a Fourth Amendment violation because the detectives lacked probable cause for his warrantless arrest. After an evidentiary hearing, the trial court sustained this motion and ruled that the statements would be inadmissible at trial.

At trial, five members of the larger group of boys testified for the State, and each made an in-court identification of the defendant. Each testified that the person responsible for the shooting had "reddish" hair, worn shoulder length in a slicked-back "butter" style. Each also recalled having seen James several weeks earlier at a parade, at which time James had the aforementioned hair color and style. At trial, however, his hair was black and worn in a "natural" style. Despite the discrepancy between the witnesses' description and his present appearance, the witnesses stood firm in their conviction that James had been present and had fired the shots.

James did not testify in his own defense. He called as a witness Jewel Henderson, a friend of his family. Henderson testified that on the day of the shooting she had taken James to register for high school and that, at that time, his hair was black. The State then sought, over James' objection, to introduce his illegally obtained statements as a means of impeaching the credibility of Henderson's testimony. After determining that the suppressed statements had been made voluntarily, the trial court overruled James' objection. One of the interrogating detectives then reported James' prior admissions that he had reddish hair the night of the shooting and he dyed and curled his hair the next day in order to change his appearance. James ultimately was convicted of both murder and attempted murder and sentenced to 30 years [of] imprisonment.

On appeal, the Illinois Appellate Court reversed James' convictions and ordered a new trial. * * * However, the Illinois Supreme Court reversed. * * * We granted certiorari.

"There is no gainsaying that arriving at the truth is a fundamental goal of our legal system." But various constitutional rules limit the means by which government may conduct this search for truth in order to promote other values embraced by the Framers and cherished throughout our Nation's history. * * * The occasional suppression of illegally obtained yet probative evidence has long been considered a necessary cost of preserving overriding constitutional values: "[T]here is nothing new in the realization that the Constitution sometimes insulates the criminality of a few in order to protect the privacy of us all."

This Court has carved out exceptions to the exclusionary rule, however, where the introduction of reliable and probative evidence would significantly further the truthseeking function of a criminal trial and the likelihood that admissibility of such evidence would encourage police misconduct is but a "speculative possibility." One exception to the rule permits prosecutors to introduce illegally obtained evidence for the limited purpose of impeaching the credibility of the defendant's own testimony. * * *

In *Harris v. New York* and *Oregon v. Hass,* the Court applied the exception to permit prosecutors to impeach defendants using incriminating yet voluntary and reliable statements elicited in violation of *Miranda* requirements. * * * [I]n *United States v. Havens,* the Court expanded the exception to permit prosecutors to introduce illegally obtained evidence in order to impeach a defendant's "answers to questions put to him on cross-examination that are plainly within the scope of the defendant's direct examination." * * *

In this case, the Illinois Supreme Court held that our balancing approach in [these cases] justifies expanding the scope of the impeachment exception to permit prosecutors to use illegally obtained evidence to impeach the credibility of defense witnesses. We disagree. Expanding the class of impeachable witnesses from the defendant alone to all defense witnesses would create different incentives affecting the behavior of both defendants and law enforcement officers. As a result, this expansion would not promote the truthseeking function to the same extent as did creation of the original exception, and yet it would significantly undermine the deterrent effect of the general exclusionary rule. Hence, we believe that this proposed expansion would frustrate rather than further the purposes underlying the exclusionary rule.

* * * [E]xpanding the impeachment exception to encompass the testimony of all defense witnesses likely would chill some defendants from presenting their best defense and sometimes any defense at all—through the testimony of others. Whenever police obtained evidence illegally, defendants would have to assess prior to trial the likelihood that the evidence would be admitted to impeach the otherwise favorable testimony of any witness they call. Defendants might reasonably fear that one or more of their witnesses, in a position to offer truthful and favorable testimony, would also make some statement in sufficient tension with the tainted

evidence to allow the prosecutor to introduce that evidence for impeachment. * * * As a result, an expanded impeachment exception likely would chill some defendants from calling witnesses who would otherwise offer probative evidence. * * *

Moreover, the proposed expansion of the current impeachment exception would significantly weaken the exclusionary rule's deterrent effect on police misconduct. * * * [E]xpanding the impeachment exception to *all* defense witnesses would significantly enhance the expected value to the prosecution of illegally obtained evidence. First, this expansion would vastly increase the number of occasions on which such evidence could be used. Defense witnesses easily outnumber testifying defendants, both because many defendants do not testify themselves and because many if not most defendants call multiple witnesses on their behalf. Moreover, due to the chilling effect identified above, illegally obtained evidence holds even greater value to the prosecution for each individual witness than for each defendant. The prosecutor's access to impeachment evidence would not just deter perjury; it would also deter defendants from calling witnesses in the first place, thereby keeping from the jury much probative exculpatory evidence. For both of these reasons, police officers and their superiors would recognize that obtaining evidence through illegal means stacks the deck heavily in the prosecution's favor. It is thus far more than a "speculative possibility" that police misconduct will be encouraged by permitting such use of illegally obtained evidence.

The United States argues that this result is constitutionally acceptable because excluding illegally obtained evidence solely from the prosecution's case in chief would still provide a quantum of deterrence sufficient to protect the privacy interests underlying the exclusionary rule. We disagree. * * * [M]uch if not most of the time, police officers confront opportunities to obtain evidence illegally after they have already legally obtained (or know that they have other means of legally obtaining) sufficient evidence to sustain a prima facie case. In these situations, a rule requiring exclusion of illegally obtained evidence from only the government's case in chief would leave officers with little to lose and much to gain by overstepping constitutional limits on evidence gathering. Narrowing the exclusionary rule in this manner, therefore, would significantly undermine the rule's ability "to compel respect for the constitutional guaranty in the only effectively available way-by removing the incentive to disregard it." So long as we are committed to protecting the people from the disregard of their constitutional rights during the course of criminal investigations, inadmissibility of illegally obtained evidence must remain the rule, not the exception.

The cost to the truth-seeking process of evidentiary exclusion invariably is perceived more tangibly in discrete prosecutions than is the protection of privacy values through deterrence of future police misconduct.

When defining the precise scope of the exclusionary rule, however, we must focus on systemic effects of proposed exceptions to ensure that individual liberty from arbitrary or oppressive police conduct does not succumb to the inexorable pressure to introduce all incriminating evidence, no matter how obtained, in each and every criminal case. Our previous recognition of an impeachment exception limited to the testimony of defendants reflects a careful weighing of the competing values. Because expanding the exception to encompass the testimony of all defense witnesses would not further the truth-seeking value with equal force but would appreciably undermine the deterrent effect of the exclusionary rule, we adhere to the line drawn in our previous cases.

Accordingly, we hold that the Illinois Supreme Court erred in affirming James' convictions despite the prosecutor's use of illegally obtained statements to impeach a defense witness' testimony. The court's judgment is reversed, and the case is remanded for further proceedings not inconsistent with this opinion.

It is so ordered.

JUSTICE KENNEDY, with whom THE CHIEF JUSTICE, JUSTICE O'CONNOR, and JUSTICE SCALIA join, dissenting.

* * * [T]oday's opinion grants the defense side in a criminal case broad immunity to introduce whatever false testimony it can produce from the mouth of a friendly witness. Unless petitioner's conviction is reversed, we are told, police would flout the Fourth Amendment, and as a result, the accused would be unable to offer any defense. This exaggerated view leads to a drastic remedy: The jury cannot learn that defense testimony is inconsistent with probative evidence of undoubted value. A more cautious course is available, one that retains Fourth Amendment protections and yet safeguards the truth-seeking function of the criminal trial.

Our precedents establish that the exclusionary rule does not apply where the interest in pursuing truth or other important values outweighs any deterrence of unlawful conduct that the rule might achieve. * * * The interest in protecting the truth-seeking function of the criminal trial is every bit as strong in this case as in our earlier cases that allowed rebuttal with evidence that was inadmissible as part of the prosecution's case in chief. Here a witness who knew the accused well took the stand to testify about the accused's personal appearance. The testimony could be expected to create real doubt in the minds of jurors concerning the eyewitness identifications by persons who did not know the accused. To deprive the jurors of knowledge that statements of the defendant himself revealed the witness' testimony to be false would result in a decision by triers of fact who were not just kept in the dark as to excluded evidence, but positively misled. The potential for harm to the truth-seeking process resulting from the majority's new rule in fact will be greater than if the defendant himself had testified. It is natural for jurors to be skeptical of self-serving testimony by the defendant. Testimony by a witness said to be independent has the greater potential to deceive. And if a defense witness can present false testimony with impunity, the jurors may find the rest of the prosecution's case suspect, for ineffective and artificial cross-examination will be viewed as a real weakness in the state's case. Jurors will assume that if the prosecution had any proof the statement was false, it would make the proof known. The majority does more than deprive the prosecution of evidence. The state must also suffer the introduction of false testimony and appear to bolster the falsehood by its own silence.

The majority's fear that allowing the jury to know the whole truth will chill defendants from putting on any defense seems to me far too speculative to justify the rule here announced. No restriction on the defense results if rebuttal of testimony by witnesses other than the defendant is confined to the introduction of excludable evidence that is in direct contradiction of the testimony. * * *

Where the jury is misled by false testimony, otherwise subject to flat contradiction by evidence illegally seized, the protection of the exclusionary rule is "perverted into a license to use perjury by way of a defense, free from the risk of confrontation with prior inconsistent utterances." The perversion is the same where the perjury is by proxy. I would affirm the judgment of the Illinois Supreme Court.

[JUSTICE STEVENS' concurring opinion has been omitted.]

WRONGLY ACCUSED: IS RACE A FACTOR IN CONVICTING THE INNOCENT?
Andrew E. Taslitz
4 Ohio St. J. Crim. L. 121 (2006)

Social psychologists widely agree that many of the interrogation techniques for judging suspect credibility taught to police officers under the rubric of science are anything but. Instead, they are based on facially implausible psychological assumptions not only not validated by empirical evidence but actually contradicted by empirical evidence. The resulting police officer judgments made about an interrogatee's credibility are thus based on little more than the investigator's subjective judgments, hunches, and a series of after-the-fact observations designed to confirm preconceptions, for example, concerning the meaning of eye movement during interrogation. Some research also suggests that the more powerless party in a situation—a black youth isolated in an interrogation room with multiple detectives clearly fitting that relatively powerless bill—is likely to adopt a style of speech perceived by observers as less credible, a phenomenon that may again feed into uninformed officers' preconceptions.

A separate line of research shows that most people are generally notoriously bad at judging other persons' credibility based on their demeanor. This same research shows, however, that those with law enforcement training and experience are more likely than those without it to see deception, to perceive guilt, and to have a high level of confidence in these judgments yet are no more likely to be right in fact. This is likely so, the researchers maintain, because prior experience, presumed base rates of behavior, stereotyping, and a system of rewards for gathering incriminating rather than exculpating evidence encourage this view. Police may thus readily interpret nervousness during interrogation—a natural reaction by anyone in that situation—as in fact only typical of the guilty. Stereotypes have more clout when cognitive resources are limited, such as by time or social pressure, and where a theory is held in great confidence; the latter also leads to neglecting further evidence-gathering or to heightened attention to confirmatory evidence and diminished attention to contradicting evidence.

When investigators expect suspect guilt, however, they use more investigative techniques, try harder, exert more pressure and, as a result, lead innocent suspects most of all to behave defensively. But that defensiveness makes them appear more guilty to observers. Indeed, in lab experiments pairing the most guilt-presumptive interrogators with the truly innocent, the harshest interrogation techniques result, in turn causing the greatest intensification of the presumption of guilt. Researchers maintain that these lab results likely underestimate real-world risks because detectives:

- are trained to have confidence in their judgments;
- are trained to use psychological interrogation techniques effectively;
- are motivated by career aspiration to solve cases; and
- typically pressure suspects over the course of hours, not, as in in the lab, just minutes of interrogation.

The innocent may also readily waive *Miranda*, believing that their innocence will set them free and not realizing that what they see as exculpatory statements may be viewed by others as inculpatory. As the time for interrogation builds, and as a suspect is increasingly confronted with manufactured or biased evidence against him—two very typical interrogation techniques—the risk of falsely confessing to escape the isolation and pressure rises dramatically; this is especially true of juveniles.

Now when we add race to the mix, the picture becomes clearer. Officers start with a presumption of the guilt of a young black male based upon one-sided and limited circumstantial evidence. The kid reacts with hostility and defensiveness. These reactions, combined with his powerless speech patterns, lead police to believe he is lying. They close off alternative theories, heightening the pressure on the kid about whose guilt they are now convinced. They make real evidence sound more inculpatory than it is, they deceive him into believing there is still more inculpatory evidence against him, they appeal to his self-interest, and they hammer away at him for hours. Young, isolated, cut off from family and friends, fearful, and rightly seeing no way out, he confesses. Falsely.

Should the youth take the stand at a suppression hearing, the judge, drawing on the same racially-stigmatizing images of black youth, won't believe him. The case goes to trial, and the jury likely sees a film just of his confession. But even if they see a video of the entire interrogation, they will see a camera focused on only the suspect, not the police, a camera angle shown in laboratory studies to enhance the perceived likelihood of guilt. Moreover, the same defensiveness and linguistic barriers that made the kid seem to be a liar to the police prod the jury toward a similar conclusion. And the same stereotypes of black criminality and duplicity again favor jurors accepting the truthfulness of the confession rather than of its retraction.

There is no reason to think that similar dynamics will have any less force at other steps in the process, and these multi-stage dynamics may be reinforcing. Thus a flawed cross-racial identification may lead to a presumption of guilt resulting in aggressive interrogation tactics that elicit a false confession. The identification of sloppy lab work further implicating the defendant is not further pursued or corrected because of the operative presumption of likely guilt. Racial code words are used by prosecutors in closing arguments to draw on images of black ill-characters. A jury skeptical of a seemingly evasive defendant convicts. No other leads or theories have been pursued. Another injustice has been done.

E. *MIRANDA* AND *MASSIAH*: CONTRASTING PERSPECTIVES

Both *Miranda* and *Massiah* recognize a right to counsel. In *Miranda*, that right is grounded in the Fifth Amendment while in the *Massiah* line of cases, that right is based on the Sixth Amendment. As the cases in this section demonstrate, these differences matter in the interrogation context. In the first case in this section, *Patterson v. Illinois*, the Court considers whether a post-indictment waiver of one's *Miranda* right to counsel also constitutes a waiver of one's Sixth Amendment right to counsel at an interrogation. In the next case, *McNeil v. Wisconsin*, the Court determines whether a defendant's invocation of the Sixth Amendment right to counsel is sufficient to invoke his *Miranda* right to counsel. Finally, in *Montejo v. Louisiana*, the Court decides whether police are prohibited from initiating an interrogation when a defendant has requested counsel at arraignment. The answer to this question may surprise you. When you read the cases in this section, pay close attention to the differences in the scope of the right to counsel based on *Miranda* and scope of the right to counsel based on the Sixth Amendment. Are these differences justifiable?

1. DOES A VOLUNTARY, KNOWING AND INTELLIGENT WAIVER OF ONE'S *MIRANDA* RIGHT TO COUNSEL SUFFICE TO WAIVE ONE'S SIXTH AMENDMENT RIGHT TO COUNSEL?

PATTERSON V. ILLINOIS
Supreme Court of the United States
487 U.S. 285, 108 S. Ct. 2389, 101 L. Ed. 2d 261 (1988)

JUSTICE WHITE delivered the opinion of the Court.

In this case, we are called on to determine whether the interrogation of petitioner after his indictment violated his Sixth Amendment right to counsel. * * *

Before dawn on August 21, 1983, petitioner and other members of the "Vice Lords" street gang became involved in a fight with members of a rival gang, the "Black Mobsters." Some time after the fight, a former member of the Black Mobsters, James Jackson, went to the home where the Vice Lords had fled. A second fight broke out there, with petitioner and three other Vice Lords beating Jackson severely. The Vice Lords then put Jackson into a car, drove to the end of a nearby street, and left him face down in a puddle of water. Later that morning, police discovered Jackson, dead, where he had been left.

That afternoon, local police officers obtained warrants for the arrest of the Vice Lords * * *. One of the gang members who was arrested gave the police a statement concerning the first fight; the statement also implicated several of the Vice Lords (including petitioner) in Jackson's murder. A few hours later, petitioner was apprehended. Petitioner was informed of his rights under *Miranda* and volunteered to answer questions put to him by the police. Petitioner gave a statement concerning the initial fight between the rival gangs, but denied knowing anything about Jackson's death. Petitioner was held in custody the following day, August 22, as law enforcement authorities completed their investigation of the Jackson murder.

On August 23, a Cook County grand jury indicted petitioner and two other gang members for the murder of James Jackson. Police Officer Michael Gresham, who had questioned petitioner earlier, removed him from the lockup where he was being held, and told petitioner that because he had been indicted he was being transferred to the Cook County jail. Petitioner asked Gresham which of the gang members had been charged with Jackson's murder, and upon learning that one particular Vice Lord had been omitted from the indictments, asked: "[W]hy wasn't he indicted, he did everything." Petitioner also began to explain that there was a witness who would support his account of the crime.

At this point, Gresham interrupted petitioner, and handed him a *Miranda* waiver form. * * * Gresham read the warnings aloud, as petitioner read along with him. Petitioner initialed each of the five warnings, and signed the waiver form. Petitioner then gave a lengthy statement to police officers concerning the Jackson murder; petitioner's statement described in detail the role of each of the Vice Lords—including himself—in the murder of James Jackson.

Later that day, petitioner confessed involvement in the murder for a second time. This confession came in an interview with Assistant State's Attorney (ASA) George Smith. At the outset of the interview, Smith reviewed with petitioner the *Miranda* waiver he had previously signed, and petitioner confirmed that he had signed the waiver and understood his rights. Smith went through the waiver procedure once again [and had petitioner] sign a waiver form. * * * Petitioner then gave another inculpatory statement concerning the crime.

Before trial, petitioner moved to suppress his statements * * *. The trial court denied these motions, and the statements were used against petitioner at his trial. The jury found petitioner guilty of murder, and petitioner was sentenced to a 24-year prison term.

On appeal, petitioner argued that he had not "knowingly and intelligently" waived his Sixth Amendment right to counsel before he gave his uncounseled postindictment confessions. Petitioner contended that the warnings he received, while adequate for the purposes of protecting his *Fifth* Amendment rights as guaranteed by *Miranda,* did not adequately inform him of his *Sixth* Amendment right to counsel. The Illinois Supreme Court, however, rejected this theory * * *. We granted this petition for certiorari * * *.

There can be no doubt that petitioner had the right to have the assistance of counsel at his postindictment interviews with law enforcement authorities. Our cases make it plain that the Sixth Amendment guarantees this right to criminal defendants. Petitioner asserts that the questioning that produced his incriminating statements violated his Sixth Amendment right to counsel * * *.

Petitioner's principal * * * claim is that questioning him without counsel present violated the Sixth Amendment because he did not validly waive his right to have counsel present during the interviews. Since it is clear that after the *Miranda* warnings were given to petitioner, he not only voluntarily answered questions without claiming his right to silence or his right to have a lawyer present to advise him but also executed a written waiver of his right to counsel during questioning, the specific issue posed here is whether this waiver was a "knowing and intelligent" waiver of his Sixth Amendment right.

In the past, this Court has held that a waiver of the Sixth Amendment right to counsel is valid only when it reflects "an intentional relinquishment or abandonment of a known right or privilege." In other words, the accused must "kno[w] what he is doing" so that "his choice is made with eyes open." * * * [T]he key inquiry in a case such as this one must be: Was the accused * * * made sufficiently aware of his right to have counsel present during the questioning, and of the possible consequences of a decision to forgo the aid of counsel? In this case, we are convinced that by admonishing petitioner with the *Miranda* warnings, respondent has met this burden and that petitioner's waiver of his right to counsel at the questioning was valid.

First, the *Miranda* warnings given petitioner made him aware of his right to have counsel present during the questioning. By telling petitioner that he had a right to consult with an attorney, to have a lawyer present while he was questioned, and even to have a lawyer appointed for him if he could not afford to retain one on his own, Officer Gresham and ASA Smith conveyed to petitioner the sum and substance of the rights that the Sixth Amendment provided him. * * *

Second, the *Miranda* warnings also served to make petitioner aware of the consequences of a decision by him to waive his Sixth Amendment rights during postindictment questioning. Petitioner knew that any statement that he made could be used against him in subsequent criminal proceedings. This is the ultimate adverse consequence petitioner could have suffered by virtue of his choice to make uncounseled admissions to the authorities. This warning also sufficed—contrary to petitioner's claim here, to let petitioner know what a lawyer could "do for him" during the postindictment questioning: namely, advise petitioner to refrain from making any such statements. By knowing what could be done with any statements he might make, and therefore, what benefit could be obtained by having the aid of counsel while making such statements, petitioner was essentially informed of the possible consequences of going without counsel during questioning. * * *

Our conclusion is supported by petitioner's inability, in the proceedings before this Court, to articulate with precision what additional information should have been provided to him before he would have been competent to waive his right to counsel. * * *

As a general matter, then, an accused who is admonished with the warnings prescribed by this Court in *Miranda,* has been sufficiently apprised of the nature of his Sixth Amendment rights, and of the consequences of abandoning those rights, so that his waiver on this basis will be considered a knowing and intelligent one. We feel that our conclusion in a recent Fifth Amendment case is equally apposite here: "Once it is determined that a suspect's decision not to rely on his rights was uncoerced, that he at all times knew he could stand mute and request a lawyer, and that he was aware of the State's intention to use his statements to secure a conviction, the analysis is complete and the waiver is valid as a matter of law." * * *

Before confessing to the murder of James Jackson, petitioner was meticulously informed by authorities of his right to counsel, and of the consequences of any choice not to exercise that right. On two separate occasions, petitioner elected to forgo the assistance of counsel, and speak directly to officials concerning his role in the murder. Because we believe that petitioner's waiver of his Sixth Amendment rights was "knowing and intelligent," we find no error in the decision of the trial court to permit petitioner's confessions to be used against him. Consequently, the judgment of the Illinois Supreme Court is

Affirmed.

[JUSTICE BLACKMUN's and JUSTICE STEVENS' dissenting opinions have been omitted.]

2. DOES INVOCATION OF THE SIXTH AMENDMENT RIGHT TO COUNSEL CONSTITUTE AN INVOCATION OF ONE'S *MIRANDA* RIGHT TO COUNSEL?

MCNEIL V. WISCONSIN
The Supreme Court of the United States
501 U.S. 171, 111 S. Ct. 2204, 115 L. Ed. 2d 158 (1991)

JUSTICE SCALIA delivered the opinion of the Court.

This case presents the question whether an accused's invocation of his Sixth Amendment right to counsel during a judicial proceeding constitutes an invocation of his *Miranda* right to counsel.

Petitioner Paul McNeil was arrested in Omaha, Nebraska, in May 1987, pursuant to a warrant charging him with an armed robbery in West Allis, Wisconsin, a suburb of Milwaukee. Shortly after his arrest, two Milwaukee County deputy sheriffs arrived in Omaha to retrieve him. After advising him of his *Miranda* rights, the deputies sought to question him. He refused to answer any questions, but did not request an attorney. The deputies promptly ended the interview.

Once back in Wisconsin, petitioner was brought before a Milwaukee County Court Commissioner on the armed robbery charge. The

Commissioner set bail and scheduled a preliminary examination. An attorney from the Wisconsin Public Defender's Office represented petitioner at this initial appearance.

Later that evening, Detective Joseph Butts of the Milwaukee County Sheriff's Department visited petitioner in jail. Butts had been assisting the Racine County, Wisconsin police in their investigation of a murder, attempted murder, and armed burglary in the town of Caledonia; petitioner was a suspect. Butts advised petitioner of his *Miranda* rights, and petitioner signed a form waiving them. In this first interview, petitioner did not deny knowledge of the Caledonia crimes, but said that he had not been involved.

Butts returned two days later with detectives from Caledonia. He again began the encounter by advising petitioner of his *Miranda* rights and providing a waiver form. Petitioner placed his initials next to each of the warnings and signed the form. This time, petitioner admitted that he had been involved in the Caledonia crimes, which he described in detail. * * *

Butts and the Caledonia Police returned two days later. * * * They again began the interview by administering the *Miranda* warnings and obtaining petitioner's signature and initials on the waiver form. * * * Petitioner * * * provided another statement recounting the events, which was transcribed, signed, and initialed as before.

The following day, petitioner was formally charged with the Caledonia crimes and transferred to that jurisdiction. His pretrial motion to suppress the three incriminating statements was denied. He was convicted of second-degree murder, attempted first-degree murder, and armed robbery, and sentenced to 60 years in prison.

On appeal, petitioner argued that the trial court's refusal to suppress the statements was reversible error. He contended that his courtroom appearance with an attorney for the West Allis crime constituted an invocation of the *Miranda* right to counsel, and that any subsequent waiver of that right during police-initiated questioning regarding *any* offense was invalid. * * * We granted certiorari * * *.

The Sixth Amendment provides that "[i]n all criminal prosecutions, the accused shall enjoy the right . . . to have the Assistance of Counsel for his defence." * * * It is undisputed, and we accept for purposes of the present case, that at the time petitioner provided the incriminating statements at issue, his Sixth Amendment right had attached and had been invoked with respect to the *West Allis armed robbery,* for which he had been formally charged.

The Sixth Amendment right, however, is offense specific. It cannot be invoked once for all future prosecutions, for it does not attach until a prosecution is commenced, that is, "'at or after the initiation of adversary judicial criminal proceedings—whether by way of formal charge, preliminary hearing, indictment, information, or arraignment.'" * * * Because petitioner provided the statements at issue here before his Sixth Amendment right to counsel with respect to the *Caledonia offenses* had been (or even could have been) invoked, that right poses no bar to the admission of the statements in this case.

Petitioner relies, however, upon a different "right to counsel," found not in the text of the Sixth Amendment, but in this Court's jurisprudence relating to the Fifth Amendment guarantee that "[n]o person . . . shall be compelled in any criminal case to be a witness against himself." * * * In *Miranda v. Arizona*, we established a number of prophylactic rights designed to counteract the "inherently compelling pressures" of custodial interrogation, including the right to have counsel present. *Miranda* did not hold, however, that those rights could not be waived. On the contrary, the opinion recognized that statements elicited during custodial interrogation would be admissible if the prosecution could establish that the suspect "knowingly and intelligently waived his privilege against self-incrimination and his right to retained or appointed counsel."

In *Edwards v. Arizona*, we established a second layer of prophylaxis for the *Miranda* right to counsel: Once a suspect asserts the right, not only must the current interrogation cease, but he may not be approached for further interrogation "until counsel has been made available to him,"— which means, we have most recently held, that counsel must be present. If the police do subsequently initiate an encounter in the absence of counsel (assuming there has been no break in custody), the suspect's statements are presumed involuntary and therefore inadmissible as substantive evidence at trial, even where the suspect executes a waiver and his statements would be considered voluntary under traditional standards. This is "designed to prevent police from badgering a defendant into waiving his previously asserted *Miranda* rights." The *Edwards* rule, moreover, is not offense specific: Once a suspect invokes the *Miranda* right to counsel for interrogation regarding one offense, he may not be reapproached regarding any offense unless counsel is present.

Having described the nature and effects of both the Sixth Amendment right to counsel and the *Miranda-Edwards* "Fifth Amendment" right to counsel, we come at last to the issue here: Petitioner seeks to prevail by combining the two of them. He contends that, although he expressly waived his *Miranda* right to counsel on every occasion he was interrogated, those waivers were the invalid product of impermissible approaches, because his prior invocation of the offense specific Sixth Amendment right with regard to the West Allis burglary was also an invocation of the non-offense-specific *Miranda-Edwards* right. We think that is false as a matter of fact and inadvisable (if even permissible) as a contrary-to-fact presumption of policy.

As to the former: The purpose of the Sixth Amendment counsel guarantee—and hence the purpose of invoking it—is to "protec[t] the unaided layman at critical confrontations" with his "expert adversary," the government, *after* "the adverse positions of government and defendant have solidified" with respect to a particular alleged crime. The purpose of the *Miranda-Edwards* guarantee, on the other hand—and hence the purpose of invoking it—is to protect a quite different interest: the suspect's "desire to deal with the police only through counsel." * * * To invoke the Sixth Amendment interest is, as a matter of *fact, not* to invoke the *Miranda-Edwards* interest. One might be quite willing to speak to the police without counsel present concerning many matters, but not the matter under prosecution. It can be said, perhaps, that it is *likely* that one who has asked for counsel's assistance in defending against a prosecution would want counsel present for all custodial interrogation, even interrogation unrelated to the charge. That is not necessarily true, since suspects often believe that they can avoid the laying of charges by demonstrating an assurance of innocence through frank and unassisted answers to questions. But even if it were true, the *likelihood* that a suspect would wish counsel to be present is not the test for applicability of *Edwards*. The rule of that case applies only when the suspect "ha[s] *expressed*" his wish for the particular sort of lawyerly assistance that is the subject of *Miranda*. It requires, at a minimum, some statement that can reasonably be construed to be an expression of a desire for the assistance of an attorney *in dealing with custodial interrogation by the police.* Requesting the assistance of an attorney at a bail hearing does not bear that construction. * * *

"This Court is forever adding new stories to the temples of constitutional law, and the temples have a way of collapsing when one story too many is added." We decline to add yet another story to *Miranda*. The judgment of the Wisconsin Supreme Court is

Affirmed.

[JUSTICE KENNEDY's concurring opinion and JUSTICE STEVENS' dissenting opinion have been omitted.]

3. DOES A REQUEST FOR COUNSEL AT AN ARRAIGNMENT TRIGGER THE PROTECTIONS OF THE *EDWARDS* RULE?

In a case called *Michigan v. Jackson*, 475 U.S. 625 (1986), the Court imported the *Edwards* rule into the Sixth Amendment context, holding that once a defendant who has been formally charged requests counsel at an arraignment or similar proceeding, the government may not interrogate him about any charged offenses in the absence of counsel, unless counsel is present or the defendant initiates further conversation about those offenses with the government. In the next case, *Montejo v. Louisiana*, 556 U.S. 778 (2009), the Court overrules *Michigan v. Jackson*, holding that merely accepting or requesting appointed counsel is not sufficient to trigger the protections of the *Edwards* rule. After *Montejo*, the *Edwards* rule applies only where a suspect has expressly stated he wants an attorney present during interrogation and no longer automatically applies whenever a suspect who has been charged retains or is appointed counsel.

MONTEJO V. LOUISIANA
Supreme Court of the United States
556 U.S. 778, 129 S. Ct. 2079, 173 L. Ed. 2d 955 (2009)

JUSTICE SCALIA delivered the opinion of the Court.

We consider in this case the scope and continued viability of the rule announced by this Court in *Michigan v. Jackson*, forbidding police to initiate interrogation of a criminal defendant once he has requested counsel at an arraignment or similar proceeding.

Petitioner Jesse Montejo was arrested on September 6, 2002, in connection with the robbery and murder of Lewis Ferrari, who had been found dead in his own home one day earlier. Suspicion quickly focused on Jerry Moore, a disgruntled former employee of Ferrari's dry cleaning business. Police sought to question Montejo, who was a known associate of Moore.

Montejo waived his rights under *Miranda*, and was interrogated at the sheriff's office by police detectives through the late afternoon and evening of September 6 and the early morning of September 7. * * * On September 10, Montejo was brought before a judge for * * * a preliminary hearing required under state law. Although the proceedings were not transcribed, the minute record indicates what transpired: "The defendant being charged with First Degree Murder, Court ordered N[o] Bond set in this matter. Further, Court ordered the Office of Indigent Defender be appointed to represent the defendant."

Later that same day, two police detectives visited Montejo back at the prison and requested that he accompany them on an excursion to locate the murder weapon (which Montejo had earlier indicated he had thrown into a lake). After some back-and-forth, the substance of which remains in dispute, Montejo was again read his *Miranda* rights and agreed to go along; during the excursion, he wrote an inculpatory letter of apology to the victim's widow. Only upon their return did Montejo finally meet his court-appointed attorney, who was quite upset that the detectives had interrogated his client in his absence. At trial, the letter of apology was admitted over defense objection. The jury convicted Montejo of first-degree murder, and he was sentenced to death.

The Louisiana Supreme Court affirmed the conviction and sentence. * * * We granted certiorari. * * *

Under the rule adopted by the Louisiana Supreme Court, a criminal defendant must request counsel, or otherwise "assert" his Sixth Amendment right at the preliminary hearing before the *Jackson* protections are triggered. If he does so, the police may not initiate further interrogation in the absence of counsel. But if the court on its own appoints counsel, with the defendant taking no affirmative action to invoke his right to counsel, then police are free to initiate further interrogations provided that they first obtain an otherwise valid waiver by the defendant of his right to have counsel present. * * *

It is worth emphasizing first what is *not* in dispute or at stake here. Under our precedents, once the adversary judicial process has been initiated, the Sixth Amendment guarantees a defendant the right to have counsel present at all "critical" stages of the criminal proceedings. Interrogation by the State is such a stage.

Our precedents also place beyond doubt that the Sixth Amendment right to counsel may be waived by a defendant, so long as relinquishment of the right is voluntary, knowing, and intelligent. * * * And when a defendant is read his *Miranda* rights (which include the right to have counsel present during interrogation) and agrees to waive those rights, that typically does the trick, even though the *Miranda* rights purportedly have their source in the *Fifth* Amendment.

> As a general matter . . . an accused who is admonished with the warnings prescribed by this Court in *Miranda* . . . has been sufficiently apprised of the nature of his Sixth Amendment rights, and of the consequences of abandoning those rights, so that his waiver on this basis will be considered a knowing and intelligent one.

The *only* question raised by this case * * * is whether courts must *presume* that such a waiver is invalid under certain circumstances. We created such a presumption in *Jackson* by analogy to a similar prophylactic rule established to protect the Fifth Amendment-based Miranda right to have counsel present at any custodial interrogation. *Edwards v. Arizona* decided that once "an accused has invoked his right to have counsel present during custodial interrogation . . . [he] is not subject to further interrogation by the authorities until counsel has been made available," unless he initiates the contact.

The *Edwards* rule is "designed to prevent police from badgering a defendant into waiving his previously asserted Miranda rights." It does this by presuming his postassertion statements to be involuntary, "even where the suspect executes a waiver and his statements would be considered voluntary under traditional standards." This prophylactic rule thus "protect[s] a suspect's voluntary choice not to speak outside his lawyer's presence."

Jackson represented a "wholesale importation of the *Edwards* rule into the Sixth Amendment." The *Jackson* Court decided that a request for counsel at an arraignment should be treated as an invocation of the Sixth Amendment right to counsel "at every critical stage of the prosecution," despite doubt that defendants "actually inten[d] their request for counsel to encompass representation during any further questioning." * * * Citing *Edwards*, the Court held that any subsequent waiver would thus be "insufficient to justify police-initiated interrogation." In other words, we presume such waivers involuntary "based on the supposition that suspects who assert their right to counsel are unlikely to waive that right voluntarily" in subsequent interactions with police. * * *

With this understanding of what *Jackson* stands for and whence it came, it should be clear that Montejo's interpretation of that decision—that no represented defendant can ever be approached by the State and asked to consent to interrogation—is off the mark. When a court appoints counsel for an indigent defendant in the absence of any request on his part, there is no basis for a presumption that any subsequent waiver of the right to counsel will be involuntary. There is no "*initial* election" to exercise the right that must be preserved through a prophylactic rule against later waivers. No reason exists to assume that a defendant like Montejo, who has done *nothing at all* to express his intentions with respect to his Sixth Amendment rights, would not be perfectly amenable to speaking with the police without having counsel present. And no reason exists to prohibit the police from inquiring. *Edwards* [was] meant to prevent police from badgering defendants into changing their minds about their rights, but a defendant who never asked for counsel has not yet made up his mind in the first instance. * * *

Although our holding means that the Louisiana Supreme Court correctly rejected Montejo's claim * * *, we think that Montejo should be given an opportunity to contend that his letter of apology should still have been suppressed under the rule of *Edwards*. If Montejo made a clear assertion of the right to counsel when the officers approached him about accompanying them on the excursion for the murder weapon, then no interrogation should have taken place unless Montejo initiated it. Even if Montejo subsequently agreed to waive his rights, that waiver would have been invalid had it followed an "unequivocal election of the right." * * *

Montejo understandably did not pursue an *Edwards* objection, because *Jackson* served as the Sixth Amendment analogy to *Edwards* and offered broader protections. Our decision today, overruling *Jackson*, changes the legal landscape and does so in part based on the protections already provided by *Edwards*. Thus we think that a remand is appropriate so that Montejo can pursue this alternative avenue for relief. Montejo may also seek on remand to press any claim he might have that his Sixth Amendment waiver was not knowing and voluntary, *e.g.*, his argument that the waiver was invalid because it was based on misrepresentations by police as to whether he had been appointed a lawyer. * * *

The judgment of the Louisiana Supreme Court is vacated, and the case is remanded for further proceedings not inconsistent with this opinion.

It is so ordered.

[JUSTICE ALITO's concurring opinion and JUSTICE STEVENS' dissenting opinion have been omitted.]

Chapter 21

Lineups and Other Pretrial Identification Procedures

■ ■ ■

Both the Sixth Amendment and the Due Process Clause of the Fourteenth Amendment place limits on the state's use of pretrial identification procedures. The first two cases in this chapter address the protections afforded to the accused by the Sixth Amendment. The last two cases address the protections afforded by the Due Process Clause.

In *United States v. Wade*, the Court considers whether to recognize a right to counsel at a pretrial lineup that occurs after the filing of the indictment. In order to answer this question, the Court examines whether a post-indictment lineup is a "critical stage" of the proceeding. In *Kirby v. Illinois*, the Court has to decide whether to extend its holding in *Wade* to an identification procedure that also takes place pretrial, but before the defendant has been formally charged with a criminal offense.

The remaining materials in this chapter involve the protections of the Due Process Clause. In *Manson v. Brathwaite*, the Court considers which of two tests should be used to admit or exclude evidence obtained by an unnecessarily suggestive pretrial identification procedure. Sandra Guerra Thompson explains and critiques the *Manson v. Brathwaite* decision in *Eyewitness Identifications and State Courts as Guardians Against Wrongful Convictions*. Next is an article from Forbes Magazine on cross-racial identification, discussing the increased likelihood of misidentification when a witness of one race tries to identify a suspect of another race. In *Using an Expert to Evaluate Eyewitness Identification Evidence*, Shirley K. Duffy examines additional problems posed by cross-racial identifications. Finally, in *Perry v. New Hampshire*, the Court considers whether the Due Process Clause is violated when a suggestive pretrial identification procedure is involved, but the police were not responsible for arranging the suggestive procedure.

UNITED STATES v. WADE
Supreme Court of the United States
388 U.S. 218, 87 S. Ct. 1926, 18 L. Ed. 2d 1149 (1967)

JUSTICE BRENNAN delivered the opinion of the Court.

The question here is whether courtroom identifications of an accused at trial are to be excluded from evidence because the accused was exhibited to the witnesses before trial at a post-indictment lineup conducted for identification purposes without notice to and in the absence of the accused's appointed counsel.

The federally insured bank in Eustace, Texas, was robbed on September 21, 1964. A man with a small strip of tape on each side of his face entered the bank, pointed a pistol at the female cashier and the vice president, the only persons in the bank at the time, and forced them to fill a pillowcase with the bank's money. The man then drove away with an accomplice who had been waiting in a stolen car outside the bank. On March 23, 1965, an indictment was returned against respondent, Wade, and two others for conspiring to rob the bank, and against Wade and the accomplice for the robbery itself. Wade was arrested on April 2, and counsel was appointed to represent him on April 26. Fifteen days later an FBI agent, without notice to Wade's lawyer, arranged to have the two bank employees observe a lineup made up of Wade and five or six other prisoners and conducted in a courtroom of the local county courthouse. Each person in the line wore strips of tape such as allegedly worn by the robber and upon direction each said something like "put the money in the bag," the words allegedly uttered by the robber. Both bank employees identified Wade in the lineup as the bank robber.

At trial the two employees, when asked on direct examination if the robber was in the courtroom, pointed to Wade. The prior lineup identification was then elicited from both employees on cross-examination. At the close of testimony, Wade's counsel moved for a judgment of acquittal or, alternatively, to strike the bank officials' courtroom identifications on the ground that conduct of the lineup, without notice to and in the absence of his appointed counsel, violated * * * [Wade's] Sixth Amendment right to the assistance of counsel. The motion was denied, and Wade was convicted. The Court of Appeals for the Fifth Circuit reversed the conviction and ordered a new trial * * *. We granted certiorari, and set the case for oral argument with *Gilbert v. State of California*, and *Stovall v. Denno*, which present similar questions.

* * * [I]n this case it is urged that the assistance of counsel at the lineup was indispensable to protect Wade's most basic right as a criminal defendant—his right to a fair trial at which the witnesses against him might be meaningfully cross-examined.

* * * [O]ur cases have construed the Sixth Amendment guarantee to apply to "critical" stages of the proceedings. The guarantee reads: "In all criminal prosecutions, the accused shall enjoy the right * * * to have the Assistance of Counsel for his defence." * * * The plain wording of this guarantee thus encompasses counsel's assistance whenever necessary to assure a meaningful "defence."

* * * [To determine whether a pretrial stage of the proceeding is critical], we scrutinize [that] pretrial confrontation of the accused to determine whether the presence of his counsel is necessary to preserve the defendant's basic right to a fair trial as affected by his right meaningfully to cross-examine the witnesses against him and to have effective assistance of counsel at the trial itself. It calls upon us to analyze whether potential substantial prejudice to defendant's rights inheres in the particular confrontation and the ability of counsel to help avoid that prejudice.

The Government characterizes the lineup as a mere preparatory step in the gathering of the prosecution's evidence, not different—for Sixth Amendment purposes—from various other preparatory steps, such as systematized or scientific analyzing of the accused's fingerprints, blood sample, clothing, hair, and the like. We think there are differences which preclude such stages being characterized as critical stages at which the accused has the right to the presence of his counsel. Knowledge of the techniques of science and technology is sufficiently available, and the variables in techniques few enough, that the accused has the opportunity for a meaningful confrontation of the Government's case at trial through the ordinary processes of cross-examination of the Government's expert witnesses and the presentation of the evidence of his own experts. * * *

But the confrontation compelled by the State between the accused and the victim or witnesses to a crime to elicit identification evidence is peculiarly riddled with innumerable dangers and variable factors which might seriously, even crucially, derogate from a fair trial. The vagaries of eyewitness identification are well-known; the annals of criminal law are rife with instances of mistaken identification. * * * A major factor contributing to the high incidence of miscarriage of justice from mistaken identification has been the degree of suggestion inherent in the manner in which the prosecution presents the suspect to witnesses for pretrial identification. * * * Moreover, "[i]t is a matter of common experience that, once a witness has picked out the accused at the line-up, he is not likely to go back on his word later on, so that in practice the issue of identity may (in the absence of other relevant evidence) for all practical purposes be determined there and then, before the trial."

The pretrial confrontation for purpose of identification may take the form of a lineup, also known as an "identification parade" or "showup," as in the present case, or presentation of the suspect alone to the witness. * * *

It is obvious that risks of suggestion attend either form of confrontation and increase the dangers inhering in eyewitness identification. But as is the case with secret interrogations, there is serious difficulty in depicting what transpires at lineups and other forms of identification confrontations. * * * [T]he defense can seldom reconstruct the manner and mode of lineup identification for judge or jury at trial. * * * [N]either witnesses nor lineup participants are apt to be alert for conditions prejudicial to the suspect. And if they were, it would likely be of scant benefit to the suspect since neither witnesses nor lineup participants are likely to be schooled in the detection of suggestive influences. Improper influences may go undetected by a suspect, guilty or not, who experiences the emotional tension which we might expect in one being confronted with potential accusers. Even when he does observe abuse, if he has a criminal record he may be reluctant to take the stand and open up the admission of prior convictions. Moreover, any protestations by the suspect of the fairness of the lineup made at trial are likely to be in vain; the jury's choice is between the accused's unsupported version and that of the police officers present. In short, the accused's inability effectively to reconstruct at trial any unfairness that occurred at the lineup may deprive him of his only opportunity meaningfully to attack the credibility of the witness' courtroom identification.

What facts have been disclosed in specific cases about the conduct of pretrial confrontations for identification illustrate both the potential for substantial prejudice to the accused at that stage and the need for its revelation at trial. A commentator provides some striking examples:

> In a Canadian case * * * the defendant had been picked out of a lineup of six men, of which he was the only Oriental. On other cases, a black-haired suspect was placed among a group of light-haired persons, tall suspects have been made to stand with short nonsuspects, and, in a case where the perpetrator of the crime was known to be a youth, a suspect under twenty was placed in a lineup with five other persons, all of whom were forty or over.

Similarly state reports, in the course of describing prior identifications admitted as evidence of guilt, reveal numerous instances of suggestive procedures, for example, that all in the lineup but the suspect were known to the identifying witness, that the other participants in a lineup were grossly dissimilar in appearance to the suspect, that only the suspect was required to wear distinctive clothing which the culprit allegedly wore, that the witness is told by the police that they have caught the culprit after which the defendant is brought before the witness alone or is viewed in jail, that the suspect is pointed out before or during a lineup, and that the participants in the lineup are asked to try on an article of clothing which fits only the suspect.

The potential for improper influence is illustrated by the circumstances, insofar as they appear, surrounding the prior identifications in the three cases we decide today. In the present case, the testimony of the identifying witnesses elicited on cross-examination revealed that those witnesses were taken to the courthouse and seated in the courtroom to await assembly of the lineup. The courtroom faced on a hallway observable to the witnesses through an open door. The cashier testified that she saw Wade "standing in the hall" within sight of an FBI agent. Five or six other prisoners later appeared in the hall. The vice president testified that he saw a person in the hall in the custody of the agent who "resembled the person that we identified as the one that had entered the bank."

The lineup in *Gilbert* was conducted in an auditorium in which some 100 witnesses to several alleged state and federal robberies charged to Gilbert made wholesale identifications of Gilbert as the robber in each other's presence, a procedure said to be fraught with dangers of suggestion. And the vice of suggestion created by the identification in *Stovall*, was the presentation to the witness of the suspect alone handcuffed to police officers. It is hard to imagine a situation more clearly conveying the suggestion to the witness that the one presented is believed guilty by the police.

The few cases that have surfaced therefore reveal the existence of a process attended with hazards of serious unfairness to the criminal accused and strongly suggest the plight of the more numerous defendants who are unable to ferret out suggestive influences in the secrecy of the confrontation. We do not assume that these risks are the result of police procedures intentionally designed to prejudice an accused. Rather we assume they derive from the dangers inherent in eyewitness identification and the suggestibility inherent in the context of the pretrial identification.
* * *

Insofar as the accused's conviction may rest on a courtroom identification in fact the fruit of a suspect pretrial identification which the accused is helpless to subject to effective scrutiny at trial, the accused is deprived of that right of cross-examination which is an essential safeguard to his right to confront the witnesses against him. And even though cross-examination is a precious safeguard to a fair trial, it cannot be viewed as an absolute assurance of accuracy and reliability. Thus in the present context, where so many variables and pitfalls exist, the first line of defense must be the prevention of unfairness and the lessening of the hazards of eyewitness identification at the lineup itself. The trial which might determine the accused's fate may well not be that in the courtroom but that at the pretrial confrontation, with the State aligned against the accused, the witness the sole jury, and the accused unprotected against the overreaching, intentional or unintentional, and with little or no effective appeal from the judgment there rendered by the witness—"that's the man."

Since it appears that there is grave potential for prejudice, intentional or not, in the pretrial lineup, which may not be capable of reconstruction at trial, and since presence of counsel itself can often avert prejudice and assure a meaningful confrontation at trial, there can be little doubt that for Wade the post[-]indictment lineup was a critical stage of the prosecution at which he was "as much entitled to such aid [of counsel] . . . as at the trial itself." Thus both Wade and his counsel should have been notified of the impending lineup, and counsel's presence should have been a requisite to conduct of the lineup, absent an "intelligent waiver." * * *

We come now to the question whether the denial of Wade's motion to strike the courtroom identification by the bank witnesses at trial because of the absence of his counsel at the lineup required, as the Court of Appeals held, the grant of a new trial at which such evidence is to be excluded. We do not think this disposition can be justified without first giving the Government the opportunity to establish by clear and convincing evidence that the in-court identifications were based upon observations of the suspect other than the lineup identification. Where, as here, the admissibility of evidence of the lineup identification itself is not involved, a per se rule of exclusion of courtroom identification would be unjustified. A rule limited solely to the exclusion of testimony concerning identification at the lineup itself, without regard to admissibility of the courtroom identification, would render the right to counsel an empty one. The lineup is most often used, as in the present case, to crystallize the witnesses' identification of the defendant for future reference. We have already noted that the lineup identification will have that effect. The State may then rest upon the witnesses' unequivocal courtroom identifications, and not mention the pretrial identification as part of the State's case at trial. Counsel is then in the predicament in which Wade's counsel found himself—realizing that possible unfairness at the lineup may be the sole means of attack upon the unequivocal courtroom identification, and having to probe in the dark in an attempt to discover and reveal unfairness, while bolstering the government witness' courtroom identification by bringing out and dwelling upon his prior identification. Since counsel's presence at the lineup would equip him to attack not only the lineup identification but the courtroom identification as well, limiting the impact of violation of the right to counsel to exclusion of evidence only of identification at the lineup itself disregards a critical element of that right.

* * * [T]he proper test to be applied in these situations is * * * "[w]hether, granting establishment of the primary illegality, the evidence to which instant objection is made has been come at by exploitation of that illegality or instead by means sufficiently distinguishable to be purged of the primary taint." * * * Application of this test in the present context

requires consideration of various factors; for example, the prior opportunity to observe the alleged criminal act,[a] the existence of any discrepancy between any pre-lineup description and the defendant's actual description, any identification prior to lineup of another person, the identification by picture of the defendant prior to the lineup, failure to identify the defendant on a prior occasion, and the lapse of time between the alleged act and the lineup identification. It is also relevant to consider those facts which, despite the absence of counsel, are disclosed concerning the conduct of the lineup. * * *

On the record now before us we cannot make the determination whether the in-court identifications had an independent origin. This was not an issue at trial, although there is some evidence relevant to a determination. That inquiry is most properly made in the District Court. We therefore think the appropriate procedure to be followed is to vacate the conviction pending a hearing to determine whether the in-court identifications had an independent source, or whether, in any event, the introduction of the evidence was harmless error, and for the District Court to reinstate the conviction or order a new trial, as may be proper. * * *

[CHIEF JUSTICE WARREN's opinion, concurring in part and dissenting in part, JUSTICE DOUGLAS' opinion, concurring in part and dissenting in part, JUSTICE FORTAS' opinion, concurring in part and dissenting in part, JUSTICE CLARK's concurring opinion, JUSTICE BLACK's opinion, dissenting in part and concurring in part, and JUSTICE WHITE's opinion, concurring in part and dissenting in part, have been omitted.]

KIRBY V. ILLINOIS
Supreme Court of the United States
406 U.S. 682, 92 S. Ct. 1877, 32 L. Ed. 2d 411 (1972)

JUSTICE STEWART announced the judgment of the Court and an opinion in which the CHIEF JUSTICE, JUSTICE BLACKMUN, and JUSTICE REHNQUIST join.

* * * In the present case we are asked to extend the *Wade-Gilbert per se* exclusionary rule to identification testimony based upon a police station showup that took place *before* the defendant had been indicted or otherwise formally charged with any criminal offense.

On February 21, 1968, a man named Willie Shard reported to the Chicago police that the previous day two men had robbed him on a Chicago street of a wallet containing, among other things, traveler's checks and a

---

[a] Since, in a case involving only one criminal act, the eyewitness would not have had a prior opportunity to view the alleged criminal act, the Court may have meant to suggest consideration of whether the eyewitness had a prior opportunity to view the defendant. If, for example, the eyewitness was familiar with the defendant and had seen him multiple times before the alleged criminal act, this would suggest that the in-court identification was independent of the lineup identification.

Social Security card. On February 22, two police officers stopped the petitioner and a companion, Ralph Bean, on West Madison Street in Chicago. When asked for identification, the petitioner produced a wallet that contained three traveler's checks and a Social Security card, all bearing the name of Willie Shard. Papers with Shard's name on them were also found in Bean's possession. When asked to explain his possession of Shard's property, the petitioner first said that the traveler's checks were "play money," and then told the officers that he had won them in a crap game. The officers then arrested the petitioner and Bean and took them to a police station.

Only after arriving at the police station, and checking the records there, did the arresting officers learn of the Shard robbery. A police car was then dispatched to Shard's place of employment, where it picked up Shard and brought him to the police station. Immediately upon entering the room in the police station where the petitioner and Bean were seated at a table, Shard positively identified them as the men who had robbed him two days earlier. No lawyer was present in the room, and neither the petitioner nor Bean had asked for legal assistance, or been advised of any right to the presence of counsel.

More than six weeks later, the petitioner and Bean were indicted for the robbery of Willie Shard. Upon arraignment, counsel was appointed to represent them, and they pleaded not guilty. A pretrial motion to suppress Shard's identification testimony was denied, and at the trial Shard testified as a witness for the prosecution. In his testimony he described his identification of the two men at the police station on February 22, and identified them again in the courtroom as the men who had robbed him on February 20. He was cross-examined at length regarding the circumstances of his identification of the two defendants. The jury found both defendants guilty, and the petitioner's conviction was affirmed on appeal. The Illinois appellate court held that the admission of Shard's testimony was not error, relying upon an earlier decision of the Illinois Supreme Court, holding that the *Wade-Gilbert per se* exclusionary rule is not applicable to preindictment confrontations. We granted certiorari, limited to this question. * * *

The *Wade-Gilbert* exclusionary rule * * * stems from * * * the guarantee of the right to counsel contained in the Sixth and Fourteenth Amendments. Unless all semblance of principled constitutional adjudication is to be abandoned, therefore, it is to the decisions construing that guarantee that we must look in determining the present controversy.

In a line of constitutional cases in this Court stemming back to the Court's landmark opinion in *Powell v. Alabama*, it has been firmly established that a person's Sixth and Fourteenth Amendment right to counsel attaches only at or after the time that adversary judicial proceedings have been initiated against him.

This is not to say that a defendant in a criminal case has a constitutional right to counsel only at the trial itself. The *Powell* case makes clear that the right attaches at the time of arraignment, and the Court has recently held that it exists also at the time of a preliminary hearing. But the point is that, while members of the Court have differed as to existence of the right to counsel in the contexts of some of the above cases, all of those cases have involved points of time at or after the initiation of adversary judicial criminal proceedings—whether by way of formal charge, preliminary hearing, indictment, information, or arraignment. * * *

The initiation of judicial criminal proceedings is far from a mere formalism. It is the starting point of our whole system of adversary criminal justice. For it is only then that the government has committed itself to prosecute, and only then that the adverse positions of government and defendant have solidified. It is then that a defendant finds himself faced with the prosecutorial forces of organized society, and immersed in the intricacies of substantive and procedural criminal law. It is this point, therefore, that marks the commencement of the "criminal prosecutions" to which alone the explicit guarantees of the Sixth Amendment are applicable.

In this case we are asked to import into a routine police investigation an absolute constitutional guarantee historically and rationally applicable only after the onset of formal prosecutorial proceedings. We decline to * * * impos[e] a *per se* exclusionary rule upon testimony concerning an identification that took place long before the commencement of any prosecution whatever.

What has been said is not to suggest that there may not be occasions during the course of a criminal investigation when the police do abuse identification procedures. Such abuses are not beyond the reach of the Constitution [since the] Due Process Clause of the Fifth and Fourteenth Amendments forbids a lineup that is unnecessarily suggestive and conducive to irreparable mistaken identification. * * *

The judgment is affirmed.

JUSTICE BRENNAN, with whom JUSTICE DOUGLAS and JUSTICE MARSHALL join, dissenting. * * *

While it should go without saying, it appears necessary, in view of the plurality opinion today, to re-emphasize that *Wade* did not require the presence of counsel at pretrial confrontations for identification purposes simply on the basis of an abstract consideration of the words "criminal prosecutions" in the Sixth Amendment. Counsel is required at those confrontations because "the dangers inherent in eyewitness identification and the suggestibility inherent in the context of the pretrial identification" mean that protection must be afforded to the "most basic right (of) a criminal defendant—his right to a fair trial at which the witnesses against him might be meaningfully cross-examined." * * * Hence, "the initiation of adversary judicial criminal proceedings," is completely irrelevant to whether counsel is necessary at a pretrial confrontation for identification in order to safeguard the accused's constitutional rights to confrontation and the effective assistance of counsel at his trial.

In view of *Wade*, it is plain, and the plurality today does not attempt to dispute it, that there inhere[s] in a confrontation for identification conducted after arrest the identical hazards to a fair trial that inhere in such a confrontation conducted "after the onset of formal prosecutorial proceedings." The plurality apparently considers an arrest, which for present purposes we must assume to be based upon probable cause, to be nothing more than part of "a routine police investigation," and thus not "the starting point of our whole system of adversary criminal justice." * * * If these propositions do not amount to "mere formalism," it is difficult to know how to characterize them. An arrest evidences the belief of the police that the perpetrator of a crime has been caught. A post-arrest confrontation for identification is not "a mere preparatory step in the gathering of the prosecution's evidence." A primary, and frequently sole, purpose of the confrontation for identification at that stage is to accumulate proof to buttress the conclusion of the police that they have the offender in hand. The plurality offers no reason, and I can think of none, for concluding that a post-arrest confrontation for identification, unlike a post-charge confrontation, is not among those "critical confrontations of the accused by the prosecution at pretrial proceedings where the results might well settle the accused's fate and reduce the trial itself to a mere formality."

The highly suggestive form of confrontation employed in this case underscores the point. This showup was particularly fraught with the peril of mistaken identification. In the setting of a police station squad room where all present except petitioner and Bean were police officers, the danger was quite real that Shard's understandable resentment might lead him too readily to agree with the police that the pair under arrest, and the only persons exhibited to him, were indeed the robbers. "It is hard to imagine a situation more clearly conveying the suggestion to the witness that the one presented is believed guilty by the police." The State had no case without Shard's identification testimony, and safeguards against [the risk of mistaken identification] were therefore of critical importance. Shard's testimony itself demonstrates the necessity for such safeguards. On direct examination, Shard identified petitioner and Bean not as the alleged robbers on trial in the courtroom, but as the pair he saw at the police station. * * *

[CHIEF JUSTICE BURGER's concurring opinion, JUSTICE POWELL's opinion concurring in the result, and JUSTICE WHITE's dissenting opinion have been omitted.]

MANSON V. BRATHWAITE

Supreme Court of the United States
432 U.S. 98, 97 S. Ct. 2243, 53 L. Ed. 2d 140 (1977)

JUSTICE BLACKMUN delivered the opinion of the Court.

This case presents the issue as to whether the Due Process Clause of the Fourteenth Amendment compels the exclusion * * * of pretrial identification evidence obtained by a police procedure that was both suggestive and unnecessary. * * *

Jimmy D. Glover, a full-time trooper of the Connecticut State Police, in 1970 was assigned to the Narcotics Division in an undercover capacity. On May 5 of that year, about 7:45 p.m., * * * and while there was still daylight, Glover and Henry Alton Brown, an informant, went to an apartment building at 201 Westland, in Hartford, for the purpose of purchasing narcotics from "Dickie Boy" Cicero, a known narcotics dealer. * * * Glover and Brown entered the building, observed by back-up Officers D'Onofrio and Gaffey, and proceeded by stairs to the third floor. Glover knocked at the door. * * * The area was illuminated by natural light from a window in the third floor hallway. The door was opened 12 to 18 inches in response to the knock. Glover observed a man standing at the door and, behind him, a woman. Brown identified himself. Glover then asked for "two things" of narcotics. The man at the door held out his hand, and Glover gave him two $10 bills. The door closed. Soon the man returned and handed Glover two glassine bags. While the door was open, Glover stood within two feet of the person from whom he made the purchase and observed his face. Five to seven minutes elapsed from the time the door first opened until it closed the second time.

Glover and Brown then left the building. This was about eight minutes after their arrival. Glover drove to headquarters where he described the seller to D'Onofrio and Gaffey. Glover at that time did not know the identity of the seller. He described him as being "a colored man, approximately five feet eleven inches tall, dark complexion, black hair, short Afro style, and having high cheekbones, and of heavy build. He was wearing at the time blue pants and a plaid shirt." D'Onofrio, suspecting from this description that respondent might be the seller, obtained a photograph of respondent from the Records Division of the Hartford Police Department. He left it at Glover's office. D'Onofrio was not acquainted with respondent personally, but did know him by sight and had seen him "[s]everal times" prior to May 5. Glover, when alone, viewed the photograph for the first time upon his return to headquarters on May 7; he identified the person shown as the one from whom he had purchased the narcotics. * * *

Respondent was charged, in a two-count information, with possession and sale of heroin. * * * At his trial in January 1971, the photograph from which Glover had identified respondent was received in evidence without objection on the part of the defense. Glover also testified that, although he had not seen respondent in the eight months that had elapsed since the sale, "there (was) no doubt whatsoever" in his mind that the person shown on the photograph was respondent. Glover also made a positive in-court identification without objection. * * *

Respondent * * * testified that on May 5, the day in question, he had been ill at his Albany Avenue apartment * * * and that at no time on that particular day had he been at 201 Westland. His wife testified that she recalled, after her husband had refreshed her memory, that he was home all day on May 5. * * *

The jury found respondent guilty on both counts of the information. He received a sentence of not less than six nor more than nine years. * * * [After his conviction was affirmed on appeal,] respondent filed a petition for habeas corpus in the United States District Court for the District of Connecticut. He alleged that the admission of the identification testimony at his state trial deprived him of due process of law to which he was entitled under the Fourteenth Amendment. The District Court * * * dismissed respondent's petition. On appeal, the United States Court of Appeals for the Second Circuit reversed. * * * We granted certiorari.

Stovall v. Denno, decided in 1967, concerned a petitioner who had been convicted in a New York court of murder. He was arrested the day following the crime and was taken by the police to a hospital where the victim's wife, also wounded in the assault, was a patient. After observing Stovall and hearing him speak, she identified him as the murderer. She later made an in-court identification. * * * On the identification issue, the Court reviewed the practice of showing a suspect singly for purposes of identification,[a] and the claim that this was so unnecessarily suggestive and conducive to irreparable mistaken identification that it constituted a denial of due process of law. The Court noted that the practice "has been widely condemned," but it concluded that "a claimed violation of due process of law in the conduct of a confrontation depends on the totality of the circumstances surrounding it." In that case, showing Stovall to the victim's spouse "was imperative." The Court then quoted the observations of the Court of Appeals, to the effect that the spouse was the only person who could possibly exonerate the accused; that the hospital was not far from the courthouse and jail; that no one knew how long she might live; that she

---

[a] Stovall was the only Black individual in the hospital room at the time. Stovall v. Denno, 388 U.S. 293, 295 (1967).

was not able to visit the jail; and that taking Stovall to the hospital room was the only feasible procedure, and, under the circumstances, "the usual police station line-up . . . was out of the question."

Neil v. Biggers, decided in 1972, concerned a respondent who had been convicted in a Tennessee court of rape, on evidence consisting in part of the victim's visual and voice identification of Biggers at a station-house showup seven months after the crime. The victim had been in her assailant's presence for some time and had directly observed him indoors and under a full moon outdoors. She testified that she had "no doubt" that Biggers was her assailant. She previously had given the police a description of the assailant. She had made no identification of others presented at previous showups, lineups, or through photographs. * * * [This] Court concluded that * * * "admission of evidence of a showup without more does not violate due process." * * * The "central question," * * * [is] "whether under the totality of the circumstances the identification was reliable even though the confrontation procedure was suggestive." * * *

Biggers well might be seen to provide an unambiguous answer to the question before us * * *. In one passage, however, the Court observed that the challenged procedure occurred pre-*Stovall* * * *. The question before us, then, is simply whether the *Biggers* analysis applies to post-*Stovall* confrontations as well to those pre-*Stovall*. * * *

Petitioner at the outset acknowledges that "the procedure in the instant case was suggestive (because only one photograph was used) and unnecessary" (because there was no emergency or exigent circumstance). The respondent * * * proposes a per se rule of exclusion that he claims is dictated by the demands of the Fourteenth Amendment's guarantee of due process. * * *

Since the decision in *Biggers*, the Courts of Appeals appear to have developed at least two approaches to such evidence. The first, or per se approach, employed by the Second Circuit in the present case, focuses on the procedures employed and requires exclusion of the out-of-court identification evidence, without regard to reliability, whenever it has been obtained through unnecessarily suggestive confrontation procedures. The justifications advanced are the elimination of evidence of uncertain reliability, deterrence of the police and prosecutors, and the stated "fair assurance against the awful risks of misidentification."

The second, or more lenient, approach is one that continues to rely on the totality of the circumstances. It permits the admission of the confrontation evidence if, despite the suggestive aspect, the out-of-court identification possesses certain features of reliability. * * * This second approach, in contrast to the other, is ad hoc and serves to limit the societal costs imposed by a sanction that excludes relevant evidence from consideration and evaluation by the trier of fact. * * *

There are, of course, several interests to be considered and taken into account. * * * [First is] the concern that the jury not hear eyewitness testimony unless that evidence has aspects of reliability. It must be observed that both approaches before us are responsive to this concern. The per se rule, however, goes too far since its application automatically and peremptorily, and without consideration of alleviating factors, keeps evidence from the jury that is reliable and relevant.

The second factor is deterrence. Although the per se approach has the more significant deterrent effect, the totality approach also has an influence on police behavior. * * *

The third factor is the effect on the administration of justice. Here the per se approach suffers serious drawbacks. Since it denies the trier reliable evidence, it may result, on occasion, in the guilty going free. Also, because of its rigidity, the per se approach may make error by the trial judge more likely than the totality approach. * * * Certainly, inflexible rules of exclusion that may frustrate rather than promote justice have not been viewed recently by this Court with unlimited enthusiasm. * * *

The standard * * * is that of fairness as required by the Due Process Clause of the Fourteenth Amendment. * * * We therefore conclude that reliability is the linchpin in determining the admissibility of identification testimony for both pre-and post-*Stovall* confrontations. The factors to be considered are set out in *Biggers*. These include the opportunity of the witness to view the criminal at the time of the crime, the witness' degree of attention, the accuracy of his prior description of the criminal, the level of certainty demonstrated at the confrontation, and the time between the crime and the confrontation. Against these factors is to be weighed the corrupting effect of the suggestive identification itself.

We turn, then, to the facts of this case and apply the analysis:

1. The opportunity to view. Glover testified that for two to three minutes he stood at the apartment door, within two feet of the respondent. The door opened twice, and each time the man stood at the door. The moments passed, the conversation took place, and payment was made. Glover looked directly at his vendor. It was near sunset, to be sure, but the sun had not yet set, so it was not dark or even dusk or twilight. * * * There was natural light. * * *

2. The degree of attention. Glover was not a casual or passing observer. * * * Trooper Glover was a trained police officer. * * * Glover himself was a Negro. * * * [A]s a specially trained, assigned, and experienced officer, he could be expected to pay scrupulous attention to detail, for he knew that subsequently he would have to find and arrest his vendor. In addition, he knew that his claimed observations would be subject later to close scrutiny and examination at any trial.

3. The accuracy of the description. Glover's description was given to D'Onofrio within minutes after the transaction. It included the vendor's race, his height, his build, the color and style of his hair, and the high cheekbone facial feature. It also included clothing the vendor wore. No claim has been made that respondent did not possess the physical characteristics so described. * * *

4. The witness' level of certainty. * * * Glover, in response to a question whether the photograph was that of the person from whom he made the purchase, testified: "There is no question whatsoever." This positive assurance was repeated.

5. The time between the crime and the confrontation. Glover's description of his vendor was given to D'Onofrio within minutes of the crime. The photographic identification took place only two days later. * * *

These indicators of Glover's ability to make an accurate identification are hardly outweighed by the corrupting effect of the challenged identification itself. * * * Although it plays no part in our analysis, all this assurance as to the reliability of the identification is hardly undermined by the facts that respondent was arrested in the very apartment where the sale had taken place * * *. Surely, we cannot say that under all the circumstances of this case there is "a very substantial likelihood of irreparable misidentification." Short of that point, such evidence is for the jury to weigh. * * *

We conclude that the criteria laid down in *Biggers* are to be applied in determining the admissibility of evidence offered by the prosecution concerning a post-*Stovall* identification, and that those criteria are satisfactorily met and complied with here.

The judgment of the Court of Appeals is reversed.

It is so ordered.

JUSTICE MARSHALL, with whom JUSTICE BRENNAN joins, dissenting.

* * * Relying on little more than a strong distaste for "inflexible rules of exclusion," the Court rejects the per se test. In so doing, the Court disregards two significant distinctions between the per se rule advocated in this case and the exclusionary remedies for certain other constitutional violations.

First, the per se rule here is not "inflexible." Where evidence is suppressed, for example, as the fruit of an unlawful search, it may well be forever lost to the prosecution. Identification evidence, however, can by its very nature be readily and effectively reproduced. * * * [W]hen a prosecuting attorney learns that there has been a suggestive confrontation, he can easily arrange another lineup conducted under scrupulously fair conditions. * * *

Second, other exclusionary rules have been criticized for preventing jury consideration of relevant and usually reliable evidence in order to serve interests unrelated to guilt or innocence, such as discouraging illegal searches or denial of counsel. Suggestively obtained eyewitness testimony is excluded, in contrast, precisely because of its unreliability and concomitant irrelevance. Its exclusion both protects the integrity of the truth-seeking function of the trial and discourages police use of needlessly inaccurate and ineffective investigatory methods.

Indeed, impermissibly suggestive identifications are not merely worthless law enforcement tools. They pose a grave threat to society at large in a more direct way than most governmental disobedience of the law. For if the police and the public erroneously conclude, on the basis of an unnecessarily suggestive confrontation, that the right man has been caught and convicted, the real outlaw must still remain at large. Law enforcement has failed in its primary function and has left society unprotected from the depredations of an active criminal.

For these reasons, I conclude that adoption of the per se rule would enhance, rather than detract from, the effective administration of justice. In my view, the Court's totality test will allow seriously unreliable and misleading evidence to be put before juries. * * * [Nonetheless,] assuming applicability of the totality test enunciated by the Court, the facts of the present case require [exclusion of Officer Glover's identification testimony.]

I consider first the opportunity that Officer Glover had to view the suspect. Careful review of the record shows that he could see the heroin seller only for the time it took to speak three sentences of four or five short words, to hand over some money, and later after the door reopened, to receive the drugs in return. The entire face-to-face transaction could have taken as little as 15 or 20 seconds. But during this time, Glover's attention was not focused exclusively on the seller's face. He observed that the door was opened 12 to 18 inches, that there was a window in the room behind the door, and, most importantly, that there was a woman standing behind the man. Glover was, of course, also concentrating on the details of the transaction—he must have looked away from the seller's face to hand him the money and receive the drugs. The observation during the conversation thus may have been as brief as 5 or 10 seconds.

As the Court notes, Glover was a police officer trained in and attentive to the need for making accurate identifications. Nevertheless, both common sense and scholarly study indicate that while a trained observer such as a police officer "is somewhat less likely to make an erroneous identification than the average untrained observer, the mere fact that he has been so trained is no guarantee that he is correct in a specific case. Police identification testimony should be scrutinized just as carefully as that of the normal witness." Moreover, "identifications made by policemen in highly competitive activities, such as undercover narcotic agents . . . , should be scrutinized with special care." Yet it is just such a searching inquiry that the Court fails to make here.

Another factor on which the Court relies, the witness' degree of certainty in making the identification, is worthless as an indicator that he is correct. Even if Glover had been unsure initially about his identification of respondent's picture, by the time he was called at trial to present a key piece of evidence for the State that paid his salary, it is impossible to imagine his responding negatively to such questions as "is there any doubt in your mind whatsoever" that the identification was correct. As the Court noted in *Wade*: "It is a matter of common experience that, once a witness has picked out the accused at the (pretrial confrontation), he is not likely to go back on his word later on."

Next, the Court finds that because the identification procedure took place two days after the crime, its reliability is enhanced. While such temporal proximity makes the identification more reliable than one occurring months later, the fact is that the greatest memory loss occurs within hours after an event. After that, the dropoff continues much more slowly. Thus, the reliability of an identification is increased only if it was made within several hours of the crime. If the time gap is any greater, reliability necessarily decreases.

Finally, the Court makes much of the fact that Glover gave a description of the seller to D'Onofrio shortly after the incident. Despite the Court's assertion that because "Glover himself was a Negro and unlikely to perceive only general features of 'hundreds of Hartford black males,' as the Court of Appeals stated," the description given by Glover was actually no more than a general summary of the seller's appearance. [Aside from describing the seller's clothing,] Glover merely described vaguely the seller's height, skin color, hairstyle, and build. He did say that the seller had "high cheekbones," but there is no other mention of facial features, nor even an estimate of age. Conspicuously absent is any indication that the seller was a native of the West Indies, certainly something which a member of the black community could immediately recognize from both appearance and accent.

From all of this, I must conclude that the evidence of Glover's ability to make an accurate identification is far weaker than the Court finds it. In contrast, the procedure used to identify respondent was both extraordinarily suggestive and strongly conducive to error. * * * By displaying a single photograph of respondent to the witness Glover under the circumstances in this record almost everything that could have been done wrong was done wrong.

In the first place, there was no need to use a photograph at all. Because photos are static, two-dimensional, and often outdated, they are "clearly inferior in reliability" to corporeal procedures. * * * [T]he poor reliability of photos makes their use inexcusable where any other means of identification is available. Here, since Detective D'Onofrio believed that he knew the seller's identity, further investigation without resort to a photographic showup was easily possible. With little inconvenience, a corporeal lineup including Brathwaite might have been arranged. * * *

Worse still than the failure to use an easily available corporeal identification was the display to Glover of only a single picture, rather than a photo array. With good reason, such single-suspect procedures have "been widely condemned." They give no assurance that the witness can identify the criminal from among a number of persons of similar appearance, surely the strongest evidence that there was no misidentification. * * *

The use of a single picture (or the display of a single live suspect, for that matter) is a grave error, of course, because it dramatically suggests to the witness that the person shown must be the culprit. Why else would the police choose the person? And it is deeply ingrained in human nature to agree with the expressed opinions of others particularly others who should be more knowledgeable when making a difficult decision. In this case, moreover, the pressure was not limited to that inherent in the display of a single photograph. Glover, the identifying witness, was a state police officer on special assignment. He knew that D'Onofrio, an experienced Hartford narcotics detective, presumably familiar with local drug operations, believed respondent to be the seller. There was at work, then, both loyalty to another police officer and deference to a better-informed colleague. * * *

The Court discounts this overwhelming evidence of suggestiveness, however. It reasons that because D'Onofrio was not present when Glover viewed the photograph, there was "little pressure on the witness to acquiesce in the suggestion." That conclusion blinks psychological reality. There is no doubt in my mind that even in D'Onofrio's absence, a clear and powerful message was telegraphed to Glover as he looked at respondent's photograph. He was emphatically told that "this is the man," and he responded by identifying respondent then and at trial "whether or not he was in fact 'the man.'"

I must conclude that this record presents compelling evidence that there was "a very substantial likelihood of misidentification" of respondent Brathwaite. The suggestive display of respondent's photograph to the witness Glover likely erased any independent memory that Glover had retained of the seller from his barely adequate opportunity to observe the criminal. * * *

[JUSTICE STEVENS' concurring opinion has been omitted.]

NOTE

The photographic identification procedure in *Manson v. Brathwaite* took place before Brathwaite was indicted. If the photographic identification had taken place after Brathwaite was indicted, would Brathwaite have been able to challenge the identification as violating his Sixth Amendment right to counsel?

In *United States v. Ash*, 413 U.S. 300 (1973), the Court answered this question in the negative, holding that a defendant has no right to have counsel present at a post-indictment photographic identification procedure in which his picture is presented to a witness. The Court explained that a photo identification is not a critical stage of the proceeding because it is not a trial-like confrontation where the guiding hand of counsel is needed. Because the defendant is not present at a photo identification procedure, "no possibility arises that the accused might be misled by his lack of familiarity with the law or overpowered by his professional adversary." *Id.* at 317. The Court further noted that equality of access to photographs "remove[s] any inequality in the adversary process." *Id.* at 319. Defense counsel can seek its own witnesses and conduct its own photographic displays. Justice Stewart, concurring, added that "there are substantially fewer possibilities of impermissible suggestion when photographs are used, and those unfair influences can be readily reconstructed at trial." *Id.* at 324. If a defendant's photograph is substantially different from the others displayed, "this unfairness can be demonstrated at trial from an actual comparison of the photographs used or from the witness's description of the display." *Id.*

In his dissent, Justice Brennan noted various ways impermissible suggestion might occur in the context of a photographic display. For example, the police officer or the prosecutor's "inflection, facial expressions, physical motions, and myriad other almost imperceptible means of communication might tend, intentionally or unintentionally, to compromise the witness's objectivity" and lead to an erroneous identification. *Id.* at 333–34. The defense, however, would not be able to reconstruct at trial the exact mode and manner of the photographic identification. *Id.* at 335. Justice Brennan also pointed out that precisely because the accused is not present at a photographic identification, this reduces "the likelihood that irregularities in the procedure will ever come to light." *Id.* at 336.

Ash is significant in light of the fact that police "have mostly stopped using live lineups because it is so difficult and time-consuming to find people who look similar to a suspect." Brandon L. Garrett, *Eyewitnesses and Exclusion*, 65 VAND. L. REV. 451, 459 (2012). Police today tend to use photo arrays rather than live lineups.

EYEWITNESS IDENTIFICATIONS AND STATE COURTS AS GUARDIANS AGAINST WRONGFUL CONVICTION

Sandra Guerra Thompson
7 Ohio St. J. Crim. L. 603 (2010)

It is fascinating to read the Supreme Court's Due Process jurisprudence on eyewitness identifications—now well over thirty years old—from a perspective which is informed by the lessons of hundreds of wrongful convictions and by the massive body of social science literature that has since developed. Long before the advent of DNA evidence and the release of so many wrongly convicted people, a rich dialogue had existed in the jurisprudence of eyewitness identifications about the risks of misidentification and the role the courts should play in protecting the innocent. In the early 1970's, federal district and circuit courts were apparently more inclined than now to exclude identification testimony on Due Process grounds. In *Manson v. Brathwaite*, the Supreme Court, clearly signaling its intent to take a hands-off approach, reversed several such decisions and, in the process, set in place a "more lenient" Due Process standard that has failed to provide any meaningful protection against wrongful convictions, despite the fact that the Court declared reliability to be the "linchpin" of its approach.

Upon a showing that the identification procedure is impermissibly suggestive, the Court then considers the "totality of the circumstances" to determine whether the identification is nonetheless reliable. To assess the totality of the circumstances, the Court instructs lower courts to consider five factors (taken from its earlier decision in *Neil v. Biggers*): "the opportunity of the witness to view the criminal at the time of the crime, the witness' degree of attention, the accuracy of his prior description of the criminal, the level of certainty demonstrated at the confrontation, and the time between the crime and the confrontation." The Court also called for the weighing of these factors against "the corrupting effect of the suggestive identification itself." However, courts have generally not undertaken to measure the extent to which suggestive practices might have undermined reliability. The Supreme Court has not revisited this jurisprudence in the three decades since it was established, so it continues to govern in federal courts and is followed in most state courts as well. * * *

The Supreme Court's Due Process test focuses first on the question of police suggestiveness before turning to the question of reliability. If there is no suggestion introduced by the police procedures, then there is no Due Process claim. The test, thus, completely ignores unreliability if there is no evidence of police suggestion. This is a gaping hole in the protection against mistaken identification and erroneous conviction. If the Due Process clause serves to protect against unfair trials due to unreliable evidence, then the *Brathwaite* test applies too narrowly. A great deal of unreliability is caused by factors inherent to the eyewitnesses (age, lighting, weapon-focus, cross-race bias, etc.). * * * However, the Supreme Court's Due Process protection only applies if the defense first crosses the threshold of suggestive police practices. * * *

The Supreme Court instructs courts to consider the "totality of the circumstances" in determining reliability, but this "totality" turns out to be restricted to a checklist of five factors (which, again, do not include suggestiveness). * * * [T]he list of factors is problematic. First, it includes the consideration of the witness's level of certainty as an indication of reliability, when scientific studies show witness certainty does not correlate with reliability. Second, it fails to include many other important * * * variables such as cross-race identification and weapon-focus, which have a strong impact on reliability. By limiting the courts to a restrictive list of factors, the Supreme Court's test has actually hamstrung the lower courts in their ability to evaluate the true "totality" of the circumstances. * * *

'THEY ALL LOOK ALIKE': THE OTHER-RACE EFFECT

Steven Ross Pomeroy
Forbes Magazine (Jan. 28, 2014)

If somebody says, "Well, they all look alike," one might assume that person to be a closet bigot. But in all likelihood, he's simply being honest about a well-known limitation that plagues people of all colors: we humans are notoriously poor at distinguishing between the members of races different from our own.

The Other-Race Effect, as this psychological shortcoming is called, has been studied for decades. Originally realized during times of mass immigration, it was first recognized by science a century ago. Theories to explain it abound, but two clearly have an edge. The first hypothesis goes something like this: we generally spend more time with people of our own race and thus gain "perceptual expertise" for the characteristics of people who look like us. For example, since Caucasians sport wide variability in hair color, they may grow accustomed to differentiating strangers by looking at their hair. On the other hand, black people show more variability in skin tone, so they might instinctively use skin tone to tell others apart.

The second hypothesis states that people think more categorically about members of other races. Basically, we take notice that they're different from us, but tune out less noticeable characteristics. "The problem is not that we can't code the details of cross-race faces—it's that we don't," Daniel Levin, a cognitive psychologist at Kent State University explained to the American Psychological Association.

Concrete evidence is often hard to come by in psychology, so it's unlikely that either theory will ever be "proven" conclusively. We can, however, switch gears and examine a couple of things that don't factor in to the Other-Race Effect.

First, it's not simply because some races are more homogenous. Available evidence suggests that humans belonging to all ethnicities differ in a multitude of ways. "Cognitive psychologists have pointed to the fact that faces are not all alike; they differ from each other in terms of specific features like width, length, size of nose, and color of eyes," Professor Lawrence White of Beloit College says.

Second, the Other Race effect is not necessarily fueled by racist thinking. "Studies have found that racial attitudes don't predict performance in cross-race identification tasks; prejudiced and non-prejudiced people are equally likely to fall victim to the other-race effect," White says.

Many might scoff at the idea of studying the Other-Race Effect, but it certainly merits examination. The effect is ubiquitous, and has real-world, life and death implications. Take eyewitness testimony, for example. The Other-Race effect suggests that witnesses of one race would not be very skilled at identifying suspects of another. Published research bears this out. In one study, investigators examined 40 participants in a racially diverse area of the United States. Participants watched a video of a crime being committed, then, over the following 24 hours, were asked to pick a suspect out of a photo line-up. The majority of participants either misidentified the suspect or stated the suspect was not in the line-up at all. However, correct identification of the suspect occurred more often when the eyewitness and the suspect were of the same race.

Is there any way to prevent or minimize the Other-Race Effect? Absolutely. Recent research points to a sensitive period in which the effect develops. If infants regularly see and interact with people of other races before nine months of age, the Other-Race Effect may never emerge. But for those who are already inept at distinguishing between people of other ethnicities, don't fret, there's still hope. According to University of London psychologist Gizelle Anzures, "The Other-Race Effect can be prevented, attenuated, and even reversed given experience with a novel race class." So broaden your horizons! Get out there any meet some new people!

This article originally appeared on RealClearScience.

USING AN EXPERT TO EVALUATE EYEWITNESS IDENTIFICATION EVIDENCE

Shirley K. Duffy[a]

83 N.Y. St. B. Ass'n J. 41 (2011)

A cross-racial identification occurs where a victim/witness of one race identifies a suspect of another race as a perpetrator. A problem exists because cross-racial identifications by witnesses are more likely to result in wrongful convictions. This greater tendency to misidentify suspects of another race has been dubbed the "other-race effect" or "own-race bias." There is some support that the own-race effect is strongest when a white witness must identify a black face. While the majority of research has been conducted using white and black subjects, a recent study has noted the other-race effect between black and Hispanic subjects. * * *

In the last 20 years, research has been conducted in an attempt to discern whether the effect has a social or cognitive explanation. Some researchers have suggested that the inability to accurately encode and recognize other-race faces stems from a simple lack of contact with persons of other races. This theory has not been heavily supported, however, and many studies have argued that it is the quality—not the quantity—of the contact that results in increased ability to recognize other-race faces. Originally, prejudice and racism were thought to be an explanation for lower recognition rates; however, recent studies have found no correlation.

A cognitive interpretation for the "other-race effect" focuses on the physiognomic variability of faces. Specifically, the type of variability in faces, and not the amount of variability, is what accounts for differences in recognition accuracy. Because different races can differ in the type of variability among their faces (e.g., hair color in whites, skin tone in blacks, etc.), relying on the facial cues that lead to variability in one's own race will be ineffective for encoding and recognition of an other-race face.

Whatever the reason for the other-race effect, it has been extensively documented in laboratory research and has been shown to exist outside the lab as well. If cross-racial identification errors cannot be precluded at the source, then they need to be identified and remedied in the courtroom. * * *

Cross-racial-identification error poses unique problems in the realm of eyewitness testimony, primarily because most witnesses either do not know it exists or do not know that they suffer from it. The problem is magnified by the fact that the potential problems with recognition and identification are lost on most jurors. Further, because traditional safeguards against the admission of inaccurate eyewitness testimony (suppression hearings, cross-examination and closing arguments) fail to

---

[a] Reprinted with permission from the New York State Bar Association Journal, June 2011, Vol. 83, No. 5, published by the New York State Bar Association, One Elk Street, Albany, New York 12207.

bring out the existence of any bias, attorneys who are aware of the other-race effect cannot educate the jurors properly. The use of expert testimony and special jury instructions has shown some promise; however, they carry an inherent ineffectiveness because they attempt to make jurors aware of the problem after the fact, with only mixed results.

PERRY V. NEW HAMPSHIRE
Supreme Court of the United States
565 U.S. 228, 132 S. Ct. 716, 181 L. Ed. 2d 691 (2012)

JUSTICE GINSBURG delivered the opinion of the Court.

* * *

Around 3 a.m. on August 15, 2008, Joffre Ullon called the Nashua, New Hampshire, Police Department and reported that an African-American male was trying to break into cars parked in the lot of Ullon's apartment building. Officer Nicole Clay responded to the call. Upon arriving at the parking lot, Clay heard what "sounded like a metal bat hitting the ground." She then saw petitioner Barion Perry standing between two cars. Perry walked toward Clay, holding two car-stereo amplifiers in his hands. A metal bat lay on the ground behind him. Clay asked Perry where the amplifiers came from. "[I] found them on the ground," Perry responded.

Meanwhile, Ullon's wife, Nubia Blandon, woke her neighbor, Alex Clavijo, and told him she had just seen someone break into his car. Clavijo immediately went downstairs to the parking lot to inspect the car. * * * [H]e discovered that the speakers and amplifiers from his car stereo were missing, as were his bat and wrench. * * *

By this time, another officer had arrived at the scene. Clay asked Perry to stay in the parking lot with that officer, while she and Clavijo went to talk to Blandon. * * * They met Blandon in the hallway just outside the open door to her apartment.

Asked to describe what she had seen, Blandon stated that, around 2:30 a.m., she saw from her kitchen window a tall, African-American man roaming the parking lot and looking into cars. Eventually, the man circled Clavijo's car, opened the trunk, and removed a large box.

Clay asked Blandon for a more specific description of the man. Blandon pointed to her kitchen window and said the person she saw breaking into Clavijo's car was standing in the parking lot, next to the police officer. Perry's arrest followed this identification.

About a month later, the police showed Blandon a photographic array that included a picture of Perry and asked her to point out the man who had broken into Clavijo's car. Blandon was unable to identify Perry.

Perry was charged in New Hampshire state court with one count of theft by unauthorized taking and one count of criminal mischief.[a] Before trial, he moved to suppress Blandon's identification on the ground that admitting it at trial would violate due process. Blandon witnessed what amounted to a one-person showup in the parking lot, Perry asserted, which all but guaranteed that she would identify him as the culprit.

The New Hampshire Superior Court denied the motion. * * * [T]he Superior Court concluded [that] Blandon's identification of Perry on the night of the crime did not result from an unnecessarily suggestive procedure "manufacture[d] . . . by the police." Blandon pointed to Perry "spontaneously," the court noted, "without any inducement from the police." * * *

The Superior Court recognized that there were reasons to question the accuracy of Blandon's identification: the parking lot was dark in some locations; Perry was standing next to a police officer; Perry was the only African-American man in the vicinity; and Blandon was unable, later, to pick Perry out of a photographic array. But "[b]ecause the police procedures were not unnecessarily suggestive," the court ruled that the reliability of Blandon's testimony was for the jury to consider. At the ensuing trial, Blandon and Clay testified to Blandon's out-of-court identification. The jury found Perry guilty of theft and not guilty of criminal mischief. On appeal, * * * [t]he New Hampshire Supreme Court rejected Perry's argument and affirmed his conviction.

We granted certiorari to resolve a division of opinion on the question whether the Due Process Clause requires a trial judge to conduct a preliminary assessment of the reliability of an eyewitness identification made under suggestive circumstances not arranged by the police. * * *

[W]e set forth in *Neil v. Biggers*, and reiterated in *Manson v. Brathwaite*, the approach appropriately used to determine whether the Due Process Clause requires suppression of an eyewitness identification tainted by police arrangement. The Court emphasized, first, that due process concerns arise only when law enforcement officers use an identification procedure that is both suggestive and unnecessary. Even when the police use such a procedure, the Court next said, suppression of the resulting identification is not the inevitable consequence.

A rule requiring automatic exclusion, the Court reasoned, would "g[o] too far," for it would "kee[p] evidence from the jury that is reliable and relevant," and "may result, on occasion, in the guilty going free."

Instead of mandating a *per se* exclusionary rule, the Court held that the Due Process Clause requires courts to assess, on a case-by-case basis,

---

[a] In order to be found guilty of criminal mischief in the state of New Hampshire, one must, when "having no right to do so nor any reasonable basis for belief of having such a right, purposely or recklessly damage property of another." N.H. REV. STAT. ANN. § 634:2 (2008).

whether improper police conduct created a "substantial likelihood of misidentification." "[R]eliability [of the eyewitness identification] is the linchpin" of that evaluation, the Court stated in *Brathwaite*. Where the "indicators of [a witness'] ability to make an accurate identification" are "outweighed by the corrupting effect" of law enforcement suggestion, the identification should be suppressed. Otherwise, the evidence (if admissible in all other respects) should be submitted to the jury.

Applying this "totality of the circumstances" approach, the Court held in *Biggers* that law enforcement's use of an unnecessarily suggestive showup did not require suppression of the victim's identification of her assailant. Notwithstanding the improper procedure, the victim's identification was reliable: She saw her assailant for a considerable period of time under adequate light, provided police with a detailed description of her attacker long before the showup, and had "no doubt" that the defendant was the person she had seen. Similarly, the Court concluded in *Brathwaite* that police use of an unnecessarily suggestive photo array did not require exclusion of the resulting identification. The witness, an undercover police officer, viewed the defendant in good light for several minutes, provided a thorough description of the suspect, and was certain of his identification. Hence, the "indicators of [the witness'] ability to make an accurate identification [were] hardly outweighed by the corrupting effect of the challenged identification."

Perry concedes that * * * law enforcement officials did not arrange the suggestive circumstances surrounding Blandon's identification. He contends, however, that it was mere happenstance that each of the [previously discussed] cases involved improper police action. The rationale underlying our decisions, Perry asserts, supports a rule requiring trial judges to prescreen eyewitness evidence for reliability any time an identification is made under suggestive circumstances. We disagree.

Perry's argument depends, in large part, on the Court's statement in *Brathwaite* that "reliability is the linchpin in determining the admissibility of identification testimony." If reliability is the linchpin of admissibility under the Due Process Clause, Perry maintains, it should make no difference whether law enforcement was responsible for creating the suggestive circumstances that marred the identification.

Perry has removed our statement in *Brathwaite* from its mooring, and thereby attributes to the statement a meaning a fair reading of our opinion does not bear. * * * The due process check for reliability, *Brathwaite* made plain, comes into play only after the defendant establishes improper police conduct. The very purpose of the check, the Court noted, was to avoid depriving the jury of identification evidence that is reliable, notwithstanding improper police conduct. * * * A primary aim of excluding identification evidence obtained under unnecessarily suggestive circumstances, the Court said, is to deter law enforcement use of improper lineups, showups, and photo arrays in the first place. * * *

Perry's argument, reiterated by the dissent, thus lacks support in the case law he cites. Moreover, his position would open the door to judicial preview, under the banner of due process, of most, if not all, eyewitness identifications. External suggestion is hardly the only factor that casts doubt on the trustworthiness of an eyewitness' testimony. As one of Perry's amici points out, many other factors bear on "the likelihood of misidentification,"—for example, the passage of time between exposure to and identification of the defendant, whether the witness was under stress when he first encountered the suspect, how much time the witness had to observe the suspect, how far the witness was from the suspect, whether the suspect carried a weapon, and the race of the suspect and the witness. There is no reason why an identification made by an eyewitness with poor vision, for example, or one who harbors a grudge against the defendant, should be regarded as inherently more reliable, less of a "threat to the fairness of trial," than the identification Blandon made in this case. To embrace Perry's view would thus entail a vast enlargement of the reach of due process as a constraint on the admission of evidence. * * *

In urging a broadly applicable due process check on eyewitness identifications, Perry maintains that eyewitness identifications are a uniquely unreliable form of evidence. We do not doubt * * * the fallibility of eyewitness identifications. * * * The fallibility of eyewitness evidence does not, without the taint of improper state conduct, warrant a due process rule requiring a trial court to screen such evidence for reliability before allowing the jury to assess its creditworthiness.

Our unwillingness to enlarge the domain of due process as Perry and the dissent urge rests, in large part, on our recognition that the jury, not the judge, traditionally determines the reliability of evidence. We also take account of other safeguards built into our adversary system that caution juries against placing undue weight on eyewitness testimony of questionable reliability. * * *

Many of the safeguards * * * were at work at Perry's trial. During her opening statement, Perry's court-appointed attorney cautioned the jury about the vulnerability of Blandon's identification. While cross-examining Blandon and Officer Clay, Perry's attorney constantly brought up the weaknesses of Blandon's identification. She highlighted: (1) the significant distance between Blandon's window and the parking lot, (2) the lateness of the hour, (3) the van that partly obstructed Blandon's view, (4) Blandon's concession that she was "so scared [she] really didn't pay attention" to what Perry was wearing, (5) Blandon's inability to describe Perry's facial features or other identifying marks, (6) Blandon's failure to pick Perry out of a photo array, and (7) Perry's position next to a uniformed, gun-bearing police officer at the moment Blandon made her identification. Perry's counsel reminded the jury of these frailties during her summation.

After closing arguments, the trial court read the jury a lengthy instruction on identification testimony and the factors the jury should consider when evaluating it. The court also instructed the jury that the defendant's guilt must be proved beyond a reasonable doubt, and specifically cautioned that "one of the things the State must prove [beyond a reasonable doubt] is the identification of the defendant as the person who committed the offense."

Given the safeguards generally applicable in criminal trials, protections availed of by the defense in Perry's case, we hold that the Due Process Clause does not require a preliminary judicial inquiry into the reliability of an eyewitness identification when the identification was not procured under unnecessarily suggestive circumstances arranged by law enforcement. Accordingly, the judgment of the New Hampshire Supreme Court is

Affirmed.

JUSTICE SOTOMAYOR, dissenting. * * *

The majority today creates a novel and significant limitation on our longstanding rule: Eyewitness identifications so impermissibly suggestive that they pose a very substantial likelihood of an unreliable identification will be deemed inadmissible at trial only if the suggestive circumstances were "police-arranged." Absent "improper police arrangement," "improper police conduct," or "rigging," the majority holds, our two-step inquiry does not even "com[e] into play." I cannot agree.

The majority does not simply hold that an eyewitness identification must be the product of police action to trigger our ordinary two-step inquiry. Rather, the majority maintains that the suggestive circumstances giving rise to the identification must be "police-arranged," "police rigg[ed]," "police-designed," or "police-organized." Those terms connote a degree of intentional orchestration or manipulation. The majority categorically exempts all eyewitness identifications derived from suggestive circumstances that were not police-manipulated—however suggestive, and however unreliable—from our due process check. The majority thus appears to graft a *mens rea* requirement onto our existing rule.

As this case illustrates, police intent is now paramount. As the Court acknowledges, Perry alleges an "accidental showup." He was the only African-American at the scene of the crime standing next to a police officer. For the majority, the fact that the police did not intend that showup, even if they inadvertently caused it in the course of a police procedure, ends the inquiry. The police were questioning the eyewitness, Blandon, about the perpetrator's identity, and were intentionally detaining Perry in the parking lot—but had not intended for Blandon to identify the perpetrator from her window. Presumably, in the majority's view, had the police asked Blandon to move to the window to identify the perpetrator, that could have made all the difference.

I note, however, that the majority leaves what is required by its arrangement-focused inquiry less than clear. In parts, the opinion suggests that the police must arrange an identification "procedure," regardless of whether they "inten[d] the arranged procedure to be suggestive." Elsewhere, it indicates that the police must arrange the "suggestive circumstances" that lead the witness to identify the accused. Still elsewhere it refers to "improper" police conduct, connoting bad faith. * * *

The arrangement-focused inquiry will sow needless confusion. If the police had called Perry and Blandon to the police station for interviews, and Blandon saw Perry being questioned, would that be sufficiently "improper police arrangement"? If Perry had voluntarily come to the police station, would that change the result? Today's opinion renders the applicability of our ordinary inquiry contingent on a murky line-drawing exercise. Whereas our two-step inquiry focuses on overall reliability—and could account for the spontaneity of the witness' identification and degree of police manipulation under the totality of the circumstances—today's opinion forecloses that assessment by establishing a new and inflexible step zero.

* * * [T]he majority emphasizes that we should rely on the jury to determine the reliability of evidence. But our cases are rooted in the assumption that eyewitness identifications upend the ordinary expectation that it is "the province of the jury to weigh the credibility of competing witnesses." As noted, jurors find eyewitness evidence unusually powerful and their ability to assess credibility is hindered by a witness' false confidence in the accuracy of his or her identification. That disability in no way depends on the intent behind the suggestive circumstances. * * *

The empirical evidence demonstrates that eyewitness misidentification is "the single greatest cause of wrongful convictions in this country." Researchers have found that a staggering 76% of the first 250 convictions overturned due to DNA evidence since 1989 involved eyewitness misidentification. Study after study demonstrates that eyewitness recollections are highly susceptible to distortion by postevent information or social cues; that jurors routinely overestimate the accuracy of eyewitness identifications; that jurors place the greatest weight on eyewitness confidence in assessing identifications even though confidence is a poor gauge of accuracy; and that suggestiveness can stem from sources beyond police-orchestrated procedures. The majority today nevertheless adopts an artificially narrow conception of the dangers of suggestive identifications at a time when our concerns should have deepened. * * *

[JUSTICE THOMAS' concurring opinion has been omitted.]

CHAPTER 22

THE PROSECUTOR'S CHARGING DISCRETION

■ ■ ■

The Supreme Court has often said that the decision whether to prosecute and what charge or charges to file rests entirely within the prosecutor's discretion. The prosecutor's charging discretion, however, is not unfettered. It is subject to constitutional constraints. *United States v. Armstrong* examines one of these constitutional constraints: the Equal Protection Clause. A defendant who believes she has been unfairly charged because of her race, gender, national origin, or other protected class status can assert a selective prosecution claim. A selective prosecution claim is an affirmative defense that can lead to a dismissal of the indictment or a reversal of a conviction. The *Armstrong* Court explains the requirements for a selective prosecution claim and decides what showing is necessary for a defendant to obtain discovery in support of a selective prosecution claim.[a]

In *Racial Fairness in the Criminal Justice System: The Role of the Prosecutor*, Angela Davis explains how racial considerations can affect prosecutorial charging decisions, even when the prosecutor is not consciously intending to discriminate based on race. Davis' article examines the traditional factors that inform the prosecutor's charging decision, and shows how race and class can have an impact on these seemingly race-neutral factors. A note on the prosecutor's charging discretion in relation to the 2012 shooting death of Trayvon Martin, an unarmed Black male teenager, by George Zimmerman, a Neighborhood Watch volunteer, follows this excerpt.

In *United States v. Goodwin*, we learn about another constitutional constraint on the prosecutor's charging discretion: the Due Process Clause. The Due Process Clause prohibits the prosecution from using its charging discretion to retaliate against a defendant for exercising a constitutional or statutory right. A defendant who believes he is being retaliated against or punished for exercising a constitutional or statutory right may assert a claim of vindictive prosecution. Because it is difficult to prove that a

---

[a] Discovery is the process in which the parties obtain information, usually before trial, about the witnesses the other side intends to call at trial and the evidence that the other side possesses. *See How Courts Work*, AM. BAR ASS'N (Nov. 28, 2021), http://www.americanbar.org/groups/public_education/resources/law_related_education_network/how_courts_work/discovery.html (https://perma.cc/PU2Y-PGG7). We will study the rules governing discovery in criminal cases in a later chapter.

prosecutor acted with retaliatory motive, courts may apply a presumption of vindictiveness in cases involving a realistic likelihood of vindictiveness. In these cases, the defendant need only show that he exercised a constitutional or statutory right, and that this was followed by an additional or more serious charge. If the court applies a presumption of vindictiveness, the prosecutor can overcome that presumption by presenting objective information supporting the additional or more serious charge. If the court does not apply a presumption of vindictiveness, the defendant must show actual vindictiveness, i.e., that the prosecutor filed the additional or more serious charge to punish the defendant for exercising a legally protected statutory or constitutional right.

It should be noted that the prosecutor is also subject to ethical constraints. As noted in the American Bar Association's *Criminal Justice Standards for the Prosecution Function*, "The primary duty of the prosecutor is to seek justice within the bounds of the law, not merely to convict." *See* Standard 3–1.2(a) in Appendix. Under these standards, "A prosecutor should ... file criminal charges only if the prosecutor reasonably believes that the charges are supported by probable cause, that admissible evidence will be sufficient to support a conviction beyond a reasonable doubt, and that the decision to charge is in the interests of justice." *See* Standard 3–4.3(a) in Appendix.

Finally, in *United States v. Batchelder*, the Court examines a case involving overlapping statutes, i.e., two statutes that are identical except for the penalty that is authorized by each statute. The *Batchelder* Court considers whether it violates the Constitution for the prosecutor to charge a defendant with violating the statute with the greater penalty. As part of this inquiry, the Court considers whether the rule of lenity and/or the void for vagueness doctrine require the prosecutor to charge the defendant with violating the offense with the lesser sentence.

UNITED STATES V. ARMSTRONG
Supreme Court of the United States
517 U.S. 456, 116 S. Ct. 1480, 134 L. Ed. 2d 687 (1996)

CHIEF JUSTICE REHNQUIST delivered the opinion of the Court. * * *

In April 1992, respondents were indicted in the United States District Court for the Central District of California on charges of conspiring to possess with intent to distribute more than 50 grams of cocaine base (crack) and conspiring to distribute the same, in violation of 21 U.S.C. §§ 841 and 846, and federal firearms offenses. For three months prior to the indictment, agents of the Federal Bureau of Alcohol, Tobacco, and Firearms and the Narcotics Division of the Inglewood, California, Police Department had infiltrated a suspected crack distribution ring by using three confidential informants. On seven separate occasions during this period, the informants had bought a total of 124.3 grams of crack from respondents and witnessed respondents carrying firearms during the sales. The agents searched the hotel room in which the sales were transacted, arrested respondents Armstrong and Hampton in the room, and found more crack and a loaded gun. The agents later arrested the other respondents as part of the ring.

In response to the indictment, respondents filed a motion for discovery or for dismissal of the indictment, alleging that they were selected for federal prosecution because they are black. In support of their motion, they offered only an affidavit by a "Paralegal Specialist," employed by the Office of the Federal Public Defender representing one of the respondents. The only allegation in the affidavit was that, in every one of the 24 § 841 or § 846 cases closed by the office during 1991, the defendant was black. Accompanying the affidavit was a "study" listing the 24 defendants, their race, whether they were prosecuted for dealing cocaine as well as crack, and the status of each case.

The Government opposed the discovery motion, arguing, among other things, that there was no evidence or allegation "that the Government has acted unfairly or has prosecuted non-black defendants or failed to prosecute them." The District Court granted the motion. It ordered the Government (1) to provide a list of all cases from the last three years in which the Government charged both cocaine and firearms offenses, (2) to identify the race of the defendants in those cases, (3) to identify what levels of law enforcement were involved in the investigations of those cases, and (4) to explain its criteria for deciding to prosecute those defendants for federal cocaine offenses.

The Government moved for reconsideration of the District Court's discovery order. With this motion it submitted affidavits and other evidence to explain why it had chosen to prosecute respondents and why respondents' study did not support the inference that the Government was singling out blacks for cocaine prosecution. The federal and local agents participating in the case alleged in affidavits that race played no role in their investigation. An Assistant United States Attorney explained in an affidavit that the decision to prosecute met the general criteria for prosecution, because

> there was over 100 grams of cocaine base involved, over twice the threshold necessary for a ten year mandatory minimum sentence; there were multiple sales involving multiple defendants, thereby indicating a fairly substantial crack cocaine ring; . . . there were multiple federal firearms violations intertwined with the narcotics trafficking; the overall evidence in the case was extremely strong, including audio and videotapes of defendants;

... and several of the defendants had criminal histories including narcotics and firearms violations.

The Government also submitted sections of a published 1989 Drug Enforcement Administration report which concluded that "[l]arge-scale, interstate trafficking networks controlled by Jamaicans, Haitians and Black street gangs dominate the manufacture and distribution of crack."

In response, one of respondents' attorneys submitted an affidavit alleging that an intake coordinator at a drug treatment center had told her that there are "an equal number of caucasian users and dealers to minority users and dealers." Respondents also submitted an affidavit from a criminal defense attorney alleging that in his experience many nonblacks are prosecuted in state court for crack offenses, and a newspaper article reporting that federal "crack criminals . . . are being punished far more severely than if they had been caught with powder cocaine, and almost every single one of them is black."

The District Court denied the motion for reconsideration. When the Government indicated it would not comply with the court's discovery order, the court dismissed the case. * * * [An] en banc panel [of the Court of Appeals] affirmed the District Court's order of dismissal, holding that "a defendant is not required to demonstrate that the government has failed to prosecute others who are similarly situated." We granted certiorari to determine the appropriate standard for discovery for a selective-prosecution claim. * * *

A selective-prosecution claim is not a defense on the merits to the criminal charge itself, but an independent assertion that the prosecutor has brought the charge for reasons forbidden by the Constitution. Our cases delineating the necessary elements to prove a claim of selective prosecution have taken great pains to explain that the standard is a demanding one. * * *

A selective-prosecution claim asks a court to exercise judicial power over a "special province" of the Executive. The Attorney General and United States Attorneys retain "broad discretion" to enforce the Nation's criminal laws. They have this latitude because they are designated by statute as the President's delegates to help him discharge his constitutional responsibility to "take Care that the Laws be faithfully executed." As a result, "[t]he presumption of regularity supports" their prosecutorial decisions and, "in the absence of clear evidence to the contrary, courts presume that they have properly discharged their official duties." In the ordinary case, "so long as the prosecutor has probable cause to believe that the accused committed an offense defined by statute, the decision whether or not to prosecute, and what charge to file or bring before a grand jury, generally rests entirely in his discretion."

Of course, a prosecutor's discretion is "subject to constitutional constraints." One of these constraints, imposed by the equal protection component of the Due Process Clause of the Fifth Amendment, is that the decision whether to prosecute may not be based on "an unjustifiable standard such as race, religion, or other arbitrary classification." A defendant may demonstrate that the administration of a criminal law is "directed so exclusively against a particular class of persons . . . with a mind so unequal and oppressive" that the system of prosecution amounts to "a practical denial" of equal protection of the law.

In order to dispel the presumption that a prosecutor has not violated equal protection, a criminal defendant must present "clear evidence to the contrary." We explained in *Wayte* why courts are "properly hesitant to examine the decision whether to prosecute." Judicial deference to the decisions of these executive officers rests in part on an assessment of the relative competence of prosecutors and courts. "Such factors as the strength of the case, the prosecution's general deterrence value, the Government's enforcement priorities, and the case's relationship to the Government's overall enforcement plan are not readily susceptible to the kind of analysis the courts are competent to undertake." It also stems from a concern not to unnecessarily impair the performance of a core executive constitutional function. "Examining the basis of a prosecution delays the criminal proceeding, threatens to chill law enforcement by subjecting the prosecutor's motives and decisionmaking to outside inquiry, and may undermine prosecutorial effectiveness by revealing the Government's enforcement policy."

The requirements for a selective-prosecution claim draw on "ordinary equal protection standards." The claimant must demonstrate that the federal prosecutorial policy "had a discriminatory effect and that it was motivated by a discriminatory purpose." To establish a discriminatory effect in a race case, the claimant must show that similarly situated individuals of a different race were not prosecuted. This requirement has been established in our case law since *Ah Sin v. Wittman*. Ah Sin, a subject of China, petitioned a California state court for a writ of habeas corpus, seeking discharge from imprisonment under a San Francisco County ordinance prohibiting persons from setting up gambling tables in rooms barricaded to stop police from entering. He alleged in his habeas petition "that the ordinance is enforced 'solely and exclusively against persons of the Chinese race and not otherwise.'" We rejected his contention that this averment made out a claim under the Equal Protection Clause, because it did not allege "that * * * there were other offenders against the ordinance than the Chinese as to whom it was not enforced."

The similarly situated requirement does not make a selective-prosecution claim impossible to prove. Twenty years before *Ah Sin*, we invalidated an ordinance, also adopted by San Francisco, that prohibited the operation of laundries in wooden buildings. The plaintiff in error [in *Yick Wo*] successfully demonstrated that the ordinance was applied against Chinese nationals but not against other laundry-shop operators. The authorities had denied the applications of 200 Chinese subjects for permits to operate shops in wooden buildings, but granted the applications of 80 individuals who were not Chinese subjects to operate laundries in wooden buildings "under similar conditions." * * *

Having reviewed the requirements to prove a selective-prosecution claim, we turn to the showing necessary to obtain discovery in support of such a claim. If discovery is ordered, the Government must assemble from its own files documents which might corroborate or refute the defendant's claim. Discovery thus imposes many of the costs present when the Government must respond to a prima facie case of selective prosecution. It will divert prosecutors' resources and may disclose the Government's prosecutorial strategy. The justifications for a rigorous standard for the elements of a selective-prosecution claim thus require a correspondingly rigorous standard for discovery in aid of such a claim.

The parties, and the Courts of Appeals which have considered the requisite showing to establish entitlement to discovery, describe this showing with a variety of phrases, like "colorable basis," "substantial threshold showing," "substantial and concrete basis," or "reasonable likelihood." However, the many labels for this showing conceal the degree of consensus about the evidence necessary to meet it. The Courts of Appeals "require some evidence tending to show the existence of the essential elements of the defense," discriminatory effect and discriminatory intent.

In this case we consider what evidence constitutes "some evidence tending to show the existence" of the discriminatory effect element. The Court of Appeals held that a defendant may establish a colorable basis for discriminatory effect without evidence that the Government has failed to prosecute others who are similarly situated to the defendant. We think it was mistaken in this view. The vast majority of the Courts of Appeals require the defendant to produce some evidence that similarly situated defendants of other races could have been prosecuted, but were not, and this requirement is consistent with our equal protection case law. As the three-judge panel explained, " '[s]elective prosecution' implies that a selection has taken place." * * *

In the case before us, respondents' "study" did not constitute "some evidence tending to show the existence of the essential elements of" a selective-prosecution claim. The study failed to identify individuals who were not black and could have been prosecuted for the offenses for which respondents were charged, but were not so prosecuted. This omission was not remedied by respondents' evidence in opposition to the Government's motion for reconsideration. The newspaper article, which discussed the discriminatory effect of federal drug sentencing laws, was not relevant to an allegation of discrimination in decisions to prosecute. Respondents' affidavits, which recounted one attorney's conversation with a drug treatment center employee and the experience of another attorney defending drug prosecutions in state court, recounted hearsay and reported personal conclusions based on anecdotal evidence. The judgment of the Court of Appeals is therefore reversed, and the case is remanded for proceedings consistent with this opinion.

It is so ordered.

JUSTICE STEVENS, dissenting.

Federal prosecutors are respected members of a respected profession. Despite an occasional misstep, the excellence of their work abundantly justifies the presumption that "they have properly discharged their official duties." Nevertheless, the possibility that political or racial animosity may infect a decision to institute criminal proceedings cannot be ignored. For that reason, it has long been settled that the prosecutor's broad discretion to determine when criminal charges should be filed is not completely unbridled. As the Court notes, however, the scope of judicial review of particular exercises of that discretion is not fully defined. * * *

The District Judge's order should be evaluated in light of three circumstances that underscore the need for judicial vigilance over certain types of drug prosecutions. First, the Anti-Drug Abuse Act of 1986 and subsequent legislation established a regime of extremely high penalties for the possession and distribution of so-called "crack" cocaine. Those provisions treat one gram of crack as the equivalent of 100 grams of powder cocaine. The distribution of 50 grams of crack is thus punishable by the same mandatory minimum sentence of 10 years in prison that applies to the distribution of 5,000 grams of powder cocaine. The Sentencing Guidelines extend this ratio to penalty levels above the mandatory minimums: For any given quantity of crack, the guideline range is the same as if the offense had involved 100 times that amount in powder cocaine. These penalties result in sentences for crack offenders that average three to eight times longer than sentences for comparable powder offenders.[a]

Second, the disparity between the treatment of crack cocaine and powder cocaine is matched by the disparity between the severity of the punishment imposed by federal law and that imposed by state law for the

---

[a] For years, the U.S. Sentencing Commission tried without success to get Congress to eliminate the 100 to 1 ratio between sentences for crack cocaine and sentences for powder cocaine because of the disproportionate impact this was having on Blacks. Ellis Cose, *Closing the Gap: Obama Could Fix Cocaine Sentencing*, NEWSWEEK, July 20, 2009, at 25. Finally, more than two decades after passage of the Anti-Drug Abuse Act of 1986, Congress passed the Fair Sentencing Act in July of 2010, reducing the 100 to 1 disparity between crack and powder cocaine to approximately 18 to 1. Fair Sentencing Act of 2010, 21 U.S.C. §§ 841, 960 (2012). *See also* Jim Abrams, *Congress Passes Bill to Reduce Disparity in Crack, Powder Cocaine Sentencing*, WASH. POST, July 29, 2010, at A9.

same conduct. For a variety of reasons, often including the absence of mandatory minimums, the existence of parole, and lower baseline penalties, terms of imprisonment for drug offenses tend to be substantially lower in state systems than in the federal system. The difference is especially marked in the case of crack offenses. The majority of States draw no distinction between types of cocaine in their penalty schemes; of those that do, none has established as stark a differential as the Federal Government. For example, if respondent Hampton is found guilty, his federal sentence might be as long as a mandatory life term. Had he been tried in state court, his sentence could have been as short as 12 years, less worktime credits of half that amount.

Finally, it is undisputed that the brunt of the elevated federal penalties falls heavily on blacks. While 65% of the persons who have used crack are white, in 1993 they represented only 4% of the federal offenders convicted of trafficking in crack. Eighty-eight percent of such defendants were black. During the first 18 months of full guideline implementation, the sentencing disparity between black and white defendants grew from preguideline levels: Blacks on average received sentences over 40% longer than whites. Those figures represent a major threat to the integrity of federal sentencing reform, whose main purpose was the elimination of disparity (especially racial) in sentencing. The Sentencing Commission acknowledges that the heightened crack penalties are a "primary cause of the growing disparity between sentences for Black and White federal defendants."

The extraordinary severity of the imposed penalties and the troubling racial patterns of enforcement give rise to a special concern about the fairness of charging practices for crack offenses. Evidence tending to prove that black defendants charged with distribution of crack in the Central District of California are prosecuted in federal court, whereas members of other races charged with similar offenses are prosecuted in state court, warrants close scrutiny by the federal judges in that district. In my view, the District Judge, who has sat on both the federal and the state benches in Los Angeles, acted well within her discretion to call for the development of facts that would demonstrate what standards, if any, governed the choice of forum where similarly situated offenders are prosecuted.

Respondents submitted a study showing that of all cases involving crack offenses that were closed by the Federal Public Defender's Office in 1991, 24 out of 24 involved black defendants. To supplement this evidence, they submitted affidavits from two of the attorneys in the defense team. The first reported a statement from an intake coordinator at a local drug treatment center that, in his experience, an equal number of crack users and dealers were caucasian as belonged to minorities. The second was from David R. Reed, counsel for respondent Armstrong. Reed was both an active court-appointed attorney in the Central District of California and one of the directors of the leading association of criminal defense lawyers who practice before the Los Angeles County courts. Reed stated that he did not recall "ever handling a [crack] cocaine case involving non-black defendants" in federal court, nor had he even heard of one. He further stated that "[t]here are many crack cocaine sales cases prosecuted in state court that *do* involve racial groups other than blacks." (emphasis in original).

The majority discounts the probative value of the affidavits, claiming that they recounted "hearsay"[b] and reported "personal conclusions based on anecdotal evidence." But the Reed affidavit plainly contained more than mere hearsay; Reed offered information based on his own extensive experience in both federal and state courts. Given the breadth of his background, he was well qualified to compare the practices of federal and state prosecutors. In any event, the Government never objected to the admission of either affidavit on hearsay or any other grounds. It was certainly within the District Court's discretion to credit the affidavits of two members of the bar of that Court, at least one of whom had presumably acquired a reputation by his frequent appearances there, and both of whose statements were made on pains of perjury.

The criticism that the affidavits were based on "anecdotal evidence" is also unpersuasive. I thought it was agreed that defendants do not need to prepare sophisticated statistical studies in order to receive mere discovery in cases like this one. Certainly evidence based on a drug counselor's personal observations or on an attorney's practice in two sets of courts, state and federal, can "ten[d] to show the existence" of a selective prosecution.

Even if respondents failed to carry their burden of showing that there were individuals who were not black but who could have been prosecuted in federal court for the same offenses, it does not follow that the District Court abused its discretion in ordering discovery. There can be no doubt that such individuals exist, and indeed the Government has never denied the same. In those circumstances, I fail to see why the District Court was unable to take judicial notice of this obvious fact and demand information from the Government's files to support or refute respondents' evidence.

* * * In this case, the evidence was sufficiently disturbing to persuade the District Judge to order discovery that might help explain the conspicuous racial pattern of cases before her court. I cannot accept the

---

[b] Black's Law Dictionary defines hearsay as:

1. Traditionally, testimony that is given by a witness who relates not what he or she knows personally, but what others have said, and that is therefore dependent on the credibility of someone other than the witness. Such testimony is generally inadmissible under the rules of evidence. 2. In federal law, a statement . . . other than one made by the declarant while testifying at the trial or hearing, offered in evidence to prove the truth of the matter asserted.

BLACK'S LAW DICTIONARY 838 (10th ed. 2014).

majority's conclusion that the District Judge either exceeded her power or abused her discretion when she did so. I therefore respectfully dissent.

[JUSTICE SOUTER's concurring opinion, JUSTICE GINSBURG's concurring opinion, and JUSTICE BREYER's concurring opinion have been omitted.]

NOTE

Does *Armstrong* make it impossible for defendants to get discovery to support a selective prosecution claim? Richard McAdams points out that the *Armstrong* Court provides only one case, *Yick Wo v. Hopkins*, as support for its claim that it is not impossible to satisfy the requirement that the defendant show that similarly situated individuals could have been, but were not prosecuted. Richard H. McAdams, *Race and Selective Prosecution: Discovering the Pitfalls of* Armstrong, 73 CHI.-KENT L. REV. 605, 615 (1998). *Yick Wo*, however, was decided in 1886, more than 100 years before *Armstrong*, and the Court was unable to find any other case in which the defendant succeeded in meeting this standard.

RACIAL FAIRNESS IN THE CRIMINAL JUSTICE SYSTEM: THE ROLE OF THE PROSECUTOR
Angela J. Davis
39 Colum. Hum. Rts. L. Rev. 202 (2007)

Prosecutors exercise a tremendous amount of discretion in charging and plea bargaining processes with no external oversight and very little accountability to the constituents they serve. Charging and plea bargaining decisions frequently predetermine the outcome of criminal cases, especially in cases involving mandatory minimum sentences. Since over ninety-five percent of criminal cases are resolved with guilty pleas, the impact of prosecutorial discretion cannot be understated. * * *

Prosecutors can, and frequently do, decide not to charge individuals who have been arrested, even if there is probable cause to believe they have committed a crime. This decision is completely within their discretion. If they do decide to charge, prosecutors have complete discretion in deciding what crime or crimes to charge and are restrained only by the criminal codes of their jurisdictions. * * *

Most prosecutors would vehemently deny that they take race into account in any way in the exercise of their prosecutorial duties, and most probably do not consciously consider race. Nonetheless, prosecutors rely on legitimate, race-neutral factors that sometimes have racial effects. The American Bar Association (ABA) Standards for the Prosecution Function have endorsed several such factors. A report to the ABA noted that legitimate factors include: the seriousness of the offense, the defendant's prior criminal record, the victim's interest in prosecution, the strength of the evidence, the likelihood of conviction, and the availability of alternative dispositions.

The factor that many prosecutors consider most important is the seriousness of the offense: the more serious the offense, the more likely the prosecutor will charge the accused. For example, a prosecutor may decide to dismiss a simple assault while zealously pursuing the prosecution of an aggravated assault involving serious injury. Few would question this decision, regardless of the race of the defendant or victim. The more difficult issue arises when two defendants are charged differently in cases involving similar facts, except with defendants or victims of different races. At this point, the issue of unconscious racism becomes relevant. If, for example, a defendant in a case involving a white victim is charged with capital murder while a similarly situated defendant in a case involving a black victim is charged with second-degree murder, questions arise about the value the prosecutors placed on the lives of the respective victims.[a] A prosecutor may unconsciously consider a case involving a white victim as more serious than a case involving a black victim, and this may influence the charging, plea bargaining, and other related decisions.[b]

If a prosecutor initially deems a particular case to be more serious than others, she will invest more time and resources investigating the case and preparing for trial. This will yield more evidence, making it less likely that the prosecutor will offer a plea bargain and more likely that she will succeed in obtaining a conviction at trial. The likelihood of conviction is another consideration endorsed by the ABA. Thus, although the strength of the evidence and the likelihood of conviction are facially race-neutral factors, they may be influenced by initial, unconscious racial valuations.[c]

The victim's interest in prosecution is another factor that prosecutors legitimately consider in making charging and plea bargaining decisions. If the victim of a crime has no interest in the prosecution of his case and no desire to see the defendant punished, the prosecutor may dismiss the case based on these views, especially if the prosecutor believes that the defendant does not pose a danger to society and that there are no other legitimate reasons for pursuing the prosecution. Few would question this

---

[a] Empirical research suggests that defendants charged with killing White victims are far more likely to receive the death penalty than defendants charged with killing Black victims. For example, the well-known Baldus study, discussed in *McCleskey v. Kemp, infra*, found that defendants charged with killing White victims received the death penalty in 11 percent of the cases, whereas defendants charged with killing Black victims received the death penalty in only 1 percent of the cases.

[b] *See* Robert J. Smith et al., *Implicit White Favoritism in the Criminal Justice System*, 66 ALA. L. REV. 871 (2015) (arguing that even if we eliminated negative stereotyping of Blacks, automatic associations of positive stereotypes with White Americans would still exist).

[c] Prosecutors are not the only actors in the criminal justice system whose decisions are influenced by unconscious racial valuations. L. Song Richardson and Phillip Atiba Goff suggest that public defenders are also influenced by implicit biases that affect their decisions about which cases to prioritize. L. Song Richardson & Phillip Atiba Goff, *Implicit Racial Bias in Public Defender Triage*, 122 YALE L.J. 2626 (2013).

decision, especially if the victim of the crime considered the prosecution process too onerous and difficult.

On the other hand, should a prosecutor pursue a prosecution in a case that she would otherwise dismiss for legitimate reasons simply because the victim demonstrates an interest in prosecution? Or should a prosecutor assume that a victim is not interested in prosecution when the victim does not appear for witness conferences or respond to a subpoena? Prosecutors are more likely to pursue prosecutions in cases involving crime victims who are comfortable navigating the criminal process and who have time to attend grand jury hearings, witness conferences, and status hearings. The poor, who are disproportionately people of color, are less able to take time off from work to attend these hearings. They may also feel less comfortable participating in the process, especially since they are more likely to have family or friends involved in the system as criminal defendants. Thus, race and class may have an unintended effect on this factor as well.

The prior record of the defendant is another seemingly race-neutral factor considered by prosecutors in the charging and plea bargaining process. Prosecutors understandably are more likely to charge and less likely to offer a favorable plea bargain to defendants with prior arrest and conviction records; defendants who are recidivists are arguably more deserving of prosecution. Race, however, may affect the existence of a prior criminal record even in the absence of recidivist tendencies on the part of the suspect because of racial profiling at the arrest stage of the process.

Race often plays a role in the decision to detain and/or arrest a suspect. In addition, policy decisions about where police officers should be deployed and what offenses they should investigate have racial ramifications. A white defendant with no criminal arrest or conviction record may have engaged in criminal behavior. If he lives in a community that resolves certain criminal offenses (drug use, assault, etc.) without police intervention, he may be a recidivist without a record. Likewise, a black defendant who lives in a designated "high crime" area may have been detained and arrested on numerous occasions even if he has not engaged in criminal behavior. Thus, the existence or nonexistence of an arrest or conviction record may not reflect criminality. A prosecutor without knowledge of or sensitivity to this issue may give prior arrests undue consideration in making charging and plea bargaining decisions.

The ABA standards also suggest that prosecutors consider the availability of alternative dispositions before bringing criminal charges. Many prosecutors' offices have diversion programs or other alternatives that allow for the dismissal of a case combined with alternative resolutions such as restitution, rehabilitative treatment or community service. Most of these alternatives are available for first offenders only and benefit not only the defendant but all parties. The victim may be compensated if restitution is involved, and the alternatives have the added benefit of eliminating the time and expense of trying another case for the prosecutor, the defense attorney, and the court. As with other seemingly legitimate considerations, however, this factor may have class and race ramifications. Wealthier defendants have a greater ability to make restitution or pay for drug, alcohol, or psychiatric treatment. Since people of color are disproportionately poor, this seemingly race neutral factor can have racial effects.

Arbitrary, unsystematic decision-making, exacerbated by unconscious race and class predilections, sometimes results in disparate treatment of similarly situated victims and defendants. That prosecutors do not intend to cause racial disparities does not excuse them from responsibility for the harmful effects of their decisions. The U.S. Supreme Court, however, has repeatedly blocked efforts to hold prosecutors accountable for unintentional discrimination. * * *

NOTE

"While the decision to arrest is often the responsibility of law enforcement personnel, the decision to institute formal criminal proceedings is the responsibility of the prosecutor."[a] The question whether to charge George Zimmerman, a white Hispanic male, with criminal homicide in the shooting death of Trayvon Martin, an unarmed Black male teenager, was wrought with much controversy, including allegations of racial bias.

The shooting took place on February 26, 2012, in Sanford, Florida. Martin had been walking back to the apartment where he was staying while visiting his father and was talking on his cell phone with a friend when Zimmerman first began following him in his car. Zimmerman called 911 and told the dispatcher that he thought Martin "looked suspicious" and was "up to no good." When Martin started running away, Zimmerman got out of his car and followed Martin on foot. A physical altercation ensued and Zimmerman found himself on the ground on his back with Martin on top. Zimmerman claimed he shot Martin in self-defense because he thought Martin was going to kill him. A haunting 911 call from a neighbor concerned about the altercation, which captured a desperate scream for help immediately before the fatal shot, initially put Zimmerman's self-defense claim into question. Zimmerman, however, claimed he was the one screaming for help because he feared for his life. Martin's parents asserted the screams were from their son.[b]

---

[a] Am. Bar Ass'n, STANDARDS FOR CRIMINAL JUSTICE: PROSECUTION AND DEFENSE FUNCTION § 3–4.2(a) (4th ed. 2015).

[b] For additional commentary on the shooting of Trayvon Martin, *see* Darren Lenard Hutchinson, *"Continually Reminded of Their Inferior Position": Social Dominance, Implicit Bias, Criminality, and Race*, 46 WASH. U. J.L. & POL'Y 23 (2014); Cynthia Lee, *Making Race Salient: Trayvon Martin and Implicit Bias in a Not Yet Post-Racial Society*, 91 N.C. L. REV. 1555 (2013); L. Song Richardson & Phillip Atiba Goff, *Self-Defense and the Suspicion Heuristic*, 98 IOWA L. REV. 293 (2012); Tamara F. Lawson, *A Fresh Cut in an Old Would—A Critical Analysis of the Trayvon Martin Killing: The Public Outcry, the Prosecutors' Discretion, and the Stand Your Ground Law*,

Once the case caught the attention of the press, it was widely covered both domestically and internationally. President Barack Obama weighed in on the shooting, saying: "I can only imagine what these parents are going through. . . . If I had a son, he'd look like Trayvon."[c] The case triggered criminal investigations by both federal and state officials. The federal investigation of the case was focused on whether to charge the case as a hate crime or a violation of Martin's civil rights. The U.S. Department of Justice ultimately concluded there was insufficient evidence to file federal charges.

The response at the state level was mixed on whether to charge Zimmerman with a criminal homicide. Although the lead detective on the case recommended that Zimmerman be arrested on charges of manslaughter, Norm Wolfinger, the State Attorney, instructed the police not to arrest Zimmerman because he had concerns about the strength of the evidence. Both the Sanford Police Department and Wolfinger were harshly criticized for the initial decision not to arrest or charge Zimmerman with any crime.

The case split the public along racial lines, at least initially. One study conducted by USA Today reported 73% of Blacks believed that George Zimmerman should have been arrested, while only 33% of Whites felt the same way.[d] As the case attracted national attention, however, individuals of all races came together to demand Zimmerman's arrest. Scores of people held vigils in honor of Trayvon Martin. Many wore T-shirts emblazoned with a photo of Martin and the words, "I am Trayvon." The case sparked a national dialogue regarding the exercise of prosecutorial discretion and race.

Professor Tamara Lawson describes the impact of the initial charging decision on Black Americans as a reinjuring of an "old wound" reminiscent of a historic era in which impunity was common for the killing of Black men and boys in America.

> [The response to] Trayvon Martin's killing [and the lack of criminal charges] was becoming a national movement * * *. Communities [across the country] were chanting the slogan: "I am Trayvon." Students of Trayvon's age group and younger were walking out of school in symbolic rage regarding the fact that nothing was being done to vindicate his killing. People from all walks of life were wearing hoodies in solidarity with the perceived injustice of the treatment of the case. Although the initial outcry was primarily led by the Black community, the expression of outrage was not limited to Black people. Joe Scarborough, a well-known white conservative

---

23 U. FLA. J.L. & PUB. POL'Y 271 (2012); Valena Elizabeth Beety, *What the Brain Saw: The Case of Trayvon Martin and the Need for Eyewitness Identification Reform*, 90 DENV. U. L. REV. 331 (2012); Josephine Ross, *Cops on Trial: Did Fourth Amendment Case Law Help George Zimmerman's Claim of Self-Defense?*, 40 SEATTLE U. L. REV. 1 (2016).

[c] Sam Stein, *Obama on Trayvon Martin Case: "If I Had a Son, He'd Look Like Trayvon,"* HUFFPOST (Mar. 23, 2012), https://www.huffpost.com/entry/obama-trayvon-martin_n_1375083 (https://perma.cc/DVY5-DBJ6).

[d] Yamiche Alcindor, *Poll on Trayvon Martin Case Shows Racial Divide*, YAMICHE ALCINDOR (Apr. 5, 2012), https://yamichealcindor.com/2012/04/05/poll-on-trayvon-martin-case-shows-racial-divide/ (https://perma.cc/WN89-5WUA).

[R]epublican [television] commentator * * * also called for charges to be filed. Scarborough * * * felt [Florida officials] should intervene to correct this injustice. Scarborough, along with * * * others * * * implored the government to do something. At that point, it was still uncertain whether or not the something would be to charge Trayvon's killer with murder.[e]

After numerous public protests, then Florida Governor Rick Scott appointed Special Prosecutor Angela Corey to take over the case and re-evaluate the charging decision. Within twenty days of being appointed as Special Prosecutor, Corey decided to charge George Zimmerman with second degree murder. Corey insisted that her charging decision was not influenced by public opinion but was governed solely by the facts of the case and the laws of the state of Florida.

After a three-week trial, a jury acquitted Zimmerman of all charges. Does the acquittal suggest that Corey made the wrong charging decision? Why was Corey's charging decision so different from Wolfinger's when both reviewed the same facts and same laws? According to the American Bar Association, the minimum requirements for filing and maintaining criminal charges are as follows: "A prosecutor should seek or file criminal charges only if the prosecutor reasonably believes that the charges are supported by probable cause, that admissible evidence will be sufficient to support conviction beyond a reasonable doubt, and that the decision to charge is in the interests of justice." Am.Bar Ass'n, STANDARDS FOR CRIMINAL JUSTICE: PROSECUTION AND DEFENSE FUNCTION, STANDARD § 3–4.3(a) (4th ed. 2015). Standard 3–1.2(c) states: "[T]he primary duty of the prosecutor is to seek justice within the bounds of the law, not merely to convict." Did Corey appropriately exercise the prosecutorial obligation to "seek justice" in the Zimmerman case? Did Wolfinger? Is it possible that both Wolfinger and Corey correctly exercised their duties even though their charging decisions were different? The Zimmerman case illustrates the breadth of prosecutorial discretion as well as the political, social, and cultural dynamics that may impact it.

UNITED STATES V. GOODWIN
Supreme Court of the United States
457 U.S. 368, 102 S. Ct. 2485, 73 L. Ed. 2d 74 (1982)

JUSTICE STEVENS delivered the opinion of the Court. * * *

Respondent Goodwin was stopped for speeding by a United States Park Policeman on the Baltimore-Washington Parkway. Goodwin emerged from his car to talk to the policeman. After a brief discussion, the officer noticed a clear plastic bag underneath the armrest next to the driver's seat of Goodwin's car. The officer asked Goodwin to return to his car and to raise

---

[e] Tamara F. Lawson, *A Fresh Cut in an Old Wound—A Critical Analysis of the Trayvon Martin Killing: The Public Outcry, the Prosecutors' Discretion, and the Stand Your Ground Law*, 23 U. FLA. J.L. & PUB. POL'Y 271, 274, 283–84 (2012).

the armrest. Respondent did so, but as he raised the armrest he placed the car into gear and accelerated rapidly. The car struck the officer, knocking him first onto the back of the car and then onto the highway. The policeman returned to his car, but Goodwin eluded him in a high-speed chase.

The following day, the officer filed a complaint in the District Court charging respondent with several misdemeanor and petty offenses, including assault. Goodwin was arrested and arraigned before a United States Magistrate. The Magistrate set a date for trial, but respondent fled the jurisdiction. Three years later Goodwin was found in custody in Virginia and was returned to Maryland.

Upon his return, respondent's case was assigned to an attorney from the Department of Justice, who was detailed temporarily to try petty crime and misdemeanor cases before the Magistrate. The attorney did not have authority to try felony cases or to seek indictments from the grand jury. Respondent initiated plea negotiations with the prosecutor, but later advised the Government that he did not wish to plead guilty and desired a trial by jury in the District Court.

The case was transferred to the District Court and responsibility for the prosecution was assumed by an Assistant United States Attorney. Approximately six weeks later, after reviewing the case and discussing it with several parties, the prosecutor obtained a four-count indictment charging respondent with one felony count of forcibly assaulting a federal officer and three related counts arising from the same incident.[2] A jury convicted respondent on the felony count and on one misdemeanor count.

Respondent moved to set aside the verdict on the ground of prosecutorial vindictiveness, contending that the indictment on the felony charge gave rise to an impermissible appearance of retaliation. The District Court denied the motion, finding that "the prosecutor in this case has adequately dispelled any appearance of retaliatory intent."

Although the Court of Appeals readily concluded that "the prosecutor did not act with actual vindictiveness in seeking a felony indictment," it nevertheless reversed. Relying on our decisions in *North Carolina v. Pearce* and *Blackledge v. Perry*, the court held that the Due Process Clause of the Fifth Amendment prohibits the Government from bringing more serious charges against a defendant after he has invoked his right to a jury trial, unless the prosecutor comes forward with objective evidence to show that the increased charges could not have been brought before the defendant

---

[2] By affidavit, the Assistant United States Attorney later set forth his reasons for this action: (1) he considered respondent's conduct on the date in question to be a serious violation of law, (2) respondent had a lengthy history of violent crime, (3) the prosecutor considered respondent's conduct to be related to major narcotics transactions, (4) the prosecutor believed that respondent had committed perjury at his preliminary hearing, and (5) respondent had failed to appear for trial as originally scheduled. The Government attorney stated that his decision to seek a felony indictment was not motivated in any way by Goodwin's request for a jury trial in District Court.

exercised his rights. Because the court believed that the circumstances surrounding the felony indictment gave rise to a genuine risk of retaliation, it adopted a legal presumption designed to spare courts the "unseemly task" of probing the actual motives of the prosecutor.

To punish a person because he has done what the law plainly allows him to do is a due process violation "of the most basic sort." In a series of cases beginning with *North Carolina v. Pearce* and culminating in *Bordenkircher v. Hayes*, the Court has recognized this basic—and itself uncontroversial—principle. For while an individual certainly may be penalized for violating the law, he just as certainly may not be punished for exercising a protected statutory or constitutional right.

* * * Motives are complex and difficult to prove. As a result, in certain cases in which action detrimental to the defendant has been taken after the exercise of a legal right, the Court has found it necessary to "presume" an improper vindictive motive. Given the severity of such a presumption, however—which may operate in the absence of any proof of an improper motive and thus may block a legitimate response to criminal conduct—the Court has done so only in cases in which a reasonable likelihood of vindictiveness exists.

In *North Carolina v. Pearce*, the Court held that neither the Double Jeopardy Clause nor the Equal Protection Clause prohibits a trial judge from imposing a harsher sentence on retrial after a criminal defendant successfully attacks an initial conviction on appeal. The Court stated, however, that "[i]t can hardly be doubted that it would be a flagrant violation [of the Due Process Clause] of the Fourteenth Amendment for a state trial court to follow an announced practice of imposing a heavier sentence upon every reconvicted defendant for the explicit purpose of punishing the defendant for his having succeeded in getting his original conviction set aside." The Court continued:

> Due process of law, then, requires that vindictiveness against a defendant for having successfully attacked his first conviction must play no part in the sentence he receives after a new trial. And since the fear of such vindictiveness may unconstitutionally deter a defendant's exercise of the right to appeal or collaterally attack his first conviction, due process also requires that a defendant be freed of apprehension of such a retaliatory motivation on the part of the sentencing judge.

In order to assure the absence of such a motivation, the Court concluded:

> [W]henever a judge imposes a more severe sentence upon a defendant after a new trial, the reasons for his doing so must affirmatively appear. Those reasons must be based upon objective information concerning identifiable conduct on the part of the defendant occurring after the time of the original sentencing

proceeding.[a] And the factual data upon which the increased sentence is based must be made part of the record, so that the constitutional legitimacy of the increased sentence may be fully reviewed on appeal.

In sum, the Court applied a presumption of vindictiveness, which may be overcome only by objective information in the record justifying the increased sentence.

In *Blackledge v. Perry*, the Court confronted the problem of increased punishment upon retrial after appeal in a setting different from that considered in *Pearce*. Perry was convicted of assault in an inferior court having exclusive jurisdiction for the trial of misdemeanors. The court imposed a 6-month sentence. Under North Carolina law, Perry had an absolute right to a trial *de novo* in the Superior Court, which possessed felony jurisdiction. After Perry filed his notice of appeal, the prosecutor obtained a felony indictment charging him with assault with a deadly weapon. Perry pleaded guilty to the felony and was sentenced to a term of five to seven years in prison.

In reviewing Perry's felony conviction and increased sentence this Court first stated the essence of the holdings in *Pearce* and the cases that had followed it:

> The lesson that emerges from *Pearce* [and other cases] is that the Due Process Clause is not offended by all possibilities of increased punishment upon retrial after appeal, but only by those that pose a realistic likelihood of "vindictiveness."

The Court held that the opportunities for vindictiveness in the situation before it were such "as to impel the conclusion that due process of law requires a rule analogous to that of the *Pearce* case." * * *

The Court emphasized in *Blackledge* that it did not matter that no evidence was present that the prosecutor had acted in bad faith or with malice in seeking the felony indictment. As in *Pearce*, the Court held that the likelihood of vindictiveness justified a presumption that would free defendants of apprehension of such a retaliatory motivation on the part of the prosecutor.[8] * * *

In *Bordenkircher v. Hayes*, the Court for the first time considered an allegation of vindictiveness that arose in a pretrial setting. In that case the Court held that the Due Process Clause of the Fourteenth Amendment did

---

[a] In a later case, the Court retreated from this statement, noting that "[r]estricting justifications for a sentence increase to *only* 'events that occurred subsequent to the original sentencing proceedings' could in some circumstances lead to absurd results." Texas v. McCullough, 475 U.S. 134, 141 (1986).

[8] The presumption again could be overcome by objective evidence justifying the prosecutor's action. The Court noted: "This would clearly be a different case if the State had shown that it was impossible to proceed on the more serious charge at the outset * * *."

not prohibit a prosecutor from carrying out a threat, made during plea negotiations, to bring additional charges against an accused who refused to plead guilty to the offense with which he was originally charged. The prosecutor in that case had explicitly told the defendant that if he did not plead guilty and "save the court the inconvenience and necessity of a trial" he would return to the grand jury to obtain an additional charge that would significantly increase the defendant's potential punishment.[9] The defendant refused to plead guilty and the prosecutor obtained the indictment. It was not disputed that the additional charge was justified by the evidence, that the prosecutor was in possession of this evidence at the time the original indictment was obtained, and that the prosecutor sought the additional charge because of the accused's refusal to plead guilty to the original charge.

In finding no due process violation, the Court in *Bordenkircher* considered the decisions in *Pearce* and *Blackledge*, and stated:

> In those cases the Court was dealing with the State's unilateral imposition of a penalty upon a defendant who had chosen to exercise a legal right to attack his original conviction—a situation "very different from the give-and-take negotiation common in plea bargaining between the prosecution and defense, which arguably possess relatively equal bargaining power."

The Court stated that the due process violation in *Pearce* and *Blackledge* "lay not in the possibility that a defendant might be deterred from the exercise of a legal right . . . but rather in the danger that the State might be retaliating against the accused for lawfully attacking his conviction."

The Court held, however, that there was no such element of punishment in the "give-and-take" of plea negotiation, so long as the accused "is free to accept or reject the prosecution's offer." The Court noted that, by tolerating and encouraging the negotiation of pleas, this Court had accepted as constitutionally legitimate the simple reality that the prosecutor's interest at the bargaining table is to persuade the defendant to forgo his constitutional right to stand trial. The Court concluded:

> We hold only that the course of conduct engaged in by the prosecutor in this case, which no more than openly presented the defendant with the unpleasant alternatives of forgoing trial or facing charges on which he was plainly subject to prosecution, did not violate the Due Process Clause of the Fourteenth Amendment.

* * *

---

[9] The prosecutor advised the defendant that he would obtain an indictment under the Kentucky Habitual Criminal Act, which would subject the accused to a mandatory sentence of life imprisonment by reason of his two prior felony convictions. Absent the additional indictment, the defendant was subject to a punishment of 2 to 10 years in prison.

This case, like *Bordenkircher*, arises from a pretrial decision to modify the charges against the defendant. Unlike *Bordenkircher*, however, there is no evidence in this case that could give rise to a claim of *actual* vindictiveness; the prosecutor never suggested that the charge was brought to influence the respondent's conduct. The conviction in this case may be reversed only if a *presumption* of vindictiveness—applicable in all cases—is warranted.

There is good reason to be cautious before adopting an inflexible presumption of prosecutorial vindictiveness in a pretrial setting. In the course of preparing a case for trial, the prosecutor may uncover additional information that suggests a basis for further prosecution or he simply may come to realize that information possessed by the State has a broader significance. At this stage of the proceedings, the prosecutor's assessment of the proper extent of prosecution may not have crystallized. In contrast, once a trial begins—and certainly by the time a conviction has been obtained—it is much more likely that the State has discovered and assessed all of the information against an accused and has made a determination, on the basis of that information, of the extent to which he should be prosecuted. Thus, a change in the charging decision made after an initial trial is completed is much more likely to be improperly motivated than is a pretrial decision.

In addition, a defendant before trial is expected to invoke procedural rights that inevitably impose some "burden" on the prosecutor. Defense counsel routinely file pretrial motions to suppress evidence; to challenge the sufficiency and form of an indictment; to plead an affirmative defense; to request psychiatric services; to obtain access to government files; to be tried by jury. It is unrealistic to assume that a prosecutor's probable response to such motions is to seek to penalize and to deter. The invocation of procedural rights is an integral part of the adversary process in which our criminal justice system operates.

Thus, the timing of the prosecutor's action in this case suggests that a presumption of vindictiveness is not warranted. A prosecutor should remain free before trial to exercise the broad discretion entrusted to him to determine the extent of the societal interest in prosecution. * * *

In declining to apply a presumption of vindictiveness, we of course do not foreclose the possibility that a defendant in an appropriate case might prove objectively that the prosecutor's charging decision was motivated by a desire to punish him for doing something that the law plainly allowed him to do. In this case, however, the Court of Appeals stated: "On this record we readily conclude that the prosecutor did not act with actual vindictiveness in seeking a felony indictment." Respondent does not challenge that finding. Absent a presumption of vindictiveness, no due process violation has been established. * * *

JUSTICE BLACKMUN, concurring in the judgment.

Like Justice Brennan, I believe that our precedents mandate the conclusion that "a realistic likelihood of 'vindictiveness'" arises in this context. The Assistant United States Attorney responsible for increasing the charges against respondent was aware of the initial charging decision; he had the means available to discourage respondent from electing a jury trial in District Court; he had a substantial stake in dissuading respondent from exercising that option; and he was familiar with, and sensitive to, the institutional interests that favored a trial before the Magistrate.

Moreover, I find no support in our prior cases for any distinction between pretrial and post-trial vindictiveness. As I have said before: "Prosecutorial vindictiveness in any context is still prosecutorial vindictiveness. The Due Process Clause should protect an accused against it, however it asserts itself." And, as Justice Brennan points out, *Bordenkircher* does not dictate the result here. In fact, in *Bordenkircher* the Court expressly distinguished and left *unresolved* cases such as this one, "where the prosecutor without notice brought an additional and more serious charge after plea negotiations relating only to the original [charges] had ended with the defendant's insistence on pleading not guilty."

The Court's ruling in *Bordenkircher* did not depend on a distinction between the pretrial and post-trial settings: rather, the Court declined to apply its prior opinions in *Blackledge* and *North Carolina v. Pearce* because those cases involved "the State's unilateral imposition of a penalty," rather than "the give-and-take negotiation common in plea bargaining." Here, as in *Pearce* and *Blackledge*, the prosecutor unilaterally imposed a penalty in response to respondent's exercise of a legal right.

* * * [T]he Due Process Clause does not deprive a prosecutor of the flexibility to add charges after a defendant has decided not to plead guilty and has elected a jury trial in District Court—so long as the adjustment is based on "objective information concerning identifiable conduct on the part of the defendant occurring after the time of the original" charging decision. In addition, I believe that the prosecutor adequately explains an increased charge by pointing to objective information that he could not reasonably have been aware of at the time charges were initially filed.

Because I find that the Assistant United States Attorney's explanation for seeking a felony indictment satisfies these standards, I conclude that the Government has dispelled the appearance of vindictiveness and, therefore, that the imposition of additional charges did not violate respondent's due process rights. Accordingly, I concur in the judgment.

JUSTICE BRENNAN, with whom JUSTICE MARSHALL joins, dissenting.
* * *

The salient facts of this case are quite simple. Respondent was originally charged with several petty offenses and misdemeanors—speeding, reckless driving, failing to give aid at the scene of an accident, fleeing from a police officer, and assault by striking a police officer—arising from his conduct on the Baltimore-Washington Parkway. Assuming that respondent had been convicted on every count charged in this original complaint, the maximum punishment to which he conceivably could have been exposed was fines of $3,500 and 28 months in prison. Because all of the charges against respondent were petty offenses or misdemeanors, they were scheduled for trial before a magistrate, who was not authorized to conduct jury trials. In addition, the case was assigned to a prosecutor who, owing to inexperience, was not even authorized to try felony cases. Thus the Government recognized that respondent's alleged crimes were relatively minor, and attempted to dispose of them in an expedited manner. But respondent frustrated this attempt at summary justice by demanding a jury trial in Federal District Court. This was his right, of course, not only under the applicable statute, but also under the Constitution.

Respondent's demand required that the case be transferred from the Magistrate's Court in Hyattsville to the District Court in Baltimore, and that the prosecution be reassigned to an Assistant United States Attorney, who was authorized to prosecute cases in the District Court. The new prosecutor sought and obtained a second, four-count indictment, in which the same conduct originally charged as petty-offense and misdemeanor counts was now charged as a misdemeanor and two felonies: assaulting, resisting, or impeding a federal officer with a deadly weapon, and assault with a dangerous weapon. If we assume (as before) that respondent was convicted on all of these charges, his maximum exposure to punishment had now become fines of $11,500 and 15 years in prison. Respondent's claim below was that such an elevation of the charges against him from petty offenses to felonies, following his exercise of his statutory and constitutional right to a jury trial, reflected prosecutorial vindictiveness that denied him due process of law. * * *

I would analyze respondent's claim in the terms employed by our precedents. Did the elevation of the charges against respondent "pose a realistic likelihood of 'vindictiveness?' " Is it possible that "the fear of such vindictiveness may unconstitutionally deter" a person in respondent's position from exercising his statutory and constitutional right to a jury trial? The answer to these questions is plainly "Yes." * * *

The truth of my conclusion, and the patent fallacy of the Court's, is particularly evident on the record before us. The practical effect of respondent's demand for a jury trial was that the Government had to transfer the case from a trial before a Magistrate in Hyattsville to a trial before a District Judge and jury in Baltimore, and had to substitute one prosecutor for another. The Government thus suffered not only administrative inconvenience: It also lost the value of the preparation and services of the first prosecutor, and was forced to commit a second prosecutor to prepare the case from scratch. Thus, just as in *Blackledge*, respondent's election had the effect of "clearly requir[ing] increased expenditures of prosecutorial resources before the defendant's conviction" could finally be achieved. And, to paraphrase *Blackledge*,

> if the prosecutor has the means readily at hand to discourage such [elections]—by "upping the ante" through a felony indictment . . . —the State can insure [sic] that only the most hardy defendants will brave the hazards of a [jury] trial.

I conclude that the facts of this case easily support the inference of "a realistic likelihood of vindictiveness." * * *

NOTE

Although *United States v. Goodwin* might be interpreted as holding that a presumption of vindictiveness can never be applied in the pretrial setting, it does not lay down such a rigid rule. Lower courts can decide that the circumstances in an individual case merit finding a realistic likelihood of vindictiveness, and then apply a presumption of vindictiveness. *See United States v. LaDeau*, 734 F.3d 561 (6th Cir. 2013) (finding that a presumption of vindictiveness was appropriately applied in the pretrial context).

UNITED STATES V. BATCHELDER
Supreme Court of the United States
442 U.S. 114, 99 S. Ct. 2198, 60 L. Ed. 2d 755 (1979)

JUSTICE MARSHALL delivered the opinion of the Court.

At issue in this case are two overlapping provisions of the Omnibus Crime Control and Safe Streets Act of 1968 (Omnibus Act). Both prohibit convicted felons from receiving firearms, but each authorizes different maximum penalties. We must determine whether a defendant convicted of the offense carrying the greater penalty may be sentenced only under the more lenient provision when his conduct violates both statutes.

Respondent, a previously convicted felon, was found guilty of receiving a firearm that had traveled in interstate commerce, in violation of 18 U.S.C. § 922(h).[2] The District Court sentenced him under 18 U.S.C.

---

[2] In pertinent part, 18 U.S.C. § 922(h) provides:

"It shall be unlawful for any person—

(1) who is under indictment for, or who has been convicted in any court of, a crime punishable by imprisonment for a term exceeding one year;

(2) who is a fugitive from justice;

(3) who is an unlawful user of or addicted to marihuana or any depressant or stimulant drug . . . or narcotic drug . . . ; or

§ 924(a) to five years' imprisonment, the maximum term authorized for violation of § 922(h).[3]

The Court of Appeals affirmed the conviction but, by a divided vote, remanded for resentencing. The majority recognized that respondent had been indicted and convicted under § 922(h) and that § 924(a) permits five years' imprisonment for such violations. However, noting that the substantive elements of § 922(h) and 18 U.S.C. App. § 1202(a) are identical as applied to a convicted felon who unlawfully receives a firearm, the court interpreted the Omnibus Act to allow no more than the 2-year maximum sentence provided by § 1202(a).[4] In so holding, the Court of Appeals relied on [several] principles of statutory construction. Because, in its view, the "arguably contradict[ory]" penalty provisions for similar conduct and the "inconclusive" legislative history raised doubt whether Congress had intended the two penalty provisions to coexist, the court first applied the doctrine that ambiguities in criminal legislation are to be resolved in favor of the defendant. Second, the court determined that since § 1202(a) was "Congress' last word on the issue of penalty," it may have implicitly repealed the punishment provisions of § 924(a). * * *

We granted certiorari, and now reverse the judgment vacating respondent's 5-year prison sentence.

This Court has previously noted the partial redundancy of §§ 922(h) and 1202(a), both as to the conduct they proscribe and the individuals they reach. However, we find nothing in the language, structure, or legislative history of the Omnibus Act to suggest that because of this overlap, a defendant convicted under § 922(h) may be imprisoned for no more than the maximum term specified in § 1202(a). As we read the Act, each

---

(4) who has been adjudicated as a mental defective or who has been committed to any mental institution; to receive any firearm or ammunition which has been shipped or transported in interstate or foreign commerce."

[3] Title 18 U.S.C. § 924(a) provides in relevant part:

"Whoever violates any provision of this chapter . . . shall be fined not more than $5,000, or imprisoned not more than five years, or both, and shall become eligible for parole as the Board of Parole shall determine."

[4] Section 1202(a) states:

"Any person who—

(1) has been convicted by a court of the United States or of a State or any political subdivision thereof of a felony, or

(2) has been discharged from the Armed Forces under dishonorable conditions, or

(3) has been adjudged by a court of the United States or of a State or any political subdivision thereof of being mentally incompetent, or

(4) having been a citizen of the United States has renounced his citizenship, or

(5) being an alien is illegally or unlawfully in the United States,

and who receives, possesses, or transports in commerce or affecting commerce, after the date of enactment of this Act, any firearm shall be fined not more than $10,000 or imprisoned for not more than two years, or both." 18 U.S.C. App. § 1202(a).

substantive statute, in conjunction with its own sentencing provision, operates independently of the other.

Section 922(h), contained in Title IV of the Omnibus Act, prohibits four categories of individuals from receiving "any firearm or ammunition which has been shipped or transported in interstate or foreign commerce." Persons who violate Title IV are subject to the penalties provided by § 924(a), which authorizes a maximum fine of $5,000 and imprisonment for up to five years. Section 1202(a), located in Title VII of the Omnibus Act, forbids five categories of individuals from "receiv[ing], possess[ing], or transport[ing] in commerce or affecting commerce . . . any firearm." This same section authorizes a maximum fine of $10,000 and imprisonment for not more than two years. * * *

In construing § 1202(a) to override the penalties authorized by § 924(a), the Court of Appeals relied, we believe erroneously, on [several] principles of statutory interpretation. First, the court invoked the well-established doctrine that ambiguities in criminal statutes must be resolved in favor of lenity. Although this principle of construction applies to sentencing as well as substantive provisions, in the instant case there is no ambiguity to resolve. Respondent unquestionably violated § 922(h), and § 924(a) unquestionably permits five years' imprisonment for such a violation. That § 1202(a) provides different penalties for essentially the same conduct is no justification for taking liberties with unequivocal statutory language. By its express terms, § 1202(a) limits its penalty scheme exclusively to convictions obtained under that provision. Where, as here, "Congress has conveyed its purpose clearly, . . . we decline to manufacture ambiguity where none exists."

Nor can § 1202(a) be interpreted as implicitly repealing § 924(a) whenever a defendant's conduct might violate both Titles. For it is "not enough to show that the two statutes produce differing results when applied to the same factual situation." Rather, the legislative intent to repeal must be manifest in the "positive repugnancy between the provisions." In this case, however, the penalty provisions are fully capable of coexisting because they apply to convictions under different statutes. * * *

In resolving the statutory question, the majority below expressed "serious doubts about the constitutionality of two statutes that provide different penalties for identical conduct." Specifically, the court suggested that the statutes might (1) be void for vagueness, (2) implicate "due process and equal protection interest[s] in avoiding excessive prosecutorial discretion and in obtaining equal justice," and (3) constitute an impermissible delegation of congressional authority. We find no constitutional infirmities.

It is a fundamental tenet of due process that "[n]o one may be required at peril of life, liberty or property to speculate as to the meaning of penal statutes." A criminal statute is therefore invalid if it "fails to give a person of ordinary intelligence fair notice that his contemplated conduct is forbidden." So too, vague sentencing provisions may post constitutional questions if they do not state with sufficient clarity the consequences of violating a given criminal statute.

The provisions in issue here, however, unambiguously specify the activity proscribed and the penalties available upon conviction. That this particular conduct may violate both Titles does not detract from the notice afforded by each. Although the statutes create uncertainty as to which crime may be charged and therefore what penalties may be imposed, they do so to no greater extent than would a single statute authorizing various alternative punishments. So long as overlapping criminal provisions clearly define the conduct prohibited and the punishment authorized, the notice requirements of the Due Process Clause are satisfied.

This Court has long recognized that when an act violates more than one criminal statute, the Government may prosecute under either so long as it does not discriminate against any class of defendants. Whether to prosecute and what charge to file or bring before a grand jury are decisions that generally rest in the prosecutor's discretion.

The Court of Appeals acknowledged this "settled rule" allowing prosecutorial choice. Nevertheless, relying on the dissenting opinion in *Berra v. United States*, the court distinguished overlapping statutes with identical standards of proof from provisions that vary in some particular [way]. In the court's view, when two statutes prohibit "exactly the same conduct," the prosecutor's "selection of which of two penalties to apply" would be "unfettered." Because such prosecutorial discretion could produce "unequal justice," the court expressed doubt that this form of legislative redundancy was constitutional. We find this analysis factually and legally unsound.

Contrary to the Court of Appeals' assertions, a prosecutor's discretion to choose between §§ 922(h) and 1202(a) is not "unfettered." Selectivity in the enforcement of criminal laws is, of course, subject to constitutional constraints. And a decision to proceed under § 922(h) does not empower the Government to predetermine ultimate criminal sanctions. Rather, it merely enables the sentencing judge to impose a longer prison sentence than § 1202(a) would permit and precludes him from imposing the greater fine authorized by § 1202(a). More importantly, there is no appreciable difference between the discretion a prosecutor exercises when deciding whether to charge under one of two statutes with different elements and the discretion he exercises when choosing one of two statutes with identical elements. In the former situation, once he determines that the proof will support conviction under either statute, his decision is indistinguishable from the one he faces in the latter context. The prosecutor may be influenced by the penalties available upon conviction, but this fact, standing alone, does not give rise to a violation of the Equal Protection or Due Process Clause. Just as a defendant has no constitutional right to elect which of two applicable federal statutes shall be the basis of his indictment and prosecution, neither is he entitled to choose the penalty scheme under which he will be sentenced.

Approaching the problem of prosecutorial discretion from a slightly different perspective, the Court of Appeals postulated that the statutes might impermissibly delegate to the Executive Branch the Legislature's responsibility to fix criminal penalties. We do not agree. The provisions at issue plainly demarcate the range of penalties that prosecutors and judges may seek and impose. In light of that specificity, the power that Congress has delegated to those officials is no broader than the authority they routinely exercise in enforcing the criminal laws. * * *

Accordingly, the judgment of the Court of Appeals is

Reversed.

CHAPTER 23

GRAND JURY

■ ■ ■

The Fifth Amendment to the U.S. Constitution provides:

No person shall be held to answer for a capital, or otherwise infamous crime, unless on a presentment or indictment of a Grand Jury . . . .

The Fifth Amendment right to an indictment[a] by a grand jury applies only to defendants in federal court. A defendant in state court does not have a right under the U.S. Constitution to an indictment by a grand jury.[b]

It is often said that the grand jury operates as both a sword and a shield. The grand jury acts as a sword when it helps the government investigate and bring charges against individuals. The grand jury acts as a shield when it declines to return an indictment, even in cases where there is probable cause to support an indictment. In this way, the grand jury can protect individuals from unjust prosecutions.

In contrast to the trial and the preliminary hearing, which are adversarial proceedings at which both the government and the defense have the right to present evidence, the grand jury proceeding is a one-sided proceeding at which the government alone presents evidence. Generally speaking, the target of the investigation (the defendant-to-be) has no right to present evidence to the grand jury, including his own testimony, unless he is called by the government to testify.[c] Unlike most criminal trials,

---

[a] An indictment is a charging document drawn up by the prosecutor. If a majority of the grand jury finds probable cause to believe the defendant committed the crimes in the indictment, it may return the indictment to the prosecutor. When the grand jury returns an indictment, this action is called returning a true bill. If a majority of the grand jury does not think the evidence presented supports a finding of probable cause, they will return a no bill. In cases involving a no bill, the indictment drawn up by the prosecutor will be considered invalid and cannot be used to commence a prosecution.

[b] Hurtado v. California, 110 U.S. 516 (1884) (declining to apply the Fifth Amendment right to indictment by a grand jury to the states through the Due Process Clause). In a majority of the states, the prosecutor can choose to proceed either by grand jury indictment or by preliminary hearing. A minority of states require a grand jury indictment in felony cases as a matter of state law. YALE KAMISAR ET AL., MODERN CRIMINAL PROCEDURE (13th ed. West).

[c] Some states permit the target of the investigation to testify before the grand jury as a matter of state law. *See* IND. CODE. ANN. § 35–34–2–9(b) (West 1999) ("A target of a grand jury investigation shall be given the right to testify before the grand jury, provided he signs a waiver of immunity"); NEV. REV. STAT. § 172.241(1) (1999) ("a person whose indictment the district attorney intends to seek . . . may testify before the grand jury if the person requests to do so . . . "); N.M. STAT. ANN. § 31–6–11(B) (LexisNexis 2000) ("the target of a grand jury investigation shall be notified in writing of . . . the target's right to testify . . . "); N.Y. CRIM. PROC. LAW § 190.50(5)(a)

which are open to the public, grand jury proceedings are closed to the public. Indeed, under Rule 6 of the Federal Rules of Criminal Procedure, grand jurors are required to keep secret anything that is said during the grand jury proceeding.

The grand jury differs in many other respects from the trial jury, also known as the petit jury. In the federal system, the grand jury consists of 16 to 23 persons whereas the petit jury usually consists of 12 persons.[d] The grand jury may sit for up to 18 months. In contrast, a petit jury will only sit for the duration of the trial. Even though the grand jury may sit for a longer period of time than a petit jury, grand jurors are not called into session every day. Some grand juries meet just once a month. Others meet once a week. A petit jury usually meets every day until the trial is concluded.[e]

The first case in this chapter, *Vasquez v. Hillery*, considers whether automatic reversal of a conviction is appropriate when racial discrimination occurs in the selection of the grand jury. The next few cases deal with questions concerning what evidence the grand jury can and should consider. *Costello v. United States* addresses whether the grand jury should be allowed to consider hearsay evidence. *United States v. Williams* discusses whether the prosecutor must advise the grand jury of any exculpatory evidence in its possession.

VASQUEZ V. HILLERY
Supreme Court of the United States
474 U.S. 254, 106 S. Ct. 617, 88 L. Ed. 2d 598 (1986)

JUSTICE MARSHALL delivered the opinion of the Court.

The Warden of San Quentin State Prison asks this Court to retire a doctrine of equal protection jurisprudence first announced in 1880. The time has come, he urges, for us to abandon the rule requiring reversal of the conviction of any defendant indicted by a grand jury from which members of his own race were systematically excluded.

In 1962, the grand jury of Kings County, California, indicted respondent, Booker T. Hillery, for a brutal murder. Before trial in Superior Court, respondent moved to quash the indictment on the ground that it had been issued by a grand jury from which blacks had been systematically

---

(Consol. 1996) ("When a criminal charge against a person is being or is about to be or has been submitted to a grand jury, such person has a right to appear before such grand jury as a witness in his own behalf").

[d] As you will learn in the chapter on the right to a trial by jury, the states are free to have as few as 6 persons on a jury. Williams v. Florida, 399 U.S. 78 (1970).

[e] For helpful information about the grand jury, *see* Jeffrey Fagan & Bernard E. Harcourt, *Professors Fagan and Harcourt Provide Facts on Grand Jury Practice in Light of Ferguson Decision*, COLUMBIA L. SCH., http://www.law.columbia.edu/media_inquiries/news_events/2014/november2014/Facts-on-Ferguson-Grand-Jury (https://perma.cc/DP94-77F2).

excluded.[a] A hearing on respondent's motion was held by Judge Meredith Wingrove, who was the sole Superior Court Judge in the county and had personally selected all grand juries, including the one that indicted respondent, for the previous seven years. Absolving himself of any discriminatory intent, Judge Wingrove refused to quash the indictment. Respondent was subsequently convicted of first-degree murder.

For the next 16 years, respondent pursued appeals and collateral relief in the state courts, raising at every opportunity his equal protection challenge to the grand jury that indicted him. Less than one month after the California Supreme Court foreclosed his final avenue of state relief in 1978, respondent filed a petition for a writ of habeas corpus in federal court, raising that same challenge. The District Court concluded that respondent had established discrimination in the grand jury, and granted the writ. The Court of Appeals affirmed, and we granted certiorari. * * *

On the merits, petitioner urges this Court to find that discrimination in the grand jury amounted to harmless error in this case,[b] claiming that the evidence against respondent was overwhelming and that discrimination no longer infects the selection of grand juries in Kings County. Respondent's conviction after a fair trial, we are told, purged any taint attributable to the indictment process. Our acceptance of this theory would require abandonment of more than a century of consistent precedent.

In 1880, this Court reversed a state conviction on the ground that the indictment charging the offense had been issued by a grand jury from which blacks had been excluded. We reasoned that deliberate exclusion of blacks "is practically a brand upon them, affixed by the law, an assertion of their inferiority, and a stimulant to that race prejudice which is an impediment to securing to individuals of the race that equal justice which the law aims to secure to all others."

Thereafter, the Court has repeatedly rejected all arguments that a conviction may stand despite racial discrimination in the selection of the grand jury. Only six years ago, the Court explicitly addressed the question whether this unbroken line of case law should be reconsidered in favor of a

---

[a] Hillery was a Black farmhand. Miles Corwin, *Man Guilty of Slaying—24 Years After Crime*, L.A. TIMES (Dec. 19, 1986), http://articles.latimes.com/1986-12-19/news/mn-3565_1_kings-county (https://perma.cc/M7GX-49VR).

[b] Under the doctrine of harmless error, a conviction may stand "where the reviewing court believes the defect in the proceeding was harmless beyond a reasonable doubt." Roger A. Fairfax, Jr., *Harmless Constitutional Error and the Institutional Significance of the Jury*, 76 FORDHAM L. REV. 2027, 2029 (2008). If, however, the reviewing court finds that the conviction was infected by structural error, the conviction is subject to automatic reversal rather than harmless error review. *Id.* The Supreme Court has recognized only a few errors as structural errors subject to automatic reversal, including *inter alia* bias of the trial judge, denial of the right to counsel, racial discrimination in the selection of the grand jury, and denial of the right to a public trial. *Id.* at 2029 n.3. All other errors—those that are not structural errors—are considered trial errors, which are subject to harmless error review. Arizona v. Fulminante, 499 U.S. 279, 306–08 (1991).

harmless-error standard, and determined that it should not. We reaffirmed our conviction that discrimination on the basis of race in the selection of grand jurors "strikes at the fundamental values of our judicial system and our society as a whole," and that the criminal defendant's right to equal protection of the laws has been denied when he is indicted by a grand jury from which members of a racial group purposefully have been excluded.

Petitioner argues here that requiring a State to retry a defendant, sometimes years later, imposes on it an unduly harsh penalty for a constitutional defect bearing no relation to the fundamental fairness of the trial. Yet intentional discrimination in the selection of grand jurors is a grave constitutional trespass, possible only under color of state authority, and wholly within the power of the State to prevent. Thus, the remedy we have embraced for over a century—the only effective remedy for this violation—is not disproportionate to the evil that it seeks to deter. If grand jury discrimination becomes a thing of the past, no conviction will ever again be lost on account of it.

Nor are we persuaded that discrimination in the grand jury has no effect on the fairness of the criminal trials that result from that grand jury's actions. The grand jury does not determine only that probable cause exists to believe that a defendant committed a crime, or that it does not. In the hands of the grand jury lies the power to charge a greater offense or a lesser offense; numerous counts or a single count; and perhaps most significant of all, a capital offense or a noncapital offense—all on the basis of the same facts. Moreover, "[t]he grand jury is not bound to indict in every case where a conviction can be obtained."[c] Thus, even if a grand jury's determination of probable cause is confirmed in hindsight by a conviction on the indicted offense, that confirmation in no way suggests that the discrimination did not impermissibly infect the framing of the indictment and, consequently, the nature or very existence of the proceedings to come.

When constitutional error calls into question the objectivity of those charged with bringing a defendant to judgment, a reviewing court can neither indulge a presumption of regularity nor evaluate the resulting harm. * * * [W]hen a petit jury has been selected upon improper criteria or has been exposed to prejudicial publicity, we have required reversal of the conviction because the effect of the violation cannot be ascertained. Like these fundamental flaws, which never have been thought harmless, discrimination in the grand jury undermines the structural integrity of the criminal tribunal itself, and is not amenable to harmless-error review.

Just as a conviction is void under the Equal Protection Clause if the prosecutor deliberately charged the defendant on account of his race, a

---

[c] When a grand jury declines to indict when there is probable cause to indict, it may be engaging in "grand jury nullification," which is within its authority and power. Roger A. Fairfax, Jr., *Grand Jury Discretion and Constitutional Design*, 93 CORNELL L. REV. 703 (2008).

conviction cannot be understood to cure the taint attributable to a charging body selected on the basis of race. Once having found discrimination in the selection of a grand jury, we simply cannot know that the need to indict would have been assessed in the same way by a grand jury properly constituted. The overriding imperative to eliminate this systemic flaw in the charging process, as well as the difficulty of assessing its effect on any given defendant, requires our continued adherence to a rule of mandatory reversal. * * *

The judgment of the Court of Appeals, accordingly, is affirmed. * * *

JUSTICE POWELL, with whom THE CHIEF JUSTICE and JUSTICE REHNQUIST join, dissenting.

Respondent, a black man, was indicted by a grand jury having no black members for the stabbing murder of a 15-year-old girl. A petit jury found respondent guilty of that charge beyond a reasonable doubt, in a trial the fairness of which is unchallenged here. Twenty-three years later, we are asked to grant respondent's petition for a writ of habeas corpus—and thereby require a new trial if that is still feasible—on the ground that blacks were purposefully excluded from the grand jury that indicted him. It is undisputed that race discrimination has long since disappeared from the grand jury selection process in Kings County, California. It is undisputed that a grand jury that perfectly represented Kings County's population at the time of respondent's indictment would have contained only one black member. Yet the Court holds that respondent's petition must be granted, and that respondent must be freed unless the State is able to reconvict, more than two decades after the murder that led to his incarceration.

It is difficult to reconcile this result with a rational system of justice. The Court nevertheless finds its decision compelled by a century of precedent and by the interests of respondent and of society in ending race discrimination in the selection of grand juries. I dissent for two reasons. First, in my view, any error in the selection of the grand jury that indicted respondent is constitutionally harmless. Second, even assuming that the harmless-error rule does not apply, reversal of respondent's conviction is an inappropriate remedy for the wrong that prompts this case.

* * * In this case, the Court misapplies *stare decisis* because it relies only on decisions concerning grand jury discrimination. There is other precedent, including important cases of more recent vintage than those cited by the Court, that should control this case. Those cases hold, or clearly imply, that a conviction should not be reversed for constitutional error where the error did not affect the outcome of the prosecution. * * *

In *Chapman v. California*, the Court held that a trial judge's improper comment on the defendant's failure to testify—a clear violation of the Fifth and Fourteenth Amendments—was not a proper basis for reversal if harmless. Since *Chapman*, "the Court has consistently made clear that it is the duty of a reviewing court to consider the trial record as a whole and to ignore errors that are harmless, including most constitutional violations." This rule has been applied to a variety of constitutional violations. * * *

In *Rose v. Mitchell*, the Court contended that the principle of these cases is inapplicable to grand jury discrimination claims, because grand jury discrimination "destroys the appearance of justice and thereby casts doubt on the integrity of the judicial process." But *every* constitutional error may be said to raise questions as to the "appearance of justice" and the "integrity of the judicial process." * * * Grand jury discrimination is a serious violation of our constitutional order, but so also are the deprivations of rights guaranteed by the Fourth, Fifth, Sixth, and Fourteenth Amendments to which we have applied harmless-error analysis or an analogous prejudice requirement. * * * The Court does not adequately explain why grand jury discrimination affects the "integrity of the judicial process" to a greater extent than the deprivation of equally vital constitutional rights, nor why it is exempt from a prejudice requirement while other constitutional errors are not. * * *

No one questions that race discrimination in grand jury selection violates the Equal Protection Clause of the Fourteenth Amendment. The issue in this case is not whether the State erred, but what should be done about it. The question is whether reversal of respondent's conviction either is compelled by the Constitution or is an appropriate, but not constitutionally required, remedy for racial discrimination in the selection of grand jurors. * * *

The Court * * * decides that discrimination in the selection of the grand jury potentially harmed respondent, because the grand jury is vested with broad discretion in deciding whether to indict and in framing the charges, and because it is impossible to know whether this discretion would have been exercised differently by a properly selected grand jury. The point appears to be that an all-white grand jury from which blacks are systematically excluded might be influenced by race in determining whether to indict and for what charge. Since the State may not imprison respondent for a crime if one of its elements is his race, the argument goes, his conviction must be set aside.

This reasoning ignores established principles of equal protection jurisprudence. We have consistently declined to find a violation of the Equal Protection Clause absent a finding of intentional discrimination. There has been no showing in this case—indeed, respondent does not even allege—that the Kings County grand jury indicted respondent because of his race, or that the grand jury declined to indict white suspects in the face of similarly strong evidence. Nor is it sensible to assume that impermissible discrimination might have occurred simply because the grand jury had no black members. This Court has never suggested that the racial composition of a grand jury gives rise to the inference that indictments are racially motivated, any more than it has suggested that a suspect arrested by a policeman of a different race may challenge his subsequent conviction on that basis. But the Court now holds that relief is justified in part because of the bare potential, unsupported by any evidence, that an all-white grand jury charged respondent because of his race.

Twenty-three years ago, respondent was fairly convicted of the most serious of crimes. * * * For that reason alone, the Court should reverse the Court of Appeals' decision. * * *

[JUSTICE O'CONNOR's concurring opinion has been omitted.]

NOTE

In a part of his dissent not included in the excerpt of *Vasquez v. Hillery* above, Justice Powell argued that, "when relief is granted many years after the original conviction . . . the State may find itself severely handicapped in its ability to carry its heavy burden of proving guilt beyond a reasonable doubt." Notwithstanding the risk that Hillery might have escaped conviction if reprosecuted so many years after the first trial, a majority of the Supreme Court affirmed the reversal of Hillery's conviction. Justice Marshall responded to Justice Powell's criticism of the majority's application of the automatic reversal rule and the risk that the Court would be letting a guilty man go free by noting, "If grand jury discrimination becomes a thing of the past, no conviction will ever again be lost on account of it."

In the end, Hillery did not go free. Despite the handicap to the State that Justice Powell feared given the more than 20 year time span between Hillery's conviction in the 1960s and the reversal of that conviction in 1986, the State secured another conviction when they reprosecuted Hillery. Miles Corwin, *Man Guilty of Slaying—24 Years After Crime*, L.A. TIMES (Dec. 19, 1986, 12:00 AM), http://articles.latimes.com/1986-12-19/news/mn-3565_1_kings-county (https://perma.cc/M7GX-49VR) (noting that "[o]ne remarkable aspect of the case [was] that the Kings County Sheriff's Department held onto more than one hundred pieces of evidence from the Hillery case, including photographs of the crime scene, fiber and paint samples and Hillery's car."); *Killer, Twice Convicted, Due Parole Hearing*, L.A. TIMES (Feb. 28, 1987, 12:00 AM), http://articles.latimes.com/1987-02-28/news/mn-6520_1_parole-hearing (https://perma.cc/SV69-SFM3). An all-white jury found Hillery guilty on December 18, 1986, and he was sentenced to life in prison. *Id.* Public outrage against Hillery for the murder of Marlene Miller, a white fifteen-year-old girl who was at home alone making a dress to wear to a party when she was stabbed to death with her own sewing scissors, remained high for many years. Miles Corwin, *Man Guilty of Slaying—24 Years After Crime*, L.A. TIMES (Dec. 19, 1986, 12:00 AM), http://articles.latimes.com/1986-12-19/news/mn-3565_1_kings-county (https://

perma.cc/M7GX-49VR). As of 1993, Hillery continued to be denied parole. *Man Who Killed Girl, 15, in 1962 is Denied Parole*, L.A. TIMES (July 30, 1993, 12:00 AM) http://articles.latimes.com/1993-07-30/news/mn-18501_1_parole-hearing (https://perma.cc/32RK-UWWY).

COSTELLO V. UNITED STATES
Supreme Court of the United States
350 U.S. 359, 76 S. Ct. 406, 100 L. Ed. 397 (1956)

JUSTICE BLACK delivered the opinion of the Court.

We granted certiorari in this case to consider a single question: "May a defendant be required to stand trial and a conviction be sustained where only hearsay evidence was presented to the grand jury which indicted him?"

Petitioner, Frank Costello, was indicted for wilfully attempting to evade payment of income taxes due the United States for the years 1947, 1948 and 1949. The charge was that petitioner falsely and fraudulently reported less income than he and his wife actually received during the taxable years in question. Petitioner promptly filed a motion for inspection of the minutes of the grand jury and for a dismissal of the indictment. His motion was based on an affidavit stating that he was firmly convinced there could have been no legal or competent evidence before the grand jury which indicted him since he had reported all his income and paid all taxes due. The motion was denied. At the trial which followed the Government offered evidence designed to show increases in Costello's net worth in an attempt to prove that he had received more income during the years in question than he had reported. To establish its case the Government called and examined 144 witnesses and introduced 368 exhibits. All of the testimony and documents related to business transactions and expenditures by petitioner and his wife. The prosecution concluded its case by calling three government agents. Their investigations had produced the evidence used against petitioner at the trial. They were allowed to summarize the vast amount of evidence already heard and to introduce computations showing, if correct, that petitioner and his wife had received far greater income than they had reported. * * *

Counsel for petitioner asked each government witness at the trial whether he had appeared before the grand jury which returned the indictment. This cross-examination developed the fact that the three investigating officers had been the only witnesses before the grand jury. After the Government concluded its case, petitioner again moved to dismiss the indictment on the ground that the only evidence before the grand jury was "hearsay," since the three officers had no firsthand knowledge of the transactions upon which their computations were based. Nevertheless the trial court again refused to dismiss the indictment, and petitioner was convicted. The Court of Appeals affirmed. * * * Petitioner here urges: (1) that an indictment based solely on hearsay evidence violates that part of the Fifth Amendment providing that "No person shall be held to answer for a capital, or otherwise infamous crime, unless on a presentment or indictment of a Grand Jury . . . ," and (2) that if the Fifth Amendment does not invalidate an indictment based solely on hearsay we should now lay down such a rule for the guidance of federal courts.

* * * [N]either the Fifth Amendment nor any other constitutional provision prescribes the kind of evidence upon which grand juries must act. * * * The basic purpose of the English grand jury was to provide a fair method for instituting criminal proceedings against persons believed to have committed crimes. Grand jurors were selected from the body of the people and their work was not hampered by rigid procedural or evidential rules. In fact, grand jurors could act on their own knowledge and were free to make their presentments or indictments on such information as they deemed satisfactory. * * * And in this country as in England of old the grand jury has convened as a body of laymen, free from technical rules, acting in secret, pledged to indict no one because of prejudice and to free no one because of special favor. * * *

In *Holt v. United States*, this Court had to decide whether an indictment should be quashed because supported in part by incompetent evidence. Aside from the incompetent evidence "there was very little evidence against the accused." The Court refused to hold that such an indictment should be quashed, pointing out that "The abuses of criminal practice would be enhanced if indictments could be upset on such a ground." The same thing is true where as [sic] here all the evidence before the grand jury was in the nature of "hearsay." If indictments were to be held open to challenge on the ground that there was inadequate or incompetent evidence before the grand jury, the resulting delay would be great indeed. The result of such a rule would be that before trial on the merits a defendant could always insist on a kind of preliminary trial to determine the competency and adequacy of the evidence before the grand jury. This is not required by the Fifth Amendment. An indictment returned by a legally constituted and unbiased grand jury, * * * is enough to call for trial of the charge on the merits. The Fifth Amendment requires nothing more.

Petitioner urges that this Court should exercise its power to supervise the administration of justice in federal courts and establish a rule permitting defendants to challenge indictments on the ground that they are not supported by adequate or competent evidence. No persuasive reasons are advanced for establishing such a rule. It would run counter to the whole history of the grand jury institution, in which laymen conduct their inquiries unfettered by technical rules. Neither justice nor the concept of a fair trial requires such a change. In a trial on the merits, defendants are entitled to a strict observance of all the rules designed to bring about a fair verdict. Defendants are not entitled, however, to a rule which would result in interminable delay but add nothing to the assurance of a fair trial.

Affirmed.

JUSTICE CLARK and JUSTICE HARLAN took no part in the consideration or decision of this case.

[JUSTICE BURTON's concurring opinion has been omitted.]

UNITED STATES V. WILLIAMS
Supreme Court of the United States
504 U.S. 36, 112 S. Ct. 1735, 118 L. Ed. 2d 352 (1992)

JUSTICE SCALIA delivered the opinion of the Court.

The question presented in this case is whether a district court may dismiss an otherwise valid indictment because the Government failed to disclose to the grand jury "substantial exculpatory evidence" in its possession.

* * * [R]espondent John H. Williams, Jr., * * * was indicted * * * [for] "knowingly mak[ing] [a] false statement or report . . . for the purpose of influencing . . . the action [of a federally insured financial institution]," * * *. According to the indictment, * * * Williams supplied four Oklahoma banks with "materially false" statements that variously overstated the value of his current assets and interest income in order to influence the banks' actions on his loan requests.

* * * [T]he District Court granted Williams' motion for disclosure of all exculpatory portions of the grand jury transcripts. Upon reviewing this material, Williams demanded that the District Court dismiss the indictment, alleging that the Government had failed to fulfill its obligation under the Tenth Circuit's prior decision in *United States v. Page* to present "substantial exculpatory evidence" to the grand jury. His contention was that evidence which the Government had chosen not to present to the grand jury * * * belied an intent to mislead the banks, and thus directly negated an essential element of the charged offense.

The District Court * * * ordered the indictment dismissed without prejudice. It found * * * that the withheld evidence was "relevant to an essential element of the crime charged," created "a reasonable doubt about [respondent's] guilt," and thus "render[ed] the grand jury's decision to indict gravely suspect." Upon the Government's appeal, the Court of Appeals affirmed the District Court's order * * *. It first sustained * * * the District Court's determination that the Government had withheld "substantial exculpatory evidence" from the grand jury. It then found that the Government's behavior "substantially influence[d]" the grand jury's decision to indict, or at the very least raised a "grave doubt that the decision to indict was free from such substantial influence." [The Court of Appeals also found that] * * * it was not an abuse of discretion for the District Court to require the Government to begin anew before the grand jury. We granted certiorari. * * *

Respondent does not contend that the Fifth Amendment itself obliges the prosecutor to disclose substantial exculpatory evidence in his possession to the grand jury. Instead, building on our statement that the federal courts "may, within limits, formulate procedural rules not specifically required by the Constitution or the Congress," he argues that imposition of the Tenth Circuit's disclosure rule is supported by the courts' "supervisory power." We think not.

* * * Because the grand jury is an institution separate from the courts, over whose functioning the courts do not preside, we think it clear that, as a general matter at least, no such "supervisory" judicial authority exists, and that the disclosure rule applied here exceeded the Tenth Circuit's authority.

"[R]ooted in long centuries of Anglo-American history," the grand jury is mentioned in the Bill of Rights, but not in the body of the Constitution. It has not been textually assigned, therefore, to any of the branches described in the first three Articles. It "is a constitutional fixture in its own right." In fact the whole theory of its function is that it belongs to no branch of the institutional Government, serving as a kind of buffer or referee between the Government and the people. Although the grand jury normally operates, of course, in the courthouse and under judicial auspices, its institutional relationship with the Judicial Branch has traditionally been, so to speak, at arm's length. Judges' direct involvement in the functioning of the grand jury has generally been confined to the constitutive one of calling the grand jurors together and administering their oaths of office.

The grand jury's functional independence from the Judicial Branch is evident both in the scope of its power to investigate criminal wrongdoing and in the manner in which that power is exercised. "Unlike [a] [c]ourt, whose jurisdiction is predicated upon a specific case or controversy, the grand jury 'can investigate merely on suspicion that the law is being violated, or even because it wants assurance that it is not.'" It need not identify the offender it suspects, or even "the precise nature of the offense" it is investigating. The grand jury requires no authorization from its constituting court to initiate an investigation, nor does the prosecutor require leave of court to seek a grand jury indictment. And in its day-to-day functioning, the grand jury generally operates without the interference of a presiding judge. It swears in its own witnesses, and deliberates in total secrecy. * * *

No doubt in view of the grand jury proceeding's status as other than a constituent element of a "criminal prosecutio[n]," we have said that certain constitutional protections afforded defendants in criminal proceedings have no application before that body. The Double Jeopardy Clause of the Fifth Amendment does not bar a grand jury from returning an indictment when a prior grand jury has refused to do so. We have twice suggested, though not held, that the Sixth Amendment right to counsel does not attach when an individual is summoned to appear before a grand jury, even if he is the subject of the investigation. And although "the grand jury may not force a witness to answer questions in violation of [the Fifth Amendment's] constitutional guarantee" against self-incrimination, our cases suggest that an indictment obtained through the use of evidence previously obtained in violation of the privilege against self-incrimination "is nevertheless valid." * * *

Respondent argues that the Court of Appeals' rule can be justified as a sort of Fifth Amendment "common law," a necessary means of assuring the constitutional right to the judgment "of an independent and informed grand jury." Respondent makes a generalized appeal to functional notions: Judicial supervision of the quantity and quality of the evidence relied upon by the grand jury plainly facilitates, he says, the grand jury's performance of its twin historical responsibilities, *i.e.,* bringing to trial those who may be justly accused and shielding the innocent from unfounded accusation and prosecution. We do not agree. The rule would neither preserve nor enhance the traditional functioning of the institution that the Fifth Amendment demands. To the contrary, requiring the prosecutor to present exculpatory as well as inculpatory evidence would alter the grand jury's historical role, transforming it from an accusatory to an adjudicatory body.

It is axiomatic that the grand jury sits not to determine guilt or innocence, but to assess whether there is adequate basis for bringing a criminal charge. That has always been so; and to make the assessment it has always been thought sufficient to hear only the prosecutor's side. As Blackstone described the prevailing practice in 18th-century England, the grand jury was "only to hear evidence on behalf of the prosecution[,] for the finding of an indictment is only in the nature of an enquiry or accusation, which is afterwards to be tried and determined." So also in the United States. According to the description of an early American court, three years before the Fifth Amendment was ratified, it is the grand jury's function not "to enquire . . . upon what foundation [the charge may be] denied," or otherwise to try the suspect's defenses, but only to examine "upon what foundation [the charge] is made" by the prosecutor. As a consequence, neither in this country nor in England has the suspect under investigation by the grand jury ever been thought to have a right to testify or to have exculpatory evidence presented. * * *

We accepted Justice Nelson's description in *Costello v. United States,* where we held that "[i]t would run counter to the whole history of the grand jury institution" to permit an indictment to be challenged "on the ground that there was inadequate or incompetent evidence before the grand jury." And we reaffirmed this principle recently in *Bank of Nova Scotia,* where we held that "the mere fact that evidence itself is unreliable is not sufficient to require a dismissal of the indictment," and that "a challenge to the reliability or competence of the evidence presented to the grand jury" will not be heard. It would make little sense, we think, to abstain from reviewing the evidentiary support for the grand jury's judgment while scrutinizing the sufficiency of the prosecutor's presentation. A complaint about the quality or adequacy of the evidence can always be recast as a complaint that the prosecutor's presentation was "incomplete" or "misleading." Our words in *Costello* bear repeating: Review of facially valid indictments on such grounds "would run counter to the whole history of the grand jury institution[,] [and] [n]either justice nor the concept of a fair trial requires [it]."

* * * For the reasons set forth above, however, we conclude that courts have no authority to prescribe such a duty pursuant to their inherent supervisory authority over their own proceedings. The judgment of the Court of Appeals is accordingly reversed, and the cause is remanded for further proceedings consistent with this opinion. * * *

JUSTICE STEVENS, with whom JUSTICE BLACKMUN and JUSTICE O'CONNOR join, and with whom JUSTICE THOMAS joins as to Parts II and III, dissenting. * * *

II

We do not protect the integrity and independence of the grand jury by closing our eyes to the countless forms of prosecutorial misconduct that may occur inside the secrecy of the grand jury room. After all, the grand jury is not merely an investigatory body; it also serves as a "protector of citizens against arbitrary and oppressive governmental action." * * * It blinks reality to say that the grand jury can adequately perform this important historic role if it is intentionally misled by the prosecutor—on whose knowledge of the law and facts of the underlying criminal investigation the jurors will, of necessity, rely.

Unlike the Court, I am unwilling to hold that countless forms of prosecutorial misconduct must be tolerated—no matter how prejudicial they may be, or how seriously they may distort the legitimate function of the grand jury—simply because they are not proscribed by Rule 6 of the Federal Rules of Criminal Procedure or a statute that is applicable in grand jury proceedings. Such a sharp break with the traditional role of the federal judiciary is unprecedented, unwarranted, and unwise. Unrestrained prosecutorial misconduct in grand jury proceedings is inconsistent with the administration of justice in the federal courts and should be redressed in appropriate cases by the dismissal of indictments obtained by improper methods.

III

What, then, is the proper disposition of this case? I agree with the Government that the prosecutor is not required to place all exculpatory evidence before the grand jury. A grand jury proceeding is an *ex parte* investigatory proceeding to determine whether there is probable cause to believe a violation of the criminal laws has occurred, not a trial. Requiring the prosecutor to ferret out and present all evidence that could be used at trial to create a reasonable doubt as to the defendant's guilt would be inconsistent with the purpose of the grand jury proceeding and would place significant burdens on the investigation. But that does not mean that the prosecutor may mislead the grand jury into believing that there is probable cause to indict by withholding clear evidence to the contrary. * * *

Although I question whether the evidence withheld in this case directly negates respondent's guilt, I need not resolve my doubts because the Solicitor General did not ask the Court to review the nature of the evidence withheld. Instead, he asked us to decide the legal question whether an indictment may be dismissed because the prosecutor failed to present exculpatory evidence. Unlike the Court and the Solicitor General, I believe the answer to that question is yes, if the withheld evidence would plainly preclude a finding of probable cause. I therefore cannot endorse the Court's opinion. * * *

NOTE

Despite the holding in *United States v. Williams*, some states require their prosecutors to present exculpatory evidence to the grand jury as a matter of state law. *See, e.g.,* Willis v. Bernini, 515 P.3d 142, 150 (Az. 2022) (prosecutor has a duty to inform the grand jury of clearly exculpatory evidence); NEV. REV. STAT. § 172.145 (2021) ("If the district attorney is aware of any evidence which will explain away the charge, the district attorney shall submit it to the grand jury"); State v. Herrera, 601 P.2d 75, 77 (N.M. Ct. App. 1979) (holding "due process requires the presentation of evidence to the grand jury which tends to negate guilt" because "the basic duty of the prosecutor is to seek a just result"); Frink v. State, 597 P.2d 154, 164 (Alaska 1979) (affirming that "the prosecutor has a duty to present exculpatory evidence to the grand jury"); Johnson v. Superior Court, 15 Cal.3d 248, 255 (1975) (holding that "when a district attorney seeking an indictment is aware of evidence reasonably tending to negate guilt, he is obligated . . . to inform the grand jury of its nature and existence."). Federal prosecutors conducting grand jury proceedings are also instructed to disclose exculpatory evidence to the grand jury. *See* U.S. DEP'T OF JUST., JUST. MANUAL § 9–11.223 (2022). ("It is the policy of the Department of Justice, . . . that when a prosecutor conducting a grand jury inquiry is personally aware of substantial evidence that directly negates the guilt of a subject of the investigation, the prosecutor must present or otherwise disclose such evidence to the grand jury before seeking an indictment against such a person.")

The 2014 deaths of Michael Brown in Ferguson, Missouri, and Eric Garner in New York City, New York, drew public attention to the use of the grand jury in charging decisions involving police officers. In each of these high profile cases, the grand jury failed to indict the officers involved. The "no bill" for Michael Brown's death in Missouri was returned first, followed a few days later by the "no bill" in New York for Eric Garner's death.

Notably, the events leading up to Garner's death—the officer putting Garner into a chokehold and Garner, who suffered from asthma, crying out, "I can't breathe; I can't breathe"—were captured on video. Thus, many were surprised when no indictment was returned by the grand jury. The no bill was particularly surprising given that the New York City Police Department prohibits its officers from using chokeholds.[a] In the Ferguson case, there were allegations of prosecutorial error, such as instructing the grand jurors on an outdated version of the use-of-force law.[b] Moreover, the prosecutor admitted he presented the grand jury with evidence he knew was false.[c]

In both cases, the decisions by each of the grand juries resulted in strong public reaction. The Pew Research Center conducted public opinion polls that gauged the public's reaction to the decisions and found that a majority of Whites (64%) felt the grand jury's decision not to indict Officer Darren Wilson in the death of Michael Brown was the right decision, while an overwhelming majority of Blacks (80%) felt the grand jury's decision in the Ferguson case was

---

[a] Alissa Scheller, *The Chokehold Is Banned by NYPD, but Complaints About Its Use Persist*, HUFFPOST (Dec. 6, 2017), https://www.huffpost.com/entry/nyc-police-chokeholds_n_6272000 (https://perma.cc/LT27-8WB9); Ian Fisher, *Kelly Bans Chokeholds by Officers*, N.Y. TIMES (Nov. 24, 1993), http://www.nytimes.com/1993/11/24/nyregion/kelly-bans-choke-holds-by-officers.html (https://perma.cc/EJ6A-6ADC).

[b] Jeffrey Fagan & Bernard E. Harcourt, *Professors Fagan and Harcourt Provide Facts on Grand Jury Practice in Light of Ferguson Decision*, COLUMBIA L. SCH. (Dec. 5, 2014), http://www.law.columbia.edu/media_inquiries/news_events/2014/november2014/Facts-on-Ferguson-Grand-Jury (https://perma.cc/DP94-77F2). It appears this criticism may have been misplaced since the initial instruction instructed grand jurors on the use of force law in effect in Missouri at the time. In 2014, Missouri was still operating under the old common law rule, which permitted police officers to use deadly force to prevent the escape of a fleeing felon even if the individual was not posing an imminent threat of death or serious bodily injury to anyone. *See* Chad Flanders & Joseph Welling, *Police Use of Deadly Force: State Statutes 30 Years After Garner*, 35 ST. LOUIS U. PUB. L. REV. 109, 124–26 (2015) (explaining that the ruling in *Tennessee v. Garner* controls in Section 1983 civil rights actions, but a state's use of force law controls in its criminal prosecutions). In 2016, Missouri finally abandoned the common law rule and changed its use of force statute to comport with *Tennessee v. Garner*. *See* H.B. 2332, 98th Gen. Assemb., 2nd Reg. Sess. (Mo. 2016).

[c] Judd Legum, *A Startling Admission by the Ferguson Prosecutor Could Restart the Case Against Darren Wilson*, THINKPROGRESS (Dec. 21, 2014, 7:32 PM), https://archive.thinkprogress.org/a-startling-admission-by-the-ferguson-prosecutor-could-restart-the-case-against-darren-wilson-ccfcc3d0adfc/ (https://perma.cc/3PCG-BTV2) (noting that prosecutor Bob McCulloch admitted in a radio interview that he presented witnesses to the grand jury who clearly were not telling the truth); Josh Levs, *One Challenge for Ferguson Grand Jury: Some Witnesses' Credibility*, CNN (Dec. 14, 2014, 3:53 PM), http://www.cnn.com/2014/12/14/justice/ferguson-witnesses-credibility/ (https://perma.cc/FY7D-AJFE).

the wrong decision.[d] In the New York case, Whites and Blacks were more aligned in feeling that the grand jury's decision not to indict the officer involved in Eric Garner's death was the wrong decision. Nonetheless, only 47% of Whites polled felt the no bill in Garner's case was the wrong decision compared to an overwhelming majority of Blacks (90%) who felt the no bill was the wrong decision.

---

[d] *Sharp Racial Divisions in Reactions to Brown, Garner Decisions*, PEW RSCH. CTR. (Dec. 8, 2014), http://www.people-press.org/2014/12/08/sharp-racial-divisions-in-reactions-to-brown-garner-decisions (https://perma.cc/GE8Z-CZ82).

CHAPTER 24

BAIL

■ ■ ■

Bail is the process of releasing a defendant from jail pending trial with conditions to ensure that the defendant will make future court appearances and not endanger the community.[a] The term "bail" is often used as shorthand for "bail bond," which is an agreement between the defendant and the court or a private bail bondsman[b] in which the defendant posts some form of security—usually a sum of money—and promises to appear in court as required. In exchange, the defendant is released from jail pending trial. The defendant agrees to forfeit the money paid to the court or the bail bondsman if he does not fulfill his promise to appear.

Since 1900, the bail system in the United States has primarily relied upon financial conditions as the means for ensuring court appearances and safety of the community. While the court can release the defendant on the defendant's own recognizance or personal promise to appear, also known as OR (own recognizance) release, in most cases, the court will set financial and other conditions for release and require the defendant to post bond before the defendant is released pending trial.

There is no express right to bail in the U.S. Constitution. The Eighth Amendment to the U.S. Constitution, however, provides that "[e]xcessive bail shall not be required." In the first case in this chapter, *Stack v. Boyle*, the Court explains when bail is excessive in violation of the Eighth Amendment.

Prior to 1984, it was understood that the purpose of setting financial conditions upon release was to secure the defendant's appearance at trial. In 1984, Congress passed the Federal Bail Reform Act of 1984, *see* Appendix, which authorizes the pretrial detention of a defendant to ensure either the appearance of the defendant or the safety of any other person or the community. When a defendant is incarcerated prior to or pending trial to assure the safety of the community, this type of detention is known as "preventive detention." In *United States v. Salerno*, the Court considers

---

[a] NATIONAL INSTITUTE OF CORRECTIONS, FUNDAMENTALS OF BAIL: A RESOURCE GUIDE FOR PRETRIAL PRACTITIONERS AND A FRAMEWORK FOR AMERICAN PRETRIAL REFORM 2 (2014).

[b] Bail is often set in an amount that is higher than most defendants can pay, which leads many defendants and their families to hire a bail bondsman. A bail bondsman usually charges the defendant a percentage of the full amount of bail set by the court, often 10 to 20 percent, and agrees to pay the full amount to the court if the defendant does not appear. The amount of money paid to the bail bondsman is nonrefundable.

whether preventive detention violates either the Due Process Clause or the Eighth Amendment's proscription against excessive bail.

The chapter ends with a Note on recent efforts to reform the bail system and an article by Cynthia Jones that summarizes the results of research studies that show Black defendants are subjected to pretrial detention at higher rates and are subjected to higher bail amounts than White defendants with similar charges and similar criminal histories.

STACK V. BOYLE
Supreme Court of the United States
342 U.S. 1, 72 S. Ct. 1, 96 L. Ed. 3 (1951)

CHIEF JUSTICE VINSON delivered the opinion of the Court.

Indictments have been returned in the Southern District of California charging the twelve petitioners with conspiring to violate the Smith Act.[a] Upon their arrest, bail was fixed for each petitioner in the widely varying amounts of $2,500, $7,500, $75,000 and $100,000. On motion of petitioner Schneiderman following arrest in the Southern District of New York, his bail was reduced to $50,000 before his removal to California. On motion of the Government to increase bail in the case of other petitioners, and after several intermediate procedural steps not material to the issues presented here, bail was fixed in the District Court for the Southern District of California in the uniform amount of $50,000 for each petitioner.

Petitioners moved to reduce bail on the ground that bail as fixed was excessive under the Eighth Amendment.[1] In support of their motion, petitioners submitted statements as to their financial resources, family relationships, health, prior criminal records, and other information. The only evidence offered by the Government was a certified record showing that four persons previously convicted under the Smith Act in the Southern District of New York had forfeited bail. No evidence was produced relating those four persons to the petitioners in this case. At a hearing on the motion, petitioners were examined by the District Judge and cross-examined by an attorney for the Government. Petitioners' factual statements stand uncontroverted.

After their motion to reduce bail was denied, petitioners filed applications for habeas corpus in the same District Court. Upon consideration of the record on the motion to reduce bail, the writs were denied. The Court of Appeals for the Ninth Circuit affirmed.

---

[a] The Smith Act, formally the Alien Registration Act of 1940, makes it a felony punishable by up to twenty years of imprisonment to advocate the overthrow of the United States government by force or violence. *See* 18 U.S.C. § 2385 (2022).

[1] "Excessive bail shall not be required, nor excessive fines imposed, nor cruel and unusual punishments inflicted." U.S. Const. Amend. VIII.

*** [F]rom the passage of the Judiciary Act of 1789 to the present Federal Rules of Criminal Procedure, Rule 46(a)(1), federal law has unequivocally provided that a person arrested for a non-capital offense shall be admitted to bail. This traditional right to freedom before conviction permits the unhampered preparation of a defense, and serves to prevent the infliction of punishment prior to conviction. Unless this right to bail before trial is preserved, the presumption of innocence, secured only after centuries of struggle, would lose its meaning.

The right to release before trial is conditioned upon the accused's giving adequate assurance that he will stand trial and submit to sentence if found guilty. Like the ancient practice of securing the oaths of responsible persons to stand as sureties for the accused, the modern practice of requiring a bail bond or the deposit of a sum of money subject to forfeiture serves as additional assurance of the presence of an accused. Bail set at a figure higher than an amount reasonably calculated to fulfill this purpose is "excessive" under the Eighth Amendment.

Since the function of bail is limited, the fixing of bail for any individual defendant must be based upon standards relevant to the purpose of assuring the presence of that defendant. The traditional standards as expressed in the Federal Rules of Criminal Procedure[3] are to be applied in each case to each defendant. *** Upon final judgment of conviction, petitioners face imprisonment of not more than five years and a fine of not more than $10,000. It is not denied that bail for each petitioner has been fixed in a sum much higher than that usually imposed for offenses with like penalties and yet there has been no factual showing to justify such action in this case. The Government asks the courts to depart from the norm by assuming, without the introduction of evidence, that each petitioner is a pawn in a conspiracy and will, in obedience to a superior, flee the jurisdiction. To infer from the fact of indictment alone a need for bail in an unusually high amount is an arbitrary act. Such conduct would inject into our own system of government the very principles of totalitarianism which Congress was seeking to guard against in passing the statute under which petitioners have been indicted.

If bail in an amount greater than that usually fixed for serious charges of crimes is required in the case of any of the petitioners, that is a matter to which evidence should be directed in a hearing so that the constitutional rights of each petitioner may be preserved. In the absence of such a showing, we are of the opinion that the fixing of bail before trial in these

---

[3] Rule 46(c). "AMOUNT. If the defendant is admitted to bail, the amount thereof shall be such as in the judgment of the commissioner or court or judge or justice will insure the presence of the defendant, having regard to the nature and circumstances of the offense charged, the weight of the evidence against him, the financial ability of the defendant to give bail and the character of the defendant."

cases cannot be squared with the statutory and constitutional standards for admission to bail. * * *

The Court concludes that bail has not been fixed by proper methods in this case and that petitioners' remedy is by motion to reduce bail, with right of appeal to the Court of Appeals. Accordingly, the judgment of the Court of Appeals is vacated and the case is remanded to the District Court with directions to vacate its order. * * * Petitioners may move for reduction of bail in the criminal proceeding so that a hearing may be held for the purpose of fixing reasonable bail for each petitioner.

It is so ordered.

* * *

By JUSTICE JACKSON, whom JUSTICE FRANKFURTER joins. * * *

The practice of admission to bail, as it has evolved in Anglo-American law, is not a device for keeping persons in jail upon mere accusation until it is found convenient to give them a trial. On the contrary, the spirit of the procedure is to enable them to stay out of jail until a trial has found them guilty. Without this conditional privilege, even those wrongly accused are punished by a period of imprisonment while awaiting trial and are handicapped in consulting counsel, searching for evidence and witnesses, and preparing a defense. To open a way of escape from this handicap and possible injustice, Congress commands allowance of bail for one under charge of any offense not punishable by death, Fed.Rules Crim.Proc. 46(a)(1) providing: "A person arrested for an offense not punishable by death shall be admitted to bail . . ." before conviction. * * *

It is complained that the District Court fixed a uniform blanket bail chiefly by consideration of the nature of the accusation and did not take into account the difference in circumstances between different defendants. If this occurred, it is a clear violation of Rule 46(c). Each defendant stands before the bar of justice as an individual. Even on a conspiracy charge defendants do not lose their separateness or identity. While it might be possible that these defendants are identical in financial ability, character and relation to the charge—elements Congress has directed to be regarded in fixing bail—I think it violates the law of probabilities. Each accused is entitled to any benefits due to his good record, and misdeeds or a bad record should prejudice only those who are guilty of them. The question when application for bail is made relates to each one's trustworthiness to appear for trial and what security will supply reasonable assurance of his appearance.

* * * [T]he defect in the proceedings below appears to be, that, provoked by the flight of certain Communists after conviction, the Government demands and public opinion supports a use of the bail power to keep Communist defendants in jail before conviction. Thus, the amount

is said to have been fixed not as a reasonable assurance of their presence at the trial, but also as an assurance they would remain in jail. There seems reason to believe that this may have been the spirit to which the courts below have yielded, and it is contrary to the whole policy and philosophy of bail. This is not to say that every defendant is entitled to such bail as he can provide, but he is entitled to an opportunity to make it in a reasonable amount. I think the whole matter should be reconsidered by the appropriate judges in the traditional spirit of bail procedure. * * *

UNITED STATES V. SALERNO
Supreme Court of the United States
481 U.S. 739, 107 S. Ct. 2095, 95 L. Ed. 2d 697 (1987)

CHIEF JUSTICE REHNQUIST delivered the opinion of the Court.

The Bail Reform Act of 1984 (Act) allows a federal court to detain an arrestee pending trial if the Government demonstrates by clear and convincing evidence after an adversary hearing that no release conditions "will reasonably assure ... the safety of any other person and the community." The United States Court of Appeals for the Second Circuit struck down this provision of the Act as facially unconstitutional, because, in that court's words, this type of pretrial detention violates "substantive due process." We granted certiorari because of a conflict among the Courts of Appeals regarding the validity of the Act. We hold that, as against the facial attack mounted by these respondents, the Act fully comports with constitutional requirements. We therefore reverse.

Responding to "the alarming problem of crimes committed by persons on release," Congress formulated the Bail Reform Act of 1984, as the solution to a bail crisis in the federal courts. The Act represents the National Legislature's considered response to numerous perceived deficiencies in the federal bail process. By providing for sweeping changes in both the way federal courts consider bail applications and the circumstances under which bail is granted, Congress hoped to "give the courts adequate authority to make release decisions that give appropriate recognition to the danger a person may pose to others if released."

To this end, § 3141(a) of the Act requires a judicial officer to determine whether an arrestee shall be detained. Section 3142(e) provides that "[i]f, after a hearing pursuant to the provisions of subsection (f), the judicial officer finds that no condition or combination of conditions will reasonably assure the appearance of the person as required and the safety of any other person and the community, he shall order the detention of the person prior to trial." Section 3142(f) provides the arrestee with a number of procedural safeguards. He may request the presence of counsel at the detention hearing, he may testify and present witnesses in his behalf, as well as proffer evidence, and he may cross-examine other witnesses appearing at the hearing. If the judicial officer finds that no conditions of pretrial release can reasonably assure the safety of other persons and the community, he must state his findings of fact in writing, and support his conclusion with "clear and convincing evidence."

The judicial officer is not given unbridled discretion in making the detention determination. Congress has specified the considerations relevant to that decision. These factors include the nature and seriousness of the charges, the substantiality of the Government's evidence against the arrestee, the arrestee's background and characteristics, and the nature and seriousness of the danger posed by the suspect's release. Should a judicial officer order detention, the detainee is entitled to expedited appellate review of the detention order.

Respondents Anthony Salerno and Vincent Cafaro were arrested on March 21, 1986, after being charged in a 29-count indictment alleging various Racketeer Influenced and Corrupt Organizations Act (RICO) violations, mail and wire fraud offenses, extortion, and various criminal gambling violations. The RICO counts alleged 35 acts of racketeering activity, including fraud, extortion, gambling, and conspiracy to commit murder. At respondents' arraignment, the Government moved to have Salerno and Cafaro detained pursuant to § 3142(e), on the ground that no condition of release would assure the safety of the community or any person. The District Court held a hearing at which the Government made a detailed proffer of evidence. The Government's case showed that Salerno was the "boss" of the Genovese crime family of La Cosa Nostra and that Cafaro was a "captain" in the Genovese family. According to the Government's proffer, based in large part on conversations intercepted by a court-ordered wiretap, the two respondents had participated in wide-ranging conspiracies to aid their illegitimate enterprises through violent means. The Government also offered the testimony of two of its trial witnesses, who would assert that Salerno personally participated in two murder conspiracies. Salerno opposed the motion for detention, challenging the credibility of the Government's witnesses. He offered the testimony of several character witnesses as well as a letter from his doctor stating that he was suffering from a serious medical condition. Cafaro presented no evidence at the hearing, but instead characterized the wiretap conversations as merely "tough talk."

The District Court granted the Government's detention motion, concluding that the Government had established by clear and convincing evidence that no condition or combination of conditions of release would ensure the safety of the community or any person:

> The activities of a criminal organization such as the Genovese Family do not cease with the arrest of its principals and their release on even the most stringent of bail conditions. The illegal

businesses, in place for many years, require constant attention and protection, or they will fail. Under these circumstances, this court recognizes a strong incentive on the part of its leadership to continue business as usual. When business as usual involves threats, beatings, and murder, the present danger such people pose in the community is self-evident.

Respondents appealed, contending that to the extent that the Bail Reform Act permits pretrial detention on the ground that the arrestee is likely to commit future crimes, it is unconstitutional on its face. Over a dissent, the United States Court of Appeals for the Second Circuit agreed. Although the court agreed that pretrial detention could be imposed if the defendants were likely to intimidate witnesses or otherwise jeopardize the trial process, it found "§ 3142(e)'s authorization of pretrial detention [on the ground of future dangerousness] repugnant to the concept of substantive due process, which we believe prohibits the total deprivation of liberty simply as a means of preventing future crimes." The court concluded that the Government could not, consistent with due process, detain persons who had not been accused of any crime merely because they were thought to present a danger to the community. It reasoned that our criminal law system holds persons accountable for past actions, not anticipated future actions. * * *

Respondents present two grounds for invalidating the Bail Reform Act's provisions permitting pretrial detention on the basis of future dangerousness. First, they rely upon the Court of Appeals' conclusion that the Act exceeds the limitations placed upon the Federal Government by the Due Process Clause of the Fifth Amendment. Second, they contend that the Act contravenes the Eighth Amendment's proscription against excessive bail. We treat these contentions in turn.

The Due Process Clause of the Fifth Amendment provides that "No person shall . . . be deprived of life, liberty, or property, without due process of law. . . ." This Court has held that the Due Process Clause protects individuals against two types of government action. So-called "substantive due process" prevents the government from engaging in conduct that "shocks the conscience," or interferes with rights "implicit in the concept of ordered liberty." When government action depriving a person of life, liberty, or property survives substantive due process scrutiny, it must still be implemented in a fair manner. This requirement has traditionally been referred to as "procedural" due process.

Respondents first argue that the Act violates substantive due process because the pretrial detention it authorizes constitutes impermissible punishment before trial. The Government, however, has never argued that pretrial detention could be upheld if it were "punishment." The Court of

Appeals assumed that pretrial detention under the Bail Reform Act is regulatory, not penal, and we agree that it is.

As an initial matter, the mere fact that a person is detained does not inexorably lead to the conclusion that the government has imposed punishment. To determine whether a restriction on liberty constitutes impermissible punishment or permissible regulation, we first look to legislative intent. Unless Congress expressly intended to impose punitive restrictions, the punitive/regulatory distinction turns on "whether an alternative purpose to which [the restriction] may rationally be connected is assignable for it, and whether it appears excessive in relation to the alternative purpose assigned [to it]."

We conclude that the detention imposed by the Act falls on the regulatory side of the dichotomy. The legislative history of the Bail Reform Act clearly indicates that Congress did not formulate the pretrial detention provisions as punishment for dangerous individuals. Congress instead perceived pretrial detention as a potential solution to a pressing societal problem. There is no doubt that preventing danger to the community is a legitimate regulatory goal.

Nor are the incidents of pretrial detention excessive in relation to the regulatory goal Congress sought to achieve. The Bail Reform Act carefully limits the circumstances under which detention may be sought to the most serious of crimes. See 18 U.S.C. § 3142(f) (detention hearings available if case involves crimes of violence, offenses for which the sentence is life imprisonment or death, serious drug offenses, or certain repeat offenders). The arrestee is entitled to a prompt detention hearing, and the maximum length of pretrial detention is limited by the stringent time limitations of the Speedy Trial Act. Moreover, * * * the conditions of confinement envisioned by the Act "appear to reflect the regulatory purposes relied upon by the" Government. * * * [T]he statute at issue here requires that detainees be housed in a "facility separate, to the extent practicable, from persons awaiting or serving sentences or being held in custody pending appeal." We conclude, therefore, that the pretrial detention contemplated by the Bail Reform Act is regulatory in nature, and does not constitute punishment before trial in violation of the Due Process Clause. * * *

Respondents also contend that the Bail Reform Act violates the Excessive Bail Clause of the Eighth Amendment. The Court of Appeals did not address this issue because it found that the Act violates the Due Process Clause. We think that the Act survives a challenge founded upon the Eighth Amendment.

The Eighth Amendment addresses pretrial release by providing merely that "[e]xcessive bail shall not be required." This Clause, of course, says nothing about whether bail shall be available at all. Respondents nevertheless contend that this Clause grants them a right to bail calculated solely upon considerations of flight. They rely on *Stack v. Boyle*, in which the Court stated that "[b]ail set at a figure higher than an amount reasonably calculated [to ensure the defendant's presence at trial] is 'excessive' under the Eighth Amendment." In respondents' view, since the Bail Reform Act allows a court essentially to set bail at an infinite amount for reasons not related to the risk of flight, it violates the Excessive Bail Clause. Respondents concede that the right to bail they have discovered in the Eighth Amendment is not absolute. A court may, for example, refuse bail in capital cases. And, as the Court of Appeals noted and respondents admit, a court may refuse bail when the defendant presents a threat to the judicial process by intimidating witnesses. Respondents characterize these exceptions as consistent with what they claim to be the sole purpose of bail—to ensure the integrity of the judicial process.

While we agree that a primary function of bail is to safeguard the courts' role in adjudicating the guilt or innocence of defendants, we reject the proposition that the Eighth Amendment categorically prohibits the government from pursuing other admittedly compelling interests through regulation of pretrial release. The above-quoted *dictum* in *Stack v. Boyle* is far too slender a reed on which to rest this argument.

*** Nothing in the text of the Bail Clause limits permissible Government considerations solely to questions of flight. The only arguable substantive limitation of the Bail Clause is that the Government's proposed conditions of release or detention not be "excessive" in light of the perceived evil. Of course, to determine whether the Government's response is excessive, we must compare that response against the interest the Government seeks to protect by means of that response. Thus, when the Government has admitted that its only interest is in preventing flight, bail must be set by a court at a sum designed to ensure that goal, and no more. We believe that when Congress has mandated detention on the basis of a compelling interest other than prevention of flight, as it has here, the Eighth Amendment does not require release on bail.

In our society liberty is the norm, and detention prior to trial or without trial is the carefully limited exception. We hold that the provisions for pretrial detention in the Bail Reform Act of 1984 fall within that carefully limited exception. The Act authorizes the detention prior to trial of arrestees charged with serious felonies who are found after an adversary hearing to pose a threat to the safety of individuals or to the community which no condition of release can dispel. The numerous procedural safeguards detailed above must attend this adversary hearing. We are unwilling to say that this congressional determination, based as it is upon that primary concern of every government—a concern for the safety and indeed the lives of its citizens—on its face violates either the Due Process Clause of the Fifth Amendment or the Excessive Bail Clause of the Eighth Amendment.

The judgment of the Court of Appeals is therefore

Reversed.

JUSTICE MARSHALL, with whom JUSTICE BRENNAN joins, dissenting.

This case brings before the Court for the first time a statute in which Congress declares that a person innocent of any crime may be jailed indefinitely, pending the trial of allegations which are legally presumed to be untrue, if the Government shows to the satisfaction of a judge that the accused is likely to commit crimes, unrelated to the pending charges, at any time in the future. Such statutes, consistent with the usages of tyranny and the excesses of what bitter experience teaches us to call the police state, have long been thought incompatible with the fundamental human rights protected by our Constitution. Today a majority of this Court holds otherwise. Its decision disregards basic principles of justice established centuries ago and enshrined beyond the reach of governmental interference in the Bill of Rights.

* * * The Eighth Amendment, as the majority notes, states that "[e]xcessive bail shall not be required." The majority then declares, as if it were undeniable, that: "[t]his Clause, of course, says nothing about whether bail shall be available at all." If excessive bail is imposed the defendant stays in jail. The same result is achieved if bail is denied altogether. Whether the magistrate sets bail at $1 million or refuses to set bail at all, the consequences are indistinguishable. It would be mere sophistry to suggest that the Eighth Amendment protects against the former decision, and not the latter. * * *

The essence of this case may be found, ironically enough, in a provision of the Act to which the majority does not refer. Title 18 U.S.C. § 3142(j) (1982 ed., Supp. III) provides that "[n]othing in this section shall be construed as modifying or limiting the presumption of innocence." But the very pith and purpose of this statute is an abhorrent limitation of the presumption of innocence. The majority's untenable conclusion that the present Act is constitutional arises from a specious denial of the role of the Bail Clause and the Due Process Clause in protecting the invaluable guarantee afforded by the presumption of innocence.

"The principle that there is a presumption of innocence in favor of the accused is the undoubted law, axiomatic and elementary, and its enforcement lies at the foundation of the administration of our criminal law." Our society's belief, reinforced over the centuries, that all are innocent until the state has proved them to be guilty, like the companion principle that guilt must be proved beyond a reasonable doubt, is "implicit in the concept of ordered liberty," and is established beyond legislative contravention in the Due Process Clause.

The statute now before us declares that persons who have been indicted may be detained if a judicial officer finds clear and convincing evidence that they pose a danger to individuals or to the community. The statute does not authorize the Government to imprison anyone it has evidence is dangerous; indictment is necessary. But let us suppose that a defendant is indicted and the Government shows by clear and convincing evidence that he is dangerous and should be detained pending a trial, at which trial the defendant is acquitted. May the Government continue to hold the defendant in detention based upon its showing that he is dangerous? The answer cannot be yes, for that would allow the Government to imprison someone for uncommitted crimes based upon "proof" not beyond a reasonable doubt. The result must therefore be that once the indictment has failed, detention cannot continue. But our fundamental principles of justice declare that the defendant is as innocent on the day before his trial as he is on the morning after his acquittal. Under this statute an untried indictment somehow acts to permit a detention, based on other charges, which after an acquittal would be unconstitutional.
* * *

It is not a novel proposition that the Bail Clause plays a vital role in protecting the presumption of innocence. Reviewing the application for bail pending appeal by members of the American Communist Party convicted under the Smith Act, Justice Jackson wrote:

> Grave public danger is said to result from what [the defendants] may be expected to do, in addition to what they have done since their conviction. If I assume that defendants are disposed to commit every opportune disloyal act helpful to Communist countries, it is still difficult to reconcile with traditional American law the jailing of persons by the courts because of anticipated but as yet uncommitted crimes. Imprisonment to protect society from predicted but unconsummated offenses is . . . unprecedented in this country and . . . fraught with danger of excesses and injustice. . . .

As Chief Justice Vinson wrote for the Court in *Stack v. Boyle:* "Unless th[e] right to bail before trial is preserved, the presumption of innocence, secured only after centuries of struggle, would lose its meaning." * * *

"It is a fair summary of history to say that the safeguards of liberty have frequently been forged in controversies involving not very nice people." Honoring the presumption of innocence is often difficult; sometimes we must pay substantial social costs as a result of our commitment to the values we espouse. But at the end of the day the presumption of innocence protects the innocent; the shortcuts we take with those whom we believe to be guilty injure only those wrongfully accused and, ultimately, ourselves. * * *

I dissent.

[JUSTICE STEVENS' dissenting opinion has been omitted.]

NOTE

According to a 2022 report by the U.S. Commission on Civil Rights, "[a]pproximately 631,000 individuals are held in jails every day and almost half a million or 74 percent of these individuals are unconvicted and awaiting trial."[a] Some of these individuals have been charged with a violent crime but "most (three quarters of them, according to the National Conference of State Legislatures) are nonviolent offenders, arrested for traffic violations or property crimes or simple drug possession."[b] "Many will end up being found not guilty of the crimes with which they are charged.[c]

Chris Ingraham notes that "this means that plenty of people sit behind bars not because they are dangerous or because they're a flight risk, but simply because they can't come up with the cash."[d] "For low-income people, the consequences of a pre-trial detention, even a brief one, can be disastrous. Miss too much work and you're out of a job. Fall behind on your rent and you're out of a home, too."[e] In contrast, wealthy defendants—even those charged with violent crimes—can be set free pending trial simply because they have the means to pay whatever amount of bail is set for them.

In addition to income and class, race also appears to play a role in the amount of bail that is set in any given case and who ends up getting released on bail. According to the U.S. Commission on Civil Rights, in "one 2018 study, researchers found that when Black defendants were assigned monetary bail, they received significantly greater amounts than White defendants."[f] "The study also showed that judges were also more likely to perceive Black defendants as more 'dangerous' compared to White defendants, and thus, [Black defendants were more often than their White counterparts] denied bail and detained pretrial."[g] Black defendants in state court were nearly 10 percentage points more likely to be detained pending trial than similarly situated White defendants.[h]

---

[a] U.S. COMM'N ON CIV. RTS., BRIEFING REPORT, THE CIVIL RIGHTS IMPLICATIONS OF CASH BAIL 2 (Jan. 2022), available at https://www.usccr.gov/reports/2021/civil-rights-implications-cash-bail (https://perma.cc/MAD5-G7MU).

[b] Chris Ingraham, *Should More Defendants Get Out of Jail Free?*, WASH. POST, June 14, 2015, at F2.

[c] *Id.* ("A 2013 Bureau of Justice Statistics report found that one-third of felony defendants in the nation's largest counties were not ultimately convicted of any crime.").

[d] *Id.*

[e] *Id.*

[f] U.S. COMM'N ON CIV. RTS., *supra* note a, at 4 (citing David Arnold, Will Dobbie, & Crystal Yang, *Racial Bias in Bail Decisions*, 133 Q. J. Econ. 1885 (2018)).

[g] *Id.*

[h] Fola Akinnibi, *How Bail Reform, Crime Surge Mix in an Angry Debate*, BLOOMBERG (Apr. 8, 2022, 3:26 PM), https://www.bloomberg.com/news/articles/2022-01-21/how-bail-reform-crime-surge-mix-in-an-angry-debate-quicktake (https://perma.cc/TA6L-Q5PH).

In recent years, bail has taken on an important role in efforts to reform the criminal justice system. Critics of cash bail argue that it goes against the presumption of innocence, acts as a penalty against poor people, and disproportionately impacts low-income defendants of color.[i] Moreover, people who are detained pending trial tend to be more likely to plead guilty than similarly situated defendants who were released pending trial.[j] This may happen not because people who are detained pending trial are more likely to be guilty than people who are released pending trial but because those who are detained pending trial just want to get out of jail and continue on with their lives.

It is also costly to keep defendants in jail pending trial. According to the New York City Comptroller's Office, it costs $1,525 per day to incarcerate a single individual.[k] These costs can add up to billions of dollars annually across the nation.[l]

Some cities and states have begun to implement changes to bail practices.[m] For example, in 2019, the state of New York passed legislation barring judges from setting bail for defendants charged with a wide-ranging number of misdemeanors and nonviolent felonies, mandating release for these defendants pending trial.[n] Bail reform has been met with pushback from those who argue that releasing most individuals pending trial has led to more crime.[o] This pushback coupled with increases in crime led New York lawmakers to

---

[i] *Id.*

[j] *Id.* (referencing a study from Harris County, Texas conducted prior to implementing changes to bail practices that found defendants detained while awaiting trial were 25 percent more likely to plead guilty than similarly situated defendants who were released).

[k] *See Comptroller Stringer: Cost of Incarceration per Person in New York City Skyrockets to All-Time High*, N.Y.C. COMPTROLLER (Dec. 6, 2021), https://comptroller.nyc.gov/newsroom/comptroller-stringer-cost-of-incarceration-per-person-in-new-york-city-skyrockets-to-all-time-high-2/ (https://perma.cc/PLR8-KDEM); N.Y.C. DEP'T OF CORR., FYS 2011–21 OPERATING EXPENDITURES, JAIL POPULATION, COST PER INCARCERATED PERSON, STAFFING RATIOS, PERFORMANCE MEASURE OUTCOMES, AND OVERTIME (2021).

[l] Ingraham, *supra* note b (estimating that "[w]e spend about $17 billion dollars annually to keep innocent people locked up as they await trial").

[m] For many years, the District of Columbia, which is viewed as a leader in bail reform efforts, has prohibited detention based upon inability to pay. KiDeuk Kim & Megan Denver, *A Case Study on the Practice of Pretrial Services and Risk Assessment in Three Cities* 3 (December 2011). If financial conditions are imposed, defendants are entitled to a bail bond they can meet, and money is not supposed to be used to ensure community safety. *Id.* As a result, the District of Columbia releases about 85 percent of all arrestees. Clifford T. Keenan, *We Need More Bail Reform* (Pretrial Services Agency for the District of Columbia Sept. 2013). About 88 percent of arrestees are not arrested again prior to trial and appear for trial. *Id.* Of those who are re-arrested, less than 1 percent are alleged to have committed a violent crime. *Id.* The use of preventive detention (pretrial detention on the basis of danger to the community) is allowed but limited to approximately 15 percent of all accused persons in the District of Columbia. *Id.*

[n] Chelsia Rose Marcius, Troy Closson & Grace Ashford, *New York's Bail Laws Are Changing Again. Here's How.* N.Y. TIMES (Apr. 11, 2022), https://www.nytimes.com/2022/04/11/nyregion/new-york-bail-laws.html (https://perma.cc/6QPQ-YQSD) (noting that the new bail reform provisions "which took effect in January 2020, were met with fierce backlash from many district attorneys, judges, law enforcement officials and Republicans").

[o] Akinnibi, *supra* note h.

revise New York's bail statute in 2020 and again in 2022, expanding the number of crimes for which defendants can be required to pay bail.[p]

"GIVE US FREE": ADDRESSING RACIAL DISPARITIES IN BAIL DETERMINATIONS
Cynthia E. Jones
16 N.Y.U. J. Legis. & Pub. Pol'y 919 (2013)

Over the last fifty years, research studies have consistently found that African American defendants receive significantly harsher bail outcomes than those imposed on white defendants. * * * [N]early every study on the impact of race in bail determinations has concluded that African Americans are subjected to pretrial detention at a higher rate and are subjected to higher bail amounts than are white arrestees with similar charges and similar criminal histories. The adverse impact of the defendant's race on the outcome of the bail determination is not a new or recent problem, nor is it confined to specific types of cases. Criminologists and researchers have published over twenty five studies documenting racial disparities in bail determinations in state cases, federal cases, and juvenile delinquency proceedings. The adverse impact of race in bail determinations also is not isolated to particular regions of the country. The problem is pervasive. Researchers documented racial disparities in bail determinations in studies of northeast urban areas, mid-western urban areas, southern counties, mid-western counties, and northern counties. Researchers also documented similar patterns of ethnic disparities in bail determinations for Latino defendants.

A. The First Generation Studies of Race and Bail: 1970–2000

In 2003, Professor Marvin D. Free, Jr. completed a meta-analysis of twenty-five different studies on the impact of race in bail determinations published between 1970 and 2000. In each study, researchers identified representative samples of criminal cases, isolated particular legal and extra-legal factors, and employed various metrics and statistical analyses to determine whether race played a role in bail determinations. In eighteen studies, researchers concluded that African American defendants were subjected to more severe treatment than white defendants. * * * For example, one major national study examined bail determinations in over 5000 felony cases adjudicated in the federal district courts in Brooklyn, Manhattan, Chicago, Philadelphia, Baltimore, Dallas, Kansas City, Atlanta, Los Angeles and Detroit. Researchers compared the bail outcomes for African American and white defendants, all of whom had prior felony convictions. * * * The researchers found that white defendants with a prior felony conviction received more favorable bail outcomes than similarly-situated African American defendants. * * *

---

[p] Marcius, Closson & Ashford, *supra* note m.

Other first generation studies found that African Americans were charged a higher money bond to secure their pretrial release than were white defendants. * * * Also, local community ties, generally viewed as a positive factor in determining risk of flight, were found to decrease the bond amount for white residents, but not African American defendants. More recent studies have likewise found that bail officials generally tend to impose higher bail amounts on African American defendants.

B. The Second Generation Studies of Race and Bail: 2001–2012

The second generation of research studies on the role of race in bail determinations relies primarily on the volume of national criminal justice data compiled by the Department of Justice as part of the State Court Processing Statistics Project (SCPS). One study examined bail determinations in over 30,000 property, drug, and violent criminal cases filed in over forty-five counties across the country. Controlling for important legal and extralegal factors relevant to bail determinations, the study found that African Americans were sixty-six percent more likely to be in jail pretrial than were white defendants, and that Latino defendants were ninety-one percent more likely to be detained pretrial. Overall, the odds of similarly-situated African American and Latino defendants being held on bail because they were unable to pay the bond amounts imposed were twice that of white defendants.

Another 2005 study examined bail determinations in over 36,000 felony state court cases across the country. The study found that "being Black increases a defendant's odds of being held in jail pretrial by 25%." Similar to earlier studies, this study also concluded that poverty plays a role in pretrial outcomes.

* * * The two most recent studies—both published since 2010—found that African American defendants face higher bail amounts than white arrestees with similar criminal charges and criminal histories and, when race is combined with other legally relevant factors, African Americans have lower odds of non-financial release and greater odds of pretrial detention.

C. The Cause of Racial Disparities in Bail Determinations

There is relative agreement among criminologists regarding the reasons for the persistent pattern of racial disparities in bail determinations. * * * [B]ail officials are vested with tremendous discretionary authority, have very few legal constraints, and possess scant relevant background information on the defendant when making bail determinations. Criminologists believe this combination of factors forces bail officials to create their own internal guidelines, relying on racial stereotypes and biases to assist them in deciding whether a defendant is dangerous or a flight risk, and what amount of bond should be imposed. Criminologist Stephen DeMuth explains:

> Legal decision making is complex, repetitive, and often constrained by information, time and resources in ways that produce considerable ambiguity or uncertainty for arriving at a "satisfactory" decision. As an adaptation to these constraints, a "perceptual shorthand" for decision making emerges that allows for more simple and efficient processing of cases by court actors.... [L]egal agents may rely on the defendant's current offense and criminal history, but also on stereotypes linked to the defendant's race.... On the basis of these stereotypes, judges may project behavioral expectations about such things as the offender's risk of recidivism or danger to the community. Once in place and continuously reinforced, such patterned thinking and acting are resistant to change and may result in the inclusion of racial and ethnic biases in criminal case processing.

CHAPTER 25

THE RIGHT TO A SPEEDY TRIAL

■ ■ ■

The defendant's right to a speedy trial is usually covered by statute or court rule. In addition to a statutory right to a speedy trial, however, a defendant has a constitutional right to a speedy trial. The Sixth Amendment to the U.S. Constitution provides, "In all criminal prosecutions, the accused shall enjoy the right to a speedy ... trial...."

In *Barker v. Wingo*, the first case in this chapter, the Supreme Court outlines the factors that a court should consider in deciding whether a defendant's Sixth Amendment right to a speedy trial has been violated. In *Betterman v. Montana*, the Court decides whether the Sixth Amendment's speedy trial right applies to a delay between conviction and sentencing.

The Sixth Amendment right to a speedy trial typically covers delays between accusation and trial. If the defendant has been subjected to a lengthy preindictment delay, the defendant cannot allege a violation of the Sixth Amendment right to a speedy trial. Instead, the defendant can allege a violation of the Due Process Clause. The last case in this chapter, *United States v. Lovasco*, examines a defendant's claim that his due process rights were violated by an 18-month delay in the Government's filing of an indictment against him and sheds light on what a defendant needs to do in order to prevail when asserting a due process violation due to preindictment delay.

BARKER V. WINGO
Supreme Court of the United States
407 U.S. 514, 92 S. Ct. 2182, 33 L. Ed. 2d 101 (1972)

JUSTICE POWELL delivered the opinion of the Court.

Although a speedy trial is guaranteed the accused by the Sixth Amendment to the Constitution,[1] this Court has dealt with that right on infrequent occasions. The Court's opinion in *Kloper v. North Carolina*, established that the right to a speedy trial is "fundamental" and is imposed

---

[1] The Sixth Amendment provides: "In all criminal prosecutions, the accused shall enjoy the right to a speedy and public trial, by an impartial jury of the State and district wherein the crime shall have been committed, which district shall have been previously ascertained by law, and to be informed of the nature and cause of the accusation; to be confronted with the witnesses against him; to have compulsory process for obtaining Witnesses in his favor, and to have the Assistance of Counsel for his defense."

by the Due Process Clause of the Fourteenth Amendment on the States. As Mr. Justice Brennan pointed out in his concurring opinion in *Dickey*, in none of these cases have we attempted to set out the criteria by which the speedy trial right is to be judged. This case compels us to make such an attempt.

On July 20, 1958, in Christian County, Kentucky, an elderly couple was beaten to death by intruders wielding an iron tire tool. Two suspects, Silas Manning and Willie Barker, the petitioner, were arrested shortly thereafter. The grand jury indicted them on September 15. Counsel was appointed on September 17, and Barker's trial was set for October 21. The Commonwealth had a stronger case against Manning, and it believed that Barker could not be convicted unless Manning testified against him. Manning was naturally unwilling to incriminate himself. Accordingly, on October 23, the day Silas Manning was brought to trial, the Commonwealth sought and obtained the first of what was to be a series of 16 continuances of Barker's trial. Barker made no objection. By first convicting Manning, the Commonwealth would remove possible problems of self-incrimination and would be able to assure his testimony against Barker.

The Commonwealth encountered more than a few difficulties in its prosecution of Manning. The first trial ended in a hung jury. A second trial resulted in a conviction, but the Kentucky Court of Appeals reversed because of the admission of evidence obtained by an illegal search. At his third trial, Manning was again convicted, and the Court of Appeals again reversed because the trial court had not granted a change of venue. A fourth trial resulted in a hung jury. Finally, after five trials, Manning was convicted, in March 1962, of murdering one victim, and after a sixth trial, in December 1962, he was convicted of murdering the other.

The Christian County Circuit Court holds three terms each year—in February, June, and September. Barker's initial trial was to take place in the September term of 1958. The first continuance postponed it until the February 1959 term. The second continuance was granted for one month only. Every term thereafter for as long as the Manning prosecutions were in process, the Commonwealth routinely moved to continue Barker's case to the next term. When the case was continued from the June 1959 term until the following September, Barker, having spent 10 months in jail, obtained his release by posting a $5,000 bond. He thereafter remained free in the community until his trial. Barker made no objection, through his counsel, to the first 11 continuances.

When on February 12, 1962, the Commonwealth moved for the twelfth time to continue the case until the following term, Barker's counsel filed a motion to dismiss the indictment. The motion to dismiss was denied two weeks later, and the Commonwealth's motion for a continuance was granted. The Commonwealth was granted further continuances in June 1962 and September 1962, to which Barker did not object.

In February 1963, the first term of court following Manning's final conviction, the Commonwealth moved to set Barker's trial for March 19. But on the day scheduled for trial, it again moved for a continuance until the June term. It gave as its reason the illness of the ex-sheriff who was the chief investigating officer in the case. To this continuance, Barker objected unsuccessfully.

The witness was still unable to testify in June, and the trial, which had been set for June 19, was continued again until the September term over Barker's objection. This time the court announced that the case would be dismissed for lack of prosecution if it were not tried during the next term. The final trial date was set for October 9, 1963. On that date, Barker again moved to dismiss the indictment, and this time specified that his right to a speedy trial had been violated. The motion was denied; the trial commenced with Manning as the chief prosecution witness; Barker was convicted and given a life sentence.

Barker appealed his conviction to the Kentucky Court of Appeals, relying in part on his speedy trial claim. The court affirmed. * * * We granted Barker's petition for certiorari.

The right to a speedy trial is generically different from any of the other rights enshrined in the Constitution for the protection of the accused. In addition to the general concern that all accused persons be treated according to decent and fair procedures, there is a societal interest in providing a speedy trial which exists separate from, and at times in opposition to, the interests of the accused. The inability of courts to provide a prompt trial has contributed to a large backlog of cases in urban courts which, among other things, enables defendants to negotiate more effectively for pleas of guilty to lesser offenses and otherwise manipulate the system. In addition, persons released on bond for lengthy periods awaiting trial have an opportunity to commit other crimes. It must be of little comfort to the residents of Christian County, Kentucky, to know that Barker was at large on bail for over four years while accused of a vicious and brutal murder of which he was ultimately convicted. Moreover, the longer an accused is free awaiting trial, the more tempting becomes his opportunity to jump bail and escape. Finally, delay between arrest and punishment may have a detrimental effect on rehabilitation.

If an accused cannot make bail, he is generally confined, as was Barker for 10 months, in a local jail. This contributes to the overcrowding and generally deplorable state of those institutions. Lengthy exposure to these conditions "has a destructive effect on human character and makes the rehabilitation of the individual offender much more difficult." At times the result may even be violent rioting. Finally, lengthy pretrial detention is costly. The cost of maintaining a prisoner in jail varies from $3 to $9 per day, and this amounts to millions across the Nation. In addition, society loses wages which might have been earned, and it must often support families of incarcerated breadwinners.

A second difference between the right to speedy trial and the accused's other constitutional rights is that deprivation of the right may work to the accused's advantage. Delay is not an uncommon defense tactic. As the time between the commission of the crime and trial lengthens, witnesses may become unavailable or their memories may fade. If the witnesses support the prosecution, its case will be weakened, sometimes seriously so. And it is the prosecution which carries the burden of proof. Thus, unlike the right to counsel or the right to be free from compelled self-incrimination, deprivation of the right to speedy trial does not per se prejudice the accused's ability to defend himself.

Finally, and perhaps most importantly, the right to speedy trial is a more vague concept than other procedural rights. It is, for example, impossible to determine with precision when the right has been denied. We cannot definitely say how long is too long in a system where justice is supposed to be swift but deliberate. As a consequence, there is no fixed point in the criminal process when the State can put the defendant to the choice of either exercising or waiving the right to a speedy trial. * * *

The amorphous quality of the right also leads to the unsatisfactorily severe remedy of dismissal of the indictment when the right has been deprived. This is indeed a serious consequence because it means that a defendant who may be guilty of a serious crime will go free, without having been tried. Such a remedy is more serious than an exclusionary rule or a reversal for a new trial, but it is the only possible remedy.

Perhaps because the speedy trial right is so slippery, two rigid approaches are urged upon us as ways of eliminating some of the uncertainty which courts experience in protecting the right. The first suggestion is that we hold that the Constitution requires a criminal defendant to be offered a trial within a specified time period. The result of such a ruling would have the virtue of clarifying when the right is infringed and of simplifying courts' application of it. Recognizing this, some legislatures have enacted laws, and some courts have adopted procedural rules which more narrowly define the right. The United States Court of Appeals for the Second Circuit has promulgated rules for the district courts in that Circuit establishing that the government must be ready for trial within six months of the date of arrest, except in unusual circumstances, or the charge will be dismissed. This type of rule is also recommended by the American Bar Association.

But such a result would require this Court to engage in legislative or rulemaking activity, rather than in the adjudicative process to which we should confine our efforts. We do not establish procedural rules for the States, except when mandated by the Constitution. We find no constitutional basis for holding that the speedy trial right can be quantified into a specified number of days or months. The States, of course, are free to prescribe a reasonable period consistent with constitutional standards, but our approach must be less precise.

The second suggested alternative would restrict consideration of the right to those cases in which the accused has demanded a speedy trial. Most States have recognized what is loosely referred to as the "demand rule," although eight States reject it. It is not clear, however, precisely what is meant by that term. Although every federal court of appeals that has considered the question has endorsed some kind of demand rule, some have regarded the rule within the concept of waiver, whereas others have viewed it as a factor to be weighed in assessing whether there has been a deprivation of the speedy trial right. We shall refer to the former approach as the demand-waiver doctrine. The demand-waiver doctrine provides that a defendant waives any consideration of his right to speedy trial for any period prior to which he has not demanded a trial. Under this rigid approach, a prior demand is a necessary condition to the consideration of the speedy trial right. This essentially was the approach the Sixth Circuit took below.

Such an approach, by presuming waiver of a fundamental right from inaction, is inconsistent with this Court's pronouncements on waiver of constitutional rights. The Court has defined waiver as "an intentional relinquishment or abandonment of a known right or privilege." Courts should "indulge every reasonable presumption against waiver," and they should "not presume acquiescence in the loss of fundamental rights." * * *

In excepting the right to speedy trial from the rule of waiver we have applied to other fundamental rights, courts that have applied the demand-waiver rule have relied on the assumption that delay usually works for the benefit of the accused and on the absence of any readily ascertainable time in the criminal process for a defendant to be given the choice of exercising or waiving his right. But it is not necessarily true that delay benefits the defendant. There are cases in which delay appreciably harms the defendant's ability to defend himself. Moreover, a defendant confined to jail prior to trial is obviously disadvantaged by delay as is a defendant released on bail but unable to lead a normal life because of community suspicion and his own anxiety.

The nature of the speedy trial right does make it impossible to pinpoint a precise time in the process when the right must be asserted or waived, but that fact does not argue for placing the burden of protecting the right solely on defendants. A defendant has no duty to bring himself to trial; the State has that duty as well as the duty of insuring that the trial is consistent with due process. Moreover, for the reasons earlier expressed, society has a particular interest in bringing swift prosecutions, and society's representatives are the ones who should protect that interest.

It is also noteworthy that such a rigid view of the demand-waiver rule places defense counsel in an awkward position. Unless he demands a trial early and often, he is in danger of frustrating his client's right. If counsel is willing to tolerate some delay because he finds it reasonable and helpful in preparing his own case, he may be unable to obtain a speedy trial for his client at the end of that time. * * *

We reject, therefore, the rule that a defendant who fails to demand a speedy trial forever waives his right. This does not mean, however, that the defendant has no responsibility to assert his right. We think the better rule is that the defendant's assertion of or failure to assert his right to a speedy trial is one of the factors to be considered in an inquiry into the deprivation of the right. Such a formulation avoids the rigidities of the demand-waiver rule and the resulting possible unfairness in its application. It allows the trial court to exercise a judicial discretion based on the circumstances, including due consideration of any applicable formal procedural rule. It would permit, for example, a court to attach a different weight to a situation in which the defendant knowingly fails to object from a situation in which his attorney acquiesces in long delay without adequately informing his client, or from a situation in which no counsel is appointed. It would also allow a court to weigh the frequency and force of the objections as opposed to attaching significant weight to a purely pro forma objection.

In ruling that a defendant has some responsibility to assert a speedy trial claim, we do not depart from our holdings in other cases concerning the waiver of fundamental rights, in which we have placed the entire responsibility on the prosecution to show that the claimed waiver was knowingly and voluntarily made. * * * We have shown above that the right to a speedy trial is unique in its uncertainty as to when and under what circumstances it must be asserted or may be deemed waived. But the rule we announce today, which comports with constitutional principles, places the primary burden on the courts and the prosecutors to assure that cases are brought to trial. * * *

We, therefore, reject both of the inflexible approaches—the fixed-time period because it goes further than the Constitution requires; the demand-waiver rule because it is insensitive to a right which [w]e have deemed fundamental. The approach we accept is a balancing test, in which the conduct of both the prosecution and the defendant are weighed.

A balancing test necessarily compels courts to approach speedy trial cases on an ad hoc basis. We can do little more than identify some of the factors which courts should assess in determining whether a particular defendant has been deprived of his right. Though some might express them in different ways, we identify four such factors: Length of delay, the reason for the delay, the defendant's assertion of his right, and prejudice to the defendant.

The length of the delay is to some extent a triggering mechanism. Until there is some delay which is presumptively prejudicial, there is no necessity for inquiry into the other factors that go into the balance. Nevertheless, because of the imprecision of the right to speedy trial, the length of delay that will provoke such an inquiry is necessarily dependent upon the peculiar circumstances of the case. To take but one example, the delay that can be tolerated for an ordinary street crime is considerably less than for a serious, complex conspiracy charge.

Closely related to length of delay is the reason the government assigns to justify the delay. Here, too, different weights should be assigned to different reasons. A deliberate attempt to delay the trial in order to hamper the defense should be weighted heavily against the government. A more neutral reason such as negligence or overcrowded courts should be weighted less heavily but nevertheless should be considered since the ultimate responsibility for such circumstances must rest with the government rather than with the defendant. Finally, a valid reason, such as a missing witness, should serve to justify appropriate delay.

We have already discussed the third factor, the defendant's responsibility to assert his right. Whether and how a defendant asserts his right is closely related to the other factors we have mentioned. The strength of his efforts will be affected by the length of the delay, to some extent by the reason for the delay, and most particularly by the personal prejudice, which is not always readily identifiable, that he experiences. The more serious the deprivation, the more likely a defendant is to complain. The defendant's assertion of his speedy trial right, then, is entitled to strong evidentiary weight in determining whether the defendant is being deprived of the right. We emphasize that failure to assert the right will make it difficult for a defendant to prove that he was denied a speedy trial.

A fourth factor is prejudice to the defendant.[a] Prejudice, of course, should be assessed in the light of the interests of defendants which the speedy trial right was designed to protect. This Court has identified three such interests: (i) to prevent oppressive pretrial incarceration; (ii) to minimize anxiety and concern of the accused; and (iii) to limit the possibility that the defense will be impaired. Of these, the most serious is the last, because the inability of a defendant adequately to prepare his case skews the fairness of the entire system. If witnesses die or disappear

---

[a] In a later case, the Court held that a showing of actual prejudice is not essential to a defendant's speedy trial claim. In *Doggett v. United States*, 505 U.S. 647 (1992), the Court held that a judge can find a violation of the Sixth Amendment right to a speedy trial based on presumptive prejudice since excessive delay may compromise the reliability of a trial in ways that the defendant cannot prove or identify.

during a delay, the prejudice is obvious. There is also prejudice if defense witnesses are unable to recall accurately events of the distant past. Loss of memory, however, is not always reflected in the record because what has been forgotten can rarely be shown.

We have discussed previously the societal disadvantages of lengthy pretrial incarceration, but obviously the disadvantages for the accused who cannot obtain his release are even more serious. The time spent in jail awaiting trial has a detrimental impact on the individual. It often means loss of a job; it disrupts family life; and it enforces idleness. Most jails offer little or no recreational or rehabilitative programs. The time spent in jail is simply dead time. Moreover, if a defendant is locked up, he is hindered in his ability to gather evidence, contact witnesses, or otherwise prepare his defense. Imposing those consequences on anyone who has not yet been convicted is serious. It is especially unfortunate to impose them on those persons who are ultimately found to be innocent. Finally, even if an accused is not incarcerated prior to trial, he is still disadvantaged by restraints on his liberty and by living under a cloud of anxiety, suspicion, and often hostility.

We regard none of the four factors identified above as either a necessary or sufficient condition to the finding of a deprivation of the right of speedy trial. Rather, they are related factors and must be considered together with such other circumstances as may be relevant. In sum, these factors have no talismanic qualities; courts must still engage in a difficult and sensitive balancing process. But, because we are dealing with a fundamental right of the accused, this process must be carried out with full recognition that the accused's interest in a speedy trial is specifically affirmed in the Constitution.

The difficulty of the task of balancing these factors is illustrated by this case, which we consider to be close. It is clear that the length of delay between arrest and trial—well over five years—was extraordinary. Only seven months of that period can be attributed to a strong excuse, the illness of the ex-sheriff who was in charge of the investigation. Perhaps some delay would have been permissible under ordinary circumstances, so that Manning could be utilized as a witness in Barker's trial, but more than four years was too long a period, particularly since a good part of that period was attributable to the Commonwealth's failure or inability to try Manning under circumstances that comported with due process.

Two counterbalancing factors, however, outweigh these deficiencies. The first is that prejudice was minimal. Of course, Barker was prejudiced to some extent by living for over four years under a cloud of suspicion and anxiety. Moreover, although he was released on bond for most of the period, he did spend 10 months in jail before trial. But there is no claim that any of Barker's witnesses died or otherwise became unavailable owing to the delay. The trial transcript indicates only two very minor lapses of memory—one on the part of a prosecution witness—which were in no way significant to the outcome.

More important than the absence of serious prejudice, is the fact that Barker did not want a speedy trial. Counsel was appointed for Barker immediately after his indictment and represented him throughout the period. No question is raised as to the competency of such counsel. Despite the fact that counsel had notice of the motions for continuances, the record shows no action whatever taken between October 21, 1958, and February 12, 1962, that could be construed as the assertion of the speedy trial right. On the latter date, in response to another motion for continuance, Barker moved to dismiss the indictment. The record does not show on what ground this motion was based, although it is clear that no alternative motion was made for an immediate trial. Instead the record strongly suggests that while he hoped to take advantage of the delay in which he had acquiesced, and thereby obtain a dismissal of the charges, he definitely did not want to be tried. Counsel conceded as much at oral argument:

> Your honor, I would concede that Willie Mae Barker probably—I don't know this for a fact—probably did not want to be tried. I don't think any man wants to be tried. And I don't consider this a liability on his behalf. I don't blame him.

The probable reason for Barker's attitude was that he was gambling on Manning's acquittal. The evidence was not very strong against Manning, as the reversals and hung juries suggest, and Barker undoubtedly thought that if Manning were acquitted, he would never be tried. Counsel also conceded this:

> Now, it's true that the reason for this delay was the Commonwealth of Kentucky's desire to secure the testimony of the accomplice, Silas Manning. And it's true that if Silas Manning were never convicted, Willie Mae Barker would never have been convicted. We concede this.

That Barker was gambling on Manning's acquittal is also suggested by his failure, following the pro forma motion to dismiss filed in February 1962, to object to the Commonwealth's next two motions for continuances. Indeed, it was not until March 1963, after Manning's convictions were final, that Barker, having lost his gamble, began to object to further continuances. At that time, the Commonwealth's excuse was the illness of the ex-sheriff, which Barker has conceded justified the further delay.

We do not hold that there may never be a situation in which an indictment may be dismissed on speedy trial grounds where the defendant has failed to object to continuances. There may be a situation in which the defendant was represented by incompetent counsel, was severely prejudiced, or even cases in which the continuances were granted ex parte.

But barring extraordinary circumstances, we would be reluctant indeed to rule that a defendant was denied this constitutional right on a record that strongly indicates, as does this one, that the defendant did not want a speedy trial. We hold, therefore, that Barker was not deprived of his * * * right to a speedy trial. * * *

[JUSTICE WHITE's concurring opinion has been omitted.]

BETTERMAN V. MONTANA
Supreme Court of the United States
578 U.S. 437, 136 S. Ct. 1609, 194 L. Ed. 2d 723 (2016)

JUSTICE GINSBURG, delivered the opinion of the Court.

The Sixth Amendment to the U.S. Constitution provides that "[i]n all criminal prosecutions, the accused shall enjoy the right to a speedy and public trial, by an impartial jury. . . ." Does the Sixth Amendment's speedy trial guarantee apply to the sentencing phase of a criminal prosecution? That is the sole question this case presents. * * *

Ordered to appear in court on domestic assault charges, Brandon Betterman failed to show up and was therefore charged with bail jumping. After pleading guilty to the bail-jumping charge, he was jailed for over 14 months awaiting sentence on that conviction. The holdup, in large part, was due to institutional delay: the presentence report took nearly five months to complete; the trial court took several months to deny two presentence motions (one seeking dismissal of the charge on the ground of delay); and the court was slow in setting a sentencing hearing. Betterman was eventually sentenced to seven years' imprisonment, with four of those years suspended.

Arguing that the 14-month gap between conviction and sentencing violated his speedy trial right, Betterman appealed. The Montana Supreme Court affirmed his conviction and sentence, ruling that the Sixth Amendment's Speedy Trial Clause does not apply to postconviction, presentencing delay.

We granted certiorari, to resolve a split among courts over whether the Speedy Trial Clause applies to such delay. Holding that the Clause does not apply to delayed sentencing, we affirm the Montana Supreme Court's judgment.

Criminal proceedings generally unfold in three discrete phases. First, the State investigates to determine whether to arrest and charge a suspect. Once charged, the suspect stands accused but is presumed innocent until conviction upon trial or guilty plea. After conviction, the court imposes sentence. There are checks against delay throughout this progression, each geared to its particular phase.

In the first stage—before arrest or indictment, when the suspect remains at liberty—statutes of limitations provide the primary protection against delay, with the Due Process Clause as a safeguard against fundamentally unfair prosecutorial conduct.

The Sixth Amendment's Speedy Trial Clause homes in on the second period: from arrest or indictment through conviction. The constitutional right, our precedent holds, does not attach until this phase begins, that is, when a defendant is arrested or formally accused. Today we hold that the right detaches upon conviction, when this second stage ends.

Prior to conviction, the accused is shielded by the presumption of innocence, the "bedrock[,] axiomatic and elementary principle whose enforcement lies at the foundation of the administration of our criminal law." The Speedy Trial Clause implements that presumption by "prevent[ing] undue and oppressive incarceration prior to trial, . . . minimiz[ing] anxiety and concern accompanying public accusation[,] and . . . limit[ing] the possibilities that long delay will impair the ability of an accused to defend himself." As a measure protecting the presumptively innocent, the speedy trial right—like other similarly aimed measures—loses force upon conviction. * * *

Reflecting the concern that a presumptively innocent person should not languish under an unresolved charge, the Speedy Trial Clause guarantees "the *accused*" "the right to a speedy . . . *trial*." At the founding, "accused" described a status preceding "convicted." And "trial" meant a discrete episode after which judgment (*i.e.,* sentencing) would follow.

This understanding of the Sixth Amendment language—"accused" as distinct from "convicted," and "trial" as separate from "sentencing"—endures today.

* * * [I]n *Marion*, addressing "the major evils protected against by the speedy trial guarantee," we observed: "Arrest is a public act that may seriously interfere with the defendant's liberty, whether he is free on bail or not, and that may disrupt his employment, drain his financial resources, curtail his associations, subject him to public obloquy, and create anxiety in him, his family and his friends." We acknowledged in *Marion* that even prearrest—a stage at which the right to a speedy trial does not arise—the passage of time "may impair memories, cause evidence to be lost, deprive the defendant of witnesses, and otherwise interfere with his ability to defend himself." Nevertheless, we determined, "this possibility of prejudice at trial is not itself sufficient reason to wrench the Sixth Amendment from its proper [arrest or charge triggered] context." Adverse consequences of postconviction delay, though subject to other checks, are similarly outside the purview of the Speedy Trial Clause.

The sole remedy for a violation of the speedy trial right—dismissal of the charges—fits the preconviction focus of the Clause. It would be an unjustified windfall, in most cases, to remedy sentencing delay by vacating validly obtained convictions. Betterman concedes that a dismissal remedy ordinarily would not be in order once a defendant has been convicted. * * *[6]

As we have explained, at the third phase of the criminal-justice process, *i.e.*, between conviction and sentencing, the Constitution's presumption-of-innocence protective speedy trial right is not engaged. That does not mean, however, that defendants lack any protection against undue delay at this stage. The primary safeguard comes from statutes and rules. The federal rule on point directs the court to "impose sentence without unnecessary delay." Many States have provisions to the same effect, and some States prescribe numerical time limits. Further, as at the prearrest stage, due process serves as a backstop against exorbitant delay. After conviction, a defendant's due process right to liberty, while diminished, is still present. He retains an interest in a sentencing proceeding that is fundamentally fair. But because Betterman advanced no due process claim here, we express no opinion on how he might fare under that more pliable standard.

The course of a criminal prosecution is composed of discrete segments. During the segment between accusation and conviction, the Sixth Amendment's Speedy Trial Clause protects the presumptively innocent from long enduring unresolved criminal charges. The Sixth Amendment speedy trial right, however, does not extend beyond conviction, which terminates the presumption of innocence. The judgment of the Supreme Court of Montana is therefore

Affirmed.

[JUSTICE THOMAS' and JUSTICE SOTOMAYOR's concurring opinions have been omitted.]

UNITED STATES V. LOVASCO
Supreme Court of the United States
431 U.S. 783, 97 S. Ct. 2044, 52 L. Ed. 2d 752 (1977)

JUSTICE MARSHALL delivered the opinion of the Court.

We granted certiorari in this case to consider the circumstances in which the Constitution requires that an indictment be dismissed because of delay between the commission of an offense and the initiation of prosecution.

On March 6, 1975, respondent was indicted for possessing eight firearms stolen from the United States mails, and for dealing in firearms

---

[6] Betterman suggests that an appropriate remedy for the delay in his case would be reduction of his sentence by 14 months—the time between his conviction and sentencing. See Tr. of Oral Arg. 6. We have not read the Speedy Trial Clause, however, to call for a flexible or tailored remedy. Instead, we have held that violation of the right demands termination of the prosecution.

without a license. The offenses were alleged to have occurred between July 25 and August 31, 1973, more than 18 months before the indictment was filed. Respondent moved to dismiss the indictment due to the delay.

The District Court conducted a hearing on respondent's motion at which the respondent sought to prove that the delay was unnecessary and that it had prejudiced his defense. In an effort to establish the former proposition, respondent presented a Postal Inspector's report on his investigation that was prepared one month after the crimes were committed, and a stipulation concerning the post-report progress of the probe. The report stated, in brief, that within the first month of the investigation respondent had admitted to Government agents that he had possessed and then sold five of the stolen guns, and that the agents had developed strong evidence linking respondent to the remaining three weapons. The report also stated, however, that the agents had been unable to confirm or refute respondent's claim that he had found the guns in his car when he returned to it after visiting his son, a mail handler, at work. The stipulation into which the Assistant United States Attorney entered indicated that little additional information concerning the crimes was uncovered in the 17 months following the preparation of the Inspector's report.

To establish prejudice to the defense, respondent testified that he had lost the testimony of two material witnesses due to the delay. The first witness, Tom Stewart, died more than a year after the alleged crimes occurred. At the hearing respondent claimed that Stewart had been his source for two or three of the guns. The second witness, respondent's brother, died in April 1974, eight months after the crimes were completed. Respondent testified that his brother was present when respondent called Stewart to secure the guns, and witnessed all of respondent's sales. Respondent did not state how the witnesses would have aided the defense had they been willing to testify.

The Government made no systematic effort in the District Court to explain its long delay. The Assistant United States Attorney did expressly disagree, however, with defense counsel's suggestion that the investigation had ended after the Postal Inspector's report was prepared. The prosecutor also stated that it was the Government's theory that respondent's son, who had access to the mail at the railroad terminal from which the guns were "possibly stolen," was responsible for the thefts. * * *

Following the hearing, the District Court filed a brief opinion and order. The court found that by October 2, 1973, the date of the Postal Inspector's report, "the Government had all the information relating to defendant's alleged commission of the offenses charged against him," and that the 17-month delay before the case was presented to the grand jury "had not been explained or justified" and was "unnecessary and unreasonable." The court also found that "[a]s a result of the delay defendant has been prejudiced by reason of the death of Tom Stewart, a material witness on his behalf." Accordingly, the court dismissed the indictment.

The Government appealed to the United States Court of Appeals for the Eighth Circuit. In its brief the Government explained the months of inaction by stating:

> [T]here was a legitimate Government interest in keeping the investigation open in the instant case. The defendant's son worked for the Terminal Railroad and had access to mail. It was the Government's position that the son was responsible for the theft and therefore further investigation to establish this fact was important. * * *

The Court of Appeals accepted the Government's representation as to the motivation for the delay, but a majority of the court nevertheless affirmed the District Court's finding that the Government's actions were "unjustified, unnecessary, and unreasonable." The majority also found that respondent had established that his defense had been impaired by the loss of Stewart's testimony because it understood respondent to contend that "were Stewart's testimony available it would support (respondent's) claim that he did not know that the guns were stolen from the United States mails." The court therefore affirmed the District Court's dismissal of the three possession counts by a divided vote.

We granted certiorari and now reverse.

In *United States v. Marion*, this Court considered the significance, for constitutional purposes, of a lengthy preindictment delay. We held that as far as the Speedy Trial Clause of the Sixth Amendment is concerned, such delay is wholly irrelevant, since our analysis of the language, history, and purposes of the Clause persuaded us that only "a formal indictment or information or else the actual restraints imposed by arrest and holding to answer a criminal charge ... engage the particular protections" of that provision. We went on to note that statutes of limitations, which provide predictable, legislatively enacted limits on prosecutorial delay, provide "the primary guarantee, against bringing overly stale criminal charges." But we did acknowledge that the "statute of limitations does not fully define (defendants') rights with respect to the events occurring prior to indictment," and that the Due Process Clause has a limited role to play in protecting against oppressive delay.

Respondent seems to argue that due process bars prosecution whenever a defendant suffers prejudice as a result of preindictment delay. To support that proposition respondent relies on the concluding sentence of the Court's opinion in *Marion* where, in remanding the case, we stated that "[e]vents of the trial may demonstrate actual prejudice, but at the present time appellees' due process claims are speculative and premature." But the quoted sentence establishes only that proof of actual prejudice makes a due process claim concrete and ripe for adjudication, not that it makes the claim automatically valid. Indeed, two pages earlier in the opinion we expressly rejected the argument respondent advances here:

> [W]e need not ... determine when and in what circumstances actual prejudice resulting from preaccusation delays requires the dismissal of the prosecution. Actual prejudice to the defense of a criminal case may result from the shortest and most necessary delay; and no one suggests that every delay-caused detriment to a defendant's case should abort a criminal prosecution.

Thus *Marion* makes clear that proof of prejudice is generally a necessary but not sufficient element of a due process claim, and that the due process inquiry must consider the reasons for the delay as well as the prejudice to the accused.

The Court of Appeals found that the sole reason for the delay here was "a hope on the part of the Government that others might be discovered who may have participated in the theft. . . ." It concluded that this hope did not justify the delay, and therefore affirmed the dismissal of the indictment. But the Due Process Clause does not permit courts to abort criminal prosecutions simply because they disagree with a prosecutor's judgment as to when to seek an indictment. Judges are not free, in defining "due process," to impose on law enforcement officials our "personal and private notions" of fairness and to "disregard the limits that bind judges in their judicial function." Our task is more circumscribed. We are to determine only whether the action complained of here, compelling respondent to stand trial after the Government delayed indictment to investigate further, violates those "fundamental conceptions of justice which lie at the base of our civil and political institutions," and which define "the community's sense of fair play and decency[.]"

It requires no extended argument to establish that prosecutors do not deviate from "fundamental conceptions of justice" when they defer seeking indictments until they have probable cause to believe an accused is guilty; indeed it is unprofessional conduct for a prosecutor to recommend an indictment on less than probable cause. It should be equally obvious that prosecutors are under no duty to file charges as soon as probable cause exists but before they are satisfied they will be able to establish the suspect's guilt beyond a reasonable doubt. To impose such a duty "would have a deleterious effect both upon the rights of the accused and upon the ability of society to protect itself." From the perspective of potential defendants, requiring prosecutions to commence when probable cause is established is undesirable because it would increase the likelihood of unwarranted charges being filed, and would add to the time during which defendants stand accused but untried. These costs are by no means insubstantial since * * * a formal accusation may "interfere with the defendant's liberty, ... disrupt his employment, drain his financial resources, curtail his associations, subject him to public obloquy, and create anxiety in him, his family and his friends." From the perspective of law enforcement officials, a requirement of immediate prosecution upon probable cause is equally unacceptable because it could make obtaining proof of guilt beyond a reasonable doubt impossible by causing potentially fruitful sources of information to evaporate before they are fully exploited. And from the standpoint of the courts, such a requirement is unwise because it would cause scarce resources to be consumed on cases that prove to be insubstantial, or that involve only some of the responsible parties or some of the criminal acts. Thus, no one's interests would be well served by compelling prosecutors to initiate prosecutions as soon as they are legally entitled to do so. * * *

We would be most reluctant to adopt a rule which would [require prosecutors to file charges as soon as they have probable cause or guilt beyond a reasonable doubt] absent a clear constitutional command to do so. We can find no such command in the Due Process Clause of the Fifth Amendment. In our view, investigative delay is fundamentally unlike delay undertaken by the Government solely "to gain tactical advantage over the accused," precisely because investigative delay is not so one-sided. Rather than deviating from elementary standards of "fair play and decency," a prosecutor abides by them if he refuses to seek indictments until he is completely satisfied that he should prosecute and will be able promptly to establish guilt beyond a reasonable doubt. Penalizing prosecutors who defer action for these reasons would subordinate the goal of "orderly expedition" to that of "mere speed." This the Due Process Clause does not require. We therefore hold that to prosecute a defendant following investigative delay does not deprive him of due process, even if his defense might have been somewhat prejudiced by the lapse of time. * * *

[JUSTICE STEVENS' dissenting opinion has been omitted.]

NOTE

The Due Process Clause of the Fifth Amendment provides, "No person shall ... be deprived of life, liberty, or property, without due process of law." *Lovasco* informs us that a defendant who claims a violation of due process stemming from preindictment delay must show: (1) actual prejudice, and (2) an unacceptable reason for the delay. Do you agree with the Supreme Court's assessment that the government's reason for the delay in filing an indictment against Lovasco was acceptable?

CHAPTER 26

DISCOVERY

■ ■ ■

Discovery is the process through which the parties in a case discover, usually before trial, what evidence the other party possesses. At common law, subject to a few limited exceptions, discovery was prohibited in criminal cases.[a] Gradually, the common law prohibition on criminal discovery was replaced by rules permitting discovery.

Today, criminal discovery in federal court is governed by Rule 16 of the Federal Rules of Criminal Procedure. Rule 16 requires the government to permit the defendant to inspect and copy certain documents and tangible objects in the government's possession, custody, and control.[b] Each state has its own rules governing discovery in state court.[c]

Separate and apart from Rule 16 and state discovery rules, the U.S. Supreme Court has held that prosecutors have a constitutional obligation to provide the defendant with "evidence favorable to the accused" that is material to guilt or punishment. *Brady v. Maryland*, the first case in the chapter, is the seminal case on the prosecutor's constitutional duty to disclose exculpatory evidence to the defense. *United States v. Bagley* elaborates on the meaning of "materiality" for purposes of the *Brady* rule.

In addition to the constitutional duty to disclose exculpatory evidence under *Brady*, prosecutors also have an ethical obligation to disclose evidence favorable to the defendant under Model Rule 3.8(d) of the Model Rules of Professional Conduct, which is reprinted in this chapter. As you read Model Rule 3.8(d), think about how it differs from the *Brady* rule. In the excerpt that follows, *Prosecutorial Discretion at the Core: The Good Prosecutor Meets Brady*, Janet Hoeffel explains why the prudent prosecutor

---

[a] Jerry E. Norton, *Discovery in the Criminal Process*, 81 J. CRIM. L. & CRIMINOLOGY 11, 12–13 (1970).

[b] Under Rule 16(a)(1)(E), the documents sought by the defendant must be (1) material to the preparation of the defense, (2) intended for use by the government in its case-in-chief, or (3) obtained from or belong to the defendant. *See* FED. R. CRIM. P. 16(a)(1)(E). If the defendant requests discovery under Rule 16, the government may, upon compliance with the defendant's discovery request, request documents and tangible objects that are in the possession, custody, or control of the defendant that the defendant intends to use at trial, excluding work product and any statements of the defendant or the defendant's witnesses. *See* FED. R. CRIM. P. 16(b).

[c] Many prosecutorial offices have voluntarily expanded their discovery obligations beyond what is specified in Rule 16. For example, some prosecutors now have "open file" discovery, "allowing the defense to review and copy all documents that are in the prosecution's file on the particular case." 5 WAYNE R. LAFAVE ET AL., CRIMINAL PROCEDURE § 20.2(c) (4th ed. 2021).

will usually choose not to disclose evidence favorable to the accused despite the duties to disclose outlined in *Brady v. Maryland* and Model Rule 3.8(d).

For many years, discovery in state court was a one-way street, permitting the defendant to obtain from the government evidence that the government planned to use against him at trial, but not permitting the government to obtain information about the defendant's case from the defense. Today, almost every state requires some sort of reciprocal discovery. The widespread acceptance of reciprocal discovery was likely encouraged by the Supreme Court's decision in *Williams v. Florida*, the last case in the chapter, which discusses a Notice-of-Alibi rule.

BRADY V. MARYLAND
Supreme Court of the United States
373 U.S. 83, 83 S. Ct. 1194, 10 L. Ed. 2d 215 (1963)

Opinion of the Court by JUSTICE DOUGLAS, announced by JUSTICE BRENNAN.

Petitioner and a companion, Boblit, were found guilty of murder in the first degree and were sentenced to death, their convictions being affirmed by the Court of Appeals of Maryland. Their trials were separate, petitioner being tried first. At his trial Brady took the stand and admitted his participation in the crime, but he claimed that Boblit did the actual killing. * * * Prior to the trial petitioner's counsel had requested the prosecution to allow him to examine Boblit's extrajudicial statements. Several of those statements were shown to him; but one dated July 9, 1958, in which Boblit admitted the actual homicide, was withheld by the prosecution and did not come to petitioner's notice until after he had been tried, convicted, and sentenced, and after his conviction had been affirmed.

Petitioner moved the trial court for a new trial based on the newly discovered evidence that had been suppressed by the prosecution. * * * [O]n appeal the Court of Appeals held that suppression of the evidence by the prosecution denied petitioner due process of law and remanded the case for a retrial of the question of punishment, not the question of guilt. The case is here on certiorari. * * *

We agree with the Court of Appeals that suppression of this confession was a violation of the Due Process Clause of the Fourteenth Amendment. * * * This ruling is an extension of *Mooney v. Holohan*, where the Court ruled on what nondisclosure by a prosecutor violates due process:

> It is a requirement that cannot be deemed to be satisfied by mere notice and hearing if a state has contrived a conviction through the pretense of a trial which in truth is but used as a means of depriving a defendant of liberty through a deliberate deception of court and jury by the presentation of testimony known to be

perjured. Such a contrivance by a state to procure the conviction and imprisonment of a defendant is as inconsistent with the rudimentary demands of justice as is the obtaining of a like result by intimidation. * * *

We now hold that the suppression by the prosecution of evidence favorable to an accused upon request violates due process where the evidence is material either to guilt or to punishment, irrespective of the good faith or bad faith of the prosecution.[a]

The principle of *Mooney* is not punishment of society for misdeeds of a prosecutor but avoidance of an unfair trial to the accused. Society wins not only when the guilty are convicted but when criminal trials are fair; our system of the administration of justice suffers when any accused is treated unfairly. A prosecution that withholds evidence on demand of an accused which, if made available, would tend to exculpate him or reduce the penalty helps shape a trial that bears heavily on the defendant. That casts the prosecutor in the role of an architect of a proceeding that does not comport with standards of justice, even though, as in the present case, his action is not "the result of guile," to use the words of the Court of Appeals. * * *

Affirmed.

[The separate opinion of JUSTICE WHITE and JUSTICE HARLAN's dissenting opinion have been omitted.]

NOTE

On remand, Brady's sentence was commuted to life and he was later released on parole. Stephanos Bibas, *Brady v. Maryland: From Adversarial Gamesmanship Toward the Search for Innocence?* in CRIMINAL PROCEDURE STORIES 137 (Steiker ed. 2006).

---

[a] As the *Brady* Court notes, its disclosure rule does not require a finding of bad faith on the part of the prosecutor. Even an accidental nondisclosure of evidence that is favorable to the accused and material to guilt or punishment can constitute a *Brady* violation. While a *Brady* violation can occur without intent, the intent of the prosecutor is not completely irrelevant. Professor Cynthia Jones notes that in deciding whether to impose sanctions for *Brady* violations, courts often consider whether the government acted in bad faith or purposely suppressed evidence it should have disclosed. *See* Cynthia E. Jones, *A Reason to Doubt: The Suppression of Evidence and the Inference of Innocence*, 100 J. CRIM. L. & CRIMINOLOGY 415 (2010). In an effort to deter intentional violations of the *Brady* rule, Professor Jones proposes that judges who discover that a prosecutor has intentionally violated the *Brady* rule should give a special jury instruction that informs the jury of the government's duties under *Brady*, tells them that the government intentionally withheld evidence favorable to the defense, explains what evidence was withheld, and advises the jury that the government's conduct may create a reasonable doubt about the defendant's guilt. Alternatively, Professor Jones urges criminal defense attorneys who find out that the prosecutor in their case intentionally withheld *Brady* material to seek to admit evidence of this misconduct to show the jury that the government was conscious that they had a weak case. In criminal cases, this type of inference is usually used by the government against a defendant who took steps after the crime to elude capture or manipulate the evidence. In such cases, the government often argues that the defendant's actions give rise to an inference that the defendant was conscious of his guilt.

UNITED STATES v. BAGLEY
Supreme Court of the United States
473 U.S. 667, 105 S. Ct. 3375, 87 L. E. 2d 481 (1985)

JUSTICE BLACKMUN announced the judgment of the Court * * *.

In *Brady v. Maryland*, this Court held that "the suppression by the prosecution of evidence favorable to an accused upon request violates due process where the evidence is material either to guilt or punishment." The issue in the present case concerns the standard of materiality to be applied in determining whether a conviction should be reversed because the prosecutor failed to disclose requested evidence that could have been used to impeach Government witnesses.

In October 1977, respondent Hughes Anderson Bagley was indicted in the Western District of Washington on 15 charges of violating federal narcotics and firearms statutes. On November 18, 24 days before trial, respondent filed a discovery motion. The sixth paragraph of that motion requested:

> The names and addresses of witnesses that the government intends to call at trial. Also the prior criminal records of witnesses, and any deals, promises or inducements made to witnesses in exchange for their testimony.

The Government's two principal witnesses at the trial were James F. O'Connor and Donald E. Mitchell. O'Connor and Mitchell were state law-enforcement officers employed by the Milwaukee Railroad as private security guards. Between April and June 1977, they assisted the federal Bureau of Alcohol, Tobacco and Firearms (ATF) in conducting an undercover investigation of respondent.

The Government's response to the discovery motion did not disclose that any "deals, promises or inducements" had been made to O'Connor or Mitchell. In apparent reply to a request in the motion's ninth paragraph for "[c]opies of all Jencks Act material,"[a] the Government produced a series of affidavits that O'Connor and Mitchell had signed between April 12 and May 4, 1977, while the undercover investigation was in progress. These affidavits recounted in detail the undercover dealings that O'Connor and Mitchell were having at the time with respondent. Each affidavit concluded with the statement, "I made this statement freely and voluntarily without any threats or rewards, or promises of reward having been made to me in return for it."

---

[a] Under the Jencks Act, after a witness for the government testifies at trial and upon defense request, the court must order the government to produce any statements of the witness in the government's possession that relate to the witness's testimony. *See* Note at the end of this chapter, *infra.*

*** At the trial, O'Connor and Mitchell testified about both the firearms and the narcotics charges. On December 23, the court found respondent guilty on the narcotics charges, but not guilty on the firearms charges.

In mid-1980, respondent filed requests for information pursuant to the Freedom of Information Act and to the Privacy Act of 1974. He received in response copies of ATF form contracts that O'Connor and Mitchell had signed on May 3, 1977. Each form was entitled "Contract for Purchase of Information and Payment of Lump Sum Therefor." The printed portion of the form stated that the vendor "will provide" information to ATF and that "upon receipt of such information by the Regional Director, Bureau of Alcohol, Tobacco and Firearms, or his representative, and upon the accomplishment of the objective sought to be obtained by the use of such information to the satisfaction of said Regional Director, the United States will pay to said vendor a sum commensurate with services and information rendered." Each form contained the following typewritten description of services:

> That he will provide information regarding T-I and other violations committed by Hughes A. Bagley, Jr.; that he will purchase evidence for ATF; that he will cut [sic] in an undercover capacity for ATF; that he will assist ATF in gathering of evidence and testify against the violator in federal court.

The figure "$300.00" was handwritten in each form on a line entitled "Sum to Be Paid to Vendor."

Because these contracts had not been disclosed to respondent in response to his pretrial discovery motion, respondent moved under 28 U.S.C. § 2255 to vacate his sentence. He alleged that the Government's failure to disclose the contracts, which he could have used to impeach O'Connor and Mitchell, violated his right to due process under *Brady v. Maryland*.

*** [T]he [District] [C]ourt found that it was "probable" that O'Connor and Mitchell expected to receive compensation, in addition to their expenses, for their assistance ***. The District Court found beyond a reasonable doubt, however, that had the existence of the agreements been disclosed to it during trial, the disclosure would have had no effect upon its finding that the Government had proved beyond a reasonable doubt that respondent was guilty of the offenses for which he had been convicted. The District Court reasoned: Almost all of the testimony of both witnesses was devoted to the firearms charges in the indictment. Respondent, however, was acquitted on those charges. The testimony of O'Connor and Mitchell concerning the narcotics charges was relatively very brief [and] tended to be favorable to respondent. Thus, the claimed impeachment evidence would not have been helpful to respondent and would not have affected the outcome of the trial. Accordingly, the District Court denied respondent's motion to vacate his sentence.

The United States Court of Appeals for the Ninth Circuit reversed. The Court of Appeals [distinguished between exculpatory evidence and impeachment evidence, treated the nondisclosure of impeachment evidence as more egregious than the nondisclosure of exculpatory evidence, and held that the Government's failure to disclose impeachment evidence required automatic reversal of the conviction.]

We granted certiorari, and we now reverse.

The holding in *Brady* requires disclosure only of evidence that is both favorable to the accused and "material either to guilt or to punishment." The Court explained in *United States v. Agurs*: "A fair analysis of the holding in *Brady* indicates that implicit in the requirement of materiality is a concern that the suppressed evidence might have affected the outcome of the trial." * * *

The *Brady* rule is based on the requirement of due process. * * * Thus, the prosecutor is not required to deliver his entire file to defense counsel, but only to disclose evidence favorable to the accused that, if suppressed, would deprive the defendant of a fair trial:

> * * * [T]he prosecutor will not have violated his constitutional duty of disclosure unless his omission is of sufficient significance to result in the denial of the defendant's right to a fair trial.

In *Brady* and *Agurs*, the prosecutor failed to disclose exculpatory evidence. In the present case, the prosecutor failed to disclose evidence that the defense might have used to impeach the Government's witnesses by showing bias or interest. Impeachment evidence * * * as well as exculpatory evidence, falls within the *Brady* rule. Such evidence is "evidence favorable to an accused," so that, if disclosed and used effectively, it may make the difference between conviction and acquittal. * * *

The Court of Appeals treated impeachment evidence as constitutionally different from exculpatory evidence. According to that court, failure to disclose impeachment evidence is "even more egregious" than failure to disclose exculpatory evidence "because it threatens the defendant's right to confront adverse witnesses." * * *

This Court has rejected any such distinction between impeachment evidence and exculpatory evidence. In *Giglio*, the Government failed to disclose impeachment evidence similar to the evidence at issue in the present case, that is, a promise made to the key Government witness that he would not be prosecuted if he testified for the Government.[b] This Court said:

> When the "reliability of a given witness may well be determinative of guilt or innocence," nondisclosure of evidence affecting credibility falls within th[e] general rule [of *Brady*]. We do not, however, automatically require a new trial whenever "a combing of the prosecutors' files after the trial has disclosed evidence possibly useful to the defense but not likely to have changed the verdict. . . ." A finding of materiality of the evidence is required under *Brady*. . . . A new trial is required if "the false testimony could . . . in any reasonable likelihood have affected the judgment of the jury. . . ."

Thus, the Court of Appeals' holding is inconsistent with our precedents.
* * *

It remains to determine the standard of materiality applicable to the nondisclosed evidence at issue in this case. Our starting point is the framework for evaluating the materiality of *Brady* evidence established in *United States v. Agurs*. The Court in *Agurs* distinguished three situations involving the discovery, after trial, of information favorable to the accused that had been known to the prosecution but unknown to the defense. The first situation was the prosecutor's knowing use of perjured testimony or, equivalently, the prosecutor's knowing failure to disclose that testimony used to convict the defendant was false. * * *

At the other extreme is the situation in *Agurs* itself, where the defendant does not make a *Brady* request and the prosecutor fails to disclose certain evidence favorable to the accused. * * *

The third situation identified by the Court in *Agurs* is where the defense makes a specific request and the prosecutor fails to disclose responsive evidence. * * * The Court did not define the standard of materiality applicable in this situation, but suggested that the standard might be more lenient to the defense than in the situation in which the defense makes no request or only a general request. The Court also noted:

---

[b] In *Giglio v. United States*, 405 U.S. 150 (1972), the Court reversed a defendant's conviction and ordered a new trial after it was discovered that the government failed to disclose to the defense a promise made to its key witness that the witness would not be prosecuted if he testified for the government. The Assistant U.S. Attorney (AUSA) who presented the case to the grand jury later admitted that he made this promise to the witness. *Id.* at 152. Prior to trial, however, that AUSA assured the AUSA who was going to try the case that no promises of immunity had been made to the witness, so the AUSA who tried the case was unaware of the promise. *Id.* at 152. Despite this unawareness, the Court found a violation of Due Process, explaining "whether the nondisclosure was a result of negligence of design, it is the responsibility of the prosecutor. The prosecutor's office is an entity and as such it is the spokesperson for the Government. A promise made by one attorney must be attributed, for these purposes, to the Government." *Id.* at 154. *Giglio* is often cited for the proposition that impeachment evidence—evidence tending to impeach the credibility of a witness—falls under the *Brady* rule as evidence favorable to the accused.

"When the prosecutor receives a specific and relevant request, the failure to make any response is seldom, if ever, excusable."

The Court has relied on and reformulated the *Agurs* standard for the materiality of undisclosed evidence in two subsequent cases arising outside the *Brady* context. In neither case did the Court's discussion * * * distinguish among the three situations described in *Agurs*. In *United States v. Valenzuela-Bernal*, the Court held that due process is violated when testimony is made unavailable to the defense by Government deportation of witnesses "only if there is a reasonable likelihood that the testimony could have affected the judgment of the trier of fact." And in *Strickland v. Washington*, the Court held that a new trial must be granted when evidence is not introduced because of the incompetence of counsel only if "there is a reasonable probability that, but for counsel's unprofessional errors, the result of the proceeding would have been different." The *Strickland* Court defined a "reasonable probability" as "a probability sufficient to undermine confidence in the outcome."

We find the *Strickland* formulation of the *Augurs* test for materiality sufficiently flexible to cover the "no request," "general request," and "specific request" cases of prosecutorial failure to disclose evidence favorable to the excused: The evidence is material only if there is a reasonable probability that, had the evidence been disclosed to the defense, the result of the proceeding would have been different. A "reasonable probability" is a probability sufficient to undermine confidence in the outcome. * * *

We agree that the prosecutor's failure to respond fully to a *Brady* request may impair the adversary process * * *. And the more specifically the defense requests certain evidence, thus putting the prosecutor on notice of its value, the more reasonable it is for the defense to assume from the nondisclosure that the evidence does not exist, and to make pretrial and trial decisions on the basis of this assumption. This possibility of impairment does not necessitate a different standard of materiality. * * * [T]he reviewing court may consider directly any adverse effect that the prosecutor's failure to respond might have had on the preparation or presentation of the defendant's case. The reviewing court should assess the possibility that such effect might have occurred in light of the totality of the circumstances and with an awareness of the difficulty of reconstructing in a post-trial proceeding the course that the defense and the trial would have taken had the defense not been misled by the prosecutor's incomplete response.

In the present case, we think that there is a significant likelihood that the prosecutor's response to respondent's discovery motion misleadingly induced defense counsel to believe that O'Connor and Mitchell could not be impeached on the basis of bias or interest arising from inducements offered by the Government. * * * Moreover, the prosecutor disclosed affidavits that stated that O'Connor and Mitchell received no promises of reward in return for providing information in the affidavits implicating respondent in criminal activity.

* * * Accordingly, we reverse the judgment of the Court of Appeals and remand the case to that court for a determination whether there is a reasonable probability that, had the inducement offered by the Government to O'Connor and Mitchell been disclosed to the defense, the result of the trial would have been different.

It is so ordered.

JUSTICE MARSHALL, with whom JUSTICE BRENNAN joins, dissenting.

When the Government withholds from a defendant evidence that might impeach the prosecution's only witnesses, that failure to disclose cannot be deemed harmless error. Because that is precisely the nature of the undisclosed evidence in this case, I would affirm the judgment of the Court of Appeals and would not remand for further proceedings.

* * * [W]itnesses O'Connor and Mitchell were crucial to the Government's case. * * * [T]heir personal credibility was potentially dispositive * * *. It simply cannot be denied that the existence of a contract signed by those witnesses, promising a reward whose size would depend "on the Government's satisfaction with the end result," might sway the trier of fact, or cast doubt on the truth of all that the witnesses allege. In such a case, the trier of fact is absolutely entitled to know of the contract, and the defense counsel is absolutely entitled to develop his case with an awareness of it. Whatever the applicable standard of materiality, in this instance it undoubtedly is well met. * * *

I begin from the fundamental premise, which hardly bears repeating, that "[t]he purpose of a trial is as much the acquittal of an innocent person as it is the conviction of a guilty one." When evidence favorable to the defendant is known to exist, disclosure only enhances the quest for truth; it takes no direct toll on that inquiry. Moreover, the existence of any small piece of evidence favorable to the defense may, in a particular case, create just the doubt that prevents the jury from returning a verdict of guilty. The private whys and wherefores of jury deliberations pose an impenetrable barrier to our ability to know just which piece of information might make, or might have made, a difference.

When the state does not disclose information in its possession that might reasonably be considered favorable to the defense, it precludes the trier of fact from gaining access to such information and thereby undermines the reliability of the verdict. Unlike a situation in which exculpatory evidence exists but neither the defense nor the prosecutor has uncovered it, in this situation the state already has, resting in its files, material that would be of assistance to the defendant. With a minimum of effort, the state could improve the real and apparent fairness of the trial enormously, by assuring that the defendant may place before the trier of fact favorable evidence known to the government.

* * * [F]requently considerable imbalance exists in resources between most criminal defendants and most prosecutors' offices. * * * [U]nlike the government, defense counsel is not in the position to make deals with witnesses to gain evidence. Thus, an inexperienced, unskilled, or unaggressive attorney often is unable to amass the factual support necessary to a reasonable defense. When favorable evidence is in the hands of the prosecutor but not disclosed, the result may well be that the defendant is deprived of a fair chance before the trier of fact, and the trier of fact is deprived of the ingredients necessary to a fair decision. * * *

My view is based in significant part on the reality of criminal practice and on the consequently inadequate protection to the defendant that a different rule would offer. * * * Our system of criminal justice is animated by two seemingly incompatible notions: the adversary model, and the state's primary concern with justice, not convictions. *Brady*, of course, reflects the latter goal of justice, and is in some ways at odds with the competing model of a sporting event. Our goal, then, must be to integrate the *Brady* right into the harsh, daily reality of this apparently discordant criminal process. * * *

[F]for purposes of *Brady*, the prosecutor must abandon his role as an advocate and pore through his files, as objectively as possible, to identify the material that could undermine his case. Given this obviously unharmonious role, it is not surprising that these advocates oftentimes overlook or downplay potentially favorable evidence. * * * One telling example, offered by Judge Newman when he was a United States Attorney, suffices:

> I recently had occasion to discuss [*Brady*] at a PLI Conference in New York City before a large group of State prosecutors. . . . I put to them this case: You are prosecuting a bank robbery. You have talked to two or three of the tellers and one or two of the customers at the time of the robbery. They have all taken a look at your defendant in a line-up, and they have said, 'This is the man.' In the course of your investigation you also have found another customer who was in the bank that day, who viewed the suspect, and came back and said, 'This is *not* the man.'
>
> The question I put to these prosecutors was, do you believe you should disclose to the defense the name of the witness who, when he viewed the suspect, said 'that is not the man'? In a room of prosecutors not quite as large as this group but almost as large, only two hands went up. There were only two prosecutors in that

group who felt they should disclose or would disclose that information. Yet I was putting to them what I thought was the easiest case—the clearest case for disclosure of exculpatory information!"

While familiarity with *Brady* no doubt has increased since 1967, the dual role that the prosecutor must play, and the very real pressures that role creates, have not changed. * * *

Once the prosecutor suspects that certain information might have favorable implications for the defense, either because it is potentially exculpatory or relevant to credibility, I see no reason why he should not be required to disclose it. After all, favorable evidence indisputably enhances the truthseeking process at trial. And it is the job of the defense, not the prosecution, to decide whether and in what way to use arguably favorable evidence. In addition, to require disclosure of all evidence that might reasonably be considered favorable to the defendant would have the precautionary effect of assuring that no information of potential consequence is mistakenly overlooked. By requiring full disclosure of favorable evidence in this way, courts could begin to assure that a possibly dispositive piece of information is not withheld from the trier of fact by a prosecutor who is torn between the two roles he must play. A clear rule of this kind, coupled with a presumption in favor of disclosure, also would facilitate the prosecutor's admittedly difficult task by removing a substantial amount of unguided discretion.

The standard for disclosure that the Court articulates today enables prosecutors to avoid disclosing obviously exculpatory evidence while acting well within the bounds of their constitutional obligation. * * *

The Court's definition poses other, serious problems. Besides legitimizing the nondisclosure of clearly favorable evidence, the standard set out by the Court also asks the prosecutor to predict what effect various pieces of evidence will have on the trial. He must evaluate his case and the case of the defendant—of which he presumably knows very little—and perform the impossible task of deciding whether a certain piece of information will have a significant impact on the trial, bearing in mind that a defendant will later shoulder the heavy burden of proving how it would have affected the outcome. At best, this standard places on the prosecutor a responsibility to speculate, at times without foundation, since the prosecutor will not normally know what strategy the defense will pursue or what evidence the defense will find useful. At worst, the standard invites a prosecutor, whose interests are conflicting, to gamble, to play the odds, and to take a chance that evidence will later turn out not to have been potentially dispositive. * * *

JUSTICE POWELL took no part in the decision of this case.

[JUSTICE WHITE's concurring opinion and JUSTICE STEVENS' dissenting opinion have been omitted.]

NOTE

In *Kyles v. Whitley*, 514 U.S. 419 (1995), the Court elaborated on the proof required for the showing of materiality, noting that "a showing of materiality does not require demonstration by a preponderance that disclosure of the suppressed evidence would have resulted ultimately in the defendant's acquittal." *Id.* at 434. The Court explained:

> *Bagley*'s touchstone of materiality is a "reasonable probability" of a different result, and the adjective is important. The question is not whether the defendant would more likely than not have received a different verdict with the evidence, but whether in its absence he received a fair trial, understood as a trial resulting in a verdict worthy of confidence. A "reasonable probability" of a different result is accordingly shown when the government's evidentiary suppression "undermines confidence in the outcome of the trial."

Id. The Court also noted that "the individual prosecutor has a duty to learn of any favorable evidence known to the others acting on the government's behalf in the case, including the police." *Id.* at 437.

RULE 3.8: SPECIAL RESPONSIBILITIES OF A PROSECUTOR
MODEL RULES OF PROFESSIONAL CONDUCT AMERICAN BAR ASSOCIATION CENTER FOR PROFESSIONAL RESPONSIBILITY (2022)

The prosecutor in a criminal case shall: * * *

(d) make timely disclosure to the defense of all evidence or information known to the prosecutor that tends to negate the guilt of the accused or mitigates the offense, and, in connection with sentencing, disclose to the defense and to the tribunal all unprivileged mitigating information known to the prosecutor, except when the prosecutor is relieved of this responsibility by a protective order of the tribunal.

* * *

(g) When a prosecutor knows of new, credible, and material evidence creating a reasonable likelihood that a convicted defendant did not commit an offense of which the defendant was convicted, the prosecutor shall:

   1) Promptly disclose that evidence to an appropriate court or authority, and

   2) If the conviction was obtained in the prosecutor's jurisdiction,

      i) promptly disclose that evidence to the defendant unless a court authorizes delay, and

ii) undertake further investigation, or make reasonable efforts to cause an investigation, to determine whether the defendant was convicted of an offense that the defendant did not commit.

(h) When a prosecutor knows of clear and convincing evidence establishing that a defendant in the prosecutor's jurisdiction was convicted of an offense that the defendant did not commit, the prosecutor shall seek to remedy the conviction.

NOTE

One of the biggest challenges of both the *Brady* rule and Model Rule 3.8(d) lies in identifying violations. Because violations of the *Brady* rule and Model Rule 3.8(d) can occur without the defendant ever knowing that evidence that should have been disclosed was not disclosed, it is the rare case when a violation is identified and an even rarer case when a prosecutor is disciplined for that violation. Apparently, fewer than 1 percent of prosecutors who have committed any kind of misconduct have been disciplined for that misconduct.[a]

Former Chief Judge Alex Kozinski of the Ninth Circuit Court of Appeals commented upon the difficulty of identifying violations of the *Brady* rule:

> Due to the nature of a *Brady* violation, it's highly unlikely wrongdoing will ever come to light in the first place. This creates a serious moral hazard for * * * prosecutors * * *. In the rare event that the suppressed evidence does surface, the consequences usually leave the prosecution no worse than had it complied with *Brady* from the outset. Professional discipline is rare, and violations seldom give rise to liability.[b]

While violations of the *Brady* rule usually go unnoticed, a few notable cases show what can happen to a prosecutor who is caught failing to disclose exculpatory evidence to the defense. First, a prosecutor who fails to disclose such evidence risks losing their license to practice law. The Duke Lacrosse case, in which former District Attorney Mike Nifong failed to disclose exculpatory evidence to the defense in a rape prosecution, provides one example of a case in which the failure to disclose resulted in the prosecutor being disbarred.[c] A summary of the *Brady* violation discovered in this case is provided below.

In March 2006, a female victim alleged that multiple members of Duke University's LaCrosse team raped her. In response to these allegations, the members of the team were suspended, the coach was forced to resign, and the

---

[a] Radley Balko, *Opinion: Why Prosecutors Get Away With Misconduct*, WASH. POST (Nov. 18, 2021), https://www.washingtonpost.com/opinions/2021/11/18/why-prosecutors-get-away-with-misconduct/ (https://perma.cc/H5Y5-JP4L).

[b] United States v. Olsen, 737 F.3d 625, 630 (9th Cir. 2013) (Kozinski, C.J., dissenting).

[c] *See* Duke Off. of News & Commc'n, *Looking Back at the Duke Lacrosse Case*, http://today.duke.edu/showcase/lacrosseincident/ (https://perma.cc/NQ8V-Y24U).

entire season was canceled. District Attorney Mike Nifong filed sexual assault charges against three members of the team.

As part of the criminal investigation, Nifong's office arranged for a private lab to conduct DNA testing. The DNA testing uncovered genetic material from several men—but no matches to members of the Lacrosse team. Nifong failed to disclose the results of the DNA testing notwithstanding defense counsel's repeated requests for the DNA results. Instead Nifong denied that these tests had been conducted and continued to pursue the rape prosecution.[d]

Nifong's failure to disclose the DNA test results was revealed when the prosecution's forensic expert testified that DNA tests were conducted and that the test results contained no matches between the victim and the accused defendants. The North Carolina State Bar charged Nifong with multiple ethics violations.[e] On June 16, 2007, Nifong was disbarred.[f]

The Attorney General of North Carolina later dropped the criminal charges against the defendants. If convicted, the players could have received up to 30 years in prison.[g]

Second, a prosecutor can face criminal contempt charges for failing to disclose exculpatory evidence to the defense. For example, in one case, a prosecutor who failed to disclose exculpatory evidence after being ordered by a judge to do so was held in contempt of court and ordered to serve 10 days in jail, pay a $500 fine, perform 500 hours of community service, and surrender his license to practice law.[h]

PROSECUTORIAL DISCRETION AT THE CORE: THE GOOD PROSECUTOR MEETS BRADY
Janet C. Hoeffel
109 Penn. St. L. Rev. 1133 (2005)

If the good prosecutor were the ethical prosecutor, he would disclose to the defense all information favorable to the defense, without hesitation. He would seek such information from any government official who touched the case. If in doubt, he would err on the side of disclosure. Consistent with

---

[d] Some speculated that Nifong was motivated to get a conviction in this high-profile case because it was an election year. McFadyen v. Duke Univ., 786 F. Supp. 2d 887, 908 (M.D.N.C. 2011).

[e] R. Michael Cassidy, *The Prosecutor and the Press: Lesson (Not) Learned from the Mike Nifong Debacle*, 71 LAW AND CONTEMP. PROB. 67, 68 (2008).

[f] Duff Wilson, *Prosecutor in Duke Case is Disbarred for Ethics Breaches*, N.Y. TIMES (June 16, 2007), http://www.nytimes.com/2007/06/16/us/16cnd-nifong.html?_r=0 (https://perma.cc/6SQC-JU6E).

[g] Susannah Meadows, *What Really Happened That Night at Duke*, NEWSWEEK, Apr. 22, 2007, http://www.newsweek.com/what-really-happened-night-duke-97835 (https://perma.cc/R2DZ-6SBD).

[h] Paul Cates, *Former Williamson County Prosecutor Ken Anderson Enters Plea to Contempt for Misconduct in Michael Morton's Wrongful Murder Conviction*, INNOCENCE PROJECT.ORG (Nov. 8, 2013, 12:00 AM), https://www.innocenceproject.org/former-williamson-county-prosecutor-ken-anderson-enters-plea-to-contempt-for-misconduct-in-michael-mortonaes-wrongful-murder-conviction/ (https://perma.cc/2MYN-LXBR).

"doing justice," such disclosure ensures that the adversarial process is fair. In reality, however, the good prosecutor must do none of these things to be a worthy adversary, according to the Supreme Court of the United States.

It may be that the Warren Court originally intended to place the prosecutor in the ethical role. In *Brady v. Maryland*, the Court broke new ground by holding that "the suppression by the prosecution of evidence favorable to an accused upon request violates due process where the evidence is material either to guilt or to punishment, irrespective of the good faith or the bad faith of the prosecution." * * * The Court emphasized the role of the ethical prosecutor, saying that "[a] prosecution that withholds evidence on demand of an accused which, if made available, would tend to exculpate him or reduce the penalty . . . casts the prosecutor in the role of an architect of a proceeding that does not comport with standards of justice[.]" Hence "[s]ociety wins not only when the guilty are convicted but when criminal trials are fair [.]"

In any event, this view of the good prosecutor as the ethical prosecutor was undone by the march of [several cases.] In [*United States v.*] *Bagley*, the Court held that favorable evidence is "material," and constitutional error results from its suppression, "if there is a reasonable probability that, had the evidence been disclosed to the defense, the result of the proceeding would have been different."

* * * *Bagley* directly places the prosecutor in the role of the architect of the proceeding. The prosecutor can withhold the evidence if he or she believes there would not be a reasonable probability that the disclosure would have affected the jury's verdict. * * *

The Court's admonishments that "the prudent prosecutor will resolve doubtful questions in favor of disclosure" and that "a prosecutor anxious about tacking too close to the wind will disclose a favorable piece of evidence" are either ignorant or disingenuous. The prudent prosecutor will do no such thing. * * *

For example, imagine that the prudent prosecutor is in possession of information that one of the two eyewitnesses to a robbery initially gave the police a description of the perpetrator of the crime that was inconsistent with the appearance of the defendant. The eyewitness described the person as 5'8" tall, with a medium build. The defendant is 5'11" tall and thin. That same eyewitness, however, picked the defendant out of a lineup and indicated she was sure that the defendant was the robber. The other eyewitness gave a general description that fit the defendant and also picked the defendant out of a lineup. The prudent prosecutor, convinced of the defendant's guilt, will not disclose that information.

Several rational reasons explain this decision. First, he is convinced of the defendant's guilt and he is certain that a defense attorney will use this information to attempt to create reasonable doubt where none exists. The prudent prosecutor believes people misgauge the actual height and weight of a person for many reasons, and a minor discrepancy should not derail the prosecution. Second, the prudent prosecutor has read *Bagley* * * * and realizes he has discretion to wait to disclose until he feels a reasonable probability exists that the information would change the outcome of the case. He does not believe this inconsistency creates a reasonable probability, and who is to fault his discretion?

Third, the prudent prosecutor also knows that, because he has no obligation to disclose this evidence, it may never be discovered and, therefore, will never make its way into an appeal of the conviction. Fourth, he knows that even if it is discovered post-trial, an appellate court is likely to view this evidence as harmless in hindsight. The burden will be on the defendant and appellate courts have shown themselves to be predisposed to upholding convictions. The remote prospect of a reversal at some point in the future is hardly a deterrent now, when faced with a discretionary decision which will help him get a conviction. In any case, a reversal simply calls for a retrial, so that the prosecutor is put in essentially the same position he was in prior to the error.

Fifth, the prudent prosecutor is unconcerned about an ethical violation. Even assuming the prosecutor is aware of his duty to disclose favorable evidence under the professional codes (which may be a stretch), he has never heard of a prosecutor being disciplined for his exercise of discretion in withholding evidence. In 1987, Richard Rosen combed the universe of written disciplinary decisions and found only nine which even involved a referral of a prosecutor for withholding exculpatory evidence. In only one of those was the prosecutor given a major sanction, and then, only a suspension. The message sent is that, although it is a rule on the books, the disciplinary authorities do not believe its violation worthy of condemnation.

The barriers to enforcement of the ethical rule are enormous. First, a third party must have the time, wherewithal, and inclination to refer the prosecutor. The only third party who might have an interest is a defendant, who likely is focused on reversing his conviction and does not have the resources to engage an attorney to handle the ethical claim. Even if referred, all incentives point in favor of letting the prosecutor off the hook. If the appellate courts have already determined that the nondisclosure did not amount to a constitutional violation, it is unlikely that the ethical board or the overseeing court will find fault with the prosecutor, despite a technical violation of the rules. Politics, separation of powers, and judicial restraint all play a role. * * *

Withholding favorable evidence * * * seems to be the norm. One recent study reported that convictions in 381 homicide cases nationwide had been reversed because prosecutors concealed evidence suggesting the defendants' innocence or presented evidence they knew to be false. Of the first seventy exonerations of prisoners through DNA testing nationwide, 34% involved prosecutorial misconduct; and of the instances of prosecutorial misconduct in the 152 exonerations occurring between 1989 and 2004, 37% were due to the suppression of exculpatory evidence. These, of course, are only the cases where somehow the nondisclosure came to light. Most cases of nondisclosure likely go undiscovered.

Therefore, we have a criminal justice system which encourages adversarial zeal in its prosecutors to the tune of withholding favorable evidence. To hold our noses at such conduct on the part of prosecutors is unrealistic. To blame the prosecutor ignores fundamental problems inherent in our adversarial system of justice that assumes the average criminal defendant is guilty and encourages prosecutors to pursue convictions in the name of justice. * * *

WILLIAMS V. FLORIDA
Supreme Court of the United States
399 U.S. 78, 90 S. Ct. 1893, 26 L. Ed. 2d 446 (1970)

JUSTICE WHITE delivered the opinion of the Court.

Prior to his trial for robbery in the State of Florida, petitioner filed a "Motion for a Protective Order," seeking to be excused from the requirements of Rule 1.200 of the Florida Rules of Criminal Procedure. That rule requires a defendant, on written demand of the prosecuting attorney, to give notice in advance of trial if the defendant intends to claim an alibi, and to furnish the prosecuting attorney with information as to the place where he claims to have been and with the names and addresses of the alibi witnesses he intends to use.[a] In his motion petitioner openly declared his intent to claim an alibi, but objected to the further disclosure requirements on the ground that the rule "compels the Defendant in a criminal case to be a witness against himself" in violation of his Fifth and Fourteenth Amendment rights. The motion was denied. * * *

Florida's notice-of-alibi rule is in essence a requirement that a defendant submit to a limited form of pretrial discovery by the State whenever he intends to rely at trial on the defense of alibi. In exchange for the defendant's disclosure of the witnesses he proposes to use to establish that defense, the State in turn is required to notify the defendant of any witnesses it proposes to offer in rebuttal to that defense. Both sides are under a continuing duty promptly to disclose the names and addresses of

---

[a] Similarly, Rule 12.1 of the Federal Rules of Criminal Procedure, reprinted in the Appendix, requires the defendant in a federal case, within 14 days of receiving a written request from an attorney for the government, to provide written notice of any intended alibi defense. That notice must state "each specific place where the defendant claims to have been at the time of the alleged offense" and "the name, address, and telephone number of each alibi witness on whom the defendant intends to rely." FED. R. CRIM. P. 12.1.

additional witnesses bearing on the alibi as they become available. The threatened sanction for failure to comply is the exclusion at trial of the defendant's alibi evidence—except for his own testimony—or, in the case of the State, the exclusion of the State's evidence offered in rebuttal of the alibi.

In this case, following the denial of his Motion for a Protective Order, petitioner complied with the alibi rule and gave the State the name and address of one Mary Scotty. Mrs. Scotty was summoned to the office of the State Attorney on the morning of the trial, where she gave pretrial testimony. At the trial itself, Mrs. Scotty, petitioner, and petitioner's wife all testified that the three of them had been in Mrs. Scotty's apartment during the time of the robbery. On two occasions during cross-examination of Mrs. Scotty, the prosecuting attorney confronted her with her earlier deposition in which she had given dates and times that in some respects did not correspond with the dates and times given at trial. Mrs. Scotty adhered to her trial story, insisting that she had been mistaken in her earlier testimony. The State also offered in rebuttal the testimony of one of the officers investigating the robbery who claimed that Mrs. Scotty had asked him for directions on the afternoon in question during the time when she claimed to have been in her apartment with petitioner and his wife.

* * * Given the ease with which an alibi can be fabricated, the State's interest in protecting itself against an eleventh-hour defense is both obvious and legitimate. Reflecting this interest, notice-of-alibi provisions, dating at least from 1927, are now in existence in a substantial number of States. The adversary system of trial * * * is not yet a poker game in which players enjoy an absolute right always to conceal their cards until played. We find ample room in that system, at least as far as "due process" is concerned, for the instant Florida rule, which is designed to enhance the search for truth in the criminal trial by insuring both the defendant and the State ample opportunity to investigate certain facts crucial to the determination of guilt or innocence.

Petitioner's major contention is that he was "compelled * * * to be a witness against himself" contrary to the commands of the Fifth and Fourteenth Amendments because the notice-of-alibi rule required him to give the State the name and address of Mrs. Scotty in advance of trial and thus to furnish the State with information useful in convicting him. No pretrial statement of petitioner was introduced at trial; but armed with Mrs. Scotty's name and address and the knowledge that she was to be petitioner's alibi witness, the State was able to take her deposition in advance of trial and to find rebuttal testimony. Also, requiring him to reveal the elements of his defense is claimed to have interfered with his right to wait until after the State had presented its case to decide how to defend against it. We conclude, however, as has apparently every other court that has considered the issue, that the privilege against self-incrimination is not violated by a requirement that the defendant give notice of an alibi defense and disclose his alibi witnesses.

The defendant in a criminal trial is frequently forced to testify himself and to call other witnesses in an effort to reduce the risk of conviction. When he presents his witnesses, he must reveal their identity and submit them to cross-examination which in itself may prove incriminating or which may furnish the State with leads to incriminating rebuttal evidence. That the defendant faces such a dilemma demanding a choice between complete silence and presenting a defense has never been thought an invasion of the privilege against compelled self-incrimination. The pressures generated by the State's evidence may be severe but they do not vitiate the defendant's choice to present an alibi defense and witnesses to prove it, even though the attempted defense ends in catastrophe for the defendant. However "testimonial" or "incriminating" the alibi defense proves to be, it cannot be considered "compelled" within the meaning of the Fifth and Fourteenth Amendments.

Very similar constraints operate on the defendant when the State requires pretrial notice of alibi and the naming of alibi witnesses. Nothing in such a rule requires the defendant to rely on an alibi or prevents him from abandoning the defense; these matters are left to his unfettered choice. That choice must be made, but the pressures that bear on his pretrial decision are of the same nature as those that would induce him to call alibi witnesses at the trial: the force of historical fact beyond both his and the State's control and the strength of the State's case built on these facts. Response to that kind of pressure by offering evidence or testimony is not compelled self-incrimination transgressing the Fifth and Fourteenth Amendments.

In the case before us, the notice-of-alibi rule by itself in no way affected petitioner's crucial decision to call alibi witnesses or added to the legitimate pressures leading to that course of action. At most, the rule only compelled petitioner to accelerate the timing of his disclosure, forcing him to divulge at an earlier date information that the petitioner from the beginning planned to divulge at trial. Nothing in the Fifth Amendment privilege entitles a defendant as a matter of constitutional right to await the end of the State's case before announcing the nature of his defense, any more than it entitles him to await the jury's verdict on the State's case-in-chief before deciding whether or not to take the stand himself.

Petitioner concedes that absent the notice-of-alibi rule the Constitution would raise no bar to the court's granting the State a continuance at trial on the ground of surprise as soon as the alibi witness is called. Nor would there be self-incrimination problems if, during that continuance, the State was permitted to do precisely what it did here prior to trial: take the deposition of the witness and find rebuttal evidence. But if so utilizing a continuance is permissible under the Fifth and Fourteenth Amendments, then surely the same result may be accomplished through pretrial discovery, as it was here, avoiding the necessity of a disrupted trial. We decline to hold that the privilege against compulsory self-incrimination guarantees the defendant the right to surprise the State with an alibi defense. * * *

CHIEF JUSTICE BURGER, concurring.

I join fully in Mr. Justice WHITE's opinion for the Court. I see an added benefit to the notice-of-alibi rule in that it will serve important functions by way of disposing of cases without trial in appropriate circumstances—a matter of considerable importance when courts, prosecution offices, and legal aid and defender agencies are vastly overworked. The prosecutor upon receiving notice will, of course, investigate prospective alibi witnesses. If he finds them reliable and unimpeachable he will doubtless re-examine his entire case and this process would very likely lead to dismissal of the charges. In turn he might be obliged to determine why false charges were instituted and where the breakdown occurred in the examination of evidence that led to a charge.

On the other hand, inquiry into a claimed alibi defense may reveal it to be contrived and fabricated and the witnesses accordingly subject to impeachment or other attack. In this situation defense counsel would be obliged to re-examine his case and, if he found his client has proposed the use of false testimony, either seek to withdraw from the case or try to persuade his client to enter a plea of guilty, possibly by plea discussions which could lead to disposition on a lesser charge.

In either case the ends of justice will have been served and the processes expedited. These are the likely consequences of an enlarged and truly reciprocal pretrial disclosure of evidence and the move away from the "sporting contest" idea of criminal justice.

JUSTICE BLACK, with whom JUSTICE DOUGLAS joins, concurring in part and dissenting in part.

The Court [today] holds that a State can require a defendant in a criminal case to disclose in advance of trial the nature of his alibi defense and give the names and addresses of witnesses he will call to support that defense. This requirement, the majority says, does not violate the Fifth Amendment prohibition against compelling a criminal defendant to be a witness against himself. Although this case itself involves only a notice-of-alibi provision, it is clear that the decision means that a State can require a defendant to disclose in advance of trial any and all information he might possibly use to defend himself at trial. This decision, in my view, is a radical and dangerous departure from the historical and constitutionally guaranteed right of a defendant in a criminal case to remain completely silent, requiring the State to prove its case without any assistance of any kind from the defendant himself.

The core of the majority's decision is an assumption that compelling a defendant to give notice of an alibi defense before a trial is no different from requiring a defendant, after the State has produced the evidence against him at trial, to plead alibi before the jury retires to consider the case. This assumption is clearly revealed by the statement that "the pressures that bear on (a defendant's) pre-trial decision are of the same nature as those that would induce him to call alibi witnesses at the trial." * * * That statement is plainly and simply wrong as a matter of fact and law, and the Court's holding based on that statement is a complete misunderstanding of the protections provided for criminal defendants by the Fifth Amendment and other provisions of the Bill of Rights.

When a defendant is required to indicate whether he might plead alibi in advance of trial, he faces a vastly different decision from that faced by one who can wait until the State has presented the case against him before making up his mind. Before trial the defendant knows only what the State's case might be. Before trial there is no such thing as the "strength of the State's case"; there is only a range of possible cases. At that time there is no certainty as to what kind of case the State will ultimately be able to prove at trial. Therefore any appraisal of the desirability of pleading alibi will be beset with guesswork and gambling far greater than that accompanying the decision at the trial itself. Any lawyer who has actually tried a case knows that, regardless of the amount of pretrial preparation, a case looks far different when it is actually being tried than when it is only being thought about.

The Florida system, as interpreted by the majority, plays upon this inherent uncertainty in predicting the possible strength of the State's case in order effectively to coerce defendants into disclosing an alibi defense that may never be actually used. Under the Florida rule, a defendant who might plead alibi must, at least 10 days before the date of trial, tell the prosecuting attorney that he might claim an alibi or else the defendant faces the real threat that he may be completely barred from presenting witnesses in support of his alibi. * * * Thus in most situations defendants with any possible thought of pleading alibi are in effect compelled to disclose their intentions in order to preserve the possibility of later raising the defense at trial. Necessarily few defendants and their lawyers will be willing to risk the loss of that possibility by not disclosing the alibi. Clearly the pressures on defendants to plead an alibi created by this procedure are not only quite different from the pressures operating at the trial itself, but are in fact significantly greater. Contrary to the majority's assertion, the pretrial decision cannot be analyzed as simply a matter of "timing," influenced by the same factors operating at the trial itself.

The Court apparently also assumes that a defendant who has given the required notice can abandon his alibi without hurting himself. Such an assumption is implicit in and necessary for the majority's argument that the pretrial decision is no different from that at the trial itself. I, however, cannot so lightly assume that pretrial notice will have no adverse effects on a defendant who later decides to forgo such a defense. Necessarily the defendant will have given the prosecutor the names of persons who may have some knowledge about the defendant himself or his activities. Necessarily the prosecutor will have every incentive to question these persons fully, and in doing so he may discover new leads or evidence. Undoubtedly there will be situations in which the State will seek to use such information—information it would probably never have obtained but for the defendant's coerced cooperation.

It is unnecessary for me, however, to engage in any such intellectual gymnastics concerning the practical effects of the notice-of-alibi procedure, because the Fifth Amendment itself clearly provides that "[n]o person * * * shall be compelled in any criminal case to be a witness against himself." If words are to be given their plain and obvious meaning, that provision, in my opinion, states that a criminal defendant cannot be required to give evidence, testimony, or any other assistance to the State to aid it in convicting him of crime. The Florida notice-of-alibi rule in my opinion is a patent violation of [the Fifth Amendment's] constitutional provision because it requires a defendant to disclose information to the State so that the State can use that information to destroy him. It seems to me at least slightly incredible to suggest that this procedure may have some beneficial effects for defendants. There is no need to encourage defendants to take actions they think will help them. The fear of conviction and the substantial cost or inconvenience resulting from criminal prosecutions are more than sufficient incentives to make defendants want to help themselves. If a defendant thinks that making disclosure of an alibi before trial is in his best interest, he will obviously do so. And the only time the State needs the compulsion provided by this procedure is when the defendant has decided that such disclosure is likely to hurt his case.

It is no answer to this argument to suggest that the Fifth Amendment as so interpreted would give the defendant an unfair element of surprise, turning a trial into a "poker game" or "sporting contest," for that tactical advantage to the defendant is inherent in the type of trial required by our Bill of Rights. The Framers were well aware of the awesome investigative and prosecutorial powers of government and it was in order to limit those powers that they spelled out in detail in the Constitution the procedure to be followed in criminal trials. A defendant, they said, is entitled to notice of the charges against him, trial by jury, the right to counsel for his defense, the right to confront and cross-examine witnesses, the right to call witnesses in his own behalf, and the right not to be a witness against himself. All of these rights are designed to shield the defendant against state power. None are designed to make convictions easier and taken together they clearly indicate that in our system the entire burden of proving criminal activity rests on the State. The defendant, under our Constitution, need not do anything at all to defend himself, and certainly he cannot be required to help convict himself. Rather he has an absolute, unqualified right to compel the State to investigate its own case, find its own witnesses, prove its own facts, and convince the jury through its own resources. Throughout the process the defendant has a fundamental right to remain silent, in effect challenging the State at every point to: "Prove it!" * * *

On the surface this case involves only a notice-of-alibi provisions, but in effect the decision opens the way for a profound change in one of the most important traditional safeguards of a criminal defendant. The rationale of today's decision is in no way limited to alibi defenses, or any other type or classification of evidence. The theory advanced goes at least so far as to permit the State to obtain under threat of sanction complete disclosure by the defendant in advance of trial of all evidence, testimony, and tactics he plans to use at that trial. In each case the justification will be that the rule affects only the "timing" of the disclosure, and not the substantive decision itself.

* * * [T]he rationale of today's decision can be used to transform radically our system of criminal justice into a process requiring the defendant to assist the State in convicting him, or be punished for failing to do so. * * *

[JUSTICE MARSHALL's opinion, dissenting in part, has been omitted.]

NOTE

In 1957, the Supreme Court held in *Jencks v. United States*, 353 U.S. 657 (1957), that the government is required to give statements of its witnesses to the defense. In response, Congress passed the Jencks Act, 18 U.S.C. § 3500(b), *see* Appendix, limiting this rule such that the government need not turn over prosecution witness statements to the defense until after the witness testifies on direct examination at trial. After the government's witness testifies and upon the defendant's request, the court shall order the government to deliver any statements of the witness in the government's possession that relate to the subject matter upon which the witness has testified. Federal Rule of Criminal Procedure 26.2(a) codified the Jencks Act and made the disclosure obligation reciprocal, requiring the defense, upon prosecution request, to deliver the statements of its witnesses to the prosecution after those witnesses testify. Rule 26.2(a) does not require the production of a testifying defendant's statements.

CHAPTER 27

PLEA BARGAINING

■ ■ ■

Although a criminal defendant has a constitutional right to a jury trial, a defendant may choose to waive this right and enter a guilty plea. When the defendant does so as the result of a plea bargain with the government, he foregoes his right to a trial usually in exchange for a lesser charge or a favorable sentencing recommendation.

The Supreme Court has noted that "[p]lea bargaining flows from 'the mutuality of advantage' to defendants and prosecutors, each with his own reason for wanting to avoid trial."[a] This chapter examines the constitutional requirements surrounding plea bargaining.

Plea bargaining is an extremely common practice. It has become such a dominant force in the criminal justice process that very few criminal cases go to trial today. Indeed "[n]inety-seven percent of all federal convictions and ninety-four percent of all state convictions are the result of guilty pleas."[b] As one judge has noted, "our entire criminal justice system has shifted far away from trials and juries and adjudication to a massive system of [plea] bargaining that is heavily rigged against the accused citizen."[c]

In the plea bargaining process, the prosecutor holds most of the cards. The prosecutor can reduce or dismiss some or all of the charges in exchange for the defendant's guilty plea. Since there is no constitutional right to a plea bargain, the prosecutor can even refuse to plea bargain with the defendant.

What if the prosecutor threatens to add a charge that will subject the defendant to a mandatory sentence of life imprisonment if the defendant does not plead guilty to the offense with which he was originally charged? The first case in this chapter, *Bordenkircher v. Hayes*, considers whether such conduct violates the Due Process Clause of the Fourteenth Amendment.

The plea agreement is often viewed as a contract that binds the prosecutor as well as the defendant. When the prosecutor breaches the plea agreement, what is the defendant's remedy? In *Santobello v. New York*, the

---

[a] Bordenkircher v. Hayes, *infra*.
[b] Missouri v. Frye, 566 U.S. 134, 143 (2012).
[c] United States v. Green, 346 F. Supp. 2d 259, 265 (D. Mass. 2004).

Court considers the various ways a defendant can be made whole when the government breaches its half of the plea bargain. In *Mabry v. Johnson*, the Court considers whether the defendant's acceptance of a prosecutor's proposed plea agreement creates an enforceable agreement. If one views plea bargaining as a contractual arrangement between the prosecutor and the defendant, one may be surprised at the Court's answer to this question.

In the chapter on discovery, we learned that the prosecutor has an ethical and constitutional duty to provide exculpatory evidence to the defense. Given this duty, can prosecutors insist that defendants waive their right to such evidence as part of a plea bargain? For many years, federal prosecutors routinely conditioned their plea agreements on defendants waiving their right to receive impeachment evidence relating to the government's informants and witnesses. In *United States v. Ruiz*, the Court considers whether this practice comports with due process.

In *Boykin v. Alabama* and *Henderson v. Morgan*, the Court outlines the requirements for a constitutionally valid guilty plea. In the last case in this chapter, *North Carolina v. Alford*, the Court considers whether a judge can accept a guilty plea from a defendant who claims he is innocent of the charge to which he is pleading guilty and what procedural safeguards are needed in this type of situation. The chapter ends with an article by John Keker, lamenting the fact that so many cases today never go to trial.

BORDENKIRCHER V. HAYES
Supreme Court of the United States
434 U.S. 357, 98 S. Ct. 663, 54 L. Ed. 2d 604 (1978)

JUSTICE STEWART delivered the opinion of the Court.

The question in this case is whether the Due Process Clause of the Fourteenth Amendment is violated when a state prosecutor carries out a threat made during plea negotiations to reindict the accused on more serious charges if he does not plead guilty to the offense with which he was originally charged.

The respondent, Paul Lewis Hayes, was indicted by a Fayette County, Ky., grand jury on a charge of uttering a forged instrument in the amount of $88.30, an offense then punishable by a term of 2 to 10 years in prison. After arraignment, Hayes, his retained counsel, and the Commonwealth's Attorney met in the presence of the Clerk of the Court to discuss a possible plea agreement. During these conferences the prosecutor offered to recommend a sentence of five years in prison if Hayes would plead guilty to the indictment. He also said that if Hayes did not plead guilty and "save the court the inconvenience and necessity of a trial," he would return to the grand jury to seek an indictment under the Kentucky Habitual Criminal Act, which would subject Hayes to a mandatory sentence of life imprisonment by reason of his two prior felony convictions. Hayes chose not to plead guilty, and the prosecutor did obtain an indictment charging him under the Habitual Criminal Act. * * *

A jury found Hayes guilty on the principal charge of uttering a forged instrument and, in a separate proceeding, further found that he had twice before been convicted of felonies. As required by the habitual offender statute, he was sentenced to a life term in the penitentiary. * * * We granted certiorari to consider a constitutional question of importance in the administration of criminal justice.

It may be helpful to clarify at the outset the nature of the issue in this case. While the prosecutor did not actually obtain the recidivist indictment until after the plea conferences had ended, his intention to do so was clearly expressed at the outset of the plea negotiations. Hayes was thus fully informed of the true terms of the offer when he made his decision to plead not guilty. This is not a situation, therefore, where the prosecutor without notice brought an additional and more serious charge after plea negotiations relating only to the original indictment had ended with the defendant's insistence on pleading not guilty. As a practical matter, in short, this case would be no different if the grand jury had indicted Hayes as a recidivist from the outset, and the prosecutor had offered to drop that charge as part of the plea bargain.

The Court of Appeals nonetheless drew a distinction between "concessions relating to prosecution under an existing indictment," and threats to bring more severe charges not contained in the original indictment—a line it thought necessary in order to establish a prophylactic rule to guard against the evil of prosecutorial vindictiveness. Quite apart from this chronological distinction, however, the Court of Appeals found that the prosecutor had acted vindictively in the present case since he had conceded that the indictment was influenced by his desire to induce a guilty plea.

We have recently had occasion to observe: "[W]hatever might be the situation in an ideal world, the fact is that the guilty plea and the often concomitant plea bargain are important components of this country's criminal justice system. Properly administered, they can benefit all concerned." The open acknowledgment of this previously clandestine practice has led this Court to recognize the importance of counsel during plea negotiations, the need for a public record indicating that a plea was knowingly and voluntarily made and the requirement that a prosecutor's plea-bargaining promise must be kept. The decision of the Court of Appeals in the present case, however, did not deal with considerations such as these, but held that the substance of the plea offer itself violated the limitations imposed by the Due Process Clause of the Fourteenth Amendment. For the reasons that follow, we have concluded that the Court of Appeals was mistaken in so ruling.

This Court held in *North Carolina v. Pearce*, that the Due Process Clause of the Fourteenth Amendment "requires that vindictiveness against a defendant for having successfully attacked his first conviction must play no part in the sentence he receives after a new trial." The same principle was later applied [in *Blackledge v. Perry*] to prohibit a prosecutor from reindicting a convicted misdemeanant on a felony charge after the defendant had invoked an appellate remedy, since in this situation there was also a "realistic likelihood of 'vindictiveness.'"

In those cases the Court was dealing with the State's unilateral imposition of a penalty upon a defendant who had chosen to exercise a legal right to attack his original conviction—a situation "very different from the give-and-take negotiation common in plea bargaining between the prosecution and defense, which arguably possess relatively equal bargaining power." The Court has emphasized that the due process violation in cases such as *Pearce* and *Perry* lay not in the possibility that a defendant might be deterred from the exercise of a legal right, but rather in the danger that the State might be retaliating against the accused for lawfully attacking his conviction.

To punish a person because he has done what the law plainly allows him to do is a due process violation of the most basic sort, and for an agent of the State to pursue a course of action whose objective is to penalize a person's reliance on his legal rights is "patently unconstitutional." But in the "give-and-take" of plea bargaining, there is no such element of punishment or retaliation so long as the accused is free to accept or reject the prosecution's offer.

Plea bargaining flows from "the mutuality of advantage" to defendants and prosecutors, each with his own reasons for wanting to avoid trial. Defendants advised by competent counsel and protected by other procedural safeguards are presumptively capable of intelligent choice in response to prosecutorial persuasion, and unlikely to be driven to false self-condemnation. Indeed, acceptance of the basic legitimacy of plea bargaining necessarily implies rejection of any notion that a guilty plea is involuntary in a constitutional sense simply because it is the end result of the bargaining process. By hypothesis, the plea may have been induced by promises of a recommendation of a lenient sentence or a reduction of charges, and thus by fear of the possibility of a greater penalty upon conviction after a trial.

While confronting a defendant with the risk of more severe punishment clearly may have a "discouraging effect on the defendant's assertion of his trial rights, the imposition of these difficult choices [is] an inevitable"—and permissible—"attribute of any legitimate system which tolerates and encourages the negotiation of pleas." It follows that, by tolerating and encouraging the negotiation of pleas, this Court has necessarily accepted as constitutionally legitimate the simple reality that the prosecutor's interest at the bargaining table is to persuade the defendant to forgo his right to plead not guilty.

It is not disputed here that Hayes was properly chargeable under the recidivist statute, since he had in fact been convicted of two previous felonies. In our system, so long as the prosecutor has probable cause to believe that the accused committed an offense defined by statute, the decision whether or not to prosecute, and what charge to file or bring before a grand jury, generally rests entirely in his discretion.[8] Within the limits set by the legislature's constitutionally valid definition of chargeable offenses, "the conscious exercise of some selectivity in enforcement is not in itself a federal constitutional violation" so long as "the selection was [not] deliberately based upon an unjustifiable standard such as race, religion, or other arbitrary classification." To hold that the prosecutor's desire to induce a guilty plea is an "unjustifiable standard," which, like race or religion, may play no part in his charging decision, would contradict the very premises that underlie the concept of plea bargaining itself. Moreover, a rigid constitutional rule that would prohibit a prosecutor from acting forthrightly in his dealings with the defense could only invite unhealthy subterfuge that would drive the practice of plea bargaining back into the shadows from which it has so recently emerged.

There is no doubt that the breadth of discretion that our country's legal system vests in prosecuting attorneys carries with it the potential for both individual and institutional abuse. And broad though that discretion may be, there are undoubtedly constitutional limits upon its exercise. We hold only that the course of conduct engaged in by the prosecutor in this case, which no more than openly presented the defendant with the unpleasant alternatives of forgoing trial or facing charges on which he was plainly subject to prosecution, did not violate the Due Process Clause of the Fourteenth Amendment.

Accordingly, the judgment of the Court of Appeals is

Reversed.

JUSTICE BLACKMUN, with whom JUSTICE BRENNAN and JUSTICE MARSHALL join, dissenting. * * *

Prosecutorial vindictiveness, it seems to me, in the present narrow context, is the fact against which the Due Process Clause ought to protect. I perceive little difference between vindictiveness after what the Court describes as the exercise of a "legal right to attack his original conviction," and vindictiveness in the "give-and-take negotiation common in plea

---

[8] This case does not involve the constitutional implications of a prosecutor's offer during plea bargaining of adverse or lenient treatment for some person other than the accused, which might pose a greater danger of inducing a false guilty plea by skewing the assessment of the risks a defendant must consider.

bargaining." Prosecutorial vindictiveness in any context is still prosecutorial vindictiveness. The Due Process Clause should protect an accused against it, however it asserts itself. The Court of Appeals rightly so held, and I would affirm the judgment. * * *

It might be argued that it really makes little difference how this case, now that it is here, is decided. The Court's holding gives plea bargaining full sway despite vindictiveness. A contrary result, however, merely would prompt the aggressive prosecutor to bring the greater charge initially in every case, and only thereafter to bargain. The consequences to the accused would still be adverse, for then he would bargain against a greater charge, face the likelihood of increased bail, and run the risk that the court would be less inclined to accept a bargained plea. Nonetheless, it is far preferable to hold the prosecution to the charge it was originally content to bring and to justify in the eyes of its public.

JUSTICE POWELL, dissenting.

Although I agree with much of the Court's opinion, I am not satisfied that the result in this case is just or that the conduct of the plea bargaining met the requirements of due process. * * *

The prosecutor's initial assessment of respondent's case led him to forgo an indictment under the habitual criminal statute. The circumstances of respondent's prior convictions are relevant to this assessment and to my view of the case. Respondent was 17 years old when he committed his first offense. He was charged with rape but pleaded guilty to the lesser included offense of "detaining a female." One of the other participants in the incident was sentenced to life imprisonment. Respondent was sent not to prison but to a reformatory where he served five years. Respondent's second offense was robbery. This time he was found guilty by a jury and was sentenced to five years in prison, but he was placed on probation and served no time. Although respondent's prior convictions brought him within the terms of the Habitual Criminal Act, the offenses themselves did not result in imprisonment; yet the addition of a conviction on a charge involving $88.30 subjected respondent to a mandatory sentence of imprisonment for life. Persons convicted of rape and murder often are not punished so severely. * * *

It seems to me that the question to be asked under the circumstances is whether the prosecutor reasonably might have charged respondent under the Habitual Criminal Act in the first place. The deference that courts properly accord the exercise of a prosecutor's discretion perhaps would foreclose judicial criticism if the prosecutor originally had sought an indictment under that Act, as unreasonable as it would have seemed. But here the prosecutor evidently made a reasonable, responsible judgment not to subject an individual to a mandatory life sentence when his only new offense had societal implications as limited as those accompanying the uttering of a single $88 forged check and when the circumstances of his prior convictions confirmed the inappropriateness of applying the habitual criminal statute. I think it may be inferred that the prosecutor himself deemed it unreasonable and not in the public interest to put this defendant in jeopardy of a sentence of life imprisonment. * * *

The plea bargaining process, as recognized by this Court, is essential to the functioning of the criminal-justice system. It normally affords genuine benefits to defendants as well as to society. And if the system is to work effectively, prosecutors must be accorded the widest discretion, within constitutional limits, in conducting bargaining. This is especially true when a defendant is represented by counsel and presumably is fully advised of his rights. Only in the most exceptional case should a court conclude that the scales of the bargaining are so unevenly balanced as to arouse suspicion. In this case, the prosecutor's actions denied respondent due process because their admitted purpose was to discourage and then to penalize with unique severity his exercise of constitutional rights. Implementation of a strategy calculated solely to deter the exercise of constitutional rights is not a constitutionally permissible exercise of discretion. I would affirm the opinion of the Court of Appeals on the facts of this case.

SANTOBELLO V. NEW YORK

Supreme Court of the United States
404 U.S. 257, 92 S. Ct. 495, 30 L. Ed. 2d 427 (1971)

CHIEF JUSTICE BURGER delivered the opinion of the Court.

We granted certiorari in this case to determine whether the State's failure to keep a commitment concerning the sentence recommendation on a guilty plea required a new trial.

The facts are not in dispute. The State of New York indicted petitioner in 1969 on two felony counts, Promoting Gambling in the First Degree, and Possession of Gambling Records in the First Degree. Petitioner first entered a plea of not guilty to both counts. After negotiations, the Assistant District Attorney in charge of the case agreed to permit petitioner to plead guilty to a lesser-included offense, Possession of Gambling Records in the Second Degree, conviction of which would carry a maximum prison sentence of one year. The prosecutor agreed to make no recommendation as to the sentence.

On June 16, 1969, petitioner accordingly withdrew his plea of not guilty and entered a plea of guilty to the lesser charge. Petitioner represented to the sentencing judge that the plea was voluntary and that the facts of the case, as described by the Assistant District Attorney, were true. The court accepted the plea and set a date for sentencing. * * *

At [sentencing], another prosecutor had replaced the prosecutor who had negotiated the plea. The new prosecutor recommended the maximum one-year sentence. In making this recommendation, he cited petitioner's criminal record and alleged links with organized crime. Defense counsel immediately objected on the ground that the State had promised petitioner before the plea was entered that there would be no sentence recommendation by the prosecution. He sought to adjourn the sentence hearing in order to have time to prepare proof of the first prosecutor's promise. The second prosecutor, apparently ignorant of his colleague's commitment, argued that there was nothing in the record to support petitioner's claim of a promise, but the State, in subsequent proceedings, has not contested that such a promise was made.

The sentencing judge ended discussion, with the following statement, quoting extensively from the pre-sentence report:

> Mr. Aronstein (Defense Counsel), I am not at all influenced by what the District Attorney says, so that there is no need to adjourn the sentence, and there is no need to have any testimony. It doesn't make a particle of difference what the District Attorney says he will do, or what he [won't] do.
>
> I have here, Mr. Aronstein, a probation report. I have here a history of a long, long serious criminal record. I have here a picture of the life history of this man. . . .
>
> "He is unamenable to supervision in the community. He is a professional criminal." This is in quotes. "And a recidivist. Institutionalization—"; that means, in plain language, just putting him away, "is the only means of halting his anti-social activities," and protecting you, your family, me, my family, protecting society. "Institutionalization." Plain language, put him behind bars.
>
> Under the plea, I can only send him to the New York City Correctional Institution for men for one year, which I am hereby doing.

The judge then imposed the maximum sentence of one year. * * *

This record represents another example of an unfortunate lapse in orderly prosecutorial procedures, in part, no doubt, because of the enormous increase in the workload of the often understaffed prosecutor's offices. The heavy workload may well explain these episodes, but it does not excuse them. The disposition of criminal charges by agreement between the prosecutor and the accused, sometimes loosely called "plea bargaining," is an essential component of the administration of justice. Properly administered, it is to be encouraged. If every criminal charge were subjected to a full-scale trial, the States and the Federal Government would need to multiply by many times the number of judges and court facilities.

Disposition of charges after plea discussions is not only an essential part of the process but a highly desirable part for many reasons. It leads to prompt and largely final disposition of most criminal cases; it avoids much of the corrosive impact of enforced idleness during pre-trial confinement for those who are denied release pending trial; it protects the public from those accused persons who are prone to continue criminal conduct even while on pretrial release; and, by shortening the time between charge and disposition, it enhances whatever may be the rehabilitative prospects of the guilty when they are ultimately imprisoned.

However, all of these considerations presuppose fairness in securing agreement between an accused and a prosecutor. * * * [A] constant factor is that when a plea rests in any significant degree on a promise or agreement of the prosecutor, so that it can be said to be part of the inducement or consideration, such promise must be fulfilled.

On this record, petitioner "bargained" and negotiated for a particular plea in order to secure dismissal of more serious charges, but also on condition that no sentence recommendation would be made by the prosecutor. It is now conceded that the promise to abstain from a recommendation was made, and at this stage the prosecution is not in a good position to argue that its inadvertent breach of agreement is immaterial. The staff lawyers in a prosecutor's office have the burden of "letting the left hand know what the right hand is doing" or has done. That the breach of agreement was inadvertent does not lessen its impact.

* * * [W]e conclude that the interests of justice and appropriate recognition of the duties of the prosecution in relation to promises made in the negotiation of pleas of guilty will be best served by remanding the case to the state courts for further consideration. The ultimate relief to which petitioner is entitled we leave to the discretion of the state court, which is in a better position to decide whether the circumstances of this case require only that there be specific performance of the agreement on the plea, in which case petitioner should be resentenced by a different judge, or whether, in the view of the state court, the circumstances require granting the relief sought by petitioner, i.e., the opportunity to withdraw his plea of guilty. * * *

The judgment is vacated and the case is remanded for reconsideration not inconsistent with this opinion.

JUSTICE DOUGLAS, concurring.

* * * [I]t is * * * clear that a prosecutor's promise may deprive a guilty plea of the "character of a voluntary act." The decisions of this Court have not spelled out what sorts of promises by prosecutors tend to be coercive,

but in order to assist appellate review in weighing promises in light of all the circumstances, all trial courts are now required to interrogate the defendants who enter guilty pleas so that the waiver of these fundamental rights will affirmatively appear in the record. The lower courts, however, have uniformly held that a prisoner is entitled to some form of relief when he shows that the prosecutor reneged on his sentencing agreement made in connection with a plea bargain, most jurisdictions preferring vacation of the plea on the ground of "involuntariness," while a few permit only specific enforcement.

* * * In choosing a remedy, however, a court ought to accord a defendant's preference considerable, if not controlling, weight inasmuch as the fundamental rights flouted by a prosecutor's breach of a plea bargain are those of the defendant, not of the State.

JUSTICE MARSHALL, with whom JUSTICE BRENNAN and JUSTICE STEWART join, concurring in part and dissenting in part.

I agree with much of the majority's opinion, but conclude that petitioner must be permitted to withdraw his guilty plea. This is the relief petitioner requested and, on the facts set out by the majority, it is a form of relief to which he is entitled.

* * * When a prosecutor breaks [a plea] bargain, he undercuts the basis for the waiver of constitutional rights implicit in the plea. This, it seems to me, provides the defendant ample justification for rescinding the plea. Where a promise is "unfulfilled," *Brady v. United States* specifically denies that the plea "must stand." Of course, where the prosecutor has broken the plea agreement, it may be appropriate to permit the defendant to enforce the plea bargain. But that is not the remedy sought here. Rather, it seems to me that a breach of the plea bargain provides ample reason to permit the plea to be vacated. * * *

MABRY V. JOHNSON

Supreme Court of the United States
467 U.S. 504, 104 S. Ct. 2543, 81 L. Ed. 2d 437 (1984)

JUSTICE STEVENS delivered the opinion of the Court.

The question presented is whether a defendant's acceptance of a prosecutor's proposed plea bargain creates a constitutional right to have the bargain specifically enforced.

In the late evening of May 22, 1970, three members of a family returned home to find a burglary in progress. Shots were exchanged resulting in the daughter's death and the wounding of the father and respondent—one of the burglars. Respondent was tried and convicted on three charges: burglary, assault, and murder. The murder conviction was set aside by the Arkansas Supreme Court. Thereafter, plea negotiations ensued.

At the time of the negotiations respondent was serving his concurrent 21- and 12-year sentences on the burglary and assault convictions. On Friday, October 27, 1972, a deputy prosecutor proposed to respondent's attorney that in exchange for a plea of guilty to the charge of accessory after a felony murder, the prosecutor would recommend a sentence of 21 years to be served concurrently with the burglary and assault sentences. On the following day, counsel communicated the offer to respondent who agreed to accept it. On the next Monday the lawyer called the prosecutor "and communicated [respondent's] acceptance of the offer." The prosecutor then told counsel that a mistake had been made and withdrew the offer. He proposed instead that in exchange for a guilty plea he would recommend a sentence of 21 years to be served consecutively to respondent's other sentences.

Respondent rejected the new offer and elected to stand trial. On the second day of trial, the judge declared a mistrial and plea negotiations resumed, ultimately resulting in respondent's acceptance of the prosecutor's second offer. In accordance with the plea bargain, the state trial judge imposed a 21-year sentence to be served consecutively to the previous sentences.

After exhausting his state remedies, respondent filed a petition for a writ of habeas corpus * * *. The District Court dismissed the petition, finding that respondent had understood the consequences of his guilty plea, that he had received the effective assistance of counsel, and that because the evidence did not establish that respondent had detrimentally relied on the prosecutor's first proposed plea agreement, respondent had no right to enforce it. The Court of Appeals reversed * * *. The majority concluded that "fairness" precluded the prosecution's withdrawal of a plea proposal once accepted by respondent. * * * [W]e granted certiorari. We now reverse. * * *

It is well settled that a voluntary and intelligent plea of guilty made by an accused person, who has been advised by competent counsel, may not be collaterally attacked. It is also well settled that plea agreements are consistent with the requirements of voluntariness and intelligence—because each side may obtain advantages when a guilty plea is exchanged for sentencing concessions, the agreement is no less voluntary than any other bargained-for exchange. It is only when the consensual character of the plea is called into question that the validity of a guilty plea may be impaired. In *Brady v. United States*, we stated the applicable standard:

> [A] plea of guilty entered by one fully aware of the direct consequences, including the actual value of any commitments made to him by the court, prosecutor, or his own counsel, must stand unless induced by threats (or promises to discontinue

improper harassment), misrepresentation (including unfulfilled or unfulfillable promises), or perhaps by promises that are by their nature improper as having no proper relationship to the prosecutor's business (e.g. bribes).

Thus, only when it develops that the defendant was not fairly apprised of its consequences can his plea be challenged under the Due Process Clause. * * * [T]he conditions for a valid plea "presuppose fairness in securing agreement between an accused and a prosecutor.... The plea must, of course, be voluntary and knowing and if it was induced by promises, the essence of those promises must in some way be made known." It follows that when the prosecution breaches its promise with respect to an executed plea agreement, the defendant pleads guilty on a false premise, and hence his conviction cannot stand.

* * * Respondent's plea was in no sense induced by the prosecutor's withdrawn offer. * * * [A]t the time respondent pleaded guilty he knew the prosecution would recommend a 21-year consecutive sentence. Respondent * * * pleaded guilty with the advice of competent counsel and with full awareness of the consequences—he knew that the prosecutor would recommend and that the judge could impose the sentence now under attack. Respondent's plea was thus in no sense the product of governmental deception; it rested on no "unfulfilled promise" and fully satisfied the test for voluntariness and intelligence.

Thus, because it did not impair the voluntariness or intelligence of his guilty plea, respondent's inability to enforce the prosecutor's offer is without constitutional significance. Neither is the question whether the prosecutor was negligent or otherwise culpable in first making and then withdrawing his offer relevant. The Due Process Clause is not a code of ethics for prosecutors; its concern is with the manner in which persons are deprived of their liberty. Here respondent was not deprived of his liberty in any fundamentally unfair way. Respondent was fully aware of the likely consequences when he pleaded guilty; it is not unfair to expect him to live with those consequences now.

The judgment of the Court of Appeals is

Reversed.

UNITED STATES v. RUIZ

Supreme Court of the United States
536 U.S. 622, 122 S. Ct. 2450, 153 L. Ed. 2d 586 (2002)

JUSTICE BREYER delivered the opinion of the Court. * * *

After immigration agents found 30 kilograms of marijuana in Angela Ruiz's luggage, federal prosecutors offered her what is known in the Southern District of California as a "fast track" plea bargain. That bargain—standard in that district—asks a defendant to waive indictment, trial, and an appeal. In return, the Government agrees to recommend to the sentencing judge a two-level departure downward from the otherwise applicable United States Sentencing Guidelines sentence. In Ruiz's case, a two-level departure downward would have shortened the ordinary Guidelines-specified 18-to-24-month sentencing range by 6 months, to 12-to-18 months.

The prosecutors' proposed plea agreement * * * specifies that "any [known] information establishing the factual innocence of the defendant" "has been turned over to the defendant" and it acknowledges the Government's "continuing duty to provide such information." At the same time it require[s] that the defendant "waiv[e] the right" to receive "impeachment information relating to any informants or other witnesses" as well as the right to receive information supporting any affirmative defense the defendant raises if the case goes to trial. Because Ruiz would not agree to this last-mentioned waiver, the prosecutors withdrew their bargaining offer. The Government then indicted Ruiz for unlawful drug possession. And despite the absence of any agreement, Ruiz ultimately pleaded guilty.

At sentencing, Ruiz asked the judge to grant her the same two-level downward departure that the Government would have recommended had she accepted the "fast track" agreement. The Government opposed her request, and the District Court denied it, imposing a standard Guideline sentence instead.

* * * Ruiz appealed her sentence to the United States Court of Appeals for the Ninth Circuit. The Ninth Circuit vacated the District Court's sentencing determination. The Ninth Circuit pointed out that the Constitution requires prosecutors to make certain impeachment information available to a defendant before trial. It decided that this obligation entitles defendants to receive that same information before they enter into a plea agreement. The Ninth Circuit also decided that the Constitution prohibits defendants from waiving their right to that information. And it held that the prosecutors' standard "fast track" plea agreement was unlawful because it insisted upon that waiver. * * *

When a defendant pleads guilty he or she, of course, forgoes not only a fair trial, but also other accompanying constitutional guarantees. Given the seriousness of the matter, the Constitution insists, among other things, that the defendant enter a guilty plea that is "voluntary" and that the defendant must make related waivers "knowing[ly], intelligent[ly], [and] with sufficient awareness of the relevant circumstances and likely consequences."

In this case, the Ninth Circuit in effect held that a guilty plea is not "voluntary" (and that the defendant could not, by pleading guilty, waive her right to a fair trial) unless the prosecutors first made the same disclosure of material impeachment information that the prosecutors would have had to make had the defendant insisted upon a trial. We must decide whether the Constitution requires that preguilty plea disclosure of impeachment information. We conclude that it does not.

First, impeachment information is special in relation to the fairness of a trial, not in respect to whether a plea is voluntary ("knowing," "intelligent," and "sufficient[ly] aware"). Of course, the more information the defendant has, the more aware he is of the likely consequences of a plea, waiver, or decision, and the wiser that decision will likely be. But the Constitution does not require the prosecutor to share all useful information with the defendant. And the law ordinarily considers a waiver knowing, intelligent, and sufficiently aware if the defendant fully understands the nature of the right and how it would likely apply in general in the circumstances—even though the defendant may not know the specific detailed consequences of invoking it. A defendant, for example, may waive his right to remain silent, his right to a jury trial, or his right to counsel even if the defendant does not know the specific questions the authorities intend to ask, who will likely serve on the jury, or the particular lawyer the State might otherwise provide. * * *

Second, we have found no legal authority embodied either in this Court's past cases or in cases from other circuits that provides significant support for the Ninth Circuit's decision. To the contrary, this Court has found that the Constitution, in respect to a defendant's awareness of relevant circumstances, does not require complete knowledge of the relevant circumstances, but permits a court to accept a guilty plea, with its accompanying waiver of various constitutional rights, despite various forms of misapprehension under which a defendant might labor. * * *

Third, due process considerations, the very considerations that led this Court to find trial-related rights to exculpatory and impeachment information in *Brady* and *Giglio*, argue against the existence of the "right" that the Ninth Circuit found here. * * * Here, * * * the added value of the Ninth Circuit's "right" to a defendant is often limited, for it depends upon the defendant's independent awareness of the details of the Government's case. And in any case, as the proposed plea agreement at issue here specifies, the Government will provide "any information establishing the factual innocence of the defendant" regardless. That fact, along with other guilty-plea safeguards, * * * diminishes the force of Ruiz's concern that, in the absence of impeachment information, innocent individuals, accused of crimes, will plead guilty. * * *

At the same time, a constitutional obligation to provide impeachment information during plea bargaining, prior to entry of a guilty plea, could seriously interfere with the Government's interest in securing those guilty pleas that are factually justified, desired by defendants, and help to secure the efficient administration of justice. The Ninth Circuit's rule risks premature disclosure of Government witness information, which, the Government tells us, could "disrupt ongoing investigations" and expose prospective witnesses to serious harm. * * *

Consequently, the Ninth Circuit's requirement could force the Government to abandon its "general practice" of not "disclos[ing] to a defendant pleading guilty information that would reveal the identities of cooperating informants, undercover investigators, or other prospective witnesses."[a] It could require the Government to devote substantially more resources to trial preparation prior to plea bargaining, thereby depriving the plea-bargaining process of its main resource-saving advantages. Or it could lead the Government instead to abandon its heavy reliance upon plea bargaining in a vast number—90% or more—of federal criminal cases. We cannot say that the Constitution's due process requirement demands so radical a change in the criminal justice process in order to achieve so comparatively small a constitutional benefit.

These considerations, taken together, lead us to conclude that the Constitution does not require the Government to disclose material impeachment evidence prior to entering a plea agreement with a criminal defendant.

For these reasons the judgment of the Court of Appeals for the Ninth Circuit is

Reversed.

[JUSTICE THOMAS' concurring opinion has been omitted.]

BOYKIN V. ALABAMA

Supreme Court of the United States
395 U.S. 238, 89 S. Ct. 1709, 23 L. Ed. 2d 274 (1969)

JUSTICE DOUGLAS delivered the opinion of the Court.

In the spring of 1966, within the period of a fortnight, a series of armed robberies occurred in Mobile, Alabama. The victims, in each case, were local shopkeepers open at night who were forced by a gunman to hand over money. While robbing one grocery store, the assailant fired his gun once, sending a bullet through a door into the ceiling. A few days earlier in a drugstore, the robber had allowed his gun to discharge in such a way that

---

[a] In *Roviaro v. United States*, 353 U.S. 53 (1957), the Supreme Court acknowledged the Government's privilege to withhold from disclosure the identity of persons who furnish information to law enforcement officers but noted that this privilege is limited. The Court explained that "[w]here the disclosure of an informer's identity, or of the contents of his communication, is relevant and helpful to the defense of an accused, or is essential to a fair determination of a cause, the privilege must give way." *Id.* at 60–61. "In these situations the trial court may require disclosure and, if the Government withholds the information, dismiss the action." *Id.*

the bullet, on ricochet from the floor, struck a customer in the leg. Shortly thereafter, a local grand jury returned five indictments against petitioner, a 27-year-old Negro, for commonlaw robbery—an offense punishable in Alabama by death.[a]

Before the matter came to trial, the court determined that petitioner was indigent and appointed counsel to represent him. Three days later, at his arraignment, petitioner pleaded guilty to all five indictments. So far as the record shows, the judge asked no questions of petitioner concerning his plea, and petitioner did not address the court.

Trial strategy may of course make a plea of guilty seem the desirable course. But the record is wholly silent on that point and throws no light on it.

Alabama provides that when a defendant pleads guilty, "the court must cause the punishment to be determined by a jury" (except where it is required to be fixed by the court) and may "cause witnesses to be examined, to ascertain the character of the offense." In the present case a trial of that dimension was held, the prosecution presenting its case largely through eyewitness testimony. Although counsel for petitioner engaged in cursory cross-examination, petitioner neither testified himself nor presented testimony concerning his character and background. There was nothing to indicate that he had a prior criminal record.

In instructing the jury, the judge stressed that petitioner had pleaded guilty in five cases of robbery, defined as "the felonious taking of money * * * from another against his will * * * by violence or by putting him in fear * * * (carrying) from ten years minimum in the penitentiary to the supreme penalty of death by electrocution." The jury, upon deliberation, found petitioner guilty and sentenced him severally to die on each of the five indictments.

It was error, plain on the face of the record, for the trial judge to accept petitioner's guilty plea without an affirmative showing that it was intelligent and voluntary.

A plea of guilty is more than a confession which admits that the accused did various acts; it is itself a conviction; nothing remains but to give judgment and determine punishment. Admissibility of a confession must be based on a "reliable determination on the voluntariness issue which satisfies the constitutional rights of the defendant." The requirement that the prosecution spread on the record the prerequisites of a valid waiver is no constitutional innovation. In *Carnley v. Cochran*, we dealt with a problem of waiver of the right to counsel, a Sixth Amendment right. We

---

[a] At the time this case was decided, robbery was a capital crime in Alabama. Leonard D. Savitz, *Capital Crimes as Defined in American Statutory Law*, 46 J. CRIM. L. & CRIMINOLOGY 355, 358–59 (1955). Today, robbery is no longer a capital offense in Alabama. *See* ALA. CODE § 13A–5–40 (not listing robbery as an aggravating circumstance for a capital offense in Alabama).

held: "Presuming waiver from a silent record is impermissible. The record must show, or there must be an allegation and evidence which show, that an accused was offered counsel but intelligently and understandingly rejected the offer. Anything less is not waiver."

We think that the same standard must be applied to determining whether a guilty plea is voluntarily made. For, as we have said, a plea of guilty is more than an admission of conduct; it is a conviction. Ignorance, incomprehension, coercion, terror, inducements, subtle or blatant threats might be a perfect cover-up of unconstitutionality. * * *

Several federal constitutional rights are involved in a waiver that takes place when a plea of guilty is entered in a state criminal trial. First, is the privilege against compulsory self-incrimination guaranteed by the Fifth Amendment and applicable to the States by reason of the Fourteenth. Second, is the right to trial by jury. Third, is the right to confront one's accusers. We cannot presume a waiver of these three important federal rights from a silent record.

What is at stake for an accused facing death or imprisonment demands the utmost solicitude of which courts are capable in canvassing the matter with the accused to make sure he has a full understanding of what the plea connotes and of its consequence. When the judge discharges that function, he leaves a record adequate for any review that may be later sought, and forestalls the spin-off of collateral proceedings that seek to probe murky memories.

The three dissenting justices in the Alabama Supreme Court stated the law accurately when they concluded that there was reversible error "because the record does not disclose that the defendant voluntarily and understandingly entered his pleas of guilty."

Reversed.

JUSTICE HARLAN, whom JUSTICE BLACK joins, dissenting.

The Court today holds that petitioner Boykin was denied due process of law, and that his robbery convictions must be reversed outright, solely because "the record (is) inadequate to show that petitioner * * * intelligently and knowingly pleaded guilty." * * * [T]he Court does all this at the behest of a petitioner who has never at any time alleged that his guilty plea was involuntary or made without knowledge of the consequences. I cannot possibly subscribe to so bizarre a result. * * *

HENDERSON V. MORGAN
Supreme Court of the United States
426 U.S. 637, 96 S. Ct. 2253, 49 L. Ed. 2d 108 (1976)

JUSTICE STEVENS delivered the opinion of the Court.

The question presented is whether a defendant may enter a voluntary plea of guilty to a charge of second-degree murder without being informed that intent to cause the death of the victim was an element of the offense.

* * * Respondent, having been indicted on a charge of first-degree murder, pleaded guilty to second-degree murder and [in 1965] was sentenced to an indeterminate term of imprisonment of 25 years to life. * * *

In 1970, respondent initiated proceedings * * * seeking to have his conviction vacated on the ground that his plea of guilty was involuntary. * * * He alleged that his guilty plea was involuntary because [among other things] he was not aware * * * that intent to cause death was an element of the offense. * * * [T]he Federal District Court denied relief. The Court of Appeals reversed summarily and directed the District Court "to conduct an evidentiary hearing on the issues raised by petitioner, including whether, at the time of his entry of his guilty plea, he was aware that intent was an essential element of the crime and was advised of the scope of the punishment that might be imposed." * * *

At the conclusion of the hearing, the District Court * * * found that respondent "was not advised by counsel or court, at any time, that an intent to cause the death or a design to effect the death of the victim was an essential element of Murder 2nd degree." On the basis of the latter finding, the District Court held "as a matter of law" that the plea of guilty was involuntary and had to be set aside. This holding was affirmed, without opinion, by the Court of Appeals.

Before addressing the question whether the District Court correctly held the plea invalid as a matter of law, we review some of the facts developed at the evidentiary hearing.

On April 6, 1965, respondent killed Mrs. Ada Francisco in her home. When he was in seventh grade, respondent was committed to the Rome State School for Mental Defectives where he was classified as "retarded." He was released to become a farm laborer and ultimately went to work on Mrs. Francisco's farm. Following an argument, she threatened to return him to state custody. He then decided to abscond. During the night he entered Mrs. Francisco's bedroom with a knife, intending to collect his earned wages before leaving; she awoke, began to scream, and he stabbed her. He took a small amount of money, fled in her car, and became involved in an accident about 80 miles away. The knife was found in the glove compartment of her car. He was promptly arrested and made a statement to the police. He was then 19 years old and substantially below average intelligence.

Respondent was indicted for first-degree murder and arraigned on April 15, 1965. Two concededly competent attorneys were appointed to represent him. The indictment, which charged that he "willfully" stabbed his victim, was read in open court. * * *

Respondent was found competent to stand trial. Defense counsel held a series of conferences with the prosecutors, with the respondent, and with members of his family. The lawyers "thought manslaughter first would satisfy the needs of justice." They therefore endeavored to have the charge reduced to manslaughter, but the prosecution would agree to nothing less than second-degree murder and a minimum sentence of 25 years. The lawyers gave respondent advice about the different sentences which could be imposed for the different offenses, but, as the District Court found, did not explain the required element of intent.

On June 8, 1965, respondent appeared in court with his attorneys and entered a plea of guilty to murder in the second degree in full satisfaction of the first-degree murder charge made in the indictment. In direct colloquy with the trial judge respondent stated that his plea was based on the advice of his attorneys, that he understood he was accused of killing Mrs. Francisco in Fulton County, that he was waiving his right to a jury trial, and that he would be sent to prison. There was no discussion of the elements of the offense of second-degree murder, no indication that the nature of the offense had ever been discussed with respondent, and no reference of any kind to the requirement of intent to cause the death of the victim.

At the sentencing hearing a week later his lawyers made a statement explaining his version of the offense, particularly noting that respondent "meant no harm to that lady" when he entered her room with the knife. The prosecutor disputed defense counsel's version of the matter, but did not discuss it in detail. After studying the probation officer's report, the trial judge pronounced sentence.

At the evidentiary hearing in the Federal District Court, respondent testified that he would not have pleaded guilty if he had known that an intent to cause the death of his victim was an element of the offense of second-degree murder.

* * * [A] plea cannot support a judgment of guilt unless it was voluntary in a constitutional sense. And clearly the plea could not be voluntary in the sense that it constituted an intelligent admission that he committed the offense unless the defendant received "real notice of the true nature of the charge against him, the first and most universally recognized requirement of due process."

The charge of second-degree murder was never formally made. Had it been made, it necessarily would have included a charge that respondent's assault was "committed with a design to effect the death of the person killed." * * * [A]n admission by respondent that he killed Mrs. Francisco does not necessarily also admit that he was guilty of second-degree murder.

There is nothing in this record that can serve as a substitute for either a finding after trial, or a voluntary admission, that respondent had the requisite intent. Defense counsel did not purport to stipulate to that fact; they did not explain to him that his plea would be an admission of that fact; and he made no factual statement or admission necessarily implying that he had such intent. In these circumstances it is impossible to conclude that his plea to the unexplained charge of second-degree murder was voluntary.

Petitioner argues that affirmance of the Court of Appeals will invite countless collateral attacks on judgments entered on pleas of guilty, since frequently the record will not contain a complete enumeration of the elements of the offense to which an accused person pleads guilty.[18] We think petitioner's fears are exaggerated.

Normally the record contains either an explanation of the charge by the trial judge, or at least a representation by defense counsel that the nature of the offense has been explained to the accused. Moreover, even without such an express representation, it may be appropriate to presume that in most cases defense counsel routinely explain the nature of the offense in sufficient detail to give the accused notice of what he is being asked to admit. This case is unique because the trial judge found as a fact that the element of intent was not explained to respondent. Moreover, respondent's unusually low mental capacity provides a reasonable explanation for counsel's oversight; it also forecloses the conclusion that the error was harmless beyond a reasonable doubt, for it lends at least a modicum of credibility to defense counsel's appraisal of the homicide as a manslaughter rather than a murder.

Since respondent did not receive adequate notice of the offense to which he pleaded guilty, his plea was involuntary and the judgment of conviction was entered without due process of law.

Affirmed.

JUSTICE REHNQUIST, with whom THE CHIEF JUSTICE joins, dissenting. * * *

Respondent was originally indicted for the crime of first-degree murder, and that indictment charged that in April 1965, he had "willfully,

---

[18] There is no need in this case to decide whether notice of the true nature, or substance, of a charge always requires a description of every element of the offense; we assume it does not. Nevertheless, intent is such a critical element of the offense of second-degree murder that notice of that element is required.

feloniously and of malice aforethought, stabbed and cut Ada Francisco with a dangerous knife . . . and that thereafter . . . the said Ada Francisco died of said wounds and injuries, said killing being inexcusable and unjustifiable." Respondent's attorney at the habeas hearing testified that respondent had stabbed his victim "many times" which suggests that experienced counsel would not consider the "design to effect death" issue to be in serious dispute. The habeas judge, in deciding that there was a factual basis for the entry of the plea, took much the same approach when he observed:

> The Court: Well the intent, I think there is a factual basis from the evidence where it, that is the jury would have a right to infer on the mere fact, I think when he hit her first and then used the knife, that there were multiple knife wounds, that the jury could infer, and as a matter of fact, I think from those same facts the Judge would have to permit the jury to decide as a question of fact whether there was premeditation on first degree murder, so that this man was a long way short of being out of the woods.
>
> So I am satisfied that there was a factual basis for the entry of the plea.

I do not see how this Court, or any court, could conclude on this state of the record that respondent was not "properly advised" at the time he entered his plea of guilty to the charge of second-degree murder.

His attorneys were motivated by the eminently reasonable tactical judgment on their part that he should plead guilty to second-degree murder in order to avoid the possibility of conviction for first-degree murder with its more serious attendant penalties. Since the Court concedes both the competence of respondent's counsel and the wisdom of their advice, that should be the end of the matter. * * *

[JUSTICE WHITE's concurring opinion has been omitted.]

NORTH CAROLINA V. ALFORD
Supreme Court of the United States
400 U.S. 25, 91 S. Ct. 160, 27 L. Ed. 2d 162 (1970)

JUSTICE WHITE delivered the opinion of the Court.

On December 2, 1963, Alford was indicted for first-degree murder, a capital offense under North Carolina law. The court appointed an attorney to represent him, and this attorney questioned all but one of the various witnesses who appellee said would substantiate his claim of innocence. The witnesses, however, did not support Alford's story but gave statements that strongly indicated his guilt. Faced with strong evidence of guilt and no substantial evidentiary support for the claim of innocence. Alford's attorney recommended that he plead guilty, but left the ultimate decision to Alford himself. The prosecutor agreed to accept a plea of guilty to a charge of second-degree murder, and on December 10, 1963, Alford pleaded guilty to the reduced charge.

Before the plea was finally accepted by the trial court, the court heard the sworn testimony of a police officer who summarized the State's case. Two other witnesses besides Alford were also heard. Although there was no eyewitness to the crime, the testimony indicated that shortly before the killing Alford took his gun from his house, stated his intention to kill the victim, and returned home with the declaration that he had carried out the killing. After the summary presentation of the State's case, Alford took the stand and testified that he had not committed the murder but that he was pleading guilty because he faced the threat of the death penalty if he did not do so.[1] In response to the questions of his counsel, he acknowledged that his counsel had informed him of the difference between second-and first-degree murder and of his rights in case he chose to go to trial. The trial court then asked appellee if, in light of his denial of guilt, he still desired to plead guilty to second-degree murder and appellee answered, "Yes, sir. I plead guilty on—from the circumstances that he (Alford's attorney) told me." After eliciting information about Alford's prior criminal record, which was a long one, the trial court sentenced him to 30 years' imprisonment, the maximum penalty for second-degree murder.

Alford sought post-conviction relief in the state court. Among the claims raised was the claim that his plea of guilty was invalid because it was the product of fear and coercion. After a hearing, the state court * * * found that the plea was "willingly, knowingly, and understandingly" made on the advice of competent counsel and in the face of a strong prosecution case. * * * On appeal, a divided panel of the Court of Appeals for the Fourth Circuit reversed on the ground that Alford's guilty plea was made involuntarily. * * * [T]he Court of Appeals ruled that Alford's guilty plea

---

[1] After giving his version of the events of the night of the murder, Alford stated:

I pleaded guilty on second degree murder because they said there is too much evidence, but I ain't shot no man, but I take the fault for the other man. We never had an argument in our life and I just pleaded guilty because they said if I didn't they would gas me for it, and that is all.

In response to questions from his attorney, Alford affirmed that he had consulted several times with his attorney and with members of his family and had been informed of his rights if he chose to plead not guilty. Alford then reaffirmed his decision to plead guilty to second-degree murder:

Q. (by Alford's attorney). And you authorized me to tender a plea of guilty to second degree murder before the court?

A. Yes, sir.

Q. And in doing that, that you have again affirmed your decision on that point?

A. Well, I'm still pleading that you all got me to plead guilty. I plead the other way, circumstantial evidence; that the jury will prosecute me on—on the second. You told me to plead guilty, right. I don't—I'm not guilty but I plead guilty.

was involuntary because its principal motivation was fear of the death penalty. * * *

We held in *Brady v. United States*, that a plea of guilty which would not have been entered except for the defendant's desire to avoid a possible death penalty and to limit the maximum penalty to life imprisonment or a term of years was not for that reason compelled. * * * The standard was and remains whether the plea represents a voluntary and intelligent choice among the alternative courses of action open to the defendant. That he would not have pleaded except for the opportunity to limit the possible penalty does not necessarily demonstrate that the plea of guilty was not the product of a free and rational choice, especially where the defendant was represented by competent counsel whose advice was that the plea would be to the defendant's advantage. The standard fashioned and applied by the Court of Appeals was therefore erroneous and we would, without more, vacate and remand the case for further proceedings with respect to any other claims of Alford which are properly before that court, if it were not for other circumstances appearing in the record which might seem to warrant an affirmance of the Court of Appeals.

As previously recounted, after Alford's plea of guilty was offered and the State's case was placed before the judge, Alford denied that he had committed the murder but reaffirmed his desire to plead guilty to avoid a possible death sentence and to limit the penalty to the 30-year maximum provided for second-degree murder. Ordinarily, a judgment of conviction resting on a plea of guilty is justified by the defendant's admission that he committed the crime charged against him and his consent that judgment be entered without a trial of any kind. The plea usually subsumes both elements, and justifiably so, even though there is no separate, express admission by the defendant that he committed the particular acts claimed to constitute the crime charged in the indictment. Here Alford entered his plea but accompanied it with the statement that he had not shot the victim.

If Alford's statements were to be credited as sincere assertions of his innocence, there obviously existed a factual and legal dispute between him and the State. Without more, it might be argued that the conviction entered on his guilty plea was invalid, since his assertion of innocence negatived any admission of guilt, which, as we observed last Term in *Brady*, is normally "[c]entral to the plea and the foundation for entering judgment against the defendant." * * *

State and lower federal courts are divided upon whether a guilty plea can be accepted when it is accompanied by protestations of innocence and hence contains only a waiver of trial but no admission of guilt. Some courts, giving expression to the principle that "[o]ur law only authorizes a conviction where guilt is shown," require that trial judges reject such pleas. But others have concluded that * * * "[a]n accused, though believing in or entertaining doubts respecting his innocence, might reasonably conclude a jury would be convinced of his guilt and that he would fare better in the sentence by pleading guilty."

* * * The fact that [Alford's] plea was denominated a plea of guilty rather than a plea of nolo contendere is of no constitutional significance with respect to the issue now before us, for the Constitution is concerned with the practical consequences, not the formal categorizations, of state law. Thus, while most pleas of guilty consist of both a waiver of trial and an express admission of guilt, the latter element is not a constitutional requisite to the imposition of criminal penalty. An individual accused of crime may voluntarily, knowingly, and understandingly consent to the imposition of a prison sentence even if he is unwilling or unable to admit his participation in the acts constituting the crime.

Nor can we perceive any material difference between a plea that refuses to admit commission of the criminal act and a plea containing a protestation of innocence when, as in the instant case, a defendant intelligently concludes that his interests require entry of a guilty plea and the record before the judge contains strong evidence of actual guilt. Here the State had a strong case of first-degree murder against Alford. Whether he realized or disbelieved his guilt, he insisted on his plea because in his view he had absolutely nothing to gain by a trial and much to gain by pleading. Because of the overwhelming evidence against him, a trial was precisely what neither Alford nor his attorney desired. Confronted with the choice between a trial for first-degree murder, on the one hand, and a plea of guilty to second-degree murder, on the other, Alford quite reasonably chose the latter and thereby limited the maximum penalty to a 30-year term. When his plea is viewed in light of the evidence against him, which substantially negated his claim of innocence and which further provided a means by which the judge could test whether the plea was being intelligently entered, its validity cannot be seriously questioned. In view of the strong factual basis for the plea demonstrated by the State and Alford's clearly expressed desire to enter it despite his professed belief in his innocence, we hold that the trial judge did not commit constitutional error in accepting it. * * *

The Court of Appeals for the Fourth Circuit was in error to find Alford's plea of guilty invalid because it was made to avoid the possibility of the death penalty. That court's judgment directing the issuance of the writ of habeas corpus is vacated and the case is remanded to the Court of Appeals for further proceedings consistent with this opinion.

It is so ordered.

Vacated and remanded.

JUSTICE BRENNAN, with whom JUSTICE DOUGLAS and JUSTICE MARSHALL join, dissenting.

Last Term, this Court held, over my dissent, that a plea of guilty may validly be induced by an unconstitutional threat to subject the defendant to the risk to death, so long as the plea is entered in open court and the defendant is represented by competent counsel who is aware of the threat, albeit not of its unconstitutionality. Today the Court makes clear that its previous holding was intended to apply even when the record demonstrates that the actual effect of the unconstitutional threat was to induce a guilty plea from a defendant who was unwilling to admit his guilt.

I adhere to the view that, in any given case, the influence of such an unconstitutional threat "must necessarily be given weight in determining the voluntariness of a plea." And, without reaching the question whether due process permits the entry of judgment upon a plea of guilty accompanied by a contemporaneous denial of acts constituting the crime, I believe that at the very least such a denial of guilt is also a relevant factor in determining whether the plea was voluntarily and intelligently made. With these factors in mind, it is sufficient in my view to state that the facts set out in the majority opinion demonstrate that Alford was "so gripped by fear of the death penalty" that his decision to plead guilty was not voluntary but was "the product of duress as much so as choice reflecting physical constraint." Accordingly, I would affirm the judgment of the Court of Appeals.

[JUSTICE BLACK's concurring opinion has been omitted.]

NOTE

North Carolina v. Alford illustrates the dilemma that a trial court judge faces when a defendant pleads guilty while protesting his innocence. Such pleas are called *Alford* pleas. The ruling in *Alford* has been understood to require a strong factual basis supporting the entry of a judgment of conviction whenever a defendant claims to be innocent of the crime to which he is pleading guilty. In such cases, the record before the judge must contain "strong evidence of actual guilt."

Apart from the unique circumstances of an *Alford* plea, a factual basis for a guilty plea is not constitutionally required even though it may be required as a matter of statute or rule of criminal procedure. *See, e.g.,* FED. R. CRIM. P. 11(b) (requiring federal trial judges to satisfy themselves that there is a factual basis for a defendant's guilty plea before accepting defendant's plea and entering judgment).

THE ADVENT OF THE "VANISHING TRIAL": WHY TRIALS MATTER

John W. Keker
29-Oct Champion 32 (2005)

"The Vanishing Trial" has everyone's attention. That trials are increasingly an oddity is certain. One study found that in 2002, only 0.6 percent of civil cases filed went to trial, down from 1.8 percent in 1976. Data for criminal jury trials is just as extreme.

* * * Sustained now by the two most powerful courtroom patrons, [*i.e.*, judges and prosecutors], plea bargaining [has become] the dominant force in criminal procedure. * * *

No one puts it more bluntly than Chief Judge Young of Boston in *United States v. Green*:

> The Department [of Justice] is so addicted to plea bargaining to leverage its law enforcement resources to an overwhelming conviction rate that the focus of our entire criminal justice system has shifted far away from trials and juries and adjudication to a massive system of sentence bargaining that is heavily rigged against the accused citizen. * * *

So who cares if we are trying fewer cases? * * *

The first reason why trials matter is that more defendants would get off, which after all is our job. Try more cases, win more cases. Most acquittals occur because the prosecution makes a mistake, either in bringing the case or during trial of the case. Taking even "unwinnable" cases to trial often leads to surprising results. * * *

But * * * there are other equally important reasons we should try more cases, and challenge the government more. Probably the most obvious reason why trials matter is that without trials the law will not develop: trials provide the meat for appellate decisions. * * *

Judge Patrick Higginbotham gave a speech entitled "So Why Do We Still Call Them Trial Courts?" It is a good question. He concluded:

> Ultimately, law unenforced by courts is no law. We need trials, and a steady stream of them, to ground our normative standards—to make them sufficiently clear that persons can abide by them in planning their affairs—and never face the courthouse—the ultimate settlement. Trials reduce disputes, and it is a profound mistake to view a trial as a failure of the system. A well conducted trial is its crowning achievement.

Guilty pleas, on the other hand, create either no law, or bad law. * * * We have people pleading guilty to crimes they weren't aware they committed, in order to avoid the draconian penalty for going to trial. * * *

Our system of justice demands trials to work. We have a "battle model" of justice. Sometimes it leans towards "due process," as in the Warren Court years, and at other times it leans towards "efficiency," as it has under Chief Justices Burger and Rehnquist. But at heart the system is based on battle, usually called, in the quaint way of the English, "the adversarial system." It works on the premise that conflict and contradiction is the way to truth. * * *

Our prosecutors are trained to represent the state in the battle model. In our system, they need resisting, they need to be kept honest—indeed, in my opinion, they need to be kept humble. The only thing defense lawyers have to keep prosecutors in check is the threat that we will embarrass them by winning at trial. If they know we won't go to trial, we have nothing. One SEC lawyer told a colleague that the SEC in the old days would not bring a case unless it had at least a 70 percent chance of winning. Now, he said, SEC lawyers bring marginal cases if they think they have a 30 percent chance of winning, because they know their cases will settle without a trial.

Without trials, the jury system will atrophy; citizens will forget how to be jurors, forget that the government can be wrong. Jurors are already showing signs of forgetting. After several recent high profile white collar cases, jurors explained their guilty verdicts not with evidence or by the burden of proof but with speculation about what the defendant "must have known." Prosecutors urge them to substitute "common sense" for proof. This development, if it continues, is serious, not just to the legal system, but to democracy itself. * * *

Other countries find it simply astonishing that citizen jurors, not judges, decide who is guilty and who is not guilty. What they don't get is that it is not so much that jurors make great decisions, rather it is that they are not judges. Judges are bureaucrats, part of the system. As G. K. Chesterton said:

> The horrible thing about all legal officials, even the best . . . is not that they are wicked . . . not that they are stupid . . . it is simply that they have got used to it.

A little appreciated aspect of the Supreme Court's *Booker* decision is that it and its predecessors *Blakely*, *Apprendi* and *Ring* represent an increasingly loud endorsement by at least the conservative block of the importance of jury trials. For example, in *Blakely v. Washington*, the Court said the right to trial by jury "is no mere procedural formality, but a fundamental reservation of power in our constitutional structure. Just as suffrage ensures the people's ultimate control in the legislative and executive branches, jury trial is meant to ensure their control in the judiciary." * * *

Another virtue of trials over pleas is that trials are public, while most of what goes into a plea is not. The Rule 11 recital is ritual, not substance.

Someday during a plea I will do something I have always wanted to do. When the judge asks, "Have any promises or threats been made to you other than those recited here?" I will burst out laughing when the defendant answers as instructed. The honest answer is always "I am pleading guilty because I understand if I go to trial and lose you will give me four times the sentence, and that scares the [expletive] out of me."

Trials let light into the process, helping keep prosecutors honest, cops more honest, judges in check. Guilty pleas and deals occur behind closed doors, away from public scrutiny, where, as Lord Acton warned: "Everything secret degenerates, even the administration of justice." * * *

The last reason why trials matter, the one most dear to me, is that only frequent trials will guarantee the survival of the warrior class: defense counsel. Being a real, *i.e.*, adversarial, defense lawyer is hard. Fear stalks you. Before the trial starts in a tough case, we all feel like the guy who whines "Mom, I don't want to go to school today." His mother asks him "Why?" "The kids aren't nice to me and they all hate me." His mother says, "Well, you have to go to school." He says "Why?" She says, "Because you are 45 years old and the principal."

Trials are nasty and, yes, confrontational. You cannot try a case without suspecting the motives, even the integrity, of your opponent. The horror of defeat looms large. Opposing the government can be terrifying, particularly when you are friendly with, and probably belong to, the same associations as the prosecutors and the judges. Many of us can confront our enemies; few can stand the obloquy of friends. * * *

It takes courage to try difficult cases, ones we will probably lose. Recently in San Francisco two terrific young federal public defenders, Shawn Halbert and Rebecca Sullivan, tried a case I admired greatly. Their client was charged with illegal entry into the United States from Mexico. He had already pleaded guilty to the same offense twice before. It was a tough case, with a guideline range of 120–150 months. After some digging, Shawn and Rebecca figured out that their client had no idea where he was born (isn't our birth always a matter of hearsay) but that family members in Mexico believed it possible that the defendant's mother had been in the United States (illegally) at the time he was born. If that were true, he would be innocent. If there were a reasonable doubt about that, he deserved an acquittal. Unfortunately the jury found it less compelling than I did, and he was convicted. But the point is they tried the case, and made a real run of it.

Another personal example of why trials matter, and why defense lawyers should try more cases, arises out of the prosecution of my friend Patrick Hallinan. Patrick is a noted defense lawyer in San Francisco who my partner Jan Little and I defended on RICO, conspiracy and obstruction charges in federal court in Reno, Nevada. A Federal Drug task force there had been rolling up drug smugglers by means of "we will go light on you if you give us the next guy" for years. Scores of people had pled guilty. Hallinan represented one of the kingpins for a while, finally made a deal for him, and turned him over to the task force. The drug kingpin, having nowhere up to point, decided to offer the task force his defense lawyer and Patrick was indicted. These prosecutors had not tried a real case for years. They had forgotten how to evaluate a witness, they had forgotten what juries thought of the deals they made, and they had forgotten how offensive their tactics were. Patrick's trial, closely watched by the press, monitored by a stern, even-handed judge, was a debacle for prosecutors, as one witness after another was exposed as a lying dog. It took the jury just a few hours to acquit Patrick. But on paper, *i.e.*, reading the DEA's 6 reports, he never had a chance. * * *

TRIALS WITHOUT JUSTICE
Daniel Harawa
Inquest.org (Sept. 21, 2021)

Carissa Byrne Hessick's *Punishment Without Trial* paints a damning picture of plea bargaining. * * * Hessick, a law professor at the University of North Carolina at Chapel Hill, comprehensively explores plea bargaining's problems. As she details, it is a system of coercion and asymmetry where, for many defendants, the benefit of pleading guilty outweighs the downsides of going to trial. Deftly weaving in anecdotes, interviews, and statistics, Hessick walks through the pressure points of the plea-bargaining system that may impel a defendant—even one who is innocent—to plead guilty. * * *

Hessick's portrayal of a plea system that's out of control is compelling. The solution that Hessick identifies—more trials—is important, but also raises additional questions and concerns that should not be ignored. As Hessick explains, the problems with plea bargaining cut across racial lines, yet Black and Brown defendants have another question they must consider before standing on their trial rights—a question that white defendants can usually breeze past: How will their race affect trial? * * * Black and Brown defendants may plead guilty because they think (or know) that they will not get a fair trial because of their race. * * *

Take the heart-wrenching story of Damian Mills, which Hessick both opens and closes *Punishment* with. Damian pleaded guilty to a murder he did not commit and spent over a decade in prison before he was exonerated. At the end of the book, Hessick recalls asking Damian if he regretted pleading guilty to a crime he did not commit. Damian's answer surprised her: He only regretted not getting a better plea deal, because, in the end, he believed that if he went to trial, he would have lost. This answer haunted Hessick, prompting her to ponder how to fix the trial process to ensure people like Damian have more faith in the system. * * *

But I wasn't as surprised by Damian's answer. Damian was a Black man facing murder charges in a North Carolina county where white people ran law enforcement. North Carolina prosecutors designed a statewide training program on how to strike Black people from juries. Studies show that this training worked: North Carolina prosecutors were far more likely to strike Black North Carolinians than white North Carolinians and suffered no recourse. And just a few years before Damian's plea, an all-white jury in the same jurisdiction sentenced a Black teen to death. Perhaps Damian's belief that he would have been convicted at trial— perceptibly or imperceptibly—stemmed from a deep-seated fear that he could never overcome the overwhelming evidence that was the color of his skin. I was not shocked to read that a Black man accused of murder in the South was doubtful that he would get justice.

While plea bargaining may have its problems, there are several truths about the trial system that, without serious reform, may make trial an equally unappealing alternative for Black and Brown defendants caught in the system. These truths may help explain, on top of all the reasons Hessick lays out, why people of color plead guilty.

Truth 1: Black and Brown people are disproportionately excluded from juries. In jurisdictions across the country, from California to Mississippi, a jury of one's "peers" usually means a jury filled with white people. First, Black and Brown people are often underrepresented in the jury pool. This can be due to source issues: like using voting rolls to compile the pool despite Black and Brown people not being registered at the same rate as white people. Qualification issues: like the fact that many states have laws in place that disqualify people with felony convictions from jury service, disproportionately affecting people of color. Or burden issues: jury service is not compensated adequately, and therefore the needed sacrifice may be prohibitive for poor people, particularly poor people of color. Then, even if Black and Brown people make it into the pool, prosecutors routinely strike them at disproportionate rates, and the law has made it easy for them to get away with this rank discrimination.

If I were a poor Black or Brown defendant, I may think twice about going to trial knowing that few of my "peers" on the jury will look like me or identify with my life experiences.

Truth 2: People hold both explicit and implicit racial biases. A Black or Brown defendant may hesitate to go to trial and instead accept a plea because they also know that racism is real. Over the past few years, the number of hate crimes against Black, Latinx, and Asian Americans have soared. A recent survey also found that people think it is increasingly more common for people to express racist or racially insensitive views, and that it is increasingly more common for those views to be seen as acceptable. This is just explicit bias. Implicit biases are just as problematic, as studies reveal that darker skin is more often associated with dangerousness, violence, and a predisposition for criminality. Thus, for Black and Brown people, sitting in the courtroom just wearing their skin can trigger a viscerally negative response—either consciously or subconsciously—in many people.

If I were a poor Black or Brown defendant, I may think twice about going to trial knowing that my skin color would be on trial too.

Truth 3: It is hard to uncover—much less fix—racial bias in the jury system. Knowing racial bias is real, there is also the problem that it is challenging to uncover bias at trial. Moreover, even if racial bias is uncovered, it is hard to remedy. It is no secret that it is tough to effectively voir dire for racial bias, and court systems across the country have not adequately implemented comprehensive procedures to address implicit bias. Then, juries deliberate in secret, so even if jurors express their bias, it is extremely difficult to discover that fact. Beyond that, even if a juror's racial bias is uncovered, it is hard to get redress.

If I were a poor Black or Brown defendant, I may think twice about going to trial knowing that the trial mechanisms designed to keep the jury impartial are ineffective and at times allow bias to flourish.

Truth 4: Racial bias can affect the jury's view of the case. I would be especially reluctant to face an all-white or predominately white jury given that we know racial bias shades white jurors' perceptions. Studies show that white jurors are more likely to believe that a Black defendant is guilty than an identically situated white defendant. White jurors are more likely to view the prosecution's case as strong against a Black defendant and more likely to view a Black person's defense as weak. When it comes to Black defendants, white jurors are also more likely to focus on aggravating evidence while ignoring evidence that is mitigating. In addition, white jurors are more likely to recommend harsher punishment for Black defendants than white defendants.

If I were a poor Black or Brown defendant, I may think twice about going to trial knowing that my race may skew the jury's view of the case.

Truth 5: Judges punish Black and Brown people more harshly. When accepting a plea, defendants have some limited control over their sentence. But once a defendant proceeds to trial, the defendant is generally at the mercy of the judge. And studies show that judges sentence Black and Brown defendants more harshly than similarly situated white defendants.
* * *

If I were a poor Black or Brown defendant, I may think twice about going to trial knowing that my race may ultimately work to increase my punishment.

To be clear, I am sympathetic to Professor Hessick's call for more jury trials. In theory, I believe in the power of juries to help advance justice, which is why my scholarship aims to make them fairer. My belief in the potential of fair jury trials comes from my own professional experience. I was a public defender in a well-resourced office where lawyers were unafraid to take cases to trial and would often win. It was also a jurisdiction where juries were diverse, the white people were mostly "progressive," and the public defenders and their investigators were unrelenting. If I were a defendant in that jurisdiction (or a similar jurisdiction), depending on the strength of my case, I may readily take my chances and go to trial. * * *

If we have a plea problem in jurisdictions across the country, we have a trial problem, too. One reinforces the other. Until we fix both, defendants, especially Black and Brown defendants, will lose out no matter which route they choose. * * * Punishment without trials is no worse than trials without justice.

CHAPTER 28

THE RIGHT TO TRIAL BY JURY

■ ■ ■

The Sixth Amendment to the U.S. Constitution provides in relevant part:

> In all criminal prosecutions, the accused shall enjoy the right to a speedy and public trial, by an impartial jury of the State and district wherein the crime shall have been committed. . . .

In *Duncan v. Louisiana*, 391 U.S. 145 (1968), the Court held that the Sixth Amendment right to trial by jury in criminal cases is "fundamental to the American scheme of justice" and thus is applicable to the states through the Due Process Clause of the Fourteenth Amendment. This means there is a right to a jury trial in both federal and state court. *Blanton v. City of North Las Vegas* examines whether this right to a jury trial applies to all criminal defendants.

The next case, *Ramos v. Louisiana*, considers whether unanimity is constitutionally required for criminal trials in both state and federal court. The text of the Sixth Amendment does not mention unanimity, so the *Ramos* Court relies primarily on history to explain its decision. The Court spends little time talking about whether or how unanimity helps to ensure a fair and impartial trial by jury. To help us think about this important question, we include an excerpt from Kim Taylor Thompson's law review article, *Empty Votes in Jury Deliberation*, which suggests ways in which unanimous verdicts help protect the voices of racial minority and female jurors. *Singer v. United States* examines whether federal criminal defendants can unilaterally waive their right to a jury trial.

The remaining cases in this chapter explore race and gender considerations in the selection of jurors. In *Taylor v. Louisiana*, the Court examines whether a fair cross section requirement is part of the Sixth Amendment's guarantee of a fair and impartial trial by jury and the constitutionality of systematically excluding women from jury service. *Duren v. Missouri* outlines the requirements for a prima facie claim that the fair cross section requirement has been violated. *Turner v. Murray* focuses on whether and when a criminal defendant has the right to question prospective jurors on racial bias. *Batson v. Kentucky* and *J.E.B. v. Alabama* address race and gender discrimination in the selection of the petit jury.

BLANTON v. CITY OF NORTH LAS VEGAS
Supreme Court of the United States
489 U.S. 538, 109 S. Ct. 1289, 103 L. Ed. 2d 550 (1989)

JUSTICE MARSHALL delivered the opinion of the Court.

The issue in this case is whether there is a constitutional right to a trial by jury for persons charged under Nevada law with driving under the influence of alcohol (DUI). We hold that there is not.

DUI is punishable by a minimum term of two days' imprisonment and a maximum term of six months' imprisonment. Alternatively, a trial court may order the defendant "to perform 48 hours of work for the community while dressed in distinctive garb which identifies him as [a DUI offender]." The defendant also must pay a fine ranging from $200 to $1,000. In addition, the defendant automatically loses his driver's license for 90 days, and he must attend, at his own expense, an alcohol abuse education course. Repeat DUI offenders are subject to increased penalties.

Petitioners Melvin R. Blanton and Mark D. Fraley were charged with DUI in separate incidents. Neither petitioner had a prior DUI conviction. The North Las Vegas, Nevada, Municipal Court denied their respective pretrial demands for a jury trial. * * * We granted certiorari to consider whether petitioners were entitled to a jury trial, and now affirm.

It has long been settled that "there is a category of petty crimes or offenses which is not subject to the Sixth Amendment jury trial provision." In determining whether a particular offense should be categorized as "petty," our early decisions focused on the nature of the offense and on whether it was triable by a jury at common law. In recent years, however, we have sought more "objective indications of the seriousness with which society regards the offense." "[W]e have found the most relevant such criteria in the severity of the maximum authorized penalty." In fixing the maximum penalty for a crime, a legislature "include[s] within the definition of the crime itself a judgment about the seriousness of the offense." The judiciary should not substitute its judgment as to seriousness for that of a legislature, which is "far better equipped to perform the task, and [is] likewise more responsive to changes in attitude and more amenable to the recognition and correction of their misperceptions in this respect." In using the word "penalty," we do not refer solely to the maximum prison term authorized for a particular offense. A legislature's view of the seriousness of an offense also is reflected in the other penalties that it attaches to the offense. We thus examine "whether the length of the authorized prison term *or the seriousness of other punishment* is enough in itself to require a jury trial." Primary emphasis, however, must be placed on the maximum authorized period of incarceration. Penalties such as probation or a fine may engender "a significant infringement of personal freedom," but they cannot approximate in severity the loss of liberty that a prison term entails. Indeed, because incarceration is an "intrinsically different" form of punishment, it is the most powerful indication whether an offense is "serious."

Following this approach, our decision in *Baldwin* established that a defendant is entitled to a jury trial whenever the offense for which he is charged carries a maximum authorized prison term of greater than six months. The possibility of a sentence exceeding six months, we determined, is "sufficiently severe by itself" to require the opportunity for a jury trial. As for a prison term of six months or less, we recognized that it will seldom be viewed by the defendant as "trivial or petty." But we found that the disadvantages of such a sentence, "onerous though they may be, may be outweighed by the benefits that result from speedy and inexpensive nonjury adjudications."

Although we did not hold in *Baldwin* that an offense carrying a maximum prison term of six months or less automatically qualifies as a "petty" offense, and decline to do so today, we do find it appropriate to presume for purposes of the Sixth Amendment that society views such an offense as "petty." A defendant is entitled to a jury trial in such circumstances only if he can demonstrate that any additional statutory penalties, viewed in conjunction with the maximum authorized period of incarceration, are so severe that they clearly reflect a legislative determination that the offense in question is a "serious" one. This standard, albeit somewhat imprecise, should ensure the availability of a jury trial in the rare situation where a legislature packs an offense it deems "serious" with onerous penalties that nonetheless "do not puncture the 6-month incarceration line."

Applying these principles here, it is apparent that petitioners are not entitled to a jury trial. The maximum authorized prison sentence for first-time DUI offenders does not exceed six months. A presumption therefore exists that the Nevada Legislature views DUI as a "petty" offense for purposes of the Sixth Amendment. Considering the additional statutory penalties as well, we do not believe that the Nevada Legislature has clearly indicated that DUI is a "serious" offense.

In the first place, it is immaterial that a first-time DUI offender may face a minimum term of imprisonment. In settling on six months' imprisonment as the constitutional demarcation point, we have assumed that a defendant convicted of the offense in question would receive the *maximum* authorized prison sentence. It is not constitutionally determinative, therefore, that a particular defendant may be required to serve some amount of jail time *less* than six months. Likewise, it is of little moment that a defendant may receive the maximum prison term because of the prohibitions on plea bargaining and probation. As for the 90-day license suspension, it, too, will be irrelevant if it runs concurrently with the prison sentence, which we assume for present purposes to be the maximum of six months.

We are also unpersuaded by the fact that, instead of a prison sentence, a DUI offender may be ordered to perform 48 hours of community service dressed in clothing identifying him as a DUI offender. Even assuming the outfit is the source of some embarrassment during the 48-hour period, such a penalty will be less embarrassing and less onerous than six months in jail. As for the possible $1,000 fine, it is well below the $5,000 level set by Congress in its most recent definition of a "petty" offense, and petitioners do not suggest that this congressional figure is out of step with state practice for offenses carrying prison sentences of six months or less. Finally, we ascribe little significance to the fact that a DUI offender faces increased penalties for repeat offenses. Recidivist penalties of the magnitude imposed for DUI are commonplace and, in any event, petitioners do not face such penalties here.

Viewed together, the statutory penalties are not so severe that DUI must be deemed a "serious" offense for purposes of the Sixth Amendment. It was not error, therefore, to deny petitioners jury trials. Accordingly, the judgment of the Supreme Court of Nevada is

Affirmed.

NOTE

What if a defendant is charged with multiple petty offenses and the maximum authorized penalty for all of the offenses added together would exceed 6 months if served consecutively? Would such a defendant have a right to a jury trial? In *Lewis v. United States*, 518 U.S. 322 (1996), the Supreme Court answered this question in the negative, holding there is no Sixth Amendment right to a trial by jury unless the defendant is charged with at least one non-petty offense. The next case examines whether unanimous verdicts are constitutionally required in both state and federal criminal trials.

RAMOS V. LOUISIANA
Supreme Court of the United States
590 U.S. ___, 140 S. Ct. 1390; 206 L. Ed. 2d 583 (2020)

JUSTICE GORSUCH announced the judgment of the Court and delivered the opinion of the Court.

Accused of a serious crime, Evangelisto Ramos insisted on his innocence and invoked his right to a jury trial. Eventually, 10 jurors found the evidence against him persuasive. But a pair of jurors believed that the State of Louisiana had failed to prove Mr. Ramos's guilt beyond reasonable doubt; they voted to acquit.

In 48 States and federal court, a single juror's vote to acquit is enough to prevent a conviction. But not in Louisiana. Along with Oregon, Louisiana has long punished people based on 10-to-2 verdicts like the one here. So instead of the mistrial he would have received almost anywhere else, Mr. Ramos was sentenced to life in prison without the possibility of parole.

Why do Louisiana and Oregon allow nonunanimous convictions? Though it's hard to say why these laws persist, their origins are clear. Louisiana first endorsed nonunanimous verdicts for serious crimes at a constitutional convention in 1898. According to one committee chairman, the avowed purpose of that convention was to "establish the supremacy of the white race," and the resulting document included many of the trappings of the Jim Crow era: a poll tax, a combined literacy and property ownership test, and a grandfather clause that in practice exempted white residents from the most onerous of these requirements.

* * * Just a week before the convention, the U.S. Senate passed a resolution calling for an investigation into whether Louisiana was systemically excluding African-Americans from juries. Seeking to avoid unwanted national attention, and aware that this Court would strike down any policy of overt discrimination against African-American jurors as a violation of the Fourteenth Amendment, the delegates sought to undermine African-American participation on juries in another way. With a careful eye on racial demographics, the convention delegates sculpted a "facially race-neutral" rule permitting 10-to-2 verdicts in order "to ensure that African-American juror service would be meaningless."

Adopted in the 1930s, Oregon's rule permitting nonunanimous verdicts can be similarly traced to the rise of the Ku Klux Klan and efforts to dilute "the influence of racial, ethnic, and religious minorities on Oregon juries." In fact, no one before us contests any of this; courts in both Louisiana and Oregon have frankly acknowledged that race was a motivating factor in the adoption of their States' respective nonunanimity rules.

We took this case to decide whether the Sixth Amendment right to a jury trial—as incorporated against the States by way of the Fourteenth Amendment—requires a unanimous verdict to convict a defendant of a serious offense. * * *

The Sixth Amendment promises that "[i]n all criminal prosecutions, the accused shall enjoy the right to a speedy and public trial, by an impartial jury of the State and district wherein the crime shall have been committed, which district shall have been previously ascertained by law." The Amendment goes on to preserve other rights for criminal defendants but says nothing else about what a "trial by an impartial jury" entails.

*** The text and structure of the Constitution clearly suggest that the term "trial by an impartial jury" carried with it *some* meaning about the content and requirements of a jury trial.

One of these requirements was unanimity. Wherever we might look to determine what the term "trial by an impartial jury trial" meant at the time of the Sixth Amendment's adoption—whether it's the common law, state practices in the founding era, or opinions and treatises written soon afterward—the answer is unmistakable. A jury must reach a unanimous verdict in order to convict.

The requirement of juror unanimity emerged in 14th century England and was soon accepted as a vital right protected by the common law. As Blackstone explained, no person could be found guilty of a serious crime unless "the truth of every accusation . . . should . . . be confirmed by the unanimous suffrage of twelve of his equals and neighbors, indifferently chosen, and superior to all suspicion." A " 'verdict, taken from eleven, was no verdict' " at all.

This same rule applied in the young American States. Six State Constitutions explicitly required unanimity. Another four preserved the right to a jury trial in more general terms. But the variations did not matter much; consistent with the common law, state courts appeared to regard unanimity as an essential feature of the jury trial.

It was against this backdrop that James Madison drafted and the States ratified the Sixth Amendment in 1791. By that time, unanimous verdicts had been required for about 400 years. If the term "trial by an impartial jury" carried any meaning at all, it surely included a requirement as long and widely accepted as unanimity.

*** This Court has, repeatedly and over many years, recognized that the Sixth Amendment requires unanimity. As early as 1898, the Court said that a defendant enjoys a "constitutional right to demand that his liberty should not be taken from him except by the joint action of the court and the unanimous verdict of a jury of twelve persons." A few decades later, the Court elaborated that the Sixth Amendment affords a right to "a trial by jury as understood and applied at common law, . . . includ[ing] all the essential elements as they were recognized in this country and England when the Constitution was adopted." And, the Court observed, this includes a requirement "that the verdict should be unanimous." In all, this Court has commented on the Sixth Amendment's unanimity requirement no fewer than 13 times over more than 120 years.

There can be no question either that the Sixth Amendment's unanimity requirement applies to state and federal criminal trials equally. This Court has long explained that the Sixth Amendment right to a jury trial is "fundamental to the American scheme of justice" and incorporated against the States under the Fourteenth Amendment. This Court has long explained, too, that incorporated provisions of the Bill of Rights bear the same content when asserted against States as they do when asserted against the federal government. So if the Sixth Amendment's right to a jury trial requires a unanimous verdict to support a conviction in federal court, it requires no less in state court.

How, despite these seemingly straightforward principles, have Louisiana's and Oregon's laws managed to hang on for so long? It turns out that the Sixth Amendment's otherwise simple story took a strange turn in 1972. That year, the Court confronted these States' unconventional schemes for the first time—in *Apodaca* v. *Oregon* and a companion case, *Johnson* v. *Louisiana*. Ultimately, the Court could do no more than issue a badly fractured set of opinions. Four dissenting Justices would not have hesitated to strike down the States' laws, recognizing that the Sixth Amendment requires unanimity and that this guarantee is fully applicable against the States under the Fourteenth Amendment. But a four-Justice plurality took a very different view of the Sixth Amendment. These Justices declared that the real question before them was whether unanimity serves an important "function" in "contemporary society." Then, having reframed the question, the plurality wasted few words before concluding that unanimity's costs outweigh its benefits in the modern era, so the Sixth Amendment should not stand in the way of Louisiana or Oregon. * * *

* * * The dissent doesn't dispute that the Sixth Amendment protects the right to a unanimous jury verdict, or that the Fourteenth Amendment extends this right to state-court trials. But it insists we must affirm Mr. Ramos's conviction anyway. Why? Because the doctrine of *stare decisis* supposedly commands it. * * *

* * * Even if we accepted the premise that *Apodaca* established a precedent, no one on the Court today is prepared to say it was rightly decided, and *stare decisis* isn't supposed to be the art of methodically ignoring what everyone knows to be true. Of course, the precedents of this Court warrant our deep respect as embodying the considered views of those who have come before. But *stare decisis* has never been treated as "an inexorable command." And the doctrine is "at its weakest when we interpret the Constitution" because a mistaken judicial interpretation of that supreme law is often "practically impossible" to correct through other means. To balance these considerations, when it revisits a precedent, this Court has traditionally considered "the quality of the decision's reasoning; its consistency with related decisions; legal developments since the decision; and reliance on the decision." In this case, each factor points in the same direction.

Start with the quality of the reasoning. Whether we look to the plurality opinion or Justice Powell's separate concurrence, *Apodaca* was gravely mistaken; again, no Member of the Court today defends either as rightly decided. * * * [T]he plurality spent almost no time grappling with the historical meaning of the Sixth Amendment's jury trial right, this Court's long-repeated statements that it demands unanimity, or the racist origins of Louisiana's and Oregon's laws. Instead, the plurality subjected the Constitution's jury trial right to an incomplete functionalist analysis of its own creation[.] * * *

Looking to *Apodaca*'s consistency with related decisions and recent legal developments compounds the reasons for concern. *Apodaca* sits uneasily with 120 years of preceding case law. * * *

When it comes to reliance interests, it's notable that neither Louisiana nor Oregon claims anything like the prospective economic, regulatory, or social disruption litigants seeking to preserve precedent usually invoke. * * * Nor does anyone suggest that nonunanimous verdicts have "become part of our national culture." It would be quite surprising if they had, given that nonunanimous verdicts are insufficient to convict in 48 States and federal court.

Instead, the only reliance interests that might be asserted here fall into two categories. The first concerns the fact Louisiana and Oregon may need to retry defendants convicted of felonies by nonunanimous verdicts whose cases are still pending on direct appeal. The dissent claims that this fact supplies the winning argument for retaining *Apodaca* because it has generated "enormous reliance interests" and overturning the case would provoke a "crushing" "tsunami" of follow-on litigation.

The overstatement may be forgiven as intended for dramatic effect, but prior convictions in only two States are potentially affected by our judgment. Those States credibly claim that the number of nonunanimous felony convictions still on direct appeal are somewhere in the hundreds, and retrying or plea bargaining these cases will surely impose a cost. But new rules of criminal procedures usually do, often affecting significant numbers of pending cases across the whole country. * * *

The second and related reliance interest the dissent seizes upon involves the interest Louisiana and Oregon have in the security of their final criminal judgments. In light of our decision today, the dissent worries that defendants whose appeals are already complete might seek to challenge their nonunanimous convictions through collateral (*i.e.*, habeas) review.

But again the worries outstrip the facts. Under *Teague* v. *Lane*, newly recognized rules of criminal procedure do not normally apply in collateral review. True, *Teague* left open the possibility of an exception for "watershed rules" "implicat[ing] the fundamental fairness [and accuracy] of the trial." But, as this language suggests, *Teague*'s test is a demanding one, so much so that this Court has yet to announce a new rule of criminal procedure capable of meeting it. * * *

Nor is the *Teague* question even before us. Whether the right to jury unanimity applies to cases on collateral review is a question for a future case where the parties will have a chance to brief the issue and we will benefit from their adversarial presentation.[a] * * *

In the final accounting, the dissent's *stare decisis* arguments round to zero. We have an admittedly mistaken decision, on a constitutional issue, an outlier on the day it was decided, one that's become lonelier with time. * * *

* * * The judgment of the Court of Appeals is

Reversed.

JUSTICE ALITO, with whom THE CHIEF JUSTICE joins, and with whom JUSTICE KAGAN joins as to all but Part III-D, dissenting.

The doctrine of *stare decisis* gets rough treatment in today's decision. Lowering the bar for overruling our precedents, a badly fractured majority casts aside an important and long-established decision with little regard for the enormous reliance the decision has engendered. * * *

Nearly a half century ago in *Apodaca v. Oregon*, the Court held that the Sixth Amendment permits non-unanimous verdicts in state criminal trials, and in all the years since then, no Justice has even hinted that *Apodaca* should be reconsidered. Understandably thinking that *Apodaca* was good law, the state courts in Louisiana and Oregon have tried thousands of cases under rules that permit such verdicts. But today, the Court does away with *Apodaca* and, in so doing, imposes a potentially crushing burden on the courts and criminal justice systems of those States. * * *

To add insult to injury, the Court tars Louisiana and Oregon with the charge of racism for permitting nonunanimous verdicts—even though this Court found such verdicts to be constitutional and even though there are entirely legitimate arguments for allowing them.

I would not overrule *Apodaca*. Whatever one may think about the correctness of the decision, it has elicited enormous and entirely reasonable reliance. And before this Court decided to intervene, the decision appeared to have little practical importance going forward. Louisiana has now abolished non-unanimous verdicts, and Oregon seemed on the verge of doing the same until the Court intervened. * * *

---

[a] In 2021, the Court held that *Ramos v. Louisiana* does not apply retroactively. Edwards v. Vannoy, 141 S. Ct. 1547, 1549 (2021) (holding that the ruling in *Ramos v. Louisiana* did not apply to retroactively to federal habeas petitioners whose state court convictions were already final when *Ramos* was decided).

Too much public discourse today is sullied by *ad hominem* rhetoric, that is, attempts to discredit an argument not by proving that it is unsound but by attacking the character or motives of the argument's proponents. The majority regrettably succumbs to this trend. At the start of its opinion, the majority asks this rhetorical question: "Why do Louisiana and Oregon allow nonunanimous convictions?" And the answer it suggests? Racism, white supremacy, the Ku Klux Klan. Non-unanimous verdicts, the Court implies, are of a piece with Jim Crow laws, the poll tax, and other devices once used to disfranchise African-Americans.

If Louisiana and Oregon originally adopted their laws allowing non-unanimous verdicts for these reasons, that is deplorable, but what does that have to do with the broad constitutional question before us? The answer is: nothing.

For one thing, whatever the reasons why Louisiana and Oregon originally adopted their rules many years ago, both States readopted their rules under different circumstances in later years. Louisiana's constitutional convention of 1974 adopted a new, narrower rule, and its stated purpose was "judicial efficiency." "In that debate no mention was made of race." * * * The majority makes no effort to show either that the delegates to the constitutional convention retained the rule for discriminatory purposes or that proponents of the new Constitution made racial appeals when approval was submitted to the people. The same is true for Oregon's revisions and reenactments. * * *

[T]he origins of the Louisiana and Oregon rules have no bearing on the broad constitutional question that the Court decides. * * *

Some years ago the British Parliament enacted a law allowing non-unanimous verdicts. Was Parliament under the sway of the Klan? The Constitution of Puerto Rico permits non-unanimous verdicts. Were the framers of that Constitution racists? Non-unanimous verdicts were once advocated by the American Law Institute and the American Bar Association. Was their aim to promote white supremacy? And how about the prominent scholars who have taken the same position? Racists all? Of course not. So all the talk about the Klan, etc., is entirely out of place. We should set an example of rational and civil discourse instead of contributing to the worst current trends.

Now to what matters.

* * * *Stare decisis* has been a fundamental part of our jurisprudence since the founding, and it is an important doctrine. But, as we have said many times, it is not an "inexorable command." There are circumstances when past decisions must be overturned, but we begin with the presumption that we will follow precedent, and therefore when the Court decides to overrule, it has an obligation to provide an explanation for its decision. * * *

What is the majority's justification for overruling *Apodaca*? * * *

The majority's primary reason for overruling *Apodaca* is the supposedly poor "quality" of Justice White's plurality opinion and Justice Powell's separate opinion. * * *

I cannot say that I would have agreed either with Justice White's analysis or his bottom line in *Apodaca* if I had sat on the Court at that time, but the majority's harsh criticism of his opinion is unwarranted. * * *

* * * What convinces me that *Apodaca* should be retained are the enormous reliance interests of Louisiana and Oregon. For 48 years, Louisiana and Oregon, trusting that *Apodaca* is good law, have conducted thousands and thousands of trials under rules allowing non-unanimous verdicts. Now, those States face a potential tsunami of litigation on the jury unanimity issue.

At a minimum, all defendants whose cases are still on direct appeal will presumably be entitled to a new trial if they were convicted by a less-than-unanimous verdict and preserved the issue in the trial court. * * * Oregon asserts that more than a thousand defendants whose cases are still on direct appeal may be able to challenge their convictions if *Apodaca* is overruled. * * * [T]here is no guarantee that all the cases affected by today's ruling can be retried. In some cases, key witnesses may not be available, and it remains to be seen whether the criminal justice systems of Oregon and Louisiana have the resources to handle the volume of cases in which convictions will be reversed.

These cases on direct review are only the beginning. Prisoners whose direct appeals have ended will argue that today's decision allows them to challenge their convictions on collateral review, and if those claims succeed, the courts of Louisiana and Oregon are almost sure to be overwhelmed. * * *

* * * *Apodaca* should not be overruled. I would therefore affirm the judgment below, and I respectfully dissent.

[JUSTICE SOTOMAYOR's, JUSTICE KAVANAUGH's, and JUSTICE THOMAS' concurring opinions have been omitted.]

NOTE

Criminal defendants in federal court must be tried before a 12-person jury. *See* FED. R. OF CRIM. P. 23. Criminal defendants in state court, however, may be tried before a jury comprised of only 6 persons. *See* Williams v. Florida, 399 U.S. 78 (1970). In *Burch v. Louisiana*, the Court explained why it held in *Williams v. Florida* that allowing states to lower the number of persons on a jury to six comported with the Sixth Amendment right to a trial by jury. Notice that the *Burch* Court looked to the purpose of the right to a trial by jury to explain its previous decision:

The purpose of trial by jury, as noted in *Duncan*, is to prevent government oppression by providing a "safeguard against the corrupt or overzealous prosecutor and against the compliant, biased, or eccentric judge." Given this purpose, the *Williams* Court observed that the jury's essential feature lies in the "interposition between the accused and his accuser of the commonsense judgment of a group of laymen, and in the community participation and shared responsibility that results from that group's determination of guilt or innocence." These purposes could be fulfilled, the Court believed, so long as the jury was of a sufficient size to promote group deliberation, free from outside intimidation, and to provide a fair possibility that a cross section of the community would be represented on it. The Court concluded, however, that there is "little reason to think that these goals are in any meaningful sense less likely to be achieved when the jury numbers six, than when it numbers 12—particularly if the requirement of unanimity is retained."

Burch v. Louisiana, 441 U.S. 130, 135 (1979) (holding that conviction by a nonunanimous six-person jury in a state criminal trial violates the rights of an accused to trial by jury guaranteed by the Sixth Amendment). While a jury of only 6 persons comports with the Sixth Amendment as long as it is required to render a unanimous verdict, the Court has drawn the line at 6 person juries. In *Ballew v. Georgia*, the Court held that conviction by a five-person jury, even if unanimous, violates the Sixth Amendment. Ballew v. Georgia, 435 U.S. 223 (1978).

The *Burch* Court also explained why in a previous case (*Apodaca v. Oregon*), it held that unanimity was not required in criminal cases with 12 person juries:

> A similar analysis led us to conclude in 1972 that a jury's verdict need not be unanimous to satisfy constitutional requirements, even though unanimity had been the rule at common law. Thus, in *Apodaca v. Oregon*, we upheld a state statute providing that only 10 members of a 12-person jury need concur to render a verdict in certain noncapital cases. In terms of the role of the jury as a safeguard against oppression, the plurality opinion perceived no difference between those juries required to act unanimously and those permitted to act by votes of 10 to 2. Nor was unanimity viewed by the plurality as contributing materially to the exercise of the jury's common-sense judgment or as a necessary precondition to effective application of the requirement that jury panels represent a fair cross section of the community.

Id. at 136.

In overruling *Apodaca v. Oregon* and *Johnson v. Louisiana*, the Court in *Ramos v. Louisiana* never directly engages with the question of whether jury unanimity contributes materially to the exercise of the jury's common-sense judgment. Nor does it discuss whether unanimity is required to ensure that the jury functions as a safeguard against oppression. Instead, the Court bases its ruling primarily on history. The next excerpt explains how requiring unanimity in jury verdicts can help achieve the underlying goals of the right to a jury trial, filling in this missing discussion.

EMPTY VOTES IN JURY DELIBERATIONS
Kim Taylor-Thompson
113 Harv. L. Rev. 1261 (2000)

For much of the past quarter-century, courts and legal scholars have devised various strategies to combat the exclusion of people of color and women from juries. Animating this effort has been the belief that to deny access to jury service based on an individual's heritage or gender offends core democratic principles. The Supreme Court has outlawed the wholesale exclusion of members of protected groups and has similarly disapproved procedural devices that function as barriers to full participation of members of these groups. For the most part, courts and litigants have tried to follow these rules. Yet the complexion and composition of juries have barely changed. Juries remain overwhelmingly white and male.

Scholars have clashed over the causes of this lack of diversity. Some blame race- and gender-based peremptory strikes exercised during *voir dire*. Many of these scholars applaud the Supreme Court's requirements of closer scrutiny of peremptory challenges excluding people of color and women. Others dispute the efficacy of prohibiting such strikes, observing that courts routinely accept lawyers' pretextual reasons for removing members of commonly targeted groups. * * *

But the picture is incomplete. Peremptory challenges may not be the only cause for concern. Another phenomenon within the jury box threatens quietly—but effectively—to deprive individuals with diverse views who actually serve on juries from exercising any real voting power. This phenomenon is the emerging acceptance of nonunanimous verdicts in criminal cases, in which ten or sometimes nine of twelve jurors are permitted to issue the verdict. The picture becomes all the more complex because, on the surface, majority rule voting seems innocuous enough. Advocates of nonunanimous voting almost reflexively equate majority rule with democracy. But for all its appearance of fairness, nonunanimous voting in this setting tends to inhibit inclusion. Jury research conducted in the past two decades reveals that eliminating the obligation to secure each person's agreement on the verdict can result in truncating or even eliminating jury deliberations. By discouraging meaningful examination of opposing viewpoints, majority rule decisionmaking impoverishes deliberations.

But an even more basic and fractious consequence looms. Nonunanimous decisionmaking in criminal trials could jeopardize the limited victories that historically excluded groups have won in cases challenging barriers to jury service. If—as is often true—the views of jurors of color and female jurors diverge from the mainstream, nonunanimous decisionmaking rules can operate to eliminate the voice of difference on the jury. Given that people of color tend to form the numerical minority on juries, the majority could ignore minority views by simply outvoting dissenters. Equally troubling is the fact that studies examining the participation rates of women in a group setting, coupled with jury research on the impact of nonunanimous voting, suggest that a majority of jurors could reach a verdict without ever hearing from women on the jury. Thus, despite the simplistic appeal of making the jury system more "democratic," nonunanimity threatens to eliminate the voices of those who have only recently secured the right to participate in the democratic process.

* * * An examination of psychological and social science research suggests that personal background and experience define and in very real ways limit individual perception. An individual's experiences influence her capacity to interpret and evaluate facts and then to make judgments about justice. More particularly, race and gender inform the processes by which individuals make decisions, especially about social justice. Until now the requirement to reach complete consensus has at least provided an impetus to stretch beyond group experiences and loyalties. But the race and gender unconsciousness inherent in majority rule would permit a jury to return a verdict without ever acknowledging or confronting gaps in its interpretation of evidence.

The United States Supreme Court [has] played a role in creating this dilemma. Over two decades ago, the Court issued a pair of decisions holding that the Constitution does not mandate jury-verdict unanimity in state criminal trials.[a] The Court's review of the constitutionality of majority rule showed little appreciation of a possible relationship between this practice and the Court's long history of battling exclusions of groups from the jury process. The Court perceived no dissonance between nonunanimous decisionmaking and the democratic aspirations it had consistently embraced. * * * All of the Justices agreed on the importance of the deliberative process, but they disagreed on the likely impact of an alteration in the voting rule, and particularly the extent to which a minority of jurors can still influence the ultimate decision. Against that backdrop, the Court granted states the opportunity to experiment with majority rule. * * *

---

[a] The author is referring to Apodaca v. Oregon, 406 U.S. 404 (1972) (upholding state rule allowing non-unanimous jury verdicts in which 10 out of 12 jurors vote to convict) and Johnson v. Louisiana, 406 U.S. 356 (1972) (upholding state rule allowing non-unanimous jury verdicts in which 9 out of 12 jurors vote to convict). In 2020, both of these cases were overruled. *See* Ramos v. Louisiana, *infra*.

In the wake of the Supreme Court's decisions in *Johnson* and *Apodaca*, researchers began to experiment with nonunanimous decision rules. They constructed jury studies to test the assumptions of both the majority and dissenting opinions. Although jury research should perhaps be viewed with some caution, its findings provide necessary insight into the operation of such rules. Indeed, the evidence that jury researchers have amassed directly contravenes the majority opinions' contentions that these decision rules have no effect on the reliability of jury decisions. A shift to majority rule appears to alter both the quality of the deliberative process and the accuracy of the jury's judgment. In the end, the data indicates that unanimity assures viewpoint diversity better than majority rule.

The heart of the problem is that nonunanimous decisionmaking constricts the flow of information. Researchers have discovered that once a vote indicates that the required majority has formed, deliberations halt in a matter of minutes. Jury research reveals how rarely juries deliberating under majority rule attain full consensus. In more than seventy percent of the cases in which a majority develops, the jury does not bother reaching consensus. This behavior reduces the amount of information considered by jurors.

* * * Jury research [also] indicates that shorter deliberation leads to less accurate judgments. At first blush, to question the accuracy of the jury's decision in a criminal trial may seem odd. The justice system tends not to expect the jury to discern the objective "truth" about the events at issue. Instead the jury must deliver its evaluation of whether the government has met its burden of proof. Still, empirical research alerts us to the fact that majority rule discourages painstaking analyses of the evidence and steers jurors toward swift judgments that too often are erroneous or at least highly questionable.

In one study individuals called for jury duty were given the opportunity to volunteer to serve on a mock jury. Researchers conducted a mock *voir dire*, showed participants a film re-enactment of a murder trial, and then divided jurors into groups governed by either unanimity or majority rule. Legal experts evaluating the murder case considered first-degree murder an untenable verdict given the evidence. According to pre-deliberation questionnaires, many individual jurors initially preferred the higher charge. Following deliberations, however, not one unanimous jury returned a first-degree murder verdict—the arguably "incorrect" choice. By contrast, twelve percent of the majority-rule juries reached this result. * * *

These findings should not be surprising. Because the jury's work largely depends on subjective interpretations of evidence, a variety of perspectives will enrich jury discussions. It is true that many facts will be readily apparent to all jurors. For example, in a homicide case, jurors may easily accept medical evidence establishing that the victim sustained a fatal injury on the day in question. But significant questions of guilt or innocence and the degrees of responsibility for conduct often hinge on a juror's personal interpretation of behavior—which other jurors may or may not share. When deciding whether the government has established the requisite mental state for the offense, for instance, the juror often must infer the actor's state of mind from conduct open to numerous interpretations. The juror must also determine whether the actor's conduct is culpable or can instead be justified or excused. And in all cases the juror must determine whether the witnesses are sufficiently credible. Like other members of society, jurors approach these responsibilities with the imperfect yet well-worn assumptions and expectations that guide their everyday evaluations of events. They often have a wide range of views regarding whose word merits trust or distrust.

So open discussion is critical. An individual juror's experience can affect her perception of and reaction to the evidence. As knowledge and expertise may be distributed unequally within any given jury, interaction among jurors will expand the range of issues to be discussed and broaden the scope of information shared by the group. * * * In the end, a deliberative process that emphasizes and maximizes consultation among individual jurors with diverse backgrounds broadens the overall perspective of the jury.

* * * Perhaps more than anywhere else in the legal system, race plays a significant role in the administration of criminal justice. * * * Although the juror of color will not necessarily sympathize with or support the accused, her presence offers the accused the best possible chance that someone in the jury room will understand the accused's world and world views. Because of the pervasiveness of racism, jurors of color, regardless of their socioeconomic position, are likely to have experienced some form of racial subordination that may provide them with a broader conceptual framework for the ensuing discussion in the deliberation room. * * *

Similar concerns arise when one considers the impact of majority rule upon the participation of women on juries. * * *

In mock-jury studies, researchers have observed that women generally speak less frequently than men in the deliberation process. When women offer comments in the course of mock deliberations, men often interrupt them or ignore their statements. This process of dismissing women's contributions frequently results in a progressive diminution of remarks from women as time passes. Women also tend to take longer than men to enter a discussion and to voice their views. In a decision scheme that demands full jury consensus, jurors may at least recognize the need to draw out the views of those who do not contribute as readily or as frequently. But under majority rule, decisions tend to be reached faster, leaving jurors without an incentive to encourage full participation in the deliberations.

* * * This would be of little practical consequence if women's perspectives were not unique. Both feminist theory and jury research suggest that gender matters in moral decisionmaking. * * *

In addition to its practical role as factfinder, the jury serves an important symbolic function: it adds legitimacy to the justice system by providing citizens with the "security ... that they, as jurors, actual or possible, being part of the judicial system of the country can prevent its arbitrary use or abuse." * * * The operation of majority rule does interfere with the participation of people of color and women. Its adoption should trigger the same concerns that prompted the Court to outlaw the wholesale exclusion of jurors who happen to be members of these groups. The jury system must find ways to build consensus and to encourage expression of and debate about divergent views. Deliberation and group agreement help to ferret out extreme views and to ensure that all jurors are engaged. By contrast, the growing disenchantment with the justice system will only become more pronounced if it adopts a decisionmaking rule that in essence excludes segments of the jury and, by extension, segments of the community.

SINGER V. UNITED STATES
Supreme Court of the United States
380 U.S. 24, 85 S. Ct. 783, 13 L. Ed. 2d 630 (1965)

CHIEF JUSTICE WARREN delivered the opinion of the Court.

Rule 23(a) of the Federal Rules of Criminal Procedure provides:

Cases required to be tried by jury shall be so tried unless the defendant waives a jury trial in writing with the approval of the court and the consent of the government.

Petitioner challenges the permissibility of this rule, arguing that the Constitution gives a defendant in a federal criminal case the right to waive a jury trial whenever he believes such action to be in his best interest, regardless of whether the prosecution and the court are willing to acquiesce in the waiver.

Petitioner was charged in a federal district court with 30 infractions of the mail fraud statute. The gist of the indictment was that he used the mails to dupe amateur songwriters into sending him money for the marketing of their songs. On the opening day of trial petitioner offered in writing to waive a trial by jury "[f]or the purpose of shortening the trial." The trial court was willing to approve the waiver, but the Government refused to give its consent. Petitioner was subsequently convicted by a jury on 29 of the 30 counts and the Court of Appeals for the Ninth Circuit affirmed. We granted certiorari.

Petitioner's argument is that a defendant in a federal criminal case has not only an unconditional constitutional right * * * to a trial by jury, but also a correlative right to have his case decided by a judge alone if he considers such a trial to be to his advantage. * * * [P]etitioner argues that the provisions relating to jury trial are for the protection of the accused. Petitioner further urges that since a defendant can waive other constitutional rights without the consent of the Government, he must necessarily have a similar right to waive a jury trial and that the Constitution's guarantee of a fair trial gives defendants the right to safeguard themselves against possible jury prejudice by insisting on a trial before a judge alone. * * *

The issue whether a defendant could waive a jury trial in federal criminal cases was * * * presented to this Court in *Patton v. United States*. The *Patton* case came before the Court on a certified question from the Eighth Circuit. The wording of the question is significant:

> After the commencement of a trial in a federal court before a jury of twelve men upon an indictment charging a crime, punishment for which may involve a penitentiary sentence, if one juror becomes incapacitated and unable to further proceed with his work as a juror, can defendant or defendants and the government through its official representative in charge of the case consent to the trial proceeding to a finality with 11 jurors, and can defendant or defendants thus waive the right to a trial and verdict by a constitutional jury of 12 men?

The question explicitly stated that the Government had agreed with the defendant that his trial should proceed with 11 jurors. The case did not involve trial before a judge alone, but the Court believed that trial before 11 jurors was as foreign to the common law as was trial before a judge alone, and therefore, both forms of waiver "in substance amount(ed) to the same thing." The Court * * * concluded that a jury trial was a right which the accused might "forego at his election." The Court also spoke of jury trial as a "privilege," not an "imperative requirement," and remarked that jury trial was principally for the benefit of the accused. Nevertheless, the Court was conscious of the precise question that was presented by the Eighth Circuit, and concluded its opinion with carefully chosen language that dispelled any notion that the defendant had an absolute right to demand trial before a judge sitting alone:

> Not only must the right of the accused to a trial by a constitutional jury be jealously preserved, but the maintenance of the jury as a factfinding body in criminal cases is of such importance and has such a place in our traditions, that, before any waiver can become effective, the consent of government counsel and the sanction of

the court must be had, in addition to the express and intelligent consent of the defendant. * * *

In *Adams v. United States ex rel. McCann*, this Court reaffirmed the position taken in *Patton* that "one charged with a serious federal crime may dispense with his Constitutional right to jury trial, where this action is taken with his express, intelligent consent, where the Government also consents, and where such action is approved by the responsible judgment of the trial court."

Thus, there is no federally recognized right to a criminal trial before a judge sitting alone, but a defendant can, as was held in *Patton*, in some instances waive his right to a trial by jury. The question remains whether the effectiveness of this waiver can be conditioned upon the consent of the prosecuting attorney and the trial judge.

The ability to waive a constitutional right does not ordinarily carry with it the right to insist upon the opposite of that right. For example, although a defendant can, under some circumstances, waive his constitutional right to a public trial, he has no absolute right to compel a private trial, although he can waive his right to be tried in the State and district where the crime was committed, he cannot in all cases compel transfer of the case to another district, and although he can waive his right to be confronted by the witnesses against him, it has never been seriously suggested that he can thereby compel the Government to try the case by stipulation. Moreover, it has long been accepted that the waiver of constitutional rights can be subjected to reasonable procedural regulations * * *.

Trial by jury has been established by the Constitution as the "normal and * * * preferable mode of disposing of issues of fact in criminal cases." As with any mode that might be devised to determine guilt, trial by jury has its weaknesses and the potential for misuse. However, the mode itself has been surrounded with safeguards to make it as fair as possible * * *.

In light of the Constitution's emphasis on jury trial, we find it difficult to understand how the petitioner can submit the bald proposition that to compel a defendant in a criminal case to undergo a jury trial against his will is contrary to his right to a fair trial or to due process. A defendant's only constitutional right concerning the method of trial is to an impartial trial by jury. We find no constitutional impediment to conditioning a waiver of this right on the consent of the prosecuting attorney and the trial judge when, if either refuses to consent, the result is simply that the defendant is subject to an impartial trial by jury—the very thing that the Constitution guarantees him. The Constitution recognizes an adversary system as the proper method of determining guilt, and the Government, as a litigant, has a legitimate interest in seeing that cases in which it believes a conviction is warranted are tried before the tribunal which the Constitution regards as most likely to produce a fair result. * * *

In upholding the validity of Rule 23(a), we reiterate the sentiment expressed in *Berger v. United States* that the government attorney in a criminal prosecution is not an ordinary party to a controversy, but a "servant of the law" with a "twofold aim . . . that guilt shall not escape or innocence suffer." It was in light of this concept of the role of prosecutor that Rule 23(a) was framed, and we are confident that it is in this light that it will continue to be invoked by government attorneys. Because of this confidence in the integrity of the federal prosecutor, Rule 23(a) does not require that the Government articulate its reasons for demanding a jury trial at the time it refuses to consent to a defendant's proffered waiver. Nor should we assume that federal prosecutors would demand a jury trial for an ignoble purpose. We need not determine in this case whether there might be some circumstances where a defendant's reasons for wanting to be tried by a judge alone are so compelling that the Government's insistence on trial by jury would result in the denial to a defendant of an impartial trial. Petitioner argues that there might arise situations where "passion, prejudice . . . public feeling" or some other factor may render impossible or unlikely an impartial trial by jury. However, since petitioner gave no reason for wanting to forgo jury trial other than to save time, this is not such a case, and petitioner does not claim that it is. * * *

The judgment of the Court of Appeals is affirmed. * * *

TAYLOR V. LOUISIANA
Supreme Court of the United States
419 U.S. 522, 95 S. Ct. 692, 42 L. Ed. 2d 690 (1975)

JUSTICE WHITE delivered the opinion of the Court.

When this case was tried, Art. VII, § 41, of the Louisiana Constitution, and Art. 402 of the Louisiana Code of Criminal Procedure provided that a woman should not be selected for jury service unless she had previously filed a written declaration of her desire to be subject to jury service. The constitutionality of these provisions is the issue in this case.

Appellant, Billy J. Taylor, was indicted by the grand jury * * * for aggravated kidnaping. On April 12, 1972, appellant moved the trial court to quash the petit jury venire drawn for the special criminal term beginning with his trial the following day. Appellant alleged that women were systematically excluded from the venire and that he would therefore be deprived of what he claimed to be his federal constitutional right to "a fair trial by jury of a representative segment of the community. . . ."

* * * The appellee has stipulated that 53% of the persons eligible for jury service * * * were female, and that no more than 10% of the persons

on the jury wheel in St. Tammany Parish were women. During the period from December 8, 1971, to November 3, 1972, 12 females were among the 1,800 persons drawn to fill petit jury venires in St. Tammany Parish. * * * In the present case, a venire totaling 175 persons was drawn for jury service beginning April 13, 1972. There were no females on the venire.

Appellant's motion to quash the venire was denied that same day. After being tried, convicted, and sentenced to death, appellant sought review in the Supreme Court of Louisiana, where he renewed his claim that the petit jury venire should have been quashed. The Supreme Court of Louisiana * * * held, one justice dissenting, that these provisions were valid and not unconstitutional under federal law.

Appellant appealed from that decision to this Court. We noted probable jurisdiction to consider whether the Louisiana jury-selection system deprived appellant of his Sixth and Fourteenth Amendment right to an impartial jury trial. * * *

The Louisiana jury-selection system does not disqualify women from jury service, but in operation its conceded systematic impact is that only a very few women, grossly disproportionate to the number of eligible women in the community, are called for jury service. In this case, no women were on the venire from which the petit jury was drawn. The issue we have, therefore, is whether a jury-selection system which operates to exclude from jury service an identifiable class of citizens constituting 53% of eligible jurors in the community comports with the Sixth and Fourteenth Amendments.

The State first insists that Taylor, a male, has no standing to object to the exclusion of women from his jury. * * * Taylor was not a member of the excluded class; but there is no rule that claims such as Taylor presents may be made only by those defendants who are members of the group excluded from jury service. In *Peters v. Kiff*, the defendant, a white man, challenged his conviction on the ground that Negroes had been systematically excluded from jury service. Six Members of the Court agreed that petitioner was entitled to present the issue and concluded that he had been deprived of his federal rights. * * * Our inquiry is whether the presence of a fair cross section of the community on venires, panels, of lists from which petit juries are drawn is essential to the fulfillment of the Sixth Amendment's guarantee of an impartial jury trial in criminal prosecutions. * * *

We accept the fair-cross-section requirement as fundamental to the jury trial guaranteed by the Sixth Amendment and are convinced that the requirement has solid foundation. The purpose of a jury is to guard against the exercise of arbitrary power—to make available the commonsense judgment of the community as a hedge against the overzealous or mistaken prosecutor and in preference to the professional or perhaps overconditioned or biased response of a judge. This prophylactic vehicle is not provided if the jury pool is made up of only special segments of the populace or if large, distinctive groups are excluded from the pool. Community participation in the administration of the criminal law, moreover, is not only consistent with our democratic heritage but is also critical to public confidence in the fairness of the criminal justice system. * * *

We are also persuaded that the fair-cross-section requirement is violated by the systematic exclusion of women, who in the judicial district involved here amounted to 53% of the citizens eligible for jury service. This conclusion necessarily entails the judgment that women are sufficiently numerous and distinct from men and that if they are systematically eliminated from jury panels, the Sixth Amendment's fair-cross-section requirement cannot be satisfied.

* * * If the fair-cross-section rule is to govern the selection of juries, as we have concluded it must, women cannot be systematically excluded from jury panels from which petit juries are drawn. This conclusion is consistent with the current judgment of the country, now evidenced by legislative or constitutional provisions in every State and at the federal level qualifying women for jury service.

There remains the argument that women as a class serve a distinctive role in society and that jury service would so substantially interfere with that function that the State has ample justification for excluding women from service unless they volunteer, even though the result is that almost all jurors are men. * * * The right to a proper jury cannot be overcome on merely rational grounds. There must be weightier reasons if a distinctive class representing 53% of the eligible jurors is for all practical purposes to be excluded from jury service. No such basis has been tendered here.

The States are free to grant exemptions from jury service to individuals in case of special hardship or incapacity and to those engaged in particular occupations the uninterrupted performance of which is critical to the community's welfare. It would not appear that such exemptions would pose substantial threats that the remaining pool of jurors would not be representative of the community. A system excluding all women, however, is a wholly different matter. It is untenable to suggest these days that it would be a special hardship for each and every woman to perform jury service or that society cannot spare any women from their present duties. This may be the case with many, and it may be burdensome to sort out those who should be exempted from those who should serve. But that task is performed in the case of men, and the administrative convenience in dealing with women as a class is insufficient justification for diluting the quality of community judgment represented by the jury in criminal trials. * * *

Accepting as we do, * * * the view that the Sixth Amendment affords the defendant in a criminal trial the opportunity to have the jury drawn from venires representative of the community, we think it is no longer tenable to hold that women as a class may be excluded or given automatic exemptions based solely on sex if the consequence is that criminal jury venires are almost totally male. * * * If it was ever the case that women were unqualified to sit on juries or were so situated that none of them should be required to perform jury service, that time has long since passed. If at one time it could be held that Sixth Amendment juries must be drawn from a fair cross section of the community but that this requirement permitted the almost total exclusion of women, this is not the case today. Communities differ at different times and places. What is a fair cross section at one time or place is not necessarily a fair cross section at another time or a different place. Nothing persuasive has been presented to us in this case suggesting that all-male venires in the parishes involved here are fairly representative of the local population otherwise eligible for jury service.

* * * The fair-cross-section principle must have much leeway in application. The States remain free to prescribe relevant qualifications for their jurors and to provide reasonable exemptions so long as it may be fairly said that the jury lists or panels are representative of the community. * * *

It should also be emphasized that in holding that petit juries must be drawn from a source fairly representative of the community we impose no requirement that petit juries actually chosen must mirror the community and reflect the various distinctive groups in the population. Defendants are not entitled to a jury of any particular composition, but the jury wheels, pools of names, panels, or venires from which juries are drawn must not systematically exclude distinctive groups in the community and thereby fail to be reasonably representative thereof.

The judgment of the Louisiana Supreme Court is reversed and the case remanded to that court for further proceedings not inconsistent with this opinion.

So ordered.

Reversed and remanded.

CHIEF JUSTICE BURGER concurs in the result.

JUSTICE REHNQUIST, dissenting.

The Court's opinion reverses a conviction without a suggestion, much less a showing, that the appellant has been unfairly treated or prejudiced in any way by the manner in which his jury was selected. * * * I disagree with the Court and would affirm the judgment of the Supreme Court of Louisiana. * * *

I cannot conceive that today's decision is necessary to guard against oppressive or arbitrary law enforcement, or to prevent miscarriages of justice and to assure fair trials. Especially is this so when the criminal defendant involved makes no claims of prejudice or bias. The Court does accord some slight attention to justifying its ruling in terms of the basis on which the right to jury trial was read into the Fourteenth Amendment. It concludes that the jury is not effective, as a prophylaxis against arbitrary prosecutorial and judicial power, if the "jury pool is made up of only special segments of the populace or if large, distinctive groups are excluded from the pool." It fails, however, to provide any satisfactory explanation of the mechanism by which the Louisiana system undermines the prophylactic role of the jury, either in general or in this case. The best it can do is to posit "a flavor, a distinct quality," which allegedly is lost if either sex is excluded. * * *

[One change] that appears to undergird the Court's turnabout is societal in nature, encompassing both our higher degree of sensitivity to distinctions based on sex, and the "evolving nature of the structure of the family unit in American society." * * * [I]t may be fair to conclude that the Louisiana system is in fact an anachronism, inappropriate at this "time or place." But surely constitutional adjudication is a more canalized function than enforcing as against the States this Court's perception of modern life.

Absent any suggestion that appellant's trial was unfairly conducted, or its result was unreliable, I would not require Louisiana to retry him (assuming the State can once again produce its evidence and witnesses) in order to impose on him the sanctions which its laws provide.

DUREN V. MISSOURI
Supreme Court of the United States
439 U.S. 357, 99 S. Ct. 664, 58 L. Ed. 2d 579 (1979)

MR. JUSTICE WHITE delivered the opinion of the Court. * * *

Petitioner Duren was indicted in 1975 in the Circuit Court of Jackson County, Mo., for first-degree murder and first-degree robbery. In a pretrial motion to quash his petit jury panel, and again in a post-conviction motion for a new trial, he contended that his right to trial by a jury chosen from a fair cross section of his community was denied by provisions of Missouri law granting women who so request an automatic exemption from jury service. Both motions were denied.

At hearings on these motions, petitioner established that the jury-selection process in Jackson County begins with the annual mailing of a questionnaire to persons randomly selected from the Jackson County voter registration list. Approximately 70,000 questionnaires were mailed in 1975. The questionnaire contains a list of occupations and other categories which are the basis under Missouri law for either disqualification or exemption from jury service. Included on the questionnaire is a paragraph prominently addressed "TO WOMEN" that states in part:

Any woman who elects not to serve will fill out this paragraph and mail this questionnaire to the jury commission at once.

A similar paragraph is addressed "TO MEN OVER 65 YEARS OF AGE," who are also statutorily exempt upon request.

The names of those sent questionnaires are placed in the master jury wheel for Jackson County, except for those returning the questionnaire who indicate disqualification or claim an applicable exemption. Summonses are mailed on a weekly basis to prospective jurors randomly drawn from the jury wheel. The summons, like the questionnaire, contains special directions to men over 65 and to women, this time advising them to return the summons by mail if they desire not to serve. The practice also is that even those women who do not return the summons are treated as having claimed exemption if they fail to appear for jury service on the appointed day. Other persons seeking to claim an exemption at this stage must make written or personal application to the court.

Petitioner established that according to the 1970 census, 54% of the adult inhabitants of Jackson County were women. He also showed that for the periods June–October 1975 and January–March 1976, 11,197 persons were summoned and that 2,992 of these, or 26.7%, were women. Of those summoned, 741 women and 4,378 men appeared for service. Thus, 14.5% (741 of 5,119) of the persons on the post-summons weekly venires during the period in which petitioner's jury was chosen were female. In March 1976, when petitioner's trial began, 15.5% of those on the weekly venires were women (110 of 707). Petitioner's jury was selected from a 53-person panel on which there were 5 women; all 12 jurors chosen were men. None of the foregoing statistical evidence was disputed. * * *

In affirming petitioner's conviction, the Missouri Supreme Court * * * [held that] "the number of female names in the wheel, those summoned and those appearing were well above acceptable constitutional standards." We granted certiorari because of concern that the decision below is not consistent with our decision in *Taylor* [*v. Louisiana*].

We think that in certain crucial respects the Missouri Supreme Court misconceived the nature of the fair-cross-section inquiry set forth in *Taylor*. In holding that "petit juries must be drawn from a source fairly representative of the community," we explained that

> jury wheels, pools of names, panels, or venires from which juries are drawn must not systematically exclude distinctive groups in the community and thereby fail to be reasonably representative thereof.

In order to establish a prima facie violation of the fair-cross-section requirement, the defendant must show (1) that the group alleged to be excluded is a "distinctive" group in the community; (2) that the representation of this group in venires from which juries are selected is not fair and reasonable in relation to the number of such persons in the community; and (3) that this underrepresentation is due to systematic exclusion of the group in the jury-selection process.

With respect to the first part of the prima facie test, *Taylor* without doubt established that women "are sufficiently numerous and distinct from men" so that "if they are systematically eliminated from jury panels, the Sixth Amendment's fair-cross-section requirement cannot be satisfied."

The second prong of the prima facie case was established by petitioner's statistical presentation. Initially, the defendant must demonstrate the percentage of the community made up of the group alleged to be underrepresented, for this is the conceptual benchmark for the Sixth Amendment fair-cross-section requirement. In *Taylor*, the State had stipulated that 53% of the population eligible for jury service was female, while petitioner Duren has relied upon a census measurement of the actual percentage of women in the community (54%). . . . * * * Petitioner's presentation was clearly adequate prima facie evidence of population characteristics for the purpose of making a fair-cross-section violation.

Given petitioner's proof that in the relevant community slightly over half of the adults are women, we must disagree with the conclusion of the court below that jury venires containing approximately 15% women are "reasonably representative" of this community. * * * Such a gross discrepancy between the percentage of women in jury venires and the percentage of women in the community requires the conclusion that women were not fairly represented in the source from which petit juries were drawn in Jackson County.

Finally, in order to establish a prima facie case, it was necessary for petitioner to show that the underrepresentation of women, generally and on his venire, was due to their systematic exclusion in the jury-selection process. Petitioner's proof met this requirement. His undisputed demonstration that a large discrepancy occurred not just occasionally, but in every weekly venire for a period of nearly a year manifestly indicates that the cause of the underrepresentation was systematic—that is, inherent in the particular jury-selection process utilized. * * *

The resulting disproportionate and consistent exclusion of women from the jury wheel and at the venire stage was quite obviously due to the system by which juries were selected. Petitioner demonstrated that the underrepresentation of women in the final pool of prospective jurors was due to the operation of Missouri's exemption criteria—whether the automatic exemption for women or other statutory exemptions—as implemented in Jackson County. Women were therefore systematically underrepresented within the meaning of *Taylor*.

The demonstration of a prima facie fair-cross-section violation by the defendant is not the end of the inquiry into whether a constitutional violation has occurred. We have explained that "States remain free to prescribe relevant qualifications for their jurors and to provide reasonable exemptions so long as it may be fairly said that the jury lists or panels are representative of the community." However, we cautioned that "[the] right to a proper jury cannot be overcome on merely rational grounds." Rather, it requires that a significant state interest be manifestly and primarily advanced by those aspects of the jury-selection process, such as exemption criteria, that result in the disproportionate exclusion of a distinctive group. * * *

[O]nce the defendant has made a prima facie showing of an infringement of his constitutional right to a jury drawn from a fair cross section of the community, it is the State that bears the burden of justifying this infringement by showing attainment of a fair cross section to be incompatible with a significant state interest. * * *

Neither the Missouri Supreme Court nor respondent in its brief has offered any substantial justification for [the automatic] exemption [from jury service for women]. In response to questioning at oral argument, counsel for respondent ventured that the only state interest advanced by the exemption is safeguarding the important role played by women in home and family life. But exempting all women because of the preclusive domestic responsibilities of some women is insufficient justification for their disproportionate exclusion on jury venires. What we stated in *Taylor* with respect to the system there challenged under which women could "opt in" for jury service is equally applicable to Missouri's "opt out" exemption:

It is untenable to suggest these days that it would be a special hardship for each and every woman to perform jury service or that society cannot spare any women from their present duties. This may be the case with many, and it may be burdensome to sort out those who should be exempted from those who should serve. But that task is performed in the case of men, and the administrative convenience in dealing with women as a class is insufficient justification for diluting the quality of community judgment represented by the jury in criminal trials.

If it was ever the case that women were unqualified to sit on juries or were so situated that none of them should be required to perform jury service, that time has long since passed.

We recognize that a State may have an important interest in assuring that those members of the family responsible for the care of children are available to do so. An exemption appropriately tailored to this interest would, we think, survive a fair-cross-section challenge. We stress, however, that the constitutional guarantee to a jury drawn from a fair cross-section of the community requires that States exercise proper caution in exempting broad categories of persons from jury service. * * *

The judgment of the Missouri Supreme Court is reversed, and the case is remanded for further proceedings not inconsistent with this opinion.

So ordered.

[JUSTICE REHNQUIST's dissenting opinion has been omitted.]

NOTE

The Supreme Court has addressed whether a criminal defendant has a right to question prospective jurors on the issue of racial bias in only a handful of cases. Initially, the Court was fairly sympathetic to the idea that a criminal defendant has a constitutional right to question prospective jurors about racial bias. In *Aldridge v. United States*, 283 U.S. 308 (1931), the Court reversed a Black defendant's murder conviction where the trial judge had refused a defense request to interrogate the venire on racial prejudice, explaining that fairness demands that inquiries into racial prejudice be allowed. In *Ham v. South Carolina*, 409 U.S. 524, 529 (1973), a case involving a Black civil rights activist charged with possession of marijuana, the Court again sided with the defendant, holding that a trial judge's refusal to question prospective jurors as to possible racial prejudice violated the defendant's constitutional rights. This time, the Court went further than it had in *Aldridge* and expressly grounded its decision in due process, holding that "the Due Process Clause of the Fourteenth Amendment requires that . . . the [defendant] be permitted to have the jurors interrogated on the issue of racial bias."

Three years later, the Court started retreating from its support for *voir dire* into racial bias. In *Ristaino v. Ross*, 424 U.S. 589, 597 (1976), the Court held that the mere fact that the defendant is Black and the victim is White is not enough to trigger the constitutional requirement that the trial court question prospective jurors about racial prejudice. The defendants in *Ristaino* were three Black men on trial for armed robbery, assault and battery by means of a dangerous weapon, and assault with intent to murder two White security guards. In holding that the trial court did not err in refusing to question the venire on racial bias, the Court established what some have called a "special circumstances" rule: a defendant has a constitutional right to have prospective jurors questioned on racial bias only if the circumstances of the case suggest a "significant likelihood" of prejudice by the jurors.

In the next case, *Turner v. Murray*, the Court once again addresses the issue of a defendant's right to have perspective jurors questioned on racial prejudice.[a]

---

[a] For more information on the Supreme Court's jurisprudence on voir dire into racial bias and ways an attorney might question prospective jurors if concerned about racial bias, *see* Cynthia Lee, *A New Approach to Voir Dire on Racial Bias*, 5 UC IRVINE L. REV. 843 (2015), cited by Justice Samuel Alito, dissenting in Pena-Rodriguez v. Colorado, 580 U.S. 206 (2017).

TURNER V. MURRAY
Supreme Court of the United States
476 U.S. 28, 106 S. Ct. 1683, 90 L. Ed. 2d 27 (1986)

JUSTICE WHITE announced the judgment of the Court and delivered the opinion of the Court. * * *

Petitioner is a black man sentenced to death for the murder of a white storekeeper. The question presented is whether the trial judge committed reversible error at *voir dire* by refusing petitioner's request to question prospective jurors on racial prejudice.

On July 12, 1978, petitioner entered a jewelry store in Franklin, Virginia, armed with a sawed-off shotgun. He demanded that the proprietor, W. Jack Smith, Jr., put jewelry and money from the cash register into some jewelry bags. Smith complied with petitioner's demand, but triggered a silent alarm, alerting the Police Department. When Alan Bain, a police officer, arrived to inquire about the alarm, petitioner surprised him and forced him to surrender his revolver.

Having learned that Smith had triggered a silent alarm, petitioner became agitated. He fired toward the rear wall of the store and stated that if he saw or heard any more police officers, he was going to start killing those in the store. When a police siren sounded, petitioner walked to where Smith was stationed behind a counter and without warning shot him in the head with Bain's pistol, wounding Smith and causing him to slump incapacitated to the floor.

Officer Bain attempted to calm petitioner, promising to take him anywhere he wanted to go and asking him not to shoot again. Petitioner angrily replied that he was going to kill Smith for "snitching," and fired two pistol shots into Smith's chest, fatally wounding him. As petitioner turned away from shooting Smith, Bain was able to disarm him and place him under arrest.

A Southampton County, Virginia, grand jury indicted petitioner on charges of capital murder, use of a firearm in the commission of a murder, and possession of a sawed-off shotgun in the commission of a robbery. Petitioner requested and was granted a change of venue to Northampton County, Virginia, a rural county some 80 miles from the location of the murder.

Prior to the commencement of *voir dire*, petitioner's counsel submitted to the trial judge a list of proposed questions, including the following:

> The defendant, Willie Lloyd Turner, is a member of the Negro race. The victim, W. Jack Smith, Jr., was a white Caucasian. Will these facts prejudice you against Willie Lloyd Turner or affect your ability to render a fair and impartial verdict based solely on the evidence?

The judge declined to ask this question, stating that it "has been ruled on by the Supreme Court." The judge did ask the venire, who were questioned in groups of five in petitioner's presence, whether any person was aware of any reason why he could not render a fair and impartial verdict, to which all answered "no." At the time the question was asked, the prospective jurors had no way of knowing that the murder victim was white.

The jury that was empaneled, which consisted of eight whites and four blacks, convicted petitioner on all of the charges against him. After a separate sentencing hearing on the capital charge, the jury recommended that petitioner be sentenced to death, a recommendation the trial judge accepted.

Petitioner appealed his death sentence to the Virginia Supreme Court. * * * The court held that "[t]he mere fact that a defendant is black and that a victim is white does not constitutionally mandate . . . an inquiry [into racial prejudice]."

Having failed in his direct appeal, petitioner sought habeas corpus relief. * * * The United States Court of Appeals for the Fourth Circuit * * * found no special circumstance in the fact that petitioner is black and his victim white.

We granted certiorari to review the Fourth Circuit's decision that petitioner was not constitutionally entitled to have potential jurors questioned concerning racial prejudice. We reverse. * * *

The Fourth Circuit's opinion correctly states the analytical framework for evaluating petitioner's argument: "The broad inquiry in each case must be . . . whether under all of the circumstances presented there was a constitutionally significant likelihood that, absent questioning about racial prejudice, the jurors would not be indifferent as [they stand] unsworn." The Fourth Circuit was correct, too, in holding that under *Ristaino* the mere fact that petitioner is black and his victim white does not constitute a "special circumstance" of constitutional proportions. What sets this case apart from *Ristaino*, however, is that in addition to petitioner's being accused of a crime against a white victim, the crime charged was a capital offense.

In a capital sentencing proceeding before a jury, the jury is called upon to make a "highly subjective, unique, individualized judgment regarding the punishment that a particular person deserves." The Virginia statute under which petitioner was sentenced is instructive of the kinds of judgments a capital sentencing jury must make. First, in order to consider the death penalty, a Virginia jury must find either that the defendant is likely to commit future violent crimes or that his crime was "outrageously or wantonly vile, horrible or inhuman in that it involved torture, depravity of mind or an aggravated battery to the victim." Second, the jury must consider any mitigating evidence offered by the defendant. Mitigating evidence may include, but is not limited to, facts tending to show that the defendant acted under the influence of extreme emotional or mental disturbance, or that at the time of the crime the defendant's capacity "to appreciate the criminality of his conduct or to conform his conduct to the requirements of law was significantly impaired." Finally, even if the jury has found an aggravating factor, and irrespective of whether mitigating evidence has been offered, the jury has discretion not to recommend the death sentence, in which case it may not be imposed. * * *

Because of the range of discretion entrusted to a jury in a capital sentencing hearing, there is a unique opportunity for racial prejudice to operate but remain undetected. On the facts of this case, a juror who believes that blacks are violence prone or morally inferior might well be influenced by that belief in deciding whether petitioner's crime involved the aggravating factors specified under Virginia law. Such a juror might also be less favorably inclined toward petitioner's evidence of mental disturbance as a mitigating circumstance. More subtle, less consciously held racial attitudes could also influence a juror's decision in this case. Fear of blacks, which could easily be stirred up by the violent facts of petitioner's crime, might incline a juror to favor the death penalty.

The risk of racial prejudice infecting a capital sentencing proceeding is especially serious in light of the complete finality of the death sentence. * * * In the present case, we find the risk that racial prejudice may have infected petitioner's capital sentencing unacceptable in light of the ease with which that risk could have been minimized. By refusing to question prospective jurors on racial prejudice, the trial judge failed to adequately protect petitioner's constitutional right to an impartial jury.

We hold that a capital defendant accused of an interracial crime is entitled to have prospective jurors informed of the race of the victim and questioned on the issue of racial bias. The rule we propose is minimally intrusive; as in other cases involving "special circumstances," the trial judge retains discretion as to the form and number of questions on the subject, including the decision whether to question the venire individually or collectively. Also, a defendant cannot complain of a judge's failure to question the venire on racial prejudice unless the defendant has specifically requested such an inquiry.

The inadequacy of *voir dire* in this case requires that petitioner's death sentence be vacated. It is not necessary, however, that he be retried on the issue of guilt. Our judgment in this case is that there was an unacceptable risk of racial prejudice infecting the *capital sentencing proceeding*. This judgment is based on a conjunction of three factors: the fact that the crime charged involved interracial violence, the broad discretion given the jury at the death-penalty hearing, and the special seriousness of the risk of improper sentencing in a capital case. At the guilt phase of petitioner's trial, the jury had no greater discretion than it would have had if the crime charged had been noncapital murder. * * *

The judgment of the Court of Appeals is reversed, and the case is remanded for further proceedings consistent with this opinion.

It is so ordered.

THE CHIEF JUSTICE concurs in the judgment.

JUSTICE BRENNAN, concurring in part and dissenting in part.

* * * [I]n my view, the decision in this case, although clearly half right, is even more clearly half wrong. After recognizing that the constitutional guarantee of an impartial jury entitles a defendant in a capital case involving interracial violence to have prospective jurors questioned on the issue of racial bias—a holding which requires that this case be reversed and remanded for new sentencing—the Court disavows the logic of its own reasoning in denying petitioner Turner a new trial on the issue of his guilt. It accomplishes this by postulating a jury role at the sentencing phase of a capital trial fundamentally different from the jury function at the guilt phase and by concluding that the former gives rise to a significantly greater risk of a verdict tainted by racism. * * * I join only that portion of the Court's judgment granting petitioner a new sentencing proceeding, but dissent from that portion of the judgment refusing to vacate the conviction. * * *

The Court's argument is simply untenable on its face. As best I can understand it, the thesis is that since there is greater discretion entrusted to a capital jury in the sentencing phase than in the guilt phase, "there is [in the sentencing hearing] a unique opportunity for racial prejudice to operate but remain undetected." However, the Court's own discussion of the issues demonstrates that the opportunity for racial bias to taint the jury process is not "uniquely" present at a sentencing hearing, but is equally a factor at the guilt phase of a bifurcated capital trial.

* * * [I]t is certainly true, as the Court maintains, that racial bias inclines one to disbelieve and disfavor the object of the prejudice, and it is similarly incontestable that subconscious, as well as express, racial fears and hatreds operate to deny fairness to the person despised; that is why we seek to insure that the right to an impartial jury is a meaningful right by providing the defense with the opportunity to ask prospective jurors questions designed to expose even hidden prejudices. But the Court never explains why these biases should be of less concern at the guilt phase than at the sentencing phase. The majority asserts that "a juror who believes that blacks are violence prone or morally inferior might well be influenced by that belief in deciding whether petitioner's crime involved the aggravating factors specified under Virginia law." But might not that same

juror be influenced by those same prejudices in deciding whether, for example, to credit or discredit white witnesses as opposed to black witnesses at the guilt phase? Might not those same racial fears that would incline a juror to favor death not also incline a juror to favor conviction?

A trial to determine guilt or innocence is, at bottom, nothing more than the sum total of a countless number of small discretionary decisions made by each individual who sits in the jury box. The difference between conviction and acquittal turns on whether key testimony is believed or rejected; on whether an alibi sounds plausible or dubious; on whether a character witness appears trustworthy or unsavory; and on whether the jury concludes that the defendant had a motive, the inclination, or the means available to commit the crime charged. A racially biased juror sits with blurred vision and impaired sensibilities and is incapable of fairly making the myriad decisions that each juror is called upon to make in the course of a trial. To put it simply, he cannot judge because he has prejudged. This is equally true at the trial on guilt as at the hearing on sentencing. * * *

The Court may believe that it is being Solomonic in "splitting the difference" in this case and granting petitioner a new sentencing hearing while denying him the other "half" of the relief demanded. Starkly put, petitioner "wins" in that he gets to be resentenced, while the State "wins" in that it does not lose its conviction. But King Solomon did not, in fact, split the baby in two, and had he done so, I suspect that he would be remembered less for his wisdom than for his hardheartedness. Justice is not served by compromising principles in this way. I would reverse the conviction as well as the sentence in this case to insure compliance with the constitutional guarantee of an impartial jury.

JUSTICE POWELL, with whom JUSTICE REHNQUIST joins, dissenting.

The Court today adopts a *per se* rule applicable in capital cases, under which "a capital defendant accused of an interracial crime is entitled to have prospective jurors informed of the race of the victim and questioned on the issue of racial bias." * * *

In effect, the Court recognizes a presumption that jurors who have sworn to decide the case impartially nevertheless are racially biased. * * * [I]t is unnecessary and unwise for this Court to rule, as a matter of constitutional law, that a trial judge *always* must inquire into racial bias in a capital case involving an interracial murder, rather than leaving that decision to be made on a case-by-case basis. * * *

Nothing in this record suggests that racial bias played any role in the jurors' deliberations. * * * The prosecutor pointed out that the case presented no racial issues beyond the fact that petitioner and his victim were of different races. * * *

There is nothing in the record of this trial that reflects racial overtones of any kind. * * * The Court does not purport to identify any such circumstance, or to explain why the facts that a capital defendant is of one race and his victim of another now create a significant likelihood that racial issues will distort the jurors' consideration of the issues in the trial. This case illustrates that it is unnecessary for the Court to adopt a *per se* rule that constitutionalizes the unjustifiable presumption that jurors are racially biased. * * *

The *per se* rule announced today may appear innocuous. But the rule is based on what amounts to a constitutional presumption that jurors in capital cases are racially biased. Such presumption unjustifiably suggests that criminal justice in our courts of law is meted out on racial grounds. * * * The manner in which petitioner was tried and sentenced, and particularly the jurors who fulfilled their civic duty to sit in his case, reflected not a trace of the racial prejudice that the Court's new rule now presumes. * * *

[JUSTICE MARSHALL's opinion, concurring in part and dissenting in part, has been omitted.]

NOTE

Unfortunately, racial bias—whether conscious or unconscious—still exists today. While *Turner v. Murray* mandates *voir dire* into racial bias only in capital cases involving an interracial crime of violence upon defense request, trial courts have the discretion to allow attorneys in any case to question prospective jurors. Even if attorneys are permitted by the court to question prospective jurors, however, it may be difficult for them to figure out which jurors are racially biased. What types of questions might an attorney concerned about racial or other bias ask prospective jurors?

BATSON V. KENTUCKY
Supreme Court of the United States
476 U.S. 79, 106 S. Ct. 1712, 90 L. Ed.2d 69 (1986)

JUSTICE POWELL delivered the opinion of the Court. * * *

Petitioner, a black man, was indicted in Kentucky on charges of second-degree burglary and receipt of stolen goods. On the first day of trial in Jefferson Circuit Court, the judge conducted *voir dire* examination of the venire, excused certain jurors for cause, and permitted the parties to exercise peremptory challenges. The prosecutor used his peremptory challenges to strike all four black persons on the venire, and a jury composed only of white persons was selected. Defense counsel moved to discharge the jury before it was sworn on the ground that the prosecutor's removal of the black veniremen violated petitioner's rights * * * under the Fourteenth Amendment to equal protection of the laws. Counsel requested a hearing on his motion. Without expressly ruling on the request for a hearing, the trial judge observed that the parties were entitled to use their peremptory challenges to "strike anybody they want to." The judge then denied petitioner's motion. * * *

The jury convicted petitioner on both counts. On appeal to the Supreme Court of Kentucky, petitioner pressed, among other claims, the argument concerning the prosecutor's use of peremptory challenges. * * * The Supreme Court of Kentucky affirmed [petitioner's conviction]. * * * We granted certiorari, and now reverse. * * *

In *Swain v. Alabama*, this Court recognized that a "State's purposeful or deliberate denial to Negroes on account of race of participation as jurors in the administration of justice violates the Equal Protection Clause." This principle has been "consistently and repeatedly" reaffirmed, in numerous decisions of this Court both preceding and following *Swain*. We reaffirm the principle today. * * *

Purposeful racial discrimination in selection of the venire violates a defendant's right to equal protection because it denies him the protection that a trial by jury is intended to secure. "The very idea of a jury is a body . . . composed of the peers or equals of the person whose rights it is selected or summoned to determine; that is, of his neighbors, fellows, associates, persons having the same legal status in society as that which he holds." The petit jury has occupied a central position in our system of justice by safeguarding a person accused of crime against the arbitrary exercise of power by prosecutor or judge. Those on the venire must be "indifferently chosen," to secure the defendant's right under the Fourteenth Amendment to "protection of life and liberty against race or color prejudice."

Racial discrimination in selection of jurors harms not only the accused whose life or liberty they are summoned to try. Competence to serve as a juror ultimately depends on an assessment of individual qualifications and ability impartially to consider evidence presented at a trial. A person's race simply "is unrelated to his fitness as a juror." * * *

The harm from discriminatory jury selection extends beyond that inflicted on the defendant and the excluded juror to touch the entire community. Selection procedures that purposefully exclude black persons from juries undermine public confidence in the fairness of our system of justice. * * *

Accordingly, the component of the jury selection process at issue here, the State's privilege to strike individual jurors through peremptory challenges, is subject to the commands of the Equal Protection Clause. Although a prosecutor ordinarily is entitled to exercise permitted peremptory challenges "for any reason at all, as long as that reason is related to his view concerning the outcome" of the case to be tried, the Equal Protection Clause forbids the prosecutor to challenge potential jurors solely on account of their race or on the assumption that black jurors as a group will be unable impartially to consider the State's case against a black defendant.

*** [In] *Swain v. Alabama,* [we also held that] a black defendant could make out a prima facie case of purposeful discrimination *** on evidence that a prosecutor, "in case after case, whatever the circumstances, whatever the crime and whoever the defendant or the victim may be, is responsible for the removal of Negroes who have been selected as qualified jurors by the jury commissioners and who have survived challenges for cause, with the result that no Negroes ever serve on petit juries." Evidence offered by the defendant in *Swain* did not meet that standard. While the defendant showed that prosecutors in the jurisdiction had exercised their strikes to exclude blacks from the jury, he offered no proof of the circumstances under which prosecutors were responsible for striking black jurors beyond the facts of his own case.

A number of lower courts following the teaching of *Swain* reasoned that proof of repeated striking of blacks over a number of cases was necessary to establish a violation of the Equal Protection Clause. Since this interpretation of *Swain* has placed on defendants a crippling burden of proof, prosecutors' peremptory challenges are now largely immune from constitutional scrutiny. *** [W]e reject this evidentiary formulation as inconsistent with standards that have been developed since *Swain* for assessing a prima facie case under the Equal Protection Clause. ***

[S]ince the decision in *Swain,* this Court has recognized that a defendant may make a prima facie showing of purposeful racial discrimination in selection of the venire by relying solely on the facts concerning its selection *in his case.* These decisions are in accordance with the proposition *** that "a consistent pattern of official racial discrimination" is not "a necessary predicate to a violation of the Equal Protection Clause. A single invidiously discriminatory governmental act" is not "immunized by the absence of such discrimination in the making of other comparable decisions." For evidentiary requirements to dictate that "several must suffer discrimination" before one could object, would be inconsistent with the promise of equal protection to all.

*** These principles support our conclusion that a defendant may establish a prima facie case of purposeful discrimination in selection of the petit jury solely on evidence concerning the prosecutor's exercise of peremptory challenges at the defendant's trial.[a] To establish such a case,

---

[a] Even though the *Batson* Court did not address whether the Equal Protection Clause imposes any limits on the exercise of peremptory challenges by criminal defense counsel, in a later case, the Court applied the *Batson* framework in a case where the prosecutor objected to a White defendant's use of the peremptory challenge to strike Black prospective jurors. *Georgia v. McCollum,* 505 U.S. 42 (1992). The Court explained that the racially discriminatory use of peremptory challenges by criminal defense counsel inflicts the same harms addressed in the *Batson* case. It also found state action, quoting from a previous Supreme Court decision where the

the defendant first must show that he is a member of a cognizable racial group, and that the prosecutor has exercised peremptory challenges to remove from the venire members of the defendant's race.[b] Second, the defendant is entitled to rely on the fact, as to which there can be no dispute, that peremptory challenges constitute a jury selection practice that permits "those to discriminate who are of a mind to discriminate." Finally, the defendant must show that these facts and any other relevant circumstances raise an inference that the prosecutor used that practice to exclude the veniremen from the petit jury on account of their race. * * *

Once the defendant makes a prima facie showing, the burden shifts to the State to come forward with a neutral explanation for challenging black jurors. Though this requirement imposes a limitation in some cases on the full peremptory character of the historic challenge, we emphasize that the prosecutor's explanation need not rise to the level justifying exercise of a challenge for cause.[c] But the prosecutor may not rebut the defendant's prima facie case of discrimination by stating merely that he challenged jurors of the defendant's race on the assumption—or his intuitive judgment—that they would be partial to the defendant because of their shared race. Just as the Equal Protection Clause forbids the States to exclude black persons from the venire on the assumption that blacks as a group are unqualified to serve as jurors, so it forbids the States to strike black veniremen on the assumption that they will be biased in a particular case simply because the defendant is black. The core guarantee of equal protection, ensuring citizens that their State will not discriminate on account of race, would be meaningless were we to approve the exclusion of jurors on the basis of such assumptions, which arise solely from the jurors' race. Nor may the prosecutor rebut the defendant's case merely by denying that he had a discriminatory motive or "affirm[ing] [his] good faith in making individual selections." If these general assertions were accepted as rebutting a defendant's prima facie case, the Equal Protection Clause "would be but a vain and illusory requirement." The prosecutor therefore must articulate a neutral explanation related to the particular case to be

---

Court explained that "the peremptory challenge system, as well as the jury system as a whole, 'simply could not exist'" without the "'overt, significant participation of the government,'" *id.* at 51, and noting that "peremptory challenges perform a traditional function of the government: 'Their sole purpose is to permit litigants to assist the government in the selection of an impartial trier of fact.'" *Id.* at 52 (quoting Edmonson v. Leesville Concrete Co., 500 U.S. 614 (1991)).

[b] In *Powers v. Ohio*, the Court held that the defendant and the prospective juror who is struck by the opposing party need not be members of the same race. 499 U.S. 400 (1991) (permitting a White defendant to object to the prosecution's use of its peremptory challenges to strike Black persons on the venire).

[c] In *Purkett v. Elem*, 514 U.S. 765 (1995), the Court noted that at this second stage, it is not necessary that the prosecutor's explanation be "minimally persuasive." *Id.* at 768. "At the third stage, however, when the trial court has to decide whether the defendant has established purposeful discrimination, 'implausible or fantastic justifications may (and probably will) be found to be pretexts for purposeful discrimination.'" *Id.*

tried. The trial court then will have the duty to determine if the defendant has established purposeful discrimination.d * * *

The State contends that our holding will eviscerate the fair trial values served by the peremptory challenge. Conceding that the Constitution does not guarantee a right to peremptory challenges and that *Swain* did state that their use ultimately is subject to the strictures of equal protection, the State argues that the privilege of unfettered exercise of the challenge is of vital importance to the criminal justice system.

While we recognize, of course, that the peremptory challenge occupies an important position in our trial procedures, we do not agree that our decision today will undermine the contribution the challenge generally makes to the administration of justice. The reality of practice, amply reflected in many state and federal court opinions, shows that the challenge may be, and unfortunately at times has been, used to discriminate against black jurors. By requiring trial courts to be sensitive to the racially discriminatory use of peremptory challenges, our decision enforces the mandate of equal protection and furthers the ends of justice. In view of the heterogeneous population of our Nation, public respect for our criminal justice system and the rule of law will be strengthened if we ensure that no citizen is disqualified from jury service because of his race. * * *

In this case, petitioner made a timely objection to the prosecutor's removal of all black persons on the venire. Because the trial court flatly rejected the objection without requiring the prosecutor to give an explanation for his action, we remand this case for further proceedings. If the trial court decides that the facts establish, prima facie, purposeful discrimination and the prosecutor does not come forward with a neutral explanation for his action, our precedents require that petitioner's conviction be reversed.

It is so ordered.

JUSTICE MARSHALL, concurring. * * *

I wholeheartedly concur in the Court's conclusion that use of the peremptory challenge to remove blacks from juries, on the basis of their race, violates the Equal Protection Clause. I would go further, however, in fashioning a remedy adequate to eliminate that discrimination. Merely allowing defendants the opportunity to challenge the racially discriminatory use of peremptory challenges in individual cases will not end the illegitimate use of the peremptory challenge.

---

[d] In *Miller-El v. Dretke*, 545 U.S. 231 (2005), the Court noted that "[i]f a prosecutor's proffered reason for striking a black panelist applies just as well to an otherwise-similar nonblack who is permitted to serve, that is evidence tending to prove purposeful discrimination to be considered at *Batson*'s third step." *Id.* at 241.

*** First, defendants cannot attack the discriminatory use of peremptory challenges at all unless the challenges are so flagrant as to establish a prima facie case. *** Prosecutors are left free to discriminate against blacks in jury selection provided that they hold that discrimination to an "acceptable" level.

Second, when a defendant can establish a prima facie case, trial courts face the difficult burden of assessing prosecutors' motives. Any prosecutor can easily assert facially neutral reasons for striking a juror, and trial courts are ill equipped to second-guess those reasons. How is the court to treat a prosecutor's statement that he struck a juror because the juror had a son about the same age as defendant, or seemed "uncommunicative," or "never cracked a smile" and, therefore "did not possess the sensitivities necessary to realistically look at the issues and decide the facts in this case." If such easily generated explanations are sufficient to discharge the prosecutor's obligation to justify his strikes on nonracial grounds, then the protection erected by the Court today may be illusory.

Nor is outright prevarication by prosecutors the only danger here. *** A prosecutor's own conscious or unconscious racism may lead him easily to the conclusion that a prospective black juror is "sullen," or "distant," a characterization that would not have come to his mind if a white juror had acted identically. A judge's own conscious or unconscious racism may lead him to accept such an explanation as well supported. As Justice Rehnquist concedes, prosecutors' peremptories are based on their "seat-of-the-pants instincts" as to how particular jurors will vote. Yet "seat-of-the-pants instincts" may often be just another term for racial prejudice. Even if all parties approach the Court's mandate with the best of conscious intentions, that mandate requires them to confront and overcome their own racism on all levels—a challenge I doubt all of them can meet. ***

The inherent potential of peremptory challenges to distort the jury process by permitting the exclusion of jurors on racial grounds should ideally lead the Court to ban them entirely from the criminal justice system. *** Some authors have suggested that the courts should ban prosecutors' peremptories entirely, but should zealously guard the defendant's peremptory as "essential to the fairness of trial by jury." I would not find that an acceptable solution. Our criminal justice system "requires not only freedom from any bias against the accused, but also from any prejudice against his prosecution. Between him and the state the scales are to be evenly held." We can maintain that balance, not by permitting both prosecutor and defendant to engage in racial discrimination in jury selection, but by banning the use of peremptory challenges by prosecutors and by allowing the States to eliminate the defendant's peremptories as well. ***

I applaud the Court's holding that the racially discriminatory use of peremptory challenges violates the Equal Protection Clause, and I join the Court's opinion. However, only by banning peremptories entirely can such discrimination be ended.

CHIEF JUSTICE BURGER, joined by JUSTICE REHNQUIST, dissenting.
* * *

Today the Court sets aside the peremptory challenge, a procedure which has been part of the common law for many centuries and part of our jury system for nearly 200 years. * * * Permitting unexplained peremptories has long been regarded as a means to strengthen our jury system in other ways as well. One commentator has recognized:

> The peremptory, made without giving any reason, avoids trafficking in the core of truth in most common stereotypes.... Common human experience, common sense, psychosociological studies, and public opinion polls tell us that it is likely that certain classes of people statistically have predispositions that would make them inappropriate jurors for particular kinds of cases. But to allow this knowledge to be expressed in the evaluative terms necessary for challenges for cause would undercut our desire for a society in which all people are judged as individuals and in which each is held reasonable and open to compromise.... [W]e have evolved in the peremptory challenge a system that allows the covert expression of what we dare not say but know is true more often than not.

For reasons such as these, this Court concluded in *Swain* that "the [peremptory] challenge is one of the most important of the rights" in our justice system. For close to a century, then, it has been settled that "[t]he denial or impairment of the right is reversible error without a showing of prejudice."

Instead of even considering the history or function of the peremptory challenge, the bulk of the Court's opinion is spent recounting the well-established principle that intentional exclusion of racial groups from jury venires is a violation of the Equal Protection Clause. * * * That the Court is not applying conventional equal protection analysis is shown by its limitation of its new rule to allegations of impermissible challenge on the basis of race; the Court's opinion clearly contains such a limitation. But if conventional equal protection principles apply, then presumably defendants could object to exclusions on the basis of not only race, but also sex. * * *

JUSTICE REHNQUIST, with whom THE CHIEF JUSTICE joins, dissenting.
* * *

I cannot subscribe to the Court's unprecedented use of the Equal Protection Clause to restrict the historic scope of the peremptory challenge, which has been described as "a necessary part of trial by jury." In my view, there is simply nothing "unequal" about the State's using its peremptory challenges to strike blacks from the jury in cases involving black defendants, so long as such challenges are also used to exclude whites in cases involving white defendants, Hispanics in cases involving Hispanic defendants, Asians in cases involving Asian defendants, and so on. This case-specific use of peremptory challenges by the State does not single out blacks, or members of any other race for that matter, for discriminatory treatment. * * *

The use of group affiliations, such as age, race, or occupation, as a "proxy" for potential juror partiality, based on the assumption or belief that members of one group are more likely to favor defendants who belong to the same group, has long been accepted as a legitimate basis for the State's exercise of peremptory challenges. Indeed, given the need for reasonable limitations on the time devoted to *voir dire*, the use of such "proxies" by both the State and the defendant may be extremely useful in eliminating from the jury persons who might be biased in one way or another. The Court today holds that the State may not use its peremptory challenges to strike black prospective jurors on this basis without violating the Constitution. But I do not believe there is anything in the Equal Protection Clause, or any other constitutional provision, that justifies such a departure from [our precedents]. I would therefore affirm the judgment of the court below.

[JUSTICE WHITE's concurring opinion, JUSTICE STEVENS' concurring opinion, and JUSTICE O'CONNOR's concurring opinion have been omitted.]

"GOOD" REVERSAL FOLLOWED "UNFAIR" TRIAL
Kay Stewart[a]
The Courier-Journal, Nov. 6, 2005

His name is used regularly in courtrooms across America, but James Kirkland Batson would be happier if everyone forgot all about him. "It's so old, they ought to let it go," Batson said of the landmark U.S. Supreme Court ruling bearing his name. But the 49-year-old Louisville construction worker still gets emotional at the mention of his 1982 conviction for burglary and receiving stolen property by an all-white Jefferson Circuit Court jury. Batson, who is black, watched as the prosecutor dismissed all four blacks from the panel. "I don't *think* it was unfair. It was unfair," he said.

In 1986, while Batson was serving a 20-year prison sentence, the U.S. Supreme Court reversed his conviction and the ruling established new

---

[a] © The Courier-Journal—USA Today Network.

standards to prevent discrimination in jury selection. Rather than risk a retrial, Batson pleaded guilty to burglary as part of a plea bargain that resulted in a five-year sentence. He subsequently got in trouble with the law several times and racked up a string of burglary, theft, receiving stolen property and persistent-felon convictions, said Lisa Lamb, a Kentucky Corrections Department spokeswoman. He was released from prison in January 2003 and will remain on parole through 2026.

Joe Gutmann, the prosecutor in Batson's 1982 trial, said in a recent interview that the Supreme Court's decision in the case was "a good one," because it prevents lawyers from discriminating in jury selection. Gutmann, who now teaches at Central High School, said he removed the blacks not because of their race but because they were young and might sympathize with Batson.

Batson said he doesn't blame Gutmann. "He was doing what he thought was necessary," Batson said. "He was the prosecutor, and he didn't want to lose."

NOTE

On Monday, April 27, 1987, less than a year following the *Batson* decision in May 1986, jury selection began in Timothy Foster's trial. Foster was charged with malice murder and burglary and faced the death penalty. Initially, there were five prospective Black jurors but after one of these prospective jurors notified the court that one of her close friends was related to Foster, the court removed that juror for cause, leaving four prospective Black jurors.

During jury selection, the State exercised its peremptory strikes against all four of the remaining Black prospective jurors. Foster objected to the prosecution's use of its peremptory challenges, alleging purposeful racial discrimination in violation of *Batson v. Kentucky*. The trial court denied Foster's *Batson* challenge. Foster was convicted and sentenced to death. His conviction and death sentence were affirmed by the Georgia Supreme Court.

In 2015, based on newly discovered evidence from the prosecutor's file obtained through Georgia's Open Records Act, Foster filed a petition for a writ of certiorari with the United States Supreme Court, repeating his claim that the government had engaged in purposeful race-based discrimination during jury selection. The newly discovered evidence in the prosecutor's file contained copies of the jury venire lists from the prosecutor's office on which the names of each Black prospective juror were highlighted in bright green with the letter "B" next to their name; a draft affidavit from an investigator comparing the Black prospective jurors and concluding, "If it comes down to having to pick one of the black jurors, [this one] might be okay;" notes identifying three of the Black prospective jurors as "B#1," "B#2," and "B#3;" notes with "N" (for "no") appearing next to the names of all five of the Black prospective jurors; a list titled "[D]efinite NO's" containing six names, including the names of all five of the Black prospective jurors; a document with notes on the Church of Christ that was annotated "*NO*. No *Black* Church;" and the questionnaires filled out by the five prospective Black jurors, on which each juror's response indicating his or her race had been circled.

The Supreme Court held in a 7–1 decision that the prosecutor had engaged in purposeful discrimination with respect to two of the dismissed jurors and remanded the case for further proceedings. Foster v. Chatman, 578 U.S. 488 (2016). The Court's opinion focused narrowly on the facts of the case and did not revise the *Batson* framework to try to prevent future *Batson* violations.[a]

Pretrial hearings in anticipation of Foster's retrial began in late 2018.[b] The government expressed its intent to again seek the death penalty.[c] Before the retrial began, Foster pled guilty and agreed to a life sentence without the possibility of parole in exchange for which the government agreed to take the death penalty off the table.[d]

J.E.B. v. ALABAMA
Supreme Court of the United States
511 U.S. 127, 114 S. Ct. 1419, 128 L. Ed. 2d 89 (1994)

JUSTICE BLACKMUN delivered the opinion of the Court.

* * * Today we are faced with the question whether the Equal Protection Clause forbids intentional discrimination on the basis of gender, just as it prohibits discrimination on the basis of race. We hold that gender, like race, is an unconstitutional proxy for juror competence and impartiality.

On behalf of relator T.B., the mother of a minor child, respondent State of Alabama filed a complaint for paternity and child support against petitioner J.E.B. in the District Court of Jackson County, Alabama. * * * The trial court assembled a panel of 36 potential jurors, 12 males and 24 females. After the court excused three jurors for cause, only 10 of the remaining 33 jurors were male. The State then used 9 of its 10 peremptory strikes to remove male jurors; petitioner used all but one of his strikes to remove female jurors. As a result, all the selected jurors were female.

---

[a] Lyle Denniston, *Telltale Files on Race-Based Jury Selection*, SCOTUSBLOG (May 23, 2016) (observing that "it is doubtful that prosecutors [in the future will] create such revealing files, with clear markings next to the names of potential black jurors to be stricken from the jury pool"), https://www.scotusblog.com/2016/05/opinion-analysis-telltale-files-on-race-based-jury-selection/ (https://perma.cc/RE2D-GBBD).

[b] *See* John Bailey, *Hearings for Foster Re-Trial Begin*, AP NEWS (Oct. 28, 2018), https://apnews.com/article/04e14c2cbd814b60908ac6e982e39e3a (https://perma.cc/92LP-GM8R).

[c] *See* John Bailey, *Resolution: Family Remembers Queen White as Her Killer Pleads Guilty, Sentenced to Life Without Parole*, ROME NEWS TRIB. (Mar. 4, 2022), https://www.northwestgeorgianews.com/rome/news/local/resolution-family-remembers-queen-white-as-her-killer-pleads-guilty-sentenced-to-life-without-parole/article_08241632-9c10-11ec-813f-9f3b8bf4117a.html (https://perma.cc/R6A6-3UCV).

[d] *Id.*

Before the jury was empaneled, petitioner objected to the State's peremptory challenges on the ground that they were exercised against male jurors solely on the basis of gender, in violation of the Equal Protection Clause of the Fourteenth Amendment. Petitioner argued that the logic and reasoning of *Batson v. Kentucky*, which prohibits peremptory strikes solely on the basis of race, similarly forbids intentional discrimination on the basis of gender. The court rejected petitioner's claim and empaneled the all-female jury. The jury found petitioner to be the father of the child, and the court entered an order directing him to pay child support. On post judgment motion, the court reaffirmed its ruling that *Batson* does not extend to gender-based peremptory challenges. * * *

We granted certiorari to resolve a question that has created a conflict of authority—whether the Equal Protection Clause forbids peremptory challenges on the basis of gender as well as on the basis of race. Today we reaffirm what, by now, should be axiomatic: Intentional discrimination on the basis of gender by state actors violates the Equal Protection Clause, particularly where, as here, the discrimination serves to ratify and perpetuate invidious, archaic, and overbroad stereotypes about the relative abilities of men and women.

Discrimination on the basis of gender in the exercise of peremptory challenges is a relatively recent phenomenon. Gender-based peremptory strikes were hardly practicable during most of our country's existence, since, until the 20th century, women were completely excluded from jury service. * * *

Many States continued to exclude women from jury service well into the present century, despite the fact that women attained suffrage upon ratification of the Nineteenth Amendment in 1920. States that did permit women to serve on juries often erected other barriers, such as registration requirements and automatic exemptions, designed to deter women from exercising their right to jury service.

The prohibition of women on juries was derived from the English common law which, according to Blackstone, rightfully excluded women from juries under "the doctrine of propter defectum sexus, literally, the 'defect of sex.'" In this country, supporters of the exclusion of women from juries tended to couch their objections in terms of the ostensible need to protect women from the ugliness and depravity of trials. Women were thought to be too fragile and virginal to withstand the polluted courtroom atmosphere.

* * * Since *Reed v. Reed*, this Court consistently has subjected gender-based classifications to heightened scrutiny in recognition of the real danger that government policies that professedly are based on reasonable considerations in fact may be reflective of "archaic and overbroad" generalizations about gender, or based on "outdated misconceptions

concerning the role of females in the home rather than in the marketplace and world of ideas."

Despite the heightened scrutiny afforded distinctions based on gender, respondent argues that gender discrimination in the selection of the petit jury should be permitted, though discrimination on the basis of race is not. Respondent suggests that "gender discrimination in this country ... has never reached the level of discrimination" against African-Americans, and therefore gender discrimination, unlike racial discrimination, is tolerable in the courtroom.

While the prejudicial attitudes toward women in this country have not been identical to those held toward racial minorities, the similarities between the experiences of racial minorities and women, in some contexts, "overpower those differences." * * * Certainly, with respect to jury service, African-Americans and women share a history of total exclusion, a history which came to an end for women many years after the embarrassing chapter in our history came to an end for African-Americans.

We need not determine, however, whether women or racial minorities have suffered more at the hands of discriminatory state actors during the decades of our Nation's history. It is necessary only to acknowledge that "our Nation has had a long and unfortunate history of sex discrimination," a history which warrants the heightened scrutiny we afford all gender-based classifications today. Under our equal protection jurisprudence, gender-based classifications require "an exceedingly persuasive justification" in order to survive constitutional scrutiny. Thus, the only question is whether discrimination on the basis of gender in jury selection substantially furthers the State's legitimate interest in achieving a fair and impartial trial. In making this assessment, we do not weigh the value of peremptory challenges as an institution against our asserted commitment to eradicate invidious discrimination from the courtroom. Instead, we consider whether peremptory challenges based on gender stereotypes provide substantial aid to a litigant's effort to secure a fair and impartial jury.

Far from proffering an exceptionally persuasive justification for its gender-based peremptory challenges, respondent maintains that its decision to strike virtually all the males from the jury in this case "may reasonably have been based upon the perception, supported by history, that men otherwise totally qualified to serve upon a jury in any case might be more sympathetic and receptive to the arguments of a man alleged in a paternity action to be the father of an out-of-wedlock child, while women equally qualified to serve upon a jury might be more sympathetic and receptive to the arguments of the complaining witness who bore the child."

We shall not accept as a defense to gender-based peremptory challenges "the very stereotype the law condemns." Respondent's rationale, not unlike those regularly expressed for gender-based strikes, is reminiscent of the arguments advanced to justify the total exclusion of women from juries. Respondent offers virtually no support for the conclusion that gender alone is an accurate predictor of juror's attitudes; yet it urges this Court to condone the same stereotypes that justified the wholesale exclusion of women from juries and the ballot box. Respondent seems to assume that gross generalizations that would be deemed impermissible if made on the basis of race are somehow permissible when made on the basis of gender.

Discrimination in jury selection, whether based on race or on gender, causes harm to the litigants, the community, and the individual jurors who are wrongfully excluded from participation in the judicial process. The litigants are harmed by the risk that the prejudice that motivated the discriminatory selection of the jury will infect the entire proceedings. The community is harmed by the State's participation in the perpetuation of invidious group stereotypes and the inevitable loss of confidence in our judicial system that state-sanctioned discrimination in the courtroom engenders.

When state actors exercise peremptory challenges in reliance on gender stereotypes, they ratify and reinforce prejudicial views of the relative abilities of men and women. * * * Discriminatory use of peremptory challenges may create the impression that the judicial system has acquiesced in suppressing full participation by one gender or that the "deck has been stacked" in favor of one side.

In recent cases we have emphasized that individual jurors themselves have a right to nondiscriminatory jury selection procedures. Contrary to respondent's suggestion, this right extends to both men and women. * * * Striking individual jurors on the assumption that they hold particular views simply because of their gender is "practically a brand upon them, affixed by the law, an assertion of their inferiority." * * *

The experience in the many jurisdictions that have barred gender-based challenges belies the claim that litigants and trial courts are incapable of complying with a rule barring strikes based on gender. As with race-based *Batson* claims, a party alleging gender discrimination must make a prima facie showing of intentional discrimination before the party exercising the challenge is required to explain the basis for the strike. When an explanation is required, it need not rise to the level of a "for cause" challenge; rather, it merely must be based on a juror characteristic other than gender, and the proffered explanation may not be pretextual.

Failing to provide jurors the same protection against gender discrimination as race discrimination could frustrate the purpose of *Batson* itself. Because gender and race are overlapping categories, gender can be used as a pretext for racial discrimination. Allowing parties to remove racial minorities from the jury not because of their race, but because of their gender, contravenes well-established equal protection principles and could insulate effectively racial discrimination from judicial scrutiny.

Equal opportunity to participate in the fair administration of justice is fundamental to our democratic system. It not only furthers the goals of the jury system. It reaffirms the promise of equality under the law-that all citizens, regardless of race, ethnicity, or gender, have the chance to take part directly in our democracy. When persons are excluded from participation in our democratic processes solely because of race or gender, this promise of equality dims, and the integrity of our judicial system is jeopardized.

In view of these concerns, the Equal Protection Clause prohibits discrimination in jury selection on the basis of gender, or on the assumption that an individual will be biased in a particular case for no reason other than the fact that the person happens to be a woman or happens to be a man. * * *

The judgment of the Court of Civil Appeals of Alabama is reversed, and the case is remanded to that court for further proceedings not inconsistent with this opinion.

It is so ordered.

JUSTICE O'CONNOR, concurring.

I agree with the Court that the Equal Protection Clause prohibits the government from excluding a person from jury service on account of that person's gender. * * * I therefore join the Court's opinion in this case. But today's important blow against gender discrimination is not costless. I write separately to discuss some of these costs, and to express my belief that today's holding should be limited to the government's use of gender-based peremptory strikes. * * * [T]oday's decision further erodes the role of the peremptory challenge. * * *

In so doing we make the peremptory challenge less discretionary and more like a challenge for cause. We also increase the possibility that biased jurors will be allowed onto the jury, because sometimes a lawyer will be unable to provide an acceptable gender-neutral explanation even though the lawyer is in fact correct that the juror is unsympathetic. Similarly, in jurisdictions where lawyers exercise their strikes in open court, lawyers may be deterred from using their peremptories, out of the fear that if they are unable to justify the strike the court will seat a juror who knows that the striking party thought him unfit. Because I believe the peremptory remains an important litigator's tool and a fundamental part of the process of selecting impartial juries, our increasing limitation of it gives me pause.

Nor is the value of the peremptory challenge to the litigant diminished when the peremptory is exercised in a gender-based manner. We know that like race, gender matters. A plethora of studies make clear that in rape cases, for example, female jurors are somewhat more likely to vote to convict than male jurors. * * * Today's decision severely limits a litigant's ability to act on this intuition, for the import of our holding is that any correlation between a juror's gender and attitudes is irrelevant as a matter of constitutional law. * * * These concerns reinforce my conviction that today's decision should be limited to a prohibition on the government's use of gender-based peremptory challenges. * * *

JUSTICE SCALIA, with whom THE CHIEF JUSTICE and JUSTICE THOMAS join, dissenting.

Today's opinion is an inspiring demonstration of how thoroughly up-to-date and right-thinking we Justices are in matters pertaining to the sexes (or as the Court would have it, the genders), and how sternly we disapprove the male chauvinist attitudes of our predecessors. The price to be paid for this display—a modest price, surely—is that most of the opinion is quite irrelevant to the case at hand. The hasty reader will be surprised to learn, for example, that this lawsuit involves a complaint about the use of peremptory challenges to exclude men from a petit jury. To be sure, petitioner, a man, used all but one of his peremptory strikes to remove women from the jury (he used his last challenge to strike the sole remaining male from the pool), but the validity of his strikes is not before us. Nonetheless, the Court treats itself to an extended discussion of the historic exclusion of women not only from jury service, but also from service at the bar (which is rather like jury service, in that it involves going to the courthouse a lot). All this, as I say, is irrelevant, since the case involves state action that allegedly discriminates against men. The parties do not contest that discrimination on the basis of sex is subject to what our cases call "heightened scrutiny," and the citation of one of those cases (preferably one involving men rather than women), is all that was needed.

* * * The extension of *Batson* to sex, and almost certainly beyond, will provide the basis for extensive collateral litigation, which especially the criminal defendant (who litigates full time and cost free) can be expected to pursue. While demographic reality places some limit on the number of cases in which race-based challenges will be an issue, every case contains a potential sex-based claim. Another consequence, as I have mentioned, is a lengthening of the *voir dire* process that already burdens trial courts. * * *

For these reasons, I dissent.

[JUSTICE KENNEDY's opinion, concurring in the judgment, and CHIEF JUSTICE REHNQUIST's dissenting opinion have been omitted.]

Chapter 29

The Role of Criminal Defense Counsel

■ ■ ■

The Sixth Amendment to the U.S. Constitution provides, "In all criminal prosecutions, the accused shall . . . have the Assistance of Counsel for his defence." In *Gideon v. Wainwright*, excerpted in Chapter 17, the U.S. Supreme Court held that the States, along with the federal government, must provide indigent defendants with appointed counsel at trial. This right to appointed counsel applies even to an indigent defendant charged with a misdemeanor who is sentenced to a term of imprisonment. *Argersinger v. Hamlin*, 407 U.S. 25 (1972). To help students understand the important role that criminal defense counsel plays in the administration of justice, the chapter starts with a short article by Barry Winston entitled, *Why I Defend Guilty Clients*.

To give the right to counsel meaning, the Court has held that the right to counsel includes the right to effective assistance of counsel. *Strickland v. Washington* elaborates on the meaning of effective assistance of counsel and outlines what a defendant must do to prevail on a claim of ineffective assistance of counsel. The next three cases apply the *Strickland* test for ineffective assistance of counsel. *Padilla v. Kentucky* examines whether an attorney's failure to inform his immigrant client that pleading guilty would subject the client to removal from the United States constitutes ineffective assistance of counsel. *Buck v. Davis* considers whether a criminal defense attorney's decision to call an expert witness to the stand in a capital case involving an African American defendant, knowing that the witness had written a report in which he opined there is an increased probability of future violence with respect to Black offenders, constitutes ineffective assistance of counsel. *Nix v. Whiteside* considers whether a criminal defense attorney's threat to withdraw if the client takes the stand and testifies in a way that the attorney thinks would be providing false testimony constitutes ineffective assistance of counsel.

The remaining cases in this chapter focus on other issues related to the right to counsel. *Wheat v. United States* examines whether the right to counsel includes a right to counsel of one's choice. *Faretta v. California* examines whether the right to counsel includes a right to proceed without counsel—in other words, a right of self-representation.

WHY I DEFEND GUILTY CLIENTS
Barry Winston[a]
Harper's Magazine (December 1986)

Let me tell you a story. A true story. The court records are all there if anyone wants to check. It's three years ago. I'm sitting in my office, staring out the window, when I get a call from a lawyer I hardly know. Tax lawyer. Some kid is in trouble and would I be interested in helping him out? He's charged with manslaughter, a felony, and driving under the influence. I tell him sure, have the kid call me.

So the kid calls and makes an appointment to see me. He's a nice kid, fresh out of college, and he's come down here to spend some time with his older sister, who's in med school. One day she tells him they're invited to a cookout with some friends of hers. She's going directly from class and he's going to take her car and meet her there. It's way out in the country, but he gets there before she does, introduces himself around, and pops a beer. She shows up after a while and he pops another beer. Then he eats a hamburger and drinks a third beer. At some point his sister says, "Well, it's about time to go," and they head for the car.

And, the kid tells me, sitting there in my office, the next thing he remembers, he's waking up in a hospital room, hurting like hell, bandages and casts all over him, and somebody is telling him he's charged with manslaughter and DUI because he wrecked his sister's car, killed her in the process, and blew fourteen on the Breathalyzer. I ask him what the hell he means by "the next thing he remembers," and he looks me straight in the eye and says he can't remember anything from the time they leave the cookout until he wakes up in the hospital. He tells me the doctors say he has post-retrograde amnesia. I say of course I believe him, but I'm worried about finding a judge who'll believe him.

I agree to represent him and send somebody for a copy of the wreck report. It says there are four witnesses: a couple in a car going the other way who passed the kid and his sister just before their car ran off the road, the guy whose front yard they landed in, and the trooper who investigated. I call the guy whose yard they ended up in. He isn't home. I leave word. Then I call the couple. The wife agrees to come in the next day with her husband. While I'm talking to her, the first guy calls. I call him back, introduce myself, tell him I'm representing the kid and need to talk to him about the accident. He hems and haws and I figure he's one of those people who think it's against the law to talk to defense lawyers. I say the D.A. will tell him it's O.K. to talk to me, but he doesn't have to. I give him the name and number of the D.A. and he says he'll call me back.

---

[a] Copyright © 1986 Harper's Magazine. All Rights Reserved. Reproduced from the December issue by special permission.

Then I go out and hunt up the trooper. He tells me the whole story. The kid and his sister are coming into town on Smith Level Road, after it turns from fifty-five to forty-five. The Thornes—the couple—are heading out of town. They say this sports car passes them, going the other way, right after that bad turn just south of the new subdivision. They say it's going like a striped-ass ape, at least sixty-five or seventy. Mrs. Thorne turns around to look and Mr. Thorne watches in the rearview mirror. They both see the same thing: halfway into the curve, the car runs off the road on the right, whips back onto the road, spins, runs off on the left, and disappears. They turn around in the first driveway they come to and start back, both terrified of what they're going to find. By this time, Trooper Johnson says, the guy whose front yard the car has ended up in has pulled the kid and his sister out of the wreck and started CPR on the girl. Turns out he's an emergency medical technician. Holloway, that's his name. Johnson tells me that Holloway says he's sitting in his front room, watching television, when he hears a hell of a crash in his yard. He runs outside and finds the car flipped over, and so he pulls the kid out from the driver's side, the girl from the other side. She dies in his arms.

And that, says Trooper Johnson, is that. The kid's blood/alcohol content was fourteen, he was going way too fast, and the girl is dead. He had to charge him. It's a shame, he seems a nice kid, it was his own sister and all, but what the hell can he do, right?

The next day the Thornes come in, and they confirm everything Johnson said. By now things are looking not so hot for my client, and I'm thinking it's about time to have a little chat with the D.A. But Holloway still hasn't called me back, so I call him. Not home. Leave word. No call. I wait a couple of days and call again. Finally I get him on the phone. He's very agitated, and won't talk to me except to say that he doesn't have to talk to me.

I know I better look for a deal, so I go to the D.A. He's very sympathetic. But. There's only so far you can get on sympathy. A young woman is dead, promising career cut short, all because somebody has too much to drink and drives. The kid has to pay. Not, the D.A. says, with jail time. But he's got to plead guilty to two misdemeanors: death by vehicle and driving under the influence. That means probation, a big fine. Several thousand dollars. Still, it's hard for me to criticize the D.A. After all, he's probably going to have the MADD mothers all over him because of reducing the felony to a misdemeanor.

On the day of the trial, I get to court a few minutes early. There are the Thornes and Trooper Johnson, and someone I assume is Holloway. Sure enough, when this guy sees me, he comes over and introduces himself and starts right in: "I just want you to know how serious all this drinking and driving really is," he says. "If those young people hadn't been drinking and driving that night, that poor young girl would be alive today." Now, I'm trying to hold my temper when I spot the D.A. I bolt across the room, grab him by the arm, and say, "We gotta talk. Why the hell have you got all those people here? That jerk Holloway. Surely to God you're not going to call him as a witness. This is a guilty plea! My client's parents are sitting out there. You don't need to put them through a dog-and-pony show."

The D.A. looks at me and says, "Man, I'm sorry, but in a case like this, I gotta put on witnesses. Weird Wally is on the bench. If I try to go without witnesses, he might throw me out."

The D.A. calls his first witness. Trooper Johnson identifies himself, tells about being called to the scene of the accident, and describes what he found when he got there and what everybody told him. After he finishes, the judge looks at me. "No questions," I say. Then the D.A. calls Holloway. He describes the noise, running out of the house, the upside down car in his yard, pulling my client out of the window on the left side of the car and then going around to the other side for the girl. When he gets to this part, he really hits his stride. He describes, in minute detail, the injuries he saw and what he did to try and save her life. And then he tells, breath by breath, how she died in his arms.

The D.A. says, "No further questions, your Honor." The judge looks at me. I shake my head, and he says to Holloway, "You may step down." One of those awful silences hangs there, and nothing happens for a minute. Holloway doesn't move. Then he looks at me, and at the D.A., and then at the judge. He says, "Can I say something else, your Honor?"

All my bells are ringing at once, and my gut is screaming at me, Object! Object! I'm trying to decide in three-quarters of a second whether it'll be worse to listen to a lecture on the evils of drink from this jerk Holloway or piss off the judge by objecting. But all I say is, "No objections, your Honor." The judge smiles at me, then at Holloway, and says, "Very well, Mr. Holloway. What did you wish to say?"

It all comes out in a rush. "Well, you see, your Honor," Holloway says, "it was just like I told Trooper Johnson. It all happened so fast. I heard the noise, and I came running out, and it was night, and I was excited, and the next morning, when I had a chance to think about it, I figured out what had happened, but by then I'd already told Trooper Johnson and I didn't know what to do, but you see, the car, it was up-side down, and I did pull that boy out of the left-hand window, but don't you see, the car was upside down, and if you turned it over on its wheels like it's supposed to be, the left-hand side is really on the right-hand side, and your Honor, that boy wasn't driving that car at all. It was the girl that was driving, and when I had a chance to think about it the next morning, I realized that I'd told Trooper Johnson wrong, and I was scared and I didn't know what to do, and that's why"—and now he's looking right at me—"why I wouldn't talk to you."

Naturally, the defendant is allowed to withdraw his guilty plea. The charges are dismissed and the kid and his parents and I go into one of the back rooms in the courthouse and sit there looking at one another for a while. Finally, we recover enough to mumble some Oh my Gods and Thank yous and You're welcomes. And that's why I can stand to represent somebody when I know he's guilty.

STRICKLAND V. WASHINGTON
Supreme Court of the United States
466 U.S. 668, 104 S. Ct. 2052, 80 L. Ed. 2d 674 (1984)

JUSTICE O'CONNOR delivered the opinion of the Court.

This case requires us to consider the proper standards for judging a criminal defendant's contention that the Constitution requires a conviction or death sentence to be set aside because counsel's assistance at the trial or sentencing was ineffective.

During a 10-day period in September 1976, respondent planned and committed three groups of crimes, which included three brutal stabbing murders, torture, kidnaping, severe assaults, attempted murders, attempted extortion, and theft. After his two accomplices were arrested, respondent surrendered to police and voluntarily gave a lengthy statement confessing to the third of the criminal episodes. The State of Florida indicted respondent for kidnaping and murder and appointed an experienced criminal lawyer to represent him.

Counsel actively pursued pretrial motions and discovery. He cut his efforts short, however, and he experienced a sense of hopelessness about the case, when he learned that, against his specific advice, respondent had also confessed to the first two murders. By the date set for trial, respondent was subject to indictment for three counts of first-degree murder and multiple counts of robbery, kidnaping for ransom, breaking and entering and assault, attempted murder, and conspiracy to commit robbery. Respondent waived his right to a jury trial, again acting against counsel's advice, and pleaded guilty to all charges, including the three capital murder charges. * * *

Counsel advised respondent to invoke his right under Florida law to an advisory jury at his capital sentencing hearing. Respondent rejected the advice and waived the right. He chose instead to be sentenced by the trial judge without a jury recommendation.

In preparing for the sentencing hearing, counsel spoke with respondent about his background. He also spoke on the telephone with respondent's wife and mother, though he did not follow up on the one unsuccessful effort to meet with them. He did not otherwise seek out character witnesses for respondent. Nor did he request a psychiatric examination, since his conversations with his client gave no indication that respondent had psychological problems.

Counsel decided not to present and hence not to look further for evidence concerning respondent's character and emotional state. That decision reflected trial counsel's sense of hopelessness about overcoming the evidentiary effect of respondent's confessions to the gruesome crimes. * * * [B]y forgoing the opportunity to present new evidence on these subjects, counsel prevented the State from cross-examining respondent on his claim and from putting on psychiatric evidence of its own.

Counsel also excluded from the sentencing hearing other evidence he thought was potentially damaging. He successfully moved to exclude respondent's "rap sheet." Because he judged that a presentence report might prove more detrimental than helpful, as it would have included respondent's criminal history and thereby would have undermined the claim of no significant history of criminal activity, he did not request that one be prepared.

At the sentencing hearing, * * * [c]ounsel argued that respondent's remorse and acceptance of responsibility justified sparing him from the death penalty. Counsel also argued that respondent had no history of criminal activity and that respondent committed the crimes under extreme mental or emotional disturbance, thus coming within the statutory list of mitigating circumstances. He further argued that respondent should be spared death because he had surrendered, confessed, and offered to testify against a codefendant and because respondent was fundamentally a good person who had briefly gone badly wrong in extremely stressful circumstances. The State put on evidence and witnesses largely for the purpose of describing the details of the crimes. Counsel did not cross-examine the medical experts who testified about the manner of death of respondent's victims.

* * * [T]he trial judge found numerous aggravating circumstances and no * * * mitigating circumstance. * * * He therefore sentenced respondent to death on each of the three counts of murder and to prison terms for the other crimes. * * *

Respondent subsequently sought collateral relief in state court on numerous grounds, among them that counsel had rendered ineffective assistance at the sentencing proceeding. Respondent challenged counsel's assistance in six respects. He asserted that counsel was ineffective because he failed to move for a continuance to prepare for sentencing, to request a psychiatric report, to investigate and present character witnesses, to seek a presentence investigation report, to present meaningful arguments to the sentencing judge, and to investigate the medical examiner's reports or cross-examine the medical experts. In support of the claim, respondent submitted 14 affidavits from friends, neighbors, and relatives stating that they would have testified if asked to do so. He also submitted one psychiatric report and one psychological report stating that respondent, though not under the influence of extreme mental or emotional disturbance, was "chronically frustrated and depressed because of his economic dilemma" at the time of his crimes. * * *

Because of the vital importance of counsel's assistance, this Court has held that, with certain exceptions, a person accused of a federal or state crime has the right to have counsel appointed if retained counsel cannot be obtained. That a person who happens to be a lawyer is present at trial alongside the accused, however, is not enough to satisfy the constitutional command. The Sixth Amendment recognizes the right to the assistance of counsel because it envisions counsel's playing a role that is critical to the ability of the adversarial system to produce just results. An accused is entitled to be assisted by an attorney, whether retained or appointed, who plays the role necessary to ensure that the trial is fair.

For that reason, the Court has recognized that "the right to counsel is the right to the effective assistance of counsel." * * *

The Court has not elaborated on the meaning of the constitutional requirement of effective assistance in * * * cases * * * presenting claims of "actual ineffectiveness." In giving meaning to the requirement, however, we must take its purpose—to ensure a fair trial—as the guide. The benchmark for judging any claim of ineffectiveness must be whether counsel's conduct so undermined the proper functioning of the adversarial process that the trial cannot be relied on as having produced a just result. * * *

A convicted defendant's claim that counsel's assistance was so defective as to require reversal of a conviction or death sentence has two components. First, the defendant must show that counsel's performance was deficient. This requires showing that counsel made errors so serious that counsel was not functioning as the "counsel" guaranteed the defendant by the Sixth Amendment. Second, the defendant must show that the deficient performance prejudiced the defense. This requires showing that counsel's errors were so serious as to deprive the defendant of a fair trial, a trial whose result is reliable. Unless a defendant makes both showings, it cannot be said that the conviction or death sentence resulted from a breakdown in the adversary process that renders the result unreliable.

As all the Federal Courts of Appeals have now held, the proper standard for attorney performance is that of reasonably effective assistance. * * * When a convicted defendant complains of the ineffectiveness of counsel's assistance, the defendant must show that counsel's representation fell below an objective standard of reasonableness.

*** In any case presenting an ineffectiveness claim, the performance inquiry must be whether counsel's assistance was reasonable considering all the circumstances. ***

Judicial scrutiny of counsel's performance must be highly deferential. It is all too tempting for a defendant to second-guess counsel's assistance after conviction or adverse sentence, and it is all too easy for a court, examining counsel's defense after it has proved unsuccessful, to conclude that a particular act or omission of counsel was unreasonable. A fair assessment of attorney performance requires that every effort be made to eliminate the distorting effects of hindsight, to reconstruct the circumstances of counsel's challenged conduct, and to evaluate the conduct from counsel's perspective at the time. Because of the difficulties inherent in making the evaluation, a court must indulge a strong presumption that counsel's conduct falls within the wide range of reasonable professional assistance; that is, the defendant must overcome the presumption that, under the circumstances, the challenged action "might be considered sound trial strategy." There are countless ways to provide effective assistance in any given case. Even the best criminal defense attorneys would not defend a particular client in the same way.

The availability of intrusive post-trial inquiry into attorney performance or of detailed guidelines for its evaluation would encourage the proliferation of ineffectiveness challenges. Criminal trials resolved unfavorably to the defendant would increasingly come to be followed by a second trial, this one of counsel's unsuccessful defense. Counsel's performance and even willingness to serve could be adversely affected. Intensive scrutiny of counsel and rigid requirements for acceptable assistance could dampen the ardor and impair the independence of defense counsel, discourage the acceptance of assigned cases, and undermine the trust between attorney and client.

Thus, a court *** must judge the reasonableness of counsel's challenged conduct on the facts of the particular case, viewed as of the time of counsel's conduct. A convicted defendant making a claim of ineffective assistance must identify the acts or omissions of counsel that are alleged not to have been the result of reasonable professional judgment. The court must then determine whether, in light of all the circumstances, the identified acts or omissions were outside the wide range of professionally competent assistance. In making that determination, the court should keep in mind that counsel's function, as elaborated in prevailing professional norms, is to make the adversarial testing process work in the particular case. At the same time, the court should recognize that counsel is strongly presumed to have rendered adequate assistance and made all significant decisions in the exercise of reasonable professional judgment. ***

An error by counsel, even if professionally unreasonable, does not warrant setting aside the judgment of a criminal proceeding if the error had no effect on the judgment. The purpose of the Sixth Amendment guarantee of counsel is to ensure that a defendant has the assistance necessary to justify reliance on the outcome of the proceeding. Accordingly, any deficiencies in counsel's performance must be prejudicial to the defense in order to constitute ineffective assistance under the Constitution.

It is not enough for the defendant to show that the errors had some conceivable effect on the outcome of the proceeding. Virtually every act or omission of counsel would meet that test, and not every error that conceivably could have influenced the outcome undermines the reliability of the result of the proceeding.

* * * [T]he appropriate test for prejudice finds its roots in the test for materiality of exculpatory information not disclosed to the defense by the prosecution * * *. The defendant must show that there is a reasonable probability that, but for counsel's unprofessional errors, the result of the proceeding would have been different. A reasonable probability is a probability sufficient to undermine confidence in the outcome.

* * * [T]he ultimate focus of inquiry must be on the fundamental fairness of the proceeding whose result is being challenged. In every case the court should be concerned with whether, despite the strong presumption of reliability, the result of the particular proceeding is unreliable because of a breakdown in the adversarial process that our system counts on to produce just results. * * *

Although we have discussed the performance component of an ineffectiveness claim prior to the prejudice component, there is no reason for a court deciding an ineffective assistance claim to approach the inquiry in the same order or even to address both components of the inquiry if the defendant makes an insufficient showing on one. In particular, a court need not determine whether counsel's performance was deficient before examining the prejudice suffered by the defendant as a result of the alleged deficiencies. The object of an ineffectiveness claim is not to grade counsel's performance. If it is easier to dispose of an ineffectiveness claim on the ground of lack of sufficient prejudice, which we expect will often be so, that course should be followed. Courts should strive to ensure that ineffectiveness claims not become so burdensome to defense counsel that the entire criminal justice system suffers as a result. * * *

Having articulated general standards for judging ineffectiveness claims, we think it useful to apply those standards to the facts of this case in order to illustrate the meaning of the general principles. * * * Application of the governing principles is not difficult in this case. The facts as described above make clear that the conduct of respondent's counsel at and before respondents sentencing proceeding cannot be found unreasonable. They also make clear that, even assuming the challenged conduct of counsel was unreasonable, respondent suffered insufficient prejudice to warrant setting aside his death sentence.

With respect to the performance component, the record shows that respondent's counsel made a strategic choice to argue for the extreme emotional distress mitigating circumstance and to rely as fully as possible on respondent's acceptance of responsibility for his crimes. Although counsel understandably felt hopeless about respondent's prospects, nothing in the record indicates * * * that counsel's sense of hopelessness distorted his professional judgment. Counsel's strategy choice was well within the range of professionally reasonable judgments, and the decision not to seek more character or psychological evidence than was already in hand was likewise reasonable.

* * * The aggravating circumstances were utterly overwhelming. Trial counsel could reasonably surmise from his conversations with respondent that character and psychological evidence would be of little help. * * * Restricting testimony on respondent's character to what had come in at the plea colloquy ensured that contrary character and psychological evidence and respondent's criminal history, which counsel had successfully moved to exclude, would not come in. On these facts, there can be little question, even without application of the presumption of adequate performance, that trial counsel's defense, though unsuccessful, was the result of reasonable professional judgment.

With respect to the prejudice component, the lack of merit of respondent's claim is even more stark. The evidence that respondent says his trial counsel should have offered at the sentencing hearing would barely have altered the sentencing profile presented to the sentencing judge. * * * [A]t most this evidence shows that numerous people who knew respondent thought he was generally a good person and that a psychiatrist and a psychologist believed he was under considerable emotional stress that did not rise to the level of extreme disturbance. Given the overwhelming aggravating factors, there is no reasonable probability that the omitted evidence would have changed the conclusion that the aggravating circumstances outweighed the mitigating circumstances and, hence, the sentence imposed. * * *

Failure to make the required showing of either deficient performance or sufficient prejudice defeats the ineffectiveness claim. Here there is a double failure. More generally, respondent has made no showing that the justice of his sentence was rendered unreliable by a breakdown in the adversary process caused by deficiencies in counsel's assistance. Respondent's sentencing proceeding was not fundamentally unfair. * * *

JUSTICE MARSHALL, dissenting. * * *

My objection to the performance standard adopted by the Court is that it is so malleable that, in practice, it will either have no grip at all or will yield excessive variation in the manner in which the Sixth Amendment is interpreted and applied by different courts. To tell lawyers and the lower courts that counsel for a criminal defendant must behave "reasonably" and must act like "a reasonably competent attorney," is to tell them almost nothing. In essence, the majority has instructed judges called upon to assess claims of ineffective assistance of counsel to advert to their own intuitions regarding what constitutes "professional" representation, and has discouraged them from trying to develop more detailed standards governing the performance of defense counsel. In my view, the Court has thereby not only abdicated its own responsibility to interpret the Constitution, but also impaired the ability of the lower courts to exercise theirs. * * *

I object to the prejudice standard adopted by the Court for two independent reasons. First, it is often very difficult to tell whether a defendant convicted after a trial in which he was ineffectively represented would have fared better if his lawyer had been competent. Seemingly impregnable cases can sometimes be dismantled by good defense counsel. On the basis of a cold record, it may be impossible for a reviewing court confidently to ascertain how the government's evidence and arguments would have stood up against rebuttal and cross-examination by a shrewd, well-prepared lawyer. The difficulties of estimating prejudice after the fact are exacerbated by the possibility that evidence of injury to the defendant may be missing from the record precisely because of the incompetence of defense counsel. In view of all these impediments to a fair evaluation of the probability that the outcome of a trial was affected by ineffectiveness of counsel, it seems to me senseless to impose on a defendant whose lawyer has been shown to have been incompetent the burden of demonstrating prejudice.

Second and more fundamentally, the assumption on which the Court's holding rests is that the only purpose of the constitutional guarantee of effective assistance of counsel is to reduce the chance that innocent persons will be convicted. In my view, the guarantee also functions to ensure that convictions are obtained only through fundamentally fair procedures. The majority contends that the Sixth Amendment is not violated when a manifestly guilty defendant is convicted after a trial in which he was represented by a manifestly ineffective attorney. I cannot agree. Every defendant is entitled to a trial in which his interests are vigorously and conscientiously advocated by an able lawyer. A proceeding in which the defendant does not receive meaningful assistance in meeting the forces of the State does not, in my opinion, constitute due process.

* * * I would thus hold that a showing that the performance of a defendant's lawyer departed from constitutionally prescribed standards

requires a new trial regardless of whether the defendant suffered demonstrable prejudice thereby. * * *

[JUSTICE BRENNAN's opinion, concurring in part and dissenting in part, has been omitted.]

NOTE

David LeRoy Washington was executed on July 13, 1984.[a] Before being executed, he said "I'd like to say to the families of all my victims, I'm sorry for all the grief and heartache I brought to them."[b]

Shaun Ossei-Owusu provides some interesting, little-known facts about Washington:

> David LeRoy Washington zigzagged across state and federal tribunals while garnering attention in legal journals and in the mainstream media. He actually was a choirboy, and although one person in his community described him as "a nonviolent young black man who did not use drugs or alcohol," he committed a series of heinous crimes. He stabbed a minister, shot an old lady, and robbed and killed a University of Miami student who was in the act of reciting the Lord's Prayer. As the Fifth Circuit noted, "Washington's victims included black and white, young and old, male and female, all intentionally murdered in tortuous ways." Washington epitomized the uncomfortable fact of black criminality.[c]

Ossei-Owusu also provides some important historical context that helps us understand how racial considerations may have encouraged the Supreme Court to pick Washington's case as the vehicle to reign in the right to counsel:

> *Strickland* provided Florida—the state that lost *Gideon* and *Argersinger*—with an opportunity to prevail nationally while advancing an ineffective assistance doctrine that would coincide with crime control imperatives. There are some important observations that have gone unstated in indigent defense scholarship. First, the case that established the modern ineffective assistance of counsel doctrine involved a murderous black man who sought leniency because of putative procedural errors. This is precisely what law in order hawks assailed against a decade and half before: actually guilty (minority) defendants walking scot-free due to technicalities. * * * The case was decided during a war on crime that scholars have shown was inextricably tied to racial considerations. * * * In its reversal of

---

[a] *Killer Tells Daughter to 'Do Better,'* CHIC. TRIB., July 14, 1984, at 3, http://archives.chicagotribune.com/1984/07/14/page/3 (https://perma.cc/C3Z2-ZXF6). To view this article, which is no longer available at the original url, please choose "screenshot" view in the perma.cc link.

[b] *Id. See also* Kenneth A. Soo, *David Leroy Washington, A Former Choir Boy Who Stabbed Three*, UPI (July 13, 1984), https://www.upi.com/Archives/1984/07/13/David-Leroy-Washington-a-former-choirboy-who-stabbed-three/3676458539200/ (https://perma.cc/D3T8-JYKN).

[c] Shaun Ossei-Owusu, *The Sixth Amendment Façade: The Racial Evolution of the Right to Counsel*, 167 U. PA. L. REV. 1161, 1224 (2019).

the appellate court, the *Strickland* court sought to limit perceived procedural excesses that benefited defendants.[d]

Ossei-Owusu continues:

> [T]he same year that the Supreme Court granted certiorari in *Strickland*, it rejected another Eleventh Circuit case involving an ineffective assistance of counsel claim. The Eleventh Circuit decision, *Goodwin v. Balkcom*, was replete with the ingredients of a high-profile criminal procedure case: a black criminal defendant accused of murder who had been diagnosed with borderline mental retardation; the failure of appointed counsel to challenge the racial composition of the grand and petit jury pool in a southern county that was sued in federal court for having racially unrepresentative juries; and aforementioned counsel's errant references to his client in his closing as a "little old n--- boy . . . [T]he kind of people that we have historically put to death year in Georgia." Although the defendant won and Georgia appealed, the Court denied certiorari. [Anthony] O'Rourke captures the implications of this choice nicely: "[o]ne need not be a legal realist to conclude [that] the ineffective assistance standard might be different today if, in 1984, the Court had been considering Terry Lee Goodwin's representation rather than David Leroy Washington's. The legal facts in *Strickland* lend themselves more easily to a restrictive right to counsel."[e]

The next three cases illustrate how the Court has applied the *Strickland* test for ineffective assistance of counsel in various contexts.

PADILLA V. KENTUCKY
Supreme Court of the United States
559 U.S. 356, 130 S. Ct. 1473, 176 L. Ed. 2d 284 (2010)

JUSTICE STEVENS delivered the opinion of the Court.

Petitioner Jose Padilla, a native of Honduras, has been a lawful permanent resident of the United States for more than 40 years. Padilla served this Nation with honor as a member of the U.S. Armed Forces during the Vietnam War. He now faces deportation after pleading guilty to the transportation of a large amount of marijuana in his tractor-trailer in the Commonwealth of Kentucky.

In this post-conviction proceeding, Padilla claims that his counsel not only failed to advise him of this consequence prior to his entering the plea, but also told him that he "did not have to worry about immigration status since he had been in the country so long." Padilla relied on his counsel's erroneous advice when he pleaded guilty to the drug charges that made his

---

[d] *Id.* at 1226.

[e] *Id.* at 1226–27 (citing Anthony O'Rourke, *The Political Economy of Criminal Procedure Litigation*, 45 GA. L. REV. 721, 764–66 (2011)).

deportation virtually mandatory. He alleges that he would have insisted on going to trial if he had not received incorrect advice from his attorney. * * *

We granted certiorari to decide whether, as a matter of federal law, Padilla's counsel had an obligation to advise him that the offense to which he was pleading guilty would result in his removal from this country. * * *

Before deciding whether to plead guilty, a defendant is entitled to "the effective assistance of competent counsel." The Supreme Court of Kentucky rejected Padilla's ineffectiveness claim on the ground that the advice he sought about the risk of deportation concerned only collateral matters, i.e., those matters not within the sentencing authority of the state trial court. In its view, "collateral consequences are outside the scope of representation required by the Sixth Amendment," and, therefore, the "failure of defense counsel to advise the defendant of possible deportation consequences is not cognizable as a claim for ineffective assistance of counsel." The Kentucky high court is far from alone in this view.

We, however, have never applied a distinction between direct and collateral consequences to define the scope of constitutionally "reasonable professional assistance" required under *Strickland*. Whether that distinction is appropriate is a question we need not consider in this case because of the unique nature of deportation. * * *

Deportation as a consequence of a criminal conviction is, because of its close connection to the criminal process, uniquely difficult to classify as either a direct or a collateral consequence. The collateral versus direct distinction is thus ill suited to evaluating a *Strickland* claim concerning the specific risk of deportation. We conclude that advice regarding deportation is not categorically removed from the ambit of the Sixth Amendment right to counsel. *Strickland* applies to Padilla's claim.

Under *Strickland,* we first determine whether counsel's representation "fell below an objective standard of reasonableness." Then we ask whether "there is a reasonable probability that, but for counsel's unprofessional errors, the result of the proceeding would have been different." The first prong—constitutional deficiency—is necessarily linked to the practice and expectations of the legal community: "The proper measure of attorney performance remains simply reasonableness under prevailing professional norms." * * *

The weight of prevailing professional norms supports the view that counsel must advise her client regarding the risk of deportation. "[A]uthorities of every stripe—including the American Bar Association, criminal defense and public defender organizations, authoritative treatises, and state and city bar publications—universally require defense attorneys to advise as to the risk of deportation consequences for non-citizen clients. . . ."

We too have previously recognized that "[p]reserving the client's right to remain in the United States may be more important to the client than any potential jail sentence." * * *

In the instant case, the terms of the relevant immigration statute are succinct, clear, and explicit in defining the removal consequence for Padilla's conviction. This is not a hard case in which to find deficiency: The consequences of Padilla's plea could easily be determined from reading the removal statute, his deportation was presumptively mandatory, and his counsel's advice was incorrect.

Immigration law can be complex, and it is a legal specialty of its own. Some members of the bar who represent clients facing criminal charges, in either state or federal court or both, may not be well versed in it. There will, therefore, undoubtedly be numerous situations in which the deportation consequences of a particular plea are unclear or uncertain. The duty of the private practitioner in such cases is more limited. When the law is not succinct and straightforward (as it is in many of the scenarios posited by Justice Alito), a criminal defense attorney need do no more than advise a noncitizen client that pending criminal charges may carry a risk of adverse immigration consequences. But when the deportation consequence is truly clear, as it was in this case, the duty to give correct advice is equally clear.

Accepting his allegations as true, Padilla has sufficiently alleged constitutional deficiency to satisfy the first prong of *Strickland*. Whether Padilla is entitled to relief on his claim will depend on whether he can satisfy *Strickland*'s second prong, prejudice, a matter we leave to the Kentucky courts to consider in the first instance.[a] * * *

In sum, we have long recognized that the negotiation of a plea bargain is a critical phase of litigation for purposes of the Sixth Amendment right to effective assistance of counsel. The severity of deportation—"the equivalent of banishment or exile,"—only underscores how critical it is for counsel to inform her noncitizen client that he faces a risk of deportation.

It is our responsibility under the Constitution to ensure that no criminal defendant—whether a citizen or not—is left to the "mercies of incompetent counsel." To satisfy this responsibility, we now hold that counsel must inform her client whether his plea carries a risk of deportation. Our longstanding Sixth Amendment precedents, the seriousness of deportation as a consequence of a criminal plea, and the

---

[a] On remand, the Court of Appeals of Kentucky found prejudice and ordered that Mr. Padilla's conviction be reversed. *See* Padilla v. Commonwealth, 381 S.W.2d 322 (Ky. App. 2012) (remanding the case to the Circuit Court for an order vacating Padilla's judgment and conviction). It is unlikely that Mr. Padilla was re-prosecuted because he had already served his full sentence. Margaret Love & Gabriel J. Chin, *The "Major Upheaval" of* Padilla v. Kentucky: *Extending the Right to Counsel to the Collateral Consequences of Conviction*, 25 CRIMINAL JUSTICE 173, 176 (2010).

concomitant impact of deportation on families living lawfully in this country demand no less. * * *

The judgment of the Supreme Court of Kentucky is reversed, and the case is remanded for further proceedings not inconsistent with this opinion.

JUSTICE ALITO, with whom THE CHIEF JUSTICE joins, concurring in the judgment.

* * * The Court * * * holds that a criminal defense attorney must provide advice in this specialized area [of immigration law] in those cases in which the law is "succinct and straightforward"—but not, perhaps, in other situations. This vague, halfway test will lead to much confusion and needless litigation.

Under *Strickland,* an attorney provides ineffective assistance if the attorney's representation does not meet reasonable professional standards. Until today, the longstanding and unanimous position of the federal courts was that reasonable defense counsel generally need only advise a client about the *direct* consequences of a criminal conviction. While the line between "direct" and "collateral" consequences is not always clear, the collateral-consequences rule expresses an important truth: Criminal defense attorneys have expertise regarding the conduct of criminal proceedings. They are not expected to possess—and very often do not possess—expertise in other areas of the law, and it is unrealistic to expect them to provide expert advice on matters that lie outside their area of training and experience.

This case happens to involve removal, but criminal convictions can carry a wide variety of consequences other than conviction and sentencing, including civil commitment, civil forfeiture, the loss of the right to vote, disqualification from public benefits, ineligibility to possess firearms, dishonorable discharge from the Armed Forces, and loss of business or professional licenses. A criminal conviction may also severely damage a defendant's reputation and thus impair the defendant's ability to obtain future employment or business opportunities. All of those consequences are "seriou[s]," but this Court has never held that a criminal defense attorney's Sixth Amendment duties extend to providing advice about such matters. * * *

The Court's new approach is particularly problematic because providing advice on whether a conviction for a particular offense will make an alien removable is often quite complex. "Most crimes affecting immigration status are not specifically mentioned by the [Immigration and Nationality Act (INA)], but instead fall under a broad category of crimes, such as *crimes involving moral turpitude* or *aggravated felonies.*" As has been widely acknowledged, determining whether a particular crime is an "aggravated felony" or a "crime involving moral turpitude [(CIMT)]" is not an easy task.

Defense counsel who consults a guidebook on whether a particular crime is an "aggravated felony" will often find that the answer is not "easily ascertained." For example, the ABA Guidebook answers the question "Does simple possession count as an aggravated felony?" as follows: "Yes, *at least in the Ninth Circuit*." After a dizzying paragraph that attempts to explain the evolution of the Ninth Circuit's view, the ABA Guidebook continues: "Adding to the confusion, however, is that the Ninth Circuit has conflicting opinions depending on the context on whether simple drug possession constitutes an aggravated felony under 8 U.S.C. § 1101(a)(43)." * * *

Determining whether a particular crime is one involving moral turpitude is no easier. See *id.*, at 134 ("Writing bad checks *may or may not* be a CIMT" (emphasis added)); *ibid.* ("[R]eckless assault coupled with an element of injury, but not serious injury, is *probably* not a CIMT" (emphasis added)); *id.*, at 135 (misdemeanor driving under the influence is generally not a CIMT, but may be a CIMT if the DUI results in injury or if the driver knew that his license had been suspended or revoked); *id.*, at 136 ("If there is no element of actual injury, the endangerment offense *may* not be a CIMT" (emphasis added)); *ibid.* ("Whether [a child abuse] conviction involves moral turpitude *may* depend on the subsection under which the individual is convicted. Child abuse done with criminal negligence *probably* is not a CIMT" (emphasis added)). * * *

The Court tries to downplay the severity of the burden it imposes on defense counsel by suggesting that the scope of counsel's duty to offer advice concerning deportation consequences may turn on how hard it is to determine those consequences. Where "the terms of the relevant immigration statute are succinct, clear, and explicit in defining the removal consequence[s]" of a conviction, the Court says, counsel has an affirmative duty to advise the client that he will be subject to deportation as a result of the plea. But "[w]hen the law is not succinct and straightforward . . . , a criminal defense attorney need do no more than advise a noncitizen client that pending criminal charges may carry a risk of adverse immigration consequences." This approach is problematic for at least four reasons.

First, it will not always be easy to tell whether a particular statutory provision is "succinct, clear, and explicit." How can an attorney who lacks general immigration law expertise be sure that a seemingly clear statutory provision actually means what it seems to say when read in isolation? What if the application of the provision to a particular case is not clear but a cursory examination of case law or administrative decisions would provide a definitive answer?

Second, if defense counsel must provide advice regarding only one of the many collateral consequences of a criminal conviction, many defendants are likely to be misled. To take just one example, a conviction for a particular offense may render an alien excludable but not removable.

If an alien charged with such an offense is advised only that pleading guilty to such an offense will not result in removal, the alien may be induced to enter a guilty plea without realizing that a consequence of the plea is that the alien will be unable to reenter the United States if the alien returns to his or her home country for any reason, such as to visit an elderly parent or to attend a funeral. Incomplete legal advice may be worse than no advice at all because it may mislead and may dissuade the client from seeking advice from a more knowledgeable source.

Third, the Court's rigid constitutional rule could inadvertently head off more promising ways of addressing the underlying problem—such as statutory or administrative reforms requiring trial judges to inform a defendant on the record that a guilty plea may carry adverse immigration consequences. As *amici* point out, "28 states and the District of Columbia have *already* adopted rules, plea forms, or statutes requiring courts to advise criminal defendants of the possible immigration consequences of their pleas." * * *

Fourth, the Court's decision marks a major upheaval in Sixth Amendment law. This Court decided *Strickland* in 1984, but the majority does not cite a single case, from this or any other federal court, holding that criminal defense counsel's failure to provide advice concerning the removal consequences of a criminal conviction violates a defendant's Sixth Amendment right to counsel. * * * [T]he Court's view has been rejected by every Federal Court of Appeals to have considered the issue thus far. * * *

[JUSTICE SCALIA's dissent has been omitted.]

NOTE

It is clear from *Padilla v. Kentucky* that a defendant has a right to effective assistance of counsel in the plea process. Claims of ineffective assistance in the plea context, just like ineffective assistance of counsel claims in other contexts, are governed by the two-part test set forth in *Strickland v. Washington* under which the defendant must show both deficient performance and prejudice to establish ineffective assistance of counsel. The prejudice prong, however, is analyzed a bit differently in the plea context.

In *Lee v. United States*, 582 U.S. ___, 137 S. Ct. 1958, 1965 (2017), the Court explained that when a defendant alleges ineffective assistance of counsel led him to accept an unfavorable plea offer and plead guilty rather than go to trial, "we do not ask whether, had he gone to trial, the result of that trial 'would have been different' than the result of the plea bargain." Instead, in order to establish prejudice, the defendant must show "a reasonable probability that, but for counsel's errors, he would not have pled guilty and would have insisted on going to trial." *Id.* (citing *Hill v. Lockhart*, 474 U.S. 52, 59 (1985)). The *Lee* Court rejected the dissent's contention "that a defendant must also show that he would have been better off going to trial." *Id.*

Lee v. United States involved defense counsel who gave bad advice by encouraging his client to accept an unfavorable plea offer. What if defense counsel advises the client to reject a favorable plea offer? In *Lafler v. Cooper*, 566 U.S. 156, 161 (2012), criminal defense counsel communicated to his client—who was charged with assault with intent to murder, possession of a firearm by a felon, possession of a firearm in the commission of a felony, misdemeanor possession of marijuana, and being a habitual offender—the prosecution's plea offer to dismiss some of the charges and recommend a sentence of 51 to 85 months for the remaining charges in exchange for a guilty plea, but advised him to reject the offer on the ground that he could not be convicted at trial. The client followed his attorney's advice, went to trial, was convicted, and received a much harsher sentence than he would have under the plea offer.

The *Lafler v. Cooper* Court noted that all parties agreed the performance of defense counsel who had advised his client to reject a favorable plea offer was deficient. *Id.* at 163. The Court then held that to establish prejudice in the context of a rejected plea offer, "a defendant must show that but for the ineffective advice of counsel there is a reasonable probability that the plea offer would have been presented to the court (*i.e.*, that the defendant would have accepted the plea and the prosecution would not have withdrawn it in light of intervening circumstances), that the court would have accepted its terms, and that the conviction or sentence, or both, under the offer's terms would have been less severe than under the judgment and sentence that in fact were imposed." *Id.* at 164.

What if defense counsel fails to communicate a favorable plea offer to his client? In *Missouri v. Frye*, 566 U.S. 134 (2012), the Court examined whether a criminal defense attorney's failure to communicate a favorable plea offer from the prosecutor to the client before its expiration constituted ineffective assistance of counsel. The Court held that defense counsel has a duty to communicate favorable plea offers from the prosecutor and that by failing to communicate a plea offer to the client before it expired, defense counsel did not render the effective assistance of counsel that the Constitution requires. The Court, however, also held that to show prejudice from such ineffective assistance of counsel, "defendants must demonstrate a reasonable probability they would have accepted the earlier plea offer had they been afforded effective assistance of counsel" and that "the plea would have been entered without the prosecution canceling it or the trial court refusing to accept it." *Id.* at 147.

In the next case, the Court has to decide whether a criminal defense attorney's decision in a capital case to call a psychologist to testify during the sentencing phase of the case, knowing that the psychologist had written a report in which he opined that there is an increased probability of future violence with Black offenders, constituted ineffective assistance of counsel.

BUCK V. DAVIS
Supreme Court of the United States
580 U.S. ___, 137 S. Ct. 759, 197 L. Ed. 2d 1 (2017)

CHIEF JUSTICE ROBERTS delivered the opinion of the Court. * * *

On the morning of July 30, 1995, Duane Buck arrived at the home of his former girlfriend, Debra Gardner. He was carrying a rifle and a shotgun. Buck entered the home, shot Phyllis Taylor, his stepsister, and then shot Gardner's friend Kenneth Butler. Gardner fled the house, and Buck followed. So did Gardner's young children. While Gardner's son and daughter begged for their mother's life, Buck shot Gardner in the chest. Gardner and Butler died of their wounds. Taylor survived.

Police officers arrived soon after the shooting and placed Buck under arrest. An officer would later testify that Buck was laughing at the scene. He remained "happy" and "upbeat" as he was driven to the police station, "[s]miling and laughing" in the back of the patrol car.

Buck was tried for capital murder, and the jury convicted. During the penalty phase of the trial, the jury was charged with deciding two issues. The first was what the parties term the "future dangerousness" question. At the time of Buck's trial, a Texas jury could impose the death penalty only if it found—unanimously and beyond a reasonable doubt—"a probability that the defendant would commit criminal acts of violence that would constitute a continuing threat to society." The second issue, to be reached only if the jury found Buck likely to be a future danger, was whether mitigating circumstances nevertheless warranted a sentence of life imprisonment instead of death.

The parties focused principally on the first question. The State called witnesses who emphasized the brutality of Buck's crime and his evident lack of remorse in its aftermath. The State also called another former girlfriend, Vivian Jackson. She testified that, during their relationship, Buck had routinely hit her and had twice pointed a gun at her. Finally, the State introduced evidence of Buck's criminal history, including convictions for delivery of cocaine and unlawfully carrying a weapon.

Defense counsel answered with a series of lay witnesses, including Buck's father and stepmother, who testified that they had never known him to be violent. Counsel also called two psychologists to testify as experts. The first, Dr. Patrick Lawrence, observed that Buck had previously served time in prison and had been held in minimum custody. From this he concluded that Buck "did not present any problems in the prison setting." Dr. Lawrence further testified that murders within the Texas penal system tend to be gang related (there was no evidence Buck had ever been a member of a gang) and that Buck's offense had been a "crime of passion" occurring within the context of a romantic relationship. Based on these considerations, Dr. Lawrence determined that Buck was unlikely to be a danger if he were sentenced to life in prison.

Buck's second expert, Dr. Walter Quijano, had been appointed by the presiding judge to conduct a psychological evaluation. Dr. Quijano had met with Buck in prison prior to trial and shared a report of his findings with defense counsel.

Like Dr. Lawrence, Dr. Quijano thought it significant that Buck's prior acts of violence had arisen from romantic relationships with women; Buck, of course, would not form any such relationships while incarcerated. And Dr. Quijano likewise considered Buck's behavioral record in prison a good indicator that future violence was unlikely.

But there was more to the report. In determining whether Buck was likely to pose a danger in the future, Dr. Quijano considered seven "statistical factors." The fourth factor was "race." His report read, in relevant part: "4. Race. Black: Increased probability. There is an overrepresentation of Blacks among the violent offenders."

Despite knowing Dr. Quijano's view that Buck's race was competent evidence of an increased probability of future violence, defense counsel called Dr. Quijano to the stand and asked him to discuss the "statistical factors" he had "looked at in regard to this case." Dr. Quijano responded that certain factors were "know[n] to predict future dangerousness" and, consistent with his report, identified race as one of them. It's a sad commentary," he testified, "that minorities, Hispanics and black people, are overrepresented in the Criminal Justice System." Through further questioning, counsel elicited testimony concerning factors Dr. Quijano thought favorable to Buck, as well as his ultimate opinion that Buck was unlikely to pose a danger in the future. At the close of Dr. Quijano's testimony, his report was admitted into evidence.

After opening cross-examination with a series of general questions, the prosecutor likewise turned to the report. She asked first about the statistical factors of past crimes and age, then questioned Dr. Quijano about the roles of sex and race: "You have determined that the sex factor, that a male is more violent than a female because that's just the way it is, and that the race factor, black, increases the future dangerousness for various complicated reasons; is that correct?" Dr. Quijano replied, "Yes." * * *

The jury deliberated over the course of two days. During that time it sent out four notes, one of which requested the "psychology reports" that had been admitted into evidence. These reports—including Dr. Quijano's—were provided. The jury returned a sentence of death.

* * * The Sixth Amendment right to counsel "is the right to the effective assistance of counsel." A defendant who claims to have been

denied effective assistance must show both that counsel performed deficiently and that counsel's deficient performance caused him prejudice.

Strickland's first prong sets a high bar. A defense lawyer navigating a criminal proceeding faces any number of choices about how best to make a client's case. The lawyer has discharged his constitutional responsibility so long as his decisions fall within the "wide range of professionally competent assistance." It is only when the lawyer's errors were "so serious that counsel was not functioning as the 'counsel' guaranteed ... by the Sixth Amendment" that Strickland's first prong is satisfied.

The District Court determined that, in this case, counsel's performance fell outside the bounds of competent representation. We agree. Counsel knew that Dr. Quijano's report reflected the view that Buck's race disproportionately predisposed him to violent conduct; he also knew that the principal point of dispute during the trial's penalty phase was whether Buck was likely to act violently in the future. Counsel nevertheless (1) called Dr. Quijano to the stand; (2) specifically elicited testimony about the connection between Buck's race and the likelihood of future violence;[a] and (3) put into evidence Dr. Quijano's expert report that stated, in reference to factors bearing on future dangerousness, "Race. Black: Increased probability."

Given that the jury had to make a finding of future dangerousness before it could impose a death sentence, Dr. Quijano's report said, in effect, that the color of Buck's skin made him more deserving of execution. It would be patently unconstitutional for a state to argue that a defendant is liable to be a future danger because of his race. No competent defense attorney would introduce such evidence about his own client.

To satisfy *Strickland*, a litigant must also demonstrate prejudice—"a reasonable probability that, but for counsel's unprofessional errors, the result of the proceeding would have been different." Accordingly, the question before the District Court was whether Buck had demonstrated a reasonable probability that, without Dr. Quijano's testimony on race, at least one juror would have harbored a reasonable doubt about whether Buck was likely to be violent in the future. The District Court concluded that Buck had not made such a showing. We disagree.

* * * [S]everal considerations convince us that it is reasonably probable—notwithstanding the nature of Buck's crime and his behavior in

---

[a] Sheri Lynn Johnson points out that trial counsel's decision to elicit the unfavorable information in the report from Dr. Quijano was not out of the ordinary as a matter of trial strategy. She explains, "Assuming that trial counsel was going to call Quijano, *of course* he elicited the unfavorable 'statistical' race factor from the witness; he was better off eliciting it himself—thereby blunting its effect—than allowing the prosecution to bring it out for the first time on cross-examination." Sheri Lynn Johnson, Buck v. Davis *from the Left*, 15 OHIO ST. J. CRIM. L. 247, 256 (2017).

its aftermath—that the proceeding would have ended differently had counsel rendered competent representation.

Dr. Quijano testified on the key point at issue in Buck's sentencing. True, the jury was asked to decide two issues—whether Buck was likely to be a future danger, and, if so, whether mitigating circumstances nevertheless justified a sentence of life imprisonment. But the focus of the proceeding was on the first question. Much of the penalty phase testimony was directed to future dangerousness, as were the summations for both sides. The jury, consistent with the focus of the parties, asked during deliberations to see the expert reports on dangerousness.

Deciding the key issue of Buck's dangerousness involved an unusual inquiry. The jurors were not asked to determine a historical fact concerning Buck's conduct, but to render a predictive judgment inevitably entailing a degree of speculation. Buck, all agreed, had committed acts of terrible violence. Would he do so again?

Buck's prior violent acts had occurred outside of prison, and within the context of romantic relationships with women. If the jury did not impose a death sentence, Buck would be sentenced to life in prison, and no such romantic relationship would be likely to arise. A jury could conclude that those changes would minimize the prospect of future dangerousness.

But one thing would never change: the color of Buck's skin. Buck would always be black. And according to Dr. Quijano, that immutable characteristic carried with it an "[i]ncreased probability" of future violence. Here was hard statistical evidence—from an expert—to guide an otherwise speculative inquiry.

And it was potent evidence. Dr. Quijano's testimony appealed to a powerful racial stereotype—that of black men as "violence prone." In combination with the substance of the jury's inquiry, this created something of a perfect storm. Dr. Quijano's opinion coincided precisely with a particularly noxious strain of racial prejudice, which itself coincided precisely with the central question at sentencing. The effect of this unusual confluence of factors was to provide support for making a decision on life or death on the basis of race.

This effect was heightened due to the source of the testimony. Dr. Quijano took the stand as a medical expert bearing the court's imprimatur. The jury learned at the outset of his testimony that he held a doctorate in clinical psychology, had conducted evaluations in some 70 capital murder cases, and had been appointed by the trial judge (at public expense) to evaluate Buck. Reasonable jurors might well have valued his opinion concerning the central question before them.

For these reasons, we cannot accept the District Court's conclusion that "the introduction of any mention of race" during the penalty phase was "*de minimis.*" There were only "two references to race in Dr. Quijano's testimony"—one during direct examination, the other on cross. But when a jury hears expert testimony that expressly makes a defendant's race directly pertinent on the question of life or death, the impact of that evidence cannot be measured simply by how much air time it received at trial or how many pages it occupies in the record. Some toxins can be deadly in small doses.

The State acknowledges, as it must, that introducing "race or ethnicity as evidence of criminality" can in some cases prejudice a defendant. But it insists that this is not such a case, because Buck's own counsel, not the prosecution, elicited the offending testimony. We are not convinced. In fact, the distinction could well cut the other way. A prosecutor is seeking a conviction. Jurors understand this and may reasonably be expected to evaluate the government's evidence and arguments in light of its motivations. When a defendant's own lawyer puts in the offending evidence, it is in the nature of an admission against interest, more likely to be taken at face value.

The effect of Dr. Quijano's testimony on Buck's sentencing cannot be dismissed as *"de minimis."* Buck has demonstrated prejudice. * * *

For the foregoing reasons, we conclude that Buck has demonstrated * * * ineffective assistance of counsel under *Strickland*.

The judgment of the United States Court of Appeals for the Fifth Circuit is reversed, and the case is remanded for further proceedings consistent with this opinion.

It is so ordered.

JUSTICE THOMAS, with whom JUSTICE ALITO joins, dissenting.

Having settled on a desired outcome, the Court bulldozes procedural obstacles and misapplies settled law to justify it. But the majority's focus on providing relief to petitioner in this particular case has at least one upside: Today's decision has few ramifications, if any, beyond the highly unusual facts presented here. The majority leaves entirely undisturbed the black-letter principles of collateral review, ineffective assistance of counsel, and Rule 60(b)(6) law that govern day-to-day operations in federal courts. * * *

The Court's application of the standard in *Strickland v. Washington,* is * * * misguided. In particular, the Court erroneously finds that petitioner's claim satisfies *Strickland's* second prong, which requires a defendant to show that his counsel's mistake materially prejudiced his defense. Prejudice exists only when correcting the alleged error would have produced a "substantial" likelihood of a different result. Here, the sentence of death hinged on the jury's finding that petitioner posed a threat of future dangerousness. Texas' standard for making such a finding is not difficult to satisfy: "The facts of the offense alone may be sufficient to sustain the jury's finding of future dangerousness," and "[a] jury may also infer a defendant's future dangerousness from evidence showing a lack of remorse."

The majority neglects even to mention the relevant legal standard in Texas, relying instead on rhetoric and speculation to craft a finding of prejudice. But the prosecution's evidence of both the heinousness of petitioner's crime and his complete lack of remorse was overwhelming. Accordingly, Dr. Quijano's *de minimis* racial testimony, did not prejudice petitioner.

First, the facts leave no doubt that this crime was premeditated and cruel. The Court recites defense testimony describing the killing spree here as a "crime of passion," but the record belies that characterization. The rampage occurred at the home of Debra Gardner, petitioner's ex-girlfriend. Prior to the shooting, petitioner called her house. His stepsister, Phyllis Taylor, answered, and petitioner asked to speak with Gardner. Gardner declined, and petitioner hung up. Petitioner then retrieved a shotgun and rifle, loaded both guns, and drove 28 miles to Gardner's house. Upon arrival, he broke down the door and opened fire without provocation. The shooting did not occur in the heat of the moment.

In addition to describing this as a crime of passion, the majority also parrots defense testimony that petitioner's violence was limited to "the context of romantic relationships." But this assertion is also quite wrong. Upon entering Gardner's house, petitioner first shot at an acquaintance, Harold Ebnezer. He next approached his stepsister, Taylor, who was seated on the couch. He said, " 'I'm going to shoot your ass too.' " She begged him, " 'Duane, please don't shoot me. I'm your sister. I don't deserve to be shot. Remember I do have children.' " Petitioner ignored her pleas, placed the gun on her chest, and shot her. Petitioner does not claim that he was in a romantic relationship with either Ebnezer or Taylor.

After shooting Taylor, petitioner cornered one of Gardner's friends, Kenneth Butler, and shot him, as well. He then exited the house and chased Gardner into the middle of the street. She turned to him and pleaded, " 'Please don't shoot me. Please don't shoot me. Why are you doing this in front of my kids?' Her son, Devon, watched from the sidewalk. Her daughter, Shennel, begged petitioner to spare her mother and even attempted to restrain him. Petitioner pointed the gun at Gardner and said, " 'I'm going to shoot you. I'm going to shoot your A[ss].' " He then did so. The flight path of the bullet suggests that Gardner was on her knees when petitioner shot her.

Second, the evidence of petitioner's lack of remorse, largely ignored by the majority, is startling. After shooting Gardner, petitioner walked back to his car and placed the firearms in the trunk. He then returned to taunt

Gardner where she lay mortally wounded and bleeding in the street. He said, " 'It ain't funny now. You ain't laughing now.' " Police arrived shortly thereafter and arrested him. In the patrol car, petitioner was "laughing and joking and taunting." He continued to smile and laugh during the drive to the police station. When one of the officers informed petitioner that he did not find the situation humorous, petitioner replied that " '[t]he bitch got what she deserved.' " He remained happy and upbeat for the remainder of the drive, even commenting that he was going to heaven because God had already forgiven him. * * *

I respectfully dissent.

NOTE

While agreeing with the outcome in *Buck v. Davis*, Sheri Lynn Johnson critiques the majority for not doing more to improve the existing law on ineffective assistance of counsel.[a] Johnson also critiques the majority for "treat[ing] the injustices apparent in Buck's sentencing as aberrational."[b] She observes that contrary to Chief Justice Roberts' suggestion that what occurred in Buck's case was extraordinary, it is not that unusual to have overtly racial references made by defense counsel, prosecutors, witnesses, and even jurors in criminal cases, explaining:

> Along with colleagues, I examined criminal cases from the first decade of this century for the presence of racial epithets. We found five cases (four of them capital) where defense counsel used a racial epithet in speaking of a client. Relatedly, we found nine cases (three capital) where jurors used a racial epithet, either in the course of jury deliberations or in describing the defendant, one capital case in which a witness did so in the course of the trial (not counting cases where the witness was testifying as to someone else's remarks) and three cases (all capital) where prosecutors used a racial epithet to describe a defendant. Considering that racial epithets are a much narrower category than are explicit references to race, I am sure what we found substantially underestimates the category of express references to race in the course of capital or other criminal proceedings. Thus, express references are hardly "extraordinary."[c]

She also notes that besides expressly racial references, unarticulated racial stereotypes also influence jurors in cases involving Black or Latino defendants.[d]

---

[a] Sheri Lynn Johnson, Buck v. Davis *from the Left*, 15 OHIO ST. J. CRIM. L. 247, 247 (2017) (agreeing with dissenting Justice Thomas' statement that the "decision has few ramifications, if any, beyond the highly unusual facts presented here" but viewing this as a regrettable downside while Justice Thomas viewed the narrowness of the majority opinion as an upside).

[b] *Id.* at 255.

[c] *Id.* at 265 (citing Sheri Lynn Johnson, John H. Blume & Patrick M. Wilson, *Racial Epithets in the Criminal Process*, 2011 MICH. ST. L. REV. 755 (2011)).

[d] *Id.* at 268–69.

CH. 29   THE ROLE OF CRIMINAL DEFENSE COUNSEL   909

Noting that the *Strickland* test for ineffective assistance of counsel "has generally been interpreted as requiring an alarmingly low level of competence,"[e] Robin Walker Sterling argues that the Supreme Court's ineffective assistance of counsel jurisprudence should be understood as merely setting the constitutional floor or the bare minimum that a criminal defense attorney must do to comply with the Sixth Amendment.[f] After highlighting the extreme racial disproportion in incarceration rates, Sterling suggests that "[b]ecause of their access to criminal defendants and their ethical mandate to represent their clients' expressed interests, defense attorneys are uniquely positioned to be an incredibly powerful weapon in the fight against invidious race bias in the criminal justice system."[g] Given "social science and empirical research suggest[ing] that calling attention to race as an issue reduces reliance on stereotypes," Sterling suggests that criminal defense attorneys should seek to inject issues of race discrimination into the courtroom conversation when doing so would help their clients.[h]

The next case deals with the question of whether it constitutes ineffective assistance of counsel for an attorney to tell his client that if the client takes the stand and says he saw a gun, he (the attorney) will have to tell the court that he thinks the client committed perjury. The Court is careful to note that "breach of an ethical standard does not necessarily make out a denial of the Sixth Amendment guarantee of assistance of counsel," yet relies heavily on the assumption that the attorney was acting ethically in concluding that the attorney rendered effective assistance to the client. Indeed, much of the opinion focuses on whether the attorney was acting ethically rather than on whether the *Strickland* test for effective assistance of counsel was satisfied even though the U.S. Supreme Court lacks authority to establish rules of ethics for attorneys practicing in state courts.

As you read the case, think about whether the attorney was rendering the effective assistance of counsel that the Sixth Amendment guarantees. Do you think counsel's assistance was reasonable when both Model Rule 3.3 and Iowa's Rule 32:3.3(b) require that the attorney *know* (not merely believe) that the client has offered false testimony?[i] Was it reasonable in light of the role

---

[e] Robin Walker Sterling, *Defense Attorney Resistance*, 99 IOWA L. REV. 2245, 2259 (2014) (providing examples where the criminal defense attorney was shockingly incompetent in failing to present mitigating evidence, sleeping during the trial, or failing to do the most basic investigation, yet the defendants' claims of ineffective assistance of counsel in these cases were unsuccessful).

[f] *Id.* at 2250 ("At the lower boundary, the minimum acceptable performance is defined by court decisions on ineffective assistance of counsel").

[g] *Id.* at 2251.

[h] *Id.* at 2264, 2265–70 (suggesting ways that defense attorneys can raise the issue of race to help their clients).

[i] Model Rule 3.3(a)(3) provides, *inter alia*, "If a lawyer, the lawyer's client, or a witness called by the lawyer, has offered material evidence and the lawyer comes to know of its falsity, the lawyer shall take reasonable remedial measures, including, if necessary, disclosure to the tribunal." Rule 3.3(a)(3) further provides that "[a] lawyer may refuse to offer evidence, *other than the testimony of a defendant in a criminal matter*, that the lawyer reasonably believes is false." (emphasis added). Similarly, Iowa Rule 32:3.3(b) provides, "If a lawyer, the lawyer's client, or a witness called by the lawyer, has offered material evidence and the lawyer comes to know of its falsity, the lawyer shall take reasonable remedial measures, including, if necessary, disclosure to the tribunal. A lawyer

criminal defense counsel play in the criminal justice system? Do you think the attorney's advice to his client not to testify that he saw a gun prejudiced the client? In other words, do you think there was a reasonable probability that, if the attorney had not given such advice, the outcome of the proceeding would have been different?

NIX V. WHITESIDE
Supreme Court of the United States
475 U.S. 157, 106 S. Ct. 988, 89 L. Ed. 2d 123 (1986)

CHIEF JUSTICE BURGER delivered the opinion of the Court.

We granted certiorari to decide whether the Sixth Amendment right of a criminal defendant to assistance of counsel is violated when an attorney refuses to cooperate with the defendant in presenting perjured testimony at his trial.

Whiteside was convicted of second-degree murder by a jury verdict * * *. The killing took place on February 8, 1977, in Cedar Rapids, Iowa. Whiteside and two others went to one Calvin Love's apartment late that night, seeking marihuana. Love was in bed when Whiteside and his companions arrived * * *. At one point, Love directed his girlfriend to get his "piece," and at another point got up, then returned to his bed. According to Whiteside's testimony, Love then started to reach under his pillow and moved toward Whiteside. Whiteside stabbed Love in the chest, inflicting a fatal wound.

Whiteside was charged with murder. * * * Gary L. Robinson was then appointed and immediately began an investigation. Whiteside gave him a statement that he had stabbed Love as the latter "was pulling a pistol from underneath the pillow on the bed." Upon questioning by Robinson, however, Whiteside indicated that he had not actually seen a gun, but that he was convinced that Love had a gun. No pistol was found on the premises; shortly after the police search following the stabbing, which had revealed no weapon, the victim's family had removed all of the victim's possessions from the apartment. Robinson interviewed Whiteside's companions who were present during the stabbing, and none had seen a gun during the incident. Robinson advised Whiteside that the existence of a gun was not necessary to establish the claim of self-defense, and that only a reasonable belief that the victim had a gun nearby was necessary even though no gun was actually present.

Until shortly before trial, Whiteside consistently stated to Robinson that he had not actually seen a gun, but that he was convinced that Love had a gun in his hand. About a week before trial, during preparation for direct examination, Whiteside for the first time told Robinson and his

---

may refuse to offer evidence, other than the testimony of a defendant in a criminal matter, that the lawyer reasonably believes is false."

associate Donna Paulsen that he had seen something "metallic" in Love's hand. When asked about this, Whiteside responded: "[I]n Howard Cook's case there was a gun. If I don't say I saw a gun, I'm dead."

Robinson told Whiteside that such testimony would be perjury and repeated that it was not necessary to prove that a gun was available but only that Whiteside reasonably believed that he was in danger. On Whiteside's insisting that he would testify that he saw "something metallic" Robinson told him * * *:

> [W]e could not allow him to [testify falsely] because that would be perjury, and as officers of the court we would be suborning perjury if we allowed him to do it; . . . I advised him that if he did do that it would be my duty to advise the Court of what he was doing and that I felt he was committing perjury; also, that I probably would be allowed to attempt to impeach that particular testimony.

Robinson also indicated he would seek to withdraw from the representation if Whiteside insisted on committing perjury.

Whiteside testified in his own defense at trial and stated that he "knew" that Love had a gun and that he believed Love was reaching for a gun and he had acted swiftly in self-defense. On cross-examination, he admitted that he had not actually seen a gun in Love's hand. Robinson presented evidence that Love had been seen with a sawed-off shotgun on other occasions, that the police search of the apartment may have been careless, and that the victim's family had removed everything from the apartment shortly after the crime. Robinson presented this evidence to show a basis for Whiteside's asserted fear that Love had a gun.

The jury returned a verdict of second-degree murder, and Whiteside moved for a new trial * * *. The Supreme Court of Iowa affirmed respondent's conviction. * * * [After Whiteside filed a petition for habeas corpus, the] United States Court of Appeals for the Eighth Circuit reversed and directed that the writ of habeas corpus be granted. * * * We granted certiorari and we reverse.

The right of an accused to testify in his defense is of relatively recent origin. Until the latter part of the preceding century, criminal defendants in this country, as at common law, were considered to be disqualified from giving sworn testimony at their own trial by reason of their interest as a party to the case. * * * Although this Court has never explicitly held that a criminal defendant has a due process right to testify in his own behalf, cases in several Circuits have so held, and the right has long been assumed.[a] * * *

---

[a] One year after deciding *Nix v. Whiteside*, the Supreme Court recognized that a defendant has a constitutional right to testify in her own behalf. *See* Rock v. Arkansas, 483 U.S. 44, 49 (1987) (noting "it cannot be doubted that a defendant in a criminal case has the right to take the witness stand and to testify in his or her own defense.").

In *Strickland v. Washington*, we held that to obtain relief by way of federal habeas corpus on a claim of a deprivation of effective assistance of counsel under the Sixth Amendment, the movant must establish both serious attorney error and prejudice. To show such error, it must be established that the assistance rendered by counsel was constitutionally deficient in that "counsel made errors so serious that counsel was not functioning as 'counsel' guaranteed the defendant by the Sixth Amendment." To show prejudice, it must be established that the claimed lapses in counsel's performance rendered the trial unfair so as to "undermine confidence in the outcome" of the trial.

In *Strickland*, we acknowledged that the Sixth Amendment does not require any particular response by counsel to a problem that may arise. Rather, the Sixth Amendment inquiry is into whether the attorney's conduct was "reasonably effective." To counteract the natural tendency to fault an unsuccessful defense, a court reviewing a claim of ineffective assistance must "indulge a strong presumption that counsel's conduct falls within the wide range of reasonable professional assistance." In giving shape to the perimeters of this range of reasonable professional assistance, *Strickland* mandates that "[p]revailing norms of practice as reflected in American Bar Association Standards and the like ... are guides to determining what is reasonable, but they are only guides."

Under the *Strickland* standard, breach of an ethical standard does not necessarily make out a denial of the Sixth Amendment guarantee of assistance of counsel. When examining attorney conduct, a court must be careful not to narrow the wide range of conduct acceptable under the Sixth Amendment so restrictively as to constitutionalize particular standards of professional conduct and thereby intrude into the state's proper authority to define and apply the standards of professional conduct applicable to those it admits to practice in its courts. In some future case challenging attorney conduct in the course of a state-court trial, we may need to define with greater precision the weight to be given to recognized canons of ethics, the standards established by the state in statutes or professional codes, and the Sixth Amendment, in defining the proper scope and limits on that conduct. Here we need not face that question, since virtually all of the sources speak with one voice.[b]

We turn next to the question presented: the definition of the range of "reasonable professional" responses to a criminal defendant client who informs counsel that he will perjure himself on the stand. We must determine whether, in this setting, Robinson's conduct fell within the wide

---

[b] Actually, state ethics rules governing criminal defense attorneys who believe their client plans to testify falsely are not uniform. As discussed in the note following this case, some states prohibit disclosure and instead allow the attorney to put the client on the witness stand where the client may testify in narrative form. The attorney, however, may not rely on anything the client said that the attorney believes to be false in the attorney's closing argument.

range of professional responses to threatened client perjury acceptable under the Sixth Amendment.

In *Strickland,* we recognized counsel's duty of loyalty and his "overarching duty to advocate the defendant's cause." Plainly, that duty is limited to legitimate, lawful conduct compatible with the very nature of a trial as a search for truth. Although counsel must take all reasonable lawful means to attain the objectives of the client, counsel is precluded from taking steps or in any way assisting the client in presenting false evidence or otherwise violating the law. This principle has consistently been recognized in most unequivocal terms by expositors of the norms of professional conduct since the first Canons of Professional Ethics were adopted by the American Bar Association in 1908. * * *

These principles have been carried through to contemporary codifications of an attorney's professional responsibility. Disciplinary Rule 7–102 of the Model Code of Professional Responsibility (1980), entitled "Representing a Client Within the Bounds of the Law," provides: "(A) In his representation of a client, a lawyer shall not: (4) Knowingly use perjured testimony or false evidence. (7) Counsel or assist his client in conduct that the lawyer knows to be illegal or fraudulent."

This provision has been adopted by Iowa, and is binding on all lawyers who appear in its courts. The more recent Model Rules of Professional Conduct (1983) similarly admonish attorneys to obey all laws in the course of representing a client: "RULE 1.2—Scope of Representation (d) A lawyer shall not counsel a client to engage, or assist a client, in conduct that the lawyer knows is criminal or fraudulent. . . ."

Both the Model Code of Professional Responsibility and the Model Rules of Professional Conduct also adopt the specific exception from the attorney-client privilege for disclosure of perjury that his client intends to commit or has committed. * * * Indeed, both the Model Code and the Model Rules do not merely *authorize* disclosure by counsel of client perjury; they *require* such disclosure.[c]

These standards confirm that the legal profession has accepted that an attorney's ethical duty to advance the interests of his client is limited by an equally solemn duty to comply with the law and standards of professional conduct; it specifically ensures that the client may not use

---

[c] Comment 10 to Rule 3.3 of the ABA Model Rules of Professional Conduct mandates disclosure to the tribunal only where an attorney has offered material evidence in the belief that it is true and "subsequently come[s] to *know* that the evidence is false," ABA MODEL RULES OF PROFESSIONAL CONDUCT (2015) (emphasis added). An attorney's mere belief, even if reasonable and supported by other evidence, is not a sufficient basis to refuse to provide assistance to the defendant client in a criminal case who wishes to testify. *United States v. Midgett*, 342 F.3d 321, 326 (4th Cir. 2003) (noting that the Model Rules of Professional Conduct, while requiring that a lawyer not knowingly offer evidence that the lawyer *knows* to be false, also states that "[a] lawyer may refuse to offer evidence, *other than the testimony of a defendant in a criminal matter*, that the lawyer *reasonably believes* is false").

false evidence. This special duty of an attorney to prevent and disclose frauds upon the court derives from the recognition that perjury is as much a crime as tampering with witnesses or jurors by way of promises and threats, and undermines the administration of justice.

The offense of perjury was a crime recognized at common law and has been made a felony in most states by statute, including Iowa. An attorney who aids false testimony by questioning a witness when perjurious responses can be anticipated risks prosecution for subornation of perjury * * *.

It is universally agreed that at a minimum the attorney's first duty when confronted with a proposal for perjurious testimony is to attempt to dissuade the client from the unlawful course of conduct. * * * The commentary [to the Model Rules] also suggests that an attorney's revelation of his client's perjury to the court is a professionally responsible and acceptable response to the conduct of a client who has actually given perjured testimony. Similarly, the Model Rules and the commentary, as well as the Code of Professional Responsibility adopted in Iowa, expressly permit withdrawal from representation as an appropriate response of an attorney when the client threatens to commit perjury. * * *

Considering Robinson's representation of respondent in light of these accepted norms of professional conduct, we discern no failure to adhere to reasonable professional standards that would in any sense make out a deprivation of the Sixth Amendment right to counsel. Whether Robinson's conduct is seen as a successful attempt to dissuade his client from committing the crime of perjury, or whether seen as a "threat" to withdraw from representation and disclose the illegal scheme, Robinson's representation of Whiteside falls well within accepted standards of professional conduct and the range of reasonable professional conduct acceptable under *Strickland*. * * * Since there has been no breach of any recognized professional duty, it follows that there can be no deprivation of the right to assistance of counsel under the *Strickland* standard.

We hold that, as a matter of law, counsel's conduct complained of here cannot establish the prejudice required for relief under the second strand of the *Strickland* inquiry. Although a defendant need not establish that the attorney's deficient performance more likely than not altered the outcome in order to establish prejudice under *Strickland,* a defendant must show that "there is a reasonable probability that, but for counsel's unprofessional errors, the result of the proceeding would have been different." According to *Strickland,* "[a] reasonable probability is a probability sufficient to undermine confidence in the outcome." * * *

Whether he was persuaded or compelled to desist from perjury, Whiteside has no valid claim that confidence in the result of his trial has been diminished by his desisting from the contemplated perjury. Even if we were to assume that the jury might have believed his perjury, it does not follow that Whiteside was prejudiced. * * *

Whiteside's attorney treated Whiteside's proposed perjury in accord with professional standards, and since Whiteside's truthful testimony could not have prejudiced the result of his trial, the Court of Appeals was in error to direct the issuance of a writ of habeas corpus and must be reversed.

Reversed.

JUSTICE BRENNAN, concurring in the judgment.

This Court has no constitutional authority to establish rules of ethical conduct for lawyers practicing in the state courts. Nor does the Court enjoy any statutory grant of jurisdiction over legal ethics.

Accordingly, it is not surprising that the Court emphasizes that it "must be careful not to narrow the wide range of conduct acceptable under the Sixth Amendment so restrictively as to constitutionalize particular standards of professional conduct and thereby intrude into the state's proper authority to define and apply the standards of professional conduct applicable to those it admits to practice in its courts." I read this as saying in another way that the Court *cannot* tell the States or the lawyers in the States how to behave in their courts, unless and until federal rights are violated.

Unfortunately, the Court seems unable to resist the temptation of sharing with the legal community its vision of ethical conduct. But let there be no mistake: the Court's essay regarding what constitutes the correct response to a criminal client's suggestion that he will perjure himself is pure discourse without force of law. * * * [T]hat issue is a thorny one, but it is not an issue presented by this case. Lawyers, judges, bar associations, students, and others should understand that the problem has not now been "decided."

I [concur] because I agree that respondent has failed to prove the kind of prejudice necessary to make out a claim under *Strickland v. Washington*.

JUSTICE STEVENS, concurring in the judgment.

Justice Holmes taught us that a word is but the skin of a living thought. A "fact" may also have a life of its own. From the perspective of an appellate judge, after a case has been tried and the evidence has been sifted by another judge, a particular fact may be as clear and certain as a piece of crystal or a small diamond. A trial lawyer, however, must often deal with mixtures of sand and clay. Even a pebble that seems clear enough at first glance may take on a different hue in a handful of gravel.

As we view this case, it appears perfectly clear that respondent intended to commit perjury, that his lawyer knew it, and that the lawyer had a duty—both to the court and to his client, for perjured testimony can ruin an otherwise meritorious case—to take extreme measures to prevent the perjury from occurring. The lawyer was successful and, from our unanimous and remote perspective, it is now pellucidly clear that the client suffered no "legally cognizable prejudice."

Nevertheless, beneath the surface of this case there are areas of uncertainty that cannot be resolved today. A lawyer's certainty that a change in his client's recollection is a harbinger of intended perjury—as well as judicial review of such apparent certainty—should be tempered by the realization that, after reflection, the most honest witness may recall (or sincerely believe he recalls) details that he previously overlooked. * * * Thus, one can be convinced—as I am—that this lawyer's actions were a proper way to provide his client with effective representation without confronting the much more difficult questions of what a lawyer must, should, or may do after his client has given testimony that the lawyer does not believe. The answer to such questions may well be colored by the particular circumstances attending the actual event and its aftermath. * * *

[JUSTICE BLACKMUN's opinion, concurring in the judgment, has been omitted.]

NOTE

The Court suggests there is no question that the attorney acted as he was required to act under the canons of legal ethics "since virtually all of the sources speak with one voice" on what an attorney must do when faced with a situation like the one the attorney in *Nix v. Whiteside* found himself in. In fact, however, there is considerable disagreement over what an attorney should do when the attorney thinks his or her client is going to commit perjury. At one extreme is the view of the late Monroe Freedman, Abbe Smith, and the National Association of Criminal Defense Lawyers (NACDL): the criminal defense attorney should proceed as normal, putting the client on the stand and examining the client as the attorney would do in any other case. Monroe H. Freedman & Abbe Smith, UNDERSTANDING LAWYER'S ETHICS 162–63 (4th ed. 2010). At the other extreme is the Model Rules approach, mandating disclosure to the tribunal if the lawyer knows that his client intends to testify falsely. In between these two extremes is another approach that recognizes the criminal defendant's right to testify as well as the obligation of defense counsel as an officer of the court not to assist in any criminal or fraudulent activity by the client. Under the narrative approach, a criminal defense attorney who believes the client intends to testify falsely may put the client on the stand and allow the client to testify in the narrative. Under this approach, the lawyer will simply ask the defendant if he or she wishes to make a statement concerning the case rather than engaging in direct examination of the client. *See e.g.*, *People v. Johnson*, 62 Cal. App. 4th 608, 630 (Cal. Ct. App. 1998) ("We conclude the narrative approach best accommodates the competing interests of the defendant's constitutional right to testify and the attorney's ethical obligations."); *People v. Bolton*, 166 Cal. App. 4th 343, 358 (Cal. Ct. App. 2008) ("We reaffirm the conclusion of the *Johnson* court that where an attorney knows or suspects that his client intends to give false testimony, the 'narrative approach' best accommodates the interests of both the defendant and the attorney, who is obligated 'not to participate in the presentation of perjured testimony.' "); *People v. Lowery*, 52 Ill. App. 3d 44, 47 (Ill. App. Ct. 1977) (approving of the narrative approach outlined in the ABA Standards Relating to the Defense Function § 7.7); *State v. Fosnight*, 679 P.2d 180 (Kan. 1984) (finding no violation of the Code of Professional Responsibility where counsel permitted his client to tell his story on the witness stand without engaging in direct examination of the client); *Sanborn v. State*, 474 So. 2d 309 (Fla. Dist. Ct. App. 1985) (noting that the procedure used when there is a chance of perjured testimony being presented by the defendant is to allow the defendant to take the stand and deliver his statement in narrative form); D.C. Rules of Prof'l Conduct R. 3.3(b) (D.C. Bar 2015) ("If the lawyer is unable to dissuade the client or to withdraw without seriously harming the client, the lawyer may put the client on the stand to testify in a narrative fashion, but the lawyer shall not examine the client in such manner as to elicit testimony which the lawyer knows to be false, and shall not argue the probative value of the client's testimony in closing argument.").

WHEAT V. UNITED STATES
Supreme Court of the United States
486 U.S. 153, 108 S. Ct. 1692, 100 L. Ed. 2d 140 (1988)

CHIEF JUSTICE REHNQUIST delivered the opinion of the Court. * * *

Petitioner Mark Wheat, along with numerous codefendants, was charged with participating in a far-flung drug distribution conspiracy. * * * Petitioner acted primarily as an intermediary in the distribution ring; he received and stored large shipments of marijuana at his home, then distributed the marijuana to customers in the region.

Also charged in the conspiracy were Juvenal Gomez-Barajas and Javier Bravo, who were represented in their criminal proceedings by attorney Eugene Iredale.[a] Gomez-Barajas was tried first and was acquitted on drug charges overlapping with those against petitioner. To avoid a second trial on other charges, however, Gomez-Barajas offered to plead guilty to tax evasion and illegal importation of merchandise. At the commencement of petitioner's trial, the District Court had not accepted the

---

[a] Eugene Iredale is considered one of the best criminal defense lawyers in San Diego, California. In 2022, Iredale's law firm was ranked in Tier 1 for Civil Rights Law, Criminal Defense: General Practice, and Criminal Defense: White Collar cases by U.S. News and World Report. *See Best Law Firms*, U.S. NEWS AND WORLD REPORT, http://bestlawfirms.usnews.com/profile/iredale-and-yoo-apc/rankings/13056 (https://perma.cc/EDU3-P6ZJ). Additionally, Iredale has also been chosen by Super Lawyers as a Super Lawyer each year from 2007 to 2022. *See Attorney Profile*, SUPERLAWYERS, http://profiles.superlawyers.com/california-san-diego/san-diego/lawyer/eugene-g-iredale/999bbee4-ba00-46e1-9a52-a13d38abc9bb.html (https://perma.cc/Q3P2-DZR5).

plea; Gomez-Barajas was thus free to withdraw his guilty plea and proceed to trial.

Bravo, evidently a lesser player in the conspiracy, decided to forgo trial and plead guilty to one count of transporting approximately 2,400 pounds of marijuana from Los Angeles to a residence controlled by Victor Vidal. At the conclusion of Bravo's guilty plea proceedings * * *, Iredale notified the District Court that he had been contacted by petitioner and had been asked to try petitioner's case as well. In response, the Government registered substantial concern about the possibility of conflict in the representation.

* * * [T]he Government objected to petitioner's proposed substitution on the ground that Iredale's representation of Gomez-Barajas and Bravo created a serious conflict of interest. The Government's position was premised on two possible conflicts. First, the District Court had not yet accepted the plea and sentencing arrangement negotiated between Gomez-Barajas and the Government; in the event that arrangement were rejected by the court, Gomez-Barajas would be free to withdraw the plea and stand trial. He would then be faced with the prospect of representation by Iredale, who in the meantime would have acted as petitioner's attorney. Petitioner, through his participation in the drug distribution scheme, was familiar with the sources and size of Gomez-Barajas' income, and was thus likely to be called as a witness for the Government at any subsequent trial of Gomez-Barajas. This scenario would pose a conflict of interest for Iredale, who would be prevented from cross-examining petitioner and thereby from effectively representing Gomez-Barajas.

Second, and of more immediate concern, Iredale's representation of Bravo would directly affect his ability to act as counsel for petitioner. The Government believed that a portion of the marijuana delivered by Bravo to Vidal's residence eventually was transferred to petitioner. In this regard, the Government contacted Iredale and asked that Bravo be made available as a witness to testify against petitioner, and agreed in exchange to modify its position at the time of Bravo's sentencing. In the likely event that Bravo were called to testify, Iredale's position in representing both men would become untenable, for ethical proscriptions would forbid him to cross-examine Bravo in any meaningful way. By failing to do so, he would also fail to provide petitioner with effective assistance of counsel. Thus, because of Iredale's prior representation of Gomez-Barajas and Bravo and the potential for serious conflict of interest, the Government urged the District Court to reject the substitution of attorneys.

In response, petitioner emphasized his right to have counsel of his own choosing and the willingness of Gomez-Barajas, Bravo, and petitioner to waive the right to conflict-free counsel. Petitioner argued that the circumstances posited by the Government that would create a conflict for Iredale were highly speculative and bore no connection to the true relationship between the co-conspirators. If called to testify, Bravo would simply say that he did not know petitioner and had no dealings with him; no attempt by Iredale to impeach Bravo would be necessary. Further, in the unlikely event that Gomez-Barajas went to trial on the charges of tax evasion and illegal importation, petitioner's lack of involvement in those alleged crimes made his appearance as a witness highly improbable. Finally, and most importantly, all three defendants agreed to allow Iredale to represent petitioner and to waive any future claims of conflict of interest. In petitioner's view, the Government was manufacturing implausible conflicts in an attempt to disqualify Iredale, who had already proved extremely effective in representing Gomez-Barajas and Bravo.

* * * [T]he District Court * * * ruled: " * * * that an irreconcilable conflict of interest exists" [and denied] Mr. Wheat's request to substitute Mr. Iredale in as attorney of record. * * * Petitioner proceeded to trial with his original counsel and was convicted * * *.

The Sixth Amendment to the Constitution guarantees that "[i]n all criminal prosecutions, the accused shall enjoy the right ... to have the Assistance of Counsel for his defence." In *United States v. Morrison* we observed that this right was designed to assure fairness in the adversary criminal process. Realizing that an unaided layman may have little skill in arguing the law or in coping with an intricate procedural system, we have held that the Sixth Amendment secures the right to the assistance of counsel, by appointment if necessary, in a trial for any serious crime. We have further recognized that the purpose of providing assistance of counsel "is simply to ensure that criminal defendants receive a fair trial," and that in evaluating Sixth Amendment claims, "the appropriate inquiry focuses on the adversarial process, not on the accused's relationship with his lawyer as such." Thus, while the right to select and be represented by one's preferred attorney is comprehended by the Sixth Amendment, the essential aim of the Amendment is to guarantee an effective advocate for each criminal defendant rather than to ensure that a defendant will inexorably be represented by the lawyer whom he prefers.

The Sixth Amendment right to choose one's own counsel is circumscribed in several important respects. Regardless of his persuasive powers, an advocate who is not a member of the bar may not represent clients (other than himself) in court. Similarly, a defendant may not insist on representation by an attorney he cannot afford or who for other reasons declines to represent the defendant. Nor may a defendant insist on the counsel of an attorney who has a previous or ongoing relationship with an opposing party, even when the opposing party is the Government. The question raised in this case is the extent to which a criminal defendant's right under the Sixth Amendment to his chosen attorney is qualified by the fact that the attorney has represented other defendants charged in the same criminal conspiracy.

In previous cases, we have recognized that multiple representation of criminal defendants engenders special dangers of which a court must be aware. While "permitting a single attorney to represent codefendants . . . is not *per se* violative of constitutional guarantees of effective assistance of counsel," a court confronted with and alerted to possible conflicts of interest must take adequate steps to ascertain whether the conflicts warrant separate counsel. As we said in *Holloway:*

> Joint representation of conflicting interests is suspect because of what it tends to prevent the attorney from doing. . . . [A] conflict may . . . prevent an attorney from challenging the admission of evidence prejudicial to one client but perhaps favorable to another, or from arguing at the sentencing hearing the relative involvement and culpability of his clients in order to minimize the culpability of one by emphasizing that of another.

Petitioner insists that the provision of waivers by all affected defendants cures any problems created by the multiple representation. But no such flat rule can be deduced from the Sixth Amendment presumption in favor of counsel of choice. Federal courts have an independent interest in ensuring that criminal trials are conducted within the ethical standards of the profession and that legal proceedings appear fair to all who observe them. * * * Not only the interest of a criminal defendant but the institutional interest in the rendition of just verdicts in criminal cases may be jeopardized by unregulated multiple representation.

For this reason, the Federal Rules of Criminal Procedure direct trial judges to investigate specially cases involving joint representation. In pertinent part, Rule 44(c) provides:

> [T]he court shall promptly inquire with respect to such joint representation and shall personally advise each defendant of his right to the effective assistance of counsel, including separate representation. Unless it appears that there is good cause to believe no conflict of interest is likely to arise, the court shall take such measures as may be appropriate to protect each defendant's right to counsel.

Although Rule 44(c) does not specify what particular measures may be taken by a district court, one option * * * is an order by the court that the defendants be separately represented in subsequent proceedings in the case. This suggestion comports with our instructions in *Holloway* and in *Glasser v. United States* that the trial courts, when alerted by objection from one of the parties, have an independent duty to ensure that criminal defendants receive a trial that is fair and does not contravene the Sixth Amendment. * * *

[W]here a court justifiably finds an actual conflict of interest, there can be no doubt that it may decline a proffer of waiver, and insist that defendants be separately represented. * * * [W]e think the district court must be allowed substantial latitude in refusing waivers of conflicts of interest not only in those rare cases where an actual conflict may be demonstrated before trial, but in the more common cases where a potential for conflict exists which may or may not burgeon into an actual conflict as the trial progresses. In the circumstances of this case, with the motion for substitution of counsel made so close to the time of trial, the District Court relied on instinct and judgment based on experience in making its decision. We do not think it can be said that the court exceeded the broad latitude which must be accorded it in making this decision. * * *

Here the District Court was confronted not simply with an attorney who wished to represent two coequal defendants in a straightforward criminal prosecution; rather, Iredale proposed to defend three conspirators of varying stature in a complex drug distribution scheme. The Government intended to call Bravo as a witness for the prosecution at petitioner's trial. The Government might readily have tied certain deliveries of marijuana by Bravo to petitioner, necessitating vigorous cross-examination of Bravo by petitioner's counsel. Iredale, because of his prior representation of Bravo, would have been unable ethically to provide that cross-examination.

Iredale had also represented Gomez-Barajas, one of the alleged kingpins of the distribution ring, and had succeeded in obtaining a verdict of acquittal for him. Gomez-Barajas had agreed with the Government to plead guilty to other charges, but the District Court had not yet accepted the plea arrangement. If the agreement were rejected, petitioner's probable testimony at the resulting trial of Gomez-Barajas would create an ethical dilemma for Iredale from which one or the other of his clients would likely suffer.

Viewing the situation as it did before trial, we hold that the District Court's refusal to permit the substitution of counsel in this case was within its discretion and did not violate petitioner's Sixth Amendment rights. * * * The District Court must recognize a presumption in favor of petitioner's counsel of choice, but that presumption may be overcome not only by a demonstration of actual conflict but by a showing of a serious potential for conflict. The evaluation of the facts and circumstances of each case under this standard must be left primarily to the informed judgment of the trial court. * * *

JUSTICE MARSHALL, with whom JUSTICE BRENNAN joins, dissenting.

* * * As the Court states, * * * the trial court must recognize a presumption in favor of a defendant's counsel of choice. This presumption means that a trial court may not reject a defendant's chosen counsel on the ground of a potential conflict of interest absent a showing that both the likelihood and the dimensions of the feared conflict are substantial. Unsupported or dubious speculation as to a conflict will not suffice. The

Government must show a substantial potential for the kind of conflict that would undermine the fairness of the trial process.

* * * In my view, a trial court that rejects a criminal defendant's chosen counsel on the ground of a potential conflict should make findings on the record to facilitate review, and an appellate court should scrutinize closely the basis for the trial court's decision. Only in this way can a criminal defendant's right to counsel of his choice be appropriately protected.

The Court's resolution of the instant case flows from its deferential approach to the District Court's denial of petitioner's motion to add or substitute counsel; absent deference, a decision upholding the District Court's ruling would be inconceivable. Indeed, I believe that even under the Court's deferential standard, reversal is in order. The mere fact of multiple representation, as the Court concedes, will not support an order preventing a criminal defendant from retaining counsel of his choice. As this Court has stated on prior occasions, such representation will not invariably pose a substantial risk of a serious conflict of interest and thus will not invariably imperil the prospect of a fair trial. The propriety of the District Court's order thus depends on whether the Government showed that the particular facts and circumstances of the multiple representation proposed in this case were such as to overcome the presumption in favor of petitioner's choice of counsel. I believe it is clear that the Government failed to make this showing. Neither Eugene Iredale's representation of Juvenal Gomez-Barajas nor Iredale's representation of Javier Bravo posed any threat of causing a conflict of interest.

At the time of petitioner's trial, Iredale's representation of Gomez-Barajas was effectively completed. As the Court notes, Iredale had obtained an acquittal for Gomez-Barajas on charges relating to a conspiracy to distribute marijuana. Iredale also had negotiated an agreement with the Government under which Gomez-Barajas would plead guilty to charges of tax evasion and illegal importation of merchandise, although the trial court had not yet accepted this plea arrangement. Gomez-Barajas was not scheduled to appear as a witness at petitioner's trial; thus, Iredale's conduct of that trial would not require him to question his former client. The only possible conflict this Court can divine from Iredale's representation of both petitioner and Gomez-Barajas rests on the premise that the trial court would reject the negotiated plea agreement and that Gomez-Barajas then would decide to go to trial. In this event, the Court tells us, "petitioner's probable testimony at the resulting trial of Gomez-Barajas would create an ethical dilemma for Iredale."

This argument rests on speculation of the most dubious kind. The Court offers no reason to think that the trial court would have rejected Gomez-Barajas' plea agreement; neither did the Government posit any such reason in its argument or brief before this Court. The most likely occurrence at the time petitioner moved to retain Iredale as his defense counsel was that the trial court would accept Gomez-Barajas' plea agreement, as the court in fact later did. Moreover, even if Gomez-Barajas had gone to trial, petitioner probably would not have testified. The record contains no indication that petitioner had any involvement in or information about crimes for which Gomez-Barajas might yet have stood trial. The only alleged connection between petitioner and Gomez-Barajas sprang from the conspiracy to distribute marijuana, and a jury already had acquitted Gomez-Barajas of that charge. It is therefore disingenuous to say that representation of both petitioner and Gomez-Barajas posed a serious potential for a conflict of interest.

Similarly, Iredale's prior representation of Bravo was not a cause for concern. The Court notes that the prosecution intended to call Bravo to the stand at petitioner's trial and asserts that Bravo's testimony could well have "necessitat[ed] vigorous cross-examination . . . by petitioner's counsel." The facts, however, belie the claim that Bravo's anticipated testimony created a serious potential for conflict. Contrary to the Court's inference, Bravo could not have testified about petitioner's involvement in the alleged marijuana distribution scheme. As all parties were aware at the time, Bravo did not know and could not identify petitioner; indeed, prior to the commencement of legal proceedings, the two men never had heard of each other. Bravo's eventual testimony at petitioner's trial related to a shipment of marijuana in which petitioner was not involved; the testimony contained not a single reference to petitioner. Petitioner's counsel did not cross-examine Bravo, and neither petitioner's counsel nor the prosecutor mentioned Bravo's testimony in closing argument. All of these developments were predictable when the District Court ruled on petitioner's request that Iredale serve as trial counsel; the contours of Bravo's testimony were clear at that time. Given the insignificance of this testimony to any matter that petitioner's counsel would dispute, the proposed joint representation of petitioner and Bravo did not threaten a conflict of interest.

Moreover, even assuming that Bravo's testimony might have "necessitat[ed] vigorous cross-examination," the District Court could have insured against the possibility of any conflict of interest without wholly depriving petitioner of his constitutional right to the counsel of his choice. Petitioner's motion requested that Iredale either be substituted for petitioner's current counsel or be added to petitioner's defense team. Had the District Court allowed the addition of Iredale and then ordered that he take no part in the cross-examination of Bravo, any possibility of a conflict would have been removed. Especially in light of the availability of this precautionary measure, the notion that Iredale's prior representation of

Bravo might well have caused a conflict of interest at petitioner's trial is nothing short of ludicrous.

The Court gives short shrift to the actual circumstances of this case in upholding the decision below. These circumstances show that the District Court erred in denying petitioner's motion to substitute or add Iredale as defense counsel. The proposed representation did not pose a substantial risk of a serious conflict of interest. The District Court therefore had no authority to deny petitioner's Sixth Amendment right to retain counsel of his choice. This constitutional error demands that petitioner's conviction be reversed. I accordingly dissent.

[JUSTICE STEVENS' dissenting opinion has been omitted.]

FARETTA V. CALIFORNIA
Supreme Court of the United States
422 U.S. 806, 95 S. Ct. 2525, 45 L. Ed. 2d 562 (1975)

JUSTICE STEWART delivered the opinion of the Court.

The Sixth and Fourteenth Amendments of our Constitution guarantee that a person brought to trial in any state or federal court must be afforded the right to the assistance of counsel before he can be validly convicted and punished by imprisonment. * * * The question before us now is whether a defendant in a state criminal trial has a constitutional right to proceed without counsel when he voluntarily and intelligently elects to do so. * * *

Anthony Faretta was charged with grand theft in an information filed in the Superior Court of Los Angeles County, Cal. At the arraignment, the Superior Court Judge assigned to preside at the trial appointed the public defender to represent Faretta. Well before the date of trial, however, Faretta requested that he be permitted to represent himself. Questioning by the judge revealed that Faretta had once represented himself in a criminal prosecution, that he had a high school education, and that he did not want to be represented by the public defender because he believed that that office was "very loaded down with ... a heavy case load." The judge responded that he believed Faretta was "making a mistake" and emphasized that in further proceedings Faretta would receive no special favors. Nevertheless, after establishing that Faretta wanted to represent himself and did not want a lawyer, the judge, in a "preliminary ruling," accepted Faretta's waiver of the assistance of counsel. The judge indicated, however, that he might reverse this ruling if it later appeared that Faretta was unable adequately to represent himself.

Several weeks thereafter, but still prior to trial, the judge *sua sponte* held a hearing to inquire into Faretta's ability to conduct his own defense, and questioned him specifically about both the hearsay rule and the state law governing the challenge of potential jurors. After consideration of

Faretta's answers, and observation of his demeanor, the judge ruled that Faretta had not made an intelligent and knowing waiver of his right to the assistance of counsel, and also ruled that Faretta had no constitutional right to conduct his own defense. The judge, accordingly, reversed his earlier ruling permitting self-representation and again appointed the public defender to represent Faretta. Faretta's subsequent request for leave to act as co-counsel was rejected, as were his efforts to make certain motions on his own behalf. Throughout the subsequent trial, the judge required that Faretta's defense be conducted only through the appointed lawyer from the public defender's office. At the conclusion of the trial, the jury found Faretta guilty as charged, and the judge sentenced him to prison.

The California Court of Appeal, relying upon a then-recent California Supreme Court decision that had expressly decided the issue, affirmed the trial judge's ruling that Faretta had no federal or state constitutional right to represent himself. Accordingly, the appellate court affirmed Faretta's conviction. A petition for rehearing was denied without opinion, and the California Supreme Court denied review. We granted certiorari.

In the federal courts, the right of self-representation has been protected by statute since the beginning of our Nation. * * * With few exceptions, each of the several States also accords a defendant the right to represent himself in any criminal case. The constitutions of 36 States explicitly confer that right. Moreover, many state courts have expressed the view that the right is also supported by the Constitution of the United States.

This Court has more than once indicated the same view. * * * "[A]n accused, in the exercise of a free and intelligent choice, and with the considered approval of the court, may waive trial by jury, and so likewise may he competently and intelligently waive his Constitutional right to assistance of counsel."

* * * "[T]he Constitution does not force a lawyer upon a defendant." Whether the Constitution forbids a State from forcing a lawyer upon a defendant is a different question. * * *

This Court's past recognition of the right of self-representation, the federal-court authority holding the right to be of constitutional dimension, and the state constitutions pointing to the right's fundamental nature form a consensus not easily ignored. "[T]he mere fact that a path is a beaten one," Mr. Justice Jackson once observed, "is a persuasive reason for following it." We confront here a nearly universal conviction, on the part of our people as well as our courts, that forcing a lawyer upon an unwilling defendant is contrary to his basic right to defend himself if he truly wants to do so.

* * * The right of self-representation finds support in the structure of the Sixth Amendment, as well as in the English and colonial jurisprudence from which the Amendment emerged. * * *

The Sixth Amendment includes a compact statement of the rights necessary to a full defense:

> In all criminal prosecutions, the accused shall enjoy the right ... to be informed of the nature and cause of the accusation; to be confronted with the witnesses against him; to have compulsory process for obtaining witnesses in his favor, and to have the Assistance of Counsel for his defence.

Because these rights are basic to our adversary system of criminal justice, they are part of the "due process of law" that is guaranteed by the Fourteenth Amendment to defendants in the criminal courts of the States. The rights to notice, confrontation, and compulsory process, when taken together, guarantee that a criminal charge may be answered in a manner now considered fundamental to the fair administration of American justice—through the calling and interrogation of favorable witnesses, the cross-examination of adverse witnesses, and the orderly introduction of evidence. In short, the Amendment constitutionalizes the right in an adversary criminal trial to make a defense as we know it.

The Sixth Amendment does not provide merely that a defense shall be made for the accused; it grants to the accused personally the right to make his defense. It is the accused, not counsel, who must be "informed of the nature and cause of the accusation," who must be "confronted with the witnesses against him," and who must be accorded "compulsory process for obtaining witnesses in his favor." Although not stated in the Amendment in so many words, the right to self-representation—to make one's own defense personally—is thus necessarily implied by the structure of the Amendment. The right to defend is given directly to the accused; for it is he who suffers the consequences if the defense fails.

The counsel provision supplements this design. It speaks of the "assistance" of counsel, and an assistant, however expert, is still an assistant. The language and spirit of the Sixth Amendment contemplate that counsel, like the other defense tools guaranteed by the Amendment, shall be an aid to a willing defendant—not an organ of the State interposed between an unwilling defendant and his right to defend himself personally. To thrust counsel upon the accused, against his considered wish, thus violates the logic of the Amendment. * * *

The Sixth Amendment, when naturally read, thus implies a right of self-representation. * * *

There can be no blinking of the fact that the right of an accused to conduct his own defense seems to cut against the grain of this Court's decisions holding that the Constitution requires that no accused can be convicted and imprisoned unless he has been accorded the right to the assistance of counsel. For it is surely true that the basic thesis of those decisions is that the help of a lawyer is essential to assure the defendant a fair trial. And a strong argument can surely be made that the whole thrust of those decisions must inevitably lead to the conclusion that a State may constitutionally impose a lawyer upon even an unwilling defendant.

But it is one thing to hold that every defendant, rich or poor, has the right to the assistance of counsel, and quite another to say that a State may compel a defendant to accept a lawyer he does not want. * * * It is undeniable that in most criminal prosecutions defendants could better defend with counsel's guidance than by their own unskilled efforts. But where the defendant will not voluntarily accept representation by counsel, the potential advantage of a lawyer's training and experience can be realized, if at all, only imperfectly. To force a lawyer on a defendant can only lead him to believe that the law contrives against him. Moreover, it is not inconceivable that in some rare instances, the defendant might in fact present his case more effectively by conducting his own defense. Personal liberties are not rooted in the law of averages. The right to defend is personal. The defendant, and not his lawyer or the State, will bear the personal consequences of a conviction. It is the defendant, therefore, who must be free personally to decide whether in his particular case counsel is to his advantage. And although he may conduct his own defense ultimately to his own detriment, his choice must be honored out of "that respect for the individual which is the lifeblood of the law."

When an accused manages his own defense, he relinquishes, as a purely factual matter, many of the traditional benefits associated with the right to counsel. For this reason, in order to represent himself, the accused must "knowingly and intelligently" forgo those relinquished benefits. Although a defendant need not himself have the skill and experience of a lawyer in order competently and intelligently to choose self-representation, he should be made aware of the dangers and disadvantages of self-representation, so that the record will establish that "he knows what he is doing and his choice is made with eyes open."[a]

Here, weeks before trial, Faretta clearly and unequivocally declared to the trial judge that he wanted to represent himself and did not want counsel. The record affirmatively shows that Faretta was literate, competent, and understanding, and that he was voluntarily exercising his informed free will. The trial judge had warned Faretta that he thought it

---

[a] While a defendant must be warned of the dangers of self-representation prior to being allowed to self-represent at trial, such a warning is not required for a defendant who chooses to self-represent at the entry of a plea. Iowa v. Tovar, 541 U.S. 77 (2004) (holding Sixth Amendment does not require trial court to warn defendant that waiving right to counsel at plea hearing entails risk that viable defenses may be overlooked and deprives defendant of independent opinion as to whether to plead guilty).

was a mistake not to accept the assistance of counsel, and that Faretta would be required to follow all the "ground rules" of trial procedure. We need make no assessment of how well or poorly Faretta had mastered the intricacies of the hearsay rule and the California code provisions that govern challenges of potential jurors on *voir dire*.[b] For his technical legal knowledge, as such, was not relevant to an assessment of his knowing exercise of the right to defend himself.[c]

In forcing Faretta, under these circumstances, to accept against his will a state-appointed public defender, the California courts deprived him of his constitutional right to conduct his own defense. Accordingly, the judgment before us is vacated, and the case is remanded for further proceedings not inconsistent with this opinion.

It is so ordered.

Judgment vacated and case remanded.

CHIEF JUSTICE BURGER, with whom JUSTICE BLACKMUN and JUSTICE REHNQUIST join, dissenting. * * *

The most striking feature of the Court's opinion is that it devotes so little discussion to the matter which it concedes is the core of the decision, that is, discerning an independent basis in the Constitution for the supposed right to represent oneself in a criminal trial. Its ultimate assertion that such a right is tucked between the lines of the Sixth Amendment is contradicted by the Amendment's language and its consistent judicial interpretation.

* * * [T]he conclusion that the right guaranteed by the Sixth Amendment are "personal" to an accused reflects nothing more than the obvious fact that it is he who is on trial and therefore has need of a defense. But neither that nearly trivial proposition nor the language of the Amendment, which speaks in uniformly mandatory terms, leads to the further conclusion that the right to counsel is merely supplementary and may be dispensed with at the whim of the accused. Rather, this Court's

---

[b] The trial court may appoint standby counsel to assist the defendant who chooses to self-represent at trial, thus relieving the judge of the need to explain and enforce basic rules of courtroom protocol, even over the defendant's objection, without violating the Sixth Amendment. *McKaskle v. Wiggins*, 465 U.S. 168 (1984).

[c] While the trial court may not deny a defendant the right to self-represent on the ground that the defendant lacks the technical knowledge of a skilled trial attorney, the trial court may consider the defendant's mental incapacity when deciding whether to grant or deny a motion to self-represent. In *Indiana v. Edwards*, 554 U.S. 164 (2008), the Court held that a defendant who wishes to self-represent and meets the standard for competence to stand trial, i.e. the defendant understands the nature of the proceedings against him and can assist in his own defense, may nonetheless be denied the right to self-represent if the defendant's mental illness would affect his ability to competently represent himself at trial. The Court, however, did not set forth a test for measuring a defendant's mental capacity to self-represent, leaving it up to the states to fashion their own standards.

decisions have consistently included the right to counsel as an integral part of the bundle making up the larger "right to a defense as we know it." * * *

The reason for this hardly requires explanation. The fact of the matter is that in all but an extraordinarily small number of cases an accused will lose whatever defense he may have if he undertakes to conduct the trial himself.[d]

* * * Nor is it accurate to suggest, as the Court seems to later in its opinion, that the quality of his representation at trial is a matter with which only the accused is legitimately concerned. Although we have adopted an adversary system of criminal justice, the prosecution is more than an ordinary litigant, and the trial judge is not simply an automaton who insures that technical rules are adhered to. Both are charged with the duty of insuring that justice, in the broadest sense of that term, is achieved in every criminal trial. That goal is ill-served, and the integrity of and public confidence in the system are undermined, when an easy conviction is obtained due to the defendant's ill-advised decision to waive counsel. * * * The system of criminal justice should not be available as an instrument of self-destruction. * * *

JUSTICE BLACKMUN, with whom THE CHIEF JUSTICE and JUSTICE REHNQUIST join, dissenting. * * *

If there is any truth to the old proverb that "one who is his own lawyer has a fool for a client," the Court by its opinion today now bestows a constitutional right on one to make a fool of himself.

---

[d] Contrary to the commonly held belief that defendants who self-represent are likely to lose, felony defendants who self-represent are actually convicted at rates equal to or lower than felony defendants who are represented by counsel. *See* Erica J. Hashimoto, *Defending the Right of Self-Representation: An Empirical Look at the Pro Se Felony Defendant*, 85 N.C. L. REV. 423 (2007).

CHAPTER 30

THE RIGHT OF PRESENCE

■ ■ ■

A criminal defendant's right to be present at trial is rooted in the Sixth Amendment's Confrontation Clause. This chapter evaluates whether the right of presence is absolute or can be limited or waived. *United States v. Gagnon* evaluates whether the right of presence includes a right to be present at an *in camera* session between the judge and a juror in judge's chambers. *Taylor v. United States* analyzes whether a defendant's failure to return to court after a mid-trial recess is sufficient to constitute a waiver of the right to presence. *Illinois v. Allen* considers the constitutionality of a judge's decision to remove a disruptive defendant from court and continue the trial without him.

UNITED STATES V. GAGNON
Supreme Court of the United States
470 U.S. 522, 105 S. Ct. 1482, 84 L. Ed.2d 486 (1985)

PER CURIAM.

The four respondents were indicted on various counts and tried together in Federal District Court for participation in a large-scale cocaine distribution conspiracy. During the afternoon recess on the first day of trial the District Judge was discussing matters of law in open court with the respondents, their respective counsel, and the Assistant United States Attorney, outside the presence of the jury. The bailiff entered the courtroom and informed the judge that one of the jurors, Garold Graham, had expressed concern because he had noticed respondent Gagnon sketching portraits of the jury. Gagnon's attorney admitted that Gagnon had been sketching jury members during the trial. The District Judge ordered that the practice cease immediately. Gagnon's lawyer suggested that the judge question the juror to ascertain whether the sketching had prejudiced the juror against Gagnon. The judge then stated, still in open court in the presence of each respondent and his counsel: "I will talk to the juror in my chambers and make a determination. We'll stand at recess." No objections were made by any respondent and no respondent requested to be present at the discussion in chambers.

The District Judge then went into the chambers and called for juror Graham. The judge also requested the bailiff to bring Gagnon's counsel to chambers. There the judge, in the company of Gagnon's counsel, discussed the sketching with the juror. The juror stated: " . . . I just thought that perhaps because of the seriousness of the trial, and because of, whichever way the deliberations go, it kind of, it upset me, because of what could happen afterwards."

The judge then explained that Gagnon was an artist, meant no harm, and the sketchings had been confiscated. The juror was assured that Gagnon would sketch no more. Graham stated that another juror had seen the sketching and made a comment to him about it but no one else seemed to have noticed, and no other jurors had discussed the matter. The judge then elicited from Graham his willingness to continue as an impartial juror. Gagnon's counsel asked two questions of the juror and then stated that he was satisfied. The *in camera* meeting broke up, and the trial resumed. A transcript of the *in camera* proceeding was available to all of the parties; at no time did any respondent mention or object to the *in camera* interview of the juror. No motions were made to disqualify Graham or the other juror who witnessed the sketching, nor did any respondent request that cautionary instructions be given to the jury. After the jury returned guilty verdicts no post-trial motions concerning the incident were filed with the District Court.

On the consolidated appeal, however, each respondent claimed that the District Court's discussion with the juror in chambers violated respondents' Sixth Amendment rights to an impartial jury and their rights under Federal Rule of Criminal Procedure 43 to be present at all stages of the trial.[a] A divided panel of the Court of Appeals for the Ninth Circuit Court of Appeals reversed the convictions of all respondents, holding that the *in camera* discussion with the juror violated respondents' rights under Rule 43 and the Due Process Clause of the Fifth Amendment. * * *

We think it clear that respondents' rights under the Fifth Amendment Due Process Clause were not violated by the *in camera* discussion with the juror. "[T]he mere occurrence of an *ex parte* conversation between a trial judge and a juror does not constitute a deprivation of any constitutional right. The defense has no constitutional right to be present at every interaction between a judge and a juror, nor is there a constitutional right to have a court reporter transcribe every such communication."

The constitutional right to presence is rooted to a large extent in the Confrontation Clause of the Sixth Amendment, but we have recognized that this right is protected by the Due Process Clause in some situations where the defendant is not actually confronting witnesses or evidence against him. In *Snyder v. Massachusetts,* the Court explained that a

---

[a] Rule 43 of the Federal Rules of Criminal Procedure provides, "A defendant who was initially present at trial, or who had pleaded guilty or nolo contendere, waives the right to be present . . . when the defendant is voluntarily absent after the trial has begun, regardless of whether the court informed the defendant of an obligation to remain during trial." *See* FED. R. CRIM. P. 43.

defendant has a due process right to be present at a proceeding "whenever his presence has a relation, reasonably substantial, to the fullness of his opportunity to defend against the charge. . . . [T]he presence of a defendant is a condition of due process to the extent that a fair and just hearing would be thwarted by his absence, and to that extent only." The Court also cautioned in *Snyder* that the exclusion of a defendant from a trial proceeding should be considered in light of the whole record.

In this case the presence of the four respondents and their four trial counsel at the *in camera* discussion was not required to ensure fundamental fairness or a "reasonably substantial . . . opportunity to defend against the charge." The encounter between the judge, the juror, and Gagnon's lawyer was a short interlude in a complex trial; the conference was not the sort of event which every defendant had a right personally to attend under the Fifth Amendment. * * * The Fifth Amendment does not require that all the parties be present when the judge inquires into such a minor occurrence.

The Court of Appeals also held that the conference with the juror was a "stage of the trial" at which Gagnon's presence was guaranteed by Federal Rule of Criminal Procedure 43. We assume for the purposes of this opinion that the Court of Appeals was correct in this regard. We hold, however, that the court erred in concluding that respondents had not waived their rights under Rule 43 to be present at the conference with the juror.

The record shows * * * that the District Judge, in open court, announced her intention to speak with the juror in chambers, and then called a recess. The *in camera* discussion took place during the recess, and trial resumed shortly thereafter with no change in the jury. Respondents neither then nor later in the course of the trial asserted any Rule 43 rights they may have had to attend this conference. Respondents did not request to attend the conference at any time. No objections of any sort were lodged, either before or after the conference. Respondents did not even make any post-trial motions, although post-trial hearings may often resolve this sort of claim. * * * The district court need not get an express "on the record" waiver from the defendant for every trial conference which a defendant may have a right to attend. * * *

We hold that failure by a criminal defendant to invoke his right to be present under Federal Rule of Criminal Procedure 43 at a conference which he knows is taking place between the judge and a juror in chambers constitutes a valid waiver of that right. The petition for certiorari and respondents' motion to supplement the record are granted, and the judgment of the Court of Appeals is

Reversed.

JUSTICE POWELL took no part in the consideration or decision of this case.

[JUSTICE BRENNAN's dissenting opinion has been omitted.]

TAYLOR V. UNITED STATES
Supreme Court of the United States
414 U.S. 17, 94 S. Ct. 194, 38 L. Ed. 2d 174 (1973)

PER CURIAM.

On the first day of his trial on four counts of selling cocaine * * *, petitioner failed to return for the afternoon session. He had been present at the expiration of the morning session when the court announced that the lunch recess would last until 2 p.m., and he had been told by his attorney to return to the courtroom at that time. The judge recessed the trial until the following morning, but petitioner still did not appear. His wife testified that she had left the courtroom the previous day with petitioner after the morning session; that they had separated after sharing a taxicab to Roxbury; that he had not appeared ill; and, finally, that she had not heard from him since. The trial judge then denied a motion for mistrial by defense counsel, who asserted that the jurors' minds would be tainted by petitioner's absence and that continuation of the trial in his absence deprived him of his Sixth Amendment right to confront witnesses against him. Relying upon Fed. Rules Crim. Proc. 43, which expressly provides that a defendant's voluntary absence "shall not prevent continuing the trial," the court found that petitioner had absented himself voluntarily from the proceedings.

Throughout the remainder of the trial, the court admonished the jury that no inference of guilt could be drawn from petitioner's absence. Petitioner was found guilty on all four counts. Following his subsequent arrest, he was sentenced to the statutory five-year minimum. The Court of Appeals affirmed the conviction, and we now grant the motion for leave to proceed in forma pauperis and the petition for certiorari and affirm the judgment of the Court of Appeals.

There is no challenge to the trial court's conclusion that petitioner's absence from the trial was voluntary, and no claim that the continuation of the trial was not authorized by Rule 43. Nor are we persuaded that Rule 43 is unconstitutional or that petitioner was deprived of any constitutional rights in the circumstances before us. Rule 43 has remained unchanged since the adoption of the Federal Rules of Criminal Procedure in 1945; and with respect to the consequences of the defendant's voluntary absence from trial, it reflects the long-standing rule recognized by this Court in *Diaz v. United States*:

> [W]here * * * the accused is not in custody, the prevailing rule has been, that if, after the trial has begun in his presence, he voluntarily absents himself, this does not nullify what has been done or prevent the completion of the trial, but, on the contrary, operates as a waiver of his right to be present and leaves the court free to proceed with the trial in like manner and with like effect as if he were present.

Under this rule, the District Court and the Court of Appeals correctly rejected petitioner's claims.

Petitioner, however, insists that his mere voluntary absence from his trial cannot be construed as an effective waiver, that is, "an intentional relinquishment or abandonment of a known right or privilege," unless it is demonstrated that he knew or had been expressly warned by the trial court not only that he had a right to be present but also that the trial would continue in his absence and thereby effectively foreclose his right to testify and to confront personally the witnesses against him.

Like the Court of Appeals, we cannot accept this position. Petitioner had no right to interrupt the trial by his voluntary absence, as he implicitly concedes by urging only that he should have been warned that no such right existed and that the trial would proceed in his absence. The right at issue is the right to be present, and the question becomes whether that right was effectively waived by his voluntary absence. Consistent with Rule 43 and *Diaz*, we conclude that it was.

It is wholly incredible to suggest that petitioner, who was at liberty on bail, had attended the opening session of his trial, and had a duty to be present at the trial, entertained any doubts about his right to be present at every stage of his trial. It seems equally incredible to us, as it did to the Court of Appeals, "that a defendant who flees from a courtroom in the midst of a trial—where judge, jury, witnesses and lawyers are present and ready to continue—would not know that as a consequence the trial could continue in his absence." Here the Court of Appeals noted that when petitioner was questioned at sentencing regarding his flight, he never contended that he was unaware that a consequence of his flight would be a continuation of the trial without him. Moreover, no issue of the voluntariness of his disappearance was ever raised. As was recently noted, "there can be no doubt whatever that the governmental prerogative to proceed with a trial may not be defeated by conduct of the accused that prevents the trial from going forward." Under the circumstances present here, the Court of Appeals properly applied Rule 43 and affirmed the judgment of conviction.

Affirmed.

ILLINOIS V. ALLEN
Supreme Court of the United States
397 U.S. 337, 90 S. Ct. 1057, 25 L. Ed. 2d 353 (1970)

JUSTICE BLACK delivered the opinion of the Court.

* * * One of the most basic of the rights guaranteed by the Confrontation Clause is the accused's right to be present in the courtroom at every stage of his trial. The question presented in this case is whether an accused can claim the benefit of this constitutional right to remain in the courtroom while at the same time he engages in speech and conduct which is so noisy, disorderly, and disruptive that it is exceedingly difficult or wholly impossible to carry on the trial.

* * * Allen's expulsion from the courtroom [is] set out in the Court of Appeals' opinion * * *:

> After his indictment [for armed robbery] and during the pretrial stage, the petitioner [Allen] refused court-appointed counsel and indicated to the trial court on several occasions that he wished to conduct his own defense. After considerable argument by the petitioner, the trial judge told him, "I'll let you be your own lawyer, but I'll ask Mr. Kelly (court-appointed counsel) [to] sit in and protect the record for you, insofar as possible."
>
> The trial began on September 9, 1957. After the State's Attorney had accepted the first four jurors following their voir dire examination, the petitioner began examining the first juror and continued at great length. Finally, the trial judge interrupted the petitioner, requesting him to confine his questions solely to matters relating to the prospective juror's qualifications. At that point, the petitioner started to argue with the judge in a most abusive and disrespectful manner. At last, and seemingly in desperation, the judge asked appointed counsel to proceed with the examination of the jurors. The petitioner continued to talk, proclaiming that the appointed attorney was not going to act as his lawyer. He terminated his remarks by saying, "When I go out for lunchtime, you're [the judge] going to be a corpse here." At that point he tore the file which his attorney had and threw the papers on the floor. The trial judge thereupon stated to the petitioner, "One more outbreak of that sort and I'll remove you from the courtroom." This warning had no effect on the petitioner. He continued to talk back to the judge, saying, "There's not going to be no trial, either. I'm going to sit here and you're going to talk and you can bring your shackles out and straight jacket and put them on me and tape my mouth, but it will do no good because there's not going to be no trial." After more abusive remarks by the petitioner, the trial judge ordered the trial to proceed in the

petitioner's absence. The petitioner was removed from the courtroom. The voir dire examination then continued and the jury was selected in the absence of the petitioner.

After a noon recess and before the jury was brought into the courtroom, the petitioner, appearing before the judge, complained about the fairness of the trial and his appointed attorney. He also said he wanted to be present in the court during his trial. In reply, the judge said that the petitioner would be permitted to remain in the courtroom if he "behaved [himself] and [did] not interfere with the introduction of the case." The jury was brought in and seated. Counsel for the petitioner then moved to exclude the witnesses from the courtroom. The [petitioner] protested this effort on the part of his attorney, saying: "There is going to be no proceeding. I'm going to start talking and I'm going to keep on talking all through the trial. There's not going to be no trial like this. I want my sister and my friends here in court to testify for me." The trial judge thereupon ordered the petitioner removed from the courtroom.

After this second removal, Allen remained out of the courtroom during the presentation of the State's case-in-chief, except that he was brought in on several occasions for purposes of identification. During one of these latter appearances, Allen responded to one of the judge's questions with vile and abusive language. After the prosecution's case had been presented, the trial judge reiterated his promise to Allen that he could return to the courtroom whenever he agreed to conduct himself properly. Allen gave some assurances of proper conduct and was permitted to be present through the remainder of the trial, principally his defense, which was conducted by his appointed counsel. * * *

The Court of Appeals felt that the defendant's Sixth Amendment right to be present at his own trial was so "absolute" that, no matter how unruly or disruptive the defendant's conduct might be, he could never be held to have lost that right so long as he continued to insist upon it, as Allen clearly did. Therefore the Court of Appeals concluded that a trial judge could never expel a defendant from his own trial and that the judge's ultimate remedy when faced with an obstreperous defendant like Allen who determines to make his trial impossible is to bind and gag him. We cannot agree that the Sixth Amendment, the cases upon which the Court of Appeals relied, or any other cases of this Court so handicap a trial judge in conducting a criminal trial. * * * We accept instead the statement of Mr. Justice Cardozo who, speaking for the Court in *Snyder v. Massachusetts*, said: "No doubt the privilege [of personally confronting witnesses] may be lost by consent or at times even by misconduct." Although mindful that courts must indulge every reasonable presumption against the loss of constitutional rights, we explicitly hold today that a defendant can lose his right to be present at trial if, after he has been warned by the judge that he will be removed if he continues his disruptive behavior, he nevertheless insists on conducting himself in a manner so disorderly, disruptive, and disrespectful of the court that his trial cannot be carried on with him in the courtroom. Once lost, the right to be present can, of course, be reclaimed as soon as the defendant is willing to conduct himself consistently with the decorum and respect inherent in the concept of courts and judicial proceedings.

It is essential to the proper administration of criminal justice that dignity, order, and decorum be the hallmarks of all court proceedings in our country. The flagrant disregard in the courtroom of elementary standards of proper conduct should not and cannot be tolerated. We believe trial judges confronted with disruptive, contumacious, stubbornly defiant defendants must be given sufficient discretion to meet the circumstances of each case. No one formula for maintaining the appropriate courtroom atmosphere will be best in all situations. We think there are at least three constitutionally permissible ways for a trial judge to handle an obstreperous defendant like Allen: (1) bind and gag him, thereby keeping him present; (2) cite him for contempt; (3) take him out of the courtroom until he promises to conduct himself properly.

Trying a defendant for a crime while he sits bound and gagged before the judge and jury would to an extent comply with that part of the Sixth Amendment's purposes that accords the defendant an opportunity to confront the witnesses at the trial. But even to contemplate such a technique, much less see it, arouses a feeling that no person should be tried while shackled and gagged except as a last resort. Not only is it possible that the sight of shackles and gags might have a significant effect on the jury's feelings about the defendant, but the use of this technique is itself something of an affront to the very dignity and decorum of judicial proceedings that the judge is seeking to uphold. Moreover, one of the defendant's primary advantages of being present at the trial, his ability to communicate with his counsel, is greatly reduced when the defendant is in a condition of total physical restraint. * * * However, in some situations * * *, binding and gagging might possibly be the fairest and most reasonable way to handle a defendant who acts as Allen did here.

* * * [C]iting or threatening to cite a contumacious defendant for criminal contempt might in itself be sufficient to make a defendant stop interrupting a trial. If so, the problem would be solved easily, and the defendant could remain in the courtroom. Of course, if the defendant is determined to prevent any trial, then a court in attempting to try the defendant for contempt is still confronted with the identical dilemma * * *. And criminal contempt has obvious limitations as a sanction when the defendant is charged with a crime so serious that a very severe sentence such as death or life imprisonment is likely to be imposed. In such a case the defendant might not be affected by a mere contempt sentence when he

ultimately faces a far more serious sanction. Nevertheless, the contempt remedy should be borne in mind by a judge in the circumstances of this case.

Another aspect of the contempt remedy is the judge's power, when exercised consistently with state and federal law, to imprison an unruly defendant such as Allen for civil contempt and discontinue the trial until such time as the defendant promises to behave himself. This procedure is consistent with the defendant's right to be present at trial, and yet it avoids the serious shortcomings of the use of shackles and gags. It must be recognized, however, that a defendant might conceivably, as a matter of calculated strategy, elect to spend a prolonged period in confinement for contempt in the hope that adverse witnesses might be unavailable after a lapse of time. A court must guard against allowing a defendant to profit from his own wrong in this way.

The trial court in this case decided under the circumstances to remove the defendant from the courtroom and to continue his trial in his absence until and unless he promised to conduct himself in a manner befitting an American courtroom. As we said earlier, we find nothing unconstitutional about this procedure. Allen's behavior was clearly of such an extreme and aggravated nature as to justify either his removal from the courtroom or his total physical restraint. Prior to his removal he was repeatedly warned by the trial judge that he would be removed from the courtroom if he persisted in his unruly conduct * * *. Allen was constantly informed that he could return to the trial when he would agree to conduct himself in an orderly manner. Under these circumstances we hold that Allen lost his right guaranteed by the Sixth and Fourteenth Amendments to be present throughout his trial. * * *

We do not hold that removing this defendant from his own trial was the only way the Illinois judge could have constitutionally solved the problem he had. We do hold, however, that there is nothing whatever in this record to show that the judge did not act completely within his discretion. Deplorable as it is to remove a man from his own trial, even for a short time, we hold that the judge did not commit legal error in doing what he did.

The judgment of the Court of Appeals is reversed. * * *

[JUSTICE BRENNAN's and JUSTICE DOUGLAS' concurring opinions have been omitted.]

CHAPTER 31

THE CONFRONTATION CLAUSE

■ ■ ■

The right of a criminal defendant to confront adversarial witnesses is rooted in the Sixth Amendment, which provides, "In all criminal prosecutions, the accused shall enjoy the right . . . to be confronted with the witnesses against him." The Confrontation Clause is vital to a defendant's ability to present an adequate defense at trial. It prevents trial by affidavit or private testimony and provides the defendant with a meaningful opportunity to challenge the evidence through the process of "face to face" cross-examination of the witnesses against him or her.

Crawford v. Washington, the first case in this chapter, is the principal case on the Confrontation Clause and articulates the current standard for determining whether a defendant's confrontation rights have been violated when an out-of-court statement is admitted at trial. Before *Crawford* was decided in 2004, a defendant's confrontation rights were governed by the rule against hearsay and its exceptions.[a] If an out-of-court statement contained adequate indicia of reliability, either by falling within a firmly rooted exception to the hearsay rule or by bearing particularized guarantees of trustworthiness, its admission at trial would not violate the defendant's confrontation rights. *See Ohio v. Roberts*, 448 U.S. 56 (1980).

Crawford abandoned the hearsay-exception-centered approach to confrontation and replaced it with a test that focuses on the availability of the witness whose statement is at issue to testify at trial and the nature of the out-of-court statement. Under *Crawford*, a defendant's confrontation rights are not implicated unless the out-of-court statement is testimonial. In *Davis v. Washington*, the Court articulates the test that is currently used to determine whether a statement is testimonial or non-testimonial for purposes of the Confrontation Clause.

This chapter also covers some of the limitations on the defendant's right of confrontation. In *Giles v. California*, the Court examines the common law doctrine of forfeiture by wrongdoing, which permits the admission of an out-of-court statement of a witness who was kept from testifying by the defendant. The *Giles* Court considers whether the

---

[a] Hearsay is often defined as "an out-of-court statement offered to prove the truth of whatever it asserts." *Hearsay*, *Legal Information Institute*, CORNELL L. SCH., https://www.law.cornell.edu/wex/hearsay (last visited June 22, 2022). Under the hearsay rule, hearsay is generally inadmissible at trial, but many exceptions to the hearsay rule apply.

Confrontation Clause requires proof that the defendant intended to keep the witness from testifying before that witness' statement can be admitted at trial under the forfeiture by wrongdoing doctrine.

Richardson v. Marsh, the last case in the chapter, examines whether the *Bruton* rule—the rule that forbids the admission of a non-testifying codefendant's confession naming the defendant as a participant in the crime—applies to a situation in which a non-testifying codefendant's confession has been redacted to omit any reference to the defendant.

CRAWFORD V. WASHINGTON
Supreme Court of the United States
541 U.S. 36, 124 S. Ct. 1354, 158 L. Ed. 2d 177 (2004)

JUSTICE SCALIA delivered the opinion of the Court.

Petitioner Michael Crawford stabbed a man who allegedly tried to rape his wife, Sylvia. At his trial, the State played for the jury Sylvia's tape-recorded statement to the police describing the stabbing, even though he had no opportunity for cross-examination. The Washington Supreme Court upheld petitioner's conviction after determining that Sylvia's statement was reliable. The question presented is whether this procedure complied with the Sixth Amendment's guarantee that, "[i]n all criminal prosecutions, the accused shall enjoy the right . . . to be confronted with the witnesses against him."

On August 5, 1999, Kenneth Lee was stabbed at his apartment. Police arrested petitioner later that night. After giving petitioner and his wife *Miranda* warnings, detectives interrogated each of them twice. Petitioner eventually confessed that he and Sylvia had gone in search of Lee because he was upset over an earlier incident in which Lee had tried to rape her. The two had found Lee at his apartment, and a fight ensued in which Lee was stabbed in the torso and petitioner's hand was cut.

Petitioner gave the following account of the fight:

Q. Okay. Did you ever see anything in [Lee's] hands?

A. I think so, but I'm not positive.

Q. Okay, when you think so, what do you mean by that?

A. I could a swore I seen him goin' for somethin' before, right before everything happened. He was like reachin', fiddlin' around down here and stuff . . . and I just . . . I don't know, I think, this is just a possibility, but I think, I think that he pulled somethin' out and I grabbed for it and that's how I got cut . . . but I'm not positive. I, I, my mind goes blank when things like this happen. I mean, I just, I remember things wrong, I remember things that just doesn't, don't make sense to me later.

Sylvia generally corroborated petitioner's story about the events leading up to the fight, but her account of the fight itself was arguably different—particularly with respect to whether Lee had drawn a weapon before petitioner assaulted him:

Q. Did Kenny do anything to fight back from this assault?

A. (pausing) I know he reached into his pocket . . . or somethin' . . . I don't know what.

Q. After he was stabbed?

A. He saw Michael coming up. He lifted his hand . . . his chest open, he might [have] went to go strike his hand out or something and then (inaudible).

Q. Okay, you, you gotta speak up.

A. Okay, he lifted his hand over his head maybe to strike Michael's hand down or something and then he put his hands in his . . . put his right hand in his right pocket . . . took a step back . . . Michael proceeded to stab him . . . then his hands were like . . . how do you explain this . . . open arms . . . with his hands open and he fell down . . . and we ran (describing subject holding hands open, palms toward assailant).

Q. Okay, when he's standing there with his open hands, you're talking about Kenny, correct?

A. Yeah, after, after the fact, yes.

Q. Did you see anything in his hands at that point?

A. (pausing) um (no).

The State charged petitioner with assault and attempted murder. At trial, he claimed self-defense. Sylvia did not testify because of the state marital privilege, which generally bars a spouse from testifying without the other spouse's consent. In Washington, this privilege does not extend to a spouse's out-of-court statements admissible under a hearsay exception, so the State sought to introduce Sylvia's tape-recorded statements to the police as evidence that the stabbing was not in self-defense. Noting that Sylvia had admitted she led petitioner to Lee's apartment and thus had facilitated the assault, the State invoked the hearsay exception for statements against penal interest.

Petitioner countered that * * * admitting the evidence would violate his federal constitutional right to be "confronted with the witnesses against him." According to our description of that right in *Ohio v. Roberts*, it does not bar admission of an unavailable witness's statement against a criminal defendant if the statement bears "adequate 'indicia of reliability.' " To meet that test, evidence must either fall within a "firmly rooted hearsay exception" or bear "particularized guarantees of trustworthiness." The trial court here admitted the statement on the latter ground, offering several reasons why it was trustworthy: Sylvia was not shifting blame but rather corroborating her husband's story that he acted in self-defense or "justified reprisal"; she had direct knowledge as an eyewitness; she was describing recent events; and she was being questioned by a "neutral" law enforcement officer. The prosecution played the tape for the jury and relied on it in closing, arguing that it was "damning evidence" that "completely refutes [petitioner's] claim of self-defense." The jury convicted petitioner of assault.

The Washington Court of Appeals reversed [the conviction on the ground that Sylvia's statement lacked particularized guarantees of trustworthiness]. * * * The Washington Supreme Court reinstated the conviction unanimously concluding that, although Sylvia's statement did not fall under a firmly rooted hearsay exception, it bore guarantees of trustworthiness * * *. We granted certiorari to determine whether the State's use of Sylvia's statement violated the Confrontation Clause.

The Sixth Amendment's Confrontation Clause provides that, "[i]n all criminal prosecutions, the accused shall enjoy the right . . . to be confronted with the witnesses against him." We have held that this bedrock procedural guarantee applies to both federal and state prosecutions. As noted above, *Roberts* says that an unavailable witness's out-of-court statement may be admitted so long as it has adequate indicia of reliability—i.e., falls within a "firmly rooted hearsay exception" or bears "particularized guarantees of trustworthiness." Petitioner argues that this test strays from the original meaning of the Confrontation Clause and urges us to reconsider it.

The Constitution's text does not alone resolve this case. One could plausibly read "witnesses against" a defendant to mean those who actually testify at trial, those whose statements are offered at trial, or something in-between. We must therefore turn to the historical background of the Clause to understand its meaning.

* * * [H]istory supports two inferences about the meaning of the Sixth Amendment. First, the principal evil at which the Confrontation Clause was directed was the civil law mode of criminal procedure, and particularly its use of *ex parte* examinations as evidence against the accused. It was these practices * * * that English law's assertion of a right to confrontation was meant to prohibit; and that the founding-era rhetoric decried. The Sixth Amendment must be interpreted with this focus in mind. * * *

The text of the Confrontation Clause reflects this focus. It applies to "witnesses" against the accused—in other words, those who "bear testimony." "Testimony," in turn, is typically "[a] solemn declaration or affirmation made for the purpose of establishing or proving some fact." An accuser who makes a formal statement to government officers bears testimony in a sense that a person who makes a casual remark to an acquaintance does not. The constitutional text, like the history underlying the common-law right of confrontation, thus reflects an especially acute concern with a specific type of out-of-court statement.

Various formulations of this core class of "testimonial" statements exist: "*ex parte* in-court testimony or its functional equivalent—that is, material such as affidavits, custodial examinations, prior testimony that the defendant was unable to cross-examine, or similar pretrial statements that declarants would reasonably expect to be used prosecutorially"; "extrajudicial statements ... contained in formalized testimonial materials, such as affidavits, depositions, prior testimony, or confessions"; "statements that were made under circumstances which would lead an objective witness reasonably to believe that the statement would be available for use at a later trial." These formulations all share a common nucleus and then define the Clause's coverage at various levels of abstraction around it. Regardless of the precise articulation, some statements qualify under any definition—for example, *ex parte* testimony at a preliminary hearing. Statements taken by police officers in the course of interrogations are also testimonial * * *.

The historical record also supports a second proposition: that the Framers would not have allowed admission of testimonial statements of a witness who did not appear at trial unless he was unavailable to testify, and the defendant had had a prior opportunity for cross-examination. The text of the Sixth Amendment does not suggest any open-ended exceptions from the confrontation requirement to be developed by the courts. Rather, the "right ... to be confronted with the witnesses against him," is most naturally read as a reference to the right of confrontation at common law, admitting only those exceptions established at the time of the founding. * * * [T]he common law in 1791 conditioned admissibility of an absent witness's examination on unavailability and a prior opportunity to cross-examine. The Sixth Amendment therefore incorporates those limitations. The numerous early state decisions applying the same test confirm that these principles were received as part of the common law in this country.

We do not read the historical sources to say that a prior opportunity to cross-examine was merely a sufficient, rather than a necessary, condition for admissibility of testimonial statements. They suggest that this requirement was dispositive, and not merely one of several ways to establish reliability. * * *

Our case law has been largely consistent with these two principles. * * * [P]rior trial or preliminary hearing testimony is admissible only if the defendant had an adequate opportunity to cross-examine. Even where the defendant had such an opportunity, we excluded the testimony where the government had not established unavailability of the witness.[a] We similarly excluded accomplice confessions where the defendant had no opportunity to cross-examine. In contrast, we considered reliability factors beyond prior opportunity for cross-examination when the hearsay statement at issue was not testimonial. * * *

Our cases have * * * remained faithful to the Framers' understanding: Testimonial statements of witnesses absent from trial have been admitted only where the declarant is unavailable, and only where the defendant has had a prior opportunity to cross-examine. Although the results of our decisions have generally been faithful to the original meaning of the Confrontation Clause, the same cannot be said of our rationales. *Roberts* conditions the admissibility of all hearsay evidence on whether it falls under a "firmly rooted hearsay exception" or bears "particularized guarantees of trustworthiness." This test departs from the historical principles identified above in two respects. First, it is too broad: It applies the same mode of analysis whether or not the hearsay consists of *ex parte* testimony. This often results in close constitutional scrutiny in cases that are far removed from the core concerns of the Clause. At the same time, however, the test is too narrow: It admits statements that *do* consist of *ex parte* testimony upon a mere finding of reliability. This malleable standard often fails to protect against paradigmatic confrontation violations. * * *

Where testimonial statements are involved, we do not think the Framers meant to leave the Sixth Amendment's protection to the vagaries of the rules of evidence, much less to amorphous notions of "reliability." Certainly none of the authorities discussed above acknowledges any general reliability exception to the common-law rule. Admitting statements deemed reliable by a judge is fundamentally at odds with the right of confrontation. To be sure, the Clause's ultimate goal is to ensure reliability of evidence, but it is a procedural rather than a substantive guarantee. It commands, not that evidence be reliable, but that reliability be assessed in a particular manner: by testing in the crucible of cross-examination. The Clause thus reflects a judgment, not only about the desirability of reliable evidence (a point on which there could be little dissent), but about how reliability can best be determined.

The *Roberts* test allows a jury to hear evidence, untested by the adversary process, based on a mere judicial determination of reliability. It thus replaces the constitutionally prescribed method of assessing reliability with a wholly foreign one. * * *

---

[a] In *Barber v. Page*, the Court held that "a witness is not 'unavailable' for purposes of [the Confrontation Clause] unless the prosecutorial authorities have made a good-faith effort to obtain his presence at trial." 390 U.S. 719, 724–25 (1968).

Dispensing with confrontation because testimony is obviously reliable is akin to dispensing with jury trial because a defendant is obviously guilty. This is not what the Sixth Amendment prescribes. * * *

Reliability is an amorphous, if not entirely subjective, concept. There are countless factors bearing on whether a statement is reliable * * *. Whether a statement is deemed reliable depends heavily on which factors the judge considers and how much weight he accords each of them. * * * The unpardonable vice of the *Roberts* test, however, is not its unpredictability, but its demonstrated capacity to admit core testimonial statements that the Confrontation Clause plainly meant to exclude. * * *

Roberts' failings were on full display in the proceedings below. Sylvia Crawford made her statement while in police custody, herself a potential suspect in the case. Indeed, she had been told that whether she would be released "depend[ed] on how the investigation continues." In response to often leading questions from police detectives, she implicated her husband in Lee's stabbing and at least arguably undermined his self-defense claim. Despite all this, the trial court admitted her statement, listing several reasons why it was reliable. In its opinion reversing, the Court of Appeals listed several *other* reasons why the statement was *not* reliable. Finally, the State Supreme Court relied exclusively on the interlocking character of the statement and disregarded every other factor the lower courts had considered. The case is thus a self-contained demonstration of *Roberts'* unpredictable and inconsistent application. Each of the courts also made assumptions that cross-examination might well have undermined. * * *

Where nontestimonial hearsay is at issue, it is wholly consistent with the Framers' design to afford the States flexibility in their development of hearsay law—as does *Roberts,* and as would an approach that exempted such statements from Confrontation Clause scrutiny altogether. Where testimonial evidence is at issue, however, the Sixth Amendment demands what the common law required: unavailability and a prior opportunity for cross-examination. We leave for another day any effort to spell out a comprehensive definition of "testimonial." Whatever else the term covers, it applies at a minimum to prior testimony at a preliminary hearing, before a grand jury, or at a former trial; and to police interrogations. These are the modern practices with closest kinship to the abuses at which the Confrontation Clause was directed.

In this case, the State admitted Sylvia's testimonial statement against petitioner, despite the fact that he had no opportunity to cross-examine her. That alone is sufficient to make out a violation of the Sixth Amendment. *Roberts* notwithstanding, we decline to mine the record in search of indicia of reliability. Where testimonial statements are at issue, the only indicium of reliability sufficient to satisfy constitutional demands is the one the Constitution actually prescribes: confrontation.

The judgment of the Washington Supreme Court is reversed, and the case is remanded for further proceedings not inconsistent with this opinion.
* * *

CHIEF JUSTICE REHNQUIST, with whom JUSTICE O'CONNOR joins, concurring in the judgment.[b]

I dissent from the Court's decision to overrule *Ohio v. Roberts*. I believe that the Court's adoption of a new interpretation of the Confrontation Clause is not backed by sufficiently persuasive reasoning to overrule long-established precedent. Its decision casts a mantle of uncertainty over future criminal trials in both federal and state courts, and is by no means necessary to decide the present case.

The Court's distinction between testimonial and nontestimonial statements, contrary to its claim, is no better rooted in history than our current doctrine. Under the common law, although the courts were far from consistent, out-of-court statements made by someone other than the accused and not taken under oath, unlike *ex parte* depositions or affidavits, were generally not considered substantive evidence upon which a conviction could be based. Testimonial statements such as accusatory statements to police officers likely would have been disapproved of in the 18th century, not necessarily because they resembled *ex parte* affidavits or depositions as the Court reasons, but more likely than not because they were not made under oath. Without an oath, one usually did not get to the second step of whether confrontation was required.

Thus, while I agree that the Framers were mainly concerned about sworn affidavits and depositions, it does not follow that they were similarly concerned about the Court's broader category of testimonial statements. As far as I can tell, unsworn testimonial statements were treated no differently at common law than were nontestimonial statements, and it seems to me any classification of statements as testimonial beyond that of sworn affidavits and depositions will be somewhat arbitrary, merely a proxy for what the Framers might have intended had such evidence been liberally admitted as substantive evidence like it is today.

I therefore see no reason why the distinction the Court draws is preferable to our precedent. * * * [W]e have never drawn a distinction between testimonial and nontestimonial statements. * * * I see little value in trading our precedent for an imprecise approximation at this late date. I am also not convinced that the Confrontation Clause categorically requires the exclusion of testimonial statements. * * *

---

[b] Chief Justice Rehnquist agreed with the majority that Sylvia's statement was inadmissible but reached this conclusion by applying the *Ohio v. Roberts* reliability test.

NOTE

Joshua Dressler and Alan Michaels explain how the Confrontation Clause works with the test set forth in *Crawford*:

> The Confrontation Clause barrier erected in *Crawford* does *not* apply if a witness is unavailable for trial and the testimonial statement was subject to cross-examination at the time it was made. So, for example, suppose W testified and was cross-examined at D's first trial, which ended in a hung jury, and then died before D's retrial. The Confrontation Clause would *not* bar admission of W's testimony from the first trial at D's second trial, because W is now unavailable and the statement (W's testimony) was subject to cross-examination.
>
> Finally, if a witness *is* available and testifies, "the Confrontation Clause places no constraints at all on the use of his prior testimonial statements." Even if they were not subject to cross-examination when they were made, the Court allows their admission because the person who made the statement can be questioned about it now.

JOSHUA DRESSLER & ALAN C. MICHAELS, UNDERSTANDING CRIMINAL PROCEDURE, VOLUME 2: ADJUDICATION § 11.02(B)(2) (4th ed. 2015 Carolina Acad. Press).

DAVIS V. WASHINGTON
Supreme Court of the United States
547 U.S. 813, 126 S. Ct. 2266, 165 L. Ed. 2d 224 (2006)

JUSTICE SCALIA delivered the opinion of the Court.

These cases require us to determine when statements made to law enforcement personnel during a 911 call or at a crime scene are "testimonial" and thus subject to the requirements of the Sixth Amendment's Confrontation Clause.

The relevant statements in *Davis v. Washington*, were made to a 911 emergency operator on February 1, 2001. When the operator answered the initial call, the connection terminated before anyone spoke. She reversed the call, and Michelle McCottry answered. In the ensuing conversation, the operator ascertained that McCottry was involved in a domestic disturbance with her former boyfriend Adrian Davis, the petitioner in this case:

911 Operator: Hello.

Complainant: Hello.

911 Operator: What's going on?

Complainant: He's here jumpin' on me again.

911 Operator: Okay. Listen to me carefully. Are you in a house or an apartment?

Complainant: I'm in a house.

911 Operator: Are there any weapons?

Complainant: No. He's usin' his fists.

911 Operator: Okay. Has he been drinking?

Complainant: No.

911 Operator: Okay, sweetie. I've got help started. Stay on the line with me, okay?

Complainant: I'm on the line.

911 Operator: Listen to me carefully. Do you know his last name?

Complainant: It's Davis.

911 Operator: Davis? Okay, what's his first name?

Complainant: Adrian.

911 Operator: What is it?

Complainant: Adrian.

911 Operator: Adrian?

Complainant: Yeah.

911 Operator: Okay. What's his middle initial?

Complainant: Martell. He's runnin' now.

As the conversation continued, the operator learned that Davis had "just r[un] out the door" after hitting McCottry, and that he was leaving in a car with someone else. McCottry started talking, but the operator cut her off, saying, "Stop talking and answer my questions." She then gathered more information about Davis (including his birthday), and learned that Davis had told McCottry that his purpose in coming to the house was "to get his stuff," since McCottry was moving. McCottry described the context of the assault, after which the operator told her that the police were on their way. "They're gonna check the area for him first," the operator said, "and then they're gonna come talk to you."

The police arrived within four minutes of the 911 call and observed McCottry's shaken state, the "fresh injuries on her forearm and her face," and her "frantic efforts to gather her belongings and her children so that they could leave the residence."

The State charged Davis with felony violation of a domestic no-contact order. "The State's only witnesses were the two police officers who responded to the 911 call. Both officers testified that McCottry exhibited injuries that appeared to be recent, but neither officer could testify as to the cause of the injuries." McCottry presumably could have testified as to whether Davis was her assailant, but she did not appear. Over Davis's objection, based on the Confrontation Clause of the Sixth Amendment, the trial court admitted the recording of her exchange with the 911 operator, and the jury convicted him. The Washington Court of Appeals affirmed. The Supreme Court of Washington * * * also affirmed concluding that the portion of the 911 conversation in which McCottry identified Davis was not testimonial, and that if other portions of the conversation were testimonial, admitting them was harmless beyond a reasonable doubt. We granted certiorari.

In *Hammon v. Indiana,* police responded late on the night of February 26, 2003, to a "reported domestic disturbance" at the home of Hershel and Amy Hammon. They found Amy alone on the front porch, appearing "somewhat frightened," but she told them that "nothing was the matter." She gave them permission to enter the house, where an officer saw "a gas heating unit in the corner of the living room" that had "flames coming out of the . . . partial glass front. There were pieces of glass on the ground in front of it and there was flame emitting from the front of the heating unit."

Hershel, meanwhile, was in the kitchen. He told the police "that he and his wife had 'been in an argument' but 'everything was fine now' and the argument 'never became physical.'" By this point Amy had come back inside. One of the officers remained with Hershel; the other went to the living room to talk with Amy, and "again asked [her] what had occurred." Hershel made several attempts to participate in Amy's conversation with the police, but was rebuffed. The officer later testified that Hershel "became angry when I insisted that [he] stay separated from Mrs. Hammon so that we can investigate what had happened." After hearing Amy's account, the officer "had her fill out and sign a battery affidavit." Amy handwrote the following: "Broke our [f]urnace & shoved me down on the floor into the broken glass. Hit me in the chest and threw me down. Broke our lamps & phone. Tore up my van where I couldn't leave the house. Attacked my daughter."

The State charged Hershel with domestic battery and with violating his probation. Amy was subpoenaed, but she did not appear at his subsequent bench trial. The State called the officer who had questioned Amy, and asked him to recount what Amy told him and to authenticate the affidavit. Hershel's counsel repeatedly objected to the admission of this evidence. At one point, after hearing the prosecutor defend the affidavit because it was made "under oath," defense counsel said, "That doesn't give us the opportunity to cross examine [the] person who allegedly drafted it. Makes me mad." Nonetheless, the trial court admitted the affidavit as a "present sense impression," and Amy's statements as "excited utterances" that "are expressly permitted in these kinds of cases even if the declarant is not available to testify." The officer thus testified that Amy informed me that she and Hershel had been in an argument. That he became irrate [sic] over the fact of their daughter going to a boyfriend's house. The argument became . . . physical after being verbal and she informed me that Mr. Hammon, during the verbal part of the argument was breaking things in the living room and I believe she stated he broke the phone, broke the lamp, broke the front of the heater. When it became physical he threw her down into the glass of the heater. . . . She informed me Mr. Hammon had pushed her onto the ground, had shoved her head into the broken glass of the heater and that he had punched her in the chest twice I believe.

The trial judge found Hershel guilty on both charges, and the Indiana Court of Appeals affirmed in relevant part. The Indiana Supreme Court also affirmed, concluding that Amy's statement was admissible for state-law purposes as an excited utterance, that "a 'testimonial' statement is one given or taken in significant part for purposes of preserving it for potential future use in legal proceedings," where "the motivations of the questioner and declarant are the central concerns;" and that Amy's oral statement was not "testimonial" under these standards. It also concluded that, although the [written] affidavit was testimonial and thus wrongly admitted, it was harmless beyond a reasonable doubt, largely because the trial was to the bench. We granted certiorari.

The Confrontation Clause of the Sixth Amendment provides: "In all criminal prosecutions, the accused shall enjoy the right . . . to be confronted with the witnesses against him." In *Crawford v. Washington* we held that this provision bars "admission of testimonial statements of a witness who did not appear at trial unless he was unavailable to testify, and the defendant had had a prior opportunity for cross-examination." A critical portion of this holding, and the portion central to resolution of the two cases now before us, is the phrase "testimonial statements." Only statements of this sort cause the declarant to be a "witness" within the meaning of the Confrontation Clause. It is the testimonial character of the statement that separates it from other hearsay that, while subject to traditional limitations upon hearsay evidence, is not subject to the Confrontation Clause.

Our opinion in *Crawford* set forth "[v]arious formulations" of the core class of "testimonial" statements, but found it unnecessary to endorse any of them, because "some statements qualify under any definition." Among those, we said, were "[s]tatements taken by police officers in the course of interrogations." * * *

Without attempting to produce an exhaustive classification of all conceivable statements—or even all conceivable statements in response to police interrogation—as either testimonial or nontestimonial, it suffices to decide the present cases to hold as follows: Statements are nontestimonial when made in the course of police interrogation under circumstances objectively indicating that the primary purpose of the interrogation is to enable police assistance to meet an ongoing emergency. They are testimonial when the circumstances objectively indicate that there is no such ongoing emergency, and that the primary purpose of the interrogation is to establish or prove past events potentially relevant to later criminal prosecution. * * *

The question before us in *Davis*, then, is whether, objectively considered, the interrogation that took place in the course of the 911 call produced testimonial statements. When we said in *Crawford*, that "interrogations by law enforcement officers fall squarely within [the] class" of testimonial hearsay, we had immediately in mind (for that was the case before us) interrogations solely directed at establishing the facts of a past crime, in order to identify (or provide evidence to convict) the perpetrator. The product of such interrogation, whether reduced to a writing signed by the declarant or embedded in the memory (and perhaps notes) of the interrogating officer, is testimonial. * * * A 911 call, on the other hand, and at least the initial interrogation conducted in connection with a 911 call, is ordinarily not designed primarily to "establis[h] or prov[e]" some past fact, but to describe current circumstances requiring police assistance.

The difference between the interrogation in *Davis* and the one in *Crawford* is apparent on the face of things. In *Davis*, McCottry was speaking about events *as they were actually happening*, rather than "describ[ing] past events." Sylvia Crawford's interrogation, on the other hand, took place hours after the events she described had occurred. Moreover, any reasonable listener would recognize that McCottry (unlike Sylvia Crawford) was facing an ongoing emergency. Although one *might* call 911 to provide a narrative report of a crime absent any imminent danger, McCottry's call was plainly a call for help against bona fide physical threat. Third, the nature of what was asked and answered in *Davis*, again viewed objectively, was such that the elicited statements were necessary to be able to *resolve* the present emergency, rather than simply to learn (as in *Crawford*) what had happened in the past. That is true even of the operator's effort to establish the identity of the assailant, so that the dispatched officers might know whether they would be encountering a violent felon. And finally, the difference in the level of formality between the two interviews is striking. Crawford was responding calmly, at the station house, to a series of questions, with the officer-interrogator taping and making notes of her answers; McCottry's frantic answers were provided over the phone, in an environment that was not tranquil, or even (as far as any reasonable 911 operator could make out) safe.

We conclude from all this that the circumstances of McCottry's interrogation objectively indicate its primary purpose was to enable police assistance to meet an ongoing emergency.[a] She simply was not acting as a *witness*; she was not *testifying*. * * *

This is not to say that a conversation which begins as an interrogation to determine the need for emergency assistance cannot, as the Indiana Supreme Court put it, "evolve into testimonial statements," once that purpose has been achieved. In this case, for example, after the operator gained the information needed to address the exigency of the moment, the emergency appears to have ended (when Davis drove away from the premises). The operator then told McCottry to be quiet, and proceeded to pose a battery of questions. It could readily be maintained that, from that point on, McCottry's statements were testimonial, not unlike the "structured police questioning" that occurred in Crawford. This presents no great problem. Just as, for Fifth Amendment purposes, "police officers can and will distinguish almost instinctively between questions necessary to secure their own safety or the safety of the public and questions designed solely to elicit testimonial evidence from a suspect," trial courts will recognize the point at which, for Sixth Amendment purposes, statements in response to interrogations become testimonial. Through *in limine* procedure, they should redact or exclude the portions of any statement that have become testimonial, as they do, for example, with unduly prejudicial portions of otherwise admissible evidence. Davis's jury did not hear the *complete* 911 call, although it may well have heard some testimonial portions. We were asked to classify only McCottry's early statements identifying Davis as her assailant, and we agree with the Washington Supreme Court that they were not testimonial. That court also concluded that, even if later parts of the call were testimonial, their admission was harmless beyond a reasonable doubt. Davis does not challenge that holding, and we therefore assume it to be correct.

Determining the testimonial or nontestimonial character of the statements that were the product of the interrogation in *Hammon* is a much easier task, since they were not much different from the statements

---

[a] In 2015, the Court addressed the admissibility under the Confrontation Clause of out-of-court statements made by a child to a private individual to meet an ongoing emergency. In *Ohio v. Clark*, 576 U.S. 237, 135 S. Ct. 2173 (2015), the government introduced the out-of-court responses of a 3-year-old child to questions by his preschool teacher about who had injured him. The defendant challenged the child's statements on confrontation grounds since he had no prior opportunity to cross-examine the child. Applying the primary purpose test articulated in *Davis v. Washington*, the Court unanimously held that the child's statements were not testimonial since they "clearly were not made with the primary purpose of creating evidence for Clark's prosecution." *Id.* at 2181. The Court noted, "statements by very young children will rarely, if ever, implicate the Confrontation Clause," *id.* at 2177, because "it is extremely unlikely that a 3-year-old child . . . would intend his statements to be a substitute for trial testimony." *Id.* at 2182. The Court also pointed out that "statements made to someone who is not principally charged with uncovering and prosecuting criminal behavior are significantly less likely to be testimonial than statements given to law enforcement officers," *id.* at 2182, but stopped short of adopting a categorical rule exempting all statements to private individuals from the Confrontation Clause's reach. The fact that teachers were mandated to report child abuse under Ohio law did not change the Court's conclusion that the child's statement was non-testimonial.

we found to be testimonial in *Crawford*. It is entirely clear from the circumstances that the interrogation was part of an investigation into possibly criminal past conduct—as, indeed, the testifying officer expressly acknowledged. There was no emergency in progress; the interrogating officer testified that he had heard no arguments or crashing and saw no one throw or break anything. When the officers first arrived, Amy told them that things were fine, and there was no immediate threat to her person. When the officer questioned Amy for the second time, and elicited the challenged statements, he was not seeking to determine (as in *Davis*) "what is happening," but rather "what happened." Objectively viewed, the primary, if not indeed the sole, purpose of the interrogation was to investigate a possible crime—which is, of course, precisely what the officer *should* have done.[b]

It is true that the *Crawford* interrogation was more formal. It followed a *Miranda* warning, was tape-recorded, and took place at the station house. While these features certainly strengthened the statements' testimonial aspect—made it more objectively apparent, that is, that the purpose of the exercise was to nail down the truth about past criminal events—none was essential to the point. It was formal enough that Amy's interrogation was conducted in a separate room, away from her husband (who tried to intervene), with the officer receiving her replies for use in his "investigat[ion]." What we called the "striking resemblance" of the *Crawford* statement to civil-law *ex parte* examinations, is shared by Amy's statement here. Both declarants were actively separated from the defendant—officers forcibly prevented Hershel from participating in the interrogation. Both statements deliberately recounted, in response to police questioning, how potentially criminal past events began and progressed. And both took place some time after the events described were over. Such statements under official interrogation are an obvious substitute for live testimony, because they do precisely *what a witness does* on direct examination; they are inherently testimonial. * * *

Respondents in both cases, joined by a number of their *amici*, contend that the nature of the offenses charged in these two cases—domestic

---

[b] In *Michigan v. Bryant*, 562 U.S. 344 (2011), the Court answered a question left open in *Davis*: whose purpose matters when assessing the primary purpose of the interrogation? The Court held that in deciding whether the primary purpose of an interrogation is to meet an ongoing emergency, "the relevant inquiry is not the subjective or actual purpose of the individuals involved in a particular encounter, but rather the purpose that reasonable participants would have had, as ascertained from the individuals' statements and actions and the circumstances in which the encounter occurred." *Id.* at 360. In a strongly worded dissent, Justice Scalia opined that the declarant's intent is the only intent that matters when applying the primary purpose test. Justice Scalia explained that in order for a statement to be testimonial, "the declarant must intend the statement to be a solemn declaration rather than an unconsidered or offhand remark; and he must make the statement with the understanding that it may be used to invoke the coercive machinery of the State against the accused." *Id.* at 381. Justice Scalia also noted that the Court's approach created a mixed motive problem: how can a court decide what constitutes the primary purpose if the police and the declarant each have motives or purposes that conflict?

violence—requires greater flexibility in the use of testimonial evidence. This particular type of crime is notoriously susceptible to intimidation or coercion of the victim to ensure that she does not testify at trial. * * * But when defendants seek to undermine the judicial process by procuring or coercing silence from witnesses and victims, the Sixth Amendment does not require courts to acquiesce. While defendants have no duty to assist the State in proving their guilt, they *do* have the duty to refrain from acting in ways that destroy the integrity of the criminal-trial system. * * * [O]ne who obtains the absence of a witness by wrongdoing forfeits the constitutional right to confrontation. * * *

We have determined that, absent a finding of forfeiture by wrongdoing, the Sixth Amendment operates to exclude Amy Hammon's affidavit. The Indiana courts may (if they are asked) determine on remand whether such a claim of forfeiture is properly raised and, if so, whether it is meritorious.

We affirm the judgment of the Supreme Court of Washington in No. 05–5224. We reverse the judgment of the Supreme Court of Indiana in No. 05–5705, and remand the case to that Court for proceedings not inconsistent with this opinion.

It is so ordered.

[JUSTICE THOMAS' opinion, concurring in the judgment in part and dissenting in part, has been omitted.]

NOTE

After *Crawford* and *Davis*, the Court decided a series of cases that tested the definitional boundaries of testimonial versus non-testimonial statements. In *Melendez-Diaz v. Massachusetts*, 557 U.S. 305 (2009), the Court considered whether a forensic lab report, prepared for use by the government at trial, was testimonial. The Court found that the lab report was akin to an affidavit, and therefore was testimonial. The Court held that because the lab report was testimonial, allowing the government to present the lab report at trial without calling the forensic analyst to testify violated the defendant's confrontation rights. *See id.* at 310–11.

In 2011, the Court extended its holding in *Melendez-Diaz* to a case in which the government offered into evidence at trial a forensic lab report and, in an attempt to satisfy the Confrontation Clause, presented an analyst from the same lab as the analyst who prepared the report to validate the report. *Bullcoming v. New Mexico*, 564 U.S. 647 (2011). The analyst who testified at trial had familiarity with the lab's testing procedures but was not involved in the testing of the defendant's blood sample. The Court found the "surrogate testimony" insufficient to satisfy the Confrontation Clause, explaining that "[t]he accused's right is to be confronted with the analyst who made the certification, unless the analyst is unavailable at trial, and the accused has an opportunity, pretrial, to cross examine that particular scientist." *Id.* at 2710.

GILES V. CALIFORNIA
Supreme Court of the United States
554 U.S. 353, 128 S. Ct. 2678, 171 L. Ed. 2d 488 (2008)

JUSTICE SCALIA delivered the opinion of the Court.

We consider whether a defendant forfeits his Sixth Amendment right to confront a witness against him when a judge determines that a wrongful act by the defendant made the witness unavailable to testify at trial.

On September 29, 2002, petitioner Dwayne Giles shot his ex-girlfriend, Brenda Avie, outside the garage of his grandmother's house. No witness saw the shooting, but Giles' niece heard what transpired from inside the house. She heard Giles and Avie speaking in conversational tones. Avie then yelled "Granny" several times and a series of gunshots sounded. Giles' niece and grandmother ran outside and saw Giles standing near Avie with a gun in his hand. Avie, who had not been carrying a weapon, had been shot six times. One wound was consistent with Avie's holding her hand up at the time she was shot, another was consistent with her having turned to her side, and a third was consistent with her having been shot while lying on the ground. Giles fled the scene after the shooting. He was apprehended by police about two weeks later and charged with murder.

At trial, Giles testified that he had acted in self-defense. Giles described Avie as jealous, and said he knew that she had once shot a man, that he had seen her threaten people with a knife, and that she had vandalized his home and car on prior occasions. He said that on the day of the shooting, Avie came to his grandmother's house and threatened to kill him and his new girlfriend, who had been at the house earlier. * * * Giles testified that after Avie threatened him at the house, he went into the garage and retrieved a gun, took the safety off, and started walking toward the back door of the house. He said that Avie charged at him, and that he was afraid she had something in her hand. According to Giles, he closed his eyes and fired several shots, but did not intend to kill Avie.

Prosecutors sought to introduce statements that Avie had made to a police officer responding to a domestic-violence report about three weeks before the shooting. Avie, who was crying when she spoke, told the officer that Giles had accused her of having an affair, and that after the two began to argue, Giles grabbed her by the shirt, lifted her off the floor, and began to choke her. According to Avie, when she broke free and fell to the floor, Giles punched her in the face and head, and after she broke free again, he opened a folding knife, held it about three feet away from her, and threatened to kill her if he found her cheating on him. Over Giles' objection, the trial court admitted these statements into evidence under a provision of California law that permits admission of out-of-court statements describing the infliction or threat of physical injury on a declarant when the declarant is unavailable to testify at trial and the prior statements are deemed trustworthy.

A jury convicted Giles of first-degree murder. He appealed. While his appeal was pending, this Court decided in *Crawford v. Washington*, that the Confrontation Clause requires that a defendant have the opportunity to confront the witnesses who give testimony against him, except in cases where an exception to the confrontation right was recognized at the time of the founding.[a] The California Court of Appeal held that the admission of Avie's unconfronted statements at Giles' trial did not violate the Confrontation Clause as construed by *Crawford* because *Crawford* recognized a doctrine of forfeiture by wrongdoing. It concluded that Giles had forfeited his right to confront Avie because he had committed the murder for which he was on trial, and because his intentional criminal act made Avie unavailable to testify. The California Supreme Court affirmed on the same ground. We granted certiorari.

* * * The State does not dispute here, and we accept without deciding, that Avie's statements accusing Giles of assault were testimonial. But it maintains (as did the California Supreme Court) that the Sixth Amendment did not prohibit prosecutors from introducing the statements because an exception to the confrontation guarantee permits the use of a witness's unconfronted testimony if a judge finds, as the judge did in this case, that the defendant committed a wrongful act that rendered the witness unavailable to testify at trial. We held in *Crawford* that the Confrontation Clause is "most naturally read as a reference to the right of confrontation at common law, admitting only those exceptions established at the time of the founding." We therefore ask whether the theory of forfeiture by wrongdoing accepted by the California Supreme Court is a founding-era exception to the confrontation right.

We have previously acknowledged that two forms of testimonial statements were admitted at common law even though they were unconfronted. The first of these were declarations made by a speaker who was both on the brink of death and aware that he was dying. Avie did not make the unconfronted statements admitted at Giles' trial when she was dying, so her statements do not fall within this historic exception.

A second common-law doctrine, which we will refer to as forfeiture by wrongdoing, permitted the introduction of statements of a witness who was "detained" or "kept away" by the "means or procurement" of the defendant. The doctrine has roots in the 1666 decision in *Lord Morley's Case*, at which

---

[a] As a general matter, a new rule of criminal procedure will only apply to cases that are not yet final, e.g., cases pending appeal, and will not be applied retroactively to cases already final and on collateral review. *See* Teague v. Lane, 489 U. S. 288, 310 (1989) (plurality opinion). Since Giles' appeal was pending when the Supreme Court decided *Crawford v. Washington*, Giles' case was not yet final. Therefore, the Court of Appeal applied the test established in *Crawford* rather than the old *Ohio v. Roberts* test.

judges concluded that a witness's having been "detained by the means or procurement of the prisoner" provided a basis to read testimony previously given at a coroner's inquest. * * *

The terms used to define the scope of the forfeiture rule suggest that the exception applied only when the defendant engaged in conduct *designed* to prevent the witness from testifying. The rule required the witness to have been "kept back" or "detained" by "means or procurement" of the defendant. Although there are definitions of "procure" and "procurement" that would merely require that a defendant have caused the witness's absence, other definitions would limit the causality to one that was *designed* to bring about the result "procured." * * *

Cases and treatises of the time indicate that a purpose-based definition of these terms governed. A number of them said that prior testimony was admissible when a witness was kept away by the defendant's "means and contrivance." * * * An 1858 treatise made the purpose requirement more explicit still, stating that the forfeiture rule applied when a witness "had been kept out of the way by the prisoner, or by someone on the prisoner's behalf, *in order to prevent him from giving evidence against him.*" * * *

The manner in which the rule was applied makes plain that unconfronted testimony would *not* be admitted without a showing that the defendant intended to prevent a witness from testifying. In cases where the evidence suggested that the defendant had caused a person to be absent, but had not done so to prevent the person from testifying—as in the typical murder case involving accusatorial statements by the victim—the testimony was excluded unless it was confronted or fell within the dying-declarations exception. * * *

The dissent closes by pointing out that a forfeiture rule which ignores *Crawford* would be particularly helpful to women in abusive relationships—or at least particularly helpful in punishing their abusers. * * * [W]e are puzzled by the dissent's decision to devote its peroration to domestic abuse cases. Is the suggestion that we should have one Confrontation Clause (the one the Framers adopted and *Crawford* described) for all other crimes, but a special, improvised Confrontation Clause for those crimes that are frequently directed against women? Domestic violence is an intolerable offense that legislatures may choose to combat through many means—from increasing criminal penalties to adding resources for investigation and prosecution to funding awareness and prevention campaigns. But for that serious crime, as for others, abridging the constitutional rights of criminal defendants is not in the State's arsenal.

The domestic-violence context is, however, relevant for a separate reason. Acts of domestic violence often are intended to dissuade a victim from resorting to outside help, and include conduct designed to prevent testimony to police officers or cooperation in criminal prosecutions. Where such an abusive relationship culminates in murder, the evidence may support a finding that the crime expressed the intent to isolate the victim and to stop her from reporting abuse to the authorities or cooperating with a criminal prosecution—rendering her prior statements admissible under the forfeiture doctrine. Earlier abuse, or threats of abuse, intended to dissuade the victim from resorting to outside help would be highly relevant to this inquiry, as would evidence of ongoing criminal proceedings at which the victim would have been expected to testify. * * *

The state courts in this case did not consider the intent of the defendant because they found that irrelevant to application of the forfeiture doctrine. This view of the law was error, but the court is free to consider evidence of the defendant's intent on remand.

The judgment of the California Supreme Court is vacated, and the case is remanded for further proceedings not inconsistent with this opinion.

It is so ordered.

JUSTICE BREYER, with whom JUSTICE STEVENS and JUSTICE KENNEDY join, dissenting.

There are several strong reasons for concluding that the forfeiture by wrongdoing exception applies here—reasons rooted in common-law history, established principles of criminal law and evidence, and the need for a rule that can be applied without creating great practical difficulties and evidentiary anomalies.

First, the language that courts have used in setting forth the exception is broad enough to cover the wrongdoing at issue in the present case (murder) and much else besides. * * * I have found no case that uses language that would not bring a murder and a subsequent trial for murder within its scope.

Second, an examination of the forfeiture rule's basic purposes and objectives indicates that the rule applies here. At the time of the founding, a leading treatise writer described the forfeiture rule as designed to ensure that the prisoner "shall never be admitted to shelter himself by such evil Practices on the Witness, that being to give him Advantage of his own Wrong." This Court's own leading case explained the exception as finding its "foundation in the maxim that no one shall be permitted to take advantage of his own wrong." What more "evil practice," what greater "wrong," than to murder the witness? And what greater evidentiary "advantage" could one derive from that wrong than thereby to prevent the witness from testifying, e.g., preventing the witness from describing a history of physical abuse that is not consistent with the defendant's claim that he killed her in self-defense?

Third, related areas of the law motivated by similar equitable principles treat forfeiture or its equivalent similarly. The common law, for example, prohibits a life insurance beneficiary who murders an insured from recovering under the policy. And it forbids recovery when the beneficiary "feloniously kills the insured, irrespective of the purpose." Similarly, a beneficiary of a will who murders the testator cannot inherit under the will. And this is so "whether the crime was committed for that very purpose or with some other felonious design."

Fourth, under the circumstances presented by this case, there is no difficulty demonstrating the defendant's intent. This is because the defendant here knew that murdering his ex-girlfriend would keep her from testifying; and that knowledge is sufficient to show the *intent* that law ordinarily demands. As this Court put the matter more than a century ago: A "man who performs an act which it is known will produce a particular result is from our common experience presumed to have anticipated that result and to have intended it."

With a few criminal law exceptions not here relevant, the law holds an individual responsible for consequences known likely to follow just as if that individual had intended to achieve them. A defendant, in a criminal or a civil case, for example, cannot escape criminal or civil liability for murdering an airline passenger by claiming that his purpose in blowing up the airplane was to kill only a single passenger for her life insurance, not the others on the same flight.

This principle applies here. Suppose that a husband, H, knows that after he assaulted his wife, W, she gave statements to the police. Based on the fact that W gave statements to the police, H also knows that it is possible he will be tried for assault. If H then kills W, H cannot avoid responsibility for intentionally preventing W from testifying, not even if H says he killed W because he was angry with her and not to keep her away from the assault trial. Of course, the trial here is not for assault; it is for murder. But I should think that this fact, because of the nature of the crime, would count as a stronger, not a weaker, reason for applying the forfeiture rule. Nor should it matter that H, at the time of the murder, may have *believed* an assault trial *more likely* to take place than a murder trial, for W's unavailability to testify at *any* future trial was a *certain* consequence of the murder. And any reasonable person would have known it. Cf. *United States v. Falstaff Brewing Corp.* (Marshall, J., concurring in result) ("[P]erhaps the oldest rule of evidence—that a man is presumed to intend the natural and probable consequences of his acts—is based on the common law's preference for objectively measurable data over subjective statements of opinion and intent").

The majority tries to overcome this elementary legal logic by claiming that the "forfeiture rule" applies, not where the defendant *intends* to prevent the witness from testifying, but only where that is the defendant's *purpose*, i.e., that the rule applies only where the defendant acts from a particular *motive*, a *desire* to keep the witness from trial. But the law does not often turn matters of responsibility upon *motive*, rather than *intent*. And there is no reason to believe that application of the rule of forfeiture constitutes an exception to this general legal principle.

Indeed, to turn application of the forfeiture rule upon proof of the defendant's *purpose* (rather than *intent*), as the majority does, creates serious practical evidentiary problems. Consider H who assaults W, knows she has complained to the police, and then murders her. H *knows* that W will be unable to testify against him at any future trial. But who knows whether H's knowledge played a major role, a middling role, a minor role, or no role at all, in H's decision to kill W? Who knows precisely what passed through H's mind at the critical moment?

Moreover, the majority's insistence upon a showing of *purpose* or *motive* cannot be squared with the exception's basically ethical objective. If H, by killing W, is able to keep W's testimony out of court, then he has successfully "take[n] advantage of his own wrong." And he does so whether he killed her *for the purpose of* keeping her from testifying, with *certain knowledge* that she will not be able to testify, or with *a belief* that rises to a *reasonable level of probability*. The inequity consists of his being able to *use* the killing to keep out of court her statements against him. That inequity exists whether the defendant's state of mind is purposeful, intentional (*i.e.*, with knowledge), or simply probabilistic. * * *

The rule of forfeiture is implicated primarily where domestic abuse is at issue. In such a case, a murder victim may have previously given a testimonial statement, say, to the police, about an abuser's attacks; and introduction of that statement may be at issue in a later trial for the abuser's subsequent murder of the victim. This is not an uncommon occurrence. Each year, domestic violence results in more than 1,500 deaths and more than 2 million injuries; it accounts for a substantial portion of all homicides; it typically involves a history of repeated violence; and it is difficult to prove in court because the victim is generally reluctant or unable to testify.

Regardless of a defendant's purpose, threats, further violence, and ultimately murder can stop victims from testifying. A *constitutional* evidentiary requirement that insists upon a showing of purpose (rather than simply intent or probabilistic knowledge) may permit the domestic partner who made the threats, caused the violence, or even murdered the victim to avoid conviction for earlier crimes by taking advantage of later ones.

In *Davis*, we recognized that "domestic violence" cases are "notoriously susceptible to intimidation or coercion of the victim to ensure that she does not testify at trial." We noted the concern that "[w]hen this occurs, the Confrontation Clause gives the criminal a windfall." And we replied to that concern by stating that "one who obtains the absence of a witness by wrongdoing forfeits the constitutional right to confrontation." To the extent that it insists upon an additional showing of purpose, the Court breaks the promise implicit in those words and, in doing so, grants the defendant not fair treatment, but a windfall. I can find no history, no underlying purpose, no administrative consideration, and no constitutional principle that requires this result.

[JUSTICE ALITO's concurring opinion, JUSTICE THOMAS' concurring opinion, and JUSTICE SOUTER's concurring opinion have been omitted.]

NOTE

On remand, the Court of Appeal reversed Giles' first degree murder conviction without prejudice, finding no evidence in the record that Giles intended to make Avie unavailable to testify. *People v. Giles* (Feb. 25, 2009, No. B166937, unpublished opinion). On retrial, the prosecutor did not seek to introduce Avie's extrajudicial statements. Giles was again convicted of first degree murder, and his conviction was affirmed on appeal. *People v. Giles*, 2012 Cal. App. Unpub. LEXIS 366 (Jan. 18, 2012, No. B224629).

RICHARDSON V. MARSH
Supreme Court of the United States
481 U.S. 200, 107 S. Ct. 1702, 95 L. Ed. 2d 176 (1987)

JUSTICE SCALIA delivered the opinion of the Court.

In *Bruton v. United States*, we held that a defendant is deprived of his rights under the Confrontation Clause when his nontestifying codefendant's confession naming him as a participant in the crime is introduced at their joint trial,[a] even if the jury is instructed to consider that confession only against the codefendant. Today we consider whether *Bruton* requires the same result when the codefendant's confession is redacted to omit any reference to the defendant, but the defendant is nonetheless linked to the confession by evidence properly admitted against him at trial.

Respondent Clarissa Marsh, Benjamin Williams, and Kareem Martin were charged with assaulting Cynthia Knighton and murdering her 4-year-old son, Koran, and her aunt, Ollie Scott. Respondent and Williams were tried jointly, over her objection. (Martin was a fugitive at the time of trial.) At the trial, Knighton testified as follows: On the evening of October 29, 1978, she and her son were at Scott's home when respondent and her

---

[a] Rule 8(b) of the Federal Rules of Criminal Procedure provides that defendants may be charged together "if they are alleged to have participated in the same act or transaction or in the same series of acts or transactions constituting an offense or offenses." FED. R. CRIM. P. 8(b).

boyfriend Martin visited. After a brief conversation in the living room, respondent announced that she had come to "pick up something" from Scott and rose from the couch. Martin then pulled out a gun, pointed it at Scott and the Knightons, and said that "someone had gotten killed and [Scott] knew something about it." Respondent immediately walked to the front door and peered out the peephole. The doorbell rang, respondent opened the door, and Williams walked in, carrying a gun. As Williams passed respondent, he asked, "Where's the money?" Martin forced Scott upstairs, and Williams went into the kitchen, leaving respondent alone with the Knightons. Knighton and her son attempted to flee, but respondent grabbed Knighton and held her until Williams returned. Williams ordered the Knightons to lie on the floor and then went upstairs to assist Martin. Respondent, again left alone with the Knightons, stood by the front door and occasionally peered out the peephole. A few minutes later, Martin, Williams, and Scott came down the stairs, and Martin handed a paper grocery bag to respondent. Martin and Williams then forced Scott and the Knightons into the basement, where Martin shot them. Only Cynthia Knighton survived.

In addition to Knighton's testimony, the State introduced (over respondent's objection) a confession given by Williams to the police shortly after his arrest. The confession was redacted to omit all reference to respondent—indeed, to omit all indication that *anyone* other than Martin and Williams participated in the crime. The confession largely corroborated Knighton's account of the activities of persons other than respondent in the house. In addition, the confession described a conversation Williams had with Martin as they drove to the Scott home, during which, according to Williams, Martin said that he would have to kill the victims after the robbery. At the time the confession was admitted, the jury was admonished not to use it in any way against respondent. Williams did not testify.

After the State rested, respondent took the stand. She testified that on October 29, 1978, she had lost money that Martin intended to use to buy drugs. Martin was upset, and suggested to respondent that she borrow money from Scott, with whom she had worked in the past. Martin and respondent picked up Williams and drove to Scott's house. During the drive, respondent, who was sitting in the backseat, "knew that [Martin and Williams] were talking" but could not hear the conversation because "the radio was on and the speaker was right in [her] ear." Martin and respondent were admitted into the home, and respondent had a short conversation with Scott, during which she asked for a loan. Martin then pulled a gun, and respondent walked to the door to see where the car was. When she saw Williams, she opened the door for him. Respondent testified that during the robbery she did not feel free to leave and was too scared to flee. She said that she did not know why she prevented the Knightons from escaping. She admitted taking the bag from Martin, but said that after

Martin and Williams took the victims into the basement, she left the house without the bag. Respondent insisted that she had possessed no prior knowledge that Martin and Williams were armed, had heard no conversation about anyone's being harmed, and had not intended to rob or kill anyone.

During his closing argument, the prosecutor admonished the jury not to use Williams' confession against respondent. Later in his argument, however, he linked respondent to the portion of Williams' confession describing his conversation with Martin in the car. (Respondent's attorney did not object to this.) After closing arguments, the judge again instructed the jury that Williams' confession was not to be considered against respondent. The jury convicted respondent of two counts of felony murder in the perpetration of an armed robbery and one count of assault with intent to commit murder. * * *

Respondent then filed a petition for a writ of habeas corpus * * *. She alleged * * * that introduction of Williams' confession at the joint trial had violated her rights under the Confrontation Clause. * * * The Court of Appeals held that in determining whether *Bruton* bars the admission of a nontestifying codefendant's confession, a court must assess the confession's "inculpatory value" by examining not only the face of the confession, but also all of the evidence introduced at trial. Here, Williams' account of the conversation in the car was the only *direct* evidence that respondent knew before entering Scott's house that the victims would be robbed and killed. Respondent's own testimony placed her in that car. In light of the "paucity" of other evidence of malice and the prosecutor's linkage of respondent and the statement in the car during closing argument, admission of Williams' confession "was powerfully incriminating to [respondent] with respect to the critical element of intent." Thus, the Court of Appeals concluded, the Confrontation Clause was violated. We granted certiorari * * *.

The Confrontation Clause of the Sixth Amendment, extended against the States by the Fourteenth Amendment, guarantees the right of a criminal defendant "to be confronted with the witnesses against him." The right of confrontation includes the right to cross-examine witnesses. Therefore, where two defendants are tried jointly, the pretrial confession of one cannot be admitted against the other unless the confessing defendant takes the stand.

Ordinarily, a witness whose testimony is introduced at a joint trial is not considered to be a witness "against" a defendant if the jury is instructed to consider that testimony only against a codefendant. * * * In *Bruton,* however, we recognized a narrow exception to this principle: We held that a defendant is deprived of his Sixth Amendment right of confrontation when the facially incriminating confession of a nontestifying codefendant is introduced at their joint trial, even if the jury is instructed to consider the confession only against the codefendant. We said:

> [T]here are some contexts in which the risk that the jury will not, or cannot, follow instructions is so great, and the consequences of failure so vital to the defendant, that the practical and human limitations of the jury system cannot be ignored. Such a context is presented here, where the powerfully incriminating extrajudicial statements of a codefendant, who stands accused side-by-side with the defendant, are deliberately spread before the jury in a joint trial. . . .

There is an important distinction between this case and *Bruton*, which causes it to fall outside the narrow exception we have created. In *Bruton*, the codefendant's confession "expressly implicat[ed]" the defendant as his accomplice. Thus, at the time that confession was introduced there was not the slightest doubt that it would prove "powerfully incriminating." By contrast, in this case the confession was not incriminating on its face, and became so only when linked with evidence introduced later at trial (the defendant's own testimony).

Where the necessity of such linkage is involved, it is a less valid generalization that the jury will not likely obey the instruction to disregard the evidence. Specific testimony that "the defendant helped me commit the crime" is more vivid than inferential incrimination, and hence more difficult to thrust out of mind. Moreover, with regard to such an explicit statement the only issue is, plain and simply, whether the jury can possibly be expected to forget it in assessing the defendant's guilt; whereas with regard to inferential incrimination the judge's instruction may well be successful in dissuading the jury from entering onto the path of inference in the first place, so that there is no incrimination to forget. In short, while it may not always be simple for the members of a jury to obey the instruction that they disregard an incriminating inference, there does not exist the overwhelming probability of their inability to do so that is the foundation of *Bruton*'s exception to the general rule. * * *

One might say, of course, that a certain way of assuring compliance would be to try defendants separately[b] whenever an incriminating statement of one of them is sought to be used. * * * It would impair both the efficiency and the fairness of the criminal justice system to require, in all these cases of joint crimes where incriminating statements exist, that prosecutors bring separate proceedings, presenting the same evidence

---

[b] Rule 14 of the Federal Rules of Criminal Procedure permits a district court to grant a severance of defendants if it appears that a defendant or the government is prejudiced by a joinder. FED. R. CRIM. P. 14 ("If the joinder of offenses or defendants in an indictment, an information, or a consolidation for trial appears to prejudice a defendant or the government, the court may order separate trials of counts, sever the defendants' trials, or provide any other relief that justice requires").

again and again, requiring victims and witnesses to repeat the inconvenience (and sometimes trauma) of testifying, and randomly favoring the last-tried defendants who have the advantage of knowing the prosecution's case beforehand. * * * The other way of assuring compliance with an expansive *Bruton* rule would be to forgo use of codefendant confessions. That price also is too high, since confessions "are more than merely 'desirable'; they are essential to society's compelling interest in finding, convicting, and punishing those who violate the law."

The rule that juries are presumed to follow their instructions is a pragmatic one, rooted less in the absolute certitude that the presumption is true than in the belief that it represents a reasonable practical accommodation of the interests of the state and the defendant in the criminal justice process. On the precise facts of *Bruton,* involving a facially incriminating confession, we found that accommodation inadequate. As our discussion above shows, the calculus changes when confessions that do not name the defendant are at issue. While we continue to apply *Bruton* where we have found that its rationale validly applies, we decline to extend it further. We hold that the Confrontation Clause is not violated by the admission of a nontestifying codefendant's confession with a proper limiting instruction when, as here, the confession is redacted to eliminate not only the defendant's name, but any reference to his or her existence. * * *

The judgment of the Court of Appeals is reversed, and the case is remanded for further proceedings consistent with this opinion. * * *

JUSTICE STEVENS, with whom JUSTICE BRENNAN and JUSTICE MARSHALL join, dissenting. * * *

The rationale of our decision in *Bruton v. United States* applies without exception to all inadmissible confessions that are "powerfully incriminating." Today, however, the Court draws a distinction of constitutional magnitude between those confessions that directly identify the defendant and those that rely for their inculpatory effect on the factual and legal relationships of their contents to other evidence before the jury. Even if the jury's indirect inference of the defendant's guilt based on an inadmissible confession is much more devastating to the defendant's case than its inference from a direct reference in the codefendant's confession, the Court requires the exclusion of only the latter statement. This illogical result demeans the values protected by the Confrontation Clause. * * *

It is a "basic premise" of the Confrontation Clause that certain kinds of hearsay "are at once so damaging, so suspect, and yet so difficult to discount, that jurors cannot be trusted to give such evidence the minimal weight it logically deserves, *whatever* instructions the trial judge might give." This constitutionally mandated skepticism undergirds the *Bruton* holding and is equally applicable to this case. The Court framed the issue in *Bruton* as "whether the conviction of a defendant at a joint trial should be set aside although the jury was instructed that a codefendant's confession inculpating the defendant had to be disregarded in determining his guilt or innocence." We answered that question in the affirmative, noting that the Sixth Amendment is violated "where the powerfully incriminating extrajudicial statements of a codefendant, who stands accused side-by-side with the defendant, are deliberately spread before the jury in a joint trial."

Today the Court nevertheless draws a line between codefendant confessions that expressly name the defendant and those that do not. The Court relies on the presumption that in the latter category "it is a less valid generalization that the jury will not likely obey the instruction to disregard the evidence." I agree; but I do not read *Bruton* to require the exclusion of *all* codefendant confessions that do not mention the defendant. Some such confessions may not have any significant impact on the defendant's case. But others will. If we presume, as we must, that jurors give their full and vigorous attention to every witness and each item of evidence, the very acts of listening and seeing will sometimes lead them down "the path of inference." Indeed, the Court tacitly acknowledges this point; while the Court speculates that the judge's instruction may dissuade the jury from making inferences at all, it also concedes the probability of their occurrence, arguing that there is no overwhelming probability that jurors will be unable to "disregard an incriminating inference." *Bruton* has always required trial judges to answer the question whether a particular confession is or is not "powerfully incriminating" on a case-by-case basis; they should follow the same analysis whether or not the defendant is actually named by his or her codefendant.

Instructing the jury that it was to consider Benjamin Williams' confession only against him, and not against Clarissa Marsh, failed to guarantee the level of certainty required by the Confrontation Clause. * * * The facts in this case are, admittedly, different from those in *Bruton* because Williams' statement did not directly mention respondent. Thus, instead of being "incriminating on its face," it became so only when considered in connection with the other evidence presented to the jury. The difference between the facts of *Bruton* and the facts of this case does not eliminate their common, substantial, and constitutionally unacceptable risk that the jury, when resolving a critical issue against respondent, may have relied on impermissible evidence.

The facts that joint trials conserve prosecutorial resources, diminish inconvenience to witnesses, and avoid delays in the administration of criminal justice have been well known for a long time. It is equally well known that joint trials create special risks of prejudice to one of the defendants, and that such risks often make it necessary to grant severances. * * * The concern about the cost of joint trials, even if valid, does not prevail over the interests of justice. * * *

I respectfully dissent.

CHAPTER 32

DOUBLE JEOPARDY

■ ■ ■

The Double Jeopardy Clause contained in the Fifth Amendment provides: "nor shall any person be subject for the same offence to be twice put in jeopardy of life or limb . . . ." The Double Jeopardy Clause protects a defendant against multiple prosecutions for the same offense. It also protects a defendant against multiple punishments for the same offense.

The Double Jeopardy Clause applies only after a defendant has been placed "in jeopardy." In a jury trial, jeopardy attaches when the jury is empaneled and sworn. In a bench trial (a trial in which a judge rather than a jury decides whether to acquit or convict the defendant), jeopardy attaches when the first witness is sworn. If the defendant pleads guilty and there is no trial, jeopardy attaches once the court accepts the defendant's guilty plea and enters a judgment of conviction.

The Double Jeopardy Clause has wide application in criminal procedure. This chapter reflects the broad reach of the doctrine and covers multiple topics, including collateral estoppel, the "same offense" limitation, the dual sovereignty doctrine, criminal versus civil punishment, retrial following a mistrial, acquittals versus dismissals, retrial following the reversal of a conviction, and jury nullification.

A. COLLATERAL ESTOPPEL

Collateral estoppel, also known as issue preclusion, is a concept that many law students learn about in Civil Procedure. Collateral estoppel in the criminal context, however, differs in significant ways from collateral estoppel in the civil context so one cannot simply take what one learned in Civil Procedure and apply it to the criminal context. The Court has explicitly stated that "any effort to transplant civil preclusion principles into the Double Jeopardy Clause would quickly meet trouble." *Currier v. Virginia*, 585 U.S. ___, 138 S. Ct. 2144, 2154, 2156 (2018) ("civil preclusion principles and double jeopardy are different doctrines, with different histories, serving different purposes"). Therefore, it is best to set aside what one learned about collateral estoppel in Civil Procedure when trying to understand collateral estoppel in the criminal context. As you read the next case, try to discern the requirements that a defendant must satisfy in order to collaterally estop the government from relitigating an issue decided in the defendant's favor in a prior case.

ASHE v. SWENSON
Supreme Court of the United States
397 U.S. 436, 90 S. Ct. 1189, 25 L. Ed. 2d 469 (1970)

JUSTICE STEWART delivered the opinion of the Court. * * *

Sometime in the early hours of the morning of January 10, 1960, six men were engaged in a poker game in the basement of the home of John Gladson at Lee's Summit, Missouri. Suddenly three or four masked men, armed with a shotgun and pistols, broke into the basement and robbed each of the poker players of money and various articles of personal property. The robbers—and it has never been clear whether there were three or four of them—then fled in a car belonging to one of the victims of the robbery. Shortly thereafter the stolen car was discovered in a field, and later that morning three men were arrested by a state trooper while they were walking on a highway not far from where the abandoned car had been found. The petitioner was arrested by another officer some distance away.

The four were subsequently charged with seven separate offenses—the armed robbery of each of the six poker players and the theft of the car. In May 1960 the petitioner went to trial on the charge of robbing Donald Knight, one of the participants in the poker game. At the trial the State called Knight and three of his fellow poker players as prosecution witnesses. Each of them described the circumstances of the holdup and itemized his own individual losses. The proof that an armed robbery had occurred and that personal property had been taken from Knight as well as from each of the others was unassailable. The testimony of the four victims in this regard was consistent both internally and with that of the others. But the State's evidence that the petitioner had been one of the robbers was weak. Two of the witnesses thought that there had been only three robbers altogether, and could not identify the petitioner as one of them. Another of the victims, who was the petitioner's uncle by marriage, said that at the "patrol station" he had positively identified each of the other three men accused of the holdup, but could say only that the petitioner's voice "sounded very much like" that of one of the robbers. The fourth participant in the poker game did identify the petitioner, but only by his "size and height, and his actions."

The cross-examination of these witnesses was brief, and it was aimed primarily at exposing the weakness of their identification testimony. Defense counsel made no attempt to question their testimony regarding the holdup itself or their claims as to their losses. Knight testified without contradiction that the robbers had stolen from him his watch, $250 in cash, and about $500 in checks. His billfold, which had been found by the police in the possession of one of the three other men accused of the robbery, was admitted in evidence. The defense offered no testimony and waived final argument.

The trial judge instructed the jury that if it found that the petitioner was one of the participants in the armed robbery, the theft of "any money" from Knight would sustain a conviction. He also instructed the jury that if the petitioner was one of the robbers, he was guilty under the law even if he had not personally robbed Knight. The jury—though not instructed to elaborate upon its verdict—found the petitioner "not guilty due to insufficient evidence."

Six weeks later the petitioner was brought to trial again, this time for the robbery of another participant in the poker game, a man named Roberts. The petitioner filed a motion to dismiss, based on his previous acquittal. The motion was overruled, and the second trial began. The witnesses were for the most part the same, though this time their testimony was substantially stronger on the issue of the petitioner's identity. For example, two witnesses who at the first trial had been wholly unable to identify the petitioner as one of the robbers, now testified that his features, size, and mannerisms matched those of one of their assailants. Another witness who before had identified the petitioner only by his size and actions now also remembered him by the unusual sound of his voice. The State further refined its case at the second trial by declining to call one of the participants in the poker game whose identification testimony at the first trial had been conspicuously negative. The case went to the jury on instructions virtually identical to those given at the first trial. This time the jury found the petitioner guilty, and he was sentenced to a 35-year term in the state penitentiary.

* * * The question is * * * whether collateral estoppel is a part of the Fifth Amendment's guarantee against double jeopardy. And if collateral estoppel is embodied in that guarantee, then its applicability in a particular case is no longer a matter to be left for state court determination within the broad bounds of "fundamental fairness," but a matter of constitutional fact we must decide through an examination of the entire record.

"Collateral estoppel" is an awkward phrase, but it stands for an extremely important principle in our adversary system of justice. It means simply that when an issue of ultimate fact has once been determined by a valid and final judgment, that issue cannot again be litigated between the same parties in any future lawsuit. Although first developed in civil litigation, collateral estoppel has been an established rule of federal criminal law at least since this Court's decision more than 50 years ago in *United States v. Oppenheimer*. As Mr. Justice Holmes put the matter in that case, "It cannot be that the safeguards of the person, so often and so rightly mentioned with solemn reverence, are less than those that protect from a liability in debt."

The federal decisions have made clear that the rule of collateral estoppel in criminal cases is not to be applied with the hypertechnical and archaic approach of a 19th century pleading book, but with realism and rationality. Where a previous judgment of acquittal was based upon a general verdict, as is usually the case, this approach requires a court to "examine the record of a prior proceeding, taking into account the pleadings, evidence, charge, and other relevant matter, and conclude whether a rational jury could have grounded its verdict upon an issue other than that which the defendant seeks to foreclose from consideration." * * *

Straightforward application of the federal rule to the present case can lead to but one conclusion. For the record is utterly devoid of any indication that the first jury could rationally have found that an armed robbery had not occurred, or that Knight had not been a victim of that robbery. The single rationally conceivable issue in dispute before the jury was whether the petitioner had been one of the robbers. And the jury by its verdict found that he had not. The federal rule of law, therefore, would make a second prosecution for the robbery of Roberts wholly impermissible.

The ultimate question to be determined * * * is whether this established rule of federal law is embodied in the Fifth Amendment guarantee against double jeopardy. We do not hesitate to hold that it is. For whatever else that constitutional guarantee may embrace, it surely protects a man who has been acquitted from having to "run the gantlet" a second time.

The question is not whether Missouri could validly charge the petitioner with six separate offenses for the robbery of the six poker players. It is not whether he could have received a total of six punishments if he had been convicted in a single trial of robbing the six victims. It is simply whether, after a jury determined by its verdict that the petitioner was not one of the robbers, the State could constitutionally hale him before a new jury to litigate that issue again.

After the first jury had acquitted the petitioner of robbing Knight, Missouri could certainly not have brought him to trial again upon that charge. Once a jury had determined upon conflicting testimony that there was at least a reasonable doubt that the petitioner was one of the robbers, the State could not present the same or different identification evidence in a second prosecution for the robbery of Knight in the hope that a different jury might find that evidence more convincing. The situation is constitutionally no different here, even though the second trial related to another victim of the same robbery. For the name of the victim, in the circumstances of this case, had no bearing whatever upon the issue of whether the petitioner was one of the robbers.

In this case the State in its brief has frankly conceded that following the petitioner's acquittal, it treated the first trial as no more than a dry run for the second prosecution: "No doubt the prosecutor felt the state had a provable case on the first charge and, when he lost, he did what every good attorney would do—he refined his presentation in light of the turn of events at the first trial." But this is precisely what the constitutional guarantee forbids.

Reversed and remanded.

JUSTICE BRENNAN, whom JUSTICE DOUGLAS and JUSTICE MARSHALL join, concurring.

I agree that the Double Jeopardy Clause incorporates collateral estoppel as a constitutional requirement and therefore join the Court's opinion. However, even if the rule of collateral estoppel had been inapplicable to the facts of this case, it is my view that the Double Jeopardy Clause nevertheless bars the prosecution of petitioner a second time for armed robbery. The two prosecutions, the first for the robbery of Knight and the second for the robbery of Roberts, grew out of one criminal episode, and therefore I think it clear on the facts of this case that the Double Jeopardy Clause prohibited Missouri from prosecuting petitioner for each robbery at a different trial. * * *

In my view, the Double Jeopardy Clause requires the prosecution, except in most limited circumstances, to join at one trial all the charges against a defendant that grow out of a single criminal act, occurrence, episode, or transaction. This "same transaction" test of "same offence" not only enforces the ancient prohibition against vexatious multiple prosecutions embodied in the Double Jeopardy Clause, but responds as well to the increasingly widespread recognition that the consolidation in one lawsuit of all issues arising out of a single transaction or occurrence best promotes justice, economy, and convenience.[a] * * *

CHIEF JUSTICE BURGER, dissenting. * * *

The essence of Mr. Justice Brennan's concurrence is that this was all one transaction, one episode, or, if I may so characterize it, one frolic, and, hence, only one crime. His approach, like that taken by the Court, totally overlooks the significance of there being six entirely separate charges of robbery against six individuals.

This "single frolic" concept is not a novel notion; it has been urged in various courts including this Court. One of the theses underlying the "single frolic" notion is that the criminal episode is "indivisible." The short answer to that is that to the victims, the criminal conduct is readily divisible and intensely personal; each offense is an offense against a person. For me it demeans the dignity of the human personality and

---

[a] The "same transaction" test favored by Justice Brennan has never been adopted by a majority of the Supreme Court.

individuality to talk of "a single transaction" in the context or six separate assaults on six individuals. * * *

I therefore join with the four courts that have found no double jeopardy in this case.

[JUSTICE BLACK's concurring opinion and JUSTICE HARLAN's concurring opinion have been omitted.]

B. THE "SAME OFFENSE" REQUIREMENT

The Double Jeopardy Clause protects a defendant from being prosecuted multiple times for the "same offense." Determining whether a subsequent prosecution is for the "same offense," however, is not always easy. Offenses may have different titles and come from different statutory provisions yet constitute the "same offense" for purposes of double jeopardy. In *United States v. Dixon*, we see the Justices arguing over how best to determine whether two offenses are the "same offense" for double jeopardy purposes.

UNITED STATES V. DIXON
Supreme Court of the United States
509 U.S. 688, 113 S. Ct. 2849, 125 L. Ed. 2d 556 (1993)

JUSTICE SCALIA announced the judgment of the Court and delivered the opinion of the Court with respect to Parts I, II, and IV, and an opinion with respect to Parts III and V, in which JUSTICE KENNEDY joins. * * *

I

Respondent Alvin Dixon was arrested for second-degree murder and was released on bond. Consistent with the District of Columbia's bail law authorizing the judicial officer to impose any condition that "will reasonably assure the appearance of the person for trial or the safety of any other person or the community," Dixon's release form specified that he was not to commit "any criminal offense," and warned that any violation of the conditions of release would subject him "to revocation of release, an order of detention, and prosecution for contempt of court."

While awaiting trial, Dixon was arrested and indicted for possession of cocaine with intent to distribute, in violation of D.C. Code Ann. § 33–541(a)(1) (1988). The court issued an order requiring Dixon to show cause why he should not be held in contempt or have the terms of his pretrial release modified. At the show-cause hearing, * * * [t]he court * * * found Dixon guilty of criminal contempt under § 23–1329(c), [and sentenced him] * * * to 180 days in jail. * * * He later moved to dismiss the cocaine indictment on double jeopardy grounds; the trial court granted the motion.

Respondent Michael Foster's route to this Court is similar. Based on Foster's alleged physical attacks upon her in the past, Foster's estranged wife Ana obtained a civil protection order (CPO) in Superior Court of the District of Columbia. The order, to which Foster consented, required that he not "molest, assault, or in any manner threaten or physically abuse" Ana Foster. * * *

Over the course of eight months, Ana Foster filed three separate motions to have her husband held in contempt for numerous violations of the CPO. Of the 16 alleged episodes, the only charges relevant here are three separate instances of threats (on November 12, 1987, and March 26 and May 17, 1988) and two assaults (on November 6, 1987, and May 21, 1988) * * *.

After issuing a notice of hearing and ordering Foster to appear, the court held a 3-day bench trial. Counsel for Ana Foster and her mother prosecuted the action; the United States was not represented at trial, although the United States Attorney was apparently aware of the action, as was the court aware of a separate grand jury proceeding on some of the alleged criminal conduct. As to the assault charges, the court stated that Ana Foster would have "to prove as an element, first that there was a Civil Protection Order, and then [that] . . . the assault as defined by the criminal code, in fact occurred." * * * [T]he court granted Foster's motion for acquittal on various counts, including the alleged threats on November 12 and May 17 * * * [but] found Foster guilty beyond a reasonable doubt of four counts of criminal contempt (three violations of Ana Foster's CPO, and one violation of the CPO obtained by her mother), including the November 6, 1987, and May 21, 1988, assaults, but acquitted him on other counts, including the March 26 alleged threats. He was sentenced to an aggregate 600 days' imprisonment.

The United States Attorney's Office later obtained an indictment charging Foster with simple assault on or about November 6, 1987 (Count I, violation of § 22–504); threatening to injure another on or about November 12, 1987, and March 26 and May 17, 1988 (Counts II–IV, violation of § 22–2307); and assault with intent to kill on or about May 21, 1988 (Count V, violation of § 22–501). Ana Foster was the complainant in all counts; the first and last counts were based on the events for which Foster had been held in contempt, and the other three were based on the alleged events for which Foster was acquitted of contempt. Like Dixon, Foster filed a motion to dismiss, claiming a double jeopardy bar to all counts, and also collateral estoppel as to Counts II–IV. The trial court denied the double jeopardy claim and did not rule on the collateral-estoppel assertion.

The Government appealed the double jeopardy ruling in *Dixon,* and Foster appealed the trial court's denial of his motion. The District of

Columbia Court of Appeals consolidated the two cases, reheard them en banc, and, relying on our recent decision in *Grady v. Corbin*, ruled that both subsequent prosecutions were barred by the Double Jeopardy Clause. * * *

II

* * * In both *Dixon* and *Foster,* a court issued an order directing a particular individual not to commit criminal offenses. (In Dixon's case, the court incorporated the entire criminal code; in Foster's case, the criminal offense of simple assault.) * * * [T]he double jeopardy issue presented here [is] whether prosecution for criminal contempt based on violation of a criminal law incorporated into a court order bars a subsequent prosecution for the criminal offense.

The Double Jeopardy Clause, whose application to this new context we are called upon to consider, provides that no person shall "be subject for the same offence to be twice put in jeopardy of life or limb." This protection applies both to successive punishments and to successive prosecutions for the same criminal offense. It is well established that criminal contempt, at least the sort enforced through nonsummary proceedings, is "a crime in the ordinary sense."

We have held that constitutional protections for criminal defendants other than the double jeopardy provision apply in nonsummary criminal contempt prosecutions just as they do in other criminal prosecutions. We think it obvious, and today hold, that the protection of the Double Jeopardy Clause likewise attaches.

In both the multiple punishment and multiple prosecution contexts, this Court has concluded that where the two offenses for which the defendant is punished or tried cannot survive the "same-elements" test, the double jeopardy bar applies. The same-elements test, sometimes referred to as the *"Blockburger"* test, inquires whether each offense contains an element not contained in the other; if not, they are the "same offence" and double jeopardy bars additional punishment and successive prosecution. * * *

We recently held in *Grady* that in addition to passing the *Blockburger* test, a subsequent prosecution must satisfy a "same-conduct" test to avoid the double jeopardy bar. The *Grady* test provides that, "if, to establish an essential element of an offense charged in that prosecution, the government will prove conduct that constitutes an offense for which the defendant has already been prosecuted," a second prosecution may not be had.

III

A

The first question before us today is whether *Blockburger* analysis permits subsequent prosecution in this new criminal contempt context, where judicial order has prohibited criminal act. If it does, we must then proceed to consider whether *Grady* also permits it.

We begin with *Dixon*. The statute applicable in Dixon's contempt prosecution provides that "[a] person who has been conditionally released . . . and who has violated a condition of release shall be subject to . . . prosecution for contempt of court." § 23–1329(a). Obviously, Dixon could not commit an "offence" under this provision until an order setting out conditions was issued. The statute by itself imposes no legal obligation on anyone. Dixon's cocaine possession, although an offense under D.C. Code Ann. § 33–541(a), was not an offense under § 23–1329 until a judge incorporated the statutory drug offense into his release order.

In this situation, in which the contempt sanction is imposed for violating the order through commission of the incorporated drug offense, the later attempt to prosecute Dixon for the drug offense resembles the situation that produced our judgment of double jeopardy in *Harris v. Oklahoma*. There we held that a subsequent prosecution for robbery with a firearm was barred by the Double Jeopardy Clause, because the defendant had already been tried for felony murder based on the same underlying felony. We have described * * * *Harris* as standing for the proposition that, for double jeopardy purposes, "the crime generally described as felony murder" is not "a separate offense distinct from its various elements." So too here, the "crime" of violating a condition of release cannot be abstracted from the "element" of the violated condition. The *Dixon* court order incorporated the entire governing criminal code in the same manner as the *Harris* felony-murder statute incorporated the several enumerated felonies. Here, as in *Harris,* the underlying substantive criminal offense is "a species of lesser-included offense." * * *

The foregoing analysis obviously applies as well to Count I of the indictment against Foster, charging assault in violation of § 22–504, based on the same event that was the subject of his prior contempt conviction for violating the provision of the CPO forbidding him to commit simple assault under § 22–504. The subsequent prosecution for assault fails the *Blockburger* test, and is barred.

B

The remaining four counts in *Foster*, assault with intent to kill (Count V; § 22–501) and threats to injure or kidnap (Counts II–IV; § 22–2307), are not barred under *Blockburger*. As to Count V: Foster's conduct on May 21, 1988, was found to violate the Family Division's order that he not "molest, assault, or in any manner threaten or physically abuse" his wife. At the contempt hearing, the court stated that Ana Foster's attorney, who prosecuted the contempt, would have to prove, first, knowledge of a CPO, and, second, a willful violation of one of its conditions, here simple assault as defined by the criminal code. On the basis of the same episode, Foster was then indicted for violation of § 22–501, which proscribes assault with intent to kill. Under governing law, that offense requires proof of specific intent to kill; simple assault does not. Similarly, the contempt offense required proof of knowledge of the CPO, which assault with intent to kill does not. Applying the *Blockburger* elements test, the result is clear: These crimes were different offenses, and the subsequent prosecution did not violate the Double Jeopardy Clause.

Counts II, III, and IV of Foster's indictment are likewise not barred. These charged Foster under § 22–2307 (forbidding anyone to "threate[n] . . . to kidnap any person or to injure the person of another or physically damage the property of any person") for his alleged threats on three separate dates. Foster's contempt prosecution included charges that, on the same dates, he violated the CPO provision ordering that he not "in any manner threaten" Ana Foster. Conviction of the contempt required willful violation of the CPO—which conviction under § 22–2307 did not; and conviction under § 22–2307 required that the threat be a threat to kidnap, to inflict bodily injury, or to damage property—which conviction of the contempt (for violating the CPO provision that Foster not "in any manner threaten") did not. Each offense therefore contained a separate element, and the *Blockburger* test for double jeopardy was not met.

IV

Having found that at least some of the counts at issue here are not barred by the *Blockburger* test, we must consider whether they are barred by the new, additional double jeopardy test we announced three Terms ago in *Grady v. Corbin*.[a] They undoubtedly are, since *Grady* prohibits "a

---

[a] In *Grady v. Corbin*, 495 U.S. 508 (1990), the Court noted that the *Blockburger* test was not the exclusive test for determining whether or not double jeopardy bars a subsequent prosecution, explaining:

> To determine whether a subsequent prosecution is barred by the Double Jeopardy Clause, a court must first apply the traditional Blockburger test. If application of that test reveals that the offenses have identical statutory elements or that one is a lesser included offense of the other, then the inquiry must cease, and the subsequent prosecution is barred.

Id. at 516. Under the *Grady v. Corbin* conduct test, if application of the *Blockburger* test suggests that the offenses in question are not the same offense, the subsequent prosecution will be barred if "the government, to establish an essential element of an offense charged in that prosecution, will prove conduct that constitutes an offense for which the defendant has already been prosecuted." *Id.* at 521.

The defendant in *Grady* pled guilty to two misdemeanor traffic offenses: driving while intoxicated and failing to keep to the right of the median. He was subsequently indicted on charges of reckless manslaughter, second-degree vehicular manslaughter, and criminally negligent homicide, and moved to dismiss the indictment on double jeopardy grounds. The bill of particulars in the subsequent prosecution stated that the prosecution would demonstrate recklessness and criminal negligence by proving that the defendant had operated a motor vehicle on a public

subsequent prosecution if, to establish an essential element of an offense charged in that prosecution [here, assault as an element of assault with intent to kill, or threatening as an element of threatening bodily injury], the government will prove conduct that constitutes an offense for which the defendant has already been prosecuted [here, the assault and the threatening, which conduct constituted the offense of violating the CPO]."

We have concluded, however, that *Grady* must be overruled. Unlike *Blockburger* analysis, whose definition of what prevents two crimes from being the "same offence," has deep historical roots and has been accepted in numerous precedents of this Court, *Grady* lacks constitutional roots. The "same-conduct" rule it announced is wholly inconsistent with earlier Supreme Court precedent and with the clear common-law understanding of double jeopardy. We need not discuss the many proofs of these statements, which were set forth at length in the *Grady* dissent.

* * * *Grady* was not only wrong in principle; it has already proved unstable in application. * * * A hypothetical based on the facts in *Harris* reinforces the conclusion that *Grady* is a continuing source of confusion and must be overruled. Suppose the State first tries the defendant for felony murder, based on robbery, and then indicts the defendant for robbery with a firearm in the same incident.[b] Absent *Grady,* our cases provide a clear answer to the double jeopardy claim in this situation. Under *Blockburger,* the second prosecution is not barred—as it clearly was not barred at common law, as a famous case establishes. In *King v. Vandercomb,* the government abandoned, midtrial, prosecution of defendant for burglary by breaking and entering and stealing goods, because it turned out that no property had been removed on the date of the alleged burglary. The defendant was then prosecuted for burglary by breaking and entering with intent to steal. That second prosecution was allowed, because "these two offences are so distinct in their nature, that evidence of one of them will not support an indictment for the other."

Having encountered today yet another situation in which the pre-*Grady* understanding of the Double Jeopardy Clause allows a second trial, though the "same-conduct" test would not, we think it time to acknowledge what is now, three years after *Grady,* compellingly clear: the case was a mistake. We do not lightly reconsider a precedent, but, because *Grady*

---

highway in an intoxicated condition and failed to keep to the right of the median. Since the government, in order to establish the *mens rea* element of the homicide charges in the subsequent prosecution, would be proving *conduct* that constituted offenses for which Grady had already been prosecuted, the Court held that the subsequent prosecution was barred by double jeopardy.

[b] In *Harris v. Oklahoma*, 433 U.S. 682 (1977), the defendant was convicted of felony murder where the underlying felony was robbery with firearms. He was then prosecuted for robbery with firearms. In a per curiam opinion, the Supreme Court held that the Double Jeopardy Clause barred the subsequent prosecution, explaining that "[w]hen, as here, conviction of a greater crime, murder, cannot be had without conviction of the lesser crime, robbery with firearms, the Double Jeopardy Clause bars prosecution for the lesser crime after conviction of the greater one." *Id.* at 682.

contradicted an "unbroken line of decisions," contained "less than accurate" historical analysis, and has produced "confusion," we do so here. Although *stare decisis* is the "preferred course" in constitutional adjudication, "when governing decisions are unworkable or are badly reasoned, 'this Court has never felt constrained to follow precedent.' " We would mock *stare decisis* and only add chaos to our double jeopardy jurisprudence by pretending that *Grady* survives when it does not. We therefore accept the Government's invitation to overrule *Grady*.c * * *

CHIEF JUSTICE REHNQUIST, with whom JUSTICE O'CONNOR and JUSTICE THOMAS join, concurring in part and dissenting in part.

* * * I do not join Part III of Justice Scalia's opinion because I think that none of the criminal prosecutions in this case were barred under *Blockburger*. * * * For the reasons set forth in the dissent in *Grady* (opinion of Scalia, J.), and in Part IV of the Court's opinion, I, too, think that *Grady* must be overruled. I therefore join Parts I, II, and IV of the Court's opinion * * *.

In my view, *Blockburger*'s same-elements test requires us to focus, not on the terms of the particular court orders involved, but on the elements of contempt of court in the ordinary sense. Relying on *Harris v. Oklahoma*, * * * Justice Scalia concludes otherwise today, and thus incorrectly finds in Part III-A of his opinion that the subsequent prosecutions of Dixon for drug distribution and of Foster for assault violated the Double Jeopardy Clause. In so doing, Justice Scalia rejects the traditional view—shared by every federal court of appeals and state supreme court that addressed the issue prior to *Grady*—that, as a general matter, double jeopardy does not bar a subsequent prosecution based on conduct for which a defendant has been held in criminal contempt. * * *

At the heart of this pre-*Grady* consensus lay the common belief that there was no double jeopardy bar under *Blockburger*. There, we stated that two offenses are different for purposes of double jeopardy if "each *provision* requires proof of a fact which the other does not." Applying this test to the offenses at bar, it is clear that the elements of the governing contempt *provision* are entirely different from the elements of the substantive crimes. Contempt of court comprises two elements: (i) a court order made known to the defendant, followed by (ii) willful violation of that order. Neither of those elements is necessarily satisfied by proof that a defendant has committed the substantive offenses of assault or drug distribution. Likewise, no element of either of those substantive offenses is necessarily

---

c Even though the *Dixon* Court overruled *Grady v. Corbin*, many states still apply a "same conduct" type of test, assessing whether the subsequent prosecution is based on the same conduct that was the subject of the prior prosecution when trying to decide whether double jeopardy bars the second prosecution. *See* Andrew Manuel Crespo, *The Hidden Law of Plea Bargaining*, 118 COLUM. L. REV. 1303, 1331 (2018). Therefore, it is still important to study *Grady v. Corbin*.

satisfied by proof that a defendant has been found guilty of contempt of court. * * *

Our double jeopardy cases applying *Blockburger* have focused on the statutory elements of the offenses charged, not on the facts that must be proved under the particular indictment at issue—an indictment being the closest analogue to the court orders in this case. * * * By focusing on the facts needed to show a violation of the specific court orders involved in this case, and not on the generic elements of the crime of contempt of court, Justice Scalia's double jeopardy analysis bears a striking resemblance to that found in *Grady*—not what one would expect in an opinion that overrules *Grady*.

Close inspection of the crimes at issue in *Harris* reveals, moreover, that our decision in that case was not a departure from *Blockburger*'s focus on the *statutory* elements of the offenses charged. * * * [T]he *ratio decidendi* of our *Harris* decision was that the two crimes there were akin to greater and lesser included offenses. The crimes at issue here, however, cannot be viewed as greater and lesser included offenses, either intuitively or logically. A crime such as possession with intent to distribute cocaine is a serious felony that cannot easily be conceived of as a lesser included offense of criminal contempt, a relatively petty offense as applied to the conduct in this case. Indeed, to say that criminal contempt is an aggravated form of that offense defies common sense. * * *

JUSTICE SOUTER, with whom JUSTICE STEVENS joins, concurring in the judgment in part and dissenting in part.

* * * I cannot join the Court in restricting the Clause's reach and dismembering the protection against successive prosecution that the Constitution was meant to provide. The Court has read our precedents so narrowly as to leave them bereft of the principles animating that protection, and has chosen to overrule the most recent of the relevant cases, *Grady v. Corbin,* decided three years ago. Because I think that *Grady* was correctly decided, amounting merely to an expression of just those animating principles, and because, even if the decision had been wrong in the first instance, there is no warrant for overruling it now, I respectfully dissent. * * *

The Double Jeopardy Clause prevents the government from "mak[ing] repeated attempts to convict an individual for an alleged offense, thereby subjecting him to embarrassment, expense and ordeal and compelling him to live in a continuing state of anxiety and insecurity." The Clause addresses a further concern as well, that the government not be given the opportunity to rehearse its prosecution, "honing its trial strategies and perfecting its evidence through successive attempts at conviction," because this "enhanc[es] the possibility that even though innocent [the defendant] may be found guilty."

Consequently, while the government may punish a person separately for each conviction of at least as many different offenses as meet the *Blockburger* test, we have long held that it must sometimes bring its prosecutions for these offenses together. If a separate prosecution were permitted for every offense arising out of the same conduct, the government could manipulate the definitions of offenses, creating fine distinctions among them and permitting a zealous prosecutor to try a person again and again for essentially the same criminal conduct. While punishing different combinations of elements is consistent with the Double Jeopardy Clause in its limitation on the imposition of multiple punishments (a limitation rooted in concerns with legislative intent), permitting such repeated prosecutions would not be consistent with the principles underlying the Clause in its limitation on successive prosecutions. The limitation on successive prosecutions is thus a restriction on the government different in kind from that contained in the limitation on multiple punishments, and the government cannot get around the restriction on repeated prosecution of a single individual merely by precision in the way it defines its statutory offenses. Thus, "[t]he *Blockburger* test is not the only standard for determining whether successive prosecutions impermissibly involve the same offense. Even if two offenses are sufficiently different to permit the imposition of consecutive sentences, successive prosecutions will be barred in some circumstances where the second prosecution requires the relitigation of factual issues already resolved by the first."

An example will show why this should be so. Assume three crimes: robbery with a firearm, robbery in a dwelling, and simple robbery. The elements of the three crimes are the same, except that robbery with a firearm has the element that a firearm be used in the commission of the robbery while the other two crimes do not, and robbery in a dwelling has the element that the robbery occur in a dwelling while the other two crimes do not.

If a person committed a robbery in a dwelling with a firearm and was prosecuted for simple robbery, all agree he could not be prosecuted subsequently for either of the greater offenses of robbery with a firearm or robbery in a dwelling. Under the lens of *Blockburger*, however, if that same person were prosecuted first for robbery with a firearm, he could be prosecuted subsequently for robbery in a dwelling, even though he could not subsequently be prosecuted on the basis of that same robbery for simple robbery.[3] This is true simply because neither of the crimes, robbery with a firearm and robbery in a dwelling, is either identical to or a lesser included offense of the other. But since the purpose of the Double Jeopardy Clause's protection against successive prosecutions is to prevent repeated trials in

---

[3] Our cases have long made clear that the order in which one is prosecuted for two crimes alleged to be the same matters not in demonstrating a violation of double jeopardy. See *Brown* v. *Ohio*, 432 U.S. 161, 168, 97 S. Ct. 2221, 53 L.Ed.2d 187 (1977) ("The sequence is immaterial").

which a defendant will be forced to defend against the same charge again and again, and in which the government may perfect its presentation with dress rehearsal after dress rehearsal, it should be irrelevant that the second prosecution would require the defendant to defend himself not only from the charge that he committed the robbery, but also from the charge of some additional fact, in this case, that the scene of the crime was a dwelling. If, instead, protection against successive prosecutions were as limited as it would be by *Blockburger* alone, the doctrine would be as striking for its anomalies as for the limited protection it would provide. Thus, in the relatively few successive prosecution cases we have had over the years, we have not held that the *Blockburger* test is the only hurdle the government must clear. * * *

In the past 20 years the Court has addressed just this problem of successive prosecution on three occasions. In *Harris v. Oklahoma* we held that prosecution for a robbery with firearms was barred by the Double Jeopardy Clause when the defendant had already been convicted of felony murder comprising the same robbery with firearms as the underlying felony. Of course the elements of the two offenses were different enough to permit more than one punishment under the *Blockburger* test: felony murder required the killing of a person by one engaged in the commission of a felony; robbery with firearms required the use of a firearm in the commission of a robbery.

In *Harris*, however, we held that "[w]hen, as here, conviction of a greater crime, murder, cannot be had without conviction of the lesser crime, robbery with firearms, the Double Jeopardy Clause bars prosecution for the lesser crime after conviction of the greater one."

* * * [T]he analysis in *Harris* turned on considering the prior conviction in terms of the conduct actually charged. While that process might be viewed as a misapplication of a *Blockburger* lesser included offense analysis, the crucial point is that the *Blockburger* elements test would have produced a different result. The case thus [shows] that the *Blockburger* test is not the exclusive standard for determining whether the rule against successive prosecutions applies in a given case.

Subsequently, in *Illinois v. Vitale*, the Court again indicated that a valid claim of double jeopardy would not necessarily be defeated by the fact that the two offenses are not the "same" under the *Blockburger* test. In that case, we were confronted with a prosecution for failure to reduce speed and a subsequent prosecution for involuntary manslaughter. * * * We held that "[i]f, as a matter of Illinois law, a careless failure to slow is always a necessary element of manslaughter by automobile, then the two offenses are the 'same' under *Blockburger* and Vitale's trial on the latter charge would constitute double jeopardy. . . ." But that was not all. Writing for the Court, Justice White went on to say that, "[i]n any event, it may be that to sustain its manslaughter case the State may find it necessary to prove a failure to slow or to rely on conduct necessarily involving such failure. . . . In that case, because Vitale has already been convicted for conduct that is a necessary element of the more serious crime for which he has been charged, his claim of double jeopardy would be substantial under * * * *Harris v. Oklahoma*."

Over a decade ago, then, we clearly understood *Harris* to stand for the proposition that when one has already been tried for a crime comprising certain conduct, a subsequent prosecution seeking to prove the same conduct is barred by the Double Jeopardy Clause. Even if this had not been clear * * *, any debate should have been settled by our decision three Terms ago in *Grady v. Corbin*, that "the Double Jeopardy Clause bars a subsequent prosecution if, to establish an essential element of an offense charged in that prosecution, the government will prove conduct that constitutes an offense for which the defendant has already been prosecuted."

* * * Whatever may have been the merits of the debate in *Grady*, the decision deserves more respect than it receives from the Court today. "Although adherence to precedent is not rigidly required in constitutional cases, any departure from the doctrine of *stare decisis* demands special justification." * * *

[JUSTICE WHITE's opinion, concurring in the judgment in part and dissenting in part, and JUSTICE BLACKMUN's opinion, concurring in the judgment in part and dissenting in part, have been omitted. Justice White believed the subsequent prosecutions in both *Dixon* and *Foster* were barred by double jeopardy and would not have overruled *Grady v. Corbin*. Justice Blackmun wrote separately because he did not see how contempt of court could be considered the "same offense" as either assault with intent to kill or possession of cocaine with intent to distribute it. Justice Blackmun also disagreed with the decision to overrule *Grady v. Corbin*.]

NOTE

In *Brown v. Ohio*, the Court recognized an exception to the usual double jeopardy rule prohibiting the government from retrying a defendant for the same offense. The Court explained that where application of its traditional double jeopardy analysis would bar a subsequent prosecution, "[a]n exception may exist where the State is unable to proceed on the more serious charge at the outset because the additional facts necessary to sustain that charge have not occurred or have not been discovered despite the exercise of due diligence." 432 U.S. 161, 169 n.7 (1977) (citing *Diaz v. United States*, 223 U.S. 442, 448–49 (1912)). This exception has been called the *Brown-Diaz* exception.

C. THE DUAL SOVEREIGNTY DOCTRINE

Notwithstanding the "same offense" limitation discussed in the previous section, a subsequent prosecution for the same offense will not be barred if brought by a different sovereign. Under the dual sovereignty doctrine, a sovereign has the right to prosecute criminal violations in its jurisdiction even if a separate sovereign has chosen to prosecute the defendant for the same criminal offense. *Heath v. Alabama* explains the rationale behind the dual sovereignty doctrine and considers whether the doctrine allows one state to prosecute a defendant who has been convicted of the same offense in another state. The note following *Heath v. Alabama* discusses the U.S. Department of Justice's Petite Policy, a policy that federal prosecutors use as a guide when deciding whether to pursue a federal prosecution following a state prosecution for the same offense.

HEATH V. ALABAMA
Supreme Court of the United States
474 U.S. 82, 106 S. Ct. 433, 88 L. Ed. 2d 387 (1985)

JUSTICE O'CONNOR delivered the opinion of the Court.

In August 1981, petitioner, Larry Gene Heath, hired Charles Owens and Gregory Lumpkin to kill his wife, Rebecca Heath, who was then nine months pregnant, for a sum of $2,000. On the morning of August 31, 1981, petitioner left the Heath residence in Russell County, Alabama, to meet with Owens and Lumpkin in Georgia, just over the Alabama border from the Heath home. Petitioner led them back to the Heath residence, gave them the keys to the Heaths' car and house, and left the premises in his girlfriend's truck. Owens and Lumpkin then kidnaped Rebecca Heath from her home. The Heath car, with Rebecca Heath's body inside, was later found on the side of a road in Troup County, Georgia. The cause of death was a gunshot wound in the head.

Georgia and Alabama authorities pursued dual investigations in which they cooperated to some extent. On September 4, 1981, petitioner was arrested by Georgia authorities. Petitioner waived his Miranda rights and gave a full confession admitting that he had arranged his wife's kidnaping and murder. In November 1981, the grand jury of Troup County, Georgia, indicted petitioner for the offense of "malice" murder. Georgia then served petitioner with notice of its intention to seek the death penalty, citing as the aggravating circumstance the fact that the murder was "caused and directed" by petitioner. On February 10, 1982, petitioner pleaded guilty to the Georgia murder charge in exchange for a sentence of life imprisonment, which he understood could involve his serving as few as seven years in prison.

On May 5, 1982, the grand jury of Russell County, Alabama, returned an indictment against petitioner for the capital offense of murder during a kidnaping. Before trial on this indictment, petitioner entered pleas of *autrefois convict* and former jeopardy under the Alabama and United States Constitutions, arguing that his conviction and sentence in Georgia barred his prosecution in Alabama for the same conduct. * * *

After a hearing, the trial court rejected petitioner's double jeopardy claims. It assumed, *arguendo*, that the two prosecutions could not have been brought in succession by one State but held that double jeopardy did not bar successive prosecutions by two different States for the same act. * * * On January 12, 1983, the Alabama jury convicted petitioner of murder during a kidnaping in the first degree. After a sentencing hearing, the jury recommended the death penalty. * * *

[On appeal of the conviction] the Alabama Supreme Court noted that "[p]rosecutions under the laws of separate sovereigns do not improperly subject an accused twice to prosecutions for the same offense," citing this Court's cases applying the dual sovereignty doctrine. The court acknowledged that this Court has not considered the applicability of the dual sovereignty doctrine to successive prosecutions by different States. It reasoned, however, that "[i]f, for double jeopardy purposes, Alabama is considered to be a sovereign entity vis-à-vis the federal government then surely it is a sovereign entity vis-à-vis the State of Georgia." * * *

Successive prosecutions are barred by the Fifth Amendment only if the two offenses for which the defendant is prosecuted are the "same" for double jeopardy purposes. Respondent does not contravene petitioner's contention that the offenses of "murder during a kidnaping" and "malice murder," as construed by the courts of Alabama and Georgia respectively, may be considered greater and lesser offenses and, thus, the "same" offense, absent operation of the dual sovereignty principle. We therefore assume, *arguendo*, that, had these offenses arisen under the laws of one State and had petitioner been separately prosecuted for both offenses in that State, the second conviction would have been barred by the Double Jeopardy Clause.

The * * * question upon which we granted certiorari is whether the dual sovereignty doctrine permits successive prosecutions under the laws of different States which otherwise would be held to "subject [the defendant] for the same offence to be twice put in jeopardy." Although we have not previously so held, we believe the answer to this query is inescapable. The dual sovereignty doctrine, as originally articulated and consistently applied by this Court, compels the conclusion that successive prosecutions by two States for the same conduct are not barred by the Double Jeopardy Clause.

The dual sovereignty doctrine is founded on the common-law conception of crime as an offense against the sovereignty of the government. When a defendant in a single act violates the "peace and dignity" of two sovereigns by breaking the laws of each, he has committed two distinct "offences." * * * Consequently, when the same act transgresses the laws of two sovereigns, "it cannot be truly averred that the offender has been twice punished for the same offence; but only that by one act he has committed two offences, for each of which he is justly punishable."

In applying the dual sovereignty doctrine, then, the crucial determination is whether the two entities that seek successively to prosecute a defendant for the same course of conduct can be termed separate sovereigns. This determination turns on whether the two entities draw their authority to punish the offender from distinct sources of power. Thus, the Court has uniformly held that the States are separate sovereigns with respect to the Federal Government because each State's power to prosecute is derived from its own "inherent sovereignty," not from the Federal Government. * * *

The States are no less sovereign with respect to each other than they are with respect to the Federal Government. Their powers to undertake criminal prosecutions derive from separate and independent sources of power and authority originally belonging to them before admission to the Union and preserved to them by the Tenth Amendment. The States are equal to each other "in power, dignity and authority, each competent to exert that residuum of sovereignty not delegated to the United States by the Constitution itself." Thus, "[e]ach has the power, inherent in any sovereign, independently to determine what shall be an offense against its authority and to punish such offenses, and in doing so each 'is exercising its own sovereignty, not that of the other.'" * * *

In those instances where the Court has found the dual sovereignty doctrine inapplicable, it has done so because the two prosecuting entities did not derive their powers to prosecute from independent sources of authority. Thus, the Court has held that successive prosecutions by federal and territorial courts are barred because such courts are "creations emanating from the same sovereignty." Similarly, municipalities that derive their power to try a defendant from the same organic law that empowers the State to prosecute are not separate sovereigns with respect to the State. These cases confirm that it is the presence of independent sovereign authority to prosecute, not the relation between States and the Federal Government in our federalist system that constitutes the basis for the dual sovereignty doctrine.

* * * The Court's express rationale for the dual sovereignty doctrine is not simply a fiction that can be disregarded in difficult cases. It finds weighty support in the historical understanding and political realities of

the States' role in the federal system and in the words of the Double Jeopardy Clause itself, "nor shall any person be subject for the same *offence* to be twice put in jeopardy of life or limb."

It is axiomatic that "[i]n America, the powers of sovereignty are divided between the government of the Union, and those of the States. They are each sovereign, with respect to the objects committed to it, and neither sovereign with respect to the objects committed to the other." It is as well established that the States, "as political communities, [are] distinct and sovereign, and consequently foreign to each other." The Constitution leaves in the possession of each State "certain exclusive and very important portions of sovereign power." Foremost among the prerogatives of sovereignty is the power to create and enforce a criminal code.[a] To deny a State its power to enforce its criminal laws because another State has won the race to the courthouse "would be a shocking and untoward deprivation of the historic right and obligation of the States to maintain peace and order within their confines." * * *

The judgment of the Supreme Court of Alabama is affirmed.

It is so ordered.

JUSTICE MARSHALL, with whom JUSTICE BRENNAN joins, dissenting.

Seizing upon the suggestion in past cases that every "independent" sovereign government may prosecute violations of its laws even when the defendant has already been tried for the same crime in another

---

[a] In *Puerto Rico v. Sanchez Valle*, 579 U.S. 59 (2016), the Supreme Court held that Puerto Rico, a territory of the United States since 1898, is not a separate sovereign from the U.S. government for purposes of the dual sovereignty doctrine despite the fact that Puerto Rico created its own criminal code and has its own local prosecutors who enforce that code by prosecuting crimes under Puerto Rico's criminal law. Justice Kagan, writing for the Court, explained:

> [T]he test we have devised to decide whether two governments are distinct for double jeopardy purposes overtly disregards common indicia of sovereignty. * * * The degree to which an entity exercises self-governance—whether autonomously managing its own affairs or continually submitting to outside direction—plays no role in the analysis. Nor do we care about a government's more particular ability to enact and enforce its own criminal laws. Rather, as Puerto Rico itself acknowledges, our test hinges on a single criterion: the "ultimate source" of the power undergirding the respective prosecutions. The inquiry is thus historical, not functional looking at the deepest wellsprings, not the current exercise, of prosecutorial authority. If two entities derive their power to punish from wholly independent sources (imagine here a pair of parallel lines), then they may bring successive prosecutions. Conversely, if those entities draw their power from the same ultimate source (imagine now two lines merging from a common point, even if later diverging), then they may not.

Id. at 67–68. The Court found that Puerto Rico was not a separate sovereign because the U.S. Congress was the ultimate source of Puerto Rico's power to prosecute. *See id.* at 78. This means that Puerto Rico is barred from prosecuting an individual after that individual has been prosecuted by the U.S. government for the same offense.

On November 3, 2020, Puerto Ricans voted in a non-binding referendum in favor of statehood for the sixth time. *See* Cristina Corujo, *Puerto Rico Votes in Favor of Statehood. But What Does It Mean for the Island?*, ABC NEWS (Nov. 8, 2020, 11:21 AM), https://abcnews.go.com/US/990uerto-rico-votes-favor-statehood-island/story?id=74055630 (https://perma.cc/A4DZ-RCXR). The final decision whether to add Puerto Rico as a state, however, resides with Congress and thus far, Congress has not indicated that it is likely to vote to make Puerto Rico a state. *See id.*

jurisdiction, the Court today gives short shrift to the policies underlying those precedents. The "dual sovereignty" doctrine, heretofore used to permit federal and state prosecutions for the same offense, was born of the need to accommodate complementary state and federal concerns within our system of concurrent territorial jurisdictions. It cannot justify successive prosecutions by different States. Moreover, even were the dual sovereignty doctrine to support successive state prosecutions as a general matter, it simply could not legitimate the collusion between Georgia and Alabama in this case to ensure that petitioner is executed for his crime.

On August 31, 1981, the body of Rebecca Heath was discovered in an abandoned car in Troup County, Georgia. Because the deceased was a resident of Russell County, Alabama, members of the Russell County Sheriff's Department immediately joined Troup County authorities in investigating the causes and agents of her death. This cooperative effort proved fruitful. On September 4, petitioner Larry Heath, the deceased's husband, was arrested and brought to the Georgia State Patrol barracks in Troup County, where he confessed to having hired other men to murder his wife. Shortly thereafter, petitioner was indicted by the grand jury of Troup County for malice murder. The prosecution's notice to petitioner that it was seeking the death penalty triggered the beginning of the Unified Appeals Procedure that Georgia requires in capital cases. But while these pretrial proceedings were still in progress, petitioner seized the prosecution's offer of a life sentence in exchange for a guilty plea. Upon entry of his plea in February 1982, petitioner was sentenced in Troup County Superior Court to life imprisonment. His stay in the custody of Georgia authorities proved short, however. Three months later, a Russell County, Alabama, grand jury indicted him for the capital offense of murdering Rebecca Heath during the course of a kidnaping in the first degree.

The murder of Rebecca Heath must have been quite noteworthy in Russell County, Alabama. By petitioner's count, of the 82 prospective jurors questioned before trial during *voir dire,* all but 7 stated that they were aware that petitioner had pleaded guilty to the same crime in Georgia. The *voir dire* responses of almost all of the remaining 75 veniremen can only be characterized as remarkable. When asked whether they could put aside their knowledge of the prior guilty plea in order to give petitioner a fair trial in Alabama, the vast majority answered in the affirmative. These answers satisfied the trial judge, who denied petitioner's challenges for cause except as to those jurors who explicitly admitted that the Georgia proceedings would probably affect their assessment of petitioner's guilt.

With such a well-informed jury, the outcome of the trial was surely a foregone conclusion. Defense counsel could do little but attempt to elicit information from prosecution witnesses tending to show that the crime was committed exclusively in Georgia. The court having rejected petitioner's constitutional and jurisdictional claims, the defense was left to spend most of its summation arguing that Rebecca Heath may not actually have been kidnaped from Alabama before she was murdered and that petitioner was already being punished for ordering that murder. Petitioner was convicted and, after sentencing hearings, was condemned to die. The conviction and sentence were upheld by the Alabama Court of Criminal Appeals and the Alabama Supreme Court.

Had the Georgia authorities suddenly become dissatisfied with the life sentence petitioner received in their courts and reindicted petitioner in order to seek the death penalty once again, that indictment would without question be barred by the Double Jeopardy Clause of the Fifth Amendment, as applied to the States by the Fourteenth Amendment. Whether the second indictment repeated the charge of malice murder or instead charged murder in the course of a kidnaping, it would surely, under any reasonable constitutional standard, offend the bar to successive prosecutions for the same offense.

The only difference between this case and such a hypothetical *volte-face* by Georgia is that here Alabama, not Georgia, was offended by the notion that petitioner might not forfeit his life in punishment for his crime. The only reason the Court gives for permitting Alabama to go forward is that Georgia and Alabama are separate sovereigns.

The dual sovereignty theory posits that where the same act offends the laws of two sovereigns, "it cannot be truly averred that the offender has been twice punished for the same offence; but only that by one act he has committed two offences, for each of which he is justly punishable." Therefore, "prosecutions under the laws of separate sovereigns do not, in the language of the Fifth Amendment, 'subject [the defendant] for the same offence to be twice put in jeopardy.'" * * *

This strained reading of the Double Jeopardy Clause has survived and indeed flourished in this Court's cases not because of any inherent plausibility, but because it provides reassuring interpretivist support for a rule that accommodates the unique nature of our federal system. Before this rule is extended to cover a new class of cases, the reasons for its creation should therefore be made clear.

Under the constitutional scheme, the Federal Government has been given the exclusive power to vindicate certain of our Nation's sovereign interests, leaving the States to exercise complementary authority over matters of more local concern. The respective spheres of the Federal Government and the States may overlap at times, and even where they do not, different interests may be implicated by a single act. Yet were a prosecution by a State, however zealously pursued, allowed to preclude further prosecution by the Federal Government for the same crime, an entire range of national interests could be frustrated. The importance of those federal interests has thus quite properly been permitted to trump a defendant's interest in avoiding successive prosecutions or multiple punishments for the same crime. Conversely, because "the States under our federal system have the principal responsibility for defining and prosecuting crimes," it would be inappropriate—in the absence of a specific congressional intent to pre-empt state action pursuant to the Supremacy Clause—to allow a federal prosecution to preclude state authorities from vindicating "the historic right and obligation of the States to maintain peace and order within their confines." * * *

Where two States seek to prosecute the same defendant for the same crime in two separate proceedings, the justifications found in the federal-state context for an exemption from double jeopardy constraints simply do not hold. Although the two States may have opted for different policies within their assigned territorial jurisdictions, the sovereign concerns with whose vindication each State has been charged are identical. Thus, in contrast to the federal-state context, barring the second prosecution would still permit one government to act upon the broad range of sovereign concerns that have been reserved to the States by the Constitution. The compelling need in the federal-state context to subordinate double jeopardy concerns is thus considerably diminished in cases involving successive prosecutions by different States. * * *

To be sure, a refusal to extend the dual sovereignty rule to state-state prosecutions would preclude the State that has lost the "race to the courthouse" from vindicating legitimate policies distinct from those underlying its sister State's prosecution. But as yet, I am not persuaded that a State's desire to further a particular policy should be permitted to deprive a defendant of his constitutionally protected right not to be brought to bar more than once to answer essentially the same charges. * * *

[JUSTICE BRENNAN's dissenting opinion has been omitted.]

NOTE

In 2018, the U.S. Supreme Court was asked to reconsider the dual sovereignty doctrine. The Court declined to overrule its precedents, explaining "[w]e have long held that a crime under one sovereign's laws is not 'the same offence' as a crime under the laws of another sovereign. Under this 'dual-sovereignty' doctrine, a State may prosecute a defendant under state law even if the Federal Government has prosecuted him for the same conduct under a federal statute." *Gamble v. United States*, 139 S. Ct. 1960, 1964 (2019).

In a strongly worded dissent, Justice Gorsuch wrote:

> A free society does not allow its government to try the same individual for the same crime until it's happy with the result. Unfortunately, the Court today endorses a colossal exception to this ancient rule against double jeopardy. My colleagues say that the

federal government and each State are "separate sovereigns" entitled to try the same person for the same crime. So if all the might of one "sovereign" cannot succeed against the presumptively free individual, another may insist on the chance to try again. And if both manage to succeed, so much the better; they can add one punishment on top of the other. * * *

Enforcing the Constitution always bears its costs. But when the people adopted the Constitution and its Bill of Rights, they thought the liberties promised there worth the costs. It is not for this Court to reassess this judgment to make the prosecutor's job easier. * * * When governments may unleash all their might in multiple prosecutions against an individual, exhausting themselves only when those who hold the reins of power are content with the result, it is "the poor and the weak," the unpopular and controversial, who suffer first—and there is nothing to stop them from being the last. The separate sovereigns exception was wrong when it was invented, and it remains wrong today.

Id. at 1996, 2009 (Gorsuch, J., dissenting).

Although the dual sovereignty doctrine permits the federal government to prosecute a defendant after a state prosecution for the same offense, the federal government disfavors such prosecutions. The U.S. Department of Justice's "Dual and Successive Prosecution Policy," also known as the "Petite Policy," establishes the following guidelines for the exercise of prosecutorial charging discretion in cases in which there has already been a previous state or federal prosecution of the defendant:

> This policy precludes the initiation or continuation of a federal prosecution, following a prior state or federal prosecution based on substantially the same act(s) or transaction(s) unless three substantive prerequisites are satisfied: first, the matter must involve a substantial federal interest; second, the prior prosecution must have left that interest demonstrably unvindicated; and third, applying the same test that is applicable to all federal prosecutions, the government must believe that the defendant's conduct constitutes a federal offense, and that the admissible evidence probably will be sufficient to obtain and sustain a conviction by an unbiased trier of fact. In addition, there is a procedural prerequisite to be satisfied, that is, the prosecution must be approved by the appropriate Assistant Attorney General.
>
> Satisfaction of the three substantive prerequisites does not mean that a proposed prosecution must be approved or brought. The traditional elements of federal prosecutorial discretion continue to apply.

U.S. DEP'T OF JUSTICE, UNITED STATES ATTORNEYS' MANUAL (1997), *available at* https://www.justice.gov/archives/usam/united-states-attorneys-manual (https://perma.cc/Y3ZT-JZSL). Since the Petite Policy is just an internal guideline, a defendant cannot use the Petite Policy to challenge a federal prosecution that follows a state prosecution for the same offense. *See* Ellen S. Podgor, *Department of Justice Guidelines: Balancing "Discretionary Justice,"* 13 CORNELL J.L. & PUB. POL'Y 167 (2004).

D. CRIMINAL VERSUS CIVIL PUNISHMENT

In addition to its prohibition against multiple prosecutions for the same offense, the Double Jeopardy Clause also bars multiple punishments—that is, *criminal* punishments—for the same offense. A penalty imposed after a civil proceeding may constitute criminal punishment under certain circumstances. In order to determine whether a penalty imposed after a civil proceeding should be considered a criminal punishment or merely a civil penalty, the infringed statute, as well as the legislative intent behind the statute, must be examined. *Hudson v. United States* examines when a penalty imposed after a civil proceeding constitutes criminal punishment for double jeopardy purposes.

HUDSON V. UNITED STATES
Supreme Court of the United States
522 U.S. 93, 118 S. Ct. 488, 139 L. Ed. 2d 450 (1997)

CHIEF JUSTICE REHNQUIST delivered the opinion of the Court.

The Government administratively imposed monetary penalties and occupational debarment on petitioners for violation of federal banking statutes, and later criminally indicted them for essentially the same conduct. * * *

During the early and mid-1980's, petitioner John Hudson was the chairman and controlling shareholder of the First National Bank of Tipton (Tipton) and the First National Bank of Hammon (Hammon). During the same period, petitioner Jack Rackley was president of Tipton and a member of the board of directors of Hammon, and petitioner Larry Baresel was a member of the board of directors of both Tipton and Hammon.

An examination of Tipton and Hammon led the Office of the Comptroller of the Currency (OCC) to conclude that petitioners had used their bank positions to arrange a series of loans to third parties in violation of various federal banking statutes and regulations. According to the OCC, those loans, while nominally made to third parties, were in reality made to Hudson in order to enable him to redeem bank stock that he had pledged as collateral on defaulted loans. * * *

In October 1989, petitioners resolved the OCC proceedings against them by each entering into a "Stipulation and Consent Order." These consent orders provided that Hudson, Baresel, and Rackley would pay assessments of $16,500, $15,000, and $12,500 respectively. In addition, each petitioner agreed not to "participate in any manner" in the affairs of any banking institution without the written authorization of the OCC and all other relevant regulatory agencies.

In August 1992, petitioners were indicted * * * [for conspiracy, misapplication of bank funds, and making false bank entries]. The violations charged in the indictment rested on the same lending transactions that formed the basis for the prior administrative actions brought by OCC. Petitioners moved to dismiss the indictment on double jeopardy grounds, but the District Court denied the motions. * * *

The Double Jeopardy Clause provides that no "person [shall] be subject for the same offence to be twice put in jeopardy of life or limb." We have long recognized that the Double Jeopardy Clause does not prohibit the imposition of all additional sanctions that could, "in common parlance," be described as punishment. The Clause protects only against the imposition of multiple *criminal* punishments for the same offense.

Whether a particular punishment is criminal or civil is, at least initially, a matter of statutory construction. A court must first ask whether the legislature, "in establishing the penalizing mechanism, indicated either expressly or impliedly a preference for one label or the other." Even in those cases where the legislature "has indicated an intention to establish a civil penalty, we have inquired further whether the statutory scheme was so punitive either in purpose or effect," as to "transfor[m] what was clearly intended as a civil remedy into a criminal penalty."

In making this latter determination, the factors listed in *Kennedy v. Mendoza-Martinez* provide useful guideposts, including: (1) "[w]hether the sanction involves an affirmative disability or restraint"; (2) "whether it has historically been regarded as a punishment"; (3) "whether it comes into play only on a finding of *scienter*"; (4) "whether its operation will promote the traditional aims of punishment-retribution and deterrence"; (5) "whether the behavior to which it applies is already a crime"; (6) "whether an alternative purpose to which it may rationally be connected is assignable for it"; and (7) "whether it appears excessive in relation to the alternative purpose assigned." It is important to note, however, that "these factors must be considered in relation to the statute on its face," and "only the clearest proof" will suffice to override legislative intent and transform what has been denominated a civil remedy into a criminal penalty. * * *

Applying traditional double jeopardy principles to the facts of this case, it is clear that the criminal prosecution of these petitioners would not violate the Double Jeopardy Clause. It is evident that Congress intended the OCC money penalties and debarment sanctions * * * to be civil in nature. As for the money penalties, * * * [the statutes] expressly provide that such penalties are "civil." While the provision authorizing debarment contains no language explicitly denominating the sanction as civil, we think it significant that the authority to issue debarment orders is conferred upon the "appropriate Federal banking agenc[ies]." That such authority was conferred upon administrative agencies is prima facie evidence that Congress intended to provide for a civil sanction.

Turning to the second stage of the * * * test, we find that there is little evidence, much less the clearest proof that we require, suggesting that either OCC money penalties or debarment sanctions are "so punitive in form and effect as to render them criminal despite Congress' intent to the contrary." First, neither money penalties nor debarment has historically been viewed as punishment. We have long recognized that "revocation of a privilege voluntarily granted," such as a debarment, "is characteristically free of the punitive criminal element." Similarly, "the payment of fixed or variable sums of money [is a] sanction which ha[s] been recognized as enforcible [sic] by civil proceedings since the original revenue law of 1789."

Second, the sanctions imposed do not involve an "affirmative disability or restraint," as that term is normally understood. While petitioners have been prohibited from further participating in the banking industry, this is "certainly nothing approaching the 'infamous punishment' of imprisonment." Third, neither sanction comes into play "only" on a finding of scienter. The provisions under which the money penalties were imposed, allow for the assessment of a penalty against any person "who violates" any of the underlying banking statutes, without regard to the violator's state of mind. * * *

Fourth, the conduct for which OCC sanctions are imposed may also be criminal (and in this case formed the basis for petitioners' indictments). This fact is insufficient to render the money penalties and debarment sanctions criminally punitive, particularly in the double jeopardy context.

Finally, we recognize that the imposition of both money penalties and debarment sanctions will deter others from emulating petitioners' conduct, a traditional goal of criminal punishment. But the mere presence of this purpose is insufficient to render a sanction criminal, as deterrence "may serve civil as well as criminal goals." For example, the sanctions at issue here, while intended to deter future wrongdoing, also serve to promote the stability of the banking industry. To hold that the mere presence of a deterrent purpose renders such sanctions "criminal" for double jeopardy purposes would severely undermine the Government's ability to engage in effective regulation of institutions such as banks.

In sum, there simply is very little showing * * * that OCC money penalties and debarment sanctions are criminal. The Double Jeopardy Clause is therefore no obstacle to their trial on the pending indictments, and it may proceed.

The judgment of the Court of Appeals for the Tenth Circuit is accordingly

Affirmed.

JUSTICE STEVENS, concurring in the judgment.

* * * [In prior cases, we have] held that sanctions imposed in civil proceedings [may constitute] "punishment" barred by the Double Jeopardy Clause. * * * [T]he Government cannot use the "civil" label to escape entirely the Double Jeopardy Clause's command, as we have recognized for at least six decades. That proposition is extremely important because the States and the Federal Government have an enormous array of civil administrative sanctions at their disposal that are capable of being used to punish persons repeatedly for the same offense, violating the bedrock double jeopardy principle of finality. "The underlying idea, one that is deeply ingrained in at least the Anglo-American system of jurisprudence, is that the State with all its resources and power should not be allowed to make repeated attempts to convict an individual for an alleged offense, thereby subjecting him to embarrassment, expense and ordeal and compelling him to live in a continuing state of anxiety and insecurity. . . ." * * *

JUSTICE BREYER, with whom JUSTICE GINSBURG joins, concurring in the judgment.

* * * I disagree with [the Court's] reasoning in two respects. First, unlike the Court I would not say that "only the clearest proof" will "transform" into a criminal punishment what a legislature calls a "civil remedy." I understand that the Court has taken this language from earlier cases. But the limitation that the language suggests is not consistent with what the Court has actually done. Rather, in fact if not in theory, the Court has simply applied factors of the *Kennedy* variety to the matter at hand. * * * The "clearest proof" language is consequently misleading. * * *

Second, I would not decide now that a court should evaluate a statute only "on its face," rather than "assessing the character of the actual sanctions imposed." * * * That said, an analysis of the *Kennedy* factors still leads me to the conclusion that the statutory penalty in this case is not on its face a criminal penalty. Nor, in my view, does the application of the statute to the petitioners in this case amount to criminal punishment. I therefore concur in the judgment.

[JUSTICE SCALIA's concurring opinion and JUSTICE SOUTER's concurring opinion have been omitted.]

NOTE

In *United States v. Ursery*, 518 U.S. 267 (1996), the Supreme Court considered whether a civil forfeiture action following a prosecution for manufacturing marijuana constituted punishment for purposes of the Double Jeopardy Clause. The Court answered this question in the negative, concluding that *in rem* civil forfeitures are neither criminal nor "punishment" for double jeopardy purposes, and therefore the subsequent civil forfeiture action was not barred. *Id.* at 292.

E. MISTRIALS

A mistrial is a trial that is terminated before its normal conclusion. Whether the defendant can be retried following a mistrial depends upon various factors, including which party requested the mistrial. *Arizona v. Washington* and *Oregon v. Kennedy* outline the tests the Court has established for determining whether and when a defendant may be retried following a mistrial.

ARIZONA V. WASHINGTON
Supreme Court of the United States
434 U.S. 497, 98 S. Ct. 824, 54 L. Ed. 2d (1978)

JUSTICE STEVENS delivered the opinion of the Court. * * *

In 1971 respondent was found guilty of murdering a hotel night clerk. In 1973, the Superior Court of Pima County, Ariz., ordered a new trial because the prosecutor had withheld exculpatory evidence from the defense. The Arizona Supreme Court affirmed the new trial order in an unpublished opinion.

Respondent's second trial began in January 1975. During the *voir dire* examination of prospective jurors, the prosecutor made reference to the fact that some of the witnesses whose testimony the jurors would hear had testified in proceedings four years earlier. Defense counsel told the prospective jurors "that there was evidence hidden from [respondent] at the last trial."

In his opening statement, he made this point more forcefully:

You will hear testimony that notwithstanding the fact that we had a trial in May of 1971 in this matter, that the prosecutor hid those statements and didn't give those to the lawyer for George saying the man was Spanish speaking, didn't give those statements at all, hid them.

You will hear that that evidence was suppressed and hidden by the prosecutor in that case. You will hear that that evidence was purposely withheld. You will hear that because of the misconduct of the County Attorney at that time and because he withheld evidence, that the Supreme Court of Arizona granted a new trial in this case.

After opening statements were completed, the prosecutor moved for a mistrial. In colloquy during argument of the motion, the trial judge expressed the opinion that evidence concerning the reasons for the new trial, and specifically the ruling of the Arizona Supreme Court, was irrelevant to the issue of guilt or innocence and therefore inadmissible. Defense counsel asked for an opportunity "to find some law" that would support his belief that the Supreme Court opinion would be admissible. After further argument, the judge stated that he would withhold ruling on the admissibility of the evidence and denied the motion for mistrial. Two witnesses then testified.

The following morning the prosecutor renewed his mistrial motion. * * * [H]e argued that there was no theory on which the basis for the new trial ruling could be brought to the attention of the jury, that the prejudice to the jury could not be repaired by any cautionary instructions, and that a mistrial was a "manifest necessity." Defense counsel * * * argued that his comment was invited by the prosecutor's reference to the witnesses' earlier testimony and that any prejudice could be avoided by curative instructions. * * *

Ultimately the trial judge granted the motion, stating that his ruling was based upon defense counsel's remarks in his opening statement concerning the Arizona Supreme Court opinion. The trial judge did not expressly find that there was "manifest necessity" for a mistrial; nor did he expressly state that he had considered alternative solutions and concluded that none would be adequate. The Arizona Supreme Court refused to review the mistrial ruling. * * * [In federal court, Respondent filed a petition for habeas corpus, alleging that a retrial would violate Double Jeopardy. His petition was granted based upon the lack of express findings by the trial judge for the mistrial. The Ninth Circuit Court of Appeals affirmed.] * * *

We are persuaded that the Court of Appeals applied an inappropriate standard of review to mistrial rulings of this kind, and attached undue significance to the form of the ruling. We therefore reverse.

A State may not put a defendant in jeopardy twice for the same offense. The constitutional protection against double jeopardy unequivocally prohibits a second trial following an acquittal. The public interest in the finality of criminal judgments is so strong that an acquitted defendant may not be retried even though "the acquittal was based upon an egregiously erroneous foundation." If the innocence of the accused has been confirmed by a final judgment, the Constitution conclusively presumes that a second trial would be unfair.

Because jeopardy attaches before the judgment becomes final, the constitutional protection also embraces the defendant's "valued right to have his trial completed by a particular tribunal." The reasons why this "valued right" merits constitutional protection are worthy of repetition. Even if the first trial is not completed, a second prosecution may be grossly unfair. It increases the financial and emotional burden on the accused, prolongs the period in which he is stigmatized by an unresolved accusation of wrongdoing, and may even enhance the risk that an innocent defendant may be convicted. The danger of such unfairness to the defendant exists whenever a trial is aborted before it is completed. Consequently, as a general rule, the prosecutor is entitled to one, and only one, opportunity to require an accused to stand trial.

Unlike the situation in which the trial has ended in an acquittal or conviction, retrial is not automatically barred when a criminal proceeding is terminated without finally resolving the merits of the charges against the accused. Because of the variety of circumstances that may make it necessary to discharge a jury before a trial is concluded, and because those circumstances do not invariably create unfairness to the accused, his valued right to have the trial concluded by a particular tribunal is sometimes subordinate to the public interest in affording the prosecutor one full and fair opportunity to present his evidence to an impartial jury. Yet in view of the importance of the right, and the fact that it is frustrated by any mistrial, the prosecutor must shoulder the burden of justifying the mistrial if he is to avoid the double jeopardy bar. His burden is a heavy one. The prosecutor must demonstrate "manifest necessity" for any mistrial declared over the objection of the defendant.

The words "manifest necessity" appropriately characterize the magnitude of the prosecutor's burden. * * * Nevertheless, those words do not describe a standard that can be applied mechanically or without attention to the particular problem confronting the trial judge. Indeed, it is manifest that the key word "necessity" cannot be interpreted literally. * * * [W]e assume that there are degrees of necessity and we require a "high degree" before concluding that a mistrial is appropriate.

The question whether that "high degree" has been reached is answered more easily in some kinds of cases than in others. At one extreme are cases in which a prosecutor requests a mistrial in order to buttress weaknesses in his evidence. * * * [T]he prohibition against double jeopardy as it evolved in this country was plainly intended to condemn this "abhorrent" practice. * * *

Thus, the strictest scrutiny is appropriate when the basis for the mistrial is the unavailability of critical prosecution evidence, or when there is reason to believe that the prosecutor is using the superior resources of the State to harass or to achieve a tactical advantage over the accused.

At the other extreme is the mistrial premised upon the trial judge's belief that the jury is unable to reach a verdict, long considered the classic basis for a proper mistrial. * * * [W]ithout exception, the courts have held that the trial judge may discharge a genuinely deadlocked jury and require the defendant to submit to a second trial. This rule accords recognition to society's interest in giving the prosecution one complete opportunity to convict those who have violated its laws.

In this case the trial judge ordered a mistrial because the defendant's lawyer made improper and prejudicial remarks during his opening statement to the jury.[a] * * * An improper opening statement unquestionably tends to frustrate the public interest in having a just judgment reached by an impartial tribunal. * * * The trial judge, of course, may instruct the jury to disregard the improper comment. In extreme cases, he may discipline counsel, or even remove him from the trial * * *. Those actions, however, will not necessarily remove the risk of bias that may be created by improper argument. Unless unscrupulous defense counsel are to be allowed an unfair advantage, the trial judge must have the power to declare a mistrial in appropriate cases. The interest in orderly, impartial procedure would be impaired if he were deterred from exercising that power by a concern that any time a reviewing court disagreed with his assessment of the trial situation a retrial would automatically be barred. The adoption of a stringent standard of appellate review in this area, therefore, would seriously impede the trial judge in the proper performance of his "duty, in order to protect the integrity of the trial, to take prompt and affirmative action to stop . . . professional misconduct." * * *

There are compelling institutional considerations militating in favor of appellate deference to the trial judge's evaluation of the significance of possible juror bias. He has seen and heard the jurors during their *voir dire* examination. He is the judge most familiar with the evidence and the background of the case on trial. He has listened to the tone of the argument as it was delivered and has observed the apparent reaction of the jurors. In short, he is far more "conversant with the factors relevant to the determination" than any reviewing court can possibly be.

Our conclusion that a trial judge's decision to declare a mistrial based on his assessment of the prejudicial impact of improper argument is entitled to great deference does not, of course, end the inquiry. * * * [R]eviewing courts have an obligation to satisfy themselves that, * * * the trial judge exercised "sound discretion" in declaring a mistrial.

Thus, if a trial judge acts irrationally or irresponsibly, his action cannot be condoned. But our review of this record indicates that this was not such a case. Defense counsel aired improper and highly prejudicial

---

[a] The Court suggests that defense counsel acted improperly by referencing the fact that the prosecutor, at the original trial, withheld evidence that he was required to disclose to the defense. As we saw in the chapter on Discovery, however, one could argue that defense counsel was simply telling the jury what in fact the prosecutor did at the previous trial. Recall that Professor Cynthia Jones suggests defense counsel should be permitted not only to inform the jury when a prosecutor has intentionally withheld *Brady* evidence but also to argue that such prosecutorial misconduct suggests consciousness of a weak case because the prosecutor is the one who has engaged in misconduct in such cases. *See* Cynthia E. Jones, *A Reason to Doubt: The Suppression of Evidence and the Inference of Innocence*, 100 J. CRIM. L. & CRIMINOLOGY 415 (2010).

evidence before the jury, the possible impact of which the trial judge was in the best position to assess. The trial judge did not act precipitately in response to the prosecutor's request for a mistrial. On the contrary, * * * he gave both defense counsel and the prosecutor full opportunity to explain their positions on the propriety of a mistrial. We are therefore persuaded by the record that the trial judge acted responsibly and deliberately, and accorded careful consideration to respondent's interest in having the trial concluded in a single proceeding. Since he exercised "sound discretion" in handling the sensitive problem of possible juror bias created by the improper comment of defense counsel, the mistrial order is supported by the "high degree" of necessity which is required in a case of this kind. Neither party has a right to have his case decided by a jury which may be tainted by bias; in these circumstances, "the public's interest in fair trials designed to end in just judgements" must prevail over the defendant's "valued right" to have his trial concluded before the first jury impaneled.

One final matter requires consideration. The absence of an explicit finding of "manifest necessity" appears to have been determinative for the District Court and may have been so for the Court of Appeals. If those courts regarded that omission as critical, they required too much. Since the record provides sufficient justification for the state-court ruling, the failure to explain that ruling more completely does not render it constitutionally defective.

Review of any trial court decision, is of course, facilitated by findings and by an explanation of the reasons supporting the decision. No matter how desirable such procedural assistance may be, it is not constitutionally mandated in a case such as this. The basis for the trial judge's mistrial order is adequately disclosed by the record, which includes the extensive argument of counsel prior to the judge's ruling. The state trial judge's mistrial declaration is not subject to collateral attack in a federal court simply because he failed to find "manifest necessity" in those words or to articulate on the record all the factors which informed the deliberate exercise of his discretion. * * *

JUSTICE BLACKMUN concurs in the result.

JUSTICE MARSHALL, with whom JUSTICE BRENNAN joins, dissenting. * * *

My disagreement with the majority is a narrow one. * * * Where I part ways from the Court is in its assumption that an "assessment of the prejudicial impact of improper argument," sufficient to support the need for a mistrial may be implied from this record. * * *

I do not propose that the Constitution invariably requires a trial judge to make findings of necessity on the record to justify the declaration of a mistrial over a defendant's objections. * * * What the "manifest necessity" doctrine does require, in my view, is that the record make clear either that there were no meaningful and practical alternatives to a mistrial, or that the trial court scrupulously considered available alternatives and found all wanting but a termination of the proceedings. The record here * * * does neither. * * *

Had the court here explored alternatives on the record, or made a finding of substantial and incurable prejudice or other "manifest necessity," this would be a different case and one in which I would agree with both the majority's reasoning and its result. On this ambiguous record, however, the absence of any such finding—and indeed of any express indication that the trial court applied the manifest-necessity doctrine—leaves open the substantial possibility that there was in fact no need to terminate the proceedings. While the Court states that a "high degree" of necessity is required before a mistrial may properly be granted, its reading of the record here is inconsistent with this principle. * * *

[JUSTICE WHITE's dissenting opinion has been omitted.]

OREGON V. KENNEDY
Supreme Court of the United States
456 U.S. 667, 102 S. Ct. 2083, 72 L. Ed. 2d 416 (1982)

JUSTICE REHNQUIST delivered the opinion of the Court. * * *

Respondent was charged with the theft of an oriental rug. During his first trial, the State called an expert witness on the subject of Middle Eastern rugs to testify as to the value and the identity of the rug in question. On cross-examination, respondent's attorney apparently attempted to establish bias on the part of the expert witness by asking him whether he had filed a criminal complaint against respondent. The witness eventually acknowledged this fact, but explained that no action had been taken on his complaint. On redirect examination, the prosecutor sought to elicit the reasons why the witness had filed a complaint against respondent, but the trial court sustained a series of objections to this line of inquiry. The following colloquy then ensued:

Prosecutor: Have you ever done business with the Kennedys?

Witness: No, I have not.

Prosecutor: Is that because he is a crook?

The trial court then granted respondent's motion for a mistrial.

When the State later sought to retry respondent, he moved to dismiss the charges because of double jeopardy. After a hearing at which the prosecutor testified, the trial court found as a fact that "it was not the intention of the prosecutor in this case to cause a mistrial." On the basis of this finding, the trial court held that double jeopardy principles did not bar retrial, and respondent was then tried and convicted.

Respondent then successfully appealed to the Oregon Court of Appeals, which sustained his double jeopardy claim. * * * The Court of Appeals accepted the trial court's finding that it was not the intent of the prosecutor to cause a mistrial. Nevertheless, the court held that retrial was barred because the prosecutor's conduct in this case constituted what it viewed as "overreaching." * * *

Where the trial is terminated over the objection of the defendant, the classical test for lifting the double jeopardy bar to a second trial is the "manifest necessity" standard first enunciated in Justice Story's opinion for the Court in *United States v. Perez*. *Perez* dealt with the most common form of "manifest necessity": a mistrial declared by the judge following the jury's declaration that it was unable to reach a verdict. While other situations have been recognized by our cases as meeting the "manifest necessity" standard, the hung jury remains the prototypical example. The "manifest necessity" standard provides sufficient protection to the defendant's interests in having his case finally decided by the jury first selected while at the same time maintaining "the public's interest in fair trials designed to end in just judgments."

But in the case of a mistrial declared at the behest of the defendant, quite different principles come into play. Here the defendant himself has elected to terminate the proceedings against him, and the "manifest necessity" standard has no place in the application of the Double Jeopardy Clause. * * *

Our cases, however, have indicated that even where the defendant moves for a mistrial, there is a narrow exception to the rule that the Double Jeopardy Clause is no bar to retrial. The circumstances under which respondent's first trial was terminated require us to delineate the bounds of that exception more fully than we have in previous cases.

Since one of the principal threads making up the protection embodied in the Double Jeopardy Clause is the right of the defendant to have his trial completed before the first jury empaneled to try him, it may be wondered as a matter of original inquiry why the defendant's election to terminate the first trial by his own motion should not be deemed a renunciation of that right for all purposes. We have recognized, however, that there would be great difficulty in applying such a rule where the prosecutor's actions giving rise to the motion for mistrial were done "in order to goad the [defendant] into requesting a mistrial." In such a case, the defendant's valued right to complete his trial before the first jury would be a hollow shell if the inevitable motion for mistrial were held to prevent a later invocation of the bar of double jeopardy in all circumstances. But the precise phrasing of the circumstances which *will* allow a defendant to interpose the defense of double jeopardy to a second prosecution where the first has terminated on his own motion for a mistrial have been stated with less than crystal clarity in our cases which deal with this area of the law.

In *United States v. Dinitz* we said:

The Double Jeopardy Clause does protect a defendant against governmental actions intended to provoke mistrial requests and thereby to subject defendants to the substantial burdens imposed by multiple prosecutions.

* * * [I]mmediately following the quoted language we went on to say:

[The Double Jeopardy Clause] bars retrials where 'bad-faith conduct by judge or prosecutor,' threatens the '[h]arassment of an accused by successive prosecutions or declaration of a mistrial so as to afford the prosecution a more favorable opportunity to convict' the defendant.

The language just quoted would seem to broaden the test from one of *intent* to provoke a motion for a mistrial to a more generalized standard of "bad faith conduct" or "harassment" on the part of the judge or prosecutor. It was upon this language that the Oregon Court of Appeals apparently relied in concluding that the prosecutor's colloquy with the expert witness in this case amount to "overreaching."

The difficulty with the more general standards which would permit a broader exception than one merely based on intent is that they offer virtually no standards for their application. Every act on the part of a rational prosecutor during a trial is designed to "prejudice" the defendant by placing before the judge or jury evidence leading to a finding of his guilt. Given the complexity of the rules of evidence, it will be a rare trial of any complexity in which some proffered evidence by the prosecutor or by the defendant's attorney will not be found objectionable by the trial court. Most such objections are undoubtedly curable by simply refusing to allow the proffered evidence to be admitted, or in the case of a particular line of inquiry taken by counsel with a witness, by an admonition to desist from a particular line of inquiry.

More serious infractions on the part of the prosecutor may provoke a motion for mistrial on the part of the defendant, and may in the view of the trial court warrant the granting of such a motion. The "overreaching" standard applied by the court below and urged today by Justice STEVENS, however, would add another classification of prosecutorial error, one requiring dismissal of the indictment, but without supplying any standard by which to assess that error.

By contrast, a standard that examines the intent of the prosecutor, though certainly not entirely free from practical difficulties, is a manageable standard to apply. It merely calls for the court to make a finding of fact. Inferring the existence or nonexistence of intent from objective facts and circumstances is a familiar process in our criminal justice system. When it is remembered that resolution of double jeopardy questions by state trial courts are reviewable not only within the state court system, but in the federal court system on habeas corpus as well, the desirability of an easily applied principle is apparent.

Prosecutorial conduct that might be viewed as harassment or overreaching, even if sufficient to justify a mistrial on defendant's motion, therefore, does not bar retrial absent intent on the part of the prosecutor to subvert the protections afforded by the Double Jeopardy Clause. A defendant's motion for a mistrial constitutes "a deliberate election on his part to forgo his valued right to have his guilt or innocence determined before the first trier of fact." Where prosecutorial error even of a degree sufficient to warrant a mistrial has occurred, "[t]he important consideration, for purposes of the Double Jeopardy Clause, is that the defendant retain primary control over the course to be followed in the event of such error." Only where the governmental conduct in question is intended to "goad" the defendant into moving for a mistrial may a defendant raise the bar of double jeopardy to a second trial after having succeeded in aborting the first on his own motion.

Were we to embrace the broad and somewhat amorphous standard adopted by the Oregon Court of Appeals, we are not sure that criminal defendants as a class would be aided. Knowing that the granting of the defendant's motion for mistrial would all but inevitably bring with it an attempt to bar a second trial on grounds of double jeopardy, the judge presiding over the first trial might well be more loath to grant a defendant's motion for mistrial. If a mistrial were in fact warranted under the applicable law, of course, the defendant could in many instances successfully appeal a judgment of conviction on the same grounds that he urged a mistrial, and the Double Jeopardy Clause would present no bar to retrial. But some of the advantages secured to him by the Double Jeopardy Clause—the freedom from extended anxiety, and the necessity to confront the government's case only once—would be to a large extent lost in the process of trial to verdict, reversal on appeal, and subsequent retrial.

* * * We do not by this opinion lay down a flat rule that where a defendant in a criminal trial successfully moves for a mistrial, he may not thereafter invoke the bar of double jeopardy against a second trial. But we do hold that the circumstances under which such a defendant may invoke the bar of double jeopardy in a second effort to try him are limited to those cases in which the conduct giving rise to the successful motion for a mistrial was intended to provoke the defendant into moving for a mistrial.

Since the Oregon trial court found, and the Oregon Court of Appeals accepted, that the prosecutorial conduct culminating in the termination of the first trial in this case was not so intended by the prosecutor, that is the end of the matter for purposes of the Double Jeopardy Clause of the Fifth Amendment to the United States Constitution. The judgment of the Oregon Court of Appeals is reversed, and the cause is remanded for further proceedings not inconsistent with this opinion. * * *

JUSTICE POWELL, concurring.

I join the Court's opinion holding that the *intention* of a prosecutor determines whether his conduct, viewed by the defendant and the court as justifying a mistrial, bars a retrial of the defendant under the Double Jeopardy Clause. Because "subjective" intent often may be unknowable, I emphasize that a court—in considering a double jeopardy motion—should rely primarily upon the objective facts and circumstances of the particular case.

In the present case the mistrial arose from the prosecutor's conduct in pursuing a line of redirect examination of a key witness. The Oregon Court of Appeals identified a single question as constituting "overreaching" so serious as to bar a retrial. Yet, there are few vigorously contested lawsuits—whether criminal or civil—in which improper questions are not asked. Our system *is* adversarial and vigorous advocacy is encouraged.

Nevertheless, this would have been a close case for me if there had been substantial factual evidence of intent beyond the question itself. Here, however, other relevant facts and circumstances strongly support the view that prosecutorial intent to cause a mistrial was absent. First, there was no sequence of overreaching prior to the single prejudicial question. Moreover, it is evident from a colloquy between counsel and the court, out of the presence of the jury, that the prosecutor not only resisted, but also was surprised by, the defendant's motion for a mistrial. Finally, at the hearing on respondent's double jeopardy motion, the prosecutor testified—and the trial found as a fact and the appellate court agreed—that there was no " 'intention . . . to cause a mistrial.' "

In view of these circumstances, the Double Jeopardy Clause provides no bar to retrial.

JUSTICE STEVENS, with whom JUSTICE BRENNAN, JUSTICE MARSHALL, and JUSTICE BLACKMUN join, concurring in the judgment. * * *

The Double Jeopardy Clause represents a constitutional policy of finality for the defendant's benefit in criminal proceedings. If the defendant is acquitted by the jury, or if he is convicted and the conviction is upheld on appeal, he may not be prosecuted again for the same offense. The defendant's interest in finality is not confined to final judgments; he also has a protected interest in having his guilt or innocence decided in one proceeding. That interest must be balanced against society's interest in affording the prosecutor one full and fair opportunity to present his evidence to the jury. Our decisions in the mistrial setting accordingly have accommodated the defendant's double jeopardy interests with legitimate prosecutorial interests.

The accommodation is reflected in two general rules that govern the permissibility of reprosecution after a mistrial. Which general rule applies turns on whether the defendant has retained control over the course to be followed once error has substantially tainted the initial proceeding. When a mistrial is declared over the defendant's objection, the general rule is that retrial is barred. An exception to this general rule exists for cases in which the mistrial was justified by "manifest necessity." The other general rule is that the defendant's motion for, or consent to, a mistrial removes any double jeopardy bar to reprosecution. There is an exception to this rule for cases in which the prosecutor intended to provoke a mistrial or otherwise engaged in "overreaching" or "harassment." The prosecutor has the burden of proving the former exception for manifest necessity, and the defendant has the burden of proving the latter exception for overreaching. * * *

Today the Court once again recognizes that the exception properly encompasses the situation in which the prosecutor commits prejudicial error with the intent to provoke a mistrial. But the Court reaches out to limit the exception to that one situation, rejecting the previous recognition that prosecutorial overreaching or harassment is also within the exception.

Even if I agreed that the balance of competing interests tipped in favor of a bar to reprosecution only in the situation in which the prosecutor intended to provoke a mistrial, I would not subscribe to a standard that conditioned such a bar on the determination that the prosecutor harbored such intent when he committed prejudicial error. It is almost inconceivable that a defendant could prove that the prosecutor's deliberate misconduct was motivated by an intent to provoke a mistrial instead of an intent simply to prejudice the defendant. The defendant must shoulder a strong burden to establish a bar to reprosecution when he has consented to the mistrial, but the Court's subjective intent standard would eviscerate the exception. * * *

To invoke the exception for overreaching, a court need not divine the exact motivation for the prosecutorial error. It is sufficient that the court is persuaded that egregious prosecutorial misconduct has rendered unmeaningful the defendant's choice to continue or to abort the proceeding. * * *

[JUSTICE BRENNAN's opinion, concurring in the judgment, has been omitted.]

F. RETRIAL FOLLOWING ACQUITTALS, DISMISSALS, AND CONVICTIONS

As a general matter, a defendant may not be subjected to retrial following an acquittal. In *United States v. Scott*, the Court explains whether and when a dismissal of the indictment counts as an acquittal for double jeopardy purposes.

Conversely, a defendant who has been convicted can usually be retried after successfully appealing a conviction. In *Burks v. United States*, the Court considers whether this rule permitting retrial following a successful appeal applies when a defendant's conviction is reversed due to insufficiency of the evidence as opposed to trial error.

UNITED STATES v. SCOTT
Supreme Court of the United States
437 U.S. 82, 98 S. Ct. 2187, 57 L. Ed. 2d 65 (1978)

JUSTICE REHNQUIST delivered the opinion of the Court.

On March 5, 1975, respondent, a member of the police force in Muskegon, Mich., was charged * * * with distribution of various narcotics. Both before his trial, and twice during the trial, respondent moved to dismiss the two counts of the indictment which concerned transactions that took place during the preceding September, on the ground that his defense had been prejudiced by preindictment delay. At the close of all the evidence, the court granted respondent's motion. * * *

The Government sought to appeal the dismissals. [The Court of Appeals], relying on our opinion in *United States v. Jenkins*, concluded that any further prosecution of respondent was barred by the Double Jeopardy Clause of the Fifth Amendment, and therefore dismissed the appeal. We granted certiorari to give further consideration to the applicability of the Double Jeopardy Clause to Government appeals from orders granting defense motions to terminate a trial before verdict. * * *

The origin and history of the Double Jeopardy Clause are hardly a matter of dispute. The constitutional provision had its origin in the three common-law pleas of *autrefois acquit, autrefois convict,* and pardon. These three pleas prevented the retrial of a person who had previously been acquitted, convicted, or pardoned for the same offense. As this Court has described the purpose underlying the prohibition against double jeopardy:

> The underlying idea, one that is deeply ingrained in at least the Anglo-American system of jurisprudence, is that the State with all its resources and power should not be allowed to make repeated attempts to convict an individual for an alleged offense, thereby subjecting him to embarrassment, expense and ordeal

and compelling him to live in a continuing state of anxiety and insecurity, as well as enhancing the possibility that even though innocent he may be found guilty.

*** At the time the Fifth Amendment was adopted, its principles were easily applied, since most criminal prosecutions proceeded to final judgment, and neither the United States nor the defendant had any right to appeal an adverse verdict. The verdict in such a case was unquestionably final, and could be raised in bar against any further prosecution for the same offense.

*** It was not until 1889 that Congress permitted criminal defendants to seek a writ of error in this Court, and then only in capital cases. Only then did it become necessary for this Court to deal with the issues presented by the challenge of verdicts on appeal.

And, in the very first case presenting the issues, *United States v. Ball,* the Court established principles that have been adhered to ever since. Three persons had been tried together for murder; two were convicted, the other acquitted. This Court reversed the convictions, finding the indictment fatally defective whereupon all three defendants were tried again. This time all three were convicted and they again sought review here. This Court held that the Double Jeopardy Clause precluded further prosecution of the defendant who had been *acquitted* at the original trial but that it posed no such bar to the prosecution of those defendants who had been *convicted* in the earlier proceeding. ***

Although *Ball* firmly established that a successful appeal of a conviction precludes a subsequent plea of double jeopardy, the opinion shed no light on whether a judgment of acquittal could be reversed on appeal consistently with the Double Jeopardy Clause. *** [I]n *United States v. Martin Linen Supply Co.,* [we] held that the Government could not appeal the granting of a motion to acquit *** where a second trial would be required upon remand. The Court, quoting language in *Ball,* stated: "Perhaps the most fundamental rule in the history of double jeopardy jurisprudence has been that '[a] verdict of acquittal ... could not be reviewed, on error or otherwise, without putting [a defendant] twice in jeopardy, and thereby violating the Constitution.'"

These, then, at least, are two venerable principles of double jeopardy jurisprudence. The successful appeal of a judgment of conviction, on any ground other than the insufficiency of the evidence to support the verdict, poses no bar to further prosecution on the same charge. A judgment of acquittal, whether based on a jury verdict of not guilty or on a ruling by the court that the evidence is insufficient to convict, may not be appealed and terminates the prosecution when a second trial would be necessitated by a reversal. *** To permit a second trial after an acquittal, however mistaken the acquittal may have been, would present an unacceptably high risk that the Government, with its vastly superior resources, might wear down the defendant so that "even though innocent, he may be found guilty." On the other hand, to require a criminal defendant to stand trial again after he has successfully invoked a statutory right of appeal to upset his first conviction is not an act of governmental oppression of the sort against which the Double Jeopardy Clause was intended to protect. * * *

Although the primary purpose of the Double Jeopardy Clause was to protect the integrity of a final judgment, this Court has also developed a body of law guarding the separate but related interest of a defendant in avoiding multiple prosecutions even where no final determination of guilt or innocence has been made. Such interests may be involved in two different situations: the first, in which the trial judge declares a mistrial; the second, in which the trial judge terminates the proceedings favorably to the defendant on a basis not related to factual guilt or innocence. * * *

We turn now to the relationship between the Double Jeopardy Clause and reprosecution of a defendant who has successfully obtained not a mistrial but a termination of the trial in his favor before any determination of factual guilt or innocence. Unlike the typical mistrial, the granting of a motion such as this obviously contemplates that the proceedings will terminate then and there in favor of the defendant. The prosecution, if it wishes to reinstate the proceedings in the face of such a ruling, ordinarily must seek reversal of the decision of the trial court. * * *

In the present case, the District Court's dismissal of the first count of the indictment was based upon a claim of preindictment delay and not on the court's conclusion that the Government had not produced sufficient evidence to establish the guilt of the defendant. Respondent Scott points out quite correctly that he had moved to dismiss the indictment on this ground prior to trial, and that had the District Court chosen to grant it at that time the Government could have appealed the ruling * * *.

* * * It is quite true that the Government with all its resources and power should not be allowed to make repeated attempts to convict an individual for an alleged offense. * * * [A] defendant once acquitted may not be again subjected to trial without violating the Double Jeopardy Clause.

But that situation is obviously a far cry from the present case, where the Government was quite willing to continue with its production of evidence to show the defendant guilty before the jury first empaneled to try him, but the defendant elected to seek termination of the trial on grounds unrelated to guilt or innocence. This is scarcely a picture of an all-powerful state relentlessly pursuing a defendant who had either been found not guilty or who had at least insisted on having the issue of guilt submitted to the first trier of fact. It is instead a picture of a defendant who chooses to avoid conviction and imprisonment, not because of his assertion that the

Government has failed to make out a case against him, but because of a legal claim that the Government's case against him must fail even though it might satisfy the trier of fact that he was guilty beyond a reasonable doubt. * * *

We have previously noted that "the trial judge's characterization of his own action cannot control the classification of the action." * * * Rather, a defendant is acquitted only when "the ruling of the judge, whatever its label, actually represents a resolution [in the defendant's favor], correct or not, of some or all of the factual elements of the offense charged." Where the court, before the jury returns a verdict, enters a judgment of acquittal * * *, appeal will be barred only when "it is plain that the District Court ... evaluated the Government's evidence and determined that it was legally insufficient to sustain a conviction." * * *

We think that in a case such as this the defendant, by deliberately choosing to seek termination of the proceedings against him on a basis unrelated to factual guilt or innocence of the offense of which he is accused, suffers no injury cognizable under the Double Jeopardy Clause if the Government is permitted to appeal from such a ruling of the trial court in favor of the defendant. * * * [W]e conclude that the Double Jeopardy Clause, which guards against Government oppression, does not relieve a defendant from the consequences of his voluntary choice.

* * * [W]here the defendant * * * obtains the termination of the proceedings against him in the trial court without any finding by a court or jury as to his guilt or innocence[,] [h]e has not been "deprived" of his valued right to go to the first jury; only the public has been deprived of its valued right to "one complete opportunity to convict those who have violated its laws." No interest protected by the Double Jeopardy Clause is invaded when the Government is allowed to appeal and seek reversal of such a midtrial termination of the proceedings in a manner favorable to the defendant. * * *

Here, "the lessons of experience" indicate that Government appeals from midtrial dismissals requested by the defendant would significantly advance the public interest in assuring that each defendant shall be subject to a just judgment on the merits of his case, without "enhancing the possibility that even though innocent he may be found guilty." * * *

JUSTICE BRENNAN, with whom JUSTICE WHITE, JUSTICE MARSHALL, and JUSTICE STEVENS join, dissenting. * * *

I dissent. * * * The Court's attempt to draw a distinction between "true acquittals" and other final judgments favorable to the accused, quite simply, is unsupportable in either logic or policy. * * *

While the Double Jeopardy Clause often has the effect of protecting the accused's interest in the finality of particular favorable determinations, this is not its objective. For the Clause often permits Government appeals from final judgments favorable to the accused. *See United States v. Wilson* (whether or not final judgment was an acquittal, Government may appeal if reversal would not necessitate a retrial). The purpose of the Clause, which the Court today fails sufficiently to appreciate, is to protect the accused against the agony and risks attendant upon undergoing more than one criminal trial for any single offense. * * * Society's "willingness to limit the Government to a single criminal proceeding to vindicate its very vital interest in enforcement of criminal laws" bespeaks society's recognition of the gross unfairness of requiring the accused to undergo the strain and agony of more than one trial for any single offense. Accordingly, the policies of the Double Jeopardy Clause mandate that the Government be afforded but one complete opportunity to convict an accused and that when the first proceeding terminates in a final judgment favorable to the defendant any retrial be barred. The rule as to acquittals can only be understood as simply an application of this larger principle.

Judgments of acquittal normally result from jury or bench verdicts of not guilty. In such cases, the acquittal represents the factfinder's conclusion that, under the controlling legal principles, the evidence does not establish that the defendant can be convicted of the offense charged in the indictment. But the judgment does not necessarily establish the criminal defendant's lack of criminal culpability; the acquittal may result from erroneous evidentiary rulings or erroneous interpretations of governing legal principles induced by the defense. Yet the Double Jeopardy Clause bars a second trial.

* * * [T]he Court's new theory [is] that a criminal defendant who seeks to avoid conviction on a "ground unrelated to factual innocence" somehow stands on a different constitutional footing from a defendant whose participation in his criminal trial creates a situation in which a judgment of acquittal has to be entered. This premise is simply untenable. * * * The rule prohibiting retrials following acquittals does not and could not rest on a conclusion that the accused was factually innocent in any meaningful sense.

* * * [T]he reasons that bar a retrial following an acquittal are equally applicable to a final judgment entered on a ground "unrelated to factual innocence." The heavy personal strain of the second trial is the same in either case. So too is the risk that, though innocent, the defendant may be found guilty at a second trial. If the appeal is allowed in either situation, the Government will, following any reversal, not only obtain the benefit of the favorable appellate ruling but also be permitted to shore up any other weak points of its case and obtain all the other advantages at the second trial that the Double Jeopardy Clause was designed to forbid.

It is regrettable that the Court should introduce such confusion in an area of the law that, until today, had been crystal clear. * * * [T]oday's decision fashions an entirely arbitrary distinction that creates precisely the evils that the Double Jeopardy Clause was designed to prevent. I would affirm the judgment of the Court of Appeals.

BURKS V. UNITED STATES
Supreme Court of the United States
437 U.S. 1, 98 S. Ct. 2141, 57 L. Ed. 2d 1 (1978)

CHIEF JUSTICE BURGER delivered the opinion of the Court.

We granted certiorari to resolve the question of whether an accused may be subjected to a second trial when conviction in a prior trial was reversed by an appellate court solely for lack of sufficient evidence to sustain the jury's verdict.

Petitioner Burks was tried in the United States District Court for the crime of robbing a federally insured bank by use of a dangerous weapon * * *. Burks' principal defense was insanity. To prove this claim petitioner produced three expert witnesses who testified, albeit with differing diagnoses of his mental condition, that he suffered from a mental illness at the time of the robbery, which rendered him substantially incapable of conforming his conduct to the requirements of the law. In rebuttal the Government offered the testimony of two experts, one of whom testified that although petitioner possessed a character disorder, he was not mentally ill. The other prosecution witness acknowledged a character disorder in petitioner, but gave a rather ambiguous answer to the question of whether Burks had been capable of conforming his conduct to the law. Lay witnesses also testified for the Government, expressing their opinion that petitioner appeared to be capable of normal functioning and was sane at the time of the alleged offense.

Before the case was submitted to the jury, the court denied a motion for a judgment of acquittal. The jury found Burks guilty as charged. * * * On appeal petitioner narrowed the issues by admitting the affirmative factual elements of the charge against him, leaving only his claim concerning criminal responsibility to be resolved. With respect to this point, the Court of Appeals agreed with petitioner's claim that the evidence was insufficient to support the verdict and reversed his conviction, [explaining that] the prosecution's evidence with respect to Burks' mental condition, even when viewed in the light most favorable to the Government, did not "effectively rebu[t]" petitioner's proof with respect to insanity and criminal responsibility. * * *

Petitioner's argument is straightforward. He contends that the Court of Appeals' holding was nothing more or less than a decision that the District Court had erred by not granting his motion for a judgment of acquittal. By implication, he argues, the appellate reversal was the operative equivalent of a district court's judgment of acquittal, entered either before or after verdict. Petitioner points out, however, that had the District Court found the evidence at the first trial inadequate, as the Court of Appeals said it should have done, a second trial would violate the Double Jeopardy Clause of the Fifth Amendment. Therefore, he maintains, it makes no difference that the determination of evidentiary insufficiency was made by a *reviewing* court since the double jeopardy considerations are the same, regardless of which court decides that a judgment of acquittal is in order.

The position advanced by petitioner has not been embraced by our prior holdings. * * * It is unquestionably true that the Court of Appeals' decision "represente[d] a resolution, correct or not, of some or all of the factual elements of the offense charged." By deciding that the Government had failed to come forward with sufficient proof of petitioner's capacity to be responsible for criminal acts, that court was clearly saying that Burks' criminal culpability had not been established. If the District Court had so held in the first instance, as the reviewing court said it should have done, a judgment of acquittal would have been entered and, of course, petitioner could not be retried for the same offense. * * * [I]t should make no difference that the *reviewing* court, rather than the trial court, determined the evidence to be insufficient. The appellate decision unmistakably meant that the District Court had erred in failing to grant a judgment of acquittal. To hold otherwise would create a purely arbitrary distinction between those in petitioner's position and others who would enjoy the benefit of a correct decision by the District Court.

The Double Jeopardy Clause forbids a second trial for the purpose of affording the prosecution another opportunity to supply evidence which it failed to muster in the first proceeding. This is central to the objective of the prohibition against successive trials. The Clause does not allow "the State . . . to make repeated attempts to convict an individual for an alleged offense," since "[t]he constitutional prohibition against 'double jeopardy' was designed to protect an individual from being subjected to the hazards of trial and possible conviction more than once for an alleged offense." * * *

United States v. Ball * * * provides a logical starting point for unraveling the conceptual confusion arising from [several] cases * * *. This is especially true since *Ball* appears to represent the first instance in which this Court considered in any detail the double jeopardy implications of an appellate reversal.

Ball came before the Court twice, the first occasion being on writ of error from federal convictions for murder. On this initial review, those defendants who had been found guilty obtained a reversal of their convictions due to a fatally defective indictment. On remand after appeal, the trial court dismissed the flawed indictment and proceeded to retry the defendants on a new indictment. They were again convicted and the defendants came once more to this Court, arguing that their second trial was barred because of former jeopardy. The Court rejected this plea in a brief statement:

> [A] defendant, who procures a judgment against him upon an indictment to be set aside, may be tried anew upon the same indictment, or upon another indictment, for the same offence of which he had been convicted.

The reversal in *Ball* was therefore based not on insufficiency of evidence but rather on trial error, *i.e.*, failure to dismiss a faulty indictment. Moreover, the cases cited as authority by *Ball* were ones involving trial errors. We have no doubt that *Ball* was correct in allowing a new trial to rectify *trial error*:

> The principle that [the Double Jeopardy Clause] does not preclude the Government's retrying a defendant whose conviction is set aside because of an *error in the proceedings* leading to conviction is a well-established part of our constitutional jurisprudence. * * *

As we have seen * * *, the cases which have arisen since *Ball* generally do not distinguish between reversals due to trial error and those resulting from evidentiary insufficiency. We believe, however, that the failure to make this distinction has contributed substantially to the present state of conceptual confusion existing in this area of the law. Consequently, it is important to consider carefully the respective roles of these two types of reversals in double jeopardy analysis. Various rationales have been advanced to support the policy of allowing retrial to correct trial error, but in our view the most reasonable justification is * * *:

> It would be a high price indeed for society to pay were every accused granted immunity from punishment because of any defect sufficient to constitute reversible error in the proceedings leading to conviction.

In short, reversal for trial error, as distinguished from evidentiary insufficiency, does not constitute a decision to the effect that the government has failed to prove its case. As such, it implies nothing with respect to the guilt or innocence of the defendant. Rather, it is a determination that a defendant has been convicted through a judicial process which is defective in some fundamental respect, *e. g.*, incorrect receipt or rejection of evidence, incorrect instructions, or prosecutorial misconduct. When this occurs, the accused has a strong interest in obtaining a fair readjudication of his guilt free from error, just as society maintains a valid concern for insuring [sic] that the guilty are punished.

The same cannot be said when a defendant's conviction has been overturned due to a failure of proof at trial, in which case the prosecution cannot complain of prejudice, for it has been given one fair opportunity to offer whatever proof it could assemble. Moreover, such an appellate reversal means that the government's case was so lacking that it should not have even been *submitted* to the jury. Since we necessarily afford absolute finality to a jury's *verdict* of acquittal—no matter how erroneous its decision—it is difficult to conceive how society has any greater interest in retrying a defendant when, on review, it is decided as a matter of law that the jury could not properly have returned a verdict of guilty.

The importance of a reversal on grounds of evidentiary insufficiency for purposes of inquiry under the Double Jeopardy Clause is underscored by the fact that a federal court's role in deciding whether a case should be considered by the jury is quite limited. Even the trial court, which has heard the testimony of witnesses first hand, is not to weigh the evidence or assess the credibility of witnesses when it judges the merits of a motion for acquittal. The prevailing rule has long been that a district judge is to submit a case to the jury if the evidence and inferences therefrom most favorable to the prosecution would warrant the jury's finding the defendant guilty beyond a reasonable doubt. Obviously a federal appellate court applies no higher a standard; rather, it must sustain the verdict if there is substantial evidence, viewed in the light most favorable to the Government, to uphold the jury's decision. While this is not the appropriate occasion to re-examine in detail the standards for appellate reversal on grounds of insufficient evidence, it is apparent that such a decision will be confined to cases where the prosecution's failure is clear. Given the requirements for entry of a judgment of acquittal, the purposes of the Clause would be negated were we to afford the government an opportunity for the proverbial "second bite at the apple."

In our view it makes no difference that a defendant has sought a new trial as one of his remedies, or even as the sole remedy. It cannot be meaningfully said that a person "waives" his right to a judgment of acquittal by moving for a new trial. * * * Since we hold today that the Double Jeopardy Clause precludes a second trial once the reviewing court has found the evidence legally insufficient, the only "just" remedy available for that court is the direction of a judgment of acquittal. To the extent that our prior decisions suggest that by moving for a new trial, a defendant waives his right to a judgment of acquittal on the basis of evidentiary insufficiency, those cases are overruled. * * *

JUSTICE BLACKMUN took no part in the consideration or decision of this case.

G. JURY NULLIFICATION

Jury nullification occurs when a jury votes to acquit the defendant despite evidence that the defendant is guilty of the charged offense. The Double Jeopardy Clause of the Fifth Amendment prohibits reversal of a jury's decision to acquit, even if there is overwhelming evidence of guilt and it appears that the jury has engaged in jury nullification. In the first excerpt below, *Racially Based Jury Nullification: Black Power in the Criminal Justice System*, Paul Butler outlines the history of jury nullification and then proposes that African-American jurors engage in racially based jury nullification. In *The Dangers of Race-Based Jury Nullification: A Response to Professor Butler*, Andrew Leipold provides a strong counter to Butler's proposal.

RACIALLY BASED JURY NULLIFICATION: BLACK POWER IN THE CRIMINAL JUSTICE SYSTEM
Paul Butler
105 Yale L.J. 677 (1995)

* * *

II. B. *Jury Nullification*

When a jury disregards evidence presented at trial and acquits an otherwise guilty defendant because the jury objects to the law that the defendant violated or to the application of the law to that defendant, it has practiced jury nullification. * * * I argue that it is both lawful and morally right that black jurors consider race in reaching verdicts in criminal cases.

1. *What Is Jury Nullification?* * * *

In the United States, the doctrine of jury nullification originally was based on the common law idea that the function of a jury was, broadly, to decide justice, which included judging the law as well as the facts. If jurors believed that applying a law would lead to an unjust conviction, they were not compelled to convict someone who had broken that law. Although most American courts now disapprove of a jury's deciding anything other than the "facts," the Double Jeopardy Clause of the Fifth Amendment prohibits appellate reversal of a jury's decision to acquit, regardless of the reason for the acquittal. Thus, even when a trial judge thinks that a jury's acquittal directly contradicts the evidence, the jury's verdict must be accepted as final. The jurors, in judging the law, function as an important and necessary check on government power.

2. *A Brief History*

The prerogative of juries to nullify has been part of English and American law for centuries. In 1670, the landmark decision in *Bushell's Case* established the right of juries under English common law to nullify on the basis of an objection to the law the defendant had violated. Two members of an unpopular minority group—the Quakers—were prosecuted for unlawful assembly and disturbance of the peace. At trial, the defendants, William Penn and William Mead, admitted that they had assembled a large crowd on the streets of London. Upon that admission, the judge asked the men if they wished to plead guilty. Penn replied that the issue was not "whether I am guilty of this Indictment but whether this Indictment be legal," and argued that the jurors should go "behind" the law and use their consciences to decide whether he was guilty. The judge disagreed, and he instructed the jurors that the defendants' admissions compelled a guilty verdict. After extended deliberation, however, the jurors found both defendants not guilty. The judge then fined the jurors for rendering a decision contrary to the evidence and to his instructions. When one juror, Bushell, refused to pay his fine, the issue reached the Court of Common Pleas, which held that jurors in criminal cases could not be punished for voting to acquit, even when the trial judge believed that the verdict contradicted the evidence. The reason was stated by the Chief Justice of the Court of Common Pleas:

> A man cannot see by another's eye, nor hear by another's ear, no more can a man conclude or inferr [sic] the thing to be resolv'd by another's understanding or reasoning; and though the verdict be right the jury give, yet they being not assur'd it is so from their own understanding, are forsworn, at least in foro conscientiae.

This decision "changed the course of jury history." It is unclear why the jurors acquitted Penn and Mead, but their act has been viewed in near mythological terms. Bushell and his fellow jurors have come to be seen as representing the best ideals of democracy because they "rebuffed the tyranny of the judiciary and vindicated their own true historical and moral purpose."

American colonial law incorporated the common law prerogative of jurors to vote according to their consciences after the British government began prosecuting American revolutionaries for political crimes. The best known of these cases involved John Peter Zenger, who was accused of seditious libel for publishing statements critical of British colonial rule in North America. In seditious libel cases, English law required that the judge determine whether the statements made by the defendant were libelous; the jury was not supposed to question the judge's finding on this issue. At trial, Zenger's attorney told the jury that it should ignore the judge's instructions that Zenger's remarks were libelous because the jury "ha[d] the right beyond all dispute to determine both the law and the facts." The lawyer then echoed the language of *Bushell's Case,* arguing that the jurors had "to see with their eyes, to hear with their own ears, and to make use of their own consciences and understandings, in judging of the lives, liberties or estates of their fellow subjects." Famously, the jury acquitted Zenger, and another case entered the canon as a shining example of the benefits of the jury system.

After Zenger's trial, the notion that juries should decide "justice," as opposed to simply applying the law to the facts, became relatively settled in American jurisprudence. In addition to pointing to political prosecutions of white American revolutionaries like Zenger, modern courts and legal historians often cite with approval nullification in trials of defendants "guilty" of helping to free black slaves. In these cases, Northern jurors with abolitionist sentiments used their power as jurors to subvert federal law that supported slavery. In *United States v. Morris,* for example, three defendants were accused of aiding and abetting a runaway slave's escape to Canada. The defense attorney told the jury that, because it was hearing a criminal case, it had the right to judge the law, and if it believed that the Fugitive Slave Act was unconstitutional, it was bound to disregard any contrary instructions given by the judge. The defendants were acquitted, and the government dropped the charges against five other people accused of the same crime. Another success story entered the canon.

3. Sparf *and Other Critiques*

In the mid-nineteenth century, as memories of the tyranny of British rule faded, some American courts began to criticize the idea of jurors deciding justice. A number of the state decisions that allowed this practice were overruled, and in the 1895 case of *Sparf v. United States,* the Supreme Court spoke regarding jury nullification in federal courts.

In *Sparf,* two men on trial for murder requested that the judge instruct the jury that it had the option of convicting them of manslaughter, a lesser-included offense. The trial court refused this request and instead instructed the jurors that if they convicted the defendants of any crime less than murder, or if they acquitted them, the jurors would be in violation of their legal oath and duties. The Supreme Court held that this instruction was not contrary to law and affirmed the defendants' murder convictions. The Court acknowledged that juries have the "physical power" to disregard the law, but stated that they have no "moral right" to do so. Indeed, the Court observed, "If the jury were at liberty to settle the law for themselves, the effect would be . . . that the law itself would be most uncertain, from the different views, which different juries might take of it." Despite this criticism, *Sparf* conceded that, as a matter of law, a judge could not prevent jury nullification, because in criminal cases "[a] verdict of acquittal cannot be set aside." An anomaly was thus created, and has been a feature of American criminal law ever since: Jurors have the power to nullify, but, in most jurisdictions, they have no right to be informed of this power.

Since *Sparf,* most of the appellate courts that have considered jury nullification have addressed that anomaly and have endorsed it. Some of these courts, however, have not been as critical of the concept of jury nullification as the *Sparf* Court. The D.C. Circuit's opinion in *United States v. Dougherty* is illustrative. In *Dougherty,* the court noted that the ability of juries to nullify was widely recognized and even approved "as a 'necessary counter to case-hardened judges and arbitrary prosecutors.'" This necessity, however, did not establish "as an imperative" that a jury be informed by the judge of its power to nullify. The D.C. Circuit was concerned that "[w]hat makes for health as an occasional medicine would be disastrous as a daily diet." Specifically:

> Rules of law or justice involve choice of values and ordering of objectives for which unanimity is unlikely in any society, or group representing the society, especially a society as diverse in cultures and interests as ours. To seek unity out of diversity, under the national motto, there must be a procedure for decision by vote of a majority or prescribed plurality—in accordance with democratic philosophy. To assign the role of mini-legislature to the various petit juries, who must hang if not unanimous, exposes criminal law and administration to paralysis, and to a deadlock that betrays rather than furthers the assumptions of viable democracy.
> * * *

C. *The Moral Case for Jury Nullification by African-Americans*

Any juror legally may vote for nullification in any case, but, certainly, jurors should not do so without some principled basis. The reason that some historical examples of nullification are viewed approvingly is that most of us now believe that the jurors in those cases did the morally right thing; it would have been unconscionable, for example, to punish those slaves who committed the crime of escaping to the North for their freedom. It is true that nullification later would be used as a means of racial subordination by some Southern jurors, but that does not mean that nullification in the approved cases was wrong. It only means that those Southern jurors erred in their calculus of justice. * * *

1. *African-Americans and the "Betrayal" of Democracy*

There is no question that jury nullification is subversive of the rule of law. It appears to be the antithesis of the view that courts apply settled, standing laws and do not "dispense justice in some ad hoc, case-by-case basis." * * * [J]ury nullification "betrays rather than furthers the assumptions of viable democracy." Because the Double Jeopardy Clause makes this power part-and-parcel of the jury system, the issue becomes whether black jurors have any moral right to "betray democracy" in this sense. I believe that they do for two reasons that I borrow from the jurisprudence of legal realism and critical race theory: First, the idea of "the rule of law" is more mythological than real, and second, "democracy," as practiced in the United States, has betrayed African-Americans far more than they could ever betray it. * * *

2. *The Rule of Law as Myth*

*** The argument, in brief, is that law is indeterminate and incapable of neutral interpretation. *** Think, for example, of the existence of slavery in a republic purportedly dedicated to the proposition that all men are created equal, or the law's support of state-sponsored segregation even after the Fourteenth Amendment guaranteed blacks equal protection. That the rule of law ultimately corrected some of the large holes in the American fabric is evidence more of its malleability than of its virtue; the rule of law had, in the first instance, justified the holes. ***

If the rule of law is a myth, or at least is not applicable to African-Americans, the criticism that jury nullification undermines it loses force. The black juror is simply another actor in the system, using her power to fashion a particular outcome; the juror's act of nullification *** exposes the indeterminacy of law, but does not create it.

3. *The Moral Obligation to Disobey Unjust Laws*

*** [T]here *** is no moral obligation to follow an unjust law. This principle is familiar to many African-Americans who practiced civil disobedience during the civil rights protests of the 1950s and 1960s. Indeed, Martin Luther King suggested that morality requires that unjust laws not be obeyed. As I state above, the difficulty of determining which laws are unjust should not obscure the need to make that determination. ***

4. *Democratic Domination*

*** Lani Guinier suggests that the moral legitimacy of majority rule hinges on two assumptions: 1) that majorities are not fixed; and 2) that minorities will be able to become members of some majorities. Racial prejudice "to such a degree that the majority consistently excludes the minority, or refuses to inform itself about the relative merit of the minority's preferences," defeats both assumptions.

*** [African Americans] are not even proportionally represented in the U.S. House of Representatives or in the Senate. As a result, African-Americans wield little influence over criminal law, state or federal. African-Americans should embrace the antidemocratic nature of jury nullification because it provides them with the power to determine justice in a way that majority rule does not.

D. *"[J]ustice must satisfy the appearance of justice": The Symbolic Function of Black Jurors*

*** [O]n several occasions, the Supreme Court has referred to the usefulness of black jurors to the rule of law in the United States. In essence, black jurors symbolize the fairness and impartiality of the law. *** [T]he Court has suggested that these jurors perform a symbolic function, especially when they sit on cases involving African-American defendants, and the Court has typically made these suggestions in the form of rhetoric about the social harm caused by the exclusion of blacks from jury service. I will refer to this role of black jurors as the "legitimization function." * * *

When blacks are excluded from juries, beyond any harm done to the juror who suffers the discrimination or to the defendant, the social injury of the exclusion is that it "undermine[s] . . . public confidence—as well [it] should." Because the United States is both a democracy and a pluralist society, it is important that diverse groups appear to have a voice in the laws that govern them. Allowing black people to serve on juries strengthens "public respect for our criminal justice system and the rule of law."

* * * In choosing [to nullify], the juror makes a decision not to be a passive symbol of support for a system for which she has no respect. Rather than signaling her displeasure with the system by breaching "community peace," the black juror invokes the political nature of her role in the criminal justice system and votes "no." In a sense, the black juror engages in an act of civil disobedience, except that her choice is better than civil disobedience because it is lawful. Is the black juror's race-conscious act moral? Absolutely. * * * [T]he doctrine of jury nullification affords African-American jurors the opportunity to control the authority of the law over some African-American criminal defendants. * * *

III. C. *Some Political and Procedural Concerns*

1. *What if White People Start Nullifying Too?*

One concern is that whites will nullify in cases of white-on-black crime. The best response to this concern is that often white people do nullify in those cases. The white jurors who acquitted the police officers who beat up Rodney King are a good example. There is no reason why my proposal should cause white jurors to acquit white defendants who are guilty of violence against blacks any more frequently. My model assumes that black violence against whites would be punished by black jurors; I hope that white jurors would do the same in cases involving white defendants.

If white jurors were to begin applying my proposal to cases with white defendants, then they, like the black jurors, would be choosing to opt out of the criminal justice system. For pragmatic political purposes, that would be excellent. Attention would then be focused on alternative methods of correcting antisocial conduct much sooner than it would if only African-Americans raised the issue. * * *

THE DANGERS OF RACE-BASED JURY NULLIFICATION: A RESPONSE TO PROFESSOR BUTLER

Andrew D. Leipold
44 UCLA L. Rev. 109 (1996)

In his provocative essay, *Racially Based Jury Nullification: Black Power in the Criminal Justice System*, Professor Paul Butler argues that African-American jurors should sometimes vote to acquit in criminal cases because the defendant is black. As every lawyer knows, juries have the unreviewable power to acquit for any reason, and Professor Butler urges black jurors to exercise this power on behalf of factually guilty African-American defendants whenever the benefits of returning the defendant to the community outweigh the harms that will be caused by incarceration. Butler claims that this use of "jury nullification"—when a jury acquits for reasons unrelated to the evidence—will diminish the racially disparate impact of the criminal law, help bring about beneficial legal reform, and improve the African-American communities that are now crippled by the excessive imprisonment of their members. * * *

Curiously, Professor Butler spends little time exploring the incentives his proposal will create for those at the source of the perceived problem: the police and prosecutors who enforce the criminal law, and the legislators who hold the keys to change. Butler's vision is that, faced with widespread nullification, convictions for drug crimes will be sharply reduced, which will, in turn, force a rethinking of the war on drugs. Perhaps, Butler believes, this will lead legislators to divert money that is now being used to warehouse "criminals" into treatment and social programs, which will attack the sickness of addiction and the poverty that breeds it.

Perhaps—but don't bet on it. A more likely, and more sinister, outcome would be that police and prosecutors would simply abandon their efforts to enforce the drug laws in black neighborhoods. In most cities, there is no shortage of criminals to pursue or charges to file, so rational police and prosecutors will spend little time on drug crimes if the probable outcome is an acquittal against the evidence. To the honest citizens of drug-ravaged neighborhoods, the notion of being abandoned by the police until a drug war erupts or until an addict actually accosts them (i.e., until there is a "victim") should be a frightening one.

A second tangible harm is that prosecutors would change the way they pick juries. Prosecutors may not excuse jurors because of their race, but may remove jurors for cause if it appears they will not apply the law as given by the judge, and may challenge jurors peremptorily if they can articulate a race-neutral reason for the strike. Black jurors who become aware of Butler's proposal could surely be questioned about it during voir dire, and those who admit that they subscribe to the plan could almost certainly be removed for cause. Even if prospective jurors lied or were undecided about the wisdom of the proposal, their hesitancy to affirm that they would follow the law might be enough to permit a peremptory strike, despite the disparate impact the strikes would have on prospective black jurors. The results could only be that fewer black jurors would be seated, and many of the benefits of culturally diverse juries would be lost. * * *

By its terms, the plan is limited to nullification by African-American jurors in cases involving nonviolent, victimless crimes. These limits are by fiat; there is no logic to them. It takes little imagination to think of other groups who might also stake a claim to the use of nullification: Hispanic defendants could tell a tale of oppression by the criminal justice system, as could those of Chinese and Japanese background. Italian Americans and, more recently, Colombians, have claimed that they are disproportionately targeted for investigation when organized crime is involved; Arabic defendants believe that they are unfairly stereotyped as terrorists. Perhaps, most significantly, women have been poorly treated by the legal system throughout much of our history. Each of these groups could claim that they too have suffered systemic discrimination, and make cogent arguments about their perceived inability to bring about legal change through the legislative process.

It is hard to believe that supporters of the Butler plan could oppose strategic nullification by these groups. It is also hard to imagine, however, that reasonable people would favor a world in which each juror would begin deliberations with a presumption that defendants who are members of his or her own group should be acquitted, regardless of the evidence. The upheaval that would follow would surely prevent unjust convictions, but would do so at the cost of preventing a huge number of justified convictions. The impact would fall most heavily on future crime victims, whose perpetrators failed to learn the lesson that a prior nullification was supposed to teach. The proposal would also leave unprotected those who belong to no identifiable group (the homeless, non-citizens, the mentally impaired) who are in great need of the law's protection, but who are unlikely to be represented on juries. Jurors who come to the box with a mandate to protect their own may have no mercy to spare for those who do not fit in anywhere. * * *

Finally, even if strictly followed, the proposal still sends the wrong message to those with an interest in the criminal justice system—in other words, to all of us. It is a sad commentary on the state of race relations and legal thinking that the most obvious problem with Butler's plan needs to be made at all: deciding whether a defendant should go to prison or be set free should not depend on the color of his skin. Urging prospective jurors to return a verdict in a criminal case based on the race of the defendant is wrong, and neither good intentions nor strategic political considerations can change that.

Race-based decisionmaking by juries is wrong on so many levels it is hard to know where to begin. It is wrong because verdicts will inevitably be based on stereotypes that are harmful to all members of the group; wrong because those who are not part of the favored group are treated more harshly for reasons unrelated to their blameworthiness; wrong because it helps polarize a society that is already struggling with racial division; and most tragically, wrong because it raises the flag of surrender in the fight for equality. Butler's inescapable message is that equal treatment will never be possible, at least in court, so African Americans should take whatever small benefits they can grab on their own and be content with that. But those who have struggled for equal justice deserve better: The tangible gains that have been made over the last few decades in reducing racial bias in the criminal system should not be so casually dismissed by those who are too impatient to continue on the current course. * * *

CHAPTER 33

SENTENCING

■ ■ ■

The Eighth Amendment to the U.S. Constitution prohibits "cruel and unusual punishments." In *Coker v. Georgia*, the Supreme Court considers whether allowing the death penalty for rape constitutes cruel and unusual punishment. In *Ewing v. California*, the Court reviews the constitutionality of California's "Three Strikes and You're Out Law" which was meant to ensure that certain repeat felony offenders would receive harsher penalties than others. Finally, in *McCleskey v. Kemp*, the Court considers whether a sophisticated statistical study, which demonstrates a risk that race discrimination may have influenced Georgia's capital sentencing scheme, should render a death sentence unconstitutional under the Eighth and Fourteenth Amendments.

COKER V. GEORGIA
Supreme Court of the United States
433 U.S. 584, 97 S. Ct. 2861, 53 L. Ed. 2d 982 (1977)

JUSTICE WHITE announced the judgment of the Court. * * *

Georgia Code Ann. § 26–2001 (1972) provides that "[a] person convicted of rape shall be punished by death or by imprisonment for life, or by imprisonment for not less than one nor more than 20 years." * * * Petitioner Coker was convicted of rape and sentenced to death. Both the conviction and the sentence were affirmed by the Georgia Supreme Court. Coker was granted a writ of certiorari * * * limited to the single claim * * * that the punishment of death for rape violates the Eighth Amendment, which proscribes "cruel and unusual punishments" * * *.

While serving various sentences for murder, rape kidnaping, and aggravated assault, petitioner escaped from the Ware Correctional Institution near Waycross, Ga., on September 2, 1974. At approximately 11 o'clock that night, petitioner entered the house of Allen and Elnita Carver through an unlocked kitchen door. Threatening the couple with a "board," he tied up Mr. Carver in the bathroom, obtained a knife from the kitchen, and took Mr. Carver's money and the keys to the family car. Brandishing the knife and saying "you know what's going to happen to you if you try anything, don't you," Coker then raped Mrs. Carver. Soon thereafter, petitioner drove away in the Carver car, taking Mrs. Carver with him. Mr. Carver, freeing himself, notified the police; and not long thereafter petitioner was apprehended. Mrs. Carver was unharmed.

Petitioner was charged with escape, armed robbery, motor vehicle theft, kidnaping, and rape. * * * The jury returned a verdict of guilty, rejecting his general plea of insanity. A sentencing hearing was then conducted * * *. The jury's verdict on the rape count was death by electrocution.

* * * It is now settled that the death penalty is not invariably cruel and unusual punishment within the meaning of the Eighth Amendment; it is not inherently barbaric or an unacceptable mode of punishment for crime; neither is it always disproportionate to the crime for which it is imposed.

* * * [T]he Eighth Amendment bars not only those punishments that are "barbaric" but also those that are "excessive" in relation to the crime committed. Under *Gregg*, a punishment is "excessive" and unconstitutional if it (1) makes no measurable contribution to acceptable goals of punishment and hence is nothing more than the purposeless and needless imposition of pain and suffering; or (2) is grossly out of proportion to the severity of the crime. A punishment might fail the test on either ground. Furthermore, these Eighth Amendment judgments should not be, or appear to be, merely the subjective views of individual Justices; judgment should be informed by objective factors to the maximum possible extent. To this end, attention must be given to the public attitudes concerning a particular sentence—history and precedent, legislative attitudes, and the response of juries reflected in their sentencing decisions are to be consulted. In *Gregg*, after giving due regard to such sources, the Court's judgment was that the death penalty for deliberate murder was neither the purposeless imposition of severe punishment nor a punishment grossly disproportionate to the crime. But the Court reserved the question of the constitutionality of the death penalty when imposed for other crimes.

That question, with respect to rape of an adult woman, is now before us. We have concluded that a sentence of death is grossly disproportionate and excessive punishment for the crime of rape and is therefore forbidden by the Eighth Amendment as cruel and unusual punishment.

As advised by recent cases, we seek guidance in history and from the objective evidence of the country's present judgment concerning the acceptability of death as a penalty for rape of an adult woman. At no time in the last 50 years have a majority of the States authorized death as a punishment for rape. In 1925, 18 States, the District of Columbia, and the Federal Government authorized capital punishment for the rape of an adult female. By 1971 * * *, that number had declined, but not substantially, to 16 States plus the Federal Government. *Furman* then invalidated most of the capital punishment statutes in this country, including the rape statutes, because, among other reasons, of the manner in which the death penalty was imposed and utilized under those laws.

With their death penalty statutes for the most part invalidated, the States were faced with the choice of enacting modified capital punishment laws in an attempt to satisfy the requirements of *Furman* or of being satisfied with life imprisonment as the ultimate punishment for *any* offense. Thirty-five States immediately reinstituted the death penalty. * * *

In reviving death penalty laws to satisfy *Furman*'s mandate, none of the States that had not previously authorized death for rape chose to include rape among capital felonies. Of the 16 States in which rape had been a capital offense, only three provided the death penalty for rape of an adult woman in their revised statutes. * * *

The current judgment with respect to the death penalty for rape is not wholly unanimous among state legislatures, but it obviously weighs very heavily on the side of rejecting capital punishment as a suitable penalty for raping an adult woman.

It was also observed in *Gregg* that "[t]he jury . . . is a significant and reliable objective index of contemporary values because it is so directly involved" and that it is thus important to look to the sentencing decisions that juries have made in the course of assessing whether capital punishment is an appropriate penalty for the crime being tried. * * *

According to the factual submissions in this Court, out of all rape convictions in Georgia since 1973, * * * 63 cases had been reviewed by the Georgia Supreme Court as of the time of oral argument; and of these, 6 involved a death sentence, 1 of which was set aside, leaving 5 convicted rapists now under sentence of death in the State of Georgia. Georgia juries have thus sentenced rapists to death six times since 1973. This obviously is not a negligible number; and the State argues that as a practical matter juries simply reserve the extreme sanction for extreme cases of rape and that recent experience surely does not prove that jurors consider the death penalty to be a disproportionate punishment for every conceivable instance of rape, no matter how aggravated. Nevertheless, it is true that in the vast majority of cases, at least 9 out of 10, juries have not imposed the death sentence.

These recent events evidencing the attitude of state legislatures and sentencing juries do not wholly determine this controversy, for the Constitution contemplates that in the end our own judgment will be brought to bear on the question of the acceptability of the death penalty under the Eighth Amendment. Nevertheless, the legislative rejection of capital punishment for rape strongly confirms our own judgment, which is that death is indeed a disproportionate penalty for the crime of raping an adult woman. * * *

Rape is without doubt deserving of serious punishment; but in terms of moral depravity and of the injury to the person and to the public, it does not compare with murder, which does involve the unjustified taking of human life. Although it may be accompanied by another crime, rape by definition does not include the death of or even the serious injury to another person. The murderer kills; the rapist, if no more than that, does not. Life is over for the victim of the murderer; for the rape victim, life may not be nearly so happy as it was, but it is not over and normally is not beyond repair. We have the abiding conviction that the death penalty, which "is unique in its severity and irrevocability," is an excessive penalty for the rapist who, as such, does not take human life. * * *

The judgment of the Georgia Supreme Court upholding the death sentence is reversed, and the case is remanded to that court for further proceedings not inconsistent with this opinion.

So ordered.

CHIEF JUSTICE BURGER, with whom JUSTICE REHNQUIST joins, dissenting. * * *

Unlike the plurality, I would narrow the inquiry in this case to the question actually presented: Does the Eighth Amendment's ban against cruel and unusual punishment prohibit the State of Georgia from executing a person who has, within the space of three years, raped three separate women, killing one and attempting to kill another, who is serving prison terms exceeding his probable lifetime and who has not hesitated to escape confinement at the first available opportunity? Whatever one's view may be as to the State's constitutional power to impose the death penalty upon a rapist who stands before a court convicted for the first time, this case reveals a chronic rapist whose continuing danger to the community is abundantly clear.

* * * [O]nce the Court has held that "the punishment of death does not invariably violate the Constitution," it seriously impinges upon the State's legislative judgment to hold that it may not impose such sentence upon an individual who has shown total and repeated disregard for the welfare, safety, personal integrity, and human worth of others, and who seemingly cannot be deterred from continuing such conduct. I therefore would hold that the death sentence here imposed is within the power reserved to the State and leave for another day the question of whether such sanction would be proper under other circumstances. * * *

[JUSTICE BRENNAN's concurring opinion, JUSTICE MARSHALL's concurring opinion, and JUSTICE POWELL's concurring opinion have been omitted.]

NOTE

Prior to the Court's decision in *Coker*, Black men were substantially more likely than other men to receive the death penalty for raping White women. Between 1930 and 1972, 455 people were executed for rape. U.S. DEP'T OF JUSTICE BUREAU OF PRISONS, NATIONAL PRISONER STATISTICS, BULLETIN No. 45, CAPITAL PUNISHMENT 1930–1968 (1969). Of those, 405 or 89.1 percent were Black. *Id.* Black men were sentenced to death for raping White women approximately 18 times more often than any other combination of defendant and victim in rape cases. Marvin E. Wolfgang & Marc Riedel, *Race, Judicial Discretion, and the Death Penalty*, 407 ANNALS OF THE AM. ACAD. OF POL. AND SOC. SCI. 119, 126–33 (1973).

In *Kennedy v. Louisiana*, 554 U.S. 407 (2008), the Supreme Court revisited the question of whether the death penalty for the crime of rape violates the Eighth Amendment's prohibition against cruel and unusual punishment. This case involved the violent rape and sodomy of an eight year old girl. In a 5 to 4 decision, Justice Kennedy explained that since there was no national consensus that the death penalty was an appropriate punishment for child rape, the death penalty was disproportionate punishment. The Court concluded that when crimes against individual people are at issue, "the death penalty should not be expanded to instances where the victim's life was not taken." *Id.* at 437.

EWING V. CALIFORNIA
Supreme Court of the United States
538 U.S. 11, 123 S. Ct. 1179, 155 L. Ed. 2d 108 (2003)

JUSTICE O'CONNOR announced the judgment of the Court and delivered an opinion in which the Chief Justice and JUSTICE KENNEDY join.

In this case, we decide whether the Eighth Amendment prohibits the State of California from sentencing a repeat felon to a prison term of 25 years to life under the State's "Three Strikes and You're Out" law. California's three strikes law reflects a shift in the State's sentencing policies toward incapacitating and deterring repeat offenders who threaten the public safety. The law was designed "to ensure longer prison sentences and greater punishment for those who commit a felony and have been previously convicted of serious and/or violent felony offenses." * * *

> [Under California's three strikes law as initially enacted, a defendant with two or more prior "serious" or "violent" felony convictions, who was convicted of a third felony (not necessarily a serious or violent felony), faced a mandatory sentence of twenty-five years to life.]

On parole from a 9-year prison term, petitioner Gary Ewing walked into the pro shop of the El Segundo Golf Course in Los Angeles County on March 12, 2000. He walked out with three golf clubs, priced at $399 apiece, concealed in his pants leg. A shop employee, whose suspicions were aroused when he observed Ewing limp out of the pro shop, telephoned the police. The police apprehended Ewing in the parking lot.

Ewing is no stranger to the criminal justice system. In 1984, at the age of 22, he pleaded guilty to theft. The court sentenced him to six months in jail (suspended), three years' probation, and a $300 fine. In 1988, he was convicted of felony grand theft auto and sentenced to one year in jail and three years' probation. After Ewing completed probation, however, the sentencing court reduced the crime to a misdemeanor, permitted Ewing to withdraw his guilty plea, and dismissed the case. In 1990, he was convicted of petty theft with a prior and sentenced to 60 days in the county jail and three years' probation. In 1992, Ewing was convicted of battery and sentenced to 30 days in the county jail and two years' summary probation. One month later, he was convicted of theft and sentenced to 10 days in the county jail and 12 months' probation. In January 1993, Ewing was convicted of burglary and sentenced to 60 days in the county jail and one year's summary probation. In February 1993, he was convicted of possessing drug paraphernalia and sentenced to six months in the county jail and three years' probation. In July 1993, he was convicted of appropriating lost property and sentenced to 10 days in the county jail and two years' summary probation. In September 1993, he was convicted of unlawfully possessing a firearm and trespassing and sentenced to 30 days in the county jail and one year's probation.

In October and November 1993, Ewing committed three burglaries and one robbery at a Long Beach, California, apartment complex over a 5-week period. He awakened one of his victims, asleep on her living room sofa, as he tried to disconnect her video cassette recorder from the television in that room. When she screamed, Ewing ran out the front door. On another occasion, Ewing accosted a victim in the mailroom of the apartment complex. Ewing claimed to have a gun and ordered the victim to hand over his wallet. When the victim resisted, Ewing produced a knife and forced the victim back to the apartment itself. While Ewing rifled through the bedroom, the victim fled the apartment screaming for help. Ewing absconded with the victim's money and credit cards.

On December 9, 1993, Ewing was arrested on the premises of the apartment complex for trespassing and lying to a police officer. The knife used in the robbery and a glass cocaine pipe were later found in the back seat of the patrol car used to transport Ewing to the police station. A jury convicted Ewing of first-degree robbery and three counts of residential burglary. Sentenced to nine years and eight months in prison, Ewing was paroled in 1999.

Only 10 months later, Ewing stole the golf clubs at issue in this case. He was charged with, and ultimately convicted of, one count of felony grand theft of personal property in excess of $400. As required by the three strikes law, the prosecutor formally alleged, and the trial court later found, that Ewing had been convicted previously of four serious or violent felonies for the three burglaries and the robbery in the Long Beach apartment complex.

At the sentencing hearing, Ewing asked the court to reduce the conviction for grand theft, a "wobbler" under California law, to a misdemeanor so as to avoid a three strikes sentence.[a] Ewing also asked the trial court to exercise its discretion to dismiss the allegations of some or all of his prior serious or violent felony convictions, again for purposes of avoiding a three strikes sentence. Before sentencing Ewing, the trial court took note of his entire criminal history, including the fact that he was on parole when he committed his latest offense. The court also heard arguments from defense counsel and a plea from Ewing himself.

In the end, the trial judge determined that the grand theft should remain a felony. The court also ruled that the four prior strikes for the three burglaries and the robbery in Long Beach should stand. As a newly convicted felon with two or more "serious" or "violent" felony convictions in his past, Ewing was sentenced under the three strikes law to 25 years to life.

The California Court of Appeal affirmed in an unpublished opinion. * * * The Supreme Court of California denied Ewing's petition for review, and we granted certiorari. We now affirm.

The Eighth Amendment, which forbids cruel and unusual punishments, contains a "narrow proportionality principle" that "applies to noncapital sentences." We have most recently addressed the proportionality principle as applied to terms of years in a series of cases beginning with *Rummel v. Estelle.*

In *Rummel,* we held that it did not violate the Eighth Amendment for a State to sentence a three-time offender to life in prison with the possibility of parole. Like Ewing, Rummel was sentenced to a lengthy prison term under a recidivism statute. Rummel's two prior offenses were a 1964 felony for "fraudulent use of a credit card to obtain $80 worth of goods or services," and a 1969 felony conviction for "passing a forged check in the amount of $28.36." His triggering offense was a conviction for felony theft—"obtaining $120.75 by false pretenses."

This Court ruled that "having twice imprisoned him for felonies, Texas was entitled to place upon Rummel the onus of one who is simply unable to bring his conduct within the social norms prescribed by the criminal law of the State." The recidivism statute "is nothing more than a societal decision that when such a person commits yet another felony, he should be

---

[a] Under California law, certain offenses can be classified as either felonies or misdemeanors. These offenses are known as "wobblers." A wobbler is presumptively a felony unless the prosecution or the trial court exercises its discretion to reduce the wobbler to a misdemeanor.

subjected to the admittedly serious penalty of incarceration for life, subject only to the State's judgment as to whether to grant him parole." We noted that this Court "has on occasion stated that the Eighth Amendment prohibits imposition of a sentence that is grossly disproportionate to the severity of the crime." But "outside the context of capital punishment, successful challenges to the proportionality of particular sentences have been exceedingly rare."

Although we stated that the proportionality principle "would . . . come into play in the extreme example . . . if a legislature made overtime parking a felony punishable by life imprisonment," we held that "the mandatory life sentence imposed upon this petitioner does not constitute cruel and unusual punishment under the Eighth and Fourteenth Amendments." * * *

Three years after *Rummel*, in *Solem v. Helm,* we held that the Eighth Amendment prohibited "a life sentence without possibility of parole for a seventh nonviolent felony." The triggering offense in *Solem* was "uttering a 'no account' check for $100." We specifically stated that the Eighth Amendment's ban on cruel and unusual punishments "prohibits . . . sentences that are disproportionate to the crime committed," and that the "constitutional principle of proportionality has been recognized explicitly in this Court for almost a century." The *Solem* Court then explained that three factors may be relevant to a determination of whether a sentence is so disproportionate that it violates the Eighth Amendment: "(i) the gravity of the offense and the harshness of the penalty; (ii) the sentences imposed on other criminals in the same jurisdiction; and (iii) the sentences imposed for commission of the same crime in other jurisdictions."

Applying these factors in *Solem*, we struck down the defendant's sentence of life without parole. We specifically noted the contrast between that sentence and the sentence in *Rummel*, pursuant to which the defendant was eligible for parole. Indeed, we explicitly declined to overrule *Rummel*: "Our conclusion today is not inconsistent with *Rummel v. Estelle.*"

Eight years after *Solem*, we grappled with the proportionality issue again in *Harmelin v. Michigan. Harmelin* was not a recidivism case, but rather involved a first-time offender convicted of possessing 672 grams of cocaine. He was sentenced to life in prison without possibility of parole. A majority of the Court rejected Harmelin's claim that his sentence was so grossly disproportionate that it violated the Eighth Amendment. The Court, however, could not agree on why his proportionality argument failed. * * *

Justice Kennedy, joined by two other Members of the Court, concurred in part and concurred in the judgment. Justice Kennedy specifically recognized that "the Eighth Amendment proportionality principle also applies to noncapital sentences." He then identified four principles of proportionality review—"the primacy of the legislature, the variety of legitimate penological schemes, the nature of our federal system, and the requirement that proportionality review be guided by objective factors"—that "inform the final one: The Eighth Amendment does not require strict proportionality between crime and sentence. Rather, it forbids only extreme sentences that are grossly disproportionate to the crime." Justice Kennedy's concurrence also stated that *Solem* "did not mandate" comparative analysis "within and between jurisdictions."

The proportionality principles in our cases distilled in Justice Kennedy's concurrence guide our application of the Eighth Amendment in the new context that we are called upon to consider.

For many years, most States have had laws providing for enhanced sentencing of repeat offenders. Yet between 1993 and 1995, three strikes laws effected a sea change in criminal sentencing throughout the Nation. These laws responded to widespread public concerns about crime by targeting the class of offenders who pose the greatest threat to public safety: career criminals. * * *

Throughout the States, legislatures enacting three strikes laws made a deliberate policy choice that individuals who have repeatedly engaged in serious or violent criminal behavior, and whose conduct has not been deterred by more conventional approaches to punishment, must be isolated from society in order to protect the public safety. Though three strikes laws may be relatively new, our tradition of deferring to state legislatures in making and implementing such important policy decisions is longstanding.

Our traditional deference to legislative policy choices finds a corollary in the principle that the Constitution "does not mandate adoption of any one penological theory." A sentence can have a variety of justifications, such as incapacitation, deterrence, retribution, or rehabilitation. Some or all of these justifications may play a role in a State's sentencing scheme. Selecting the sentencing rationales is generally a policy choice to be made by state legislatures, not federal courts.

When the California Legislature enacted the three strikes law, it made a judgment that protecting the public safety requires incapacitating criminals who have already been convicted of at least one serious or violent crime. Nothing in the Eighth Amendment prohibits California from making that choice. To the contrary, our cases establish that "States have a valid interest in deterring and segregating habitual criminals." Recidivism has long been recognized as a legitimate basis for increased punishment.

California's justification is no pretext. Recidivism is a serious public safety concern in California and throughout the Nation. According to a recent report, approximately 67 percent of former inmates released from state prisons were charged with at least one "serious" new crime within three years of their release. In particular, released property offenders like

Ewing had higher recidivism rates than those released after committing violent, drug, or public-order offenses. * * *

The State's interest in deterring crime also lends some support to the three strikes law. We have long viewed both incapacitation and deterrence as rationales for recidivism statutes * * *. Four years after the passage of California's three strikes law, the recidivism rate of parolees returned to prison for the commission of a new crime dropped by nearly 25 percent. Even more dramatically:

> [A]n unintended but positive consequence of "Three Strikes" has been the impact on parolees leaving the state. More California parolees are now leaving the state than parolees from other jurisdictions entering California. This striking turnaround started in 1994. It was the first time more parolees left the state than entered since 1976. This trend has continued and in 1997 more than 1,000 net parolees left California.

To be sure, California's three strikes law has sparked controversy. Critics have doubted the law's wisdom, cost-efficiency, and effectiveness in reaching its goals. This criticism is appropriately directed at the legislature, which has primary responsibility for making the difficult policy choices that underlie any criminal sentencing scheme. We do not sit as a "superlegislature" to second-guess these policy choices. It is enough that the State of California has a reasonable basis for believing that dramatically enhanced sentences for habitual felons "advances the goals of [its] criminal justice system in any substantial way."

Against this backdrop, we consider Ewing's claim that his three strikes sentence of 25 years to life is unconstitutionally disproportionate to his offense of "shoplifting three golf clubs." We first address the gravity of the offense compared to the harshness of the penalty. At the threshold, we note that Ewing incorrectly frames the issue. The gravity of his offense was not merely "shoplifting three golf clubs." Rather, Ewing was convicted of felony grand theft for stealing nearly $1,200 worth of merchandise after previously having been convicted of at least two "violent" or "serious" felonies. * * *

In weighing the gravity of Ewing's offense, we must place on the scales not only his current felony, but also his long history of felony recidivism. Any other approach would fail to accord proper deference to the policy judgments that find expression in the legislature's choice of sanctions. In imposing a three strikes sentence, the State's interest is not merely punishing the offense of conviction, or the "triggering" offense: "It is in addition the interest . . . in dealing in a harsher manner with those who by repeated criminal acts have shown that they are simply incapable of conforming to the norms of society as established by its criminal law." To give full effect to the State's choice of this legitimate penological goal, our proportionality review of Ewing's sentence must take that goal into account.

Ewing's sentence is justified by the State's public-safety interest in incapacitating and deterring recidivist felons, and amply supported by his own long, serious criminal record. * * * To be sure, Ewing's sentence is a long one. But it reflects a rational legislative judgment, entitled to deference, that offenders who have committed serious or violent felonies and who continue to commit felonies must be incapacitated. * * *

We hold that Ewing's sentence of 25 years to life in prison, imposed for the offense of felony grand theft under the three strikes law, is not grossly disproportionate and therefore does not violate the Eighth Amendment's prohibition on cruel and unusual punishments. The judgment of the California Court of Appeal is affirmed.

It is so ordered.

[JUSTICE SCALIA's concurring opinion, JUSTICE THOMAS' concurring opinion, JUSTICE STEVENS' dissenting opinion, and JUSTICE BREYER's dissenting opinion have been omitted.]

NOTE

In 2012, California voters passed Proposition 36, which amended the Three Strikes law to require the third felony, as well as the first and second, to be a "serious" or "violent" felony. Tracey Kaplan, *Proposition 36: Voters overwhelmingly ease Three Strikes law*, SAN JOSE MERCURY NEWS, Nov. 6, 2012, http://www.mercurynews.com/ci_21943951/prop-36-huge-lead-early-returns?source=infinite or https://perma.cc/X6CT-UH89; *see also* CAL. PENAL CODE §§ 667, 1170.12, 1170.125, 1170.126 (West 2014).

MCCLESKEY V. KEMP

Supreme Court of the United States
481 U.S. 279, 107 S. Ct. 1756, 95 L. Ed. 2d 262 (1987)

JUSTICE POWELL delivered the opinion of the Court.

This case presents the question whether a complex statistical study that indicates a risk that racial considerations enter into capital sentencing determinations proves that petitioner McCleskey's capital sentence is unconstitutional under the Eighth or Fourteenth Amendment.

McCleskey, a black man, was convicted of two counts of armed robbery and one count of murder in the Superior Court of Fulton County, Georgia, on October 12, 1978. McCleskey's convictions arose out of the robbery of a furniture store and the killing of a white police officer during the course of the robbery. The evidence at trial indicated that McCleskey and three accomplices planned and carried out the robbery. All four were armed. * * * During the course of the robbery, a police officer, answering a silent alarm, entered the store through the front door. As he was walking down the center aisle of the store, two shots were fired. Both struck the officer. One hit him in the face and killed him.

Several weeks later, McCleskey was arrested in connection with an unrelated offense. He confessed that he had participated in the furniture store robbery, but denied that he had shot the police officer. At trial, the State introduced evidence that at least one of the bullets that struck the officer was fired from a .38 caliber Rossi revolver. This description matched the description of the gun that McCleskey had carried during the robbery. The State also introduced the testimony of two witnesses who had heard McCleskey admit to the shooting.

The jury convicted McCleskey of murder. * * * The jury in this case found two aggravating circumstances to exist beyond a reasonable doubt: the murder was committed during the course of an armed robbery; and the murder was committed upon a peace officer engaged in the performance of his duties. * * * McCleskey offered no mitigating evidence. The jury recommended that he be sentenced to death on the murder charge and to consecutive life sentences on the armed robbery charges. The court followed the jury's recommendation and sentenced McCleskey to death.

On appeal, the Supreme Court of Georgia affirmed the convictions and the sentences. * * * McCleskey next filed a petition for a writ of habeas corpus in the Federal District Court for the Northern District of Georgia. His petition raised 18 claims, one of which was that the Georgia capital sentencing process is administered in a racially discriminatory manner in violation of the Eighth and Fourteenth Amendments to the United States Constitution. In support of his claim, McCleskey proffered a statistical study performed by Professors David C. Baldus, Charles Pulaski, and George Woodworth (the Baldus study) that purports to show a disparity in the imposition of the death sentence in Georgia based on the race of the murder victim and, to a lesser extent, the race of the defendant. The Baldus study is actually two sophisticated statistical studies that examine over 2,000 murder cases that occurred in Georgia during the 1970's. The raw numbers collected by Professor Baldus indicate that defendants charged with killing white persons received the death penalty in 11% of the cases, but defendants charged with killing blacks received the death penalty in only 1% of the cases. The raw numbers also indicate a reverse racial disparity according to the race of the defendant: 4% of the black defendants received the death penalty, as opposed to 7% of the white defendants.

Baldus also divided the cases according to the combination of the race of the defendant and the race of the victim. He found that the death penalty was assessed in 22% of the cases involving black defendants and white victims; 8% of the cases involving white defendants and white victims; 1% of the cases involving black defendants and black victims; and 3% of the cases involving white defendants and black victims. Similarly, Baldus found that prosecutors sought the death penalty in 70% of the cases involving black defendants and white victims; 32% of the cases involving white defendants and white victims; 15% of the cases involving black defendants and black victims; and 19% of the cases involving white defendants and black victims.

Baldus subjected his data to an extensive analysis, taking account of 230 variables that could have explained the disparities on nonracial grounds. One of his models concludes that, even after taking account of 39 nonracial variables, defendants charged with killing white victims were 4.3 times as likely to receive a death sentence as defendants charged with killing blacks. According to this model, black defendants were 1.1 times as likely to receive a death sentence as other defendants. Thus, the Baldus study indicates that black defendants, such as McCleskey, who kill white victims have the greatest likelihood of receiving the death penalty.

The District Court * * * denied the petition * * *. The Court of Appeals for the Eleventh Circuit, sitting en banc, * * * affirmed the denial by the District Court of McCleskey's petition for a writ of habeas corpus * * *. We granted certiorari and now affirm.

McCleskey's first claim is that the Georgia capital punishment statute violates the Equal Protection Clause of the Fourteenth Amendment.[7] He argues that race has infected the administration of Georgia's statute in two ways: persons who murder whites are more likely to be sentenced to death than persons who murder blacks, and black murderers are more likely to be sentenced to death than white murderers. As a black defendant who killed a white victim, McCleskey claims that the Baldus study demonstrates that he was discriminated against because of his race and because of the race of his victim. * * * We agree with the Court of Appeals, and every other court that has considered such a challenge, that this claim must fail.

Our analysis begins with the basic principle that a defendant who alleges an equal protection violation has the burden of proving "the existence of purposeful discrimination." A corollary to this principle is that a criminal defendant must prove that the purposeful discrimination "had a discriminatory effect" on him. Thus, to prevail under the Equal Protection Clause, McCleskey must prove that the decisionmakers in *his* case acted with discriminatory purpose. He offers no evidence specific to his own case that would support an inference that racial considerations played a part in

---

[7] * * * As did the Court of Appeals, we assume the study is valid statistically without reviewing the factual findings of the District Court. Our assumption that the Baldus study is statistically valid does not include the assumption that the study shows that racial considerations actually enter into any sentencing decisions in Georgia. Even a sophisticated multiple-regression analysis such as the Baldus study can only demonstrate a *risk* that the factor of race entered into some capital sentencing decisions and a necessarily lesser risk that race entered into any particular sentencing decision.

his sentence. Instead, he relies solely on the Baldus study. McCleskey argues that the Baldus study compels an inference that his sentence rests on purposeful discrimination. McCleskey's claim that these statistics are sufficient proof of discrimination, without regard to the facts of a particular case, would extend to all capital cases in Georgia, at least where the victim was white and the defendant is black.

The Court has accepted statistics as proof of intent to discriminate in certain limited contexts. First, this Court has accepted statistical disparities as proof of an equal protection violation in the selection of the jury venire in a particular district. Although statistical proof normally must present a "stark" pattern to be accepted as the sole proof of discriminatory intent under the Constitution, "because of the nature of the jury-selection task, . . . we have permitted a finding of constitutional violation even when the statistical pattern does not approach [such] extremes." Second, this Court has accepted statistics in the form of multiple-regression analysis to prove statutory violations under Title VII of the Civil Rights Act of 1964.

But the nature of the capital sentencing decision, and the relationship of the statistics to that decision, are fundamentally different from the corresponding elements in the venire-selection or Title VII cases. Most importantly, each particular decision to impose the death penalty is made by a petit jury selected from a properly constituted venire. Each jury is unique in its composition, and the Constitution requires that its decision rest on consideration of innumerable factors that vary according to the characteristics of the individual defendant and the facts of the particular capital offense. Thus, the application of an inference drawn from the general statistics to a specific decision in a trial and sentencing simply is not comparable to the application of an inference drawn from general statistics to a specific venire-selection or Title VII case. In those cases, the statistics relate to fewer entities, and fewer variables are relevant to the challenged decisions.

* * * McCleskey's statistical proffer must be viewed in the context of his challenge. McCleskey challenges decisions at the heart of the State's criminal justice system. "One of society's most basic tasks is that of protecting the lives of its citizens and one of the most basic ways in which it achieves the task is through criminal laws against murder." Implementation of these laws necessarily requires discretionary judgments. Because discretion is essential to the criminal justice process, we would demand exceptionally clear proof before we would infer that the discretion has been abused. The unique nature of the decisions at issue in this case also counsels against adopting such an inference from the disparities indicated by the Baldus study. Accordingly, we hold that the Baldus study is clearly insufficient to support an inference that any of the decisionmakers in McCleskey's case acted with discriminatory purpose.

McCleskey also suggests that the Baldus study proves that the State as a whole has acted with a discriminatory purpose. He appears to argue that the State has violated the Equal Protection Clause by adopting the capital punishment statute and allowing it to remain in force despite its allegedly discriminatory application. But "discriminatory purpose ... implies more than intent as volition or intent as awareness of consequences. It implies that the decisionmaker, in this case a state legislature, selected or reaffirmed a particular course of action at least in part because of, not merely in spite of, its adverse effects upon an identifiable group." For this claim to prevail, McCleskey would have to prove that the Georgia Legislature enacted or maintained the death penalty statute *because of* an anticipated racially discriminatory effect. * * * There [is] no evidence * * * that the Georgia Legislature enacted the capital punishment statute to further a racially discriminatory purpose.

Nor has McCleskey demonstrated that the legislature maintains the capital punishment statute because of the racially disproportionate impact suggested by the Baldus study. * * * Accordingly, we reject McCleskey's equal protection claims.

McCleskey also argues that the Baldus study demonstrates that the Georgia capital sentencing system violates the Eighth Amendment. * * * [McCleskey] contends that the Georgia capital punishment system is arbitrary and capricious in *application*, and therefore his sentence is excessive, because racial considerations may influence capital sentencing decisions in Georgia. * * *

To evaluate McCleskey's challenge, we must examine exactly what the Baldus study may show. Even Professor Baldus does not contend that his statistics *prove* that race enters into any capital sentencing decisions or that race was a factor in McCleskey's particular case. Statistics at most may show only a likelihood that a particular factor entered into some decisions. There is, of course, some risk of racial prejudice influencing a jury's decision in a criminal case. There are similar risks that other kinds of prejudice will influence other criminal trials. The question "is at what point that risk becomes constitutionally unacceptable." McCleskey asks us to accept the likelihood allegedly shown by the Baldus study as the constitutional measure of an unacceptable risk of racial prejudice influencing capital sentencing decisions. This we decline to do. * * *

McCleskey's argument that the Constitution condemns the discretion allowed decisionmakers in the Georgia capital sentencing system is antithetical to the fundamental role of discretion in our criminal justice system. Discretion in the criminal justice system offers substantial benefits to the criminal defendant. Not only can a jury decline to impose the death sentence, it can decline to convict or choose to convict of a lesser offense. * * * Similarly, the capacity of prosecutorial discretion to provide individualized justice is "firmly entrenched in American law." * * * Of course, "the power to be lenient [also] is the power to discriminate," but a capital punishment system that did not allow for discretionary acts of leniency "would be totally alien to our notions of criminal justice."

At most, the Baldus study indicates a discrepancy that appears to correlate with race. Apparent disparities in sentencing are an inevitable part of our criminal justice system. * * * In light of the safeguards designed to minimize racial bias in the process, the fundamental value of jury trial in our criminal justice system, and the benefits that discretion provides to criminal defendants, we hold that the Baldus study does not demonstrate a constitutionally significant risk of racial bias affecting the Georgia capital sentencing process.

Two additional concerns inform our decision in this case. First, McCleskey's claim, taken to its logical conclusion, throws into serious question the principles that underlie our entire criminal justice system. The Eighth Amendment is not limited in application to capital punishment, but applies to all penalties. Thus, if we accepted McCleskey's claim that racial bias has impermissibly tainted the capital sentencing decision, we could soon be faced with similar claims as to other types of penalty. Moreover, the claim that his sentence rests on the irrelevant factor of race easily could be extended to apply to claims based on unexplained discrepancies that correlate to membership in other minority groups, and even to gender. * * * Also, there is no logical reason that such a claim need be limited to racial or sexual bias. If arbitrary and capricious punishment is the touchstone under the Eighth Amendment, such a claim could—at least in theory—be based upon any arbitrary variable, such as the defendant's facial characteristics, or the physical attractiveness of the defendant or the victim, that some statistical study indicates may be influential in jury decisionmaking. As these examples illustrate, there is no limiting principle to the type of challenge brought by McCleskey. * * *

Second, McCleskey's arguments are best presented to the legislative bodies. It is not the responsibility—or indeed even the right—of this Court to determine the appropriate punishment for particular crimes. It is the legislatures, the elected representatives of the people, that are "constituted to respond to the will and consequently the moral values of the people." * * * Despite McCleskey's wide-ranging arguments that basically challenge the validity of capital punishment in our multiracial society, the only question before us is whether in his case the law of Georgia was properly applied. We agree with the District Court and the Court of Appeals for the Eleventh Circuit that this was carefully and correctly done in this case.

Accordingly, we affirm the judgment of the Court of Appeals for the Eleventh Circuit.

It is so ordered.

JUSTICE BRENNAN, with whom JUSTICE MARSHALL joins, and with whom JUSTICE BLACKMUN and JUSTICE STEVENS join * * *, dissenting.

* * * Since *Furman v. Georgia*, the Court has been concerned with the *risk* of the imposition of an arbitrary sentence, rather than the proven fact of one. * * * Defendants challenging their death sentences thus never have had to prove that impermissible considerations have actually infected sentencing decisions. We have required instead that they establish that the system under which they were sentenced posed a significant risk of such an occurrence. McCleskey's claim does differ, however, in one respect from these earlier cases: it is the first to base a challenge not on speculation about how a system *might* operate, but on empirical documentation of how it *does* operate.

The Court assumes the statistical validity of the Baldus study, and acknowledges that McCleskey has demonstrated a risk that racial prejudice plays a role in capital sentencing in Georgia. Nonetheless, it finds the probability of prejudice insufficient to create constitutional concern. Close analysis of the Baldus study, however, in light of both statistical principles and human experience, reveals that the risk that race influenced McCleskey's sentence is intolerable by any imaginable standard.

The Baldus study indicates that, after taking into account some 230 nonracial factors that might legitimately influence a sentencer, the jury *more likely than not* would have spared McCleskey's life had his victim been black. * * * [In cases] in which the jury has considerable discretion in choosing a sentence * * * death is imposed in 34% of white-victim crimes and 14% of black-victim crimes, a difference of 139% in the rate of imposition of the death penalty. In other words, just under 59%—almost 6 in 10—defendants comparable to McCleskey would not have received the death penalty if their victims had been black.

Furthermore, even examination of the sentencing system as a whole, factoring in those cases in which the jury exercises little discretion, indicates the influence of race on capital sentencing. For the Georgia system as a whole, race accounts for a six percentage point difference in the rate at which capital punishment is imposed. Since death is imposed in 11% of all white-victim cases, the rate in comparably aggravated black-victim cases is 5%. The rate of capital sentencing in a white-victim case is thus 120% greater than the rate in a black-victim case. Put another way, over half—55%—of defendants in white-victim crimes in Georgia would not have been sentenced to die if their victims had been black. * * *

These adjusted figures are only the most conservative indication of the risk that race will influence the death sentences of defendants in Georgia. Data unadjusted for the mitigating or aggravating effect of other factors show an even more pronounced disparity by race. The capital sentencing rate for all white-victim cases was almost *11 times* greater than the rate for black-victim cases. Furthermore, blacks who kill whites are sentenced to death at nearly *22 times* the rate of blacks who kill blacks, and more than *7 times* the rate of whites who kill blacks. In addition, prosecutors seek the death penalty for 70% of black defendants with white victims, but for only 15% of black defendants with black victims, and only 19% of white defendants with black victims. Since our decision upholding the Georgia capital sentencing system in *Gregg*, the State has executed seven persons. All of the seven were convicted of killing whites, and six of the seven executed were black. Such execution figures are especially striking in light of the fact that, during the period encompassed by the Baldus study, only 9.2% of Georgia homicides involved black defendants and white victims, while 60.7% involved black victims. * * *

The statistical evidence in this case thus relentlessly documents the risk that McCleskey's sentence was influenced by racial considerations. This evidence shows that there is a better than even chance in Georgia that race will influence the decision to impose the death penalty: a majority of defendants in white-victim crimes would not have been sentenced to die if their victims had been black. In determining whether this risk is acceptable, our judgment must be shaped by the awareness that "the risk of racial prejudice infecting a capital sentencing proceeding is especially serious in light of the complete finality of the death sentence," and that "it is of vital importance to the defendant and to the community that any decision to impose the death sentence be, and appear to be, based on reason rather than caprice or emotion." In determining the guilt of a defendant, a State must prove its case beyond a reasonable doubt. That is, we refuse to convict if the chance of error is simply less likely than not. Surely, we should not be willing to take a person's life if the chance that his death sentence was irrationally imposed is *more* likely than not. In light of the gravity of the interest at stake, petitioner's statistics on their face are a powerful demonstration of the type of risk that our Eighth Amendment jurisprudence has consistently condemned.

Evaluation of McCleskey's evidence cannot rest solely on the numbers themselves. We must also ask whether the conclusion suggested by those numbers is consonant with our understanding of history and human experience. Georgia's legacy of a race-conscious criminal justice system, as well as this Court's own recognition of the persistent danger that racial attitudes may affect criminal proceedings, indicates that McCleskey's claim is not a fanciful product of mere statistical artifice.

For many years, Georgia operated openly and formally precisely the type of dual system the evidence shows is still effectively in place. The criminal law expressly differentiated between crimes committed by and against blacks and whites, distinctions whose lineage traced back to the time of slavery. During the colonial period, black slaves who killed whites in Georgia, regardless of whether in self-defense or in defense of another, were automatically executed.

By the time of the Civil War, a dual system of crime and punishment was well established in Georgia. The state criminal code contained separate sections for "Slaves and Free Persons of Color" and for all other persons. The code provided, for instance, for an automatic death sentence for murder committed by blacks, but declared that anyone else convicted of murder might receive life imprisonment if the conviction were founded solely on circumstantial testimony *or* simply if the jury so recommended. The code established that the rape of a free white female by a black "shall be" punishable by death. However, rape by anyone else of a free white female was punishable by a prison term not less than 2 nor more than 20 years. The rape of *blacks* was punishable "by fine and imprisonment, at the discretion of the court." A black convicted of assaulting a free white person with intent to murder could be put to death at the discretion of the court, but the same offense committed against a black, slave or free, was classified as a "minor" offense whose punishment lay in the discretion of the court, as long as such punishment did not "extend to life, limb, or health." Assault with intent to murder by a white person was punishable by a prison term of from 2 to 10 years. * * *

The ongoing influence of history is acknowledged, as the majority observes, by our " 'unceasing efforts' to eradicate racial prejudice from our criminal justice system." These efforts, however, signify not the elimination of the problem but its persistence. Our cases reflect a realization of the myriad of opportunities for racial considerations to influence criminal proceedings * * *.

The discretion afforded prosecutors and jurors in the Georgia capital sentencing system creates such opportunities. No guidelines govern prosecutorial decisions to seek the death penalty, and Georgia provides juries with no list of aggravating and mitigating factors, nor any standard for balancing them against one another. * * * The Georgia sentencing system therefore provides considerable opportunity for racial considerations, however subtle and unconscious, to influence charging and sentencing decisions.

History and its continuing legacy thus buttress the probative force of McCleskey's statistics. Formal dual criminal laws may no longer be in effect, and intentional discrimination may no longer be prominent. Nonetheless * * * "subtle, less consciously held racial attitudes" continue to be of concern and the Georgia system gives such attitudes considerable room to operate.

* * * Enhanced willingness to impose the death sentence on black defendants, or diminished willingness to render such a sentence when blacks are victims, reflects a devaluation of the lives of black persons. When

confronted with evidence that race more likely than not plays such a role in a capital sentencing system, it is plainly insufficient to say that the importance of discretion demands that the risk be higher before we will act—for in such a case the very end that discretion is designed to serve is being undermined. * * *

The Court next states that its unwillingness to regard petitioner's evidence as sufficient is based in part on the fear that recognition of McCleskey's claim would open the door to widespread challenges to all aspects of criminal sentencing. Taken on its face, such a statement seems to suggest a fear of too much justice. Yet surely the majority would acknowledge that if striking evidence indicated that other minority groups, or women, or even persons with blond hair, were disproportionately sentenced to death, such a state of affairs would be repugnant to deeply rooted conceptions of fairness. The prospect that there may be more widespread abuse than McCleskey documents may be dismaying, but it does not justify complete abdication of our judicial role. The Constitution was framed fundamentally as a bulwark against governmental power, and preventing the arbitrary administration of punishment is a basic ideal of any society that purports to be governed by the rule of law. * * *

The Court also maintains that accepting McCleskey's claim would pose a threat to all sentencing because of the prospect that a correlation might be demonstrated between sentencing outcomes and other personal characteristics. Again, such a view is indifferent to the considerations that enter into a determination whether punishment is "cruel and unusual." Race is a consideration whose influence is expressly constitutionally proscribed. We have expressed a moral commitment, as embodied in our fundamental law, that this specific characteristic should not be the basis for allotting burdens and benefits. * * * That a decision to impose the death penalty could be influenced by *race* is thus a particularly repugnant prospect, and evidence that race may play even a modest role in levying a death sentence should be enough to characterize that sentence as "cruel and unusual." * * *

Finally, the Court justifies its rejection of McCleskey's claim by cautioning against usurpation of the legislatures' role in devising and monitoring criminal punishment. The Court is, of course, correct to emphasize the gravity of constitutional intervention and the importance that it be sparingly employed. * * * [However t]he judiciary's role in this society counts for little if the use of governmental power to extinguish life does not elicit close scrutiny.

* * * "[T]he methods we employ in the enforcement of our criminal law have aptly been called the measures by which the quality of our civilization may be judged." Those whom we would banish from society or from the human community itself often speak in too faint a voice to be heard above

society's demand for punishment. It is the particular role of courts to hear these voices, for the Constitution declares that the majoritarian chorus may not alone dictate the conditions of social life. The Court thus fulfills, rather than disrupts, the scheme of separation of powers by closely scrutinizing the imposition of the death penalty, for no decision of a society is more deserving of "sober second thought."

It is tempting to pretend that minorities on death row share a fate in no way connected to our own, that our treatment of them sounds no echoes beyond the chambers in which they die. Such an illusion is ultimately corrosive, for the reverberations of injustice are not so easily confined. "The destinies of the two races in this country are indissolubly linked together," and the way in which we choose those who will die reveals the depth of moral commitment among the living. * * *

[JUSTICE BLACKMUN's dissenting opinion has been omitted.]

APPENDIX

■ ■ ■

I. THE CONSTITUTION OF THE UNITED STATES OF AMERICA
(selected Amendments)

Amendment IV

The right of the people to be secure in their persons, houses, papers, and effects, against unreasonable searches and seizures, shall not be violated, and no Warrants shall issue, but upon probable cause, supported by Oath or affirmation, and particularly describing the place to be searched, and the persons or things to be seized.

Amendment V

No person shall be held to answer for a capital, or otherwise infamous crime, unless on a presentment or indictment of a Grand Jury, except in cases arising in the land or naval forces, or in the Militia, when in actual service in time of War or public danger; nor shall any person be subject for the same offense to be twice put in jeopardy of life or limb; nor shall be compelled in any criminal case to be a witness against himself, nor be deprived of life, liberty, or property, without due process of law; nor shall private property be taken for public use, without just compensation.

Amendment VI

In all criminal prosecutions, the accused shall enjoy the right to a speedy and public trial, by an impartial jury of the State and district wherein the crime shall have been committed, which district shall have been previously ascertained by law, and to be informed of the nature and cause of the accusation; to be confronted with the witnesses against him; to have compulsory process for obtaining witnesses in his favor, and to have the Assistance of Counsel for his defense.

Amendment VIII

Excessive bail shall not be required, nor excessive fines imposed, nor cruel and unusual punishments inflicted.

Amendment XIV

Section 1

All persons born or naturalized in the United States, and subject to the jurisdiction thereof, are citizens of the United States and of the State wherein they reside. No State shall make or enforce any law which shall abridge the privileges or immunities of citizens of the United States; nor shall any State deprive any person of life, liberty, or property, without due process of law; nor deny to any person within its jurisdiction the equal protection of the laws. * * *

II. FEDERAL RULES OF CRIMINAL PROCEDURE

RULE 6: THE GRAND JURY
Federal Rules of Criminal Procedure
U.S. Gov't Printing Office, 2021

(a) Summoning a Grand Jury.

(1) In General. When the public interest so requires, the court must order that one or more grand juries be summoned. A grand jury must have 16 to 23 members, and the court must order that enough legally qualified persons be summoned to meet this requirement.

(2) Alternate Jurors. When a grand jury is selected, the court may also select alternate jurors. Alternate jurors must have the same qualifications and be selected in the same manner as any other juror. Alternate jurors replace jurors in the same sequence in which the alternates were selected. An alternate juror who replaces a juror is subject to the same challenges, takes the same oath, and has the same authority as the other jurors.

(b) Objection to the Grand Jury or to a Grand Juror.

(1) Challenges. Either the government or a defendant may challenge the grand jury on the ground that it was not lawfully drawn, summoned, or selected, and may challenge an individual juror on the ground that the juror is not legally qualified.

(2) Motion to Dismiss an Indictment. A party may move to dismiss the indictment based on an objection to the grand jury or on an individual juror's lack of legal qualification, unless the court has previously ruled on the same objection under Rule 6(b)(1). The motion to dismiss is governed by 28 U.S.C. § 1867(e). The court must not dismiss the indictment on the ground that a grand juror was not legally qualified if the record shows that at least 12 qualified jurors concurred in the indictment.

(c) Foreperson and Deputy Foreperson. The court will appoint one juror as the foreperson and another as the deputy foreperson. In the foreperson's absence, the deputy foreperson will act as the foreperson. The foreperson may administer oaths and affirmations and will sign all indictments. The foreperson—or another juror designated by the foreperson—will record the number of jurors concurring in every indictment and will file the record with the clerk, but the record may not be made public unless the court so orders.

(d) Who May Be Present.

(1) While the Grand Jury Is in Session. The following persons may be present while the grand jury is in session: attorneys for the government, the witness being questioned, interpreters when needed, and a court reporter or an operator of a recording device.

(2) During Deliberations and Voting. No person other than the jurors, and any interpreter needed to assist a hearing-impaired or speech-impaired juror, may be present while the grand jury is deliberating or voting.

(e) Recording and Disclosing the Proceedings.

(1) Recording the Proceedings. Except while the grand jury is deliberating or voting, all proceedings must be recorded by a court reporter or by a suitable recording device. But the validity of a prosecution is not affected by the unintentional failure to make a recording. Unless the court orders otherwise, an attorney for the government will retain control of the recording, the reporter's notes, and any transcript prepared from those notes.

(2) Secrecy.

(A) No obligation of secrecy may be imposed on any person except in accordance with Rule 6(e)(2)(B).

(B) Unless these rules provide otherwise, the following persons must not disclose a matter occurring before the grand jury:

(i) a grand juror;

(ii) an interpreter;

(iii) a court reporter;

(iv) an operator of a recording device;

(v) a person who transcribes recorded testimony;

(vi) an attorney for the government; or

(vii) a person to whom disclosure is made under Rule 6(e)(3)(A)(ii) or (iii).

(3) Exceptions.

(A) Disclosure of a grand-jury matter—other than the grand jury's deliberations or any grand juror's vote—may be made to:

(i) an attorney for the government for use in performing that attorney's duty;

(ii) any government personnel—including those of a state, state subdivision, Indian tribe, or foreign government—that an attorney for the government considers necessary to assist in performing that attorney's duty to enforce federal criminal law; or

(iii) a person authorized by 18 U.S.C. § 3322.

(B) A person to whom information is disclosed under Rule 6(e)(3)(A)(ii) may use that information only to assist an attorney for the government in performing that attorney's duty to enforce federal criminal law. An attorney for the government must promptly provide the court that impaneled the grand jury with the names of all persons to whom a disclosure has been made, and must certify that the attorney has advised those persons of their obligation of secrecy under this rule.

(C) An attorney for the government may disclose any grand-jury matter to another federal grand jury.

(D) An attorney for the government may disclose any grand-jury matter involving foreign intelligence, counterintelligence (as defined in 50 U.S.C. § 3003), or foreign intelligence information (as defined in Rule 6(e)(3)(D)(iii)) to any federal law enforcement, intelligence, protective, immigration, national defense, or national security official to assist the official receiving the information in the performance of that official's duties. An attorney for the government may also disclose any grand-jury matter involving, within the United States or elsewhere, a threat of attack or other grave hostile acts of a foreign power or its agent, a threat of domestic or international sabotage or terrorism, or clandestine intelligence gathering activities by an intelligence service or network of a foreign power or by its agent, to any appropriate federal, state, state subdivision, Indian tribal, or foreign government official, for the purpose of preventing or responding to such threat or activities.

> **(i)** Any official who receives information under Rule 6(e)(3)(D) may use the information only as necessary in the conduct of that person's official duties subject to any limitations on the unauthorized disclosure of such information. Any state, state subdivision, Indian tribal, or foreign government official who receives information under Rule 6(e)(3)(D) may use the information only in a manner consistent with any guidelines issued by the Attorney General and the Director of National Intelligence.
>
> **(ii)** Within a reasonable time after disclosure is made under Rule 6(e)(3)(D), an attorney for the government must file, under seal, a notice with the court in the district where the grand jury convened stating that such information was

disclosed and the departments, agencies, or entities to which the disclosure was made.

(iii) As used in Rule 6(e)(3)(D), the term "foreign intelligence information" means:

(a) information, whether or not it concerns a United States person, that relates to the ability of the United States to protect against—

- actual or potential attack or other grave hostile acts of a foreign power or its agent;
- sabotage or international terrorism by a foreign power or its agent; or
- clandestine intelligence activities by an intelligence service or network of a foreign power or by its agent; or

(b) information, whether or not it concerns a United States person, with respect to a foreign power or foreign territory that relates to—

- the national defense or the security of the United States; or
- the conduct of the foreign affairs of the United States.

(E) The court may authorize disclosure—at a time, in a manner, and subject to any other conditions that it directs—of a grand-jury matter:

(i) preliminarily to or in connection with a judicial proceeding;

(ii) at the request of a defendant who shows that a ground may exist to dismiss the indictment because of a matter that occurred before the grand jury;

(iii) at the request of the government, when sought by a foreign court or prosecutor for use in an official criminal investigation;

(iv) at the request of the government if it shows that the matter may disclose a violation of State, Indian tribal, or foreign criminal law, as long as the disclosure is to an appropriate state, state-subdivision, Indian tribal, or foreign government official for the purpose of enforcing that law; or

(v) at the request of the government if it shows that the matter may disclose a violation of military criminal law under the Uniform Code of Military Justice, as long as the disclosure is to an appropriate military official for the purpose of enforcing that law.

(F) A petition to disclose a grand-jury matter under Rule 6(e)(3)(E)(i) must be filed in the district where the grand jury convened. Unless the hearing is ex parte—as it may be when the government is the petitioner—the petitioner must serve the petition on, and the court must afford a reasonable opportunity to appear and be heard to:

(i) an attorney for the government;

(ii) the parties to the judicial proceeding; and

(iii) any other person whom the court may designate.

(G) If the petition to disclose arises out of a judicial proceeding in another district, the petitioned court must transfer the petition to the other court unless the petitioned court can reasonably determine whether disclosure is proper. If the petitioned court decides to transfer, it must send to the transferee court the material sought to be disclosed, if feasible, and a written evaluation of the need for continued grand-jury secrecy. The transferee court must afford those persons identified in Rule 6(e)(3)(F) a reasonable opportunity to appear and be heard.

(4) Sealed Indictment. The magistrate judge to whom an indictment is returned may direct that the indictment be kept secret until the defendant is in custody or has been released pending trial. The clerk must then seal the indictment, and no person may disclose the indictment's existence except as necessary to issue or execute a warrant or summons.

(5) Closed Hearing. Subject to any right to an open hearing in a contempt proceeding, the court must close any hearing to the extent necessary to prevent disclosure of a matter occurring before a grand jury.

(6) Sealed Records. Records, orders, and subpoenas relating to grand-jury proceedings must be kept under seal to the extent and as long as necessary to prevent the unauthorized disclosure of a matter occurring before a grand jury.

(7) Contempt. A knowing violation of Rule 6, or of any guidelines jointly issued by the Attorney General and the Director of National Intelligence under Rule 6, may be punished as a contempt of court.

(f) Indictment and Return. A grand jury may indict only if at least 12 jurors concur. The grand jury—or its foreperson or deputy foreperson—must return the indictment to a magistrate judge in open court. To avoid unnecessary cost or delay, the magistrate judge may take the return by video teleconference from the court where the grand jury sits. If a complaint or information is pending against the defendant and 12 jurors do not concur in the indictment, the foreperson must promptly and in writing report the lack of concurrence to the magistrate judge.

(g) Discharging the Grand Jury. A grand jury must serve until the court discharges it, but it may serve more than 18 months only if the court, having determined that an extension is in the public interest, extends the grand jury's service. An extension may be granted for no more than 6 months, except as otherwise provided by statute.

(h) Excusing a Juror. At any time, for good cause, the court may excuse a juror either temporarily or permanently, and if permanently, the court may impanel an alternate juror in place of the excused juror.

(i) "Indian Tribe" Defined. "Indian tribe" means an Indian tribe recognized by the Secretary of the Interior on a list published in the Federal Register under 25 U.S.C. § 479a–1.

RULE 7: THE INDICTMENT AND THE INFORMATION
Federal Rules of Criminal Procedure
U.S. Gov't Printing Office, 2021

(a) When Used.

    (1) Felony. An offense (other than criminal contempt) must be prosecuted by an indictment if it is punishable:

        (A) by death; or

        (B) by imprisonment for more than one year.

    (2) Misdemeanor. An offense punishable by imprisonment for one year or less may be prosecuted in accordance with Rule 58(b)(1).

(b) Waiving Indictment. An offense punishable by imprisonment for more than one year may be prosecuted by information if the defendant—in open court and after being advised of the nature of the charge and of the defendant's rights—waives prosecution by indictment.

(c) Nature and Contents.

    (1) In General. The indictment or information must be a plain, concise, and definite written statement of the essential facts constituting the offense charged and must be signed by an attorney for the government. It need not contain a formal introduction or conclusion. A count may incorporate by reference an allegation made in another count. A count may allege that the means by which the defendant committed the offense are unknown or that the defendant committed it by one or more specified means. For each count, the indictment or information must give the official or customary citation of the statute, rule, regulation, or other provision of law that the defendant is alleged to have violated. For purposes of an indictment referred to in section 3282 of title 18, United States Code, for which the identity of the defendant is unknown, it shall be sufficient for the indictment to describe the defendant as an individual whose name is unknown, but who has a particular DNA profile, as that term is defined in that section 3282.

(2) Citation Error. Unless the defendant was misled and thereby prejudiced, neither an error in a citation nor a citation's omission is a ground to dismiss the indictment or information or to reverse a conviction.

(d) Surplusage. Upon the defendant's motion, the court may strike surplusage from the indictment or information.

(e) Amending an Information. Unless an additional or different offense is charged or a substantial right of the defendant is prejudiced, the court may permit an information to be amended at any time before the verdict or finding.

(f) Bill of Particulars. The court may direct the government to file a bill of particulars. The defendant may move for a bill of particulars before or within 14 days after arraignment or at a later time if the court permits. The government may amend a bill of particulars subject to such conditions as justice requires.

RULE 11: PLEAS
Federal Rules of Criminal Procedure
U.S. Gov't Printing Office, 2021

(a) Entering a Plea.

(1) In General. A defendant may plead not guilty, guilty, or (with the court's consent) nolo contendere.

(2) Conditional Plea. With the consent of the court and the government, a defendant may enter a conditional plea of guilty or nolo contendere, reserving in writing the right to have an appellate court review an adverse determination of a specified pretrial motion. A defendant who prevails on appeal may then withdraw the plea.

(3) Nolo Contendere Plea. Before accepting a plea of nolo contendere, the court must consider the parties' views and the public interest in the effective administration of justice.

(4) Failure to Enter a Plea. If a defendant refuses to enter a plea or if a defendant organization fails to appear, the court must enter a plea of not guilty.

(b) Considering and Accepting a Guilty or Nolo Contendere Plea.

(1) Advising and Questioning the Defendant. Before the court accepts a plea of guilty or nolo contendere, the defendant may be placed under oath, and the court must address the defendant personally in open court. During this address, the court must inform the defendant of, and determine that the defendant understands, the following:

(A) the government's right, in a prosecution for perjury or false statement, to use against the defendant any statement that the defendant gives under oath;

(B) the right to plead not guilty, or having already so pleaded, to persist in that plea;

(C) the right to a jury trial;

(D) the right to be represented by counsel—and if necessary have the court appoint counsel—at trial and at every other stage of the proceeding;

(E) the right at trial to confront and cross-examine adverse witnesses, to be protected from compelled self-incrimination, to testify and present evidence, and to compel the attendance of witnesses;

(F) the defendant's waiver of these trial rights if the court accepts a plea of guilty or nolo contendere;

(G) the nature of each charge to which the defendant is pleading

(H) any maximum possible penalty, including imprisonment, fine, and term of supervised release;

(I) any mandatory minimum penalty;

(J) any applicable forfeiture;

(K) the court's authority to order restitution;

(L) the court's obligation to impose a special assessment;

(M) in determining a sentence, the court's obligation to calculate the applicable sentencing-guideline range and to consider that range, possible departures under the Sentencing Guidelines, and other sentencing factors under 18 U.S.C. § 3553(a);

(N) the terms of any plea-agreement provision waiving the right to appeal or to collaterally attack the sentence; and

(O) that, if convicted, a defendant who is not a United States citizen may be removed from the United States, denied citizenship, and denied admission to the United States in the future.

(2) Ensuring That a Plea Is Voluntary. Before accepting a plea of guilty or nolo contendere, the court must address the defendant personally in open court and determine that the plea is voluntary and did not result from force, threats, or promises (other than promises in a plea agreement).

(3) Determining the Factual Basis for a Plea. Before entering judgment on a guilty plea, the court must determine that there is a factual basis for the plea.

(c) Plea Agreement Procedure

(1) In General. An attorney for the government and the defendant's attorney, or the defendant when proceeding pro se, may discuss and reach a plea agreement. The court must not participate in these discussions. If the defendant pleads guilty or nolo contendere to either a charged offense or a lesser or related offense, the plea agreement may specify that an attorney for the government will:

(A) not bring, or will move to dismiss, other charges;

(B) recommend, or agree not to oppose the defendant's request, that a particular sentence or sentencing range is appropriate or that a particular provision of the Sentencing Guidelines, or policy statement, or sentencing factor does or does not apply (such a recommendation or request does not bind the court); or

(C) agree that a specific sentence or sentencing range is the appropriate disposition of the case, or that a particular provision of the Sentencing Guidelines, or policy statement, or sentencing factor does or does not apply (such a recommendation or request binds the court once the court accepts the plea agreement).

(2) Disclosing a Plea Agreement. The parties must disclose the plea agreement in open court when the plea is offered, unless the court for good cause allows the parties to disclose the plea agreement in camera.

(3) Judicial Consideration of a Plea Agreement.

(A) To the extent the plea agreement is of the type specified in Rule 11(c)(1)(A) or (C), the court may accept the agreement, reject it, or defer a decision until the court has reviewed the presentence report.

(B) To the extent the plea agreement is of the type specified in Rule 11(c)(1)(B), the court must advise the defendant that the defendant has no right to withdraw the plea if the court does not follow the recommendation or request.

(4) Accepting a Plea Agreement. If the court accepts the plea agreement, it must inform the defendant that to the extent the plea agreement is of the type specified in Rule 11(c)(1)(A) or (C), the agreed disposition will be included in the judgment.

(5) Rejecting a Plea Agreement. If the court rejects a plea agreement containing provisions of the type specified in Rule 11(c)(1)(A) or (C), the court must do the following on the record and in open court (or, for good cause, in camera):

(A) inform the parties that the court rejects the plea agreement;

(B) advise the defendant personally that the court is not required to follow the plea agreement and give the defendant an opportunity to withdraw the plea; and

(C) advise the defendant personally that if the plea is not withdrawn, the court may dispose of the case less favorably toward the defendant than the plea agreement contemplated.

(d) Withdrawing a Guilty or Nolo Contendere Plea. A defendant may withdraw a plea of guilty or nolo contendere:

(1) before the court accepts the plea, for any reason or no reason; or

(2) after the court accepts the plea, but before it imposes sentence if:

(A) the court rejects a plea agreement under Rule 11(c)(5); or

(B) the defendant can show a fair and just reason for requesting the withdrawal.

(e) Finality of a Guilty or Nolo Contendere Plea. After the court imposes sentence, the defendant may not withdraw a plea of guilty or nolo contendere, and the plea may be set aside only on direct appeal or collateral attack.

(f) Admissibility or Inadmissibility of a Plea, Plea Discussions, and Related Statements. The admissibility or inadmissibility of a plea, a plea discussion, and any related statement is governed by Federal Rule of Evidence 410.

(g) Recording the Proceedings. The proceedings during which the defendant enters a plea must be recorded by a court reporter or by a suitable recording device. If there is a guilty plea or a nolo contendere plea, the record must include the inquiries and advice to the defendant required under Rule 11(b) and (c).

(h) Harmless Error. A variance from the requirements of this rule is harmless error if it does not affect substantial rights.

Rule 12.1: Notice of an Alibi Defense
Federal Rules of Criminal Procedure
U.S. Gov't Printing Office, 2021

(a) Government's Request for Notice and Defendant's Response.

(1) Government's Request. An attorney for the government may request in writing that the defendant notify an attorney for the government of any intended alibi defense. The request must state the time, date, and place of the alleged offense.

(2) Defendant's Response. Within 14 days after the request, or at some other time the court sets, the defendant must serve written notice on an attorney for the government of any intended alibi defense. The defendant's notice must state:

(A) each specific place where the defendant claims to have been at the time of the alleged offense; and

(B) the name, address, and telephone number of each alibi witness on whom the defendant intends to rely.

(b) Disclosing Government Witnesses.

(1) Disclosure.

(A) In General. If the defendant serves a Rule 12.1(a)(2) notice, an attorney for the government must disclose in writing to the defendant or the defendant's attorney:

(i) the name of each witness—and the address and telephone number of each witness other than a victim—that the government intends to rely on to establish that the defendant was present at the scene of the alleged offense; and

(ii) each government rebuttal witness to the defendant's alibi defense.

(B) Victim's Address and Telephone Number. If the government intends to rely on a victim's testimony to establish that the defendant was present at the scene of the alleged offense and the defendant establishes a need for the victim's address and telephone number, the court may:

(i) order the government to provide the information in writing to the defendant or the defendant's attorney; or

(ii) fashion a reasonable procedure that allows preparation of the defense and also protects the victim's interests.

(2) Time to Disclose. Unless the court directs otherwise, an attorney for the government must give its Rule 12.1(b)(1) disclosure within 14 days after the defendant serves notice of an intended alibi defense under Rule 12.1(a)(2), but no later than 14 days before trial.

(c) Continuing Duty to Disclose.

(1) In General. Both an attorney for the government and the defendant must promptly disclose in writing to the other party the name of each additional witness—and the address and telephone number of each additional witness other than a victim—if:

(A) the disclosing party learns of the witness before or during trial; and

(B) the witness should have been disclosed under Rule 12.1(a) or (b) if the disclosing party had known of the witness earlier.

(2) Address and Telephone Number of an Additional Victim Witness. The address and telephone number of an additional victim witness must not be disclosed except as provided in Rule 12.1(b)(1)(B).

(d) Exceptions. For good cause, the court may grant an exception to any requirement of Rule 12.1(a)–(c).

(e) Failure to Comply. If a party fails to comply with this rule, the court may exclude the testimony of any undisclosed witness regarding the defendant's alibi. This rule does not limit the defendant's right to testify.

(f) Inadmissibility of Withdrawn Intention. Evidence of an intention to rely on an alibi defense, later withdrawn, or of a statement made in connection with that intention, is not, in any civil or criminal proceeding, admissible against the person who gave notice of the intention.

RULE 16: DISCOVERY AND INSPECTION
Federal Rules of Criminal Procedure
U.S. Gov't Printing Office, 2021

(a) Government's Disclosure.

(1) Information Subject to Disclosure.

(A) Defendant's Oral Statement. Upon a defendant's request, the government must disclose to the defendant the substance of any relevant oral statement made by the defendant, before or after arrest, in response to interrogation by a person the defendant knew was a government agent if the government intends to use the statement at trial.

(B) Defendant's Written or Recorded Statement. Upon a defendant's request, the government must disclose to the defendant, and make available for inspection, copying, or photographing, all of the following:

(i) any relevant written or recorded statement by the defendant if:

- the statement is within the government's possession, custody, or control; and
- the attorney for the government knows—or through due diligence could know—that the statement exists;

(ii) the portion of any written record containing the substance of any relevant oral statement made before or after arrest if the defendant made the statement in response to interrogation by a person the defendant knew was a government agent; and

(iii) the defendant's recorded testimony before a grand jury relating to the charged offense.

(C) Organizational Defendant. Upon a defendant's request, if the defendant is an organization, the government must disclose to the defendant any statement described in Rule 16(a)(1)(A) and (B) if the government contends that the person making the statement:

(i) was legally able to bind the defendant regarding the subject of the statement because of that person's position as the defendant's director, officer, employee, or agent; or

(ii) was personally involved in the alleged conduct constituting the offense and was legally able to bind the defendant regarding that conduct because of that person's position as the defendant's director, officer, employee, or agent.

(D) Defendant's Prior Record. Upon a defendant's request, the government must furnish the defendant with a copy of the defendant's prior criminal record that is within the government's possession, custody, or control if the attorney for the government knows—or through due diligence could know—that the record exists.

(E) Documents and Objects. Upon a defendant's request, the government must permit the defendant to inspect and to copy or photograph books, papers, documents, data, photographs, tangible objects, buildings or places, or copies or portions of any of these items, if the item is within the government's possession, custody, or control and:

(i) the item is material to preparing the defense;

(ii) the government intends to use the item in its case-in-chief at trial; or

(iii) the item was obtained from or belongs to the defendant.

(F) Reports of Examinations and Tests. Upon a defendant's request, the government must permit a defendant to inspect and to copy or photograph the results or reports of any physical or mental examination and of any scientific test or experiment if:

(i) the item is within the government's possession, custody, or control;

(ii) the attorney for the government knows—or through due diligence could know—that the item exists; and

(iii) the item is material to preparing the defense or the government intends to use the item in its case-in-chief at trial.

(G) Expert witnesses. At the defendant's request, the government must give to the defendant a written summary of any testimony that the government intends to use under Rules 702, 703, or 705 of the Federal Rules of Evidence during its case-in-chief at trial. If the government requests discovery under subdivision (b)(1)(C)(ii) and the defendant complies, the government must, at the defendant's request, give to the defendant a written summary of testimony that the government intends to use under Rules 702, 703, or 705 of the Federal Rules of Evidence as evidence at trial on the issue of the defendant's mental condition. The summary provided under this subparagraph must describe the witness's opinions, the bases and reasons for those opinions, and the witness's qualifications.

(2) Information Not Subject to Disclosure. Except as permitted by Rule 16(a)(1)(A)–(D), (F), and (G), this rule does not authorize the discovery or inspection of reports, memoranda, or other internal government documents made by an attorney for the government or other government agent in connection with investigating or prosecuting the case. Nor does this rule authorize the discovery or inspection of statements made by prospective government witnesses except as provided in 18 U.S.C. § 3500.

(3) Grand Jury Transcripts. This rule does not apply to the discovery or inspection of a grand jury's recorded proceedings, except as provided in Rules 6, 12(h), 16(a)(1), and 26.2.

(b) Defendant's Disclosure.

(1) Information Subject to Disclosure.

(A) Documents and Objects. If a defendant requests disclosure under Rule 16(a)(1)(E) and the government complies, then the defendant must permit the government, upon request, to inspect and to copy or photograph books, papers, documents, data, photographs, tangible objects, buildings or places, or copies or portions of any of these items if:

> **(i)** the item is within the defendant's possession, custody, or control; and
>
> **(ii)** the defendant intends to use the item in the defendant's case-in-chief at trial.

(B) Reports of Examinations and Tests. If a defendant requests disclosure under Rule 16(a)(1)(F) and the government complies, the defendant must permit the government, upon request, to inspect and to copy or photograph the results or reports of any physical or mental examination and of any scientific test or experiment if:

> **(i)** the item is within the defendant's possession, custody, or control; and
>
> **(ii)** the defendant intends to use the item in the defendant's case-in-chief at trial, or intends to call the witness who prepared the report and the report relates to the witness's testimony.

(C) Expert witnesses. The defendant must, at the government's request, give to the government a written summary of any testimony that the defendant intends to use under Rules 702, 703, or 705 of the Federal Rules of Evidence as evidence at trial, if—

> **(i)** the defendant requests disclosure under subdivision (a)(1)(G) and the government complies; or
>
> **(ii)** the defendant has given notice under Rule 12.2(b) of an intent to present expert testimony on the defendant's mental condition.

This summary must describe the witness's opinions, the bases and reasons for those opinions, and the witness's qualifications[.]

(2) Information Not Subject to Disclosure. Except for scientific or medical reports, Rule 16(b)(1) does not authorize discovery or inspection of:

> **(A)** reports, memoranda, or other documents made by the defendant, or the defendant's attorney or agent, during the case's investigation or defense; or
>
> **(B)** a statement made to the defendant, or the defendant's attorney or agent, by:
>
>> **(i)** the defendant;

(ii) a government or defense witness; or

(iii) a prospective government or defense witness.

(c) Continuing Duty to Disclose. A party who discovers additional evidence or material before or during trial must promptly disclose its existence to the other party or the court if:

(1) the evidence or material is subject to discovery or inspection under this rule; and

(2) the other party previously requested, or the court ordered, its production.

(d) Regulating Discovery.

(1) Protective and Modifying Orders. At any time the court may, for good cause, deny, restrict, or defer discovery or inspection, or grant other appropriate relief. The court may permit a party to show good cause by a written statement that the court will inspect ex parte. If relief is granted, the court must preserve the entire text of the party's statement under seal.

(2) Failure to Comply. If a party fails to comply with this rule, the court may:

(A) order that party to permit the discovery or inspection; specify its time, place, and manner; and prescribe other just terms and conditions;

(B) grant a continuance;

(C) prohibit that party from introducing the undisclosed evidence; or

(D) enter any other order that is just under the circumstances.

RULE 26.2: PRODUCING A WITNESS'S STATEMENT

Federal Rules of Criminal Procedure
U.S. Gov't Printing Office, 2021

(a) Motion to Produce. After a witness other than the defendant has testified on direct examination, the court, on motion of a party who did not call the witness, must order an attorney for the government or the defendant and the defendant's attorney to produce, for the examination and use of the moving party, any statement of the witness that is in their possession and that relates to the subject matter of the witness's testimony.

(b) Producing the Entire Statement. If the entire statement relates to the subject matter of the witness's testimony, the court must order that the statement be delivered to the moving party.

(c) Producing a Redacted Statement. If the party who called the witness claims that the statement contains information that is privileged or does not relate to the subject matter of the witness's testimony, the court must inspect the statement in camera. After excising any privileged or unrelated portions, the court must order delivery of the redacted statement to the moving party. If the defendant objects to an excision, the court must preserve the entire statement with the excised portion indicated, under seal, as part of the record.

(d) Recess to Examine a Statement. The court may recess the proceedings to allow time for a party to examine the statement and prepare for its use.

(e) Sanction for Failure to Produce or Deliver a Statement. If the party who called the witness disobeys an order to produce or deliver a statement, the court must strike the witness's testimony from the record. If an attorney for the government disobeys the order, the court must declare a mistrial if justice so requires.

(f) "Statement" Defined. As used in this rule, a witness's "statement" means:

(1) a written statement that the witness makes and signs, or otherwise adopts or approves;

(2) a substantially verbatim, contemporaneously recorded recital of the witness's oral statement that is contained in any recording or any transcription of a recording; or

(3) the witness's statement to a grand jury, however taken or recorded, or a transcription of such a statement.

(g) Scope. This rule applies at trial, at a suppression hearing under Rule 12, and to the extent specified in the following rules:

(1) Rule 5.1(h) (preliminary hearing);

(2) Rule 32(i)(2) (sentencing);

(3) Rule 32.1(e) (hearing to revoke or modify probation or supervised release);

(4) Rule 46(j) (detention hearing); and

(5) Rule 8 of the Rules Governing Proceedings under 28 U.S.C. § 2255.

RULE 29: MOTION FOR A JUDGMENT OF ACQUITTAL

Federal Rules of Criminal Procedure
U.S. Gov't Printing Office, 2021

(a) Before Submission to the Jury. After the government closes its evidence or after the close of all the evidence, the court on the defendant's motion must enter a judgment of acquittal of any offense for which the evidence is insufficient to sustain a conviction. The court may on its own consider whether the evidence is insufficient to sustain a conviction. If the court denies a motion for a judgment of acquittal at the close of the government's evidence, the defendant may offer evidence without having reserved the right to do so.

(b) Reserving Decision. The court may reserve decision on the motion, proceed with the trial (where the motion is made before the close of all the evidence), submit the case to the jury, and decide the motion either before the jury returns a verdict or after it returns a verdict of guilty or is discharged without having returned a verdict. If the court reserves decision, it must decide the motion on the basis of the evidence at the time the ruling was reserved.

(c) After Jury Verdict or Discharge.

  (1) Time for a Motion. A defendant may move for a judgment of acquittal, or renew such a motion, within 14 days after a guilty verdict or after the court discharges the jury, whichever is later.

  (2) Ruling on the Motion. If the jury has returned a guilty verdict, the court may set aside the verdict and enter an acquittal. If the jury has failed to return a verdict, the court may enter a judgment of acquittal.

  (3) No Prior Motion Required. A defendant is not required to move for a judgment of acquittal before the court submits the case to the jury as a prerequisite for making such a motion after jury discharge.

(d) Conditional Ruling on a Motion for a New Trial.

  (1) Motion for a New Trial. If the court enters a judgment of acquittal after a guilty verdict, the court must also conditionally determine whether any motion for a new trial should be granted if the judgment of acquittal is later vacated or reversed. The court must specify the reasons for that determination.

  (2) Finality. The court's order conditionally granting a motion for a new trial does not affect the finality of the judgment of acquittal.

  (3) Appeal.

    (A) Grant of a Motion for a New Trial. If the court conditionally grants a motion for a new trial and an appellate court later reverses the judgment of acquittal, the trial court must proceed with the new trial unless the appellate court orders otherwise.

    (B) Denial of a Motion for a New Trial. If the court conditionally denies a motion for a new trial, an appellee may assert that the denial was erroneous. If the appellate court later reverses the judgment of acquittal, the trial court must proceed as the appellate court directs.

III. FEDERAL STATUTES

FEDERAL BAIL REFORM ACT OF 1984
18 U.S.C.S. §§ 3141, 1342
LexisNexis 2022

18 U.S.C.S. § 3141—Release and Detention Authority Generally

(a) Pending trial. A judicial officer authorized to order the arrest of a person under section 3041 of this title [18 USCS § 3041] before whom an arrested person is brought shall order that such person be released or detained, pending judicial proceedings, under this chapter. [18 USCS §§ 3141 et seq.].

(b) Pending sentence or appeal. A judicial officer of a court of original jurisdiction over an offense, or a judicial officer of a Federal appellate court, shall order that, pending imposition or execution of sentence, or pending appeal of conviction or sentence, a person be released or detained under this chapter. [18 USCS §§ 3141 et seq.]

18 U.S.C.S. § 3142—Release or Detention of a Defendant Pending Trial

(a) In general. Upon the appearance before a judicial officer of a person charged with an offense, the judicial officer shall issue an order that, pending trial, the person be—

(1) released on personal recognizance or upon execution of an unsecured appearance bond, under subsection (b) of this section;

(2) released on a condition or combination of conditions under subsection (c) of this section;

(3) temporarily detained to permit revocation of conditional release, deportation, or exclusion under subsection (d) of this section; or

(4) detained under subsection (e) of this section.

(b) Release on personal recognizance or unsecured appearance bond. The judicial officer shall order the pretrial release of the person on personal recognizance, or upon execution of an unsecured appearance bond in an amount specified by the court, subject to the condition that the person not commit a Federal, State, or local crime during the period of release and subject to the condition that the person cooperate in the collection of a DNA sample from the person if the collection of such a sample is authorized pursuant to section 3 of the DNA Analysis Backlog Elimination Act of 2000 (42 U.S.C. 14135a), unless the judicial officer determines that such release will not reasonably assure the appearance of the person as required or will endanger the safety of any other person or the community.

(c) Release on conditions.

(1) If the judicial officer determines that the release described in subsection (b) of this section will not reasonably assure the appearance of the person as required or will endanger the safety of any other person or the community, such judicial officer shall order the pretrial release of the person—

(A) subject to the condition that the person not commit a Federal, State, or local crime during the period of release and subject to the condition that the person cooperate in the collection of a DNA sample from the person if the collection of such a sample is authorized pursuant to section 3 of the DNA Analysis Backlog Elimination Act of 2000 (42 U.S.C. 14135a); and

(B) subject to the least restrictive further condition, or combination of conditions, that such judicial officer determines will reasonably assure the appearance of the person as required and the safety of any other person and the community, which may include the condition that the person—

(i) remain in the custody of a designated person, who agrees to assume supervision and to report any violation of a release condition to the court, if the designated person is able reasonably to assure the judicial officer that the person will appear as required and will not pose a danger to the safety of any other person or the community;

(ii) maintain employment, or, if unemployed, actively seek employment;

(iii) maintain or commence an educational program;

(iv) abide by specified restrictions on personal associations, place of abode, or travel;

(v) avoid all contact with an alleged victim of the crime and with a potential witness who may testify concerning the offense;

(vi) report on a regular basis to a designated law enforcement agency, pretrial services agency, or other agency;

(vii) comply with a specified curfew;

(viii) refrain from possessing a firearm, destructive device, or other dangerous weapon;

(ix) refrain from excessive use of alcohol, or any use of a narcotic drug or other controlled substance, as defined in section 102 of the Controlled Substances Act (21 U.S.C. 802), without a prescription by a licensed medical practitioner;

(x) undergo available medical, psychological, or psychiatric treatment, including treatment for drug or alcohol dependency, and remain in a specified institution if required for that purpose;

(xi) execute an agreement to forfeit upon failing to appear as required, property of a sufficient unencumbered value, including money, as is reasonably necessary to assure the appearance of the person as required, and shall provide the court with proof of ownership and the value of the property along with information regarding existing encumbrances as the judicial office may require;

(xii) execute a bail bond with solvent sureties; who will execute an agreement to forfeit in such amount as is reasonably necessary to assure appearance of the person as required and shall provide the court with information regarding the value of the assets and liabilities of the surety if other than an approved surety and the nature and extent of encumbrances against the surety's property; such surety shall have a net worth which shall have sufficient unencumbered value to pay the amount of the bail bond;

(xiii) return to custody for specified hours following release for employment, schooling, or other limited purposes; and

(xiv) satisfy any other condition that is reasonably necessary to assure the appearance of the person as required and to assure the safety of any other person and the community.

In any case that involves a minor victim under section 1201, 1591, 2241, 2242, 2244(a)(1), 2245, 2251, 2251A, 2252(a)(1), 2252(a)(2), 2252(a)(3), 2252A(a)(1), 2252A(a)(2), 2252A(a)(3), 2252A(a)(4), 2260, 2421, 2422, 2423, or 2425 of this title [18 USCS § 1201, 1591, 2241, 2242, 2244(a)(1), 2245, 2251, 2251A, 2252(a)(1), (2), (3), 2252A(a)(1), (2), (3), (4), 2260, 2421, 2422, 2423, or 2425], or a failure to register offense under section 2250 of this title [18 USCS § 2250], any release order shall contain, at a minimum, a condition of electronic monitoring and each of the conditions specified at subparagraphs (iv), (v), (vi), (vii), and (viii).[a]

---

[a] In 2006, Congress enacted the Adam Walsh Act, which, among other things, mandates specific conditions for the pretrial release of persons charged with certain offenses, including child pornography, sexual exploitation, offenses involving a minor victim, and the offense of failing to register as a sex offender. In these cases, a release order "shall contain, at a minimum, a condition of electronic monitoring" even if the Magistrate Judge does not make a specific finding that electronic monitoring is necessary to assure the defendant's appearance or the safety of the

(2) The judicial officer may not impose a financial condition that results in the pretrial detention of the person.

(3) The judicial officer may at any time amend the order to impose additional or different conditions of release.

(d) Temporary detention to permit revocation of conditional release, deportation, or exclusion. If the judicial officer determines that—

(1) such person—

(A) is, and was at the time the offense was committed, on—

(i) release pending trial for a felony under Federal, State, or local law;

(ii) release pending imposition or execution of sentence, appeal of sentence or conviction, or completion of sentence, for any offense under Federal, State, or local law; or

(iii) probation or parole for any offense under Federal, State, or local law; or

(B) is not a citizen of the United States or lawfully admitted for permanent residence, as defined in section 101(a)(20) of the Immigration and Nationality Act (8 U.S.C. 1101(a)(20)); and

(2) the person may flee or pose a danger to any other person or the community;

such judicial officer shall order the detention of the person, for a period of not more than ten days, excluding Saturdays, Sundays, and

---

community. Several U.S. district courts have struck down the electronic monitoring provision of the Adam Walsh Act as violating the Due Process Clause of the Fifth Amendment and/or the Eighth Amendment's prohibition against excessive bail. *See, e.g.* United States v. Polouizzi, 697 F. Supp. 2d 381, 394 (E.D.N.Y. 2010) (finding that the Adam Walsh Act's mandatory pretrial release condition of electronic monitoring for all defendants charged with possession or receipt of child pornography violated defendant's procedural due process rights and the Eighth Amendment's prohibition against excessive bail); United States v. Arzberger, 592 F. Supp. 2d 590, 601 (S.D.N.Y. 2008) (finding that imposition of electronic monitoring on certain defendants without providing the defendant with any opportunity to contest whether such monitoring is necessary to ensure his return to court or the safety of the community violates the Due Process Clause of the Fifth Amendment); United States v. Karper, 847 F. Supp. 2d 350, 360 (N.D.N.Y. 2011) (finding that the provision of the Adam Walsh Act that mandates conditions, such as electronic monitoring, on certain pretrial detainees without affording them an opportunity to contest the restriction on their freedom of movement violates procedural due process); United States v. Torres, 566 F. Supp. 2d 591 (W.D. Tex. 2008) (finding that the provision of the Adam Walsh Amendments to the Federal Bail Reform Act, mandating electronic monitoring, as set forth in 3142(c)(1)(B), violates the Due Process Clause of the Fifth Amendment and the Eighth Amendment's prohibition against excessive punishment); United States v. Smedley, 611 F. Supp. 2d 971 (E.D. Mo. 2009) (finding that provision of Adam Walsh Act imposing home detention with electronic monitoring as a condition of pretrial release violates due process); United States v. Merritt, 612 F. Supp. 2d 1074 (D. Neb. 2009) (finding that the Adam Walsh Amendments violate the Due Process Clause because they mandate certain release conditions in child pornography cases, such as electronic monitoring and a curfew, without a judicial determination of whether such restrictions are necessary to ensure the defendant's appearance at trial or to protect the public).

holidays, and direct the attorney for the Government to notify the appropriate court, probation or parole official, or State or local law enforcement official, or the appropriate official of the Immigration and Naturalization Service. If the official fails or declines to take the person into custody during that period, the person shall be treated in accordance with the other provisions of this section, notwithstanding the applicability of other provisions of law governing release pending trial or deportation or exclusion proceedings. If temporary detention is sought under paragraph (1)(B) of this subsection, the person has the burden of proving to the court such person's United States citizenship or lawful admission for permanent residence.

(e) Detention.

(1) If, after a hearing pursuant to the provisions of subsection (f) of this section, the judicial officer finds that no condition or combination of conditions will reasonably assure the appearance of the person as required and the safety of any other person and the community, such judicial officer shall order the detention of the person before trial.

(2) In a case described in subsection (f)(1) of this section, a rebuttable presumption arises that no condition or combination of conditions will reasonably assure the safety of any other person and the community if such judicial officer finds that—

> **(A)** the person has been convicted of a Federal offense that is described in subsection (f)(1) of this section, or of a State or local offense that would have been an offense described in subsection (f)(1) of this section if a circumstance giving rise to Federal jurisdiction had existed;
>
> **(B)** the offense described in subparagraph (A) was committed while the person was on release pending trial for a Federal, State, or local offense; and
>
> **(C)** a period of not more than five years has elapsed since the date of conviction, or the release of the person from imprisonment, for the offense described in subparagraph (A), whichever is later.

(3) Subject to rebuttal by the person, it shall be presumed that no condition or combination of conditions will reasonably assure the appearance of the person as required and the safety of the community if the judicial officer finds that there is probable cause to believe that the person committed—

> **(A)** an offense for which a maximum term of imprisonment of ten years or more is prescribed in the Controlled Substances Act (21 U.S.C. 801 et seq.), the Controlled Substances Import and Export Act (21 U.S.C. 951 et seq.), or chapter 705 of title 46 [46 USCS § 70501 et seq.];

(B) an offense under section 924(c), 956(a), or 2332b of this title [18 USCS § 924(c), 956(a), or 2332b];

(C) an offense listed in section 2332b(g)(5)(B) of title 18, United States Code [18 USCS § 2332b(g)(5)(B)], for which a maximum term of imprisonment of 10 years or more is prescribed;

(D) an offense under chapter 77 of this title [18 USCS §§ 1581 et seq.] for which a maximum term of imprisonment of 20 years or more is prescribed; or

(E) an offense involving a minor victim under section 1201, 1591, 2241, 2242, 2244(a)(1), 2245, 2251, 2251A, 2252(a)(1), 2252(a)(2), 2252(a)(3), 2252A(a)(1), 2252A(a)(2), 2252A(a)(3), 2252A(a)(4), 2260, 2421, 2422, 2423, or 2425 of this title [18 USCS § 1201, 1591, 2241, 2242, 2244, (a)(1), 2245, 2251, 2251A, 2252(a)(1), 2252(a)(2), 2252(a)(3), 2252A(a)(1), 2252A(a)(2), 2252A(a)(3), 2252A(a)(4), 2260, 2421, 2422, 2423, or 2425].

(f) **Detention hearing.** The judicial officer shall hold a hearing to determine whether any condition or combination of conditions set forth in subsection (c) of this section will reasonably assure the appearance of such person as required and the safety of any other person and the community—

(1) upon motion of the attorney for the Government, in a case that involves—

(A) a crime of violence, a violation of section 1591 [18 USCS § 1591], or an offense listed in section 2332b(g)(5)(B) [18 USCS § 2332b(g)(5)(B)] for which a maximum term of imprisonment of 10 years or more is prescribed;

(B) an offense for which the maximum sentence is life imprisonment or death;

(C) an offense for which a maximum term of imprisonment of ten years or more is prescribed in the Controlled Substances Act (21 U.S.C. 801 et seq.), the Controlled Substances Import and Export Act (21 U.S.C. 951 et seq.), or chapter 705 of title 46 [46 USCS §§ 70501 et seq.];

(D) any felony if such person has been convicted of two or more offenses described in subparagraphs (A) through (C) of this paragraph, or two or more State or local offenses that would have been offenses described in subparagraphs (A) through (C) of this paragraph if a circumstance giving rise to Federal jurisdiction had existed, or a combination of such offenses; or

(E) any felony that is not otherwise a crime of violence that involves a minor victim or that involves the possession or use of a firearm or destructive device (as those terms are defined in section

921 [18 USCS § 921]), or any other dangerous weapon, or involves a failure to register under section 2250 of title 18, United States Code [18 USCS § 2250]; or

(2) upon motion of the attorney for the Government or upon the judicial officer's own motion, in a case that involves—

(A) a serious risk that such person will flee; or

(B) a serious risk that such person will obstruct or attempt to obstruct justice, or threaten, injure, or intimidate, or attempt to threaten, injure, or intimidate, a prospective witness or juror.

The hearing shall be held immediately upon the person's first appearance before the judicial officer unless that person, or the attorney for the Government, seeks a continuance. Except for good cause, a continuance on motion of such person may not exceed five days (not including any intermediate Saturday, Sunday, or legal holiday), and a continuance on motion of the attorney for the Government may not exceed three days (not including any intermediate Saturday, Sunday, or legal holiday). During a continuance, such person shall be detained, and the judicial officer, on motion of the attorney for the Government or sua sponte, may order that, while in custody, a person who appears to be a narcotics addict receive a medical examination to determine whether such person is an addict. At the hearing, such person has the right to be represented by counsel, and, if financially unable to obtain adequate representation, to have counsel appointed. The person shall be afforded an opportunity to testify, to present witnesses, to cross-examine witnesses who appear at the hearing, and to present information by proffer or otherwise. The rules concerning admissibility of evidence in criminal trials do not apply to the presentation and consideration of information at the hearing. The facts the judicial officer uses to support a finding pursuant to subsection (e) that no condition or combination of conditions will reasonably assure the safety of any other person and the community shall be supported by clear and convincing evidence. The person may be detained pending completion of the hearing. The hearing may be reopened, before or after a determination by the judicial officer, at any time before trial if the judicial officer finds that information exists that was not known to the movant at the time of the hearing and that has a material bearing on the issue whether there are conditions of release that will reasonably assure the appearance of such person as required and the safety of any other person and the community.

(g) Factors to be considered. The judicial officer shall, in determining whether there are conditions of release that will reasonably assure the appearance of the person as required and the safety of any other person and the community, take into account the available information concerning—

(1) the nature and circumstances of the offense charged, including whether the offense is a crime of violence, a violation of section 1591 [18 USCS § 1591], a Federal crime of terrorism, or involves a minor victim or a controlled substance, firearm, explosive, or destructive device;

(2) the weight of the evidence against the person;

(3) the history and characteristics of the person, including—

(A) the person's character, physical and mental condition, family ties, employment, financial resources, length of residence in the community, community ties, past conduct, history relating to drug or alcohol abuse, criminal history, and record concerning appearance at court proceedings; and

(B) whether, at the time of the current offense or arrest, the person was on probation, on parole, or on other release pending trial, sentencing, appeal, or completion of sentence for an offense under Federal, State, or local law; and

(4) the nature and seriousness of the danger to any person or the community that would be posed by the person's release. In considering the conditions of release described in subsection (c)(1)(B)(xi) or (c)(1)(B)(xii) of this section, the judicial officer may upon his own motion, or shall upon the motion of the Government, conduct an inquiry into the source of the property to be designated for potential forfeiture or offered as collateral to secure a bond, and shall decline to accept the designation, or the use as collateral, of property that, because of its source, will not reasonably assure the appearance of the person as required.

(h) **Contents of release order.** In a release order issued under subsection (b) or (c) of this section, the judicial officer shall—

(1) include a written statement that sets forth all the conditions to which the release is subject, in a manner sufficiently clear and specific to serve as a guide for the person's conduct; and

(2) advise the person of—

(A) the penalties for violating a condition of release, including the penalties for committing an offense while on pretrial release;

(B) the consequences of violating a condition of release, including the immediate issuance of a warrant for the person's arrest; and

(C) sections 1503 of this title [18 USCS § 1503] (relating to intimidation of witnesses, jurors, and officers of the court), 1510

[18 USCS § 1510] (relating to obstruction of criminal investigations), 1512 [18 USCS § 1512] (tampering with a witness, victim, or an informant), and 1513 [18 USCS § 1513] (retaliating against a witness, victim, or an informant).

(i) Contents of detention order. In a detention order issued under subsection (e) of this section, the judicial officer shall—

(1) include written findings of fact and a written statement of the reasons for the detention;

(2) direct that the person be committed to the custody of the Attorney General for confinement in a corrections facility separate, to the extent practicable, from persons awaiting or serving sentences or being held in custody pending appeal;

(3) direct that the person be afforded reasonable opportunity for private consultation with counsel; and

(4) direct that, on order of a court of the United States or on request of an attorney for the Government, the person in charge of the corrections facility in which the person is confined deliver the person to a United States marshal for the purpose of an appearance in connection with a court proceeding.

The judicial officer may, by subsequent order, permit the temporary release of the person, in the custody of a United States marshal or another appropriate person, to the extent that the judicial officer determines such release to be necessary for preparation of the person's defense or for another compelling reason.

(j) Presumption of innocence. Nothing in this section shall be construed as modifying or limiting the presumption of innocence.

THE JENCKS ACT: DEMANDS FOR PRODUCTION OF STATEMENTS AND REPORTS OF WITNESSES
18 U.S.C.A. § 3500
West 2022

(a) In any criminal prosecution brought by the United States, no statement or report in the possession of the United States which was made by a Government witness or prospective Government witness (other than the defendant) shall be the subject of subpoena, discovery, or inspection until said witness has testified on direct examination in the trial of the case.

(b) After a witness called by the United States has testified on direct examination, the court shall, on motion of the defendant, order the United States to produce any statement (as hereinafter defined) of the witness in the possession of the United States which relates to the subject matter as to which the witness has testified. If the entire contents of any such statement relate to the subject matter of the testimony of the witness, the court shall order it to be delivered directly to the defendant for his examination and use.

(c) If the United States claims that any statement ordered to be produced under this section contains matter which does not relate to the subject matter of the testimony of the witness, the court shall order the United States to deliver such statement for the inspection of the court in camera. Upon such delivery the court shall excise the portions of such statement which do not relate to the subject matter of the testimony of the witness. With such material excised, the court shall then direct delivery of such statement to the defendant for his use. If, pursuant to such procedure, any portion of such statement is withheld from the defendant and the defendant objects to such withholding, and the trial is continued to an adjudication of the guilt of the defendant, the entire text of such statement shall be preserved by the United States and, in the event the defendant appeals, shall be made available to the appellate court for the purpose of determining the correctness of the ruling of the trial judge. Whenever any statement is delivered to a defendant pursuant to this section, the court in its discretion, upon application of said defendant, may recess proceedings in the trial for such time as it may determine to be reasonably required for the examination of such statement by said defendant and his preparation for its use in the trial.

(d) If the United States elects not to comply with an order of the court under subsection (b) or (c) hereof to deliver to the defendant any such statement, or such portion thereof as the court may direct, the court shall strike from the record the testimony of the witness, and the trial shall proceed unless the court in its discretion shall determine that the interests of justice require that a mistrial be declared.

(e) The term "statement", as used in subsections (b), (c), and (d) of this section in relation to any witness called by the United States, means—

(1) a written statement made by said witness and signed or otherwise adopted or approved by him;

(2) a stenographic, mechanical, electrical, or other recording, or a transcription thereof, which is a substantially verbatim recital of an oral statement made by said witness and recorded contemporaneously with the making of such oral statement; or

(3) a statement, however taken or recorded, or a transcription thereof, if any, made by said witness to a grand jury.

IV. AMERICAN BAR ASSOCIATION STANDARDS

PROSECUTION FUNCTION

CRIMINAL JUSTICE STANDARDS FOR THE PROSECUTION FUNCTION
AM. BAR ASS'N, 4th ed. 2017

Standard 3-1.2: Functions and Duties of the Prosecutor

(a) The prosecutor is an administrator of justice, a zealous advocate, and an officer of the court. The prosecutor's office should exercise sound discretion and independent judgment in the performance of the prosecution function.

(b) The primary duty of the prosecutor is to seek justice within the bounds of the law, not merely to convict. The prosecutor serves the public interest and should act with integrity and balanced judgment to increase public safety both by pursuing appropriate criminal charges of appropriate severity, and by exercising discretion to not pursue criminal charges in appropriate circumstances. The prosecutor should seek to protect the innocent and convict the guilty, consider the interests of victims and witnesses, and respect the constitutional and legal rights of all persons, including suspects and defendants.

(c) The prosecutor should know and abide by the standards of professional conduct as expressed in applicable law and ethical codes and opinions in the applicable jurisdiction. The prosecutor should avoid an appearance of impropriety in performing the prosecution function. A prosecutor should seek out, and the prosecutor's office should provide, supervisory advice and ethical guidance when the proper course of prosecutorial conduct seems unclear. A prosecutor who disagrees with a governing ethical rule should seek its change if appropriate, and directly challenge it if necessary, but should comply with it unless relieved by court order.

(d) The prosecutor should make use of ethical guidance offered by existing organizations, and should seek to establish and make use of an ethics advisory group akin to that described in Defense Function Standard 4-1.11.

(e) The prosecutor should be knowledgeable about, consider, and where appropriate develop or assist in developing alternatives to prosecution or conviction that may be applicable in individual cases or classes of cases. The prosecutor's office should be available to assist community efforts addressing problems that lead to, or result from, criminal activity or perceived flaws in the criminal justice system.

(f) The prosecutor is not merely a case-processor but also a problem-solver responsible for considering broad goals of the criminal justice system. The prosecutor should seek to reform and improve the administration of criminal justice, and when inadequacies or injustices in the substantive or procedural law come to the prosecutor's attention, the prosecutor should stimulate and support efforts for remedial action. The prosecutor should provide service to the community, including involvement in public service and Bar activities, public education, community service activities, and Bar leadership positions. A prosecutorial office should support such activities, and the office's budget should include funding and paid release time for such activities.

Standard 3-1.6: Improper Bias Prohibited

(a) The prosecutor should not manifest or exercise, by words or conduct, bias or prejudice based upon race, sex, religion, national origin, disability, age, sexual orientation, gender identity, or socioeconomic status. A prosecutor should not use other improper considerations, such as partisan or political or personal considerations, in exercising prosecutorial discretion. A prosecutor should strive to eliminate implicit biases, and act to mitigate any improper bias or prejudice when credibly informed that it exists within the scope of the prosecutor's authority.

(b) A prosecutor's office should be proactive in efforts to detect, investigate, and eliminate improper biases, with particular attention to historically persistent biases like race, in all of its work. A prosecutor's office should regularly assess the potential for biased or unfairly disparate impacts of its policies on communities within the prosecutor's jurisdiction, and eliminate those impacts that cannot be properly justified.

Standard 3-1.12: Duty to Report and Respond to Prosecutorial Misconduct

(a) The prosecutor's office should adopt policies to address allegations of professional misconduct, including violations of law, by prosecutors. At a minimum such policies should require internal reporting of reasonably suspected misconduct to supervisory staff within the office, and authorize supervisory staff to quickly address the allegations. Investigations of allegations of professional misconduct within the prosecutor's office should be handled in an independent and conflict-free manner.

(b) When a prosecutor reasonably believes that another person associated with the prosecutor's office intends or is about to engage in misconduct, the prosecutor should attempt to dissuade the person. If such attempt fails or is not possible, and the prosecutor reasonably believes that misconduct is ongoing, will occur, or has occurred, the prosecutor should promptly refer the matter to higher authority in the prosecutor's office including, if warranted by the seriousness of the matter, to the chief prosecutor.

(c) If, despite the prosecutor's efforts in accordance with sections (a) and (b) above, the chief prosecutor permits, fails to address, or insists upon an action or omission that is clearly a violation of law, the prosecutor should take further remedial action, including revealing information necessary to address, remedy, or prevent the violation to appropriate judicial, regulatory, or other government officials not in the prosecutor's office.

Standard 3–4.2: Decisions to Charge are the Prosecutor's

(a) While the decision to arrest is often the responsibility of law enforcement personnel, the decision to institute formal criminal proceedings is the responsibility of the prosecutor. Where the law permits a law enforcement officer or other person to initiate proceedings by complaining directly to a judicial officer or the grand jury, the complainant should be required to present the complaint for prior review by the prosecutor, and the prosecutor's recommendation regarding the complaint should be communicated to the judicial officer or grand jury.

(b) The prosecutor's office should establish standards and procedures for evaluating complaints to determine whether formal criminal proceedings should be instituted.

(c) In determining whether formal criminal charges should be filed, prosecutors should consider whether further investigation should be undertaken. After charges are filed the prosecutor should oversee law enforcement investigative activity related to the case.

(d) If the defendant is not in custody when charged, the prosecutor should consider whether a voluntary appearance rather than a custodial arrest would suffice to protect the public and ensure the defendant's presence at court proceedings.

Standard 3–4.3: Minimum Requirements for Filing and Maintaining Criminal Charges

(a) A prosecutor should seek or file criminal charges only if the prosecutor reasonably believes that the charges are supported by probable cause, that admissible evidence will be sufficient to support conviction beyond a reasonable doubt, and that the decision to charge is in the interests of justice.

(b) After criminal charges are filed, a prosecutor should maintain them only if the prosecutor continues to reasonably believe that probable cause exists and that admissible evidence will be sufficient to support conviction beyond a reasonable doubt.

(c) If a prosecutor has significant doubt about the guilt of the accused or the quality, truthfulness, or sufficiency of the evidence in any criminal case assigned to the prosecutor, the prosecutor should disclose those doubts to supervisory staff. The prosecutor's office should then determine whether it is appropriate to proceed with the case.

(d) A prosecutor's office should not file or maintain charges if it believes the defendant is innocent, no matter what the state of the evidence.

Standard 3-4.4: Discretion in Filing, Declining, Maintaining, and Dismissing Criminal Charges

(a) In order to fully implement the prosecutor's functions and duties, including the obligation to enforce the law while exercising sound discretion, the prosecutor is not obliged to file or maintain all criminal charges which the evidence might support. Among the factors which the prosecutor may properly consider in exercising discretion to initiate, decline, or dismiss a criminal charge, even though it meets the requirements of Standard 3-4.3, are:

(i) the strength of the case;

(ii) the prosecutor's doubt that the accused is in fact guilty;

(iii) the extent or absence of harm caused by the offense;

(iv) the impact of prosecution or non-prosecution on the public welfare;

(v) the background and characteristics of the offender, including any voluntary restitution or efforts at rehabilitation;

(vi) whether the authorized or likely punishment or collateral consequences are disproportionate in relation to the particular offense or the offender;

(vii) the views and motives of the victim or complainant;

(viii) any improper conduct by law enforcement;

(ix) unwarranted disparate treatment of similarly situated persons;

(x) potential collateral impact on third parties, including witnesses or victims;

(xi) cooperation of the offender in the apprehension or conviction of others;

(xii) the possible influence of any cultural, ethnic, socioeconomic or other improper biases;

(xiii) changes in law or policy;

(xiv) the fair and efficient distribution of limited prosecutorial resources;

(xv) the likelihood of prosecution by another jurisdiction; and

(xvi) whether the public's interests in the matter might be appropriately vindicated by available civil, regulatory, administrative, or private remedies.

(b) In exercising discretion to file and maintain charges, the prosecutor should not consider:

(i) partisan or other improper political or personal considerations;

(ii) hostility or personal animus towards a potential subject, or any other improper motive of the prosecutor; or

(iii) the impermissible criteria described in Standard 1.6 above. * * *

(d) The prosecutor should not file or maintain charges greater in number or degree than can reasonably be supported with evidence at trial and are necessary to fairly reflect the gravity of the offense or deter similar conduct. * * *

(f) The prosecutor should consider the possibility of a noncriminal disposition, formal or informal, or a deferred prosecution or other diversionary disposition, when deciding whether to initiate or prosecute criminal charges. The prosecutor should be familiar with the services and resources of other agencies, public or private, that might assist in the evaluation of cases for diversion or deferral from the criminal process.

Standard 3-4.5: Relationship with a Grand Jury

(a) In presenting a matter to a criminal grand jury, and in light of its *ex parte* character, the prosecutor should respect the independence of the grand jury and should not preempt a function of the grand jury, mislead the grand jury, or abuse the processes of the grand jury.

(b) Where the prosecutor is authorized to act as a legal advisor to the grand jury, the prosecutor should appropriately explain the law and may, if permitted by law, express an opinion on the legal significance of the evidence, but should give due deference to the grand jury as an independent legal body.

(c) The prosecutor should not make statements or arguments to a grand jury in an effort to influence grand jury action in a manner that would be impermissible in a trial.

(d) The entirety of the proceedings occurring before a grand jury, including the prosecutor's communications with and presentations and instructions to the grand jury, should be recorded in some manner, and that record should be preserved. The prosecutor should avoid off-the-record communications with the grand jury and with individual grand jurors.

Standard 3-4.6: Quality and Scope of Evidence Before a Grand Jury

(a) A prosecutor should not seek an indictment unless the prosecutor reasonably believes the charges are supported by probable cause and that there will be admissible evidence sufficient to support the charges beyond reasonable doubt at trial. A prosecutor should advise a grand jury of the prosecutor's opinion that it should not indict if the prosecutor believes the evidence presented does not warrant an indictment.

(b) In addition to determining what criminal charges to file, a grand jury may properly be used to investigate potential criminal conduct, and also to determine the sense of the community regarding potential charges.

(c) A prosecutor should present to a grand jury only evidence which the prosecutor believes is appropriate and authorized by law for presentation to a grand jury. The prosecutor should be familiar with the law of the jurisdiction regarding grand juries, and may present witnesses to summarize relevant evidence to the extent the law permits.

(d) When a new grand jury is empanelled, a prosecutor should ensure that the grand jurors are appropriately instructed, consistent with the law of the jurisdiction, on the grand jury's right and ability to seek evidence, ask questions, and hear directly from any available witnesses, including eyewitnesses.

(e) A prosecutor with personal knowledge of evidence that directly negates the guilt of a subject of the investigation should present or otherwise disclose that evidence to the grand jury. The prosecutor should relay to the grand jury any request by the subject or target of an investigation to testify before the grand jury, or present other non-frivolous evidence claimed to be exculpatory.

(f) If the prosecutor concludes that a witness is a target of a criminal investigation, the prosecutor should not seek to compel the witness's testimony before the grand jury absent immunity. The prosecutor should honor, however, a reasonable request from a target or subject who wishes to testify before the grand jury.

(g) Unless there is a reasonable possibility that it will facilitate flight of the target, endanger other persons, interfere with an ongoing investigation, or obstruct justice, the prosecutor should give notice to a target of a grand jury investigation, and offer the target an opportunity to testify before the grand jury. Prior to taking a target's testimony, the prosecutor should advise the target of the privilege against self-incrimination and obtain a voluntary waiver of that right.

(h) The prosecutor should not seek to compel the appearance of a witness whose activities are the subject of the grand jury's inquiry, if the witness states in advance that if called the witness will claim the constitutional privilege not to testify, and provides a reasonable basis for such claim. If warranted, the prosecutor may judicially challenge such a claim of privilege or seek a grant of immunity according to the law.

(i) The prosecutor should not issue a grand jury subpoena to a criminal defense attorney or defense team member, or other witness whose testimony reasonably might be protected by a recognized privilege, without considering the applicable law and rules of professional responsibility in the jurisdiction.

(j) Except where permitted by law, a prosecutor should not use the grand jury in order to obtain evidence to assist the prosecution's preparation for trial of a defendant who has already been charged. A prosecutor may, however, use the grand jury to investigate additional or new charges against a defendant who has already been charged.

(k) Except where permitted by law, a prosecutor should not use a criminal grand jury solely or primarily for the purpose of aiding or assisting in an administrative or civil inquiry.

Standard 3–5.4: Identification and Disclosure of Information and Evidence

(a) After charges are filed if not before, the prosecutor should diligently seek to identify all information in the possession of the prosecution or its agents that tends to negate the guilt of the accused, mitigate the offense charged, impeach the government's witnesses or evidence, or reduce the likely punishment of the accused if convicted.

(b) The prosecutor should diligently advise other governmental agencies involved in the case of their continuing duty to identify, preserve, and disclose to the prosecutor information described in (a) above.

(c) Before trial of a criminal case, a prosecutor should make timely disclosure to the defense of information described in (a) above that is known to the prosecutor, regardless of whether the prosecutor believes it is likely to change the result of the proceeding, unless relieved of this responsibility by a court's protective order. (Regarding discovery prior to a guilty plea, see Standard 3–5.6(f) below.) A prosecutor should not intentionally attempt to obscure information disclosed pursuant to this standard by including it without identification within a larger volume of materials.

(d) The obligations to identify and disclose such information continue throughout the prosecution of a criminal case.

(e) A prosecutor should timely respond to legally proper discovery requests, and make a diligent effort to comply with legally proper disclosure obligations, unless otherwise authorized by a court. When the defense makes requests for specific information, the prosecutor should provide specific responses rather than merely a general acknowledgement of discovery obligations. Requests and responses should be tailored to the case and "boilerplate" requests and responses should be disfavored.

(f) The prosecutor should make prompt efforts to identify and disclose to the defense any physical evidence that has been gathered in the investigation, and provide the defense a reasonable opportunity to examine it.

(g) A prosecutor should not avoid pursuit of information or evidence because the prosecutor believes it will damage the prosecution's case or aid the accused.

(h) A prosecutor should determine whether additional statutes, rules or caselaw may govern or restrict the disclosure of information, and comply with these authorities absent court order.

Standard 3–5.5: Preservation of Information and Evidence

(a) The prosecutor should make reasonable efforts to preserve, and direct the prosecutor's agents to preserve, relevant materials during and after a criminal case, including

> **(i)** evidence relevant to investigations as well as prosecutions, whether or not admitted at trial;
>
> **(ii)** information identified pursuant to Standard 3–5.4(a); and
>
> **(iii)** other materials necessary to support significant decisions made and conclusions reached by the prosecution in the course of an investigation and prosecution.

(b) The prosecutor's office should develop policies regarding the method and duration of preservation of such materials. Such policies should be consistent with applicable rules and laws (such as public records laws) in the jurisdiction. These policies, and individual preservation decisions, should consider the character and seriousness of each case, the character of the particular evidence or information, the likelihood of further challenges to judgments following conviction, and the resources available for preservation. Physical evidence should be preserved so as to reasonably preserve its forensic characteristics and utility.

(c) Materials should be preserved at least until a criminal case is finally resolved or is final on appeal and the time for further appeal has expired. In felony cases, materials should be preserved until post-conviction litigation is concluded or time-limits have expired. In death penalty cases, information should be preserved until the penalty is carried out or is precluded.

(d) The prosecutor should comply with additional statutes, rules or caselaw that may govern the preservation of evidence.

Standard 3–6.3: Selection of Jurors

(a) The prosecutor's office should be aware of legal standards that govern the selection of jurors, and train prosecutors to comply. The prosecutor should prepare to effectively discharge the prosecution function in the selection of the jury, including exercising challenges for cause and peremptory challenges. The prosecutor's office should also be aware of the process used to select and summon the jury pool and bring legal deficiencies to the attention of the court.

(b) The prosecutor should not strike jurors based on any criteria rendered impermissible by the constitution, statutes, applicable rules of the jurisdiction, or these standards, including race, sex, religion, national origin, disability, sexual orientation or gender identity. The prosecutor should consider contesting a defense counsel's peremptory challenges that appear to be based upon such criteria.

(c) In cases in which the prosecutor conducts a pretrial investigation of the background of potential jurors, the investigative methods used should not harass, intimidate, or unduly embarrass or invade the privacy of potential jurors. Absent special circumstances, such investigation should be restricted to review of records and sources of information already in existence and to which access is lawfully allowed. If the prosecutor uses record searches that are unavailable to the defense, such as criminal record databases, the prosecutor should share the results with defense counsel or seek a judicial protective order.

(d) The opportunity to question jurors personally should be used solely to obtain information relevant to the well-informed exercise of challenges. The prosecutor should not seek to commit jurors on factual issues likely to arise in the case, and should not intentionally present arguments, facts or evidence which the prosecutor reasonably should know will not be admissible at trial. Voir dire should not be used to argue the prosecutor's case to the jury, or to unduly ingratiate counsel with the jurors.

(e) During voir dire, the prosecutor should seek to minimize any undue embarrassment or invasion of privacy of potential jurors, for example by seeking to inquire into sensitive matters outside the presence of other potential jurors, while still enabling fair and efficient juror selection.

(f) If the court does not permit voir dire by counsel, the prosecutor should provide the court with suggested questions in advance, and request specific follow-up questions during the selection process when necessary to ensure fair juror selection.

(g) If the prosecutor has reliable information that conflicts with a potential juror's responses, or that reasonably would support a "for cause" challenge by any party, the prosecutor should inform the court and, unless the court orders otherwise, defense counsel.

Standard 3–7.2: Sentencing

(a) The severity of sentences imposed should not be used as a measure of a prosecutor's effectiveness.

(b) The prosecutor should be familiar with relevant sentencing laws, rules, consequences and options, including alternative non-imprisonment sentences. Before or soon after charges are filed, and throughout the pendency of the case, the prosecutor should evaluate potential consequences of the prosecution and available sentencing options, such as forfeiture, restitution, and immigration effects, and be prepared to actively advise the court in sentencing.

(c) The prosecutor should seek to assure that a fair and informed sentencing judgment is made, and to avoid unfair sentences and disparities.

(d) In the interests of uniformity, the prosecutor's office should develop consistent policies for evaluating and making sentencing recommendations, and not leave complete discretion for sentencing policy to individual prosecutors.

(e) The prosecutor should know the relevant laws and rules regarding victims' rights, and facilitate victim participation in the sentencing process as the law requires or permits.

DEFENSE FUNCTION
CRIMINAL JUSTICE STANDARDS FOR THE DEFENSE FUNCTION
AM. BAR ASS'N, 4th ed. 2017

Standard 4–1.1: The Scope and Function of These Standards

(a) As used in these Standards, "defense counsel" means any attorney—including privately retained, assigned by the court, acting *pro bono* or serving indigent defendants in a legal aid or public defender's office—who acts as an attorney on behalf of a client being investigated or prosecuted for alleged criminal conduct, or a client seeking legal advice regarding a potential, ongoing or past criminal matter or subpoena, including as a witness. These Standards are intended to apply in any context in which a lawyer would reasonably understand that a criminal prosecution could result. The Standards are intended to serve the best interests of clients, and should not be relied upon to justify any decision that is counter to the client's best interests. The burden to justify any exception should rest with the lawyer seeking it.

(b) These Standards are intended to provide guidance for the professional conduct and performance of defense counsel. They are not intended to modify a defense attorney's obligations under applicable rules, statutes or the constitution. They are aspirational or describe "best practices," and are not intended to serve as the basis for the imposition of professional discipline, to create substantive or procedural rights for clients, or to create a standard of care for civil liability. They may be relevant in judicial evaluation of constitutional claims regarding the right to counsel. For purposes of consistency, these Standards sometimes include language taken from the Model Rules of Professional Conduct; but the Standards often address conduct or provide details beyond that governed by the Model Rules of Professional Conduct. No inconsistency is ever intended; and in any case a lawyer should always read and comply with the rules of professional conduct and other authorities that are binding in the specific jurisdiction or matter, including choice of law principles that may regulate the lawyer's ethical conduct.

(c) Because the Standards for Criminal Justice are aspirational, the words "should" or "should not" are used in these Standards, rather than mandatory phrases such as "shall" or "shall not," to describe the conduct of lawyers that is expected or recommended under these Standards. The Standards are not intended to suggest any lesser standard of conduct than may be required by applicable mandatory rules, statutes, or other binding authorities.

(d) These Standards are intended to address the performance of criminal defense counsel in all stages of their professional work. Other ABA Criminal Justice Standards should also be consulted for more detailed consideration of the performance of criminal defense counsel in specific areas.

Standard 4–1.2: Functions and Duties of Defense Counsel

(a) Defense counsel is essential to the administration of criminal justice. A court properly constituted to hear a criminal case should be viewed as an entity consisting of the court (including judge, jury, and other court personnel), counsel for the prosecution, and counsel for the defense.

(b) Defense counsel have the difficult task of serving both as officers of the court and as loyal and zealous advocates for their clients. The primary duties that defense counsel owe to their clients, to the administration of justice, and as officers of the court, are to serve as their clients' counselor and advocate with courage and devotion; to ensure that constitutional and other legal rights of their clients are protected; and to render effective, high-quality legal representation with integrity.

(c) Defense counsel should know and abide by the standards of professional conduct as expressed in applicable law and ethical codes and opinions in the applicable jurisdiction. Defense counsel should seek out supervisory advice when available, and defense counsel organizations as well as others should provide ethical guidance when the proper course of conduct seems unclear. Defense counsel who disagrees with a governing ethical rule should seek its change if appropriate, and directly challenge it if necessary, but should comply with it unless relieved by court order.

(d) Defense counsel is the client's professional representative, not the client's alter-ego. Defense counsel should act zealously within the bounds of the law and standards on behalf of their clients, but have no duty to, and may not, execute any directive of the client which violates the law or such standards. In representing a client, defense counsel may engage in a good faith challenge to the validity of such laws or standards if done openly.

(e) Defense counsel should seek to reform and improve the administration of criminal justice. When inadequacies or injustices in the substantive or procedural law come to defense counsel's attention, counsel should stimulate and support efforts for remedial action. Defense counsel should provide services to the community, including involvement in public service and Bar activities, public education, community service activities, and Bar leadership positions. A public defense organization should support such activities, and the office's budget should include funding and paid release time for such activities.

(f) Defense counsel should be knowledgeable about, and consider, alternatives to prosecution or conviction that may be applicable in individual cases, and communicate them to the client. Defense counsel should be available to assist other groups in the community in addressing problems that lead to, or result from, criminal activity or perceived flaws in the criminal justice system.

(g) Because the death penalty differs from other criminal penalties, defense counsel in a capital case should make extraordinary efforts on behalf of the accused and, more specifically, review and comply with the ABA Guidelines for the Appointment and Performance of Defense Counsel in Death Penalty Cases.

Standard 4–1.3: Continuing Duties of Defense Counsel

Some duties of defense counsel run throughout the period of representation, and even beyond. Defense counsel should consider the impact of these duties at all stages of a criminal representation and on all decisions and actions that arise in the course of performing the defense function. These duties include:

(a) a duty of confidentiality regarding information relevant to the client's representation which duty continues after the representation ends;

(b) a duty of loyalty toward the client;

(c) a duty of candor toward the court and others, tempered by the duties of confidentiality and loyalty;

(d) a duty to communicate and keep the client informed and advised of significant developments and potential options and outcomes;

(e) a duty to be well-informed regarding the legal options and developments that can affect a client's interests during a criminal representation;

(f) a duty to continually evaluate the impact that each decision or action may have at later stages, including trial, sentencing, and post-conviction review;

(g) a duty to be open to possible negotiated dispositions of the matter, including the possible benefits and disadvantages of cooperating with the prosecution;

(h) a duty to consider the collateral consequences of decisions and actions, including but not limited to the collateral consequences of conviction.

Standard 4–1.6: Improper Bias Prohibited

(a) Defense counsel should not manifest or exercise, by words or conduct, bias or prejudice based upon race, sex, religion, national origin, disability, age, sexual orientation, gender identity, or socioeconomic status. Defense counsel should strive to eliminate implicit biases, and act to mitigate any improper bias or prejudice when credibly informed that it exists within the scope of defense counsel's authority.

(b) Defense counsel should be proactive in efforts to detect, investigate, and eliminate improper biases, with particular attention to historically persistent biases like race, in all of counsel's work. A public defense office should regularly assess the potential for biased or unfairly disparate impacts of its policies on communities within the defense office's jurisdiction, and eliminate those impacts that cannot be properly justified.

Standard 4–4.1: Duty to Investigate and Engage Investigators

(a) Defense counsel has a duty to investigate in all cases, and to determine whether there is a sufficient factual basis for criminal charges.

(b) The duty to investigate is not terminated by factors such as the apparent force of the prosecution's evidence, a client's alleged admissions to others of facts suggesting guilt, a client's expressed desire to plead guilty or that there should be no investigation, or statements to defense counsel supporting guilt.

(c) Defense counsel's investigative efforts should commence promptly and should explore appropriate avenues that reasonably might lead to information relevant to the merits of the matter, consequences of the criminal proceedings, and potential dispositions and penalties. Although investigation will vary depending on the circumstances, it should always be shaped by what is in the client's best interests, after consultation with the client. Defense counsel's investigation of the merits of the criminal charges should include efforts to secure relevant information in the possession of the prosecution, law enforcement authorities, and others, as well as independent investigation. Counsel's investigation should also include evaluation of the prosecution's evidence (including possible re-testing or re-evaluation of physical, forensic, and expert evidence) and consideration of inconsistencies, potential avenues of impeachment of prosecution witnesses, and other possible suspects and alternative theories that the evidence may raise.

(d) Defense counsel should determine whether the client's interests would be served by engaging fact investigators, forensic, accounting or other experts, or other professional witnesses such as sentencing specialists or social workers, and if so, consider, in consultation with the client, whether to engage them. Counsel should regularly re-evaluate the need for such services throughout the representation.

(e) If the client lacks sufficient resources to pay for necessary investigation, counsel should seek resources from the court, the government, or donors. Application to the court should be made *ex parte* if appropriate to protect the client's confidentiality. Publicly funded defense offices should advocate for resources sufficient to fund such investigative expert services on a regular basis. If adequate investigative funding is not provided, counsel may advise the court that the lack of resources for investigation may render legal representation ineffective.

Standard 4–5.2: Control and Direction of the Case

(a) Certain decisions relating to the conduct of the case are for the accused; others are for defense counsel. Determining whether a decision is ultimately to be made by the client or by counsel is highly contextual, and counsel should give great weight to strongly held views of a competent client regarding decisions of all kinds.

(b) The decisions ultimately to be made by a competent client, after full consultation with defense counsel, include:

    (i) whether to proceed without counsel;

    (ii) what pleas to enter;

    (iii) whether to accept a plea offer;

    (iv) whether to cooperate with or provide substantial assistance to the government;

    (v) whether to waive jury trial;

    (vi) whether to testify in his or her own behalf;

    (vii) whether to speak at sentencing;

    (viii) whether to appeal; and

    (ix) any other decision that has been determined in the jurisdiction to belong to the client.

(c) If defense counsel has a good faith doubt regarding the client's competence to make important decisions, counsel should consider seeking an expert evaluation from a mental health professional, within the protection of confidentiality and privilege rules if applicable.

(d) Strategic and tactical decisions should be made by defense counsel, after consultation with the client where feasible and appropriate. Such decisions include how to pursue plea negotiations, how to craft and respond to motions and, at hearing or trial, what witnesses to call, whether and how to conduct cross-examination, what jurors to accept or strike, what motions and objections should be made, what stipulations if any to agree to, and what and how evidence should be introduced.

(e) If a disagreement on a significant matter arises between defense counsel and the client, and counsel resolves it differently than the client prefers, defense counsel should consider memorializing the disagreement and its resolution, showing that record to the client, and preserving it in the file.

Standard 4-5.4: Consideration of Collateral Consequences

(a) Defense counsel should identify, and advise the client of, collateral consequences that may arise from charge, plea or conviction. Counsel should investigate consequences under applicable federal, state, and local laws, and seek assistance from others with greater knowledge in specialized areas in order to be adequately informed as to the existence and details of relevant collateral consequences. Such advice should be provided sufficiently in advance that it may be fairly considered in a decision to pursue trial, plea, or other dispositions.

(b) When defense counsel knows that a consequence is particularly important to the client, counsel should advise the client as to whether there are procedures for avoiding, mitigating or later removing the consequence, and if so, how to best pursue or prepare for them.

(c) Defense counsel should include consideration of potential collateral consequences in negotiations with the prosecutor regarding possible dispositions, and in communications with the judge or court personnel regarding the appropriate sentence or conditions, if any, to be imposed.

Standard 4-5.5: Special Attention to Immigration Status and Consequences

(a) Defense counsel should determine a client's citizenship and immigration status, assuring the client that such information is important for effective legal representation and that it should be protected by the attorney-client privilege. Counsel should avoid any actions that might alert the government to information that could adversely affect the client.

(b) If defense counsel determines that a client may not be a United States citizen, counsel should investigate and identify particular immigration consequences that might follow possible criminal dispositions. Consultation or association with an immigration law expert or knowledgeable advocate is advisable in these circumstances. Public and appointed defenders should develop, or seek funding for, such immigration expertise within their offices.

(c) After determining the client's immigration status and potential adverse consequences from the criminal proceedings, including removal, exclusion, bars to relief from removal, immigration detention, denial of citizenship, and adverse consequences to the client's immediate family, counsel should advise the client of all such potential consequences and determine with the client the best course of action for the client's interests and how to pursue it.

(d) If a client is convicted of a removable offense, defense counsel should advise the client of the serious consequences if the client illegally returns to the United States.

Standard 4-8.3: Sentencing

(a) Early in the representation, and throughout the pendency of the case, defense counsel should consider potential issues that might affect sentencing. Defense counsel should become familiar with the client's background, applicable sentencing laws and rules, and what options might be available as well as what consequences might arise if the client is convicted. Defense counsel should be fully informed regarding available sentencing alternatives and with community and other resources which may be of assistance in formulating a plan for meeting the client's needs. Defense counsel should also consider whether consultation with an expert specializing in sentencing options or other sentencing issues is appropriate.

(b) Defense counsel's preparation before sentencing should include learning the court's practices in exercising sentencing discretion; the collateral consequences of different sentences; and the normal pattern of sentences for the offense involved, including any guidelines applicable for either sentencing and, where applicable, parole. The consequences (including reasonably foreseeable collateral consequences) of potential dispositions should be explained fully by defense counsel to the client.

(c) Defense counsel should present all arguments or evidence which will assist the court or its agents in reaching a sentencing disposition favorable to the accused. Defense counsel should ensure that the accused understands the nature of the presentence investigation process, and in particular the significance of statements made by the accused to probation officers and related personnel. Defense counsel should cooperate with court presentence officers unless, after consideration and consultation, it appears not to be in the best interests of the client. Unless prohibited, defense counsel should attend the probation officer's presentence interview with the accused and meet in person with the probation officer to discuss the case.

(d) Defense counsel should gather and submit to the presentence officers, prosecution, and court as much mitigating information relevant to sentencing as reasonably possible; and in an appropriate case, with the consent of the accused, counsel should suggest alternative programs of service or rehabilitation or other non-imprisonment options, based on defense counsel's exploration of employment, educational, and other opportunities made available by community services.

(e) If a presentence report is made available to defense counsel, counsel should seek to verify the information contained in it, and should supplement or challenge it if necessary. Defense counsel should either provide the client with a copy or (if copying is not allowed) discuss counsel's knowledge of its contents with the client. In many cases, defense counsel should independently investigate the facts relevant to sentencing, rather than relying on the court's presentence report, and should seek discovery or relevant information from governmental agencies or other third-parties if necessary.

(f) Defense counsel should alert the accused to the right of allocution. Counsel should consider with the client the potential benefits of the judge hearing a personal statement from the defendants as contrasted with the possible dangers of making a statement that could adversely impact the sentencing judge's decision or the merits of an appeal.

(g) If a sentence of imprisonment is imposed, defense counsel should seek the court's assistance, including an on-the-record statement by the court if possible, recommending the appropriate place of confinement and types of treatment, programming and counseling that should be provided for the defendant in confinement.

(h) Once the sentence has been announced, defense counsel should make any objections necessary for the record, seek clarification of any unclear terms, and advise the client of the meaning and effects of the judgment, including any known collateral consequences. Counsel should also note on the record the intention to appeal, if that decision has already been made with the client.

(i) If the client has received an imprisonment sentence and an appeal will be taken, defense counsel should determine whether bail pending appeal is appropriate and, if so, request it.

Standard 4–9.6: Challenges to the Effectiveness of Counsel

(a) If appellate or post-appellate counsel is satisfied after appropriate investigation and legal research that another defense counsel who served in an earlier phase of the case did not provide effective assistance, new counsel should not hesitate to seek relief for the client.

(b) If defense counsel concludes that he or she did not provide effective assistance in an earlier phase of the case, counsel should explain this conclusion to the client. Unless the client clearly wants counsel to continue, counsel in this situation should seek to withdraw from further representation of the client with an explanation to the court of the reason, consistent with the duty of confidentiality to the client. Counsel should recommend that the client consult with independent counsel if the client desires counsel to continue with the representation. Counsel should continue with the representation only if the client so desires after informed consent and such further representation is consistent with applicable conflict of interest rules.

(c) Defense counsel whose conduct in a criminal case is drawn into question is permitted to testify concerning the matters at issue, and is not precluded from disclosing the truth concerning the matters raised by his former client, even though this involves revealing matters which were given in confidence. Former counsel must act consistently with applicable confidentiality rules, and ordinarily may not reveal confidences unless necessary for the purposes of the proceeding and under judicial supervision.

(d) In a proceeding challenging counsel's performance, counsel should not rely on the prosecutor to act as counsel's lawyer in the proceeding, and should continue to consider the former client's best interests.

INDEX

References are to Pages

ADMINISTRATIVE SEARCHES
Generally, 371
Drug Testing, 371
Inventory Searches, 372–377
Strip Searches, 388–403
Vehicle Checkpoints, 377–388

AERIAL SURVEILLANCE
Generally, 18–23

APPEALS
Generally, 8

ARRAIGNMENT
Generally, 4–5
On Complaint, 4
On Information or Indictment, 5
Start of Adversarial Judicial Criminal
    Proceedings, 512, 517, 627, 666, 681

ARRESTS
Generally, 2–3, 117
Arrest Warrant, When Needed, 117–123
In Home, 120–123, 406
Material Witness, 128–131
Public Places, 117–120
Third Party's Home, 123–128

AUTOMOBILE EXCEPTION
Generally, 169–200
Containers and, 175–189
Justifications for, 169–174
Mobile Homes and, 169–174
Privacy, Reduced Expectation of, 171
Ready Mobility, 170–173, 186, 194
Scope of, 175–189

BAIL
Generally, 747–762
Class and, 758–760
Excessive, 748–750
Factors Courts Consider, 748, 1077
Federal Bail Reform Act of 1984, 747, 751–758, 1070–1078
Preventive Detention, 747–749, 751–758
Race and, 758–759, 760–762

BENCH TRIALS
Generally, 851–854

BRADY RULE
See Discovery
Waiver of the Right to Impeachment
    Evidence as Part of Plea Bargain,
    814–817

BRUTON RULE
Generally, 963–969

CELL PHONE SEARCHES
Generally, 161–167

COLLATERAL REVIEW
Generally, 8, 958

CONFESSIONS
Generally, 487–671
See also Interrogations
Due Process Voluntariness Test, 487–502
Miranda Rule, 531–671
Right to Counsel Approach, 503–529

CONFRONTATION CLAUSE
Generally, 941–969
Bruton Rule, 963–969
Forfeiture by Wrongdoing Doctrine, 957–963
Primary Purpose Test, 949–956
Testimonial Evidence, Examples of, 945, 947, 954, 956
Unavailability, 946

CONSENT SEARCHES
Generally, 351–369
Acquiescence to a Claim of Lawful
    Authority, 357
Scope, 357–358
Third-Party Consent, 358–369
Voluntariness, 351–356

CONTAINER SEARCHES
Automobile Exception, 169, 172–174, 175–183, 183–189, 189–192
Consent Searches, 357–358
Container, Definition of, 147
Container Doctrine (*Chadwick v. United States*), 35, 172, 173–174, 177–178
Containers, No Distinction Between
    "Worthy" and "Unworthy," 35, 172
Inventory Searches, 373, 376
Searches Incident to Arrest, 137–140, 145–160, 165
Terry Frisk of the Car (*Michigan v. Long*), 239
Trash Bags, 32–38

1100 INDEX

COUNSEL, THE SIXTH AMENDMENT RIGHT TO
    Generally, 467–486
Applicability of to the States, 468–472, 473–476
Counsel of One's Choice, 917–924
Effective Assistance of, 883, 887–894, 895–900, 900–901, 902–908, 908–910, 910–917
Gender and, 482, 483–486
Interrogations and, 503–529
Lineups and, 673, 674–683
Presumption of Adequate Assistance of Counsel, 887–894
Race and, 472–473, 476–477, 481–482, 483–486, 894–895, 902–908, 908–909
Waiver of, 924–929

CURTILAGE
    Generally, 17–26, 75–82, 192–199
Common Areas of Multi-Occupant Dwellings, 24–26
Definition of (and *Dunn* Factors), 19, 24
Driveway of Home as Part of, 192–199
Front Porch as Part of, 75–82

CUSTODY
See Miranda, Custody

DEFENSE COUNSEL
    Generally, 883–929
See Counsel, the Sixth Amendment Right to

DISCOVERY
    Generally, 779–801
ABA Model Rule 3.8, 790–791
Brady Rule, 779, 780–781, 782–790, 791–792, 792–795
Jencks Act, 782, 801, 1078–1079
Notice of Alibi Defense, 795–801, 1062–1063
Rule 16, 1063–1067

DOG SNIFFS
    Generally, 74–75
Common Areas of Apartment Building, of, 24–26
Front Porch of Home, of, 75–82
Luggage at Airport, of, 74
Vehicle During Traffic Stop, of, 74–75

DOUBLE JEOPARDY
    Generally, 971–1025
Blockburger Test, 517, 976–986
Brown-Diaz Exception, 986
Civil Forfeiture, 998–999
Collateral Estoppel, 971–972
Criminal Punishment v. Civil Penalty, 995–999
Department of Justice's Petite Policy, 994–995
Dual Sovereignty Doctrine, 987–995
Intent to Goad Defendant into Moving for a Mistrial, 1004–1009

Jury Nullification, 1019–1027
Manifest Necessity, 999–1004
Mistrials, 999–1009
Retrial Following Acquittals, Dismissals, and Convictions, 1010–1018
Same Conduct Test (*Grady v. Corbin*), 978, 980–981, 982, 983, 986
Same Offense Limitation, 976–986

DRUG TESTING
Generally, 371, 384

DUE PROCESS
    Generally, 1051–1052
Interrogations and the Due Process Voluntariness Test, 487–502
Lineups and, 683–690, 692–693, 696–702
Pre-Indictment Delay and, 774–778
Procedural Due Process, 753
Shocks the Conscience, 753
Substantive Due Process, 335, 337, 338, 751, 753

ELECTRONIC SURVEILLANCE
    Generally, 43–74
Cell Site Location Information (CSLI), 63–74
Electronic Eavesdropping, 44–48
GPS Tracking Devices, 53–62
Thermal Imaging Devices, 48–53

EMERGENCY AID
Generally, 406, 412–415

EXCLUSIONARY RULE
    Generally, 421–465
Good Faith Exception, 436–448
Mapp v. Ohio, 421, 425–431, 432–436

EXIGENT CIRCUMSTANCES EXCEPTION
    Generally, 405–420
Driving Under the Influence (DUI) and, 406–411, 411–412
Emergency Aid Doctrine, 412–415
Nature or Gravity of the Offense, 406–411
Police-Created Exigency Doctrine, 415–420

FAIR CROSS SECTION REQUIREMENT
Generally, 854–862

FEDERAL RULES OF CRIMINAL PROCEDURE
Generally, 1052–1070

FIFTH AMENDMENT
    Generally, 5, 1051
Due Process, 487, 778, 1051
Privilege Against Self-Incrimination, 5, 531, 569, 602–603, 615, 1051

FOURTH AMENDMENT
See Arrests, Searches, Search Warrants, Seizures

FRUIT OF THE POISONOUS TREE
Generally, 449–465
Attenuation Doctrine, 456, 457–465
Fruit of the Poisonous Tree Doctrine, 404–420
Independent Source, 421, 448, 452, 453, 455–456, 458, 459
Inevitable Discovery, 421, 448, 453–456
Wong Sun v. United States, 421, 449–453, 462, 637, 645

GARBAGE, SEARCHES OF
Generally, 32–38

GPS TRACKING DEVICES
Generally, 53, 54–62

GRAND JURY
Generally, 5, 731–746
Exculpatory Evidence, 740–744, 744–745
Hearsay, 738–740
Indictment, 731
Racial Discrimination in the Selection of, 732–737

HABEAS CORPUS
Generally, 8

HARMLESS ERROR
Generally, 733

IDENTIFICATION PROCEDURES (LINEUPS)
Generally, 673–702
Cross-Racial Identification, 693–696
Due Process Test, 683–690, 692–693, 696–702
Photo Identification, 691
Right to Counsel at, 674–683

INEFFECTIVE ASSISTANCE OF COUNSEL
Generally, 883
Client Perjury and, 910–917
Immigration Consequences, 895–900
Plea Bargains, 900–901
Race and, 902–908, 908–909
Strickland v. Washington Two Part Test, 887–895

INFORMANTS
Anonymous Tipsters, 222–225
Impeachment Evidence Relating to, 814–817
Probable Cause and Confidential Informants, 89–99
Sixth Amendment Right to Counsel and Jailhouse Informants, 521–529

INTERROGATIONS
Generally, 487–671
Due Process Voluntariness Test, 487–502
Gender and, 587–590
Miranda Rule, 531–671
Race and, 587–590, 658–660

Sixth Amendment Right to Counsel Approach, 503–529

JURY NULLIFICATION
Generally, 1019–1022
Grand Jury and, 734
Race-Based, 1019–1027

JURY TRIAL, RIGHT TO
Generally, 835–882
Batson Challenges, 868–882
Equal Protection, 868–882
Fair Cross-Section, 854–862
Petty Offense Limitation, 836–838
Size of Jury, 845–847
Unanimity, 838–845, 846, 847–851
Voir Dire into Racial Bias, 862–868
Waiver of, 851–854

LINEUPS
See Identification Procedures (Lineups)

***MIRANDA* RULE**
Generally, 531–671
Can Congress Overrule *Miranda*?, 626–632
Compared to *Massiah* and Sixth Amendment Approach, 660–671
Custody, the Meaning of, 548–559
Edwards Rule, 579–582, 583, 583–587, 587–590, 590–596, 667–671
Impeachment Exception, 578, 651–658
Initiation, the Meaning of, 583
Interrogation, the Meaning of, 559–573
Miranda v. Arizona, 531–547, 547–548
Physical Fruits of a *Miranda* Violation, Admissibility of, 632–635
Public Safety Exception, 619–626
Right to Silence, Invocation of, 609–615
Two-Stage Interrogations, 636–650
Undercover Exception, 568–573
Waiver of, 597–618

MISTRIALS
Generally, 999–1009

NEW TECHNOLOGIES
Generally, 48–74

OPEN FIELDS DOCTRINE
Generally, 17–26
Class, and, 24–26, 85–88

ORIGINALISM, THE NEW FOURTH AMENDMENT
Generally, 189–192

PEN REGISTERS
Generally, 27–32

PEREMPTORY CHALLENGES
Generally, 847, 868–882, 1087–1088
Batson Challenges, 868–882

PERJURY
Counsel's Ethical Obligations, 909–910, 910–916, 916–917

PETITE POLICY
Generally, 994–995

PLAIN FEEL DOCTRINE
Generally, 249–254

PLAIN VIEW DOCTRINE
Generally, 241–254

PLEA BARGAINING
Generally, 803–834
Admissibility of Plea Discussions, 1061
Alford Pleas, 823–827, 827
Breach by Prosecutor, 809–812
Critiques of, 828–831, 831–834
Nolo Contendere, 5, 1058–1061
Race and, 712–715, 831–834
Requisites of a Valid Plea, 817–823
Rule 11: Pleas, 1058–1061
Vindictive Prosecution, and, 717–726, 804–810
Waiver of Right to Impeachment Information, and, 814–817
Withdrawal of Guilty or Nolo Contendere Plea, 1061

POLICE USE OF FORCE
Generally, 329–349

PRESENCE, RIGHT OF
Generally, 931–939
Disruptive Defendant, 936–939
Rule 43, 931–935
Voluntary Absence, 931–935
Waiver of the Right, 931–935

PRESUMPTIONS
Coercion or Compulsion in *Miranda* Context, 630, 634, 635, 639
Constitutionality, Acts of Congress, 118
Counsel of Choice, 920, 922
Criminality, 231, 301
Danger to the Community (Federal Bail Reform Act of 1984), 1074
Edwards, 590, 593, 595
Guilt, 659, 660
Innocence, 749, 756, 757, 759, 773, 774, 1078
Involuntariness re: Waiver of *Miranda* Right to Counsel, 590, 593, 595
Jurors Follow Jury Instructions, 967, 968
Petty Offense, 837
Reasonable or Adequate Performance by Criminal Defense Counsel, 890, 892, 912
Regularity in Prosecutorial Charging Decisions, 706, 707, 709, 719
Stare Decisis, 844
Unreasonableness, Warrantless Home Searches, 408
Vindictiveness, 704, 719, 720, 722, 725
Waiver, 669, 767

PROBABLE CAUSE
Generally, 89–101
Arrest and, 2, 119
Confidential Informants and, 90–99
Grand Jury and, 5, 731
Judicial Determination of, 3, 151
Plain View Doctrine and, 219–226
Preliminary Hearing and, 4
Race and, 89

PROFILING
Generally, 255–281
See also Racial Profiling
Driving While Black, 270–274, 274–278
Drug Courier Profile, 277, 320
Ethnic Profiling, 261–269, 283–286
Walking While Black, 278–283
Walking While Trans, 283

PROSECUTOR'S CHARGING DISCRETION
Generally, 703–729
Overlapping Statutes, 725–729
Race, and, 712–717
Selective Prosecution, 704–712
Vindictive Prosecution, 717–725, 804–810

QUALIFIED IMMUNITY
Generally, 129, 389

RACIAL PROFILING
Generally, 152, 231, 255–286
Driving While Black, 274–278
Walking While Black, 278–283
Whren v. U.S., 270–274

REASONABLE EXPECTATION OF PRIVACY TEST
Generally, 9–88

REASONABLE SUSPICION
Generally, 212–215, 234–235
Terry v. Ohio, 201–211

RIGHT TO COUNSEL
Generally, 467–486
See also Counsel, the Sixth Amendment Right to

SEARCH INCIDENT TO ARREST
Generally, 133–167
Automobiles and, 145–160
Cell Phones, 161–167
Container, Defined, 147
Effect of State Law Prohibiting Arrest, 140–141
Home, Search of, 133–136, 141–145
Persons, 137–141
Protective Sweep, 135
Scope, 133–167
Substantially Contemporaneous Requirement, 142, 149

INDEX

SEARCHES
Generally, 9–88
Administrative Searches (*see* Administrative Searches)
Automobile Searches (*see* Automobile Exception, Search Incident to Arrest, Automobiles and, *Terry* Stops and Frisks, Vehicles and)
Consent Searches (*see* Consent Searches)
Container Searches (*see* Container Searches)
Cross-Gender Searches, 400–403
Katz Test, 10–17
Reasonable Expectation of Privacy Test, 10–17, 82–88
Searches Incident to Arrest (*see* Search Incident to Arrest)
Stops and Frisks (*see Terry* Stops and Frisks)
Warrants and (*see* Search Warrants)

SEARCH WARRANTS
Generally, 103–116
Knock and Announce Requirement, 110–116
No Knock Warrants, 110–112
Particularity Requirement, 103–111

SEIZURES OF PROPERTY
Generally, 59, 241

SEIZURES OF THE PERSON
Generally, 287–327
Age and, 311–313
Bus Sweeps and, 294–308
Disability and, 313
Explained, 289
"Free to Leave" Test, 288–293, 293–294, 308–311
Modified Test for Seizure, 294–299, 299–303, 304–308
Physical Force and, 289, 320–327
Race and, 293–294, 299–303, 308–313
Stops v. Arrests, 313–320
Submission to Assertion of Authority, 287, 289

SELECTIVE PROSECUTION
Generally, 704–712

SENTENCING
Generally, 1029–1049
Cruel and Unusual Punishment Discussed, 1029–1032, 1033–1039, 1048, 1051
Death Penalty and Race, 1033, 1039–1049
Death Penalty and Rape, 1029–1032, 1033
Proportionality Principle for Non-Capital Sentences, 1033–1039
Three Strikes Law, and Eighth Amendment, 1033–1039, 1039

SIXTH AMENDMENT RIGHT TO COUNSEL
Generally, 467–486
See also Right to Counsel and Counsel, the Sixth Amendment Right to
Interrogations, 503–529
Race and, 472–473, 476–477, 481–482, 483–486, 894–895, 902–908, 908–909

SPECIAL NEEDS SEARCHES
See Administrative Searches

SPEEDY TRIAL
Generally, 763–778
Barker v. Wingo Four Factor Balancing Test, 763–772
Due Process and, 774–778
Pre-Indictment Delay, 774–778
Sentencing, Delay in, 772–774

STRUCTURAL ERROR
Generally, 733

***TERRY* STOPS AND FRISKS**
Generally, 201–239
Flight from Police, 225–231, 233–235
NYPD (*Floyd v. City of New York*), 211–212
Race and, 211–222, 231, 232
Terry v. Ohio, 201–219
Vehicles and, 235–239

THIRD PARTY CONSENT
Generally, 358–369
Illinois v. Rodriquez, 358–361

TRESPASS DOCTRINE
Generally, 9, 11–12, 15–17
Florida v. Jardines, 75–82
United States v. Jones, 54–62

VINDICTIVE PROSECUTION
Generally, 717–725, 804–810

VOIR DIRE
Racial Bias and, 862–868

VOLUNTARINESS
Consent and, 351–358
Due Process Voluntariness Test, 487–502

WAIVER
Alford Pleas and, 825–826
Miranda Rights, of, 532, 540–546, 579–582, 585, 590–596, 597–618, 661–664
Plea Bargaining and, 814–817, 817–819
Right to Conflict-Free Counsel, of, 917–924
Sixth Amendment Right to Counsel, Generally, of, 924–929
Sixth Amendment Right to Counsel (Interrogation Context), of, 513–521, 524, 661–664, 668–671
Sixth Amendment Right to Jury Trial, of, 851–854, 817–819

Sixth Amendment Right to Speedy Trial
 and Rejection of Demand-Waiver
 Rule, 767–768

WARRANTS
See Search Warrants